Handbook on Crime

Handbook on Crime

Edited by

Fiona Brookman, Mike Maguire, Harriet Pierpoint, Trevor Bennett

WILLAN
PUBLISHING

Published by

Willan Publishing
Culmcott House
Mill Street, Uffculme
Cullompton, Devon
EX15 3AT, UK
Tel: +44(0)1884 840337
Fax: +44(0)1884 840251
e-mail: info@willanpublishing.co.uk
website: www.willanpublishing.co.uk

Published simultaneously in the USA and Canada by

Willan Publishing
c/o ISBS, 920 NE 58th Ave, Suite 300
Portland, Oregon 97213-3644, USA
Tel: +001(0)503 287 3093
Fax: +001(0)503 280 8832
e-mail: info@isbs.com
website: www.isbs.com

First published 2010

ISBN   978-1-84392-371-8 paperback
        978-1-84392-372-5 hardback

British Library Cataloguing-in-Publication Data

A catalogue record for this book is available from the British Library

FSC
Mixed Sources
Product group from well-managed
forests and other controlled sources
Cert no. SGS-COC-2482
www.fsc.org
© 1996 Forest Stewardship Council

Project management by Deer Park Productions, Tavistock, Devon
Typeset by GCS, Leighton Buzzard, Beds
Printed and bound by T.J. International, Padstow, Cornwall

Contents

List of abbreviations   *ix*

List of figures and tables   *xvii*

Table of statutes   *xix*

Notes on contributors   *xxiii*

Introduction   *xxxv*
Fiona Brookman, Mike Maguire, Harriet Pierpoint and Trevor Bennett

Part I: 'Conventional' property crime

Introduction   1

1   **Domestic burglary**   3
     Mike Maguire, Richard Wright and Trevor Bennett

2   **Vehicle crime**   26
     Rick Brown

3   **Shoplifting**   48
     Nick Tilley

4   **Understanding and tackling stolen goods markets**   68
     Mike Sutton

Part II: Fraud and Fakes

Introduction   85

5   **Income tax evasion and benefit fraud**   87
     John Minkes and Leonard Minkes

6   **Theft and fraud by employees**   100
     Martin Gill and Janice Goldstraw-White

7   **Fakes**   120
     Simon Mackenzie

8   **Scams**   137
     Simon Mackenzie

9   **Credit fraud**   153
     Michael Levi

10   **Identity theft and fraud**   172
     Natasha Semmens

11   **Cybercrime**   191
     Matthew Williams

Part III: Violent Crime
Introduction   215

12   **Homicide**   217
     Fiona Brookman

13   **Domestic violence**   245
     Amanda Robinson

14   **Street robbery**   270
     Trevor Bennett and Fiona Brookman

15   **Stealing commercial cash: from safe-cracking to armed robbery**   290
     Dick Hobbs

16   **Youth gang crime**   308
     Jennifer Maher

17   **Violence in the night-time economy**   331
     Simon Winlow

18   **Hate crime**   351
     Paul Iganski

19   **Stalking and harassment**   366
     Victoria Heckels and Karl Roberts

20   **Arson**   380
     Emma J. Palmer, Clive R. Hollin, Ruth M. Hatcher and
     Tammy C. Ayres

21   **Blackmail, kidnapping and threats to kill**   393
     Keith Soothill and Brian Francis

22   Elder abuse   415
     John Williams

23   School bullying: risk factors, theories and interventions   427
     Maria M. Ttofi and David P. Farrington

24   Institutional abuse and children's homes   458
     Jonathan Evans

25   Animal abuse   480
     Harriet Pierpoint and Jennifer Maher

Part IV: Sex-Related Crime
Introduction   503

26   Sexual offences against adults   505
     Clive R. Hollin, Ruth M. Hatcher and Emma J. Palmer

27   Sexual offences against children   525
     Clive R. Hollin, Emma J. Palmer and Ruth M. Hatcher

28   Sex work   542
     Belinda Brooks-Gordon

Part V: Drug-Related Crime
Introduction   577

29   Drug- and alcohol-related crime   579
     Trevor Bennett and Katy Holloway

30   Drug supply and possession   598
     Tim McSweeney, Paul J. Turnbull and Tiggey May

31   Drug trafficking   626
     Letizia Paoli, Toine Spapens and Cyrille Fijnaut

Part VI: Organised and Business Crime
Introduction   651

32   Corporate financial crimes   653
     John Minkes

33   Middle-range business crime: rogue and respectable businesses,
     family firms and entrepreneurs   678
     Hazel Croall

34   Human trafficking   698
     Jo Goodey

35 **Money laundering**   712
    David C. Hicks

36 **Extortion**   726
    Dick Hobbs

Part VII: State, Political and War Crimes
Introduction   739

37 **State crime**   741
    Katherine S. Williams

38 **Genocide and 'ethnic cleansing'**   762
    Andy Aitchison

39 **Torture**   785
    Rod Morgan

40 **Crimes of the global state**   801
    Maureen Cain

41 **Political protest and crime**   825
    P.A.J. Waddington

42 **Terrorism**   846
    Nicola Weston and Martin Innes

Part VIII: Harms, Health and Safety
Introduction   865

43 **Eco-crime and air pollution**   867
    Reece Walters

44 **Corporate violence and harm**   884
    Steve Tombs

45 **Driving offences**   904
    Claire Corbett

Index   *930*

List of abbreviations

AAIPT	Alliance Against Intellectual Property Theft
ACF	Arson Control Forum
ACFE	Association of Certified Fraud Examiners
ACMD	Advisory Council on the Misuse of Drugs
ACPO	Association of Chief Police Officers
ADHD	Attention-Deficit Hyperactivity Disorder
ADL	Anti-Defamation League
AIDS	acquired immune deficiency syndrome
AML	anti-money laundering
ANPR	Automatic Number Plate Recognition
APA	American Psychological Association
APACS	Association for Payment Clearing Services
APPG	All Party Parliamentary Group
AQMA	Air Quality Management Area
ARA	Assets Recovery Agency
ASBO	Anti-Social Behaviour Order
ASRO	Addressing Substance Related Offending
ATM	automated teller machine
AUC	area under the curve
BAC	blood alcohol concentration
BARK	Brent Action for Responsible K9s
BAT	best available techniques
BATNEEC	best available techniques not entailing excessive cost
BCCI	Bank of Credit and Commerce International
BCS	British Crime Survey
BCU	basic command unit
BDSM	bondage, domination, sadism and masochism
BERR	Department for Business, Enterprise and Regulatory Reform
BiH	Bosnia and Herzegovina
BJS	Bureau of Justice Statistics (US)

BKA	Bundeskriminalamt (German Federal Police)
BMA	British Medical Association
BME	black and minority ethnic
BMK	benzyl methyl ketone
BPEO	best practicable environmental option
BPI	British Phonographic Industry
BPM	best practicable means
BPS	British Psychological Society
BRC	British Retail Consortium
BSA	Bank Secrecy Act 1970 (US)
BSA	British Software Agency
BVQ	Bully/Victim Questionnaire [Revised]
C/P	counterfeit/pirated [goods]
CAADA	Coordinated Action Against Domestic Abuse
CAP	Common Agricultural Policy
CARAT	Counselling, Assessment, Referral, Advice and Throughcare
CARS	Comprehensive Auto-Theft Research System (Australia)
CATW	Coalition against Trafficking in Women
CBT	cognitive-behavioural therapy
CCAL	Campaign for Clear Air in London
CCTV	closed-circuit television
CD	conduct disorder
CDPA	Copyright, Designs and Patents Act 1988
CEDAW	Convention on the Elimination of all forms of Discrimination Against Women
CEOP	Child Exploitation and Online Protection Centre
CID	Criminal Investigation Department
CIFAS	Credit Industry Fraud Avoidance System
CIT	cash in transit
CITES	Convention on International Trade in Endangered Species of Wild Fauna and Flora
CMCHA	Corporate Manslaughter and Corporate Homicide Act 2007
CNP	card-not-present [transaction]
COE	Council of Europe
COMEAP	Committee on the Medical Effects of Air Pollutants
CONADEP	National Commission on the Disappearance of Persons (Argentina)
CONSORT	Consolidated Standards of Reporting Trials
COTES	Control of Trade in Endangered Species (Enforcement) Regulations 1997
CPS	Crown Prosecution Service
CPT	Committee for the Prevention of Torture
CRAVED	concealable, removable, available, valuable, enjoyable and disposable
CSI	Computer Security Institute
CSJ	Centre for Social Justice
CtC	Communities that Care

CTR	currency transaction report
CVS	Commercial Victimisation Survey
CWASU	Child and Woman Abuse Studies Unit
DCPCU	Dedicated Cheque and Plastic Crime Unit
DDoS	distributed denial of service
Defra	Department for Environment, Food and Rural Affairs
DfT	Department for Transport
DIP	Drug Interventions Programme
DMCA	Digital Millenium Copyright Act 1998
DoS	denial of service
DPC	Drug Policy Commission (UK)
DRR	Drug Rehabilitation Requirement
DSS	Department of Social Security
DTI	Department of Trade and Industry
DTLR	Depart for Transport, Local Government and the Regions
DTOA	Drug Trafficking Offences Act 1986
DTTO	Drug Treatment and Testing Order
DVLC	Driver and Vehicle Licensing Centre
DWP	Department of Work and Pensions
EA	Environment Agency
ECJ	European Court of Justice
ECPAT	End Child Prostitution, Child Pornography and the Trafficking of Children
EEA	European Environmental Agency
ELSPA	Entertainment and Leisure Software Producers Association
EMCDDA	European Monitoring Centre for Drugs and Drug Addiction
EPA	Environmental Protection Agency (US)
EU	European Union
FACE	Fire Awareness Child Education Programme
FACT	Federation Against Copyright Theft
FARC	Revolutionary Armed Forces of Columbia
FAST	Family Systems Test
FAST	Federation Against Software Theft
FATF	Financial Action Task Force
FBI	US Federal Bureau of Investigation
FEMA	Federal Emergency Management Agency
FIU	financial intelligence unit
FPN	fixed penalty notice
FRA	EU Agency for Fundamental Rights
FSA	Financial Services Authority
FSE	fire safety education
FTC	Federal Trade Commission (US)
GAATW	Global Alliance Against Trafficking in Women
GATT	General Agreement on Tariffs and Trade

GDP	gross domestic product
GMO	genetically modified organism
GREAT	Gang Resistance Education and Training
GSS	General Security Services (Israel)
HDI	Human development Index
HGV	heavy goods vehicle
HIPC	Highly Indebted Poor Countries Initiative
HIV	human immunodeficiency virus
HMCS	Her Majesty's Court Service
HMIC	Her Majesty's Inspectorate of Constabulary
HMRC	Her Majesty's Revenue and Customs
HMSO	Her Majesty's Stationery Office
HO	Home Office
HSE	Health and Safety Executive
HSUS	Humane Society of the United States
HVF	home visit from a firefighter
ICCPR	International Covenant on Civil and Political Rights
ICJS	Institute of Criminal Justice Studies
ICRC	International Committee of the Red Cross
ICTs	information communication technologies
ICTR	International Criminal Tribunal for Rwanda
ICTY	International Criminal Tribunal for the former Yugoslavia
IDTS	Integrated Drug Treatment System
IDVA	Independent Domestic Violence Advisor
IGO	intergovernmental organisation
ILO	International Labour Organisation
IMF	International Monetary Fund
IMT	International Military Tribunal
INCB	International Narcotics Control Board
IOM	International Organisation for Migration
IP	intellectual property
IPC	intellectual property crime/integrated pollution control
IPCC	Independent Police Complaints Commission
IPPC	Integrated Pollution Prevention and Control
ISA	Intelligent Speed Adaptation
ISBS	Information Security Breaches Survey
ISP	Internet service provider
IUSW	International Union of Sex Workers
IWF	Internet Watch Foundation
KFOR	(NATO-led) Kosovo Force
KSI	killed or seriously injured
KYC	know your customer
LAAPC	Local Authority Air Pollution Control
LCV	light commercial vehicle

LFS	Labour Force Survey
LGBT	lesbian, gay, bisexual and transgender
LRP	lifetime recourse to prostitution
MARAC	multi-agency risk assessment conference
MMAGS	Manchester Multi-Agency Gang Strategy
MoJ	Ministry of Justice
MRA	market reduction approach
MTIC	missing trader intra-community [fraud]
NAD	Not Another Drop
NAO	National Audit Office
NAPO	National Association of Probation Officers
NAQS	National Air Quality Strategy
NASUWT	National Association of Schoolmasters and Union of Women Teachers
NatCen	National Centre for Social Research
NATO	North Atlantic Treaty Organisation
NCC	National Consumer Council
NCCT	Non-Cooperative Countries and Territories
NCIS	National Criminal Intelligence Service
NCS	National Crime Squad
NCVCCO	National Council of Voluntary Child Care Organisations
NCVS	National Crime Victimization Survey (US)
NeET	National e-Crime Enforcement Team
NFER	National Foundation for Education Research
NFIB	National Fraud Intelligence Bureau
NFRC	National Fraud Reporting Centre
NGO	non-governmental organisation
NHTCU	National High-Tech Crime Unit
NIBRS	National Incident-Based Reporting System (US)
NIEA	Northern Ireland Environment Agency
NOMS	National Offender Management Service
NOP	National Opinion Poll
NPIA	National Police Improvement Agency
NSCA	National Society for Clean Air
NSPCC	National Society for the Prevention of Cruelty to Children
NSW	New South Wales
OBPP	Olweus Bullying Prevention Programme
OCJR	Office for Criminal Justice Reform
OCJS	Offending, Crime and Justice Survey
ODD	Oppositional Defiant Disorder
ODIHR	Office for Democratic Institutions and Human Rights
OECD	Organisation for Economic Cooperation and Development
OFT	Office of Fair Trading
OJJDP	Office of Juvenile Justice and Delinquency Prevention (US)
ONDCP	Office of National Drug Control Policy

ONS	Office for National Statistics
OPM	Office for Public Management
OSAP	Offender Substance Abuse Programme
OSCE	Organisation for Security and Cooperation in Europe
OTC	over-the-counter (medicine etc.)
PACE	Police and Criminal Evidence Act 1984
PAW	Partnership for Action Against Wildlife Crime
PCeU	Police Central e-Crime Unit
PICS	Platform for Internet Content Selection
PIN	personal identification number
PMK	piperonyl methyl ketone
POCA	Proceeds of Crime Act 2002
PPC	pollution prevention and control
PPG	penile plethysmograph
PRA	Prostitution Reform Act 2003 [New Zealand]
PRAQ	Peer Relations Assessment Questionnaire
PRQ	Peer Relations Questionnaire
PTSD	post-traumatic stress disorder
R&D	research and development
RCEP	Royal Commission on Environmental Pollution
RCN	Royal College of Nursing
RCT	randomised control trial
RFID	radio frequency identification
RICO	Racketeer-Influenced Corrupt Organizations Act 1970 (US)
RIDDOR	Reporting of Injuries, Diseases and Dangerous Occurrences Regulations 1995
RoB	Restrictions on Bail
ROC	return on capital
RSPCA	Royal Society for the Prevention of Cruelty to Animals
RST	Reintegrative Shaming Theory
RTA	Road Traffic Act
SAP	structural adjustment programme
SAPRIN	Structural Adjustment Participatory Review International Network
SCI	Street Crime Initiative
SCPO	Serious Crime Prevention Order
SDVC	Specialised Domestic Violence Court
SEPA	Scottish Environment Protection Agency
SGC	Sentencing Guidelines Council
SIP	Social Information Processing Theory
SME	small and medium enterprise
SMR	Standard Minimum Rules (for the Treatment of Prisoners)
SOA	Sexual Offences Act 2003
SOCA	Serious Organised Crime Agency
SOTEP	Sex Offender Treatment and Evaluation Programme

SOTP	Sex Offender Treatment Programme
SPOC	single point of contact
SSPCA	Scottish Society for the Prevention of Cruelty to Animals
SSPCC	Scottish Society for the Prevention of Cruelty to Children
TDPF	Transform Drug Policy Foundation
TGAP	Tackling Gangs Action Plan
THC	tetrahydrocannabinol
TKAP	Tackling Knives Action Programme
TLC	Teaching Love and Compassion
TMA	Trade Marks Act 1994
ToM	Theory of Mind
TOMPs	toxic organic micro-pollutants
TRL	Transport Research Laboratory
UDHR	Universal Declaration of Human Rights
UKDPC	UK Drug Policy Commission
UK-IPO	UK Intellectual Property Office
UKTA	UK Threat Assessment
UN	United Nations
UN.GIFT	UN Global Initiative to Fight Human Trafficking
UNCTAD	UN Conference on Trade and Development
UNESCO	UN Educational, Social and Cultural Organisation
UNGA	UN General Assembly
UNHCR	UN High Commission for Refugees
UNICRI	UN Interregional Crime and Justice Research Institute
UNIFEM	UN Development Fund for Women
UNMIK	UN Mission in Kosovo
UNODC	UN Office on Drugs and Crime
USEPA	US Environmental Protection Agency
vCJD	variant Creutzfeld-Jakob Disease
VCRAT	Vehicle Crime Reduction Action Team
VIN	Vehicle Identification Number
VOC	volatile organic compound
WAG	Welsh Assembly Government
WHO	World Health Organisation
WIDER	World Institute for Development Economics Research
WIPO	World Intellectual Property Organisation
YJB	Youth Justice Board
YJCEA	Youth Justice and Criminal Evidence Act 1999

List of figures and tables

Figures

1.1	Trends in police recorded domestic burglary, 1981 to 2008/9	5
2.1	Trend in police recorded vehicle crime, 1977 to 2007/8	29
3.1	Trends in recorded shop theft in England and Wales, 1934–2008	49
3.2	Indexed trends in shop theft and other theft 1945–2008	49
11.1	The government Cabinet Office website hacked in August 2000	196
11.2	Prevalence of business cybercrime (1998–2008)	201
11.3	Cybercrime prevalence by type 2004	203
12.1	Annual totals of recorded homicide in England and Wales, 1967–2007/8	221
12.2	Victim–offender relationship, 1998–2007/8	226
14.1	Trends in violent crime by type of violence, 1995 to 2007/8 BCS	273
21.1	Recorded offences and convictions by year	403
21.2	Mean age at conviction by year	405
21.3	Proportion of sentences which are custodial by year	410
25.1	Total convictions recorded by the RSPCA	487
25.2	Phone calls and complaints made to the RSPCA and rescues and collections made by the RSPCA	488
25.3	Court statistics on gender of offenders	489
25.4	Court statistics on age of offenders	489
30.1	Number of UK seizures by class (1980–2000)	605
30.2	Market share and seizure rates (2003/4)	607
30.3	Persons found guilty, cautioned, fined or dealt with by compounding for drug dealing or supply offences (1980–2000)	613

Tables

3.1	Most stolen items by type of store	51
3.2	Types of shop and items shoplifted in Exeter	52
3.3	Attributes and shop theft results of major British self-report studies	54

3.4	Motives for shop theft as found among Milton Keynes novices	58
3.5	Motive for shoplifting among CPS cases	59
9.1	Summary of fraud statistics	166
12.1	The number and rates of homicides in the UK in 2007/8	221
12.2	Homicide rates per 100,000 population, selected countries of the world by region, 2004–6	223
12.3	Gender 'mix' of suspect and victims of homicide in England and Wales: 1998–2008	225
19.1	Stalker–victim relationships	376
21.1	Prevalence of the three offences per 100,000 population in England and Wales and Australia in 2006	401
21.2	Offenders convicted of blackmail, kidnapping and threats to kill in 1999–2001 – previous convictions (standard list)	406
21.3	Offenders convicted of blackmail, kidnapping and threats to kill in 1979–81 – subsequent convictions (standard list)	408
25.1	Legislation listed in the RSPCA's Inspector's Legal Handbook	483
25.2	The number of persons cautioned, proceeded against at magistrates' courts and found guilty at all courts, by result, under selected offences of cruelty to wildlife, 2002 to 2007	490
26.1	Sexual offences in 2003 Act	506
26.2	Implicit theories of rapists	511
27.1	Sexual offences in 2003 Act (after Sentencing Guidelines)	526
27.2	Recorded crime 2007/8: sexual offences against children (adapted from Home Office n.d.)	529
28.1	Offences associated with sex work	543
28.2	Trafficking for 'sexual exploitation'	546
28.3	Prostitution offences in England and Wales 1997–2007/8	548
28.4	Policy responses to prostitution and their effects	557
30.1	Use of illicit drugs among EU citizens aged between 15 and 64 years	599
30.2	Classification of drugs	602
30.3	Maximum sentences for possession, supply and production	602
38.1	Definitions of genocide	770
38.2	Proposed genocides 1933–99	777
40.1	Earnings of those employed in Trinidad and Tobago 1987–91	805
40.2	Serious offences reported to the police (excluding traffic offences) in Trinidad and Tobago 1980–92	807
45.1	Numbers of speed limit offences dealt with by official action (in thousands) and the proportions detected by speed cameras: 1996–2006	912
45.2	Bad driving offences dealt with by official police action: England and Wales (thousands of offences)	916
45.3	Gender and age profile of bad driving offenders: England and Wales	917
45.4	Estimates of all GB road accident casualties where illegal alcohol levels were found among drivers and riders, adjusted for under-reporting	922
45.5	Findings of guilt for drink- or drug-driving offences by age and sex	922

Table of statutes

Abandonment of Animals Act 1960
Adult Support and Protection (Scotland) Act 2007
Aggravated Vehicle-Taking Act 1992
Agriculture Act 1947
Agriculture (Miscellaneous Provisions) Act 1972
Alkali Works Regulation Act 1906
Animal (Cruel Poisons) Act 1962
Animal Welfare Act 2006
Animals (Scientific Procedures) Act 1986
Anti-Social Behaviour Act 2003
Asylum and Immigration Act 2004
Care Standards Act 2000
Child Abduction Act 1984
Children Act 1908
Children Act 1948
Children Act 1984
Children Act 1989
Children Act 2004
Children and Young Persons Act 1933
Children and Young Persons Act 1969
Clean Air Act 1956
Clean Air Act 1968
Computer Misuse Act 1990
Conservation of Seals Act 1970
Contagious Diseases Acts 1964–9
Copyright, Designs and Patents Act 1988
Corporate Manslaughter and Corporate Homicide Act 2007
Crime (Sentences) Act 1997
Crime and Disorder Act 1998
Criminal Attempts Act 1981
Criminal Code 2004 (Ethiopia)

Criminal Damage Act 1971
Criminal Justice Act 1998
Criminal Justice Act 2003
Criminal Justice and Police Act 2001
Criminal Justice and Public Order Act 1994
Criminal Law Act 1967
Criminal Law Act 1977
Criminal Law Amendment Act 1885
Data Protection Act 1998
Deer Act 1991
Destructive Imported Animals Act 1932
Disorderly Houses Act 1751
Docking and Nicking of Horses Act 1949
Domestic Violence Crime and Victims Act 2004
Drug Trafficking Offences Act 1986
Endangered Species (Import and Export) Act 1976
Enterprise Act 2002
Environment Act 1995
Environmental Protection Act 1990
Farriers (Registration) Act 1975
Forgery and Counterfeiting Act 1981
Fraud Act 2006
Freedom of Information Act 2000
Game Act 1831
Genocide Act 1969
Ground Game Act 1880
Hares Preservation Act 1892
Homicide Act 1957
Hunting Act 2004
Identity Cards Act 2006
Industrial Schools Act 1857
Industrial Schools Act 1866
Infanticide Act 1938
Insolvency Act 1986
International Criminal Court Act 2001
International Criminal Court (Scotland) Act 2001
International Convention on the Prevention and Punishment of the Crime of
    Genocide 1948
International Convention on the Elimination of All Forms of Racial
    Discrimination 1965
Law on the Establishment of Extraordinary Chambers 2004 (Cambodia)
Law Reform (Year and a Day Rule) Act 1996
Leaving Care Act 2000
London and Local Authorities Act 1991
Lotteries and Amusements Act 1976
Medicines Act 1968
Mental Capacity Act 2005
Mental Health Act 1983

Metropolitan Police Act 1839
Misuse of Drugs Act 1971
Motor Car Act 1903
Murder (Abolition of the Death Penalty) Act 1965
National Health Service and Community Care Act 1990
Nationality, Immigration and Asylum Act 2002
Night Poaching Act 1828
Obscene Publications Act 1959
Offences Against the Person Act 1861
Parliament Act 1911
Penal Code 1957 (Ethiopia)
Pests Act 1954
Police and Criminal Evidence Act 1984
Police and Criminal Justice Act 2001
Pollution Prevention and Control Act 1999
Proceeds of Crime Act 2002
Protection from Harassment Act 1997
Protection of Animals (Amendment) Act 1954
Protection of Animals Act 1911
Protection of Badgers Act 1992
Public Order Act 1986
Road Safety Act 1967
Road Safety Act 2006
Road Traffic Act 1930
Road Traffic Act 1988
Road Traffic Act 1991
Road Traffic Offenders Act 1988
Serious Crime Act 2007
Serious Organised Crime and Police Act 2005
Sexual Offences (Amendment) Act 2000
Sexual Offences Act 1956
Sexual Offences Act 1959
Sexual Offences Act 1967
Sexual Offences Act 1985
Sexual Offences Act 2003
Strafgesetzbuch 1998 (Germany)
Street Offences Act 1959
Taking of Hostages Act 1982
Theft Act 1968
Theft Act 1978
Trade Descriptions Act 1968
Trade Marks Act 1994
Vagrancy Acts (various)
Vagrants Act 1898
Veterinary Surgeons Act 1966
Video Recordings Act 1984
Violent Crime Reduction Act 2006
Wild Mammals (Protection) Act 1996

Wildlife and Countryside Act 1981
Youth Justice and Criminal Evidence Act 1999

UK Regulations

Consumer Protection (Cancellation of Contracts Concluded away from
  Business Premises) Regulations 1987
Control of Misleading Advertisements Regulations 1988
Control of Trade in Endangered Species (Enforcement) Regulations 1997
Money Laundering Regulations 2003/2007
Motor Vehicle (Type Approval) (Amendment) Regulations 1975
Pollution Prevention and Control (England and Wales) Regulations 2000
Town and Country Planning (Control of Advertisements) Regulations 1992
Welfare of Animals (Slaughter and Killing) (Amendment) Regulations 1999

EU

Council Directive 74/61/EEC
Directive 2001/29/EC [Copyright Directive]
IPPC Directive
Regulation 1383/2003 Customs Actions Against Goods Suspected of
  Infringing Intellectual Property Rights
L'Regulation 1891/2004
Statute of the International Criminal Court (1998) (Rome)
Statute of the ICTR 2007
Statute of the ICTY 2008

US

Bank Secrecy Act 1970
Digital Millennium Copyright Act 1998
Federal Kidnapping Act
Hate Crime Statistics Act 1990
Identity Theft and Assumption Deterrence Act 1998
Local Law Enforcement Hate Crimes Prevention Act 2007
Money Laundering Control Act 1986
Motor Vehicle Theft Law Enforcement Act 1984
Organized Crime Control Act 1970
Racketeer-Influenced Corrupt organizations Act 1970
Violent Crime Control and Law Enforcement Act 1994

Notes on contributors

Andy Aitchison is Lecturer in Social Policy at the School of Social and Political Science, University of Edinburgh, where he co-directs the MSc programme in Global Crime, Justice and Security. His most significant publications to date focus on post-war criminal justice reform in Bosnia and Herzegovina.

Tammy C. Ayres is University Tutor in the Department of Criminology at the University of Leicester and a PhD student in the Department of Health Sciences. Her research interests include the link between drugs and crime, substance-using offenders, and the use of drugs in prison and its subsequent treatment.

Trevor Bennett is Professor of Criminology and Director of the Centre for Criminology, which he established in 2001, at the University of Glamorgan. He has worked mainly in the areas of offender decision-making, policing, crime prevention and drug misuse and his recent work has focused on the connection between drug use and crime. Recent books include *Understanding Drugs, Alcohol, and Crime* (Open University/McGraw-Hill) and *Drug-Crime Connections* (Cambridge University Press). His current research includes analysis of an ESRC project database on violent street crime and data collection for a study on prescription drug misuse.

Fiona Brookman is Reader in Criminology and Deputy Director of the Centre for Criminology, University of Glamorgan, which she helped to establish in 2001. She has published principally in the areas of homicide and violence and is author of *Understanding Homicide* (Sage, 2005). She is currently researching and publishing on street violence and undertaking research into difficult to detect and unsolved homicides. Her research on homicide forms part of the Murder Investigation Manual.

Belinda Brooks-Gordon is a Reader in Psychology and Social Policy at Birkbeck, University of London. A chartered psychologist, the particular focus of Belinda's research is sex work with an emphasis on the civil liberties, human rights, safety, health and welfare of those in sex work. Belinda's book *The Price of Sex: Prostitution, Policy and Society* (Willan, 2006) was shortlisted for the British Society of Criminology Book Prize 2007. Belinda is currently working on the effects of state violence on migration; see, for example, 'State Violence Towards Sex Workers', *BMJ* (2008).

Rick Brown is Managing Director of Evidence Led Solutions Limited, a consultancy that specialises in criminal justice and community safety issues. He has written widely on vehicle crime and previously worked on vehicle crime and roads policing research for the Home Office. His current research interests are in policing and organised crime.

Maureen Cain's early interest in policing has broadened over the years into a more general concern with the sociology of law and crime. In Trinidad, where she served as Professor of Sociology from 1987 to 1995, she developed a course in 'Caribbean Criminology'. This subsequently shaped her current concerns with the impact on crime and victimisation of globalisation in general and of global economic policies in particular. Already in her seventies, she is now retired, albeit still writing and supervising graduate students at the University of Birmingham. She was President of the British Society of Criminology from 2002 to 2005.

Claire Corbett is Director of the Criminal Justice Research Group at Brunel University and a Reader in the Brunel Law School, Brunel University. Her research interests largely lie in the field of road crime and traffic law enforcement, and in particular on speeding, speed cameras and public perceptions of these. The enforcement of a wide range of traffic offences is one aspect researched in her book *Car Crime* (Willan, 2003). She has recently been an invited member of various government scientific advisory groups related to road safety improvement.

Hazel Croall is Professor of Criminology at Glasgow Caledonian University where she set up the BA programme in Criminology. She has published widely in the area of white-collar and corporate crime, including the 2001 text *Understanding White Collar Crime*. She is currently researching issues involved in the regulation of corporate crime and preparing the second edition of her text, *Crime and Society*.

Jonathan Evans is a qualified social worker with experience of both practice and management in the probation service. He is currently a senior lecturer in the Centre for Criminology at the University of Glamorgan. His main research interests and publications are in the area of children, young people and youth policy. He is particularly interested in the relationship between welfare and criminal justice systems. Since 2006 he has been a member of the European Network of Experts on Youth Research (Council of Europe and European Commission Partnership). He is the co-editor of a forthcoming book entitled *Youth Employment and the Future of Work* (Strasbourg: CoE Publications).

David P. Farrington, OBE, is Professor of Psychological Criminology at the Institute of Criminology, Cambridge University, and Adjunct Professor of Psychiatry at Western Psychiatric Institute and Clinic, University of Pittsburgh. He is a Chartered Forensic Psychologist and has been President of the American Society of Criminology, President of the European Association of Psychology and Law, President of the British Society of Criminology, President of the Academy of Experimental Criminology and Chair of the Division of Forensic Psychology of the British Psychological Society. His major research interest is in developmental criminology and he is Director of the Cambridge Study in Delinquent Development. He has received the Sellin-Glueck and Sutherland awards of the American Society of Criminology and the prize for distinguished scholarship of the American Sociological Association Criminology Section. In addition to 490 published journal articles and book chapters on criminological and psychological topics, he has published 70 books, monographs and government publications.

Cyrille Fijnaut is Professor of International and Comparative Criminal Law at the Law School of Tilburg University. He is a member of the Global Law School Faculty of the New York University School of Law. His main research interests are related to organised crime and terrorism, international police and judicial cooperation, comparative criminal procedure and police law, the history of European criminology and of policing in Europe, and police and judicial cooperation in the Benelux countries. In these fields he has written and edited some 75 books and published hundreds of articles in learned and professional journals and edited books. In addition he has worked in the last 15 years as an expert for a number of governmental and parliamentary committees of inquiry in Belgium and the Netherlands with regard to organised and professional crime problems and in relation to security issues. Since 2005 he has held a special chair, sponsored by the Dutch State Lottery, on the regulatory aspects of gambling.

Brian Francis is Professor of Social Statistics at Lancaster University and Director of an ESRC National Centre for Research Methods node. He has over 30 years of experience of statistical consultancy and applied statistical research and has focused recently on the analysis of criminal careers and risk factors for serious crime. His publications span statistics, health, sociology and criminology, developing analytic approaches. His research interests include quantitative methods in criminology, latent class methods and analysis of ranked data.

Martin Gill is Director of Perpetuity Research and Consultancy International, a spin-out company from the University of Leicester and a Professor of Criminology. Martin has been actively involved in a range of studies relating to different aspects of business crime and its prevention including why fraudsters steal, staff dismissed for dishonesty, the effectiveness of CCTV, how companies protect their brand image and the generators of illicit markets and stolen goods, to name but a few. He has written and edited 13 books including *The Handbook of Security* (2006). He is a Fellow of the Security Institute, Chair of the ASIS Research Council and co-editor of the *Security Journal*.

Janice Goldstraw-White is an independent criminologist running her own management and research consultancy, Goldstraw-White Associates, working with academic, private and public sector bodies. Janice is also an accountant and as such is interested in the area of white-collar criminology. Her PhD thesis was on the accounts of white-collar criminals including a number of interviews with white-collar crime offenders. She is currently writing a book entitled *White-Collar Crime: Opportunity, Motivation and Morality*, and is also interested in the area of gender and white-collar crime. She is a member of the British Society of Criminology.

Jo Goodey is Head of Department 'Freedoms and Justice' at the European Union Agency for Fundamental Rights in Vienna. She previously worked as a research fellow in the field of trafficking, migration and crime at the United Nations Office on Drugs and Crime, and before this was a university lecturer in criminology and criminal justice at the universities of Sheffield and Leeds. She is the author of *Victims and Victimology: Research, Policy and Practice* and co-editor of *Integrating a Victim Perspective in Criminal Justice*, and has written many journal articles and book chapters on subjects ranging from hate crime to trafficking.

Ruth M. Hatcher is Lecturer in Forensic Psychology at the University of Leicester. Her research interests include interventions with offenders to reduce crime, victimisation within prisons, offender perspectives of the offender management system in England and Wales, and the effect on staff of working with forensic populations. She has published a range of reports and academic publications on these topics.

Victoria Heckels is a Forensic Psychologist and is a Senior Lecturer in Psychology at the University of Teesside. Victoria is accredited as a Behavioural Investigative Advisor (BIA) by the Association of Chief Police Officers (ACPO). In this role she has provided psychological advice on a significant number of major police investigations since 1993. Victoria is currently carrying out research examining stalking behaviour, which focuses on the tactics utilised by stalkers and the effects that various tactics have upon victims. The research also aims to identify various risk factors for violence.

David C. Hicks is Lecturer in Criminology at the Cardiff University School of Social Sciences. He received his PhD from Cardiff for his study 'Thinking About the Prevention of Organised Crime'. His current research focuses on financial crimes and the elaboration of anti-money laundering (AML) regimes. He has published work on financial crimes, serious and organised crimes, crime prevention, and drugs policy. He worked with academic, intelligence, nongovernment and government institutions in Canada prior to joining the staff at Cardiff.

Dick Hobbs is Professor of Sociology at the London School of Economics. His interests focus on ethnographic work, working-class entrepreneurship, the sociology of deviance, professional and organised crime, violence, drug markets, the night-time economy and the sociology of East London. He is currently working on a book looking at the sociology of organised crime in the UK, *Populating the Underworld* (Polity, 2011) He is also working on a four-volume edited collection on ethnography (Sage, 2011) and a collaborative book on the policing and security implications of the 2012 Olympics, *Securing the Olympic Neighbourhood* (Ashgate).

Clive R. Hollin is Professor of Criminological Psychology in the Department of Health Sciences at the University of Leicester. His primary research interest lies in the design and evaluation of initiatives to reduce crime. He wrote the best-selling textbook *Psychology and Crime: An Introduction to Criminological Psychology* (Routledge, 1989). His most recent book, edited with Graham Davies and Ray Bull, is *Forensic Psychology* (John Wiley & Sons, 2008). In all, he has published 21 books alongside 300 other academic publications; he is also co-editor of the journal *Psychology, Crime and Law*.

Katy Holloway is Reader in Criminology at the Centre for Criminology, University of Glamorgan. She has worked mainly in the area of drugs and crime and has recently published two books on the subject: *Understanding Drugs, Alcohol and Crime* (Open University/McGraw-Hill) and *Drug–Crime Connections* (Cambridge University Press). Her current research includes an evaluation of the Take Home Naloxone project for the Welsh Assembly Government and a survey on prescription drug misuse among university staff and students.

Paul Iganski is a Senior Lecturer in Social Justice at Lancaster University, UK. He specialises in research and writing on 'hate crime' and is the co-ordinator of The Hate Crime Research Group – an alliance of academics, activists, policymakers at various levels of governance, practitioners, researchers and students. His books include *Hate Crime and the City* (2008), the edited volumes *Hate Crime: The Consequences of Hate Crime* (2009) and *The Hate Debate* (2002), and *Hate Crimes Against London's Jews* (2005) (with Vicky Kielinger and Susan Paterson).

Martin Innes is Professor and Director of the Universities' Police Science Institute at Cardiff University. He is the author of the books *Investigating Murder* (Oxford University Press, 2003) and *Understanding Social Control* (Open University Press, 2003) as well as a large number of scholarly articles and reports. Innes is also the serving editor of the journal *Policing and Society* published by Routledge. His current research includes empirical and theoretical studies of social reactions to crime and disorder and the police role in counterterrorism.

Michael Levi is Professor of Criminology at Cardiff University School of Social Sciences. His most recent books are the second edition (2008) of *The Phantom Capitalists: The Organisation and Control of Long-Firm Fraud* (Andover: Ashgate), and (with Petrus van Duyne) *Drugs and Money* (2005). He has published widely on fraud, organised crime, and money laundering in the *British Journal of Criminology*, *Crime and Justice*, *Criminology and Criminal Justice* and the *Journal of Financial Crime*. He currently holds a three-year ESRC Professorial Fellowship (RES-051-27-0208), researching fraud networks, public-private partnerships against financial crimes, and the global governance of financial crimes.

Simon Mackenzie is Reader in Criminology at the Scottish Centre for Crime and Justice Research, University of Glasgow. His research interests are in white-collar crime, organised crime, international criminal markets and policing. He is currently working on the prevention of trafficking in cultural heritage (United Nations), threat assessment in organised crime (SCDEA), the drivers of perceptions of anti-social behaviour (Home Office) and community policing (AHRC). He is author of *Going, Going, Gone: Regulating the Market in Illicit Antiquities* (2005) and editor of *Criminology and Archaeology: Studies in Looted Antiquities* (2009).

Mike Maguire is a Professor of Criminology and Criminal Justice, now based part-time at Cardiff University and the University of Glamorgan. He has conducted research on numerous crime and justice related topics, especially burglary, victims, policing, prisons and probation. His main current interests are in the resettlement of prisoners, reducing reoffending and the devolution of crime control. He has over 100 publications to his name, including co-editing (with Rod Morgan and Robert Reiner) *The Oxford Handbook of Criminology* (4th edn, 2007). He also edits a book series for the Open University Press. He is a member of the Correctional Services Accreditation Panel and academic advisor to the Home Office crime reduction team based in the Welsh Assembly Government.

Jennifer Maher is a Lecturer in Criminology at the University of Glamorgan. She was awarded her PhD in 2007 for her study 'Angels with Dirty Faces: Youth Gangs and Troublesome Youth Groups in South Wales'. She has since researched and published on youth gangs, youth violence, weapon use among young people and the link between animal abuse and interpersonal violence. Her current research on 'the use and abuse of animals among youth gangs and groups' links together many of these research interests.

Tiggey May is a Senior Research Fellow at the Institute for Criminal Policy Research, King's College London. To date her research and published work has focused on mapping local drug markets, the policing of cannabis, drug dealing and distribution systems, sex work, the police complaints system and more recently young black and minority people's experience of interventions in the youth justice system. Tiggey is currently examining the differential treatment of ethnic minority young people in the youth justice system.

Tim McSweeney is a Senior Research Fellow at the Institute for Criminal Policy Research based at King's College London. He has ten years' experience of conducting and managing social science research with local, national and international dimensions using both quantitative and qualitative methodologies. His research activities to date have focused on substance misuse, its treatment and the role played by criminal justice interventions in tackling these and related issues. He has served as an advisor on 'coerced' drug treatment options to both the Council of Europe and UN Office on Drugs and Crime. He is a PhD candidate under scholarship with both the Drug Policy Modelling Programme and the University of New South Wales in Sydney, Australia.

John Minkes is a Lecturer in Criminology and Criminal Justice at the Centre for Criminal Justice and Criminology, Swansea University. He was previously a probation officer, a researcher at Cardiff and Bristol universities and a social worker. He has published articles on corporate crime, youth justice and the history of criminal justice and probation and, with Professor Leonard Minkes, edited *Corporate and White-Collar Crime* (Sage, 2008). Current research includes a case study of the *E. coli* outbreak in South Wales and the early history of the Court of Criminal Appeal.

Leonard Minkes is Emeritus Professor of Business Organisation in the University of Birmingham. He has lectured in universities, management centres in industry and other organisations, and has acted as a consultant on business topics and management training in Britain and overseas. He also spent part of his career in the Economic Commission for Europe of the United Nations. From 1974 to 1980, he was a non-executive member of the Midlands Postal Board and from 1975 to 1983 he served on the Council of the Birmingham Chamber of Industry and Commerce. He has published widely in the areas of corporate behaviour and strategic management.

Rod Morgan is Professor Emeritus, University of Bristol, and Visiting Professor at the London School of Economics and the Universities' Police Science Institute, University of Cardiff. He has been HM Chief Inspector of Probation and Chairman of the Youth Justice Board for England and Wales. He has for many years been an expert advisor to Amnesty International and the Council of Europe on custodial conditions and the prevention of torture and is co-author (with Evans) of *Preventing Torture* (OUP, 1998), *Protecting Prisoners* (OUP, 1999) and the Council of Europe's official guide to the European Convention for the Prevention of Torture and Inhuman or Degrading Treatment or Punishment, *Combating Torture in Europe* (Council of Europe, 2001). He often acts as an expert witness in extradition proceedings involving a possible breach of Article 3 of the ECHR.

Emma J. Palmer is Reader in Forensic Psychology at the University of Leicester. Her research interests include the design and evaluation of interventions with offenders, risk/need assessment, and the role of parenting and social cognition in the development of offending. She has published widely on these topics and recently co-edited with Clive Hollin the book *Offending Behaviour Programmes: Development, Applications, and Controversies* (John Wiley & Sons, 2006).

Letizia Paoli is Full Professor of Criminology at the K.U. Leuven Faculty of Law, Belgium. Italian by birth, she served during the 1990s as consultant to the Italian Ministries of the Interior and Justice and several UN bodies and worked for eight years up to 2006 at the Max Planck Institute for Foreign and International Criminal Law in Freiburg, Germany. Since the early 1990s she has published extensively on organised crime, drugs and related control policies, including *Mafia Brotherhoods: Organised Crime, Italian Style* (Oxford University Press, 2003), *Organised Crime in Europe: Concepts, Patterns and Policies in the European Union and Beyond* (edited with Cyrille Fijnaut, Springer, 2004) and, together with Victoria Greenfield and Peter Reuter, *The World Heroin Market: Can the Supply Be Cut?* (Oxford University Press, 2009).

Harriet Pierpoint is a Reader in Criminology and Criminal Justice at the Centre for Criminology at University of Glamorgan in Wales. Her research interests relate to criminal justice processing and vulnerable people in the criminal justice system and alternatives to prosecution and imprisonment, and, more recently, animal abuse. She has undertaken several funded research projects (including research for the Home Office, Ministry of Justice and National Offender Management Service Cymru) and published widely in nationally and internationally recognised journals including *Policing and Society and Criminology and Criminal Justice*. She is the Chair of the British Society of Criminology Wales Branch.

Karl Roberts is a Forensic Psychologist and Associate Professor of Policing at the Australian Graduate School of Policing at Charles Sturt University in Sydney. He has published widely on the topics of stalking and harassment, counterterrorism policing and police interviewing. He is a consultant to various police forces and international governmental bodies on police interviewing, terrorism and stalking and harassment and is actively involved in police training in these areas.

Amanda L. Robinson received her PhD in Interdisciplinary Social Science from Michigan State University. She is currently a Senior Lecturer in Criminology and Criminal Justice at Cardiff University. She has conducted empirical research into the American and British criminal justice systems. She has recently published in *Violence Against Women*, the *Howard Journal* and *Contemporary Justice Review*, and co-edited a special issue of the *International Journal of Applied and Comparative Criminal Justice* entitled 'Responding to Violence Against Women Across the Globe'. She has recently completed research into advocacy services for victims of domestic and sexual violence in the UK and Sexual Assault Referral Centres.

Natasha Semmens is a lecturer and researcher in the Centre for Criminological Research at the University of Sheffield. Her research interests include the fear of crime, crime survey methodology, white-collar crime and identity and personal data. Her publications include a series of articles on plastic card fraud and identity theft. Her recent research has focused on neighbourhood policing and confidence/satisfaction in the police.

Keith Soothill is Emeritus Professor of Social Research and is currently attached to the Centre for Applied Statistics, Lancaster University. His recent co-edited books *Questioning Crime and Criminology* and *Handbook of Forensic Mental Health* and the co-authored book *Understanding Criminal Careers* (all Willan) span the areas of crime and health. His current research interests are in the areas of criminal careers, sex offending, serious offending and white-collar offenders.

Toine Spapens is a senior research fellow at the Department of Criminal Law at Tilburg University. He previously worked at an institute for policy research in the Netherlands. He specialises in empirical research on organised crime and transnational law enforcement cooperation and is also involved in the research programme 'Regulation of Gambling in Europe' at Tilburg University, focusing on the relationship between gambling and (organised) crime. His current research relates to trafficking in illicit firearms, the role of organised crime groups in cannabis cultivation in the Netherlands, and police and judicial cooperation, particularly in European border regions. Spapens wrote his PhD thesis on the interaction between organised crime and law enforcement, based on the case of ecstasy-production and trafficking in the Netherlands.

Mike Sutton is Reader in Criminology and Founding Director of Nottingham Centre for the Study and Reduction of Hate Crimes, Bias and Prejudice at Nottingham Trent University. He is General Editor of the *Internet Journal of Criminology*. Mike is the originator of the Market Reduction Approach, which seeks to reduce theft by tackling stolen goods markets. Among his most recent work on this subject is a Problem Oriented Policing (USA National Institute of Justice) guide for police, *Tackling Stolen Goods Markets* (http://www.cops.usdoj.gov/RIC/ResourceList.aspx?lt=Series&SID=1&srt=Title&pn=1) which has passed peer review and is in press and expected to be published online in November 2009. He has recently completed several journal articles on the Far Right and on hate crimes against those in interracial relationships. Mike has recently completed a Report for the UK Department of Government and Local Communities, *Getting the Message Across: Using Media to Reduce 'Racial' Prejudice* (http://www.communities.gov.uk/documents/communities/pdf/611667.pdf).

Nick Tilley is visiting professor in the Department of Security and Crime Science at University College London. He is interested in theoretically informed applied social science, especially as this relates to the prevention of crime and disorder. He has published a dozen books and more than 150 reports, chapters and journal articles, mostly relating to policing, crime reduction and programme evaluation methodology. His most recent books include *Crime Prevention* (Willan, 2009) and *Evaluating Crime Reduction Initiatives* (edited with Johannes Knutsson, Willan, 2009).

Steve Tombs is Professor of Sociology at Liverpool John Moores University. Recent publications include *A Crisis of Enforcement: The Decriminalisation of*

Death and Injury at Work (Centre for Crime and Justice Studies, 2008) and *Safety Crimes* (Willan, 2007), both co-authored with Dave Whyte. He is editor, with Roy Coleman, Joe Sim and Dave Whyte, of *State, Power, Crime* (Sage, 2009). He has a long-standing interest in the incidence, nature and regulation of corporate crime, and in particular the regulation and management and health and safety at work.

Maria M. Ttofi is the Leverhulme Early Career Fellow at the Institute of Criminology, Cambridge University. She completed her MPhil in Criminological Research and her PhD at the Institute of Criminology, under the supervision of Professor D. P. Farrington. She also holds two Bachelors degrees in Educational Sciences and Sociology. Her PhD research focused on the effectiveness of anti-bullying programmes (based on a systematic and meta-analytic review that was completed for the Swedish National Council for Crime Prevention) and on the empirical testing of theories of teacher victimisation, school bullying and aggressive behaviour in general. She has had papers published in *Aggressive Behavior, Journal of Aggression, Conflict and Peace Research, Victims and Offenders* and *Crime and Justice*. Maria's main interests are in systematic/meta-analytic reviews, experimental research, bullying and delinquency.

Paul J. Turnbull is Co-Director of the Institute for Criminal Policy Research at King's College London. He has 20 years' experience of researching issues relating to drugs and criminal policy for a range of government departments and non-governmental organisations. He led the teams evaluating the pilot Drug Treatment and Testing Orders and London Arrest Referral Schemes. He heads a team conducting a number of research projects on criminal policy in the UK and Europe. He is currently undertaking a national study assessing the relative effectiveness of the different types of institutions that form the secure estate for juvenile offenders. He is also conducting work on the impact of the changes in the classification of cannabis on policing and of drug treatment on drug supply in prisons. He has written many articles and reports on interventions based within the criminal justice system for drug-using offenders

P.A.J. Waddington is Professor of Social Policy at the University of Wolverhampton. He has published widely on policing issues, especially public order policing and the police use of force and firearms. He was a founder member of a 13-country consortium on public use of force, and co-editor (with Chris Birkbeck) of a special issue of *Crime, Law and Social Change* and lead author of an article therein reporting research on how officers in six countries normatively assess the police use of force. He is currently a member of the Independent Expert Panel advising Her Majesty's Chief Inspector of Constabulary in his report on the policing of the G20 protests. His current research is on public perceptions of police behaviour in routine encounters.

Reece Walters is Professor of Criminology at the Open University. He has published widely on the politics and governance of criminological knowledge, including *Deviant Knowledge – Criminology, Politics and Policy* (2003) and *Critical Thinking About the Uses of Research* (with Tim Hope, 2008). His research focuses on crimes of the powerful, notably the ways in which corporate and government officials abuse their authority for personal or political gain. His more recent work, including *Crime is in the Air – Air Pollution Regulations in the UK* (2009) and *Eco Crime and GM Food* (2010), seeks to push existing criminological horizons to include notions of environmental harm and justice. In doing so, his research examines the political economy of water, air and food and how these essential ingredients for human and non-human life are constantly threatened and exploited by the harmful acts of governments and corporations.

Nicola Weston is a Researcher at the Universities' Police Science Institute at Cardiff University where her current research interests include theoretical understanding of human behaviour and cognition and the application to police practice. She has authored and co-authored a number of scholarly articles in international psychology related journals covering areas such as decision-making, human memory and perception. Her recent work investigates how understandings of human behaviour contribute to the role of the police in counterterrorism, crime and disorder and investigation.

John Williams is Professor of Law and head of the Department of Law and Criminology at Aberystywth University. He has published widely on the law relating to older people and vulnerable adults with particular reference to the criminal justice system. He has presented papers at international conferences in America, Kenya, Canada, Australia, China and Malaysia. Currently he is researching the impact of imprisonment on older people in the United Kingdom and America and the extent to which prison systems fail to address their needs and their human rights.

Katherine S. Williams is a Senior Lecturer in Criminology in the Department of Law and Criminology, Aberystwyth University. She is well known for her *Textbook on Criminology*, published by Oxford University Press (now in its sixth edition). She is also the author of reports and numerous papers in high-quality legal and social science academic journals. Much of her work has focused on the protection of rights against breach, especially by the state. She acted as expert adviser to the Council of Europe in the preparation of the Cybercrime Convention. Her recent research and publications have concerned the control of child pornography and her current research is exploring the effectiveness of antisocial behaviour and looking at the effects of domestic violence on young people.

Matthew Williams is a senior lecturer at the Cardiff School of Social Sciences and was the independent academic advisor on E-crime to the Welsh Assembly Government. He has published and conducted research in the areas of cybercrime, online and digital research methodologies and sexuality, policing and criminal justice. He is co-editor of *Criminology and Criminal Justice* and is on the editorial board for *Sociological Research Online* and the *Internet Journal* *of Criminology*. He was also on the board of directors for the Association of Internet Researchers (AoIR). Publications include *Virtually Criminal: Crime, Deviance and Regulation Online* (Routledge, 2006), 'Policing and Cybersociety: The Maturation of Regulation in an Online Community', *Policing and Society* (2006) and 'Policing Diversity in the Digital Age: Maintaining Order in Virtual Communities', *Criminology and Criminal Justice*. Recent research includes 'E-crime Rapid Evidence Assessment' (Welsh Assembly Government), 'Ethnography for the Digital Age' (ESRC) and 'Methodological Issues for Qualitative Data Sharing and Archiving' (ESRC).

Simon Winlow is Senior Lecturer in the Department of Sociology at the University of York. He is the author of *Badfellas: Crime, Tradition and New Masculinities* (Berg, 2001) and co-author of *Bouncers: Violence and Governance in the Night-time Economy* (Oxford University Press, 2003), *Violent Night: Urban Leisure and Contemporary Culture* (Berg, 2006) and *Criminal Identities and Consumer Culture: Crime, Exclusion and the New Culture of Narcissism* (Willan, 2008).

Richard Wright is Curators' Professor of Criminology and Criminal Justice at the University of Missouri-St Louis and Editor-in-Chief of the *British Journal of Sociology*. He has been studying active urban street criminals, including residential burglars, armed robbers, carjackers and drug dealers, for over two decades. His research has been funded by the US National Institute of Justice, the Harry Frank Guggenheim Foundation, the Icelandic Research Council, the US National Consortium on Violence Research, the US National Science Foundation and the Irish Research Council for the Humanities and Social Sciences. His most recent book, co-authored with Bruce Jacobs, is *Street Justice: Retaliation in the Criminal Underworld* (Cambridge University Press, 2006).

Introduction

Fiona Brookman, Mike Maguire,
Harriet Pierpoint and Trevor Bennett

Criminologists publish surprisingly little about specific forms of criminal activity: when, how, by whom and in what contexts they are carried out, whether and why they are increasing or declining, what particular issues they raise for the police or criminal justice agencies, and so on. Despite a major expansion in criminology in universities since the mid-1990s, the empirical research base remains quite thin in relation even to some of the most common crimes, including those which attract regular media and political attention. Moreover – albeit for very good reasons – general texts in the subject tend to be organised around broad social, cultural or psychological explanations of 'crime' or 'criminality', and/or around social and criminal justice responses to offences and offenders. This often means that what may be markedly different types of behaviour in markedly different contexts are conflated and discussed only under catch-all categories such as 'violence' or 'sex offending'. In addition, little may be said about what might be called 'emerging' crime problems: for example, new illegal ways of taking advantage of developments in technology, or types of criminal behaviour which appear to be growing in frequency or seriousness. Examples include various forms of Internet fraud, identity theft and, of course, global terrorism.

It was discussions along these lines that initially sparked the idea for this book. In essence, we and our contributors have adopted the highly unusual strategy of, in each chapter, *using a specific type of crime as the starting point for discussion and analysis*. Of course, there are significant risks and challenges attached to such an approach. Most obviously, there is a danger of failing to go beyond the purely descriptive and hence producing no more than a catalogue of 'facts' about each offence type. Conversely, if this problem is avoided by engaging in every chapter in etiological debates, there is a risk of excessive repetition: many offenders commit a range of different offences, doubtless often for similar underlying reasons. In addition, there are difficult judgments to be made about how to define, divide up and select the 'types of crime' to be covered: for example, to what extent they should be categorised according to legal or social categories (e.g. 'robbery' or 'mugging'), victim characteristics or environmental context (e.g. 'elder abuse' or 'crime in closed institutions') or the status of offenders (e.g. 'state' or 'corporate' crime, as opposed to crime by individuals). This raises further questions about how far to include actions at the blurred borderlines between 'crime', 'breaches of regulations' and 'accidents', in some of which those responsible may be protected from criminalisation by powerful political or financial interests (train crashes, deaths at work, environmental pollution, and so on).

While such issues have caused difficulties, these were much less severe than we first feared. Most authors have been comfortable with a broad template which allows them to present a balance of (a) historical and definitional issues relating to the type of crime concerned; (b) statistical and other descriptive information about its nature, extent and trends; (c) theoretical debates around its etiology; (d) social and criminal justice responses and (e) any recent academic, political or policy debates which have been particularly relevant to this type of crime. In order to minimise repetition in sections on etiology, we have generally encouraged authors to focus more on 'proximal' factors which may help to explain specific patterns of offending behaviour than on 'distal' factors which may be more appropriate to explanations of why individuals become involved in crime at all. This is, however, more appropriate for some types of offending than others and there are several exceptions.

As far as the categorisation of crime types is concerned, we have not adopted a rigid framework, and chapter headings range from legal to popular classifications of crime. Generally speaking, we have favoured more 'socially contextualised' terms which highlight the location or environment in which offences occur (e.g. shoplifting, cybercrime, violence in the night-time economy) and/or the type of victim or the nature of the offender–victim relationship involved (e.g. sexual offences against children, hate crime, animal abuse, theft and fraud by employees).

Inevitably, even in a book with 45 chapters, there are some glaring gaps. For example, there is no chapter on one of the most common recorded offences of all, 'criminal damage'. However, comprehensiveness – especially where standard police recorded offences are concerned – was never our priority. Rather, we set out to illustrate as wide as possible a range of broad categories of criminal (and potentially criminal) behaviour, including those which receive relatively little attention from criminologists or indeed the criminal justice system. This is reflected in the structure of the book, which is divided into eight parts. It begins in Part I with what we refer to as 'conventional' crimes against property – including the major 'volume' crimes of theft of and from vehicles, domestic burglary and shoplifting. Parts II–IV cover other groups of offences with headings that are similar to those used in the official criminal statistics in England and Wales: fraud and fakes, violent crime and sex-related crime. However, they cover a much wider variety of individual forms of criminal behaviour types than are reflected in the legally based categories used in the official figures. For example, the fraud and fakes part includes chapters on 'cybercrime', 'scams', and 'tax and benefit fraud', none of which are prominent among recorded offences (the first two often go unreported and the latter is usually dealt with by agencies other than the police). The violent crime part includes behaviour as diverse as gang violence, stalking, animal abuse, school bullying and abuse in children's homes.

Part V covers drug-related (including some forms of alcohol-related) crime, with chapters on trafficking and dealing in drugs, as well as one on crimes committed either under the influence of substance abuse or in order to support a drugs habit. It should also be noted that the issue of alcohol-fuelled violence in the 'night time economy' is discussed in depth by Simon Winlow in Part III.

In the final three parts the focus shifts from crimes committed by individuals to those committed by organised groups or institutions. There is also a much stronger international dimension than in most of the earlier chapters. Part VI covers various forms of organised and business crime, including human trafficking, money laundering and extortion. Part VII focuses on major crimes committed either by or against the state, including global terrorism, torture, genocide and ethnic cleansing. Finally, Part VIII examines examples of both corporate and individual behaviour regarded by many as criminal but often dealt with via various forms of regulatory law (such as health and safety legislation), namely 'eco-crime', corporate violence and some kinds of driving offences.

Part I

'Conventional' Property Crime

This opening part of the book covers what we describe as 'conventional' forms of property crime: in essence, 'volume' offences which are prominent in official crime statistics and the investigation of which forms part of 'bread-and-butter' police work. Less frequently reported or researched forms of crime involving property, including 'scams', corporate and business crime, and state corruption, are covered in later sections. The use of the term 'conventional' also reflects the fact that the crime categories included in this part are closer to official and legal classifications than is the case with many of the other types of criminal behaviour discussed later.

The first three chapters deal with crimes against specific types of property: Maguire, Wright and Bennett focus on domestic burglary, Brown on vehicle crime, and Tilley on shoplifting. The fourth chapter by Sutton reviews what is known about a wide range of activities that are officially classified under the heading of 'handling stolen goods'.

In combination, these four chapters provide many insights into modern forms of property crime. Maguire, Wright and Bennett reconsider, three decades after their original work on this topic, the current state of knowledge and thinking about domestic burglary. Since their research in the early 1980s, domestic burglary rates in England and Wales have more than doubled and then more than halved, and are now back roughly to where they started. Over that time, the nature of burglary has changed considerably, with new forms of the offence emerging, such as the growth in distraction burglaries (entry by trickery), car key burglaries (with the objective of car theft) and new forms of items being stolen (such as mobile phones). Moreover, the extent to which drug addiction acts as a motivating factor for burglary appears to have increased significantly. Extensive changes over time are also identified by Brown in his study of vehicle crime. Like burglary, car-related crime has seen a significant increase followed by a similar decrease. At the same time, there now exist more sophisticated methods of exporting vehicles and vehicle parts into Europe and beyond, while methods of enacting the theft have changed in response to changes in security technology.

By contrast, Tilley provides a trend curve for shoplifting which shows a gradual and sustained increase over time. However, he warns that official data are not good measures of shoplifting. The research evidence is also limited in that there is a strong correlation between the types of customers and types of shoplifters, both of which might change over time in response to changes in shops and shopping habits. Sutton has an equally difficult task in uncovering the characteristics of hidden markets in stolen goods. The kinds of goods traded reflect closely the types of goods that are fashionable and in demand.

The most striking theme that emerges from this collection of papers is that property crime is in itself innovative and changes in nature and form in response to broader social and cultural changes. It would appear that some of the most 'conventional' crimes that we might expect to know well from the past have in fact changed dramatically over the last two or three decades and may well continue to do so in the future.

Chapter 1

Domestic burglary

Mike Maguire, Richard Wright and
Trevor Bennett

Background and definitions

'Burglary' in its modern guise in England and Wales is an offence defined under section 9 of the Theft Act 1968, which brought together under one umbrella the ancient offence of burglary (which referred only to forced entry into a dwelling by night with intent to commit a felony) with a variety of other offences which had accumulated over time, including house-breaking (which included entry in daylight), breaking into other kinds of building (shop-breaking, factory-breaking and so on) and non-forced entry into all kinds of building with intent to commit any of a number of named crimes. A person is now guilty of burglary under the above-mentioned Act if:

(1) (a) he enters any building or part of a building as a trespasser and with intent to commit any such offence as is mentioned in subsection (2) below; or (b) having entered any building or part of a building as a trespasser he steals or attempts to steal anything in the building or that part of it or inflicts or attempts to inflict on any person therein any grievous bodily harm

(2) The offences referred to in subsection 1(a) above are offences of stealing anything in the building or part of a building in question, of inflicting on any person therein any grievous bodily harm or raping any woman therein, and of doing unlawful damage to the building or anything therein.

In addition, a person is guilty of 'aggravated burglary' if he or she 'commits any burglary and at the time has with him any firearm or imitation firearm, any weapon of offence, or any explosive'.

'Burglary in a dwelling' (also referred to as domestic burglary or residential burglary) is hence not a separate offence in law, although it is a Home Office classification used in the official recording and counting of criminal offences.

Burglary – and particularly residential burglary – has always been treated very seriously by legislators and the courts. Night-time forced entry into houses carried the death penalty until the early nineteenth century, and the current maximum penalty for burglary is 14 years, rising to life for aggravated burglary. There is also a minimum sentence of three years for a third burglary (unless there are exceptional circumstances) under the 'three strikes and you're out' rule of the Crime (Sentences) Act 1997. As Chappell (1965: 3–9) argues, the origins of the severe penalties attached to burglary lie in the fact that it was attacks upon the security of a building or settlement – and hence of its occupants – rather than theft of the contents that the law was principally designed to punish. One of the earliest known definitions, recorded by Britton in about 1300, referred not only to housebreaking but also to the breaking of the walls or gates of cities. The emotional impact on victims of modern-day residential burglary can reflect similar anxieties about security, victims reporting fear, a sense of violation and no longer feeling safe in their own home; it is this, rather than the scale of financial loss, that motivates judges to continue to pass relatively heavy sentences on burglars.

This chapter presents a broad descriptive and (to a limited extent) explanatory overview of the offence and its perpetrators and victims, drawing on published statistics and a range of academic and government literature. It begins with a summary of trends in burglary rates over the past thirty or so years, together with an outline of common characteristics of the offence and the kinds of household most at risk. This is followed by a discussion of research findings on burglars' perceptions of what they do and why, addressing questions about their general motives as well as their decision-making behaviour in specific circumstances. The chapter ends with a consideration of responses to burglary by various key actors: victims, police and other agencies concerned with crime prevention, and sentencers. The main focus is on domestic burglary in England and Wales, but evidence from the United States and elsewhere is also included.

Patterns and trends

In 2008/9 there were over 280,000 recorded offences of burglary in a dwelling in England and Wales (Walker *et al.* 2009). This represents 48 per cent of all burglaries (including commercial burglaries), 8 per cent of all property crimes, and 6 per cent of all recorded crimes. Domestic burglary ranked fifth in numbers of crimes recorded behind 'other theft offences' (approximately 1.1 million), criminal damage (940,000), vehicle crime (600,000) and burglary in a building other than a dwelling (300,000).

The long-term annual trends in police recorded 'burglary dwelling' show a gradual increase over the 1980s and a particularly steep rise in the early 1990s, but then a lengthy and sustained decrease from the peak in 1993 until 2007/8 (see Figure 1.1). This trend is largely mirrored in British Crime Survey (BCS) findings on reported domestic burglaries, which also show a peak in the mid-1990s, followed by a marked decline until the mid-2000s. Indeed, according to the BCS, the numbers of such offences have more than halved since 1995. Large

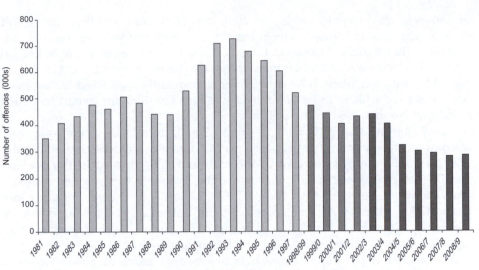

Figure 1.1 Trends in police recorded domestic burglary, 1981 to 2008/9
Source: Walker *et al.* (2009).

falls have also been observed in several other western countries (Bernasco, 2009). However, there is some current concern in England and Wales that this trend may have come to an end. The Home Office Statistical Bulletin for 2008/9 showed that there had been an increase of 1 per cent in police recorded residential burglaries from the previous year, which represented the first annual increase in the offence since the introduction of the National Crime Recording Standard in 2002.[1] BCS figures also rose marginally over the same period, as they had done in 2007/8. The media has seized upon such figures as evidence for the idea that property crimes, such as residential burglary, are likely to increase during a recession (Field 1990, 1999). However, the increase in both cases is modest, and whether it really marks a break in the long-term declining trend and the beginning of a recession-fuelled rise will not be known until further evidence becomes available.

Some significant variations in domestic burglary are apparent across different areas. As with many other types of volume crime, higher rates tend to be found in major cities than elsewhere. BCS figures for 2007/8 show that the rate of burglaries per household in London was 411 offences per 10,000 households, while in Wales it was only 226. At the same time, they indicate that, over the past few years, domestic burglaries have declined more rapidly in deprived areas than in more wealthy areas. For example, over the period 2001/2 to 2007/8, there was a reduction of 38 per cent in the 20 per cent most deprived areas, compared with one of only 9 per cent in the 20 per cent least deprived areas (Kershaw *et al.* 2008).

Characteristics of the offence

The regular Home Office statistical publications give few details about offences of domestic burglary. However, in 2007 a special Home Office analysis of BCS results was published which went some way towards addressing this omission (Kent 2007). In this section, we briefly summarise what is known from this document and elsewhere about the times at which burglaries are most likely to take place, how entry is most frequently made and the types of household most likely to be victimised. We also consider the extent to which burglaries are reported to the police.

According to the 2005/6 BCS (Kent 2007), burglaries were relatively uncommon in the mornings (8 per cent) but fairly evenly distributed during the rest of the day (24 per cent in the afternoon, 25 per cent in the evening and 25 per cent overnight). The front of the property was a more common entry point (48 per cent) than the back (40 per cent) or the side (9 per cent). Doors (70 per cent) were also more common entry points than windows (28 per cent). Although the majority of entries were forced, over a quarter of all reported cases involved entry through an unlocked door.

The 2007/8 BCS further shows that the median value of goods stolen in domestic burglaries was £360. The most common group of items stolen was 'purse/wallet/money etc.' (51 per cent of all reported burglaries in which entry was achieved), followed by 'jewellery' (29 per cent) and 'electrical goods/cameras' (24 per cent). Mobile phones have also become a target in a significant proportion of burglaries, rising from about one per cent in 1993 to almost 20 per cent in 2003/4, although since then falling back to around 15 per cent. By contrast, there has been a major reduction in a type of burglary that was common twenty or thirty years ago: cases involving theft of the cash contents of gas or electricity pre-payment meters. This phenomenon, which was often regarded cynically by police officers as 'do-it-yourself' crime by members of the household (Maguire and Bennett 1982), has virtually disappeared with the introduction of token systems and other non-cash payment methods.

Finally, apparent increases in two specific types of burglary have caused concern in recent years. One is 'distraction burglary', particularly when committed against older people. This is defined as gaining entry by 'a falsehood, trick or distraction' (Home Office 2003), and often involves offenders posing as officials to 'talk their way' into the house or to distract the victim's attention in order to steal (Thornton *et al.* 2003). Estimates based on samples of police reports suggest that in 2003/4 distraction burglary accounted for 4 per cent of all recorded burglaries in England and Wales (Ruparel 2004). This is similar to a finding from the 2005/6 BCS that 5 per cent of burglaries involved entry by 'false pretences'. The other phenomenon causing concern is 'car key' burglary, where the offender enters the house in order to steal the victim's keys and drive off in their car. Recent police figures indicate that the numbers of such cases are rising, and in 2008/9 occurred in 7 per cent of domestic burglaries (Walker *et al.* 2009).

Victims and repeat victimisation

According to the BCS, the annual risk of an average household in England and Wales being a victim of burglary has been fairly stable over the last few years at around 2.5 per cent (Walker *et al.* 2009). However, this risk varies considerably with the type of area, characteristics of the occupants and levels of household security.

As with most crime, those living in urban areas are more likely to be victimised (2.8 per cent) than rural dwellers (1.1 per cent), while those living in areas which they perceive as having high levels of 'social disorder' are more often burgled (5.4 per cent) than those where disorder is perceived to be low (2.2 per cent). In terms of demographics, the most significant variables are age and level of income. For example, in 2008/9, households in which the person responsible for the accommodation was aged between 16 and 24 had an annual burglary rate of 7.2 per cent, compared with just over one per cent for those aged 65 or over. Social renters (4.2 per cent) were more likely to be burgled than owner-occupiers (1.7 per cent), while particularly high rates were found among households comprising a single adult with one or more children (6.8 per cent), and those where the person responsible for the accommodation was a student (6.4 per cent) or unemployed (5.7 per cent). Ironically, too, Flatley *et al.* (2009) found that occupants who had no household insurance were significantly more likely to be burgled than those who had. In broad terms, then, the young and the less well-off are more vulnerable than the older and the wealthier.

The 2008/9 BCS further found that 15 per cent of all victims of domestic burglary were 'repeat' victims, in the sense that they reported two or more burglaries in the same 12-month survey period (Walker *et al.* 2009). This proportion has remained fairly stable over time, with no more than a 4 percentage point variation over the last quarter of a century. Understanding of this issue expanded considerably during the 1980s and 1990s, particularly as a result of work conducted by Ken Pease and others for the Home Office. During this time, several important findings emerged about the nature of repeat victimisation in general and domestic burglary in particular. In a re-analysis of the results of the 1992 British Crime Survey, it was found that 4 per cent of all respondents accounted for 44 per cent of all crime incidents reported (Farrell and Pease 1993). The same authors also used data from Canada and elsewhere to show that, in the period immediately after a burglary, the chance of being victimised increased substantially. They calculated that the probability of being burgled in the month following a burglary was over twelve times the normal rate, and that half of the offences occurring in the first month did so within seven days of the initial crime. Furthermore, the probability of being burgled remained higher than average for at least six months after a burglary, during which time it gradually reduced back to slightly under twice the normal rate. This and other findings helped to change the course of crime prevention theory and practice for several years to come, reinforcing an increasing interest in 'hot spot' analysis and in targeted policing and prevention initiatives, including the prioritisation of responses to calls from recent victims (see, for example, Anderson *et al.* 1995; Pease 1998: Laycock 2001).

Reporting to the police

Burglary is a crime that is usually reported to the police. The findings of the 2005/6 BCS showed that about 65 per cent of all residential burglaries known to victims were reported to the police. This figure was even higher for burglaries with loss (81 per cent were reported) compared with burglaries with no loss (53 per cent). The high reporting rate – considerably above that for theft – may be linked to the need to make a police report in order to claim insurance, but is also likely to reflect a general public view of burglary as a serious offence.

Characteristics of offenders and explanations of the crime

What kinds of people break into others' houses and why? Clearly, there is no simple answer: as with any other type of crime, offenders vary in age, background, motivation, persistence, skills and levels of organisation. However, a number of strong patterns are evident.

First of all, the available evidence suggests that residential burglars in the UK and the US – and indeed, as far as can be ascertained, in every country in the world – are disproportionately young, male and poor. Kent's (2007) analysis of the 2005/6 BCS shows that victims were able to describe the offender's characteristics in 43 per cent of domestic burglaries;[2] in 83 per cent of such cases, the suspect or suspects were male and in nearly two-thirds they were thought to be under 25 years old. Among sentenced burglars, too, young males are prominent: in 2007, over 95 per cent of all those sentenced for burglary (of any kind) in England and Wales were male and 43 per cent were under the age of 21 (Ministry of Justice 2008).[3] Where social class is concerned, few relevant official statistics are produced, but academic studies of burglars based on prison interviews or ethnographic fieldwork in the community (some of which have used 'snowball' techniques to find subjects rather than relying on samples of those known to the authorities) strongly suggest that the great majority are from lower-class backgrounds (see, for example, Maguire and Bennett 1982; Shover 1991; Wright and Decker 1994; Cromwell and Olson 2004).

Secondly, people convicted of domestic burglary tend to have high reoffending rates, including a high likelihood of committing more burglaries. Hence, while it is acknowledged that a significant minority of burglaries are committed by 'one-off' or 'occasional' offenders, including children experimenting with crime by breaking into houses within their immediate neighbourhood, the 'burglary problem' is associated first and foremost with people (many of them still quite young) who have developed a pattern of frequent, and in some cases prolific, offending. It is on this group – some of whom are considerably more skilled, selective or 'professional' than others – that the primary focus will be placed in this section.

Thirdly, for many, burglary is not the only type of crime they commit, nor is it necessarily one that they continue to commit throughout their whole offending career. Many recidivist adult offenders describe house burglary as a 'phase' they went through in their younger days, before discovering what they claim to be more lucrative and less risky ways of illegally making money. Even those who continue to burgle houses over many years tend to do so as part of a broader 'repertoire' of offending behaviour. For example, among a sample of 40 prisoners interviewed by Maguire and Bennett (1982) who had been convicted of residential burglary and were known to staff or other prisoners (or self-described) as 'burglars', all but five had recently committed other kinds of offence: the authors concluded that a more accurate label would be 'thieves whose main line is burglary' (for other evidence on criminal versatility and specialisation, see for example Blumstein *et al.* 1986; Wolfgang *et al.* 1987).

As to why people commit burglary (and especially those who do so persistently), there is no reason to believe that the *distal* causes differ significantly from those put forward by generations of criminologists to explain the roots of offending behaviour in general: social deprivation, individual pathology, poor parenting, the influence of subcultures and so on. However, while such factors are clearly important in shaping the interactional contexts in which burglary is contemplated or enacted, broad explanations of this kind offer little insight either into how offenders perceive and reflect upon their own behaviour, nor into the *proximal* causes of specific acts of offending – i.e. the processes that motivate and sustain individuals' decisions to commit a residential burglary in the run-up to and during the offending moment. In order to gain a better understanding of these issues, several researchers have conducted in-depth interviews with incarcerated or currently active offenders (see, among others, Walsh 1980; Maguire and Bennett 1982; Bennett and Wright 1984; Wright and Logie 1988; Nee and Taylor 1988; Shover 1972, 1991; Cromwell *et al.* 1991; Wright and Decker 1994; Hearnden and Magill 2004).

'Occupation', 'survival' or 'partying'?

In most of the above studies, the factor most often identified by offenders as underpinning their involvement in burglary is a need or desire for money: claims that they burgle 'for the thrill' are much less common and restricted mainly to young offenders. In other words, although victims of burglary often experience the intrusion into their home as much more threatening and disturbing than a plain act of theft (see later), to most offenders breaking into a house is simply one among a number of illegal options for financial gain. However, there are considerable variations in the circumstances in which they use this 'option' and in the nature, scale and urgency of the financial needs they seek to meet, ranging from those who treat burglary to some degree as an 'occupation' providing a fairly regular source of income to those who offend mainly when they experience an urgent need for cash – for example, to feed a drug habit or simply to eat. This, of course, also has implications for how they choose targets, and hence for crime prevention strategies.

During the 1970s and early 1980s, much of the focus of criminologists who researched burglars (or offenders who committed burglary among a range of property offences) was on interviewees' own accounts of how they perceived and organised their criminal activities. A common finding was that many saw them as a form of 'work' and regarded themselves to some extent as 'professionals' – though in many cases this involved a highly inflated image of their actual behaviour and skills. This focus is clearly reflected in the titles of Letkemann's (1973) book, *Crime as Work* and Shover's (1971) PhD thesis, 'Burglary as an Occupation'. Other comparable studies were conducted in the United States (e.g. Irwin 1970; Reppetto 1974), Canada (Waller and Okihiro 1978) and the UK (Walsh 1980; Maguire and Bennett 1982; Bennett and Wright 1984).

As an example, Maguire and Bennett's (1982) study of burglary in medium-sized English towns found that a substantial proportion of residential burglaries were committed by what they called 'medium range' (as opposed to 'low' or 'high' level[4]) offenders local to the town. These were persistent offenders, many of whom knew each other and in some cases offended together, who tended to identify themselves – and to be known by the police – as 'thieves' or 'burglars' attempting to make much of their living through crime. Many had in their minds an image of a successful criminal 'career', involving careful selections of targets, lucrative hauls of stolen goods, and avoidance of arrest. However, the reality was that they often committed burglaries without much planning, gleaned relatively little reward per offence, and ended up in prison on a frequent basis. (Maguire and Webster, in an earlier unpublished paper, used a phrase from a Snoopy cartoon to encapsulate this gap between image and reality: 'Why can't you guys get organised like that?') The problem from their point of view was not that they were likely to be 'caught in the act' – many, in fact, were technically quite skilled – but that they often lacked the social skills and organisation to keep their activities from the notice of the police. They rarely made substantial amounts of money from individual burglaries ('fences' buying stolen goods at very low prices), leading them to commit high numbers of offences and thereby to increase their chances of being identified and convicted. They were also vulnerable to informers (often fellow burglars, as well as receivers), and as they tended to spend a considerable amount of time drinking in public with other known offenders, the police had a good picture of their networks of associates.

Later studies began to move away from the model of burglary as an 'occupation'. For example, Wright and Decker (1994) found that the majority of offenders they interviewed (a 'snowball' sample outside prison containing a mixture of adjudicated and unadjudicated burglars) described their offending more as a response to immediate needs. Most claimed not to have been seeking money for its own sake or to achieve some sort of long-term goal, but rather as a solution to a pressing problem. As they saw it, burglary was a means of 'survival'. In some cases, this was meant literally, the offenders claiming to use the proceeds of crime to meet daily subsistence needs. An active residential burglar interviewed by Wright and Decker (1994: 37) put it this way: 'I'm poor and I'm raggedy and I need some food and I need some shoes … So I got to have some money some kind of way. If it's got to be the wrong way, then so be it.'

However, the authors note that whereas offenders may phrase their reasons for burgling in terms of 'survival', when questioned closely about how they actually use the money from their crimes, many if not most persistent burglars admit that much of it is spent on various sorts of so-called 'party pursuits' such as heavy drinking and drug-taking. The decision to commit a break-in often emerges during an intense round of partying with the explicit aim of sustaining it. A prisoner interviewed by Bennett and Wright (1984: 32), for example, reported that the burglary that led to his arrest came about because 'We were slowly running out of drugs and this guy mentioned getting some money to get some more.' Lemert (1953: 304) refers to self-perpetuating activities such as this as 'dialectical self-enclosed systems of behavior' with an internal logic or 'false structure' that calls for more of the same. Once caught up in such a cycle, Lemert maintains, participants experience considerable psychic pressure to keep it going, even if doing so necessitates risking imprisonment.

In the United States in particular, this hedonistic lifestyle is emblematic of the values of urban street culture, a culture that lionises the open-ended pursuit of illicit action, to which many burglars have become strongly committed (see Katz 1988). Seen from that perspective, the offenders' often heard claim that they commit their burglaries to survive does not seem quite so far-fetched. Most of them see their fate as inextricably bound up with the imperatives of street culture and therefore are prepared to 'keep the party going' by any means necessary, including burglary (Wright and Decker 1994: 38–42).

Of course, the use of the term 'partying' in this context should not be taken to mean that those involved lead a continually happy and carefree existence. First, despite the generally low clear-up rates for burglary, anyone who commits large numbers of offences has a high risk of making a mistake at some point, so persistent burglars tend to get caught frequently and to serve a fair number of prison sentences. Secondly, frequent substance abuse is likely to lead to addiction, and offenders may find themselves increasingly driven to steal – sometimes in a state of desperation that leads them to take excessive risks – in order to feed a habit that they cannot control. Indeed, based on fieldwork in the United States in the late 1980s, Cromwell *et al.* (1991) argued that drug addiction had become the most important factor behind burglary, and this theme has been prominent in subsequent literature. For example, Hearnden and Magill (2004) found that 'money for drugs' was the main reason given by offenders for committing burglaries (see also Bennett 1999; Bennett and Sibbitt 2000; Rengert and Wasilchick 2000; Bernasco 2009). This is in strong contrast to most of the studies undertaken in the 1970s, which placed relatively little emphasis on drug abuse, and in some cases argued that burglars formed a distinctly different group or type of offender from those whose crimes were drug-related. Even so, as Mawby (2001: 65–8) argues, while there is evidence that a growing proportion of those arrested for burglary have a drug problem, the relationship between substance misuse and burglary is complex and not necessarily causal.

Target selection

Turning now to the selection of specific properties to burgle, a broad distinction is sometimes made between 'planners', 'searchers' and 'opportunists' (see, especially, Bennett and Wright 1984) – i.e. those who set out to burgle specific houses they have previously identified as targets, those who travel around with the intention of finding a convenient house to burgle and those who (with no previous intent) respond spontaneously to the tempting sight of, for example, an insecurely locked window. In reality, there are many overlaps: the same offender may act in all of the above ways on different occasions, or even the same occasion. For example, 'planners' may abandon the plan they set out with and change to a 'searching' mode, while 'searchers' may suddenly remember a house they know from past experience and decide to head for it. Moreover, the concept of 'opportunist' burglaries needs some unpacking. An insecure window would not be interpreted as a 'tempting sight' or an 'opportunity' by most people; those with a predisposition to steal, or with previous experience of burgling, are more likely than others to recognise and interpret such sights in this way, so in a sense they too might be described as 'searchers', albeit in a more passive mode – i.e. even when not actively looking for a suitable property to burgle, they are always 'keeping an eye out' for an easy opportunity to steal (Maguire 1988; Logie *et al.* 1991). This does not necessarily mean that they will take advantage of the opportunity then and there – they may store up the knowledge for future use.

Despite these complications, the extent to which burglars behave in each of the above ways has important implications for crime prevention policy and practice. For example, simple security measures such as locking all windows or simulating signs of occupancy may be effective in avoiding victimisation by a burglar in 'opportunist' (or 'passive searching') mode, but are unlikely to stop someone who has targeted a particular property in advance. They may also fail to deter an experienced 'searcher', whose decisions are less likely to be based on whether houses are properly locked than on, for example, whether the rewards appear sizeable or whether there is sufficient cover to give them time to break in unobserved (Bennett and Wright 1984; Maguire 1988; Bernasco and Luykx 2006).

Interview-based studies suggest that the great majority of persistent burglars operate either in the searching or planning mode, or a combination of the two. For example, only 20 of Hearnden and Magill's (2004) snowball sample of 73 burglars from a number of deprived housing estates reported that their most recent burglary had been a spur of the moment decision. Indeed, Wright and Decker (1994) concluded from their interviews with American burglars that a large proportion already have a target in mind when they decide to commit a break-in and thus have little need to search for one. They acquire information about potential targets in a variety of ways, including receiving tips and keeping their eyes open during their day-to-day activities; many, too, are able to gather information about possible targets simply because they know the occupants or at least are familiar with their movements. In many cases, this means that they burgle properties quite close to where they live.

There is some support for this view in British research, though mainly in relation to burglaries committed in deprived areas. For example, over half of Hearnden and Magill's sample reported that they often committed offences close to home and had at some time burgled people they knew.[5] They explained this in terms of the need to obtain funds for drugs quickly, problems with transporting heavy goods over long distances and/or familiarity with the area. Again, in a study of 76 offenders convicted of burglaries in a housing estate in Kirkholt, Forrester *et al.* (1988) found that 53 per cent had travelled less than two miles to get to their most recent offending location and over three-quarters had walked there. Wiles and Costello (2000) likewise showed that over half of a sample of burglars in Sheffield had travelled less than a mile to commit their latest offence. These findings all fit well with the patterns of burglary mapped in middle-sized towns by Maguire and Bennett (1982), which showed that around half occurred on large council estates, and that most of these were thought by the police to have been committed by people living on the same estate who would be likely to know something about their victims.

At the same time, Maguire and Bennett (1982) found rather different patterns of offending in more middle-class areas, with a preponderance of targets close to road junctions, particularly just off main roads: this suggested that the main reasons for the choice of target were to do with accessibility and the availability of rapid escape routes rather than prior knowledge of the property or residents and hence a 'searcher' mode of target selection practised by (possibly more 'professional') burglars prepared to travel beyond their local area. This kind of interpretation also fits with Hearden and Magill's (2004) finding that those in their sample who regularly travelled longer distances to commit offences – a minority, but a substantial minority – tended to be more experienced adult burglars with a more 'professional' self-image. Again, the activities of 'searchers' appear to be reflected in the results of a recent analysis by Bernasco and Luykx (2006) of the details of over 25,000 burglaries in Den Haag in the Netherlands. The spatial patterns identified suggest that three factors were prominent in the burglars' choices of neighbourhoods in which to steal: opportunity, attractiveness and accessibility.

More direct evidence about burglars' ways of thinking in this mode of operation was gleaned by Bennett and Wright (1984), who used a variety of visual and experimental methods, including showing them detailed videos of residential streets, to explore with interviewees what 'cues' they used when searching for a target to help them decide which properties to burgle and which to avoid. The factor of greatest importance, mentioned by over 90 per cent of those interviewed, was whether or not the property was occupied. In most cases, the offender did not know conclusively at the point of selection whether anyone one was in. Instead, they based their assessments on whether there were signs of occupancy, such as lights on, the sounds of a television or a car in the drive. This could then be confirmed by knocking on the door or looking through the window (or less frequently, in cases where they knew the occupants, by telephoning the house). Most offenders said that an alarm would deter them: the main reason given was that they lacked the skill or knowledge to disarm them. The majority of burglars also mentioned that they were deterred by informal surveillance such as the presence of neighbours, the property being overlooked by other properties, or visibility to passers by. Relatively few offenders said that they were deterred by security locks. These findings accord quite well with the results of other research carried out around the same period, including an interview-based study in Ireland by Nee and Taylor (1988) and research on target choice by 'young burglars' conducted by Wright and Logie (1988). However, a later study by Hearnden and Magill (2004) found wider variety between individuals in the factors they took into account in selecting targets.

To conclude, while they give somewhat different messages about the relative frequencies of 'planning' and 'searching' (or hybrids between them), the authors of virtually all the studies mentioned seem to agree that purely 'opportunist' burglaries are in a minority and that most offenders are determined enough not to be deterred by low-level target-hardening alone. They also learn to 'read' cues about the likelihood of the house being occupied, the point of entry being visible to passers-by, the presence of items worth stealing and so on. This in turn suggests that traditional approaches to burglary prevention should be supplemented by consideration of alternatives based on an understanding of burglars' modes of thinking and behaviour (and of how these may vary in different kinds of neighbourhood); examples might include various forms of community surveillance and environmental design.

Enactment

Once would-be residential burglars have settled on a potential target, they still face the task of breaking into the dwelling, carrying out a search and leaving undetected. Many offenders state that the act of breaking in is usually in itself not technically difficult, although it is made problematic by having to be undertaken under considerable pressure in an environment alive with potential risks (Shover 1991; Wright and Decker 1994).

In approaching targets and effecting an entry to them, offenders usually seek to project a conventional appearance in order to avoid attracting suspicion from occupants, police or passers-by. Many do this using the simplest of tactics, such as walking up to residences dressed as they are and armed with a plausible excuse for being on the property should anyone challenge them. Once they have reassured themselves that nobody is at home, they can set about breaking into the dwelling, a process that seldom requires specialised knowledge or sophisticated equipment. Indeed, a majority of residential burglaries are accomplished using nothing more than common household tools like a hammer or screwdriver to break a window, overcome a lock or pry open a door (see Wright and Decker 1994, for a detailed examination of this process).

The problem, of course, is that offenders must do all of this under the constant threat of apprehension and punishment. How do they manage to remain calm and focused in spite of such risks? Most do so by trying not to dwell on the possibility of getting caught, a form of mental gymnastics that serves to rob threatened penalties of their deterrence potential, making it easier for them to concentrate on the job at hand (see Bennett and Wright 1984; Wright and Decker 1994). As a currently active residential burglar explained to Wright and Decker (1994: 128): 'I mean, I already know that there's a chance of getting caught so, when you doin' something like that, you try and keep that off your mind.'

Having successfully entered a dwelling, the first concern of most offenders is to reassure themselves yet again that no one is home. They do this in a variety of ways, including remaining still and listening for suspicious sounds, making a quick check of every room or calling out something like 'Is anybody home?' With that done, many offenders report a marked reduction in anxiety, perhaps because once they actually have broken into the residence, a burglary has been committed and there is no undoing it. But that is not to say that they stop worrying altogether, with the length of time they are willing to remain inside offering a reasonable estimate of the strength of their concern. Few want to linger. As Wright and Decker (1994: 141) observe: 'The outside world does not stand still while offenders are burglarizing targets ... and [their] vulnerability to discovery increases the longer they remain inside them.' Offenders know this and most respond by searching dwellings as quickly as possible so they can make good their escape.

In doing this, offenders almost invariably rely on a so-called cognitive script, a tried and tested method of searching targets which, they believe, results in 'the maximum yield in cash and goods per unit of time invested' (Wright and Decker 1994: 142). Adherence to such a script guides offenders' movement through dwellings almost automatically, avoiding the need for them to stop periodically to figure out which room to search next (Nee and Meenaghan 2006). These scripts, of course, vary somewhat from offender to offender, mostly because some are willing to remain inside a residence longer than others. That said, almost all residential burglars are agreed that it is best to search the master bedroom first, as this is where the most valuables are likely to be located. In fact, given even a modicum of success therein, some offenders do not bother to look in other rooms, sacrificing the possibility of greater reward so they can make good their escape. Most, however, conduct at least a cursory search of the rest of the dwelling, often avoiding children's bedrooms which they regard as unlikely to be lucrative. The last place to be searched typically is the living room because the items kept here tend to be bulky and thus are best left to the last minute (see Wright and Decker 1994, for an in depth examination of the cognitive scripts employed).

The fact that offenders typically are reluctant to remain inside dwellings for more than a few minutes, foregoing the prospect of increased reward in favour of reducing the risk of being discovered, has important implications for both criminological theory and crime prevention policy. In the realm of criminological theory, it demonstrates that deterrence threats continue to shape the actions of offenders throughout the residential burglary process and long after a burglary technically has been committed (see Wright 2001). And in regard to crime prevention policy, it shows that even after it is too late to prevent the break-in itself, it still may be possible to reduce the loss of cash and goods by keeping them in areas outside the cognitively scripted space wherein burglars tend to concentrate their searches.

Reactions and responses to burglary

We end the chapter with necessarily brief comments on three kinds of responses to burglary: those of victims and agencies that support them, of the police and other agencies concerned with crime prevention and detection and of sentencers and legislators.

Victims: impact, needs and rights

As noted earlier, burglary can have a considerable impact on victims, not only in terms of financial loss but in terms of emotional impact. During the 1980s a number of victim surveys and interview-based studies in both Britain and North America demonstrated that victims of burglary reported reactions such as fear, anger and upset at similar levels to those experienced by victims of robbery and other serious offences (see, for example, Maguire 1980, 1984, 1991; Brown and Yantzi 1980; Friedman *et al.* 1982). In England and Wales, Victim Support – whose 'bread and butter' work entails visiting burglary victims in their homes to offer practical assistance and emotional support – grew from a small cluster of local voluntary groups to a major national organisation attracting substantial government funding (Reeves 1985; Maguire and Corbett 1987; Mawby and Gill 1987). Similar organisations grew up across North America, many acting not only as support agencies, but as pressure groups campaigning for victims' rights, including compensation from offenders and a voice in court – issues which have continued to fuel debate ever since (Shapland 1984, 1988; Walklate 1989; Lurigio *et al.* 1990; Maguire 1991; Roach 1999; Rock 2002). Periodically, too, questions come to the fore about how far victims can go in protecting themselves from burglars. In Britain, argument on this topic reached a crescendo in 1999 when a householder (Tony Martin) who shot and killed a teenager who was burgling his house was convicted of murder and sentenced to life imprisonment. Although this was reduced on appeal to five years for manslaughter, the judges ruled that a claim of self-defence was insufficient to justify such a drastic response. Even so, Martin's arguments that it was have received a considerable amount of support in the popular press and among right-wing political groups (for further discussion, see McVicar 2004).

Detection and prevention

Detection rates for burglary have always been among the lowest of all offence types and – despite some improvement over the last five years – in some police force areas in Britain the 'sanction detection' rate[6] remains below 10 per cent (Kershaw *et al.* 2008). There are a number of reasons for this, most obviously that most burglaries occur when nobody is at home so are infrequently witnessed and in many cases not reported until hours have passed and 'the trail is cold'. Identifiable fingerprints are also found in a small minority of cases (Steer 1980). Indeed, one of the most comprehensive and influential studies of crime investigation, carried out in the 1970s in California by Greenwood *et al.* (1977), led the researchers to conclude that, unless an offender is apprehended in the first 24 hours after a burglary, the chances of a detection are reduced to as low as one per cent. Over the following decades, these and similar findings fuelled widespread changes in police investigation strategies, including the introduction of 'crime screening' (immediate closure of cases in which there are no promising leads: Eck 1983) and greater integration into investigative practice of proactive or 'intelligence-led' approaches, such as targeting either known offenders or high-risk areas on the basis of intelligence and crime pattern or 'hot spot' analysis (Maguire

2000; Jacobson *et al.* 2003; Ratcliffe 2008). A variant on this theme is giving priority attention to repeat victims, including issuing them with silent alarms and building in a rapid response resource (Farrell and Pease 1993).

However, although such methods may well have contributed to improvements in detection rates, as well as the overall fall in burglary, their impact is inevitably limited, and it remains a truism that the best response to burglary is to prevent it before it occurs. In fact, domestic burglary has been prominent in many of the debates and developments in crime prevention that have taken place over the last three decades. During this time, the greatest influence has been exercised by variations of so-called 'situational' crime prevention. This emerged in the early 1980s as a theoretical and empirical approach to crime reduction led by Ron Clarke and colleagues in the Home Office Research Unit and others at linked universities (Clarke 1980; see also Clarke 2005). Their starting point was that many offences involve the exploitation of opportunities for gain by more or less rational actors and that the three main 'proximal' determinants of crimes such as burglary relate to the *ease or difficulty of commission*, the *risk of detection* and the *likely rewards*. Designers of burglary prevention programmes began to embrace such ideas and to seek ways of influencing these determinants by making the offence more difficult and less worthwhile to commit from the offender's point of view.

The main method of increasing the difficulty of commission involves 'target hardening': that is, increasing the level of security of a dwelling, mainly through additional door and window locks. Some support for such a strategy comes from survey findings which suggest that victims of burglary tend to have lower levels of security than non-victims (Mayhew *et al.* 1993; Kent 2007). The results of evaluations of systematic hardening initiatives have also been generally favourable (see especially Forrester *et al.* 1988; on 'alley-gating', which protects the backs of rows of terraced houses, see Millie and Hough 2004; Hamilton-Brown and Kent 2005). However, the problem of 'displacement' to less well protected properties (reflecting, as discussed earlier, the determination of many burglars to continue 'searching') remains a major obstacle to the effectiveness of individual target-hardening.

Attempts to prevent burglary by increasing the perceived risk of detection have relied mainly on raising levels of surveillance over potential targets. Surveillance is usually conceptualised on a continuum with formal surveillance such as police patrols and security guards at one end and informal surveillance by passers-by and neighbours at the other. One of the classic programmes based on police surveillance was the Kansas City Preventive Patrol Experiment (Kelling *et al.* 1974), which found that increasing the number of vehicle patrols by two to three times their normal level made no discernible difference to levels of crime (although later studies found that visible policing may impact on fear of crime). However, surveillance by neighbours or passers-by appears rather more promising. The most systematic means of exploiting its potential in residential areas has been through Neighbourhood Watch. A recent systematic review and meta-analysis of Neighbourhood Watch evaluations concluded that it was associated with a small favourable effect on burglary, although the results across studies and across different types of area were variable (Bennett *et al.* 2006).

Reducing the likely rewards from burglary is difficult to achieve in practice. The most common method is to encourage householders to mark valuable items with their postcode. It is believed that this will deter offenders from taking their valuables as the resale price of marked items will be greatly reduced. One of the earliest evaluations of property marking in the UK, which received wide media attention, found that burglary rates decreased significantly in the first year of operation (Laycock 1985). However, the project was located in a small rural area and it was argued at the time that its success may have been due to the special characteristics of the area and its close-knit community. Other evaluations have produced mixed results and suggest that property-marking is effective mainly as part of a coordinated 'package' of interventions in a particular area, which includes publicity warning potential burglars that it has been implemented (Hamilton-Brown and Kent 2005).

Situational crime prevention, of course, is only one of a number of possible approaches to preventing burglary. It has come under strong attack from some commentators as an atheoretical, technicist strategy based on dubious assumptions about the motives and 'rationality' of offenders, which distracts attention from the deeper causes of crime (see, for example, Young 1994; Hughes 1998; Von Hirsch *et al*. 2000; for a refutation, see Clarke 2005). Instead, some argue, more resources should be put into 'social' or 'community' crime prevention (e.g. initiatives to strengthen communities or give young people positive alternatives to engaging in crime). Others claim that burglary reduction is best achieved through either deterrent or rehabilitative measures aimed at persistent offenders, who as we have seen are responsible for a significant proportion of all burglaries. For example, Trasler (1986: 24) wrote that 'Policies of crime reduction really demand two strategies: deterring occasional or low-rate offenders from committing crimes; and identifying and incapacitating high-rate, persistent offenders. Situational crime control offers effective measures for the first, but is likely to have little impact on the second group.' While his stark conclusion is questionable, Trasler's simple basic message – that different kinds of approach are more appropriate for different kinds of offender – is an important one. Hence we would argue that the most effective anti-burglary strategies are likely to be those which combine (in a conscious and planned fashion) a variety of aims and approaches.

Sentencing and legislation

Finally, it would be remiss of us to discuss responses to burglary without at least a brief mention of sentencing. As noted earlier, domestic burglary has always been treated by the courts as more serious than most other forms of non-violent property crime and attracts relatively heavy sentences. It is instructive that when in 1980 the Court of Appeal in England made a landmark general statement about types of offence for which judges should consider lowering tariffs, burglary in a dwelling was identified as one where this was not appropriate:

Many offenders can be dealt equally justly and effectively by a sentence of six or nine months' imprisonment as by one of 18 months or three years....

> [For example,] the less serious forms of factory or shopbreaking; the minor cases of sexual indecency; the more petty frauds ... There are, on the other hand, some offences for which, generally speaking, only the medium or longer sentences will be appropriate. For example, most robberies; most offences involving serious violence; use of a weapon to wound; burglary of private dwelling-houses... (*R v. Bibi*, 21 July 1980, cited in Maguire and Bennett 1982: 154)

Since then, attitudes have hardened further, not just in the courts, but among legislators. Most notably, domestic burglary – along with serious violent and sexual offences – was the subject of a new mandatory sentencing policy brought into English law through the Crime (Sentences) Act 1997, similar to the 'three strikes and you're out' laws in force in several US states. This required judges to pass a sentence of at least three years on anyone over 18 convicted of domestic burglary on three separate occasions, unless 'it would be unjust to do so in all the circumstances'. Although this general 'escape clause' – along with guidance from the Court of Appeal to reduce sentences in the light of mitigating circumstances, including guilty pleas – has been used quite often by the judiciary to pass sentences lower than three years, the Act has contributed to a continuing increase in the average sentence for burglary. For example, between 1993 and 1998 in the Crown Court, this rose from to 15.3 to 20.9 months, and over the next five years (during which the new law was implemented) it rose again to 24.5 months. The equivalent figures for 'burglary in a building other than a dwelling' were 13.6, 16.4 and 17.8, respectively – a much slower rate of increase (Sentencing Guidelines Council 2005). Moreover, in January 2009, a Court of Appeal judgment gave further momentum to the trend by stating that sentences for domestic burglary should take into account the impact on the victim as well as the culpability of the offender, adding that the mandatory minimum of three years for a third offence should be treated not as a guideline but simply as a minimum sentence: where the offence was characterised by 'significant or seriously raised culpability or impact', longer sentences would be appropriate.[7]

Ironically, despite the beliefs of judges, politicians and the media that the public want heavy sentences for burglars, there is some research evidence that ordinary people are not as punitive as assumed. Maguire and Bennett (1982: 156) found that, when asked in general terms about sentencing, most victims saw imprisonment as the only suitable sentence for an adult recidivist burglar. Yet at the same time, relatively few wanted 'their' burglar to go to prison. This suggests that when they consider the reality of an individual offence, despite its emotional impact, people tend to see it as less serious than the image of burglary in their mind. A more recent contribution to this debate was made by Hough and Roberts (1999), whose analysis of survey data suggested that the general public significantly underestimates the lengths of sentences passed by judges; moreover, when asked to suggest the appropriate sentence in a specific case of burglary described to them, most respondents chose disposals that were little different from – and if anything more lenient than – current sentencing practice.

Concluding comments

Despite significant falls since the mid-1990s, domestic burglary still ranks as one of the top five property crimes in the UK in terms of numbers of offences. Although the average amount stolen is modest, and few householders actually confront or are attacked by burglars (who are mainly young lower-class males whose motives are financial, typically to feed a substance misuse habit or to fund a pleasure-oriented lifestyle), it is an offence that can have a considerable impact on victims as well as causing substantial levels of fear and concern among the general public. Its impact also falls disproportionately on the most vulnerable members of society, especially those living in urban deprived areas. It is afforded high priority by the police and policymakers and attracts relatively high – and increasing – prison sentences, especially for persistent offenders. It would seem that the ancient legislation that gave special significance to entry into private homes reflected common perceptions and as such it is likely to continue to be one of the offences at the centre of crime control policy.

Suggested further reading

Relatively little qualitative research has been conducted in recent years on burglary or burglars and for comprehensive empirical studies of the offence one has to look mainly to the 1980s and 1990s, including books by the co-authors of this chapter. Maguire and Bennett's 1982 study *Burglary in a Dwelling* remains the most wide-ranging British study, with statistical and interview-based data on the nature of the offence and on the perspectives of both victims and offenders. Bennett and Wright's *Burglars on Burglary* (1984) offers a detailed analysis of how burglars think about the crime and select their targets. Wright and Decker's ethnographic study *Burglars on the Job* (1994), based substantially on accounts by offenders not known to the police, provides a rich picture of American burglars 'in the wild'. An interesting alternative picture can be found in Cromwell *et al.*'s *Breaking and Entering* (1991), which emphasises the need for money to buy drugs as a key driver of burglary.

By contrast, there is a much more extensive recent literature on burglary prevention, well summarised in Hamilton-Brown and Kent's (2005) essay on 'The prevention of domestic burglary' in the *Handbook of Crime Prevention and Community Safety*. Particularly important are the results of the Crime Reduction Programme's Reducing Burglary Initiative, discussed by Millie and Hough (2004), as well as the many ramifications of the influential findings on repeat victimisation reported by Farrell and Pease (1993).

There is also a wide range of literature on victims' rights and the provision of services to victims. For overviews of early work in this field, see Maguire's (1991) review 'The needs and rights of victims of crime' and Mawby and Gill's (1987) book *Crime Victims: Needs, Services and the Voluntary Sector*, while useful recent discussions of victim rights include Rock's (2002) essay on 'Victims' rights in England and Wales at the beginning of the 21st Century'.

Finally, for general reviews of issues relating to burglary, among the most comprehensive and thoughtful are Shover's (1991) essay, entitled simply 'Burglary' and Mawby's (2001) book of the same name, while Kent's (2007) *Key Domestic Burglary Crime Statistics* provides a wealth of statistical data on the topic.

Notes

1 It should also be noted that there were changes to the counting rules in 1998/9. The two changes have made comparisons with earlier figures problematic, but their overall effect has been to produce higher recording rates and hence an under-representation of the 'real' extent of the fall in burglary figures (see Simmons *et al.* 2003).

2 They were able to do this because they or another household member had contact with the offender during the incident, because the police identified the offender or because they thought they knew who the offender was.

3 It is likely that the percentage under 21 is higher for residential burglary than commercial burglary.

4 While the research found examples of more successful offenders living in the towns in question who tended to travel greater distances to offend and kept their activities more secret, it was concluded that these were in the minority. At the other end of the scale, a significant minority of burglaries were committed by 'occasional' or 'one-off' offenders – in many cases children.

5 Both Wright and Decker (1994) and Shover (1991) argue that, in the USA, instances of victim and offender knowing each other (albeit not well) are much more common than is usually thought, and may be in the region of 40 per cent of all cases. Wright and Decker (1994: 64) quote a 'typical' case in which the burglar stated: 'I knew [the victim] before anyway. We was all just on the street getting high and drinking. [The soon-to-be victim] said, "We can go to my house and smoke this shit." That's how I ended up over at his house … He wasn't a friend of mine, just somebody I knew. I was at their house getting high and it was, like, three days later I wanted to get high [again] and I needed some money. I was thinking, "Where can I make some money at?" I said, "I can go over to John's house."' British Crime Survey results indicate that at least 21 per cent of all victims were able to describe 'their' burglar had known him or her prior to the offence, though only half of these had known him/her well (Kent 2007).

6 The proportion of all recorded offences which are cleared up through a formal sanction (including charges or summonses which do not ultimately lead to a conviction).

7 *R* v. *Saw and others*, reported in *Times Online*, 26 January 2009.

References

Anderson, D., Chenery, S. and Pease, K. (1995) *Biting Back: Tackling Repeat Burglary and Car Crime*, Crime Detection and Prevention Series, Paper No. 58. London: Home Office. Online at: http://www.homeoffice.gov.uk/rds/prgpdfs/cdp58bf.pdf.

Bennett, T. H. (1999) *Drugs and Crime: The Results of Drug Testing and Interviewing Arrestees*, Home Office Research Study No. 183. London: Home Office.

Bennett, T. H. and Sibbitt, R. (2000) *Drug Use Among Arrestees*, Research Findings No. 119. London: Home Office, Home Office Research and Statistics Directorate.

Bennett, T. H. and Wright, R. (1984) *Burglars on Burglary*. Aldershot: Gower.

Bennett, T. H., Holloway, K. and Farrington, D. P. (2006) 'Does neighborhood watch reduce crime? A systematic review and meta-analysis', *Journal of Experimental Criminology*, 2 (4): 437–58.

Bernasco, W. (2009) 'Burglary', in M. Tonry (ed.), *The Oxford Handbook of Crime and Public Policy*. Oxford: Oxford Unversity Press.

Bernasco, W. and Luykx, F. (2006) 'Effects of attractiveness, opportunity and accessibility to burglars on residential burglary rates of urban neighbourhoods', *Criminology*, 41 (3): 981–1002.

Blumstein, A., Cohen, J., Roth, J. and Visher, C. (1986) *Criminal Careers and Career Criminals*, Vol. 1. Washington, DC: National Academic Press.

Brown, S. and Yantzi, M. (1980) *Needs Assessment for Victims and Witnesses of Crime.* Kitchener, ON: Mennonite Central Committee.

Chappell, D. (1965) *The Development and Administration of the English Criminal Law Relating to Offences of Breaking and Entering.* Doctoral dissertation, University of Cambridge.

Clarke, R. V. (1980) 'Situational crime prevention: its theoretical basis and practical scope', *British Journal of Criminology*, 20: 136–47.

Clarke, R. V. (2005) 'Seven misconceptions of situational crime prevention', in N. Tilley (ed.), *Handbook of Crime Prevention and Community Safety.* Cullompton: Willan.

Cromwell, P. and Olson, J. (2004) *Breaking and Entering: Burglars on Burglary.* Belmont, CA: Wadsworth.

Cromwell, P., Olson, J. and Avary, D. (1991) *Breaking and Entering: An Ethnographic Analysis of Burglary.* Newbury Park, CA: Sage.

Eck, J. (1983) *Solving Crime: A Study of the Investigation of Burglary and Robbery.* Washington, DC: Police Executive Research Forum.

Farrell, G. and Pease, K. (1993) *Once Bitten, Twice Bitten: Repeat Victimisation and Its Implications for Crime Prevention*, Crime Prevention Unit Paper No. 46. London: Home Office.

Field, S. (1990) *Trends in Crime and Their Interpretation: A Study of Recorded Crime in Post-War England and Wales*, Home Office Research Study No. 119. London: Home Office.

Field, S. (1999) *Trends in Crime Revisited*, Home Office Research Study No. 195. London: Home Office.

Flatley, J., Moon, D., Roes, S., Hall, P. and Moley, S. (2009) *Home Security, Mobile Phone Theft and Stolen Goods: Supplementary Volume 3 to Crime in England and Wales 2007/8*, Home Office Statistical Bulletin 10/09. London: Home Office.

Forrester, D., Chatterton, M. and Pease, K. (1988) *The Kirkholt Burglary Prevention Project, Rochdale*, Crime Prevention Unit Paper No. 13. London: Home Office.

Friedman, K., Bischoff, K., Davis, R. and Person, A. (1982) *Victims and Helpers: Reactions to Crime.* New York: Victim Services Agency.

Greenwood, P., Chaiken, J. and Petersilia, J. (1977) *The Criminal Investigation Process.* Lexington, MA: D. C. Heath.

Hamilton-Brown, N. and Kent, A. (2005) 'The prevention of domestic burglary', in N. Tilley (ed.), *Handbook of Crime Prevention and Community Safety.* Cullompton: Willan.

Hearnden, I. and Magill, C. (2004) *Decision-making by Burglars: Offenders' Perspectives*, Findings No. 249. London: Home Office.

Home Office (2003) *Counting Rules for Recorded Crime.* London: Home Office.

Hough, J. J. M. and Roberts, J. (1999) 'Sentencing trends in Britain', *Punishment and Society*, 1 (1): 11–26.

Hughes, G. (1998) *Understanding Crime Prevention.* Milton Keynes: Open University Press.

Irwin, J. (1970) *The Felon.* Englewood Cliffs, NJ: Prentice-Hall.

Jacobson, J., Maitland, L. and Hough, M. (2003) *The Reducing Burglary Initiative: Investigating Burglary*, Home Office Research Study No. 264. London: Home Office.

Katz, J. (1988) *Seductions of Crime: Moral and Sensual Attractions in Doing Evil*. New York: Basic Books.

Kelling, G., Pate, T., Dieckman, D. and Brown, C. (1974) *Kansas City Preventive Patrol Experiment: A Summary Report*. Washington, DC: Police Foundation.

Kent, A. (2007) *Key Domestic Burglary Crime Statistics (at January 2007)*. London: Home Office, Crime Reduction Effectiveness Group.

Kershaw, C., Nicholas, S. and Walker, A. (2008) *Crime in England and Wales 2007/08: Findings from the British Crime Survey and Police Recorded Crime*, Home Office Statistical Bulletin Home 07/08: London: Home Office.

Laycock, G. (1985) *Property Marking: A Deterrent to Domestic Burglary?*, Crime Detection and Prevention Series, Paper No. 3. London: Home Office.

Laycock, G. (2001) 'Hypothesis-based research: the repeat victimisation story', *Criminology and Criminal Justice*, 1 (1): 59–2.

Lemert, E. M. (1953) 'An isolation and closure theory of naïve check forgery', *Journal of Criminal Law, Criminology, and Police Science*, 44: 296–07.

Letkemann, P. (1973) *Crime as Work*. Englewood Cliffs, NJ: Prentice-Hall.

Logie, R., Wright, R. and Decker, S. (1991) 'Recognition memory performance and residential burglary', *Applied Cognitive Psychology*, 6 (2): 109–23.

Lurigio, A. J., Skogan, W. G. and Davis, R. C. (eds) (1990) *Victims of Crime: Problems, Policies and Programs*. Newbury Park, CA: Sage.

McVicar, J. (2004) *Tony Martin: A Right to Kill?* London: Artnik.

Maguire, M. (1980) 'The impact of burglary upon victims', *British Journal of Criminology*, 20 (3): 261–75.

Maguire, M. (1984) 'Meeting the needs of burglary victims: some questions for the police and the criminal justice system', in R. Clarke and T. Hope (eds), *Coping with Burglary*. Boston: Kluwer-Nijhoff.

Maguire, M. (1988) 'Searchers and opportunists: offender behaviour and burglary prevention', *Journal of Security Administration*, Special Issue on Situational Prevention, 11 (2): 70–7.

Maguire, M. (1991) 'The needs and rights of victims of crime', in M. Tonry (ed.), *Crime and Justice*, Vol. 14. Chicago: University of Chicago Press, pp. 363–433.

Maguire, M. (2000) 'Policing by risks and targets: some dimensions and implications of intelligence-led crime control', *Policing and Society*, 9: 1–22.

Maguire, M. and Bennett, T. (1982) *Burglary in a Dwelling: The Offence, the Offender and the Victim*. London: Heinemann.

Maguire, M. and Corbett, C. (1987) *The Effects of Crime and the Work of Victims Support Schemes*. Aldershot: Gower.

Mawby, R. I. (2001) *Burglary*. Cullompton: Willan.

Mawby, R. I. and Gill, M. L. (1987) *Crime Victims: Needs, Services and the Voluntary Sector*. London: Tavistock.

Mayhew, P., Aye-Maung, N. and Mirrlees-Black, C. (1993) *The 1992 British Crime Survey*, Home Office Research Study No. 132. London: Home Office.

Millie, A. and Hough, J. J. M. (2004) *Assessing the Impact of the Reducing Burglary Initiative in Southern England and Wales*, Home Office Online Report 42/04. Online at: http://www.crimereduction.homeoffice.gov.uk/burglary/burglary78.htm.

Ministry of Justice (2008) *Sentencing Statistics 2007, England and Wales*. http://www.justice.gov.uk/publications/docs/sentencing-statistics-2007-revised.pdf.

Nee, C. and Meenaghan, A. (2006) 'Expert decision making in burglars', *British Journal of Criminology*, 46: 935–49.

Nee, C. and Taylor, M. (1988) 'Residential burglary in the Republic of Ireland: a situational perspective', *Howard Journal of Criminal Justice*, 27 (2): 105–16.

Pease, K. (1998) *Repeat Victimisation: Taking Stock*, Crime Detection and Prevention Series, Paper No. 90. London: Home Office.

Ratcliffe, J. (2008) *Intelligence-Led Policing*. Cullompton: Willan.

Reeves, H. (1985) 'Victim support schemes: the United Kingdom model', *Victimology*, 10: 679–86.

Rengert, G. and Wasilchick, J. (2000) *Suburban Burglary*. Springfield, IL: Charles C. Thomas.

Reppetto, T. (1974) *Residential Crime*. Cambridge, MA: Ballinger.

Roach, K. (1999) *Due Process and Victims' Rights: The New Law and Politics of Criminal Justice*. Toronto: University of Toronto Press.

Rock, P. (2002) 'Victims' rights in England and Wales at the beginning of the 21st century', in J. Ermisch, D. Gallie and A. Heath (eds), *Understanding Social Change*. Oxford: British Academy and Oxford University Press.

Ruparel, C. (2004) *Distraction Burglary: Recorded Crime Data*, Online Supplement to Home Office Statistical Bulletin No. 14/04. London: Home Office.

Sentencing Guidelines Council (2005) *The Sentence*. May.

Shapland, J. (1984) 'The victim, the criminal justice system and compensation', *British Journal of Criminology*, 24: 131–49.

Shapland, J. (1988) 'Fiefs and peasants: accomplishing change for victims in the criminal justice system', in M. Maguire and J. Pointing (eds), *Victims of Crime: A New Deal*. Milton Keynes: Open University Press.

Shover, N. (1971) 'Burglary as an Occupation'. Unpublished PhD thesis, University of Illinois.

Shover, N. (1972) 'Structures and careers in burglary', *Journal of Criminal Law, Criminology and Police Science*, 63: 540–49.

Shover, N. (1991) 'Burglary' in M. Tonry (ed.), *Crime and Justice: A Review of Research*, Vol. 14. Chicago: University of Chicago Press.

Simmons, J., Legg, C. and Hosking, R. (2003) *National Crime Recording Standard (NCRS): An Analysis of the Impact on Recorded Crime*, Home Office Online Report 31/03. Online at: http://www.homeoffice.gov.uk/rds/pdfs2/rdsolr3103.pdf.

Steer, D. (1980) *Uncovering Crime: The Police Role*, Royal Commission on Criminal Procedure, Research Study No. 7. London: HMSO.

Thornton, A., Walker, D. and Erol, R. (2003) *Distraction Burglary Amongst Older Adults and Minority Ethnic Communities*, Home Office Findings No. 197. London: Home Office. Online at: http://www.homeoffice.gov.uk/rds/pdfs2/r197.pdf.

Trasler, G. (1986) 'Situational crime control and rational choice: a critique', in K. Heal and G. Laycock (eds), *Situational Crime Prevention: From Theory into Practice*. London: HMSO.

Von Hirsch, A., Garland, D. and Wakefield, A. (eds) (2000) *Ethical and Social Issues in Situational Crime Prevention*. Oxford: Hart.

Walker, A., Flatley, J., Kershaw, C. and Moon, D. (2009) *Crime in England and Wales 2008/09: Findings from the British Crime Survey and Police Recorded Crime*, Vol. 1, Home Office Statistical Bulletin 11/09. London: Home Office.

Walklate, S. (1989) *Victimology: The Victim and the Criminal Justice System*. London: Unwin Hyman.

Waller, I. and Okihiro, N. (1978) *Burglary: The Victim and the Public*. Toronto: University of Toronto Press.

Walsh, D. (1980) *Break-Ins: Burglary from Private Houses*. London: Constable.

Wiles, P. and Costello, A. (2000) *The Road to Nowhere: The Evidence for Travelling Criminals*, Home Office Research Study No. 207. London: Home Office

Wolfgang, M. (1958) *Patterns of Criminal Homicide*. Philadelphia: University of Pennsylvania Press.

Wolfgang, M., Thornberry, T. P. and Figlio, R. (1987) *From Boy to Man, From Delinquency to Crime.* Chicago: University of Chicago Press.

Wright, R. (2001) 'Searching a house: deterrence and the undeterred residential burglar', in H. Pontell and D. Shichor (eds), *Contemporary Issues in Crime and Criminal Justice: Essays in Honor of Gilbert Geis.* Englewood Cliffs, NJ: Prentice-Hall.

Wright, R. and Decker, S. H. (1994) *Burglars on the Job.* Boston: Northeastern University Press.

Wright, R. and Logie, R. (1988) 'How young house burglars choose targets', *Howard Journal of Criminal Justice,* 27 (2): 92–104.

Young, J. (1994) 'Incessant chatter: recent paradigms in criminology', in M. Maguire, R. Morgan and R. Reiner (eds), *The Oxford Handbook of Criminology.* Oxford: Oxford University Press.

Chapter 2

Vehicle crime

Rick Brown

Introduction

Vehicle crime was a significant problem in the latter part of the twentieth century. The dawning of the twenty-first century has seen some marked improvements in some aspects of vehicle crime, although other aspects of this type of offending persist. In this chapter, we look at what we mean by vehicle crime and its various attributes and examine how these have changed over time.

What do we mean by vehicle crime?

The term 'vehicle crime' consists of a wide range of different behaviours with different motivations. We need to articulate the different facets of this activity if we are to understand what constitutes vehicle crime. In its widest sense, vehicle crime encompasses offending that involves acquisitive forms of property crime associated with a 'conveyance'. In law, a 'conveyance' means 'any conveyance constructed or adapted for the carriage of a person or persons whether by land, water, or air' (section 12(7) of the Theft Act 1968. This excludes bicycles which are not defined as a 'conveyance' for the purposes of the Theft Act (1968). The other distinguishing feature of vehicle crime is that the acquisitive property crime involved can be associated with the vehicle itself being the target of the theft (known as theft of vehicles), or items that may be found in, or on, the vehicle (known as theft from vehicles).

Thefts of vehicles

In the year to March 2008, there were 170,182 thefts of vehicles recorded by the police in England and Wales. Thefts of vehicles tend to have a high rate of reporting to the police due to most vehicles being insured for theft and the fact that a crime reference number is required to claim on insurance. The British Crime Survey estimates that 93 per cent of thefts of vehicles are reported to the police (Kershaw *et al*. 2008: 22).

These thefts can involve a number of different motivations. One key differentiation is between thefts for temporary use and thefts for permanent use. This is also the basis by which thefts of vehicles are differentiated legally. The following sections examine each of these in turn.

Temporary thefts of vehicles

Theft for temporary use is legally defined in England and Wales as *unauthorised taking* under section 12(1) of the Theft Act 1968. This states that:

> … a person shall be guilty of an offence if, without having the consent of the owner or other lawful authority, he takes any conveyance for his own or another's use, or knowing that any conveyance has been taken without such authority, drives it or allows himself to be carried in or on it.

The key aspect of this definition is that it does not require one to prove that there was an intention to permanently deprive the owner of the item, as would be the case for theft. It is sufficient to prove that the vehicle had been taken by the accused without the owner's permission. In 1992, at the height of the vehicle crime problem in the UK, the offence of *aggravated vehicle taking* was introduced.[1] This took account of situations in which stolen vehicles were driven dangerously, involved in accidents or damaged and the growing problem associated with stolen vehicles being driven dangerously and subsequently involved in accidents.

Temporary thefts can have a number of different motivations. Most commonly, vehicles will be taken for so called 'joyriding' in which the motivation behind the theft is the exhilaration of stealing a car and driving it around – often at high speed and in a dangerous manner. In other cases, the motivation may be more instrumental, such as to get home from the pub on a rainy night! Vehicles will also sometimes be used in the commission of other crimes – such as for use in ram raids or as getaway cars in robberies.

An obvious key feature of temporary thefts is that the owner might eventually get the vehicle back. However, that doesn't mean that the vehicle will be in a drivable condition. With improvements in forensic investigations, car thieves now sometimes set fire to stolen vehicles once they have finished with them, regardless of whether the risk of detection is real or perceived.

Permanent thefts of vehicles

Permanent thefts of vehicles are those that are stolen with the intent of permanently depriving the owner of them. These are covered by section 1(1) of the Theft Act 1968. This states that:

> A person is guilty of theft if he dishonestly appropriates property belonging to another with the intention of permanently depriving the other of it; and 'theft' and 'steal' shall be construed accordingly.

There can be a number of different motivations for permanent vehicle crime. In some cases, vehicles will be stolen for their component parts. Some vehicles will also be subject to insurance fraud. In these cases, the vehicle will not actually have been stolen, but will be disposed of by the owner who then claims on insurance for the theft of the vehicle. This is thought to be particularly prevalent among older vehicles, where the insurance value may exceed the maintenance costs of repairing a vehicle. Webb and Laycock (1992) estimated that 8 per cent of all thefts in 1990 were insurance frauds (this equates to 23 per cent of permanent thefts using their figures).

Vehicle interference and tampering

Vehicle interference and tampering offences were introduced in the Criminal Attempts Act 1981 and relate to offences in which a vehicle or anything carried in a vehicle is interfered with and where the intention is to commit an offence of theft of a vehicle, theft from a vehicle or taking without consent. This has been shown as a separate category of crime in published criminal statistics since 1998.

Thefts from vehicles

Unlike thefts of vehicles, thefts from vehicles tend to have a relatively low rate of reporting. Figures from the British Crime Survey estimate that just 45 per cent of thefts from vehicle are reported to the police (Walker *et al.* 2006: 52). This will be due to the relatively low value of many thefts, the lack of expectation that the stolen items will be recovered and the lack of insurance for thefts from vehicles.

Patterns and trends in vehicle crime

Figure 2.1 shows the trends in vehicle crime between 1977 and 2007/8. This shows the trends in thefts from vehicles, thefts of vehicles and vehicle interference and tampering. The figures for thefts of vehicles combine temporary and permanent thefts. They also include aggravated vehicle-taking offences, which account for approximately 10,000 offences per year.

Thefts from vehicles accounted for 66 per cent of vehicle crime in 2007/8, with 432,377 offences recorded by the police. In the late 1970s the level of thefts from vehicle offences was similar to thefts of vehicles. However, the 1980s saw a sharp increase in these offences. Between 1980 and 1992, thefts from vehicles increased by 224 per cent, peaking at 954,200 offences. Since 1992, there have been steady reductions in this type of offence, which now stands at levels similar to those in the early 1980s.

Thefts of vehicles (including unauthorised takings) have followed a similar, if somewhat more conservative, path. Between 1980 and 1992, there was an 81 per cent increase, peaking at 587,900 thefts of vehicles in 1992. Since then, there has been a steady decline, with just 170,182 thefts of vehicles recorded by the police in 2008/9 – a fall of 71 per cent from its peak. This is a level not seen since the late 1960s.

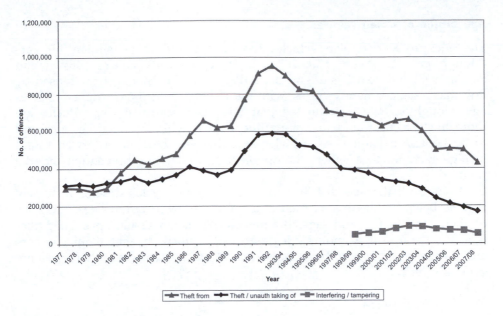

Figure 2.1   Trend in police recorded vehicle crime: 1977 to 2007/8

The trend in vehicle interference and tampering offences recorded by the police has also seen reductions, with a fall of 42 per cent since 2002/3, to stand at 53,990 offences in 2008/9.

Although the pattern of thefts from vehicles is more marked than thefts of vehicles, and account for a greater proportion of vehicle crime, relatively little research has been focused on this type of offending and it is generally treated as similar to other types of theft. However, this is an area that would warrant further analysis in future, not least to understand what has brought about the significant reductions in recent years.

The remainder of this chapter will focus on exploring the nature of thefts of vehicles and discussing some of the possible reasons for these patterns.

Characteristics of the offence, offenders and victims

When we think of vehicle crime, we tend to think of thefts of *cars*. However, there are also relatively large numbers of other types of vehicle stolen too. Sallybanks and Brown (1999) estimated that in 1996, 81 per cent of vehicles stolen were cars. The remainder were motorcycles (9 per cent), light commercial vehicles (LCVs) (9 per cent) and heavy goods vehicles (HGVs) (1 per cent).[2] While cars, LCVs and HGVs had relatively similar rates of theft per 1,000 vehicles registered, the rates for motorcycle theft were much higher. Braun and Wilkinson (2005) estimated that the rate of motorcycle theft in 2003 was 37 thefts per 1,000 registered, at a time when the theft rate for cars was just 10 per 1,000 registered.

29

Age profile of stolen vehicles

The age profile of stolen vehicles has been found to be similar for cars (Houghton 1992; Webb *et al.* 2004), light commercial vehicles (Brown and Saliba 1998) and heavy goods vehicles (Brown 1995). This is characterised by low theft rates for new vehicles, with the risks of theft increasing as vehicles age. Houghton (1992) speculated that this was because newer vehicles are more likely to be found in more affluent areas with lower crime rates and to be kept in a garage. As vehicles age, they are more likely to be found in higher crime areas, where the opportunities for crime prevention may be reduced.

By contrast, the age distribution of stolen motorcycles differs, with new models being at higher risk than older models. With motorcycles, the risks of theft tend to fall with age. Braun and Wilkinson (2005) speculated that this was because new motorcycles tend to be much cheaper than new cars and so are more likely to be found in less affluent areas where theft risks are generally higher.

Models of car stolen

Where the types of car that tend to be stolen are concerned,[3] the Home Office published the Car Theft Index until 2003. This provided a guide to the theft risks associated with different models of car registered in the UK. This index was an empirical guide, based on reports of cars stolen and reported to the police and recorded on the Police National Computer. The last index, produced in 2003 (and based on thefts in 2002), showed that the models most at risk of being stolen were those that were the older versions of popular, mass-market cars, such as Austin/Rover Metros, Ford Escorts, Ford Fiestas, Ford Sierras, Vauxhall Astras, Vauxhall Cavaliers and Vauxhall Novas. This accords with Light *et al.*'s (1993) observation that the vehicles most likely to be stolen are those that are the most popular models in the legitimate market. Furthermore, there would appear to be a preference for models that are traditionally perceived to be 'British' built (even if they were in reality built abroad), such as Fords and Vauxhalls, rather than, for example, Japanese (Nissan, Toyota, Honda) or German (Volkswagen, Audi, BMW) models.

Houghton (1992) also showed how theft rates were higher for sportier variants of popular models. This preference was also noted by the car thieves interviewed by Spencer (1992). Given a choice of targets, those that are viewed as faster tend to be more at risk of theft.

Theft risk by car segment

The Home Office Car Theft Index allowed analysis to be undertaken of the theft risks associated with different market segments. Data from the 2002 Index (based on cars stolen in 2001) showed that, while the average theft rate was 13 thefts per 1,000 cars registered, the highest theft risks were associated with small saloons (such as Ford Escorts and Vauxhall Astras), which had a rate of 15 thefts per 1,000 registered. By contrast, the lowest theft risks were associated with 4 x 4s and people carriers, with 10 per 1,000 registered being stolen in 2001.

Locations of thefts

Thefts of vehicles have been shown to vary considerably from one geographical location to another. This seems to hold at every level, from differences at the international level down to the particular parking space that one leaves one's car in.

At the international level, comparisons are hard to find due to the different ways in which vehicle crime is recorded by the police. However, findings from the International Crime Victimisation Survey undertaken in 2000 showed that England and Wales had the highest rate of thefts of cars (with 2.6 per cent of owners experiencing a theft[4]) among 17 industrialised countries examined (van Kesteren *et al.* 2000). This was followed by Australia (2.1 per cent of owners experiencing a theft) and France (1.9 per cent). By contrast, theft risks were lowest in countries such as the Netherlands, Finland, USA, Catalonia (Spain), Switzerland and Japan. In these countries, 0.5 per cent or fewer owners had had a car stolen. Given the large changes in theft risks in recent years, it is unknown whether these rankings still hold.

Within England and Wales, there are disparities in the number of thefts from one region to another. Criminal statistics for 2007/8 (Kershaw *et al.* 2008) show that theft and unauthorised taking of vehicles recorded by the police are highest in London (45 offences per 10,000 head of population) and Yorkshire and the Humber (38 offences per 10,000 population) and lowest in the South West (23 offences per 10,000 population), South East (24 offences per 10,000 population) and East of England (26 offences per 1,000 population), compared to a national rate of 32 offences per 10,000 population in England and 33 per 10,000 in Wales.

Where individual police force areas are concerned, the rates of theft appear to be highest in South Yorkshire (50 offences per 10,000 population), Greater Manchester (49 per 10,000), South Wales (47 per 10,000) and Metropolitan London (45 per 10,000). They are lowest in Dyfed Powys (12 per 10,000), Cumbria (15 per 10,000), Devon and Cornwall (16 per 10,000) and Dorset (16 per 10,000). These findings suggest that theft rates may be higher in the more urban areas. Indeed, Kershaw *et al.* (2008) show that the risks of vehicle-related theft[5] are higher in urban areas (7 per cent of the population are victims) than in rural areas (4 per cent of the population are victims). They are also higher among those that live in an area ranked as in the 20 per cent most deprived areas (9 per cent are victims) compared to those living in an area ranked as in the 20 per cent least deprived (5 per cent are victims).

Furthermore, areas assessed to have high levels of physical disorder have higher levels of vehicle-related theft (11 per cent are victims) than areas with low physical disorder (6 per cent are victims).

One of the interesting features of thefts of vehicles is that the risks of theft will vary according to where the vehicle is parked. This means that the risks of theft of any one vehicle can vary throughout a given day, depending on the area and specific location in which a vehicle is parked. Findings from the 2005/6 British Crime Survey (Walker *et al.* 2006) showed that 68 per cent of vehicle-related thefts occurred in areas close to the victim's home. However, risks at particular locations appear to vary according to the time of day.

During the day (6 a.m. to 6 p.m.), the largest proportion of vehicle-related thefts (31 per cent) occurred in car parks, while during the night (6 p.m. to 6 a.m.), the largest proportion (50 per cent) occurred in the street outside the victim's home.

Where the specific risks in the area close to the owner's home are concerned, Clarke and Mayhew (1994) showed that cars parked in a domestic garage were 20 times less likely to be stolen than cars parked in a driveway. Furthermore, they were 50 times less likely to be stolen than those parked in a street near the owner's home.

The analysis of theft risks at specific locations presented so far takes no account of how long a vehicle is parked at a particular location. Indeed, vehicles parked near the owner's home may be stolen most often because that is the location where they are parked for the longest periods of time. Analysis of theft risk, taking into account the length of time a vehicle was parked in a location was undertaken in the 1994 British Crime Survey (Mirrlees-Black *et al.* 1996; Clarke and Mayhew 1998). This found that cars parked in car parks were four times more likely to be stolen than cars parked in the street outside the driver's home and 40 per cent more likely to be stolen than cars parked in any other street. Furthermore, cars parked in car parks were 200 times more likely to be stolen than those parked in a garage at home.

Mayhew and Braun (2004) provided a summary of research on the factors that affected theft risks in car parks. They found that those car parks with higher risks were:

- city-centre car parks;
- long-stay park-and-ride commuter and shopping car parks;
- car parks used around the clock;
- communal bays on housing estates;
- car parks catering for young people, such as on a university campus;
- surface car parks (compared to lower risk multi-storey car parks);
- car parks with no access control;
- car parks with no security guard presence;
- car parks with pedestrian throughways.

Those with lower risks included:

- car parks with valet parking;
- car parks with CCTV;
- car parks with good lighting;
- car parks near shops, vending facilities and active commercial enterprise.

Destinations of stolen vehicles

As noted by Spencer (1992) many vehicles stolen for temporary use will be recovered close to the owner's home (and probably the offender's home too) and will have been used in most cases for 'joyriding'.

The remaining vehicles will usually have been stolen for some form of financial gain. As noted above, Webb and Laycock (1992) have highlighted how some of these will not have been thefts at all, but insurance fraud cases. In these cases, the vehicles will be destroyed in some way, whether it be by setting them on fire, dropping them in a canal or taking them to a scrapyard.

Apart from these insurance frauds, there are a variety of outlets for stolen vehicles. These include stripping vehicles for the use of their component parts, resale of the whole vehicle within the domestic market and export of the whole vehicle to foreign markets.

Stripping vehicles for their components

So far as stripping vehicles for their component parts is concerned, this will occur where there is a high demand for component parts, where the cost of replacement parts is high or where components are in short supply. With regard to the demand for component parts, there is a market for some older vehicles where the replacement parts are required due to wear and tear. The extent of this particular market, however, is likely to be relatively small because legitimate used parts, especially for older vehicles, are often available from local salvage yards where prices tend to be fairly low.

Obtaining component parts may be more problematic where newer cars are concerned. Often, there will not be a ready supply of used parts as few of these models will have reached the end of their life, so are therefore not available from salvage yards. In these cases, those maintaining vehicles may have to rely on buying new components. However, the price of such new components can be extremely high, especially where parts are only available from the original manufacturer. Indeed, this is an essential element of the business model of motor manufacturers and their network of dealerships, which rely on making high margins from the replacement parts market. Indeed, if one were to price the cost of buying the major components associated with a new vehicle, one will find the cost will often far outweigh the cost of buying a whole new vehicle. For example, work undertaken in 2001 as part of an evaluation of the NCIS Organised Vehicle Crime Programme (see Brown *et al.* (2004) for further details on the evaluation) found that the retail price of a new Honda CBR 600F motorcycle was £6,550. However, the price of the individual component parts totalled £41,100. Under these circumstances, one can see that the economic gains may outweigh the risk of detection for those needing to purchase such components. The demand for such parts can come from either owners looking for the cheapest way to repair their vehicles or from mechanics looking to improve their profit margin by passing off stolen parts as new, legitimate parts.

In some cases, mechanics may turn to the illegitimate market to obtain parts that are not available on the legitimate market. In the late 1990s the author observed a police test purchase operation in Detroit, Michigan, in which undercover officers attempted to sell a car airbag that was reputed to be stolen to local car repair businesses. Local intelligence had shown that Ford Mustang airbags were in short supply and this had led to a spate of thefts of these components from cars in Detroit. The police approached the Ford Motor Company to request use of a Mustang airbag. However, they were in such demand that the police were told that one could not be spared. In the event, the operation went ahead with a Chrysler airbag. Unsurprisingly, the undercover officers found that no one was interested in buying readily available Chrysler airbags.

In an attempt to combat the theft of vehicles for their parts, the USA introduced the Motor Vehicle Theft Law Enforcement Act 1984 which required manufacturers to mark the major sheet metal parts of high-theft cars with Vehicle Identification Numbers (VINs). However, Harris and Clarke (1991) concluded that the role played by thefts for component parts (especially for the sheet metal parts) was overstated in the US market and that the Act would have little impact on theft rates.

Thefts for resale in the domestic market

Resale into the domestic market is likely to be the destination for the majority of the vehicles that are stolen for professional gain. This requires vehicles to be reintroduced to the legitimate market (known as 'ringing') and typically this will require two changes. Firstly, the vehicle's physical identity will need to be changed so that it does not obviously appear to be stolen. Secondly, the documentation accompanying the vehicle will need to be changed to give it a legitimate provenance.

So far as the vehicle's physical identity is concerned, this can vary from the simple to the elaborate. In its most basic form, this can simply mean changing number plates (often using a number plate similar to that of a similar legitimate vehicle) on the understanding that many buyers will not check physical identity features beyond this. In other cases, efforts will be made to change all identifying features, such as the VIN plate on the engine housing, visible VIN under the windscreen, engine numbers and other identifying numbers. At its most extreme, changing the physical identity can involve creating a 'cut and shut' vehicle, in which the front half of one vehicle (often an insurance write off – see below) is welded to the back half of a stolen vehicle. This preserves the legitimate identity of the written off car thereby creating a new identity for the stolen half.

Obtaining legitimate registration documentation for a stolen vehicle is in many respects the more difficult aspect of the ringing operation. Indeed, some organised car thieves are known to obtain the documentation first and then steal a vehicle to match the paperwork as this can be easier than working the opposite way around. There are a number of methods that have commonly been used to obtain documentation. These are listed below.

- **Selling a vehicle with no documentation.** The simplest method is to sell a vehicle claiming that the documentation has been lost and telling the purchaser to obtain replacements from the DVLA. In these circumstances, the purchaser may suspect or know that the vehicle is stolen but still buys it because it is cheap.

- **Forging documentation.** Another method is to sell a vehicle with documentation that has been forged. This can be the documents relating to scrapped vehicles that had been doctored to show the new vehicle's identity, new documents produced on high-quality photocopiers or blank registration documents stolen from vehicle licensing offices.

- **Fraudulently obtaining the identity of a registered keeper.** In some cases, organised crime groups have obtained the identity of registered keepers and then arranged for the replacement vehicle registration to be sent to a different address.

- **Bribing a local official.** Rung vehicles have also been registered by bribing a member of staff in a local vehicle registration office.

- **Re-registering salvage.** A common method of ringing is to buy a car that is an insurance write-off and then to use the identity of that vehicle on a stolen vehicle whose identifying features have been changed to match those of the written-off vehicle. The stolen vehicle is then re-registered under the guise of being a written-off vehicle that has been rebuilt and made roadworthy.

- **Creating Euro-clones.** A Euro-clone involves obtaining the identity of a similar model in another European country and then pretending it has been imported into the UK for registration here. This relies on local vehicle registration officers being unused to seeing foreign registration documents, which will have been forged. A simpler version of this method is to invent the details of the European vehicle before registering it in the UK.

These are among the most common methods of ringing vehicles and there are no doubt many others that are used effectively.

Theft for export

The final destination for stolen vehicles is the export market. However, given the fact that we in the UK drive on the left-hand side of the road and most of the rest of the world drive on the right, where do these exported vehicles go? The first response to this question is that there are in the region of 75 countries around the world that actually drive on the left. Many of these are part of the Commonwealth, with whom there are good trading links and which historically were a market for British manufacturers. This can mean that these countries have an infrastructure for maintaining vehicles from Britain and, given that they drive on the left, will not stand out as unusual. Brown (1995) noted how Bedford trucks were commonly stolen in the UK and pointed to the fact that such vehicles were still popular in Africa which had at one time been an important market for the company.

The second response to where stolen right-hand drive (therefore designed to be driven on the left) vehicles go is that this does not appear to be a blockage to vehicles being exported to left-hand drive countries. For example, there are news stories of cars stolen in the UK and exported to Poland and other central European countries and to the United Arab Emirates, all of which are left-hand drive countries. There have also been examples of cars stolen in Hong Kong (who drive on the left) and taken to mainland China (who drive on the right).

Unlike other types of smuggling (such as drugs and people trafficking), where goods move from the poorer south to the richer north, stolen vehicles tend to move in the opposite direction. However, the scale of exported stolen vehicles may not be as large as official estimates. Law enforcement estimates of the number of permanently stolen vehicles in the UK that have been exported range from 10 to 20 per cent. However, estimates by Clarke and Brown (2003) suggested that the figure may be closer to 0.2 per cent of unrecovered stolen vehicles being exported.

Methods of theft

Methods of theft have changed over time, in response to improvements in security by motor manufacturers. Southall and Ekblom (1985) likened this to an arms race in which vehicle thieves have adapted their methods to overcome increasingly sophisticated security technologies.

At one time, vehicles could be easily started with the use of a screwdriver or similar implement inserted in the barrel of the ignition (Spencer 1992). The introduction of steering locks on all new vehicles in the early 1970s provided an extra challenge for the vehicle thief and is heralded as having had an impact on temporary thefts (Webb 1994). However, many thieves found ways to overcome this form of security and thefts continued to rise in the 1980s. As Spencer (1992) noted, a scaffold bar could be used as leverage to break a steering column lock.

Electronic immobilisation, introduced in the early 1990s meant that cars have become practically impossible to start without obtaining the key. This has led to methods of theft that focus on the obtaining of the key. Levesley *et al.* (2004) showed that, for cars built after 1997, a key was known to have been used in 85 per cent of cases. One method of obtaining the key has involved carjacking, in which the car is targeted by a thief while the driver is still in it. This has been a greater problem in other countries, such as the USA (Klaus 1999) and South Africa (Minnaar and Zinn 2000), than in the UK. Here, there appears to have been little systematic research on the subject, although there continue to be small numbers reported by the media. The work of Levesley *et al.* (2004) showed that just 4 per cent of car thefts involved robbery for the key, including carjackings. Of greater concern are burglaries that are undertaken in order to obtain the keys. Levesley *et al.* (2004) showed that burglaries were the most common method for obtaining the key, accounting for 37 per cent of thefts.

Profile of victims of vehicle theft

The British Crime Survey provides the best profile of victims of car theft in the UK. The mostly recently available figures (Kershaw *et al.* 2008) show a number of socio-demographic factors are associated with higher risk. For example, younger households tend to be at greater risk than older households. Indeed, 9.4 per cent of 16–24 year olds experienced a vehicle-related theft[6] compared to 1.9 per cent of those aged over 75 years.

Households in areas with high levels of physical disorder were more likely to be victims of vehicle-related theft (10.5 per cent) than areas where the level was not high (6.2 per cent). Furthermore, those with three or more vehicles were also more likely to be victims (10.2 per cent) than those owning one vehicle (5.3 per cent).

Profile of vehicle crime offenders

The Offending, Crime and Justice Survey (2006) showed that 1 per cent of young people aged 10–25 had engaged in a theft of a motor vehicle (Roe and Ashe 2008). However, the sample sizes of this group were too small for further analysis, which meant that offences were grouped to create a vehicle-related theft category, of which 2 per cent of 10–25 year olds had committed such an offence.

Three per cent of young men aged 10–25 years were found to have committed a vehicle-related theft in the previous year, compared to 1 per cent of young women. Furthermore, the age of males committing vehicle-related theft peaked at 14–15 years, with 6 per cent of this age group committing such an offence, compared to 5 per cent of 16–17 year olds, 4 per cent of 18–19 year olds and 2 per cent of 20–21 year olds. Light *et al.* (1993) similarly found that almost half of their sample first engaged in thefts of vehicles when they were 14 or 15 years old. These findings indicate that vehicle-related thefts are most likely to be committed by teenage boys.

Analysis of the Offenders Index by Rose (2000) found that those convicted of a theft of a vehicle tended to be slightly older, with 31 per cent aged 18–20 years and 23 per cent aged 21–25 years. Rose also found that 70 per cent of the vehicle thieves appearing on the Offenders Index in 1996 had previous convictions (of any kind) and 48 per cent had previous convictions for other vehicle theft offences. This group had an average of 15 previous offences. Furthermore, 52 per cent of offenders convicted of a car theft were reconvicted of another offence within 12 months. These figures suggest that, while, overall, the prevalence of involvement in vehicle crime is low, those that do engage in such behaviour often continue to engage in such offending over a period of time. Indeed, the risk of detection and sanction does not necessarily appear to be a sufficient deterrent to prevent car thieves from engaging in this type of crime. Taken to its extreme, in the 1980s and 1990s there were examples of joyriders who had suffered punishment beatings at the hands of paramilitaries in Northern Ireland who still continued to steal cars (McCullough *et al.* 1990).

Explanations of the crime

In explaining the causes behind thefts of vehicles, we again need to differentiate between temporary thefts and permanent thefts as each are likely to involve quite different motivations. This is not to deny that motivations may change over time, with those involved in temporary thefts later using the skills they gained to more financially profitable ends by engaging in thefts for permanent use.

Explanations for temporary thefts

So far as temporary thefts are concerned, many of the vehicles stolen will be for joyriding and in these cases the explanations are largely expressive in nature. Vehicle thieves (mostly teenage boys as outlined above) will often commit such offences for the thrill and excitement of stealing cars and driving them at high speed. This will be an antidote to feelings of boredom. Excitement and boredom are therefore often expressed as key motivations for involvement in joyriding (Light *et al.* 1993).

However, another key motivation often cited is the influence of peers. Light *et al.* (1993) showed how peers were important in the decision to engage in car theft and that it was considered important to impress a group of friends and to be accepted by the group. This was often a gradual process with new members being drawn into the offending over time, often starting with going along as a passenger at first, before graduating to stealing the car.

There are a number of criminological theories relevant to this explanation for involvement in crime. Key among these is differential associated theory (Sutherland 1942), which explains how offending behaviour is often learned from a group already involved in offending. Such groups will provide the attitudes and rationalisation for involvement in offending and bestow status on those involved in offending. In addition, they will provide the means by which methods of committing crime can be learned. Given the fact that joyriding appears to be largely a group activity, differential associated theory may be relevant for explaining how young people are introduced to, and become proficient in, this type of behaviour.

However, differential association does not necessarily explain why young people turn to vehicle theft in the first instance. Why should this be popular as an activity among some individuals rather than other potential activities? Part of the explanation here may be the status given to the motor car in our society. It is generally recognised to be the second largest purchase that one makes in one's life (after buying a house) and the type of car one drives bestows status on the driver. For example, one is likely to view differently a driver of a 15-year-old Ford Escort with a body-kit and big exhaust, from a Volvo driver, or Aston Martin driver. With cars, we make snap judgments about the characteristics of the driver and motor manufacturers have exploited this by segmenting the market according to different types of driver. Cars have therefore become a powerful symbol of success and one's status in terms of wealth and power (as bestowed by others) will, to some degree, be shaped by the car that one drives.

The fact that the car has become so important as a status symbol should be viewed as a major success for motor manufacturers, who spend millions of pounds annually to promote their latest models. Indeed, the fact that much of the advertising of cars is associated with the lifestyle characteristics of the driver rather than the specification of the vehicle points to the importance of the car as a status symbol.

There is, however, an inbuilt dilemma for young people in this regard. Indeed, they may recognise the importance of cars as a status symbol at a point in their lives when they may be exploring their own position and status in society. However, they will also come to recognise that the symbols of success that are most valued are also those that they are least likely to acquire. Expensive or high-performance cars that they are unlikely to obtain through legitimate means any time soon will also be viewed highly among many young men in particular. This holds not only for car thieves but for young men in general. Faced with this dilemma, some young people may decide to steal cars as a way of achieving status among their peers, even if it is for a limited period of time. This may explain why sportier models of car tend to be preferred by joyriders, as they bestow a greater degree of status on the driver (although they will also be more exciting to drive too!).

Although it has largely fallen into disuse generally in criminology, the specific motivation for joyriding described here would suggest there may be something anomic (Merton 1938) about the desire for cars. Faced, on the one hand, by powerful prescribed cultural goals to exhibit success through the car one drives (a goal that may be even more important among teenage male subcultures) and, on the other hand, with the inability to achieve that success through institutionalised, legitimate means, some young people may choose to make an 'innovative' response to this problem by stealing cars to obtain status.

Explanations for permanent thefts

Explanations for permanent thefts can be considered more instrumental than those for temporary thefts as the motive is far more likely to be about profit. Here, rationale choice theory (Cornish and Clarke 1986) would seem particularly pertinent. The theft of vehicles becomes a rational decision based on the alternative legitimate and illegitimate opportunities, taking into account the costs associated with detection and possible sanction. On this basis, one can assume that the gains to be made from stealing vehicles for stripping, resale or export outweigh the costs associated with these endeavours.

This decision-making process is also aided by the fact that vehicles tend to meet the criteria of *hot-products* (Clarke 1999). Clarke established that the likelihood of theft of a product depended on the extent to which it was Concealable, Removable, Available, Valuable, Enjoyable and Disposable (giving an acronym of CRAVED).

Vehicles are particularly good at meeting the CRAVED criteria. They are Concealable in the sense that their identity can be changed to appear like any other vehicle on the road. In this sense, they are hidden by their ordinariness. The fact that the majority of cars that are stolen are the high-volume models lends support to this argument. One is unlikely to take any notice of a Ford Mondeo parked outside a garage because of its ubiquity – one expects to find such cars in such places so a stolen one is unlikely to stand out. However, a Ferrari is likely to draw more attention because such cars are not so commonplace. Therefore stolen cars with changed identities are concealable by the fact that they can be hidden within the general vehicle parc. Under these circumstances, finding one that has been stolen becomes like looking for a needle in a haystack. So far as stripping cars for their component parts is concerned, they will be concealable by the fact that one used stolen component will look just like a used legitimate item. Moreover, unless a stolen component has serial numbers that can be traced to an individual vehicle, there is no way of proving whether a part has been stolen.

Vehicles are by definition Removable in the sense that they are designed to be moved from one place to another. For a vehicle to be removable for the thief, this relies on overcoming the security, although (as noted above) this is becoming easier by the increasing trend towards acquiring the keys. In the worst case scenario, should a thief fail to overcome the security on a car, it can always be towed away or loaded onto the back of a lorry.

Vehicles are also abundantly Available. In, 2007, there were 34 million vehicles registered in Great Britain, according to the Department for Transport (2008). This provides plenty of targets for theft.

Vehicles are Valuable in the sense that they will have a market price which is widely known. There are a number of price guides for cars that are published on a regular basis and these provide the average market value of vehicles for different conditions. This means that prospective buyers will generally have a good idea how much a vehicle is worth and know when they are offered a bargain, as may well be the case when stolen vehicles are on offer. They also represent a major purchase for most consumers and therefore will often provide a good return for a car thief given the effort expended to obtain a vehicle. As noted earlier, component parts for vehicles are often expensive and this can make the sale of stolen components profitable.

Vehicles are also generally Enjoyable in the sense that many people will enjoy the sensation of driving at speed, or may simply enjoy the comfort that comes from driving a newer car.

Finally, vehicles are Disposable by the fact that there is a market in which they can be traded. The fact that there is ready demand for vehicles and their component parts means that they can often be introduced into the legitimate market and sold to unsuspecting buyers.

Response to the crime

Since the peak of the vehicle crime problem in the early 1990s, governments have taken a number of steps to tackle the problem. One of the key steps was the publication of the first Home Office Car Theft Index in 1992 (Houghton 1992). At that time, car security was not considered to be a major concern of motor manufacturers, who were more focused on comfort and performance. Laycock (2004) has shown how the Car Theft Index was used to publicise for the first time the vehicles that were most at risk of theft and to encourage manufacturers to improve the security on their models. This led to rapid improvements in the security of new models.

The government's approach from this point forward was to build partnerships with industry representatives and there followed a series of multi-agency working groups designed to tackle vehicle crime from a range of perspectives. In 1993, the Vehicle Crime Prevention Group was established as a subcommittee of the National Board for Crime Prevention. This later continued as a subcommittee of the Crime Prevention Agency when that was formed in 1995. In 1998, the Vehicle Crime Prevention Group was disbanded and a new Vehicle Crime Reduction Action Team (VCRAT) was established. This published a five-year vehicle crime reduction strategy under the auspices of the Home Office. A number of further multi-agency subgroups were also formed to tackle specific aspects of vehicle theft. These included the Joint

Action Group on Lorry Theft and the Construction Plant Action Group, each of which developed its own programmes of work to tackle thefts of vehicles.

This multi-agency approach was generally regarded to be successful. A report by the National Audit Office (Comptroller and Auditor General 2005) showed that the Home Office and the work of VCRAT had succeeded in reducing vehicle crime (although the fact that other forms of property crime, such as burglary, fell significantly over the same period and that UK trends were repeated in many other industrialised countries calls into question whether the Home Office can take full credit for the reductions observed in vehicle crime).

The specific responses to thefts of vehicles can be seen in the work that has been undertaken in relation to three key areas – social crime prevention, enforcement and situational crime prevention.

Social crime prevention

Social crime prevention associated with vehicle thefts has concentrated on tackling the motivations for engaging in vehicle crime among those already engaged in such offending and those at risk of doing so. During the 1980s and 1990s many areas introduced motor projects in which participants were provided with a mix of education and practical experience of working on cars. These were designed to channel young people's interests in cars into more legitimate aspects, such as providing mechanic skills. Some also offered the opportunity to replicate the thrill of driving at high speed by entering into banger races. The results of evaluations of these schemes were mixed, although there was relatively little evidence of effectiveness (Wilkinson 1997; Sugg 1998; Smith 1999).

Enforcement

A range of enforcement approaches has been tried to increase the risk of detection associated with vehicle theft. For example, the use of decoy vehicles by the police has been shown to be effective (Sallybanks 2001) as a method of both detecting and preventing crime. This method involves the deployment of a vehicle that is placed under surveillance by the police in the expectation that it will become the target of a theft. Brown *et al.* (2004) reported on an evaluation of an intelligence-led vehicle crime reduction approach, in which police resources at the Basic Command Unit level were focused on addressing vehicle crime in one particular area, using a mix of targeted enforcement and crime prevention advice. The results were, however, equivocal, with a relatively small impact being demonstrated given the level of resources devoted to the operation.

Many police forces in England and Wales have in the past also operated vehicle crime units to target organised groups involved in stealing vehicles. However, with the decline in vehicle crime over the last decade, many of these have been disbanded.

Enforcement activity has also been undertaken in relation to salvage yards. Since October 2002, motor salvage yards in England and Wales have been required to register with the local authority and to agree to regular inspections by the police.

New technology has also played a role in police enforcement. For example, Automatic Number Plate Recognition (ANPR) has been used in conjunction with CCTV systems to identify vehicles that have been flagged by the police for further attention. These have been used with specialist police units to increase detections associated with thefts of vehicles as well as in relation to a host of other types of crime. A national evaluation of ANPR showed that use of the technology had resulted in 20,592 arrests, the identification of 52,037 document offences and the identification and recovery of 2,021 stolen vehicles (PA Consulting 2007).

Much of the current police enforcement work associated with vehicle crime has involved more generic targeting of prolific offenders (Dawson and Cuppleditch 2007), in the recognition that most vehicle-related offenders are not specialist – they are likely to be involved in a range of different types of offending simultaneously. As such, the focus has been more on the individual rather than on the offence.

Situational crime prevention

The use of situational crime prevention measures to reduce the thefts of cars represents one of the most successful examples of crime control. These approaches have been widely used in the UK and have paid significant dividends in terms of vehicle crime reduction.

Where the vehicle itself is concerned, there has been a steady development in new technology designed to prevent thefts. In 1975, steering column locks became a mandatory requirement for type-approval on all new cars (under the Motor Vehicle (Type Approval) (Amendment) Regulations 1975) following an earlier European Directive (Council Directive 74/61/EEC). These steering column locks were shown to have an impact on temporary thefts of vehicles by preventing amateur thieves from stealing cars (Mayhew and Hough 1976), although there was also shown to be a degree of displacement towards older, unprotected cars. The way in which steering column locks were introduced, with new vehicles only being installed with the new technology, left a large number of unprotected vehicles on the road and it took more than a decade before a sizable proportion of the vehicle parc was protected. Webb (1994) compared the patterns in the UK to Germany, where steering column locks were introduced to the entire vehicle parc. This was found to have the effect of immediate and sustained reductions in vehicle theft.

In the late 1980s electronic immobilisers began to be available on new models of car, although at first these were an optional extra. These immobilisers prevented a vehicle from being started without a key (some early versions required a separate immobiliser key as well as the standard ignition key) which meant vehicles could not be hot-wired or started with a screwdriver.

With the falling cost and increasing use of this new technology, new European Union regulations were introduced in 1995 requiring all vehicles registered from October 1998 to be installed with an electronic immobiliser. Brown and Thomas (2003) and Brown (2004) showed how these immobilisers had been particularly effective in reducing thefts – especially temporary thefts – although there were signs of displacement to older vehicles.

Other forms of vehicle security have also seen large increases in usage, although without a statutory requirement. For example, according to the British Crime Survey, 35 per cent of households reported that their car had central locking in 1992. This had increased to 87 per cent by 2005/06. Similarly, the proportion of households reporting a car with an alarm increased from 23 per cent in 1992 to 63 per cent in 2005/06.

Improved security has not been restricted to vehicles. The Secured Car Park initiative (later rebranded as the Safer Parking Initiative and administered by the British Parking Association) introduced an award scheme for car parks, which established criteria based largely on situational crime prevention measures. An evaluation of the scheme by Smith *et al.* (2003) showed that these car parks reduced the risks of vehicle crime significantly. This has helped to tackle some of the most vulnerable locations for thefts, although the majority of car parks in the UK are still not covered by this scheme.

Discussion and conclusions

Vehicle crime in the UK experienced large increases during the 1980s, followed by declines from 1992 onwards. This seems to have held for thefts of vehicles (both permanent and temporary) and thefts from vehicles. The last two decades have been marked by a great deal of action that has been undertaken to reduce the risks of theft, especially in relation to thefts of vehicles. Arguably the most successful measure has been the introduction of electronic immobilisation which has made the theft of cars built since 1998 practically impossible without a key. Furthermore, the 'passive' nature of this crime prevention measure means that it works without the need for the vehicle owner to do anything other than look after the key. This feature is preferable to more 'active' crime prevention measures that rely on vehicle owners taking positive action.

Looking forward, the introduction of immobilisers is also likely to change the nature of vehicle theft. Temporary thefts of vehicles are likely to continue to decline because of the difficulty in starting a car. This may herald the end of joyriding by all but the most persistent of offenders. Anecdotally, we now seldom hear reports in the media of joyriding which were at one time commonplace. This raises an issue about the notion of joyriding being an adaptive response to anomic pressures involving an excess of aspiration over expectation. If young people are no longer able to steal cars as a way of achieving status, to what alternative responses are they likely to turn? This may be in terms of other forms of acquisitive property crime as a means of acquiring the resources with which to conspicuously consume the goods that will bestow status among their peers. Alternatively, it may involve the acquisition of status through involvement in other forms of crime, such as robbery and violence. The key here is that if anomic pressures were previously a factor for joyriding, one would expect them still to exist, with an expectation that such pressures would need to be channelled in some way.

Where the theft of vehicles for professional gain is concerned, we can expect to see this persist as long as there is a viable profit to be made from such endeavours. Enforcement efforts may continue, but with low detection rates and potentially large profit margins, thefts of vehicles are likely to continue. In particular, ringing of vehicles is likely to persist as long as there continue to be loopholes in the vehicle registration system that allows stolen vehicles to be recycled into the legitimate market. While work is being undertaken to address this issue, there would still appear to be much that could be done.

Furthermore, one is likely to continue to see a rise in the number of burglaries as a means to obtain car keys. This represents the most viable way to steal cars with electronic immobilisation. As a result, it is possible that one will see an increase in the average value of the vehicles that are stolen in future. Faced with the opportunity to steal two new cars – a low-value one and a high-value one – one can expect that a vehicle thief will seek to maximise profits by stealing the new car, given that the effort involved in stealing each is likely to be similar (both requiring a burglary to obtain the keys). Brown and Thomas (2003) pointed towards evidence that this was beginning to occur. This pattern is amplified by the fact that older, low-value vehicles are increasingly being secured as electronic immobilisation works through the vehicle parc, meaning they are no longer available as targets of theft employing 'traditional' methods.

One final point worth making is in relation to the trends in thefts from vehicles. It is beyond question that a great deal of work has been undertaken to address thefts of vehicles with a focus of attention by successive governments and intervention from a range of perspectives – both crime prevention and detection. It is also clear that thefts of vehicles have fallen sharply during the very time when this activity was being undertaken. Yet there remains a doubt about what brought this reduction in thefts of vehicles about. If we look at the pattern of thefts from vehicles, we see that such offences have, according to police recorded figures, also declined significantly since 1992.[7] This large reduction was achieved without anything like the effort that was devoted to thefts of vehicles. This raises a number of possibilities. Either the work that has gone into reducing thefts of vehicles has in some way had a protective effect on thefts from vehicles, the limited effort focused on thefts from vehicles has been much more effective than that expended on thefts of vehicles, or reductions in both thefts of and thefts from vehicles have been due to some other external factor (such as other economic or social forces). It therefore remains unclear what has brought about the reduction in vehicle crime in recent years. However, one can predict that the reduction in thefts of vehicles (given the types of interventions that have been undertaken) is more sustainable than reductions in thefts from vehicles.

Selected further reading

A useful overview of many of the issues associated with vehicle crime can be found in *Understanding and Preventing Car Theft* edited by Maxfield and Clarke (2004). There are also a number of useful websites with vehicle crime-related publications, including the Home Office in England and Wales (http://www.homeoffice.gov.uk/rds/), the Comprehensive Auto-Theft Research System (CARS) in Australia (http://www.ncars. on.net/publish.asp) and the National Insurance Crime Bureau (http://www.nicb.org) in the USA.

Notes

1 This was introduced in the Aggravated Vehicle-Taking Act 1992.
2 Note that this analysis has not been repeated since 1996.
3 As cars make up 80 per cent of vehicles stolen, we will concentrate solely on the models of car that are stolen.
4 The average across all countries examined was 1.2 per cent of owners having a car stolen.
5 Including thefts of vehicles, thefts from vehicles, aggravated vehicle taking and vehicle interference.
6 Including thefts of vehicles, thefts from vehicles, aggravated vehicle taking and vehicle interference.
7 Between 1992 and 2008/9, thefts from vehicles declined by 54 per cent while theft and unauthorised taking of vehicles declined by 71 per cent.

References

Braun, G. and Wilkinson, M. (2005) *The Extent of Motorcycle Theft*, Home Office Research Findings No. 269. London: Home Office.

Brown, R. (1995) *The Nature and Extent of Heavy Goods Vehicle Theft*, Crime Detection and Prevention Series Paper No. 66. London: Home Office.

Brown, R. (2004) 'The effectiveness of electronic immobilisation: changing patterns of temporary and permanent vehicle theft', in M.G. Maxfield and R.V. Clarke (eds), *Understanding and Preventing Car Theft*, Crime Prevention Studies Vol. 17. Monsey, NY: Criminal Justice Press.

Brown, R. and Saliba, J. (1998) *The Nature and Extent of Light Commercial Vehicle Theft*, Crime Detection and Prevention Series Paper No. 88. London: Home Office.

Brown, R. and Thomas, N. (2003) 'Aging vehicles: evidence of the effectiveness of new car security from the Home Office Car Theft Index', *Security Journal*, 16 (3): 45–54.

Brown, R., Cannings, A. and Sherriff, J. (2004) *Intelligence-Led Vehicle Crime Reduction: An Evaluation of Operation Gallant*, Home Office Online Report No. 47/04. London: Home Office.

Brown, R., Clarke, R. V., Sheptyki, J. and Rix, B. (2004) *Tackling Organised Vehicle Crime: The Role of NCIS*, Home Office Findings No. 238. London: Home Office.

Clarke, R. V. (1999) *Hot Products: Understanding, Anticipating and Reducing Demand for Stolen Goods*, Crime Detection and Prevention Series Paper 112. London: Home Office.

Clarke, R. V. and Brown, R. (2003) 'International trafficking in stolen vehicles', in M. Tonry (ed.), *Crime and Justice: A Review of Research*, Vol. 30. London: University of Chicago Press.

Clarke, R. V. and Mayhew, P. (1994) 'Parking patterns and car theft risks: policy relevant findings from the British Crime Survey', in R. V. Clarke (ed.), *Crime Prevention Studies*, Vol. III. Monsey, NY: Criminal Justice Press.

Clarke, R. V. and Mayhew, P. (1998) 'Preventing crime in parking lots: what we know and need to know', in M. Felson and R. Peiser (eds), *Crime Prevention Through Real Estate Management and Development*. Washington, DC: Urban Land Institute.

Comptroller and Auditor General (2005) *Home Office: Reducing Vehicle Crime*. London: National Audit Office.

Cornish, D. and Clarke, R. V. (1986) 'Introduction', in D. Cornish and R. Clarke (eds), *The Reasoning Criminal*. New York: Springer-Verlag. pp. 1–16.

Dawson, P. and Cuppleditch, L. (2007) *An Impact Assessment of the Prolific and Other Priority Offender Programme*, Home Office Online Report No. 08/07. London: Home Office.

Department for Transport (2008) *Transport Trends: 2008 Edition*. London: Department for Transport.

Harris, P. M. and Clarke, R. V. (1991) 'Car chopping, parts marking and the Motor Vehicle Theft Law Enforcement Act of 1984', *Sociology and Social Research*, 74 (4): 228–33.

Houghton, G. (1992) *Car Theft in England and Wales: The Home Office Car Theft Index*, Crime Prevention Unit Paper No. 33. London: Home Office.

Kershaw, C., Nicholas, S. and Walker, A. (2008) *Crime in England and Wales 2007/08: Findings from the British Crime Survey and Police Recorded Crime*, July 2008. London: Home Office.

Klaus, P. (1999) *Carjackings in the United States, 1992–96*, Bureau of Justice Statistics Special Report. Washington, DC: US Department of Justice, Office of Justice Reform.

Laycock, G. (2004) 'The UK Car Theft Index: an example of government leverage', in M. G. Maxfield and R. V. Clarke (eds), *Understanding and Preventing Car Theft*, Crime Prevention Studies, Vol. 17. Monsey, NY: Criminal Justice Press.

Levesley, T., Braun, G., Wilkinson, M. and Powell, C. (2004) *Emerging Methods of Car Theft – Theft of Keys*, Research Findings No. 239. London: Home Office.

Light, R., Nee, C. and Ingham, H. (1993) *Car Theft: The Offenders' Perspective*, Home Office Research Study No. 130. London: Home Office.

McCullough, D., Schmidt, T. and Lockhart, B. (1990) *Car Theft in Northern Ireland*, Cirac Paper No. 2. Belfast: Extern Organisation.

Mayhew, P. and Braun, G. (2004) 'Parking lot security', in Michael G. Maxfield and Ronald V. Clarke (eds), *Understanding and Preventing Car Theft*, Crime Prevention Studies Vol. 17. Monsey, NY: Criminal Justice Press.

Mayhew, P. and Hough, M. (1976) *Crime as Opportunity*, Home Office Research Study No. 34. London: Home Office.

Maxfield, M. G. and Clarke, R. V. (2004) *Understanding and Preventing Car Theft*, Crime Prevention Series Vol. 17. Monsey, NY: Criminal Justice Press.

Merton, R. K. (1938) 'Social structure and anomie', *American Sociological Review*, 3: 672–82.

Minnaar, A. and Zinn, R. (2000) *Vehicle Hijacking in South Africa: An Examination of Victimisation Patterns and an Evaluation of Current Prevention/Interventionist Strategies with Specific Reference to Gauteng Province, South Africa*. Online at: http://bcpf.homestead.com/Vehicle_Hijackings_-_Zinn__Minnaar.pdf.

Mirrlees-Black, C., Mayhew, P. and Percy, A. (1996) *The 1996 British Crime Survey: England and Wales*, Home Office Statistical Bulletin No. 19/96. London: Home Office.

PA Consulting (2007) *Evaluation of Automatic Number Plate Recognition 2006/07*. London: Police Standard Unit, Home Office.

Roe, S. and Ashe, J. (2008) *Young People and Crime: Findings from the 2006 Offending, Crime and Justice Survey*, Home Office Statistical Bulletin No. 09/08. London: Home Office.

Rose, G. (2000) *The Criminal Histories of Serious Traffic Offenders*, Home Office Research Study No. 206. London: Home Office.

Sallybanks, J. (2001) *Assessing the Police Use of Decoy Vehicles*, Police Research Series Paper 137. London: Home Office.

Sallybanks, J. and Brown, R. (1999) *Vehicle Crime Reduction: Turning the Corner*, Police Research Series Paper No. 119. London: Home Office.

Smith, A. (1999) *Motor Projects Reviewed: Current Knowledge of Good Practice*. London: Home Office.

Smith, D. G., Gregson, M. and Morgan, J. (2003) *Between the Lines: An Evaluation of the Secured Car Park Award Scheme*, Home Office Research Study No. 266. London: Home Office.

Southall, D. and Ekblom, P. (1985) *Designing for Car Security: Towards a Crime-Free Car*, Crime Prevention Unit Paper No. 4. London: Home Office.

Spencer, E. (1992) *Car Crime and Young People on a Sunderland Housing Estate*, Crime Prevention Unit Series No. 40. London: Home Office.

Sugg, D. (1998) *Motor Projects in England and Wales: An Evaluation*, Research Findings No. 81. London: Home Office.

Sutherland, E. H. (1942) 'Development of the theory', in Karl Schuessler (ed.), *On Analyzing Crime*. Chicago: University of Chicago Press.

van Kesteren, J. N., Mayhew, P. and Nieuwbeerta, P. (2000) *Criminal Victimisation in Seventeen Industrialised Countries: Key Findings from the 2000 International Crime Victims Survey*. The Hague: Ministry of Justice, WODC.

Walker, A., Kershaw, C. and Nichols, S. (2006) *Crime in England and Wales 2005/06*, July 2006. London: Home Office.

Webb, B. (1994) 'Steering column locks and motor vehicle theft: evaluations from three countries', in R. V. Clarke (ed.), *Crime Prevention Studies*, Vol. 2. London: Willow Tree Press.

Webb, B. and Laycock, G. (1992) *Tackling Car Crime: The Nature and Extent of the Problem*, Crime Prevention Unit Paper No. 32. London: Home Office.

Webb, B., Smith, M. and Laycock, G. (2004) 'Designing out crime through vehicle licensing and registration systems', in M. G. Maxfield and R. V. Clarke (eds), *Understanding and Preventing Car Theft*, Crime Prevention Studies Vol. 17. Monsey, NY: Criminal Justice Press.

Wilkinson, J. (1997) 'The impact of the Ilderton Motor Project on Motor Vehicle Crime and Offending', *British Journal of Criminology*, 32 (4): 568–81.

Chapter 3

Shoplifting

Nick Tilley

The Oxford English Dictionary indicates that the term 'shoplifting' goes back to 1680. Some people prefer the term 'shop theft' on the grounds that shoplifting might seem to trivialise the offence, which is indeed that of theft, although from shops rather than any other target. What distinguishes shoplifting from burglary is that the perpetrator has legitimate access to the premises from which the stolen goods are taken. What distinguishes it from robbery is that no use or threat of violence is involved. What distinguishes it from staff theft is that the person committing the offence is not employed by the shop. In short, shoplifting refers to the crime of theft, where customers (or those posing as customers) steal from retail outlets to which they have legitimate access.

In this chapter the terms 'shoplifting', 'shop theft' and 'customer theft' will be used interchangeably, although shoplifting will generally be preferred on account of its brevity, common usage and long history. Issues of the seriousness, or triviality, of the offence will be considered in due course.

Patterns of shoplifting and their measurement

What can be said with some confidence is that shoplifting is a high-volume offence. It is tricky to determine exactly how much of it there is. Different methods of measurement yield widely varying estimates. Problems of measurement mean that estimates of trends and distributions by victim, target and offender are subject to substantial uncertainty.

An obvious starting point is recorded crime trends. Theft from shops has been returned as a separate offence in England and Wales since 1934, although there are earlier reports of shoplifting as a common offence in London from the eighteenth century and also in Paris, Boston and New York from the nineteenth century (Segrave 2001). Figure 3.1 shows the trends in recorded shop theft since 1934 in England and Wales. It shows that numbers of incidents grew rapidly from the 1950s to the mid-1980s. There was a substantial dip between

1985 and 1989, which was largely an artefact of the informal means then used to deal with shoplifters (Farrington and Burrows 1993), after which numbers of recorded incidents rose rapidly once more, before levelling off from the early 1990s. Since the Second World War the volume of recorded shop theft incidents has grown more quickly than other types of property/acquisitive crime. Figure 3.2 shows the trends in each, indexed to 100 in 1945.

There are distinct difficulties in using recorded shop thefts as an indicator of the real level of shop theft. Many incidents will not be noticed, and of those noticed many will not be reported to the police. The police may then,

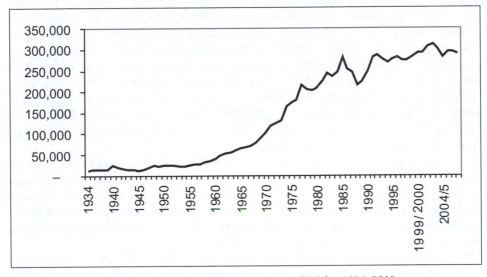

Figure 3.1 Trends in recorded shop theft England and Wales 1934–2008

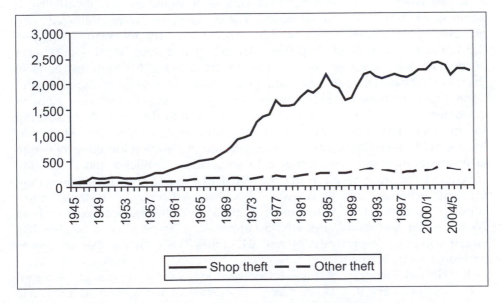

Figure 3.2 Indexed trends in shop theft and other theft 1945–2008

of course, not record all incidents reported to them. What is distinctive about shop theft, as compared to other incidents where crime may not be reported or recorded, is the fact that many incidents may not be noticed. The retailer may know that they have suffered 'shrinkage', but will generally be unable to distinguish shop thefts from other sources such as theft by shop workers, shortfalls in delivery and wastage.

Commercial victimisation surveys comprise one alternative to recorded crime data for measuring levels of shop theft. These ask a randomly selected sample of businesses about the crimes they have suffered in the previous year. The Commercial Victimisation Survey (CVS) of 2002 found that shops in England and Wales had experienced an average (median) of 25 incidents of shop theft each over the previous 12 months (Shury et al. 2005). Based on the survey findings it was estimated that there were 11,493,000 incidents of shop theft in 2002. To put this in perspective, that figure is close to the BCS estimate for all crime against individuals and households in the same year, which stood at 12,618,000, and more than twice the total for all recordable crime in 2001–2, which stood at 5,525,000 (Nicholas et al. 2007). There were just 306,596 recorded shop thefts in 2001/2, one in 37 of those estimated to have taken place according to the CVS.

Commercial victimisation surveys have their own weaknesses. As already indicated, owners and managers of shops may not know the composition of their shrinkage. They have no way of being sure of the number of shop theft incidents they have suffered. In replying to questions in commercial victimisation surveys they are making estimates which may be systematically skewed in one direction or the other.

One alternative to recorded crime data and survey findings for estimating levels of shop theft is to observe shoppers and count the numbers who engage in shoplifting. This method was adopted by Buckle and Farrington in a painstaking study of a random sample of shoppers in a small British department store in Peterborough. These shoppers were followed and observed by two researchers working together to try to ensure that they did not miss instances of shop theft. Altogether just over 500 shoppers were observed while they were in the store for an average 6.9 minutes. Nine of the 503 shoppers (1.8 per cent) stole at least one item while in the store and none was apprehended. The authors estimate that, given the throughput of customers, over 500 items per week were taken from the store. By comparing the number of recorded crime incidents in the area in which the store was located with the estimate for the store and roughly estimating the proportion of incidents that could be attributed to this one store, Buckle and Farrington concluded that the police record 'between 1 in 100 and 1 in 1,000 shoplifting incidents' (Buckle and Farrington 1984: 69). Assuming that these ratios continue to apply, this would mean that the real figures for shop theft in 2001/2 in England and Wales would fall between 30,659,600 and 306,596,000, which comprise respectively 24 and 243 times the total number of crimes covered by the BCS.

Buckle and Farrington's (1984) intensive study was meticulous in its design and execution. Yet it was, perforce, small-scale. They looked at only one store over a short period (three weeks) in one town and tracked only 500 shoppers. Questions might therefore be asked about its representativeness. However, a later study in Bedford using the same basic methods, although finding differences in the details of the patterns of offending, came to a similar conclusion about the ratio of recorded to actual numbers of shoplifting incidents (Farrington 1999). There appear to be few positive reasons to doubt Buckle and Farrington's basic findings. All the available evidence indicates that there is an eye-watering volume of shop theft in England and Wales, dwarfing all other crime.

What gets stolen?

Clarke (1999) uses the acronym CRAVED to describe the attributes of goods that tend to be stolen. CRAVED refers to Concealable, Removable, Available, Valuable, Enjoyable and Disposable. Expensive, small, high-demand, consumer goods fit the bill. Clarke quotes an American study (Hayes 1997) of what tends to be taken from various types of shop. Table 3.1 provides some examples.

In Britain, Walsh (1978) paints a picture of what was stolen in Exeter in 1975. He distinguishes between high risk, medium risk and low risk shops, and what is taken from them, as shown in Table 3.2.

As part of a project looking at differing means of preventing shoplifting Farrington *et al.* (1994) explored items stolen from Dixons and Currys stores in 1990. Using a method of 'repeated, systematic counting of specified items' they gauge the rate at which products are stolen by shoplifters. The technique involves attaching sticky labels to specified items and removing the labels from those sold at the till. This provides a count of the number sold. The relevant items on the shop floor are also counted at least once a day. The difference between the numbers sold and the change in numbers displayed (and put on display) provides an estimate of the number stolen by shoplifters. Farrington *et al.* found substantial variation by store and by product type among those for which measurements were made. Ten of the 29 stores included in the study lost at least 10 per cent of the specified items through customer theft. One store lost as much as 35 per cent of items and 36 per cent by value in this way. Across the 15 Dixons stores stolen items accounted for 11 per cent

Table 3.1 Most stolen items by type of store

Types of store	Most stolen items
Bookshops	Cassette tapes, magazines
Department stores	Clothing, shirts, jeans, Hilfiger and Polo items
Discount stores	Clothing, undergarments, CDs
Groceries, supermarkets, convenience stores	Medicines, beauty aids, cigarettes, video cassettes
Drug stores, pharmacies	Medicines, beauty aids, cigarettes, batteries, birth control
Hardware, DIY stores	Tools

Source: Clarke (1999), citing Hayes (1997).

Table 3.2 Types of shop and items shoplifted in Exeter

Level of risk	Shop type	Most stolen items
High (daily shoplifting)	Department stores	Most small items
	Food shops	Pre-packaged foodstuffs
	Confectioners	Cigars, chocolate bars
	Electrical and radio	Cassette tapes
	Ironmongers	Tools, especially power tools
	Motor accessories	Gloves, sunglasses, instruments
	Ladies clothing	Tights
	Booksellers	Stationery
Medium (intermittent shoplifting)	Chinaware	Ornaments
	Wine and spirits	Miniatures of spirits
	House furnishers	Display objects
	Chemists	Sundries (not medicines)
	Men's clothing	Ties, trousers
Low (virtually no shoplifting)	Butchers	Negligible
	Fishmongers	Negligible
	Greengrocers	Negligible
	Jewellers	Rings
	Office equipment	Negligible
	Shoe shops	Footwear
	Tailors	Small items

Source: Walsh (1978: 73).

of the audiotapes, 14 per cent of the films and a massive 24 per cent of the headphones that left the stores.

Who shoplifts?

Data on convicted shoplifters are liable to be highly biased. We have seen that rather a small proportion of all offences are noticed and of those noticed only a fraction are reported, dealt with by the police and proceeded with. The subset of incidents that come to official attention will reflect the patterns of suspicion that lead some rather than others to be watched and to some rather than others being processed as criminals when they leave a shop without paying for an item. Notwithstanding the small numbers formally processed in relation to the total number of incidents, shoplifting represents a high proportion of all cases of theft and the handling of stolen goods: almost three in five defendants (58 per cent) proceeded against for theft and handling stolen goods in England and Wales in 2005 were for shoplifting.

Speed and Burrows (2006) examined the Crown Prosecution Service case files relating to 1,563 cases of shoplifting in eight areas in the second half of 2004 and early 2005. Three-quarters of the offenders were male (76 per cent) and a quarter female, in line with Table 3.3 below, although given the sample all were aged 18 or over. The age range went from 18 to 69, with half aged between 18 and 29. Around 90 per cent were white Europeans, and the proportion of White European and non-White European offenders closely matched that of the local communities. Only 10 per cent were employed. Only 2 per cent had an address away from the area in which the offence took place, although a further 8 per cent were of no fixed abode. Each offender had an average of 19 previous convictions. Only 5 per cent had no previous convictions and only 2 per cent neither convictions nor a caution.

Because of the intrinsic weaknesses in data on those caught and processed through the criminal justice system for shoplifting, other sources have been sought. Research findings on the attributes of shoplifters, however, throw up mixed and contradictory results. Buckle and Farrington's observational studies in Peterborough and Bedford found higher rates for males than females (2.8 per cent as against 1.4 per cent in Peterborough and 2.2 per cent and 0.6 per cent in Bedford), and higher rates for older than younger shoppers in Peterborough (4.9 per cent for those judged to be aged over 55 compared to 1.0 per cent for the rest), but not for Bedford, where the 17–25 year olds were most likely to shoplift (Buckle and Farrington 1984: 67; Farrington 1999: 18). Buckle and Farrington also found that males tended to steal more items than females: 5.3 compared to 1.1 per 10 customer hours in Peterborough with 1.1 compared to 0.4 items in Bedford (Farrington 1999: 18).

A self-report study of 417 shoppers in Northampton by Tonglet found that shop theft tended to be more common among younger people (Tonglet 1998). She found that 14 per cent of under 20 year olds (18 of 130), 8 per cent of 20–29 year olds (7 of 90), but only 1 per cent of those aged 30 or over (2 of 197) admitted to shoplifting in the past year. Her findings did, however, accord with Buckle and Farrington's in finding a higher rate of shoplifting among males than females (9 per cent compared to 5 per cent over the previous year).

Farrington (2001) helpfully summarised the findings of a number of British self-report studies where questions about shoplifting were asked of young people, as shown in Table 3.3, to which two more recent studies have now been added. The range of responses is bewildering!

Reports from earlier times, which were not based on systematic empirical research, produce different impressions of who had been involved in shop theft. In the nineteenth and early twentieth centuries, Segrave (2001) reports recurrent concerns over posh ladies shoplifting in significant numbers from posh shops. Segrave refers, for example, to a newspaper article of 1908 quoting a Leslie Graff, Secretary of the Retail Dry Goods Association of New York City, saying that:

> The professional shoplifters don't bother us much … nor is it the poor people who rob the stores, in most cases. Wives of prominent business men, wives of clergymen, well-to-do supposedly respectable women whose husbands make $5,000 to $15,000 a year are those who prey upon the stores. They don't need to take the things; they just take them, and when they are detected and brought before proprietors of the store they weep and beg for mercy. They say their husbands will leave them if

Table 3.3 Attributes and shop theft results of major British self-report studies

Researcher and date of study	Sample characteristics	Shoplifting findings
Willcock (1963)	808 M aged 15–21 from England and Wales. Individual interview. 71% response.	6% ever stole from small shop, 3% ever stole from big store. Av. onset 13. Av. offences per offender 4.3 (small shop), 4.0 (big store).
Belson (1967)	1,425 M aged 13–16 from London. Individual interview. 86% response.	70% ever shoplifted. Av. onset 10. Av. offences per offender 9.7. Av. duration 4.2 years.
Mawby (1975)	327 M and 267 F aged 13–15 from one Sheffield school. Group self-completion. 80% response.	56.3% M and 38.6% F shoplifted in past year.
Riley and Shaw (1983)	378 M and 373 F aged 14–15 from England and Wales. Individual interview. 71% response.	2.4% M and 1.3% F stole item worth £1 or more. 12.4% M and 5.9% F stole item worth less than £1.
Anderson *et al.* (1989)	465 M and 427 F aged 11–15 from four Edinburgh schools. Group self-completion. Response rate not stated.	40% M and 30% F shoplifted in last 9 months.
McQuoid (1990)	149 M and 161 F aged 14–21 from Belfast. Individual interview. 95% response.	21.5 % M and 22.4% F ever shoplifted. Median age of onset 13. Av. offences per offender last year 2.3.
McQuoid (1992–3)	456 M and 427 F aged 14–21 from Belfast. Individual interview. 92% response.	26.8% ever shoplifted. 5.7% M and 3.3% F shoplifted in last year. Av. offences per offender ever 10.2.
Graham and Bowling (1992–3)	738 M and 910 F aged 14–25 from England and Wales. Individual interview. 64% response.	23.9% M and 15.5% F ever shoplifted. 4.5% M and 2.4% F shoplifted in last year.
Flood-Page *et al.* (1998–9)	4,848 persons aged 12–30 from England and Wales. Computer Interview. 69% response.	2% M and 2% F shoplifted in last year.

Table 3.3 continues opposite

Table 3.3 continued

Researcher and date of study	Sample characteristics	Shoplifting findings
Wikström and Butterworth (2006)	2,118 persons aged 14–15 from Peterborough. Self-completion questionnaire. 92% response rate.	11.8% M and 16.1% F shoplifted in last year. Av. offences per offender 3 for boys and 2.6 for girls.
Roe and Ashe (2008)	5,000 persons aged 10–25 from England and Wales. Computer interview. 67% response rate for fresh respondents (799 in all) and 85% (4,554 in all).	2% M and 3% F, and 3% aged 10–17 and 2% aged 18–25 had shoplifted in last year.

Source: Farrington (2001: 25); Farrington (1999: 15); Wikström and Butterworth (2006); Roe and Ashe (2008).

> they find it out, and usually the merchants let it pass. They will not do
> so in the future. (Segrave 2001: 14, quoting the *New York Times*, 1908: 3)

While it is clear from systematic research that shoplifters do not reflect the general population or the customers going into shops, equally it would seem that the shoplifters in any shop are partly a function of what is sold and who goes to the shops. The shoplifters in New York presumably reflect the kinds of people going to the stores. Where women are the main shoppers then they are likely to be the main shoplifters too, which explains why women appear to have been the main culprits in the nineteenth and early twentieth centuries (Segrave 2001: 9). Where more men come to shop, more will steal, which goes some way to explaining the patterns that seem more recently to have emerged.

Explanations for shoplifting

Patterns of shop theft

Shoplifting has a very long history, as the origins of the term show. It is not difficult to understand why. Shops bring wanted goods together to market. It is in the interests of consumers to obtain those goods as cheaply as possible. Theft makes them free. Shops provide a concentrated supply of desired goods. Anyone unable to pay for them or whose moral principles are insufficient to dissuade them is liable to steal them if the risks and difficulties of doing so seem sufficiently low. In Brantingham and Brantingham's terms shops act as 'crime generators' and 'crime attractors' (Brantingham and Brantingham 1995). They are crime generators in that a proportion of those in shops take the goods they want without paying for them should the opportunity arise.

They are crime attractors in that a proportion of those who go to the shops will do so with a view to committing shop theft because of the expected opportunities.

Changes in methods of retailing create changes in patterns of opportunity. Segrave (2001) refers to the growth of department stores with the large numbers of customers milling around, the open display of goods and consequent difficulties for shop assistants to watch what was happening as conditions in the United States in the nineteenth century favouring the growth of wide-scale shop theft. Walsh (1978) describes the mutual adjustments made in the development of retail and the development in shoplifting. He suggests that shop theft was common in medieval fairs, where goods were readily accessible to the thief. Structures then developed as a means of keeping the thief from the goods that might be taken. Eventually the counter emerged as a conventional barrier between the customer and the shopkeeper and his or her wares. This is a style that still operates in jewellers who sell archetypal CRAVED goods.

In the nineteenth century there were efforts to keep members of the 'lower social orders', who were believed most likely to steal, out of many shops, which will have affected the population available to steal. Determined shoplifters then had to adopt ruses to obtain access to the goods they wished to steal. Shop theft was a 'craft' crime. Walsh (1978) refers to shop theft in jewellers, where the thief would pose as a fussy customer and ask to look at a large number of items which would be put on the counter. At that point they would employ legerdemain, perhaps using an accomplice to provide distraction, to pocket one without being noticed before leaving the shop. 'T.W.' in a letter to *The Times* in 1818 paints a vivid picture:

> Some years since a lady came into a silk warehouse in the city with which I was then connected, by making use of the name of a customer as an introduction, and asked to see some silk shawls. Having no suspicion from her appearance and manners that she could be a thief, the young man who served her placed before her a large variety; she gave him much trouble, and finally left without buying. Scarcely had she quitted the warehouse when he missed several shawls of a peculiar pattern, and, being sent after the lady, requested her to return, to which she consented with evidently very suspicious reluctance. One of the principals of the house then charged her with taking these shawls, and, as you may suppose, she affected great surprise and indignation at the imputation. However, the young man being positive to the fact, she was requested to permit herself to be searched in a private room by one of the female servants of the establishment, or otherwise, she was told, she must be placed in the hands of the police. She chose the milder alternative, and after various attempts to conceal the stolen property, by removing it from one side to the other under her clothes during examination, it was found and she no longer denied her guilt. Being asked her name, she gave it without further attempt at evasion, and to our great surprise we found that she was the lady of one of the most eminent and benevolent physicians of the day. (T.W. 1844: 6)

Although F. W. Woolworth operated stores from 1879 in the US selling inexpensive goods on open display (Segrave 2001: 18), it took time for this pattern to become the norm. Walsh (1978) stressed the fundamental changes in retail in Britain following the Second World War, which expanded opportunities for shoplifting and led to rapid increases in it. Shops became larger with fewer staff in relation to the turnover. Self-service became the norm. The counter which once stood between the customer and the goods being purchased has now largely disappeared from almost all types of shop. The specialist butcher, fishmonger and jeweller are, of course, examples of exceptions, but they are relatively uncommon. Large-scale self-service shops, where the customer has direct access to the goods, where he or she is anonymous and where CRAVED goods are on display, provide plentiful temptations and opportunities. In these circumstances it is to be expected that levels of shop theft will rise dramatically. Notwithstanding the weaknesses in the recorded shop theft figures, they do suggest a dramatic rise in shop theft in the postwar years which coincided with changes in the prevailing form of retailing. Moreover, shoplifting no longer depended on craft skills. It became more straightforward to pick items up and leave the shop without paying for some or all of them.

Shoplifters

The most obvious explanation for shoplifting is rational choice. Customers in shops try to obtain what they want at least cost and, if no cost is an option, then they will just take them. At the same time suppliers will try to prevent customers from taking goods without payment. Opportunities for shop theft have altered over time, with changes in goods produced, in forms of retail and in those who habitually go shopping. The rates of shoplifting and the attributes of shoplifters have changed accordingly. In posh stores selling luxury goods, which are frequented by posh ladies, for example, posh ladies are the shoplifters. The disincentive to shoplifting, where the opportunity for it arises, is the prospect of a penalty that more than outweighs the potential benefit. Where apparent risks are low and where this is confirmed by very low rates of detection, many people will be tempted to obtain goods by shoplifting rather than by paying for them.

An objection to this account is that although there is an enormous amount of shoplifting many neither pursue opportunities nor take advantage of them as they arise. The rational choice response is a simple one. First, although the chances of being caught from shoplifting on any single occasion are very small, the chance of getting caught at some time, if shoplifting is engaged in routinely over a sustained period, is very high. Even where the costs in terms of formal penalty might be low enough in relation to the utilities from the stolen goods, the costs in terms of reputation are liable to be much higher. Those with relatively little to lose by way of reputation, at least in the eyes of people with whom they most closely identify, will have little disincentive. Those with more to lose have a greater disincentive. Second, estimating costs and benefits separately in relation to each individual point where choices are to be made is complex and difficult. Paralysis would follow if individuals undertook a bespoke calculation of the full range of likely short and long-term positive and negative consequences of all the alternatives that might be open to them before they decided what to do. Much that is done is therefore habitual and this includes paying for goods in shops. For many people being caught shoplifting would be very costly in terms of their reputation. It will therefore be rational for them routinely to pay for goods, even if on any particular occasion the chances of being caught stealing them are very low.

In the nineteenth century, where many female shoplifters appeared to be living in affluent family circumstances, need may have played a part alongside opportunity in stimulating shoplifting. Segrave (2001: 27) points out that though the women involved may have lived well they often lacked disposable discretionary income to spend to satisfy their own wants. Likewise, those who are drug dependent have less to lose by way of reputation, especially if they have previous convictions for shop theft. They also have high short-term wants or needs for income to satisfy their habits. Others are drawn into shop theft at impressionable ages when peer-group pressures, either to obtain lifestyle goods (for example particular types of footwear) or to join in criminal behaviour, are at work. In these cases perceived rewards for shop theft from salient peer group approval are liable to outweigh any distant (apparently unlikely) costs of being caught and brought to book.

McCulloch (1996) summarises the apparent major motivation for 265 shoplifters who were interviewed by the police in Milton Keynes in 1994. Her findings are shown in Table 3.4. This suggests that peer group influences are more important for younger, novice shoplifters, accounting for almost half of those who were under 16 but only one in six of those aged 16 and over. Greed was deemed the main motive in a little under a third, regardless of age. External needs (lack of money and illness) appeared to be more significant for the over 16 year olds, accounting for close to a third of them but less than one in ten of those aged less than 16.

Table 3.4 Motives for shop theft as found among Milton Keynes novices

	Under 16 %	16 & over %	Total %
Threat/coercion/peer pressure	46	18	35
Greed	31	32	31
No clear motive	13	18	15
Lack of money	6	21	12
Illness	1	10	5
Family break-up	1	1	1
Bereavement	1	0	1
Total	99*	100	100
Number of individuals	156	109	265

Source: McCulloch (1996: 13).

*The percentages add to 99 due to rounding

Table 3.5 shows what Speed and Burrows (2006) found to be the main motives for shoplifting as they emerged from an examination of Crown Prosecution Service (CPS) files relating to cases sentenced in 2004. Here the shoplifters will, of course, tend to be more experienced than those included in McCulloch's study. In Speed and Burrows' study drugs emerge as the most significant motivating factor for a quarter of the cases, with 'need' accounting for just less than 1 in 10. Peer group pressure was the key factor for fewer than one in 25.

Table 3.5 Motives for shoplifting among CPS cases

Motivation	%
Drugs	24
Need	9
Status/pressure	4
Enterprise	3
Other	23
Don't know	36
Total	99*
Number of cases	1,563

Source: Speed and Burrows (2006: 27).
*The percentages add to 99 due to rounding.

Many young people appear to embark on shoplifting as a result of peer group influences but the same pressures are not found among older offenders and in particular among those who become more serious offenders. This impression is reinforced in Schneider's study of 50 prolific burglars in and around Shrewbury (Schneider 2005). She found that 44 of them also undertook shoplifting. Of these 26 did so on a daily basis and a further eight did so 'several times a week'. That is, these prolific burglars tended also to be prolific shoplifters. She associates this pattern of offending with drug habits. Shop theft, in particular, yields a reliable income to meet the need for drugs.

Responses to shoplifting

By shops

Early responses of shops, from at least 1878, typically involved the employment of store detectives in an effort to catch offenders (Segrave 2001). There was, however, some reluctance to prosecute for fear of loss of reputation. This continues to be the case. Most shopkeepers have evidently not wanted the adverse publicity that goes with adopting a heavily punitive response. Let us return to the 1844 case described by T.W. which occurred without store detectives but nevertheless illustrates the chronic difficulties faced by shops in dealing with some offenders and also the unfairness of the responses:

> ... Her husband [remember: the eminent and benevolent physician] being then sent for promptly attended and was much affected by the humiliating situation of his wife. Upon his representation that she must to a certain extent be insane, as she had a handsome income and establishment of her own, which placed her beyond the reach of temptation, we were willing to believe that she was not a responsible agent, and permitted her to drive off in her carriage without further trouble to herself or her worthy, but distressed partner in life ... As far as personal feeling and inconvenience are concerned we were right; for, by so doing, we were spared the impudent insinuations of hired advocates as to our character and motives, and the constant fire of newspaper invective, to say nothing of expense and loss of time ... But there is another circumstance connected with this case which may have had its influence in favour of non-prosecution, and that is, that in all cases of alleged shoplifting by persons moving in a high sphere of society, no search of the residence takes place, so that the traces of similar depredations which such search might disclose, are not afforded. Not so the poor shoplifter; no sooner is she delivered over to the police, than her person and lodgings are examined, and the result adduced as collateral evidence for or against her. (T.W. 1844: 6)

In determining what to do with shoplifting suspects there have also been fears of litigation for wrongful arrest or of violence against staff from those held against their will. Shopkeepers therefore have often let suspects go. There have been periodic commitments to press for prosecution of all cases, although in practice this has rarely, if ever, been followed through.

There are, indeed, dilemmas for those in shops when faced by shop theft. As much as many might like the idea of enforcement, in practice they also very often sidestep it. One strategy that has sometimes been adopted is that of asking those caught to sign a document admitting the offence as a condition for non-prosecution. This document might then be drawn on in the event of a repeat incident for which the offender is taken to court or as a basis for excluding the individual from the shop. In the latter case, should the individual return, they would be open to prosecution for burglary, which is a much more serious offence attracting higher penalties. Another strategy has been to issue a severe rebuke to offenders in the hope that this will be enough to dissuade them from further offending.

There is much that shopkeepers can do and often have done to try to prevent shoplifting, other than simply trying to detect offenders and hand them over to the criminal justice agencies. The following lists some of the measures routinely taken in many shops, with indications for many of the earliest dates at which records of them were found:

- admitting only one child at a time;
- bag checking (1944);

- closed circuit television (1956);
- convex mirrors (1957);
- crackdowns (routine prosecution/heavy penalty) (1930);
- customer meet and greet practices (1953);
- designing goods that can be remotely disabled;
- display of CD/records/cassette tapes cases without the CDs for CRAVED items;
- display of goods away from entrances and exits;
- display of single shoes rather than pairs;
- dye tags on CRAVED clothes;
- erecting signs to discourage shop theft;
- exclusion of known shoplifters;
- hidden peepholes (1967);
- improved lighting;
- locked cabinets for CRAVED goods;
- name and shame (1921; Segrave 2001: 32);
- one-way mirrors to changing rooms (1967);
- packaging CRAVED items in ways that make them difficult to conceal (1967);
- placing CRAVED items (such as tobacco products, razors and instant coffee) behind the counter;
- providing over-the-counter sales for very high-value items such as watches and jewellery;
- putting CRAVED items near checkouts;
- restricting numbers of items taken into changing rooms;
- routinely asking customers at checkout, 'Is that all?';
- store layout to allow surveillance (1967);
- tags and alarms for CRAVED goods (1961);
- tethering CRAVED display items (such as mobile phones);
- uniformed guards (1925);
- use of RFID (Radio Frequency IDentification);
- warning leaflets (1967);
- warning signs (1930s).

Most of these comprise situational measures of the sort described by Clarke (2008). They are designed to make the offence more difficult (for example, putting high-value goods in locked cabinets), more risky (for example alarming high value goods) or less rewarding (for example, by attaching dye tags). They may also comprise rule reminders at the point of sale (for example, by asking customers, 'Is that all?' when they reach the till) or even reductions in provocation (for example, when only one child at a time is admitted to the shop and they are unable to egg one another on).

There is no hard evidence of the outcome effectiveness of many of the measures adopted by shops (Clarke 2002). In some instances, however, it is difficult to believe that they have no effect, for example putting cigarettes out of reach. In others effectiveness is less certain and these have attracted more research attention. CCTV in particular has been subject to some interesting evaluation studies. Gill and Turbin (1999) found that the effects of CCTV and how it worked depended on the circumstances. They conclude, for example, that:

> [S]taff attitudes and management with the system [are] far more important than has previously been recognised. A system introduced to a store where staff welcome the CCTV and want to work with it may create the appropriate context for triggering crime-reducing mechanisms. Equally, a store where staff resent the system may trigger different mechanisms, with the potential to increase the losses (by reducing staff vigilance or concern about shop theft). (Gill and Turpin 1999: 194–5)

Paul Ekblom (1986) highlights the shortcomings of the traditional response to shoplifting: the employment of store detectives. He notes the risk of assault against shop staff, the time taken to process suspects within stores (which also takes detectives away from the shop floor where they can try to protect the goods on display), the costs to the public from formally dealing with the offenders and risks of accusation of false arrest. He takes Oxford Street's HMV store as a case study from which 39 per cent (420 of the 1,074) of arrests for shop theft dealt with by the Marylebone Street Police Station came over a two-month period. HMV employed a large number of store detectives and sold audio cassettes on display in their boxes, which at the time were CRAVED items: 'light, easily pocketable, attractive to the young for their own use as well as resale, and having a relatively high unit cost' (Ekblom 1986: 4). Ekblom suggests that use of store detectives is an inefficient method of trying to control shop theft. The four store detectives, he calculates, were likely to catch and process fewer than five of the estimated 200 shop thieves stealing from the shop each day. Through an analysis of the items most at risk (audio and computer cassettes), the locations of the thefts (rock and pop, soul and disco and computer zones of the store) and the modus operandi (slipping the goods into pockets), he suggests a variety of targeted situational measures that will be less costly and more effective in reducing shop theft. These included the design of the goods (for example packaging to prevent pocketing), the layout of the store (for example, realigning stands to improve line of sight), CCTV (targeted at key areas), alarms (triggered at exits of high risk zones where high value CRAVED items would be tagged) and management systems allowing patterns of theft readily to be identified and addressed in informed ways.

Both Gill and Turbin and Ekblom bring out the ways in which the situational measures that may be used by shops to respond to shoplifting require careful thought and sensitive implementation if they are to be effective. They are unable to provide magic bullets whose success can be taken for granted. Farrington *et al*. (1994) conducted an experiment in the Dixons Group, comparing the relative effectiveness of electronic tagging, uniformed guards and store redesign as means of preventing shoplifting. They concluded that electronic tagging produced sustained falls, store redesign an immediate but fading fall and uniformed guards no effect. Alongside Ekblom (1986), and consistent with Gill and Turbin (1999) and Clarke (2002), they also stress the need for crime analysis to work out crime prevention needs.

In addition to their own individual security measures, retailers have been encouraged to take part in cooperative efforts at reducing their vulnerability. There are many Shop Watch schemes, for example, where retailers work together. These often include 'Retail Radio Links' which may or may not also have the local police and CCTV operators as participants. Retail Radio Links involve retailers joining a radio network by means of which they can communicate with one another (and maybe police and CCTV operators) to elicit help where needed in dealing with offenders or to forewarn one another of the presence of suspects to be looked out for (see Wright and Gibson 1995). The effects on levels of shop theft are uncertain.

By the criminal justice system

Formal criminal justice responses to shop theft have varied widely throughout history. When it was deemed a very serious offence capital punishment was an option and some were executed in the eighteenth century, although in practice transportation was more generally the most severe sentence passed. The execution of the impoverished 19 year old, Mary Jones, for shoplifting in 1771 was used as part of the case persistently put by Sir William Meredith to reform the law as it related to capital punishment, though he was unsuccessful at the time. As he put it, 'This woman was hanged for the comfort and satisfaction of some shopkeepers in Ludgate-street' (*The Times*, 26 December 1818: p. 3).

Kleptomania was 'discovered' in France as a distinctive condition in 1816, though prior to that 'mental imbalance' had evidently been used as a basis for releasing some female shoplifters before that time (Segrave 2001: 20). The 'diagnosis' was applied through the nineteenth century and into the early twentieth century, especially to well-to-do women who stole from shops. It provided a way for them to escape prosecution or the impugnment of their character. It traded on an image of women as weak and incompetent. Menstrual disorders were sometimes invoked as particular causes of shoplifting: 'ovarian insanity' was a specific form of kleptomania and these broad concerns lasted till after the Second World War (see Epps 1982: 134–5; Segrave 2001: 25). In the late 1890s, Dr (later Sir) Arthur Conan Doyle wrote a letter to *The Times*, saying:

> Might I implore your powerful intercession on behalf of the unfortunate American lady, Mrs Castle, who was condemned yesterday to three months imprisonment upon a charge of theft? Apart from the evidence of medical experts, it is inconceivable that any woman of her position in her sane senses would steal duplicates and triplicates – four toast racks, if I remember right. Small articles of silver with the hotel mark upon them, so that they could be neither sold nor used, were among the objects she had packed away in her trunk. It can surely not be denied there is at least doubt as to her moral responsibility, and if there is a doubt then the benefit of it should be given to one whose sex and whose position as a visitor amongst us give her a double claim to our consideration. It is to a consulting room not to a cell, that she should be sent. (Conan Doyle 1896: 10)

Attempts to identify some underlying medical and psychological condition that will explain, excuse or provide a basis for treatment of shoplifters have a long history as we saw earlier in the case of kleptomania. They can still be found, at least in popular psychological discourse (for example, Byron 2007).

Presently there is a range of criminal justice responses to customer theft, depending in particular on the amount stolen and the previous criminal career of the offender. Shop theft falls under section 1(1) of the Theft Act 1978, which provides for a maximum penalty of seven years' imprisonment on indictment and six months' imprisonment or a fine not exceeding the statutory maximum, or both, summarily, although sentencing guidelines suggest that these maxima will rarely be warranted (Sentencing Advisory Panel 2008). In 2007–8 there were 290,625 reported incidents of shop theft in England and Wales. In relation to these there were 185,840 sanction detections (64 per cent). In 2007, there were 45,146 fixed penalty notices (FPNs) for shoplifting (FPNs of £80 have been available since late 2004 to deal with first-time offenders where the value of goods stolen is less than £200). A total of 67,544 individuals were sent to trial, of whom 62,565 were found guilty. Of those found guilty a third (33 per cent) received community sentences, a quarter were given conditional discharges (24 per cent), about a fifth were sentenced to immediate custody (18 per cent) and one in six were fined (16 per cent). The remainder were spread across a range of other disposals.

The relative effects of different disposals on the overall rates of shop theft or on rates of reoffending among varying subsets of shoplifter are unclear. There are periodic calls for tougher penalties. In July 2008, for example, Anne McIntosh, MP for the Vale of York, attempted to bring in a ten-minute Bill, with the support of the Federation of Small Businesses, 'to replace FPNs with custodial sentences' (*Hansard*, 15 July 2008: col. 125). Likewise a press release from the British Retail Consortium, to coincide with the publication of its annual Retail Crime Survey, states that it 'believes that a combination of weak penalties and poor enforcement has led to the proliferation of shop crime' (British Retail Consortium 2006).

For the police shop theft is a time-consuming and frustrating offence, often with repeat offenders. Many have been keen to find more effective responses to offenders. In Milton Keynes in the mid-1990s, for example, a Retail Theft Initiative, which was aimed at first-time offenders, was put in place in an effort to improve responses (McCulloch 1996). The scheme involved interviewing eligible, mostly juvenile offenders about the motive for the offence and then assigning them to appropriate 'modules' in the initiative. For most of the offenders this would include an interview with the store manager, who impressed on them the impact that shop theft has on the business, staff and customers. It could also include group guidance on ways of resisting the pressure from peers to steal from shops without losing face. Of the 422 offenders in the experimental period who took part in the scheme 13 per cent reoffended over the two-month to two-year period covered by the evaluation. This compared to 16 per cent for the 50 who dropped out of the scheme, 30 per cent for the 26 given a 'normal caution' and 70 per cent for those who were charged, although these comparison groups clearly differ from those who were eligible for the scheme.

Conclusion: does shoplifting matter?

For public policy

Adherents of the strong displacement (or 'hydraulic') hypothesis would have it that there is a fixed amount of crime and all that is achieved by blocking opportunities for one crime is that it will be diverted to another. For such folk, shop theft is presumably to be welcomed. If it draws crime from other victims on whom incidents will have a more substantial impact, the more shop theft there is, in particular in large multiple stores, the better. The costs of such shop theft are shared among us all, roughly in proportion to the amount we spend.

The hydraulic theory of crime, though widely held in some circles, has, however, by now been discredited (Hesseling 1994). Research evidence and a small dose of common sense show that it is mistaken. It must be doubted whether anyone really believes that if all routine situational precautions were removed there would be no change in the volume of crime.

Even if the strong hydraulic theory of crime is mistaken, it might still be the case that some shop theft is undertaken by determined offenders who find it a relatively easy offence and would otherwise commit more serious offences. Schneider (2005) argues that one reason for the police to focus on shoplifting by prolific offenders is its association with burglary, an intrinsically more serious offence. Her argument is that shop theft is more readily detected than burglary and that searching the homes of shoplifters who are caught might provide a fruitful way of catching and convicting burglars when stolen goods from burglaries are found. Another view would be that cutting off relatively reliable sources of illegal income among such offenders, who are typically feeding a drug habit, would drive them to more serious offending that would create greater public harms.

For retailers

Proprietors of shops show some ambivalence towards shop theft. If it takes place they tend understandably to be indignant. They call for stronger action by the authorities to deal with it because of its costs to them and ultimately to the honest consumer. Yet collectively they continue to operate retail in ways that facilitate crime and build expected rates of shrinkage, including that from shop theft, into their business models. They have also tended to be reluctant in practice to act as tough as they talk. This is not to say that shopkeepers do not attempt to contain shop theft. They certainly do, as indicated earlier. Their extensive efforts can be seen in the way they run their businesses, and this almost certainly reduces the volume of theft that would otherwise occur. Indeed, if retailers fail to control shoplifting sufficiently well their businesses are put in jeopardy. But the methods of retail to which the public have become accustomed facilitate shoplifting and it is likewise unlikely that many retailers could run their businesses profitably in ways that would eliminate shop theft. And the claims that we all pay for it ring rather hollow.

Shoppers' rational choices for cheap goods they can see and handle in advance of purchase leads to forms of retail that tend to facilitate shop theft.

The small price we all pay for this covers the costs that remain once reasonable retailer efforts, consistent with our shopping preferences, are put in place.

Selected further reading

For an accessible historical account of shoplifting that discusses changing rates, costs, responses and types of people who steal from shops, see Segrave (2001). The focus is mainly on the United States although there are some references to patterns elsewhere also. For a thorough overview of late twentieth-century British research, see Farrington (1999). For recent data on criminal justice responses to shoplifters, see Speed and Burrows (2006). Walsh (1978) may be relatively difficult to get hold of. It is, however, an interesting and very thoughtful account of developments in shoplifting and responses to it. This short and very readable book reports empirical research undertaken at the time it was published. The theoretical discussion anticipates various later developments in situational crime prevention. Clarke (2002) provides a brief but excellent evidence-based guide for those trying to address specific shoplifting problems.

References

Brantingham, P. and Brantingham, P. (1995) 'Criminality of place: crime generators and crime attractors', *European Journal of Criminal Policy and Research*, 3 (3): 5–26.

British Retail Consortium (2006) 'Shopkeepers Feel Abandoned by Government and Police – BRC Survey'. Press Release, available online at: http://www.brc.org.uk/details04.asp?id=1010&kCat=&kData=1 (accessed 24 October 2008).

Buckle, A. and Farrington, D. (1984) 'An observational study of shoplifting', *British Journal of Criminology*, 34 (1): 63–73.

Byron, T. (2007) 'It's not the new pair of shoes, it's the "high"', *Timesonline*, 27 November. Online at: http://women.timesonline.co.uk/tol/life_and_style/women/the_way_we_live/article2923565.ece.

Cameron, M. (1964) *The Booster and the Snitch*. New York: Free Press.

Clarke, R. (1999) *Hot Products: Understanding, Anticipating and Reducing Demand for Stolen Goods*, Police Research Series Paper No. 112. London: Home Office.

Clarke, R. (2002) *Shoplifting*, Problem-Oriented Guides for Police Series No. 11. Washington, DC: US Department of Justice Office of Community Oriented Policing Services.

Clarke, R. (2008) 'Situational crime prevention', in R. Wortley and L. Mazerolle (eds), *Environmental Criminology and Crime Analysis*. Cullompton: Willan.

Conan Doyle, A. (1896) 'The case of Mrs Castle', *The Times*, 8 November, p. 10.

Ekblom, P. (1986) *The Prevention of Shop Theft: An Approach through Crime Analysis*, Crime Prevention Unit Paper No. 5. London: Home Office.

Epps, P. (1982) 'Women shoplifters in Holloway Prison', in T. Gibbens and J. Prince, *Shoplifting*. London: ISTD.

Farrington, D. P. (1999) 'Measuring, explaining and preventing shoplifting: a review of British research', *Security Journal*, 12 (1): 9–27.

Farrington, D. P. (2001) *What Has Been Learned from Self-Report Studies about Criminal Careers and the Causes of Offending*, Report to the Home Office. Online at: http://www.homeoffice.gov.uk/rds/pdfs/farrington.pdf.

Farrington, D. P. and Burrows, J. (1993) 'Did shoplifting really decrease?', *British Journal of Criminology*, 33 (1): 57–69.

Farrington, D., Bowen, S., Buckle, A., Burns-Howell, T., Burrows, J. and Speed, M. (1994) 'An experiment on the prevention of shoplifting', in R. Clarke (ed.), *Crime Prevention Studies*, Vol. 1. Monsey, NY: Criminal Justice Press.

Gibbens, T. and Prince, J. (1962) *Shoplifting*. London: Institute for the Study and Treatment of Delinquency.

Gill, M. and Turbin, V. (1999) 'Evaluating "realistic evaluation": evidence from a study of CCTV', in K. Painter and N. Tilley (eds), *Surveillance of Public Space: CCTV, Street Lighting and Crime Prevention*, Crime Prevention Studies, Vol. 10. Monsey, NY: Criminal Justice Press.

Hayes, R. (1997) 'Retail theft: an analysis of apprehended shoplifters', *Security Journal*, 8: 233–46.

Hesseling, R. (1994) 'Displacement: a review of the empirical literature', in R. Clarke (ed.), *Crime Prevention Studies*, Vol. 3. Monsey, NY: Criminal Justice Press.

McCulloch, H. (1996) *Shop Theft: Improving the Police Response*, Crime Prevention and Detection Series Paper No. 76. London: Home Office.

Moore, R. H. (1984) 'Shoplifting in Middle America: patterns and motivational correlates', *International Journal of Offender Therapy and Comparative Criminology*, 28 (1): 53–64.

New York Times (1908) 'War on shoplifters', 15 February, p. 3.

Nicholas, S., Kershaw, C. and Walker, A. (2007) *Crime in England and Wales 2006/7*, Home Office Statistical Bulletin No. 11/07. London: Home Office.

Roe, S. and Ashe, J. (2008) *Young People and Crime: Findings from the 2006 Offending, Crime and Justice Survey*, Home Office Statistical Bulletin No. 09/08. London: Home Office.

Schneider, J. (2005) 'The link between shoplifting and burglary: the booster burglar', *British Journal of Criminology*, 45 (3): 395–401.

Segrave, K. (2001) *Shoplifting: A Social History*. Jefferson, NC: McFarland.

Sentencing Advisory Panel (2008) *Advice to the Sentencing Guidance Council: Sentencing for Theft from a Shop*. London: Sentencing Advisory Panel.

Shury, J., Speed, M., Vivian, D., Kuechel, A. and Nicholas, S. (2005) *Crime Against Retail and Manufacturing Premises: Findings from the 2002 Commercial Victimisation Survey*, Home Office Online Report No. 57/05. London: Home Office.

Speed, M. and Burrows, J. (2006) *Sentencing in Cases of Theft from Shops*, Research Report 3 for the Sentencing Advisory Panel. Online at: http://www.sentencing-guidelines. gov.uk/docs/researchreport-theft0806.pdf.

T.W. (1844) 'Shoplifting', *The Times*, 14 December, p. 6.

Tonglet, M. (1998) 'Consumers' perceptions of shoplifting and shoplifting behaviour', in M. Gill (ed.), *Crime at Work: Increasing the Risk for Offenders*. Leicester: Perpetuity Press.

Walsh, D. (1978) *Shoplifting: Controlling a Major Crime*. London Macmillan.

Wikström, P.-O. and Butterworth, D. (2006) *Adolescent Crime: Individual Differences and Lifestyles*. Cullompton: Willan.

Wright, M. and Gibson, C. (1995) *Radio Links: Communities Linked Together by Two-way Radios and with the Police*, Home Office PRG Report. London: Home Office.

Chapter 4

Understanding and tackling stolen goods markets

Mike Sutton

Introduction

This chapter examines the law on handling stolen goods and discusses findings from a number of crime surveys, studies of stolen goods markets and policing initiatives to tackle them. Handling stolen goods is a gateway crime to other offending. Those who buy stolen goods motivate others to begin and continue stealing. Evaluations from past anti-fencing operations in the USA and wider Market Reduction Approach initiatives in the UK reveal what works, what doesn't work and what is promising for those seeking to tackle the very roots of theft.

Ever since the Industrial Revolution fuelled the mass production of desirable identical goods and improved redistribution systems, theft has switched from being an activity that predominantly involves stealing items for personal use to one of stealing to sell both near and far (Blakey and Goldsmith 1976: 1514). The very existence and proliferation of professional fencing operations, where businesses 'knowingly' buy and sell stolen goods, added to the various ways that thieves sell directly to other criminals and otherwise law-abiding citizens, provides money-making opportunities that motivate thieves to begin and continue stealing (Sutton 1996, 2003, 2008; Sutton *et al.* 2001; Sutton *et al.* 2008).

The six markets for stolen goods

In the first ever systematic analysis of stolen goods markets (Sutton 1998), I triangulated findings from the British Crime Survey (BCS) and the general literature on stolen goods markets with 45 in-depth interviews with thieves and fences and found five main market types for stolen goods:

1 *Commercial fence supplies*. Stolen goods are sold by thieves to commercial fences operating out of shops – such as jewellers, pawnbrokers and second-hand dealers.

2 *Residential fence supplies.* Stolen goods (particularly electrical goods) are sold by thieves to fences, usually at the home of the fence.

3 *Network sales.* Stolen goods are passed on and each participant adds a little to the price until a consumer is found; this may involve a *residential* fence, and the buyer may be the final consumer or may sell the goods on again through friendship networks.

4 *Commercial sales.* Commercial fences most usually pose openly as legitimate business owners while secretly selling stolen goods for a profit, either directly to the (innocent) consumer or to another distributor who thinks the goods can be sold again for additional profit. More rarely, such sales are made to another distributor.

5 *Hawking.* Thieves sell directly to consumers in places such as bars and pubs or door to door in residential areas (e.g. shoplifters selling cigarettes, toiletries, clothes or food).

Crime is constantly evolving and this is evidenced here by the fact that to these five market types we should now add a sixth type, namely eSelling, which involves trading in stolen goods online on the Internet:

6 *eSelling.* This involves selling stolen goods through private websites such as Craig's List or through online auction sites such as eBay.

It is important to emphasise that the six stolen goods markets, do not necessarily work like some kind of criminal dealing career options (Harris *et al.* 2003). Thieves and fences alike do specialise for periods of time, but others also pick and mix between these markets. For example, fences operating in *commercial fence supplies* markets may deal at home as *residential fences*, or else be involved in *network sales* (Steffensmeier and Ulmer 2005) or even *eSelling* – particularly where stolen items not sold through their legitimate retail business are being traded.

Handling stolen goods and the law

The offence of handling stolen goods is triable either way, with a penalty for 'handling' of 14 years' imprisonment in the Crown Court and six months' imprisonment in the magistrates' court. Professor Martin Wasik (2001), Chairman of the Sentencing Advisory Panel, in his guidelines to the UK Court of Appeal explains the range of issues that magistrates and the judiciary should take into account when deciding how serious is a case of stolen good 'handling' they have before them. The relevant law is, for the most part, contained within the Theft Act 1968, section 22, which states that the offence can be committed in a number of distinct ways:

A person handles stolen goods if (otherwise than in the course of the stealing), knowing or believing them to be stolen goods, he [a] dishonestly receives the goods, or [b] dishonestly undertakes or assists in their retention, removal, disposal or realisation by or for the benefit of another person, or if he arranges to do so.

The panel go on to distinguish between various types of 'handler', the value of goods, the frequency of known involvement in handling and how close they are to the original thief in terms of deciding upon the seriousness of the offence before them.

These UK sentencing *guidelines* take no account of criminological concerns regarding research which reveals that all knowing purchasers – regardless of whether they buy from a middleman (fence) or directly from the thief – are part of the very roots of theft that motivate thieves to begin and continue stealing. Indeed, it is the extent of the involvement in, and tolerance towards, trading in stolen goods that represents the biggest challenge to law enforcement taking a proactive problem-solving approach to crime reduction and policing.

The law treats the offence of handling stolen goods with particular caution. Section 22(1) of the Theft Act 1968 requires guilt to be established on the basis of knowledge or belief that goods are stolen and the jury or magistrate must infer from the circumstances of the case whether the defendant had such knowledge or belief.

Judicial interpretation of the statute has been such that a mere suspicion that goods are stolen is not enough to lead to a conviction for handling unless the defendant either knows or is virtually certain that they are stolen goods (Hall 1952). In this connection, the eminent jurisprudentialist Glanville Williams (1985) stressed the need to understand the meaning of *belief* within section 22 that goods are stolen as: the sort of belief we would associate with a devout religious believer not as a belief that the goods are probably stolen. In supporting such a strictly narrow interpretation Williams argues: people must be allowed a margin of safety. If they cannot buy goods that they know to be probably stolen then they cannot safely buy goods when there is an appreciable possibility that they are stolen, because no one knows when lawyers, judges and juries between them may not turn possibilities into probabilities. This consideration, above all others, places severe constraints on what can be achieved in the way of controlling theft and burglary by purely legal measures aimed at receiving. That said, perhaps police services should make more use of the little used section 27 of the Theft Act 1968 when dealing with known and previously convicted prolific thieves and handlers. This section allows for joint prosecution of those suspected of stealing and/or handling stolen goods. More importantly under section 27 it is possible, for the purpose of proving that a person knew or believed goods to be stolen, to present evidence of earlier convictions for theft or handling stolen goods. In this way section 27 can be used to streamline the process of proving criminal intent of theft or handling for those who have been convicted of theft or handling within a five-year period prior to a current charge and who has in their possession stolen goods from a theft occurring no more than 12 months prior to that current charge.

Wasik's (2001) sentencing guidelines take account of findings from the 1994 BCS of the extent of public involvement in knowingly consuming the proceeds of theft. In fact, the statistical findings quoted but not referenced in the sentencing *guidelines* are from my own published analysis of the data (Sutton 1998) that were collected in response to the questions on the 1994

BCS, which I drafted following my earlier work in this area (Sutton 1993, 1995). One of the most notable findings from that work is that 11 per cent of the population of England and Wales admitted buying goods in the past five years which they knew or believed to be stolen.

While the criminal justice system in England and Wales is undoubtedly keen to ensure that the occasional handler of stolen goods is not treated as seriously as the professional fence, it does seem that the law might have forgotten, or perhaps strangely neglected, a lesson learned much earlier regarding the importance of the handler as the underlying motivational force for thieves: prior to the 2003 Criminal Justice Act the maximum penalty for domestic burglary was 12 years' imprisonment – while handling carried a maximum of 14 years. The 2003 Act increased the maximum sentence for domestic burglary to 14 years and left the maximum for handling unchanged. This departure from treating handling more seriously than theft – or at least retaining the sentencing power to do so – passed seemingly without notice and in the face of a growing body of criminological research that will be examined in this chapter. This research suggests that crime-facilitating business people and other so-called general 'respectable' citizens who buy, deal in and consume stolen goods have for too long passed under the radar of a predominantly reactive criminal justice system that continues to focus on the usual suspects while ignoring the root causes of their offending that is so often instigated and facilitated by those we should, arguably, call *crimemongers*.

Patterns and trends

One way to begin to better understand the extent of the stolen goods trading problem is to find out as far as possible how many citizens appear to be willing to buy *hot products*, and whether those that do so have any defining characteristics. With that aim, 9,646 people were interviewed for the nationally representative 1994 British Crime Survey (BCS) and asked about their involvement in buying stolen goods (Sutton 1998). I wrote the questions for the stolen goods segment in the BCS in 1994 and again for the 2003 Offending, Crime and Justice Survey (OCJS) (Sutton *et al.* 2008). Quite frankly, I was amazed by what I found, because the figures for self-reported handling were much higher than I anticipated. As mentioned above, the 1994 BCS revealed that in the past five years: 11 per cent of the population of England and Wales admitted buying goods which they knew or believed to be stolen. Further, 11 per cent had been offered stolen goods in the past 12 months, and a staggeringly large 70 per cent thought that at least some of their neighbours had stolen goods in their homes, while 21 per cent thought a lot of their neighbours had the same. In the more recent 2003 OCJS we found, from a nationally representative sample of 10,079 respondents – comprising 2,704 10 to 17 year olds and 7,375 18 to 65 year olds – that 7.2 per cent of adults in England and Wales admitting buying stolen goods in the past 12 months and 2.7 per cent admitted selling stolen goods, while 1.3 per cent of children had bought a stolen mobile phone. The reason why fewer people admitted to buying stolen goods in England and Wales 2003, compared to

1994, is, I would suggest, most probably due to the fall in acquisitive crime rates between surveys, coupled with the fact that respondents in the 2003 OCJS were asked about their buying activities in the past year as opposed to past five years in the BCS.

The importance of stolen goods markets simply cannot be ignored once the data on citizen involvement is examined. This is particularly so since the authors of the nationally representative Youth Lifestyle Survey for England and Wales (Graham and Bowling 1995) found that handling stolen goods was the most prevalent offence committed by their respondents – with 49 per cent of people aged 14 to 25, who admitted offending in the past year, admitting that they had either bought or sold (handled) stolen goods during the same period.

The extent of self-reported offending in the USA is likely to be equally high. While no national figures exist, a US postal survey of 739 adult respondents in Texas, conducted by Cromwell and McElrath (1994), found that 13 per cent had bought stolen goods while 36 per cent had been offered stolen goods for purchase in their lifetimes. In Australia, Allen (2000), commissioned a telephone survey of 5,419 adult respondents on behalf of the New South Wales (NSW) Australian Bureau of Crime Statistics and Research, which asked people whether they had been offered stolen goods. From her data, Allen estimates that over a quarter of a million people in NSW were offered stolen goods in the 12 months prior to the survey. She calculated also that it is likely, on the basis of her survey findings, that some 700,000 people would have been offered stolen goods at some point in their lifetime in NSW – which represents 14 per cent of that population. Clearly, then, it is not only professional fences who are knowingly providing the market for theft. But what do we know, exactly, about the characteristics of 'citizen' buyers of stolen goods?

The 1994 BCS (Sutton 1998) found that almost half of all males interviewed aged 16–24 had been offered and/or had bought stolen goods. That research found also the following: that more than twice as many males are offered stolen goods as females and that nearly twice as many males buy stolen goods; 30 per cent of all males living in areas characterised by three adverse area factors (such as high crime or incivility etc.) and 40 per cent of all males living in areas with three adverse personal wealth factors, knowingly bought stolen goods; and living in a household where the head is self-employed significantly increases the likelihood of buying stolen goods – a finding supported by in-depth interviews that revealed small business owners are repeatedly targeted by thieves asking them to buy stolen goods. These findings were followed by Sutton et al.'s (2008) analysis between contrasting groups in England and Wales, which found that buying stolen goods, like many other offences, is a crime most often committed by those who are young, single, male, poorly qualified and living in relatively deprived areas. These findings are supported also by other research (see Pease 1994 for an overview) that shows the extent to which burglary and other theft is concentrated in particular areas and that thieves prey more often upon particular people in those areas.

However, it is important to point out that those in the very lowest income group, or those finding it difficult to manage on their income, are *not* significantly more likely to buy than those in higher income groups. A likely explanation for this is that while many stolen goods markets are concentrated in the least affluent areas, spare and readily available cash is required to buy stolen goods that are non-essential luxury items (Sutton 1998; Sutton *et al.* 2008).

Characteristics of offenders

Research in the UK (Bennett *et al.* 2001) reveals that some 29 per cent of arrested thieves are heroin or cocaine users and that these are the most prolific offenders, probably responsible for more than three-fifths of illegal income generated by thieves selling stolen goods in England and Wales. Not surprisingly, therefore, many crime experts now see illegal problem drug use as a serious root cause of theft. However, interviews with prolific burglars and other thieves (Sutton 1998, 2003, 2008) reveal also that drug dealers are often reluctant to exchange drugs for stolen goods. Generally, drug dealers do not want to be in possession of hot goods and thieves know they can get more drugs if they buy with cash, having first sold their stolen haul. This means that stolen goods markets play at least as important a part as regular illegal hard drug use in explaining high theft rates and, therefore, represent an equally important opportunity for crime reduction initiatives.

Motivation and explanations

The role of demand for stolen goods

The original reason for enabling the judiciary to treat *handling* more seriously than domestic burglary was to reflect old 'knowledge' that stems from the often quoted phrase: '… if there were no [professional] receivers there would be no thieves' (Colquhoun 1796). However, Colquhoun's simple words no longer ring quite so true in the modern world where there is a much wider range of options for converting stolen property into cash than ever before. On eBay for example, thieves can sell directly to the public as well as through a middleman – unless that is you deem eBay to be the fence – and thieves regularly hawk stolen goods door to door around poorer neighbourhoods. That said dealers in stolen goods do remain key players in many types of stolen goods market today. As middlemen, or *middlewomen*, and through professional marketing they create demand for stolen goods as well as respond to it (Sutton 1998). Yet the role of the public as *knowing buyers* is arguably of equal importance in creating even these *middleman* markets in stolen goods – because if there were no bargain hunting citizens most outlets for stolen goods would shrink enormously.

To quote Henry (1977), for example:

… public demand for stolen goods shares some of the responsibility for maintaining the fence.[1] The role of the consumer in a capitalist society requires him, like the businessman, to buy goods at the cheapest possible price. Advertising persuades him of the advantages of the 'bargain'. He needs little if any encouragement when presented with 'cheap' or 'bargain goods'.

Having completed an evaluation of a major anti-fencing operation in the USA, Weiner et al. (1981) write about the need to look further at what the wider public is knowingly involved in if we are to have any hope of tackling theft by targeting markets for stolen goods:

> Where previously it was thought that affecting the stolen property market through the apprehension of major fences would aid agencies in combating property crime, there is now evidence to suggest that the general public is responsible for a much greater proportion of the problem. This increased awareness may contribute substantially to law enforcement's understanding of the stolen property distribution system. It would concomitantly add to what has already been established concerning the profile of the property crime offender. In essence, this knowledge would force us to direct our attention to those 'legitimate' citizens who are engaged in purchasing stolen property. Also, this type of knowledge can be utilized for altering the techniques and focus of future 'anti-fencing' operations.

The existence of a causal relationship between the demand for stolen goods and their supply makes intuitive sense because personal possessions are always at risk of being stolen when thieves know or believe other people will buy them (Tremblay et al. 1994). However, the relationship between the willingness of individuals to buy stolen goods and the readiness of others to steal them is complex (Ferman et al. 1987). This complexity is revealed by the fact that it is difficult to determine the degree to which thieves cultivate a market for things they have stolen and to what extent their offending is motivated by the existence of ready markets.

Sometimes thieves steal to order. But issues of demand and supply are not always this simple and linear. For example, small business owners are frequently offered stolen goods by strangers, and those who have never bought stolen goods before are also offered them (Sutton 1998). Consequently, until research can find ways to unravel the complexity of demand and supply in this area, markets for stolen goods should be seen equally as both a downstream consequence of theft and also as an underlying motivational force for much theft.

Handling stolen goods as middleman or consumer is what might be termed a *precursor* or *gateway* crime, because knowledge of the very existence of ready markets for stolen goods motivates thieves to begin and continue stealing. This is because most prolific thieves want to sell for cash – whatever it is that they want to spend that cash on. This is what is described by criminologists as 'preparatory knowledge' in that it is information that is often picked up by young people within families, neighbourhoods and peer groups before they begin stealing. Preparatory knowledge about the fact that people buy stolen goods and who those people are and how to go about safely dealing with them is what makes acquisitive offending a rational choice for some young people growing up in less wealthy areas (see Steffensmeier and Ulmer 2005: 30).

Whereas the police will generally have the support of the public in their efforts to catch stereotypical offenders such as thieves and some types of low-level drug dealer, levels of public tolerance towards the buyers and middlemen selling 'hot bargains' are going to be much higher. This is because oftentimes they are seen as entrepreneurs providing a valuable local service (Pengelly 1996). On this theme, Henry (1978: 22) describes the street hustler selling new, legitimate goods as though they were stolen to explain their cheap price, and people buy from him because they think his wares are stolen. Such peddlers can be observed in many cities in many countries (Sutton 1995) – they talk fast and pretend to be nervous. They employ young lookouts to warn of approaching police officers. As Steffensmeier (1986: 241) explains in the words of Sam, a professional fence:

The public wants a story. They think they're getting something for nothing, a special deal. Many times, now, I've sold what was really junk for a good price 'cause they thought it was stolen.

Time and again over the years prolific burglars and other thieves have relayed the role played by the public as willing and knowing buyers of stolen stuff. The following pertinent quote from one of my interviewee subjects, a young male Nottingham burglar in his early twenties, typically sums things up (Sutton 2008):

I suppose it's wrong, but if you're not living well you gonna want a bargain, y'know what I mean, and if you can't afford something then you gonna want it cheap y'know what I mean? I suppose if you see it like that then you're not doing no wrong. If you can't afford it you're not really bothered where it's coming from.

Amazingly, apart from one reference to war, what Marshall Clinard tellingly wrote in 1952 (see Clinard 1969: 330–1) – about the problems of illicit black market dealings in the USA during the Second World War being very deeply rooted in the high level of public tolerance towards them – could have been written about stolen goods markets today:

The relative nature of social values in modern society, with its emphasis on individual choice, has put great strains, even in wartime, on social organization and democracy, both conditions resting essentially on general agreement about fundamental social objectives. Under these conditions the significance of laws becomes relative, some to be selectively obeyed according to whether one believes in them; others to be disobeyed if one does not. This absence of consensus on fundamental values in our society is illustrated in these pulls between group objectives and individual self-interest and disregard for personal integrity, and between national welfare and individual materialism. On one side has been respect for law and on the other side disrespect for law if it stood in the way of individual material success, as in the case of the black market.

This tolerance of illegality can best be understood by distinguishing between what the public sees as *licit* and *illicit* activity. Abraham and van Schendel (2005: 18) use public tolerance of soft illegal drug use to provide an excellent telling example here that might also equally be substituted by public tolerance of stolen goods dealing:

> When we shift our nomenclature [from legal and illegal] to the distinction between 'licit' and 'illicit', we refer less to the letter of the law than to social perceptions of activities defined as criminal. To take the example of drugs again, there is a growing agreement that the moderate consumption of some narcotic drugs, marijuana in particular, is no more dangerous than the moderate consumption of liquor and cigarettes, which are legal; moreover the private consumption of marijuana is extremely widespread around the world.

Clearly the role of the public as knowing buyers cannot be left out of the theft/market equation. To better understand tolerance of illegal but socially *licit* dealing in stolen goods and of the roles that the general public plays in stolen goods markets, it is important to have up-to-date knowledge about why and how people knowingly consume stolen goods. Qualitative research conducted with thieves and buyers is essential for this, and so too is quantitative information.

Consumer society

We all own certain items that we know we must be careful to protect because they are top of the thieves' shopping lists. Knowledge of these latest 'hot products' (Clarke 1999) means that thieves are just as likely to 'steal to offer' as they are to steal to order (see: Sutton 1998). As one interviewee from a study I conducted of prolific thieves in Nottingham and Mansfield (Sutton 2008) said in this regard: 'If I come across something, the first thing I think of before I take it is can I sell it. I mean I'm not going to take it if I can't sell it, it's no good to me. So when I'm taking that, I know exactly where it's going.'

In terms of where we live and what our home looks like, the car we drive, the clothes and accessories that we wear and where we vacation it is undeniable that in modern life, identity and self-worth are in no small part defined first by being a consumer and only secondly by what one produces or does besides consuming (Bauman 1998). While this drive to own *stuff* seems unending some writers suggest it is less than rewarding. Hayward (2004), for example, presents evidence to support the common-sense argument that pleasures associated with style purchases such as gadgets and clothes are short lived, while the purchaser becomes haunted by a *must have neurosis* of fashion and the need to define themselves by patterns of consumption within wealthy nations that have economies buoyed up by these predominantly urban and consumer oriented societies. The problem that challenges both critical and 'administrative', *problem-oriented*, criminology (Sutton 2007) is that while many people wish to own aspirational merchandise, they either cannot afford – or else do not wish – to pay for it at legitimate prices (Henry 1977).

The emergence and spread of popular demand for the latest 'must have' hi-tech items in society, then, is often fuelled by rapid changes in technology and the constant advertising and demand for new desirable, but expensive, mass-produced consumer goods at less than high street prices, which then drives the trade in stolen goods markets.

Henry's work was groundbreaking in taking forward our understanding of dodgy-dealing in society. The pioneering work of Henry (1978), Parker *et al.* (1988), Hobbs (1989), Foster (1990) and Sutton (1995) has emphasised the role of the consumer rather than the professional middleman 'fence' as what should the most important focus of criminal justice and criminological attention for those seeking to tackle the problem of demand for stolen goods fuelling theft. The compelling logic of the thinking here is that tackling theft by cracking down on stolen goods trading will adversely affect both consumers and middlemen and have the potential for reducing the motivation of offenders (Pease 1994; Sutton 1995, 1996). This idea has now been taken on board by other criminologists – most notably by the hugely influential Clarke (1999) and Felson (2002) – who like me are problem-oriented criminologists keen to try out and evaluate new situational-oriented ways to reduce crime.

What works and what doesn't work?

A Home Office-funded academic evaluation of the MRA (Market Reduction Approach) in two UK police constabularies (Harris *et al.* 2003; Hale *et al.* 2004) revealed that certain approaches in the implementation of the MRA and several of the theoretical recommendations in two of my earlier Home Office reports (Sutton 2008 and Sutton *et al.* 2001) should be avoided now that they have been tried out and found wanting. Although it is beyond the scope of this chapter to go into great depth and detail about what we know about previous attempts at cracking down on stolen goods markets in the UK and USA, what follows next, therefore, is a fairly extensive overview of just some key practices to avoid and of others that appear promising. These recommendations are taken from evaluations conducted by Walsh (1976), Cotter and Burrows (1981), Weiner *et al.* (1981), Harris *et al.* (2003) and Hale *et al.* (2004).

Some things to avoid in market-targeted anti-theft initiatives

- *Simple awareness-raising is not crime-reducing.* So avoid 'blowing the budget' on marketing initiatives to the press, the public and within a police force.

- *Avoid conducting local surveys of victims and the general public.* This is because they are expensive, time-consuming and offer little useful information for local initiatives.

- *Don't seek to identify stolen goods dealers through classified advertisements in newspapers.* This is so even though those with convictions who repeatedly advertise probably do so. This is a resource-intensive method that does not appear to pay dividends because thieves do it too irregularly.

- *Don't underestimate the complexity and extent of the stolen goods market problem.* Theoretically feasible targets such as taxi drivers, bars and pubs and residential fences may not be realistically actionable targets. For example, evidentiary footage of *residential fences* dealing, which would be shown during any court case, might only have been shot from one place – revealing the identity of neighbours who helped the police. Taxi drivers may be particularly vulnerable to intimidation by criminal customers. Bar owners may rely upon criminal customers for business and even for maintaining 'peace and order' in their establishments.

- *Don't expect offenders to deal only in one type of market at any one time.* The main point to be got from this is that offenders are not rigid in how they choose to use the available markets for stolen goods, particularly those operating within *network sales markets*.

- *Don't spend resources for market reduction on seeking to return property to rightful owners.* Research suggests that this is very resource-intensive and is not at all cost-effective in reducing theft or apprehending thieves.

- *Don't seek to employ TV, radio or printed media such as posters, beer mats, stickers, etc. in untested attitude change initiatives.* What works in the use of media to change attitudes is complex and likely to be counter-intuitive (Sutton *et al.* 2007). Attempts to convince the public not to buy stolen goods with print, film and broadcasting media may actually backfire and make the problem worse. As Harris *et al.* (2003) note, while these measures have been compared by Sutton to successful drink-drive campaigns those were implemented on a national basis, including prime-time TV footage and accompanied by a change in the law: 'It seems unlikely that small-scale projects can hope to inspire the kind of widespread mindset change which would result in measurable changes in people's willingness to buy potentially stolen goods.'

- *Don't maintain a fence in the community as an informant.* Research with a career fence (Steffensmeier and Ulmer 2005: 100) reveals that police sometimes provide professional fences with 'immunity' from arrest so long as they provide them with intelligence about thieves. Clearly this is beneficial to career criminals and to police careers but it is harmful to the community. Research (Sutton 1998, 2003, 2008) reveals how fences recruit, encourage, promote and provide motivation for local thieves to begin stealing and to steal more frequently.

- *Don't set up a police storefront sting operation.* Research reveals they increase theft levels in the local vicinity and help to support local illegal drugs markets with taxpayer's money.

- *Don't perpetually play catch-up with theft trends.* Instead, study the markets to employ foresight to be proactive in anticipating and gearing up for the next big stolen goods crime wave.

- *Avoid property marking like 'the plague'.* Despite the bold assertions made recently by commercial companies for the success of their products in reducing crime, at the time of writing at least, all genuinely independent academic research evidence continues to suggest otherwise and this has not changed since Knutsson (1984) and Sutton (1998) conducted their research in this area. Property marking has never been proven to reduce theft because thieves steal marked property and fences and citizens will buy it.

  Although property marking such as Smartwater is one of the easiest initiatives to undertake, it is unlikely to be effective and should not be undertaken as part of a crime-reduction initiative unless it is integral to a wider initiative that will realistically and significantly increase the likelihood of thieves/buyers being caught in possession of marked goods or proven to have criminally handled them. Any arguments that property marking schemes work by projecting some form of paranoia into the minds of thieves and buyers remain completely untested by independent research and are completely unfounded and should, therefore, be treated with what is best described as extremely healthy scientific scepticism. No matter how plausible the commercial marketers of these systems appear, at the time of writing – without fully and genuinely independent evaluation – their products are arguably no better than expensive crime reduction quackery (Bent Society 2008).

  In the latest research into this hard to kill *quack cure for crime* Harris *et al.* (2003: 175) and Hale *et al.* (2004) found that property marking, even as an integral part of an MRA scheme does not seem to be a worthwhile option:

  > ... identifiable features on property are rarely noted and victims often do not know the identifiable features – such as serial numbers – that manufacturers put on items. Property-marking schemes have a low take-up rate and it is difficult to market them to improve this when so little property is recovered. Property marking at point of sale was arranged with shop managers in South Town but each arrangement lasted for only short periods because of shop staff turnover. Very little property-marked property is recovered – so little in fact in South Town that the torches distributed to patrol cars to check recovered property for ultraviolet pen marks were allowed to run out of power and not used. (Harris *et al.* 2003)

- *Do not deploy the media without expert assistance from specialist psychologists.* In many areas of crime reduction it is possible for a policy to be ineffective, but rarely does an ineffective policy or practice that involves making changes to policing, toughening crime targets or altering the environment, with an aim to make things safer, actually completely backfire and make things worse – unless, that is, you begin to seek to calculate how wasted and scarce money might have been better spent to actually reduce crime (but then that's a separate issue). Marking property with the latest in a long line of property marking products, for example, may not reduce burglary (Sutton 2003) but it is also highly unlikely to turn people into burglars, make property more vulnerable to theft or increase the rate at which burglars offend. With media-based campaigns to change attitudes, however, there is a very real danger of policy-backfire that will actually make things worse – at least according to research on the psychology of attitude change (Sutton *et al.* 2007). Therefore, any media initiatives that seek to change attitudes among general citizens to buying stolen goods should be adopted with extreme caution since they might normalise the problem rather than stigmatise it and they might actually advertise the bargain opportunities that others are cashing in on – or they might encourage offending in other ways that we do not yet know of. The natural conclusion here then is that, without expert design and expert independent evaluation, using media to advertise property marking, as many police forces and community partnerships currently do, appears to be *doubly dangerous crime reduction quackery.*

- *Anti-fencing or wider MRA initiative?* It is essential to appreciate the big difference between feasibility and practicality. This key lesson was made very clear in the published findings of the evaluation by Harris *et al.* (2003), which revealed many examples where theoretical MRA techniques appeared feasible and compelling on paper but proved un-actionable in reality. For example, my earlier (Sutton 1998) and Sutton *et al.*'s (2001) MRA recommendation that *residential fences* should be covertly filmed during their doorstep dealing activities was not possible because (1) these fences invariably took counter-surveillance precautions and (2) the camera angle of evidence presented in court would have implicated which neighbours house was used – placing cooperative neighbours in serious danger of reprisals from criminals. This, like many of the – what not to do – lessons outlined in the bullet points above appeared feasible on paper, which just goes to prove the importance of independent evaluation of crime reduction initiatives if crime reduction quackery is to be avoided.

What follows next is a selection of promising ideas for tackling stolen goods markets. As with the *'what not to do'* pointers above, the following recommendations are drawn from a variety of research and evaluation studies.

Some things to do in a market-targeted anti-theft initiative

- *Establish multi-agency partnership to tackle markets.* The police working alone will be less effective than working with agencies that can bring into play other intelligence from their case files and employ trading, environmental, tax and other criminal and civil regulations and remedies against business and residential fences. Most importantly, for effective crime reduction partnership working, establish an advisory group headed by one agency – such as the relevant police service (Sutton 1996).

- *Because local fences deal directly with thieves the thief is an important investigative tool in finding fences.* Simply following the thief, or interviewing thieves who claim to have gone straight, and interviewing registered informants can lead to the fence and wider markets for stolen goods.

- *Set up specialist anti-fencing or MRA units.* As a dying career professional fence explains in his last testimony (Steffensmeier and Ulmer 2005: 121), non-specialists often cannot get the required evidence to convict a professional fence: 'The cops can spend a lotta time for nothing – checking it out, then come up empty. Ordinary cops doesn't have the know-how "up here"…'

- *Use foresight to gear up to tackle market-driven crime before it fuels the next big crime wave.* Keep abreast of international, national and local (*glocal*) changes in market conditions of supply, demand and price. For example, global shortages of various metals have in the past preceded crime harvests many times. Keep abreast of consumer trends to determine what are likely to be the next hot CRAVED (Clarke 1999) products.

- *Changes in the overall rate of theft should be a long-term hope rather than a short-term result.*

- *An increase in fences and other handlers of stolen goods arrested is a much more valid indicator of short-term success than theft reduction – which can be almost impossible to prove.*

- *Plan an exit strategy for future integration of the anti-fencing or MRA as a core enforcement target.* Ensure that stolen goods market targeting is someone's job – someone's sole job and their specialty area in your organisation.

Conclusion

It should go without saying that it is important that lessons are learned and successes built upon if anti-fencing and wider market reduction is to become an effective tool in the ongoing struggle to deliver justice to those who motivate thieves and, ultimately, to reduce thefts.

Despite the earlier published optimistic recommendations of criminologists such as myself, theft reduction through stolen goods market targeted initiatives is extremely difficult to measure and prove. It is important therefore for anyone implementing a theft market targeted initiative to set main aims that are realistically achievable and measurable. Aiming to increase the number of successful prosecutions against handlers may be the most achievable option – but it is one that should ideally be supported with a longer-term secondary aim to reduce theft levels.

Tackling stolen goods markets is not just a logically compelling crime reduction initiative, not just the right thing to do, it is an essential way forwards because, as this chapter has shown, stolen goods markets are not just the roots of theft, they are also a gateway to and facilitator of other offending such as problem illegal drug use and dealing and associated problems. As leading criminologist Marcus Felson (2002) poignantly notes in his summary of what we know about stolen goods markets: 'The process for marketing stolen goods is much more important than previously thought and could be the driving force for property crime. It even has an indirect impact on other types of crime.'

Finally, in our drive to tackle theft we must be careful not to squander money on crime reduction quack cures. Criminologists need to be vigilant and advise and, where necessary, speak out against those who do. When seeking to tackle theft, it is all very well focusing upon the usual and not so usual suspects, but criminologists are trained also to recognise harmful, immoral and other illicit activities within police services and other institutions of the criminal justice system as well.

Selected further reading

Clarke's work *Hot Products* (1999) and Felson's (2002) insightful forays into this area are both essential texts. These should all be read critically alongside the telling evaluation of the Market Reduction Approach (Hale *et al.* 2004).

At the time of writing, no one text comprehensively discusses how best to tackle stolen goods markets. However, that will shortly change as the Centre for Problem Oriented Policing (http://www.popcenter.org/) will shortly be including on its website (Sutton 2009) a practitioner's guide for police officers wishing to tackle stolen goods markets that is based upon the most comprehensive review of the literature in this area ever undertaken.

Note

1 Fence = dealer in stolen goods.

References

Abraham, I. and van Schendel, W. (2005) 'Introduction: the making of illicitness', in W. van Schendel and I. Abraham (eds), *Illicit Flows and Criminal Things: States, Borders and the Other Side of Globalization.* Bloomington and Indianapolis, IN: Indiana University Press.

Allen, J. (2000) 'Community survey of willingness to receive stolen goods', *Crime and Justice Bulletin: Contemporary Issues in Crime and Justice,* 51: 1–16.

Bauman, Z. (1998) *Consumerism, Work and the New Poor.* Buckingham: Open University Press.

Bennett, T., Holloway, K. and Williams, T. (2001) *Drug Use and Offending: Summary Results from the First Year of the NEW-ADAM Research Programme,* Research Findings No. 148. London: Home Office.

Bent Society (2008) 'Smartwater – dumb idea?', *Bent Society: The Origin of Curmudgeonly Criminology.* Online at: http://bentsocietyblog.blogspot.com/search/label/Smartwater%20-%20Dumb%20Idea%3F.

Blakey, G. and Goldsmith, M. (1976) 'Criminal redistribution of stolen property: the need for law reform', *Michigan Law Review,* 74: 1511–65.

Clarke, R. V. (1999) *Hot Products: Understanding, Anticipating and Reducing Demand for Stolen Goods,* Police Research Series Paper No. 112. London: Home Office, Policing and Reducing Crime Unit, Research, Development and Statistics Directorate.

Clinard, M. B. (1969) *The Black Market: A Study of White Collar Crime.* Montclair, NJ: Patterson Smith.

Colquhoun, P. (1796) *A Treatise on the Police of the Metropolis; Containing a detail of the various crimes and Misdemeanours by which Public and Private Security are, at present, injured and endangered: and suggesting Remedies for their prevention*, 3rd edn. Poultry, London: C. Dilly.

Cotter, C. and Burrows, J. (1981) *Property Crime Program: A Special Report Overview of the Sting Program and Project Summaries*. Washington, DC: US Department of Justice, Law Enforcement Assistance Administration.

Cromwell, P. and McElrath, K. (1994) 'Buying stolen property: an opportunity perspective', *Journal of Research in Crime and Delinquency*, 13 (3): 295–310.

Felson, M. (2002) *Crime and Everyday Life*, 3rd edn. Thousand Oaks, CA: Pine Forge Press.

Ferman, L., Henry, S. and Hoyman, M. (1987) 'The informal economy,' *Annals of the American Association of Political and Social Science*, 493: 154–72.

Foster, J. (1990) *Villains: Crime and Community in the Inner City*. London. Routledge.

Graham, J. and Bowling, B. (1995) *Young People and Crime*, Home Office Research Study No. 145. London: Home Office.

Hale, C., Harris, C., Uglow, S., Gilling, L. and Netton, A. (2004) *Targeting the Markets for Stolen Goods – Two Targeted Policing Initiative Projects*, Home Office Development and Practice Report No. 17. London: Home Office.

Hall, J. (1952) *Theft, Law and Society*, 2nd edn. Indianapolis, IN: Bobbs-Merrill.

Harris, C., Hale, C. and Uglow, S. (2003) 'Theory into practice: implementing a market reduction approach to property crime', in K. Bullock and N. Tilley (eds), *Crime Reduction and Problem-Oriented Policing*. Cullompton: Willan.

Hayward, K. J. (2004) *City Limits: Crime, Consumer Culture and the Urban Experience*. London: Glasshouse Press/Cavendish.

Henry, S. (1977) 'On the fence', *British Journal of Law and Society*, 4: 124–33.

Henry. S. (1978) *The Hidden Economy: The Context and Control of Borderline Crime*. London: Martin Robertson.

Hobbs, D. (1989) *Doing the Business: Entrepreneurship, the Working Class and Detectives in the East End of London*. Oxford: Oxford University Press.

Knutsson, J. (1984) *Operation Identification: A Way to Prevent Burglaries?*, Report No. 14. Stockholm: National Council for Crime Prevention Sweden, Research Division.

Parker, H., Bakx, K. and Newcombe, R. (1988) *Living with Heroin: The Impact of Drugs 'Epidemic' on an English Community*. Milton Keynes: Open University Press.

Pease, K. (1994) 'Crime prevention', in M. Maguire, R. Morgan and R. Reiner (eds), *The Oxford Handbook of Criminology*. Oxford: Oxford University Press.

Pengelly, R. (1996) 'The black economy boom: handlers play a big role in criminal activity but current performance indicators mean little is being done to target those involved in the market for stolen goods', *Police Review*, 13 December, pp. 14–16.

Steffensmeier, D. J. (1986) *The Fence: In the Shadow of Two Worlds*. Totowa, NJ: Rowman & Littlefield.

Steffensmeier, D. J. and Ulmer, J. T. (2005) *Confessions of a Dying Thief: Understanding Criminal Careers and Illegal Enterprise*. New Brunswick, NJ: Transaction Publishers.

Sutton, M. (1993) *From Receiving to Thieving: The Market for Stolen Goods and the Incidence of Theft*, Home Office Research Bulletin No. 34. London: Home Office.

Sutton, M. (1995) 'Supply by theft: does the market for second-hand goods play a role in keeping crime figures high?', *British Journal of Criminology*, 38 (3): 400–16.

Sutton, M. (1996) *Implementing Crime Prevention Schemes in a Multi-Agency Setting: Aspects of Process in the Safer Cities Programme*, Home Office Research Study No. 160. London: Home Office.

Sutton, M. (1998) *Handling Stolen Goods and Theft: A Market Reduction Approach*, Home Office Research Study No. 178. London: Home Office.

Sutton, M. (2003) 'How burglars and shoplifters sell stolen goods in Derby: describing and understanding the local illicit markets: a dynamics of offending report for Derby Community Safety Partnership', *Internet Journal of Criminology*. Online at: http://www.internetjournalofcriminology.com/Sutton%20-%20Stolen%20Goods%20in%20Derby.pdf.

Sutton, M. (2007) 'Improving national crime surveys: with a focus upon strangely neglected offenders and their offences, including fraud, high-tech crimes, and handling stolen goods', in M. Hough and M. Maxfield (eds), *Surveying Crime in the 21st Century*, Crime Prevention Studies, Vol. 22. Monsey, NY and Cullompton: Criminal Justice Press and Willan Publishing.

Sutton, M. (2008) 'How prolific thieves sell stolen goods: describing, understanding and tackling the local markets in Mansfield and Nottingham: a market reduction approach study', *Internet Journal of Criminology*. Online under primary research papers at: http://www.Internetjournalofcriminology.com; or directly at: http://www.internetjournalofcriminology.com/Sutton%20-%20How%20Prolific%20Thieves%20Sell%20Stolen%20Goods.pdf.

Sutton, M. (2009 forthcoming) *Stolen Goods Markets: Tackling the Roots of Theft*. Problem-Oriented Guides for Police, Problem-Specific Guides Series No. [xx]. Online at: http://www.popcenter.org/.

Sutton, M., Hodgkinson, S. and Levi, M. (2008) 'Handling stolen goods: findings from the 2003 Offending, Crime and Justice Survey', *Internet Journal of Criminology*. Online under primary research papers at: http://www.Internetjournalofcriminology.com; or directly at: http://www.internetjournalofcriminology.com/Sutton,%20Hodgkinson%20and%20Levi%20-%20Handling%20Stolen%20Goods.pdf.

Sutton, M., Schneider, J. L. and Hetherington, S. (2001) *Tackling Theft with the Market Reduction Approach*, Home Office Crime Reduction Research Series Paper No. 8. London: Home Office.

Sutton, M., Perry, B., Parke, J. and John-Baptiste, C. (2007) *Getting the Message Across: Using Media to Reduce Racial Prejudice and Discrimination*. Department of Communities and Local Government. Online at: http://www.communities.gov.uk/documents/communities/pdf/611667.pdf.

Talamo, J. (2007) 'Organized retail crime: setting the stage for an ORC strategy', *Loss Prevention*, 6 (1): 22–30.

Tremblay, P., Clermont, Y. and Cusson, M. (1994) 'Jockeys and joyriders: changing patterns in car theft opportunity structures', *British Journal of Criminology*, 34 (3): 307–21.

Tuckey, S. (2007) 'Stolen art is sold online: expert', *National Underwriter/Property & Casualty Risk & Benefits Management*, 111 (18): 26.

Walsh, M. (1976) *Strategies for Combating the Criminal Receiver of Stolen Goods. Organised Crime Anti-Fencing Manual*. Washington, DC: US Department of Justice, Office of Regional Operations, Law Enforcement Assistance Administration.

Wasik, M. (2001) 'Handling Stolen Goods: Advice to the Court of Appeal'. Online at: http://www.sentencing-guidelines.gov.uk/docs/stolen_goods.pdf.

Weiner, K., Besachuck, D. and Stephens, C. (1981) *Detroit Police Department Anti-Fencing Project: January 1977 through January 1981: Final Evaluation*. Detroit, MI: Detroit Police Department.

Wilbur, D. (2004) 'D.C. cracks down as stolen-goods dealers evolve: fencing becomes more sophisticated, disciplined', *Washington Post*, 16 August, p. A1.

Williams, G. (1985) 'Handling, theft and the purchaser who takes a chance', *Criminal Law Review*, pp. 432–9.

Part II

Fraud and Fakes

The crimes discussed in the following chapters – income tax evasion and benefit fraud, theft and fraud by employees, fakes, scams, credit fraud, identity theft and fraud, and cybercrime – are united by the characteristic that they contain elements of 'fraud' or the obtaining of goods and/or money by deception. All of these crimes have long histories (e.g. the Romans engaged in tax evasion). Nevertheless, industrialisation, globalisation and technological advances (most notably in relation to the Internet) have resulted in changes in the modus operandi of these offences and the range of victims affected by them, making it difficult for legislators and law enforcers to keep up. As a result of this, together with the fact that victims might not come forward for fear of bad publicity for their company or from personal embarrassment about being 'scammed', the criminal justice system deals with only a small proportion of these incidents.

The authors in this part of the book explore a range of issues which to date have received little attention in the criminological literature. Minkes and Minkes explore the different attitudes towards tax evaders and benefit fraudsters and the stigmatisation of claimants as scroungers. Gill and Goldstraw-White consider what organisations can and should do to prevent workplace crime and, in particular, note the role of gender in this type of crime. Mackenzie explores the influence of industrialisation and globalisation on the nature and prevalence of faking and scams. Levi notes that long-firm and payment card frauds are at the lower end of a spectrum of economic conduct involving insolvency with 'reckless' lending at the top. Semmens breaks down identity crime into its several forms and argues that the issue of conceptualisation needs urgent attention. Williams highlights the speed with which 'traditional' crimes develop and new crimes emerge in cyberspace.

Social attitudes to these crimes are often quite different to those of other crimes discussed elsewhere in this book. Fraud offences are often seen as more acceptable because of a belief that 'everybody does it' (e.g. CD burning and file sharing); there tends to be less sympathy for victims, who may be seen as 'bringing it on themselves' through stupidity or greed, or as able to afford the loss (e.g. large companies which have insurance to cover losses); in some cases, there appears to be no tangible 'victim' (e.g. tax fraud); the crimes can be perceived as demonstrating resistance to unpopular or oppressive government (e.g. avoiding VAT, hacking government websites); the offenders are more skilled (e.g. forgeries) and operate according to 'old-school' criminal codes; or there is often no tangible loss (e.g. intellectual property crime). Nevertheless, the costs are ultimately passed on to the taxpayer and consumer.

Chapter 5

Income tax evasion and benefit fraud

John Minkes and Leonard Minkes

This chapter deals with income tax evasion and benefit fraud, two types of crime which have one obvious characteristic in common: they both involve cheating the government, either by failing to pay money due in income tax or by claiming benefits to which there is no entitlement. It might be assumed that there is an obvious difference in that income tax evaders are in employment and benefit claimants are not, but this does not always hold good: people who are not in paid employment may evade tax by concealing or understating income from investments, rents or other sources, while some benefits (e.g. for people with disabilities) may be claimed regardless of employment status and others such as Housing Benefit may also be paid to those in work, subject to a means test. It will be shown, however, that the key difference between tax evasion and benefit fraud is not in the nature of the offences but in social attitudes to the two crimes which vary considerably, as demonstrated in particular by the work of Cook (1989a, 1989b, 1997): in short, tax evasion can be portrayed as resistance to oppressive government restraints on liberty and enterprise while benefit fraud is castigated as 'scrounging'.[1]

The present authors have emphasised elsewhere the multidisciplinary character of the study of corporate and white-collar misconduct and the critical importance of placing it within a context of economic, social and organisational considerations (Minkes and Minkes 2008). This chapter too will be multi-disciplinary in nature; the study of taxation and tax evasion has long evoked the interest of economists, psychologists and social scientists generally. In fact, such interest can be traced back into ancient history. The Romans and the ancient Egyptians were seriously concerned with the problem, as was Hammurabi, and Slemrod (2007: 25) remarks that:

> The history of taxation is replete with episodes of evasion, often notable for their inventiveness. During the third century, many wealthy Romans buried their jewellery or stocks of gold coins to evade the luxury tax, and homeowners in eighteenth century England temporarily bricked up their fireplaces to escape notice of the hearth tax collector …

Similarly, medieval European monarchs were concerned with such matters because of the effect on their revenues, and in more modern times:

> In Britain, the select committees of 1851 and 1861 heard evidence on tax avoidance and others have since. In 1981, yet another House of Commons committee took evidence on the whole of the unofficial economy, tax avoidance and evasion included. (Heertje *et al.* 1982: 61)

This government concern continues: the National Audit Office published a report on tackling tax evasion in 2003 (NAO 2003a) and the House of Commons Committee of Public Accounts has since returned to the subject of the hidden economy (Committee of Public Accounts 2008).

The idea of the state paying allowances to some of its citizens is a much more recent development and consequently benefit fraud has a shorter history than tax evasion. Although frequently decried in the media and by politicians, it has received very little attention from social scientists. But it too has been the subject of reports by the National Audit Office (NAO 2003b, 2008).

Criminologists have not paid a great deal of attention to either type of offence, as distinct from any other form of property crime. Economists have long considered the question of taxation; much of their writing on it has dealt with its effects on incentives to effort, willingness to invest, consumer expenditure and redistribution effects. They have also, however, paid attention to malpractice. Adam Smith in *The Wealth of Nations*, published in 1776, saw high taxation as a temptation to smuggling and Alfred Marshall, writing towards the end of the nineteenth century, considered that high taxation led to false returns (Cowell 1985). In more recent times, there has been a considerable development of writing by economists and econometricians on the economics of taxation as such. This has been, in some measure, the result of the importance of the taxation system in the much expanded area of public expenditure. As will be seen, though, many of these writers rely on an essentially rational model of the taxpayer; in contrast, some criminologists, psychologists and sociologists have stressed the importance of attitudes towards taxation and also people's broader morals and values. Similar work also exists in relation to benefit fraud.

Nature of offending

The main criminological work on tax evasion and benefit fraud is that of Cook (1989a, 1989b, 1997). She identifies (1989b: 55) five types of tax evasion: moonlighting, ghosting, subcontracting in the building industry, fiddling expenses, allowances and benefits-in-kind, and fiddling the accounts.[2] (She noted that another common form of fraud, claiming false allowances, had reduced in significance with the abolition of child tax allowances and other changes in legislation). The first three, she argues, constitute the 'hidden economy', while the last two represent alternative opportunities. However, there are overlaps between the categories: for example, doctors and architects may moonlight and builders may understate profits.

To categorise types of benefit fraud, Cook (1989b) drew on government statistics for cases considered for prosecution in 1984: nearly half involved claimants failing to declare relevant earnings and another 12 per cent related to failure to declare a dependant's earnings. Other frauds included fictitious desertion or failing to declare co-habiting, making multiple claims, falsely claiming to have lost benefit cheques and people with no fixed address claiming from more than one benefits office. More recently, the NAO (2003b) noted that the relative frequencies of fraud types varied depending on the benefit recipient. For lone parents receiving Income Support, the most common fraud was failing to declare that they were living with someone 'as husband and wife'. For pensioners receiving the Minimum Income Guarantee (now Pension Credit), however, it was incorrect declaration of capital, and for those claiming Jobseeker's Allowance it was failure to disclose earnings from work. But they also noted that significant amounts were lost to organised frauds, involving, for example, multiple claims or fraudulent Housing Benefit scams, where many people falsely claim to be paying rent to a 'landlord' who orchestrates the claims.

Fraudulent claims for disability benefits are less commonly reported but recent press coverage has highlighted a number of cases by people who were receiving them while apparently fit enough to referee football matches (*Daily Mail* 2008; *Daily Telegraph* 2008). Rather than faking disabilities, these cases appear to involve continuing to claim after recovering from a disabling illness or injury. Another phenomenon reported from the United States involves false claims in the wake of disasters; following the devastation caused by Hurricane Katrina in 2005, many frauds were alleged, including use of fake Social Security numbers or false addresses (Heath 2007).

Amounts involved and prevalence

As with all forms of crime, it is extremely difficult to establish accurately the prevalence and costs of tax evasion and benefit fraud. Doig (2006) discusses a number of estimates in relation to tax evasion but concludes that it is impossible to estimate the actual amount, while Grabiner (2000) gives no figures at all, preferring instead to state that it is a major problem involving billions of pounds. Doig (2006) reaches a similar conclusion in relation to benefit fraud because official estimates are based on challengeable assumptions about the amounts saved by the investigation and prosecution of suspect claims. Nevertheless, the following estimates are cited to give some indication of the scale of the problem.

According to figures cited by the National Audit Office (2003b), the Department of Work and Pensions (DWP) was at that time spending £100 billion a year on benefits and estimated the total losses to fraud at £2 billion. Three quarters of this total represented nationally administered benefits (mainly Income Support and Jobseeker's Allowance) and the remainder was due to fraudulent claims for Housing Benefit (which is administered by local authorities). Following a previous White Paper in 1999 which had concluded that not enough attention was being paid to fraud and error, fraud had been reduced but it still represented 4.1 per cent of expenditure on Income Support and Jobseeker's Allowance.[3] In terms of the proportion of claims which are fraudulent, in 2000–1 an estimated 5.4 per cent of people claiming Income Support (204,000 individuals) and 8.6 per cent of people claiming Jobseeker's Allowance (86,000 individuals) were identified as claiming the benefits fraudulently at any one time. Interestingly, when the NAO (2008) reported on progress five years later, the overall total was estimated to have fallen from £2 billion to £800 million.

In relation to tax offences, the amounts involved are even harder to estimate; fraudulent benefit claims by their nature involve paper trails since forms must be completed in order to make a claim, but tax evasion is committed by people who conceal some or all of their income or simply do not register for income tax. Estimates therefore tend to be extrapolated from those cases which have been investigated. On this basis, the Inland Revenue's annual report for 2001 (cited by Carrabine *et al.* 2002) identified £4.5 billion as the total additional tax liability identified by non-compliance actions. Doig (2006: 44–5) cites a number of figures on the cost of Inland Revenue fraud which vary widely: one study in 2000 used Inland Revenue estimates to arrive at a figure of between £1.8 and £19.4 million a year but the NAO (2003a) stated that investigations had resulted in the recovery of £1.4 billion in tax, interest and penalties in a four-year period; the problem here is in establishing how much tax is actually due, let alone how much of the 'tax gap' (the difference between 100 per cent compliance and the amount actually paid) is the result of fraud. In terms of prevalence, they refer to an earlier finding that 15 per cent of cases selected for random checking yielded over £500 in additional tax liability, but as only 3.5 per cent of cases examined resulted in penalties, they conclude that levels of fraud and negligence are low.

The most recent published estimate of tax evasion relates specifically to the 'hidden economy'. The Committee of Public Accounts (2008), while acknowledging that there are no reliable estimates of the scale and nature of the hidden economy, quotes HM Revenue and Customs as estimating that income tax unpaid by ghosts and moonlighters amounts to £1.5 billion per year.

In terms of prevalence, the Committee of Public Accounts was advised that an EU survey across 27 countries showed that 5 per cent of people admitted doing undeclared work in the previous year, with a range across countries from 1 per cent to 18 per cent; the figure for the UK was 2 per cent. However, HM Revenue & Customs stated that they believed 80 per cent of those working in the hidden economy (and therefore with particular opportunities to offend) to be avoiding small amounts of tax. Finally, figures from the 2003 Offending, Crime and Justice survey show that 2 per cent of those in a position to commit income tax fraud reported doing so, compared with a very similar 1.8 per cent of benefit claimants (Allen *et al.* 2005).

Causes

Criminologists have given little attention to the causes of tax evasion as opposed to acquisitive crime in general. This remains true despite the growth of interest in white-collar crime. Tax evasion is included in the definition of white-collar crime employed by Weisburd and his colleagues, but their work is based on court records and is therefore concerned with statutory responses (Weisburd *et al.* 1991) or the criminal careers of white-collar offenders (Weisburd *et al.* 2001) rather than causes. Furthermore, tax evasion is not referred to in any of the 50 chapters in Pontell and Geis's *International Handbook of White-Collar and Corporate Crime* (2007).

In contrast, recent decades have seen substantial interest in the study of taxation by economists and econometricians. The characteristic problems with which they have been concerned are: why do individuals (and corporate bodies) pay taxes? Why do some seek to evade taxes, and what means are likely to be effective in restraining tax evasion? In understanding their approach, it should be appreciated that economists very generally think in terms of models of economic behaviour. A seminal example of a 'modelling' approach was provided in 1968 by Nobel Laureate in Economics, Gary Becker. In his paper, Becker (1968) did not deal specifically with taxation, but he did include white-collar crime. He made the striking statement that:

> It is suggested, for example, that a useful theory of criminal behaviour can dispense with special theories of anomie, psychological inadequacies, or inheritance of special traits and simply extend the economist's usual analysis of choice.

And he went on to specify his assumption:

> ... that a person commits an offense if the expected utility to him exceeds the utility he could get by using his time and other resources at other activities.

Criminologists and students of eighteenth- and nineteenth-century thought will recognise here the utilitarian argument and Becker (1968: 209) himself makes this connection:

> Lest the reader be repelled by the apparent novelty of an 'economic' framework for illegal behaviour, let him recall that two important contributors to criminology during the eighteenth and nineteenth century, Beccaria and Bentham, explicitly applied an economic calculus.

This view of criminal behaviour essentially assumes that individuals are rational actors who apply an economic calculus of potential benefits and costs with due regard to the factor of risk. Such an approach has certainly influenced other economists, leading Allingham and Sandmo (1972) to develop a model in which, according to Slemrod (2007: 35–6):

... taxpayers decide whether and how much to evade taxes in the same way they would approach any risky decision or gamble – by maximising expected utility – and are influenced by possible legal penalties in just the same way they are influenced by any other contingent cost.

More recent studies, notably econometric analyses, have made perhaps more sophisticated assumptions but still tend to treat the taxpayer as a utility-seeking decision-maker. However, it will come as no surprise to criminologists or to social scientists generally that the idea that illegal behaviour can be explained solely in terms of the economic theory of choice has been criticised as inadequate. Thus, for example, Dean *et al.* (1980: 29) remark of the Allingham/Sandmo model:

This analytically convenient model is behaviourally unpromising because its assumptions are naive and far removed from reality.

The critique of the standard economic models is carried forward by Kirchler (2007). He notes that the four parameters of the tax decisions in the standard economic model are probability of detection of evasion, punishment of evasion, tax rates and income level. But, he says, empirical research shows that the model does not work, e.g. the probability of detection does not have much effect on non-compliant behaviour. He goes on to argue that we have to consider the interaction between the taxpaying authorities and the taxpayers: thus he considers that trust between them leads to compliance and absence of trust has adverse effects. If there is, as he expresses it, a 'cops and robbers' relationship, it will tend to produce the rational economic pattern; on the other hand, if the climate is one of positive trust, there will be a greater willingness to comply voluntarily.

Ariel (2009) also found little empirical support for the rational actor model. He systematically reviewed 15 large random controlled tests carried out in a number of countries since the 1960s to test the effectiveness of different administrative tax tools in increasing compliance. The results were inconsistent but the overall finding was that there was no impact, positive or negative. There was an indication that increasing taxpayers' perception of the likelihood of detection led to some of them making greater disclosure of income (in contrast, changing the wording of letters to explain taxation better had a negative effect). Ariel (2009) concluded that different subgroups of taxpayers may behave differently but responding with differential treatment raises questions of fairness.

Other empirical work also highlights the importance of taxpayers' attitudes to taxation, albeit with somewhat conflicting findings. James and Nobes (1992) reported on a survey of taxpayers in European countries (including Britain) which indicated that a positive attitude by taxpayers towards the tax system and a negative attitude towards offenders can contribute to the control of evasion. Brooks and Doob (1990) interviewed Canadian taxpayers in order to test out the rational actor model and concluded that it was a poor predictor of evasion because taxpayers' perceptions of the risks and costs were not necessarily accurate and different taxpayers had different motivations.

However, they found no evidence that attitudes to the government and taxation influenced taxpayers. Some years later, Varma and Doob (1998) again interviewed taxpayers, some of whom admitted having evaded tax or being willing to do so. They concluded this time that some of the evaders were concerned about the likely penalties, but the strongest association was between compliance and personal standards: evaders were much less likely to feel obliged to be honest on income tax returns. Thus for many, personal beliefs lay behind the decision to pay or avoid income tax rather than calculation of the benefits and potential costs.

The suggestion that there are differences among taxpayers is supported by Slemrod (2007). Although not unsympathetic to the deterrence model of tax evasion, he points out that there is considerable experimental (and anecdotal) evidence that tax evasion involves more than amoral cost-benefit calculation. Thus, for example, there may be a distinction between intrinsic and extrinsic motivation: some taxpayers may meet their liabilities through 'civic virtue' and others through deference to the threat of penalties.

A similar conclusion to that of Varma and Doob (1998) about the importance of personal standards is reached by Braithwaite and Braithwaite (2006) who surveyed Australian taxpayers. Previous surveys had shown that

> ... over 60 per cent of Australians either have doubts or do not believe that the public goods and services they receive are fair compared with the tax they pay. (2006: 1112)

This raised the question of why they would comply with taxation. In responses to the new survey, over 90 per cent expressed pride in being honest taxpayers and said that they believed that paying taxes benefited everyone because it enabled the government to fund worthwhile services. In addition, 70 per cent thought it was wrong to cheat and that the authorities should take action to catch cheats. But some respondents also felt that Australia was moving towards a profit-oriented society and the privileged and wealthy were not paying their share. Thus Braithwaite and Braithwaite stress the importance of ethics and the desire to avoid the community disapproval which may follow prosecution, but they also caution that if evaders are seen to escape, others will copy their example.

Cook (1989b) denotes a more politically charged version of the view that attitudes to taxation lead to evasion. Conservative commentators and employers' organisations (and her own interviewees) complained that they were subjected to excessive taxation which punishes effort and enterprise and drives the 'honest' taxpayer to fiddles. Moonlighters offered a slightly different argument, justifying their conduct by reference to their low pay (a similar argument to that put forward by many of the 'occupational cheats' described by, among others, Ditton (1977) and Mars (1982)). Some of Cook's (1989b) interviewees also used the argument that 'everybody does it' but this is probably more a rationalisation than an explanation. It is also likely to be something of an exaggeration: Doig (2006) notes that the British Social Attitudes Surveys show that 70 per cent of people think lying to avoid paying tax is wrong, which only leaves 30 per cent who do not.

Cook (1989b) also interviewed benefit fraudsters. They blamed poverty, hardship and frustration. Like the tax fraudsters, they cited economic imperatives. They also sometimes blamed the system: for example, people who had intermittent income (irregular maintenance payments, part-time work) stopped declaring it because their benefit payments were disrupted and delayed as a result – fraud then appears as a 'legitimate response to a capricious system' (1989b: 95). They also used the 'everyone does it' argument.

Reenoy (1990), in a qualitative study of workers in the informal economy in the Netherlands, found evidence of reluctance to give up benefits as a reason for fraud as well as perceived pressure of taxation, though one of his respondents laid the blame very forcefully on the impossibility of keeping a family on state benefits. Rowlingson *et al.* (1997, cited by Doig 2006) also emphasised financial necessity: those who committed benefit fraud knew that it was unlawful but did not see it as criminal; it was the lesser of two evils if money was needed and the alternative was crime. There are echoes here of Becker's model of rational choice but with the important qualification that these actors see their choices as very much constrained by financial pressures. Thus Hessing *et al.* (1993: 227) refer to benefit fraud as 'a defective behaviour within a social dilemma'. And Evason and Woods (1995: 48) found that claimants in Belfast

> … felt trapped by inadequate benefits, scarcity of employment, an awareness that if work was secured, they might be little further forward and an understanding of the hazards of moving into work and then, at a later date, back on to benefit.

Dean and Melrose (1997) interpret benefit fraud rather differently, as a form of limited resistance to social control. The claimants they surveyed were not particularly knowledgeable about the benefit system. Their predominant reason for fraud was economic need, but their offences were not necessarily planned; often they had just taken the opportunity to earn small amounts and not declared them. They thought that fiddling was common and they distinguished between what they did (which they saw as harmless) and serious fraud. Some fraudsters had no scruples (most of these had been involved in other types of crime) while for others, more concerned and anxious about their offending, it was a 'rather poorly calculated act of desperation' (1997: 106). Other writers, Dean and Melrose stated, had argued that changes in the benefit system had led to a culture of resistance, but their conclusion was that although their interviewees did resist the increasing parsimony of the system, this did not amount to a culture. Instead, they drew on Foucault to analyse the way claimants had become subject to increased regulation and control and the ways in which they resisted. Essentially, people did not challenge the dominant order but sought autonomy and opportunistic gain within it.

Official responses

These diverse attitudes are reflected in differing official responses. While it is true that both tax and benefit authorities tend to emphasise compliance above prosecution, prosecutions are consistently more common for benefit fraud than for tax evasion. For instance, Cook (1989a, 1989b) obtained information from the Inland Revenue on tax prosecutions between 1982 and 1988. She found that they adopted a sympathetic approach towards tax evaders and regarded prosecution as a last resort, preferring to negotiate settlements, which might include an agreed penalty for evasion. They had collected over £2 billion in such settlements. Only 322 convictions had been obtained in 1987/8 (including just 24 for fraudulent tax returns). In her later work (Cook 1997) she notes that the average annual number of prosecutions from 1991 to 1996 was 240, while during the same period, the number of prosecutions for benefit fraud rose from 4,379 to 10,677.

This picture of reluctance to prosecute tax evaders is confirmed by information supplied to the NAO (2003a) when the Inland Revenue again stated that they regarded civil settlements as efficient at producing revenue. Prosecutions were still reserved for the most serious cases; there were only 183 convictions between 1998/9 and 2001/2.

Current policy was described to the Committee of Public Accounts (2008) by the successor to the Inland Revenue, HM Revenue & Customs. Criminal investigation is usually reserved for cases where the amount involved is over £10,000 and there are other features such as repeated offending or the evader is a professional person who advises on tax matters.[4] The most recent figures for prosecutions were still very small: 69 cases (of which 65 resulted in convictions) in 2006/7. This represents only two out of every thousand cases detected; the comparable figure for the Department of Work and Pensions is 60 out of every thousand.

In contrast to the Inland Revenue's policy, Cook (1989b) reported that the Department of Health and Social Security prosecuted over 20,000 Supplementary Benefit claimants in 1980/1[5] and although policy changed in the 1980s to emphasise checking abuse and recovering money, there were still nearly 10,000 prosecutions in 1987/8. Many involved very small amounts of money and one claimant was sent to prison for a fraud involving only £67. In 1983 268 benefit fraudsters were imprisoned compared to only 32 tax law offenders.

Again, this trend continues. According to Grabiner (2000), the DSS prosecuted around 6,000 people in 1998/9 for failing to declare earnings, and the total number of prosecutions for benefit fraud was nearly 10,000. This represented 7 per cent of cases where a fraudulent benefit overpayment had been identified. Most recently, the DWP told the NAO (2003b) that most cases of fraud were dealt with by reducing or withdrawing benefits; in 15 per cent of cases, they also imposed an administrative penalty, but only in cases involving less than £1,500, a limit which had not increased since 1997. More serious cases were taken to court: in 2001/2, 11,183 convictions were obtained, 646 people were sent to prison and a further 175 received suspended sentences.[6]

Conclusion

This chapter started by pointing out that the net results of tax evasion and benefit fraud are identical: the state is deprived of money by offenders. Indeed, while estimates vary, the total amounts involved appear to be not greatly dissimilar. In effect, all citizens are victims, because the state must either tax them more to cover the losses or spend less on services. But, as Cook (1989a, 1989b, 1997) in particular has pointed out, attitudes towards the two different types of offence are radically different. She argues (1989a) that two centuries of prejudice against the poor translates itself into the stigmatisation of all claimants as scroungers who take from the state and are evidence of a dependency culture. Taxpayers, in contrast, give to the state and are members of an enterprise culture. Benefit fraudsters steal money from others while tax evaders are simply keeping their own money. Although in her view benefit fraud is usually motivated by poverty and tax evasion by greed, the ideological construction of the poor and the rich means that 'poverty ... inculpates the poor, while wealth and "enterprise" exculpate the rich' (1989b: 126).

Although she relates this specifically to the 1980s, a period characterised by the promotion of individual enterprise, the analysis still holds good twenty years later. Public attitudes towards genuine benefit claimants, let alone fraudulent ones, remain largely negative (Bamfield and Horton 2009). Despite a series of articles in the *Guardian* drawing attention to the scale of corporate tax avoidance (*Guardian* 2009), tax evasion fails to attract the same stigma. Government attitudes can be exemplified by the comparative length of the two documents published by the National Audit Office in 2003 (NAO 2003a, 2003b): their plans for tackling tax evasion were set out in 11 pages, but their work on benefit fraud ran to 68. And, as detailed above, enforcement policies are consistently much more severe towards benefit fraudsters than tax evaders.

As a focus of academic research, this chapter has emphasised the interdisciplinary character of the study of taxpayer and benefit recipient behaviour and has indicated various lines along which significant study might be pursued. Thus economists and econometricians have been developing models which aim to identify the factors underlying tax evasion, some of them seeking to go beyond the assumptions that drove the pioneering economic interpretation of crime by Becker. As is characteristic of a good deal of work by economists, emphasis has been placed on the ability of their models to predict behaviour in order to maximise tax returns, and this makes them vulnerable to criticism by other social scientists such as Kirchler, who devote more attention to attempting to explain the complex phenomenon of fraudulent behaviour. Nevertheless, critics of rational actor approaches should keep in mind that economic motivation is likely to be a significant factor.

Few criminologists other than Cook have investigated either tax evasion or benefit fraud and it has largely been left to other disciplines to carry out empirical work. And although Allen *et al.* (2005) found that tax evaders were more likely than non-evaders to report having committed other types of offence as well, this appears to be the only attempt to link explanations of these offences to offending in general, although their commonness and the ambivalent attitudes expressed in particular by tax evaders suggests that they might be included in the category of 'everyday offences' described by Karstedt and Farrall (2006).

Criminologists may be tempted to see the most important aspect of these offences as the differing responses to them, indicative of bias in the system and discrimination against the disadvantaged, but their lack of engagement with the subject leaves them short of evidence with which to challenge the stereotypes.

Selected further reading

As noted above, there is very little criminological work on this topic. Cook's work (Cook 1989a, 1989b, 1997) stands more or less alone. The various government publications referred to in this chapter (e.g. NAO 2003a 2003b; Committee of Public Accounts 2008) summarise current concerns and policies and include estimates of the scale of the problem. Kirchler (2007) provides a valuable introduction to and summary of non-criminological literature.

Notes

1 In this context, it is worth noting the distinction between tax avoidance and tax evasion, both for individuals and companies, which is essentially between lawful (avoidance) and unlawful (evasion) behaviour. Both result in reduced government income, but while avoidance, which merges into the area of tax planning, may in some circumstances raise ethical considerations, it is evasion, by virtue of its illegality, which is the subject of this chapter.
2 The literature generally refers only to the first two of these types of tax evaders: moonlighters, who pay tax on their main source of income but do not declare additional earnings, and ghosts, who are not registered for tax at all.
3 These benefits generated the highest amounts of fraud, hence the percentage here is higher than the overall 2 per cent suggested by the figures for all benefits.
4 Other professionals not directly involved in tax matters can apparently escape prosecution. HMRC reported to the Committee of Public Accounts (2008) that they had investigated 57 barristers, of whom 36 had settled privately, paying a total of over £600,000 between them in assessed tax and penalties. Not only did these barristers avoid prosecution, they were also spared publicity – HMRC told the Committee that they could not name them as tax affairs are confidential.
5 The DHSS subsequently became the Department of Social Security (DSS) and then the DWP; Supplementary Benefit has also been replaced by Income Support.
6 Of the remainder, over 2,000 were fined, over 3,000 received conditional discharges and nearly 4,000 received community sentences.

References

Allen, J., Forrest, S., Levi, M., Roy, H. and Sutton, M. (ed. Wilson, D.) (2005) *Fraud and Technology Crimes*: *Findings from the 2002/03 British Crime Survey and 2003 Crime and*

Justice Survey, Home Office Online Report 34/05. Online at: http://www.homeoffice. gov.uk/rds/pdfs05/rdsolr3405.pdf .

Allingham, M. and Sandmo, A. (1972) 'Income tax evasion: a theoretical analysis', *Journal of Public Economics*, 1: 323–38.

Ariel, B. (2009) *What Works in Tax Compliance: Systematic Review of Research on Administrative Tax Tools*. Paper given to the British Society of Criminology annual conference, Cardiff, 30 June.

Bamfield, L. and Horton, T. (2009) *Understanding Attitudes to Tackling Economic Inequality*. York: Joseph Rowntree Foundation.

Becker, G. (1968) 'Crime and punishment: an economic approach', *Journal of Political Economy*, 76 (2): 169–217.

Braithwaite, V. and Braithwaite, J. (2006) 'Democratic sentiment and cyclical markets in vice', *British Journal of Criminology*, 46 (6): 1110–27.

Brooks, N. and Doob, A. (1990) 'Tax evasion: searching for a theory of compliant behaviour', in M. L. Friedland (ed.), *Securing Compliance: Seven Case Studies*. Toronto: University of Toronto Press.

Carrabine, E., Cox, P., Lee, M. and South, N. (2002) *Crime in Modern Britain*. Oxford: Oxford University Press.

Committee of Public Accounts (2008) *HMRC: Tackling the Hidden Economy*. London: The Stationery Office.

Cook, D. (1989a) 'Fiddling tax and benefits: inculpating the poor, exculpating the rich', in P. Carlen and D. Cook (eds), *Paying for Crime*. Milton Keynes: Open University Press.

Cook, D. (1989b) *Rich Law, Poor Law: Differential Responses to Tax and Supplementary Benefit Fraud*. Milton Keynes: Open University Press.

Cook, D. (1997) *Poverty, Crime and Punishment*. London: Child Poverty Action Group.

Cowell, F. (1985) 'The economic analysis of tax evasion', *Bulletin of Economic Research*, 37: 163–93.

Daily Mail (2008) 'Benefits cheat who claimed £17,000 disability allowance caught out refereeing football match', 24 July. Online at: http://www.dailymail.co.uk/ news/article-1037542/Benefits-cheat-claimed-17-000-disability-allowance-caught-refereeing-football-match.html (accessed 15 April 2009).

Daily Telegraph (2008) 'Football referee mayor claimed disability benefit', 21 April. Online at: http://www.telegraph.co.uk/news/1896614/Football-referee-mayor-claimed-disability-benefit.html (accessed 15 April 2009).

Dean, H. and Melrose, M. (1997) 'Manageable discord: fraud and resistance in the social security system', *Social Policy and Administration*, 31 (2): 103–18.

Dean, P., Keenan, T. and Kenney, F. (1980) 'Taxpayers' attitudes to income tax evasion: an empirical study', *British Tax Review*, 1: 28–44.

Ditton, J. (1977) *Part-time Crime: An Ethnography of Fiddling and Pilferage*. London: Macmillan.

Doig, A. (2006) *Fraud*. Cullompton: Willan.

Evason, E. and Woods, R. (1995) 'Poverty, deregulation of the labour market and benefit fraud', *Social Policy and Administration*, 29 (1): 40–54.

Grabiner, Lord (2000) *The Informal Economy*. London: HM Treasury.

Guardian (2009) 'The price of avoidance', 2 February. Online at: http://www.guardian. co.uk/commentisfree/2009/feb/02/tax-gap-series-avoidance.htm (accessed 17 March 2009).

Heath, B. (2007) 'Katrina fraud swamps system', *USA Today*, 6 July. Online at: http:// www.usatoday.com/news/nation/2007-07-05-katrina-fraud_N.htm (accessed 28 May 2009).

Heertje, A., Allen, M. aand Cohen, M. (1982) *The Black Economy*. London: Pan Books (trans. and revised from the Dutch, originally published 1980).

Hessing, D., Elffers, H., Robben, H. and Webley, P. (1993) 'Needy or greedy: the social psychology of individuals who fraudulently claim unemployment benefit', *Journal of Applied Social Psychology*, 23 (3): 226–43.

James, S. and Nobes, C. (1992) *The Economics of Taxation*, 4th ed. Hemel Hempstead: Prentice Hall.

Karstedt, S. and Farrall, S. (2006) 'The moral economy of everyday crime: markets, consumers and citizens', *British Journal of Criminology*, 46 (6): 1011–36.

Kirchler, E. (2007) *The Economic Psychology of Tax Behaviour*. Cambridge: Cambridge University Press.

Mars, G. (1982) *Cheats at Work: An Anthropology of Workplace Crime*. London: Allen & Unwin.

Minkes, J. and Minkes, L. (2008) 'Introduction', in J. Minkes and L. Minkes (eds), *Corporate and White Collar Crime*. London: Sage.

National Audit Office (2003a) *Tackling Fraud Against the Inland Revenue*. London: The Stationery Office.

National Audit Office (2003b) *Tackling Benefit Fraud*. London: The Stationery Office.

National Audit Office (2008) *Department for Work and Pensions: Progress in Tackling Benefit Fraud*. London: NAO.

Pontell, H. and Geis, G. (eds) (2007) *International Handbook of White-Collar and Corporate Crime*. New York: Springer.

Reenoy, P. (1990) *The Informal Economy: Meaning, Measurement and Social Significance*. Utrecht: Elmkwijk.

Rowlingson, K., Whyley, C., Newburn, T. and Berthoud, R. (1997) *Social Security Fraud: The Role of Penalties*. London: The Stationery Office.

Slemrod, J. (2007) 'Cheating ourselves: the economics of tax evasion', *Journal of Economic Perspectives*, 21 (1) 25–48.

Varma, K. N. and Doob, A. N. (1998) 'Deterring economic crimes: the case of tax evasion', *Canadian Journal of Criminology*, 40 (2): 165–84.

Weisburd, D. and Waring, E. with Chayet, E. (2001) *White-Collar Crime and Criminal Careers*. Cambridge: Cambridge University Press.

Weisburd, D., Wheeler, S., Waring, E. and Bode, N. (1991) *Crimes of the Middle Classes: White-Collar Offenders in the Federal Courts*. New Haven, CT: Yale University Press.

Chapter 6

Theft and fraud by employees

Martin Gill and Janice Goldstraw-White

Introduction

As will be shown, the topic of employee theft and fraud incorporates a wide range of behaviours, relates to a diverse range of theories and involves many different preventive remedies. Even within this book there are overlaps with many other chapters, for example corporate crimes (Minkes, Chapter 32), middle-range business crimes (Croall, Chapter 33), corporate violence (Tombs, Chapter 44) and extortions (Hobbs, Chapter 36). There are also overlaps with shop theft (see Tilley, Chapter 3) and robbery (see Hobbs, Chapter 15) because these and many other offences (Ones 2002) are facilitated by 'insiders'. Of course any offence can take place at a workplace and any offence therefore can be committed (or facilitated) by employees.

This chapter will focus on theft and fraud by employees. Specifically, it sets out to show that there is much that organisations can and should do to prevent workplace crime. Organisations can choose who they employ and the working environment and governance arrangements which they allow employees to work in. The discussion begins with an exploration of the breadth of the topic of workplace theft and fraud; it encompasses a wide range of activities only some of which can be discussed in the space available. It will move on to explore levels of theft and fraud among employees where an attempt is made to throw some light on what is widely regarded as a 'dark figure'; we will suggest that employee dishonesty is not a rare event. The chapter then moves on to consider why people are dishonest, and here we have highlighted what might be done to prevent it. We will also introduce a research note about gender and staff dishonesty, a traditionally neglected research area. We will highlight research studies which show that common reasons for offending are ones that can, and should be controlled by effective organisational policies. This is explored in the final section, where we draw from both criminological research and security management studies (another area largely neglected by criminologists) to highlight where prevention efforts should appropriately be focused and where future studies may usefully fill important gaps in knowledge.

Definition and context

Employee dishonesty can take a variety of forms from the petty fiddle, which can be on the margins of criminal activity, to large-scale frauds that have brought down major institutions (for example, see Fay 1996; Leeson 1996). This includes studies of both 'blue-collar' (see Ditton 1977; Henry 1978, 1982; Levi 1981, 2008; Mars 1973, 1974, 1982) and white-collar offences (see Benson 1985; Cressey 1953; Levi 1981, 2008; Punch 1996). As will be demonstrated, workplace crimes can be committed by staff working at any level in an organisation. For the purposes of this chapter, we will utilise an offence-based (as opposed to offender-based) approach to considering fraud and theft at work (Clinnard and Quinney 1973), examining both blue-collar and white-collar offending.

The type of offences a dishonest employee may be guilty of varies considerably. There are perhaps two general categories that merit attention here: those that relate to theft and those that relate to fraud. In UK legislative terms, theft is defined in the Theft Act 1968, sections 1 to 6. It states that: 'A person is guilty of theft if he dishonestly appropriates property belonging to another with the intention of permanently depriving the other of it' (Section 1).

The property may be tangible or intangible but the principles have been fairly easy to follow. Not so with fraud, which has been characterised by a lack of clarity. Indeed, various reviews led to the passing of the Fraud Act 2006 (for a discussion of the background see Doig 2006). This stiplulates that a person is guilty of fraud if he or she is in breach of any one of three areas: fraud by false representation, fraud by failing to disclose information or fraud by abuse of position (which should make it easier to prosecute dishonest staff).

The Association of Certified Fraud Examiners (ACFE 2008: 6) define occupational fraud as: 'The use of one's occupation for personal enrichment through the deliberate misuse or misapplication of the employing organization's resources or assets.' Hollinger and Clark (1983: 1) define dishonest workplace activity as 'the unauthorised taking, control, or transfer of money and/or property of the formal work organisation perpetrated by an employee during the course of occupational activity which is related to his or her employment'.

What is taken can include cash (e.g. Bamfield 2006b; Beck 2006) and inexpensive items such as tools or office stationery, while theft of services may include the unauthorised use of assets such as the telephone, photocopier and Internet (Salinger 2005; Hollinger et al. 1992). Sometimes losses can result from a form of sabotage, either of property or in the form of purposeful poor performance of service that impacts negatively on the organisation (e.g. Harris and Ogbonna 2002). Certainly slack behaviour by staff has helped credit card fraudsters (Levi 2003) by not properly checking details on cards for example.

Patterns and trends

There is still a dearth of good information on financial crime generally as well as staff theft and fraud offences specifically. Uncovering the dark figure is a problem. Levi *et al*. (2007) recently reviewed the level of fraud losses in the UK for 2005 and found that they amounted to at least £13 billion. Their summary of a range of studies on loss, covering organisations in the public and private sectors, is instructive and a worthy reference point for those interested in assessing and understanding the impact of financial crime. As the authors note, there are real problems in measuring financial crime losses and this is true of dishonesty offences generally. A low response to surveys and poor accounting by companies provide a less than adequate source of information. Moreover, the use of various classifications for similar offence types, covering different periods and using different units of analysis at different points in time in different countries, further complicate comparisons. These limitations need to be borne in mind.

Yet, over time and across surveys, researchers have reported that employee dishonesty involving theft and fraud is rarely a minor contributor to loss. For example, the ACFE (2008) survey – which was based on data compiled from 959 cases of occupational fraud that were investigated between January 2006 and February 2008 – reported that organisations lose 7 per cent of their annual revenues to fraud, estimated to translate into approximately a $994 billion loss. And often offences are committed by insiders. Indeed, Bussmann and Werle's (2006) global economic crime survey of more than 5,500 companies found that half of the offenders identified were internal staff.

In the retailing sector, annual surveys have elicited details about levels of crime. In the USA the National Retail Security Survey from the University of Florida has consistently shown that employee theft is perceived to account for at least 40 per cent of 'shrinkage' (the total losses suffered by a retailer), the largest single loss factor. Indeed, the most recent figures for 2007 (Hollinger and Adams 2008) put employee theft at 44 per cent, way above customer or shop theft at 34 per cent.

Surveys from Europe and the rest of the world have tended to note that customer theft is higher but employee dishonesty remains an issue. Bamfield (2008) reported on global retail crime trends and found that disloyal or fraudulent employees were thought to account for 36.5 per cent of shrinkage, which he estimates costs retailers $38,150 million per annum. He found that North and Latin American retailers reported employee theft as the main cause of shrinkage. In Europe there was an increase in the percentage share of shrinkage retailers accorded to employee theft.

The most recent British Retail Consortium (BRC) Crime Survey (2008) that reported on 2007 offences noted a welcome decrease in the incidence of many offence types. The largest source of crime in terms of value was shop theft by customers (64 per cent), followed by burglary (16 per cent), robbery (8 per cent) and employee theft (8 per cent). The latter showed a 56 per cent reduction on the previous year's figures, which is low and much lower than other survey findings. The BRC credited better detection methods including more sophisticated technology as contributory reasons. Moreover, the average value of goods stolen per incident reduced from £597 to £235. However, the report warns that 'retailers are already reporting a rise in offences' and theft (it is not specified whether this applies to internal, external or both) is one example (British Retail Consortium 2008: 42).

Although there is a tendency to discuss internal and external theft and fraud separately, in practice the two overlap. Theft and fraud by employees is frequently undertaken with non-employees. And again there is some evidence that the problem is a significant one. For example, Bussmann and Werle (2006) reported that 28 per cent of known incidents were believed to involve collusion. Similarly, Bamfield (2008) found that 1 in 10 of employee-related thefts was believed to involve collusion. When Gill and Loveday (2003) interviewed credit card fraudsters, 9 of the 18 admitted to having at some point worked in collusion with staff (see also Duffin and Gill 2007). One review of cases of 'insider attacks' in the government sector concluded (Kowlaski *et al.* 2008: 34):

> Government sector insiders conspired with others to carry out their illicit activities in just over a third of the cases examined, and most of this activity was initiated prior to the incident. In these cases, the insiders were not the only beneficiaries of the incidents. Co-workers, friends, family members, and other individuals paid the insiders to gain information or to have information altered in their files. For example, a husband and wife who were co-workers in a motor vehicle department conspired to collect payment from individuals with suspended licenses to re-issue the licenses and clear the records.

There is one other point we wish to make about patterns of theft and fraud at work and this concerns the different levels of commitment shown by staff thieves to their offending. Some who pilfer may steal frequently but not a great deal on each occasion (Ditton 1977; Mars 1982) while others may steal a lot on fewer occasions or intensely over a short timescale (ACFE 2008; Gill 2005a; Levi *et al.* 2007).

Bamfield (1998) has attempted to classify levels of commitment to staff dishonesty taking account of the impact of the loss to an organisation. He identified four types of staff who commit offences whom he refers to as angels, baboons, jackdaws and crocodiles. Angels do not commit any crime at all. Their moral values will not allow it and so being honest is not a workplace decision as much as an approach to life. Baboons are described as friendly colleagues who would describe their thefts as normal behaviour, as the sort of thing everyone does. They would work in collusion with others and although their thefts are small they are regular and could be costly for their employers.

Jackdaws steal for themselves. Sometimes this will involve small amounts for personal consumption and on other occasions the theft of cash. It will be justified by the belief that offences are rarely discovered and anyway the rewards are viewed as a valuable perk of the job. Some jackdaws are small-time thieves but others approach 'semi-professional' status. Finally, crocodiles can work alone, in a team and with customers. They are typically both good employees and good thieves. They are often in a senior position so have the business acumen alongside job autonomy which makes them a serious threat to the organisation they work for.

Bamfield's classification, as he readily concedes, provides only a generalised assessment and was based on the behaviour of shop workers, but it has a more general application in recognising that commitment varies among dishonest staff who offend in different ways.

Characteristics of theft and fraud at work

There are some excellent discussions of offences that occur at work (see, for example, Croall 2001; Doig 2006; Levi 1987; Levi et al. 2007) and the impact these have on victims. Given the diverse range of activities that can be discussed under the umbrella of staff dishonesty it may be helpful to identify some key characteristics. There are seven that merit a comment.

First, as noted above, the costs are by all accounts high. These are not always recognised, but a succession of surveys has suggested that staff may account for some significant losses to companies and in rare cases contribute to its downfall. Second, there is relatively little information on employees who cheat, partly because companies often deal with them in-house and therefore there is little information in the public domain and partly because there is relatively little research. Third, the victim, the organisation, is frequently seen as either 'deserving' because the staff member feels he or she has been treated badly or that the organisation is 'not really a victim' because, for example, it has insurance to cover any crime losses or because it allows for some crime losses as a consequence of doing business which are accounted for in the way the organisation prices its good and services. This point is raised again later. Fourth, companies themselves have often been reluctant to discuss staff dishonesty for fear of courting bad publicity.

Five, the inside cheat is a serious threat to company security. Insiders have important knowledge about what protection measures are in place and more crucially their weak points and how they might be circumvented. In order to operate organisations have to trust their employees (see Shapiro 1984, 1990; see also Levi 1981, 1987), but this trust can easily be breached. And this overlaps the sixth point, offences are not very visible (Davies et al. 1999) in that most often no one sees an offence take place. If goods or cash are stolen it is not always noticed, and even if it is, it could easily be attributed to a factor other than theft or fraud such as an administrative error (see Beck forthcoming). A seventh point is that even if a loss is detected and it is recognised as the consequence of an offence committed by an employee it will not always be easy to determine who is responsible: the complexity of organisations and business systems, the autonomy of many workers and the fact that staff are often good at covering their tracks contribute to making detection and then prosecution a challenge. It is against this background we attempt to explain workplace dishonesty.

Explaining and responding to staff dishonesty

The literature on white-collar crime – and this includes work that covers different types of staff dishonesty – has revealed a range of motivations (e.g. Alalehto 2003; Friedrichs 1996; Holtfreter 2005; Paternoster and Simpson 1993; Shover and Hochstetler 2006). In one fairly recent review of employee theft and staff dishonesty Hollinger and Davis (2006) argued that the most recognised explanations for offending related either to the individual or to a lack of fairness at work or to cultural influences. Specifically they focused on rational choice theories, workplace equity theories and subcultures within organisations that breed dishonest intentions. In all, the study of workplace theft and fraud is replete with explanations or theories that have also been used to explain non-workplace crimes. After all, theft and fraud take place outside work too. However, it is possible to identify more specific explanations that have evolved from research and understanding these is an important precursor for considering preventive options.

Ekblom (2000, 2001) has written about distal and proximal causes of crime. Distal explanations focus on those causes that influence offences that occur away from the scene (including therefore a range of social explanations of crime from divided neighbourhoods to poor parenting and schooling). Proximal explanations focus on what influences offences that occur at the scene. In organisations proximal explanations are generally bigger priorities.

Frameworks to guide practice can be found in the world of criminology and management studies. Criminology offers a range of ways of evaluating what makes a locale a likely place for crime and also guides thinking on tackling the characteristics that make that place criminogenic. There is considerable potential to apply the principles of environmental criminology (see Bottoms and Wiles 2002), the conjunction of crime and opportunity (Ekblom 2001; 2002, 2003) and the routine activities of daily life (Felson 1998) to workplace crime generally and staff theft and fraud especially.

However, research in this area is more developed in the area of situational crime prevention. This is based on the premise that when the opportunity to commit crime is taken away, then a crime is less likely to take place (Cornish and Clarke 2005). This has considerable applicability to tackling workplace offending, including theft and fraud. Indeed, Weisburd and Waring (2001: 149) note from their study of white-collar criminals – which includes dishonest staff – that:

> Our approach does not simply recognize the importance of the crime situation in explaining a criminal event: we argue that for many criminals, situational components of crisis and opportunity are in fact the main explanations for their involvement in crime.

In practice, reducing the opportunity includes not just making it impossible to take goods (by eradicating the opportunity – if there is no access to goods then they cannot easily be stolen), it may also include making it difficult to steal assets. Cornish and Clarke (2005) have developed 25 situational techniques based around five key principles. These involve: increasing the effort it will take for an offender to be successful; increasing the risks offenders will have to take and so increase the chances of them being caught (or believing they might be); making the rewards less attractive; reducing the provocations that induce people to commit offences; and removing any excuses that workplace theft and fraud are somehow justified. It is important not to accept the value of situational measures uncritically; they sometimes don't work (see, for example, Gill 2006) for all sorts of reasons that go beyond the focus here, and they are not always economically justified. Nevertheless, situational measures are a way in which all organisations can change the degree to which they render themselves vulnerable to offences, including those committed by their own employees.

Our review of the research on explanations for staff dishonesty suggests that there are nine key tactics to responding.

1. Treat employees well: don't allow discontent to fester

Many offences committed against organisations often occur as a result of workers having some sort of dissatisfaction with their employer. Jeyasingh (1986) studied 50 convicted white-collar offenders. He found that they were not satisfied in their work for reasons which included not believing someone else's promotion was justified and feeling they were paid less than their perceived worth (Jeyasingh 1986: 21). Similarly, Hollinger and Clark (1983) identified a link between those unhappy in their jobs and searching for alternative employment and those engaged in stealing from work, while Thoms et al. (2001) found a relationship between theft and turnover in a fast-food chain.

2. Pay them fairly

This is related to the first point but emerges as a major specific issue within the literature where research has shown that some employees consider stealing, from work as a perk, typically justified by the low level of rewards (Greenberg 1990, 1997). For example, Mars noted how pilferage by dock workers was seen as 'a morally justified addition to wages' or 'an entitlement due from exploiting employers' (Mars 1974: 222). And Ditton's (1977) study of fiddles at work similarly highlights how thefts can be seen as recompense for low wages.

3. Find out whether staff have problems/expectations and manage them

One early writer described a major pressure to commit offences (including those relating to workplace dishonesty) was a worker with what was called a 'non-shareable problem' (Cressey 1953). This may take a variety of forms and may involve offenders at all levels in some kind of face-saving action (Ting-Toomey 1994). Some writers from the field of psychology have noted the relevance of low level cognitive abilities that can account for dishonesty, such as having limited ability to control one's actions (Dilchert *et al.* 2007).

Some people have problems outside work that can spill over into the workplace. Some offenders are greedy (see Braithwaite 1992), and by their own admission theft and fraud are means of fulfilling that greed (Gill 2005a; see also Croall 2001; Doig 2006). Sometimes the need for money is brought about by debt or life changes and this can cause workplace pressures. Noticing and managing these may prevent offences from occurring (Gill 2005a).

Some workers commit offences because they are searching for a particular status in life. Very early research by Spencer (1959) with white-collar offenders characterised some of their behaviour as 'reckless and ambitious' due to what he saw as their desire to mix with people of higher social status and to live similar lifestyles to them. Nelken (1994: 368) terms this striving to gain status as 'over-investment'. Similarly, Weisburd *et al.* (1991: 65) reported that 'many of our offenders have the material goods associated with successful people, but may be barely holding their financial selves together'. Coleman's (1994: 195) work provides a variation on this theme, noting that white-collar offenders are often driven by the fear of losing what they have rather than a desire for more and suffer from the strain of 'keeping up with the Joneses'. Such traits may be apparent to the observant manager. Good management is the key to properly identifying vulnerable workers and intervening as appropriate.

4. Recruit the right people

Employing the right individuals is not only important for performance, but also to ensure that employees do not pose risks to the organisation, for example through the perpetration of theft and fraud (see Duffin and Gill 2007; Hayes 2008). Some people join organisations in order to steal from them, certainly some spies have done (for example, see Philby 1968).

Asking staff whether they take part in crime is not likely to generate honest answers (not if they are guilty of offending at work) but one recent study asked representatives from businesses in high crime areas whether staff had been approached about crime opportunities. It reported: '50 per cent had been offered stolen or counterfeit goods (44 per cent were offered counterfeit goods and 33 per cent stolen goods), 22 per cent smuggled tobacco and seven per cent smuggled alcohol' (Hopkins and Tilley 2008: 29). And businesses believed that at least some of the criminal activity was linked to 'loosely' organised crime since, for example, 13 per cent believed they had been victims of organised shop theft. Clearly, the need to recruit the right people is crucial since they may well be subject to temptations.

5. Foster positive workplace cultures

Clearly the points about recruiting the right people apply equally to ensuring that they remain honest. Sometimes the culture of the organisation breeds dishonesty. One of the early pioneers of the study of 'white-collar crime', Edwin Sutherland, argued that a cause of deviant behaviour at work was excessive contact with negative influences, that is people who in different ways and for different reasons supported offending at work. This approach, 'differential association', has been subject to extensive discussion over the years, not always finding wholehearted support (Wheeler 1992).

There is a range of characteristics that can influence the culture of an organisation and therefore either encourage or facilitate dishonesty. Cultures can vary by industry and organisation, and methods of theft can be contingent upon industry, culture or job role. And, in a different way, cultures can influence whether theft and fraud are shared experiences or lone activities. The complexities here have been helpfully summarised by Mars (1982). He identified four occupational work groups who may pilfer. He called these hawks, donkeys, wolves and vultures. He described hawks as individuals who existed unhappily within organisations, bending the rules to suit themselves, in order to develop themselves as individual entrepreneurs and to 'make it' in their career. Donkeys were viewed as isolated individuals who were constrained by the rules and therefore involved in minor rule-breaking, sabotage and fiddling.

Whereas the previous two groups consisted of those individuals who tended to work alone in organisations, in contrast the other two types needed direct or indirect support from their group affiliations. He termed wolves as individuals who tended to steal in packs and who had strong group ethics. They clearly knew who the leader was and were self-regulating, punishing anyone who was deviant in their group. Finally, vultures, although needing the support of a group, tended to act alone when committing their illegal acts.

6. Eliminate or reduce opportunities

One reason why employees are dishonest is because they can be, that is they are provided with an opportunity and they take it. It is an important point that more recent developments in explaining crime have explicitly linked the availability of an opportunity with the cause of offending. That is, without the existence of an opportunity the crime would not have taken place (Felson and Clarke 1998). As Shover and Hochstetler (2006: 5) point out, 'opportunity is in the eye of the beholder, but there is an objective and commonsense aspect to many criminal opportunities'. As noted above the very nature of business life relies on trust. As Tilley (1993: 23) states, 'accounting and security controls often do not inhibit white-collar crime perpetrated by senior staff, because high-level employees can override controls'. The fact that workers have to be trusted means there are opportunities and, unchecked, these can facilitate crime.

7. Set clear guidelines as to what is acceptable

Some of those who are accused of dishonesty at work deny that their behaviour constitutes criminal activity. This can be for a variety of reasons. An act which may seem criminal or wrong to one person may be considered normal custom and practice to another person, or a 'legitimate entitlement' (Mars and Nicod 1981). Although clear in legal terms, in the eyes of a perpetrator, the dividing line between what may be viewed as everyday business behaviour and what is in fact an illegal activity is sometimes blurred. Incentives and bonus payments feature in this grey area (Goldstraw-White forthcoming). Duffin and Gill (2007) interviewed 35 staff who had been dismissed by retailers for being dishonest. They found that some interviewees claimed that they did not realise they were committing offences in the way they were using store discount cards and called for greater clarification and communication of company policies in this area.

8. Make it clear that the organisation is a victim

As noted above, some of those accused of theft and fraud at work claim that there was no victim. Sykes and Matza (1957: 668) described this type of criminal accounting as 'denial of the victim', where an individual challenges the actual nature and action of the offence and believes that, under such circumstances, it is not wrong. As Sykes and Matza note, in some cases the denial takes a different form, in that the offender sees the victim as deserving and this can help to neutralise their guilt, widely referred to as 'techniques of neutralisation' (Matza 1964). Or, as Coleman (1992: 72–3) notes, it helps the individual to solve a contradiction 'between the desire for maximum individual reward and the desire to maintain a positive construction of ourselves and our behaviour'. Removing excuses is a key situational technique and relevant to discussions about preventing workplace dishonesty.

9. Ensure crime prevention measures work

Offenders' accounts often suggest that it is fairly easy to circumvent crime prevention measures (Gill 2005b) and this is also the case with staff thieves and fraudsters. Duffin and Gill (2007) found that dismissed staff were disparaging about the security in place, even though some had been caught because of such measures, for example on CCTV. Beck (2006) found that the absence of CCTV was a precursor for stealing and Gill (2005a) found that fraudsters who had stolen from their employers stated that anti-fraud strategies were not much in evidence and could be circumvented. Even auditors were often not seen as a serious impediment because the fraudster knew how to outwit them. As one interviewee from Gill's (2005a: 4–5) study noted:

> Accountants can only work on the figures they have got, audit the same. Auditors came to see me and I just lied to them and gave them false pieces of paper and that was that. The checking process was abysmal. I was not worried because I have 20 years experience of auditors. Had they been better at their job I would have been in trouble. What I was doing was simple, but the lack of process enabled me to do what I did, the absence of systems, the lack of attention to detail, the lack of knowledge in auditing and accounting. I had three audits in that 18 months. And I recall a balance sheet did not balance. Now there was a good reason but I did not want it interrogated too much because that could highlight the bit I had taken. And so I worked hard at sorting this, I worked intensely for half a day. I gave the auditor the information and he said, 'thank goodness for that', and my thought was 'you complete

Muppet'. I really went through that with a passion just in case it was something involving me. There was no interrogation from audit and that was good for me.

Some interesting findings (although not derived from either an experimental design or realist evaluation) emerged from the survey results reported by ACFE (2008: 5). They examined 15 different types of fraud controls and found that in each case the absence of a fraud control resulted in higher levels of fraud:

Lack of adequate internal controls was most commonly cited as the factor that allowed fraud to occur. Thirty-five percent of respondents cited inadequate internal controls as a primary contributing factor in the frauds they investigated. Lack of management review and override of existing controls were each cited by 17 per cent of respondents.

Hayes (2008: 7) summarised the evidence as follows:

In summary, persons prone to negativity, unable to control impulses, with a perceived need for money, surrounded by uncaring or dishonest peers, under pressure, believing theft is acceptable under certain conditions, believing their boss is a jerk, and with access to unguarded assets are likely to steal.

From explanations to prevention: a research note on the issue of gender

Gender and its relationship to employee theft and fraud has received little attention, a gap that needs to be filled. For this reason, and because one of us (Goldstraw-White) has spent some time considering the issue, we have chosen to devote a little space to offering some insights.

The activity rate for people of working age in the UK is projected to reach 79.8 per cent in 2020. However, the working-age activity rate for men is projected to fall to 83.2 per cent in 2020 compared with 83.4 per cent in 2005, while for women it is projected to increase to 76.1 per cent in 2020 from 73.4 per cent in 2005 (Office for National Statistics 2006), a trend which has been evident for some years. Even with the increasing proportion of women in the workplace though, little research has been carried out about women as workplace offenders. The majority of research that has been conducted in this area, such as that by Zietz (1981) on female embezzlers and Daly (1989) on gender and varieties of white-collar crime, has tended to define criminality by women predominantly from the perspective of need as opposed to greed.

However, as Davies (2003: 18) notes, crimes committed by male offenders tend to be characterised by motives such as greed, supplementing paid work, something that is exciting, to overcome boredom or to achieve status and respect. In contrast, crimes committed by women have been depicted by them being labelled as mad or bad. Sometimes crime by women is characterised as a selfless act, undertaken not for themselves but for the benefit of others, such as men and children. Davies (2003: 18) therefore challenges us to question why we are so reluctant to recognise that women's crime is real crime and that the women who commit it are real criminals. This is a pertinent consideration in the context of the subject of this chapter. Much of the research that does exist, such as that undertaken by Dodge (2007) on high-profile female white-collar offenders, Goldstraw et al. (2005) on serious fraud offenders and Goldstraw-White (forthcoming) on general white-collar offenders, has demonstrated that females engage in workplace crimes for a variety of reasons.

Dodge examined a number of high-profile cases involving women and white-collar crime and noted that there were similarities between men and women in the way they exploited embezzlement opportunities (Dodge 2007), although she lamented the lack of research (Dodge 2007: 396). Goldstraw et al. (2005) studying sentencing reports of serious white-collar crime offenders in Australia and New Zealand and Goldstraw-White (forthcoming) found that the backgrounds of female offenders and the methods used for committing similar offences were no different than those used by men. However, both studies found that women were more likely to commit offences alone.

Goldstraw-White (forthcoming) interviewed over 40 male and female offenders convicted of white-collar crimes serving their sentences in prisons across England. Although the sample was drawn from a wide spectrum of white-collar offenders, a fifth had committed workplace crimes against their employers. Goldstraw-White recorded offenders' accounts of criminality and analysed their motives into three types of acts: rational (planned and opportunistic), pressurised (through desperate, aspiring or threatened situations) and seduced (either by close others or associates). She found that women revealed similar reasons to men for their offending and found no major differences between classification groups.

Women admitted to planned and opportunistic acts in the workplace, especially where internal controls were found to be weak and they had been left in situations which allowed them to exploit these. For example, a female management accountant who had embezzled over £250,000 from her employer believed her boss had very little idea what was going on in the business, either administratively or financially. She claimed that she had not gone out of her way to hide the money she had stolen, but neither management nor external auditors had picked up discrepancies in the figures she presented to them. Another female offender discussed how she had been able to defraud large amounts of money because institutions were, in her words, 'too mean' to implement satisfactory crime prevention measures and surveillance procedures.

Similarly, women were just as susceptible as men to attacks on their self-esteem and the need to retain their status either in society generally or in the workplace. With regard to workplace crime, they offered explanations in terms of feeling taken for granted by their employers, not believing they were paid their worth and being overlooked for promotion as well as not being given the opportunity to progress further in their jobs and careers.

Where men and women do appear to differ in workplace and white-collar crimes is in the area of morality and acceptance of criminal labels. For example, proportionately more women pleaded guilty than men and were more likely to accept their criminal label. It may be that men were more tactical than women when it came to making their plea and working out how to either reduce or avoid a custodial sentence depending on the circumstances and evidence they believed were available. Clearly, there are small numbers here which underscores the need for more research (but see, Goldstraw-White forthcoming).

Discussion

Employees offer a challenge to crime prevention. They have access to company assets and at least some insights into how they are protected. They are well placed to identify any weaknesses and will often have the inside knowledge required to circumvent whatever security is in place. At the same time, the organisation has to place a level of trust in its employees. It is in reality the only way of doing business, and it is all the more important, therefore, that employees should be encouraged to be honest. As noted above, there are nine (overlapping) key tactics – based on research evidence – that should guide practice here.

1 Treat employees well: don't allow discontent to fester
2 Pay them fairly
3 Find out whether staff have problems/expectations and manage them
4 Recruit the right people
5 Foster positive workplace cultures
6 Eliminate or reduce opportunities
7 Set clear guidelines as to what is acceptable
8 Make it clear that the organisation is a victim
9 Ensure crime prevention measures work

And these need to be considered in the context of good risk assessments of potential organisational vulnerabilities, and a well implemented strategic approach supported by effective information and intelligence gathering and analysis and an engaged audit and investigative function. The key point though is that the list presented is of types of situational measures proximal to the workplace that can be used to tackle dishonesty. And they can be provided by at least two routes.

The first is via good business practice – this applies to the first five points in particular. There are parallels between a well-run organisation and an organisation that promotes and engages in good security. After all, treating employees well, paying them fairly, following effective recruitment procedures that match them appropriately to the task, taking an interest in their work in order to support them and identifying any problems to effectively manage them while creating a positive, ethical and honest culture are all features of a well-run organisation. These approaches alone will help eliminate many of the circumstances that give rise to dishonesty (see Bamfield 2006b; Beck 2006; Hayes 2008; Kidwell and Martin 2005; Litzky et al. 2006; Punch 1996). There is one important point to emphasise here, it is not just a case of having the appropriate management strategies in place – sometimes they exist and are not effective (Ghiselli and Ismail 1998). They have to be fit for purpose and implemented appropriately – they have to work.

The second route applies to points 6, 7, 8 and 9 in the list above and concerns initiatives by the crime prevention arm of the organisation. This involves the world of corporate security management, which has largely been ignored by criminologists (but see, Button 2008; Gill 2006; Levi 2003). Security management – sometimes called by other names such as loss prevention, asset protection, profit protection, resilience, to name but a few – focuses on the prevention of workplace crimes by strategies to identify the risks, and prevent them from occurring. So situational measures to eliminate opportunities, setting clear guidelines via policies and procedures, raising awareness about security and the implications of crime, and the implementation of effective security measures are all common approaches to good security management and this includes tackling staff theft and fraud (e.g. Bamfield 2006b; Hayes 2007, 2008).

In summary there are three points that we would wish to make. The first is to highlight that we still know relatively little about the scale of the 'insider threat'. Many organisations do not have good systems for collecting information and thus it is sometimes difficult to tell whether offences have taken place, let alone identify offenders. And even when they do, they do not always see merit in reporting the matter to the police (Bussmann and Werle 2006). Moreover, in the past, workplace offences have not been categorised separately in official crime statistics. So in all, it is difficult to access the true level of employee dishonesty. What we have hopefully shown is that the available evidence (and it is patchy) suggests that theft and fraud by staff (sometimes working in collusion with outsiders), is responsible for a significant amount of illegal loss suffered by organisations.

Second, we have attempted to highlight, by drawing from a range of studies, common explanations for offending. There are often overlaps in the reasons why people commit petty fiddles and the reasons why they commit more major frauds. Weak organisational structures, dishonest cultures, easy opportunities and ineffective crime prevention measures all play their part and organisations can manage these if they choose to do so.

The third point we wish to make is that our coverage of this topic has been limited by the space available. There are many other issues that are worthy of attention and indeed some in particular merit further research. These include a wider analysis of deterrence strategies and their limitations (see Goldstraw-White, forthcoming; Paternoster and Simpson 1993; Shover and Hochstetler 2006; Stotland 1977); a broader consideration of the characteristics of organisations that makes them conducive to theft and fraud (Hollinger and Adams 2006); a better understanding of offenders and how they become engaged in workplace theft and fraud (see Gill 2005a; Levi 1981, 1998, 2008); the study of rules and compliance and the extent to which workplace behaviour and this includes different types of staff dishonesty can be governed by regulation (see Doig 2006; Levi 1987; Punch 1996); and the potential of technologies and databases to prevent dishonesty (see CERT 2007;

Jones 2008). Indeed, this is a major topic within the study of crime prevention generally as well as the prevention of theft and fraud among staff specifically. And there is still more we need to understand about collusion. We need to know more about how dishonest relationships are formed, about how and why some people join an organisation specifically to steal and why and how others are corrupted along the way. We also need to know more about the role of former staff who will often leave with insider knowledge and will have had the opportunity to cultivate internal links.

When an organisation becomes a victim, a range of stakeholders suffer, especially if it is forced to close or reduce some of its activities as a consequence. These may include shareholders and owners, but also workers who can lose jobs and customers who are deprived of services or subjected to increased costs. In some cases, for example in the closure of local shops or services, it is those who can least easily locate alternatives, often the poor and marginalised, who will suffer the most. Organisations can choose how vulnerable they are to crime. What is crucial is that organisations understand what their assets are and where they are, that they assess the risks to them and that they then develop a response plan which is implemented effectively, managed well and is subject to ongoing evaluation. Organisations need to recognise the role employees could play not only as potential offenders, but also as potential victims and, most importantly, as allies in ensuring that risks are minimised. It is yet another reason why treating employees well and ensuring their engagement with the aims of the organisation is so important: it is not just good business, it is also good crime prevention.

Selected further reading

A good review of literature on staff thieves is provided by Hollinger and Adams, 'Employee theft and staff dishonesty', in Gill (2006) *The Handbook of Security*. A summary of measures that can be useful in tackling dishonesty is provided by Hayes (2008) *Strategies to Detect and Prevent Workplace Dishonesty*. Two old texts that have stood the test of time provide scholarly insights into workplace dishonesty: Mars (1982) *Cheats at Work: An Anthology of Workplace Crime*, and Ditton (1977) *Part-Time Crime: An Ethnography of Fiddling and Pilferage*. Good insights into the world of fraud and white-collar crime are provided by Levi (2008) *The Phantom Capitalists: The Organisation and Control of Long-Firm Fraud*, and Shover and Hochstetler (2006) *Choosing White-Collar Crime*.

References

Alalehto, T. (2003) 'Economic crime: does personality matter?', *International Journal of Offender Therapy and Comparative Criminology*, 47 (3): 335–55.
Association of Certified Fraud Examiners (ACFE) (2008) *Report to the Nation on Occupational Fraud and Abuse*. Online at: http://www.acfe.com/documents/2008-rttn.pdf.
Bamfield, J. (1998) 'A breach of trust: employee collusion and theft from major retailers', in M. Gill (ed.), *Crime at Work: Increasing the Risks for Offenders*. Leicester: Perpetuity Press.

Bamfield, J. (2006a) 'Management', in M. Gill (ed.), *The Handbook of Security*. Basingstoke: Palgrave.

Bamfield, J. (2006b) 'Sed quis custodiet? Employee theft in UK retailing', *International Journal of Retail and Distribution Management*, 34 (11): 845–59.

Bamfield, J. (2008) *Global Retail Theft Barometer 2008*. Nottingham: Centre for Retail Research.

Beck, A. (2006) *Staff Dishonesty in the Retail Sector: Understanding the Opportunities*, ECR Europe White Paper. Brussels: ECR Europe. Available from bna@le.ac.uk.

Beck, A. (forthcoming) *New Loss Prevention: Redefining Shrinkage Management*. Basingstoke: Palgrave.

Benson, M. L. (1985) 'Denying the guilty mind: accounting for involvement in a white-collar crime', *Criminology*, 23 (4): 583–608.

Bottoms, A. E. and Wiles, P. (2002) 'Environmental criminology', in M. Maguire, R. Morgan and R. Reiner (eds), *The Oxford Handbook of Criminology*, 3rd edn. Oxford: Oxford University Press, pp. 620–56.

Braithwaite, J. (1992) 'Poverty, power and white-collar crime', in K. Schlegel and D. Weisburd (eds), *White-Collar Crime Reconsidered*. Boston: Northeastern University Press.

British Retail Consortium (2008) *Retail Crime Survey 2007–8*. London: British Retail Consortium.

Bussmann, K. and Werle, M. (2006) 'Addressing crime in companies: first findings from a global survey of economic crime', *British Journal of Criminology*, 46 (6): 1128–44.

Button, M. (2008) *Doing Security: Critical Reflections and an Agenda for Change*. Basingstoke: Palgrave.

CERT (2007) *Research Annual Report*. Software Engineering Institute, Carnegie Mellon University. Online at: http:www.cert.org/cert/information/researchers.html.

Clinard, M. B. and Quinney, R. (1973) *Criminal Behaviour Systems: A Typology*. New York: Holt, Rinehart & Winston.

Coleman, J. W. (1992) 'The theory of white-collar crime: from Sutherland to the 1990s', in K. Schlegel and D. Weisburd (eds), *White-Collar Crime Reconsidered*. Boston: Northeastern University Press.

Coleman, J. W. (1994) *The Criminal Elite: The Sociology of White-Collar Crime*, 3rd edn. New York: St. Martin's Press.

Cornish, D. and Clarke, R. (2005) 'Opportunities, precipitators and criminal decisions', in *Theory for Practice in Situational Crime Prevention*, Crime Prevention Studies, Vol. 16. Monsey, NY: Criminal Justice Press.

Cressey, D. R. (1953) *Other People's Money: A Study in the Social Psychology of Embezzlement*. New York: Free Press.

Croall, H. (2001) *Understanding White-Collar Crime*. Milton Keynes: Open University Press.

Daly, K. (1989) 'Gender and varieties of white-collar crime', *Criminology*, 27: 769–94.

Davies, P. A. (1997) 'Women, crime and an informal economy: female offending and crime for gain', in M. Brogden (ed.), *British Criminology Conferences: Selected Proceedings Vol. 2*. Papers from the British Society of Criminology Conference, Belfast.

Davies, P. A. (2003) 'Women, crime and work: gender and the labour market', *Criminal Justice Matters*, 53: 18–19.

Davies, P., Francis, P. and Jupp, V. (eds) (1999) *Invisible Crimes*. Basingstoke: Macmillan.

Dilchert, S., Ones, D. S., Davis, R. D. and Rostow, C. D. (2007) 'Cognitive ability predicts objectively measured counterproductive work behaviors', *Journal of Applied Psychology*, 92 (3): 616–27.

Ditton, J. (1977) *Part-Time Crime: An Ethnography of Fiddling and Pilferage*. London: Macmillan.

Dodge, M. (2007) 'From pink to white with various shades of embezzlement: women who commit white-collar crimes', in H. N. Pontell and G. Geis (eds), *International Handbook of White-Collar and Corporate Crime*. New York: Springer.

Doig, A. (2006) *Fraud*. Cullompton: Willan.

Duffin, M. and Gill, M. (2007) *Staff Dishonesty*. Leicester: Perpetuity Research and Consultancy International.

Ekblom, P. (2000) 'The conjunction of criminal opportunity – a tool for clear, "joined-up" thinking about community safety and crime reduction', in S. Ballintyne, K. Pease and V. McLaren (eds), *Secure Foundations: Key Issues in Crime Prevention, Crime Reduction and Community Safety*. London: Institute for Public Policy Research.

Ekblom, P. (2001) 'The Conjunction of Criminal Opportunity: A Framework for Crime Reduction Toolkits'. Online at the Crime Reduction website: http://www.crimereduction.gov.uk/learningzone/cco.htm.

Ekblom, P. (2002) 'From the source to the mainstream is uphill: the challenge of transferring knowledge of crime prevention through replication, innovation and anticipation', in N. Tilley (ed.), *Analysis for Crime Prevention*, Crime Prevention Studies, Vol. 13. Monsey, NY: Criminal Justice Press, pp. 131–203.

Ekblom, P. (2003) 'Organised crime and the conjunction of criminal opportunity framework', in A. Edwards and P. Gill (eds), *Transnational Organised Crime: Perspectives on Global Security*. London: Routledge, pp. 241–63.

Ekblom, P. and Tilley, N. (2000) 'Going equipped', *British Journal of Criminology*, 40: 376–98.

Fay, S. (1996) *The Collapse of Barings*. London: Arrow Business Books.

Felson, M. (1998) *Crime and Everyday Life*, 2nd edn. Newbury Park, CA: Pine Forge Press.

Felson, M. and Clarke, R.V. (1998) *Opportunity Makes the Thief: Practical Theory for Crime Prevention*, Police Research Series No. 98. London: Home Office.

Friedrichs, D. O. (1996) *Trusted Criminals: White-collar Crime in Contemporary Society*, 1st edn. Belmont, CA: Wadsworth.

Ghiselli, R. and Ismail, J. (1998) 'Employee theft and efficacy of certain control procedures in commercial food service operations', *Journal of Hospitality and Tourism Research*, 22 (2): 174–87.

Gill, M. (2005a) *Fraudsters on Fraud*, Report for Protiviti. Leicester: Perpetuity Research and Consultancy International.

Gill, M. (2005b) 'Reducing the capacity to offend: restricting resources for offending', in N. Tilley (ed.), *Handbook of Crime Prevention and Community Safety*. Cullompton: Willan, pp. 306–28.

Gill, M. (2006) 'Introduction', in M. Gill (ed.), *The Handbook of Security*. Basingstoke: Palgrave.

Gill, M. and Loveday, K. (2003) 'What do offenders think about CCTV?', in *Crime Prevention and Community Safety: An International Journal*, 5 (3): 17–25.

Goldstraw, J. E., Smith, R. G. and Sakurai, Y. (2005) 'Gender and serious fraud in Australia and New Zealand', *Trends and Issues in Crime and Criminal Justice*, No. 292. Canberra: Australian Institute of Criminology.

Goldstraw-White, J. E. (forthcoming) *White-Collar Crime: Opportunity, Motivation and Morality*. London: Palgrave Macmillan.

Green, G. (1993) 'White-collar crime and the study of embezzlement', in G. Geis and P. Jesilow (eds), *White-Collar Crime: The Annual of the American Academy of Political and Social Science*, Vol. 525. January.

Greenberg, J. (1990) 'Employee theft as a reaction to underpayment equality: the hidden cost of pay cuts', *Journal of Applied Psychology*, 75: 561–8.

Greenberg, J. (1997) 'The STEAL motive: managing the social determinants of employee theft', in R. Giacalone and J. Greenberg (eds), *Antisocial Behaviour in Organisations*. Thousand Oaks, CA: Sage, pp. 85–100.

Harris, L. C. and Ogbonna, E (2002) 'The antecedents, types and consequences of frontline, deviant, antiservice behaviors', *Journal of Service Research*, 4 (3): 163–83.

Hayes, R. (2007) *Retail Security and Loss Prevention*, 2nd edn. Basingstoke: Palgrave.

Hayes, R. (2008) *Strategies to Detect and Prevent Work-place Dishonesty*, CRISP Report, ASIS Foundation. Online at: http://www.asisonline.org/foundation/noframe/research/crisp.html.

Henry, S. (1978) *The Hidden Economy*. Oxford: Martin Robertson.

Henry, S. (1982) 'The working unemployed: perspectives on the informal economy and unemployment', *Sociological Review*, New Series, 30: 460–77.

Hollinger, R. and Adams, A. (2008) *National Retail Security Survey Final Report*. University of Florida. Online at: http://www.crim.ufl.edu/research/srp/finalreport_2007.pdf.

Hollinger, R. and Clark, J. P. (1983) *Theft by Employees*. Lexington, MA: Lexington Books.

Hollinger, R. and Davis, J. (2006) 'Employee theft and staff dishonesty', in M. Gill (ed.), *Handbook of Security*. London: Palgrave Macmillan, pp. 203–28.

Hollinger, R., Slora, K. and Terris, W. (1992) 'Deviance in the fast-food restaurant: correlates of employee theft, altruism, and counter productivity', *Deviant Behavior*, 13 (2): 155–84.

Holtfreter, K. (2005) 'Is occupational fraud "typical" white-collar crime? A comparison of individual and organizational characteristics', *Journal of Criminal Justice*, 33: 353–65.

Hopkins, M. and Tilley, N. (2008) *Business Views of Organised Crime*. London: Home Office.

Jeyasingh, J. V. (1986) 'Inside white-collar crime', *Social Defence*, 21 (82): 17–24.

Jones, P. (2008) 'Loss prevention 2012: cutting-edge technology and highly qualified talent', *Integrated Retail Solutions*, December.

Kidwell, R. and Martin, C. (eds) (2005), *Managing Organizational Deviance*. Thousand Oaks, CA: Sage, pp. 211–36.

Kleinig, J. (2005) 'Gratuities and corruption', in T. Newburn (ed.), *Policing: Key Readings*. Cullompton: Willan.

Kowalski, E., Conway, T., Keverline, S., Williams, M., Cappelli, D. and Willke, B. (2008) *Insider Threat Study: Illicit Cyber Activity in the Government Sector*, Report from the CERT Program, Carnegie Mellon University.

Leeson, N. (1996) *Rogue Trader*. London: Little, Brown.

Levi, M. (1981) *The Phantom Capitalists: The Organisation and Control of Long-Firm Fraud*. London: Heinemann.

Levi, M. (1987) *Regulating Fraud*. London: Routledge.

Levi, M. (1998) 'The craft of the long-firm fraudster: criminal skills and commercial responses', in M. Gill (ed.), *Crime at Work*, Vol. II. Leicester: Perpetuity Press, pp. 155–68.

Levi, M. (2003) 'Organising and controlling payment card fraud: fraudsters and their operational environment', *Security Journal*, 16 (2): 21–30.

Levi, M. (2008) *The Phantom Capitalists: The Organisation and Control of Long-Firm Fraud*, 2nd edn. Aldershot: Ashgate.

Levi, M., Burrows, J., Fleming, M. and Hopkins, M. (2007) *The Nature, Extent and Economic Impact of Fraud in the UK*, Report for the Association of Chief Police Officers' Economic Crime Portfolio.

Litzky, B. E., Eddleston, K. A. and Kidder, D. L. (2006) 'The good, the bad, and the misguided: how managers inadvertently encourage deviant behaviors', *Academy of Management Perspectives*, 20: 91–103.

Mars, G. (1973) 'Hotel pilferage: a case study in occupational theft', in M. Warner (ed.), *Sociology of the Workplace*. London: George Allen & Unwin.

Mars, G. (1974) 'Dock pilferage', in P. Rock and M. McIntosh (eds), *Deviance and Social Control*. London: Tavistock.

Mars, G. (1982) *Cheats at Work: An Anthology of Workplace Crime*. London: George Allen & Unwin.

Mars, G. and Nicod, M. (1981) 'Hidden rewards at work: the implications from a study of British hotels', in S. Henry (ed.), *Can I Have It in Cash? A Study of Informal Institutions and Unorthodox Ways of Doing Things*. London: Astragal Books.

Matza, D. (1964) *Delinquency and Drift*. New York: Wiley.

Nasheri, H. (2004) *Economic Espionage and Industrial Spying*. Cambridge: Cambridge University Press.

Nelken, D. (1994) *The Futures of Criminology*. London: Sage.

Office for National Statistics (2006) *Labour Force Projections 2006–2020*. London: Office for National Statistics.

Ones, D. (2002) 'Introduction to the Special Issue: counterproductive behaviours at work', *International Journal of Selection and Assessment*, 10: 1–4.

Paternoster, R. and Simpson, S. S. (1993) 'A rational choice theory of corporate crime', in R. V. Clarke and M. Felson (eds), *Routine Activities and Rational Choice*. New Brunswick, NJ: Transaction.

Philby, K. (1968) *My Silent War*. London: Macgibbon & Kee.

Pontell, H. N. and Geis, G. L. (eds) (2007) *International Handbook of White-Collar and Corporate Crime*. New York: Springer.

Punch, M. (1996) *Dirty Business: Exploring Corporate Misconduct*. London: Sage.

Salinger, L. M. (ed.) (2005) *Encyclopedia of White-Collar and Corporate Crimes*, Vols 1 and 2. Thousand Oaks, CA: Sage.

Shapiro, S. (1984) *Wayward Capitalists*. New Haven, CT: Yale University Press.

Shapiro, S. P. (1990) 'Collaring the crime, not the criminal: re-considering the concept of white-collar crime', *American Sociological Review*, 55: 346–65.

Shover, N. and Hochstetler, A. (2006) *Choosing White-Collar Crime*. Cambridge: Cambridge University Press.

Silverman, D. (1993) *Interpreting Qualitative Data: Methods for Analysing Talk, Text and Interaction*. London: Sage.

Spencer, J. C. (1959) 'A study of incarcerated white-collar offenders', in G. Geis (ed.), *White-collar Criminal*. New York: Atherton Press.

Stotland, E. (1977) 'White-collar criminals', *Journal of Social Issues*, 33: 179–96.

Sykes, G. M. and Matza, D. (1957) 'Techniques of neutralisation: a theory of delinquency', *American Sociological Review*, 43: 643–56.

Thoms, P., Wolper, P., Scott, K. S. and Jones, D. (2001) 'The relationship between immediate turnover and employee theft in the restaurant industry', *Journal of Business and Psychology*, 15 (4): 561–77.

Tilley, N. (1993) *The Prevention of Crime Against Small Businesses: The Safer Cities Experience*, Crime Prevention Unit Series Paper No. 45. London: Home Office.

Tilley, N. and Hopkins, M. (2008) *Business Views of Organised Crime*, Research Report No. 10. London: Home Office.

Ting-Toomey, S. (1994) *The Challenge of Facework, Cross-cultural and Interpersonal Issues*. Albany, NY: State University of New York Press.

Weisburd, D. and Waring, E. (2001) *White-Collar Crime and Criminal Careers*. Cambridge: Cambridge University Press.

Weisburd, D., Wheeler, S., Waring, E. and Bode, N. (1991) *Crimes of the Middle Classes: White-Collar Offenders in the Federal Courts*. New Haven, CT: Yale University Press.

Wheeler, S. (1992) 'The problem of white-collar crime motivation', in K. Schlegel and D. Weisburd (eds), *White-Collar Crime Reconsidered*. Boston: Northeastern University Press.

Zietz, D. (1981) *Women Who Embezzle or Defraud: A Study of Convicted Felons*. New York: Praeger.

Chapter 7

Fakes

Simon Mackenzie

Introduction: what is a fake?

A fake is something that purports to be what it is not. The essence of a fake is therefore in a manifestation of a misrepresentation, or confusion, over authenticity or authorship. People can be fakes, as is demonstrated by many of the confidence games detailed in the scams chapter of this volume. More often, however, the label 'fake' is applied to an object, and usually this is to suggest that it has been designed to appear to have been made by a certain person or organisation while in fact it has not.

Objects that are especially amenable to faking include: currency and financial instruments (especially banknotes); identity documents and stamps, such as passports, visas and ID cards; historical or cultural 'collectibles'; branded and designer consumer goods; industrial parts; pharmaceuticals; entertainment products such as music and video in various formats (especially at the moment CDs and DVDs); and objects of literal consumption such as food, alcohol and cigarettes.

Terminologically, the field of 'faking' can be confusing. In law, in England and Wales at least, the term 'counterfeiting' refers only to banknotes, and 'forgery' is restricted to written instruments which are made by someone other than the purported drawer. There has always been a tendency for lay people to operate these terms in a much more relaxed way, referring to forged artwork and counterfeit goods, among other things. The idea of 'counterfeit' goods in particular has caught on in business circles and the development of the idea of intellectual property crime (IPC) has cemented this use of the language of counterfeiting beyond the realm of banknotes. IPC is a generic term used to describe various individual infringements contained in IP-related legislation. In the policy (rather than strictly legal) language of those who discuss IPC, 'counterfeiting' is the unauthorised reproduction of branded goods, involving trademark infringement, while 'piracy' is the unauthorised copying of other copyright-protected works such as music and video. We will use the shorthand C/P goods for these counterfeit/pirated goods for the rest of the chapter.

While faking is, on a general view, a timeless problem that has affected various fields of social and economic activity since records began, there are some features of contemporary socio-economic organisation rendering faking an increasingly salient problem in relation to the intellectual property (IP) large corporations have in their branded goods. The subject of fakes presents us with the opportunity to describe and analyse the pressing contemporary issue represented by the global trade in fake goods which, while much discussed in policy and trade circles, has not been given extensive criminological treatment to date.

This focus will inevitably mean that other types of fake receive light, or no, treatment in this chapter. Readers who want to know more about financial fraud and forgery can refer to the many comprehensive publications on the subject by Michael Levi as well as a variety of classic and specific sources (Lemert 1958; Sternitsky 1955; Sutherland 1937). For fake identity documents, phone calls, e-mails and websites (typically pretending to be from lotteries and banks), and other related fake issues, readers are referred to the chapters on identity theft, scams and cybercrime in this volume. Fake art is another under-analysed area. It is slightly harder to refer readers to sources on art fakery, given the dearth of criminological writing there, but a good start can be found in something of a 'bookending' fashion by consulting the first (Conklin 1994) and at the time of writing last (Polk and Chappell forthcoming) criminological engagements with the topic and thereafter trying to work out why criminology had so little to say about the matter in the intervening decade and a half. Fake and forged documents may be used in money laundering schemes, and are also central to the transit and sale of illicit commodities in transnational criminal markets where shipments are designed to appear, and be sold as, legitimate, such as international markets in antiquities (Mackenzie 2005) and protected species of wildlife (Warchol 2004). One could go on, but the point is that while there is a large amount of faking around, we will try to achieve some depth here in relation to the current 'hot topic' of the international trade in C/P goods at the expense of some breadth of coverage of other faking issues.

While it is not always unlawful to make a fake, where the goods in question are subject to IP restrictions simple copying and non-fraudulent sales do involve legal infringements. The law protects IP 'rights-holders', in other words those who 'own' the relevant ideas underpinning designs and inventions. IP is a legal right of property held by an individual or organisation in relation to the 'intellectual' effort put into developing these ideas.

Patterns and trends

The industrialisation and globalisation of faking

The contemporary landscape of international economy is notable for featuring the extraordinary aggregation of wealth in very limited segments of the world's population. These are the more industrialised nations and, within them, a very small core of 'super-rich'. These industrialised nations, which have increasingly become characterised by consumption rather than production, provide the major markets for the world's goods. These goods are now produced disproportionately in countries with 'developing' economies – and therefore low-cost labour and infrastructure – such as China and India. This is also true for luxury goods, which have recently been 'democratised', as the boutique labels of small-quantity, high-quality, family designer workshops have been bought out by multinational corporations. This has involved the application of rationalisation strategies and shrewd business methods, in many cases shifting production to the Far East and working with much lower-cost materials (Thomas 2007). An aggregate view of faking shows the same pattern: brand imitations and other fake goods produced in poor countries in order to feed demand in rich ones (Grossman and Shapiro 1989).

In fact, the pattern identified here could be called 'the industrialisation of faking' and one country features as its main protagonist: China. That country has taken on the mantle of the global centre for the production of counterfeit goods on an industrial scale. Other countries are certainly notable for their production of certain types of fake – a significant proportion of fake pharmaceuticals come from India, for example – but a range of evidence points to China as the centre of the global faking industry. This is supported by EU seizure statistics which show nearly 60 per cent of the seizures in 2007 to have been in respect of articles originating in China. This is in fact a large drop on the seizures in 2006 where the figure was 79 per cent.

The corporatisation of boutique fashion labels, together with a general trend towards 'outsourcing' or relocating core parts of the businesses of commodity producers in rich countries, has led in the era of corporate globalisation to a heavy reliance by western companies on cheap labour in the Far East. In many cases this reliance is so heavy that it has effectively changed the business models of many corporations that originated in, and once produced their goods in, the rich countries of the West. Now these corporations tend to be considerably more 'global' and ethereal. They also now are increasingly transforming themselves into middlemen rather than producers of commodities, selling on goods produced abroad at low cost to consumers at home at considerable mark-up. In some cases the big corporations own the factories where production occurs in the poor countries, while in others they buy from an independent supplier. These independent suppliers will in many cases produce goods only for one major corporate customer, blurring the line between corporate ownership and corporate supply.

With the relocation of production abroad in the era of corporate globalisation has come a subsidiary stream of production: fakes. Low-paid factory owners and workers in countries which attracted outsourcing were entrusted with product designs by the large corporations who wanted their goods made cheaply, and these designs have been used as the basis for the establishment of a massive industry in fakes. This industry ranges from very poor quality imitations, which can easily be told apart from the originals, to 'fakes' which are made on the same production line as the originals, during hours of unofficial 'overtime'. These latter are therefore only 'fake' in the sense of 'unauthorised', being on all other measures identical to the originals. Somewhat ironically, the lower quality of materials now used in 'luxury' goods make them considerably easier to fake.

Although corporate profits are clearly diluted by these practices, and brand reputations may suffer injury, the labels are so heavily dependent on legitimate foreign-outsourced production in supporting the profitability of their businesses that they, and indeed the host of international regulatory bodies charged with dealing with the faking problem, have been reluctant to make accusations or take decisive action that might embarrass the governments of supply countries.

This pattern (eastern/southern production linking with western/northern consumption) is complemented by a significant uptake of the purchase of fakes in their countries of production and other developing countries. China consumes a lot of the fakes that it makes; indeed its population is mostly too poor to buy the original items. In 2001, for example, China recorded 192,000 deaths due to counterfeit medicines and closed down 1,300 factories producing these fakes (UNICRI 2007: 71). While fake lifestyle drugs such as Viagra and steroids are pumped into western consumer markets where these drugs are bought in large enough quantities to make the sale of counterfeits worthwhile (HMRC reported seizures of 735,000 pharmaceuticals in 2006), developing nations have been flooded with replicated drugs for the treatment of more serious conditions such as malaria and HIV. There have been instances of fake medicinal drugs for illness being inserted into European and US markets, but to nowhere near the extent with which they have appeared in developing countries. Developing countries are characterised by high demand for these medicines combined with difficulty in paying the prices demanded by the pharmaceutical companies, creating opportunities to be exploited by producers of counterfeit drugs who can undercut the conventional market.

Statistical evidence of the problem

There is a general dearth of reliable statistical evidence on most aspects of faking. Fakes in all markets are notoriously under-reported. Many fakes will never be discovered, even when they cause accidents: the sorts of forensic investigations which might link an aircraft crash to a fake part, or a death to a fake medicine, are not usually undertaken for more common accidents and injuries, such as motor vehicle crashes, let alone where the fake in the end does its job well enough and does not cause an accident. Where one receives an electrical shock from a faulty appliance it will be more likely to be thrown away than examined to see if it is fake. It might, if reported, be kept as data by a trading standards body, but the various processes of attrition in the likelihood of such reporting gives an indication of just how partial a view of the market will be held in such datasets. Many fakes are bought by willing buyers and will therefore not lead to reporting, and even some buyers who are duped into buying a fake will not draw attention to the fact for fear of seeming stupid or (in the case of specialist markets like the art market) having their expertise called into question. In a 1999 report on the counterfeiting of medicines, the WHO made a point of calling attention to the reluctance of pharmaceutical companies to report the known presence of counterfeits in the market (World Health Organisation 1999). While the companies claim this is to avoid consumer alarm, it has been alleged that it is more likely fuelled by a desire to protect their brand image. Recent statements have been made by trade bodies such as the Royal Pharmaceutical Society to the effect that companies are now encouraged to make their knowledge public (Cockburn *et al.* 2005).

There are various estimates available of the size of the counterfeit segments of a range of markets, many of them unreliable. UNICRI has asserted that counterfeits may make up as much as 10 per cent of the legal market for aircraft parts in the USA, a similar percentage of the motor vehicle parts market in the UK and in relation to pharmaceuticals around 1 per cent in developed countries, 10 to 30 per cent in Africa, Asia and parts of Latin America, more than 20 per cent in ex-Soviet republics and more than half of all drugs sold on the Internet (UNICRI 2007: 55, 58, 68–9).

Case studies can give us accurate local pictures of the scale and effects of some harmful faking. For example, a multinational survey in 2004 found 53 per cent of antimalarials in South East Asia to be fakes containing incorrect levels of the active ingredient (Dondorp *et al.* 2004).

Seizure statistics are also available and can give us a partial indication of the scale of the problem. Data from customs seizures in OECD countries has been used to estimate that the global trade in C/P goods 'could have been up to USD 200 billion in 2005' (OECD 2007) which would represent about 2 per cent of world trade.

In the EU, Regulation 1383/2003 (Customs Actions Against Goods Suspected of Infringing Intellectual Property Rights) sets the relevant regulatory framework for the enforcement of border measures and Regulation 1891/2004 contains provisions for implementation (Vrins and Schneider 2006). The number of EU seizures has increased year on year from 5,056 in 2001 to 43,671 in 2007 (EU Taxation and Customs Union 2007).

In the UK, the number of people sentenced for IPC has fluctuated over the last decade, with a notable rise since 2002. In 2002, 441 people were sentenced in the UK for IPC, with 25 imprisoned. By 2005, the number of people sentenced had more than doubled to 995, with 195 imprisoned (IP Crime Group 2007: 73). The increasing use of imprisonment for IP criminals suggests an increase in the seriousness with which IPC is viewed by the criminal justice system. The IP Crime Group also surveyed all trading standards services in the UK (although not all responded, rendering the data only a partial picture) in relation to their activities in 2006. By far the highest numbers of C/P goods seized by responding trading standards services (by unit) in 2006 were DVDs and software (217,274 items), followed by clothing (116,594). The next largest categories to these two were cigarettes (13,200 items) and CDs (12,719 items). The street value of the clothing seized was estimated at around £2.5 million, as against £1.1 million for the DVDs and software.

Characteristics of IPC

'Leisure' IPC and 'business' IPC

Although we have been focusing here on the 'industrial' and 'global' trade in C/P goods, the picture is considerably more complex than the one-way trade this model implies.

There is of course also much of what we might call 'leisure' IPC, to distinguish it from 'business' IPC. By leisure IPC, I mean the sort of CD-burning and file-sharing which is undertaken at home by many consumers as opposed to the organised larger-scale production of C/P goods. These two categories are ideal types, or at least extremes of a continuum of IPC; there is a considerable grey area in the middle where, for example, Internet-based file-sharing becomes organised through key portals connecting individuals with networks far beyond their friends. Accepting the limitations of the two categories, it remains useful to separate IPC for home or close-network use from larger-scale IPC for sale in the pursuit of profit. This important distinction is in fact rarely made, resulting in much clouded analysis which discusses motivation for IPC based either on interviews and surveys with samples of students (without acknowledging that this is only 'leisure' IPC and says nothing about 'business' IPC) or focuses on allegations of the organised crime threat, lumping the somewhat more benign leisure IPC in with serious transnational illicit business enterprise.

Not everyone can successfully engage in IPC: a minimum level of expertise is necessary (Piquero 2005). In some cases, such as fake art, medicines or machine parts, this expertise is rather specialist and certainly does limit entry to the field of criminal fakers. In others, however, such as music or film piracy, the 'expertise' required is only a level of competence with computers and the Internet which is increasingly commonly held, to the point that piracy by way of file-sharing or CD-burning is part of the 'routine activities' of computer users who may perform these or similar tasks on their machines for legitimate purposes all the time (Cohen and Felson 1979). In this sense, therefore, some forms of IPC are criminal simply by the nature of what you are copying and do not necessitate the deliberate evolution of new routines in order to perform criminal acts. To use Matza's terminology (1964), this makes them easy to 'drift' into. These routine activities' considerations can be combined with various ethical observations to explain why many individuals view IPC as an acceptable pursuit. Many rationalisations and neutralisations are reasonable on the level of individuals sharing IP-protected music and software with their friends, but when extended to global counterfeiting networks they become less plausible. There is a perception that 'nobody loses' through IPC; no one is being deprived of tangible property as would be the case in other forms of theft (Seale *et al.* 1998).

Many patterns emerge from analysis of the global economy of faking, among which some are clearly calculated to minimise detection. Foreign manufacturers make counterfeit clothing 'blanks' which follow brand designs but bear no labels so that fake trademarks can be attached to them once they cross the customs barrier into the market country. Even without these kinds of tactics, it is well known that the customs barriers in consumer nations balance surveillance against the hampering of expeditious trade, with the result that only a very small minority of shipments can be searched. Perhaps most mundanely, individual end sellers from market countries have been found to go abroad to pick up counterfeit stock from foreign manufacturers: a DIY approach to international trade which cuts out middlemen and depletes the overblown impression of counterfeit markets being dominated by organised criminals who specialise in illicit commodity transit. Alongside this exists the development of the Internet-aided mechanism known as 'drop shipping' in which an order for counterfeit goods is taken by a UK-based advertiser, often through an online auction site, who then sends the order to an overseas supplier to be shipped direct to the customer. Drop shipping reduces the risk to the UK seller should the goods be seized at customs: the UK seller is not easily connected to the shipment and the overseas supplier will be more difficult for the UK authorities to trace and prosecute than a UK resident.

Explaining IPC

IPC is a low-risk, high-reward crime. It can generate significant profits and is policed and regulated ineffectively. It attracts lighter sentences and other forms of punishment than many other forms of crime, including most forms of trafficking (in narcotics, humans, etc.). It is, therefore, in terms of rational choice theory, a type of crime that presents good opportunity for unlawful profits with minimal 'costs' to weigh against the profits it can generate.

The pursuit of profit makes the faking of some items more attractive than others. Faking is therefore structured such that the most prolific instances of faking are to be found either in markets for items which can be easily replicated in bulk at very low costs (for example CDs and DVDs burned on easily available electronic systems) or where items are more costly or difficult to fake, in markets where these items sell for high prices (for example, aviation parts).

Where an item is known to be fake, a consumer will pay less for it than they would for the original. Thus there arises a lure for fakers to insert their product into licit markets to be sold as apparent originals and therefore at the highest price possible. This again invites a cost-benefit and opportunity analysis. Clearly there subsist markets in fakes where no effort is made to dupe the consumer – fake Rolexes sold in street markets in the developing world would be an example – but there is also evidence that many designer clothing and luxury item fakes are being made to increasingly high standards to aid their passing off as genuine.

As well as price-maximisation, some markets display other structural pressures towards passing fakes off as genuine. In the pharmaceuticals market, end consumers are hard to reach other than through the licit market, production is tightly regulated, and production can be automated to the point that once the initial costs of setting up a factory have been met, fake drugs can be produced in bulk. Fakers, as well as legitimate businesses, are attracted by the economies of scale. Thus we have seen the development of highly expertly faked packaging, security labels, holograms and other brand paraphernalia which allow fake drugs to be inserted into licit chains of supply. There have in the last few years been an increasing number of instances of such fakes being discovered having been prescribed over the counter in western countries including the UK, and these brand-infringing and sometimes highly dangerous products confirm that fakes in this market, as in others, are often all but indistinguishable from the real thing. The profit motive here has a particularly pernicious effect: medicines which cost the most tend to be those designed to treat very serious illness. In attracting counterfeiters with the promise of high profit margins these drugs when faked and supplied without active ingredients, or with positively harmful ingredients, can be lethal.

Counterfeiters are able to 'compete' with legitimate business in heavily regulated markets since they are not constrained with the costs of having to meet the high safety standards imposed on legitimate businesses producing items for these markets. The costs involved in meeting these safety standards are passed on to consumers by way of highly priced end products, making attractive opportunities for counterfeiters who can produce at low cost and sell at high. In some markets, like that in replacement motor vehicle parts, legitimate businesses have something of a monopoly over the production of genuine spares for their vehicles, and in addition to binding the costs of meeting safety standards into these parts, choose to exploit their monopoly by keeping prices high. These choices increase the attraction of the market for counterfeiters and enable them to easily undercut the legitimate market while still turning a good profit. Counterfeiters in spare parts markets tend to focus on the high-volume sale parts, i.e. those that are most often required by consumers (Brut 1999: 10). They are not, after all, in the business of catering for consumers looking for obscure parts; that sort of relatively cost-ineffective customer aftercare is left to the legitimate trade.

Adverse effects of faking

C/P goods cause financial loss to the companies that hold the IP rights to the goods in question. For example, the British Phonographic Industry estimated physical music piracy lost the industry £16.5 million in 2006. The Business Software Agency conduct an annual Global Software Piracy Study which in its 2007 sweep estimated 38 per cent of software used worldwide to be pirated, representing losses to industry, they say, of USD 48 billion. The median piracy rate was 61 per cent, meaning half of the 108 countries in the survey had a software piracy rate of 61 per cent or higher (BSA 2008). Poor-quality brand counterfeits also deplete consumer faith in markets generally, and individual brands specifically, thereby lowering the amount of 'goodwill' a particular brand has among its customers. The ease with which counterfeiters can copy new designs may discourage businesses from research and development, and the diversion of their profits towards counterfeiters may mean they have less money available for inward investment anyway (International Chamber of Commerce 2005).

Against this argument that faking has an adverse effect on innovation through discouraging R&D, there is a more critical argument that the enforcement of IP rights themselves stifles invention (Lessig 2001; Moohr 2003) such as by restricting the capacity of some product designers to build on and improve the ideas of others. While, therefore, the World Intellectual Property Organisation (WIPO) considers IP protection an essential cornerstone of 'all social, economic and cultural development' (WIPO 2001: 41), this is a somewhat dubious, if widely accepted, position.

Fakes can sometimes also cause physical harm. Medicines, industrial machine parts, auto and aviation parts, food and beverage products (including alcohol) and the like which misleadingly purport to be made by a certain manufacturer are sometimes of significantly lower quality than the originals and can pose serious health risks to users. Therefore, although IP infringement is often seen as a matter primarily of economic loss for the brand-holder, the practice can involve serious risk to the health and safety of the public (Yar 2005a). For example, diethylene glycol (antifreeze) in counterfeit medicines has killed hundreds of people in a series of tragedies in Haiti, Nigeria and Bangladesh (Hanif *et al.* 1995). In 2002 the International Federation of Pharmaceutical Manufacturers Associations estimated that 40 per cent of antimalarial drugs in South East Asia did not contain an active ingredient (UNICRI 2007: 71). As well as causing physical or psychological harm by underperforming or containing harmful substances, counterfeit drugs containing under-dosages can foster resistance to the active ingredients, compounding the problems experienced by developing countries suffering epidemics (Morris and Stevens 2006).

Faking is suggested to equate to lost tax revenue for governments by way of corporation tax (a tax on legitimate profits), VAT and excise duties. The latest IPC report from the UK-IPO, which is the lead administrative body responsible for the government's overall IPC strategy, notes that in 2006, HMRC estimated a loss in government revenue (portrayed as a 'cost to the taxpayer') of £2.9 billion as a result of an estimated trade in 18.5 billion non-UK duty paid cigarettes (IP Crime Group 2007: 8). Of these, 2 billion (11 per cent) were thought to be counterfeit. Lost tax revenue to counterfeits is not always so clear-cut, however. In his various studies of counterfeiting in China, Daniel Chow has observed that the majority of counterfeits, which are 'home-grown' so to speak, are sold in street market stalls whose core business is no secret. Local government condones these sites and the traders pay flat-rate taxes to local officials which make up a not inconsiderable proportion of regional state income (Chow 2000, 2003, 2006). This also gives some indication of the complexities of the interests involved in the global market in counterfeits and the problems inherent in trying to achieve market reduction.

It is important to remember, however, that although faking has many victims, and effects many varieties of harm, quite often the most obvious supposed 'victims' – the buyers – do not see themselves as victims at all. Many C/P goods are bought quite willingly by buyers who know they are fake. Sugden's ethnographic study of the underground economy surrounding Manchester United's brand provides good examples of this. While fake replica shirts sold to fans cause considerable economic loss to the club, the counterfeit salesmen are viewed as 'Robin Hoods' by 'the impoverished mothers of fanatical kids from Manchester's run-down estates' who see the club that sells exorbitantly priced originals as 'robbing bastards' (Sugden 2007: 251).

Responses to the crime

Legal responses

The concept of faking is underpinned by a very wide range of legal provisions and the acts of producing and dealing in a single type of fake can often trigger several different criminal offences. Among these are offences contained in the Forgery and Counterfeiting Act 1981 (for example for faking banknotes or fake signatures on cheques), and the Fraud Act 2006. We will focus here on the legal and regulatory response to C/P goods, however.

Where consumers are duped (as opposed to knowing buyers of fakes), C/P goods sold to them will trigger an offence under the Fraud Act 2006. If goods adopt trademarks without authorisation they will breach the Trade Marks Act 1994 (TMA), which under s.92 makes the unauthorised use of a trademark a criminal offence. Even if there is no trademark infringement in such a case the fake items will still probably breach copyright in the clothes design under the Copyright, Designs and Patents Act 1988 (CDPA), which in s.107 criminalises making or dealing with infringing articles.

The provisions of the CDPA and the TMA are supplemented by a range of complementary provisions in other statutes which, while not designed specifically to deal with IPC, have proven useful in addressing the problem. These include confiscation orders under the Proceeds of Crime Act 2002 (POCA), in terms of which convicted IP criminals have been required to repay to the court sums of money representing estimates of their illicit profits. The Serious Crime Act 2007 includes IP crimes in its remit and enables a court to make a Serious Crime Prevention Order (SCPO). These Orders are somewhat like ASBOs for 'serious' crime, being granted on a civil, rather than criminal, standard of proof, and setting out various injunction-type prohibitions on elements of the subject's behaviour thought relevant such as place of work and association with specified individuals. The Money Laundering Regulations (2003 and now 2007) have also been successfully, if occasionally, used to convict operators of market venues such as those who hire out stall pitches. Where they know, or suspect, that the rent they receive for these pitches is the result of IPC, they are open to prosecution.

As well as other relevant criminal offences, such as those contained in the Video Recordings Act 1984 and the Trade Descriptions Act 1968, much faking is also governed by a variety of civil statutory and common law provisions which give consumers and rights-holders a right of redress against sellers and manufacturers of fakes. Such civil provisions give rights-holders, for example, the right to compensation from those who (mis)use IP-protected designs without permission. The remedies in these cases include injunction and damages: the former a court order to the defendant to desist in the IP infringement and the latter an award of financial compensation to the plaintiff.

Who does the 'policing'?

IPC is a good example of a field which is the subject of 'plural policing'. In the UK, investigation and/or enforcement of IPC laws tends to be performed by one of five categories of person or organisation. These are: the police; local trading standards officers; in-house corporate anti-counterfeiting teams or (often IP specialist) private investigation agencies; government-established regulatory bodies; and non-governmental industry regulatory bodies. In the UK the front-line agency addressing IPC is trading standards.

While certain products have their own regulatory body, such as the Medicines and Healthcare Products Regulatory Agency, there also exist a large number of industry bodies which perform no legal regulatory function. These bodies have formed useful alliances with trading standards where their members' interests have been threatened by fakes. This has happened, for example, with the International Federation of Spirit Producers UK, who have helped trading standards in addressing the problem of licensed premises where branded spirit bottles are refilled with cheaper alcohol and where consumers are therefore sold drinks that are 'fake' in the sense of being labelled something they are not. Others among the most relevant 'whole-industry' bodies are the Entertainment and Leisure Software Producers Association (ELSPA) and the British Phonographic Industry (BPI). Examples of industry bodies set up specifically to address IPC are the Federation Against Software Theft (FAST), the Federation Against Copyright Theft (FACT) and the Industry Trust for IP Awareness which represents the film industry and is behind public awareness campaigns such as those mentioned below.

The police and other state agencies of control also play a role in the governance of counterfeiting. The Metropolitan Police has a Film Piracy Unit, set up in 2006 and funded by FACT. This Unit sits within the Money Laundering Team of the Specialist Crime Directorate. Observations (and assertions) of links to organised crime have brought the matter onto the agenda of the Serious Organised Crime Agency (SOCA), and customs is also a key player in effecting (mostly reactive) seizures: while 20 per cent of seizures in 2007 were based on customs' own suspicions in relation to shipments, 80 per cent were the result of 'applications for action' they received (EU Taxation and Customs Union 2007). These normally originate from industry rights-holders, who can apply to have action taken by one or more Member States if they become aware their product is being faked.

Detecting, regulating and preventing fakes

There is a variety of obstacles which stand in the way of the effective regulation of fakes. Rights-holders are sometimes unable to identify fakes, resulting in abandoned prosecutions. There are several reasons for this (Vagg and Harris 2000). First, as noted, some 'fakes' are actually unauthorised factory over-runs: in other words they are identical to the 'authentic' goods except that they were not made with the consent of the rights-holder. Other than where goods are stamped with serial numbers or other systems of identification, these unauthorised products will be very hard to tell apart from the originals. Second, supply chains have become attenuated through processes of outsourcing and subcontracting to the point that a rights-holder may not have direct knowledge of the factories involved in producing their goods. The range of subcontractors in an outsourced production chain means there will be variations in the end products depending on where they were made, and this again makes it difficult for a rights-holder to say that a given product is fake as opposed to an authorised product suffering incidental variation from the core design. Third, parallel trading results sometimes in goods with different specifications being designed for markets in different countries. This means that where, for example, a UK subsidiary of a multinational company is approached by trading standards to pass judgment on whether a seized product is counterfeit, they may not have the information to decide whether it is a fake or a legitimate design from a different market. Counterfeiters can abuse this uncertainty by claiming their fakes to be parallel imports, setting off time-consuming and costly investigations to determine whether this is the case. As Vagg and Harris note, where seized goods do turn out to be legitimate parallel imports, trading standards can be sued for wrongful seizure and consequent loss of earnings. Where trading standards bear the risk of these legal recriminations rather than the rights-holder who mistakenly claimed the goods to be fake, they are best advised to err on the side of caution when there is doubt over the legitimacy of goods.

Markets in counterfeits were traditionally policed by way of arresting sellers and seizing products. This practice continues to a great extent, but it has now been supplemented by other approaches which seek to negotiate the major flaws in the traditional approach. Among these flaws, the most serious were/are (a) that where fakes are easily and cheaply produced, seizing them does not impose a major cost on criminals and they can be rapidly replaced in the market, and (b) where sellers are linked to transnational supply chains they are unlikely to be in key positions in the network, meaning removing a selection of these visible points will do little to destabilise the activity of producing and selling fakes itself.

Target hardening has been one of the most common industry responses to IPC. This kind of response fits with the high level of responsibilisation in this field. This responsibilisation, in terms of which law enforcement agencies have tended to see industry as charged with addressing its own IPC problems so far as possible, can be linked to the perception that IPC is a 'business issue' rather than a 'crime issue'. Business has responded in a variety of ways to this perception of IPC as only a matter of trade-related concern. Most major corporations have taken self-help measures, including employing anti-counterfeiting investigators and dedicated legal teams, and attempting to crime-proof their products through a range of target-hardening measures. There are too many such measures to list here: they include such things as identification codes, holographic labels and encryption technologies.

The common theme of these measures is that they aim to make faking harder. The continuing rise in the problem of global IPC demonstrates that these measures cannot solve the problem of this type of crime, at least while other components of situational crime prevention theory (Clarke 1992) such as risks and rewards remain effectively ignored. Some fakers have taken up the challenge of duplicating the safety features of various consumer products, increasing the sophistication of their fakes in response to upgraded security features in the originals. Studies of offender motivation in student samples of software pirates have also revealed that some people positively relish the challenge of breaking the codes that encrypt protected material (Sims et al. 1996).

Fitting with the underlying philosophy of the Market Reduction Approach (Sutton 1998) we also see public education playing a role in attempts to tackle markets in fakes. The rationale is that reducing the uptake of illicit purchase opportunities will lower the economic incentives for those trafficking and manufacturing counterfeits. Various strategies of intervention in this vein have been attempted, including alerting consumers to the idea that their seemingly relatively innocuous purchases of copied DVDs may be funding serious organised crime, and shaming purchasers by associating their actions with 'real' crime or otherwise trying to attach social stigma to such purchases. An example of the 'it's a crime' approach is the addition to front-end DVD material: 'you wouldn't steal a car … etc.; so don't buy a counterfeit DVD'. An example of the social stigma approach is the 'don't be a Knock-off Nigel' campaign which has recently been rolled out nationally on television and in cinemas. The problem with the 'it's a crime' approach is that surveys reveal that around 80 per cent of the public now know counterfeiting and piracy are criminal. Unfortunately the hitherto-assumed next step – that this knowledge would lead them not to purchase C/P goods – has not in fact materialised to a satisfactory degree. According to a MORI poll, 40 per cent of people would still consider buying counterfeits. Thus we see the new strategy emerging, moving from appeals to the legal and moral status of the act of theft itself, to attempts to use social stigma and embarrassment.

Other recent developments include attempts to influence purchasing routines by educating the public as to the nature of the harms counterfeits cause, but again these are somewhat hamstrung by the need to frame counterfeits as defective products (which is not always true), to highlight physical injury to consumers (which is only a risk in relation to certain categories of fake) and to suggest links to organised crime (a term never used in its more empirically nuanced sense of networked entrepreneurs and grey markets in this discourse), while strategically ignoring the driving force behind the development of the concept of IPC (businesses' lost profits) which remains a harm to which the public appear consistently unsympathetic. The latest appeals include harm to 'local communities' (IP Crime Group 2007) which again tends to operate through references to harms associated with, rather than caused by, counterfeiting, such as that people who sell fake goods are 'also engaged in defrauding the benefit system', 'are using illegal immigrants to sell pirated goods' and 'are also shown to be exploiting children and grooming them into a criminal lifestyle' (IP Crime Group 2007: 7).

Conclusion: the global political economy of faking and authenticity as culturally relativist

An important point to note in relation to the intellectual property restrictions which currently populate the field of design and branding is that it was not always thus. The industrialism of the nineteenth century was notable for the absence of any restrictions on copying the designs of others, and indeed copying industrial designs from whatever source one could, particularly overseas, tended to be encouraged as a useful tool for the development of domestic trade. The criminal law paid no attention to the matter of faking, which was presumed to be a commercial matter in which the buyer should take responsibility for his or her own decisions: caveat emptor.

As well as some questions of authorship and authenticity, such as brand protectionism, requiring to be understood on a historical view as quite specific emanations of a particular structure of global political economy, the seemingly straightforward and important question of who created a certain thing can also be seen to be culturally relativist. Just as common endeavour was a feature of the artisan's studios of previous centuries, with associated muddying of the waters of authorship, so the art of Australia's Aboriginal population can be seen to be produced in comparably communal ways. Aboriginal art tends to be a visual form of narrative – the culture has no writing, and therefore art is a traditional way for 'stories' about tribes and tribal identity to be passed down generations. Often, elders are considered custodians of the stories and therefore 'owners' or part-authors of paintings about the stories. Younger members are included in the process of the creation of what are effectively joint-authored works as a way of learning and becoming involved in the social narrative (Polk 1999). These traditional processes create confusion in western buyers of Aboriginal art who expect answers to questions of 'whose work this is' which dealers may not be able to answer, at least honestly (Alder 1999).

The important issue here for a discussion of 'wrongful faking' is that at some previous times, and still in some other cultures, the question of who made an object is not seen as central to its social importance. The relatively strict legal prohibitions on copying ideas and designs currently persisting in developed post-industrial 'knowledge economies' are intricately bound up with the economic imperatives of late-modern capitalism, and associated cultural constructions of individual merit and ownership.

Selected further reading

IP crime has not been extensively studied by criminologists. We must therefore be quite eclectic in the sources we use to gather data on the subject. The literature is spread across fields as diverse as business ethics and medicine, and therefore analytical papers are found peppered among the other submissions to journals in those fields, as well as law, economics and psychology. For an in-depth focus on China, the work of Daniel Chow is a good place to start (see his papers referenced throughout the chapter). Yar (2005a, 2005b, 2008a, 2008b) takes on the subject from the perspective of critical social theory, and a more pragmatic approach is taken towards the 'causes and prevention' of IP crime by Piquero (2005). See also Wall and Yar (2009) which was published just as the present volume was going to press. There is a large amount of data on the web, including the Business Software Alliance's annual piracy surveys at http://www.bsa.org, European Union customs statistics available at http://ec.europa.eu/taxation_customs/index_en.htm, and a collection of the UK Intellectual Property Office's reports and resources at http://www.ipo.gov.uk/crime.htm. Other useful online information is available at the websites of the World Health Organisation, the OECD and UNICRI.

References

Alder, C. (1999) *Challenges to Authenticity in the Aboriginal Art Market*. Paper presented at the Art Crime: Protecting Artists and Protecting Consumers conference convened by the Australian Institute of Criminology, Sydney, 2–3 December (online). Online at: http://www.aic.gov.au/conferences/artcrime/alder.html (accessed 17 February 2008).

Brut, J.-P. (1999) 'Car parts counterfeiting', in R. E. Kendall (ed.), *International Criminal Police Review: Special Issue on Counterfeiting*. Lyon: ICPO/Interpol.

BSA (2008) *Fifth Annual BSA and IDC Global Software Piracy Study*. Business Software Alliance (online). Online at: http://global.bsa.org/idcglobalstudy2007/studies/2007_global_piracy_study.pdf (accessed 23 May 2008).

Chow, D. C. K. (2000) 'Counterfeiting in China', *Washington University Law Quarterly*, 78 (1): 1–57.

Chow, D. C. K. (2003) 'Organized crime, local protectionism, and the trade in counterfeit goods in China', *China Economic Review*, 14: 473–84.

Chow, D. C. K. (2006) 'Why China does not take commercial piracy seriously', *Ohio Northern University Law Review*, 32: 203–25.

Clarke, R. V. (1992) *Situational Crime Prevention*. New York: Harrow & Heston.

Cockburn, R. D., Newton, P. N., Agyarko, E. K., Akunyili, D. and White, N. J. (2005) 'The global threat of counterfeit drugs: why industry and governments must communicate the dangers', *PLoS Medicine*, 2 (4): e100.

Cohen, L. E. and Felson, M. (1979) 'Social change and crime rate trends: a routine activity approach', *American Sociological Review*, 44: 588–608.

Conklin, J. E. (1994) *Art Crime*. Westport, CT: Praeger.

Dondorp, A., Newton, P., Mayxay, M., Van Damme, W., Smithuis, F., Yeung, S., Petit, A., Lynam, A., Johnson, A., Hien, T., McGready, R., Farrar, J., Looareesuwan, S., Day, N., Green, M. and White, N. (2004) 'Fake antimalarials in Southeast Asia are a major impediment to malaria control: multinational cross-sectional survey on the prevalence of fake antimalarials', *Tropical Medicine and International Health*, 9 (12): 1241.

EU Taxation and Customs Union (2007) *Report on Community Customs Activities on Counterfeit and Piracy: Results at the European Border – 2007*. European Commission (online). Available at: http://ec.europa.eu/taxation_customs/resources/documents/customs/customs_controls/counterfeit_piracy/statistics2007.pdf (accessed 23 May 2008).

Grossman, G. M. and Shapiro, C. (1989) 'Foreign counterfeit of status goods', *Quarterly Journal of Economics*, 103: 79–100.

Hanif, M., Mobarak, M., Ronan, A., Rahaman, D. and Donovan, J. (1995) 'Fatal renal failure caused by diethylene glycol in paracetamol elixir: the Bangladesh epidemic', *British Medical Journal*, 311: 88–91.

International Chamber of Commerce (2005) *Intellectual Property: Source of Innovation, Creativity, Growth and Progress*. ICC (online). Available at: http://www.iccwbo.org/uploadedFiles/ICC/policy/intellectual_property/Statements/BASCAP_IP_pub.pdf (accessed 25 May 2008).

IP Crime Group (2007) *Intellectual Property Crime Report 2007*. Newport, South Wales: UK-IPO.

Lemert, E. M. (1958) 'The behavior of the systematic check forger', *Social Problems*, 6 (2): 141–9.

Lessig, L. (2001) *The Future of Ideas: The Fate of the Commons in a Connected World*. New York: Random House.

Mackenzie, S. (2005) *Going, Going, Gone: Regulating the Market in Illicit Antiquities*. Leicester: Institute of Art and Law.

Matza, D. (1964) *Delinquency and Drift*. New York: John Wiley.

Moohr, G. S. (2003) 'The crime of copyright infringement: an inquiry based on morality, harm, and criminal theory', *Boston University Law Review*, 83 (4): 731–83.

Morris, J. and Stevens, P. (2006) *Counterfeit Medicines in Less Developed Countries: Problems and Solutions*. London: International Policy Network.

OECD (2007) *The Economic Impact of Counterfeiting and Piracy: Executive Summary*. Organisation for Economic Co-operation and Development (online). Online at: http://www.oecd.org/dataoecd/13/12/38707619.pdf (accessed 23 May 2008).

Piquero, N. L. (2005) 'Causes and prevention of intellectual property crime', *Trends in Organized Crime*, 8 (4): 40–61.

Polk, K. (1999) *Who Wins and Who Loses When Art is Stolen or Forged?* Paper presented at the conference Art Crime: Protecting Artists and Protecting Consumers, convened by the Australian Institute of Criminology, Sydney, 2–3 December, available at the AIC (online). Online at: http://www.aic.gov.au/conferences/artcrime/polkwho.html (accessed 17 February 2008).

Polk, K. and Chappell, D. (forthcoming) 'Fakers and forgers, deception and dishonesty: an exploration of the murky world of art fraud', *Current Issues in Criminal Justice*.

Seale, D. A., Polakowski, M. and Schneider, S. (1998) 'It's not really theft! Personal and workplace ethics that enable software piracy', *Behaviour and Information Technology*, 17: 27–40.

Sims, R. R., Cheng, H. K. and Teegen, H. (1996) 'Toward a profile of student software pirates', *Journal of Business Ethics*, 15: 839–49.

Sternitsky, J. L. (1955) *Forgery and Fictitious Checks*. Springfield, IL: Charles C Thomas.

Sugden, J. (2007) 'Inside the grafters' game: an ethnographic examination of football's underground economy', *Journal of Sport and Social Issues*, 31 (3): 242–58.

Sutherland, E. H. (1937) *The Professional Thief*. Chicago: University of Chicago Press.

Sutton, M. (1998) *Handling Stolen Goods and Theft: A Market Reduction Approach*, Home Office Research Study No. 178. London: Home Office.

Thomas, D. (2007) *Deluxe: How Luxury Lost Its Lustre*. New York: Penguin.

UNICRI (2007) *Counterfeiting: A Global Spread, a Global Threat*. United Nations Interregional Crime and Justice Research Institute.

Vagg, J. and Harris, J. (2000) 'False profits: why product counterfeiting is increasing', *European Journal on Criminal Policy and Research*, 8: 107–15.

Vrins, O. and Schneider, M. (eds) (2006) *Enforcement of Intellectual Property Rights Through Border Measures: Law and Practice in the EU*. Oxford: Oxford University Press.

Wall, D. S. and Yar, M. (2009) 'Intellectual property crime and the Internet: cyber-piracy and "stealing" informational intangibles', in Y. Jewkes and M. Yar (eds), *The Handbook of Internet Crime and Criminal Justice*. Cullompton: Willan.

Warchol, G. L. (2004) 'The transnational illegal wildlife trade', *Criminal Justice Studies*, 17: 57–73.

WIPO (2001) *WIPO Intellectual Property Handbook: Policy, Law and Use*, World Intellectual Property Organisation Publication No. 489(E). Geneva: WIPO.

World Health Organisation (1999) *Guidelines for the Development of Measures to Combat Counterfeit Drugs*. Geneva: WHO.

Yar, M. (2005a) 'A deadly faith in fakes: trademark theft and the global trade in counterfeit automotive components', *Internet Journal of Criminology*. Online at: http://www.internetjournalofcriminology.com.

Yar, M. (2005b) 'The global "epidemic" of movie "piracy": crime-wave or social construction?', *Media, Culture and Society*, 27 (5): 677–96.

Yar, M. (2008a) 'The *other* global drugs crisis: assessing the scope, impacts and drivers of the trade in dangerous counterfeit pharmaceuticals', *International Journal of Social Inquiry*, 1 (1): 151–66.

Yar, M. (2008b) 'The rhetorics and myths of anti-piracy campaigns: criminalization, moral pedagogy and capitalist property relations in the classroom', *New Media and Society*, 10 (2): 457–75.

Chapter 8

Scams

Simon Mackenzie

Introduction

A 'scam' has lately become the most commonly applied term to a particular type of consumer-oriented, often mass-marketed, fraud. Other terms used in this area include cons, swindles and stings. The essence of a classic scam is in encouraging a victim to take up an offer that presents itself as loaded in their favour when it is in fact loaded against. A slightly more diluted definition of a scam might be an operation that makes a rip-off seem like legitimate business. Scams therefore involve orchestrated deception in the service of profit-taking. While noting that there is no commonly accepted or legal definition of a scam, the Office of Fair Trading (OFT) defines a scam as:

> A misleading or deceptive business practice where you receive an unsolicited or uninvited contact (for example by email, letter, phone or ad) and false promises are made to con you out of money. (OFT 2006: 12)

While encompassing the most common contemporary mass-marketed scams – and these are also the types most commonly reported to the OFT, which exists to police (un)fair trading – this is in fact quite a narrow definition of scamming. Scams are not always 'business practices', they do not have to begin with 'unsolicited or uninvited contact' (think of fake websites which sit waiting to be discovered) and they may not even involve 'false promises' (a promise can be misleading without being false: think of premium rate telephone scams that promise you have won a prize, which for almost all callers will turn out to be true but effectively worthless). In cases where there has been clear fraud, the application of the term 'scam' to a crime may not add much analytical value. The boundaries of the concept of a scam are, however, wider than those of criminal fraud. There are many 'sharp practices' employed by businesses which are either legal, barely legal, borderline legal or illegal-but-not-prosecutable for various practical reasons (Passas and

Goodwin 2004). Many people would call all such practices 'scams' or 'rip-offs'. Even where no criminal law is broken or threatened (i.e. where there is no suggestion of fraud) there is a range of civil law provisions which apply to scams. These are mostly contained in consumer protection legislation and cover such things as mis-selling and misdescription of goods, selling items that are not fit for purpose, false advertising and trying to subject consumers to unfair contract terms in the contract of sale. Thus we can observe that a scam may be a crime, a civil wrong or an act which, while technically legal, is generally thought to infringe upon moral normative principles of good conduct.

In criminological analysis, scams have hitherto been subsumed in the study of fraud, a fraud being 'in essence … the obtaining of goods and/or money by deception' (Levi 2008a). There has been considerable research done on fraud generally, and on some specific categories within that headline crime (e.g. Levi 1981, 1987, 1993, 1999, 2003, 2005, 2006; Levi *et al.* 2007 and some of the chapters in this volume). Yet there may be some merit in treating scams as worthy of more detailed study against the background of fraud research. Scams appear to be emerging as a specific crime problem within policy and media discourse, evidenced in new 'scambusters' trading standards teams being funded around the UK at the time of writing and prime-time television programmes of the same ilk. The review of the history and contemporary practice of scamming in this chapter supports a view of this (quite admittedly ill-defined) conceptual category as having both continuities and discontinuities with other types of fraud, and it may be that there is scope for developing a particular 'criminology of scams' without attempting to overwrite prior research on fraud but rather complementing it.

Excepting the fraud research mentioned then, the modest criminological attention paid to scams has been a particular oversight when we consider that for most readers of this book, scams (not other types of fraud) are probably the crimes or would-be crimes encountered most frequently. This is certainly the case for regular users of e-mail or the Internet. Anyone on e-mail is likely to receive several scam e-mails a day, which is significantly more interaction with the world of crime than most of us have with street crime, for example.

Common scams

Grabosky, Smith and Dempsey have proposed a four-fold classification of consumer fraud (Grabosky *et al.* 2001: 105–29). First, they identify 'advance fee fraud', which involves pretending to sell something you do not have while taking money in advance. Advance fee fraud and variants on it covers many of the common forms of modern-day scams. This is the purpose of 'Nigerian' e-mails and fake lottery schemes, in both of which 'marks' (i.e. potential victims) are asked to pay money for the supposed legal or technical costs of releasing a fictitious pot of money to them. Advance fee frauds have become known as 419s, after the number of the provision in the Nigerian criminal code which addresses them.

'Work from home' scams are also often a variant on advance fee scams, in that those who apply are required to pay registration fees or other costs up front before the unprofitable nature of the 'work' involved is discovered. In premium rate telephone prize scams, marks receive a letter, SMS text or e-mail inviting them to ring a costly telephone number to claim a prize, which turns out to be worth less than the cost of the call or involves the payment of a further 'delivery charge' which is more than its value. Premium rate telephone scams do not always involve prizes: all sorts of lures are used, many of which are legal but of dubious ethical standing, such as a range of 'keep 'em talking' business models including sex chatlines and blind-date chatlines in which (usually male) callers are led by a (usually female) conversationalist to believe she will meet them for a date which never materialises but involves them in a lot of expensive phone chat. Pyramid schemes are an advance fee scam where a person pays to join a scheme in the hope that he or she can persuade enough others to join to recoup the expenditure and turn a profit. New membership fees cascade up the pyramid, rewarding older members with the fees paid by new recruits. The 'greater fool' principle underpins new recruits' decision to join: they often realise the pyramid nature of the scheme but rationalise (correctly) that so long as the scheme lasts they stand to make money. The problem is that the schemes can only be sustained by ever greater numbers of members joining, and since they are not underpinned by actually selling anything other than the hope of a continuing influx of new recruits, they inevitably fold, leaving those last in the door nursing losses.

The above are all members of Grabosky *et al.*'s first category: advance fee frauds or closely related variants. Their second category is non-delivery and defective products and services. This category includes selling useless educational diplomas, a variety of online auction frauds, bogus health products (again often sold online) and misleading credit and loan terms. The difference between the first and second categories is not always immediately clear. However, advance fee scams are generally unsolicited and do not involve representations made in the course of a business or other retailer–consumer relationship. Non-delivery/defective products scams tend to operate in the latter kind of environment. Property investment scams, for example, would fall in the second category. Here, consumers pay for seminars and/or join investment clubs in order to have 'privileged' access to rewarding property investment techniques. These techniques are typically rather mundane and usually involve buying, or buying-to-let, properties sourced by the company running the scheme. Sometimes the whole show is a charade put on to get the joining fee; sometimes property is sold at an overvaluation; sometimes promises of guaranteed returns from tenants are made which are later discovered to have been false. There are many permutations.

Third, we have unsolicited and unwanted goods and services, where consumers are persuaded to buy something they do not really want through oppressive or deceptive marketing techniques. The classic case here would be boiler-room selling of worthless stocks – usually part of the so-called 'pump and dump' scheme (Stevenson 2000). In pump and dump, victims are persuaded to buy into a company in which the persuader already holds shares. The new purchases temporarily inflate the share price, allowing the boiler-room to sell at a profit before the share price collapses again. Regulatory activity in target countries like the US and UK has made boiler-rooms hard to sustain on a domestic basis, but they do not of course need to be located in the same countries as their victims and many now operate telemarketing bases in countries with weaker regulation (Shover *et al.* 2003), exploiting the difficulties posed to regulators of operating across jurisdictions. This is a form of criminal 'forum shopping'; currently many scammers targeting UK consumers, including those selling shares, operate from Spain (Levi 2008b: 395).

Grabosky *et al.*'s final category is identity fraud, which is not dealt with further here as it has full treatment in its own chapter in this volume.

Patterns and trends

The OFT has estimated that UK consumers lose in the region of £3.5 billion to scams each year (OFT 2006). The greatest losses have been found in bogus holiday club scams (£1.17 billion), high-risk investment scams (£490 million), pyramid and chain letter scams (£420 million) and foreign lottery scams (£260 million). The OFT's 2006 survey asked scam-related questions to 11,200 adult respondents. Of these, 48 per cent reported having been targeted by a scam at some point in the past (OFT 2006). The survey has led the OFT to estimate that 6.5 per cent of the UK adult population, or 3.2 million people, fall victim to a scam every year. These patterns of UK victimisation appear to bear similarity to comparative data available in respect of complaints made to consumer protection organisations in the US and Australia (Levi 2008a, 2008b; Smith 2007: 2).

The available reporting/complaint data suggests that scams are increasing in ubiquity (Levi 2008b). There have always been scams, of course, but scams require the communication of tempting offers as one of their key components, and the increasing connectedness of the global population has meant that the capacity of offenders to make such offers to potential victims has greatly increased. One of the very attractive features of sending e-mail scams for offenders is that the mode of delivery is effectively free and the number of people who can be reached with the communication is enormous. The Internet has therefore given individuals the ability to commit crimes previously well beyond their financial and organisational means (Wall 2007b).

In some ways these technological changes have considerably rewritten the story of the scam in the era of globalisation, but some fundamentals of the principle of the scam remain the same. Maurer's classic ethnographic history of the emergence of 'big cons' in the US from the late nineteenth century until their decline in the 1930s provides a good base for a study of the changing trends in scams up to the present day. Maurer's informants differentiated between 'short cons', which they saw as markers of the birth of the confidence trick, and the subsequent development of 'big cons'. Whereas short cons worked in various ways to fleece a 'mark' of whatever funds he had in his possession, and to do so quickly, big cons were considerably more elaborate, tended to involve the use of a 'big store', and 'touched' marks for very large sums of money which they were sent away during the course of the con to gather ('the send') often by liquidating assets in order to put together a stake to invest in the con. There were three classic variants of the big store con, called 'the wire', 'the payoff' and 'the rag'.[1] Each of these involved roles that were common across the different formats. A 'roper' would initially win the mark's confidence and bring him to the big store. The 'insideman' was the brains behind the big store and would play a key role in ultimately winning the confidence of the mark in a manoeuvre skilfully coordinated with the roper ('the switch'). The big store was an artificial bookmakers or stockbrokers (depending on the con), set up purely for the 'benefit' of the mark and populated by all the expected props of such an establishment, including a manager and actors who would pretend to bet money ('shills') to add to the store's apparent authenticity. In this carefully scripted elaborate charade, the mark would be led to believe he was privy to a tip-off or system for beating the big store (at the races, on stocks, etc.) and be lured into eventually placing extravagant bets on these 'sure things', which he would lose as the whole event was in fact rigged against him.

In respect of the psychology at the heart of the big con, we see both points of continuity and points of difference between 'old school' and contemporary methods. Consider, for example, the idea that 'you can't cheat an honest man' which was central to the operation of big store cons in the pre-war US. At the same time that the ego of the mark was flattered by an unending wave of compliments, suggesting that he was a man of some considerable character, someone who could be depended upon and such like, he was always offered the opportunity to be complicit in an illegal enterprise of some sort, generally defrauding the big store by placing a bet on a race that was fixed or some other kind of sure thing. This was in fact the fundamental paradox at the heart of the big con: the massaging of the mark's impression of his own admirable character and the simultaneous lure with which his greed was ensnared in an illicit temptation. Both of these emotional ploys live on in current scams: see, for example, the presence in 419 e-mails of suggestions that you are to be trusted and that you are thought by the sender (who doesn't know you!) to be a person of honest and upstanding character – surely such a person will want to help out? At the same time, most marks who take up 419 or 'work from home' invitations must suspect that a millionaire's fortune could not be there for the taking unless illicit activity were involved at some stage.

Not all contemporary scams operate on the principle that you can't cheat an honest man/woman, though. Some indeed play on the honesty of the mark, such as overpayment scams. These involve a purchase of an item for sale, often nowadays on eBay, by way of a cheque in excess of the sale price (either supposedly by accident or along with a plausible story). The cheque is banked and clearance is notified by the seller's bank, at which point she is happy to wire the 'overpayment' back to the buyer. But she does not have the money: the cheque is fraudulent and on discovery of this the bank can withdraw the credit it has made to her account. Many variants of the overpayment scam can be observed: they can form part of 'work from home' (i.e. in some cases 'let us use your bank account') scams as well as Internet dating scams. Romances which flourish on the Internet are sometimes rather one-sided: you find a soulmate who declares themselves in need of funds to make the trip to see you, leading to a type of advance fee fraud, or where they send you cheques and request wired money in return, an overpayment variant.

Characteristics of the offence, offenders and victims

There are several interesting aspects to the phenomenon of scamming in terms of the characteristics of offence, offenders and victims. Most jarring, perhaps, is the evidence which suggests that white-collar fraudsters have backgrounds in which 'the disadvantages and pathologies commonplace in the early lives of most street criminals are in scant evidence' (Shover *et al.* 2003: 495). Since Sutherland first drew attention to the illogic in suggesting that the law-breaking companies he studied could have had dysfunctional early family lives, white-collar crime research has failed to find the correlations between crime and poverty/disadvantage in the early life course of the individual offender that has become so central a part of criminology based on studies of street-crime offenders. Further, studies of telemarketing scam offenders (Doocy *et al.* 2001; Shover *et al.* 2003), as well as studies of white-collar criminals more generally (Weisburd *et al.* 2001), have revealed that many such offenders have a history of criminal offending, and often not in relation to white-collar crime.

While the motivation for boiler-room salespeople tends to be reported by them, unsurprisingly, as money, they also fit broader cultural narratives such as the satisfaction achieved from feeling that one is a success in a career structure which mirrors legitimate business, as well as the highs achieved from successful 'sales' which are precisely those similarly achieved by legitimate salespeople, including the competitive kick which leads to delight in 'beating' both fellow team-members and victims (Shover *et al.* 2003; Shover *et al.* 2004). In this sense, there are 'seductions' (Katz 1988) in this type of crime beyond the most obvious financial motivation (cf. Levi 2008c) and a key seduction is the sense of power which results from being able to bend others to your own will through strategies of persuasion (Duffield and Grabosky 2001).

Some scams are obviously illegal, in the sense that what they invite the mark to do is participate in an illegal enterprise. Knowledge or suspicion of the illegality of the scheme can operate to dissuade a mark, once scammed, from notifying the authorities (Smith *et al.* 1999). Some e-mail based 'work from home' scams operate in this way, inviting participants to earn a percentage fee for receiving and paying out funds from their bank account. Most participants must suspect that there is illegality involved, and indeed where the funds are collected and paid out in this way they will often be the proceeds of advance fee frauds, paid into a bank account by an unwitting mark and then paid out by way of untraceable Western Union transfer by the account holder. If the victim of the advanced fee fraud reports the crime to the police the trail will stop with the bank account of the second mark, who now realises they have been a money mule for a fraudster. Invitations to earn money by receiving money into one's bank account are not always of this type; they can also be precursors to identity theft, or variants on the 'overpayment' scam as is the case where cheques which will ultimately bounce are paid into the mark's account and the amount of the funds, less commission, wired onwards by them.

Some scams are not in fact illegal, and many operate in a grey area around the borderline of illegality. An example here might be the congratulations that individuals, often in business, receive on making the ranks of a 'Who's Who' roster due to their great achievements. After much flattery, which leads them to feel quite puffed up, they are invited to submit their biography along with a payment for their membership fee.

The central role of emotion in scams

In 1959 Erving Goffman wrote 'On cooling the mark out' which dealt with 'some aspects of adaptation to failure' (Goffman 1959). Cooling the mark out meant trying to manage the emotions of a victim of a scam, to ensure that they 'adapted to failure' in a way that did not present a risk to the scammers. Most people do not like to think of themselves as suckers. This invites a process of 'cognitive dissonance', whereby instead of the victim seeing the scam for what it is, they may readjust their view of the situation to neutralise the perception that they are being scammed. So instead of adjusting their definition of the situation to fit reality, they may adjust (their perception of) reality to fit their self-image as someone who is too smart to be taken in by a scam. When they are finally presented with the unavoidable conclusion that they have been caught in a scam, it is the rapid destruction of this positive self-impression that requires what Goffman called 'adaptation to failure'.

Victims of scams can, upon such realisation, manifest a range of emotions. They require to be 'cooled out' since if they are left to their own devices they may become angry and attempt to take measures of redress like calling the police. The ideal response, as far as the scammers are concerned, is for the victim to see him or herself as foolish for having been taken in by the scam and to want to repair the integrity of their savvy image of self by putting the incident behind them. The victim is therefore encouraged in the cooling out process to chalk it up to experience and not to accept the label 'victim' by involving the authorities and dragging out the process of poring over the precise ways in which they were taken in by the scam: 'the mark is given instruction in the philosophy of taking a loss' (Goffman 1959: 452).

Cooling marks out does not seem to be a practice that has wholly survived the transition from the old-school con games to the new mass-marketed scams of the information society. In part this is because it is now possible, through e-mail, telephone and postal scams, to effect scams while retaining a high degree of anonymity. Victims of scams still under-report them, however, due to feelings of embarrassment, either at being perceived as stupid or greedy, and in some cases denial that they have been scammed at all (OFT 2006). Sometimes the absence of cooling out can lead to more severe victimisation: in their 1999 review of 419s, the Australian Institute of Criminology reported that since 1992, 17 people had been killed in Nigeria attempting to recover their funds (Smith *et al.* 1999: 3).

This is not to say that marks are never cooled out any more. Indeed, the point of Goffman's essay was to observe that cooling out was practised as part of many social routines beyond the tricks played by conmen: as he put it, it is 'part of a very basic social story' which is replayed every time friendships are broken, girlfriends and boyfriends are dumped, and so on. It is also the case that the transition to technology-based mass market scamming highlighted in this chapter has not entirely removed 'old-school' scams from the social scene: 'mock auctions', for example, still take place in Britain's coastal resorts in the holiday season and involve a carefully crafted pitch designed to employ all of the emotional triggers of Maurer's US big cons, including attention to encouraging a form of self-cooling-out in a crowd of marks through a variety of techniques including raising ambiguity around the legality of the sale items, thereby making customers unsure whether they are complicit in wrongdoing (Clark and Pinch 1992).

Victim demographics

It is abiding conventional wisdom that scams adversely affect the vulnerable to the greatest extent. It is very interesting then to note that the limited available evidence does not suggest that especially vulnerable groups make up a large proportion of scam victims (Muscat *et al.* 2002). To the contrary, Goffman's observations on the human defects of greed and self-delusion seem to have been prescient in light of contemporary victim demographics which suggest that most victims are fairly normal individuals whose greed got the better of them. Old, young, sick and otherwise vulnerable groups tend not to be electronically or economically active enough to come into contact with the full gamut of scams, although there is some evidence that when older people do fall victim to scams, they are likely to lose more than younger victims. Holtfreter *et al.* have recently found no correlation between risk-taking financial behaviour and consumer fraud victimisation, explained it seems by the fact that evidence of a cavalier attitude to investment is not easy for fraudsters to gather (Holtfreter *et al.* 2008).

According to the OFT data, certain demographic groups are more attracted by certain types of scam. Women are disproportionately represented in miracle health scams, clairvoyant mailing scams and career opportunity (such as 'become a model') scams. Men are disproportionately the victim of high-risk investment scams, property investment scams, African advance fee scams and Internet dialler scams (and see Trahan *et al.* 2005; Holtfreter *et al.* 2008). While older people (over 55) were more likely to have been targeted by scams, the highest victimisation rates were found in the 35–44 age range, suggesting that there is a greater uptake of scam invitations in that age range than among older scam targets. No strong trend was found in the social class of victims, although again there was differentiation in the types of scams different classes were likely to have been the victim of: loan, clairvoyant and lottery scams at the lower end of the class spectrum, investment and advance fee scams at the higher end.

A pattern of repeat victimisation is evident in the field of scams, as it is in other types of crime (Smith *et al.* 1999; Smith 2007). The OFT survey found that the victims in its sample had a 30 per cent chance of being a victim of a scam again in the next 12 months. Victims names are put on 'suckers lists' – sometimes also called 'lead' or 'mooch' lists (Shover *et al.* 2003) – which then make them more likely to be targeted again in the future (Levi 2008b), and this combined with their susceptibility to the temptation of scams (as perhaps demonstrated by their first victimisation) means that particularly promising marks are 'lined up' again in a contemporary manifestation of the tendency of the big con to repeatedly sting the same clients. The reluctance of victims to acknowledge they have been scammed, outlined in our discussion of Goffman above, can influence repeat victimisation. It leads to a 'rationalisation trap' (Pratkanis and Shadel 2005) in terms of which people experience pressure to delude themselves in order to avoid the psychologically painful realisation that they have been scammed, and this manifests as an increased willingness to respond to further scam invitations in the hope that these will prove the first event to have been legitimate.

Explanations of the crime

Victims of scams offer a variety of explanations when asked why they responded to the scam. Popular explanations include that they thought the scam was legitimate, due to its being marketed in a way that suggested a respectable business was behind it; they were caught off guard, sometimes because the scammer presented the 'golden opportunity' as time-limited to encourage an unreflective response; they suspected a scam but the investment required was so small and the potential return so large it was worth the risk; and they responded to the persuasive or individualised manner in which the scam was presented (OFT 2006).

It is not possible in the space available here to offer much analysis of which criminological theory might offer up the best explanation for the phenomenon of scams, but there are clear indicators that some elements of classic theories would need to be part of any attempt to create an integrated theoretical model here. Social learning and differential association theories would be required to explain the sometimes arcane rules and roles required to be learned for the effective performance of bygone big cons. These theories perhaps have less to offer Internet mass-mailers where the techniques are more easily acquired, but as many of the examples given in this chapter show the most popular scams are still not entirely obvious in design (not least to victims) so some level of transmission of techniques among offenders remains likely. The focus differential association brings to alternative normative reference systems is reflected to some extent in the 'othering' of victims by scammers, the creation of an in-group/out-group divide between grifters and their marks which helps deny the need to care about them as victims (Maurer 1940): one of the original techniques of neutralisation (Sykes and Matza 1957). Strain theory, and its associated concept of anomie, would clearly be relevant (Merton 1938): scams are after all attempts to achieve cultural financial success goals via illegitimate means, and in their contemporary Internet manifestations this might be thought to take place in a medium whose novelty has rendered norms of e-conduct comparatively attenuated or unclear (Wall 2005; Ogino 2007). Perhaps most obviously, routine activities, rational choice and opportunity theories are central in helping us to make sense of the links between social and technological changes and the associated changing pattern of crimes of misrepresentation and deceit (Cohen and Felson 1979; Felson 1994; Felson and Clarke 1998). As with cybercrimes (Wall 2005), what small amount of criminological discussion of scams there has been has tended to focus on offences rather than offenders, detailing the new ways offences are being committed rather than empirically investigating who is doing them in terms of their traits, backgrounds, socio-economic status, etc.

Responses to the crime

The OFT survey revealed that less than 5 per cent of victims in its sample had reported the scam to the authorities (the OFT, the police or local authority trading standards services). This low level of reporting matches the similarly low reporting of the overlapping category of Internet victimisation (Wall 2005). The usual complaints-driven processes of law enforcement agencies seem inadequate in this field. In addition to reasons of embarrassment mentioned above, victims do not report scams because they feel it is not worth taking any action or enforcement agencies will not be interested or will not be able to do anything about the problem. This is especially so if individual losses have been small and in fact is a reasonably accurate interpretation of police response to complaints in such cases. Enforcement agencies need to take account of this, moving beyond discounting as unimportant individual cases where small losses have been incurred towards linking all of these individual losses together to create a picture of a network of victimisation in which a single scammer or group of scammers may have substantially profited overall (Wall 2007a: ch. 8).

Responsibilisation strategies have formed the most obvious reply to the continuing encroachment of scams into everyday life. One finds a strong line of rhetoric in this field which aims to 'raise public awareness' (Smith and Akman 2008) among consumers rather than solve the problem of scams at source, as it were. Thus, it is suggested that 'consumers are their own best defence against scams' (Smith 2007). The OFT ran a 'Scams Awareness Month' in February 2007, and again in February 2008, aimed at educating consumers about the various risks. This approach fits with a general progression towards responsibilisation of populations in relation to crime prevention generally, but it also recognises that the number of scammers, their location in other legal jurisdictions and the difficulty of tracking them through their correspondence all make the task of cracking down on this category of criminals through arrest and prosecution extremely difficult. Nonetheless, the major difficulty with responsibilisation strategies is in encouraging people to look out for themselves where some people are not able to do this.

Some scams may be so 'serious and complex' that they fall within the Serious Fraud Office's investigation remit: an independent government department that investigates serious and complex fraud, with jurisdiction over England, Wales and Northern Ireland. More often, however, consumer scams are not dealt with by the SFO, nor do they usually merit the attention of the Serious and Organised Crime Agency (Levi 2008b). Scams are another area (like fakes: see Chapter 7 in this volume) in which enforcement rests for the most part in the hands of a range of regulatory bodies. The main relevant UK bodies that deal with consumer scams are trading standards services, the OFT and the Advertising Standards Agency, and there also exists an International Consumer Protection and Enforcement Network, which draws together regulatory agencies in different countries. In 2005 the OFT set up a Scambusters team (and website) together with a Scams Enforcement Group with partner organisations, focusing on 'law enforcement, consumer education and co-operation with private sector businesses to disrupt scammers' routes to market'. It has also set up a consumer helpline, Consumer Direct, which offers advice and assistance in relation to consumer frauds and other issues but does not take legal action against traders. As with many other business-related crimes and unethical practices, scams are of more interest to the Department of Trade and Industry than the Ministry of Justice, producing an institutional structure which makes effective governance of scams as a criminal issue somewhat harder to achieve. Other bodies, besides the police, can and do exert control functions through their places in the infrastructure used to transmit scam adverts and invitations. For instance, in the case of Internet scams these organisations will include ISPs and 'virtual environment security managers' who police behaviour and representations in specific Internet domains, such as chatrooms and bulletin boards, over which they have control (Wall 2007b).

The regulatory agencies involved tend towards a compliance model of enforcement in their work: prosecution tends only to ensue if initial warnings and requests for cessation are ignored or undertakings given by the subject of regulation are breached. Such compliance strategies are quite usual in the regulation of business conduct (Cranston 1979; Croall 1988; Braithwaite 1993). An example of such an outcome can be seen in the results of the OFT's recent investigation into clairvoyants. All sorts of outlandish claims were found in advertisements placed by clairvoyants, including that people who responded to an advert would 'in the next few days … have the very tidy sum of £169,000 in your possession', and that the homes of recipients of a mailing had been 'booby trapped by negative waves'. The OFT response was to write letters to the 'clairvoyants' concerned, drawing attention to the 'potentially misleading content of their mailings' (OFT 2007).

There is a wide range of legal provisions potentially applicable to the regulation of scams. In addition to the Fraud Act 2006, notable among these are the Consumer Protection (Cancellation of Contracts Concluded away from Business Premises) Regulations 1987 (the 'doorstep selling regulations', which provide a seven-day cooling off period for such sales and require sellers to notify buyers about it in writing at the time of sale), the Control of Misleading Advertisements Regulations 1988, the Lotteries and Amusements Act 1976 (all unauthorised lotteries are unlawful) and the Enterprise Act 2002 (gives increased powers to enforcement bodies to obtain undertakings from, and court orders against, traders in relation to a range of scam-type consumer issues).

As well as prosecution in a minority of cases, tools available to regulatory bodies in terms of these statutes include injunctions (i.e. court orders to stop doing something). The Enterprise Act 2002 is particularly interesting in that it addresses to a limited extent the perennial problems of jurisdiction which are met by enforcement agencies in relation to transnational or global crimes such as scams which have their origin in one country but their effects in others. The 2002 Act gives the OFT and some other enforcers the power to take action against businesses in other European countries where those businesses are infringing certain European-based consumer protection laws. The OFT used this power for the first time in 2004, successfully obtaining an injunction from a Belgian court against a Belgian trader which had targeted UK consumers with misleading catalogue sales leading consumers to believe they would be guaranteed a cash prize when in fact they were only entered into a draw.

In the end, the number of agencies charged with dealing with aspects of scamming leaves victims unsure which to contact. They tend either not to report at all, or to go to an organisation they see as offering some tangible benefit, such as their bank or insurance company. The police and other legal regulators such as the OFT are not always made aware of these cases of scamming (especially where they reveal some potentially embarrassing weakness in a bank's security systems, for example). Situational crime prevention is also used – for Internet scams, spam filters might be an example of this – but currently the massive rise in invitations to be scammed seems to be viewed as an acceptable, if unfortunate, cost of better communication systems.

Conclusion

We have seen that some scams try to perform illegal acts of fraud and theft while masquerading as legal enterprises. Perhaps the most effective scams, however, are those which so closely skirt the line between what is lawful and what is not that they succeed in contravening popular or institutional moral standards without breaking the law. We might call such activities 'borderline legal' insofar as they tend to purposively identify the point at which a profitable activity becomes illegal and aim their operations as close to that line as possible. Sometimes, indeed, they will cross the line, and often this is because they have identified that although a certain action is technically illegal, it is impossible or highly unlikely that it will be prosecuted in practice. There is an interesting line of literature studying such 'illicit but not illegal' activity (Passas and Goodwin 2004; Passas 2005; McBarnet 2003, 2006). Operating in a purely rational and effectively entirely amoral relationship with the law is revealed in these studies to be a core value of late modern capitalist business models.

Climate change, for example, has proven a ripe environment for scamming. Global warming has resulted in the establishment of many new institutional frameworks which, not unexpectedly, have been exploited for profit in ways which rather obviously contravene their spirit. One example of this is the so-called 'splash and dash' scam which exploits US agricultural subsidies. At the time of writing, the US grants a subsidy of 11p a litre to biofuel exports to the EU. Agricultural trading firms exploit this subsidy by shipping biodiesel from Europe to the US, where a 'dash' of US fuel is added to the mix. The new 'blended' biofuel is then shipped back to Europe for use and the subsidy is claimed on the whole batch. This operation is legal but clearly contravenes the spirit of the green ideal of biofuels.

More generally, we might observe that the psychology and sociology employed by scams from the days of the big con to the onset of consumer Internet fraud bears a close parallel to sales techniques used in legitimate commerce. Current advertising and PR plays very strongly on concepts key to scams: the idea of something for nothing, of getting a bargain, of a super-product that will solve a range of problems in one go and at a discount price, available for one week only, while stocks last, pseudo-health products, oil companies that pretend to be the front line in environmental regeneration, politicians who pretend to be on everyone's side at once. These techniques and representations can clearly be seen to be geared to encouraging certain emotional responses from their 'marks': trust, deference to someone who seems to know more about the situation than you do, reassurance that your grifter is really on your side all the way, a sense of urgency in closing the deal. We are all widely scammed, so much so that the line between licit and illicit in relation to the hustles and shakedowns we encounter each day becomes sometimes quite hard to discern: in accepting this legitimate face of current aggressive PR and marketing techniques we make it more difficult to discern a truly criminal scam when it presents itself, since we have become immunised in some measure to sharp and misleading business practice. Winning a mark's confidence remains a technique central to the working of our social world at all levels.

Selected further reading

For an entertaining and informative introduction to the routines of US con-men during the heyday of the 'big store', David Maurer's *The Big Con* (1940) is guaranteed to hook the reader with its highly detailed description of these scams presented in the fraudsters' own colourful jargon, in an ethnographic vein. Among Levi's many writings on fraud, some of the most important for students of scams are his (2005) chapter on 'International fraud' in Mangai Natarajan's textbook *Introduction to International Criminal Justice*, his (2008a) chapter on 'Financial crimes' in Michael Tonry's *Handbook on Crime and Public Policy*, and his research with others for the Association of Chief Police Officers on the 'Nature, extent and economic impact of fraud in the UK' (Levi *et al.* 2007). Neal Shover's two journal articles, with colleagues, on telemarketing (2003, 2004) are instructive subjective accounts of the sociological and psychological forces which normalise deviance or exert pressure on people to offend in a contemporary context. Useful resources on the web for scams include the websites of the Office of Fair Trading at http://www.oft.gov.uk and the Australian Institute of Criminology at http://www.aic.gov.au.

Note

1 Current e-mail scams share an architecture with the big cons here, whereby manifold minor variants and twists are applied to only a very few basic models of the con.

References

Braithwaite, J. (1993) 'Responsive regulation in Australia', in P. N. Grabosky and J. Braithwaite (eds), *Business Regulation and Australia's Future*. Canberra: Australian Institute of Criminology, pp. 81–96.

Clark, C. and Pinch, T. (1992) 'The anatomy of a deception: fraud and finesse in the mock auction sales "con"', *Qualitative Sociology*, 15 (2): 151–75.

Cohen, L. E. and Felson, M. (1979) 'Social change and crime rate trends: a routine activity approach', *American Sociological Review*, 44: 588–608.

Cranston, R. (1979) *Regulating Business: Law and Consumer Agencies*. London: Macmillan.

Croall, H. (1988) 'Mistakes, accidents, and someone else's fault: the trading offender in court', *Journal of Law and Society*, 15 (3): 293–315.

Doocy, J., Shichor, D., Sechrest, D. and Geis, G. (2001) 'Telemarketing fraud: who are the tricksters and what makes them trick?', *Securities Journal*, 14: 7–26.

Duffield, G. and Grabosky, P. N. (2001) *The Psychology of Fraud*, Trends and Issues in Crime and Criminal Justice No. 199. Canberra: Australian Institute of Criminology.

Felson, M. (1994) *Crime and Everyday Life*. Thousand Oaks, CA: Pine Forge Press.

Felson, M. and Clarke, R. V. (1998) *Opportunity Makes the Thief: Practical Theory for Crime Prevention*, Police Research Series Paper 98. London: Policing and Reducing Crime Unit, Home Office.

Goffman, E. (1959) 'On cooling the mark out: some aspects of adaptation to failure', *Psychiatry*, 15: 451–63.

Grabosky, P. N., Smith, R. G. and Dempsey, G. (2001) *Electronic Theft: Unlawful Acquisition in Cyberspace*. Cambridge: Cambridge University Press.

Holtfreter, K., Reisig, M. and Pratt, T. (2008) 'Low self-control, routine activities and fraud victimization', *Criminology*, 46 (1): 189–220.

Katz, J. (1988) *Seductions of Crime: Moral and Sensual Attractions in Doing Evil*. New York: Basic Books.

Levi, M. (1981) *The Phantom Capitalists: The Organisation and Control of Long-firm Fraud*. London: Heinemann.

Levi, M. (1987) *Regulating Fraud: White-collar Crime and the Criminal Process*. London: Tavistock.

Levi, M. (1993) *The Investigation, Prosecution, and Trial of Serious Fraud*, Royal Commission on Criminal Justice Research Study No. 14. London: HMSO.

Levi, M. (ed.) (1999) *Fraud: Organization, Motivation and Control*. Brookfield, VT: Ashgate.

Levi, M. (2003) 'Organising and controlling payment card fraud: fraudsters and their operational environment', in M. Gill (ed.), *Managing Security*. Leicester: Perpetuity Press.

Levi, M. (2005) 'International fraud', in M. Natarajan (ed.), *Introduction to International Criminal Justice*. New York: McGraw-Hill.

Levi, M. (2006) *Sentencing Frauds: A Review*. Paper commissioned by the Government Fraud Review. London: Legal Secretariat to the Law Officers.

Levi, M. (2008a) 'Financial crimes', in M. Tonry (ed.), *Handbook on Crime and Public Policy*. New York: Oxford University Press.

Levi, M. (2008b) 'Organized fraud and organizing fraud: unpacking research on networks and organization', *Criminology and Criminal Justice*, 8 (4): 379–409.

Levi, M. (2008c) *The Phantom Capitalists: The Organisation and Control of Long-firm Fraud*, 2nd edn. Aldershot: Ashgate.

Levi, M., Burrows, J., Fleming, M. H. and Hopkins, M. (2007) *The Nature, Extent and Economic Impact of Fraud in the UK*. Report for the Association of Chief Police Officers' Economic Crime Portfolio. London: ACPO.

McBarnet, D. (2003) 'When compliance is not the solution but the problem: from changes in law to changes in attitude', in V. Braithwaite (ed.), *Taxing Democracy: Understanding Tax Avoidance and Evasion*. Aldershot: Ashgate.

McBarnet, D. (2006) 'After Enron will "whiter than white collar crime" still wash?', *British Journal of Criminology*, 46 (6): 1091–109.

Maurer, D. W. (1940) *The Big Con: The Story of the Confidence Man and the Confidence Game*. New York: Bobbs-Merrill.

Merton, R. K. (1938) 'Social structure and anomie', *American Sociological Review*, 3: 672–82.

Muscat, G., James, M. and Graycar, A. (2002) *Older People and Consumer Fraud*, Trends and Issues in Crime and Criminal Justice No. 220. Canberra: Australian Institute of Criminology.

OFT (2006) *Research on Impact of Mass Marketed Scams: A Summary of Research into the Impact of Scams on UK Consumers*, Report No. 883. London: Office of Fair Trading.

OFT (2007) *A Gloomy Picture Predicted for Clairvoyants*. Office of Fair Trading Online at: http://www.oft.gov.uk/news/press/2007/18-07 (accessed 5 June 2008).

Ogino, M. (2007) *Scams and Sweeteners: A Sociology of Fraud*. Melbourne: Trans-Pacific Press.

Passas, N. (2005) 'Lawful but awful: "legal corporate crimes"', *Journal of Socio-economics*, 34: 771–86.

Passas, N. and Goodwin, N. R. (eds) (2004) *It's Legal But It Ain't Right: Harmful Social Consequences of Legal Industries*. Ann Arbor, MI: University of Michigan Press.

Pratkanis, A. and Shadel, D. (2005) *Weapons of Fraud: A Sourcebook for Fraud Fighters*. Seattle, WA: AARP Washington.

Shover, N., Coffey, G. S. and Hobbs, D. (2003) 'Crime on the line: telemarketing and the changing nature of professional crime', *British Journal of Criminology*, 43: 489–505.

Shover, N., Coffey, G. S. and Sanders, C. R. (2004) 'Dialling for dollars: opportunities, justifications, and telemarketing fraud', *Qualitative Sociology*, 27 (1): 59–75.

Smith, R. G. (2007) *Consumer Scams in Australia: An Overview*, Trends and Issues in Crime and Criminal Justice No. 331. Canberra: Australian Institute of Criminology.

Smith, R. G. and Akman, T. (2008) *Raising Public Awareness of Consumer Fraud in Australia*, Trends and Issues in Crime and Criminal Justice No. 349. Canberra: Australian Institute of Criminology.

Smith, R. G., Holmes, M. N. and Kauffman, P. (1999) *Nigerian Advance Fee Fraud*, Trends and Issues in Crime and Criminal Justice No. 121. Canberra: Australian Institute of Criminology.

Stevenson, R. J. (2000) *The Boiler Room and Other Telephone Scams*. Chicago: University of Illinois Press.

Sykes, G. M. and Matza, D. (1957) 'Techniques of neutralisation: a theory of delinquency', *American Sociological Review*, 22: 664–70.

Trahan, A., Marquart, J. and Mullings, J. (2005) 'Fraud and the American dream: towards an understanding of fraud victimization', *Deviant Behavior*, 26: 601–20.

Wall, D. S. (2005) 'The Internet as a conduit for criminals', in A. Pattavina (ed.), *Information Technology and the Criminal Justice System*. Thousand Oaks, CA: Sage.

Wall, D. S. (2007a) *Cybercrime: The Transformation of Crime in the Information Age*. Cambridge: Polity.

Wall, D. S. (2007b) *Hunting, Shooting and Phishing: New Cybercrime Challenges for CyberCanadians in the 21st Century*. The Second Eccles Centre for American Studies Plenary Lecture given at the British Association of Canadian Studies Annual Conference 2007. London: British Library.

Weisburd, D., Waring, E. and Chayet, E. (2001) *White-collar Crime and Criminal Careers*. New York: Cambridge University Press.

Chapter 9

Credit fraud

Michael Levi

Introduction

In this chapter, we will examine some aspects of fraud involving the criminal use of credit. Some facets of this are intriguing but very under-researched, for example frauds in which criminals obtain credit from each other to purchase illegal drugs or other commodities for which they have no intention of paying or for which they are unable to pay when 'stuff happens' (e.g. the drugs or money are confiscated by the police or fellow criminals) and then lie to defer payment. Others are somewhat better studied, such as 'identity fraud' (Semmens this volume). But in general such frauds lie at the blue-collar end of the 'white-collar crime' spectrum, often involving the active manipulation of expectations and perceptions, but sometimes merely exploiting the routines of commerce, for example when using someone else's credit card or credit card number to buy goods. Whether we are individuals or banks, it would be very hard to function in contemporary society if we needed to verify every single act of commerce on the assumption that it could be fraudulent. Most of the chapter will be concerned with how people commit frauds involving use of credit and how they organise themselves to do so, but we will also more briefly examine the control process – both commercial and criminal justice – and show how this interacts with levels and organisation of credit crimes. Finally, we should note that *fraud* is only one mechanism through which lenders of money, and vendors of goods who offer credit facilities, can lose their money. Risk of credit loss and its management have always been built into this process since the earliest times, and we have seen in the financial collapses of 2007–9 how critical credit is to the lubrication of everyday life: without some level of trust that people and institutions are both willing and able to repay, commerce is impossible on the scale of late modern life.

It is helpful to think of the tasks that need to be performed to commit major frauds (and other serious crimes) over a long period, most of these tasks being as easily accomplished at a local level as transnationally. These are as follows:

1 Obtain finance for crime.

2 Find people willing and technically/socially competent to commit frauds (though it may not always be necessary to find people who know that these are crimes).

3 Obtain equipment and transportation necessary to commit the frauds.

4 Convert, where necessary, products of crime into money or other usable assets.

5 Find people and places willing to store proceeds (and perhaps transmit and conceal their origin).

6 Neutralise law enforcement by technical skill, by corruption and/or by legal arbitrage, using legal obstacles to enforcement operations and prosecutions which vary between states.

Although fraud is often depicted as crime caused by ill-defined 'globalisation', the activity goes back centuries and has been criminalised for centuries (Levi 2008a).

During the past 70 years, since the end of the first phase of the 'professional crime' and 'white-collar crime' traditions Sutherland tried to stimulate in his books *The Professional Thief* and *White-Collar Crime*, 'crime as work' has been a largely neglected part of the criminological enterprise. Where a form of behaviour is considered to present 'acceptable risks' and is hard and expensive to eliminate without impacting significantly on the core marketing functions of commercial organisations, it will be tolerated, however much companies may prefer to do without it. In other words, in the terminology of situational crime prevention, 'increasing the risks for offenders' might not always be possible cost-effectively and – in the absence of any strong governmental/police interest in reducing opportunities to defraud as a matter of 'state interest' (except when tied to financing of terrorism) – companies are seldom interested in reducing crime for its own sake or even in reducing the risks for their competitors, an approach exacerbated by the tendency towards separate cost-centres within companies. Improvements in the professionalism of credit controllers, in the speed and breadth of commercial credit and in computer modelling of credit risks have reduced the opportunities for fast 'get credit and run' tactics that were so popular during the 1960s. However, as with other sorts of fraud such as plastic fraud, the skills to defraud are omnipresent and, if and when commercial controls are relaxed, they are likely to re-emerge, if not to the same extent. Moreover, it is never possible to eliminate the 'slippery-slope' fraudster who simply carries on trading at the risk of his or her creditors, hoping without realistic foundation – like Mr Micawber in Dickens' *David Copperfield* – that 'something will turn up', the something that *actually* turns up being large-scale insolvency.

Changes in any of these components will affect the level of fraud, as will the relative attractiveness of other methods of obtaining money, legal and illegal, which are within the perceived reach of potential offenders. The top-class fraudster is able to obtain goods on credit *and* avoid imprisonment; the middle-range fraudster succeeds on the first but not the second count; and the incompetent fraudster fails on both counts. I will focus here upon two forms of credit fraud: first, long-firm fraud – a kind of bankruptcy fraud involving companies obtaining credit when they do not intend to repay or are dishonestly reckless about the risks of non-repayment (Levi 2008a); and second, payment card fraud. Both of these forms of credit fraud create difficulties of identification and control by businesses, individuals and the criminal justice process. Criminal justice sees only a very small proportion of cases because of its low resourcing of fraud policing and mismatched inter-agency cooperation (Levi 1987; Doig 2006; Doig and Levi 2009); and because of the heavy resource implications the criminal justice process creates for those making reports. Instead, the latter 'manage the problem' on a commercial basis of appetite for risk, and filter into the courts only the clearest-cut cases that they wish to make symbolic display of to 'send a message' to offenders and present some downside consequences for criminal attempts. Although identity theft and fraud create alarm requiring a response from 'reassurance policing' (and the purchase of services to alert consumers to possible compromise of their credit facilities) – connecting them to 'fear of crime' issues (Levi 2009a) – frauds against card issuers and industrial companies almost never generate the moral panic seen in the more spectacular 'widows and orphans' frauds in savings and investments (Levi 2009b).

Long-firm fraud

Financing and setting up long-firm fraud

As will be discussed later in the chapter, both the techniques and the kinds of people involved in 'long-firm' fraud have changed considerably over the years – as seen, for example, in the growing use of the Internet, and in the increasing involvement of 'respectable' business people without previous convictions or 'gangster' connections. However, some of the basic elements of the activity remain constant. By contrast with credit card fraud, the establishment or purchase of a firm that will obtain large quantities of goods on credit requires some start-up capital for the business and for initial purchases, as well as sufficient funds for maintenance of lifestyle before the fraud comes to fruition. Success at obtaining goods on credit may be attained in a number of ways but there are two essential components to this process: first, the provision of a confidence-inspiring front for the fraud; and second, the negotiation of credit within the framework provided by this front.

From the fraudster's perspective, the ideal long-firm fraud is one that does not require the manufacture of a 'front', for example a company with a good established credit rating. For then, the fraudster can allow the reputation of the company to provide him (or, very rarely, even during the 2000s, and almost non-existent in the 1960s and 1970s, her) with credit without his having to do anything further in the way of specific confidence trickery. Some long-firm fraudsters are fortunate enough to be generously financed, sometimes by means of tax-evaded funds from professional people in search of profitable activities that beat inflation, perhaps even stimulated by contact with the illicit (at least until they are defrauded in turn!); others must work on shoestring budgets.

We begin with an account of the kinds of long-firm fraud most prevalent in the early and mid-1960s, when the most common technique – practised by the Kray and Richardson gangs in London – was the setting up of a number of apparently independent but actually linked companies (Levi 2008a). These companies might all be trading companies, or some might exist solely on paper: for the price of £25 each, any number of companies could be bought 'off the shelf' with 'no questions asked' from agencies specialising in company formation. By 2009, the price had risen with inflation, but Internet adverts offer 'Same day company start-up for £32.00: new limited companies establishment usually completed in 4–6 hours using electronical companies registration software' (http://www.ukincorp.co.uk/); a 'standard ready-to-trade package' including minutes of first board meeting costs £59.90; or a 'business package' including guaranteed bank account 'no interviews … we do everything' costs £199.90 (https://www.easyformations.net/form/1-prduct.asp, all accessed 18 January 2009). Incorporation elsewhere could rise to thousands of pounds: the price is a function of the level of secrecy from the authorities offered by the 'offshore finance centre' (sometimes described as 'tax haven'), and companies can still be bought with few or no questions asked from firms advertising weekly in *The Economist*, in the *International Herald Tribune*, in airline magazines and on the Internet. Due to changes driven by anti-money laundering and financing of terrorism legislation, some verification of identity is legally required, but these are not always checked out in great depth, especially for companies and their beneficial owners (i.e. the people who *really* control the firms).

Continuities and discontinuities in establishing credit: the arts of deception

In the simpler type of operation, the 'front man'[1] – recruited from underworld or commercial contacts – would be installed in rented or leased accommodation and would order goods from lists of suppliers who advertise in trade directories or from those mentioned by other fraudsters as a 'good touch'. If asked for a reference regarding his creditworthiness, he would refer a supplier to his own 'paper' companies.

These 'paper' companies might be real trading companies – perhaps indeed other frauds in the same group – or they might exist purely on paper, operating from accommodation addresses such as (then) newsagents or (now) offices, sometimes with fancy addresses, or from rooms rented by fraudsters as 'mail drops'. The mail would be collected and brought to the main premises and the trader would write out the references himself. One small firm with a paid-up capital of £2 – still the legal minimum in 2009 – at the beginning of the 1960s was provided with the following 'in-house' reference: 'Have dealt with this firm for five years, and have always found them very prompt payers and very reliable. I would consider them good for credit up to £5,000.' This very crude effort was often successful at that time, because few firms had any sophisticated form of credit control or were sensitised to the possibility of their being defrauded. However, even then, a credit inquiry agency might well have picked up the similarity in the typeface used in the references, check the dates of registration of the companies involved and check the places of work of the referees. In these circumstances, the 'front' would prove inadequate to withstand the most superficial checks and there would be clear evidence of deception if the fraudsters were caught. However, they would generally use false names and fingerprinting was not at that time standard in police investigations of fraud. Consequently, unless the police were alerted during the operation of the fraud, the chances of escaping unidentified were quite high. The more subtle operator, again within this basic technique, would use different typewriters, have headed notepaper printed for each firm by a different printer, and give a more sensible estimate of the creditworthiness of his trading firm than the one quoted above. In this way he would hope to pass the superficial scrutiny of investigators, and since he often obtained the typewriters and printing on credit, he would have to pay out little more than the crude fraudster. Even now, though large commercial credit bureaux such as Dun & Bradstreet, Experian and Equifax have large, computerised databases which can quickly cross-correlate references and check whether the telephone number corresponds to the firm and/or the location given (mobile phone numbers being suspect because they are not tied to any particular area), such deceptions remain possible, though harder. Moreover, the advent of multi-font computers has made the visual detection of self-referencing (similar typefaces on the same paper) much harder, provided that the offenders are disciplined: forensic laboratories might be able to pick up the similarities, but this is of little use to commercial debtors who have to make rapid decisions and would seldom be willing to pay a substantial sum for such technical advice when the ratio of frauds to genuine trades is so low.

If the fraudster was part of, or had access to, a wider circle of 'villains', he might extend this technique of self-reference-writing to a number of *actual* trading firms. The organiser or organisers would buy anything up to six 'off the peg' companies (or, if the price was right, existing trading companies). Each company would write to or telephone creditors, giving the other companies as referees, and in this way, a chain of long-firm frauds could be created. Although this method had the advantage over the cruder ones that the integrity of the would-be debtor could not be falsified simply by physical examination of the business premises of the referees, it had the disadvantage that it provided clear evidence of conspiracy to defraud if the police were able to detect the perpetrators (and if the crime was perceived and reported as such).

In order to surmount these 'little legal difficulties', the more subtle operators adopted two refinements. First, they would carry out 'dummy' transactions between the companies, so that there would be a record of trading to which they could refer the police for 'authentication' of the references. All of these transactions would be purely paper ones: they would not relate to any actual transfer of goods which such payments would normally represent, but this fact could not be (in)validated unless the police or some other body were conducting contemporaneous surveillance or could get an insider to turn

Queen's Evidence against the other conspirators. Secondly, operators would give slightly more ambiguous references, such as 'I have done business with the owner of this firm for a number of years, and I feel sure that he would not enter into any transaction which he would be unable to fulfil.' References such as this might make it difficult to prove a substantive deception.

In the early 1960s, a large number of such cross-referenced frauds were operated by people connected with the Kray and Richardson gangs, both inside and outside London. Their normal practice was to set up the companies in mid or late summer, pay the first few bills in cash, and gradually to increase orders 'for the Christmas trade', thus mirroring the patterns of trading of legitimate businesses. Then, as Christmas approached, there would be a large increase in orders, the goods would be sold virtually overnight and the premises closed down. The timing of the frauds was done in this way because it provided a 'normal' context in which large orders could be justified and goods could easily be resold as part of the pre-Christmas spending spree. This technique continues to the present day, since its underlying logic remains: the more enthusiastic the supplier to maximise sales or the more desperate the victim is to unload the stock – particularly in a depressed retailing climate – the less likely they are to look carefully at the 'borrower', since the opportunity cost of rejecting the 'sale' rises under such circumstances.

The cross-referencing technique was (and to a lesser extent still is) normally used for relatively small operations, but was and is sometimes used in the larger ones. They may be operated in two basic forms: first, the owner of the business builds it up and then extends his credit in the classic long-firm manner; and second, the organiser of the fraud builds up his business 'as if' it were legitimate, resigns as director in favour of his 'front man', and gets the long firm to 'take off' under his *covert* control. The objective here is for the organiser to disclaim culpability, given that his or her involvement in the firm is unlikely to be known to the police (without informant leaks) or, even if the police become aware, prior business and criminal records will not be communicated to the jury.

Where they have bought a legitimate business, the organisers usually attempt to conceal from the suppliers the fact that there has been a change in control. Sometimes they are able to persuade the vendor to stay on in an advisory capacity, 'to help them find their way around the business'. Sometimes fraudsters put in their own 'front man' with the same name as the vendor, who claims to be a relative. In most cases, to give the impression of continuity, they keep on existing staff in all departments save that of accounts. They might try to find ways of getting the vendor to delay informing Companies House of the change in ownership, or indeed tying in the previous owner to help to make the firm 'a success'. In some large travel agency frauds, people looking to retire have been persuaded to be paid in instalments for their business and told by way of apparent reassurance that they don't need to hand over the company shares until the final instalment. Meanwhile, the business has been milked by the fraudsters with liberally issued tickets and fraud upon the cards of holidaymakers, and creditors do not know anything is wrong because no notification has been made to Companies House about a change in ownership. In e-crime, this would be labelled 'social engineering', but it is the essence of the offline fraudster's art. As McIntosh (1975) argues in a more general context, society creates the venue for its own victimisation: in this instance, trade newspapers advertising businesses for sale provide the opportunity, and when their owners are trying to get out, they tend not to be 'capable guardians'. The fraudster is literally a 'phantom capitalist', for his capital is wholly illusory, an entity woven into the imagination of his suppliers.

The final category of 'fronts' comprises firms which are run for a period of time in a respectable fashion before their owners turn them into long firms. These may have been wholly straight firms, part-time 'fences' of long-firm goods which can be merged into their normal stock, or built up from the start with the intention of being turned into long firms. Whatever the case, the credit rating will have been generated by earlier trading experiences with the long firm itself in its legitimate or pseudo-legitimate phase, and the fraudster makes use of the unwillingness of creditors to suspect people whom they know. For example, when business people seek to delay payment, their creditors will question them about their reasons for delay in such a manner that they seem to be seeking reassurance rather than conflict or the turning down of orders (perhaps especially in recessionary times, when firms are desperate for customers). Tales of 'phoenix' companies where different firms rise from the ashes of the old, with the same owners and even similar names, are regularly imparted as 'sad tales' on consumer programmes, reflecting the anonymity offered to traders in a larger-scale urban society in late modernity.

Since the 1990s, bankers – especially in headquarters fraud and security departments – have become very wary of 'funny money' scams generally, partly as a consequence of money-laundering requirements (see Hicks this volume; Levi and Reuter 2006). But these understandings may not be trans-mitted perfectly throughout the banking system to local managers, even though in an economic climate of risk aversion to loans, managers who 'screw up' may find themselves higher in the redundancy queue. As banking has been depersonalised by the widespread use of credit scoring and tighter loan limits, corrupt or misled discretion by managers has been reduced, but there is still some scope in the area of business lending and, if the fraudsters do not want to borrow money from the bank, the scope for deception remains. In still more sophisticated instances, stolen shares and bonds are used as collateral against bank loans since not all banks always check the standing of such certificates, but more commonly may be used to create an illusion of affluence by the customer by *not* using them as collateral, thereby reducing the risk of exposure to the bank and of their reporting the matter to the police. Banker awareness has increased, not least because false collateral may be used by the customer to inveigle the bank into unwittingly providing legitimacy for 'advance fee fraud' on other customers. Foreign banks can be used to delay payments, since they are outside the clearing system, but by the late 1990s, harmonisation of regulatory controls and anti-laundering provisions made it harder to start up or buy crooked banks in Western Europe.

However, these developments in financial services regulation trouble the long-firm fraudster very little since there is almost no control over who may set up in business and transfer liability to the company. All s/he must do is to tell a good story, and this is done both to banks and to trade victims in a way that has witnessed few changes in the past thirty years as each new set of potential victims seeks to make its sales and in turn is lured into false optimism. For example, in the late 1960s, a man with an American accent arrived at a South Wales coastal resort and announced that he represented an American syndicate (*sic*!) which wished to purchase a leisure and amusement arcade in the town. He offered a generous price, which was accepted gratefully by the owners. Unfortunately, however, there was a small snag preventing immediate completion: the money was temporarily tied up. However, he asked the owners if, pending completion of the sale, they would allow him to order goods for the coming season; this request was acceded to, the owners even going so far as to give him their headed notepaper to use in ordering. He wrote off to a number of suppliers as if he already owned the arcades and obtained some £350,000 (at historic prices) worth of fancy goods, toiletries and groceries on credit. One night all of these goods were covertly taken away and the man disappeared for good. His identity was never discovered. Such scams would be quite feasible today, though more information about people's backgrounds is available on the Internet than was the case then, an example of how globalisation and electronic surveillance *could* cut crime opportunities rather than increase them.

In order to be successful, fraudsters have to adapt their techniques to the methods of control: they have to simulate the style of the sharp business person and yet obtain large quantities of goods. Some trade representatives, however commission-hungry they may be, will not sell goods to people who appear to them to order recklessly, for this is a sign that payment is not intended; others are not so particular, especially when they are under pressure to hit sales targets. In many cases, representatives do not seem to question why a firm should want such large quantities of their products and believe that they have 'pulled a fast one' over on the purchasers. This 'kidology' is part of the long-firm fraudster's tradecraft.

A further crucial aspect of skill is the way the long-firm merchant organises the 'fronting' of the fraud. Some prefer their 'front men' to use their own names, because this gives a better impression if the business is investigated and court proceedings ensue. In other cases, however, particularly when the 'front man' has a criminal record, elaborate measures are taken to build up a false identity which will withstand all but the most thorough scrutiny by the police and by credit inquiry agencies. The aim here is twofold: to generate a respectable image for the 'front man' and to make it difficult for him to be traced after the fraud has been carried out. Until 2008, it was easy to obtain a birth certificate in the name of a dead child and use this to develop a false identity: this loophole is now far more difficult to get through.

One organiser would find people who were prepared to front a fraud in their own names, start up a business and train them *in situ*. He would place a tape recorder in the office and get them to record every single conversation that they had, whether on the telephone or in person. At the end of the day the 'front man', making sure that he was not followed, would bring over the tapes and they would go over them in detail, pointing out mistakes and making suggestions for improvements in technique. The length of these evening classes depended upon the ability and experience of the 'front man'. In general, however, there is some coaching with regard to the market for the goods, trade jargon and other allied matters: the 'front man' has to appear to be a principal.

Banks, tradespeople and credit inquiry agents may ask the 'front man' about his previous business experience, so he may have to put on a very convincing cover story, though modern developments in electronic databases and computer searches make the generation of false fronts that will withstand examination substantially harder in the 2000s than in previous times. Where such cover is not readily available, there may have to be a false explanation for his taking up business, such as 'I have just come back from Zimbabwe: there's no future there any more for us whites.' However well he builds up a false identity though, he cannot be proof against chance contingencies which may penetrate his cover. It is the ability to withstand tests of cool and of character such as this which distinguishes classes of long-firm fraudster. It is a major element in their status system, as well as a source of considerable personal satisfaction.

Strategies to avoid arrest and conviction

The crudest strategy is simply to disappear, often overseas to a hard-to-penetrate jurisdiction such as Pakistan, PRC/Taiwan or the Middle East. The number of countries that are extradition-free has diminished over time (and most spectacularly in Europe), but there remain some in law and/or in practice.

More subtly, typically, goods are sold by ambiguous presentation; that is, the sale is accomplished by a gloss which relies on the fact that the purchaser will supply his own explanation of their origin ... With goods presented in this way, a person may feel morally free to go ahead and make a purchase. This ambiguous presentation is far easier to carry out in the case of long-firm (and many other) frauds than in more traditional types of property crime because the vendor has an apparently genuine trading concern and has a genuine title to the goods that he is selling. Even if goods are offered at below cost price, there are many circumstances in which traders do this quite lawfully, for example to get rid of unwanted stock when their cash flow is tight. In many cases, however, the goods are sold to people who do know that they are buying from a long firm and who are protected by false invoices. In many countries, throughout the last century, a false or genuine burglary, robbery or a fire is sometimes used as a means of hiding the true nature of the fraudulent enterprise; in Northern Ireland, it used to be put down to terrorist attacks, though this might attract unwelcome police interest. Burglary and truck hijacking have the advantage over arson that they require no capital outlay on the goods to be burned, but they can generate greater police suspicion than arson, particularly if the police are unable to pick up any trace of the allegedly stolen goods.

The final technique for avoiding conviction to be discussed here is the use of the voluntary liquidation to 'con' creditors. This is used only by the more sophisticated long-firm merchants and was particularly popular during the

1950s. After the mid-1970s, it gradually came to be replaced by the Individual Voluntary Agreement. The firm's deficiency will be explained by 'bad debts': the fraudster may arrange to receive cheques from a dummy company or even another long firm which conveniently bounce and remain unpaid. He may claim that a 'trusted employee' has disappeared with his funds or stock, or put the losses down to 'stock pilferage'. Finally, he may provide a rationale in the form of a fire or burglary, as mentioned above. Carried out with nerve and panache, and sometimes aided by corrupt insolvency practitioners (who now have to be licensed under the Insolvency Act 1986, for example as members of the Insolvency Practitioners Association), this can be a highly profitable and risk-free technique. Much later the creditors will find out that the stock is not worth the book value, but after all, valuation is a difficult matter and values change! Mostly, creditors will 'put it down to experience', unless the police intervene on their own initiative on the basis of information received elsewhere. Even if the police try to do something about the suspected fraud, they may be unable to find a complainant. The voluntary liquidation long firm requires the ability to handle creditors and others 'upfront' and the acceptance of a lower *percentage* profit than the cruder 'bust-out' techniques. However, it can combine profitability with relative safety to a degree that other modus operandi cannot.

The changing nature of long-firm and other credit frauds

In order to become a top-class long-firm fraudster, the skills described in this chapter have to be refined until they become almost 'second nature' to the person concerned. Top-class fraudsters can judge within moments the strengths and weaknesses of the people with whom they are dealing, can sense when one of their partners is trying to 'con' them, and can adjust their public persona to the environment in which they operate. They will have had to improvise schemes and stories for the benefit of creditors, backers, partners and 'front men': social skills for the human jungle. The skills that he or she must have vary according to the routines of social and economic control – for example, credit scoring has reduced discretion and therefore certain forms of fraud that depend on interpersonal skills – but the amount of pain caused by long-firm fraudsters to any one victim (however 'multiple') is usually modest and this conditions overall industry and police responses. In particular, the replacement of gangster-connected fraudsters – which attracted police interest in the 1960s and 1970s – by business people with no previous convictions for serious crime, combined with cutbacks in fraud squad strength, has reduced the likely downside risk from the criminal justice system, placing more of a burden upon the commercial sector. (The Metropolitan Police, for example, had a dedicated long-firm fraud section within the Fraud Squad into the 1980s: now there is no longer a Fraud Squad at all but rather a set of detectives and risk-managers in Specialist Crime Department 6 mainly involved in public-private partnership initiatives such as Operation Sterling.) Unlike shop thieves, long-firm fraudsters' pictures are seldom captured on CCTV on business premises (though they are as vulnerable as everyone in the UK to being 'captured' on public space CCTV), and they are more varied in their choice of victims and geographical areas of operation, so they are not amenable so readily to 'hot spot' prevention strategies. In the final analysis, their social skills also make raising the stakes harder, except where the estimated probability of being defrauded leads victim companies to make sufficiently frequent credit rating requests to trigger industry-wide judgments of suspiciousness. The chances of this happening are inhibited by the lack of long-term memory in most corporate credit divisions, leading to a cyclical pattern in which the lessons of the past have periodically to be relearned, since *unless one does happen to be defrauded*, credit status requests will always be more expensive than making judgments internally, and the system needs larger patterns of data to improve its predictive judgments of bankruptcy fraud. Contemporary long-firm frauds require more money and sophistication for build-ups than was the case before the 1980s, but there will always be scope for those who are bored by the routines of ordinary business struggles and prefer to defraud. They can always change their identities afterwards and do the same thing again.

Those businesses that during the 1960s and 1970s deceived their creditors on the basis that they needed larger orders to supply their expanding 'mail order' trade would now do the same on the basis that they have a booming Internet business. Thus Lithuanian or Russian fraudsters can use credit card numbers skimmed from unsuspecting cardholders to order hundreds of computers on the net from different suppliers, have them delivered to 'drop addresses' in the UK or the US and then forwarded to addresses elsewhere for resale – all of this before the cardholder and card issuer becomes aware that there is anything wrong. There are also large-scale credit card and loan 'bust outs' using people's own and stolen identities, and dishonest merchants who pass large quantities of fake (or genuine on stolen card) transactions through their commercial accounts, claim reimbursement from merchant acquirer card companies, and then disappear before the card issuer or cardholder realises that the frauds have happened (though this is more difficult since the introduction of Chip & PIN to European payment cards).

One significant change in the UK since the 1990s has been in the area of fraudulent corporate identities used to obtain credit in the name of real firms or in the name of similar-name firms. Among the more novel e-techniques (see Levi 2008a) were the following:

- Corporate hijack:
  - Criminals research existing genuine business and change directors' names and addresses without their knowledge by submitting correct but forged forms to Companies House, moving the registered office to their own nominated one.

  - Identity hijackers might appoint genuine people as directors without their knowledge as unaware 'front men': foreign or impecunious students are sometimes paid to sign company documents as directors but otherwise have no involvement in company activities.

- Phishing may be carried out by simulating/diverting genuine corporate websites and extracting information about corporate and individual users.

- Carousel frauds are committed defrauding HM Revenue and Customs by manipulating new or existing firms, sometimes known as Missing Trader Intra-Community (MTIC) frauds. In such cases, some firms reclaim the value-added tax they have allegedly paid, while the firms that were officially paid and owe the VAT to the government go 'bust'. The extent of this type of fraud was sufficient to raise serious questions over the validity of UK import-export statistics in 2004–5, with billions of pounds being lost in the UK alone. Following this, prevention measures were introduced and fraud levels dropped.

Corporate identity hijack can also be used as a gateway to other forms of identity fraud. Proof of a directorship could be used for a work permit, for benefit or as a form of token-based identifier. This could then be used to obtain a credit card or bank account, increasing the credibility of the false identity. Alternatively the company could provide worthless guarantees or references to allow the criminal access to property or other forms of finance.

Payment card and cheque fraud

Plastic card and cheque frauds take a wide range of different forms. The financial services industry has identified the principal forms of abuse. In relation to 'plastic cards' (credit or charge cards, debit cards and guaranteed cheque cards – as contrasted with cheques without cards or whose values exceed the guarantee limits), the main frauds are as follows:

- *Counterfeit card fraud* – involving cards that have been printed, embossed or encoded without permission from the issuer, or cards that have been validly issued and then altered or recoded. Most cases involve 'skimming', a process where the genuine data on a card's magnetic strip are electronically copied onto another, without the legitimate cardholder's knowledge.

- *Fraudulent possession of card details ('card-not-present' – CNP – frauds)* – carried out on the phone, or via mail order, fax or Internet transactions, where fraudulently obtained card details are used to make a purchase.

- *Fraud using lost and stolen cards* – which are generally carried out before the cardholder has reported the loss.

- *'Mail non-receipt' frauds* – carried out with new cards that have been intercepted before they reach the cardholder.

- *Identity theft fraud* – which tends to involve either 'application frauds', where a criminal uses stolen or false details to open an account in someone else's name, or 'account takeovers', where the offender masquerades as the genuine cardholder and uses the account as if it were their own.

In relation to cheques, the main frauds are as follows:

- *Counterfeiting of cheques* – i.e. the unauthorised manufacture of cheques that appear to be genuine.

- *Fraudulently altered cheques* – i.e. the changing of payment details such as payee or amount of cheque.

- *Forged cheques* – i.e. the imitation of signatures.

- *Withdrawal against uncleared effects* – sometimes known as 'kiting', in which conspirators issue cheques to each other and aim to draw against the accounts before the cheque has been cleared (or, in this case, has 'bounced').

- *Identity fraud* – in which counterfeit or stolen documentation is used to open an account or take over an existing account, and this account is used for non-plastic fraud (rather than for laundering the proceeds of drugs trafficking or for terrorist finance).

Plastic or payment card fraud is often treated as if it were a subset of 'identity fraud' (Home Office 2006) in ways that are not particularly helpful for clarity of problem definition. However, it is doubtful that frauds in which someone (a) steals a card or (b) copies the electronic data from the magnetic stripe onto another card, and then just uses it in a retail outlet should be properly regarded as 'identity fraud' or as 'identity theft'. The UK banking industry rightly does not regard it as such, differentiating this from the obtaining of new credit facilities by impersonation and the construction of completely false individual and corporate identities: 'Card ID theft occurs when a criminal uses a fraudulently obtained card or card details, along with stolen personal information, to open or take over a card account held in someone else's name' (APACS 2008: 17).

Table 9.1 shows a summary of the statistics and the number of fraud cases recorded by members of the not-for-profit fraud prevention body CIFAS during the first half of 2008, broken down by the type of fraud identified (see http://www.cifas.org.uk). Definitions are given as footnotes to the table.

In the payment card arena, tensions exist between the interests of card issuers, acquirers (who receive fees in exchange for early reimbursement to merchants of their card transactions), merchants, card schemes (principally Visa, MasterCard and American Express), cardholders and governmental regulators (the Financial Services Authority in the UK). The relationships between them, plus the effort and imagination of anti-fraud entrepreneurs, shapes the nature of the measures that are taken and the speed of their implementation. These patterns of control are not fixed over time and space, however, and the UK experience is instructive as a view of how opportunities to defraud can be reduced (see further Levi 2008b).

The replacement of 'traditional' card theft and use of stolen cards by card-not-present fraud reflects the ways in which the industry, responding to evidence on absolute and rising levels of fraud (Levi *et al.* 1991; Webb 1996; Levi and Handley 1998), introduced controls that have reduced conventional

Table 9.1 Summary of fraud statistics

	Jan to Dec 2007	Jan to Dec 2008	% change
Fraud cases identified	185,003	214,342	15.86
Financial benefit/losses avoided	£987,829,077	£848,304,084	−14.12
Identity fraud – granted	32,175	34,011	5.71
Identity fraud – not granted	45,418	43,631	−3.93
Identity fraud – total	77,593	77,642	0.06
Application fraud – granted	14,515	15,055	3.72
Application fraud – not granted	62,355	61,968	−0.62
Application fraud – total	76,870	77,023	0.02
False insurance claim	390	433	11.03
Facility takeover fraud	6,272	19,275	207.32
Asset conversion	478	522	9.21
Misuse of facility	23,400	39,447	68.58
Victims of impersonation	65,066	62,658	−3.70
Victims of takeover	6,106	19,290	215.92
Protective registrations	32,982	49,061	48.75

- *Fraud cases identified* refers to each proven instance of fraud identified by CIFAS members and filed to the CIFAS database. Members must have sufficient evidence to take the case to the police although it is not mandatory that they do so. A fraud case can involve multiple subjects and multiple addresses.
- *Financial benefits* refer to the amount of money that members of CIFAS reported that they have saved through being alerted to previous frauds by CIFAS warnings.
- *Identity fraud* is the use of a misappropriated identity in criminal activity to obtain goods or services by deception. This usually involves the use of stolen or forged identity documents such as a passport or driving licence. Identity fraud cases include cases of false identity and identity theft. Identity theft is the misappropriation of the identity (such as the name, date of birth, current address or previous addresses) of another person, without their knowledge or consent. These identity details are then used to obtain goods and services in that person's name.
- *Application fraud/false insurance claim* relates to applications or claims with material falsehood (lies) or false supporting documentation where the name has not been identified as false.
- *Facility takeover fraud* occurs where a person (the 'facility hijacker') unlawfully obtains access to details of the 'victim of takeover', namely an existing account holder or policy holder (or of an account or policy of a genuine customer or policy holder) and fraudulently operates the account or policy for his own (or someone else's) benefit.
- *Asset conversion* relates to the sale of assets subject to a credit agreement where the lender retained ownership of the asset (for example a car or a lorry).
- *Misuse of facility* is where an account, policy or other facility is used fraudulently.

card crime opportunities that were the softest targets with the largest share of losses before the twenty-first century. In 2006–7, total UK card fraud losses increased by 25 per cent to £535 million. However, the introduction of chip & PIN meant that losses on transactions on the UK high street have reduced by 67 per cent from £218.8 million in 2004 to £73.0m in 2007. Between 2006 and 2007, fraud arising from cards intercepted in the mail or after delivery dropped 34 per cent, and fraud on lost and stolen cards fell 18 per cent. By contrast, in 2007, counterfeit card fraud increased by 46 per cent to £144.3 million. However, illustrating the impact of globalisation on risk, counterfeit card fraud decreased by 32 per cent in 2006–7 within the UK, but the overall figure increased due to fraudsters copying UK cards and using these stolen cards in countries which do not yet have Chip & PIN. Card-not-present (CNP) fraud increased by 37 per cent compared with 2006. However, though since 2000, CNP losses have risen by 298 per cent, the vastly larger total value of online shopping transactions increased by 87 per cent. In 1997, CNP losses were £10 million; in 2007, they were £290.5 million. Altogether, in the UK, fraudulent transactions make up 0.12 per cent of all transactions, by value. So looking at frauds as a ratio of commerce and opportunities changes the way in which we look at this as a problem.

There is evidence of Chinese, Romanian, Russian and Italian Mafia involvement in plastic fraud – including counterfeiting factories and using their reputations for violence to pressurise merchants to process phoney or counterfeit card transactions through their stores. East European groups have performed some sophisticated operations involving interference with ATMs and 'spyhole' cameras to record PINs. There is also evidence of payment card fraud being used to fund the Sri Lankan LTTE ('Tamil Tigers') and some Islamic terrorist groups operating in the UK and elsewhere. However, there is no evidence that a great proportion of payment card fraud is organised on hierarchical lines or is a crucial component of terrorism financing overall (though if other sources of terrorist finance dry up, it may attain a greater significance in future). Indeed, even where many people are recruited and go out and use counterfeit cards or card data at the same time, there is no *need* for participants to be members of long-term groups. Inertia plays a part in how criminals behave, provided that their opportunities are not reduced or eliminated. Mativat and Tremblay (1997) suggested that Canadian Quebecois fraudsters were reluctant to shift from using stolen cards to altering cards, despite the ready availability of cheap and compact encoding and embossing equipment. Some offender techniques and profiles reviewed by Levi (1998) on the basis of offender and industry interviews have therefore become partly redundant. For many contemporary payment card fraudsters in Europe, the shift to Chip & PIN altered drastically their local crime opportunities and forced them to 'go international' or get out of the business altogether. Currently, the reluctance of North America and some other parts of the world to adopt Chip & PIN means that some opportunities remain even for 'card present' transactions, but the future technological battle lies in card-not-present transactions. In 2009, Visa Europe introduced a PINcard – a credit card with a 12-button keypad and a display powered by a battery that lasts up to three years. Users have to input their PIN every time they make an online purchase. The card then displays a security code, which must be entered into the website. If the code is authorised by Visa's servers, the purchase is approved. To place this in context, in Europe, there are over 350 million Visa debit, credit and commercial cards. In the year ending December 2007, those cards were used to make purchases and cash withdrawals to the value of over €1.3 trillion; 11.4 per cent of consumer spending at point of sale in Europe is with a Visa card. The rest of the market will doubtless follow suit, as technological prevention in one area concentrates losses in the others.

The response to fraud discussed here is mainly commercial, but since 2004, the UK banking industry has financed a special police unit – the Dedicated Cheque and Plastic Crime Unit (DCPCU) – which (with the Irish Garda Bureau of Fraud Investigation) won the 2008 European Investigation Unit of the Year award. The aim is to combat 'organised cheque and payment card fraud' – a term of art – and the reason it has been financed by the private sector is that there is insufficient confidence that these cases will be investigated by a police force stretched by other demands to hit the government's Key Performance Indicators, especially since banks themselves are not 'deserving victims' in populist policing campaigns. For both bankruptcy frauds and payment card frauds, criminal justice is a last rather than first resort, and technological risk profiling and monitoring is seen as the primary route for crime reduction. Indeed, it is arguable that for most credit crimes against most businesses and even against individuals, the issue is seen more as loss reduction than as crime reduction: creditors feel that they cannot afford to be too moralistic about issues that are not 'signal crimes' (Innes 2004) and must use the police – when willing and able – as an instrument to communicate to offenders a greater downside risk than merely their own variable investment in a failed attempt to defraud.

Investment frauds: a different form of credit

Whereas long-firm fraudsters had to be able to sell large quantities of goods to commercial purchasers (often without the latter knowing they were doing anything illegal, since they could give invoices, etc.), it is even more common now than it was then to commit investment frauds that require no such transformation of goods into money. Some of these scams on individuals are discussed by McKenzie (this volume) but a brief treatment follows. Telemarketers such as 'boiler room' operators develop 'sucker lists' of individuals who are deemed likely to fall for 'get rich quick', 'market-beating', 'inside track' investment schemes, which are then passed on to others in regular trading relationships, or to other salespeople in their own next 'boiler room' scheme, operating out of any jurisdiction with good telecommunications facilities and relatively inactive police or regulators. Sometimes e-mail is used but the personal touch from loosely scripted 'front men' on the phone or from people who infiltrate faith or other communities is preferable to fraudsters (see Holtfreter et al. 2008; Shover et al. 2003, 2004).

The most upmarket example of this was the case exposed in late 2008 involving Bernie Madoff, who stole over US $20 billion from mainly wealthy individuals and Jewish charities (including New York University). Such 'Ponzi' money tree or similar pyramid schemes, in which people are recruited from communities who improve their own income flows by recruiting others into the scheme, did exist in the 1960s and 1970s. However, the rise in disposable wealth, lump-sum retirement and redundancy schemes affecting large communities such as former miners and steelworkers, and the opening up of former Communist countries, most of whose citizens had little idea of how capitalism worked, have all contributed to the generation of target sectors for such schemes. In recent years such schemes have been observed in Albania, Romania and Colombia, with enormous losses and distress and some high-level political involvement. More common still are the outright '419' frauds most commonly associated with Nigerians, whether living there or in the multifarious places that they have settled overseas. Initial contacts used to be by letter, often using counterfeit postal stamps to reduce business costs. Nowadays our e-mail in-boxes are full of such invitations to assist the families of corrupt dictators who are deceased or in serious trouble, requiring our help to loan them our bank details to enable them to transfer the money, in return for which we will obtain a large percentage of the illicit millions. As far as one can tell, none of these schemes is genuine. Many of these offenders become fugitives, moving to other jurisdictions where media and police interest and sentences are low, or where there are ample corruption possibilities. Nigeria has an unenviable reputation as a location for fraud and corruption. However, with the creation of the Financial and Economic Crimes Commission in the aftermath of Nigeria's 'blacklisting' by the Financial Action Task Force, the Nigerian justice system has become more efficient and less corrupt over time. Its cooperation with other jurisdictions, for example with the UK Serious and Organised Crime Agency, has been significant in recent years. Nevertheless, the chances of successful action by victims – who are in effect often conspirators to commit bribery – are low. And the Nigerian police and justice system have no control over Nigerian fraudsters overseas.

The development of tax avoidance schemes and artificial tax-driven business locations has facilitated the credibility of strange addresses so that no one thought it odd that an Internet-only European Union bank with guaranteed 'discretion' towards tax authorities should be operating out of Antigua. (Sadly for its many tax-evading depositors, it was a complete scam: see Blum *et al*. 1998. Antigua itself was further rocked in February 2009 by *civil* and later *criminal* allegations by the US Securities and Exchange Commission of a $5 billion plus fraud by Sir Allen Stanford, a prominent Texan who had developed excellent relations with the previous Antiguan government, who conferred a knighthood upon him.) Technological changes in call and fax-forwarding, allied to the continuing use of multi-business 'accommodation addresses', means that without some GPS tracking system, actual or potential creditors have no idea whether the business people they are speaking to are in London or Lagos. On the basis of such deposits, credit is leveraged via the banking system into much larger total sums, with the sorts of catastrophic consequences noted in the economic recession of 2008. Though some 'reckless' lending may be later interpreted as fraudulent, however, it should not be concluded that credit and investment fraud is the principal cause of economic damage. Rather, long-firm and payment card frauds are at the lower end of a spectrum of economic conduct involving insolvency: crime is not the only route into economic hardship.

Selected further reading

Credit fraud is part of a much wider set of work on white-collar and organised crime motivations and career trajectories. The most direct (and almost the only) work on business credit fraud is my own: Levi (2008a) *The Phantom Capitalists: The Organisation and Control of Long-Firm Fraud*. On plastic fraud, McNally and Newman's (2008) *Perspectives on Identity Theft* is a useful collection.

The strongest works in the white-collar criminal career field arise from a wealth of longitudinal research on a dataset of US Federal offenders in the 1970s and from a wealth of understanding of decision-making among offenders. The former is well represented in Piquero and Weisburd's contribution to a fine edited collection by Simpson and Weisburd (2009) *The Criminology of White-Collar Crime*: Piquero and Weisburd summarise and develop their earlier work on white-collar criminal careers. Shover and Hochstetler (2006) examine a broad range of white-collar criminality and the factors that influence its decision-making.

Note

1 The gendered language here is a potentially contentious issue. At the time of the original research, female involvement in small business in the UK was much rarer than it is today. Nevertheless, officials report that it remains rare for women to play a significant role in identified long-firm frauds. (It remains an unexplored question whether stereotypes reduce the chance of women being identified as fraudsters rather than incompetents in the business sphere, notwithstanding long-standing images of 'women as deceivers' in the sexual sphere). The term 'front man' should be regarded as a technical term in common use irrespective of sex.

References

APACS (2008) *Fraud: The Facts 2008*. London: Association for Payment Clearing Services.

Blum, J., Levi, M., Naylor, T. and Williams, P. (1998) *Financial Havens, Banking Secrecy and Money-Laundering*, Issue 8, UNDCP Technical Series. New York: United Nations document V.98-55024.

Doig, A. (2006) *Fraud*. Cullompton: Willan.

Doig, A. and Levi, M. (2009) 'Inter-agency work and UK public sector investigation of fraud, 1996–2006: joined up rhetoric and disjointed reality', *Policing and Society*, 19(3): 199–215.

Holtfreter, K., Reisig, M. and Pratt. T. (2008) 'Low self-control, routine activities, and fraud victimization', *Criminology*, 49 (1): 189–220.

Home Office (2006) *Identity Fraud Update*. London: Home Office. Online at: http://www.identity-theft.org.uk/ID%20fraud%20table.pdf.

Innes, M. (2004) 'Crime as a signal, crime as a memory', *Journal for Crime, Conflict and the Media*, 1 (2): 15–22.

Levi, M. (1987) *Regulating Fraud*. London: Routledge.

Levi, M. (1998) 'Organising plastic fraud: enterprise criminals and the side-stepping of fraud prevention', *Howard Journal of Criminal Justice*, 37 (4): 423–38.

Levi, M. (2008a) *The Phantom Capitalists: The Organisation and Control of Long-Firm Fraud*, 2nd edn. Aldershot: Ashgate.

Levi, M. (2008b) 'Combating identity and other forms of payment fraud in the UK: an analytical history', in M. McNally and G. Newman (eds), *Perspectives on Identity Theft*, Crime Prevention Series Vol. 23. Monsey, NJ: Criminal Justice Press.

Levi, M. (2009a) 'White-collar crimes and the fear of crime: a review', in S. S. Simpson and D. Weisburd (eds), *The Criminology of White-Collar Crime*. New York: Springer.

Levi, M. (2009b) 'Suite revenge? The shaping of folk devils and moral panics about white-collar crimes', *Moral Panics 36 Years On*, Special Issue of *British Journal of Criminology*, 49 (1): 48–67.

Levi, M. and J. Handley, J. (1998) *The Prevention of Plastic and Cheque Fraud Revisited*, Home Office Research Study No. 182. London: Home Office.

Levi, M. and Reuter, P. (2006) 'Money laundering', *Crime and Justice*, 34: 289–376.

Levi, M., Bissell, P. and Richardson, T. (1991) *The Prevention of Cheque and Credit Card Fraud*, Crime Prevention Unit Paper No. 26. London: Home Office.

McIntosh, M. (1975) *The Organisation of Crime*. London: Macmillan.

McNally, M. M. and Newman, G. R. (eds) (2008) *Perspectives on Identity Theft*, Crime Prevention Studies Vol. 23. Monsey, NY: Criminal Justice Press.

Mativat, F. and Tremblay, P. (1997) 'Counterfeiting credit cards', *British Journal of Criminology*, 37: 165–83.

Piquero, N. L. and Weisburd, D. (2009) 'Developmental trajectories of white-collar crime', in S. S. Simpson and D. Weisburd (eds), *The Criminology of White-Collar Crime*. New York: Springer.

Shover, N. and Hochstetler, A. (2006) *Choosing White-Collar Crime*. Cambridge: Cambridge University Press.

Shover, N., Coffey, G. S. and Hobbs, D. (2003) 'Crime on the line: telemarketing and the changing nature of professional crime', *British Journal of Criminology*, 43: 489–505.

Shover, N., Coffey, G. S. and Sanders, C. R. (2004) 'Dialing for dollars: opportunities, justifications, and telemarketing fraud', *Qualitative Sociology*, 27 (1): 59–75.

Simpson, S. S. and Weisburd, D. (eds) (2009) *The Criminology of White-Collar Crime*. New York: Springer.

Sutherland, E. (1937) *The Professional Thief*. Chicago: University of Chicago Press.

Sutherland, E. (1983) *White-Collar Crime: The Uncut Version*. Princeton, NJ: Yale University Press.

Webb, B. (1996) 'Preventing plastic card fraud in the UK', *Security Journal*, 7 (1): 23–5.

Chapter 10

Identity theft and fraud

Natasha Semmens

Introduction

While it is often heralded as a new crime, identity theft has in fact been committed throughout history.[1] However, as identity theft emerges as a growing crime problem in the twenty-first century, it has new features which are closely linked with changes in modern society. Globalisation has brought with it a faster, more mobile way of life and this has brought significant new opportunities for the criminal. Technological advances, including the advent of the Internet, e-mail, and mobile phone technology, have transformed the ways in which we live our everyday lives and, in many ways, have facilitated the criminal enterprise. With all of these changes come new risks and, with them, new challenges.

Identity theft is a contemporary criminological concept. The aim of this chapter is to provide an overview of what we know about identity theft, focusing on conceptual ambiguities, the nature of the offence(s), explanations, patterns and trends and, finally, responses. I will conclude by emphasising that we currently have an insufficient understanding of the extent, nature and consequences of identity theft and that there are strong reasons for maintaining a criminological interest in it and building a knowledge base.

Definition

Although it is widely accepted as a contemporary crime threat and has been the subject of legal codification in some countries, there is no universally accepted definition of 'identity theft'. It is commonly understood as an umbrella concept, embracing a range of offences which involve the criminal acquisition and misuse of an individual's personal data to gain an advantage.[2] The concept is, then, conceived very broadly. The result is that a myriad of offences including passport theft, phishing, counterfeit credit card production, election fraud, illegal immigration, benefit fraud and terrorism are all brought together under one concept, all united by the fact that the tool used to commit the offence is an another individual's personal data.

It would be fair to say identity theft is a concept still in its infancy. In the academic literature, it has been subject to very little scrutiny, with authors focusing mainly on the distinction between two different types of identity theft: *full/permanent* identity thefts and *partial/temporary* identity thefts (Jones and Levi 2000; Finch 2002). In my own work in this field, I have previously labelled these types *identity theft* and *identity fraud* respectively (Semmens 2005). However, formal conceptual development has not really extended beyond this point. The creation of typologies and definitions has been left, in the main, to agencies responsible for educating the public about the threat posed by identity thieves (including a range of government agencies and institutions in the financial sector). As a result, we have seen the rather disorganised introduction of new terminology and the creation of sub-concepts in both the marketing and policy fields over the last decade which has muddied the waters, despite the best intentions. In a recent report on identity theft, the All Party Parliamentary Group (APPG 2007) acknowledged the urgent need for conceptual clarity, agreeing that in order for education, enforcement and prevention strategies to be successful, there needs to be an agreed definition.

One of the key points to realise is that 'identity theft' can be broken down conceptually into two parts, each representing different stages in a process: the acquisition of the identity[3] and the subsequent theft/fraud using the identity. This is an important distinction to make if we are to properly investigate the incidence, nature and consequences of the crime (as will hopefully become apparent later in this chapter). It was encouraging, then, to see the introduction of a new working definition by the Home Office's Identity Fraud Steering Committee in 2006 (APPG 2007: 35):

1 Identity Crime is a generic term for Identity Theft, creating a False Identity or committing Identity Fraud.

2 False Identity is:
   (a) a fictitious (i.e. invented) identity; or
   (b) an existing (i.e. genuine) identity that has been altered to create a fictitious identity.

3 Identity Theft occurs when sufficient information about an identity is obtained to facilitate Identity Fraud, irrespective of whether, in the case of an individual, the victim is alive or dead.

4 Identity Fraud occurs when a False Identity or someone else's identity details are used to support unlawful activity, or when someone avoids obligation/liability by falsely claiming that he/she was the victim of Identity Fraud.

This is a good definition inasmuch as it seeks to remedy the confusion caused by the terms 'identity theft' and 'identity fraud', introducing a new umbrella concept of 'identity crime'. Also, it makes a clear distinction between the assumption of and subsequent misuse of another person's personal information (labelling the two stages of the process as identity theft and identity fraud respectively). However, the definition only takes us far enough to remedy some basic (but important) terminology issues and, although it probably results in a workable concept in law enforcement terms, it fails to provide a framework for in-depth criminological analysis. Most importantly, it fails to recognise an important distinction between two types of identity misuse. Temporary/partial assumptions of identity can be visualised as a linear process – the data are acquired and then used as a tool for fraud, usually in the short term. Full/permanent immersions of identity can be visualised as a circular or spiralling process – the data are acquired and then used to acquire more data (which are then used to acquire more etc.). The emphasis is on building a portfolio of information over the long term. Clearly, while these two types of misuse have some similarities, they are very different in terms of the skills needed, the motivations and the impact on the victims.

As the chapter progresses, I hope that the shortcomings in the current conceptualisation of identity theft will become clear. I will begin by considering how we measure the extent and impact of identity theft. Later in the chapter, I will discuss the complexities of the offence in more detail, describing the different characteristics of the offence, the offenders and the impact on the victims.

Patterns and trends

Since it was first formally recognised as a new crime threat in the USA in the mid-1990s, identity theft has swiftly emerged as a key issue on the crime agendas of governments across the western world, being hailed as the fastest growing crime in a number of jurisdictions (Brin 1998). National estimates are routinely published to illustrate the size of the problem in different countries. For example, the Federal Trade Commission estimates the cost of identity theft in the US to be $50 billion annually; in Australia losses are thought to be in the region of $3 billion and in Canada $2.5 billion (APPG 2007). The most recent UK estimates place the figure at approximately £1.3 billion. These are, indeed, striking headlines. But there is a serious question mark hanging over these claims because very few countries (including the UK) are in a position to accurately assess the numbers of identity thefts committed, the number of victims and the ultimate cost to the economy.

In the UK, the traditional sources of statistics about crime, notably the Recorded Crime Statistics and Criminal Statistics are of limited use because they do not feature identity crimes as a separate, identifiable category. It is also unclear how many cases actually get reported to and investigated by the police (the Credit Industry Fraud Avoidance System (CIFAS), estimate that the police investigate only 1 per cent of cases (APPG 2007: 42)). The British Crime Survey, which can be used to detect those crimes not reported to/ recorded by the police, has recently included questions about identity theft but these produce rather superficial conclusions due to the restricted nature of the questions. So, we must currently rely on data supplied by institutions in the private and public sectors which is an approach which is steeped in methodological problems.[4]

In 2002, the Cabinet Office conducted a major study which attempted for the first time to survey the costs of identity theft to a number of government agencies and private institutions. The report estimated the cost of identity fraud to be in excess of £1.3 billion per annum. However, it was acknowledged that these were likely to be underestimates due to the problems of under-reporting, low detection rates and offence classification (Cabinet Office 2002). Later, in 2006, the Home Office Identity Fraud Steering Committee presented an updated estimate of £1.72 billion per annum, based on a series of estimates provided by associations from within the financial industry and government departments (some of which were not included in the 2002 study).

Public sector agencies have widely acknowledged that identity theft is a significant problem but there is often insufficient statistical evidence to allow for accurate estimates of the true extent of the problem in different contexts. It does not help matters that there is no clear definition of identity theft and thus it is unclear what activities should and should not be included. As identity theft becomes more firmly placed on policy agendas and the need to collect and share information is becoming more apparent, it is likely that the definition issue will cause significant problems. For present purposes, though, the following figures give an idea of the kind of estimates currently being made and demonstrate clearly the gaps in current data recording practices:

- The Department of Constitutional Affairs estimates £35.8 million was lost in unpaid fines (many fines get issued to false or inaccurate identities).
- The Department of Work and Pensions estimates that £20–50 million was lost through benefit claims made with false identities.
- The Driver and Vehicle Licensing Agency estimates that £2.5 million was spent on preventing the abuse of driving licences in identity crime.
- The Home Office estimates that £56.2 million was spent on undertaking enforcement activity against individuals involved in identity theft/fraud.
- The Police service estimates that £1.73 million was spent dealing with bogus callers, the only identity crime measureable.
- The UK Passport Service estimates £62.8 million was spent on measures to counter identity fraud in the processing of passport applications.

(Estimates drawn from Home Office Steering Group Report 2006, cited in evidence to the APPG 2007.)

We do, however, have a more accurate picture of the level of identity theft experienced within the private sector. The plastic card industry (incorporating those institutions issuing credit, debit and store cards) has had a particularly good record of measuring and monitoring levels of fraud since 1992 and thus is one of the best sources of statistical data on identity theft/fraud at this time in the UK. From the data published annually by APACS, we are able to extract information relating to the location, the method and the costs of plastic card fraud, telling us not only about the myriad of identity thefts and frauds being committed but also about the effectiveness of crime prevention initiatives. For example, following the introduction of the Chip and PIN (personal identification number) system in 2003/4, the data showed that it had become significantly harder for criminals to use lost/stolen cards in face-to-face transactions (fraud losses dropped from £114.5 million in 2004 to £89 million in 2005 and, subsequently, to £56.2 million in 2007). However, the data also shows how these criminals turned to alternative methods in response to the Chip and PIN system. So, we see a huge increase in fraud on card-not-present (CNP) transactions (where no PIN is required) and on counterfeit cards between 2004 and 2007 (CNP fraud has nearly doubled in this time from £150.8 million in 2004 to £290.5 million in 2007) (APACS 2008).

As with other fraud offences, the measurement of identity theft is always going to be fraught with methodological problems (Levi and Burrows 2008). There is, however, a clear need for better information gathering and data sharing between public and private institutions if we are to properly understand the scale of the problem. It is hard to see how this can be achieved without a much clearer definition of identity theft and the establishment of a centrally coordinated counting system. In the meantime, we can do little more than view all claims about the size of the problem with (healthy) scepticism.

Characteristics of the offence

As we have already seen, the breadth of the definition of identity theft allows for the inclusion of a wide range of different offence-types. Each is different in terms of the purpose/intention, the level of immersion, the methods used by the criminal and the impact on the victims. In this section, I will discuss the different characteristics of these offences, dealing in turn with the types of data targeted, the methods of acquiring data, methods of using the data and the characteristics of the offenders and victims.

Types of data targeted: identifiers

Up until this point, I have been referring to the theft and misuse of 'identity' and 'personal data' without paying close attention to what these terms actually mean. Now is an appropriate time to consider this issue in more detail. 'Identity' is a concept which has a number of possible meanings depending on the perspective adopted (social, cultural, legal, etc.) but when we talk about 'identity theft', we are usually using the term in a narrow way to describe the portfolio of personal data which we use to prove who we are when interacting with state agencies and private institutions and in commercial contexts. Personal data, then, is any data which relates to an individual and when that data is linked in a specific way to that individual it becomes an 'identifier'.

There are three types of identifier together forming this portfolio which builds throughout a person's lifetime (Jones and Levi 2000; Cabinet Office 2002):

1 *Attributed identifiers.* Attributed identifiers are the components of an individual's identity which are established or assigned at birth. These include name, date and place of birth and parents' names and are permanently associated with the individual.

2 *Biographical identifiers.* Biographical identifiers are the elements of identity which are accumulated after birth as an individual progresses through life. They include educational achievements and qualifications, financial records, property ownership, marriage and employment history, thus representing an individual's interactions with public and private institutions.

3 *Biometric identifiers.* Biometric identifiers are biological characteristics which relate to an individual's physical make-up. These may then relate to the physical appearance (e.g. fingerprints or facial structure) or the bio-molecular profile (e.g. DNA) of an individual. Some will be permanent characteristics and some will change as an individual ages.

We will look at how these identifiers are used in the process of identification later in the chapter. For now, though, it is important to recognise that these identifiers are targets for the criminal due to their instrumental value (Grabosky *et al.* 2001; Semmens 2006). Identifiers have a specific commercial value in the sense that they can be exchanged either for goods and services or for more information. Thus they are described by Jones and Levi (2000) as 'persuasive' data. In practice, different identifiers have different levels of exchange value in different contexts. Some identifiers are highly persuasive in a number of different contexts (for example, birth details are requested when applying for a whole range of interactions including claiming benefits, voting, getting a bank account, registering at university, opening an e-mail account, etc.) but others are only persuasive in specific contexts (for example a library card). Of course, there are also many instances when different identifiers are combined to form a set which has a higher persuasive value than its component parts.

One might assume, then, that identifiers which are higher in persuasive value will be better protected and harder for the criminal to acquire. This is not, however, always the case for reasons which will become clear later when we examine the process of identification in more depth. The point to recognise here is that the type of identifier targeted will depend on the intended use in the second stage of the identity theft process. So, for example, if the criminal simply wishes to have a shopping spree on someone else's credit card, all he or she needs is the relevant account details. Similarly, if he or she intends to open a loan account in another person's name the criminal will need to target the information required in that process (usually name, address, date of birth, evidence of income, etc.). As we move on to the next section and look at the methods of acquiring data, we must keep this in mind.

Methods of acquiring data

The identity thief will need to target specific identifiers in an individual's portfolio. What needs to be considered now is how he or she does this. Our starting point is to think in more detail about the portfolio itself – what it contains and where information is kept. Let us pause for a moment and try to visualise a portfolio of personal data. Imagine a fictional person and consider the range of identifiers that are contained in his portfolio. Next, consider the different formats these identifiers exist in and where they are stored. They might include:

- information kept on his personal computer (passwords, usernames, account numbers);
- information kept in his wallet (driving licence, credit cards, receipts, loyalty cards, membership cards);
- important documents kept in his safe (birth certificate, marriage certificate, passport);
- statements, letters, payslips and bills delivered to his house;
- information he posted on his Facebook profile (name, occupation, phone number, photos).

This is simply an example, but it is useful to think about the whole range of different identifiers which are stored in different places. We tend to store the majority of identifiers in both electronic and paper/plastic formats, either physically (on our person or in our house) or in virtual spaces (online accounts and databases). The individual has control of his portfolio and needs to decide when it is necessary and safe to release elements of it to other people. Importantly, though, other agencies will hold a copy of part of his portfolio. So, for example, his bank will have part of his portfolio on file, containing his name, address, date of birth, account details and, of course, transaction records. Even identifiers which we choose not to store physically ourselves (such as memorised passwords or PIN) are usually held by a third party.

An identity thief who wishes to seize control of part of the victim's portfolio (whichever part the thief needs to commit the next stage of the fraud) will do so in one of two ways: either by taking the identifier(s) directly from the individual or by gaining access to the partial portfolio held by another party.

Taking the identifier(s) directly from the individual's possession
When the target identifiers are in plastic or paper form, four main methods are available to the criminal. The first option is to commit a simple theft, either from a person or from property (house, car, etc.). This does, though, carry a high risk of detection. An alternative, then, is to target other documents which are more easily accessible and less likely to be missed. In our everyday lives, most of us receive and produce paper records of our transactions. Shopping receipts, bill payments, credit card statements and even junk mail are all examples of paper-based records which contain varying amounts of personal data and many of us discard them without thinking about the potential for misuse. So, a popular approach, colloquially referred to as 'dumpster diving', involves rifling through people's dustbins seeking discarded letters, bills or statements which contain the details of the victims. These documents can then be used to open new accounts or make purchases. The third and most complex method is known as 'mail intercept fraud' or 'address impersonation fraud' and is particularly associated with plastic card fraud. The criminal intercepts documents (including the card and PIN) before they are delivered to the genuine customer. So, it might be the case that someone working in the postal system is able to intercept the documents or, in properties of multiple occupation where deliveries are not always secure, people are vulnerable to having their mail stolen by co-residents. Alternatively, the fraudster might

target previous occupants of the property, usually by taking receipt of post which has been sent to the old address by mistake, or he or she might adopt the name and current address of another individual and then register his or her own address as if that individual has moved house (Jones and Levi 2000). Finally, the fourth method, which applies specifically to the plastic card payments system, is known as 'skimming'. This is where the criminal, usually a shop employee or similar, swipes a credit or debit card into a special reader which records the electronic data held on the magnetic strip (including the PIN). This information can then be used to make card-not-present purchases or to clone the card.

Data held on computers are also vulnerable, both data contained on the hard drive and in online personal spaces. Indeed, developments in technology have created more opportunities for the theft of data and criminals have been quick to adapt to these new opportunities. There are three main methods of gaining access to data on another person's computer hard drive. First, one can simply steal the computer. The second method involves the purchase of a second-hand computer which has not been properly cleaned of data by the vendor.[5] The third method is more technically complex, involving the use of spyware, a type of software which takes control of the victim's computer. It can monitor behaviour (for example, logging online shopping habits) or it can interfere with user control by changing the computer's settings, redirecting the user to specific websites or downloading programs. In all cases, some technical knowledge of computers is, of course, a significant advantage. But it is not just data stored on the hard drive that is vulnerable. Individuals also store or log important data online on websites, social network sites and on password protected account management pages (such as online bank accounts). Even the password protected accounts are vulnerable if the criminal is able to find out (or guess) an individual's username and password. There are many individuals, especially young people, who make their personal data publically available on sites such as Facebook, Bebo or Friends Reunited. These include full name, date of birth, address, phone number, employer, hobbies and photographs. Even information posted through 'status updates' and other forms of 'micro-blogging' can be useful as it informs people of someone's activities, purchases and interactions.

There is one final method which needs to be discussed in this section. An arguably easier option for the criminal is to dupe the victim into giving away the relevant data voluntarily as part of a seemingly normal transaction within an existing commercial relationship. This is commonly achieved by a method called 'phishing' where the criminal acquires personal details by sending an e-mail masquerading as a company or bank and duping the victim into disclosing their security details.

Gaining access to the partial portfolio held by another party

As mentioned earlier, sections of an individual's portfolio of identifiers will be held on file by other parties. This puts an important responsibility on that party to store and protect that information. Of course, some documents are publicly available and are therefore easy for the criminal to obtain. For example, in the UK, anyone can legitimately acquire a copy of the birth certificate of another person. But in most situations, we expect our important personal data to be kept secure by third parties.

However, it is widely recognised that there are serious problems associated with the safe storage and disposal of individuals' personal data. A recent report suggested that in 2007, 37 million items of personal data were lost by government agencies and businesses (Harrison 2008). There have been numerous cases involving CDs being lost in the post and laptops left on trains. There have also been cases of businesses disposing of old computers without removing data. A case was recently reported in which a man purchased a computer on eBay for £77 and later discovered that it contained the bank details of millions of customers of three major banks. Once these data have got into criminal hands, there is a risk that they will be used or sold on. There is a growing market in personal data which are often advertised in online chatrooms and discussion forums. Credit card and bank account details are particularly popular, but there is also a market for utility bills, passports and driving licences (Charles 2007).

Methods of using data

Once the relevant identifiers have been acquired, there are a number of different methods for using data to gain an advantage, all slightly different in terms of the nature of the advantage itself and the level of immersion into the false identity. Some offences are only intended to be short term and the offender will only intend to mask his real identity for the purposes of a single or short series of transactions. These are sometimes referred to as temporary/partial identity thefts (Jones and Levi 2000; Finch 2002). In contrast, there are cases when the offender has a much longer-term strategy in place and will adopt the new identity fully, living as the victim in everyday life. These are referred to as full/permanent identity thefts (ibid.). Let us move on to consider both types of identity theft in more detail.

Temporary/partial immersion

In these cases, the motivation tends to be financial, either to obtain goods or services or to establish credit or a loan, and the impersonation is temporary. The most common offences in this category are purchases made using another person's credit/debit card and the opening of accounts.

The targeted personal data in most cases is credit/debit card details which will usually be used in the short term until the credit limit is reached or the card is reported lost or stolen. In face-to-face transactions, the criminal will need to be in possession of the card itself and the personal identification number (PIN). There will usually be no need for the criminal to verify any further personal details at the point of sale. However, in the online environment, the situation is slightly different because the fraudster does not have to produce the card (online/telephone transactions are referred to as *card-not-present* (CNP) transactions). Often, though, he or she will need to supply further details such as the billing address, the start/end dates of the card and the security code. In these cases, the criminal will benefit from having access to some of the victim's receipts or card statements, which will allow the criminal to break through the security barriers.

Accounts are also open to abuse by criminals, including bank accounts, credit accounts (loans, mortgages, etc.) and even customer loyalty accounts (supermarket loyalty cards, etc.). There are two types of account abuse. The first is commonly referred to as 'account takeover'. This is where the criminal simply takes control of the account, usually by acquiring the account details and then registering a change of address so that he can continue to use the account masquerading as the victim. The second type of takeover involves the opening of a new account in the victim's name. This is where the criminal opens new accounts in the victim's name, again registering a different contact address so that the victim receives no communications that would alert him to the fraud. This process takes longer and involves more effort than the purchases described above, but this can yield more money for the fraudster. Once an account has been set up, this also makes it easier for additional accounts to be initiated. This will be possible up until the point that the victim realises what is happening.

It is important to recognise that temporary assumptions of a false identity may also be driven by a non-financial motive. It is possible that the criminal wishes to use the false identity to deceive the police or other regulatory agencies. Examples include giving a false name/driving licence when stopped by the police or issued with a fine.

Full/permanent immersion

In cases of full, permanent immersion into the identity (sometimes referred to as 'identity hijack') the criminal wishes to leave his or her own identity behind. These cases are rare as the new identity will need to be meticulously developed over time and requires considerable effort on the part of the fraudster. As noted by Jones and Levi (2000), the motivations for a permanent change of identity may be legitimate (for example, change of name by deed poll following gender reassignment or victim/witness protection schemes), but may also be criminal in nature, for example to remain unlawfully in the country or to fake a death to claim insurance policies. False passports and other identification documents are essential tools in the illegal immigration trade.

The immersion into the new identity is most easily achieved where the victim is deceased, especially where the victim died in infancy and has not already built a portfolio of biographical data (Jones and Levi 2000). In such a case, the fraudster may find the details of a deceased child in a graveyard, selecting one with a date of birth close to his or her own (Cabinet Office 2002). From this point, it is relatively easy to obtain a birth certificate which then becomes an important 'breeder document'. The fraudster can then begin the process of building a portfolio of data, leaving his or her own original identity behind completely.

Offenders

Due to the lack of research into identity theft, very little is known about the characteristics of the offenders. We can, though, be sure that the complex nature of the different offences described above means that the offenders will be drawn from a wide range of social groups and backgrounds, bridging across collarless, blue-collar and white-collar categories (Friedrichs 2004).

There are many examples of criminals engaging in identity-related crimes at street level, stealing credit/debit cards and using them either in person or online. We also know that employees at all levels in organisations are well placed to access the data needed to commit identity crimes. There have been many cases of clerical staff, administrators and shop workers stealing data either to use themselves or, more often, to sell on to someone else. Those further up the professional/organisational ladder are also potential offenders. Whatever their status, these criminals may work as individuals or in small groups or networks. Indeed, identity theft is commonly linked with organised crime networks and their activities which include money laundering, people and drug trafficking, and terrorism.

Victims

For each episode of identity theft/fraud there will be multiple victims: the individual whose information is borrowed or appropriated (the *primary* victim) and any individual, business or institution that is subsequently defrauded or duped by the perpetrator (the *secondary* victim(s)). It might also be said that victims exist at the wider (tertiary) level, through costs passed on by the secondary victims.

The primary victims may experience a range of different forms of harm, including physical, psychological, financial and social harm. Although the immediate loss of large sums of money is a commonly held fear, it is actually quite unlikely for the primary victim to be held liable for hefty debts incurred where an identity theft has taken place. More likely is the damage caused to the victim's credit history which will have a negative impact on his/her future financial autonomy. Also, the primary victims of identity theft face the challenge of restoring their personal identity profiles, a process which can be costly in terms of time and effort and a source of major emotional stress. It has been shown that the loss of control of personal information is potentially damaging to an individual's sense of self and quality of life and may have a serious effect on psychological and physical health. Victims report feeling frustration at the legal responses and the failures of third parties to protect individuals' data, helplessness, embarrassment and a fear of future victimisation (APPG 2007).

For the secondary victims, the loss suffered will, more often than not, be directly financial. Indeed, it is widely accepted that the costs of identity theft are absorbed by members of the retail, communications and finance industries. Of course, these costs are usually passed on to the consumer and, where government agencies are concerned, the taxpayer.

Explanations

Again, there has been very little exploration of the explanations for identity theft in the literature. Existing theories of offending may, of course, be applied to many of the criminal acts described above; similarly we might apply theories of situational crime prevention and victimisation. But in the absence of solid empirical research on identity theft offenders and victims, there seems little point in speculating here. There is, however, an area of theory which is highly relevant to these crimes and that is Clarke's theory of identification (1994). By examining the process of identification we are able to understand how identifiers are associated with individuals, how criminals are able to infiltrate the process and how the crimes might ultimately be prevented.

The process of identification

Clarke's (1994) theory of identification firmly establishes human identification as a process of association of data with a particular human being. The process begins with the registration of the individual and data associated with him or her on the identifior's database. Then, whenever the individual wishes to interact with the identifior, evidence of identity will need to be produced which can be checked with the original record. Thus, in a transaction, the identifier is attempting to establish that a person who is the subject of one observation is also the subject of a previous observation (LoPucki 2001).

The process is described by Clarke (1994) as multilayered, starting with the establishment of a base layer in which the identifying characteristics are recorded as belonging to a specific individual. Once the base layer has been established, new layers can be constructed as further interactions and transactions take place. Crucially, the identification process lies at the heart of an individual's interactions with state agencies and private companies/ institutions. Every time you visit the doctor, claim a state benefit, use a credit card, board a plane and login to your e-mail account, the process is instigated to check that you are the person you say you are and that you are entitled to conduct the transaction.

It is important to recognise that layers will differ in construction, depending on the nature of the identification process. Where the identifior is a state agency, the purpose of identification is to monitor and control access to public services and to regulate the movement of citizens. The base layer, then, is commonly constructed of birth details – the name, date, time, parents' names and hospital are all recorded on the Register of Births and a birth certificate is issued. Subsequent (secondary) layers are developed by specific agencies, often with reference to the base layer but usually with additional identifiers required (current address, income, health status, credit history, etc.). So, for example, applications for passports require birth records (or equivalent adoption certificate or certificate of registration or naturalisation), plus photographs which are certified to be a true likeness of the applicant. In order to claim benefits, evidence of identity is required (birth certificate, National Insurance number), plus an 'evidence of identity' interview. It is increasingly the case that these subsequent layers are interlinked through data sharing between agencies.

Private sector institutions operate similar processes but are driven by slightly different aims. The identification process is less about control of citizens and more about protecting the financial interests of the business or service provider. Put simply, private sector institutions need to ensure the identity of an individual before entering into a contract or business relationship in order to reduce the risk of non-payment or fulfilment of a contractual obligation. Accordingly, the institution will develop its own base layer by setting up an individual customer account or profile. This may require state-issued details such as birth registration details and National Insurance number. These will be accompanied by a raft of additional details, usually biographical in nature. So, for example, in order to open a credit card account, you are likely to be asked for employment details, bank account details and address details and to be subjected to a credit reference check.

Within the process, evidence of identity is essential because it is the tool that is used to link the data to an individual. Without evidence, the process cannot take place and if that evidence is weak then the process is vulnerable to attack. Evidence may take one of three forms: *token-based identification* (where documents or other tokens are used to prove identity), *knowledge-based identification* (information only the individual would know) and *biometric identification* (where physiological characteristics are used to identify an individual). Clarke (1994) demonstrates that in order for an identifier to be effective, it must fulfil five different requirements. These are:

- universality of coverage (all individuals must possess the identifier);
- uniqueness;
- permanence;
- precision; and
- acceptability (the collection and use of identifiers must be socially and ethically acceptable).

The problem is that no single identifier can be said to satisfy all requirements. Token-based identifiers are likely to be of varying effectiveness. A passport, for example, would fulfil the requirements of uniqueness, precision and acceptability but not universality and permanence. A utility bill (often used as proof of address) is less robust in terms of universality, uniqueness, permanence and precision. Knowledge-based identifiers are similarly problematic. A PIN is not universal, unique or permanent; one's mother's maiden name, however, is much more robust as it is universal and permanent. Biometric identifiers are often seen as highly effective identifiers but some caution is necessary. Studies looking at the use of retina scanning and fingerprint technology reveal serious deficiencies in our current ability to accurately measure physiological characteristics (Identity Project 2005). DNA is assumed to be universal and permanent but it is not yet clear how precise and permanent it is. An effective system of identification, then, must combine different types of identifiers, each bringing strengths in one or more of the requirements to work together as a complete set.

Once we understand how the process of identification operates, we are able to identify potential weaknesses within it. The identity thief must penetrate the process of identification at some point by acquiring enough evidence of identity to be able to either successfully masquerade as the real owner in a transaction or to establish a new base layer with an institution. Also, by understanding what makes strong identifiers, we are able to avoid/remedy breaches and build more secure identification processes. A good example of this would be the introduction of Chip and PIN technology in the UK. Previous to this, the process of identification in a card transaction was relatively weak. Studies showed that the method of checking a customer's signature with that on the card was worryingly unreliable and that a more secure method was needed (Levi *et al.* 1991). Chip and PIN was rolled out nationally in 2005 and was shown to be successful in reducing the amount of fraud committed by £60 million in the first year. However, this example illustrates that the process of identification is constantly under attack. Evidence clearly shows that fraudsters found other ways of committing plastic card frauds, targeting different processes with different weaknesses (in this case, they targeted card-not-present transactions which do not require the inputting of a PIN).

Responses

The USA was the first country to take significant action against the problem of identity theft, putting into place a series of legal, administrative and enforcement mechanisms aimed at tackling the crime and providing support for the victims. The Identity Theft and Assumption Deterrence Act was enacted in 1998, establishing identity theft as a criminal offence and requiring the Federal Trade Commission (FTC) to set up a central repository for identity theft complaints and to provide a national integrated support system for the victims of identity theft (Federal Trade Commission 2003). This has proved to be a very successful approach but the response strategy is in constant need of review as the identity theft problem evolves. In 2006, President Bush set up a new Identity Theft Task Force to make further improvements to law enforcement, education and the storage of personal data by government agencies and private sector institutions (President's Identity Theft Task Force 2007). The US approach is, though, a useful response model because it includes preventative measures to protect citizens and businesses, measures to improve policing and enforcement, mechanisms to help victims and legal measures to enable successful prosecutions. In the UK, responses to identity theft have been reactive and slow in comparison and are described in the following sections.

Prevention strategies

A heavy emphasis has been placed on the need to educate individual consumers/citizens to better protect their personal data. Thus significant efforts have been made to provide education and guidance in the fight against identity theft and fraud. Credit card holders, for example, are repeatedly told to keep their card details and PIN confidential and to shred or burn their statements and receipts. To what extent this message is getting through, though, is unclear. Businesses, too, are being encouraged to think more seriously about the threat of identity theft and the safety of their customers. In a report by the Fraud Advisory Panel (2003), a number of recommendations were made aimed at improving business practices to prevent identity thefts and frauds. Businesses were criticised for failing to monitor employees, to store and dispose of customers' personal data responsibly and to share important information relating to frauds with market competitors. They called for improvements in personnel management, data storage practices (both off and online) and data-sharing practices (within both the public and private sectors) and recommended the establishment of a national fraud database together with a register of stolen identities. However, as we have seen in the discussion earlier, there is still a lot of work to be done here.

There have also been significant levels of investment in prevention technologies, particularly those aimed at making identification systems more secure. Large amounts of money are being spent on research into microchip processes and biometrics. We should not, however, allow technology to lure us into a false sense of security. Experience shows that we should never underestimate the creativity and adaptability of the identity thief.

Policing and prosecution

Until recently, one of the main complaints raised regarding the policing of identity theft was the inadequacy of the Theft Acts (1968 and 1978) for dealing with the myriad of offences being experienced (Semmens 2005). There have been numerous calls for a specific offence of identity theft to be created as in other countries, including the US and Australia. However, following recent developments in the law of fraud, it seems unlikely that this will happen in the near future.

The Fraud Act 2006 was introduced with the aim of tidying up and simplifying the law by repealing the deception offences under the Theft Acts 1968 and 1978 and replacing them with a single offence of fraud. The new Act establishes a single offence of fraud which can be committed in three ways:

1 by false representation;
2 by failure to disclose information where there is a legal duty to do so;
3 by abuse of a position.

In each case, the defendant's conduct must be dishonest and his intention must be to make a gain.

Because the intention of this legislation was to create the single offence of fraud, it seems unlikely then that a specific offence of 'identity theft' will be necessary. All of the examples of identity theft described earlier do seem to fall within this broadly defined offence and there are several aspects which make a prosecution under the legislation attractive.[6] Furthermore, the Act establishes an offence of 'being in possession of articles for use in fraud' (section 6), which includes information in hard copy and data form and 'making or supplying articles for use in frauds' (section 7).

In addition to the new offences created by the Fraud Act, additional offences do exist under two other pieces of legislation. Firstly, the Identity Cards Act 2006 created a new offence of being in possession or control of false documents issued to another person without reasonable cause. Secondly, the Data Protection Act 1998 gives an individual the right to know what information is held about them, ensures that information is held securely and criminalises the misuse of personal information. Given these provisions, there is a real question as to whether we need to create a new single offence of identity theft.

As with other fraudulent offences, there are some questions to be raised as to how well equipped the police are to deal with the offences. Evidence suggests that the majority of police forces take limited action against identity theft and that there are inconsistencies between forces in the types of responses taken (APPG 2007). The reasons for this are linked with funding and expertise; forces complain that they do not have enough resources to train dedicated officers. A recent initiative to improve consistency has been the development of a network of SPOCs[7] across forces which may be able to work more closely in the future to allow for greater sharing of information and good practice.

To conclude this review of UK responses, it is clear that a more proactive and coordinated response strategy is needed if identity theft is to be effectively reduced. More work is needed to improve prevention and response strategies and this requires collaboration between the government, the police, the business sector and the public. In the last few years the UK government has established a number of dedicated advisory groups and fora[8] to deal with the problem, but there remains little evidence of strong leadership and a clear set of objectives at a national level. What is needed is a set of solutions based on clear evidence and not summations and estimates which have emerged from a politically driven climate of fear.

Conclusion

I hope that this discussion has illustrated that we are only just beginning to form an understanding of the nature, extent and effects of identity theft/fraud. Although it is certainly not a new crime, there are clearly aspects of the phenomenon which are unique to the Information Age and which are constantly changing. There are many aspects to it that we are yet to explore and understand and there is a lot of scope for research into the nature, incidence and effects of identity crimes. Before any of this research can take place, however, the issue of conceptualisation needs to be resolved. It is unhelpful for academics, politicians, the media and the financial/retail industries to adopt different conceptual interpretations. Ultimately this can only serve to hinder the public debate about the challenges faced.

There is a serious question to be asked as to whether identity theft should even be maintained and developed as a separate criminological concept or whether it is best absorbed into other existing concepts. Is there a real danger of pandering to 'popular concerns and a barrage of media interest' (Levi and Burrows 2008: 304)? I would argue that there is a need to maintain it for the following reasons. First and foremost, although we are talking about the misuse of *personal data* (identifying information), this can (as we have seen) have a significant impact on the victim's *identity*. If we were to group identity thefts together with other crimes of fraud or false representation, we are in danger of overlooking one of the most important and interesting characteristics of these crimes – the impact on the victims and the links with privacy, autonomy and well-being. Second, identity theft/fraud has now become a concept familiar to the public. We know that the public do not find it easy to grasp the complexities of fraud, so it makes some sense to avoid extra confusion if possible. Thirdly, and finally, identity theft is now established as an international crime problem. It features on the agendas of governments around the world and is driving international policy. It is extremely important that criminologists contribute to this debate.

Selected further reading

As mentioned earlier, there is little academic literature in this field at present. However, a recent book edited by McNally and Newman (2008) provides a useful overview of identity theft and includes discussion of definition, measurement, the scarcity of data, the role of technology and the importance of cooperation in combating the problem. Readers interested in knowing more about plastic card fraud are referred to Levi's leading work in the field (his chapter in McNally and Newman's book is a useful starting point and numerous additional sources are listed in the reference list). Inevitably, anyone interested in these topics must turn to electronic sources to gain the essential policy and industry perspectives. Various reports (many of which have been utilised in this article) are available from the following organisations:

- Cardwatch: http://www.cardwatch.org.uk/
- CIFAS: http://www.cifas.org.uk/
- Federal Trade Commission: http://www.ftc.gov/bcp/edu/microsites/idtheft/
- Home Office: http://www.identitytheft.org.uk/

Notes

1 Throughout history, criminals have used false identities to commit their crimes and their motivations have ranged from social control through to commercial exploitation, financial gain, voyeurism, political protest, stalking and harassment (Grabosky *et al.* 2001; Garfinkel 2001).
2 That advantage will often be financial, but sometimes the identity thief will be seeking to leave behind his or her existing identity and start a new life for non-financial reasons.
3 This first stage is referred to as the 'enabling offence' (Finch 2002).
4 Indeed, the problems associated with measuring the impact of fraud are well documented. For an excellent analysis see Levi and Burrows (2008).
5 CapitalOne recently published research which suggests that as many as half of the computers sold via legitimate channels contain information which could be used by an identity thief (including bank details, correspondence with a bank and details of a CV outlining academic and professional history) (APPG 2007).
6 Theft carries a lower minimum sentence, the *actus reus* requirement for fraud is far less stringent, it is not necessary to prove or demonstrate any consequences of fraud and the fraud offences do not require an intent permanently to deprive.

7 Single points of contact.
8 Examples include the Identity Fraud Steering Committee, the Identity Fraud Consumer Awareness Group and the Public Private Forum on Identity Management.

References

All Party Parliamentary Group (APPG) (2007) *All Party Parliamentary Group Report on Identity Fraud*. Online at: http://idfraud.org.uk/ (accessed 19 September 2008).

APACS (2008) *Fraud: The Facts 2008*. Online only at: http://www3.secure-ssl-server. com/cardwatch/images/uploads/publications/Fraud%20the%20Facts%202008_ links.pdf (accessed 19 September 2008).

Brin, D. (1998) *The Transparent Society: Will Technology Force Us to Choose Between Privacy and Freedom?* Reading, MA: Perseus Books.

Cabinet Office (2002) *Identity Fraud: A Study*. London: HMSO.

Charles, J. (2007) 'Criminals sell credit card details online for only 25p each', *The Times*, 17 September. Online at: http://business.timesonline.co.uk/tol/business/industry_ sectors/support_services/article2469139.ece (accessed 19 September 2008).

Clarke, R. (1994) 'Human identification in information systems: management challenges and public policy issues', *Information, Technology and People*, 7 (4): 6–37.

Federal Trade Commission (2003) *Federal Trade Commission Overview of the Identity Theft Program*. Online at: http://www.ftc.gov/os/2003/09/timelinereport.pdf (accessed 21 May 2009).

Finch (2002) 'What a tangled web we weave: identity theft and the internet', in Y. Jewkes (ed.), *Dot.con: Crime, Deviance and Identity on the Internet*. Cullompton: Willan.

Fraud Advisory Panel (2003) *Identity Theft: Do You Know the Signs?* Online at: http:// www.fraudadvisorypanel.org/newsite/PDFs/advice/Identity%20Theft%20Final%20 Proof%2011-7-03.pdf (access 21 May 2009).

Friedrichs, D. (2004) *Trusted Criminals: White-Collar Crime in Contemporary Society*. Belmont, CA: Thomson Wadsworth.

Garfinkel, S. (2001) *Database Nation: The Death of Privacy in the 21st Century*. Sebastopol, CA: O'Reilly & Associates.

Grabosky, P., Smith, R. G. and Dempsey, G. (2001) *Electronic Theft: Unlawful Acquisition in Cyberspace*. Cambridge: Cambridge University Press.

Harrison, D. (2008) 'Government's record year of data loss', *The Telegraph*, 7 January. Online at: http://www.telegraph.co.uk/news/newstopics/politics/1574687/ Government%27s-record-year-of-data-loss.html (accessed 19 September 2008).

Identity Project (2005) *An Assessment of the UK Identity Cards Bill and Its Implications*. London: London School of Economics.

Jones, G. and Levi, M. (2000) *The Value of Identity and the Need for Authenticity*, DTI Office of Science and Technology Crime Foresight Panel Essay for *Turning the Corner*.

Levi, M. and Burrows, J. (2008) 'Measuring the impact of fraud in the UK: a conceptual and empirical journey', *British Journal of Criminology*, 48: 293–318.

Levi, M., Bissell, P. and Richardson, T. (1991) *The Prevention of Cheque and Credit Card Fraud*, Crime Prevention Unit Paper No. 26. London: Home Office.

LoPucki, L. (2001) 'Human identification theory and the identity theft problem', *Texas Law Review*, 80: 89–136.

McNally, M. M. and Newman, G. R. (eds) (2008) *Perspectives on Identity Theft*, Crime Prevention Studies Vol. 23. Monsey, NY: Criminal Justice Press.

President's Identity Theft Task Force (2007) *Combatting Identity Theft: A Strategic Plan.* Online at: http://www.idtheft.gov/reports/StrategicPlan.pdf (accessed 19 September 2008).

Semmens, N. (2005) 'When the world knows your name: identity theft and fraud in the UK', *Scottish Journal of Criminal Justice Studies*, 11: 80–91

Semmens, N. (2006) 'Identity theft and fraud', in T. Thompson and S. Black (eds), *Forensic Human Identification: An Introduction.* Boca Raton, FL: Taylor & Francis.

Chapter 11

Cybercrime

Matthew Williams

Introduction

The relative ubiquity of the Internet has created unprecedented criminal opportunities. In 1997 only 2 per cent of the UK's population had access to the Internet compared to 65 per cent in 2008 (ONS 2009). Currently 21.9 per cent of the world's population have Internet access.[1] For the first time in 2005 online sales rivalled those of terrestrial high-street retail (DTI 2006). Capella (2001) states the specific characteristics of the Internet have opened up a new virtual criminal field that facilitates 'terrestrial' criminal activities as well as creating avenues for new forms of deviance. These opportunities are being taken up by 'career' criminals as well as previously ill-equipped potential offenders. Online sexual deviance (paedophile networks, sexual harassment, grooming, etc.), ID theft, online stalking, intellectual property theft, online fraud, malware attacks, spamming, denial of service attacks, hacktivism and online hate crime (to name a few) are now the purview of the many compared to the few only a decade ago. The escalation of these crimes not only in prevalence but in the volume of 'new' offenders has transformed the public's perception of the Internet from a new social space associated with unprecedented freedoms into a 'dangerous place' riddled with rising, often misunderstood, risks.

Defining cybercrime

The prevalence of cybercrimes, along with their definition and impact, continue to be controversial (Levi 2001). The myriad of criminal and sub-criminal acts that come under the umbrella term cybercrime means that their incidence remains deeply embedded within a dark figure (Williams 2006a). In its infancy cybercrime was the avocation of a small number of computer programmers adept at the illegal practice of hacking. The impetus behind hacking during these early years was usually non-malignant and based on a utopian idealism of non-centralised computer hardware and software access (Levy 1984). The illicit activities of these individuals were not widely detected or publicised. During this time law enforcement was far from capable of either proactively or reactively tackling the problem. More so, hacking was not considered a problem by the authorities until the mid-1990s. During this later period there were increasing reports of the misuse of the Internet and similar technologies. Businesses and domestic users were beginning to witness instances of online credit card fraud, systems sabotage and identity and data theft. A clear shift occurred from the relatively benign cyber-deviant activity of the 1980s to the malicious cyber-criminal activity of the mid to late 1990s. The current decade has seen the problem take centre stage, especially following the events of 9/11. Governments across the globe now consider the cybercrime problem as so acute that specialist law enforcement agencies are being established and contingency plans are being put in place to counter cyber-terrorist attacks.

Before categorising types of cybercime, it is important to distinguish what is criminal behaviour and what is not in relation to computer use/misuse. As advances in technology escalate at a rate unparalleled by everyday institutional mechanisms, it is no surprise that the law is slow to respond to cybercrime. Since the introduction of the Council of Europe's Convention on Cybercrime in 2001 only half of the states that signed the convention have integrated its procedures into domestic law.[2] Where advances have been made, it is questionable whether the scope of new and adapted bodies of jurisprudence can remain ahead of deviant enterprise. While existing cybercrimes such as hacking, denial of service attacks and website defacement have been met with legal regulation, many newer forms of computer-related activity escape regulation due to their esoteric nature. New and emerging technologies, such as wireless networking, mobile computing and ambient intelligence, pose a significant challenge to policymakers and law enforcement.

In attempting to define crimes that take place on computer networks, it is important to consider spatial and temporal dimensions. Traditional or terrestrial crimes exhibit certain general characteristics. Often they are static in terms of time and space. Perpetrators very often have to be present at a certain time and in a certain place to carry out a crime. The same might be said for the target of crime; targets of crime (victims, property, etc.) must share the same temporal-spatial dimensions as their perpetrator.[3] For a crime to be committed it must also be recognised as a crime within these temporal-spatial constraints. Therefore the law and conventional social understanding at the time and place must recognise behaviour as illicit for it to be labelled as criminal (Becker 1963).

The characteristics of cybercrimes vary from those of terrestrial crimes. There is little adherence to the spatial-temporal restrictions characteristic of conventional crimes. This is primarily due to the burgeoning growth of new information communication technologies (ICTs) (Woolgar 2002). Networked societies allow for time and space to be distantiated, meaning that an action in one spatial-temporal boundary may have an effect outside of that jurisdiction (Giddens 1990). In relation to criminal activity this means that individuals are able to attack their victims at a distance. The temporal dimension of crime is also affected; new ICTs allow criminals to make deals or hack systems in compressed periods of time, given the distance covered. A fraudulent transaction can take place over thousands of miles in milliseconds while a hacker can illicitly appropriate proprietary information from a business over national boundaries. Finally, unlike the 'typical' characteristics of the terrestrial offender, the virtual criminal is more likely to exhibit traits attributable to those from a more affluent and well-educated background. Partial evidence to corroborate this can be found in the findings of the 2002/03 British Crime Survey and 2003 Offending, Crime and Justice Survey. Both surveys show that peak Internet usage was among middle-income households, and that there was a significant correlation between increased Internet use and increased household income. Correspondingly, Internet use was low between those living in council estate and other low-income areas. The level of physical disorder in the immediate area also impacted on levels of Internet use, where those living in areas categorised as having relatively high physical disorder were less likely to use the Internet. Those in full-time education, compared to those in full-time employment, were also significantly more likely to admit to sending viruses, engaging in hacking activities and sending threatening e-mails.[4]

Given these inconsistencies, there is contentious debate over what constitutes cybercrime. This uncertainty is further reflected in legal discourse, where issues over jurisdiction inflate the debate. As cybercrimes can span national boundaries and legal jurisdictions, questions over what body of law should apply complicate issues of retribution. The contention surrounding legal discourse in relation to cybercrime is mirrored in other political and social arenas. Three multilateral organisations are currently involved in shaping cybercrime policy: the European Union (EU), the Council of Europe (COE) and the G8. Other organisations, such as the Organisation for Economic Cooperation and Development (OECD), the United Nations, Interpol and Europol have been involved to a lesser extent. None of the organisations has offered a definitive definition of cybercrime. The United Nations highlighted the problem of definition in its *Manual on the Prevention and Control of Computer-Related Crime* (UN Commission on Crime and Criminal Justice 1995) stating that while there is consensus among experts, these definitions have been functional and hence too specific. A similar position was held by the Council of Europe. The Committee on Crime Problems decided to leave out any definition of cybercrime in its 2001 Convention on Cybercrime, allowing individual jurisdictions to apply their own definitions based on their specific body of law. The Council of Europe does, however, provide a working definition for Europol, the European law enforcement organisation responsible for fostering effective co-operation among member states in order to tackle organised crime. However, this definition is narrow in that it only relates to attacks on automated data-processing systems (Council of the European Union 2000). This is in part due to Europol's existing mandate which already covers certain crimes that can be committed over computer networks (drug and arms trafficking, counterfeiting, trafficking in human beings, child pornography, illegal immigration networks, etc.), nullifying the necessity for a more comprehensive definition of cybercrime.

To better understand cybercrime it can be disaggregated into three forms (Wall 2007a). First, technology has provided a vehicle for the further facilitation of existing criminal activities. Computer networks have become a communications vehicle which facilitates the commission of 'traditional' criminal activities. A typical example might be the use of the Internet to appropriate restricted information to facilitate a terrestrial crime, such as gaining access to sensitive company records to facilitate extortion. The second category of computer-related crime involves the creation of new opportunities for criminal activity that are currently recognised by existing criminal or civil law. Everyday crimes have then migrated or have been re-engineered to function online. Examples would be the use of the Internet by fraudsters to trick victims into divulging their online bank password, username and security information (known as phishing and pharming). Third, entirely new forms of harmful activities that are of dubious legal status have emerged with the increased use of the Internet. Essentially the Internet has allowed for the creation of a new environment within which novel forms of misbehaviour are engineered. Examples include forms on online violence, virtual vandalism and creation of bot networks (Williams 2001, 2004, 2006a; Wall and Williams 2007). These kinds of computer-related deviant activities are posing the greatest challenge to legal systems, law enforcement and businesses and are undergoing constant evaluation in terms of understanding and interpreting the kinds of potential harms they can cause.

Cybercrime types

Denial of service

A denial of service (DoS) attack is an incident in which a business resource (such as a website) is temporarily made unavailable to customers or clients. This kind of event can occur accidentally due to systems or software failure or can be the result of a malicious hacker's actions. All recent cybercrime surveys focus upon the latter form of DoS incident. Most typically, services such as e-mail, network connectivity and access to software are adversely affected. In extreme cases consumer websites (such as those utilised by many large retail chains) that usually attract the custom of millions of people can occasionally be forced to temporarily cease operation. A DoS attack can also destroy data and files on a computer system.

While DoS attacks are a type of security breach that does not usually result in the theft of proprietary information they can result in high financial losses. These are usually as a result of loss of customer or client business, but also include the costs of technical repair and the loss of positive reputation. More sophisticated and co-ordinated attacks, known as *distributed* denial of service attacks (DDoS) where multiple compromised systems target a business's technical recourse, are far more malicious in nature and can cause much higher financial losses (beyond that of the targeted business). To date almost all large businesses have been subject to either a DoS or a DDoS attack, including eBay, Yahoo, Amazon, CNN.com and Microsoft. Due to the increasing take-up of broadband by large and small businesses, and the adoption of more powerful personal computers, DoS and DDoS attacks are predicted to increase dramatically over the coming years (Newman and Clarke 2003).

Virus attacks

A computer virus is malignant computer code that self-replicates and spreads by inserting copies of itself into other executable code or documents on a computer, network or software package. The infected hardware and software become 'hosts' to the computer virus. For viruses to spread they have to attach to known computer code on the host (such as common code within operating systems such as Windows Vista). Viruses can be written to perform a vast array of functions, from disrupting everyday computer software to destroying or manipulating proprietary data, resulting in financial losses. They typically take up computer memory used by legitimate programs. As a result, they often cause erratic behaviour and can result in system crashes. Viruses form part of a family of malicious code known as *malware*.

Other types of malware include worms and trojans. Worms, unlike viruses, can self-propagate without attaching to known code on a host computer. They usually take advantage of computer and network file transmission capabilities and as a result harm business networks and stifle bandwidth. In extreme cases worms are used by cyber criminals to subvert whole networks of computers, bringing them under their illicit control. Often these networks, known as bot-nets, are used to send out spam e-mail over the entire Internet. Cyber criminals have also been known to hold companies to ransom using worms and associated bot-nets to threaten DoS attacks. Cryptoviral extortion is also common where proprietary information is encrypted and companies are instructed to hand over funds before the cyber criminal decrypts the data. The most damaging worm to date Mydoom almost brought the Internet to a standstill in 2004. The worm was responsible for creating bot-nets and sending spam to targeted companies in DDoS attempts.

Trojans are malicious computer programs that masquerade as something harmless or interesting. Often distributed via e-mail, once executed the program can perform an array of illicit functions including sending viruses, creating bot-nets and uploading or downloading files. Most significant is the ability of trojans to install spyware on host computers and networks. Such spyware is capable of logging users' keystrokes and taking screenshots in an attempt to access sensitive information and data. Users' bank details, passwords and security information can easily be recorded and sent back to the cyber criminal.

All cybercrime surveys record the prevalence of malware infection. Not surprisingly malware infection is the most common type of domestic and business security breach. Technical security measures are least effective against malware infection and incidents are on the increase. The most notorious virus the Love Bug cost businesses over £5 billion globally (Computer Economics 2005). The average cost per UK business of recovering from virus infection in 2003 was £120,000 (Corporate IT Forum 2003). The cost for small and medium enterprises (SMEs) in 2005 was also significant. The majority of SMEs stated they spent at least £500 a year on cleaning up the aftermath of virus infections, while 1 in 20 reported spending over £10,000 (Bank of Scotland Business Banking 2005). Such significant costs clearly jeopardise the financial security of small firms.

Website and systems hacking

Hacking websites and other computer systems is considered cyber trespass (Wall 2007a). Three categories of illicit activity are conducted by hackers. The first type of activity is the deliberate manipulation of data, such as web pages, so that they misrepresent the targeted organisation. Several political party websites have been targeted by hackers on the run up to general elections in the UK and manifestos have been rewritten in sarcastic and satiric fashion (Reuters 2003). In particular *hacktivists* attempt to draw attention to their ideological position by defacing websites, such as those representing commercial or governmental interests. Notable attacks upon UK government websites occurred in the August of 2000 when a well known hacktivist going under the name 'Herbless' was successful at defacing over ten government websites with an aim to criticise official policy on smoking. 'Herbless' had already achieved some notoriety, having hacked the UK Cabinet Office website a month previously (see Figure 11.1).

Terrestrial forms of vandalism are material crimes because they have a physical presence. Conversely acts of online vandalism have no tangible element, making them immaterial. Although the defacement inflicted by a hacker on a website is visual, there is actually no physical damage – and

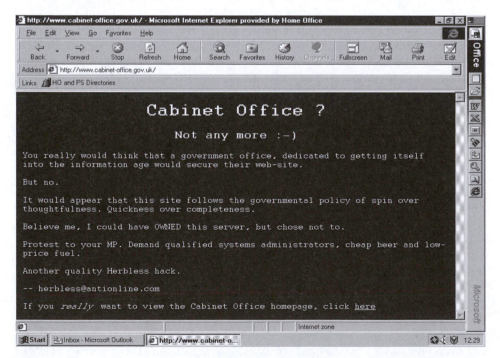

Figure 11.1 The government Cabinet Office website hacked in August 2000

repairing the damage done usually involves nothing more than downloading the original file of computer code to replace the corrupted one. The effects of online vandalism, however, are said to be disproportionate because the damage to either corporate or political reputation can be substantial (Williams 2004).

The remaining two kinds of activity associated with hackers are cyber-espionage and cyber-terrorism. Cyber-spies break access codes and passwords to enter classified areas on computer networks. The primary aim of the cyber-spy is to appropriate classified knowledge. In comparison cyber-terrorism can take many forms including DoS attacks where entire servers are brought to a standstill, halting business and sometimes even whole economies. The US was victim to the most recent national case of cyber-espionage previously known as *Titan Rain*. In 2003 several US computer networks, including Lockheed Martin, Sandia National Laboratories, Redstone Arsenal and NASA, were hacked from a source originating in China. It is suspected that Chinese officials were attempting to gather intelligence on US defences (Thornburgh 2005). The Estonian Cyberwar of 2007 was the first coordinated attack on a nation's critical national infrastructure. The attacks, supposedly originating from Russia, targeted the Estonian parliament, banks, ministries, newspapers and broadcasters. Distributed denial of service attacks, facilitated by the use of bot-nets, were used to bring websites and internal server systems to a standstill.

It is no secret that military strategists are preparing to counter 'information warfare', so defined when intruders enter major computer systems and cause damage to their contents thus causing considerable damage to the target. It is known that such intruders can infiltrate and tamper with national insurance numbers and tax codes, bringing economies to a standstill (Wall 2001). Such evidence suggests a gap seems to be opening between society's increasing dependence upon ICTs and its ability to maintain and control them. Given the vast array of illicit activities associated with hacking it is difficult to adequately approximate the potential impacts to domestic users and businesses.

Online fraud

Financial fraud is an umbrella term for a myriad of illicit activities. Computer networks and the Internet have facilitated financial fraud and have allowed previously ill-equipped would-be criminals to illicitly appropriate funds. There are currently three common methods that facilitate this type of cybercrime. The first, trojans, has already been discussed. Briefly, these malware programs surreptitiously record computer activity, via key loggers and screen grabbers, to identify and communicate back to the cyber criminal sensitive security information. The other two methods are phishing and pharming. Phishing attacks use both social engineering and technical subterfuge to steal consumers' personal identity data and financial account credentials. Such schemes use 'spoofed' e-mails to lead consumers to counterfeit websites designed to trick recipients into divulging financial data such as credit card numbers, account usernames and passwords. By hijacking brand names of banks, e-retailers and credit card companies, these cyber criminals often convince recipients to respond. Pharming removes the social engineering element with a technological fix. Usually via a trojan malware is installed on a victim's computer that automatically directs the user to the spoof website address when the original bookmark is selected.

In 2004 overall annual costs to banks in the US as a result of phishing varied between $500 million (Ponemon Institute 2004) and $1.2 billion (Gartner Research 2004). UK data show that there were over ten thousand phishing attacks in the first quarter of 2008, a 200 per cent increase on the same period in 2007. However, the costs of phishing have decreased by a third from £33.5 million in 2006 to £22.6 million in 2007 (APACS 2008a). This is due to a range of new technologies implemented by the banking sector since 2006. It must be noted that these amounts are significantly less than those resulting from 'traditional' credit card fraud. However, given the significant rise in online banking since the start of the decade (3.5 million online bankers in 2000 compared to 21 million in 2007 – a 505 per cent increase) phishing attempts and their associated losses will continue to rise (APACS 2008b).

Intellectual property violations and online theft

Intellectual property (IP) theft has increased exponentially since the introduction of the domestic Internet. Illegally downloading copyright music, television programmes and movies are the most common form of IP theft online. Barlow (1994: 1) was one of the first writers to alert the legal community to the potential problems the Internet may pose to patent and copyright law:

> If our property can be infinitely reproduced and instantaneously distributed all over the planet without cost, without our knowledge, without it even leaving our possession, how can we protect it?

It is claimed that annually the audio-visual industry loses £800 million through copyright theft with the music industry losing £1.1 billion between 2003 and 2006 due to illegal downloading (AAIPT 2009). The case of *A&M Records, Inc.* v. *Napster, Inc.* (2000)[5] was the most notorious successful prosecution for the theft of music online. The defendant, the owner of the Napster music website, was accused of distributing and selling copyright musical material. The Offending, Crime and Justice Survey (2003) found that of all online crime copyright theft was by far the most prevalent among respondents – 20 per cent of males and 9 per cent of females admitted to illegally downloading copyright material. Prosecuting these individuals is complex given the lack of resources available, the technology used and the inadequacy of law. To counter these hurdles legislation updating existing copyright laws has proliferated over the past decade. In particular the Digital Millennium Copyright Act 1998 (DMCA) was introduced to update US law for the digital age. Certain aspects of the Act made Internet service providers (ISPs) liable for copyright violations. While the DMCA was comprehensive enough to satisfy the World Intellectual Property Organisation's (WIPO) treaties, there were still concerns over its inadequate protection for copyright owners. In Europe, the European Parliament Directive 2001/29/EC harmonised copyright law in relation to the

Internet. It stresses that while no new concepts for the protection of intellectual property are needed in the information age, current laws in member states need to be adapted to respond to new technologies and forms of exploitation.

Laws relating to online theft lack the international coordination of copyright regulations. A particular challenge to non-IP-related theft online are Web 3.0 platforms such as the virtual world Second Life and the gaming world World of Warcraft. Within these online spaces community members and players own and exchange virtual property which has actual monetary value offline. The case of the Shanghai gamers Qiu Chengwei and Zhu Caoyuan in 2005 provides a lucid example of the inadequacies of law in relation to non-IP online theft. Both were players of the online game *Legends of Mir 3* which allows thousands of users from all over the globe to participate synchronously. In this game items can be used to enhance the power and status of players. In this case Chengwei loaned his 'dragon sabre' to Caoyuan shortly after acquiring it. Caoyuan then proceeded to sell the sabre on eBay without permission for the sum of 7,200 yuan (£460). Chengwei informed the police of this theft. However, the authorities claimed it could not be reported as theft as the sabre did not physically exist. As a result of this unsatisfactory response Chengwei murdered Caoyuan in real life (BBC 2005). While some countries such as South Korea do have laws that govern the theft of virtual property many do not noting that theft is only possible if the item is physically tangible.

Online violence

Online violence is the term used to describe online activities which have the potential to harm others via text and other 'digital performances'. These activities manifest in textual, visual and audio form, meaning the violence is not actually physically experienced (though psychological harm is possible). Online violence can be delineated by its perceived seriousness. Least serious are heated debates on message boards and e-mail, often referred to as flaming (Joinson 2003). At worst, a defamatory remark may be made about someone's inferior intellect or flawed argument. These exchanges are considered minor in terms of online violence due to the fact that their consequences never mount to anything more than a bruised ego.

More serious are 'digital performances' that are hate motivated. To take two examples, racial and homophobic hate-related online violence is in abundance in the form of extremist web pages (Mann *et al.* 2003). Protected under freedom of speech laws in the US, these sites employ shocking tactics to drum up support for their extremist viewpoints. In particular, some sites go as far as to display images of hate-related homicide victims in distasteful ways to heighten their very often misguided outlook on society's minorities (Schafer 2002). The use of derogatory homophobic and racist text on these sites, combined with the use of inappropriate imagery and sound, results in a digital performance which is violent and potentially psychologically harmful, not only to the victim's families but also to the wider community.

Of potentially more harm are the violent activities of online stalkers. Cyberstalking involves the use of electronic mediums, such as the Internet, to pursue, harass or contact another in an unsolicited fashion (Petherick 2000).

Most often, given the vast distances that the Internet spans, this behaviour may never manifest itself in the physical sense, but this does not mean that the pursuit is any less distressing. Petherick (2000: 1) states that 'there are a wide variety of means by which individuals may seek out and harass individuals even though they may not share the same geographic borders, and this may present a range of physical, emotional, and psychological consequences to the victim'. Yet there still remains some concern that cyberstalking might be a prelude to its physical manifestation (Reno 1997).

A more contentious debate in the online violence literature exists around the phenomenon that has become known as 'virtual rape' (MacKinnon 1997). These cases of virtual violence have completely escaped any legal rationalisation. In the most famous case a hacker was able to enter an online community and take control over community members' actions (Dibbell 1993). Because movement and action within virtual communities is expressed through text, the 'virtual rapist' was able to manipulate avatars' actions against their will. What essentially followed was a salacious depiction of violent rape upon several individuals in real time. While no one was physically harmed, community members reported being traumatised by the event. This case was taken so seriously that the whole community (over 1,000 members) voted on what action should be taken against the perpetrator. The imperative point to be made here is that the physical self of the perpetrator, the individual that exists in the offline world, could not be physically harmed, and only his online persona could be punished.

Prevalence and impact of cybercrime

Attempts to quantify computer-related offences are difficult due to a lack of reporting and recording. In most cases individuals or businesses may not realise an offence has occurred, and indeed it may not have, given the dubious legal status of some cyber acts. Others may feel the acts are not serious enough, that the police would not be interested or that an alternative method of mediation is required. When cybercrime is reported to the police current record keeping and crime recording practices within individual forces preclude the identification of an electronic element in the modus operandi (Hyde-Bales *et al.* 2004). Such poor recording practices preclude any detailed official source analysis on the prevalence of cybercrime in England and Wales.

However, these complexities have not prevented other organisations from attempts at quantification. Since the turn of the century there has been a burgeoning of surveys attempting to measure the extent of the cybercrime problem. Governments as well as voluntary and public organisations are now collecting data on the incidence of business and personal cybercrimes. In particular the now disbanded UK National High-Tech Crime Unit (NHTCU) in conjunction with National Opinion Poll (NOP) conducted an annual cybercrime business survey between 2002 and 2004. Notably the Department for Business, Enterprise and Regulatory Reform – BERR (formerly the Department for Trade and Industry) – has published its Information Security Breaches Survey (ISBS) since 1997. Less systematically the British Chambers of Commerce, the Audit Commission and the Federation of Small Businesses have also commissioned research into the prevalence of business cybercrime victimisation. Recently the British Crime Survey (BCS) and the Offending, Crime and Justice Survey (OCJS) have for the first time shed light upon cybercrime victimisation and offending among the general population. Overseas the US Federal Bureau of Investigation (FBI) in arrangement with the Computer Security Institute (CSI) conduct an annual computer crime and security survey, targeting over 700 public and private businesses. The Australian government also conducts its own survey. Beyond national boundaries, transnational organisations and societies have begun to survey their clients and members to uncover the dark figure of cybercrime – the Global Security Survey being the most prominent. Combined, these efforts help lift the veil on the true extent of cybercrime activity.

Trends in business cybercrime

The data presented in Figure 11.2 show a synthesis of four key national and international surveys of business cybercrime. Data available on the prevalence and impact of business cybercrime in the UK dates back to the first of BERR's Information Security Breaches Surveys in 1998. The Global Information Security Survey in 2002 was the first comparable systematic international survey. Overseas national surveys, such as the CSI/FBI survey, precede this but are of less relevance to the UK and function more as a comparison. BERR's ISBS shows a steady increase in cybercrime in the UK from a low of 18 per cent in 1998 to a high of 74 per cent in 2004. The prevalence then decreases steadily to 43 per cent in 2008.

National High-Tech Crime Unit surveys show a similar pattern of increase between 2003 and 2004. The unexpected high of 97 per cent of businesses

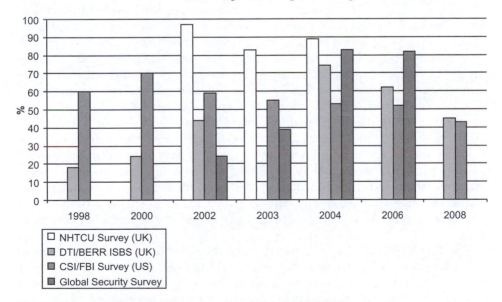

Figure 11.2 Prevalence of business cybercrime (1998–2008)

reporting cybercrime in 2002 is likely to have been inflated by a smaller sample (25 per cent less than subsequent years) and categorisation anomalies.[6] The 2004 survey included a sample of 200 companies (30 per cent from the critical national infrastructure) and revealed a victimisation rate of 89 per cent. International trends mimic the early rise in UK national cybercrime levels. The Global Information Security Survey shows a threefold increase in the prevalence of cybercrime over just three years. Globally just over four out of every five financial businesses reported suffering cybercrime in 2004 compared to only one in four in 2002. These figures represent a near exponential growth in cybercrime victimisation on a global scale.

The CSI and the FBI in the US conduct an annual computer crime and security survey, gathering information from over 700 corporations, government agencies, financial institutions, medical facilities and universities. Each year the survey provides data on the prevalence of cybercrime covering hacking, fraud and denial of service attacks, among many others. Contrary to UK and global trends this survey has shown a steady decrease in the overall incidence of cybercrime (from a high of 70 per cent in 2000 to a low of 44 per cent in 2008). The Australian Computer Crime and Security Survey paints a less severe picture than both the US and UK. It also focuses upon public and private companies and its latest incarnation included over 389 respondents. Over all sectors only 22 per cent had experienced a computer-related attack in 2006, down from highs of 67 per cent in 2002, 49 per cent in 2004 and 35 per cent in 2005.

Specific business cybercrime trends

Four key UK national surveys provided partial data on cybercrime type. Figure 11.3 shows a UK-wide breakdown of cybercrime for the year 2004.[7] Breaking down the figures in the NHTCU survey shows that viruses, worms and trojans affected 83 per cent of companies, 15 per cent reported the use of their systems for illegitimate purposes, denial of service attacks impacted upon 14 per cent of companies, 11 per cent suffered unauthorised access to systems, 10 per cent reported theft of data and 9 per cent were victim of financial fraud via computer systems. Analysis by business size indicated that larger companies (those with over 1,000 employees) were more likely to encounter financial fraud and theft of information compared to smaller organisations (less than 1,000 employees). Small organisations were also less likely compared to larger firms to become victim to DoS attacks and telecoms fraud. The financial and telecoms sectors were more likely to have suffered from financial fraud – phishing (illegitimately obtaining and utilising consumers' personal identity data and financial account credentials), fraudulent use of stolen data and keylogging (the use of spyware to record PC-user activity). Both sectors were also more likely than others to have suffered theft of information or data.

The DTI's ISBS 2005 shows that the majority of breaches were a result of virus infection (50 per cent), misuse of information systems (22 per cent), hacking attempts (17 per cent) and fraud involving computers (11 per cent). Analysis by business size revealed large companies were more likely than

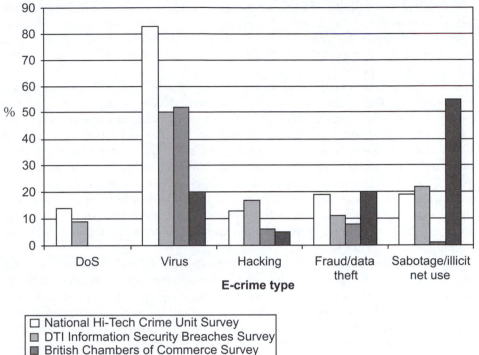

The chart shows cybercrime prevalence by type.

Figure 11.3 Cybercrime prevalence by type 2004

SMEs to receive viruses and to experience system failure and data corruption. Compared to SMEs large firms were also three times as likely to have had incidents involving staff misusing information systems and over four times as likely to have experienced theft or fraud involving computers. Medium-sized companies were more likely than others to experience website and system hacking attempts. Financial services were most likely to have received the most viruses, experienced staff misuse of information systems, experienced a website or systems hack attempt, experienced theft and fraud involving computers and experienced systems failure and data corruption.

The British Chambers of Commerce has conducted several general crime surveys that have incorporated specific questions on cybercrime. *Setting Businesses Free from Crime* (2004) found that 84 per cent of the 2,788 respondents had experienced a malicious ICT incident. Disaggregated figures show that 52 per cent were subject to virus attacks, 1 per cent experienced theft of company data, 6 per cent experienced hacking, 1 per cent experienced malicious deletion of critical data, and 6 per cent experienced credit card fraud. Analysis by business revenue revealed that organisations with a turnover of between £1 million and £5 million were more likely than those with a lower turnover to experience virus attacks. Sectoral analysis found that the hotel and catering sector was more likely than other sectors to experience credit card fraud. Hacking was found to be a greater issue for those in the professional services compared to other sectors. Uniquely this survey also conducted a geographical analysis and found statistically significant differences in the rates of virus infection. Firms in the North East and West Midlands reported the greatest occurrence of virus infection (63 per cent and 61 per cent respectively), while Wales and Scotland reported the lowest (19 per cent and 27 per cent respectively).

The Audit Commission has conducted research into ICT misuse since its inception. The 2004 report *ICT Fraud and Abuse*, which relates to the public sector only, revealed that 46 per cent of respondents had experienced cybercrime. Of those reporting victimisation, 20 per cent had experienced virus attacks, system or website hacking had been experienced by 5 per cent of respondents, 20 per cent had experienced financial fraud and theft of data and 55 per cent experienced sabotage or illicit net use. Given the nature of the sample it is reasonable to assume that in 2004 the public sector was less likely than the private sector to have experienced virus attacks and hacking attempts, but were more likely to have experienced fraud or theft of data and sabotage or illicit net use.

In comparison to UK national surveys the US CSI/FBI survey in 2005 uncovered that 56 per cent of respondents suffered computer security breaches within the previous twelve months. The most prevalent incidents were virus attacks followed by access to unauthorised information and denial of service attacks. The Australian survey of the same year found that virus, worm and trojan infection affected 64 per cent of companies, 24 per cent were victim to denial of service attacks, 15 per cent reported unauthorised access to information, 14 per cent had confidential information stolen, 2 per cent were subject to telecommunications fraud and 8 per cent had their websites defaced (AusCERT 2005).

The findings from UK national and overseas surveys are illuminating and paint quite distinct pictures of the cybercrime problem. It is likely that dramatic variance in cybercrime trends are the result of several factors. First, many companies, especially those in the financial sector, prefer to keep knowledge of victimisation to a minimum given the damage security breaches have on customer confidence and new business. As a result incidents are rarely reported to the police (unless concerning large financial losses which involve insurance claims) and are possibly not divulged to researchers working on victimisation surveys. Second, methodological differences such as the categorisation of cybercrimes and sample selection impact upon the types of data collected. Last, many cybercrimes go unnoticed and unrecorded by IT security managers and their staff meaning the data collected via surveys should be interpreted with a degree of caution. Like some crimes it is likely a large dark figure exists in relation to cybercrime.

Personal cybercrime

Assessing for the impact of cybercrimes on businesses and the national critical infrastructure has become commonplace. However, quantifying the prevalence and impact of similar acts on domestic Internet users began as late as 2003 in the UK. The 2003 British Crime Survey was the first to include a technology crimes module. Credit card fraud, mobile phone theft, mobile text harassment, online harassment and access to obscene electronic materials were some of the areas covered by the new module. This was the first systematic attempt in the UK to understand the extent of Internet-related victimisation. In relation to credit card fraud 75 per cent of the sample admitted to being anxious about using their credit card online. This is not surprising given persistent media attention on Internet-related fraud and alarming figures indicating a continued increase in credit card losses (APACS 2004). Virus victimisation affected just over 18 per cent of households. While this is much lower than reported in business surveys, it is more likely that domestic users fail to recognise infection or neglect to report their victimisation. Hacking affected just over 2 per cent of Internet-using households, 12 per cent were victim to e-mail harassment and 21 per cent had accessed or been sent offensive or upsetting unsolicited material via the Internet.

The UK-based Offending, Crime and Justice Survey (2003) gathered data on cyber offenders rather than victims. While self-report studies have their methodological flaws, the data reported on is still marginally reliable and worthy of note. Only one per cent of 18–65 year olds admitted to taking part in Internet-related fraud. Similar low offending figures were evident for virus sending (0.9 per cent), hacking (0.9 per cent), e-mail harassment (0.7 per cent), visiting racist websites (0.7 per cent) and visiting websites to obtain information on how to commit a crime (1.5 per cent). The only significant rate of online offending was copyright theft – over 20 per cent of males and over 9 per cent of females admitted to illegally downloading copyright material. However, when analysed by age group younger people were significantly more likely to become involved in all the above crime types compared to older age groups. Overall almost 11 per cent of respondents who said they used the Internet admitted to committing a technology crime.

Governance of cybercrime

Wall and Williams (2007) promote a nodal governance perspective as one way of mapping the regulation of cybercrime. They identify 'proximal' (online) and 'distal' (offline) forms of control. Methods of 'policing' online behaviour that are exercised by proximal (online) nodes such as online reputation management systems, virtual 'police' services and vigilante groups that employ 'online shaming' are juxtaposed to the more 'traditional' forms of distal (offline) nodes such as offline policing and criminal justice processes. Both forms of governance interact to produce a highly ordered space where online behaviours are constantly being monitored and controlled via technological, social, legal and market forces.

Distal governance

The economic drive to take advantage of networked information technologies has resulted in calls for the regulation and control of certain forms of electronic information. Technically the Internet is difficult to regulate. Its capacity to span the globe, ignorant of national boundaries, means that no one body of law has precedence. Barlow (1996: 1) describes how this proves problematic for policymakers:

> ... the Internet is too widespread to be easily dominated by any single government. By creating a seamless global-economic zone, borderless and unregulatable, the Internet calls into question the very idea of a nation-state.

However, it is a misnomer to state that the Internet and other forms of computer-mediated communication are not subject to any form of regulation. In fact, it may be more appropriate to talk of the governance of the Internet instead of regulation, as the discourse of governance lends itself to the very nature of the technology. Governance refers to the regulation of relationships in complex systems which can be performed by a wide variety of public and private, state and non-state, national and international, institutions and practices. The Internet is a complex system of interconnections between technologies, organisations and individuals. Any attempt to govern such a complex system of interconnectivities requires a diverse and dynamic approach. Walker and Akdeniz (1998) provide an overview of a governing framework that is both diverse in its constituent components and dynamic in its approach that is currently in operation:

- Global international regulatory solutions by the likes of the OECD and the United Nations.

- Regional supranational legislation such as by the European Union.

- Regulations by individual governments at a national or local level, such as through police squads and customs control units.

- Self-imposed regulation by the ISPs with industry-wide codes of conduct, which would transcend national boundaries.

- Transnational and national pressure groups made up of end-users.

- Rating systems such as the Platform for Internet Content Selection (PICS).

- Self-imposed regulation, such as through software filters, to be used by end users.

- Hotlines and pressure organisations to report illegal content such as child pornography. The Internet Watch Foundation (IWF) is one such incarnation in the UK.

Despite this framework criminal justice systems have been slow to react adequately to cybercrime. In the UK the advent of the National High-Tech Crime Unit (NHTCU) in 2001 was a welcome addition to the policing cybercrime arsenal. During its operation the unit provided cybercrime prevention information to UK businesses and successfully investigated an array of serious cybercrimes. The Serious Organised Crime and Police Act 2005 disbanded the NHTCU and relocated part of its operation in the newly formed Serious Organised Crime Agency (SOCA) which also combined the National Crime Squad and National Criminal Intelligence Service. In 2008 the Police Central e-Crime Unit (PCeU) was formed to work in conjunction with SOCA, the National Fraud Reporting Centre and Intelligence Bureau (NFRC/NFIB) and Police Service High-Tech Crime Units. PCeU is located within the Metropolitan Police Service and is comprised of six units. The Computer Crime Team deal with investigations and prosecutions, the National e-Crime Enforcement Team (NeET) gather evidence and intelligence, the Intelligence Team communicate intelligence to forces and NFIB, the Co-ordination and Communication Team are responsible for research, development and policy, the Partnership Development Team foster links with government and industry and the Prevention Team communicate prevention information to industry.

Unlike the PCeU local police services are less able to deal with cybercrime reports. While almost each of the 43 police services has some form of computer crime or economic crime unit, a significant number of them are not currently dealing with cybercrime incidents adequately. A recent Home Office study exposed the serious gaps in recording and dealing with cybercrime at the local police service level (Hyde-Bales *et al.* 2004). The study found that there were no formal recording practices for crimes that involve computers and the Internet. In relation to cybercrime the only legal framework available to crime control agencies is the Computer Misuse Act 1990. This Act does not define specific offence categories for the majority of the current cybercrime threats. The law currently takes a technology neutral stance to offences (for example, theft is theft whatever the modus operandi). This is a flexible approach that ensures the law does not fall behind the rapidly changing technological landscape. However, such provisions are inadequate when attempts are made to accurately quantify the instances of crime facilitated by computers. In an attempt to combat this shortfall some local forces attach a computer crime marker to command and control incident records, crime desk records and crime-related intelligence logs. These practices, however, are far from systematic and significant gaps still remain in the recording process.

At the transnational level the Convention on Cybercrime (2001) might be considered one of the most systematic attempts at regulating 'harmful' and criminal activities that employ the use of computers. The aim of the European Commission was to approximate substantive law in the area of cybercrime. It was considered that with common definitions, incriminations and sanctions, cybercrime could be successfully regulated. Four areas were focused upon: offences against the confidentiality and integrity of computer data and systems; computer-related offences; content-related offences; and offences related to infringements of copyright and related rights. Further protocols to the convention concerning content that is xenophobic and racist have also been added.[8] However, there are still major concerns that the Convention jeopardises certain civil liberties and places an unreasonable burden on Internet service providers. If and when these concerns are overcome the integration of the convention into the legal system in England and Wales will significantly strengthen the ability of the criminal justice system to regulate cybercrime.

Proximal governance

Technological control

Technology is 'native' to the environment within which cybercrimes take place. The idea that technology is a more effective regulator of cyberspace than laws has been advanced by Lessig (1999) and others (see discussion in Wall 2007a: 190–2). It was Lessig's (1999) aim to counter the technologically deterministic view that the Internet could not be regulated. Instead he subscribed to a 'digital realism' that recognised the disruptive capacity of technology within cyberspace. Rejecting Boyle's (1997) notion of an Internet Holy Trinity – that regulation was impossible due to the *technology of the medium*, the *geographical distribution of its users* and the *nature of its content* – Lessig (1999) found that the thread that links all of the Internet's characteristics together – code or architecture – could be used to control behaviour.

The effectiveness of technology as a regulator can be accounted for in several ways. First, technology can disrupt human action, forcing individuals to renegotiate paths and goals (Latour 2000). Second, technology, code or architecture is malleable; it is easily shaped by actors that have access to its control. Third, the way in which technology imposes constraints on how people can behave is more pervasive and immediate than other modes of regulation. Fourth, technology is more readily and rapidly adaptive than laws, norms or markets to cyber-criminal threats, allowing it to control both criminal and sub-criminal behaviour. Fifth, changes to system architecture incorporate a preventative approach. It is far more effective to prevent an online offence as opposed to reactively identifying and apprehending an offender. Finally, it is a native form of regulation making it less contentious. Often the origins of the technology are concealed, and hence its regulatory practice is perceived as less coercive than a state-sponsored regime. Technology is then perceived to be more benign, merely shaping – or even facilitating – individual choices (Boyle 1997). The effectiveness of technology as a regulator then lies in its ability to alter behaviours, its ability to be shaped, its rapid adaptability, its *ex ante* approach, its wide-reaching scope, its sensitivity towards criminal and sub-criminal activity and its less visible approach to social control.

However, some writers argue that this rather uncritical approach to techno-mediated regulation is short-sighted. Instead of being a self-executing benign regulator, Hosein *et al.* (2003) talk of technology as a biased cultural artefact, which is embedded with subjectivity. For this reason alone, there can be no certainty that technology will produce a particular behaviour. Hosein *et al.* (2003) continue to complicate this relationship. Instead of claiming it is the technology that determines freedom and rights, they take a non-technologically deterministic approach, arguing instead that individuals (codewriters) become the alternative sovereign. Concerns are raised about the accountability of these new masked regulators, and the basis or root of their authority is questioned.

Social control

Collections of Internet users have begun to regulate themselves as their online social formations have expanded and matured. Users of newsgroups, Web

2.0 platforms (e.g Facebook), auction sites (e.g. eBay) and virtual worlds (e.g. Second Life) have developed complex codes of conduct that exist alongside formal legal and technological systems. Williams (2006a) shows how social control within one virtual world developed over time. In Cyberworlds deviant behaviour rapidly matured over several years from an oligarchic and vigilante-based system to a formal policing model. In the early years of Cyberworlds, social control was organised around a *community involvement* model, in that the community took responsibility for the policing on a non-structured basis (Gill 1994). World creators would monitor behaviour, forming regulations that were specific to their environment. Implementation of these regulations was ad hoc, and there was no formalised method for dealing with troublesome individuals. In a response to the increasing sophistication and proliferation of deviant acts, it was recognised that an equivalent organised response had to be developed if Cyberworlds were to maintain cohesion. As a result the Peacekeepers, the community voluntary police, were established. This development was considered a progression to a *volunteer community policing* model where the community provides some limited structure to policing (Gill 1994).

Other online spaces utilise similar social control mechanisms. Amazon and eBay utilise reputation management systems to shame those who break rules. A late payment or misleading description of an item can result in negative *feedback* reducing the overall 'reputation' score of buyers and sellers. Those with poor reputations then find it more difficult to buy and sell their items online. Instances of vigilante justice have emerged in other text-based virtual worlds. Reid (1999) recounts an instance of 'virtual rape' in the multi-user domain named JennyMUSH, an environment created for the purpose of counselling women who had suffered offline sexual abuse. The harasser taunted and verbally abused several of the online visitors while performing acts of sexual violence through text. Given the nature of the environment the assailant's actions were considered exceptionally harmful. Members of the community were encouraged to textually harass the assailant in an attempt to deliver punishment. These examples show how *proximal* social control forms part of a complex matrix of online governance which continuously monitors and moulds the behaviour of Internet users.

Conclusion

Terrestrial crimes have been re-engineered to take advantage of new information communication technologies. The transformative effects of these technologies on crime are both temporal and spatial. These effects change the modus operandi of 'traditional' crimes carried out over the Internet while also altering their potential prevalence and impact upon victims. These transformations have challenged what we understand as crime, leading to debate about quantification and new forms and partnerships of control. However, efforts to understand the nature, prevalence and governance of cybercrime lag behind exponential technological advancement. As legal and criminal justice systems catch up with new ways of committing crimes alternative more sophisticated methods are being developed in the wings. An ideal example is the continued failure of legal and criminal justice systems in relation to the prevention of online copyright theft. As legislation is introduced new technologies emerge that escape regulation (e.g. torrent technology replaced peer-to-peer technology in the downloading of copyright material). Given the failures of law it has become favourable to control cybercrime via a matrix of governance featuring both proximal and distal nodes of regulation. This complex assemblage of social, technological, legal and market forces is as rapidly adaptable as the cybercrimes it seeks to regulate.

Selected further reading

Recently several key texts have emerged that provide one-stop-shop overviews of cybercrime. These include: Wall (2007a), *Cybercrime: The Transformation of Crime in the Information Age*; Yar (2006), *Cybercrime and Society*; Fafinski (2009), *Computer Misuse: Response, Regulation and the Law*; and Jewkes and Yar (2009) *Handbook of Internet Crime*. Other relevant texts include: Williams (2006a), *Virtually Criminal*; Wall (2003), *Cyberspace Crime*; and Jewkes (2007), *Crime Online*. In relation to policing the Internet the following journal articles are relevant: Wall and Williams (2007), 'Policing diversity in the digital age: maintaining order in virtual communities'; Williams (2006b), 'Policing and cybersociety: the maturation of regulation within an online community'; Wall (2007b) 'Policing cybercrime: situating the public police in networks of security in cyberspace'; and Wall (1998) 'Catching cyber-criminals: policing the Internet'. Exponential advances in the technological landscape result in rapidly outdated statistics on cybercrime. For up-to-date figures on business cybercrime victimisation in the UK readers are advised to regularly check the website of the Department for Business, Innovation and Skills. Their Information Security Breaches Survey which is carried out every two years is the definitive source on business cybercrime victimisation. Recent versions of the British Crime Survey have included questions on cybercrime which has resulted in some publications (see Allen *et al.* (2005), *Fraud and Technology Crimes: Findings from the 2002/3 British Crime Survey and 2003 Offending, Crime and Justice Survey*). Regularly check the RDS website for similar future Home Office BCS publications.

Notes

1 Based on Nielsen Ratings: Internet World Stats (2009), online at: http://www.internetworldstats.com/stats.htm.
2 To date only 23 of the 46 member and non-member states of the Council of Europe who signed the Convention have ratified it. Member states that have ratified the convention include: Albania, Armenia, Bosnia and Herzegovina, Bulgaria, Croatia, Cyprus, Denmark, Estonia, Finland, France, Hungary, Iceland, Italy, Latvia, Lithuania, Netherlands, Norway, Romania, Slovakia, Slovenia, the former Yugoslav Republic of Macedonia, Ukraine and the United States. States yet to ratify the convention include: Austria, Azerbaijan, Belgium, the Czech Republic, Georgia, Germany, Greece, Ireland, Liechtenstein, Luxembourg, Malta, Moldova, Montenegro, Poland, Portugal, Serbia, Spain, Sweden, Switzerland, the United Kingdom, Canada, Japan and South Africa. Why?

3 It is acknowledged that a small volume of terrestrial criminal activity is not dependent upon perpetrator-victim/target temporal-spatial coalescence, e.g. certain white-collar crimes.

4 However, the OCJS survey also indicated that those from council estates and other low-income areas were more likely to admit to these crimes compared to those from affluent family, suburban and rural areas. This contrary evidence may be a result of the nature of the self-report methodology utilised. However, it is worth noting that the so called 'digital divide' is subject to erosion, due in part to governments' (at both national and European levels) eInclusive initiatives.

5 A&M Records, Inc. v. Napster, Inc. (2000) 239 F.3d 1004.

6 The 2002 survey found a high prevalence of hardware theft that may have artificially inflated overall figures.

7 The year 2004 was taken as a comparison as it was the last year the NHTCU survey was run.

8 Additional Protocol to the Convention on Cybercrime, concerning the criminalisation of acts of a racist and xenophobic nature committed through computer systems, CETS No. 189.

References

Allen, J., Forrest, S., Levi, M., Roy, H. and Sutton, M. (2005) *Fraud and Technology Crimes: Findings from the 2002/3 British Crime Survey and 2003 Offending, Crime and Justice Survey*. London: Home Office.

Alliance Against IP Theft (AAIPT) (2009), available at: http://www.allianceagainstiptheft.co.uk/ff.htm.

APACS (2004) *Online Banking Survey 2004*. Online at: http://www.apacs.org.uk/.

Association for Payment Clearing Services (APACS) (2008a) Online at: http://www.apacs.org.uk/08_04_15.html.

Association for Payment Clearing Services (APACS) (2008b) Online at: http://www.apacs.org.uk/08_07_24.htm.

Audit Commission (2004) *ICT Fraud and Abuse 2004*. Online at: http://www.audit-commission.gov.uk/SiteCollectionDocuments/AuditCommissionReports/NationalStudies/ictfraudabuse2004.pdf.

AusCERT (2005) *Computer Crime and Security Survey*. Online at: http://www.auscert.org.au/crimesurvey.

Bank of Scotland Business Banking (2005) *Small Business Survey*. Edinburgh: Bank of Scotland.

Barlow, J. P. (1994) 'The economy of ideas: a framework for rethinking patents and copyrights in the digital age (everything you know about intellectual property is wrong)', *Wired*, 2/3: 84.

Barlow, J. P. (1996) *A Cyberspace Independence Declaration*. Online at: http://www.eff.org/~barlow.

BBC (2005) *'Game theft' led to fatal attack*. Online at: http://news.bbc.co.uk/1/low/technology/4397159.stm.

Becker, H. (1963) *Outsiders: Studies in the Sociology of Deviance*. New York: Free Press.

Boyle, J. (1997) 'Foucault in cyberspace: surveillance, sovereignty and hard-wired censors', *University of Cincinnati Law Review*, 177. Online at: http://www.law.duke.edu/boylesite/foucault.htm#N_1_.

British Chambers of Commerce (2004) *Setting Businesses Free from Crime*. Online at: http://www.chamberonline.co.uk/policy/issues/businesscrime/crimereport.pdf.

Capella, W. (2001) 'Not such a neat net: some comments on virtual criminality', *Social and Legal Studies*, 10: 229–49.

Computer Economics (2005) *Malware Report: The Impact if Malicious Code Attacks*. Online at: http://www.computereconomics.com/article.cfm?id=1090.

Corporate IT Forum (2003) *Cost of Security Incident Response Survey*. Hertfordshire: Corporate IT Forum.

Council of the European Union (2000) *Proposal for the Extension of Europol's Mandate to the Fight against Cybercrime*, Note from Presidency to Article 36 Committee. Online at: http://www.xs4all.nl/~respub/europol/cyberpol.html.

CSI/FBI (2005) *Computer Crime and Security Survey*. Online at: http://www.gocsi.com/forms/fbi/csi_fbi_survey.jhtml;jsessionid=CCK2I04WC5VJCQSNDBGCKH0CJUMEKJVN.

Dibbell, J. (1993) 'A rape in cyberspace; or, how an evil clown, a Haitian trickster spirit, two wizards, and a cast of dozens turned a database into a society', *The Village Voice*. Online at: http://www.juliandibbell.com/texts/bungle_vv.html.

DTI (2006) *Information Security Breaches Survey*. London: PriceWaterhouseCoopers.

European Committee on Crime Problems (2001) *Convention on Cybercrime*. Brussels: Council of Europe.

Fafinski, S. (2009) *Computer Misuse: Response, Regulation and the Law*. Cullompton: Willan.

Federation of Small Businesses (2006) *Lifting the Barriers to Growth in UK Small Businesses*. London: FSB.

Gartner Research (2004) Online at: http://www.gartner.com/DisplayDocument?doc_cd=120804.

Giddens, A. (1990) *The Consequences of Modernity*. Oxford: Polity Press.

Gill, M. (1994) *Crime at Work: Studies in Security and Crime Prevention*. Leicester: Perpetuity Press.

Hosein, G., Tsavios, P. and Whitley, E. (2003) 'Regulating architecture and architectures of regulation: contributions from information systems', *International Review of Law, Computers and Technology*, 17 (1): 85–98.

Hyde-Bales, K., Morris, S. and Charlton, A. (2004) *The Police Recording of Computer Crime*. London: Stationery Office.

Jewkes, Y. (ed.) (2007) *Crime Online*. Cullompton: Willan.

Jewkes, Y. and Yar, M. (eds) (2009) *Handbook of Internet Crime*. Cullompton: Willan.

Joinson, A. N. (2003) *Understanding the Psychology of Internet Behavior*. New York: Palgrave Macmillan.

Latour, B. (2000) 'When things strike back: a possible contribution of science studies to the social sciences', *British Journal of Sociology*, 51 (1): 231–55.

Lessig, L. (1999) *Code and Other Laws of Cyberspace*. New York: Basic Books.

Levi, M. (2001) '"Between the risk and the reality falls the shadow": evidence and urban legends in computer fraud', in D. S. Wall (ed.), *Crime and the Internet*. London: Routledge.

Levy, S. (1984) *Hackers: Heroes of the Computer Revolution*. New York: Bantam Doubleday Dell.

Mackinnon, R. C. (1997) 'Virtual rape', *Journal of Computer Mediated Communication*, 2 (4). Online at: http://jcmc.indiana.edu/vol2/issue4/mackinnon.html.

Mann, D., Sutton, M. and Tuffin, R. (2003) 'The evolution of hate: social dynamics in white racist newsgroups', *Internet Journal of Criminology* (n.p.).

Newman, G. R. and Clarke, R. V. (2003) *Superhighway Robbery: Preventing e-commerce Crime*. Cullompton: Willan.

Office for National Statistics (ONS) (2009) Online at: http://www.statistics.gov.uk/statbase/prep/5672.asp.

Petherick, W. (2000) *Cyber-Stalking: Obsessional Pursuit and the Digital Criminal*. Online at: http://www.trutv.com/library/crime/criminal_mind/psychology/cyberstalking/1.html.

Ponemon Institute (2004) *National Spoofing and Phishing Study*. Michigan: Ponemon Institute.

Reid, E. (1999) 'Hierarchy and power: social control in cyberspace', in P. Kollock and A. Smith (eds), *Communities in Cyberspace*. London: Routledge.

Reno, Rt Hon. J. (1997) *Keynote Address to the Meeting of the G8 Senior Experts Group on Transnational Organised Crime*. Chantilly, VA. Online at: http://www.usdoj.gov/criminal/cybercrime/agfranc.htm.

Reuters (2003) 16 June. Online at: http://www.reuters.co.uk/newsArticle.jhtml?type=searchNews&storyID=293676.

Schafer, J. A. (2002) 'Spinning the web of hate: web-based hate propagation by extremist organisations', *Journal of Criminal Justice and Popular Culture*, 9 (2): 69–88.

Thornburgh, N. (2005) 'Inside the Chinese hack attack', *Time*. Online at: http://www.time.com/time/nation/article/0,8599,1098371,00.html.

Walker, C. and Akdeniz, Y. (1998) 'The governance of the Internet in Europe with special reference to illegal and harmful content', *Criminal Law Review*, Special Edition on Crime, Criminal Justice and the Internet, pp. 5–18.

Wall, D. S. (1998) 'Catching cyber-criminals: policing the Internet', *International Review of Law Computers and Technology*, 12 (2): 201–18.

Wall, D. S. (2001) 'Maintaining order and law on the Internet', in D. S. Wall (ed.), *Crime and the Internet*. London: Routledge.

Wall, D. S. (ed.) (2003) *Cyberspace Crime*. Aldershot: Dartmouth/Ashgate.

Wall, D. S. (2007a) *Cybercrime: The Transformation of Crime in the Information Age*. Cambridge: Polity.

Wall, D. S. (2007b) 'Policing cybercrime: situating the public police in networks of security in cyberspace', *Police Practice and Research: An International Journal*, 8 (2): 183–205.

Wall, D. S. and Williams, M. (2007) 'Policing diversity in the digital age: maintaining order in virtual communities', *Criminology and Criminal Justice*, 7 (4): 391–415.

Williams, M. (2001) 'The language of cybercrime', in D. S. Wall (ed.), *Crime and the Internet*. London: Routledge, pp. 152–66.

Williams, M. (2004) 'Understanding King Punisher and his Order: vandalism in an online community – motives, meanings and possible solutions', *Internet Journal of Criminology*. Online at: http://www.internetjournalofcriminology.com/Williams%20-%20Understanding%20King%20Punisher%20and%20his%20Order.pdf.

Williams, M. (2006a) *Virtually Criminal: Crime, Deviance and Regulation Online*. London: Routledge.

Williams, M. (2006b) 'Policing and cybersociety: the maturation of regulation within an online community', *Policing and Society*, 17 (1): 59-82.

Woolgar, S. (2002) *Virtual Society? Technology, Cyberbole, Reality*. Oxford: Oxford University Press.

Yar, M. (2006) *Cybercrime and Society*. London: Sage.

Part III

Violent Crime

It might seem surprising that violent crime (which accounts for a relatively small proportion of officially recorded crime) comprises the largest section of the book, spanning 14 chapters. However, it is less surprising when the huge diversity of offences covered by the phrase is taken into account. Violence ranges from mass murder to fleeting drunken brawls. It covers different forms of physical harm or threat of harm, emotional and psychological abuse and a range of sexual offences, committed with a wide diversity of motives or in some cases through neglect or incompetence. Violent crime is also a special category of crime in terms of the profound effects it can have on victims. Violent attacks can result in long-term psychological damage, permanent disability and even death. As with many other offences covered in this book, violent crime has also changed over time and has been shaped to some extent by changes in late modern society.

These themes and others have been discussed by the authors of these 14 chapters. Many of the chapters draw attention to the definitional issues involved and the gap between the legal definition of the offence and the practical reality of violent attacks. Brookman, for example, points to the socially constructed nature of homicide and the fine and somewhat artificial dividing line between murder, manslaughter and accidental killings, while Williams draws attention to the wide range of actions covered under the heading of 'elder abuse', including physical, sexual, financial and emotional harms. Iganski makes a similar point when he discusses the nature of hate crime and the forms that it takes, as do Heckels and Roberts in their chapter on stalking and harassment. The point that all of these authors make is that these are not single types of offence but complex combinations of actions and motives that fit into the same legal offence category.

Several of the chapters draw attention to changes in the nature of violent offences over time and the impact that economic, social, cultural and technological changes have had on the characteristics of these offences. For example, Hobbs demonstrates how technological innovation and the shift away from a cash to a credit-based economy has led to significant changes in the modus operandi of commercial armed robbers, a recent variant (known as tiger kidnapping) involving the kidnapping of the family of a bank employee. Soothill and Francis likewise show how the ancient crimes of blackmail, kidnapping and threats to kill have changed over time as a result of developments in the Internet which have provided opportunities to commit modern variations of these offences. More broadly, Winlow discusses ways in which macro socio-economic changes and the emergence of consumerism are linked to the generation of violence in the night-time economy.

The problem of lack of reliable data is also a common theme in this section. This is compounded by the reluctance of many victims to report acts of violence against them (a particular problem with domestic violence, as discussed by Robinson), as well as the failure of organisations or staff to recognise actions as abuse or violence – the latter a key theme in the chapters on abuse in children's homes (Evans) and elder abuse (Williams). Several authors also comment on the lack of national-level data on some important offences. In particular, little is known at the national level about youth gang crime (Maher), hate crime (Iganski), school bullying (Ttofi and Farrington) or animal abuse (Pierpoint and Maher). There are also few rigorous evaluations of programmes designed to reduce the incidence of many of the offences discussed. This is emphasised particularly in relation to street robbery (Bennett and Brookman), hate crime (Iganski) and arson (Palmer and colleagues).

Finally, what clearly emerges from this section is not so much that violent crime is diverse, but that its diversity is under-represented in public debate and criminological research. While the most gruesome murders or audacious robberies will guarantee headlines, the longer-term corrosive abuse of many vulnerable groups remains neglected.

Chapter 12

Homicide

Fiona Brookman

Introduction

Homicide is a relatively rare yet high-impact event. Its consequences are deadly for the victim but also devastating for those intimately connected to the victim and offender and, often, the offender too. At the same time it is an act that captivates many and is the subject of sustained media attention and of numerous popular works of fiction. These depictions rarely reflect the reality of homicide. Rather, they tend to focus on the more (statistically) unusual forms of homicide such as those with a sexual or unknown motive, serial or spree killings or those involving young children (see Peelo *et al.* 2004; Soothill *et al.* 2004). In stark contrast, homicides among intimates and those involving young men in fights are much more prevalent, while deaths caused by corporate negligence or neglect (corporate homicide – albeit often not officially recognised and recorded as such) dwarf all of these other forms of homicide combined (see Brookman 2005; Tombs this volume).

I begin this chapter by briefly considering the legal categories of unlawful homicide in England and Wales, paying particular attention to some of the limitations of the legal framework and recent proposals to amend the law surrounding homicide. This is followed by a consideration of patterns and trends of homicide before moving on to an evaluation of some of the most important theoretical explanations of homicide and some reflections upon how homicide has been tackled in the UK context.

Deconstructing homicide

The term 'homicide' refers to the killing of a human being, whether the killing is lawful or unlawful. Examples of lawful homicide would include the killing of another human being during wartime combat, the implementation of the death penalty or the accidental killing of a boxer by his opponent. Unlawful homicide is legally classified, in England and Wales,[1] as murder, manslaughter or infanticide.[2] Each of these categories share a common *actus reus* (guilty act).

What distinguishes them is the extent to which the offender is deemed to have *intended* to cause the death of the victim or, in legal terminology, the perpetrator's *mens rea* (guilty mind).[3]

The most serious category of unlawful homicide is murder in the UK and carries a mandatory penalty of life imprisonment.[4] The classic definition of murder, generally accepted both academically and in practice, is that of Lord Chief Justice Coke from the early seventeenth century:

> When a person of sound memory, and of the age of discretion, unlawfully killeth within any county of the realm any reasonable creature in rerum natura under the kings peace, with malice aforethought, either expressed by the party or implied by law, so as the party wounded, or hurt, etc., die of the wound or hurt, etc., within a year and a day after the same.[5] (Card 1998: 184).

The phrase *rerum natura* refers to the notion that one can only be held to have killed someone who is 'in being' (as opposed to an unborn child for example) and the term 'malice aforethought' refers to the notion that a conviction for murder requires proof of intention to kill. However, what is not clear from the above extract is that intent to cause grievous bodily harm (that ultimately results in death) is also sufficient for a conviction for murder.

The liability to conviction for murder may be reduced to manslaughter if the killing stemmed from provocation, diminished responsibility or a suicide pact (Homicide Act 1957). These are commonly referred to as forms of 'voluntary manslaughter'. Alternatively, where there is no apparent intent to murder, an individual may be liable to conviction for 'involuntary manslaughter' if it is shown that they acted in a reckless or grossly negligent manner or that death resulted from an unlawful and dangerous act (adapted from Ashworth and Mitchell 2000). Finally, the defence of infanticide applies when a woman causes the death of her biological child (who is less than twelve months old) while suffering from some kind of psychological imbalance linked to childbirth (e.g. postnatal depression). The Infanticide Act 1938 provides that a woman found guilty of infanticide should be dealt with as though guilty of voluntary manslaughter. Manslaughter and infanticide carry a maximum penalty of life imprisonment though often attract much lower sentences.

The circumstances surrounding homicide vary enormously, as does public, media and ultimately the criminal justice response to them. In England and Wales during the last decade (1998–2008) 35–40 per cent of suspects indicted for homicide offences were convicted of murder and around a third received a conviction for manslaughter (figures for infanticide are negligible). The bulk of the remainder of cases resulted in acquittals (20 per cent) with a small number resulting in convictions for lesser offences (see Povey *et al.* 2009: 26). Hence, while around 800 individuals are indicted for homicide each year in England and Wales, approximately 60 per cent are seen to have done so under some sort of mitigating circumstances or not to have committed the homicide at all.

Although legal categories of homicide may appear clear cut, in reality a fine line separates 'murder' from 'manslaughter' or 'accident' or, as Croall (1998: 179) notes, 'licensed killings' by law enforcers or euthanasia. As I have pointed out elsewhere (see Brookman 2005), the divide between acceptable and unacceptable killings is socially, historically and culturally constructed, and what 'counts' (both literally and metaphorically) as murder or unlawful homicide is the product of a complex legislative history.

It is pertinent to acknowledge at this point the introduction, in April 2008, of the Corporate Manslaughter and Corporate Homicide Act 2007. This Act introduced a new offence across the UK for prosecuting companies and other organisations where there has been a gross failing throughout the organisation in the management of health and safety with fatal consequences (see http://www.justice.gov.uk/publications/corporatemanslaughter2007.htm). The introduction of this legislation is promising in that it recognises the importance of holding corporations to account for their lethal actions. Nevertheless, the maximum penalty, if found guilty, is an unlimited fine. This contrasts starkly with the maximum penalty for other forms of manslaughter in the UK of life imprisonment and seems to indicate that corporate crime is still not viewed as 'real crime' (see Box 1983; Tombs this volume). It is too early to determine whether the legislation will have any real impact upon the number of prosecutions launched or their success. It will, nevertheless, be interesting to see if corporate homicides begin to find their way into the annual homicide statistics in future years.[6]

For many years there has been criticism of the law surrounding homicide, often directed at the very broad category of manslaughter which, it has been argued, ranges in gravity from cases that only just fall short of murder right down to cases that are difficult to distinguish from accidental death (Law Commission 1996). In addition, scholars have pointed to the complexities in establishing the presence or absence of 'intent' (crucial to determining whether the defendant should be found guilty of murder) and the difficulties of interpretation surrounding the defences of provocation and diminished responsibility.

Most recently the Law Commission called for an overhaul of the law governing homicide in England and Wales suggesting that it is a 'rickety structure set upon shaky foundations' with several rules 'unaltered since the seventeenth century' (Law Commission 2006b: 3; see also http://www.lawcom.gov.uk/murder.htm). The current proposal is to create a three-tier law of homicide that would comprise:

- First degree murder:[7] (a) intentional killings; (b) killing with intent to cause serious injury where the killer was aware that his/her conduct involved a serious risk of causing death (mandatory sentence of life imprisonment).

- Second degree murder: (a) killings intended to cause serious injury; (b) killings intended to cause injury or fear or risk of injury where the killer was aware that his or her conduct involved a serious risk of causing death; (c) the result of a successful partial defence plea to first degree murder (discretionary life sentence, with guidelines).

- Manslaughter: (a) causing death by gross negligence; (b) causing death through a criminal act intended to cause injury, or in the awareness of a serious risk that injury may be caused (discretionary life sentence).

(Adapted from Law Commission, 2006b:
172–6, and Horder 2007: 19)

There is insufficient space here to deal in any detail with the potential benefits and limitations of the proposed new structure, suffice it to say that second degree murder would incorporate the worse kinds of killing by recklessness (that currently fall under manslaughter) as well as those committed as a result of provocation or diminished responsibility. It would also capture some offenders who would currently be convicted of murder.

A number of the more specific proposals for reform include extending the provocation defence to those who have overreacted in response to a fear of serious violence. Advocates of this reform suggest that it 'arises out of longstanding concerns that the law is too generous for those who kill in anger and too harsh for those who kill out of fear of serious violence' (Northern Ireland Human Rights Commission 2008: 4). Moreover, the defence of provocation has been seen to be gender biased in that it requires evidence of a sudden loss of self-control that often characterises circumstances where men kill (and in particular when a man kills an intimate partner). In contrast, female victims of domestic violence who kill their abusers often do so as a result of cumulative provocation or long-term abuse and there may be a 'cooling-off' time between provocation and reaction to it – which has undermined the case for using this defence. At the other end of the spectrum is a proposal to reconsider the law on complicity in relation to homicide. The Commission recommends that individuals be found guilty of complicity to murder if they have helped or encouraged a fatal attack, provided that they realised murder might be committed by the perpetrator. This proposal aims to tackle some of the difficulties involved in successfully prosecuting all members involved in a lethal joint-venture attack – notably gangs of young men (see Law Commission 2006a).

As Horder (2007: 29) points out, '[T]here are no easy or perfect solutions to be found in this hinterland between murder and lesser homicide offences.' For him, however, the creation of the three-tier structure 'takes some heat out of the debate'. To what extent and precisely when the new legislative powers will come into being is currently unknown. What is clear, however, is that – if and when it comes into law – this will be the first substantial overhaul of the legal framework of homicide in England and Wales for over 500 years.

Patterns and trends of homicide

Compared to most other forms of violent crime, homicide is relatively rare. There were, for example, less than 800 homicides recorded in England and Wales in 2007/8 (see Table 12.1 below) compared to almost 10,000 recorded cases of threat or conspiracy to murder, over 15,000 acts involving serious wounding or endangerment to life, over 17,000 offences involving a firearm,

Table 12.1 The number and rates of homicides in the UK in 2007/8

Jurisdiction	Number	Rate per 100,000 population
England and Wales	763	1.4
Scotland	114	2.2
Northern Ireland*	30	2.0

Sources: Pavey *et al*. 2009; Scottish Government (2008) and Tavares and Thomas (2008). The Northern Ireland figure is an average for the three-year period 2004–6.

84,000 robberies, and over 41,000 serious sexual crimes (see Kershaw *et al*. 2008: 25). Provisional data for 2008/9 show the police recorded 648 incidents of homicide, a decrease of 17 per cent on the previous year and the lowest recorded level in the last 20 years. The number of attempted murders also decreased (Walker *et al*. 2009).[8]

As Figure 12.1 illustrates there has been a steady increase in the number of homicides in England and Wales since the mid-1960s. There was also a sudden spike in 2003, with over 950 homicides recorded. However, this peak is almost wholly artificial – the result of 172 homicides attributed to the serial killer Harold Shipman being coded to this time period.[9] This and other unusual events can artificially inflate the overall figures and particular characteristics of homicide for that period. For example, the vast majority of Shipman's victims were elderly females whom he killed by administering lethal doses of (in the main) morphine and diamorphine and so for 2002/3 the proportion of female victims of homicide is unusually elevated, as is death by poisoning (see Cotton and Bibi 2005). Overall, the offences attributable to Shipman artificially inflated the homicide rate by 20 per cent during 2002–3. While this one-off peak is artificial, the general upward trend is not. Homicide has increased since the mid-1960s in Britain and this is characteristic of homicide across Europe (see Spierenburg 2008: 208).[10] For example, the homicide rate has almost doubled from 7.3 per million population in 1967 to 14.1 per million

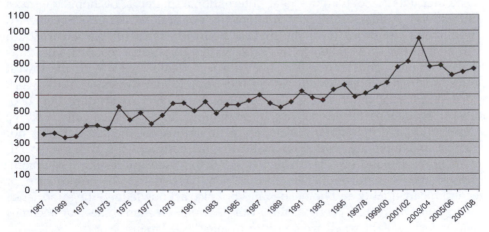

Source: Home Office Homicide Index.

Figure 12.1 Annual totals of recorded homicide in England and Wales, 1967–2007/8

population in 2007/8 in England and Wales. On the other hand, the rise appears to have been abating across some parts of Europe and the US (see Miethe and Regoeczi 2004, regarding US rates). This pattern has not yet been reflected in England and Wales, unless the above-mentioned fall in homicides in 2008/9 represents the first signs of a trend reversal.

International homicide rates

Comparative analysis of homicide statistics needs to be approached cautiously due to differences in legal definitions of homicide across countries and differences in the criteria adopted to collect and record homicide. For example, some jurisdictions include attempted homicide in their figures while others, such as Japan, exclude robbery homicide (see Finch 2001). In terms of recording homicide, this is partly dependent upon the capacity of national institutions to gather data and accurately record events (Aebi 2004). Moreover, there is some evidence that variations in crime reporting rates are strongly related to measures of institutional stability and police presence and, in some instances, to 'a subjective index of corruption' (see Soares 2004, cited in Krause et al. 2008: 69).

There are also numerous difficulties in explaining homicide trends. For example, despite a proliferation of lethal weapons in developing countries since the 1960s, the lethality of assaults has decreased due to developments in medical technology and care (Krause et al. 2008). Hence, assessment of long-term trends needs to take account of improvements in health care and, when drawing international comparisons, one needs to be mindful of differences in healthcare systems across countries and regions. With these caveats in mind, Krause et al. (2008) indicate that the world average homicide rate for 2004 is 7.6 per 100,000 population. The highest homicide rates are concentrated in Africa (excluding North Africa) and Central and South America (20–30,000 homicides per 100,000 population). East and South East Asia and West and Central Europe (which includes the UK) exhibit the lowest levels – with rates generally lower than 2 per 100,000 population (see Table 12.2 below).

Reiner (2007: 367) argues that international patterns of homicide rates correspond systematically to variations in political economies. Specifically, 'neo-liberal' countries have the highest homicide rates (in particular South Africa and the USA) followed by 'conservative corporatist' countries (such as Italy, Germany and France) and finally 'social democracies' with the lowest rates (such as Sweden, Denmark and Norway). Reiner draws upon the work of a number of authors (e.g. Currie 1998; Hall 1997) in arguing that neo-liberal economies foster violence through high levels of inequality, relative deprivation and involuntary unemployment.[11] However, the association is not perfect and there are several anomalies to this pattern – for example, social-democratic Finland (see Savolainen et al. 2008, for an interesting discussion). Jacobs and Richardson (2008), like Reiner, have noted the importance of economic inequality and homicide rates but also acknowledged the importance of the proportions of young males in the population – an issue that becomes particularly salient when we consider homicide in Japan.

Table 12.2 Homicide rates per 100,000 population, from selected countries of the world by region, 2004–6

Country	Rate	Country	Rate
Southern Africa		**Near & Middle East/South**	
Botswana	21.5	**West Asia**	
South Africa	69.0	Afghanistan	3.4
Zimbabwe	32.9	Iraq	6.7
North Africa		Israel	4.7
Algeria	9.6	Pakistan	6.3
Egypt	1.3	Saudi Arabia	3.2
Morocco	1.1	India	5.5
East Africa		Sri Lanka	7.2
Kenya	20.8	**East & South East Europe**	
Mauritius	2.7	Russian Federation	29.7
Uganda	25.2	Ukraine	12.0
West & Central Africa		Albania	6.6
Cameroon	16.1	Bulgaria	2.6
Gambia	13.5	Croatia	1.8
Senegal	14.2	Serbia	1.4
Americas – Caribbean		Turkey	6.2
Bahamas	22.5	**West & Central Europe**	
Barbados	15.1	Austria	0.7
Cuba	6.0	Belgium	1.8
Dominican Republic	24.2	Cyprus	1.9
Jamaica	55.2	Czech Republic	2.2
Trinidad & Tobago	19.6	Demark	1.1
Central America		Estonia	7.3
El Salvador	57.5	France	1.6
Panama	13.4	Germany	1.0
North America		Greece	1.0
Canada	2.0	Iceland	0.7
Mexico	11.2	Ireland	1.5
United States of America	5.9	Italy	1.2
South America		Netherlands	1.2
Argentina	5.5	Norway	0.7
Brazil	30.8	Poland	1.5
Colombia	61.1	Spain	1.1
Uruguay	6.0	Sweden	1.0
Central & East Asia		England & Wales	1.5
Kazakhstan	16.2	Northern Ireland	1.8
China	2.2	Scotland	2.3
Japan	0.5	**Oceania**	
Thailand	9.0	Australia	1.5
		New Zealand	1.5

World average homicide rate: 7.6 per 100,000 population.

Source: Adapted from UNODC (United Nations Office on Drugs and Crime) (2008), International Homicide Statistics and (for EU countries) Table 2, Tavares and Thomas (2008) Crime and Justice Statistics. The former cover the period 2004 only and the high estimate has been included here.

Japan has fewer homicides per capita than almost any other nation and the rate has dropped some 70 per cent in the last 50 years (Johnson 2008). Moreover, the demographic group most responsible for the dramatic decline is young men aged 20–24; the murder rate among them is now one tenth of what it was 50 years ago. The 'vanishing young male killer' (Johnson 2008) has been described as unprecedented (Uchiyama 2003). There are no clear answers yet as to what factors have brought about the dramatic decline of homicide in Japan. Johnson speculates that Japan's post-war commitment to anti-war values (including a pacifist constitution) may have strengthened inhibitions against killing in Japanese culture. Alternatively, growing affluence in Japan in the absence of pockets of poverty and, thereby, relative deprivation (that often characterises other developed nations) may be significant. What is also striking about Japanese culture is that it has the highest suicide rates in the developed world. Males commit almost three-quarters of suicides in Japan and it is now the second leading cause of death among young Japanese people aged 15–24 and the leading cause of death among those aged 25–39 prompting Johnson (2008: 155) to urge that the possible links between suicide and homicide be explored.

Moving to the other extreme, Krause et al. suggest that high homicide rates in Africa may be associated with a series of social and economic indicators often linked to crime including 'a low overall Human Development Index[12] (HDI), low economic performance, high levels of income inequality, a youthful population, rapid rates of urbanization, poorly resourced criminal justice systems, and a proliferation of firearms, related in part to the recurrence of conflict in all regions of the continent' (UNODC 2005: ix, cited in Krause et al. 2008: 72). Moreover, there is a plausible link between armed conflict and homicide rates both during and after hostilities in that the psychological, social and economic impact of war combined with an increased availability of weapons may contribute to homicide levels (UNODC 2005).

McAlister (2006) has found some evidence to suggest that international variation in homicide rates may be attributable to cultural differences in acceptance of moral justifications for killing. In combined data from four surveys of young people and adults in 19 nations, McAlister found that national and regional attitudes toward killing were strongly related to homicide rates. Association does not, of course, mean that the two are causally related. Rather, a third (unknown) variable might explain the presence of both high rates of homicide and high levels of acceptance of killing. Moreover, even if there is a causal connection, it is not clear in which direction it works. For example, high homicide rates in a particular jurisdiction may affect residents' acceptance of homicide (they may become desensitised), or pro-violence sentiments may indeed affect levels of homicide (see subcultural explanations later).

Offender, victim and offence characteristics[13]

This section will include brief consideration of the socio-demographic characteristics of those who become involved in homicide as well as some details of the homicide event.[14] It is important to note that while the data available on homicide are more comprehensive than is generally the case for other offence categories, certain kinds of killings are not routinely included in the Home Office homicide statistics – such as those that arise as a result of dangerous driving or corporate negligence or neglect (Brookman 2005). This has important implications regarding the overall shape or picture of homicide and skews it in certain directions – not least in terms of the social class and ethnicity of those involved.

Offenders and victims

Gender and age

One of the most significant 'facts' about homicide is that it is dominated by males or, to be more precise, young men. Over 90 per cent of offenders are male, over 70 per cent of victims are male and, as illustrated in Table 12.3, 60 per cent of homicides over the last decade were male-on-male. In stark contrast, only 3 per cent of homicides occur among females. Forty-four per cent of *all* homicides in England and Wales between 1998 and 2008 (for which age and gender of suspect are known) were committed by young males aged less than 30.

Both gender and age also have a considerable impact upon the likelihood of falling victim to homicide. For example, males are three to four times more likely to fall victim to homicide than females and comprise 70–80 per cent of the victims in an average year. Somewhat peculiar to homicide, the age group most at risk are infants under one year old (at 36 per million population). This group are followed by young adults aged 16–29 (at 24 per million population) (Povey *et al.* 2009: 13).

Ethnicity

It is now well established that black and Asian people are over-represented as both victims and offenders of homicide. For example, for the period 2003–5, black people were 5.5 times more likely to fall victim to homicide than whites and Asian people were 1.8 times more likely than white people to become victims of a homicide (CJS Race Unit 2006: 7).[15] Black individuals comprise 14 per cent of homicide victims despite comprising less than 3 per cent of the population of England and Wales (Census 2001). Whites make up over 90 per cent of the population but only 73 per cent of homicide victims. Homicides involving a black victim exhibit some distinct qualities. For example, during

Table 12.3 Gender 'mix' of suspect and victims of homicide in England and Wales: 1998–2008

Main suspect	Main victim	
	Male	Female
Male	61% (4,900)	29% (2,359)
Female	7% (589)	3% (228)

the last decade (1998–2008) almost a third of black victims were shot, compared to 5 per cent of white victims, 9 per cent of Asians and 7 per cent of other ethnic groups. Blacks are also more likely than other ethnic groups to be killed with a sharp instrument (40 per cent of black victims compared to around a third of all other groups). Finally, it is more common for homicides involving black victims to remain unsolved (28 per cent) in comparison with white or Asian victims (11 per cent) (CJS Race Unit 2006). This may be a reflection of particular difficulties associated with investigating shooting incidents or, as is widely perceived within minority ethnic communities, because such cases are investigated less rigorously (see Phillips and Bowling 2007).

Finally, non-white people are over-represented as homicide offenders, with blacks comprising 12 per cent of offenders, Asians 7 per cent and other non-white groups 3 per cent. More than one-fifth (21 per cent) of all homicide suspects between 1998 and 2008 were non-white males. We will explore later in the chapter the possible reasons for the over-representation of ethnic minority groups in homicide.

Social class and occupation

There is little reliable information in the UK regarding the social class and employment status of offenders and victims of homicide. What is clear from the limited data available on the Homicide Index is that at least 28 per cent of victims of homicide over the last decade were unemployed at the time of their death (this figure excludes students and retired individuals) and a quarter were in employment. The employment status of a quarter of victims was unknown/not recorded and it is likely that many if not most of these cases involved unemployed victims (see Brookman 2003).

Dobash et al. (2002), in the Homicide in Britain study, discovered that almost 70 per cent of the 786 male offenders that they studied were usually unemployed and that most had left school without qualifications. Overall, the available evidence indicates that homicide is dominated by offenders from the lower classes and a significant number are unemployed at the time of the offence. However, this finding is, in part, a reflection of the kinds of killings that are routinely included in the statistics and those that are generally not (as outlined earlier).

Victim-offender relationship

Around a quarter of homicides occur among friends or social acquaintances, 16 per cent among intimate partners/ex-partners and 15 per cent among strangers. Seven per cent involve the murder of a son or daughter and a further 5 per cent involve the killing of another kind of family member (e.g. an in-law or sibling). Business and criminal associates comprise a further 7 per cent (see Figure 12.2).

Unsurprisingly perhaps, these patterns vary by gender. For example, of the 208 females killed in England and Wales in 2007–8, 35 per cent were killed by a partner or ex-partner (compared to just 6 per cent of male victims), 22 per cent by another family member (compared to just 11 per cent of males) and only 13 per cent of female victims were killed by a stranger (compared

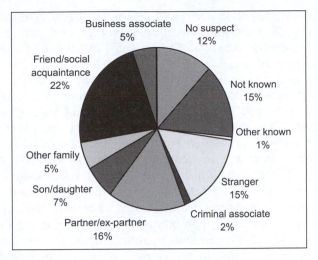

Figure 12.2 Victim–offender relationship, 1998–2007/8

to 36 per cent of male victims). Clearly, homicides involving females (as killer, victim or both) tend to occur between intimates, whereas male-on-male homicides are more likely to involve strangers or acquaintances. The basic patterns of victim–offender relationship have remained relatively stable over the last decade with just two exceptions; the number of 'no suspect' cases has increased over time (more than doubled in ten years from 7 per cent to 15 per cent) and homicides among 'partners/ex-partners' have decreased from 20 per cent to 13 per cent.

Features of the homicide event

The homicide event refers to the micro-environment in which the homicide takes place and includes 'the social context that unites offenders and victims' (Miethe and Meier 1994: 3) and the 'setting and props' (Block 1977: 74) that facilitate homicide. These include temporal and spatial features of homicide, the characteristics of a particular social setting, the availability of weapons and the role of drugs and alcohol – to name but a few. Due to the limitations of space, I will deal here only with weapons and the role of drugs and alcohol.

Weapons and method of kill

In the UK, homicide is most likely to be perpetrated with a knife or other sharp instrument (around a third of cases in England and Wales and almost 50 per cent of cases in Scotland). The number of homicides perpetrated with a sharp instrument in England and Wales in 2007/8 was the highest recorded during a financial year since the Homicide Index was introduced in 1977. The use of sharp instruments is perhaps unsurprising given that knives are routinely found in people's homes and, therefore, easily accessible. At the same time, there is some evidence of an increasing 'knife culture' (Eades *et al.* 2007) so that both indoors and outdoors knives become a readily available weapon of choice. Stabbings are followed in frequency by lethal fights involving hitting and kicking (an average of 13 per cent over the last decade) and assaults with blunt instruments (8 per cent average). An average of 6 per cent of victims are strangled (generally female victims of male attacks) and a further 4 per cent of victims are suffocated (generally infants).

Despite increased concern and attention to shooting incidents, there has not been an upward trend in the number of fatal shootings in the UK. Firearms-related homicides ranged between 6 and 12 per cent in the last decade in England and Wales (an average of 8 per cent and 64 cases each year). Most recently fatal shootings accounted for 7 per cent of homicides in England and Wales (and 4 per cent in Scotland) (Povey *et al.* 2009; and Scottish Government 2008). While there has been a certain level of exaggerated media (and government) coverage of fatal shootings, this should not distract from the fact that lethal weapons permeate sections of certain cities in the UK and particular contexts much more than others, thereby making it more likely that minor disputes end lethally. Shootings almost always occur among young males and sometimes emerge in the context of rival gang activity (whether in relation to the protection of lucrative drug dealing 'turf' or 'status' and reputation confrontations – see section on making sense of seemingly senseless acts below). Despite the high profile of such killings they present the police with particular challenges in terms of identifying suspects – i.e. suspects have not been identified in one-third of fatal shootings recorded during the last decade. In stark contrast, suspects remain unidentified in just 8 per cent of homicides that were not perpetrated with a firearm.

Drugs and alcohol

Evidence from a range of studies illustrates that both alcohol and/or drugs play a significant role in homicide events and, often, the lives of offenders and victims. For example, Shaw *et al.* (2006) found that over half of the 1,579 homicides that they examined involved offenders who were misusing either alcohol or drugs in the 12 months prior to the homicide and that overall in 45 per cent of cases that they examined, alcohol or drugs contributed to the homicide in that the offender was intoxicated in some way at the time of the offence (Shaw *et al.* 2006: 1119–20). Brookman (2003) found that alcohol had been consumed (often to excess) by either the offender or victim in over half of all cases of male-on-male homicide that she examined in England and Wales, while Dobash *et al.* (2002) found that 38 per cent of male homicide offenders were drunk or very drunk at the time of the offence and 14 per cent were using illegal drugs. Furthermore they discovered that a quarter of the men in their study (786 in total) had problems with alcohol before the age of 16 and 17 per cent had abused drugs. By adulthood these figure rose to 49 per cent for alcohol and 25 per cent for drugs.

While alcohol and/or drug consumption permeates many situations in which homicide occurs, it is nevertheless rare for people to become violent every time they consume such substances. Hence, while alcohol and/or drug consumption is doubtless frequently implicated, it is not on its own a sufficient or necessary explanation for violence. There are various ways in which the consumption of drugs and alcohol may be related to homicide (some of which will be explored in the following section). For example, in the case of drugs and violence, Goldstein (1985) suggests that there are at least three distinct levels at which one might uncover a relationship; (a) psychopharmacological (i.e. the effects upon one's mind and body); (b) economic compulsive (the notion that individuals commit violent crimes, such as robbery, to secure the funds to sustain a drug habit); and (c) 'systemic' (which refers to the violence associated with the often very lucrative supply and distribution of drugs that can lead to territorial disputes within the drugs trade (see Bennett and Holloway, this volume). Moreover, the links between alcohol and homicide and drugs and homicide are somewhat distinct. For example, recent research by Chapple (2008) indicates some interesting differences between alcohol-related homicides, drug-related homicides and non-substance related homicides in England and Wales. Alcohol-related homicides were more likely than other homicides to involve a friend or former friend, no weapon use and some kind of quarrel or dispute. Drug-related homicides were more likely than other homicides to involve an acquaintance, shooting the victim and economic motivation.

Making sense of seemingly senseless acts

There are many explanations of homicide which is unsurprising, given the diversity of homicide itself (e.g. infanticide at one extreme, serial killing at another) and the different sorts of questions posed regarding its aetiology (e.g. a focus on patterns and trends on the one hand or the situational dynamics of a particular case on the other). It is not possible to do justice to the plethora of theories here.[16] I am going to pay particular attention to structural, cultural and situational explanations of male-on-male homicide and will end this section with a consideration of gang-related homicide in a UK context. I will suggest that in order to understand homicide it is crucial to recognise the combined importance of all three approaches.

In focusing upon structural, cultural and situational factors, I pay no real attention to explanations that look 'inside' the offender. While there is no doubt that some homicides are committed by individuals with some enduring or transient individual pathology (e.g. a neurological or biochemical dysfunction or a personality disorder), and some evidence that certain people simply enjoy hurting and killing other people and commit violence for violence sake (see Schinkel 2004) most criminologists would agree that these represent the exception rather than the rule. Moreover, there is clear evidence that any individual-based factors that play a role in homicide must be understood in combination with environmental precursors or facilitators – otherwise such individuals would presumably be violent most or all of the time. Hence, the most pertinent work in this area acknowledges the link between the individual and environmental stimuli and cues (see, for example, Denno 1990; Niehoff 1999; Freedman and Hemenway 2000).

The seeds of homicide: structural forces

Structural theorists have been concerned primarily to explain certain striking patterns to be found in the social characteristics of offenders (and sometimes victims) of both violence in general and homicide in particular. They try to unravel, for example, how and why certain factors or conditions such as poverty, deprivation and inequality or social disorganisation may explain homicide patterns. To these ends, structural researchers often rely upon the statistical analysis of aggregated data. As discussed earlier, when considering international homicide patterns and trends, there is a great deal of evidence correlating poverty (Pridemore 2008), inequality and social disorganisation (Messner and Rosenfeld 1999; Jacobs and Richardson 2008), population turnover and population demographics (Jacobs and Richardson 2008) with homicide rates. Most recently, McCall *et al.* (2008) highlighted a number of contemporary social and economic factors relevant to the sharp increase in US homicides (from the mid-1980s to the early 1990s) followed by its equally dramatic decline – including, recession, illicit drug market activity, incarceration rates and police presence.

Cultural influences

While structural theories focus upon the social conditions that can foster crime, cultural theorists focus upon the ideas and values that particular groups hold and how these can generate involvement in crime. For example, the 'subculture of violence' theory (Wolfgang and Ferracuti 1967) starts from the premise that homicide predominantly occurs among individuals from the lowest socio-economic groups in society and that the lethal encounters in which they become embroiled often arise from trivial incidents – such as minor insults or scuffles. These findings can apparently be explained by the fact that the vast majority of these people share beliefs that are conducive to the use of force and violence when insulted or challenged such an exaggerated sense of honour, courage and manliness (see Curtis 1975). Research in this area has burgeoned recently with various criminologists exploring 'codes of the street' (Anderson 1999) and how these codes demand violent responses to interpersonal confrontation and vengeance and retaliation for certain infractions (Anderson 1999; Jacobs and Wright 1999; Hochstetler and Copes 2003; Wright *et al.* 2006). These accounts provide rich descriptions of the circumstances under which such violence is approved or even demanded and, to varying degrees, acknowledge that such cultures are formed as a result of the marginalisation of certain sections of society. For the most part, the theories that have developed focus upon street cultures and fit well with Bourgois' definition of street culture (2003: 8): 'a complex and conflictual web of beliefs, symbols, modes of interaction, values and ideologies that have emerged in the opposition to exclusion from mainstream society'. For Bourgois, street culture is an alternative forum for autonomous personal dignity where power in mainstream society has been denied (see also Sandberg 2008). These accounts, then, recognise the critical link between structural forces and the development of violent street cultures.

Both cultural and structural explanations suffer from the age-old problem of over-prediction. Explanations of relative deprivation or poverty and homicide, for example, cannot account for the fact that most people suffering from economic inequality do not engage in violence. This point is particularly pertinent when gender is entered into the equation. How might we explain the very low rates of female homicide while acknowledging that women are among the most disadvantaged of citizens (see Wilson 1993)? Similarly, not all members of a violent subculture engage in violence all of the time and few become embroiled in lethal violence (leading some critics to challenge the notion of a distinct violent subculture that approves of violence in general – see Corzine et al. 1999). As Levi (1997: 860) notes, such accounts 'seldom generate anything close to a causal account which makes sense of non-violence as well as of violence'. This is because, in isolation, both cultural and structural approaches fail to specify the situational conditions that channel particular dispositions for violence into concrete lines of action. Incorporating situational analyses into the equation helps to overcome this weakness. As Luckenbill and Doyle (1989: 421) state: 'Violence is performed by individuals in the context of face-to-face interactions and therefore involves a number of psychological and interpersonal processes.'

Foreground factors: the micro-environment and situational dynamics

The micro-environment of crime can be defined as 'the social context that unites offenders and victims and comprises both physical and social dimensions' (Miethe and Meier 1994: 3). Research into the micro-environment of homicide is vast and includes studies exploring victim–offender relationships (Wolfgang 1958; Polk 1994a; Decker 1996), the interactional dynamics of offenders, victims and third parties where relevant (Luckenbill 1977; Decker 1995), the lethality of situations dependent upon temporal and spatial aspects of the environment, the routine activities of those who inhabit particular locations (Weaver et al. 2004; Pizarro 2008), the lethality of situations dependent upon access to weapons (Phillips and Maume 2007) and the situational role of drugs and alcohol (Parker 1995; Parker and Auerhahn 1999). The overall aim of this approach is to provide a 'contextualised account of homicide in action' (Chapple 2008: 20). What this approach, more than any other, acknowledges is that homicide is a dynamic and evolving event where the 'actors' mould each other's behaviour.

The major substantive approach that has guided this work comes from symbolic interactionism that stresses the role of situational identities or self-images in interaction (e.g. Becker 1962; Goffman 1967; Toch 1969; Athens 1977; Tedeschi and Felson 1994). One illuminating analysis of lethal interactions is Luckenbill's (1977) paper 'Criminal homicide as a situated transaction'. Luckenbill's research, based on the analysis of 70 murders, documents the dynamic interchange of moves and countermoves between offenders, victims and oftentimes bystanders of homicide. During these interactions (which he places into six major stages) the key players develop lines of action shaped in part by the actions of each other and predominantly focused towards saving or maintaining 'face' and reputation and demonstrating character.

More recently, Polk (1994a 1995) has built upon this work drawing upon qualitative data from homicides in Australia in the 1980s. Most notably, he manages, through the use of discrete homicide scenarios (disaggregated by victim–offender relationship and situational circumstances), to unravel the dynamic nature of homicide situations while also acknowledging the importance of social class and masculinity in the evolution of homicide events (see also Brookman 2003). For example, Polk argues that confrontational homicide (where the offender and victim become involved in a spontaneous dispute and engage *together* in a violent confrontation) has its source 'in the willingness of males, first, to lay down challenges to the honour of other males, and second, the masculine readiness to engage in physical violence in response to such challenges' (Polk 1994b: 169). He notes, however, that such violent encounters are much more likely to occur among young, working-class (or underclass) males, which he relates to the manifestation of a particular kind of masculinity in response to economic marginality:

> Males who are well integrated into roles of economic success are able to ground their masculinity through methods other than physical confrontations and violence. For economically marginal males, however, physical toughness and violence become a major vehicle for the assertion of their masculinity and a way of defending themselves against what they see as challenges from other males. (Polk 1994b: 187)

Other researchers, particularly throughout the 1980s and 1990s, developed ideas around the relationship between social class, race and age and the development and expression of particular kinds of masculinity in explaining violence (see Segal 1990; Messerschmidt 1993), though this line of research seems to have abated recently with a resurgence of interest in street (or 'corner'[17]) cultures.

Despite this important body of work, there is still very little research that helps us to unravel why particular acts of homicide occur at particular moments in time – i.e. why here? why now? why this victim? Someone who has made an important contribution to this conundrum is Athens (1980, 1997), a symbolic interactionist who carefully analysed the accounts of violent offenders focusing upon the interpretations they made of situations in which they committed violent acts, their interpretations of situations in which they almost committed such acts, the self-images that they held and their violent criminal careers. Athens discovered that individuals who had committed violent criminal acts (including homicide) formed one of four possible interpretations of the situation: (a) physically defensive; (b) frustrative; (c) malefic; or (d) frustrative-malefic. On those occasions when these same individuals almost resorted to violence they formed a 'restraining judgement', escaping the tunnel vision that characterised the violent events and redefining the situation as not requiring violence. There were various reasons for the change of interpretation and sentiment such as: perceiving that the attack would fail, fear of jeopardising an important intimate or social relationship, deference to the other person or fear of legal sanctions. Finally, other individuals indicated that they re-evaluated the situation in light of a change in the course of action of the other person (e.g. the potential victim conceded in some way or apologised). Athens' work moves us much closer to the moment of the interaction than most other research in this area.

Unsurprisingly, people form restraining judgements far more often than they form overriding ones or become locked in fixed lines of indication. Consequently – and fortunately – far more violent criminal acts are begun than are ever completed. (Athens 1997: 52–3)

Integrated approaches

It is not possible to do justice to the complexity of homicide without acknowledging the interplay of structural, cultural and situational factors. For example, Luckenbill's work, while valuable in unpacking the micro-situational dynamics of homicide, failed to look outward from the encounter to the social and economic forces that set the context for such lethal violence to occur. What occurs in specific settings, while in part a product of that particular environment, is also a product of wider structural forces that themselves pave the way for the development of particular cultural adaptations and values that may support violence as a way of dealing with conflict; in short, arenas of interaction are not hermetically sealed from the outer world. Untangling the relative effects of structure, culture and situational factors is a complex business but increasingly researchers are moving away from unidimensional approaches. Bernard (1990), for example, charts the mechanisms that mediate between negative structural conditions and expressions of 'angry aggression' among the 'truly disadvantaged'. Bowling (1999) similarly linked the macro-structural forces of economic recession and poverty to the emergence of despair and relative deprivation at the community and individual level while also acknowledging the importance of the development of lucrative crack and heroin markets and the widespread availability of guns (situational) in his exploration of the dramatic surge in New York murder in the 1980s. Furthermore, some theorists focus upon particular types of homicide, allowing them, arguably, to be more context-specific (Polk 1994a; Brookman 2005). For example, Kubrin and Weitzer (2003) examined the intersection of structural and cultural influences upon retaliatory homicide in St Louis, Missouri, while Williams and Flewelling (1988) found that different cultural and structural factors had varied impacts upon different types of homicide. Finally, recent analysis of the emergence of gang-related homicides in particular parts of the UK also provides a clear illustration of the value of adopting an integrated approach.

Gang-related homicide: the influence of structural, cultural and situational factors

Gang-related homicide refers to homicides committed by or among gang members. A gang is taken to mean 'children and young people who see themselves and are seen by others as affiliates of a discrete, named, group with a discernable structure and a recognised territory' (Pitts 2008: 6). It is difficult to determine, with any degree of accuracy, the proportion of homicides attributable to gangs. The Home Office (2009) recently suggested increases in gang violence and shooting incidents linked to gangs and organised criminal groups (see also McLagan 2006). However, analysis of data from the Homicide Index indicates that no more than 3 per cent of all homicides are linked to gangs.[18]

There is a good deal of evidence from international research that street gangs emerge and flourish where inequality and marginality prevail. Vigil (2006: 22), for example, argues that 'the street gang is an outcome of marginalization, that is, the relegation of certain persons or groups to the fringes of society where social and economic conditions result in powerlessness'. He used the term 'multiple marginality' to express the extent and complexity of the forces that set the context for the emergence of street gangs. These include macro-historical forces (racism, social and cultural repression and fragmented institutions) and macrostructural (immigration and migration and the development of migrant poor barrios/ghettos) (pp. 22–3).

Pitts' (2008) research into armed youth gangs in London neatly illustrates the powerful role of structural changes in Britain in the emergence of violent gangs. Pitts (2008: 56) suggests that there have been 'seismic economic and political changes' in the UK in the past two decades that have led to the emergence of US-style armed youth gangs. These changes include: (a) the widening gap between rich and poor; (b) the concentration of the poorest sections of the population in social housing; and (c) structural youth unemployment (due to the decline of Britain's industrial base). Ultimately, segregation, marginalisation and the creation of 'discredited populations' (Baum 1996, cited in Pitts 2008: 63) set the scene for the development of gangs and gang violence. How, precisely? Some theorists have suggested that frustration and rage born of injustice (see Bernard 1990) breed 'norms and narratives supportive of gang violence' (Kennedy 2007, cited in Pitts 2008). Other researchers focus more upon the psychological strain that negative neighbourhood conditions foster noting that stress strips those affected of their coping skills and can impact negatively upon their assessment of risk; minor insults are seen as major threats (see Bernard 1990; Niehoff 1999; Vigil 2006) and a 'soldier mentality' characterised by heightened sensitivity to threats and a constant preparedness for action prevails (Sampson and Lauritsen 1994). Still others make reference to competition over scarce resources, observing that individuals raised in impoverished environments learn that they must be aggressive in their efforts to compete for scarce resources (see Sánchez-Jankowski 2003; see also Daly and Wilson 1988, 1990, for an evolutionary twist on this position). What each of these theorists agree upon is that material conditions establish the foundations for a 'culture of force' that can ultimately be labelled a 'culture of violence' (Sánchez-Jankowski 2003: 209). Specific situational contexts then promote the enactment of these cultural codes or, as Copes and Hochstetler (2003: 301) put it: 'Certain settings and activities trigger cognitive frames that make offending seem reasonable.' An example of such an activity would be drug dealing and the setting would include particular housing estates or neighbourhoods where gangs compete to control the sales of drugs. Involvement in drug dealing inevitably heightens the risk of gang violence and victimisation as members' routine activities expose them to volatile and unpredictable situations (Maher this volume; Chapple 2008). Where firearms or other lethal weapons are readily available the chances of minor disputes ending fatally is, of course, considerably enhanced. Moreover, the nature of their illicit activities (e.g. drug dealing and the carrying of firearms) places gang members outside formal avenues of redress so that they are not in a position to call upon the criminal justice system to assist when they fall victim to violence – even if they wanted to. As Topalli *et al.* (2002: 341) state: 'As drug dealers conduct their trade outside the limits of legal protection, a reputation for formidability represents one of the only mechanisms available to them for deterring victimization.' In short, a 'menacing and capable' street reputation is especially critical for men inhabiting this social setting and they are particularly sensitive to challenges to their courage and character (pp. 340–3). What these kinds of accounts clearly demonstrate is the intersection between structural disadvantage, cultural adaptations and micro-action on the street (see also Rosenfeld *et al.* 2003).

In conclusion, making sense of homicide requires that we unravel the structural, economic and social forces that constrain individuals' chances and choices (Pitts 2008) as well as the cultural and micro-situational pushes and pulls towards violence. Putting all the pieces of the puzzle together is a complex task. However, there is little doubt that such endeavours lead to richer and more meaningful accounts of homicide (and violence generally) than those that remain more narrowly focused.

Responding to homicide

Just as explanations of homicide are many and varied, so too are responses to it. Moreover, there is something of a debate regarding the extent to which homicide should be conceived as a distinct phenomenon (requiring very specific kinds of explanations and control strategies) or whether, on the other hand, it can be understood as an extreme manifestation of serious violence. It has been argued by a number of writers that the dynamics of homicide are basically identical to those of other forms of violence (Fyfe *et al.* 1997), differing in outcome rather than process. Whether the victim dies, according to this viewpoint, is often happenstance. Others note that there are some homicides in which the perpetrator fully intends to kill (as opposed to injure) the victim and ensure his or her death (see Felson and Messner 1996; Fyfe *et al.* 1997). Ultimately the two arguments are not incompatible. Clearly, there are homicides which are similar in dynamics to other acts of violence and homicides which are not (Brookman and Maguire 2005).

Broadly speaking, approaches to reduce or prevent homicide fall into one of the following categories:

1   Strategies to reduce the overall frequency of interpersonal violence (the assumption being that a decrease in violence will automatically bring about a decrease in homicide). Examples would include efforts to reduce domestic violence (see Robinson this volume) or violence in the context of the night-time economy (see Winlow this volume) or, more broadly, programmes to tackle poverty and social exclusion.

2   The identification of people, locations or situations with an exceptionally high risk of serious violence/homicide in order to 'target' these for preventative interventions (the basic assumption similar to that above, however, with the potential benefit of a greater reduction in homicide

through a more focused use of resources). Examples include 'risk factor' research to identify infants most at risk of being killed by a parent or specialist strategies to target gang-related shootings (such as Operation Trident in London).

3   The use of measures that reduce the likelihood that an assault will end lethally (the aim being to reduce the degree of violence or its impact upon the victim without necessarily aiming to reduce the overall numbers of violent incidents). Examples include the use of toughened or plastic drinking vessels in pubs and clubs or improvements in the speed and efficiency of emergency medical treatment for victims of serious violence.

Given the relative infrequency, diversity and apparently low predictability of homicide incidents, reducing or preventing it is no simple task (Brookman and Maguire 2005). For example, domestic violence has been the subject of sustained Home Office attention and funding with a number of multi-agency programmes flourishing across the UK (see Robinson this volume). A key plank of the work in this area revolves around trying to identify and intervene with the women or men who are especially vulnerable to lethal violence. However, despite considerable energy having been expended to identify 'risk factors' for domestic homicide it remains a very difficult offence to predict (category 2 above). The presence even of those factors that appear particularly salient as risk factors (and which may be good predictors of violence), such as threats to kill or the recent termination of the intimate relationship, do *not* lead to homicide in the great majority of cases (Brookman and Maguire 2005). Nevertheless, as noted earlier, domestic homicide has decreased over the last decade and it is possible that this is the result of the growth of a number of innovative multi-agency initiatives to combat domestic violence more generally.

Specific efforts to reduce homicide are relatively rare in the UK – rather there are efforts to reduce particular kinds of violence – from which lethal violence can emerge (category 1 above). A recent example of one such strategy is the Tackling Knives Action Programme (TKAP), which was launched in response to a number of high-profile knife-related murders and serious stabbings among young people. This Home Office-led intensive ten-month initiative aimed to reduce the carrying of knives, related homicide and serious stabbings among teenagers aged 13–19 (Ward and Diamond 2009). Interventions, implemented initially in ten police force areas, included increased use of intelligence-led patrolling of weapon-related violence 'hot spots' and increased use of stop and searches, the targeting of gangs and the return of at-risk, unsupervised children to their homes. Police forces also ran weapons-awareness courses and many produced posters or DVDs highlighting the dangers of knives. Focus groups, youth crime forums and youth conferences were used to engage young people and involve them in the programme (Ward and Diamond 2009). The evaluation of phase 1 found that while the programme led to a decrease of sharp-instrument related violence generally, there was no change in the number of provisionally recorded sharp-instrument-related homicides among victims aged 19 and under and a slight increase among victims aged 20 and over. Clearly, even fairly intensive interventions that combine enforcement with education and youth engagement are only partially effective.

A unique example of an initiative specifically developed to reduce and prevent homicide is Operation Trident (see http://www.stoptheguns.org/index.php), a major coordinated strategy based in London but with a national brief, which was launched in 1998. This has both an intelligence-gathering and analysis function and an operational arm. Although there has been no independent research conducted to date to assess the work of Operation Trident, there are indications that it is performing well in terms of detecting offenders. This apparently high level of success has been attributed by officers, in part, to the close working of key members of the black community in London with the police, which has permitted officers to bridge gaps with black victims and witnesses who were previously afraid to give evidence against offenders (see also the Manchester Gun Project, modelled on the Boston Gun Project – Bullock and Tilley 2008).

While it could be argued that efforts to reduce homicide are multifarious, critics point to a failure to invest in long-term strategies, such as programmes of social and economic change, in favour of short-term 'fixes' that have more political appeal (Buvinic and Morrision 2000).

As Polk (1994a: 210) aptly noted over fifteen years ago:

A society which is serious about the reduction of violence should look above all else to its economy, and to ways of providing for the deflection of individuals from the economic traps involved in under-class life.

This message is all the more pertinent given the current climate of global economic recession and the widening gap between rich and poor.

Concluding comments

Our journey began, in this chapter, by considering the legal definition of homicide through to its patterns, characteristics, causes and, briefly, responses to this crime. It should be apparent at this juncture that homicide comes in numerous guises. Understanding why around 900 people die each year in the UK and around 490,000 worldwide (Krause *et al.* 2008: 71) as the result of unlawful homicide requires careful consideration. There is a growing recognition among homicide researchers of the need to disaggregate homicide into conceptually meaningful subtypes if one is to develop worthwhile explanations. Simultaneously it is necessary to consider both offenders and victims of homicide and to explore their actions in relation to both the physical and social contexts within which they interact and the broader social and cultural environment that they inhabit (Brookman 2005; Chapple 2008). The 'official' picture of unlawful homicide is clearly just the tip of the iceberg of actual lives lost due to interpersonal violence. The moment we include deaths due to corporate negligence and neglect or genocide the figures increase dramatically. It is, therefore, something of a puzzle as to why the bulk of homicide research, media and government attention focuses on relatively uncommon homicide situations – such as gang shootings, fatal knife attacks among children or teenagers, and stranger, serial and female killers (Miethe and Regoeczi 2004). As Box (1983: 9) aptly notes:

> We are encouraged to see murder as a particular act involving a very limited range of stereotypical actors, instruments, situations and motives. Other types of avoidable killing are either defined as a less serious crime than murder, or as matters more appropriate for administrative or civil proceedings, or as events beyond the justifiable boundaries of state interference.

This is not simply a matter of distorted public consciousness. Rather, as Miethe and Regoeczi (2004) acknowledge, it can lead to the misdirecting of criminal justice and other resources away from the most deserving.

Suggested further reading

Until relatively recently there was not a great deal written by the academic community about homicide in the UK. Rather, the literature was dominated by research and theory from the USA and, to a lesser extent, Australia and some parts of Europe. The most recent comprehensive overview of homicide in the UK can be found in Brookman's *Understanding Homicide* (2005). Polk's (1994a) *When Men Kill* is also a valuable text to consult and is broader than the title suggests while Spierenburg's (2008) *A History of Murder* is an essential read for those wishing to locate murder in its historical context – he charts the changing patterns of homicide across Western Europe since the late Middle Ages. The annual homicide statistics published by the Home Office and available online provide a useful overview of patterns and trends on homicide in England and Wales. The most recent are available at: http://www.homeoffice.gov.uk/rds/pdfs09/hosb0209.pdf (they tend to be released in February each year). The Scottish Government provide a similar set of annual statistics on their website (http://www.scotland.gov.uk). The most recent are available at: http://www.scotland.gov.uk/Publications/2008/12/15155727/0. In terms of the investigation and detection of homicide, by far the best text is Innes' (2003) *Investigating Murder: Detective Work and the Police Response to Criminal Homicide*. A useful overview of the scope for reducing and preventing homicide can be found in Brookman and Maguire (2005) 'Reducing Homicide: A Review of the Possibilities'. Finally, the journal *Homicide Studies* (Sage) is worth consulting on a regular basis and is the only journal dedicated to research papers from various parts of the world dealing specifically with homicide.

Notes

1 Of the four countries that make up the United Kingdom, England and Wales share a common legal system and are treated as a single entity for the purposes of recording crime. Scotland has a very different legal system based on Roman law whereby offence definitions are often inconsistent with those of England and Wales. Northern Ireland has a separate criminal justice system that has been profoundly affected by terrorist troubles. Due to these anomalies, and for the sake of clarity, it will be necessary to deal mainly with the law related to homicide in England and Wales, referring separately to Scotland and Northern Ireland where necessary.

2 Scottish law makes a similar distinction between murder and common law culpable homicide but does not have separate legislation for the killing of infants.

3 Deaths caused by dangerous or careless driving or while under the influence of alcohol or drugs are dealt with by separate legislation (see Road Traffic Acts 1988 and 1991).

4 Prior to 1965, with the passing of the Murder (Abolition of the Death Penalty) Act, murder was a capital offence.

5 Until 1996 an individual could not be prosecuted for murder if the individual they had harmed died after a year and a day of the original attack. One of the original rationales for this rule lay in the difficulty in proving a causal connection between old injuries and subsequent death. However, this rule came under increasing criticism, especially as modern medicine and life-support machines meant that a murderer could avoid liability simply because of lengthy medical attempts to save someone's life. Hence in 1995 the House of Commons' Select Committee on Home Affairs and the Law Commission produced papers recommending the abolition of the rule, and Parliament did so in the Law Reform (Year and a Day Rule) Act 1996.

6 There have been just five recorded cases of corporate manslaughter since 2000 in the homicide statistics for England and Wales which bears no resemblance to the number of lives lost due to corporate negligence and neglect (see Tombs this volume).

7 In their original proposals the Law Commission restricted first degree murder to intentional killings only (see Law Commission 2005: 249–58).

8 Caution is needed when interpreting these preliminary figures because deaths that are not initially believed to be suspicious may be recategorised as homicides at a later date. Hence these unconfirmed data have not been included in Figure 12.1.

9 Harold Shipman was convicted in January 2000 of murdering 15 of his patients while he was a general practitioner in Hyde, Greater Manchester. The independent public inquiry identified a further 172 victims – believed to have been killed over an estimated 25-year period. These additional homicides were recorded by Greater Manchester Police in 2002/3 and thus appear in the 2002/3 homicide figures (see Smith 2002). Other events of note include the 52 victims of the 7th July London bombings (recorded in 2005/6), the 20 cockle pickers who drowned in Morecambe Bay (recorded 2003/4) and the 58 Chinese nationals who collectively suffocated in a lorry en route in the UK (recorded 2000/1).

10 That said, current homicide rates are insignificant when compared to the incidence in the Middle Ages or 1700s (see Spierenburg 2008).

11 For further discussion of longer-term homicide trends and their links to the political economy see Eisner (2001) and Spierenburg (2008).

12 The HDI combines measures of life expectancy, literacy, education and gross domestic product (GDP) per capita as a means of measuring the comparing levels of human development (Krause et al. 2008: 72).

13 This section focuses principally upon England and Wales and includes analysis of the Home Office Homicide Index 1998–2008 as well as relying upon the most recent homicide statistics published by the Home Office (see Povey et al. 2009).

14 The Home Office and Scottish Government publish annual homicide statistics that are generally much more detailed and informative than those that are available for other offences. The reader is referred to these publications as well as Brookman (2005) for further detailed analysis of offender, victim and offence characteristics.

15 This excludes 172 homicides of white people killed by Harold Shipman and the 20 Morecambe Bay homicides as these cases unusually skew the data.

16 More detailed coverage can be found in Brookman (2005).
17 Simon and Burns' (1997) *The Corner* is a highly illuminating depiction of an inner-city drug culture.
18 The Home Office began recording gang-related homicides on the Homicide Index in 2007. However, the data are not comprehensive due, in part, to incomplete returns made to the Home Office and an inevitable lack of certainty in some cases as to whether gang members were involved, e.g. unsolved shooting incidents.

References

Aebi, M. (2004) 'Crime trends in Western Europe from 1990 to 2000', *European Journal on Criminal Policy and Research*, 10 (2–3): 163–86.

Anderson, E. (1999) *Code of the Street: Decency, Violence and the Moral Life of the Inner City*. New York: W. W. Norton.

Ashworth, A. and Mitchell, B. (2000) *Rethinking English Homicide Law*. Oxford: Oxford University Press.

Athens, L. H. (1977) 'Violent crime: a symbolic interactionist study', *Symbolic Interaction*, 1: 56–70.

Athens, L. H. (1980) *Violent Criminal Acts and Actors: A Symbolic Interactionist Study*. London: Routledge & Kegan Paul.

Athens, L. H. (1997) *Violent Criminal Acts and Actors Revisited*. Chicago: University of Illinois Press.

Baum, D. (1996) 'Can integration succeed? Research into urban childhood and youth in a deprived area of Koblenz', *Social Work in Europe*, 3 (2): 30–5.

Becker, E. (1962) 'Anthropological notes on the concept of aggression', *Psychiatry*, 23: 328–38.

Bernard, T. J. (1990) 'Angry aggression among the truly disadvantaged', *Criminology*, 28 (1): 73–96.

Block, R. (1977) *Violent Crime*. Lexington, MA: D. C. Heath.

Bourgois, P. (2003) *In Search of Respect: Selling Crack in El Barrio*. Cambridge: Cambridge University Press.

Bowling, B. (1999) 'The rise and fall of New York murder', *British Journal of Criminology*, 39 (4): 531–54.

Box, S. (1983) *Power, Crime and Mystification*, Tavistock Studies in Sociology. London: Routledge.

Brookman, F. (2003) 'Confrontational and grudge revenge homicides in England and Wales', *Australian and New Zealand Journal of Criminology*, 36 (1): 34–59.

Brookman, F. (2005) *Understanding Homicide*. London: Sage.

Brookman, F. and Maguire, M. (2005) 'Reducing homicide: a review of the possibilities', *Crime, Law and Social Change*, 42: 325–403.

Bullock, K. and Tilley, N. (2008) 'Understanding and tackling gang violence', *Crime Prevention and Community Safety*, 10 (1): 36–47.

Buvinic, M. and Morrison, A. R. (2000) 'Living in a more violent world', *Foreign Policy*, 118: 58–72.

Card, R. (1998) *Criminal Law*. London: Butterworths.

Central Statistics Unit, PSNI (2008) *PSNI Annual Report, Recorded Crime and Clearances April 2007 – March 2008*, Central Statistics Branch, Operational Support Department. Belfast: PSNI. Online at: http://www.psni.police.uk/1._recorded_crime-2.pdf.

Chapple, C. (2008) 'Substance-Related Homicide in England and Wales: Pathways, Processes and Events'. Unpublished PhD Thesis, University of Manchester, School of Law.

Coleman, K. (2007) 'Homicide', in D. Povey (ed.), *Homicides, Firearm Offences and Intimate Violence 2006/07, Supplementary Vol. 2 to Crime in England and Wales 2006/7*, Home Office Statistical Bulletin 03/08. London: Home Office.

Copes, H. and Hochstetler, A. (2003) 'Situational construction of masculinity among male street thieves', *Journal of Contemporary Ethnography*, 32 (2): 279–304.

Corzine, J., Huff-Corzine, L. and Whitt, H. P. (1999) 'Cultural and subcultural theories of homicide', in M. D. Smith and M. A. Zahn (eds), *Homicide: A Sourcebook of Social Research*. London: Sage.

Cotton, J. and Bibi, N. (2005) 'Homicide', in D. Povey (ed.), *Crime in England and Wales 2003/2004: Supplementary Volume 1: Homicide and Gun Crime*. London: Home Office.

Criminal Justice System Race Unit (2006) *Race and the Criminal Justice System: An Overview to the Complete Statistics 2004–2005*. London: CJS Race Unit.

Croall, H. (1998) *Crime and Society in Britain*. London: Longman.

Currie, E. (1998) *Crime and Punishment in America*. New York: Holt.

Curtis, L. A. (1975) *Violence, Race and Culture*. Lexington, MA: Heath.

Daly, M. and Wilson, M. (1988) *Homicide*. New York: Aldine De Gruyter.

Daly, M. and Wilson, M. (1990) 'Killing the competition: female/female and male/male homicide', *Human Nature*, 1 (1): 81–107.

Decker, S. (1995) 'Reconstructing homicide events: the role of witnesses in fatal encounters', *Journal of Criminal Justice*, 23 (5): 439–50.

Decker, S. (1996) 'Deviant homicide: a new look at the role of motives and victim–offender relationships', *Journal of Research in Crime and Delinquency*, 33: 427–49.

Denno, D. (1990) *Biology and Violence: From Birth to Adulthood*. Cambridge: Cambridge University Press.

Dobash, R. E., Dobash, R. P., Cavanagh, K. and Lewis, R. (2002) *Homicide in Britain: Risk Factors, Situational Contexts and Lethal Interventions (Focus on Male Offenders)*, Research Bulletin No.1. Department of Applied Social Science, DASS, University of Manchester.

Eades, C., Grimshaw, R., Silvestri, A. and Solomon, E. (2007) *'Knife Crime': A Review of Evidence and Policy*. London: Centre for Crime and Justice Studies.

Eisner, M. (2001) 'Modernisation, self-control and lethal violence: the long-term dynamics of European homicide rates in theoretical perspective', *British Journal of Criminology*, 41: 618–38.

Felson, R. B. and Messner, S. F. (1996) 'To kill or not to kill? Lethal outcomes in injurious attacks', *Criminology*, 34 (4): 519–45.

Finch, A. (2001) 'Homicide in contemporary Japan', *British Journal of Criminology*, 14: 219–35.

Freedman, D. and Hemenway, D. (2000) 'Precursors of lethal violence: a death row sample', *Social Science and Medicine*, 50: 1757–70.

Fyfe, J., Goldkamp, J. and White, M. (1997) *Strategies for Reducing Homicide: The Comprehensive Homicide Initiative in Richmond, California*. Washington, DC: US Department of Justice.

Goffman, E. (1967) *Interaction Ritual: Essays on Face-to-Face Behaviour*. New York: Doubleday.

Goldstein, P. J. (1985) 'The drugs/violence nexus: a tripartite conceptual framework', *Journal of Drug Issues*, 15: 493–506.

Hall, S. (1997) 'Visceral cultures and criminal practice', *Theoretical Criminology*, 1: 453–78.

Hochstetler, A. and Copes, H. (2003) 'Situational construction of masculinity among male street thieves', *Journal of Contemporary Ethnography*, 32: 279–304.

Home Office (2009) *Extending Our Reach: A Comprehensive Approach to Tackling Serious Organised Crime*. London: HMSO. Online at: http://www.cabinetoffice.gov.uk/media/222240/seriouscrime.pdf.

Horder, J. (2007) *Homicide Law in Comparative Perspective*. Oxford: Hart.

Innes, M. (2003) *Investigating Murder: Detective Work and the Police Response to Criminal Homicide*. Oxford: Clarendon Press.

Jacobs, B. and Wright, R. (1999) 'Stick-up, street culture, and offender motivation', *Criminology*, 37: 149–74.

Jacobs, D. and Richardson, A. M. (2008) 'Economic inequality and homicide in the developed nations from 1975 to 1995', *Homicide Studies*, 12 (1): 28–45.

Johnson, D. T. (2008) 'The homicide drop in postwar Japan', *Homicide Studies*, 12 (1): 146–60.

Kershaw, C., Nicholas, S. and Walker, A. (2008) *Crime in England and Wales 2007/08. Findings from the British Crime Survey and Police Recorded Crime*. London: Home Office. Online at: http://www.homeoffice.gov.uk/rds/pdfs08/hosb0708.pdf.

Krause, K., Muggah, R. and Wennmann, A. (eds) (2008) *Global Burden of Armed Violence*, Secretariat of the Geneva Declaration on Armed Violence and Development. Geneva: Geneva Declaration Secretariat.

Kubrin, C. E. and Weitzer, R. (2003) 'Retaliatory homicide: concentrated disadvantage and neighbourhood culture', *Social Problems*, 50 (2): 157–80.

Law Commission (1996) *Legislating the Criminal Code: Involuntary Manslaughter*, Report No. 237. London: HMSO.

Law Commission (2005) *A New Homicide Act for England and Wales? An Overview*, Consultation Paper No. 177. London: Stationery Office. Online at: http://www.lawcom.gov.uk/docs/cp177_overview_web.pdf.

Law Commission (2006a) *Report on Murder, Manslaughter and Infanticide*, Law Commission Report No. 304, Press Briefing Paper. London: Stationery Office.

Law Commission (2006b) *Murder, Manslaughter and Infanticide*, Project 6 of the Ninth Programme of Law Reform: Homicide, Law Commission Report No. 304. London: Stationery Office. Online at: http://www.lawcom.gov.uk/docs/lc304.pdf.

Levi, M. (1997) 'Violent crime', in M. Maguire, R. Morgan and R. Reiner (eds), *The Oxford Handbook of Criminology*, 2nd edn. Oxford: Oxford University Press.

Luckenbill, D. F. (1977) 'Criminal homicide as a situated transaction', *Social Forces*, 25: 176–86.

Luckenbill, D. F. and Doyle, D. P. (1989) 'Structural position and violence: developing a cultural explanation', *Criminology*, 27 (3): 419–35.

McAlister, A. L. (2006) 'Acceptance of killing and homicide rates in nineteen nations', *European Journal of Public Health*, 16 (3): 259–65.

McCall, P., Parker, K. F. and MacDonald, J. (2008) 'The dynamic relationship between homicide rates and social, economic and political factors from 1970 to 2000', *Social Science Research*, 37: 721–35.

McLagan, G. (2006) *Guns and Gangs*. London: Alison & Busby.

Messerschmidt, J. (1993) *Masculinities and Crime*. Lanham, MA: Rowman & Littlefield.

Messner, S. F. and Rosenfeld, R. (1999) 'Social structure and homicide', in M. D. Smith and M. A. Zahn (eds), *Homicide: A Sourcebook of Social Research*. London: Sage.

Miethe, T. D. and Meier, R. F. (1994) *Crime and Its Social Context: Towards an Integrated Theory of Offenders, Victims and Situations*. Albany, NY: State University of New York Press.

Miethe, T. D. and Regoeczi, W. C. (2004) *Rethinking Homicide*. Cambridge: Cambridge University Press.

Niehoff, D. (1999) *The Biology of Violence*. New York: Free Press.

Northern Ireland Human Rights Commission (2008) *Response to Murder, Manslaughter and Infanticide: Proposals on the Reform of the Law*. Belfast: Human Rights Commission.

Parker, R. N. (1995) 'Bringing "booze" back in: the relationship between alcohol and homicide', *Journal of Research in Crime and Delinquency*, 32 (1): 3–38.

Parker, R. N. and Auerhahn, K. (1999) 'Drugs, alcohol and homicide: issues in theory and research', in M. D. Smith and M. A. Zahn (eds), *Homicide: A Sourcebook of Social Research*. London: Sage.

Peelo, M., Francis, B., Soothill, K., Pearson, J. and Ackerley, E. (2004) 'Newspaper reporting and the public construction of homicide', *British Journal of Criminology*, 44: 256–75.

Phillips, C. and Bowling B. (2007) 'Ethnicities, racism, crime and criminal justice', in M. Maguire, R. Morgan and R. Reiner (eds), *The Oxford Handbook of Criminology*. Oxford: Oxford University Press.

Phillips, S. and Maume, M. O. (2007) 'Have gun will shoot? Weapon instrumentality, intent, and the violent escalation of conflict', *Homicide Studies*, 11 (4): 272–94.

Pitts, J. (2008) *Reluctant Gangsters: The Changing Face of Youth Crime*. Cullompton: Willan.

Pizzaro, J. M. (2008) 'Reassessing the situational covariates of homicides: is there a need to disaggregate?', *Homicide Studies*, 12 (4): 323–49.

Polk, K. (1994a) *When Men Kill: Scenarios of Masculine Violence*. Cambridge: Cambridge University Press.

Polk, K. (1994b) 'Masculinity, honour and confrontational homicide', in T. Newburn and E. A. Stanko (eds), *Just Boys Doing the Business?* London: Routledge.

Polk, K. (1995) 'Lethal violence as a form of masculine conflict resolution', *Australian and New Zealand Journal of Criminology*, 28 (1): 93–115.

Povey, D., Coleman, K., Kaiza, P. and Roe, S. (eds) (2009) *Homicides, Firearms Offences and Intimate Violence 2007/08*, Home Office Statistical Bulletin 02/09. London: Home Office.

Pridemore, W. A. (2008) 'A methodological addition to the cross-national empirical literature on social structure and homicide: a first test of the poverty-homicide thesis', *Criminology*, 46: 133–54.

Reiner, R. (2007) 'Political economy, crime and criminal justice', in M. Maguire, R. Morgan and R. Reiner (eds), *The Oxford Handbook of Criminology*, 4th edn. Oxford: Oxford University Press.

Rosenfeld, R., Jacobs, B. and Wright, R. (2003) 'Snitching and the code of the streets', *British Journal of Criminology*, 43 (2): 291–309.

Sampson, R. and Lauritsen, J. (1994) 'Violent victimization and offending: individual-, situational-, and community-level risk factors', in A. J. Reiss and J. A. Roth (eds), *Understanding and Preventing Violence: Vol. 3, Social Influences*. Washington, DC: National Academy Press.

Sánchez-Jankowski, M. (2003) 'Gangs and social change', *Theoretical Criminology*, 7 (2): 191–216.

Sandberg, S. (2008) 'Street capital: ethnicity and violence on the streets of Oslo', *Theoretical Criminology*, 12 (2): 153–71

Savolainen J., Lehti, M. and Kivivuori, K. (2008) 'Historical origins of a cross-national puzzle: homicide in Finland, 1750 to 2000', *Homicide Studies*, 12 (1): 67–89.

Schinkel, W. (2004) 'The will to violence', *Theoretical Criminology*, 8 (1): 5–31.

Scottish Government (2008) *Homicide in Scotland 2007–08*. Edinburgh: Scottish Government. Online at: http://www.scotland.gov.uk/Publications/2008/12/15155727/0.

Segal, L. (1990) *Slow Motion: Changing Masculinities, Changing Men*. London: Virago.

Shaw, J., Hunt, I. M., Flynn, S., Amos, T., Meehan, J., Robinson, J., Bickley, H., Parsons, R., McCann, K., Burns, J., Kapur, N. and Appleby, L. (2006) 'The role of alcohol and drugs in homicides in England and Wales', *Addiction*, 101: 1117–24.

Simon, D. and Burns, E. (1997) *The Corner: A Year in the Life of an Inner-City Neighbourhood*. Edinburgh: Canongate.

Smith, J. (Dame) (2002) *The Shipman Enquiry*, First Report, Vol. One: *Death Disguised*. Norwich: HMSO. Online at: http://www.the-shipman-inquiry.org.uk/reports.asp.

Soares, R. R. (2004) 'Crime reporting as a measure of institutional development', *Economic Development and Cultural Change*, 52: 851–71.

Soothill, K., Peelo, M., Pearson, J. and Francis, B. (2004) 'The reporting trajectories of top homicide cases in the media: a case study of *The Times*', *Howard Journal*, 43 (1): 1–14.

Spierenburg, P. (2008) *A History of Murder*. Cambridge: Polity Press.

Tavares, C. and Thomas, G. (2008) *Crime and Criminal Justice*, Eurostat 19/2008. Luxembourg: European Communities.

Tedeschi, J. T. and Felson, R. B. (1994) *Violence, Aggression and Coercive Actions*. Washington: American Psychological Association.

Toch, H. (1969) *Violent Men: An Inquiry into the Psychology of Violence*. Chicago: Aldine.

Topalli, V., Wright, R. and Fornango, R. (2002) 'Drug dealers, robbery and retaliation', *British Journal of Criminology*, 42: 337–51.

Uchiyama, Y. (2003) '"Heitai san Moderu" kara Toku' [translated for the *International Herald Tribune* on 16 April as 'Peace motive: are Japanese men more timid? Or is the low murder rate a product of postwar culture?'], *Asahi Shimbun* (evening edition), 5 April, p. 3.

UNODC (United Nations Office on Drugs and Crime) (2005) *Crime and Development in Africa*. Vienna: UNODC. Online at: http://www.unodc.org/pdf/African_report.pdf.

UNODC (United Nations Office on Drugs and Crime) (2008) *International Homicide Statistics*. Online at: http://www.unodc.org/documents/data-and-analysis/IHS-rates-05012009.pdf.

Vigil, J. D. (2006) 'A multiple marginality framework of gangs', in A. Egley., C. Maxson, J. Miller and M. Klein (eds), *The Modern Gang Reader*, 3rd edn. Oxford: Oxford University Press.

Walker, A., Flatley, J., Kershaw, C. and Moon, D. (eds) (2009) *Crime in England and Wales 2008–09*, Vol. 1: Findings from the British Crime Survey and Police Recorded Crime, Home Office Statistical Bulletin 11/09. London: Home Office. Online at: http://www.homeoffice.gov.uk/rds/pdfs09/hosb1109vol1.pdf.

Ward, L. and Diamond, A. (2009) *Tackling Knives Action Programme (TKAP) Phase 1: Overview of Key Trends from a Monitoring Programme*, Research Report No. 18. London: Home Office.

Weaver, G. S., Wittekind, J. E. C., Huff-Corzine, L., Corzine, J., Petee, T. A. and Jarvis, J. P. (2004) 'Violent encounters: a criminal event analysis of lethal and non-lethal outcomes', *Journal of Contemporary Criminal Justice*, 20 (4): 348–68.

Williams, K. R. and Flewelling, R. L. (1988) 'The social production of criminal homicide: a comparative study of disaggregated rates in American cities', *American Sociological Review*, 53 (3): 421–31.

Wilson, N. K. (1993) 'Gendered interaction in criminal homicide', in A. V. Wilson (ed.), *Homicide: The Victim/Offender Connection*. Cincinnati, OH: Anderson.

Wolfgang, M. (1958) *Patterns in Criminal Homicide*. Montclair, NJ: Patterson Smith.

Wolfgang, M. E. and Ferracuti, F. (1967) *The Subculture of Violence: Towards an Integrated Theory in Criminology*. London: Tavistock.

Wright, R., Brookman, F. and Bennett, T (2006) 'The foreground dynamics of street robbery in Britain', *British Journal of Criminology*, 46: 1–15.

Chapter 13

Domestic violence

Amanda Robinson

Introduction

What is interesting and unique about 'domestic violence' in comparison with other types of crime? It covers a wide range of criminal and deviant behaviours, but a common theme – setting it apart from other crimes – is that it is defined by the nature of the victim/offender relationship. A number of terms are used to describe this phenomenon: wife abuse, battered women, domestic violence, domestic abuse, spousal assault, family violence, violence against women, intimate partner violence, gender-based violence. Historically, 'domestic violence' meant violence or abuse perpetrated by husbands against wives. This necessitated both a heterosexual relationship and one that had been formalised with a marriage contract. In recent years, in many different countries, definitions of domestic violence have broadened, for example to include non-married and/or same-sex intimates and to acknowledge its physical, psychological, sexual and financial components (Sandis 2006). These different components are now explicitly referred to in the shared Association of Chief Police Officers (ACPO), Crown Prosecution Service (CPS) and UK government definition:

> Any incident of threatening behaviour, violence or abuse (psychological, physical, sexual, financial or emotional) between adults, aged 18 or over, who are or have been intimate partners or family members, regardless of gender and sexuality. (National Police Improvement Agency (NPIA) 2008)

Beneficially, this definition specifies that physical violence is just one of many types of abuse that may be perpetrated and thus more truthfully reflects victims' experiences, as we will see. As a term, however, 'domestic violence' is limited, as it favours naming the violence over all the other types of abusive actions that produce harm. For this very reason, government documents in both Wales and Scotland instead refer to 'domestic abuse'. Even this can be criticised, however, as 'domestic' implies that the abuse always takes place in a domestic setting (and one shared by the victim and perpetrator), which is not always true. Others would argue that all of these actions constitute 'violence' in some regard and should therefore be named as such. The use of various terms, and different definitions being offered for the same term, 'plagues researchers and policy makers alike as information gathered for one purpose where a particular definition is appropriate is used for another where it is inappropriate and may be misleading' (Dobash 2003: 313). There is no easy way around these definitional issues, all of which have implications for our understanding of, and responses to, 'domestic violence'.

In the UK definition, 'family members' include parents, children, siblings and grandparents, whether directly related, in-laws or step-family. Therefore this definition combines violence perpetrated by intimate partners with that committed by other family members. It may be considered beneficial to provide a broad definition to alert officials to the various forms that domestic violence may take, particularly as more 'new' types, such as honour-based violence, are brought to public attention. On the other hand, it is problematic because one generic intervention will never be equally effective for every possible expression of 'domestic violence'. For example, a brother assaulting his sister might not be the kind of perpetrator envisioned in the creation of Specialist Domestic Violence Courts, yet as a 'domestic offender' (according to the official definition) these are the interventions in place to respond to his criminal behaviour (see the section on responses to domestic violence below). This chapter will use the term 'domestic violence' to be consistent with government terminology, although most of the research reviewed here (mainly from the UK and US) refers to violence perpetrated by intimate partners rather than by family members.

Patterns of domestic violence

There are ample statistics available indicating the widespread prevalence of domestic violence and that it disproportionately affects women rather than men. In 2002, the Council of Europe stated that domestic violence is the primary cause of death and disability for European women aged 16–44 (more than cancer or traffic accidents). The World Health Organisation reported that up to 70 per cent of female murder victims worldwide are killed by their male partners (Krug *et al.* 2002). Of British female homicide victims acquainted with the suspect, 65 per cent were killed by their partner, ex-partner or lover (the corresponding figure for men is 11 per cent) (Coleman 2008).

A recent literature review found over 80 prevalence studies from more than 50 countries (Ellsberg and Heise 2005). Most of these studies estimated a lifetime prevalence of domestic violence for between 20 per cent and 50 per cent of women who have ever married or been in an intimate relationship. In the UK the figures are 33 per cent for women and 22 per cent for men (Hoare and Jansson 2008). The high prevalence of this crime reveals 'the particular and specialised nature of domestic violence as a coercive course of conduct, usually involving a series of related occurrences, rather than a one-off event'

(Walby 2005: 4). Unfortunately the accepted conceptualisation of domestic violence as an enduring condition or course of conduct is at odds with official measures of crime and criminal justice. For example, crime statistics tend to be based on counts of incidents, although there might be several events involved in one 'incident'. This makes it easy for the repetitious nature of domestic violence to disappear from view, unless care is taken to collect measures of both incidence and prevalence. Using the most recent British Crime Survey (BCS) figures from 2006–7 as an example, 7 per cent of people interviewed reported experiencing domestic violence within the past year. Of these, 59 per cent suffered abuse on more than one occasion and 9 per cent said they had been victimised more than 20 times in the last year (Hoare and Jansson 2008). Indeed, the repetitious nature of domestic violence is 'one of its most traumagenic aspects' (Hamby 2004: 22) (see the section on the characteristics of domestic violence offences, offenders and victims below).

In Europe, 27 countries have carried out representative national surveys or survey modules, many of which are published only in the language of the country (Hagemann-White 2008). To date, most of these surveys are not comparable (cf. the International Violence Against Women Survey that has been employed in six European countries to date). Comparisons across national borders are difficult, because, as Sylvia Walby (2005) explained to the UN, there are at least five ways that like-for-like comparisons are routinely compromised in research on domestic violence: first, the range of perpetrators; second, the range of types of violence; third, the threshold at which it is considered 'violence' and the measurement of its severity; fourth, the focus on prevalence or incidents; fifth, experiences over the whole lifetime or during the last year (p. 3). The BCS deals with these issues by collecting data on the broadest range of perpetrators (partners and family members); types of behaviours and their severity (non-physical abuse (emotional, financial), threats, force (minor, severe), sexual assault (differentiated by type and attempted/completed), stalking); resulting injuries and emotional effects; prevalence (within last year and since age 16) and incidence (within last year). Its main drawback is that respondents are limited to those between the ages of 16 and 59, so information about domestic violence among older people is not captured.

In the UK, for the last several years, domestic violence has accounted for nearly a quarter of all recorded violent crime. This proportion would rise drastically if this crime was not so under-reported. Recent BCS figures indicated that following an incident of domestic violence, most victims spoke to someone regarding what had occurred, but only a small proportion (13 per cent) reported the abuse to the police (Hoare and Jansson 2008). The gap between the more representative 'dark figure of crime' (as distinguished from the 'tip of the iceberg' that is visible to the authorities) has always been particularly worrisome in the field of domestic violence. The fact that police remain unaware of the vast majority of domestic violence victims has pronounced implications for how effectively the criminal justice system can respond to this crime (see the section on responses to domestic violence below).

Characteristics of domestic violence offences, offenders and victims

Characteristics of domestic offences

A key characteristic of domestic violence is its multifaceted nature. As mentioned in the introduction, myriad behaviours and criminal offences may constitute 'domestic violence', including violent offences, harassment, property offences and/or sexual offences. Research with 222 women experiencing domestic violence in Cardiff (Robinson 2003) illustrated that several distinct types of behaviour are used by perpetrators, usually in combination, against the same victim:

- *93 per cent reported physical abuse.* This included being hit with a fist (30 per cent), kicked (24 per cent) and/or being choked or strangled (17 per cent). A majority of the women also felt that the pattern of abuse was escalating in severity (73 per cent) and frequency (68 per cent).

- *98 per cent reported emotional abuse.* For example, 22 per cent reported that their partner threatened their family or friends and 22 per cent said their current partner threatened to take the children away. Nearly half had been questioned about their activities. As one woman explained, 'throughout the relationship he controlled the clothes I wore and the food I ate.'

- *64 per cent reported financial abuse.* Financial abuse was not limited to arguments over bills or spending but was another tactic of control used by perpetrators. Women reported that their partners would refuse to work, generate shared debts and steal from them. One woman explained that 'when I left he'd been to the bank and cleared the account.'

- *25 per cent reported sexual abuse.* Sexual abuse could include rape, other forms of sexual assault and pressure to have unwanted sex. One woman said her husband would 'insinuate that I was a whore and sleeping with other men if I refused.'

Taking a longitudinal perspective of victims' experiences over their lifetimes illustrates the overlapping and intersecting nature of many forms of abuse (Romito 2008). One person could perpetrate many of these offences against a single partner. Experiencing one type of abuse can make a victim more susceptible to experiencing another (Hamby 2004). Each of the distinct behavioural elements described produces its own form of harm to the victim. When experienced in combination (as they usually are) the consequences for victims of even the least damaging abuses can be significant, as will be discussed in the next section.

Since the victim/offender relationship has been central to defining domestic violence, it has often been assumed in the past that by ending the relationship the abuse will also cease. Unfortunately, this is not always the case. Although in the recent BCS most (74 per cent) victims who had split up from an abusive partner reported that the violence had stopped completely when their relationships ended, 7 per cent said that the violence continued (but decreased in severity) and 9 per cent said that the abuse continued (but changed form). Furthermore, for 6 per cent of victims the abuse only started when the relationship ended (Hoare and Jansson 2008). Other recent BCS data showed that separated/divorced women had the highest likelihood of experiencing domestic violence (Coleman *et al.* 2007). This is consistent with Wilson and Daly's (1992) seminal research, which found that women were at greatest risk of homicide after they separated from a violent partner. Child contact can also provide an opportunity for conflict (and violence) to continue, even after the relationship has ended. For example, more than three-quarters of a sample of separated women suffered further abuse or harassment from their former partners and child contact was a point of particular vulnerability for both the women and their children (Humphreys and Thiara 2003).

Victims of domestic violence

There is a common assertion that domestic violence affects all types of people, can be found in every type of household, and is prevalent in every community. Whilst this may be true, the demographics of domestic violence victims are not representative of society at large. Prevalence varies by demographic and socio-economic indicators. The most obvious of these is gender. As already mentioned, women are more likely to experience domestic violence. But they also experience it differently compared to men. Research on male and female victims of domestic violence showed that experiencing domestic violence made women significantly more afraid compared to men (Robinson and Rowlands 2009). Specifically, a much higher proportion of women expressed the fear of being killed, of being subjected to further injury or violence, or of their children being harmed. This is consistent with BCS data indicating that women were much more likely to be frightened, and to stay frightened, than men (Mirrlees-Black 1999). Thus experiential outcomes from experiencing domestic violence are clearly linked to the gender of the victim.

Age is also a factor. As with violent crime generally, those in the younger age categories are more likely to experience domestic violence than older people. This is true for both men and women (Coleman *et al.* 2007). There is little evidence of differences in prevalence across different ethnic groups in the UK, although this is not true in the US, where African-American women report more domestic violence than do white women (Bureau of Justice Statistics (BJS) 1998).

Socio-economic indicators are also important for understanding the profile of domestic violence victims, and similar trends are observed in the US and UK. BCS data showed that women living in households with lower incomes had a higher than average risk of domestic violence compared to women living in more affluent households, and that there is more domestic violence in the social rental housing sector than in the owner-occupied sector (Coleman *et al.* 2007). In addition, women with children in their households were at significantly higher risk of experiencing domestic violence. One interpretation may be that these women are at increased risk because they are less reluctant to break up the family (Walby and Allen 2004). These findings are echoed in research from the US. The National Crime Victimization Survey (NCVS – the US equivalent of the British Crime Survey) found that the risk for victimisation was highest among young, single women with children, particularly those who have lived in their homes for relatively short periods, within disadvantaged areas (Lauritsen and Schaum 2004).

Consequences of domestic violence for victims can be pronounced. Negative impacts on women's livelihoods and employability include missing work due to immediate physical abuse as well as long-term ailments (Moe and Bell 2004). One British study found that 1 in 10 victims had missed work due to physical or emotional abuse perpetrated by their current partners, and one in four had missed work at some point in their lifetimes due to abuse (Robinson 2005). Recent BCS figures also showed that women were more likely than men to have to take time off work due to domestic violence (Hoare and Jansson 2008)

In the US, domestic violence accounts for between a quarter and half of all women presenting for treatment in emergency rooms (Bureau of Justice Statistics 1998). A study using NCVS data revealed that women had significantly higher odds of both injury and disability from a serious injury due to domestic violence, compared to men (Carbone-Lopez *et al.* 2006). Recent BCS figures showed that women were more likely (58 per cent) than men (48 per cent) to have experienced injuries as a result of domestic abuse (Hoare and Jansson 2008). The British Medical Association (BMA) has stated that there is growing evidence to confirm that domestic violence 'has serious and long-lasting consequences on the health and wellbeing of the victim and their family members', such as chronic pain, arthritis, hearing or sight deficits, seizures or frequent headaches, stress, stomach ulcers and hypertension (BMA 2007).

It should not be forgotten that while the physical injuries may in some cases be severe, the effects of emotional and psychological abuse may be equally, if not more, damaging to victims. Studies have shown that emotional pain has more lasting negative impacts when compared to physical pain (Chen *et al.* 2008). As one victim explained to the Home Affairs Select Committee (2008),

> Having experienced many kinds of abuse the physical abuse is horrible but the verbal and emotional abuse are far worse – no one sees that and often people think you are the one with the problem, not the abuser (p. 11).

Mental health effects from domestic violence have been extensively documented in the literature, for example anxiety, depression, post-traumatic stress disorder (PTSD), low self-esteem and suicide ideation (Hastings and Kantor 2004). Women responding to the most recent BCS indicated twice the level of mental or emotional problems, due to domestic violence, than men (33 per cent and 14 per cent respectively) (Hoare and Jansson 2008). It is the chronic, multidimensional nature of domestic violence that produces such harmful cumulative mental and physical health effects in victims.

Domestic violence offenders

What are the characteristics of domestic violence offenders? As with victims, gender, age and socio-economic status are distinguishing characteristics of domestic offenders. Young men are more likely to commit domestic violence than older men (Straus *et al.* 1980). In addition, many studies show that measures of lower socio-economic status (e.g. income, manual labour and common-law marriage) are linked to an increased likelihood of committing domestic violence (Hilton and Harris 2005; Straus *et al.* 1980).

Many researchers have attempted to reduce the monolithic category 'domestic violence offenders' into groups, subtypes or typologies. This is important in order to better explain and understand this type of offending and to tailor responses accordingly. A review of studies supports the notion that domestically violent men are a heterogeneous group (Dixon and Browne 2003). Despite identifying different numbers of subgroups, existing studies consistently identify one group of especially severe offenders who also commit other violent antisocial acts (Hilton and Harris 2005). Their proportion of the total varies according to the type of sample studied (e.g. court-referred or volunteer) from 23 per cent to 60 per cent. Characteristics of this group include previous convictions, alcohol dependency, 'macho' attitudes, narcissism, and psychopathology (Johnson *et al.* 2006). As psychopathology and alcohol/ substance use in particular have been found to be consistent and distinguishing features of domestic offenders, each will be discussed more fully.

Psychopathology is characterised by superficial charm, need for stimulation, callousness, manipulation, antisocial history and criminal versatility (Hilton and Harris 2005). A diagnosis of psychopathy is one of the strongest predictors of violence recidivism, including serious domestic violence (Harris *et al.* 2001). Although a great deal of overlap has been found between the characteristics of serious domestic violence offenders and psychopathy, Huss and Langhinrichsen-Rohling (2006) concluded that psychopathy alone cannot explain domestic violence as this condition itself is multidimensional.

Extant research indicates that domestic offenders with substance abuse problems are especially persistent offenders. Coker *et al.* (2000) found the male partner's drug or alcohol use to be the strongest correlate of domestic violence. Two British studies found that offenders who used drugs were more likely to inflict injuries, to emotionally abuse their partners and to escalate the frequency or severity of the domestic violence (Robinson 2003, 2006a). It also appears that perpetrators with substance abuse problems will be less likely to comply with criminal justice sanctions. An analysis of 2,438 violent offenders on probation in the Chicago area found that domestic offenders with substance abuse problems were significantly more likely to repeatedly violate the technical conditions of their sentence, such as missing treatment or not paying fines (Olson and Stalans 2001).

Exhibiting jealousy, being possessive and trying to control their partners are other trademark characteristics of domestic violence offenders (Dobash and Dobash 1979; Gelles 1974). Robinson (2006b) found that offenders who were reported to be jealous/controlling by victims were also more likely to injure the victim, to have threatened to kill, to have choked or strangled the victim, to have increased the severity of abuse over time and/or to have threatened suicide. In cases where the intimate relationship was over, the more jealous perpetrators also prompted conflict over child contact. These findings are consistent with theoretical notions of power and control which underpin many domestic violence policies and responses in western countries, as described below.

Explanations for domestic violence

As Dobash (2003) explained, 'proposals for actions aimed at solutions always contain underlying ideas about why the violence might occur' (p. 314). Before discussing current responses to domestic violence, it is therefore necessary to examine the explanations and reasons given for why this type of behaviour is committed in the first place.

This is not as straightforward as it may sound. The multifaceted nature of domestic violence and its varying conception as a crime, pathological condition or social problem means that theoretical insights have been offered from many different disciplines. A comment made 25 years ago is still applicable today: '… there is little agreement on the presumed causes and correlates of violent behavior. No single theory or discipline has been able to explain adequately domestic or stranger violence' (Fagan *et al.* 1983: 49). Likewise, 'predicting violence is quite a different task from explaining it' (Hilton and Harris 2005). Just because two events or characteristics are correlated does not mean that one explains the other. It is fair to say that we know much more about the correlates of domestic violence than the causes behind it.

Individual level

This set of explanations focuses on the pathology of individual perpetrators as a key reason behind the occurrence of domestic violence. These perspectives view violence as resulting from offenders' psychological problems such as inadequate self-control, sadism or psychopathology, abnormal personality traits (low frustration tolerance, depression) or substance use/abuse. Psychopathy and substance abuse are particularly strong factors linked to the onset, commission and severity of domestic violence, as discussed in the previous section.

Although there is ample evidence suggesting domestic violence and alcohol/drug abuse are interrelated, most evidence does not support a *causal* link. While research has shown that men who are violent towards their partners are more likely to abuse alcohol or other drugs than are non-abusive men, this cannot lead to the conclusion that substance abuse *causes* domestic violence. Not all intoxicated people commit domestic violence, and substance use alone cannot explain why or how these violent tendencies originate. Some researchers have even proposed that substance abuse is used as an excuse by offenders to justify their behaviour (Gelles 1974). Likewise, psychopathology might be more likely among domestic offenders, but not all abusive men are psychopaths, as the research on typologies described earlier has shown.

Another body of research identifies family dysfunction as an important contributor to domestic violence. This perspective views violence as essentially learned behaviour. Children who witness or are subjected to violence in their family of origin will begin to see violence as an acceptable way to address problems and resolve conflict. This viewpoint is alternatively described as the intergenerational transmission of violence, the cyclical hypothesis or the cycle of violence. The association between exposure to violence as a child and commission of violence as an adult is a strong one that has been replicated in different study samples (Hilton and Harris 2005). A frequently reported finding is that men who witnessed domestic violence as children, or who experienced physical abuse themselves as children, are more likely to commit domestic violence later in life (Hines and Saudino 2002). In one of the first studies, Straus *et al.* (1980) found that children who witnessed parental violence were three times more likely to be violent to their own partners. A more recent study found remarkably similar results. Following a sample of 543 children in New York over a 20-year period demonstrated that exposure to childhood abuse doubled the chances of using violence toward a partner, and that exposure to parent-to-parent violence tripled the odds of using violence toward a partner (Ehrensaft *et al.* 2003).

The problem with individual-level explanations (psychopathology and substance abuse in particular) is that many studies use samples of offenders court-referred for treatment, leading to results which may over-represent the amount of psychological problems among offenders. Furthermore, many studies use samples exclusively comprised of offenders, so results cannot be compared to men with similar characteristics who do not commit domestic violence. Perhaps most importantly, 'psychologising' the problem of domestic violence prevents a 'political analysis of the violence', thereby neglecting a crucial focus on 'dominant power relationships' (Romito 2008: 69). Dobash and Dobash (1990) criticise these approaches as too narrow as they exclude questions about the context of the violence – what actually happens and why. Even accepting the intergenerational transmission of violence hypothesis, we must ask why the effect of exposure is stronger for male compared to female children, in addition to producing different outcomes over time (boys becoming abusers and girls becoming victims). Individual-level explanations can offer a glimpse at the reasons behind why some people might go on to commit domestic violence, but these explanations alone cannot tell the whole story.

Social-structural level

Macro-level or structural explanations of domestic violence, informed by feminist research, focus on the pervasive subordination of women in patriarchal societies. The historical toleration, and in some cases encouragement, of abuse against women by male partners and family members continues to the present day and propagates a misogynist social context whereby men see women as their personal property, to be subjected to abuse if they misbehave (Pleck 1987). This patriarchal ideology is reinforced by social institutions (for example family, church, schools, police, courts) when they 'turn a blind eye' to the issue. In short, domestic violence, rape and other forms of violence against women have been viewed as tools that can be used by men to reinforce their position of power (Brownmiller 1975; Dobash and Dobash 1979; Romito 2008; Stanko 1985). In contrast to individual-level approaches, these explanations explicitly reject 'gender-blind' explanations for domestic violence.

Several themes are apparent in social-structural explanations for domestic violence, and 'power' is a key explanatory concept within each. First, there is abundant evidence of historically unequal power relations between women and men. Political, economic and social processes keep men in a position of power and keep women politically and economically disadvantaged. Straus *et al.* (1980) found the highest rates of domestic violence in families where power was concentrated in the hands of the husband (i.e. he had final decision-making authority on the majority of issues) rather than shared democratically. This perspective has been extended by research that focuses on the economic dependence of women on men, and the role that income and employment opportunities play in decision-making and in the ability of an individual to leave an abusive relationship. In the same large-scale study of US families, the highest rates of domestic violence were found in households where the woman was a full-time housewife (Straus *et al.* 1980). In the UK, Pahl (1985) found that husbands used control of money as one of their techniques to control and subordinate their wives.

Cultural ideology is also seen as a contributing factor, as culture defines gender roles. Customs, traditions and religious values can be used to justify domestic violence. Control over women is maintained in different societies through established cultural concepts such as romantic love, duty or notions of 'honour' and shame (Gill 2008). Doctrines of privacy have also contributed to the prevalence of domestic violence globally, as there has been a persistent belief in most societies that violence within the family or intimate relations is a private matter. This contributes to an environment where perpetrators are able to act with impunity and helps to create a culture of silence and shame, discouraging victims from seeking support and protection.

As with the individual-level explanations, structural explanations cannot offer a comprehensive theory for domestic violence. Their obvious weakness is that not all men perpetrate domestic violence (although some would argue that even non-abusive men benefit from the 'patriarchal dividend', meaning they do not have to commit the violence themselves to reap the same rewards from their dominant social status). Hoyle (2007) questioned the value of patriarchy as a core explanatory variable for domestic violence, particularly as other structural and cultural variables may intersect with patriarchy in various ways that are only beginning to be explored. Mills (2003) further argued against 'mainstream feminists [who] have consistently taken the position that patriarchy is the sole influence on women, and that it dictates how and why they act as they do' (p. 64). Thus there is an increasingly vocal recognition of the limits of patriarchy as an explanation for domestic violence, although its relevance cannot be ignored.

Social-structural approaches have the advantage of acknowledging the context, history and structural issues that contribute to the continued and widespread prevalence of domestic violence across the globe. It is not simply individual cases of 'troubled' perpetrators or conflict-ridden families in need of help. Structural explanations are now the most likely type found in contemporary national policy documents. Council of Europe documents regularly reaffirm that 'violence against women is the result of power imbalances between women and men'. As Hagemann-White (2008) stated, 'the problem is no longer linked to the family, and it is no longer framed as societal responsibility for unfortunate victims, but firmly anchored in a rights discourse' (p. 152). As the next section shows, however, it is less clear that these structural explanations consistently inform contemporary responses to domestic violence.

Responses to domestic violence

In most western countries, the primary response to domestic violence has been located in the criminal justice system. In other words, once brought to public attention, domestic violence has been defined as a crime problem rather than, say, a public health problem. This section provides an overview of the contemporary criminal justice response to domestic violence in the UK, drawing upon other international experiences where appropriate. The UK approach is primarily a criminal justice-led strategy but has implications for other institutions and support systems. In fact, as will be shown, these outside actors are pivotal for the success of the key initiatives within the government's current approach.

Policy context

The Home Office's national domestic violence plan (2006)[1] has a tripartite structure whereby 'one-stop-shops' for victims, specialised domestic violence courts (SDVCs) and multi-agency risk assessment conferences (MARACs) for very high-risk victims come together in a coordinated way to assist victims, hold perpetrators accountable and target resources to the most vulnerable families. This plan capitalises on local innovation and documented evidence that such approaches can make a positive difference in the lives of victims and their children. The government's *Action Plan for Tackling Violence 2008–11* further supports this three-pronged approach, setting out the intention to dramatically expand the availability of these programmes (HM Government 2008).

Other national developments include new guidance for police on investigating domestic violence published by ACPO in 2004 (and recently revised by the National Police Improvement Agency (NPIA), on behalf of ACPO, in 2008), a revised prosecution policy published by the Crown Prosecution Service (CPS) in 2005 and a joint national training programme for police and prosecutors developed by CENTREX in 2005. Recent developments in policing must be placed against the backdrop of steady change since the 1980s. Today, police agencies in the UK, and also in the US, operate with pro-arrest policies for domestic violence. In contrast to the non-interventionist approach historically favoured by the police, these policies are presumptive in favour of officers making arrests when probable cause exists. There can be no doubt that a new culture has arisen within policing that identifies domestic incidents as calls that may be potentially scrutinised by the public and/or supervisors, with higher liability for officers who shirk their duties. Today, in most western countries, for police not to intervene is now tantamount to their condoning crime.

In the UK, domestic violence is now considered part of 'Public Protection', which enjoys a high profile within police forces, comes under the command of detective constables and is well supported. Domestic violence officers are not marginalised within the police service; rather, their work is related to government targets associated with the 'core business' of policing. Training on domestic violence, including how to effectively investigate and respond to these crimes, is now incorporated into standard curricula, and many forces require supplemental domestic violence workshops along with other continuous training exercises. As the recently revised NPIA guidance for investigating domestic violence makes clear, the first priority of the police is to protect the lives of both adults and children who are at risk. They are meant to achieve this by investigating all reports, by taking effective action against offenders so that they can be held accountable through the criminal justice system and by adopting a multi-agency approach.

Finally, the government provided £2 million to underpin a new national training and accreditation programme for Independent Domestic Violence Advisors (IDVAs) beginning in 2005.[2] IDVAs are trained support workers who provide assistance and advice to victims of domestic violence. They work closely with criminal justice and statutory partners in many different settings to coordinate a range of services across agencies on behalf of victims. These innovative, recently established posts are discussed further in the subsection on supporting victims below.

Specialist domestic violence courts

Before discussing the implementation and expansion of SDVCs in the UK, it is necessary to understand the challenges of progressing cases of domestic violence through the criminal courts. Research has shown these cases progress differently from comparable cases where the crime was not committed in a domestic context. Sanders (1988) looked at prosecution practices in England and Wales and found that, compared to non-domestic violence cases, domestic violence cases were less likely to be prosecuted. When they were brought to court, more defendants were found not guilty. Cretney and Davis (1997) examined 296 cases of assault (both domestic and non-domestic) and found routine charge reductions and high rates of withdrawals and bind overs in the progression of domestic assault cases. More recent research highlights the high rate of attrition (cases dropping out of the system) for domestic violence. Hester (2006) found that only 31 offenders were eventually convicted out of a starting sample of 869 incidents.

A large part of what makes case progression in domestic violence cases unique is the important role ascribed to – and evidenced by – victim participation (or conversely, victim retraction). The influence of the victim's willingness to participate in the case cannot be overstated, and there is a well documented and significant relationship between victim participation and the progression of domestic violence cases through the system (Cretney and Davis 1997; Davis et al. 1997; Hirschel and Hutchison 2001; Schmidt and Steury 1989; Ventura and Davis 2005). The conundrum for the criminal justice system is that it relies heavily on victim participation in the type of case where victims would appear to be the most unwilling to participate.

Research has shown that, understandably, victims of any crime are often reluctant to be witnesses in court for a range of reasons, but these are exacerbated when the defendant and victim have once had, or continue to have, an intimate relationship. Research in the UK, US and Australia has illustrated how the decision of victims to retract their statements is taken in the context of a range of pressures, many of which derive from the actions or 'controlling behaviours' of perpetrators (Ford 1991; Holder 2006; Hoyle and Sanders 2000; Robinson and Cook 2006). Factors influencing victims' decisions to engage with the criminal justice process include: fear of the perpetrator and/or repercussions from his family, her own family and/or the community; the extent and nature of her injuries; fear of damaging family status or honour; fear of losing children; a lack of information about and fear of criminal and civil processes, particularly for women who do not speak or read English; lack of information about, and delays to, the progress of their case; whether the defendant offers an initial plea of guilty; changes to bail conditions; and immigration status. The extent to which victims' choices facilitate case progression and sentencing has to be seen as a secondary consideration to their overriding goal of resolving a difficult personal situation as safely as they know how.

To acknowledge the difficulties facing victims of domestic violence, as well as the criminal justice officials trying to respond to these cases, specialist domestic violence courts (SDVCs) have been implemented in many countries. The first British SDVC was established in Leeds in 1999 and by 2003 four more courts were developed from existing local multi-agency partnerships: Cardiff, Derby, West London and Wolverhampton. These first five SDVCs were subject to an evaluation (Cook et al. 2004), the results of which led the CPS to pilot two more courts: one in a rural area (Gwent, Wales) and one in an ethnically diverse urban area (Croydon, London) (Vallely et al. 2005). The evidence garnered from these evaluations led the government to launch an expansion programme that assisted nearly 100 such courts to become operational by 2008. According to the government's *Action Plan for Tackling Violence 2008–11* (2008) this number is set to double by 2011.

So what is so 'special' about these courts? Unlike other courts, SDVCs deal exclusively with cases involving domestic violence. Their guiding philosophy is that this crime poses particular difficulties for both the victim and the criminal justice system, therefore a specialised method of dealing with these cases is necessary. Basic features of British SDVCs include: a focus on criminal (not civil) matters heard in magistrates' courts; dealing mainly with pre-trial hearings rather than trials; identifying domestic violence cases and thereafter either 'clustering' or 'fast-tracking' them; having an advocate (IDVA) present to support victims; having a specialist police officer present to provide information to the court; and relying on multi-agency partnerships. Existing research, along with a recent government review of 23 SDVCs, has shown that they have higher rates of successful prosecutions, more victims being supported via IDVAs, and produce better confidence among victims, practitioners and community members.

Even within SDVCs, however, victim participation remains a crucial determinant of case outcomes. For example, a study in Toronto found that prosecutors were seven times more likely to prosecute a case when victims were perceived to be cooperative (Dawson and Dinovitzer 2001). In a study of victim retraction in five British SDVCs Robinson and Cook (2006) found that even with the support provided to victims from advocates (IDVAs) and the multi-agency partnerships within which the courts were embedded, half of victims still chose to retract. Thus case progression in SDVCs still depends in large part on the perceived and actual willingness or credibility of the victim to act as a prosecution witness. For the reasons already discussed, this is likely to be a persistent challenge for the courts, whether specialised or not.

What is the most common sentence handed down in domestic violence cases? In the US, Ventura and Davis (2005) found that the most common sanction in a sample of 204 offenders was probation with all or part of a jail sentence suspended. About one-third were sentenced and actually spent some time in jail. A fraction (7 per cent) received only a suspended jail sentence or fine and court costs. One of the few studies looking at this issue in the UK found that conditional discharges were the preferred penalties imposed on convicted domestic violence offenders (Cretney and Davis 1997). Research on several British demonstration projects aimed at reducing domestic violence found that sentencing practices varied considerably: the use of custodial sentences ranging from 11 per cent to 50 per cent (Hester and Westmarland 2005).

One of the aims of court specialisation is to produce more consistent, appropriate sentencing practices. Although there is evidence from the US of success in this regard (Keilitz 2001), this has been difficult to achieve in the UK. An analysis of sentencing in the first seven British SDVCs found that custody was used infrequently and fines were handed down at the rate of magistrates courts thirty years ago (in about two-thirds of cases) (Robinson 2008). Given the aims of SDVCs, this was seen to be a disappointing finding, especially since the use of financial penalties in cases of domestic violence has always drawn criticism. More than a decade ago, Hoyle (1998) found that domestic violence victims felt that the sentence received by their ex/partners (usually fines) was often not worth the 'pain' of prosecution. To be fair, it remains unclear what specific penalties should be used, and for which offenders. It is also uncertain what effects specific penalties might have on victims' levels of satisfaction, safety and quality of life. This lack of clarity surrounding the aims of sentencing can be seen as a significant challenge for SDVCs.

A final challenge for SDVCs derives from their focus on criminal matters. Victims of domestic violence might be involved in criminal cases (as witnesses) or civil cases (as applicants) in an attempt to seek protection from either, or both, jurisdictions. Indeed, many victims would require both criminal and civil justice to keep themselves and their children safe. As Jordan (2004) explained, 'Although most aspects of the criminal justice system are distinct from civil law, domestic violence is unique in that the response crafted by advocates and legal professionals to this area of the law includes a combination of civil and criminal remedies' (p. 1423). However, the civil justice system is not routinely included in contemporary multi-agency approaches. One study found that the 'interface' between civil and criminal courts was completely dependent upon the advocates (IDVAs) that support victims through the legal process, rather than any formal policies or procedures (Robinson 2007). In an attempt to address this issue an 'integrated' court is currently being piloted in Croydon.

Multi-agency approaches

As has been shown, domestic violence is a particularly difficult issue to resolve using criminal law alone. Multi-agency partnerships emerged as a way to address the inherent limitations of the criminal justice response to many different crimes, including domestic violence. Undeniably the most well known, the Duluth 'coordinated community response' model (Shepard and Pence 1999), was initiated in Minnesota in 1980 and its tenets are now common parlance among many types of practitioners working in many different countries. Multi-agency approaches require coordinating the actions of a variety of agencies that deal with domestic violence. The implication is that criminal justice agencies cannot, and should not be expected to, effectively deal with domestic violence on their own. Partnerships between criminal justice agencies and health care, social services, local government, education and the voluntary sector are needed to provide a holistic response to this multifaceted problem. These approaches seek to adopt a coordinated and problem-solving approach in an effort to meet the needs of victims, their families and the community. Some refer to the current emphasis on multi-agency approaches as representing a new period of 'collaborative empowerment' which has the potential to move the response beyond the institutions of the criminal justice system (Lutze and Symons 2003).

Many local and national governments have explicitly endorsed multi-agency approaches for domestic violence and have linked funding to interventions that are consistent with this ethos. Multi-agency approaches are seen to be 'visions of effective policy' across Europe (Hagemann-White 2008). In the UK, the Home Office concluded that 'local policy and practice has been transformed in some areas by multi-agency domestic violence work' and the recent Home Affairs Select Committee (2008) reaffirmed this by stating that 'multi-agency responses are needed to respond effectively to domestic violence' (p. 110).

Research with 1,509 victims in the US documented that when the victims perceived that agencies were working together, improvements were evident in both criminal justice outcomes (arrests, convictions) as well as victim outcomes (satisfaction, confidence) (Zweig and Burt 2003). Research on multi-agency risk assessment conferences (MARACs) in the UK has shown that taking a multi-agency approach can reduce repeat victimisation, even amongst the most at-risk and vulnerable victims and their children (Robinson 2006b; Robinson and Tregidga 2007). More recent and ongoing research in eight locations across the UK confirms that MARACs can produce dramatic reductions in victimisation even among the most severe cases (CAADA 2008).

The MARAC model of intervention follows a process of risk assessment by police in all reported cases of domestic violence, to identify those at highest risk so that a specialist multi-agency approach may be implemented. At the meetings, the circumstances of individual victims (mostly, but not all, women) are discussed, and plans are created to help promote their safety.

Representatives from various agencies contribute information and often this process reveals discrepancies in the information held across agencies. For example, the police might have knowledge of one woman as a repeat, high-risk victim, but probation might only know about her partner's drug offending. Only in a multi-agency framework can these loopholes be identified and closed. Acknowledging their effectiveness, in 2007 the government invested £1.85m to set up MARACs in over 100 areas.

Despite the successes that arise from multi-agency initiatives, it must also be acknowledged that they are only as effective as their composite members. Criminal justice agencies play a vital role, yet they might not always recognise this to be the case, or they may shirk from carrying out their responsibilities to victims. Conversely, but equally problematically, they might seek to invoke a legal response to the exclusion of all other possibilities for remedying the situation. Valuing criminal justice above all else undoubtedly puts a strain on multi-agency partnerships, in addition to pigeonholing victims and limiting the possible solutions to their situations. As noted by Römkens and Lünnemann (2008) police must 'learn how to better position themselves as part of a multi-disciplinary intervention chain' (p. 187).

Another challenge for multi-agency work is that concepts such as 'justice' and 'fairness' are formulated and perceived in different ways by different audiences. Any criminal justice intervention, with its concomitant focus on arrest and prosecution, will have to be reconciled with the victim's safety in order to develop a realistic prospect of what counts as, and how to measure, success (Robinson 2008; Römkens 2006). It is clear that 'success' can take many different forms as there is not one single purpose to criminal justice intervention but a number of purposes (Holder 2006). Furthermore, the importance of recognising the subjective nature of success can be a useful reminder that the law is only one element of a wider social response to domestic violence that must also include community-based, rehabilitative and preventative strategies (Lewis 2004).

Supporting victims

One of the most progressive aspects of the current UK strategy is that it explicitly recognises the unique needs faced by victims of domestic violence. Supporting them is not seen as an 'extra' to be provided when it can, but rather is considered to be essential to their engagement with criminal justice and other systems that can provide help.

Providing community-based support and advice for victims of domestic violence is not a new concept, originating in refuges in the 1960s. In these refuges, women willing to flee their homes were able to access support. The next stage was to offer services to women living in the community via 'outreach' or 'floating support' units that were based within refuges. 'Advocacy' emerged in several areas in the 1990s to provide support and advice to *all* types of victims in the community, even those still in relationships with the perpetrator. The workers who provide advocacy services to victims of domestic violence have come to be known (since circa 2005), via current government policies and funding arrangements, as independent domestic violence advisors or 'IDVAs'. Thus the label is newer than the type of work.

The UK approach draws upon work conducted in the US pointing to the benefits of providing support and advice to women in community-based settings. For example, Sullivan and Bybee (1999) studied the effects of an advocacy intervention on future violence in a longitudinal, experimental-design study. Battered women were randomly assigned to one of two groups (one group receiving one-on-one assistance from an advocate who helped them obtain resources such as housing, employment, legal assistance, education, child care and health care, and the other group receiving no such assistance). Findings from this research showed that the intervention was successful at reducing women's risks of further or more severe abuse. Moreover, women who had worked with advocates were more successful at terminating abusive relationships.

An evaluation of one of the earlier IDVA projects in Cardiff showed how providing a central point of access for victims improved the amount and quality of services they received. IDVAs at the Women's Safety Unit provided victims with advice, advocacy, information, counselling, legal services, housing services and target hardening and, importantly, also collected case evidence (Robinson 2003). A similar project in Glasgow also provided a range of services in a 'one-stop-shop' style, leading to enhanced multi-agency responses and similar positive outcomes among victims (Robinson 2006a). Providing victims with an effective, immediate and consistent range of support services at one referral point is one of the strengths of community-based advocacy. Crucially, these projects, by being responsive to the unique needs of each individual, deliver 'woman-defined' rather than 'service-defined' advocacy (Davies *et al.* 1998).

A national evaluation of four IDVA projects funded by the Home Office found that the key ingredients of effective IDVA services were independence, a focus on victims' safety and the ability to coordinate a range of services across agencies on behalf of victims (Robinson 2009). The research showed that the IDVA role offered a unique opportunity to provide independent, objective advice to victims about their options, an opportunity that is not duplicated by any other agency. IDVAs navigated multiple systems and were crucial contributors to multi-agency initiatives, especially MARACs. Their specialist skills and ability to provide both individual and institutional advocacy were very highly valued by victims and partner agencies. IDVAs were viewed as vital contributors to the 'coordinated community response' model, yet they were only one part: their success depended on the local availability of other necessary support services (e.g. outreach/long-term support, specialist sexual violence services, etc.).

The recent proliferation of advocacy in the UK is largely due to the expansion of SDVCs and MARACs in the last few years. Despite the evidence of IDVAs' centrality to the government's current strategy, funding of these services remains a key challenge. The Home Office Select Committee (2008) recognised the uncertainty of their funding beyond the current three-year plan and recommended that the government increase its funding for IDVA services. The long-term consequences of 'under-serving' victims have to be recognised and addressed by both local and national governments if the multi-agency initiatives they promote are to have any lasting effect.

Critical analysis of the current UK approach

As we have seen, in the last few years there has been a dramatic shift in the British response to domestic violence. While once treated as a private matter best dealt with in the home, it is now an issue that receives widespread attention. Taking a more proactive, interventionist and legal approach has been heralded by many victim advocates, criminal justice officials and scholars as a great advance, as progress. A formal response is seen to reinforce this message: domestic violence is a crime that will not be tolerated by society. Criminalising domestic violence encourages the legal system to treat violence between intimates in the same manner as violence between strangers (Stark 1996). The nature of the criminal justice response can send abusers 'either a green light or a red light for the continuation of their violent actions' (Dobash 2003: 316).

Despite these well-founded and hard-won changes to policy and practice, there is now a growing chorus of voices questioning the efficacy of approaches to domestic violence that are based wholly in the criminal justice system. Interestingly, and illustrating the complexity of the issues involved, some of these voices belong to the same people that were fighting so hard for the criminal justice system to treat these behaviours as crimes in the first place. Why? As Davis et al. (2003) note, 'good intentions do not always result in good public policy' (p. 280).

A body of evidence indicates several compelling arguments against a formalised, legalistic approach to domestic violence. Firstly, they rest upon the assumption that victims who do not want to cooperate with police or prosecutors are not capable of making decisions in their own best interests (Hanna 1996). Secondly, actions taken by police or prosecutors might ignore or even conflict with the goals of victims (Ford 1991; Mills 1998), who use the criminal justice system to satisfy several different goals over time (e.g. protection, prevention, reform and justice) (Lewis et al. 2000). A prosecution-centred approach can be seen to be paternalistic when it overrides a victim's autonomy or conflicts with her wishes (Hoyle and Sanders 2000; Mills 1998). Finally, these initiatives may be distorted because they emerged from 'a masculine interpretation of how to improve the plight of domestic violence victims' and are implemented by gendered institutions that undermine their effectiveness (Lutze and Symons 2003: 322).

None of the elements of the current strategy specifically addresses prevention despite this being identified in the Home Office (2003) *Safety and Justice* consultation as one of three key priorities. The conclusion of the Home Affairs Select Committee (2008) was that the government's response remains disproportionately focused on criminal justice with too little emphasis on prevention. Even the Parliamentary Under-Secretary of State at the Home Office, Vernon Coaker MP, stated that

Simply responding in a criminal justice sense will not be sufficient. What are we doing in our schools? What are we doing to support victims when they come forward?

Others who gave evidence considered the current approach not only overly legalistic, but also overly focused on high-risk victims to the exclusion of longer-term support services and prevention programmes. In other words, the approach is flawed because it is only responding to the tip of the iceberg.

The disagreement regarding the extent to which criminal justice can 'solve' domestic violence is best understood as a discourse about the probable causes of domestic violence. A criminal justice approach reflects individual or situational explanations, whereas those calling for more prevention, awareness raising and education are implying that a structural, societal explanation is at the root of domestic violence. Therefore over-reliance on criminal justice is seen to be problematic because it promotes a 'movement away from a critique of underlying social, legal, and political structures that underpin male privilege and use of violence' (Miller and Meloy 2006: 108).

Finally, regardless of how admirable the intentions and how well-designed and thought out an intervention might be, it will always be difficult to endorse one particular approach that can be equally appropriate and effective for all victims. The challenge of recognising the sociocultural context surrounding the violence and the impact of structural inequalities on victims' experiences, choices and needs is an issue that is becoming only more pertinent as time passes.

Research has documented that 'less deserving' victims, such as lesbians, rural women, immigrants, the homeless, the elderly, the mentally ill and black/minority ethnic (BME) women experience less responsive social service agencies (Donnelly *et al.* 1999). The responses of these institutions may be hindered by the racism present in their own structures as well as in society at large. In addition, BME communities attempting to deal with domestic violence have special problems because feminist politics may be viewed as out of place or even conflicting with their social context. Established community norms may discourage women from seeking outside help; subsequently, addressing this problem is made more difficult as 'people of colour often must weigh their interests in avoiding issues that might reinforce distorted public perceptions against the need to acknowledge and address intra-community problems' (Crenshaw 1991: 1256). Furthermore, a reliance on traditional gender roles within certain cultural contexts has led to a greater tolerance of domestic violence within some BME communities (Bui and Morash 1999) and its manifestation in forms that are new and different to responding agencies. For example, Gill (2008) discussed the trauma imposed by 'honour-based violence' and the difficulties of responding effectively to this problem in South Asian communities in the UK.

Improving resources and outreach to BME women experiencing domestic violence and other underserved populations is an important part of any holistic, community-wide response to domestic violence. Clearly, these women should not be further victimised by hostile or ignorant staff, a lack of awareness regarding appropriate or culturally specific food or clothing or a lack of bilingual written materials or counselling services. Embedding 'cultural competence' into domestic violence service provision is a current and emerging challenge for all types of agencies. Research shows that 'culturally competent' agencies are more effective and produce better outcomes for victims from marginalised communities (Gillum 2008; Morash and Bui 2008). However, there is a dilemma faced by agencies attempting to embed 'cultural competency' into their responses. Of course properly trained professionals will want to respect and understand each victim's particular geo-historical background and the cultural values that inform her thinking and behaviour, but some cultural beliefs will place the preservation of the family unit or a husband's 'honour' over a woman's right to live free from abuse. The dilemma is thus how to empathise with a woman's culture while at the same time empowering her to live free from abuse, which may necessitate challenging her cultural beliefs. This is most likely to be achieved via diverse, multi-disciplinary and multi-agency support interventions. While the government's current strategy is not antithetical to this *per se*, only time will tell whether it is flexible enough to produce positive outcomes across a range of victim experiences, needs and expectations.

Selected further reading

Over the past 20 years a wealth of research has been published on domestic violence. A good starting point is the book written by Eva and Carl Buzawa (2003), *Domestic Violence: The Criminal Justice Response* (a fourth edition is currently in press), which provides an easily accessible yet comprehensive account of the American context. A contemporary British perspective is provided by *Tackling Domestic Violence: Theories, Policies and Practice* by Harne and Radford (2008). Three recently published monographs are key sources for anyone seeking to understand domestic violence: Mills' (2003) *Insult to Injury*, Stark's (2007) *Coercive Control* and Romito's (2008) *A Deafening Silence*. A special issue published in 2008 of the *International Journal of Comparative and Applied Criminal Justice* on responding to intimate partner violence across the globe includes original research conducted in the US, the UK, Europe, Australia and Central Asia on both legal and non-legal interventions. There are several academic journals dedicated to the topic which can also be consulted – see in particular the *Journal of Interpersonal Violence* and *Violence Against Women*.

Notes

1 Online at: http://www.crimereduction.gov.uk/domesticviolence/domesticviolence41. pdf.
2 The accredited training programme for IDVAs is provided by CAADA (Coordinated Action Against Domestic Abuse). For more information see: http://www.caada.org. uk.

References

British Medical Association (2007) *Domestic Abuse: A Report from the BMA Board of Science*. London: British Medical Association.
Brownmiller, S. (1975) *Against Our Will: Men, Women and Rape*. New York: Bantam Books.

Bui, H. N. and Morash, M. (1999) 'Domestic violence in the Vietnamese immigrant community', *Violence Against Women*, 5 (7): 769–95.

Bureau of Justice Statistics (1998) *Violence by Intimates*. Washington, DC: US Department of Justice, Office of Justice Programs.

Buzawa, E. S. and Buzawa, C. G. (2003) *Domestic Violence: The Criminal Justice Response*, 3rd edn. Thousand Oaks, CA: Sage.

CAADA (2008) *A Multi-site Evaluation of the Impact of IDVA Services on High Risk Survivors of Domestic Abuse*, Fact Sheet 1. Online at: http://www.caada.org.uk.

Carbone-Lopez, K., Kruttschnitt, C. and Macmillan, R. (2006) 'Patterns of IPV and their associations with physical health, psychological distress, and substance use', *Public Health Reports*, 121 (4): 382–92.

Chen, Z., Williams, K. D., Fitness, J. and Newton, N. C. (2008) 'When hurt will not heal: exploring the capacity to relive social and physical pain', *Psychological Science*, 19 (8): 789–95.

Coker, A. L., Smith, P. H., McKeown, R. E. and King, M. J. (2000) 'Frequency and correlates of intimate partner violence by type: physical, sexual and psychological battering', *American Journal of Public Health*, 90 (4): 553–9.

Coleman, K. (2008) 'Homicide', in D. Povey (ed.), *Homicide, Firearms Offences, and Intimate Violence 2006/07*, Home Office Statistical Bulletin 03/08. London: Home Office.

Coleman, K., Jansson, K., Kaiza, P. and Reed, E. (2007) *Homicides, Firearm Offences and Intimate Violence 2005/06 (Supplementary Volume 1 to Crime in England and Wales 2005/06)*, Home Office Statistical Bulletin 02/07. London: Home Office.

Cook, D., Burton, M., Robinson, A. and Vallely, C. (2004) *Evaluation of Specialist Domestic Violence Courts/Fast Track Systems*. London: Crown Prosecution Service and Department of Constitutional Affairs.

Council of Europe (2002) *Domestic Violence Against Women*. Parliamentary Assembly Recommendation 1582.

Crenshaw, K. (1991) 'Mapping the margins: intersectionality, identity politics, and violence against women of color', *Stanford Law Review*, 43: 1241–99.

Cretney, A. and Davis, G. (1997) 'Prosecuting domestic assault: victims failing courts, or courts failing victims?', *Howard Journal of Criminal Justice*, 36 (2): 146–57.

Davies, J., Lyon, E. and Monti-Catania, D. (1998) *Safety Planning with Battered Women: Complex Lives/Difficult Choices*. Thousand Oaks, CA: Sage.

Davis, R. C., Smith, B. E. and Nickles, L. (1997) *Prosecuting Domestic Violence Cases with Reluctant Victims: Assessing Two Novel Approaches in Milwaukee*. Washington, DC: National Institute of Justice.

Davis, R. C., Smith, B. E. and Taylor, B. (2003) 'Increasing the proportion of domestic violence arrests that are prosecuted: a natural experiment in Milwaukee', *Criminology and Public Policy*, 2 (2): 263–82.

Dawson, M. and Dinovitzer, R. (2001) 'Victim cooperation and the prosecution of domestic violence in a specialized court', *Justice Quarterly*, 18 (3): 593–622.

Dixon, L. and Browne, K. (2003) 'The heterogeneity of spouse abuse: a review', *Aggression and Violent Behaviour*, 8: 107–30.

Dobash, R. E. (2003) 'Domestic violence: arrest, prosecution and reducing violence', *Criminology and Public Policy*, 2 (2): 313–18.

Dobash, R. E. and Dobash, R. P. (1979) *Violence Against Wives*. New York: Free Press.

Dobash, R. E. and Dobash, R. P. (1990) 'How theoretical definitions and perspectives affect research and policy', in D. J. Besharov (ed.), *Family Violence: Research and Public Policy Issues*. Washington, DC: AEI Press, pp. 108–29.

Donnelly, D. A., Cook, K. J. and Wilson, L. A. (1999) 'Provision and exclusion: the dual face of services to battered women in three deep south states', *Violence Against Women*, 5: 710–41.

265

Ehrensaft, M. K., Cohen, P., Brown, J., Smailes, E., Chen, H. and Johnson, J. G. (2003) 'Intergenerational transmission of partner violence: a 20-year prospective study', *Journal of Consulting and Clinical Psychology*, 71 (4): 741–53.

Ellsberg, M. and Heise, L. (2005) *Researching Violence Against Women: A Practical Guide for Researchers and Activists*. Geneva: World Health Organisation.

Fagan, J. A., Stewart, D. K. and Hansen, K. V. (1983) 'Violent men or violent husbands? Background factors and situational correlates', in D. Finkelhor *et al.* (eds), *The Dark Side of Families*. Beverly Hills, CA: Sage, pp. 49–67.

Ford, D. A. (1991) 'Prosecution as a victim power resource: a note on empowering women in violent conjugal relationships', *Law and Society Review*, 25: 313–34.

Gelles, R. J. (1974) *The Violent Home*. Beverly Hills, CA: Sage.

Gill, A. (2008) '"Crimes of honour" and violence against women in the UK', *International Journal of Comparative and Applied Criminal Justice*, 32 (2): 243–63.

Gillum, T. L. (2008) 'The benefits of a culturally specific intimate partner violence intervention for African American survivors', *Violence Against Women*, 14 (8): 917–43.

Hagemann-White, C. (2008) 'Measuring progress in addressing violence against women across Europe', *International Journal of Comparative and Applied Criminal Justice*, 32 (2): 149–72.

Hamby, S. L. (2004) 'The spectrum of victimization and the implications for health', in K. A. Kendall-Tackett (ed.), *Health Consequences of Abuse in the Family*. Washington, DC: American Psychological Association, pp. 7–27.

Hanna, C. (1996) 'No right to choose: mandated victim participation in domestic violence prosecutions', *Harvard Law Review*, 109: 1850–910.

Harne, L. and Radford, J. (2008) *Tackling Domestic Violence: Theories, Policies and Practice*. Princeton, NJ: Princeton University Press.

Harris, G. T., Skilling, T. A. and Rice, M. E. (2001) 'The construct of psychopathy', in M. Tonry (ed.), *Crime and Justice: An Annual Review of Research*. Chicago: University of Chicago Press.

Hastings, D. P. and Kantor, G. K. (2004) 'Screening for family violence with perioperative patients', in K. A. Kendall-Tackett (ed.), *Health Consequences of Abuse in the Family*. Washington, DC: American Psychological Association, pp. 33–44.

Hester, M. (2006) 'Making it through the criminal justice system: attrition and domestic violence', *Social Policy and Society*, 5 (1): 79–90.

Hester, M. and Westmarland, N. (2005) *Tackling Domestic Violence: Effective Interventions and Approaches*, Home Office Research Study No. 290. London: Home Office.

Hilton, N. Z. and Harris, G. T. (2005) 'Predicting wife assault: a critical review and implications for policy and practice', *Trauma, Violence and Abuse*, 6 (1): 3–23.

Hines, D. A. and Saudino, K. J. (2002) 'Intergenerational transmission of intimate partner violence', *Trauma, Violence and Abuse*, 3: 210–25.

Hirschel, D. and Hutchison, I. W. (2001) 'The relative effects of offence, offender, and victim variables on the decision to prosecute domestic violence cases', *Violence Against Women*, 7 (1): 46–59.

HM Government (2008) *Saving Lives. Reducing Harm. Protecting the Public: An Action Plan for Tackling Violence 2008–11*. London: Home Office.

Hoare, J. and Jansson, K. (2008) 'Extent of intimate violence, nature of partner abuse and serious sexual assault, 2004/05, 2005/06 and 2006/07 British Crime Survey', in D. Povey (ed.), *Homicide, Firearms Offences, and Intimate Violence 2006/07*, Home Office Statistical Bulletin 03/08. London: Home Office.

Holder, R. (2006) 'The emperor's new clothes: justice and court initiatives on family violence', *Australian Journal of Judicial Administration*, 16 (30): 30–47.

Home Affairs Select Committee (2008) *Domestic Violence, Forced Marriage and 'Honour'-Based Violence*, Sixth Report of Session 2007–08. London: House of Commons.

Home Office (2003) *Safety and Justice: The Government's Proposals on Domestic Violence*, Cm 5487. London: Home Office.

Hoyle, C. (1998) *Negotiating Domestic Violence*. Oxford: Clarendon Press.

Hoyle, C. (2007) 'Feminism, victimology and domestic violence', in S. Walklate (ed.), *Handbook of Victims and Victimology*. Cullompton: Willan, pp. 146–74.

Hoyle, C. and Sanders, A. (2000) 'Police response to domestic violence: from victim choice to victim empowerment?', *British Journal of Criminology*, 40: 14–36.

Humphreys, C. and Thiara, R. K. (2003) 'Neither justice nor protection: women's experiences of post-separation violence', *Journal of Social Welfare and Family Law*, 25: 195–214.

Huss, M. and Langhinrichsen-Rohling, J. (2006) 'Assessing the generalization of psychopathy in a clinical sample of domestic violence perpetrators', *Law and Human Behavior*, 30 (5): 571–86.

Johnson, R., Gilchrist, E., Beech, A. R., Weston, S., Takriti, R. and Freeman, R. (2006) 'A psychometric typology of UK domestic violence offenders', *Journal of Interpersonal Violence*, 21 (10): 1270–85.

Jordan, C. E. (2004) 'Intimate partner violence and the justice system', *Journal of Interpersonal Violence*, 19 (12): 1412–34.

Keilitz, S. (2001) *Specialization of Domestic Violence Case Management in the Courts: A National Survey*. Washington, DC: US Department of Justice.

Krug, E. G., Dahlberg, L. L., Mercy, J. A., Zwi, A. B. and Lozano, R. (2002) *World Report on Violence and Health: Summary*. Geneva: World Health Organisation.

Lauritsen, J. L. and Schaum, R. J. (2004) 'The social ecology of violence against women', *Criminology*, 42 (2): 323–57.

Lewis, R. (2004) 'Making justice work: effective legal interventions for domestic violence', *British Journal of Criminology*, 44: 204–24.

Lewis, R., Dobash, R. P., Dobash, R. E. and Cavanagh, K. (2000) 'Protection, prevention, rehabilitation or justice? Women's use of the law to challenge domestic violence', *International Review of Victimology*, 7: 179.

Lutze, F. E. and Symons, M. L. (2003) 'The evolution of domestic violence policy through masculine institutions: from discipline to protection to collaborative empowerment', *Criminology and Public Policy*, 2 (2): 319–28.

Miller, S. and Meloy, M. L. (2006) 'Women's use of force: voices of women arrested for domestic violence', *Violence Against Women*, 12 (1): 89–115.

Mills, L. G. (1998) 'Killing her softly: intimate abuse and the violence of state intervention', *Harvard Law Review*, 113: 550–613.

Mills, L. G. (2003) *Insult to Injury: Rethinking Our Responses to Intimate Abuse*. Princeton, NJ: Princeton University Press.

Mirrlees-Black, C. (1999) *Domestic Violence: Findings from a New British Crime Survey Self-Completion Questionnaire*, Home Office Research Study No. 191. Home Office.

Moe, A. M. and Bell, M. P. (2004) 'Abject economies: the effects of battering and violence on women's work and employability', *Violence Against Women*, 10 (1): 29–55.

Morash, M. and Bui, H. (2008) 'The connection of US best practices to outcomes for abused Vietnamese-American women', *International Journal of Comparative and Applied Criminal Justice*, 32 (2): 221–41.

National Police Improvement Agency (2008) *Guidance on Investigating Domestic Abuse*. Bedfordshire: National Police Improvement Agency.

Olson, D. E. and Stalans, L. J. (2001) 'Violent offenders on probation: profile, sentence, and outcome differences among domestic violence and other violent probationers', *Violence Against Women*, 7 (10): 1164–85.

Pahl, J. (1985) *Private Violence and Public Policy*. London: Routledge.

Pleck, E. (1987) *Domestic Tyranny: The Making of Social Policy Against Family Violence from Colonial Times to the Present*. New York: Oxford University Press.

Robinson, A. L. (2003) *The Cardiff Women's Safety Unit: A Multi-Agency Approach to Domestic Violence*. Cardiff: School of Social Sciences, Cardiff University.

Robinson A. L. (2005) *The Cardiff Women's Safety Unit: Understanding the Costs and Consequences of Domestic Violence*. Cardiff: School of Social Sciences, Cardiff University.

Robinson, A. L. (2006a) *Advice, Support, Safety and Information Services Together (ASSIST): The Benefits of Providing Assistance to Victims of Domestic Abuse in Glasgow*. Cardiff: School of Social Sciences, Cardiff University.

Robinson, A. L. (2006b) 'Reducing repeat victimisation among high-risk victims of domestic violence: the benefits of a coordinated community response in Cardiff, Wales', *Violence Against Women*, 12 (8): 761–88.

Robinson, A. L. (2007) 'Improving the civil–criminal interface for victims of domestic violence', *Howard Journal of Criminal Justice*, 46 (4): 356–71.

Robinson, A. L. (2008) *Measuring What Matters in Specialist Domestic Violence Courts*, Cardiff School of Social Sciences Working Paper 102. Cardiff: School of Social Sciences, Cardiff University.

Robinson, A. L. (2009) *Independent Domestic Violence Advisors: A Process Evaluation*. Cardiff: School of Social Sciences, Cardiff University.

Robinson, A. L. and Cook, D. (2006) 'Understanding victim retraction in cases of domestic violence: specialist courts, government policy, and victim-centred justice', *Contemporary Justice Review*, 9 (2): 189–213.

Robinson, A. L. and Rowlands, J. (2009) 'Assessing and managing risk amongst different victims of domestic abuse: limits of a generic model of risk assessment?', *Security Journal*, 22 (3): 190–204.

Robinson, A. L. and Tregidga, J. (2007) 'The perceptions of high-risk victims of domestic violence to a coordinated community response in Cardiff, Wales', *Violence Against Women*, 13 (11): 1130–48.

Romito, P. (2008) *A Deafening Silence: Hidden Violence Against Women and Children*. Bristol: Policy Press.

Römkens, R. (2006) 'Protecting prosecution: exploring the powers of law in an intervention program for domestic violence', *Violence Against Women*, 12 (2): 160–86.

Römkens, R. and Lünnemann, K. (2008) 'Getting behind closed doors: new developments in legislation to prevent domestic violence', *International Journal of Comparative and Applied Criminal Justice*, 32 (2): 173–94.

Sanders, A. (1988) 'Personal violence and public order: the prosecution of "domestic" violence in England and Wales', *International Journal of the Sociology of Law*, 16: 359.

Sandis, E. E. (2006) 'United Nations measures to stop violence against women', *Annals New York Academy of Sciences*, 1087: 370–83.

Schmidt, J. and Steury, E. (1989) 'Prosecutorial discretion in filing charges in domestic violence cases', *Criminology*, 27: 487–510.

Shepard, M. F. and Pence, E. L. (1999) *Coordinating Community Responses to Domestic Violence: Lessons from Duluth and Beyond*. London: Sage.

Stanko, E. (1985) *Intimate Intrusions: Women's Experiences of Male Violence*. London: Routledge & Kegan Paul.

Stark, E. (1996) 'Mandatory arrest of batterers: a reply to its critics', in E. S. Buzawa and C. G. Buzawa (eds), *Do Arrests and Restraining Orders Work?* Thousand Oaks, CA: Sage, pp. 115–49.

Stark, E. (2007) *Coercive Control: How Men Entrap Women in Personal Life*. New York: Oxford University Press.

Straus, M. A., Gelles, R. J. and Steinmetz, S. (1980) *Behind Closed Doors: Violence in the American Family*. New York: Anchor.

Sullivan, C. M . and Bybee, D. I. (1999) 'Reducing violence using community-based advocacy for women with abusive partners', *Journal of Consulting and Clinical Psychology*, 67 (1): 43–53.

Vallely, C., Robinson, A. L., Burton, M. and Tregidga, J. (2005) *Evaluation of Domestic Violence Pilot Sites at Caerphilly (Gwent) and Croydon*. London: Crown Prosecution Service.

Ventura, L. A. and Davis, G. (2005) 'Domestic violence: court case conviction and recidivism', *Violence Against Women*, 11: 255.

Walby, S. (2005) *Improving the Statistics on Violence Against Women*. Geneva: UN Division for the Advancement of Women.

Walby, S. and Allen, J. (2004) *Domestic Violence, Sexual Assault and Stalking: Findings from the British Crime Survey*, Home Office Research Study No. 276. London: Home Office.

Wilson, M. and Daly, M. (1992) *Homicide*. New York: Aldine de Gruyter.

Zweig, J. M. and Burt, M. (2003) 'Effects of interaction among community agencies on legal system responses to domestic violence and sexual assault in stop-funded agencies', *Criminal Justice Policy Review*, 14: 249–72.

Chapter 14

Street robbery

Trevor Bennett and Fiona Brookman

Introduction

Robbery is an offence in which the legal definition does little to identify the complexity of forms that it might take. In response to this, policy-makers, criminologists and the media have devised different kinds of robbery that aim to reflect the variations involved. These variants are not always properly defined and are often only loosely connected to the law. They include mugging, bag-snatching, carjacking, armed robbery, robbery with violence and pickpocketing. There has also been some discussion about whether the offence should be broken down further into subcategories based on location (public places, on the street, convenience stores or petrol stations), the ownership of the goods stolen (personal or business), whether there was violence or just the threat of violence (robbery with violence) and whether the victim was in any form of transport at the time (carjacking).

The starting point for a discussion on the particular form of robbery considered in this chapter on 'street robbery' is to examine the law relating to robbery in general. Robbery is legally defined under the Theft Act 1968 section 8(1) as follows:

> A person is guilty of robbery if he steals, and immediately before or at the time of doing so, and in order to do so, he uses force on any person, or puts or seeks to put any person in fear of being then and there subjected to force.

This definition alone has resulted in substantial discussion in the academic literature. The word 'steals' is used within the context of the Theft Act to refer to theft. This means that the person must intend to permanently deprive the victim of the items taken. Where this is in doubt (such as when the accused intended to obtain property that they thought they owned) then the offence would not be a robbery but assault (Griew 1995). The word 'force' requires a certain amount of subjectivity to define in practice. How much force constitutes 'force'? This might range from a gentle nudge to a full-blown attack. Putting or seeking to put a person in fear of being subjected to force is another difficult concept. This requires an action on behalf of both the offender and the victim in that one must intend it and the other must perceive it. If an offender sought to induce fear of force but failed to convey this to the victim then the activity could not be defined as a robbery (Griew 1995). Ashworth (2002) was concerned that the courts had to try what amounted to two offences simultaneously in that robbery involves both a theft or attempted theft and an assault or attempted assault. He suggested that one solution would be to abolish the offence altogether and to try the person for the two offences from which it is derived. He concluded that '... the offence of robbery is objectionable ... too vague and too liable to stereotypical interpretations' (p. 856).

The problem of definition becomes even more muddied when looking at some of the terminology used to describe the variants of robbery. The Home Office recorded crime counting rules distinguish between 'robbery of business property' (where the goods stolen belong to a business or other corporate body) and 'robbery of personal property' (where the goods stolen belong to an individual or group of individuals). This distinction introduces the problem of identification when property owned by a business is treated as personal property, such as mobile phones, laptop computers and pagers (Home Office 2002).

'Mugging' is one of the most common and popular forms of robbery referred to in the news media. According to Pratt (1980), the term 'mugger' was used in this country at the beginning of the nineteenth century to mean a blow to the face. Later, the usage broadened to refer to a 'swindler', especially one who operates on the street, or a strangler or a garrotter. It has been used more recently to mean 'street robbery' or 'personal robbery' (Smith 2003). The British Crime Survey regularly reports on the rate of 'muggings' in the country and it does this by combining 'personal robbery' and 'snatch thefts'. One reason for using the term is that it is supposed to capture the stereotypical image of a robbery that occurs on the street. The only problem with this is that other research conducted by the Home Office suggests that almost 40 per cent of personal robberies occur in locations other than the street (Smith 2003). So it is a little uncertain what kind of offence we end up with when personal robberies and snatch thefts are combined.

'Snatch thefts' are part of the offence 'theft from the person' and are covered under the Theft Act 1968. The term aims to conjure up the image of an offender snatching property away from the victim that is currently in his or her personal possession. The offence is more difficult to define in practice because the offence is on the borderline with robbery (Ashworth 2002). It is sometimes argued that in the case of snatch thefts the force is applied to the property rather than the person. The Home Office counting rules address this problem by giving some practical examples. A man who has his pocket picked but cannot prevent it is the victim of a theft from the person. A man who has his pocket picked and becomes involved in a tussle is a victim of a robbery (Home Office 2002).

'Carjacking' falls between theft or unauthorised taking of a motor vehicle and robbery. The term is not recognised as a separate offence in the UK but is included under the offence of robbery. The distinction is clarified in the Home Office counting rules which state that, 'If the circumstances of the taking of the vehicle amount to a robbery then the crime should be classified as a robbery' (Home Office 2002). Until recently, the Home Office had no record of robbery offences that might be classified as 'carjacking'. Since 2007/08 supplementary data have been collected on the number of 'unauthorised taking of vehicles' that occur during robberies (Kershaw *et al.* 2008).

The concept of 'street robbery', the subject of this chapter, is no easier to define. In one sense, it is used as a synonym for robbery or to refer to the location of robbery. A 'street robbery' is simply a robbery on the street. Smith (2003) noted that 'street robbery' is often used by police forces to describe the offences of robbery, attempted robbery and snatch theft from the person irrespective of location. He also noted that it is sometimes used as a synonym for 'mugging' and means personal robbery including or excluding snatch thefts. In this chapter, we will use the term in a broad sense to include personal robbery and snatch thefts. These two offences serve to cover all of the variants above including 'mugging', 'bag-snatching', 'pickpocketing' and 'carjacking'. However, the focus of the chapter will be on the offence of personal robbery. The remainder of the chapter will follow the broad structure of the other chapters in the book in that we will look at patterns and trends, characteristics of the offence, explanations and motivations, and responses.

Patterns and trends

There is much speculation in the media and government reports about whether robbery rates are going up or going down. The answer depends, of course, on the period of time involved, the type of robbery offence considered and the source of the data used. Changing any of these criteria can produce different results.

Police recorded crime data on personal robberies (robberies involving personal property) show that over the last year (2006/7 to 2007/8) the number of robberies has fallen by 18 per cent (from 91,922 to 75,565 recorded offences) (Kershaw *et al.* 2008). Over the last ten years (1998/99 to 2007/8), it has risen by 34 per cent. In other words, according to police crime data, personal robbery is going down in the short term, but going up in the long term. British Crime Survey (BCS) estimates for personal robbery over the last year show that the number of reported crimes has reduced by 2 per cent (from 320,000 to 313,000 incidents) (Kershaw *et al.* 2008). Over the last ten years, the number of these offences has reduced by 6 per cent. BCS estimates show therefore that personal robbery is going down in both the short term and the long term (see Figure 14.1).

The question remains whether robbery is increasing (as shown by the police data) or decreasing (as suggested by BCS estimates). Overall, it is widely thought that the BCS provides a more robust measure of change over time than police data because there is more consistency in the methods used

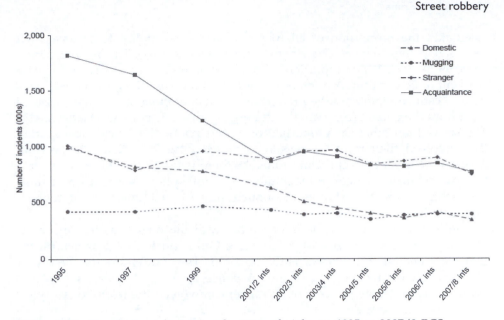

Figure 14.1 Trends in violent crime by type of violence, 1995 to 2007/8 BCS
Source: Kershaw *et al.* (2008: 72).

and the questions asked. Conversely, the coding rules for recording crimes by the police have tended to change quite regularly over time and changed fundamentally in 2002.[1] Nevertheless, they measure slightly different things. Before drawing a conclusion it might be useful to investigate trends in some of the variants of robbery such as mugging, mobile phone robberies and robberies with weapons.

It is possible that trends in some of the variants of robbery discussed above might be different from these general trends. One particular form of robbery that is currently of some concern is robbery with a weapon. Information on offences that involve the use of a knife or other sharp object has been collected quarterly by the Home Office since April 2007 (Kershaw *et al.* 2008). The first comparison over time using these data showed that between July to September 2007 and July to September 2008 the number of recorded robberies involving knives and sharp instruments increased by 18 per cent. This compares with an overall decrease in personal robbery over the same period of 3 per cent.

Data have also been published recently on the number of robberies involving firearms. This has shown that the number of firearm robberies fell by 3 per cent in 2006/7, having risen by 10 per cent in the previous year (Povey *et al.* 2008). Conversely, the number of firearm robberies committed on public highways (37 per cent of the total) increased by 1 per cent from 2005/6 to 2006/7. Having said this, the number of robberies involving firearms has been fairly stable over the previous ten years changing by no more than a few per cent each year. In 1997, there were 3,029 such offences recorded compared with 3,979 in 2006/7.

Another robbery variant that has created some interest in recent years is robbery involving mobile phones. One of the early reports on the topic calculated the proportion of all robberies across six police force areas that involved mobile phones (Harrington and Mayhew 2001). During the period 1998/99 to 2000/1 the proportion of mobile phone robberies increased from 8 per cent to 28 per cent. A more recent study on mobile phone thefts used BCS data to estimate trends in the proportion of mobile phone thefts that involved theft from the person (compared with burglary or vehicle thefts) (Flatley 2007). The study found that the proportion of mobile phone theft incidents reported that involved theft from the person increased from 2001/2 to 2005/6 from 25 per cent to 30 per cent. Unfortunately, there is no published national data that can estimate changes in the number of mobile phone robberies over time. Nevertheless, the two studies mentioned suggest that this type of robbery might be increasing.

There is very little reliable information available on trends in carjacking. Data has only been collected by the Home Office since 2007/8 which means that no trend analysis is currently possible. The data from the first year of collection received for 42 of the 44 police forces in England and Wales showed that overall 3 per cent of all robberies involved the taking of a vehicle (Kershaw *et al.* 2008).

Overall, the data suggests that there has been a long-term increase in the number of robberies committed in the UK with some indication of a more recent reduction. However, this reduction is less apparent in relation to more serious forms of robbery involving knives and firearms which instead might be increasing.

Characteristics

Since the demise of 'crime-specific analysis' (Pope 1977) from its peak in the 1970s and early 1980s, there are no longer any regular sources of updated information covering the detailed characteristics of offences. There are of course occasional studies that plot the details of specific offences as they become of policy relevance. The most recent detailed summary of the characteristics of personal robbery were published in 2003 by the Home Office (Smith 2003). In the remainder of this section, this and other studies are reviewed to examine what is known about *types of offence*, *types of offender* and *types of victim*.

Types of offence

Location
Perhaps surprisingly (considering that personal robbery and street robbery are sometimes regarded as synonymous) the Home Office robbery study found that only 50 per cent of all personal robberies were committed on the street (Smith 2003). A further 11 per cent were committed in public places other than a street (such as subways, underpasses, parks, alleyways and footpaths). The remainder occurred in the area of commercial premises (including public houses, night clubs, retail premises, schools and other public buildings) (25 per cent), on transport or in other locations (14 per cent).

The author found some variations in the locations of robberies across the areas studied. In Birmingham City Centre, for example, 40 per cent of personal robberies occurred close to one shopping mall and a nearby amusement arcade. In Stockport, over one-fifth of robberies occurred in a single shopping arcade, which included a bowling alley, leisure complex and amusement arcade. In Westminster, public houses, nightclubs and fast-food restaurants were the common locations for robberies.

Some additional information can be found in a more recent Home Office report on robberies involving firearms (Povey *et al.* 2008). The report used police recorded crime data to show that armed robberies were less frequently conducted on the street or in public places and more frequently committed in commercial areas including shops. In 2006/7, 37 per cent of all robberies involving a firearm (the largest group) were committed on public highways, whereas 25 per cent were committed in shops. This was followed in decreasing order by residential robberies, other robberies, robberies in garages or post offices and robberies in banks or building societies.

Time of day

The stereotypical street robbery is commonly thought of as occurring during the daytime as compared with the stereotypical burglary which is often thought of as occurring at night. In fact, neither view is supported by the evidence (see Chapter 1 on burglary). According to the Home Office study on personal robbery (Smith 2003), the most common time for robberies to occur is in the evening and night-time. Over 50 per cent of all personal robberies were recorded between the hours of 6 p.m. and 2 a.m. A quarter of robberies occurred in the afternoon between the hours of 2 p.m. and 6 p.m. and only 16 per cent were reported in the daytime period between 6 a.m. and 2 p.m.

The research found some differences between the areas studied. In Birmingham, there were slightly more robberies in the daytime (53 per cent) compared with at night (47 per cent) and in some areas (such as Bristol) the proportion of night-time robberies was only slightly higher than those in the daytime. There were other areas where the proportion of night-time robberies was far greater than those in the day. In London (Westminster) almost three-quarters of robberies occurred at night. The author speculated that areas with a higher proportion of night robberies might be those with a more active night-time economy.

Items stolen

The commonsense view is that robberies are usually committed to obtain cash. This view also fits the notion of the dependent drug user who selects robbery as the offence of choice because it yields immediate cash for drug purchases. The Home Office robbery study provided some support for this idea in showing that the *most common* item stolen (comprising 25 per cent of all property taken) was cash (Smith 2003). However, the *majority* of all items stolen were items other than cash. These included a range of personal accessories including mobile phones, purses and wallets, handbags, rucksacks, jewellery, watches and miscellaneous documents. The study found that the choice of items varied by gender in that male victims were typically associated with thefts of cash, mobile phones and jewellery and watches, whereas female victims were more commonly linked to losses of handbags, personal accessories and debit and credit cards.

The most striking feature of the list is that the most commonly stolen non-cash items were mobile phones. Mobile phones were the second most frequent item of property taken (18 per cent of all property taken). A study of mobile phone thefts in various police force areas found that the proportion of mobile phone thefts in robbery was higher in metropolitan forces than other forces (Harrington and Mayhew 2001). The research also found that within police force areas the proportion of robberies involving mobile phones was higher in city centre areas than elsewhere. An important issue is whether the robberies were 'phone-only' robberies or whether phones were taken along with other items. The research found that approximately one-third of all mobile phone robberies were 'phone-only' robberies. In total, 8 per cent of all robberies were 'phone-only' robberies.

Use of weapons

The Home Office personal robbery study found that weapons were present in 33 per cent of all robberies and were most frequently involved in offences involving confrontation (Smith 2003). Knives were the most common weapon type involved and were used in over 20 per cent of personal robberies. Guns were used in 3 per cent of personal robberies and blunt instruments (including hammers, coshes and baseball bats) were also used in 3 per cent of personal robberies. Men were more likely to be threatened with a weapon (37 per cent) than women (21 per cent).

Other research provides details on the use of firearms in robbery. A study of police recorded crimes covering the period 2006/7 showed that 4 per cent of all robberies involved a firearm of some kind (Povey et al. 2008). Handguns were used in 67 per cent of robberies involving firearms, whereas 12 per cent of incidents involved unidentified firearms, 5 per cent imitation firearms and 2 per cent air weapons.

Types of offender

Gender

The research tends to support conventional knowledge that the overwhelming majority of robbery offenders are male. The Home Office personal robbery study found that 94 per cent of all suspects identified in the research were male (Smith 2003). This varied from 90 per cent to 97 per cent across the various locations studied. The study of mobile phone thefts from a sub-sample of persons accused of robberies involving the theft of a mobile phone in 2000 to 2001 showed that the proportion of male offenders ranged from 88 per cent to 90 per cent across the areas studied (Harrington and Mayhew 2001). The proportion of male offenders in the city centre Basic Command Units (BCUs) of the three forces investigated were slightly higher, ranging from 92 to 97 per cent. The authors speculated on whether there might be a real gender difference in city centre and non-city centre phone robberies.

Age

There is some concern that at least some robbery might be committed by very young people. The personal robbery study found that suspects charged with robbery were generally younger than those charged with burglary dwelling and violence against the person (Smith 2003). The research showed that 36 per cent of people charged with robbery in the Metropolitan Police District in 2001 were aged 11–15 years compared with only 8 per cent of those charged with burglary dwelling and 7 per cent of those charged with violence against the person. Conversely, only 8 per cent of those charged with robbery were aged over 31 years compared to 32 per cent and 40 per cent respectively for burglary and violence against the person. The mobile phone robbery study found that the peak age of those accused of phone robbery was 16, whereas only 1 per cent were aged 40 or more (Harrington and Mayhew 2001).

Ethnicity

Research on the ethnicity of robbery offenders tends to show a higher than expected involvement among ethnic minorities. According to the Home Office personal robbery study, the proportion of suspects who were white ranged from 9 per cent to 99 per cent depending on the research location. The proportion exceeded 50 per cent (showing that the majority were white) in just three of the ten sites studied. In other words, in most cases, the majority of robbery suspects were non-white and the largest proportion of non-white suspects were black. The key issue is whether the proportion of black robbery suspects recorded is disproportionate when compared with the general population. The study showed that in some cases the ethnic composition of robbery suspects reflected the ethnic composition of the community. Lambeth, for example, had the largest proportion of black robbery suspects and the largest proportion of black residents in the general population. However, the proportion of suspects in the first survey was 86 per cent compared with 31 per cent in the general population as a whole. In other words, the number of black robbery suspects was disproportionately from ethnic minority groups. In other areas, the differences in distribution were even greater. In Birmingham, 64 per cent of robbery suspects were black compared with 6 per cent in the general population. The author concludes that ethic minorities are over-represented among robbery suspects in at least some of the areas investigated. The writer acknowledges that there are difficulties involved in making comparisons between non-matched samples. Similar findings were reported in the Home Office mobile phone robbery report. The majority of persons accused of phone robbery in the Metropolitan Police District and West Midlands were black (71 per cent and 56 per cent respectively). The authors concluded that the disparity in ethnic composition between those accused of robbery and those in the general population was marked (Harrington and Mayhew 2001, p.40).

Types of victim

Gender

Recent research has shown that over three-quarters of robbery victims are male (Smith 2003). In most cases, the majority of both offenders and victims are male. In 71 per cent of incidents reported the offence involved a male suspect and male victim. Twenty-one per cent involved male suspects and female victims and 1 per cent female suspects and male victims. Three per cent comprised female suspects and female victims. The remainder included combinations of more than one offender or victim. There was some variation shown across study sites ranging from a low of 56 per cent male (Lambeth) to a high of 93 per cent (London Underground).

Age

Robbery victims and offenders are also fairly similar in terms of age. The Home Office research found that one-fifth of all robbery victims surveyed in the research sites were aged 11–15 (Smith 2003). This was close to the proportion of suspects of the same age. Twenty-three per cent of victims were aged 16–20. Combining the two shows that over two-fifths of robbery victims were under the age of 21. The research also found that female victims tended to be older than male victims. The peak age for female victimisation was in the 21–25 and 26–30 age groups, together accounting for 34 per cent of female victims. The peak age for male victims was in the 11–15 and 16–20 age groups, which together accounted for 51 per cent of male victims. Overall, there were few elderly victims (5 per cent) aged 61 and over. However, female elderly victims were much more likely to be the victims of robbery (14 per cent) than male elderly victims (2 per cent).

Ethnicity

There is less similarity between robbery offender and victim characteristics in relation to ethnicity. The research on the ethnicity of suspects showed that the majority of robbery suspects were black (Smith 2003). The same research showed that the majority of robbery victims were white. The proportion ranged from a low of 67 per cent white to a high of 99 per cent white. A more accurate comparison can be made across the individual research sites. In Lambeth, 86 per cent of suspects identified in the first survey were black whereas only 12 per cent of the victims were black. In the London Underground site, 82 per cent of suspects were black compared with 4 per cent of victims. A similar finding was shown in the Home Office mobile phone robbery study (Harrington and Mayhew 2001). The research found that the vast majority of victims of mobile phone robberies in each of the six police forces investigated were white, ranging from 68 per cent to 91 per cent. Asians were next most frequently victimised group, ranging from 5 per cent to 23 per cent.

Explaining street robbery

Research on robbery in the United Kingdom has tended to focus on armed robbery against banks and other commercial organisations. There are very few studies on the motivation of street robbers. The Home Office study on personal robbery showed that the main motive for robbery was financial advantage for the suspect (Smith 2003). However, when robbery was committed by groups of young offenders, it also served to enhance personal reputation and status. Another UK study that acknowledged the influence of cultural factors in the motivation for robbery was conducted in London by FitzGerald *et al.* (2003). This study involved focus group interviews with 103 schoolchildren and 17 young people of a similar age given non-custodial sentences for street crime. Some gave instrumental reasons, including the need for money for everyday expenditure, and a few said that they robbed to order. However, others offered more expressive reasons. Some said that they spent money from robbery on status objects, designer clothes, and drink and drugs. Others said that they committed robberies for fun and excitement and mentioned the buzz or adrenaline rush inherent in such offences. They also mentioned that they committed street crime as a way of settling scores or to protect themselves by generating a reputation for being tough.

The research is divided on the nature of the motivation for robbery. Some researchers see robbery as a rational choice, informed primarily by the need for financial gain and a desire to minimise the risk of detection. Others see robbery as a cultural pursuit in which the costs and rewards take second place to the emotional immediacy of the offence and its benefits for the offender's lifestyle.

Rational choice explanations

The rational choice perspective gives prominence to the role of decision-making and the achievement of identifiable objectives. Its origins lie in economic theory on decision-making (e.g. Becker 1968). The rational choice perspective has been interpreted to take both a 'narrow' and 'wide' form (Opp 1997). The 'narrow' version of the model is associated with classical economic theory and is based on the principle that a person commits an offence when the expected utility of the crime exceeds the costs of committing it (Becker 1968). The 'wide' version of the model is associated with the view that people do not make exhaustive and complex calculations prior to action, but act on the basis of a few simple facts or guesswork that in most cases fall short of optimal (Carroll 1978).

The approach gained ascendance in the 1970s and 1980s through the work of Carroll (1978) in psychology and Clarke and Cornish (1985) in criminology. Clarke and Cornish (1985) acknowledged that they built their perspective on the economic analysis of criminal behaviour and the concept of evaluating costs and rewards. However, they adopted what they referred to as a 'limited' approach to rationality in which decision-making was seen as imperfect. They argued against expressing concepts in mathematical terms, as was the case in Becker's economic model, and preferred instead to draw upon decision diagrams that included concepts from psychology and sociology to explain decision-making (Clarke 1992). In this way, offenders' utilities could be extended beyond financial reward to include social status and excitement. Nevertheless, the key principle of the approach remained the same in that behaviour was viewed as goal-oriented and could be understood as an outcome of an assessment of costs and rewards.

Cultural explanations

The cultural perspective gives importance to general lifestyle and individual needs and has its origins in sociological theory of subcultures (e.g. Wolfgang and Ferracuti 1967). The perspective has grown in popularity in recent years and is based on the principle that the motivation to offend arises out of shared values rather than personal utilities. The first substantial text devoted to this topic was by Cohen (1955) who saw delinquency as a collective response among working-class youths to the strains placed upon them by the values of middle-class society. In particular, they attempted to restore the lack of status experienced in conventional society by achieving status within a deviant subculture. Miller (1958) developed the ideas of Cohen, but argued that the delinquent subcultures drew almost wholly from lower-class values. In particular, boys were expected to be tough and 'street wise' and to value action and excitement. This idea was developed further by Wolfgang and Ferracuti (1967) who invented the term 'the subculture of violence' to describe social groups who resolved conflicts through physical attack and who valued fighting and displays of 'toughness'.

In more recent times, the role of culture and value systems in the use of violence has been developed further by criminologists through the concept of 'street culture'. One hallmark of street culture is the pursuit of pleasure and status through conspicuous consumption and living a lifestyle characterised as 'life as a party' (Shover and Honaker 1992: 283). According to Jacobs and Wright (1999) the lifestyle of street offenders typically involves pleasure pursuits such as drinking, drug use, gambling, sexual conquest, fighting, assaults, and other forms of expressive violence.

Empirical support

There is some empirical support for both perspectives. Thornton (2002) reviewed explanations for carjacking found in previous research and noted both rational and cultural explanations. The most frequent motive found was monetary gain to obtain a vehicle that could be sold as parts or as a whole for cash. He noted that vehicles acquired through carjacking are sometimes referred to as 'crack rentals' in that drug users sometimes committed carjacking to obtain money and other valuables for drugs. Carjacking was also a means to another end in that cars might be stolen for transportation to be used in the commission of another crime. In addition to what appear to be 'rational' motives the author also mentions some of the social and cultural objectives of this form of robbery. He noted that carjacking is a way for individuals to prove their self-worth or otherwise enhance their authority or power. For many young people who are starting out in gangs, carjacking is used as a rite of passage or initiation to gain entry into the gang. He also noted the desire for thrill-seeking in that youths might engage in carjacking for the sheer thrill of forcefully stealing a car and driving it around with their friends.

Wright *et al.* (2006) investigated the motives for street robbery and found that it was sometimes conducted as a means of achieving money or goods. They also found that violence in robbery was used in a rational way to ensure compliance of the victim and to overcome resistance. In other cases, street robbery performed other functions such as enhancing the status of the offender, generating a reputation for toughness, providing a response to challenges to masculinity, giving an outlet for aggression and the desire to fight, and as a means of administering retaliation and revenge through informal justice. Motives of these kinds were more consistent with a cultural approach which viewed street crime as an expression of a value system that condones violent behaviour.

The empirical research tends to show that offenders' accounts are consistent with both the rational choice perspective which depicts motives as purposive and goal oriented and the cultural perspective which emphasises the role of values and normative systems. In order to understand the motives for street robbery it is necessary to reconcile these different sets of accounts.

Towards a resolution

The main research question is whether the motives for street robbery are mainly rational and the pursuit of financial advantage or mainly cultural and the pursuit of social status. One plausible answer is that it is a combination of both. But this would not deal with secondary questions such as how they are combined, whether one takes precedence over the other, or the role of situational factors in determining the type of motive. Disparate theories of these kinds cannot simply be combined but need to be integrated in some additive and convincing way. There have been some early attempts to do this.

Katz (1988, 1991) discussed the integration of rationality and street culture indirectly in his depiction of street robbers. In his description of the 'ways of the badass', he explains that 'badasses' are neither irrational nor stupid. In fact, they understand precisely the nature of rationality. They will use violence in a utilitarian and wholly instrumental manner when it suits them. However, it is also necessary to show to others that they can 'transcend rationality'. In other words, the 'badass' (in order to be a 'badass') must demonstrate '... a commitment to violence that is beyond any reason comprehensible to others' (1988: 100). In other words, rationality can be used to achieve material goals through financial gain and social goals through convincing others of its absence.

Anderson (1999) investigated street robbery in black urban areas in Philadelphia and found that both rational and cultural factors played a part. He thought that the primary motivation of the street robber was to obtain money. However, robbers also wanted their undisputed power over the victim to be recognised. Anderson showed that enactment of the offence often included rational components in the sense that the offence was often based on calculations of the costs and rewards involved and aimed to identify the right setting and the right victim. At the same time, the robbery would be conducted in a way that achieved cultural objectives. The assailant would expect deference and respect from the victim to confirm his status on the street. The outcome is similar to the position taken by Katz. Some elements of rational decision-making involve the efficient accomplishment of the crime while others involve the specific intention of appearing to be irrational in order to ensure respect from the victim and admiration from peers.

Response to street robbery

What attempts have been made to prevent street robbery? Broadly speaking, the main methods used to date are deterrent sentencing, situational crime prevention, social crime prevention, policing strategies and combined approaches.

Deterrent sentencing

According to Ashworth (2002), appellate judgments on sentencing for robbery provide clear evidence that judges are thinking about deterrence when they determine sentences. In other words, sentences for robbery can include a 'deterrent premium'. He notes that the justifications in many cases refer to the special problems of post offices, petrol stations and other outlets that hold cash but do not possess high security. The courts take the view that they can provide that extra level of security by indicating that the perpetrators will receive severe sentences.

The maximum penalty for robbery is life imprisonment. In practice, the courts decide the length of sentence according to the nature and gravity of the offence. The tariff for robbery has been established through case law. Ashworth (2002) summarises the kinds of robberies that might receive certain sentence lengths. In practice, the longest sentences are reserved for professional robberies involving additional elements such as kidnapping and these might receive up to 20 years' imprisonment. Using a gun to threaten someone in a commercial setting might receive 10 to 12 years. Non-professional robberies of post offices and small businesses that involve small sums of money might receive seven years. The least serious form of robbery in the eyes of the courts, resulting in the shortest sentence lengths of between three and five years, is street robbery. The upper end of street robbery involving, say, a robbery of a taxi driver with a knife might receive four or five years. The lower end of street robbery such as bag-snatching with only slight indication of the threat of violence might result in three years.

To what extent are the courts successful in deterring future robberies through 'deterrent premiums'? The research evidence on the effectiveness of deterrents generally is not very encouraging (Beyleveld 1980). The main finding of deterrence research is that the certainty of punishment can have a marginal deterrent effect but there is little evidence that the severity of punishment can influence outcomes. In order to be deterred, offenders have to believe that they stand a very good chance of getting caught for any particular offence. Unless they believe this, then the threat of penalties following capture is of little relevance to them (Bennett and Wright 1984).

Situational crime prevention

Situational crime prevention is based on the principle of reducing crime by reducing the opportunities for crime (Clarke 1992). In practice, this usually means changing the environment in which crimes such as robbery typically occur. It is based on several criminological theories including what is sometimes referred to as the 'triangle of crime' or the opportunities created by the interaction between a likely offender, a suitable target and the lack of a capable guardian (Felson 2002). Situational crime prevention aims to reduce the chance of these three elements coming together.

Tilley *et al.* (2004) recommend several situational measures for reducing street robbery including increasing risks of identification and capture through the use of CCTV cameras, increasing the effort by improving late-night transport to remove potential targets, and decreasing rewards by encouraging vulnerable people to avoid carrying high-value items. Barker *et al.* (1993) also offered a list of potential situational measures for tackling street robbery including advising women not to carry handbags in high-risk areas and encouraging people to 'dress down' and to avoid wearing expensive jewellery. The authors found from their own research that robbery offenders claimed they would tend not to select victims who looked 'poor'. They also proposed that some benefits might be gained if people were generally alerted to the risks of robbery in their area and were encouraged to take risk avoidance action.

Social crime prevention

Social crime prevention aims to reduce crime by reducing the motivation for crime. This can be achieved by focusing on young people at risk who have never offended with a view to discouraging them from starting offending and by focusing on those who have already offended by discouraging them from continuing their criminal careers (Graham and Bennett 1995).

One of the early social prevention programmes aimed specifically at robbery was the 'Brixton Against Robbery' initiative established in the early 1990s. This was a community-based initiative which aimed to 'help young people on the fringes of crime by discussing problems and prospects, ... to offer suitable and attractive alternatives to crime, ... to provide long-term support and to work in the interests of referred youth with other agencies' (Barker *et al.* 1993). The initiative focused on young people aged 11 to 18 involved in street robbery or believed to be becoming involved who were referred to the project team. The team gave support and advice to the family, 'befriended' the teenagers, helped to reintegrate 'school-refusers' into education, provided support for one-parent families and established a parents group. Unfortunately, the programme was not formally evaluated and it is unknown whether the project achieved any of its outcome objectives.

Policing strategies

Policing strategies aim to reduce crime by detecting and capturing offenders and deterring potential offenders. They are sometimes referred to as 'enforcement' approaches because they are based on the police doing their job (perhaps with greater intensity or concentration than usual) and enforcing the law. In practice, policing strategies designed to combat street robbery mainly comprise low-density regular patrols and high-density hot-spot and saturation patrols.

Low-density patrols

There is relatively little research on routine or general police patrols in the UK. One of the exceptions is a study by Bright (1969) who conducted an experiment which required changing the number of patrol officers in an area of London from zero officers to four. The study found that increasing the number from zero officers to one officer produced a reduction in crime. However, increasing the level further than this had no additional effect (with the exception of changing the number of officers from three to four officers which the author discounted as spurious). There is much more research on the effectiveness of police patrols in reducing street crime in the US. The classic study by Kelling *et al.* (1974) showed that increasing the number of vehicle patrols in experimental beat areas had no effect on the crime rate of those areas. Another classic study was the evaluation of the Newark Foot Patrol experiment. This showed that increasing the number of foot patrol officers in experimental beat areas resulted in no change in victimisation rates (Pate *et al.* 1986). Interestingly, the research also showed no changes in victimisation rates in the areas in which patrol officers were removed. Overall, research on the effectiveness of general-purpose patrols on street crime such as robbery is not very encouraging.

High-density patrols

Research on high-density patrols such as saturation policing, hot-spot patrols and high-visibility patrols is more positive in its ability to reduce street crime. There have been several studies conducted in the UK which have used some form of high-density policing. Burney (1990) describes a number of policing methods used in Lambeth in the 1980s and 1990s that aimed to reduce street robbery such as hot-spot patrols and saturation policing. The programmes were typically based on providing a heavy police presence to deter and detect street robbers and to target robbery suspects. Unfortunately, the programmes were not formally evaluated. However, the author reported that the police claimed that the programme was successful in reducing the rate of street robbery and improving robbery clear-up rates.

Barker *et al.* (1993) also described the use of high-density policing as part of the Battersea initiative against street robbery in 1986. The police identified the areas with the highest rate of robbery in the division over a 12-month period and established a squad of 20 dedicated police officers to tackle robbery in those areas. In the two years following the start of this operation, the number of street crimes reported to the police dropped by 58 per cent and the clear-up rate increased from 5 per cent to 23 per cent (Barker *et al.* 1993).

Research on hot-spot and saturation patrols conducted in the US has also shown that they can be effective in reducing street crime. Chaiken *et al.* (1974) found that substantial increases in the number of police officers patrolling the New York subway system resulted in a reduction in both minor violations and felonies. Sherman and Weisburd (1995) reported on the results of an experiment conducted in Minneapolis in which patrol officers were instructed to visit 55 randomly assigned crime hot spots when they were not responding to other calls for service. A further 55 hot spots were used as control locations and police patrolled these as normal. These results showed that crime calls reduced in the experimental areas and the rate of street crime and disorder was significantly lower during periods of police presence at the hot spot than during police absence.

Combined approaches

In practice, crime prevention methods used to reduce street crime have been based mainly on multi-agency approaches which result in a combination of methods being applied to a particular area. One of the early combined approaches designed specifically to reduce street robbery was Operation Eagle Eye launched in the early 1990s in the Metropolitan Police District.

Operation Eagle Eye was formally launched in August 1995 with the aim of reducing street robbery and increasing the detection rate. The scheme involved implementing six main measures: (1) target hardening; (2) installation of CCTV in high-risk areas; (3) high-profile policing; (4) advice to victims; (5) diversionary projects to reduce the chance of young people becoming involved in robbery; and (6) design improvements including improved street lighting (Stockdale and Gresham 1998). The evaluation of the programme concluded that there were small improvements in both the incidence and detection of street robbery. However, the authors were sceptical that the programme was responsible for these effects on the grounds that there were wide variations across the areas investigated and the early improvements in the areas were not maintained.

In March 2002, the government launched a multi-agency approach to robbery called the Street Crime Initiative (SCI) (Tilley *et al.* 2004). The initiative covered ten police force areas that together accounted for 83 per cent of recorded robbery in 2001/02. The SCI involves a wide range of agencies working in partnership to implement a programme of practical measures developed to reduce street crime. The programme was built around a problem-solving approach. There was no stated requirement that specific schemes should be implemented. Instead, the areas were encouraged to identify the nature of the problems experienced and to implement appropriate responses. However, the Home Office provided examples of the kinds of strategies that might be implemented including covert surveillance, CCTV, safe design features, targeted patrols, advertising campaigns, better victim handling protocols and school education programmes. The evaluation showed that in the first six months of the scheme robbery reduced in the ten police force areas by 10 per cent and in the first two years of the programme robbery reduced by 24 per cent. It is difficult to determine, of course, whether this reduction was the result of the programme or particular aspects of it.

Discussion and conclusion

This brief summary of 'street robbery' leads to one important conclusion that it is hard to define and hard to measure. There has been some doubt expressed in the literature about whether the offence of robbery should exist at all as it comprises a combination of theft and assault offences already provided in law. It has been shown that its legal definition is unclear and the various operational forms of the offence are equally confusing. This does not help in deciding whether the offence is increasing or decreasing. Police recorded crime shows that robbery is increasing over time, whereas the British Crime Survey results show that it is decreasing over time. It is difficult to know therefore whether street robbery is a growing problem or not. The latest short-term figures for specific forms of street robbery suggest that its general form might be decreasing but its most serious forms might be increasing.

We know a little about the characteristics of robbery from a small number of research studies. There have been no national level analyses of robbery that might help show the representativeness of these studies. Nevertheless, it appears from what we know that robbery is largely a night-time phenomenon, committed by quite young people who are mainly male. In areas with ethnic concentrations, the offender is likely also to be from an ethnic minority group. The motives for robbery are largely to obtain cash or goods that can be converted to cash. However, they are also committed to impress friends, to obtain status and to encourage respect on the streets.

It is difficult to know how to respond to the offence when there is so little high-quality evaluative research available. It seems unlikely, from what we do know, that deterrent sentences can reduce street robbery. It is also unlikely that routine police patrols can have an effect when the visibility of the police is held at a low level. It is more likely that targeted policing involving hot-spot patrols or saturation policing can be effective against robbery. This would be consistent with the results of deterrence research which show that the certainty of punishment has a greater effect than the severity of punishment. There is also some evidence that some multi-agency programmes might divert some youths from crime. However, these are often poorly evaluated which makes definitive statements about effectiveness difficult.

Overall, our understanding of street robbery and what to do about it is surprisingly limited. In part, this is a result of the diverse nature of the offence. It might help our understanding and our response to it if the current enthusiasm to metamorphose offences into more interesting but less comprehensible offence groups were restrained. This is slightly less of a problem in relation to street robbery as it results in part in a reduction rather than an expansion of the original offence. Nevertheless, the exact nature of the offence remains unclear and should be clarified if it is believed to be a useful subcategory. Attempts should also be made to find better ways of measuring the offence. Recent efforts by the Home Office to record separately robberies involving knives and guns and robberies that were committed as part of a vehicle crime are a step in the right direction. More also needs to be done in terms of determining the effectiveness of robbery prevention strategies. Evaluation should be rigorous and based on the best methods available. The current conflict between quantitative and qualitative research does not help in this respect. The solution would ideally use both types of method. The best quantitative research uses random allocation, randomised controlled trials and high-quality quasi-experimental designs. The best qualitative evaluations monitor the pathways of causal mechanisms and the processes that link preventative inputs with crime reduction outcomes. The future of our understanding of street robbery and the methods for tackling it will depend in part on some of these problems being solved.

Selected further reading

The best overview of official statistics on street robbery is currently Kershaw *et al.* (2008) *Crime in England and Wales 2007/08: Findings from the British Crime Survey and Police Recorded Crime.* It is likely that this series of compilations on crime will continue to be the main single source of data on this topic in the future. More detailed information on the characteristics of the offence can be found in the dedicated Home Office publications by Smith (2003), Harrington and Mayhew (2001) and Flatley (2007). A good summary of the motivation of robbers can be found in Katz (1991) and in the paper by Wright *et al.* (2006) on the dynamics of street robbery. There is no single volume that deals with the wide range of responses to robbery, but it would be worth looking at Stockdale and Gresham (1998) and Barker *et al.* (1993) for an overview of situational and policing methods.

Note

1 'There have been two major changes to the recording of crimes. In April 1998 the Home Office Counting Rules for Recorded Crime were expanded to include certain additional summary offences and counts became more victim-based (the number of victims was counted rather than the number of offences). In April 2002 the National Crime Recording Standard was introduced to ensure greater consistency between forces in recording crime and to take a more victim-oriented approach to crime recording with the police being required to record any allegation of crime unless there was credible evidence to the contrary. Both these changes resulted in an increase in the number of crimes recorded. Certain offences, such as the more minor violent crimes, were more affected by these changes than others' (Kershaw *et al.* 2008: 30).

References

Anderson, E. (1999) *Code of the Street: Decency, Violence and the Moral Life of the Inner City.* New York: Norton.

Ashworth, A. (2002) 'Robbery reassessed', *Criminal Law Review*, 851–72.

Barker, M., Geraghty, J., Webb, B. and Key, T. (1993) *The Prevention of Street Robbery*, Crime Prevention Unit Series Paper 44. London: Home Office.

Becker, G. (1968) 'Crime and punishment: an economic approach', *Journal of Political Economy*, 76 (2): 169–217.

Bennett, T. and Wright, R. (1984) *Burglars on Burglary.* Aldershot: Gower.

Beyleveld, D. (1980) *A Bibliography on General Deterrence Research.* Farnborough: Saxon House.

Bright, J. A. (1969) *The Beat Patrol Experiment.* London: Home Office Police Research and Development Branch.

Burney, E. (1990) *Putting Street Crime in Its Place: A Report to the Community/Police Consultative Group for Lambeth*. London: Goldsmiths' College.

Carroll, J. S. (1978) 'A psychological approach to deterrence: the evaluation of crime opportunities', *Journal of Personality and Social Psychology*, 36: 1512–20.

Chaiken, J. M., Lawless, M. W. and Stevenson, K. (1974) *The Impact of Police Activity on Crime: Robberies on the New York City Subway System*. New York: Rand Institute.

Clarke, R. (1992) *Situational Crime Prevention: Successful Case Studies*. New York: Harrow & Heston.

Clarke, R. V. and Cornish, D. B. (1985) 'Modelling offenders' decisions: a framework for research and policy', *Crime and Justice*, 6: 147–85.

Cohen, A. K. (1955) *Delinquent Boys. The Culture of the Gang*. New York: Free Press.

Felson, M. (2002) *Crime and Everyday Life*. Thousand Oaks, CA: Sage.

FitzGerald, M., Stockdale, J. and Hale, C. (2003) *Young People and Street Crime*. London: Youth Justice Board for England and Wales.

Flatley, J. (2007) *Mobile Phone Theft, Plastic Card and Identity Fraud: Findings from the 2005/06 British Crime Survey*, Home Office Research Bulletin 10/07. London: Home Office.

Graham, J. and Bennett, T. H. (1995) *Crime Prevention Strategies in Europe and North America*. Helsinki: HEUNI.

Griew, E. (1995) *Theft Acts 1968 & 1978*. London: Sweet & Maxwell.

Harrington, V. and Mayhew, P. (2001) *Mobile Phone Theft*, Home Office Research Study No. 235. London: Home Office.

Home Office (2002) *Home Office Counting Rules for Recorded Crime*. London: Home Office.

Jacobs, B. and Wright, R. (1999) 'Stick-up, street culture, and offender motivation', *Criminology*, 37 (1): 149–73.

Katz, J. (1988) *Seductions of Crime: Moral and Sensual Attractions in Doing Evil*. New York: Basic Books.

Katz, J. (1991) 'The motivation of the persistent robber', in M. Tonry (ed.), *Crime and Justice: A Review of Research*. Chicago: University of Chicago Press, pp. 277–306.

Kelling, G. L., Pate, T., Dieckman, D. and Brown, C. E. (1974) *The Kansas City Preventive Patrol Experiment: A Technical Report*. Washington, DC: Police Foundation.

Kershaw, C., Nicholas, S. and Walker, A. (2008) *Crime in England and Wales 2007/08: Findings from the British Crime Survey and Police Recorded Crime*, Home Office Statistical Bulletin 07/08. London: Home Office.

Miller, W. B. (1958) 'Lower-class culture as a generating milieu of gang delinquency', *Journal of Social Issues*, 14: 5–19.

Opp, K. D. (1997) 'Limited rationality and crime', in G. Newman, R. Clarke and S. Shoham (eds), *Rational Choice and Situational Crime Prevention*. Dartmouth: Ashgate, pp. 47–63.

Pate, A. M., Wycoff, M. A., Skogan, W. G. and Sherman, L. W. (1986) *Reducing Fear of Crime in Houston and Newark: A Summary Report*. Washington, DC: Police Foundation.

Pope, C. E. (1977) *Crime-Specific Analysis*. Washington, DC: US Department of Justice, Law Enforcement Assistance Administration, National Criminal Justice Information and Statistics Service.

Povey, D., Coleman, K., Kaiza, P., Hoare, J. and Jansson, K. (2008) *Homicides, Firearm Offences and Intimate Violence 2006/07*, Home Office Statistical Bulletin 03/08. London: Home Office.

Pratt, M. (1980) *Mugging as a Social Problem*. London: Routledge & Kegan Paul.

Sherman, L. W. and Weisburd, D. (1995) 'General deterrent effects of police patrol in crime hot spots: a randomized, controlled trial', *Justice Quarterly*, 12 (4): 635–48.

Shover, N. and Honaker, D. (1992) 'The socially-bounded decision making of persistent property offenders', *Howard Journal of Criminal Justice*, 31: 276–93.

Smith, J. (2003) *The Nature of Personal Robbery*, Home Office Research Study No. 254. London: Home Office.

Stockdale, J. E. and Gresham, P. J. (1998) *Tackling Street Robbery: A Comparative Evaluation of Operation Eagle Eye*, Crime Detection and Prevention Series Paper 87. London: Home Office, Police Research Group.

Thornton, W. (2002) 'Carjacking', in D. Levinson (ed.), *Encyclopedia of Crime and Punishment*. London: Sage.

Tilley, N., Smith, J., Finer, S., Erol, R., Charles, C. and Dobby, J. (2004) *Problem-Solving Street Crime: Practical Lessons from the Street Crime Initiative*. London: Home Office.

Wolfgang, M. E. and Ferracuti, F. (1967) *The Subculture of Violence*. London: Tavistock.

Wright, R., Brookman, F. and Bennett, T. H. (2006) 'The foreground dynamics of street robbery in Britain', *British Journal of Criminology*, 46 (1): 1–15.

Chapter 15

Stealing commercial cash: from safe-cracking to armed robbery

Dick Hobbs

Go where the money is … and go there often. (Willie Sutton)

Introduction

This chapter explores some of the main ways in which professional criminals steal cash from banks, commercial companies and other organisations. The focus here is on the more visible kinds of crime (rather than, for example, computer crime or company fraud – for which see Chapters 6 and 11), committed for the most part by people external to the organisations they target. The bulk of the chapter is about the rise and subsequent decline of *commercial armed robbery* during the late modern era, an era when this iconic crime succeeded in capturing the febrile imaginations of the public and the mass media alike. Armed robbers have traditionally occupied a unique position in the hierarchy of professional criminality. Normally depicted as violent professionals, they are also a staple of fictional accounts of crime and lend a piratical aura to what is usually a crude act, albeit one riddled with romantic overtones of fantastical banditry. Indeed, modern armed robbers can be seen to some extent as the successors to criminal groups which captured the public imagination in previous centuries using methods such as highway robbery (Sharpe 2004) or piracy (Gosse 1932). Indeed, the current definition of armed robbery in the UK, as a robbery where the use or threat of force involves a firearm, an imitation firearm or an offensive weapon, could easily have been applied to these pre-industrial transgressions. Thus in order to gain deeper insight into armed robbery today, it is important to analyse it within a broader historical and sociological perspective, as part of a developing portfolio of criminal strategies designed to target cash and other valuables, all of which rise and fall in prominence over time in reaction to social and technological change.

The chapter begins with a brief account of what was one of the most common strategies used by professional criminals to steal commercial cash during the middle part of the twentieth century but declined rapidly from the 1970s, that of safe-cracking. It then explores the rise of the alternative strategy of armed robbery, its emergent subculture, and the pragmatics of carrying out the crime. The chapter then explores those factors that contributed to the decline of armed robbery as an elite form of criminality and its current standing as a comparatively low-status crime.

The growth and decline of safe-cracking

During the post Second World War years, western economies blossomed on the back of reconstruction, full employment and a booming consumer economy. Property crime followed suit (Reiner 2005, 2007), and professional burglars plundered shops and the homes of the rich and famous for cash and high-value goods, (Scott 1995; Hobbs 1997; Reynolds 2000: 239). They also turned their attention to the safes of businesses relying solely upon cash, such as pawnbrokers and scrap metal merchants, as well as cinemas and departmental stores who would keep their takings overnight, and factories and warehouses, particularly on the night before payday (Hobbs 1995: 13–19).

Safe-cracking was a form of craft crime (McIntosh 1971, 1975), a transgressive version of normative industrial era employment for men (Davis 1990: 304–6).

Before a mid-nineteenth century flurry of innovation, safes were little more than iron boxes. However, innovative 'fireproof' technology rendered the safe vulnerable to 'picking', drilling, cutting or having their doors or backs levered (see http://www.safeman.org.uk or http://www.peterman.org.uk). While these tactics never really disappeared, they were extremely time-consuming, and constant innovation, particularly in the field of lock technology, inspired the increasing use of explosives (Chapman 1966; Chambliss 1972), a tactic that reached its heyday from the end of the Second World War to the late 1960s (for the most detailed discussion see Letkemann 1973: 56–86). Using explosives made safe-breaking a more complex task, and practical knowledge was hard to come by. Safe-crackers were often apprenticed to older villains as a result of sharing a prison cell (Hobbs 1995: 18; Macintyre 2007: 7), and during this apprenticeship, techniques and strategies could be absorbed.

Yet to create or come to terms with the 'risk society', during this pre-terrorism era explosives were easy to acquire: 'We rented a car ... and drove down to Mousehole in Cornwall and broke into a quarry to get gelignite and detonators' (Reynolds 2000: 128; see also Hobbs 1995: 14–15; Chapman 1966).

A top safe-cracker of the era explains:

It's called Polo Ammond (Polar Ammon Gelignite) and it was like mincemeat, red with all little red globules in it and it was powerful enough to knock a door off a safe. The detonators were of a size that just used to fit into the keyhole of the safe so you would take the baffle plate off the safe, load it up with enough explosive, put it all round in the lock. Then you press your detonator in, run the wires off if it had wires or if it had a fuse you just light the fuse and get out the way and the explosion occurs and you run back in. The door's usually laying on the floor ... (Chambliss 1972; Hobbs 1995: 15)

Bruce Reynolds, who was later to make his name as the key player in the Great Train Robbery, here explains the sensual enjoyment to be gleaned from a successful safe blowing. 'I couldn't believe the buzz blowing a safe gave me. It was the ultimate power trip. Unless you've been there, you can't understand how a little block of gelly and a handful of detonators can make you feel almost omnipotent. I couldn't wait to try again.' (Reynolds 2000: 130). Yet this was a hard won sensation: 'I discovered that it was far more technical than most people imagine. So many things can affect it – the atmosphere, the temperature, the positioning and the vagaries of metal' (ibid.: 158).

The decline of safe-cracking was brought about partly by technological innovations that made successful attacks on safes not impossible but extremely awkward and time-consuming, thus increasing the chances of apprehension (Letkemann 1973: 86–9). Again Dick Pooley explains.

They used to cement them down so you'd blow the door off. But if they weren't cemented down, 20 minutes you could have the back off. So Milner, who I could open their safes quite easy, joined up with Chatsworth Milner, and they now had a safe which was virtually blow-proof. In fact when you blew it, you blew it and it set off on springs a secondary mechanism so the bolts were shot home again. You'd made a lot of noise so you couldn't blow it again, you had to get out of there ... lot of effort, lot of noise. (Hobbs 1995: 18)

Some committed and technically adept criminals embraced technical innovations of their own to counter safe technology, but the vast amount of heavy equipment required restricted the use of devices such as the thermic lance and the oxyacetylene cutter (see Ostler 1969; Walsh 1986: 171; Punch 1991). 'Our equipment included about six suitcases and several oxyacetylene gas bottles weighing two hundredweight each' (Foreman 1996: 105). Although such methodologies have never been made completely redundant, the skill, time and equipment required led to cruder, quicker and more lucrative methodologies being employed.

Another key element in hastening the demise of the safe-cracker was to be found in the gradual shift away from a cash economy towards a credit-based, more risk-averse society. 'The cash targets who had made their lot during and after the war were changing with the times, becoming more accustomed to using banks and safety deposits' (Reynolds 2000: 239). These technological and commercial innovations accelerated the demise of craft crime and marked the emergence of team-based project crime, featuring precision and efficiency (Mannheim 1965: 656–9), along with planning and the designation of specialised roles to its participants (McIntosh 1975). 'See people graduated during my time from safes to banks, or to jugs as they'd call them. It was quicker to go and get it out with a shotgun, and they used to take all the money. That was the easy way ...' (Hobbs 1995: 18).

Wage snatches and bank robberies

Before the criminal fraternity turned their attention fully to banks, post offices and building societies, robbery with violence in the form of wage snatches was a popular and startlingly simplistic way of accessing considerable sums of money. With full employment and the post-war consumer boom, workers were often paid in cash on a weekly basis, and as a consequence clerks collecting the firms' weekly wages became ripe and easy targets for predatory robbers armed with blunt instruments (McVicar 1974: 181; Fraser 1994: 48–9). While some of the more ambitious wage snatchers were already interested in larger hauls of cash and began operating in teams (Reynolds 2000: 247–50, 269–76), generally armed raids (seldom featuring firearms) were newsworthy spectaculars (Hill 1955: 162–7, 217–19; Murphy 1993: 95–7), yet to become routinised.

Attention turned to the banks and building societies as robbers attacked the money where it was most vulnerable. Security was virtually non-existent, banks having barely changed from Victorian times and constituting little more than a large room with a counter separating customers from staff and cash. Importantly, the traditional reluctance of British criminals to use firearms was gradually being eroded. 'From my point of view, I could never believe that guns were efficient devices in the hands of criminals. Guns being so foreign to our culture, people were inclined to panic when confronted with a firearm and the results were occasionally tragic' (Reynolds 2000: 203). However, this attitude was rapidly becoming outdated. In the early 1960s robbers targeting security vans armed with crowbars, pick axe handles and other blunt instruments could, in exceptional circumstances, find themselves confronted by bank clerks armed with pistols and police accompanied by dogs. After one robber was shot and allegedly killed, the robbers upped the stakes: 'Next time we'll be armed as well' (Foreman 1996: 132). In addition robbers had become for the criminal justice system the most valued target. 'It's OK to nick a motorist; but the prize, the mythological prize is a bank robber. For a policeman to catch a bank robber is like a fisherman catching a 20 lb trout' (bank robber, quoted by Taylor 1984: 76).

A palpable moral panic concerning 'organised crime' went into full swing in the wake of the £2 million plus Great Train Robbery in 1963, and although firearms did not feature in this project crime par excellence and the minimal violence used against the train driver resulted in only minor injuries (Campbell 1994: 129–30; Reynolds 2000: 329–30), the sentences of 30 years that were awarded to the robbers penalised them in a similar manner to that of murderers (Campbell 1994: 140). Both the hazards and the rewards for robbery had clearly increased, and robbers embraced the opportunities with enthusiasm, an enthusiasm that was assisted by minimal levels of security and compounded by the tendency of the CID and its various specialist squads to guard jealously the intelligence that they had acquired. Armed robbers were able to thrive on the insularity of these CID fiefdoms, resulting in waves of armed robbery across police boundaries and the wholesale plundering of banks all over London, the south east and beyond (Ball *et al.* 1978).

Armed robbery as subculture

The 1960s marked the commencement of a golden age for armed robbers, who were the elite of the criminal community.[1] Bank security was almost non-existent, and with little planning a small team of determined robbers armed with a sawn-off shotgun, a handgun, a sledgehammer and a fast car had little trouble in cleaning up (McClintock and Gibson 1961; Ball *et al.* 1978). Armed robbery blossomed (Mannheim 1965: 657), and although this blossoming was oddly played down by criminologists (McClintock and Gibson 1961), it was afforded levels of precision and efficiency often associated with the military (Mannheim 1965: 656–7). The use of the military metaphor (Read 1979: 291–312; Reynolds 2000: 320), coupled with a tendency to regard 'Big Hits' as requiring both conception and direction from a 'Mind' (Fordham 1965: 29) or 'Mr Big' (Read 1979: 12; Biggs 1981: 217–23), both mirror the hierarchical organisation of policing (Stelfox 1996) and shift the public gaze away from the essential ingenuity of armed robbers as proletarian practitioners, often originating from locales that have been bypassed by the disciplining functions of industrial society (R. Smith 2005; T. Smith 2005). Unlike the craftsman, the self-identity of the robber was located not in skill or in the acquisition of an intricate arcane craft, but in personal, idealised masculine qualities (Hobbs 1995: 21) featuring elements of physicality, fortitude and endurance. This essentially cultural approach lends little credence either to the military metaphor or the 'Mr Big' assertion (Mason 1994: 126–33; Hobbs 1995: 47).

Sutherland (1937) presented professional crime as a distinct behaviour system (Hollingshead 1939), characterised by technical skill, consensus via a shared ideology, differential association, status and most importantly informal organisation (see Maurer 1955). Although Letkemann (1973) did not entirely disregard Sutherland's model, he emphasised that commitment (Becker 1960) to crime as a means of making a living was the most accurate way of distinguishing professional criminals. The most unambiguously subcultural analysis of professional crime appears in Einstadter's study of armed robbery (1969). The author unravelled consistency of practice and some ideological coherence but could find no evidence of a system of tutelage or relationships with quasi-legitimate agents such as receivers of stolen goods. Of course, cash robberies do not necessarily require commercial intermediaries, but for commodities such as bullion (Hogg *et al.* 1988; Pearson 2006) access to specialised expertise is crucial. This point was stressed by Mack and Kerner (1975) who indicated that to concentrate upon 'The front line operators ... or the van or bank robbers' (p. 178) was to distort the reality of professional crime. For Mack and Kerner the 'background operators', the lawyers and accountants, utilise their legal status to structure frameworks of legitimacy, and it is these frameworks that enable professional criminals to manufacture enduring careers (Pearson 2006).

Armed robbery is a crime that is usually avoided by liberal academics intent on locating external drivers for engagement with crime. However, beyond the youth, who remain the bread and butter of so much criminological theory, the fallback positions of, for instance, labelling theory provide little explanatory capital. As Walton points out, 'where is the bank robber ... who is unaware that he is engaged in the social act of stealing?' (Walton 1973: 162). The identity of the armed robber, in particular that of the 'professional' bank robber, lies in the essence of the act of armed robbery, and the meaning of armed robbery is to be found in the overt unambiguous act of robbery itself. What Katz has called the ' "professional", "business" and "accounting" metaphors ...' (1988: 236) situates the chaos which is often framed around little other than hedonism. But these metaphors are important; they ascribe competence to an individual, help to mediate risk and ascribe, certainly in western capitalist societies, key qualities of inclusivity and acceptance and an impression of communality (Hobbs 1991). The 'professional' armed robber belonged to an exclusive club which, as I shall suggest later, has become increasingly mythological with the emergence of criminal trading cultures.

Lifestyle

There is a tendency to regard crime as a highly rational activity, driven purely by commercial imperatives. Certainly, particularly in the case of iconic crimes such as armed robbery, we should carefully consider the pursuit of pleasure that provides not only the initial spur to engage in robbery but, particularly during the 'golden age', drove many individuals to gain sufficient levels of competence and consistency to maintain a lifestyle which most non-criminals can only aspire to at designated times, within regulated spaces and with highly restricted moral and material resources.

> Restaurants were prompt in their attention, a twenty-pound note to the *maître d'* ensuring that there was never any problem getting a table. Pruniers in St. James's, Bentleys, and Sheekeys were our fish places ... Wheeler's in Duke of York Street off Jermyn Street: you could have a small dining-room to yourself there, very private and intimate. The Rib Room at the Carlton Towers was an innovative fashion for a while, serving great beef at a time when beef was synonymous with strength: we all ate plenty of that, thinking that we needed it for our work. (Reynolds 2000: 241)

These essentially hedonistic lifestyle choices, compulsions and commitments singled out professional armed robbers from the mundane rhythms of legitimate employment and its attendant routines. In addition their competence marked them out as professionals which in turn gave them access to the sensual delights of 'irrational consumption' (Katz 1988: 198).

Hedonism is central to our understanding of the underworld, and both Bruce Reynolds and Freddie Foreman neatly express this sense of a criminal fraternity that marked out committed criminal hedonists from mere dilettantes:

> There were nights when we would be celebrating at the Astor or the Embassy and we would spy another group of crims supping magnums of champagne. Bottles would be exchanged as we toasted each other's

success amid much rivalry. It was exciting. This was the recognition I had always craved. (Reynolds 2000: 194)

You could go from one club to the other and see the same faces. We could easily tell which pavement firm had a touch on a particular day by the way they were celebrating in the afternoon. They'd be walking around with bottles of vodka or scotch. Money just flowed. (Foreman 1996: 93)

The hedonistic aspect of the underworld in which professional armed robbers lived is crucial and is exemplified by the narcissistic drive that is implicit to a 'Life lived without a safety net' (Pileggi 1987: 39). Numerous first hand accounts of 'life as party' (Shover and Honaker 1991) confirm the centrality of 'earning and burning money' (Katz 1988: 215) as a way of authenticating the professional criminal's commitment to a subcultural identity defined by conspicuous consumption and funded by crime (Hohimer 1981: 19; Wideman 1985: 131). The professional criminal cited by Taylor sums it up: 'Well I'm a natural. I mean, I am a natural. I love it, I love the high life … I love the … going out to wine and dine, the fucking champagne and the birds, and living it up, and first class on the airplanes. Champagne fucking Charlie. You know. Ducking and diving; and, you know, wining and dining' (Taylor 1984: 121).

For the professional armed robber, the straight world did not offer comparable financial rewards, nor did it offer the same frisson of excitement and exclusivity as they shared with their peers the ambience of 'spontaneity, autonomy, independence and resourcefulness' (Shover and Honaker 1992: 283) that is integral to outlaw status.

Buzz

Hedonism also plays a part in the commission of the crime and is exemplified in the following quote from convicted bank robber, Bertie Smalls:

The nervous tension I used to feel before a job didn't stay with me all the time, only till I got started. Once I start I feel completely calm, one hundred per cent, everything comes brilliant to me … I might be fogged up a minute or two before but the minute its on its like the sun coming out from behind a cloud. (Ball *et al.* 1978: l83)

One of the key features of the study of armed robbery is the rich seam of biographical literature that is provided by the autobiographies of retired robbers. Partly perhaps due to the inordinately long sentences awarded to robbers, enabling some deep reflection on what was and what might have been, a number of robbers have produced autobiographies that suggest levels of sensitivity that tempers the brutality that is so necessary for the commission of a successful 'blag'. The most famous is probably Willie Sutton's frequently cited ghost-written account of robbery and prison escape (Sutton 1976). Bruce Reynolds edges into this category by virtue of the cosh used against the train driver during the Great Train Robbery, and his highly literate rendition of criminal culture in the 1950s and 1960s is lucid and especially insightful with regard to the status of the professional criminal and the composition of the underworld.

John McVicar's autobiography, although he later partly disowns it as part of his plea for mitigation, is a stunning piece of work (McVicar 1974). McVicar succeeds in situating his criminal choices within a class and family context, while never seeking to shift responsibility for his actions. He also outlines a clear demarcation between robbers and gangsters, and had much to say about the relationship between masculinities and crime many years before academics had created that particular niche. Terry Smith's autobiography shows how criminal traditions are passed on through the generations, and how much was risked for relatively small sums of money often with little or no planning, and often almost at a whim (T. Smith 2005). Razor Smith's view of armed robbery, like that of his namesake, involves aspiration, but is far more explicitly connected to hedonism and in particular drug culture (R. Smith 2005). The prizes were often small, and there is little sense of skill and virtually none of foresight, but he does retain a certain pride in restraining his violence and not hurting 'civilians'. Most importantly, his work bears close comparison to McVicar's in expressing his ambition as a young man to be recognised as a 'face', a respected man whose defining characteristic is his nerve.

The sheer pleasure that robbers gleaned from their trade is a constant feature of most professional armed robbers' accounts. Indeed, as a form of edgework (Lyng 1990), armed robbery can be regarded as an exciting and pleasurable activity that sits nicely with the hedonistic opportunities that can be purchased with the proceeds. The clarity and sensual awareness identified above by Bertie Smalls (see also T. Smith 2005: 148) is not dissimilar to that described by participants of dangerous sports (Hardie-Bick 2005). The analogy is taken a step further by Razor Smith:

> I live a whole lifetime in minutes, aware of every breath that leaves my body and every beat of my heart. The world seems to suddenly pop into clear focus and my every sense is heightened … You psyche yourself up to step out of a plane thousands of feet up in the air, knowing that something could go wrong and you are jumping to your death. But you step out anyway, spitting in the face of death and knowing that once you leave the plane there is no changing your mind and turning back. And in the five minutes of free fall, you're aware of everything, but you cannot stop. (R. Smith 2005: 83–4)

Linked to this fiercely hedonistic underworld (Viccei 1993; Foreman 1996; Reynolds 2000) is the fact that few armed robbers of the 'golden age' were able to construct anything resembling permanent criminal structures from their vast ill-gotten gains (for a couple of intriguing exceptions see Jennings et al. 1990 and the career of Foreman 1996). Most of the professional robbers of the golden era were more concerned with taking their families to Spain (Ball et al. 1978) and leading a 'Lord Snooty' lifestyle of conspicuous excess (Taylor 1984).

Armed robber Robby Wideman explains:

Straight people don't understand. I mean, they think dudes is after the things straight people got. It aint that at all. People in the life aint looking for no home and grass in the yard and shit like that. We the show people. The glamour people. Come on the set with the finest car the finest woman, the finest wines. Hear people talking about you. Hear the bar get quiet when you walk in the door. Throw down a yard and tell everybody drink up ... You make something out of nothing. (Wideman 1985: 131)

A superior competence

Skill (Inciardi 1976), craft (Mcintosh 1971) and competence (Shover 1973) are the everyday methodologies inherent in the commission of crime as work (Letkemann 1973), and in the case of armed robbery in particular combined to create 'a superior competence to control the interaction' (Katz 1988: 170). Competent performance is central to Luckenbill's (1981) study of armed robbery. The central problem for the robber is how to gain and maintain the compliance of victims, and Luckenbill perceives robbery as a series of transactions managed by the robber, involving his victims in the accomplishment of four interrelated tasks. On establishing his presence with the victim, the interaction is transformed into 'the robbery frame', the goods are transferred to the robber and finally the robber leaves the scene. For Luckenbill offenders and victims must share a common definition of what is going on, and the key is the creation of 'the illusion of impending death' (Wright and Decker 1997).

For Wright and Decker the robber creates this illusion by catching victims in a state of unawareness, presenting a fierce demeanour and displaying a deadly weapon. All of this is designed to scare victims into a state of total compliance for as long as possible without carrying through with the threat. (See Goffman 1952 for an in-depth exploration of the maintenance of compliance. See also Schur 1957; Katz 1988: 176–9). However, despite the highly rational rhetoric offered up by armed robbers in retrospect, and usually from the confines of a prison cell, as Cook explains, there is often a 'Russian roulette' aspect to armed robbery (1987: 300) where there is always a chance of victims being wounded or murdered. Cook argues that this risk is related to the victims' levels of resistance during the offence as well as to the assailants' momentary murderous impulses. Cook suggests that gun robberies yield far more dangerous outcomes than those featuring other types of weapons, and that the types of guns used in robberies have implications for the degree of injury and lethality (see Matthews 2002: 68–74).

O'Donnell and Morrison, in their examination of armed robbery and the types of firearms used, successfully demystify the crime by highlighting that while armed robbery has increased in the UK, 'the majority of robbers choose not to carry live firearms' (1997: 265), and instead tend to select replica/ imitation firearms. Taylor and Hornsby (2000) support these findings, reporting that victims of armed robbery found it difficult to differentiate between real and replica handguns. This analysis gels with that of other researchers who have noted that the impression of weapon possession ensures compliance and usually circumvents actual violence (Wright and Rossi 1985).

Control

Of course, banks and security companies colluded to place as many obstacles as possible in the path of 'blaggers', and, as in the case of safe-breaking, armed robbers were faced with constant technological innovation designed to make their task more difficult. Robbers who had previously been able to jump the counter and snatch the cash were faced with glass screens necessitating the use of a sledgehammer. The glass was hardened. The money was then attacked as it was being delivered or removed by security guards who were subsequently issued with protective helmets and batons, instigating pitched battles on the pavement. The robbers used ammonia sprays to disable the guards, who were then issued with visors for their helmets. Eventually guns, usually a sawn-off shotgun, became an essential tool to intimidate guards, bank staff and customers. A blast from a sawn-off into the ceiling of a bank, shouts, threats and in less than two minutes a huge haul of used notes had been stolen (Cox *et al.* 1977: 11–17). When banks tightened their security further, the prize was attacked in transit (Gill 2000; Matthews 2002) and when the security vans became virtually impregnable, the robbers turned to chainsaws, and increased levels of brutality (Clarkson 2004). The van makers merely fought back, inventing airlocks and interlocking doors which further delayed the robbers obtaining their hands on the prize.[2]

By the summer of 1972 armed robberies in London were being committed at the rate of one every five days, and since 1969 more than £3m had been stolen. Convictions were rare, only a tiny fraction of the loot was recovered, and there can be little doubt that the robbers were assisted, in more ways than one, by both the culture and organisation of the police.

Supergrasses and police corruption

Bertie Smalls was a respected figure in London's high-spending, hedonistic robber fraternity. In 1972 he was part of a seven-handed team who, in 90 seconds inside the Wembley branch of Barclays bank, stole £138,000. An informant had named the Wembley robbers and a golfing partner of the head of Wembley CID was arrested. This success inspired the formation of a specialist Robbery Squad that combined officers from previously competing units such as the Regional Crime Squad and the Flying Squad. Despite interviewing some of the robbers and visiting Spain, the 25-strong team had no further success.

However, Smalls' name was being increasingly linked with a portfolio of robberies across London. Eventually, he was arrested and negotiated to 'do a deal', offering to give up 'every robber in London' in exchange for immunity.

Eventually a deal was struck, and the term 'supergrass' entered the public lexicon. Smalls confessed to 15 robberies and named 32 bank robbers and a number of associates. The Wembley robbers were sentenced to a total of 106 years, and over the next 14 months a further 21 men received sentences totalling 308 years.

The Chief Superintendent of Wembley CID was accused of stealing £25,000 from the safety deposit box of one of the robbers. The subsequent police investigation cleared the officer who then retired from the force. A related police inquiry into accusations that the Chief Superintendent and another senior officer had 'fiddled' a reward claim for the provision of information naming two of the Wembley robbers also found in favour of the accused officers. The second policeman promptly left the police to become a security officer for Barclays Bank. By 1973 two officers a week were voluntarily leaving the Met as a result of a general anti-corruption purge led by Commissioner Robert Mark, and in the same year the number of bank robberies in London fell from 65 in 1972 to 26.

Perhaps the most significant aspect of Smalls' criminal career was the way in which he broke for ever the myth of an underworld code of silence (Hobbs 1997). Although the law lord Lord Justice Lawton subsequently said that the arrangement between Smalls and the Director of Public Prosecutions should not be repeated, other 'supergrasses' followed in his wake. Until Smalls broke rank, great store had been placed upon the notion of a code of ethics that structured the actions of professional criminal action and could be sourced to an underworld (Benney [1936] 1981: 194), but it is clear from the Smalls case, and from subsequent studies, that this golden era could only have been sustained by embedded and highly lucrative institutionalised police corruption (Cox *et al.* 1977; Mark 1978; Hobbs 1988: 62–83; Jennings *et al.* 1990; Short 1992; see also Foreman 1996: 144–5).

Particularly for armed robbers, the underworld functioned as a network of exchange, controlling and disseminating information (McIntosh 1971; Hobbs 1995: 21). However, the old underworld was breaking down and the unwritten criminal code that provided an ethical framework for a community of professional criminals was proving inadequate to cope with the new market free for all (Sutherland 1937: 197; Irwin 1970: 8; cf. Cohen and Taylor 1972: ch. 7; Taylor 1984: 79–84, 89–90).

Big hits

If the emergence of the supergrass destroyed the honorific myth of the underworld and undoubtedly damaged the armed robber community, armed robbery did not disappear, 'indeed, raids against banks, building societies and cash in transit had doubled between 1983 and 1986' (Matthews 2002: 53). In addition, professional robbers turned their attention to huge iconic targets, targeting the depots where bullion and cash were stored. In 1983 a highly experienced team of robbers from east and south London robbed the Security Express depot of seven million pounds in cash in a crime that involved careful and extensive planning and a security guard having petrol poured over him (Knight *et al.* 2002: 10–40). A man responsible for minding some of the money became an informant and the robbery team were convicted. Six months later £26 million of gold bullion was stolen from the Brinks-Mat depot at Heathrow (Darbyshire and Hilliard 1993). The impact of this robbery, which like the Security Express raid involved petrol being poured over security guards as a means of gaining compliance (Cater and Tullett 1991), was global. The world's gold markets reacted immediately and within twelve hours of the heist the haul's value had increased by a million pounds. The insider who had provided keys and information turned informer, arrests were made and the violent aftermath of the robbery continues to this day (T. Smith 2005: 149; Pearson 2006: 262–66).

In the ten years preceding the Brinks-Mat raid armed robberies had risen from 380 to 1,772 per annum, an increase of 340 per cent, and while the importation of the supergrass system from Northern Ireland to the British mainland clearly had failed to eliminate armed robbery, it did serve to place an even higher premium upon trust among the robbery teams. Free-floating teams of the Bertie Smalls era gave way to tight-knit firms, often with family or neighbourhood connections. Further, the belief among robbers that the police were operating a shoot to kill policy had an understandable impact upon anyone considering a career in armed robbery. In July 1987 two men were shot dead by police during an attempted robbery of a wages van at an abattoir in south London. In November 1987 a robber was shot dead in a wages snatch at a supermarket in south-east London while a television crew filmed. In April 1989 two men were shot dead during a post office robbery in suburban north London, and in 1990 a robber was shot dead by police in Surrey during an attempted raid on a security van. In a shoot-out near the post office in Brockham, near Dorking, in August 1992, police injured both the robbery gang and members of the public. The officer in charge was quoted as stating that while he was sorry for any injuries to the public, 'sometimes it was necessary to fight fire with fire' (see Waddington 1991: 24).

Decline

As with craft criminals, improvements in security technology took their toll. Alarm systems connected to police stations, time-worked safes, 'voice speaking alarms, exploding boxes with red dye, inaccessible locked safes and satellite tracking devices ... CCTV, witness identification techniques and DNA evidence ... the risks involved were very real and were not worth it' (T. Smith 2005: 296–7). Improvements in police tactics (Matthews 1996, 2002) and, most importantly, the disintegration of the 'criminal code' via the emergence of the supergrass in the 1970s (Hobbs 1995: 1997) all impacted upon this iconic criminal activity. Further, firearms became easier to acquire and careless non-professionals targeted shops, garages and off-licences for disdainful reward (Morrison and O'Donnell 1994).

Only 11 per cent of Walsh's sample of robbers provided a self-description of thief or robber (Walsh 1986: 57). Armed robbery, which was previously central to the concept of professional status, became haphazard, essentially amateur excursions (Walsh 1986: ch. 3; Katz 1988: 164; Morrison and O'Donnell 1994), performed with minimal planning, base levels of competence and, most importantly, no commitment to specialised criminality (Matthews 2002; Walsh 1986: 57). However, also key to understanding the decline of professional armed robbery is the fact that the rewards from entrepreneurial pursuits, and in particular drugs, were now so much greater. Criminal entrepreneurship marked the destruction of all but the highly symbolic debris of the 'underworld', and flagged the inauguration of a mutant variety of enterprise that is fundamentally similar to legitimate commerce, spawning a highly flexible criminal equipped for entrepreneurial engagements and committed not to a hedonistic self-contained subculture but to the manipulation of markets and the maximisation of profit (Hobbs 1995: 106–24).

Convicted robbers came into contact with drug-savvy cellmates, and fugitive robbers basking in the late 1970s suspension of the extradition treaty between Spain and the UK quickly latched on to the opportunities of the cannabis trade just a short speedboat trip away across the straits of Gibraltar. The elite of British armed robbers were at the forefront of the drugs trade, investing in a relatively low-risk business that emerged as central to the concept of contemporary organised crime.[3]

Roger Matthews has clearly shown that the impact of drug use as a lubricant to the relatively controlled and sober edgework of the golden age robbers has significantly increased (2002: 33–5). R. Smith (2005) exemplifies the inevitable impact of drug use on what his namesake (T. Smith (2005) calls 'the art of armed robbery'. He explains the allure of the crime and the attraction of attempting to emulate heroes from the golden age, 'the Great Train Robbers, John McVicar, the Wembley bank Robbers, John Dillinger and Willie Sutton … they were violent robbers who controlled their violence and used just enough to get the prize' (T. Smith 2005: 59). Although his own drug-addled career as a robber did not measure up to that of his heroes, Razor Smith describes a violent subculture where weapons are used recreationally and as a way of settling scores. The spoils are less, the risks are higher and their preferred mode of hedonism locates these bandits as part of the drug culture rather than part of a specialist criminal elite.

However, armed robbery has yet to go the way of highway robbery. There were 7,926 robberies of commercial premises in England and Wales in 2004/5, and in 2005 there were 837 cash-in-transit (CIT) robberies, resulting in losses of £15.4 million. For a fourth consecutive year the British Security Industry Association reported a rise in CIT robberies, although improved security features, such as smoke and dye boxes and vehicle tracking systems, have reduced the number of significant losses and may have acted as a deterrent to the more established serious and organised criminals (UKTA 2006). Most CIT robberies are planned and executed as hijacks or attacks at a point of transfer by groups of criminals armed with firearms, 'only' 75 per cent of which are capable of firing (Gill 2000, 2001). Attacks on automated telling machines have also risen, including when they are being refilled. In contrast, large-value cash robberies of commercial premises, including banks, have declined, while robberies at convenience stores, garages, supermarkets and restaurants have increased (Gill 2000; Matthews 2002; UKTA 2006).

The 'deskilled' (Matthews 2002), 'dangerous amateur' (Taylor 1984: 92) falls someway short of an elite criminal, and armed robbery is now more than ever before strongly influenced by social factors and economic inequality (Schwaner 2000: 279). For instance, Schwaner stresses that the younger the offender at the time of his first offence and the deeper he is pushed into the criminal justice system, the more likely he is to reoffend. Released back into society and into environments where legitimate moneymaking opportunities are sparse within a culture dominated by the 'code of the street' (Anderson 1999), a continuous cycle of robbery where 'recidivism is hinged upon several structural factors related to the development of identity and lifestyle' (Schwaner 2000: 381) often results.

Fantasy and innovation

Despite the decline in professional armed robbery as a routinised specialism, the lure of the 'big one' continues to attract committed criminals. For instance, the spectacular failed attempt at stealing the 'millennium diamonds' in 2000 (Hollington 2004; Shatford and Doyle 2004) that involved a JCB digger was caught on camera by a waiting armed police squad. An organised attack on a cash storage facility in Kent in February 2006 yielded the biggest ever cash haul, reportedly £53 million (Campbell 2007; Sounes 2008). At the time of writing, a number of men have been convicted while approximately £30 million is still missing. Like an earlier cash robbery at a bank in Northern Ireland in 2004 (Jenkins 2004), the Kent robbery involved a 'tiger kidnap' (Control Risks 2008) in which the family of an employee was taken hostage and threatened in order to force the employee to help the robbers gain access to the storage facility. The tiger kidnap is the latest variation on armed robbery (BBC News 24 2004, 2006). A hybrid term, the offences that constitute a tiger kidnap are robbery (Theft Act 1968) and kidnapping (Taking of Hostages Act 1982). It has been suggested that tiger kidnap is so-called due to the way in which the victim of the crime is 'stalked' (Control Risks 2007).

Summary

It was just like going to work, but easier. (Taylor 1984: 88)

The decline in armed robbery as part of organised/professional crime, and its emergence as a deskilled, disorganised activity has been well documented by academic researchers, and in particular by Roger Matthews, who has been especially effective in stressing the ramshackle and spontaneous nature of its contemporary manifestation (Matthews 2002), often resembling a drug-addled Ealing comedy.

It is an easy conceit to dismiss armed robbers as mere dinosaurs: wide-lapelled denizens of central casting destined to reside for eternity on a 1970s copshow loop. However, these throwbacks offer to scholars a prime example of a criminal subculture generated by proletarian opportunity structures, and featuring classic, stereotypical masculine traits defined by the dominant class arrangements of industrial society. In turn we can also see the relevance of both economic shifts and control theory in the way in which the storage, distribution and protection of cash and other high-level goods have driven transgressive innovation through eras of craft and technical invention via hedonistic camaraderie, teamwork and brute strength to deskilling, fragmentation and individualisation.

With the noted exception of the occasional newsworthy spectacular attempt at obtaining fantasy riches, armed robbery has become deskilled and relegated from the Premier League of villainry. While armed robbery has not of course disappeared, establishments unable to afford the target hardening that partially defines powerful late-modern commercial and financial institutions present relatively easy pickings for the desperate or unambitious.

Selected further reading

The roots of a full understanding of armed robbery can be found in Einstadter (1969), who takes his cue from Sutherland's (1937) establishment of the armed robber as part of a distinct deviant subculture. This theme is taken up historically by McIntosh (1971) and sociologically by Hobbs (1995, 1997). For a flavour of a unique era where armed robbery was to the fore of professional criminal practice, both Ball *et al.* (1978) and Taylor (1984) provide engaging accounts that complement the first-hand accounts of McVicar (1979) and R. Smith (2005). While Katz (1988) emphasises the complex sensuality of the crime, this complexity is expertly explored by Reynolds (2000), who deals with the hedonistic aftermath of robbery. For a wider analysis of both the crime and attempts to control it Gill (2000) and particularly Matthews (2002) are essential, while the mechanics of the crime are also covered by Luckenbill (1981).

Notes

1 For a personal account of a career in armed robbery that spanned this era, see Hobbs (1995: 19–23).
2 For an illuminating overview of this contest between robbers and security industry see the TV programme *How to Rob a Bank* (RDF Television, trans. Channel 4, March 2003) which lends vivid evidence to complement Matthews (2002).
3 For an outstanding overview of this shift from predatory crime towards the drug trade see Dorn *et al.* (1992)

References

Anderson, E. (1999) *The Code of the Street*. New York: Norton.
Ball, J., Chester, L. and Pewott, R. (1978) *Cops and Robbers*. London: André Deutsch.
BBC News 24 (2004) 'The Human Factor in Bank Robbery', 21 December.
BBC News 24 (2006) 'The Security Weak Link – The Boss', 23 February.
Becker, H. (1960) 'Notes on the concept of commitment', *American Journal of Sociology*, LXVI, pp. 32–40.
Benney, M. ([1936] 1981) *Low Company*, facsimile edn. Sussex: Caliban Books.

Biggs, R. (1981) *His Own Story*. London: Sphere Books.

Campbell, D. (1994) *The Underworld*. London: BBC Books.

Campbell, D. (2007) 'Greed, pure and simple – court told of gang's motive for £53m robbery', *Guardian*, 27 June.

Cater, F. and Tullett, T. (1991) *The Sharp End*. London: Grafton.

Chambliss, W. (1972) *Box Man*. New York: Harper & Row.

Chapman, E. (1966) *The Real Eddie Chapman Story*. London: Library 33.

Clarkson, W. (2004) *Moody*. London: Mainstream Publishing.

Cohen, S. and Taylor, L. (1972) *Psychological Survival*. Harmondsworth: Penguin.

Control Risks (2007) *Tiger Kidnap – The Threat to the UK Banking Sector*. London: Control Risks.

Cook, P. J. (1987) 'Robbery violence', *Journal of Criminal Law and Criminology*, 78: 357–76.

Cox, B., Shirley, J. and Short, M. (1977) *The Fall of Scotland Yard*. Harmondsworth: Penguin.

Darbyshire, N. and Hilliard, B. (1993) *The Flying Squad*. London: Headline.

Davis, M. (1990) *City of Quartz*. London: Verso.

Dorn, N., South, N. and Murji, K. (1992) *Traffickers*. London: Routledge.

Einstadter, W. (1969) 'The social organisation of armed robbery', *Social Problems*, 17: 64–83.

Fordham, P. (1965) *The Robbers' Tale*. London: Hodder & Stoughton.

Foreman, F. (1996) *Respect*. London: Century.

Fraser, F. (1994) *Mad Frank*. London: Little, Brown.

Gill, M. (2000) *Commercial Robbery*. Leicester: Perpetuity Press.

Gill, M. (2001) 'The craft of robbers of cash-in-transit vans: crime facilitators and the entrepreneurial approach', *International Journal of the Sociology of Law*, 29: 283.

Goffman, E. (1952) 'On cooling the mark out: some aspects of adaptation to failure', *Psychiatry*, 15: 451–63.

Gosse, P. (1932) *The History of Piracy*. London: Longmans.

Hardie-Bick, J. (2005) *Dropping Out and Diving In: An Ethnography of Skydiving*. PhD thesis, University of Durham.

Hill, B. (1955) *Boss of Britain's Underworld*. London: Naldrett Press.

Hobbs, D. (1988) *Doing the Business: Entrepreneurship, Detectives and the Working Class in the East End of London*. Oxford: Clarendon Press.

Hobbs, D. (1991) 'Business as a master metaphor', in R. Burrows (ed.), *Deciphering the Enterprise Culture*. London: Routledge.

Hobbs, D. (1995) *Bad Business: Professional Criminals in Modern Britain*. Oxford: Oxford University Press.

Hobbs, D. (1997) 'Professional crime: change continuity and the enduring myth of the underworld', *Sociology*, 31 (1): 57–72.

Hogg, A., McDougall, J. and Morgan, R. (1988) *Bullion Brinks-Mat*. Harmondsworth: Penguin.

Hohimer, F. (1981) *Violent Streets*. London: Star.

Hollingshead, A. (1939) 'Behaviour systems as a field for research', *American Journal of Sociology*, 4: 816–22.

Hollington, K. (2004) *Diamond Geezers – The Inside Story of the Crime of the Millennium*. London: Michael O'Mara Books.

Inciardi, J. (1976) 'The pickpocket and his victim', *Victimology*, 1: 141–9.

Irwin, J. (1970) *The Felon*. Englewood Cliffs, NJ: Prentice Hall.

Jenkins, R. (2004) 'Gang seizes family in bank robbery', *The Times*, 23 September.

Jennings, A., Lashmar, P. and Simson, V. (1991) *Scotland Yard's Cocaine Connection*. London: Arrow.

Katz, J. (1988) *Seductions of Crime*. New York: Basic Books.

Knight, R., Knight, J. and Wilton, P. (2002) *Gotcha: The Untold Story of Britain's Biggest Cash Robbery*. London: Pan.

Letkemann, P. (1973) *Crime as Work*. Englewood Cliffs, NJ: Prentice Hall.

Luckenbill, D. (1981) 'Generating compliance: the case of robbery', *Urban Life*, 10: 25–46.

Lyng, S. (1990) 'Edgework: a social psychological analysis of voluntary risk-taking', *American Journal of Sociology*, 95 (4): 876–921.

McClintock, F. H. and Gibson, E. (1961) *Robbery in London*. London: Macmillan.

McIntosh, M. (1971) 'Changes in the organisation of thieving', in S. Cohen (ed.), *Images of Deviance*. Harmondsworth: Penguin.

McIntosh, M. (1975) *The Organisation of Crime*. London: Macmillan.

Macintyre, B. (2007) *Agent Zig-Zag*. London: Bloomsbury.

Mack, J. (1964) 'Full-time miscreants, delinquent neighbourhoods and criminal networks', *British Journal of Sociology*, 15: 38–53.

Mack, J. and Kerner, H. (1975) *The Crime Industry*. Lexington: Saxon House, Levington Books.

McVicar, J. (1974) *McVicar by Himself*. London: Arrow.

Mannheim, H. (1965) *Comparative Criminology*, Vol. 2. London: Routledge & Kegan Paul.

Mark, R. (1978) *In the Office of Constable*. London: Collins.

Mason, E. (1994) *Inside Story*. London: Pan.

Matthews, R. (1996) *Armed Robbery: Two Police Responses*, Crime Detection and Prevention Series Paper 78. London: Home Office.

Matthews, R. (2002) *Armed Robbery*. Cullompton: Willan.

Maurer, D. W. (1955) *The Whizz Mob*. New Haven, CT: College and University Press.

Morrison, S. and O'Donnell, I. (1994) *Armed Robbery: A Study in London*, Occasional Paper No. 15. Oxford: Oxford Centre for Criminological Research.

Murphy, R. (1993) *Smash and Grab*. London: Faber & Faber.

O'Donnell, I. and Morrison, S. (1997) 'Armed and dangerous? The use of firearms in robbery', *Howard Journal*, 36: 305–20.

Ostler, R. (1969) 'The thermic lance', *Police Journal*, XLII, July: 286–92.

Pearson, W. (2006) *Death Warrant*. London: Orion.

Pileggi, N. (1987) *Wise Guy*. London: Corgi.

Punch, M. (1991) 'In the underworld: an interview with a Dutch safebreaker', *Howard Journal*, 30 (2): 121–39.

Read, P. P. (1979) *The Train Robbers*. London: Coronet.

Reiner, R. (2005) 'Be tough on a crucial cause of crime – neoliberalism', *Guardian*, 24 November.

Reiner, R. (2007) *Law and Order: An Honest Citizen's Guide to Crime and Control*. London: Polity Press.

Reynolds, B. (2000) *The Autobiography of a Thief*. London: Virgin.

Schur, E. (1957) 'A sociological analysis of confidence swindling', *Journal of Criminal Law, Criminology and Police Science*, 48: 296–304.

Schwaner, S. L. (2000) '"Stick 'em up, buddy": robbery, lifestyle, and specialization within a cohort of parolees', *Journal of Criminal Justice*, 28: 371–84.

Scott, P. (1995) *Gentleman Thief*. London: Harper Collins.

Sharpe, J (2004) *Dick Turpin – The Myth of the English Highwayman*. London: Profile Books.

Shatford, J. and Doyle, W. (2004) *Dome Raiders – How Scotland Yard Foiled the Greatest Robbery of All Time*. London: Virgin Books.

Short, M. (1992) *Lundy*. London: Grafton.

Shover, N. (1973) 'The social organisation of burglary', *Social Problems*, 20: 499–514.

Shover, N. and Honaker, D. (1992) 'The socially bounded decision making of persistent property offenders', *Howard Journal*, 31: 276–93.

Smith, R. (2005) *A Few Kind Words and a Loaded Gun*. London: Penguin.

Smith, T. (2005) *The Art of Armed Robbery*. London: Blake.

Sounes, H. (2008) *Heist: The Inside Story of the World's Biggest Robbery*. London: Simon & Schuster.

Stelfox, P. (1996) *Gang Violence: Strategic and Tactical Options*. London: Home Office, Police Research Group.

Sutherland, E. (1937) *The Professional Thief*. Chicago: University of Chicago Press.

Sutton, W. (1976) *Where the Money Was: The Memoirs of a Bank Robber*. New York: Viking Press.

Taylor, I. and Hornsby, R. (2000) *Replica Firearms: A New Frontier in the Gun Market*. Department of Sociology and Social Policy, University of Durham.

Taylor, L. (1984) *In the Underworld*. Oxford: Blackwell.

Thomas, W. and Znaniecki, F. (1927) *The Polish Peasant in Europe and America*, 2nd edn, 2 vols. New York: Knopf.

UKTA (2003) *United Kingdom Threat Assessment*. London: NCIS.

UKTA (2006) *United Kingdom Threat Assessment*. London: NCIS.

Viccei, V. (1993) *Knightsbridge: The Robbery of the Century*. London: Blake.

Waddington, P. A. J. (1991) *The Strong Arm of the Law*. Oxford: Oxford University Press.

Walsh, D. (1986) *Heavy Business*. London: Routledge.

Walton, P. (1973) 'The case of the Weathermen: social reaction and radical commitment', in I. Taylor and L. Taylor (eds), *Politics and Deviance*. Harmondsworth: Pelican.

Wideman, J. (1985) *Brothers and Keepers*. New York: Penguin.

Wright, J. D. and Rossi, P. H. (1985) *The Armed Criminal in America: A Survey of Incarcerated Offenders*. Washington, DC: US Department of Justice, National Institute of Justice.

Wright, R. and Decker, S. (1997) *Armed Robbers in Action: Stick-Ups and Street Culture*. Boston: Northeastern University Press.

Chapter 16

Youth gang crime

Jennifer Maher

Introduction

One of the most widely held beliefs about gangs is that they are involved in criminal behaviour. 'Committing crimes together' is the most commonly defined gang characteristic reported in the US National Youth Gang Survey (National Youth Gang Center 2007). Many influential gang researchers (Decker and Van Winkle 1996; Huff 1996; Klein 2001; Maxson *et al.* 1985; Yablonsky 1967) argue that criminality is central to the gang identity and provides a key distinction between gangs and other youth collectives. As a result, most gang definitions include participation in crime as a key identifier. The Eurogang definition, for example, proposes 'a street gang is any durable, street oriented youth group whose own *identity* includes involvement in *illegal activity*' (emphasis added) (Gemert and Fleisher 2005: 12).

Not all writers believe that criminal behaviour is a central characteristic of gangs. Thrasher (one of the pioneering researchers on gangs) did not assume that gang members were necessarily involved in delinquency and defined them instead in terms of their social and behavioural characteristics (Thrasher 1963). Hallsworth and Young (2008) challenge the proposition that the current UK problem with youth criminality and violence is a 'problem of gangs or a burgeoning gang culture'. Pearson (1995: 1194) more generally argues that researchers 'simply do not have the evidence – in the form of government-sponsored statistics, social surveys, reliable self-report studies, etc. – to state with any confidence the actually existing relationship between youth and crime/violence'. One of the strongest criticisms of the idea that gangs cause crime was made by Sullivan (2006). During an unprecedented rise in reported US gang membership in the 1990s, youth violence in fact decreased sharply (Harrell 2005).

The link between gangs and criminality is widely supported and a large body of evidence exists which shows that gangs are frequently involved in many types of criminal behaviour. In particular, Brandt and Russell (2002: 25) argued that research has repeatedly shown in the US that 'the intrinsic nature of gangs promotes violent behaviours' and violence is an important factor in providing access to gang membership. What is more in doubt is the gang-specific nature of members' criminality. This distinction is sometimes referred to as the difference between gang-motivated and gang-affiliated crime (Rosenfeld *et al.* 1999). Individual gang members may engage in specific types of illegal activity such as selling drugs – but this may not be the function or outcome of the gang. This distinction has a measurable impact on our understanding of gang crime: as identified by Maxson and Klein (1990) the rate of Los Angeles gang homicides was half as great or twice as great depending on whether they looked at gang-motivated or gang-affiliated homicide.

Whether gangs cause criminality or are merely units of individuals with a high propensity for criminal behaviour has also been questioned. Many studies verify that gang membership results in an increase in criminal behaviour. Esbensen and Lynskey (2001) found that gang members engaged in more antisocial and criminal behaviour than non-gang members. Bennett and Holloway (2004: 317) identified that gang members committed over five times the number of offences of non-gang members. Gang members were responsible for a fifth of all offences recorded by Sharp *et al.* (2006), even though they comprised only 6 per cent of the study. Other US longitudinal studies have shown that gang membership contributes to offending above and beyond the individual level of propensity (e.g. Seattle Social Development Project – Battin *et al.* 1997; Denver Youth Study – Esbensen and Huizinga 1993; Rochester Youth Development Study – Thornberry *et al.* 1993; and the National Evaluation of the Gang Resistance Education and Training (GREAT) programme – Esbensen *et al.* 2001). Perhaps the strongest evidence comes from the study by Esbensen and Huizinga (1993) which showed that gang members committed 2–3 times more delinquency than non-gang offenders, and members committed more crime during periods of gang membership than at times when they were not gang members.

UK research identifies that gangs are more criminal than non-gang members and while most offence types have been recorded at some point, there is some consensus on the common types of offending gang members are involved in. Sharp *et al.* (2006) found that the most common UK gang offences involved drug sales or use and antisocial behaviour. Involvement in more serious offences were reported less often (34 per cent) but still remained considerably higher and more frequent than those of non-gang youths (13 per cent). Gang members were significantly more likely than non-gang youths to be involved in 'core offences',[1] (63 per cent compared to 26 per cent of non-gang youths) although weapons were relatively uncommon (only 4 per cent had carried a gun) (Sharp *et al.* 2006). Smith and Bradshaw (2005) identified similar types of gang criminality and found female gang members were involved in more prolific offending than non-gang males and females. Gang members in the Communities that Care (CtC) (2005) study were more likely to have a previous arrest than non-gang members and most commonly reported engaging in vandalism, carrying a knife or other weapon, drug use or sales. Bennett and Holloway (2004: 317) reported that gang members were more likely to report engaging in criminality (for example higher rates of weapon and gun possession) and violence in the previous 12 months (Bennett and

Holloway 2004). Bullock and Tilley (2002: 37) found gangs to be territorial and heavily involved in crime and violence (half admitted to carrying guns). With the exception of a small number of high-profile inner-city gangs, UK gang criminality appears to follow Klein's (2001) 'cafeteria-style'[2] offending – it being chronic rather than serious (Maher 2007).

Patterns of gang crime

The major gaps in official and academic research make it extremely difficult to assess the number of gangs in the UK. Much of what we understand about the nature and extent of gangs comes from the media and popular culture. To date there has been no national survey to record the prevalence of gang membership. Curry (2001: 90) reminds us that 'until agreement is achieved on defining gangs, gang-related crime, and the like, gang proliferation estimates remain just that – estimates'. Therefore, caution must be exerted when looking at the gang patterns and trends reported.

US researchers have measured gang prevalence since Thrasher's (1963) study in the US during the 1930s, which identified 1,313 youth gangs. National prevalence estimates began in the US in 1975 when Miller reported 55,000 youth gang members. By 2007, this increased to 788,000 gang members and 27,000 gangs (Egley and O'Donnell 2009). In England, the first attempt to count gangs failed to find any (Downes 1966), while early studies of gangs in Scotland identified a small number of them (Patrick 1973).

Journalistic research has helped to fill the void in UK gang research (although the accuracy of the information and methodological validity is unknown). Thompson (2003) claimed in 2003 that up to 30,000 youth gang members existed in England and Wales, while Lawrence (2003) suggested that geographically 'every British city and town has its roving gangs'. Academic research estimates have located gangs in a small number of UK cities (e.g. London, Manchester, Birmingham, Glasgow), and estimate a minimum of 20,000 gang members in England and Wales (Bennett and Holloway 2004). Bullock and Tilley (2002) identified four prominent gangs in Manchester in 2002 and Mares (2001) identified two formative groups (Gooch and Doddington) a year earlier in the same location. Research conducted in various parts of London in 2008 found 172 youth gangs (Pitts 2008). Six per cent of youths aged 10–19 were classed as members of a delinquent youth group in the first national school survey in England and Wales (Sharp et al. 2006). Twenty per cent of 13 year olds and 5 per cent of 17 year olds surveyed in Edinburgh reported belonging to a gang (Smith and Bradshaw 2005). Most recent estimates from a report by the government think-tank the Centre for Social Justice (CSJ) (2009) have suggested there are up to 50,000 gang members in the UK.

It is difficult to determine whether there are any demographic differences in gang membership and gang behaviour. Maher (2007), for example, noted that males and females engaged in similar types of violence (e.g. assault, territorial combat). However, they tended to commit these offences at different rates and levels of seriousness. There is little known in the UK about the extent to which criminality varies by age or ethnicity. Hayden (2008) concluded that 'real gangs', who had an older membership, were more likely to use 'unacceptable levels of violence'. The Youth Justice Board (YJB) (2007: 14) concluded that: 'while there are gangs that use serious violence and threats to assert control locally (often in competition with similar groups), these are more likely to involve young adults than 10 to 17 year olds'. Most US studies point towards ethnic minority gangs as the most criminal and violent; however, this focus on ethnicity is not widely replicated in European studies (Gemert et al. 2008). That said, three UK studies which identified high rates of serious violent crime and weapon use also identified large numbers of ethnic minority gang members. Ethnic minority arrestees made up 34 per cent of gang members (Bennett and Holloway 2004) and both Mares (2001) and Bullock and Tilley (2002) identified a majority of black gang members among their violent gangs.

Characteristics of gang crime

It is widely suggested that gangs are identifiable by their willingness to engage more frequently in more serious types of criminality (Fagan 1996; Moore 1978; Short and Strodtbeck 1965; Spergel 1990). In particular, certain types of crimes have been closely linked to gangs. Violent crime, territorial disputes and drug sales are frequently identified as specific gang offences in the US. In the UK, the increase in weapon use, territorial disputes, youth homicide and drug distribution has been tied to a rise in youth gangs. A selection of gang offences is discussed in detail below: homicide, weapon use and ownership, territorial disputes, in-group violence and core offences (including drug sale).

Gang homicide

The double homicide of two teenage girls in Birmingham in 2003 brought national attention to the link between UK gangs and homicide (Morris and Hopkins 2003). Media reports on youth homicide reached a high point in 2008 as gang and youth violence left 26 young males dead in London alone (Laville 2008). Nonetheless, the UK gang homicide rate is significantly lower than that in the US (Bullock and Tilley 2002). Rosenfeld et al. (1999) found between a quarter and a third of all US homicides since the early 1990s were gang related. Maxson et al. (1985) established that gang homicides differed from non-gang homicide in terms of the more public setting, the higher number of participants and the presence of firearms. Additionally, gang motivated homicide differed from gang-affiliated and non-gang homicide in that participants were closer in age and involved significantly less illicit drug use/sales (Rosenfeld et al. 1999). Maxson and Klein (1990: 10) conducted a survey to assess the number of homicides involving gang members. Among the 792 cities reporting gang activity, 60 per cent reported no gang homicides, 12 cities made up 40 per cent of reported homicides, while 80 per cent identified fewer than 10 incidents. Similar findings are evident in the UK with the majority of 'gang'-related homicides and gangs located in three cities: London, Manchester and Birmingham. As identified in the UK, the increase in US youth homicide has been attributed to increased access to weapons (specifically firearms) (Goldstein 1991; Howell 1999).

Weapons

In general, firearm offences in England and Wales peaked at 24,094 in 2003/04 and have fallen since (Povery *et al.* 2008). Conversely, fatal injury from non-air weapons rose from 49 (all injury was 864) to 77 (all injury 3,856) during the period 1998–2005 (Coleman *et al.* 2006). More recently, a decrease in firearm offences and injury from firearm offences has been reported by the Home Office (HO) (2008a). Since 2000, one-fifth of those convicted of unlawfully carrying a knife were young people aged 10 to 17 (HMSO 2006). Additionally, the number of under 16 year olds admitted to hospital with serious stab wounds has risen by 89 per cent over the past five years (Bennett 2008).

A number of UK studies have linked gang membership with the possession of firearms and other weapons (Bennett and Holloway 2004; Bullock and Tilley 2002; Hales *et al.* 2006). According to the CSJ gang members are three times more likely to carry a weapon than non-gang members (Bennett 2008). In a study involving 18–30 year olds convicted for firearm offences in three hot spots of recorded gun crime, almost half of interviewees reported they had been in a 'gang' or 'crew' (Hales *et al.* 2006). Bullock and Tilley (2002) identified an estimated 60 per cent of all shootings involved gang members as victim, offender or both. Eighty percent of deaths were a result of gang shootings, as were 70 per cent of the most serious offences. Additionally, those aged between 16 and 25 years experienced 53 per cent of all crimes involving firearms and were most likely to be the victims of the most serious firearm offences. The serious nature of weapon use identified appears as grave as but less frequent than many US gang studies (Yablonsky 1997). School surveys and official statistics portray a less serious but active problem among younger youths more generally (not specifically gangs). CtC (2005) found London pupils aged 11–15 years claiming to have carried a gun (6 per cent), knife (10 per cent) or some other type of weapon (7 per cent) in the previous 12 months. The Offending Crime and Justice Survey (OCJS) found that 7 per cent of 16-17 year olds have carried a knife and 1 per cent carried a gun in the last 12 months (Wilson *et al.* 2006). Nearly one in five 11–15 year olds in London reported that they could 'easily' get hold of a replica gun or airgun and 8 per cent said they could 'easily' access a handgun (CtC 2005).

The first experience of firearms for the majority of interviewees identified by Hales *et al.* (2006) was usually with criminal friends or with airgun and BB gun use (25 per cent). The most common reason for carrying a gun was self-defence (CtC 2005). This may be explained by the fact that once a youth becomes a victim of a shooting, the risk of repeat victimisation greatly increases (Bullock and Tilley 2002). Also, the similarities between those shot and those doing the shooting suggest fear of becoming a victim of a weapon offence is realistic for some gang youths. That those most likely to offend were also the most likely to become a victim was recognised across both gender (males were three times more likely to be a victim and all homicide victims were male) and ethnicity (ethnic minority youths were five times more likely to be victims of murder, five times more likely to be victims of attempted murder and almost twice as likely to be victims of serious wounding than white youths) (Bullock and Tilley 2002: 10). Although weapons were common in all sites in Aldridge and Medina's (2007) study, gangs in the predominantly black locality were linked with firearm offences, while the white gang sites were more likely to involve physical fights. Limited use of lethal weapons among white gang members was also found by Maher (2007).

US research establishes that weapon use is facilitated by the gang; while gun ownership increases with gang membership, it decreases again upon departure (Bjerregaard and Lizotte 1995). Drive-by[3] shootings, one of the most publicised means of gang violence, is a good example of a gang-specific weapon offence. As documented in the US, drive-bys tend not to result in a high rate of homicide but have a significant symbolic purpose in the gang (e.g. to deter rival gangs, to build status and reputation, for revenge). Hales *et al.* (2006) suggest the UK is developing *a complex gun culture* (instrumental and symbolic), which differs from the traditional instrumental criminal gun culture. This change is facilitated by gang culture, illegal drugs and the ascendancy of criminal role models.

Territorial disputes

Out-group conflict has a significant role in the formation and development of gangs. Thrasher (1963) and Sheldon (1898) both identified the natural progression from street group to gang under the threat of adversarial relations with out-groups. Researchers (Kintrea *et al.* 2008) recently documented a strong territorial instinct among Scottish youth – often passed down through generations – which is thought to encourage gangs to control and protect territory with violence. Many British cities have a history of endemic conflicts between rival groups in defence of territory, for example, among Glasgow gangs (Patrick 1973), Manchester Scuttler gangs (Davies 1998) and London Hooligan gangs (Pearson 1983). Unlike US territorial battles, ethnic conflict is not as significant a characteristic of UK rivalries (Aldridge and Medina 2007). Territorial disputes, which commonly occur in public and social venues such as nightclubs, are often related to status and respect; the presence of weapons can make even trivial disputes result in a fatality (Hales *et al.* 2006). Technology and the media facilitate organised encounters between gangs (Maher 2007). Known as 'netbanging' in the US, gangs are increasingly likely to use the Internet to recruit members, communicate their activities, lay down challenges and organise combat with rivals (Young 2009).

US gangs are identified as conflict-oriented when violent encounters with rival gangs are a major focus of group activity and a major source of status within the gang (Short and Strodtbeck 1965). As Thrasher (1963) noted, gangs developed through strife and flourish on conflict, thus out-group violence is documented as integral to life in the gang; it enhances cohesion and status (Decker and Van Winkle 1996) and provides a constant 'myth system' which stimulates the violent nature of the gang (Klein 1971). Loftin suggests 'contagion' – the subsequent acts of retaliation – can explain the spikes or sudden growth of violent conflict in gangs (1984, cited in Decker 1996). The reciprocal nature of territorial violence may be important for explaining a spike in UK gang violence and weapon use, as gang members arm themselves in the belief that other gangs are doing the same.

In-group violence

Violence among gang members has been identified in a number of UK gang studies (Maher 2007). Bullock and Tilley (2002) observed that some Manchester gangs formed as a result of in-group conflict. Aldridge and Medina (2007) identified jealousy and debt as significant sources of in-group conflict. Gangs are 'theatres of hostility' (Davies 1998: 349) in which in-group violence plays an important role. Gang membership is associated with gang-specific violent rituals – such as 'jumping in' (initiation), 'hazing'[4] and 'jumping out'. Ritualised violence serves many functions in the life of the gang (Decker and Van Winkle 1996), such as increasing solidarity, integrating members into the norms of the gang, conferring masculinity and status to members and reinforcing the gang identity, regulating violent behaviour and member's willingness to use it. Violent rituals are largely documented in US research. In some cases initiation has involved committing serious offences such as a drive-by shooting, homicide and gang-rape (documented female member's initiation – Decker and Van Winkle 1996). Over 90 per cent of Decker and Van Winkle's (1996) sample participated in a 'jumping in' ritual, similar numbers to those identified by Vigil (1988) and Hagedorn (1988). UK research found local (Huddersfield) gang initiation involved 'bagging a student' – in which a new member would attack and steal from students (Asthana 2008). Initiation rituals among two gangs were also recorded by Maher (2007), which involved new members engaging in combat with the 'best gang fighter'. Unlike out-group violence, rules reportedly regulate in-group violent encounters.

Core offences

US and UK gang research shows that gangs engage in a long list of core offences including violence, burglary, criminal damage, intimidation, vandalism, theft, vehicle crime and drug use and sales (Klein 2001; Sharp et al. 2006). Bennett and Holloway (2004) found UK gang members were more likely than non-gang members to have engaged in car theft, robbery and drug supply offences in the previous 12 months. These findings are consistent with US findings on gang criminality, specifically that gangs do not appear to specialise in a particular offence. Nonetheless, of these offences, drug sales and distribution has become synonymous with the organised US gang image (Padilla 1992). The link between gangs and drugs is unclear (Esbenson and Huizinga 1993; Klein et al. 1991; Maxson 1995). US research suggests gang involvement in drug sales is less organised and serious in nature than originally thought. Klein et al. (1991: 623) argue that gang members may become inner-city drug dealers; however, this 'connection seems in most respects to have been considerably overstated'. Drug distribution in gangs, like other core offences, is linked to opportunity rather than organisation. UK gangs are found to be involved in drug-related offences, but as only one of a spectrum of offences (Bullock and Tilley 2002; Bennett and Holloway 2004). In fact, drug sales have been reported as predominantly gang-affiliated rather than gang-motivated (Aldridge and Medina 2007; Maher 2007). There is little evidence in the UK that gang violence is linked to control of the drug market. Thus Yablonsky (1997) suggests lethal gang violence is more frequently turf-related than drug-related. Drug use, rather than sales, is commonly identified in UK research, with cannabis, other recreational drugs and alcohol consumption most prevalent among gangs (Aldridge and Medina 2007; Bennett and Holloway 2004; Maher 2007). Research confirms that gang members are more likely to engage in drug use than non-gang members; however, US research identifies more prolific involvement in serious drug use (crack, cocaine, heroin) (Fagan 1990), while UK research reports gang members were less likely than non-gang members to engage in serious drug use (Bennett and Holloway 2004).

Explaining gang crime

Theories of gang criminality span a number of dimensions and factors. There are several ways of explaining gang crime. It can be understood in terms of the background factors that might generate a general disposition to offend or join peer group subcultures or it can be explained in terms of the factors that lead to the commission of specific crimes. In the following section, I will outline only those explanations that relate to the motivation to commit the particular offences of in-group and out-group violence, territorial rivalries and weapon use. These theories identify the ways in which gangs promote violence and crime through specific gang functions and the risky routine activities of the gang.

Subcultural theory

The subcultural theory of violence is a useful perspective from which to examine both male and female gang violence. The influence of the code of the streets, the code of honour, crisis masculinity and machismo can be identified in UK gang research. Under the code of the street, gang members are eager to demonstrate their intolerance for interpersonal transgressions lest they too become targets (Anderson 1999). Acceptance of this code is evident in the wider society, evidenced by youths' reported exposure to violent events (Aldridge and Medina 2007) and their inherited normalisation and accepted dislike for outsiders (Groebel and Hinde 1989) and mainstream authority (Anderson 1999). Female gang members reinforce the 'code' and masculinity as witnesses and storytellers, through the expectation that male members defend their honour and through their central role in organising rival conflict (Maker 2007, forthcoming). The code of the street prescribes violence as the means to resolve conflict among male gang members and enforces avoidance of mainstream conflict resolution, such as agencies of the criminal justice system. Demonstration of the code is apparent in the 'wall of silence' which often characterises UK gang homicides (Attewill and Tran 2007). Although levels of US lethal violence exceed UK experiences, many of the rules found in these violent incidents are related to the same idea – a code of honour (Blok 2001). Rule books and gang tenets are commonly reported in US research, similar to the European *Code Duello* (duelling rule book). In contrast to the US, some UK gang studies have reported that local codes of honour and traditional values require limited weapon use in violent encounters (Aldridge and Medina 2007; Maher 2007) with masculinity demonstrated by physical prowess rather than the ability to use a gun.

Traditional working-class values (toughness and status) are adopted by many youths. However, dislocation from culture, community and traditional roles means there are fewer opportunities for males, in particular, to develop and retain honour and respect – leading to a crisis of masculinity. In the absence of traditional means, the need to establish masculinity, physical prowess and toughness as a form of social capital is evident among youths (see Messerschmidt 1993 (male honour); Polk 1994). Gang membership can provide marginalised and alienated youths with honour and respect as the gang confers its status to even the weakest members under its 'halo' of masculinity. While gang members look to their peers to grant them manhood, masculinity is not a consistent variable and must constantly be proved for others. Machismo (performing the gang identity through body language) is a useful concept for understanding how gang members construct masculinity and develop status, power and control within the gang (Yablonsky 1997). Machismo establishes a direct link between violent conflict (against hostile forces) and the objective reality of the gang, thereby reinforcing the use of violent processes. For example, Klein's concept of 'tipping points' may explain why UK youths (adopting the gang persona) must display and defend their masculinity as they begin to see themselves as a group that requires violence. Lethal weapon use and ownership is clearly part of the US subculture of violence, affirming the exaggerated view of maleness and honour in gangs (Wolfgang and Ferracuti 1967). This is reinforced by storytelling and myth-making (gangsta rap lyrics are a good example of this) (Horowitz 1983). Machismo is a useful concept for understanding how gang members establish patterns to control and dominate female and other male members (often through in-group violence), through notions of honour and respect within the gang (Bessant and Watts 1998).

Situational explanations

The routine activities of gang members can expose them to situational factors which exacerbate gang criminality and violence – for example, weapon availability, the presence of alcohol and drugs and gang rivalry. The availability of weapons has repeatedly been identified as a factor in the growth of gang violence (Goldstein 1991; Howell 1999). The real or apparent availability of weapons can affect gang violence in three ways: fear of victimisation can result in youths joining gangs and arming themselves; a change in the cultural norms controlling weapon ownership may facilitate use; and lethal violence may escalate due to weapon use. Victimisation and offending emerge out of closely linked processes and interactions. In fact the experience of being a victim of crime or delinquency is one of the most powerful predictors of offending in 12 or 13 year olds (Smith and Bradshaw 2005). Estimates indicate that US firearm ownership is eight to ten times the rate of that in the UK (Graduate Institute of International Studies, Geneva 2003). In 2000, 75,685 people (27/100,000) suffered non-fatal firearm gunshot injuries in the US (Federal Bureau of Investigation 2001) compared with 3,203 in England and Wales. However, comparisons between weapon ownership in the US and Canada and the lethal use of firearms suggests that weapon use may be less about availability and more about cultural norms around the use of weapons. The traditional culture of violence apparent in the UK – winning respect from an honourable fight – while promoting violence on one level, acts as an inhibitor for more lethal types of violence and weapon use among certain age groups. However, as masculinity is constantly reconstructed, this norm may reverse (as is the case in the US). In particular, youths internalise the growing threat reported by UK media of gang-related weapon fatalities and may choose to acquire weapons for 'self-defence' (Maher and Williamson 2009). The use of weapons among youths is clearly influenced by the belief that other groups have weapons. Once weapon ownership increases, so too does the risk of verbal or physical encounters escalating to lethal violence.

Alcohol use among youths is commonly linked to youth offences and may explain both in-group and out-group violence. Monahan and Klassen (1982) identify extensive literature which indicates that alcohol consumption is associated with the occurrence of serious crime, particularly violent offences. Alcohol can be used to facilitate machismo as youths use substances in 'doing masculinity' as a face-saving excuse for any weakness displayed (Brookman 2005). Alcohol acted as a dis-inhibitor and confidence builder during gang criminality and violence. For example, Maher (2007) identified increased alcohol consumption prior to engaging in rival gang encounters and participation in core offences. Although UK youth gangs are seldom involved in the control of the drug market, both US and UK research identifies a significant change in youth gangs in localities influenced by the drug market (Mares 2001 in Manchester; Padilla 1992 in Chicago; Decker and Van Winkle 1996 in St Louis). Involvement in drug sales heightens the risk of gang violence and victimisation as members' routine activities expose them to volatile and unpredictable situations. Drug use in the gang strengthens cohesion and adds entertainment to what is often a tedious existence. Psychopharmacological-driven crime may result from the buzz (core offences) or paranoia (violence) that is often associated with drug use (Goldstein 1989).

The transition from friendship networks to youth gangs is commonly associated with threats from rival groups; simply, gangs develop and thrive in the presence of rival gangs (Hagedorn 1998). Decker and Van Winkle (1996) argue that the central role of violence in the gang is often motivated by the need for protection from such real or perceived threats. One UK city with a developing gang problem points to the fear of victimisation as a significant issue; 65 per cent of youths aged 10–15 years reported being worried about the threat of gangs and 33 per cent were victims of a peer attack (Crimestoppers 2002). Ethnic and immigrant rivalries often appear in gang research (in the

UK, Europe and US) as these groups may feel a particular need to protect themselves and their identity from 'foreign' groups (see social comparison theory – Festinger 1954). In the UK, area rivalries appear to account for much out-group gang violence (Kintrea *et al.* 2008; Maher 2007) as gangs compete for control over resources (females, drug distribution and facilities) and power (status, reputation, identity). Rivalries, similar to US territoriality, are a quintessential group process, central to the development of gang cohesion. High-cohesion in a gang can lead to deindividuation – a feeling of anonymity – which is linked to increased aggression and violence (Festinger *et al.* 1952; Wyrick 2002). Rival gang encounters provide a favourable environment for gang members to incite and normalise violence and cross thresholds (e.g. gang homicide), under the cover of collective violence. These battles are a display of 'real' masculine virtues, which include risk-taking and the display of physical prowess equivalent to 'real-world' combat.

Responding to gang crime

A number of responses to gangs are evident internationally; strategies often involve a number of different phases. For example, the World Health Organisation (2002) focuses on primary, secondary or tertiary responses. The CJS (2009) identifies the immediate response, medium-term response and long-term approach. The US study by Spergel *et al.* (1994) focused on community organisation, suppression, organisational change/development, opportunity provision and social intervention.

Typically, most responses will fall into one of three categories: prevention, intervention or suppression, which are discussed below. *Prevention* generally comprises social programmes that aim to prevent the formation of gangs (anti-gang) and gang behaviour (anti-gun, anti-violence). This can include targeted prevention which focuses on 'at risk' youths and communities in order to prevent gangs from developing in high-risk areas. *Intervention* involves community and social projects aimed at working with gangs after they have developed, to reduce crime by targeting problem behaviours and encouraging members to leave the gang. *Suppression* is based on targeting serious and chronic offenders and removing the problem from the community through legislation and police intervention. In combination, these responses focus either on restricting the development of gangs or on restricting the criminal behaviour of gangs. The most successful programmes, it is believed, are those which combine multiple approaches and emphasise multi-agency involvement (e.g. the police, community, school, family, prisoners, ex-gang members, youth workers, peers and health practitioners) (Butler 2004; Young *et al.* 2007). Examples of programmes which feature each of these responses are detailed below.

Prevention

Gang crime prevention is often school and community based but national in scope. UK programmes are frequently focused on the negative behaviour rather than the gang itself. The UK government introduced 'Be Safe', a national crime programme to tackle youth involvement in knife crime through educating youths on the dangers of weapons, raising the age at which a knife can be purchased from 16 to 18, increasing police methods of knife detection and implementing tougher sentences and prosecution of offenders (Home Office 2008b). '2 Smart' is an award winning multi-agency initiative by the Essex Police that focuses on alcohol, drugs, bullying and knife issues. The combination of the '2 Smart Roadshow', 'Westley's Weapons Awareness' and Safer Schools Officers delivers a formidable message on the hazards of the aforementioned risky behaviours to 11–12 year olds in schools around Essex. These prevention programmes, like most UK programmes aimed at gang crime, are in their infancy. It is impossible to comment on how effective they are.

US programme evaluations suggest that curriculum-based gang prevention initiatives, such as GREAT, effect modest short-term change, especially among high-risk youths (Esbensen *et al.* 2001). GREAT is a school-based strategy implemented in 1992 to minimise delinquency and violence and to prevent and reduce gang membership. Delivered by the police, this cognitive approach consists of eight lessons teaching youths life skills and problem-solving strategies to resist violence, gangs and offending. Like 'Leap' (discussed below) the programme challenges attitudes by presenting facts and offering solutions to youths. Evidence suggests there is an impact upon certain types of crimes but not past or present membership of gangs. Essentially, participants are as likely as non-participants to become gang members in the long-term (Esbensen and Osgood 1999). Prevention measures are unlikely to be successful long-term if used on their own. Situational measures such as target hardening may displace the problem rather than resolve it, while social prevention, as identified above, will have limited impact so long as the social and community conditions conducive to gang formation are not addressed.

Intervention

Intervention programmes involving local and national pressure groups, offering education, alternative activities and opportunities to 'at risk' youths or current gang members, have developed across the UK in reaction to gang crime. Intervention is identified by Huff (1996) as particularly important between members' first arrest (often property crime) and their subsequent involvement in more serious offences – this period lasts about 1.5 to 2 years. Many initiatives work on the premise that the problem is not belonging to the gang, but the negative behaviours commonly linked to the gang. A good example of this is the conflict resolution programme central to the UK project Leap Confronting Conflict (known as 'Leap' 2008). Leap has five schemes targeted at different age groups, youths involved in different levels of offending and gang membership and those who work closely with gangs: gangs and territorialism, the Quarrel Shop, Peerlink, Confronting Conflict in Schools and leadership skills. Leap is a cognitive approach which challenges the normative system of the gang that prescribes violence as the only way to communicate. The overall aim is to 'enable young people to explore the creative potential of conflicts in their personal and social lives; learning new approaches to conflict through structured group work, and rehearsing alternatives to violence using enactive, experiential learning methods' and to train adults who work with gang youths (Ofsted 2004: 2).

A lack of social opportunity and high levels of social disorganisation often characterise the communities in which gangs develop (Spergel *et al.* 1994). Intervention strategies often focus on improving communities' resources and opportunities through multi-agency work and projects. Disarm Trust (BBC 2005) was set up in 2003 in the aftermath of two youth gang homicides. Initially the programme used music events to spread an anti-gun message but has since used £1.2 million recovered from criminals to support community groups like the Street Pastors, Bringing Hope, Young Disciples and First Class Youth Network to work together to reduce the high levels of social exclusion through poor education, lack of formal qualifications, poor health and lack of employment opportunities which typify the area (BBC 2005). School- and community-based projects such as the Waltham Forest Gangs Intervention Project provide education and intervention strategies through outreach youth engagement programmes via a mobile youth venue. They provide an accredited music workshop, self-development programmes, mediation programmes, peer or adult mentors from the community and information, advice and guidance (London Borough of Waltham Forest 2009; see also Pitts 2008). The STEPS programme, which helps youths gain work in the construction industry, AWAC, which targets inter-generational and inter-ethnic understanding of crime, and Defending Da Hood, which focuses on the experience of young people at the 'hard end', are examples of the intervention strategies run. Many US projects similarly focus on education and opportunity – such as remedial education for targeted youth gang members and job orientation, training, placement and mentoring for older youth gang members (Spergel *et al.* 1994). It is difficult to infer the success of UK intervention strategies as very few programmes have been evaluated.

Suppression

The political and criminal justice system approach to gangs in the UK is to use the more general suppression methods used to control general youth offending. Some of the most recent efforts include: increased stop and searches to take weapons off the street, harsher penalties for those caught, increased use of ASBOs (Anti-Social Behaviour Orders) and parenting orders, enforcement of existing police powers and legislation to remove youths from the streets at night, public consultation to identify if community sentences work and provision of youth offending team workers in police custody (HO 2008b). The recently implemented Policing and Crime Act 2009 introduces gang injunctions and other restrictions to England and Wales. A further injunction has been proposed for 14–17 year olds (HO 2009).

In addition to the above, the UK has some of the most restrictive firearm laws in Europe and indeed the world (Hales *et al.* 2006). Nonetheless, the link between youth homicide, weapon use and gangs has led to a resurgence in the effort to prevent weapon availability. A UK firearms amnesty in 2003, for example, resulted in 43,908 guns and 1,039,358 rounds of ammunition being surrendered to the police (Hales *et al.* 2006). The Anti-Social Behaviour Act 2003 has brought about tighter controls on air weapon use among youths and the Criminal Justice Act 2003 aims to introduce a five-year minimum mandatory sentence for the illegal possession of prohibited firearms.

In response to changing perceptions of gang membership in the UK, a number of multi-agency responses have emerged, such as the Manchester Multi-Agency Gang Strategy (MMAGS) developed by Manchester City Council (2009) and the Not Another Drop (NAD) (Metropolitan Police n.d.) programme in London. The MMAGS is largely modelled on the successful US Boston Ceasefire (see below), which reduced violent crime by approximately 50 per cent and 'reclaimed the streets' from gangs within two years of implementation in 1995. Recently, the Tackling Gangs Action Programme (TGAP) was set up in Birmingham, Liverpool, London and Manchester (these cities account for over half of all gun crime in the UK) to tackle serious gangs and firearm-related injuries (Dawson 2008). Overall, gang suppression measures have had mixed results – although they can effectively remove gang members and decrease gang-related crime, the impact is often short term. Essentially gang suppression alone fails to address the significant underlying conditions in which gangs emerge.

In the US, there have been many more programmes aimed at controlling gang violence. The Boston Ceasefire intervention strategy involved a partner-ship between criminal justice officials and academics to prevent gang violence and homicide through focused law enforcement deterrence. It involved a multi-agency and multi-level response: engagement with gangs to elicit information and provide diversionary activities, enhancing community relations and support for the scheme and coordinating highly publicised crackdowns on specific behaviours (e.g. possession or use of knives and firearms, harassment and serious assaults). Reed and Decker (2002) identify that the programme's combination of theory-driven evaluation, careful attention to data collection, concern for measurement issues, use of a large and diverse sample and attention to the conceptual issues facilitated the great success of the programme. Another successful gang violence reduction programme, the Little Village Project: A Community Approach to the Gang Problem (Spergel and Grossman 1997) demonstrated effective control and reduction of serious gang violence through suppression in addition to other key interrelated strategies (e.g. community mobilisation, social intervention, opportunities provision and organisational development). The four-year programme targeted both chronic and emerging gangs with the aid of former gang members, some of whom were police tactical officers and community youth workers. Overall, the project successfully reduced gang crime and violence, in particular among serious and older gang members (Spergel and Grossman 1997). Further evaluation highlighted that this success more specifically affected violent gang members rather than general gang or community life, partially due to the poor programme implementation and problems establishing successful inter-agency collaborations (Spergel *et al.* 2003).

Discussion and conclusion

Three issues in particular arise from the discussion around gang crime. First, one of the pressing issues confronting UK gang research is how gangs and gang crime should be defined. Second, systematic and national collection of data on gangs and gang crime is required; simply, not enough is known about UK gangs. Third, despite the absence of a universally applied gang definition and the constraints of a paucity of data, official bodies and agencies are increasingly reacting to the gang problem. How do they determine which response will be effective for dealing with gangs and gang crime? Each of these issues is interlinked, and focus on one issue alone will provide only limited understanding of and responses to the gang problem.

There are many ways to define a gang (see Ball and Curry 1995 for an in-depth discussion). In the US, rather than openly disregarding prior research and definitions, researchers have simply devised their own gang definition based on their experiences. The resulting quagmire of definitions has limited data collection and comparison and the subsequent responses to gangs. The influence of the definer and context of the research inevitably impacts upon the definition. For example, gang definitions can be either overly narrow (Miller 1982) or broad (Interpol 1965, cited in Hazlehurst and Hazlehurst 1998). A similar problem is evident in definitions of gang crime. Some definitions only require the offender to be a member of a gang, while others require the offender to be committing the crime for or as part of the gang.

Regrettably, although perhaps unavoidably, similar definitional problems are evident in the UK. The media, who, as aforementioned, contribute considerably to what we know about British gangs, rarely identify a definition and confusingly refer to many different types of groups (e.g. youths, adult criminals) as gangs. The Eurogang definition has been adopted by some UK definers (e.g. Maher 2007). Sharp et al. (2006) use the definition with additional requirements (gang members must have offended together in the past 12 months). The CSJ (2009) has recently built upon this definition with the additional characteristics of gangs being territorial, involved in gang rivalries and having an identifying structural feature. It is worth considering that each of these definitions refer to variations of the same thing.

More recently in the US (Klein 2001) and UK (Hallsworth and Young 2004; Maher 2007; Pitts 2008), typologies have been developed to refocus the definitional issue and account for the variations in gangs observed. Typologies consist of mutually exclusive, distinct categories based on several dimensions, such as behaviour (delinquency and street presence) and characteristics (organisation, structure and level of development). It is commonly found that gangs, for example, develop from friendship groups (Thrasher 1963; CSJ 2009). What promotes this change? Often the structure remains similar (fluid but durable) but the behaviour changes. Youth gangs exist at one end of a continuum of youth collectives, the continuum being composed of levels of disruptive or criminal behaviour and group characteristics (Klein et al. 2001). The development of groups into gangs lies at the heart of Maher's (2007) typology, with each stage representing different levels of development and as a result different responses to gangs.

The dearth of UK gang research is glaring, especially in light of the prolific sensationalised media coverage and the general acceptance that the UK has a gang problem. What is clear from the limited studies available is that youth gangs exist in a small number of UK cities, with inner-city areas presenting a particular problem. However, existing studies are largely restricted to large cities in England, usually narrowly focused on extremely violent youth groups. The Chrome Project (Manchester), for example, is commendable as it involved systematic collection of information on the nature of the gang problem prior to formulating practical proposals to deal with gangs (Bullock and Tilley 2002). However, this project is area specific, aimed at 'high-profile' cases and therein limited in its impact on the national problem.

In order to adequately address the issue of gangs and gang crime in the UK, systematic research is required which uses comparative and rigorous methodologies for collecting information. Data collection must involve both depth (e.g. youth and expert interviews and observation) and breadth (e.g. school and expert surveys) in order to establish accurately the prevalence and nature of UK gangs. Caution should be taken to avoid common stereotypes evident in many gang studies. In particular, the participation of girls and white youths in gangs needs to be explored, while the focus on particular criminal behaviours (drugs and weapons) needs to be expanded upon. As demonstrated in this chapter, the information available on gang crime is largely American in origin or extracted piecemeal from non-gang UK studies. That said, both the Edinburgh Study of Youth Transitions and Crime (Smith and Bradshaw 2005) and the Offending Crime and Justice Survey (Sharp *et al*. 2006) must be recognised for their efforts to collect longitudinal and broad data on gang members.

There is an urgent need to determine an effective response to gangs and negative gang behaviours. In May 2008 the UK government recommended a range of approaches for tackling gangs (TGAP) (Dawson 2008). The report – more of a guide than definitive strategy – is similar to the recommendations of the US Office of Juvenile Justice and Delinquency Prevention (OJJDP). The OJJDP recommend conducting some form of research before initiating any project to ensure 'a comprehensive and systematic assessment of the gang problem' (Burch and Chemers 1997: n.p.). This can ascertain the nature and extent of the problem and identify specific targets for local agency and inter-agency work. The CSJ (2009) criticises the 'inadequacy of central and local government responses' to gangs, for their focus on suppression rather than social influences, failure to support grass roots charities tackling gangs and failure to identify and support a long-term approach to gangs. In contrast, the CSJ suggested a national response to gangs with over 190 policy recommendations focusing on the causes of social breakdown responsible for gang development. The 'blueprint' emphasises the need to address '(1) the immediate response, (2) medium-term proposals for building trust and positive relations between the police and young people and (3) a long-term approach to prevent future generations of young people from becoming gang-involved' (CJS 2009: 28). These recommendations result from a national consultation with charities, social enterprises, academics, practioners and policy-makers.

A large number of local and grass root gang prevention and intervention initiatives are evident in the UK (CJS 2009), although the majority have not been evaluated. It is crucial to evaluate rigorously the various gang prevention strategies that are being suggested for implementation (e.g. in the Policing and Crime Bill), in order to direct resources towards the areas that need them most and have the best chance of success. For example, the majority of gang research suggests that most youths join gangs during adolescence – intervention at this level could stop gang membership or prevent more serious gang behaviours from developing. Early intervention necessitates identifying the environments in which gangs develop. Schools, for example, should play an important part in identifying and responding to gangs (e.g. the GREAT programme). Yet recent research by the National Association of Schoolmasters and Union of Women Teachers (NASUWT) found that schools were more likely to conceal or avoid acknowledging the gang problem to avoid being stigmatised (Goddard 2009).

Overall, evaluations of successful American gang strategies identify that efforts should be focused on local problem analysis as the gang problem is often area specific. Clear management and strong leadership are necessary to implement successful strategies. Importance is also placed on investment in protective factors (e.g. resources, education, job orientation, training, placement, family, community) while reducing risk factors (e.g. access to weapons or drugs). Finally, successful gang strategies should focus on the problematic behaviour rather than the affiliation to the gang (Butler 2004); the gang can be an integral part of the community and an essential part of youth development. As Pearson (1995) argues, the gang is a broader concept than the delinquent group and criminality is a broader concept than the gang.

Selected further reading

While there is plenty of literature available on gangs and gang violence, there is no all-inclusive academic text. For a general overview, the following edited volumes offer the most accessible introduction to the main themes relating to youth gangs in the UK and abroad: *The Eurogang Paradox* (Klein *et al.* 2001), *European Street Gangs and Troublesome Youth Groups* (Decker and Weerman 2005), *The Modern Gang Reader* (Egley *et al.* 2007) and *Street Gangs, Migration and Ethnicity* (Gemert *et al.* 2008). As the definitional debate continues, Ball and Curry's (1995) article provides a useful discussion on defining gangs. An excellent and interesting way to quickly grasp the essence of gang research is through the varied (predominantly US) ethnographic studies of Thrasher (1963), Yablonsky (1967), Hagedorn (1988), Decker and Van Winkle (1996) and Patrick (1973), to name a few.

Gang texts specific to the UK are surprisingly limited: the best to date are Pitts' (2008) informative book based on his research in London and the small, but notable, body of gang literature which appears in journals (such as Bennett and Holloway, 2004, 'Gang membership, drugs and crime in the UK') and research reports (such as 'Groups, gangs and weapons' by Young *et al.* 2007; Aldridge and Medina 2008 'Youth Gangs in an English City' and Bullock and Tilley 2002). Given the scarcity of UK gang literature, the Internet is an important tool for accessing gang literature and research. Particularly informative are the various websites dedicated to understanding gangs, gang violence and gang legalisation – there are many government (www.homeoffice.

gov.uk; http://www.iir.com/nygc/), academic (http://www.gangresearch.net/) and practitioner (http://www.leaplinx.com/) websites. National and local newspapers available online (see the BBC and *The Times*) also provide an accessible and useful source of information on gang-related incidents (historical and current) and initiatives around the UK.

Notes

1 Including assault, burglary, criminal damage, theft, vehicle crime and drug sales.
2 Involvement in an array of offences, often opportunistic rather than organised criminality.
3 Originated in gangs after the Second World War – taken from Japanese soldiers – called japing. One gang drives to another rival gang's turf and pulls up to shoot a target.
4 Hazing – making initiation difficult for new members – usually this act is used to degrade or humiliate 'members'.

References

Aldridge, J. and Medina, J. (2007) *Youth Gangs in an English City: Social Exclusion, Drugs and Violence: Full Research Report*, ESRC End of Award Report, RES-000-23-0615. Swindon: ESRC.

Anderson, E. (1999) *Code of the Street: Decency, Violence and the Moral Life of the Inner City*. New York: W. W. Norton.

Asthana, A. (2008) 'Students fall prey to gang initiation rites', *The Observer*. Available online at: http://www.guardian.co.uk/uk/2008/jul/13/ukcrime.highereducation (accessed 13 July 2008).

Attewill, F. and Tran, M. (2007) 'Police arrest youth over 11-year-old's murder', *Guardian Online*. Online at: http://www.guardian.co.uk/uk/2007/aug/24/ukcrime.ukguns1 (accessed 10 October 2008).

Ball, R. A. and Curry, D. G. (1995) 'The logic of definition in criminology: purposes and methods for defining "gangs"', *Criminology*, 33 (2): 225–45.

Battin, S. B., Hill, K. G., Abbot, R. D., Catalano, R. F. and Hawlins, J. D. (1997) 'The contribution of gang members to delinquency beyond delinquent friends', *Criminology*, 36 (1): 93–115.

BBC (2005) *Community Features: Disarm Trust – It's Time for Change*. Online at: http://www.bbc.co.uk/birmingham/content/articles/2005/07/29/disarm_trust_feature.shtml (accessed 9 March 2008).

Bennett, A. (2008) 'Huge rise in stab wound admissions', *Children and Young People Now*. Online at: http://www.cypnow.co.uk/Archive/862366/Huge-rise-stab-wound-admissions/ (accessed 30 December 2008).

Bennett, T. and Holloway, K. (2004) 'Gang membership, drugs and crime in the UK', *British Journal of Criminology*, 44: 305–23.

Bessant, J. and Watts, R. (1998) 'Media depictions and public discourses on juvenile "gangs" in Melbourne, 1989–1991', in K. M. Hazlehurst and C. Hazlehurst (eds), *Gangs and Youth Subcultures: International Explorations*. New Brunswick, NJ: Transaction Publishers.

Bjerregaard, B. and Lizotte, A. J. (1995) 'Gun ownership and gang membership', *Journal of Criminal Law and Criminology*, 86: 37–58.

Blok, A. (2001) *Honour and Violence*. Cambridge: Polity Press.

Brandt, G. A. and Russell B. (2002) 'Differentiating factors in gang and drug related homicide', *Journal of Gang Research*, 9 (2): 21–40.

Brookman, F. (2005) *Understanding Homicide*. London: Sage Publications.

Bullock, K. and Tilley, N. (2002) *Shootings, Gang and Violent Incidents in Manchester: Developing a Crime Reduction Strategy*. London: Home Office.

Burch, J. H. and Chemers, B. M. (1997) *A Comprehensive Response to America's Youth Gang Problem*, Fact Sheet #40. Washington, DC: Office of Juvenile Justice and Delinquency Prevention.

Butler, G. (2004) *Evidence-Based Approaches to Reducing Gang Violence*, presentation given for Home Office RRT & GOWM. London: Home Office. Available online at: http://www.crimereduction.homeoffice.gov.uk/gp/gpvca06c.ppt (accessed 09 June 2008).

Centre for Social Justice (CSJ) (2009) *Dying to Belong: An In-Depth Review of Street Gangs in Britain*. Online at: http://www.centreforsocialjustice.org.uk/client/downloads/DyingtoBelongEXECUTIVESUMMARY.pdf (accessed 10 March 2009).

Coleman, K., Hird, C. and Povey, D. (eds.) (2006) *Violent Crime Overview, Homicide and Gun Crime 2004/2005* 2nd edn. (Supplementary Volume to Crime in England and Wales 2004/2005). Home Office Statistical Bulletin 02/06. London: Home Office. Available at: http://www.homeoffice.gov.uk/rds/pdfs06/hosb0206.pdf (accessed 10 February 2009).

Communities that Care (CtC) (2005) *Findings from the Safer London Youth Survey 2004*. London: Communities that Care.

Crimestoppers (2002) *Youth Survey 2002*. London: Crimestoppers Trust.

Curry, D. (2001) 'The proliferation of gangs in the United States', in M. W. Klein, H. J. Kerner, C. L. Maxson and E. G. Weitekamp (eds), *The Eurogang Paradox: Street Gangs and Youth Groups in the U.S. and Europe*. Dordrecht: Kluwer Academic Press.

Davies, A. (1998) 'Youth gangs, masculinity and violence in late Victorian Manchester and Salford', *Journal of Social History*, 32 (2): 349–69.

Dawson, P. (2008) *Monitoring Data from the Tackling Gangs Action Programme*. London: Home Office. Online at: http://www.crimereduction.homeoffice.gov.uk/testbed/violentstreet011a.pdf (accessed 3 February 2009).

Decker, S. H. (1996) 'Collective and normative features of gang violence', *Justice Quarterly*, 13 (2): 243–64.

Decker, S. H. and Van Winkle, B. (1996) *Life in the Gang: Family, Friends, and Violence*. Cambridge: Cambridge University Press.

Decker, S. H. and Weerman, F. M. (2005) *European Street Gangs and Troublesome Youth Groups*. Oxford: AltaMira Press.

Downes, D. (1966) 'The gang myth', *The Listener*, 75: 534–7.

Egley, A. and O'Donnell, C. E. (2009) *Highlights of the 2007 National Youth Gang Survey*. Washington, DC: Office of Juvenile Justice and Delinquency Prevention. Online at: http://www.ncjrs.gov/pdffiles1/ojjdp/225185.pdf (accessed 18 April 2009).

Egley, A., Maxson, C. L., Miller, J. and Klein, M. (2007) *The Modern Gang Reader*, 3rd edn. Oxford: Oxford University Press.

Esbenson, F.-A. and Huizinga, D. (1993) 'Gangs, drugs, and delinquency in a survey of urban youth', *Criminology*, 31: 565–89.

Esbensen, F.-A. and Lynskey, D. P. (2001) 'Youth gang members in a school survey', in M. W. Klein, H. J. Kerner, C. L. Maxson and E. G. Weitekamp (eds), *The Eurogang Paradox: Street Gangs and Youth Groups in the U.S. and Europe*. Dordrecht: Kluwer Academic Press.

Esbensen, F.-A. and Osgood, W. D. (1999) 'Gang Resistance Education and Training (G.R.E.A.T.): results from the national evaluation', *Journal of Research in Crime and Delinquency*, 36 (2): 194–225.

Esbensen, F.-A., Osgood, W. D., Taylor, T. J., Peterson, D. and Freng, A. (2001) 'How great is G.R.E.A.T.? Results from a longitudinal quasi-experimental design', *Criminology and Public Policy*, 1 (1): 87–118.

Fagan, J. A. (1990) 'Social processes of delinquency and drug use among urban gangs', in C. R. Huff (ed.), *Gangs in America*. Newbury Park, CA: Sage.

Fagan, J. (1996) 'Gangs, drugs, and neighborhood change', in R. C. Huff (ed.), *Gangs in America*. Newbury Park, CA: Sage, pp. 39–74.

Federal Bureau of Investigation (2001) *Uniform Crime Reports for the United States: Crime in the United States 2000*. Washington, DC: US Department of Justice.

Festinger, L. (1954) 'A theory of social comparison processes', *Human Relations*, 7 (2): 117–40.

Festinger, L., Pepitone, A. and Newcomb, T. (1952) 'Some consequences of deindividuation in a group', *Journal of Abnormal and Social Psychology*, 47: 382–9.

Gemert, F. and Fleisher, M. S. (2005) 'In the grip of the group', in S. Decker and F. M. Weerman (eds), *European Street Gangs and Troublesome Youth Groups*. Oxford: Rowman & Littlefield.

Gemert, F., Peterson, D. and Lien, I.-L. (2008) *Street Gangs, Migration and Ethnicity*. Cullompton: Willan.

Goddard, C. (2009) 'Union calls for schools to recognise gang problem', *Children and Young People Now*. Available online at: http://www.cypnow.co.uk/news/ByDiscipline/Education/874579/Union-calls-schools-recognise-gang-problem/ (accessed 20 January 2009).

Goldstein, A. P. (1991) *Delinquent Gangs*. Champaign, IL: Research Press.

Goldstein, P (1989) 'Drugs and violent crime', in N. A. Weiner and M. E. Wolfgang (eds), *Pathways to Criminal Violence*. Beverly Hills, CA: Sage.

Graduate Institute of International Studies, Geneva (2007) *The Small Arms Survey 2007: Guns and the City*. Cambridge: Cambridge University Press.

Groebel, J. and Hinde, R. A. (eds) (1989) *Aggression and War: Their Biological and Social Bases*. Cambridge: Cambridge University Press.

Hagedorn, J. M. (1988) *People and Folks: Gangs, Crime and the Underclass in a Rustbelt City*. Chicago: Lakeview Press.

Hagedorn, J. M. (1998) *People and Folks: Gangs, Crime and the Underclass in a Rustbelt City*, 2nd edn. Chicago: Lakeview Press.

Hales, G., Lewis, C. and Silverstone, D. (2006) *Gun Crime: The Market in and Use of Illegal Firearms*, Research Study No. 298. London: Home Office.

Hallsworth, S. and Young, T. (2004) 'Getting real about gangs', *Criminal Justice Matters* 55 (1): 12–13.

Hallsworth, S. and Young, T. (2008) 'Gang talk and gang talkers: a critique', *Crime Media Culture*, 4: 175–95.

Harrell, E. (2005) *Violence by Gang Members, 1993–2003*. Bureau of Justice Statistics. Online at: http://www.ojp.usdoj.gov/bjs/pub/pdf/vgm03.pdf (accessed 26 June 2008).

Hayden, C. (2008) *'Staying Safe and Out of Trouble': A Survey of Young People's Perceptions and Experiences*. Portsmouth: ICJS, University of Portsmouth.

Hazlehurst, K. and Hazlehurst, C. (1998) *Gangs and Youth Subcultures*. London: Transaction Publishers.

Her Majesty's Stationery Office (2006) *Violent Crime Reduction Act 2006*. Online at: http://www.opsi.gov.uk/acts/acts2006/ukpga_20060038_en.pdf (accessed 10 January 2008).

Home Office (2006) *Anti-Social Behaviour Orders*. Available online at: http://www.crimereduction.homeoffice.gov.uk/antisocialbehaviour/antisocialbehaviour55.htm (accessed 26 March 2008).

Home Office (2008a) *Crime in England and Wales Quarterly Update to June 2008*. London: Home Office.

Home Office (2008b) *Saving Lives. Reducing Harm. Protecting the Public: An Action Plan for Tackling Violence 2008–11*. Online at: http://www.homeoffice.gov.uk/documents/ violent-crime-action-plan-08/violent-crime-action-plan-180208?view=Binary (accessed 23 January 2009).

Home Office (2009) *Stronger Power to Tackle Gangs*. Online at: http://press.homeoffice. gov.uk/press-releases/stronger-power-tackle-gangs (accessed 5 February 2009).

Home Office (2009) *Crime Reduction, The Crime and Security Bill*. Available at: http:// www.crimereduction.homeoffice. gov.uk/legislation044.htm (Accessed 30 November 2009).

Horowitz, R. (1983) *Honor and the American Dream: Culture and Identity in a Chicano Community*. New Brunswick, NJ: Rutgers University Press.

Howell, J. C. (1999) 'Youth gang homicides: a literature review', *Crime Delinquency*, 45: 208–41.

Huff, C. R. (1996) 'The criminal behavior of gang members and nongang, at-risk youth', in *Gangs in America*. Newbury Park, CA: Sage.

Kintrea, K., Bannister, J., Pickering, J., Reid, M. and Suzuki, N. (2008) *'It's an area – we all represent it': Young People and Territoriality in British Cities*. York: Joseph Rowntree Foundation.

Klein, M. (1971) *Street Gangs and Street Workers*. Englewood Cliffs, NJ: Prentice Hall.

Klein, M. W. (2001) 'Resolving the Eurogang paradox', in M. W. Klein, H.-J. Kerner, C. L. Maxson and E. G. Weitekamp (eds), *The Eurogang Paradox: Street Gangs and Youth Groups in the U.S. and Europe*. Dordrecht: Kluwer Academic.

Klein, M. W., Maxson, C. L. and Cunningham, L. C. (1991) 'Crack, street gangs, and violence', *Criminology*, 29 (4): 623–50.

Klein, M. W., Kerner, H.-J., Maxson, C. L. and Weitekamp, E. G. (eds) (2001) *The Eurogang Paradox: Street Gangs and Youth Groups in the U.S. and Europe*. Dordrecht: Kluwer Academic.

Laville, S. (2008) 'Teenage killings: "arms race" warning as another youth is killed', The *Guardian*, 15 September. Online at: http://www.guardian.co.uk/uk/2008/ sep/15/knifecrime (accessed 20 October 2008).

Lawrence, S. (2003) 'We take drugs, we drink, we fight. What else is there to do?', *Times Online*. Online at: www.timesonline.co.uk/printFriendly/0,,1-7-907882-7,00. html (accessed 15 March 2007).

LEAP (2008) *Youth Projects*. Online at: http://www.leaplinx.com/youth/index.htm (accessed 12 December 2008).

London Borough of Waltham Forest (2009) *Waltham Forest Gangs Intervention Project*. Online at: http://csd.walthamforest.gov.uk/kbroker/waltham/csd/search.ladv?fl0=_ _dsid%3A&raction=view&sm=0&ha=24&as=1&sf=&sp_scope=wfsvact&sc=waltham &nh=10&tx0=732544&sr=0&cs=UTF-8 (accessed 3 March 2009).

Maher, J. (2007) 'Angels with Dirty Faces: Youth Gangs and Troublesome Youth Groups in South Wales'. Unpublished dissertation, University of Glamorgan.

Maher, J. and Williamson, H. (2009) 'Street-based Youth Groups and Subcultural Clashes in a Post-Industrial Working Class Area: Trewaun, Wales', in H. Williamson and B. Riepl. *Peer Portraits of Peer Violence in Public Space*. Vienna: Austria. Austrian Institute of Youth Research.

Maher, J. (2009) 'Gangs? What gangs? A profile of street-based youth groups in South Wales', in *Contemporary Wales*. Cardiff: University of Wales Press.

Manchester City Council (2009) *Manchester's Crime and Disorder Partnership: The Manchester Multi-Agency Gang Strategy (MMAGS)*. Online at: http://www.manchester. gov.uk/site/scripts/documents_info.php?categoryID=200030&documentID=720&pa geNumber=6 (accessed 3 March 2009).

Mares, D. (2001) 'Gangstas or lager louts: working class street gangs in Manchester', in M. W. Klein, H.-J. Kerner, C. L. Maxson and E. G. Weitekamp (eds), *The Eurogang Paradox: Street Gangs and Youth Groups in the U.S. and Europe*. Dordrecht: Kluwer Academic.

Maxson, C. L. (1995) *Street Gangs and Drug Sales in Two Suburban Cities*. Washington, DC: Office of Juvenile Justice and Delinquency Prevention. Online at: http://www.ncjrs.gov/pdffiles/strtgang.pdf (accessed 23 January 2006).

Maxson, C. L. and Klein, M. W. (1990) 'Street gang violence: twice as great, or half as great?', in C. R. Huff (ed.), *Gangs in America*. Newbury Park, CA: Sage.

Maxson, C. L., Gordon, M. A. and Klein, M. W. (1985) 'Differences between gang and nongang homicides', *Criminology*, 23 (2): 209–22.

Messerschmidt, J. W. (1993) *Masculinities and Crime: Critique and Reconceptualization of Theory*. Lanham, MD: Rowman & Littlefield.

Metropolitan Police (n.d.) *Not Another Drop Campaign*. Available online at: http://cms.met.police.uk/met/boroughs/brent/03working_with_the_community/not_another_drop_campaign (accessed 3 February 2009).

Miller, W. B. (1982) *Crime by Youth Gangs and Groups in the United States*. Washington, DC: Office of Juvenile Justice and Delinquency Prevention.

Monahan, J. and Klassen, D. (1982) 'Situation approaches to understanding and predicting individual violent behaviour', in M. E. Wolfgang and N. A. Weiner (eds), *Criminal Violence*. London: Sage.

Moore, J. W. (1978) *Homeboys*. Philadelphia: Temple University Press.

Morris, S. and Hopkins, N. (2003) 'Caught in the crossfire of gang violence' The *Guardian*. Online at: http://www.guardian.co.uk/uk/2003/jan/03/ukguns.nickhopkins (accessed 15 March 2007).

National Youth Gang Center (2007) *National Youth Gang Survey Analysis*. Online at: http://www.iir.com/nygc/nygsa/ (accessed 10 November 2008).

Ofsted (2004) *National Voluntary Youth Organisations Inspecting Youth Work*, Leap Extended Monitoring Report. Online at: http://www.leaplinx.com/pdfs/Ofsted%20Report%202004.pdf (accessed 12 December 2008).

Padilla, F. (1992) *The Gang as an American Enterprise*. New Brunswick, NJ: Rutgers University Press.

Patrick, J. (1973) *A Glasgow Gang Observed*. London: Eyre Methuen.

Pearson, G. (1983) *Hooligan: A History of Respectable Fears*. London: Macmillan.

Pearson, G. (1995) 'Youth, crime and society', in M. Maguire, R. Morgan and R. Reiner (eds), *Oxford Handbook of Criminology*. Oxford: Clarendon Press.

Pitts, J. (2008) *Reluctant Gangsters: The Changing Face of Youth Crime*. Cullompton: Willan.

Polk, K. (1994) *When Men Kill: Scenarios of Masculine Violence*. Cambridge: Cambridge University Press.

Povery, D., Coleman, K., Kaiza, P., Hoare, J. and Jansson, K. (2008) *Homicides, Firearm Offences and Intimate Violence 2006/07*. London: Home Office.

Reed, W. L. and Decker, S.H. (eds) (2002) *Responding to Gangs: Evaluation and Research*. Washington, DC: National Institute of Justice.

Rosenfeld, R., Bray, T. and Egley, A. (1999) 'Facilitating violence: a comparison of gang-motivated, gang-affiliated and nongang youth homicide', *Journal of Quantitative Criminology*, 15 (4): 495–516.

Sharp, C., Aldridge, J. and Medina, J. (2006) *Delinquent Youth Groups and Offending Behaviour: Findings from the 2004 Offending, Crime and Justice Survey*. London: Home Office.

Sheldon, H. D. (1898) 'The institutional activities of American children', *American Journal of Psychology*, 9 (4): 425–48.

Short, J. F. and Strodtbeck, F. L. (1965) *Group Process and Gang Delinquency*. London: University of Chicago Press.

Smith, D. and Bradshaw, P. (2005) *Gang Membership and Teenage Offending: The Edinburgh Study of Youth Transitions and Crime: No. 8*. Edinburgh: Centre for Law and Society, University of Edinburgh.

Spergel, I. A. (1990) *Youth Gangs: Problem and Response: A Review of the Literature*. Washington, DC: US Department of Justice, National Youth Gang Suppression and Intervention Project with the Office of Juvenile Justice and Delinquency Planning.

Spergel, I. A., and Grossman, S. F. (1997) 'The Little Village Project: a community approach to the gang problem', *Social Work*, 42: 456–70.

Spergel, I. A., Curry, D., Chance, R., Kane, C., Ross, R., Alexander, A., Simmons, E. and Oh, S. (1994) *Gang Suppression and Intervention: Problem and Response*. Washington, DC: US Department of Justice.

Spergel, I. A., Wa, K. W., Choi, S. E., Grossman, S. F., Jacob, A., Spergel, A. and Barrios, E.M. (2003) *Evaluation of the Gang Violence Reduction Project in Little Village: Final Report Summary*. Chicago: University of Chicago, School of Social Service Administration.

Sullivan, M. L. (2006) 'Are "gang" studies dangerous? Youth violence, local context, and the problem of reification', in J. F. Short and L. A. Hughes (eds), *Studying Youth Gangs*. New York: Rowman & Littlefield.

Thompson, T. (2003) 'Girls are in half of crime gangs', *The Observer*, 8 June.

Thornberry, T. P., Krohn, M. D., Lizotte, A. J. and Chard-Wierschem, D. (1993) 'The role of juvenile gangs in facilitating delinquent behaviours', *Journal of Research in Crime and Delinquency*, 30 (1): 55–87.

Thrasher, F. (1963) *The Gang: A Study of 1313 Gangs in Chicago*. London: University of Chicago Press.

Vigil, J. D. (1988) *Barrio Gangs*. Austin, TX: University of Texas Press.

Wilson, D., Sharp, C. and Patterson, A. (2006) *Young People and Crime: Findings from the 2005 Offending, Crime and Justice Survey*. London: Home Office.

Wolfgang, M. E. and Ferracuti, F. (1967) *Subcultures of Violence Theory. The Subculture of Violence: Towards an Integrated Theory in Criminology*. London: Tavistock.

World Health Organisation (2002) *World Report on Violence and Health: Summary*. Geneva: World Health Organisation. Online at: http://www.who.int/violence_injury_prevention/violence/world_report/en/ (accessed 22 August 2005).

Wyrick, P. A. (2002) 'Organisational features as facilitators of youth gang aggression and antisocial behaviour', *Criminology*. Claremont, CA: Claremont Graduate University.

Yablonsky, L. (1967) *The Violent Gang*. Middlesex: Pelican Books.

Yablonsky, L. (1997) *Gangsters: Fifty Years of Madness*. New York: New York University Press.

Young, R. I. (2009) *Net Banging: Street Gangs Answer the Digital Craze*. National Crime Prevention Council. Online at: http://www.ncpc.org/publications/catalyst-newsletter-2008/volume-29-number-6/net-banging-street-gangs-answer-the-digital-craze (accessed 10 January 2009).

Young, T., Fitzgerald, M., Hallsworth, S. and Joseph, I. (2007) *Groups, Gangs and Weapons*. London: Youth Justice Board.

Youth Justice Board (2007) *Groups, Gangs and Weapons*. Online at: http://www.yjb.gov.uk/Publications/Resources/Downloads/Gangs%20Guns%20and%20Weapons%20Summary.pdf (accessed 10 August 2008).

Chapter 17

Violence in the night-time economy

Simon Winlow

Introduction

This chapter will address problems of violence and disorder in Britain's night-time economy, but rather than leaping straight into a discussion of the highly emotive foreground of interpersonal violence that is such a dazzling feature of Britain's urban drinking strips, we will take a circuitous route that will critically consider the development of Britain's night-time economy and its predominant cultural forms. Our goal here is to examine the rich contextual background that shapes eruptions of interpersonal violence that occur frequently in the night-time economy. Despite the current fashion for addressing the foreground of the criminal act, it is also incumbent upon the critical criminologist to drag herself away from the compelling nature of subjective violence (that is, violence conducted by an identifiable social agent) which often appears to demand micro-analysis of 'pathological' individuals, and think again about the forces that structure our social, cultural and economic life. We will begin by critically considering the growth of the night-time economy and its place in popular culture before moving on to investigate more directly the nature and meaning of alcohol-related violence.

The crime problems that followed in the wake of the rapid growth of Britain's night-time, alcohol-based leisure economy should have been entirely predictable. In the early years of its development the concentration of intoxicated young people at particular times and in particular places produced astonishing rises in localised violent crime (Hobbs *et al.* 2000, 2003) and contributed to the atmosphere of aggressive hedonism that came to typify Britain's urban drinking strips. Assessing the actual scale of the problem is particularly difficult as the forms of violent crime that tend to predominate in the night-time economy frequently fail to find their way into the statistical analyses of local police services or the British Crime Survey. Even Accident and Emergency statistics, often a useful supplement to police and BCS violence statistics, fail to incorporate those young men who simply woke up on a Sunday morning with a hangover and a bruised face and decided it was better to forget about the incident rather than seek medical attention or inform the police.

The BCS uses the term 'alcohol-related violence' to describe 'assaults and muggings in which the victim judged the offender to be under the influence of alcohol' (Budd 2003: 4) and in 2000 estimates that there were around 1.2 million incidents of alcohol-related violence. In 2007/8 around 45 per cent of all violent assaults were believed to have been committed by a perpetrator under the influence of alcohol (Kershaw *et al.* 2008). This statistic is of course heavily reliant upon the ability of the victim – who may also have been drunk – being able to identify drunken characteristics in his assailant, who more often than not is a stranger (Budd 2003). Single men aged between 18 and 29 who are regular consumers of the night-time leisure experience are the most common victims of alcohol-related violence and the BSC suggests 'around a half of the alcohol-related assaults took place in or around pubs, clubs or discos, with 70 per cent of these on weekend evenings' (ibid.: iv). Places where consumers gather for night-time services, especially taxi queues and fast-food outlets, also appear to be 'hot spots' for alcohol-related violence (Hobbs *et al.* 2003) and arrests for public order offences often occur directly outside drinking establishments, a fact that partially reflects the sterling work of door security teams whose job it is to eject troublemakers onto the public highway.

These statistics are useful as an initial indication of key trends in alcohol-related violence and the sheer scale of the problem faced by Britain's overstretched police service, but they cannot reveal the 'truth' of alcohol-related disorder amid the hustle and bustle of Britain's night-time economy. The true extent of violence and disorder in the night-time economy is almost impossible to map statistically and the BSC's definition of 'alcohol-related violence' is itself quite limited. Of course, not all forms of disorder that occur within the night-time economy can be easily defined as 'assaults or muggings' and more serious forms of violence are omitted. Accounts offered by police officers and street ethnographers tend to confirm that many violent incidents are not formalised and are destined to forever remain part of the dark figure of unrecorded crime. The incorporation of victim accounts into the British Crime Survey does not fully resolve this problem and we might add that these statistics often mask subtle spatial variations in alcohol-related violence. What we can say with a good degree of certainty is that the police, the government and the general public appear to be increasingly concerned about violence and disorder within the night-time economy and, given the sheer scale of the problem, their concerns appear entirely justified.

Context

The huge expansion of alcohol-based night-time leisure in the final decade of the twentieth century is best understood as a reflection of sweeping change in British society, economy and culture. Made up of bars and nightclubs and apparently populated by a new breed of 'mass volume vertical drinker' (Hobbs *et al.* 2000; Hadfield 2006), Britain's vigorous new night-time economy appeared to expand the staid repertoire of modernist leisure cultures and, amid the flashing lights, pounding music and impending hangovers, offer a new and beguiling consumer experience that drew young people towards it like moths to a flame.

Mass intoxication, disorder and aggressive sexuality have been cultural activities favoured by urban denizens for generations (Engels 1987; Porter 1999) and, even during the regimented era of industrial modernism, the business of pleasure has regularly taken place under the cloak of darkness (Hobbs *et al.* 2003; Hadfield 2006). However, there are many compelling reasons to suggest that the night-time economy is more than simply an updated version of a very old pastime. There now exists a considerable amount of evidence to suggest that the rapid growth of the night-time economy has significantly restructured areas of the inner city (Bianchini 1995; Zukin 1998), made a major contribution to Britain's national economy (Hobbs *et al.* 2003) and transformed British drinking cultures and mainstream youth cultural practices (Winlow and Hall 2006). As the night-time economy was gradually recognised as an economic and cultural space in its own right it became increasingly apparent that this particular aspect of urban leisure is inextricably tied to the economic logic of liberal capitalism (ibid.; Hobbs *et al.* 2003), and the cultural behaviours displayed within it are a telling indication of the shifting structures of identity and sociability in late modern society (Hayward 2004). Intoxication and hedonism, the pervasive atmosphere of danger and promise, the blandness of corporate expansionism coupled with the seductive allure of consumer excess, and of course the violence that for many came to define their experience, were all woven into the very fabric of Britain's new night-time leisure scene, appearing emblematic of the broader social, cultural and economic forces that were reshaping British society with such profundity and rapidity.

Given the scale and significance of this transformation, it is no surprise that the night-time economy has grabbed the attention of numerous commentators interested in various aspects of intoxication and disorder in Britain's town and city centres (Monaghan 2002; Chatterton and Hollands 2003; Measham 2004; Hayward and Hobbs 2007). The vast majority of this literature has focused on the cultural practices of young people between the ages of 18 and 30 and, while some acknowledge diversity in the night-time economy and the development of niche markets catering to more seasoned or discerning drinkers, there continues to be a general agreement that a large part of the night-time economy is reliant upon the custom of the young and the restless.

The drinking practices of young people are now a topic of considerable public and governmental concern (Pincock 2003; POST 2005; Prime Minister's Strategy Unit 2004;), and the spectacle of youthful excess and 'binge drinking' (Plant and Plant 2006; Hayward and Hobbs 2007) appears to have merged with a diverse range of other practices that are now seen as quasi-autonomous cultural forms liberated from economic imperatives, historical processes and traditional class and politics (Žižek 2007). The anxious and judgmental condemnation of 'binge drinking' is often connected in subtle ways to the growing discourse about 'chavs' and the disreputable elements of Britain's previously functional white working class (Hayward and Yar 2006; Webster 2008), but because this condemnation deals with nothing more serious than 'culture', the standard rules of political correctness appear to have been suspended and broadsheet commentators feel free to offer the kind of crude stereotyping and aggressive denunciation rarely seen in our supposedly tolerant and multicultural society (Eagleton 1994; Žižek 2007, 2008). Predictably enough, this surge of popular interest in youthful excess is intimately connected to the well-worn narrative of declinism offered by the right-wing press, who have once again quickly fulfilled their moral obligation to inform the nation of just how undisciplined, disrespectful and downright tawdry the 'youth of today' really are (Pearson 1983; Cohen 2002). Despite the conservative commentary that usually structures these popular debates about binge drinking, it's too easy for the critical criminologist to neatly arrive at the conclusion that our interest in and anxieties about youthful disorder in the night-time economy are simply the latest in a long and seemingly inexhaustible line of 'moral panics', the usual function of which is to camouflage the interventionist tendencies of a controlling state keen to institute a new regime of punitive criminal justice policies (Hall *et al.* 1978; Cohen 2002). However, violence in the night-time economy is serious and widespread and there is copious evidence (see, for example, Hutchinson *et al.* 1998; Bromley and Nelson 2002) to suggest that social anxiety about the violence and disorder that occur there cannot be dismissed as a mere ideological construction that distorts reality for entirely ignoble ends. Furthermore, it also appears increasingly reasonable to suggest that 'the youth of today' are experiencing a range of vague but quite profound forms of anxiety, insecurity and social competition that are closely related to the commercialised hedonism and disorder that characterise the alcohol-based leisure experience. This requires hard thinking about the structural contexts of identity formation and the way we live and interact with one another in an increasingly competitive and thoroughly consumerised world. The fascinating thing about youthful drunkenness and disorder in the night-time economy is not the social and political reactions that these behaviours have provoked, but the actual behaviours themselves, their underlying causes, meanings and motivations. Why is it that so many young people see drunkenness as a goal in itself (Plant and Plant 2006; Hayward and Hobbs 2007)? Why are the cultural activities available in the night-time economy so attractive to young people? And more importantly for our purposes: if there is no direct, causal link between alcohol and violence (Riches 1986; McDonald 1997), why is it that the night-time economy is plagued by persistently high levels of it? We will tentatively explore these issues in the coming pages.

If the press has veered towards conservative condemnation, a number of academic accounts have taken the opposite route and become trapped in the compulsory optimism of left-liberalism, proclaiming the cultures of the contemporary night-time economy to be bursting with the boundless creativity of young people who possess the natural ability to independently fashion novel cultural practices that reflect their own subcultural 'values' (Thorton 1995; Skelton and Valentine 1997). In the rush to revel in the cultural innovations of everyday young people and refocus our attention upon those groups with the power to label their social behaviours, many left-liberals find it difficult to break free from the mistaken assumption that the human subject is ultimately free, rational and creative and can never be truly captured by ideology or compelled by consumer culture. Many of the commentators working from this perspective (see Jayne *et al*. 2006, 2008) seem to be committed to the belief that youthful consumers are magically aware of consumer culture's symbolic possibilities, and that the task of the social scientist is simply to describe the various cultural practices of youthful consumers without becoming bogged down in convoluted theories about the deep values and psychosocial tendencies that structure human experience. The worst excesses of this naive liberal paradigm are clearly displayed in the unremitting desire to identify the 'positive' role of consumerism in the establishment of 'new' identities (Jayne 2006). Untroubled by epistemological or ontological doubt they ignore the problems of atomisation, social competition, debt, insecurity, instability and anxiety that might indeed accompany 'consumerised' identity, and instead content themselves with shallow descriptions of the supposed liberating benefits of consumer symbolism. Their failure to consider the power of late-capitalism's mass-mediated hegemony, the ubiquity of consumer symbolism or compulsory involvement in consumerism's acquisitive and competitive cultures does not suggest objectivity and the absence of an ideological position. Rather, it suggests a hidden liberal ideological position that contributes to the continued vitality of the current social and political order (Hall and Winlow 2007). By avoiding penetrative theory and concerning themselves only with the sunny side of capitalism's street, they either directly or indirectly validate the decidedly lightweight claims of Mary Douglas (especially Douglas and Isherwood 1996), who maintained that there are no such things as 'false consciousness' or 'false needs' (ibid.; see also Marx 1999) and the miserableness of the left shouldn't dissuade us from considering all cultural and consumer behaviour to be essentially communicative and functional, a kind of 'natural' order that exists free from the myths of ideological interpellation (Althusser 2008) and cultural hegemony (Gramsci 1998). In this chapter I hope to steer a course between the gaping flaws of conservative declinism and the guileless optimism of left-liberalism by taking a critical look at the development and cultures of Britain's night-time economy with a view to shedding some light on the causes and meanings of alcohol-related violence in and around the pubs and clubs of our city centres.

Structural change and the rise of consumer cultures

While there are many interesting observations to be made about the social significance of drinking cultures throughout our history (Lender and Martin 1982; Bakhtin 1984), it makes sense to start our story during the economic turbulence of the 1970s. Amid the chaos of the energy crisis, stagflation and the International Monetary Fund's bail-out of the British economy (Harvey 2007), a new sheriff rode into town. Brandishing a copy of Hayek's *The Constitution of Freedom*, reciting the traditional mantra of cultural conservatism and extolling the virtues of economic liberalism, Mrs Thatcher transformed British politics and presided over a period of epochal social, cultural and economic reconfiguration. Her desire to vanquish the peril of organised labour, reduce taxation and sell off state-owned industries reflected her belief that the broad panorama of the social democratic 'nanny state' impinged upon individual freedoms and curtailed the entrepreneurial spirit that was essential if Britain was to modernise its economy and thrive in the vigorous new cut-and-thrust world of the global free market. Protectionism and support for traditional industries were withdrawn as Britain opened the floodgates to cheap foreign imports and relentless economic competition. From this point forward consumerism replaced industrialism as the bedrock of Britain's economy. This key historical shift shaped the three interconnected issues that influenced the development of Britain's new night-time economy.

The first and most obvious factor relates to the role of local government and the management of local economies. Thatcher's reforming zeal impacted significantly upon forms of local governance as she, and those who followed, shifted the principal remit of local authorities from the provision of services to income generation and the attraction of inward investment (Hall and Hubbard 1998). Local councils would now be required to facilitate economic growth by attracting employers, tourists and those with the money and skills that could enable specific localities to survive and hopefully prosper in the new world of the global free market. One way of doing this was to encourage the growth of new 'culturo-economic spheres' (Zukin 1998) that appeared to indicate a forwarding-thinking mentality and a desire for progressive urban and economic change. The creation of local 24-hour economies was a product of this new imperative, and the grand dream of local bureaucrats and town planners was to construct a continental-style evening economy of lively after-dark street activity that would attract diverse populations away from their suburban hibernation and back into the city centre to reinvigorate its cultural and commercial life (Montgomery 1994; Bianchini 1995).

However, the belief that the central business districts of Hull, Hartlepool or Huddersfield could be transformed into a beacon of cosmopolitan elegance displayed a profound misunderstanding of British culture and history. Despite the sterling efforts of many city bureaucrats, the relaxed civility and ambience of Barcelona or the refined cafe culture of Paris could not easily be transposed into Britain's deindustrialised city centres as a means of regenerating urban space (Tierney 2006). The wine and cafe bars that quickly sprang up throughout Britain certainly had some impact upon the general aesthetic of Britain's developing night-time economy, but the actual drinking cultures that existed in these settings remained unswervingly British. Britain's night-time economy would not be characterised by museums, theatres, restaurants and art galleries but by bars and nightclubs serving up mass intoxication, bacchanalian excess and persistently high levels of violence and disorder.

Second, the shift from industrialism to consumerism transformed British labour markets and work cultures. The organised work practices of industrialism virtually evaporated during the 1980s as traditional Western workforces were gradually downsized and eventually replaced by the new flexible, insecure and downgraded world of service employment (Byrne 1989, 2005). Cities were recast as sites of leisure and consumption rather than work and production, and the economic viability of these cities became tied to their ability to rebrand themselves as fashionable sites of culturo-economic activity (Zukin 1998; Byrne 2005; Harvey 2006). These 'culturo-economic activities' were indications of the gradual commodification of everyday public culture as 'cultural' pastimes, such as dining in a new restaurant or enjoying an evening out with friends, became inextricably connected to *economic* activity as capitalism's profit motive began to seep through traditional demarcations and permeate social and cultural life to a degree not seen since early industrialism. The rebranding of the city also saw a push toward the (re)commercialisation of city centre space as flagship shopping precincts sought to upgrade and reinvigorate Britain's flagging high streets. The corporatised and homogenised shopping experiences on offer in Britain's main shopping thoroughfares would, in time, be mirrored in the night-time economy as new and corporately-owned theme bars came to dominate local drinking strips, becoming key indicators of post-industrial urban prosperity (Hobbs *et al.* 2003).

As Britain moved into the 1990s, service sector employment became increasingly important to the British economy. The workers who were dependent upon this new economic sector appeared to approach the general insecurity of their employment in an increasingly instrumental way (Winlow and Hall 2009). Evidence suggests that for many young employees, work increasingly became something to be done and forgotten, and the symbolism usually associated with the work identity appears to have been transplanted into the shiny new technicolour world of leisure and consumption. For many of these young worker-consumers, who they were ceased to be a reflection of class, occupation, locality, history or biography; the essence of self was increasingly structured by involvement in commercialised leisure cultures and, as time wore on, the most important social activity for many young people was regular involvement in the night-time economy (Winlow *et al.* 2003).

The third key shift related to the growing importance of leisure within western society and culture. Western society has long been committed to the mistaken assumption that leisure is an idyllic and malleable social arena that can be endlessly reconfigured to meet our needs and desires (Rojek 1995). In fact there is a great deal of evidence to suggest that leisure has played an important role in the progression and expansion of capitalism in both its industrial and consumer phases (Clark and Critcher 1985; Veblen 1994; Cross 2000). Throughout the industrial period leisure was positioned as something external to the practical/economic world. Leisure lives appeared to offer the individual the opportunity to freely express idiosyncratic elements of the core identity, free from the malign influence of exploitative and alienating labour practices. However, it seems leisure time operated as a functional respite that enabled industrial workers to recuperate after the travails of the working week, comforting them with the myth that their lives were not simply a monotonous cycle of work and rest and could provide periodic bouts of relaxation and enjoyment on the journey to ultimate self-becoming (Clark and Critcher 1985).

As the twentieth century progressed and active consumption was at least partially democratised, people began to see themselves as something other than the sum of their social and economic roles (Cross 2000). Aspirations grew, and they were often connected to rapidly developing consumer markets. Many citizen-consumers (ibid.) began to view the traditional features of identity as restrictive and saw the world of leisure as an opportunity to fashion aspects of themselves that were, they believed, entirely of their own creation. The dour world of industrialism and necessity gave way to a new world of affluence and commodified leisure possibilities that seemed to expand exponentially as the market sought to continually renew itself in order to maintain its dynamic image of fashionable consumerism, luxury, convenience and technological innovation. For most socially included westerners, the new and expanding vista of commercialised leisure reinforced the belief that the social changes that typified the final decade of the twentieth century were essentially progressive, carrying the majority of the population towards a new world of freedom and opportunity in which leisure constitutes an increasingly important and fulfilling part of life. More people began to believe work was merely a burdensome obligation rather than a self-determined social activity, and in comparison to work, leisure seemed like freedom itself.

As the twentieth century came to a close it became increasingly obvious that capitalism had pushed its interests beyond the workplace and into aspects of social and cultural life that had previously been able to maintain a degree of autonomy from the logic of the market. The relatively diverse leisure cultures of the first two-thirds of the twentieth century increasingly found themselves either obsolete or marshalled by the logic of profit accumulation as leisure as a cultural sphere was rapidly commercialised. Time spent away from work became integral to the continued expansion of Britain's consumer markets and the leisure activities and consumer trends we attached ourselves to became far more important than they had ever been as markers of cultural inclusion and self-identity (Bauman 2001). Increasingly, to consume was to be at leisure and to be at leisure was to consume; shopping became a pastime in itself and an escalating number of popular leisure activities became impossible without spending money. Critical sociologists during the industrial modern period tended to focus on the exploitation of the industrial worker in the interests of capital, but now it appeared reasonable to suggest that worker-consumers were compelled by powerful social pressure and seductive cultural symbolism to engage in activities that directly benefited capital both at work and at leisure.

One cultural transformation in particular has led to a continued and insistent cultural preoccupation with leisure and consumerism: the arrival of what Slavoj Žižek (2007, 2008) has called the new cultural 'injunction to enjoy'. Žižek argues that we have witnessed a crucial historical shift in the cultural constitution of the superego. He maintains that internal motivations and controls have been significantly reoriented, and the fundamental force of the superego – guilt – now has less energy to carry out its traditional duty of bearing down upon the failure of the individual to be civilised and sociable. The guilt that resides within the superego is now more likely to come to the fore if the individual fails to actively enjoy the seemingly endless opportunities offered by contemporary culture to experience indulgence and hedonistic excess. We are thus compelled to feel guilt as a result of our failure to enjoy all the consumer and leisure opportunities laid out for our delectation by the culture industries. We appraise our lives negatively and may feel culturally irrelevant if we fail to puncture what feels like the dull normality of the everyday with bouts of hedonistic excess, and this guilt-driven commitment to indulgence, which is not solely the preserve of the young, binds the individual to consumer culture (Kivetz and Simonson 2002; Barber 2007). Žižek's suggestion can, therefore, be used as a means of interpreting the commitment many young people have to the commercialised excess that is the core business of the night-time economy.

For many young people the night-time economy has the potential to help them momentarily forget the significant social pressures they face. Plunging headlong into what can be a deeply involving and genuinely gratifying consumer spectacle allows them to put aside the world of work, debt, relationships, career planning, housing and so on as they become temporarily captivated by the visceral pleasures on offer in the night-time economy. The binge-drinking and/or drug-taking that usually structures the weekly big night out seems to display a barely conscious commitment to the excess and indulgence that seems to be a key constitutive element of the consumer identity (Measham 2004; Measham and Brain 2005). To lives one's life without regular bouts of hedonism, aside from having a significant impact upon the individual's place in friendship groups (Winlow and Hall 2006), is understood by subjects to condemn them to a bland shadow existence in which the existential pleasures and personal freedoms that seem to accompany consumer indulgence are notably absent. Much like the now virtually extinct industrial worker, contemporary research suggests that for many young consumers the weekly night out is understood as a functional respite from the daylight world, a reward that lies at the end of the working week, an opportunity for fun and liminal release. However, unlike the industrial worker, many of the young consumers who populate the night-time economy also appear to consider their leisure lives to represent the essence of self-identity, and some appear to regard the hedonistic pleasure associated with a big night out as a growing daily need rather than a functional bout of unrestrained indulgence (Presdee 2000). In what follows below we will investigate more directly the attractions of the night-time economy for young consumers.

Young people and the attractions of the night-time economy

Despite recent and ongoing attempts to broaden its consumer base, it is crucial to acknowledge that the night-time economy continues to be heavily reliant upon 16–30 year olds. If we are to investigate why the night-time economy is so attractive to this group it is necessary to acknowledge that the nature of youth transitions and the structures of youth identities have changed quite markedly in line with the broader historical changes mentioned above. Committing to a career, moving into a home of one's own, getting married and accepting the responsibilities of family life used to clearly demonstrate arrival at a socially acceptable point of 'adulthood', but now achieving these biographical milestones is fraught with difficulty.

The nature of committed relationships appears to have evolved to fit in with our increasingly instrumental times (Beck and Beck-Gernsheim 2001; Bauman 2001) and the huge growth in university education has meant that a great many young people are not beginning their careers until later in life and as a direct consequence remain financially insecure for much longer. The huge rise in house prices has also impeded the easy transition to adulthood as a whole generation of socially included young people find it more difficult to find their way onto the property ladder. Many rent with friends or live with parents until well into their thirties.

The unstable nature of the labour market also appears to have impacted upon youth transitions. While some have been keen to stress the potential benefits of fluid labour markets, the reality is more likely to be that many young people find dealing with the here and now sufficiently taxing and thus postpone biographical planning, or implementing biographical plans, and fall into a pattern of 'taking one day at a time' and 'seeing how things go', a process that can be endlessly prolonged and come to define the whole life course (Bauman 2001). These and many other trends have challenged traditional aspects of identity formation, strengthened commitment to individualism and consumerism and subtly reinforced the allure of alcohol-based leisure.

As political commitment and mutual obligation continue to decline, individualism continues to rise and youth labour markets continue to be typified by uncertainty, alienation and exploitation, it makes sense to commit to the most pleasurable cultural activities available. The night-time economy markets itself as a temple of decadent indulgence and it appears that many young people are dedicated to the particular kinds of commodified excess that are available within it. What consumers get when they visit the night-time economy often falls some way short of their expectations. However, it appears that many regular visitors to the night-time economy construct a powerful hierarchy of remembrance that allows them to ignore the distinct possibility that they will be standing alone, broke and disappointed at the end of a huge taxi queue at three o'clock in the morning, clinging on to nothing more alluring than a rapidly cooling kebab, having spent a considerable amount of money on yet another run-of-the-mill night out. The night-time economy does, however, occasionally yield a deeply enjoyable and highly memorable drinking experience, and it is the desire to replicate these magical evenings that keeps customers coming back for more. Although they appear to constitute the norm, the mediocre nights in between appear forgotten (Conner 2008) as the subject is drawn back to the doors of desire by a powerful belief that another great night lies within reach. As they head towards the first bar and hear the reverberation of bass-heavy dance music, an air of expectancy descends.

Identifying what it is specifically that renders a big night out so appealing for young consumers is rather difficult, but a number of interesting theoretical observations have been made. A number of studies have drawn on Turner's (1969) concept of liminality (Hobbs *et al.* 2000, 2003; Monaghan 2002, 2004) and Bakhtin's (1984; see also Presdee 2000) work on the carnivalesque (Hobbs *et al.* 2003; Monaghan 2002, 2004; Measham 2004) as a means of making sense of what often appears to be an inherently disorderly cultural space. Turner's work on liminality conceptualises a condition in which established identities are dissolved and the normative order of social and cultural conduct is suspended. Bakhtin's work is primarily concerned with the inversion of the traditional hierarchical order and cultural forms that come to the fore during times of carnival. For example, Hobbs *et al.* (2000, 2003, 2005) argue that the cultures of the night-time economy are at least partly liminal as normative social and cultural protocols appear to be suspended. The night-time economy regularly displays social behaviours that, had they occurred only a few hours earlier during daylight hours, would have been met by significant social disapproval and legal sanction. Not all of these behaviours are demonstrably 'criminal', but many of them do breach the established norms of social conduct. For example, in the night-time economy public urination is quite common, but during daylight hours it is usually considered wholly inappropriate. People also seem to feel free to sing at the top of their voices, blithely step out in front of moving vehicles, make gratuitous sexual comments to passers-by and so on.

Commentators who have deployed the concept of liminality in their studies of the night-time economy tend to argue that this is not simply a matter of individuals becoming drunk and ignoring the standard 'rules' of social behaviour. Rather, they suggest, the night-time economy as a cultural space is structured by the suspension of such rules. Bakhtin's (1984) concept of the carnivalesque is often deployed in a rather general way as a means of grasping the 'anything goes' ethic of the night-time economy. Throughout history carnivals have been loaded with political and symbolic significance and appear to have contributed to periodic social renewal. Carnival was a time of liberation, carnality, drunkenness and overt sexuality, and a time in which the usual order of things was temporarily challenged, mocked and theatrically inverted. At first glance these structural and cultural inversions may appear to be manifested in the contemporary night-time economy, but crudely transposing culturo-political practices from another era onto this uniquely late-modern phenomenon tends to ignore the perversely conformist nature of much night-time leisure. The types of hedonistic excess regularly on display are clearly connected to business imperatives. Here, drunkenness is regimented and normalised rather than transgressive and, while aggressive sexuality and violence are very much part of the cultures of the night-time economy, there is no real inversion of the normative order or mocking of the dominant ideology and its elite representatives. If we are to consider the night-time economy to be a carnivalesque cultural space then it is necessary to qualify this with some acknowledgment that what is actually on offer is a distinctly commodified carnival, deprived of its traditional air of liberation and resistance and tightly harnessed to the interests of the economy.

What we get from these brief theoretical excursions is some insight into the seductions of night-time leisure for young people. The night-time economy is attractive to young consumers not simply because it offers them the opportunity to see friends and engage in the deeply symbolic field of commodified leisure. The partial suspension of normative behaviours exhorts a powerful allure to many young people as this 'anything goes' culture offers young consumers the ability to explore social behaviours that would otherwise lie just out of reach. In comparison to the humdrum everyday world of work and home, the night-time economy appears to offer endless possibilities to transgress normative boundaries and experience real pleasure and excitement.

The power of the night-time economy's liminal melody for young people is of course greatly enhanced by the harmonious and enduring appeal of getting pissed. Alcohol is the night-time economy's primary commodity and it plays an active role in shaping the cultural forms that exist within it. In western societies there appears to be a general agreement that alcohol reveals a 'culture-free' or 'truthful' self that is not restricted by obligatory politeness, consideration for others or the sober desire to manage the impressions others have of the self. When drunk, many believe our true feelings seep out as psychocultural mechanisms of inhibition and restraint become dulled by alcohol. There also appears to be a general agreement that social behaviours that occur while under the influence of alcohol are at least partially excusable after the event. Who among us has not uttered the immortal line: 'sorry, I was drunk'? Here the subject is attempting to mobilise an established excuse for problematic behaviour while drunk, and although the person at whom the apology is directed may not fully buy into this excuse as a realistic justification for the act, society still seems more willing to pardon bad behaviour while drunk than it is to pardon bad behaviour while sober. As there is no clear causal link between alcohol and inconsiderate or violent behaviour (Riches 1986; McDonald 1997), we should consider drunken behaviour to be primarily social and cultural behaviour, even if we perceive a reduction in restraint to be an unavoidable by-product of imbibing alcohol. Here the established social excuse that connects alcohol to bad behaviour contributes to a cultural climate that expects and partially sanctions such behaviours. Within the cultures of the night-time economy therefore we are encouraged to behave in ways that may often appear totally disconnected from our normative identity, and exploring unusual social behaviours, free from daylight forms of social control, contributes to the attractions of a drunken night out. We are consciously and subconsciously drawn to the prospect of momentarily breaking free from the standard rules of social conduct, letting our normal identity slip and being excused what are often prohibited social behaviours. The night-time economy encourages us to do things we wouldn't normally do and actively markets itself as a culturo-economic environment where 'anything goes'. However, *anything doesn't go here*. Rather, the night-time economy is a contrived, ordered culturo-economic environment where *something else* goes.

There is a yawning chasm between the advertised *laissez-faire* attitude of the night-time economy and its actuality. Despite the powerful marketing image of the night-time economy as a cultural space free from regulation, there are rules here. The profusion of CCTV cameras, the periodic sighting of a police van and of course the army of intimidating private security operatives policing licensed premises suggest that, while the night-time economy is structured upon the expectation of disorder, it is intent on allowing this lucrative form of disorder only if it is contained within a tight order whose parameters are based on a refined knowledge of what is good and what is bad for business. The regular consumer of night-time alcohol-based leisure is actively encouraged to engage in expressive hedonism as long as it is contained within ill-defined limits. A central problematic of the night-time economy is therefore the deliberate promotion of disorderly behaviour existing alongside a durable need to control disorder in order to maintain commercial viability.

Subjective violence in the night-time economy

If we are to offer a basic assessment of the contours of interpersonal violence in the night-time economy we must start with a general acknowledgment that the key components are hardly conducive to civility and order. Targeting the age group most likely to commit acts of crime and violence, filling them with high-strength alcohol and encouraging them to value its hedonistic and 'transgressive' cultures was never likely to produce another micro-community that fitted easily into the pacified and highly regulated world of late modernity. However, suggesting that the night-time economy experiences high levels of violence simply because it is populated by a large number of social agents who may be predisposed towards violence severely underestimates the influence of the cultures of the night-time economy upon the social behaviours that occur within it. Is it any wonder that in a cultural space with a deliberately constructed yet misleading 'anything goes' ethos intoxicated social agents occasionally misconstrue the temporary modification of rules for the absence of rules, or at least act in the belief that the vagueness of rules means the likelihood of being caught and punished for stepping outside the rules is minimal? As many authors have acknowledged, an atmosphere of dangerous adventure exists within the night-time economy. Many consumers find this edgy atmosphere attractive and appear to believe that the cultural attractions on offer outweigh the potential dangers. Most regular consumers are pragmatic; they have been to these places many times before and the actual chances of being drawn into a physical conflict appear minimal. Violence does happen quite regularly but most consumers pass through the night-time economy intact. While many view violence as a tasteless distraction from the central business of pleasure-seeking, others appear to quite enjoy their proximity to actual physical violence, marvelling at the blood and gore and experiencing a mild thrill as the Lacanian Real intrudes upon the general artificiality of the consumer experience. Individualised consumers are compelled to manage risk, and as long as they can pass through the disorderly cultures of the night-time economy without actually having violence inflicted directly upon them, most appear satisfied. Rather than challenging the business imperatives of the alcohol industry or complaining about the state's apparent inability to adequately protect leisure consumers, many regular patrons tend to deploy the standard narrative of the disorderly consumer when addressing violence in the night-time economy: violence is an unavoidable result of ill-considered levels of intoxication and the presence of 'uncivilised' individuals hell-bent on trouble (Winlow and Hall 2006). In this way many consumers join the government in their deeply flawed belief that the problem of violence in the night-time economy is best addressed by encouraging innately 'rational' individuals to alter their 'disorderly' behaviour.

While the cultural and economic structures of the night-time economy subtly encourage disorder and transgression, they do not in themselves produce violence. Only a small percentage of those who regularly attend bars and nightclubs find themselves embroiled in violent conflicts, and in order to produce a realistic assessment of the causes of violence it is necessary to briefly leave city-centre drinking cultures and explore the background issues of masculinity and identity and the practical environments in which both are formed.

Men who carry with them the deeply ingrained visceral dispositions that are the product of socialisation within micro-climates of insecurity, aggression and domination often come to value violence and place its enactment close to the centre of self-identity. These dispositions are not purely a product of the traditional working class *habitus* (Bourdieu 1986), but many of its masculine cultural forms shape the self-identity of persistently violent men. For example the desire not to be dominated by another is a traditional aspect of this particular masculine *habitus*: for generations, working-class men have been told 'look after yourself' and 'don't take any shit', and these injunctions are a practical and encultured response to everyday life in a particular cultural environment. In most cases these injunctions are understood to be primarily defensive and cautionary, but unfolding social interaction can be interpreted in many different ways, and these interpretations tend to reflect the psychosocial dimensions of *habitus* and the subject's immediate biographical narrative. Evidence seems to indicate that persistently violent men often abandon the original defensive context of these edicts and instead deploy them as an instrumental means of enhancing status and policing traditional moral and behavioural codes or addressing unresolved events in their personal history (Winlow and Hall forthcoming). Here the cultural logic of 'not taking any shit' transcends its original contextual meaning and can instead manifest itself in a compulsion to find threats or challenges within what others might consider unproblematic everyday interactions. This suggests that men attuned to the symbolism of physical violence often find themselves drawn into conflicts by an elaborate subconscious desire to resolve the emotional trauma caused by previous biographical events that produced feelings of humiliation or in which they believe their behaviours 'didn't measure up' to the exacting standards of their moral codes and their encultured self-images (ibid.). These men may then seek aspects of social interaction in which they can address their previously 'flawed' social behaviour by enacting idealised aggressive responses to behaviours they interpret as threat or challenge. Thus the stereotype of the violent Other waiting for some form of social interaction that can then be construed as a challenge or slight necessitating immediate violent resolution resonates in some cultural fields.

For many violent men, violence is a logical response to an external world populated by nakedly instrumental others who would attempt to wrestle dignity from the self. They tend to face the everyday in the stoic belief that challenges are inevitable, but must be faced down in a valiant attempt to retain dignity and self-respect. Many justify their violence by claiming it to be reactive: they become violent as a response to the aggressive or domineering behaviour of others. At first glance this explanation may appear to be a simple technique of neutralisation (Sykes and Matza 1957), but we must supplement this assessment with some acknowledgment that, in reality, the night-time economy is poorly regulated by the forces of law and order and encountering instrumental and violent others is always a distinct possibility. Here there is a strong connection between the real and the perceptual as there also exists a convincing amount of evidence to suggest that western societies are actually becoming more competitive and individualistic (Hall *et al.* 2008). A number of researchers have acknowledged that the night-time economy is a thoroughly consumerised space where the traditional social and moral orders are stretched to breaking point and aggressive and antisocial behaviours are widespread. This suggests that persistently violent men who understand and justify their own violence as a response to the threatening antisocial behaviours of others may be doing more than simply concocting an excuse to cover up their own unbridled aggression. Indeed, some appear keen to weave a beguiling tale in which they are cast as the fearless urban knight who takes it upon himself to punish the aggressive and instrumental behaviours of antisocial others who seek to impose their will upon peaceful consumers of the night-time leisure experience. In this way 'piss-takers', 'arseholes' and 'bullies' feel the wrath of violence specialists who believe their own violence possesses a restorative function and is targeted at those who deserve it (Winlow and Hall 2006). Of course, those cast in these aggressive roles are likely to interpret these events very differently and may justifiably see themselves as the passive victim of an instrumental, irrational and aggressive other. The disparity that exists between different interpretations of the same violent incident appears to demand a penetrative psychosocial reading of the gendered *habitus* of both protagonists if we aim to actually uncover the complex root causes of this kind of subjective violence.

The night-time economy's deserved reputation for interpersonal violence also appears to produce a perverse self-fulfilling prophecy. Young men are often keenly aware that violence does actually occur here and those keen to construct a no-nonsense ready-to-fight image may be called upon to back up their claims with action. This contextual expectation of violence can lead some to draw upon violence as a resource far earlier in a conflict than would otherwise be the case, and many young men with a history of violence are painfully aware that the first blow is usually the decisive one (Hobbs 1995). The night-time economy eschews traditions of codified violence and instead cuts straight to the chase: no requests to step outside, no removing of jackets or the rolling-up of sleeves, no anxieties about the cowardice of cheap shots, no faith that a beating will stop if you find yourself lying prostrate on the pavement.

Some men also appear to be drawn towards the sensual dynamics of interpersonal violence. Katz (1988) claims that masculine violence is often the result of a desire to transgress the oppressive norm and pursue existential passion and excitement but, despite receiving a significant amount of popularity within the social sciences, his theory fails to acknowledge cultural diversity and changes in human sensibilities throughout history (Elias 2000; Hall 2007). While it is certainly true that persistently violent men are drawn toward the adrenalising aspects of physical conflict, the 'buzz' they receive from these encounters cannot, on its own, account for violence. A range of encultured dispositions needs to be in place in order for the subject to feel thrilled rather than terrified by the prospect of violence. Furthermore, the night-time economy is structured on the cultural expectation of disorder and transgression and so the standard 'oppressive norm' that produces a desire to transgress doesn't appear to be operational in this context. As we discussed above, disorder, antisocial behaviour and violence are all woven into the very fabric of the night-time economy and the norm itself is commodified transgression.

Control in the night-time economy

Numerous studies have criticised the state's failure to adequately regulate the night-time leisure scene and deal with the crime problems that appear to be its almost inevitable by-product. British city centres attract many thousands of weekend revellers and policing levels are often irresponsibly low (Hobbs *et al.* 2003). Those police officers who are on duty often find themselves overwhelmed as CCTV operators identify problems throughout the city centre that necessitate an immediate police response. This 'fire brigade policing' is hardly conducive to good police work and the piecemeal crime control strategies that have been implemented to address social anxieties about drunken violence have consistently failed to tackle root causes. The New Labour leitmotif of responsibilisation acts as the foundation for numerous crime control 'innovations' that have attempted to persuade 'rational' consumers that the creation of a civilised society and night-time economy is essentially their responsibility. Of course this push towards personal responsibility suggests the resurgence of a brand of classical liberalism that is deeply indicative of contemporary governance rather than an innovative and forward-thinking development in crime control. The introduction of fixed-penalty fines for antisocial behaviour is a particularly clear example of this kind of thinking. Here the expectation is that once rational consumers become aware of the existence of civilised conduct norms and formal prohibitions they will curtail their disorderly behaviour and recognise the responsibilities that come with civilised consumer life. This assumption of rational self-regulation is of course totally at odds with the cultural injunction to *cease to regulate one's behaviour and embrace the forms of incivility and disorder* that constitute the principle marketing message of the night-time economy.

The government has also attempted to 'responsiblise' the network of bars that make up the bulk of local night-time economies. The threat to withdraw the licences of premises that display consistently high levels of disorder is believed to act as impetus for better management and regulation (Hobbs *et al.* 2003; Hadfield 2006), but of course fails entirely to address the complex causes of such disorder. A similar rationale can be detected lurking behind the glut of new initiatives that have resulted in the creation of management groups that are usually composed of 'key stakeholders', local planning and licensing officials and the police. The basic underlying principle of these groups is to facilitate inclusive management of the night-time economy and to establish clear lines of communication between the managers of licensed premises and the local police in order to clamp down on underage drinkers and violent or disorderly patrons. Those who behave inappropriately may now be subject to exclusion orders, banning them from pubs and clubs or indeed entire city centres. These strategies of course fail to address the embedded cultures of mass intoxication and disorder upon which Britain's night-time economy rests.

The government's attempt to stem the tide of 'problem drinking' also reaffirms the sanctity of the rational agent. Current state-funded advertising campaigns inform young consumers of the perils of excessive drinking, despite the government's long-standing commitment to promoting an alcohol industry that aggressively promotes drinking and drunkenness. The message of these advertisements is of course that young people should drink and engage with the night-time economy in a responsible way. We might reasonably conclude that these are worthy messages that deserve to be heard by young people but they operate on the mistaken assumption that consumers are always judicious and rational and simply need more information about the perils of drunkenness in order to adjust their behaviour. They are also directly at odds with the plethora of powerful cultural messages that encourage young consumers to embrace hedonism at every opportunity.

The inevitable conclusion is that governmental responses to alcohol-related violence are rather half-hearted and flawed in conception. The government's long-standing desire to expand the alcohol industry and their continued need to use alcohol-based urban leisure as a means of regenerating local economies creates a situation in which the growth of the night-time economy is encouraged at the same time as attempts are made to curb drunkenness. In such a situation, the government is compelled to find fault with the social behaviours of individuals rather than address complex structural issues, and this results in a renewed focus upon 'bad apples' that need to be dispensed with in order for the market to find a civilised equilibrium. The only way to appease public disquiet about urban disorder and allow the blind dance of amoral market forces to continue is to pathologise the uncivilised individual who 'doesn't know his limits' and 'oversteps the mark'. The message is clear: the problem, if one exists, lies with individual consumers rather than the cultural and economic foundations of night-time leisure.

Conclusion

Violence in Britain's night-time economy is an incredibly complex social phenomenon; what I have offered above is merely a basic guide to a number of key issues. Spectacular eruptions of subjective violence occur with alarming regularity in the night-time economy, shaping its image and establishing and reproducing its internal cultures. We appear almost naturally drawn towards this visceral, subjective violence and its accompanying discourse of pathological individuals and flawed social groups. However, what we understand as sudden 'eruptions of violence' that appear to arise 'out of nowhere' are in fact entirely predictable and emblematic of a cultural environment grounded upon drunkenness, commodified hedonism and disorder. The night-time economy deliberately promotes aggressive hedonism, mass intoxication and personal indulgence and thus creates the ground upon which immediate subjective violence occurs. My point here is essentially to suggest that a form of objective violence is present in the actual creation of the zero-level of violence against which we judge subjective violence (Žižek 2008). Our uncritical belief that the peaceful operation of the night-time economy is shattered by a sudden outbreak of immediate physical violence tends to ignore the fact that disorder actually structures and sustains this environment in its present form. While many interesting observations have been made about the causes and meanings of subjective violence, to truly appreciate its broader dimensions we must take a step back from this absorbing foreground and reaffirm our critical commitment to understand the social, cultural and economic structures of the world in which we live.

Selected further reading

Hadfield (2006) offers an interesting critical account of the development of Britain's night-time economy and the various attempts that have been made to control this inherently disorderly cultural environment. Plant and Plant (2006) have written an accessible introduction to the history of British drinking patterns and the recent rise of 'binge drinking'. Hobbs *et al.*'s (2003) book is, first and foremost, an attempt to understand the occupational culture of 'bouncers' but actually offers the reader much more than this. Packed with vivid ethnographic data, this book is perhaps the most comprehensive analysis of Britain's night-time leisure scene yet written. Winlow and Hall (2006) focus upon the lives of the young people who populate the night-time economy but their book can also be read as an original and highly critical account of the contemporary nature of consumerised youth identities.

References

Althusser, L. (2008) *On Ideology*. London: Verso.
Bakhtin, M. (1984) *Rabelais and his World*. Indianapolis, IN: Indiana University Press.
Barber, B. (2007) *Consumed: How Markets Corrupt Children, Infantilize Adults and Swallow Citizens Whole*. London: Norton.
Bauman, Z. (2001) *The Individualized Society*. Cambridge: Polity.
Beck, U. and Beck-Gernsheim, E. (2001) *Individualization: Institutionalized Individualism and Its Social and Political Consequences*. London: Sage.
Bianchini, F. (1995) 'Night cultures, night economies', *Planning Practice and Research*, 10 (2): 121–6.
Bourdieu, P. (1986) *Distinction: A Social Critique of the Judgement of Taste*. London: Routledge.
Bromley, R. D. and Nelson, A. L. (2002) 'Alcohol-related crime and disorder across urban space and time: evidence from a British city', *Geoforum*, 33: 239–54.
Budd, T. (2003) *Alcohol-related Assault: Findings from the British Crime Survey*, Home Office Online Report 35/03. London: Home Office.
Byrne, D. (1989) *Beyond the Inner City*. Buckingham: Open University Press.
Byrne, D. (2005) *Social Exclusion*. Buckingham: Open University Press.

Chatterton, P. and Hollands, R. (2003) *Urban Nightscapes*. London: Routledge.

Clark, J. and Critcher, C. (1985) *The Devil Makes Work*. London: Macmillan.

Cohen, S. (2002) *Folk Devils and Moral Panics*. London: Routledge.

Conner, S. (2008) 'Why drinkers do it all again – they only recall the good bits', *The Independent*, 10 September.

Cross, G. (2000) *An All-Consuming Century*. New York: Columbia University Press.

Douglas, M. and Isherwood, B. (1996) *The World of Goods: An Anthropological Theory of Consumption*, 2nd edn. London: Routledge.

Eagleton, T. (1994) *Ideology*. London: Longman.

Elias, N. (2000) *The Civilising Process*. London: Wiley/Blackwell.

Engels, F. (1987) *The Condition of the Working Class in England*. London: Penguin.

Gramsci, A. (1998) *Prison Notebooks: Selections*. London: Lawrence & Wishart.

Hadfield, P. (2006) *Bar Wars*. Oxford: Oxford University Press.

Hall, S. (2007) 'The emergence and breakdown of the pseudo-pacification process', in K. Watson (ed.), *Assaulting the Past*. Cambridge: Cambridge Scholars Press.

Hall, S. and Winlow, S. (2007) 'Cultural criminology and primitive accumulation: a formal introduction for two strangers who should really become more intimate', *Crime, Media, Culture*, 3 (1): 82–90.

Hall, S., Winlow, S. and Ancrum, C. (2008) *Criminal Identities and Consumer Culture: Crime, Exclusion and the New Culture of Narcissism*. Cullompton: Willan.

Hall, S., Critcher, C., Jefferson, T., Clarke J. and Roberts, B. (1978) *Policing the Crisis*. London: Macmillan.

Hall, T. and Hubbard, P. (1998) *The Entrepreneurial City*. Chichester: Wiley & Sons.

Harvey, D. (2006) *Spaces of Global Capitalism*. London: Verso.

Harvey, D. (2007) *A Brief History of Neoliberalism*. Oxford: Oxford University Press.

Hayward, K. (2004) *City Limits*. London: Glasshouse.

Hayward, K. and Hobbs, D. (2007) 'Beyond the binge in booze Britain: market-led liminalization and the spectacle of binge drinking', *British Journal of Sociology*, 58 (3): 437–56.

Hayward, K. and Yar, M. (2006) 'The "chav" phenomenon: consumption, media and the construction of a new underclass', *Crime, Media, Culture*, 2 (1): 9–28.

Hobbs, D. (1995) *Bad Business*. Oxford: Oxford University Press.

Hobbs, D., Hadfield, P., Lister, S. and Winlow, S. (2003) *Bouncers: Violence and Governance in the Night-time Economy*. Oxford: Oxford University Press.

Hobbs, D., Winlow, S., Hadfield, P. and Lister, S. (2005) 'Violent hypocrisy: governance in the night-time economy', *European Journal of Criminology*, 2 (2): 161–83.

Hobbs, D., Lister, S., Hadfield, P., Winlow, S. and Hall, S. (2000) 'Receiving shadows: governance and liminality in the night-time economy', *British Journal of Sociology*, 51 (4): 701–17.

Hutchinson, I., Magennis, P., Shepard, J. and Brown, A. (1998) 'B.A.O.M.S. United Kingdom Survey of Facial Injuries, Part 1: aetiology and the association with alcohol consumption', *British Journal of Maxillofacial Surgery*, 36 (3): 3–13.

Jayne, M. (2006) *Cities and Consumption*. London: Routledge.

Jayne, M., Holloway, S. and Valentine, G. (2006) 'Drunk and disorderly: alcohol, urban life and public space', *Progress in Human Geography*, 30 (4): 451–68.

Jayne, M., Valentine, G. and Holloway, S. (2008) 'Geographies of alcohol, drinking and drunkenness: a review of progress', *Progress in Human Geography*, 32 (2): 247–63.

Katz, J. (1988) *The Seductions of Crime*. New York: Basic Books.

Kershaw, C., Nicholas, S. and Walker, A. (eds) (2008) *Crime in England and Wales 2007/08: Findings from the British Crime Survey and Police Recorded Crime*. London: Home Office.

Kivetz, R. and Simonson, I. (2002) 'Self-control for the righteous: toward a theory of precommitment to indulgence', *Journal of Consumer Research*, 29 (2): 199–217.

Lender, M. and Martin, J. (1982) *Drinking in America*. London: Macmillan.

Marx, K. (1999) *Capital* (abridged). Oxford: Oxford Paperbacks.

McDonald, M. (ed.) (1997) *Gender, Drink and Drugs*. Oxford: Berg.

Measham, F. (2004) 'The decline of ecstasy, the rise of binge-drinking and the persistence of pleasure', *Probation Journal*, 51 (4): 309–26.

Measham, F. and Brain, K. (2005) '"Binge" drinking, British alcohol policy and the new culture of intoxication', *Crime, Media, Culture*, 1 (3): 262–83.

Monaghan, L. (2002) 'Regulating "unruly" bodies: work tasks, conflict and violence in Britain's night-time economy', *British Journal of Sociology*, 53 (3): 403–29.

Monaghan, L. (2004) 'Doorwork and legal risk: observations from an embodied ethnography', *Social and Legal Studies*, 13 (4): 453–80.

Montgomery, J. (1994) 'The evening economy of cities', *Town and Country Planning*, 63 (11): 302–7.

Pearson, G. (1983) *Hooligan: A History of Respectable Fears*. London: Macmillan.

Pincock, S. (2003) 'Binge drinking on rise in UK and elsewhere', *The Lancet*, 362 (9390): 1126–7.

Plant, M. and Plant, M. (2006) *Binge Britain*. Oxford: Oxford University Press.

Porter, D. (1999) *Health, Civilization and the State*. London: Routledge.

POST (2005) *Binge Drinking and Public Health*, No. 244. London: Parliamentary Office of Science and Technology.

Presdee, M. (2000) *Cultural Criminology and the Carnival of Crime*. London: Routledge.

Prime Minister's Strategy Unit (2004) *Alcohol Harm Reduction Strategy for England*. London: Cabinet Office.

Riches, D. (ed.) (1986) *The Anthropology of Violence*. Oxford: Basil Blackwell.

Rojek, C. (1995) *Decentring Leisure*. London: Sage.

Skelton, T. and Valentine, G. (1997) *Cool Places*. London: Routledge.

Sykes, G. and Matza, D. (1957) 'Techniques of neutralization: a theory of delinquency', *American Sociological Review*, 22 (6): 664–70.

Thorton, S. (1995) *Club Cultures: Music, Media and Sub-cultural Capital*. Cambridge: Polity.

Tierney, J. (2006) '"We want to be more European": the 2003 Licensing Act and Britain's night-time economy', *Social Policy and Society*, 5: 453–60.

Turner, V. (1969) *The Ritual Process*. London: Routledge & Kegan Paul.

Veblen, T. (1994) *The Theory of the Leisure Class*. London: Dover.

Webster, C. (2008) 'Marginalized white ethnicity, race and crime', *Theoretical Criminology*, 12 (3): 293–312.

Winlow, S. and Hall, S. (2006) *Violent Night: Urban Leisure and Contemporary Culture*. Oxford: Berg.

Winlow, S. and Hall, S. (2009) 'Living for the weekend: instrumentalism, consumption and "individualism" in youth identities in the North East of England', *Ethnography*, 10 (1): 91–113.

Winlow, S. and Hall, S. (forthcoming) 'Retaliate first: memory, humiliation and male violence'.

Winlow, S., Hobbs, D., Lister, S. and Hadfield, P. (2003) 'Bouncers and the social context of violence: masculinity, class and violence in the night-time economy', in E. Stanko (ed.) *The Meanings of Violence*. London: Routledge.

Žižek, S. (2007) *The Universal Exception*. London: Continuum.

Žižek, S. (2008) *Violence*. London: Profile Books.

Zukin, S. (1998) 'Urban lifestyles: diversity and standardisation in spaces of consumption', *Urban Studies*, 35 (5): 825–39.

Chapter 18

Hate crime

Paul Iganski

Introduction: the growth of the 'hate crime' policy domain

The notion that there is such a thing as 'hate crime' has been wholeheartedly adopted by the criminal justice system in the United Kingdom within the last decade. It has been eagerly imported from the United States where the idea has a much longer provenance. The foundations of the 'hate crime' policy domain – the convergence of activism, policy and legislation on the problem – were laid in the United States in the 1970s when an emergent anti-'hate crime' movement was built on the strategies of mobilisation of civil rights and victims' rights movements in the 1960s and 1970s. Since then, so-called 'hate crime' laws have been enacted by most states and at the federal level, and since 1992 the Federal Bureau of Investigation has been publishing what it calls 'hate crime statistics' as part of its uniform crime reports.[1]

In the UK the foundations of the 'hate crime' policy domain were laid in the 1990s by the inquiry into the racist murder of Stephen Lawrence and the provisions against racially aggravated offences of the 1998 Crime and Disorder Act – one of the UK's earliest 'hate crime' laws. While in the United States the birth and maturation of the 'hate crime' policy domain occurred across the late 1970s to the late 1990s (Jenness and Grattet 2001), in the UK it is very much still in its adolescence in terms of the energetic burst of institutional arrangements being initiated to manage the problem. Most police forces have designated 'hate crime' officers who specialise in the investigation and monitoring of 'hate crime'. Many local authorities employ specialist 'hate crime' officers to coordinate local policy and practice against 'hate crime'. The Crown Prosecution Service (CPS) has established what it calls 'Hate Crime Scrutiny Panels' in all police force areas in England and Wales to engage with local community 'stakeholders' to scrutinise and draw lessons from 'hate crime' prosecutions in their areas. Probation services have established programmes to work with offenders in prisons and in the community to try to reduce reoffending. In total, there has been a considerable investment of public resources in the UK channelled into confronting and managing the problem of 'hate crime'. However, what is lacking is the sharing of good practice and policy learning. This point will be returned to below.

Elsewhere in Europe the 'hate crime' policy domain is beginning to be established. At cross-national level the Organisation for Security and Cooperation in Europe (OSCE) has been coordinating policy initiatives on monitoring and policing 'hate crime'.[2] International non-governmental organisations (NGOs), such as Human Rights First,[3] have incorporated the notion of 'hate crime' into their vernacular of human rights concerns.

But what is 'hate crime'? Who are the perpetrators? What are the consequences? How prevalent is it? These are the questions to be addressed in this chapter.

Conceptualising 'hate crime'

The UK Home Office states on its website that: 'A hate crime is any criminal offence that is motivated by hostility or prejudice based upon the victim's: disability, race, religion or belief, sexual orientation, transgender.'[4] The UK Association of Chief Police Officers (ACPO) slips the word 'prejudice' into their definition (as a number of scholars do as will be discussed below) by defining 'hate crime' as: 'Any incident, which constitutes a criminal offence, perceived by the victim or any other person, as being motivated by prejudice or hate' (ACPO 2005: 9).

As with all conceptual labels though, 'hate', or 'hatred', does not mean very much until it is further defined into its constituent parts. Over five decades ago Gordon Allport provided a very clear conceptualisation of 'hate' in his influential book *The Nature of Prejudice*. He drew a distinction between 'hate' and 'anger'. Anger, according to Allport, 'is a transitory emotional state, aroused by thwarting some ongoing activity'. 'Hatred', on the other hand, is a 'sentiment', not an emotion. Allport defined it as 'an enduring organization of aggressive impulses toward a person or toward a class of persons. Since it is composed of habitual bitter feeling and accusatory thought, it constitutes a stubborn structure in the mental-emotional life of the individual' (Allport 1954/1979: 363). To emphasise the difference between anger and hate, in drawing from Allport's conceptualisation, we might think in terms of the heat of anger, and by contrast think of 'cold hatred': not a short-lived emotional condition but an enduring state of mind.

Yet, if our notion of 'hate crime' is informed solely by Allport's conceptualisation of hatred and its stress on 'aggressive impulses' then 'hate crime' offenders would most likely be confined to the most extreme bigots who either deliberately set out to victimise the targets of their hate or alternatively seize upon any opportunity that presents itself to do so. Yet a number of studies have demonstrated that while bigotry is present in some form in all incidents of 'hate crime', other impulses and motivations than 'hate' are often at work (McDevitt et al. 2002; Iganski et al. 2005), such as a sense of grievance, a desire for retaliation or just the fun of it.

It is perhaps because of the conceptual ambiguities of the notion of 'hate crime' that scholarly texts on the subject generally open with a chapter exploring the concept and agonising over the causal nexus between 'hate' and crime. In opening their book *Hate Crimes: Criminal Law and Identity Politics* (1998) Jacobs and Potter argue that '"Hate crime' is not really about hate, but about bias or prejudice' (Jacobs and Potter 1998: 11). Fred Lawrence, early on in his book *Punishing Hate* (1999), states that he prefers to use the term 'bias' rather than 'hate' to stress that 'the key factor in a bias crime is not the perpetrator's hatred of the victim per se, but rather his bias or prejudice toward that victim' (Lawrence 1999: 9). British scholar Nathan Hall also prefers the label 'prejudice', stating in the opening chapter to his book *Hate Crime* (2005) that 'for the most part it is prejudice and not hate that we refer to when we talk about hate crime' (Hall 2005: 9). While there is evident agreement amongst these texts that 'hate' rarely makes an appearance in so-called 'hate crime', and that the more inclusive terms of 'prejudice' and 'bias' are preferred, ambiguities unfortunately remain. 'Prejudice' and 'bias' are only slightly less slippery concepts than 'hate' to pin down, and they introduce a new problem not shared by the notion of 'hate' – prejudice and bias can go either way, they can either be for or against something.

There is a further problem. Those conceptualisations that look for the defining characteristics of 'hate crime' inside offenders' minds arguably pathologise acts of 'hate crime' in terms of the consequence of disturbed individual psychology. However, in her text *In the Name of Hate* (2001) Barbara Perry takes one step outside of offenders' minds and steps into the collective social conscience to conceptualise 'hate crime' as 'doing difference'. The notion of 'doing difference' situates the offender's mind, and their actions, in ideological structures of societal oppression that are marked, to use Perry's words, by 'deeply embedded notions of difference' (Perry 2001: 46) concerning 'race', ethnicity, gender, sexuality, disability and class. These notions of difference are characterised by negative, deviant, inferior evaluations of the 'Other' relative to the dominant norm – what some might alternatively call bigotry, bias or prejudice – and they serve to legitimise acts of violence against the 'Other'. Consequently, those communities from which the perpetrators are drawn arguably share a collective responsibility for offenders' actions.

Barbara Perry goes a step further by arguing that as well as 'doing difference' 'hate crime' offenders consciously and instrumentally 'do difference' by proposing that 'hate crime' is *'intended to marginalize'* (Perry 2001: 214) and intended to sustain the social hierarchies which serve to legitimise victimisation (Perry 2001: 3). However, such a perspective attributes a degree of instrumentalism on the part of offenders for consequences that they might not themselves intend. While there are often unintended consequences of intentional action, it is difficult to conceive (and Perry doesn't offer any empirical evidence to help) that many 'hate crime' offenders knowingly and consciously act to reproduce hierarchies of oppression.

'Hate crime' as a domain of activism

Given the conceptual ambiguities affecting the notion of 'hate crime',[5] ambiguities that lie in the depths of offenders' mental states, it is arguably fruitful to step further outside of offenders' minds to conceptualise 'hate crime' – while not ignoring altogether the offender's motivating impulses, or the sentiments they convey in committing their offence. Once free of the confinement of offender psychology a more sociological eye can be cast on the phenomenon. From such a view point 'hate crime' might be regarded as a domain of activism, or to borrow Jenness and Grattet's (2001) term, a 'policy domain' – an arena in which elements of the political system and criminal justice process have converged and focused on the substantive issue of offences and incidents where some bigotry against the victim plays a part. From this standpoint, the concept of 'hate crime' provides an emotive banner under which is now rallied a once disparate field of concerns with oppression and bigotry in various guises and victimisation on the basis of a person's 'race', religion, sexual orientation, gender or disability. The criminal justice system in the UK along with institutions of local government, have perhaps more readily embraced the notion of 'hate crime' than victims' rights campaigners. However, within the last few years a strong campaigning movement has emerged which has explicitly appropriated the label of 'hate crime' in throwing a spotlight on the problem of violence and other incidents against disabled people and the shortcomings of the criminal justice system in addressing the problem.

A legislative approach to defining 'hate crime'

Greater clarity about conceptualising 'hate crime' will be found if we step further still out of offenders' minds and consider the legislative provisions established in response to their actions. Unfortunately, though, consistency will not be found in the terms used or assumptions about the causal nexus between offender mental states and their related acts. In the United States, the Anti-Defamation League (ADL) provides text for model legislation for penalty enhancement in what it calls 'bias-motivated crimes'. The ADL's wording has been influential in shaping the text of 'hate crime' statutes across a number of states. According to the ADL, 'A person commits a Bias-Motivated Crime if, *by reason of* [emphasis added] the actual or perceived race, color, religion, national origin, sexual orientation or gender of another individual or group of individuals, he violates Section _____ of the Penal Code (insert code provisions for criminal trespass, criminal mischief, harassment, menacing, intimidation, assault, battery and or other appropriate statutorily proscribed criminal conduct).'[6] Those three carefully chosen words 'by reason of' arguably stress the discriminatory selection of victims on account of their particular identity, rather than the motivating impulses of offenders.

At the Federal level in the United States, the 1990 Hate Crime Statistics Act does though introduce an element of the offender's mental state into the conceptualisation of 'hate crime' in requiring the US Attorney General to collect and annually publish a summary of data on crimes 'that manifest *evidence of prejudice* [emphasis added] based on race, religion, sexual orientation, or ethnicity' and the list of censored prejudices was expanded to include 'disability' by the 1994 Violent Crime Control and Law Enforcement

Act. It is notable that apart from the title of the 1990 Act the word 'hate' is not used elsewhere in the text of the Act with 'prejudice' being the preferred word instead. The 1994 Act added a further twist by highlighting the act of discriminatory selection of crime victims rather than the evident impulses or sentiments of the offender, but using slightly different words than the ADL's model legislation by defining 'hate crime' as 'a crime in which the defendant intentionally selects a victim … *because of* [emphasis added] the actual or perceived race, color, religion, national origin, ethnicity, gender, disability, or sexual orientation of any person.' That definition was adopted by subsequent federal hate crime legislation: the 2007 Local Law Enforcement Hate Crimes Prevention Act.

The emphasis in the US provisions on the discriminatory selection of victims is echoed in the Office for Democratic Institutions and Human Rights (ODIHR) working definition of 'hate crime' adopted in 2005 for use across the OSCE region. The ODIHR defines 'hate crime' as 'Any criminal offence, including offences against persons or property, where the victim, premises, or target of the offence are *selected because of* [emphasis added] their real or perceived connection, attachment, affiliation, support, or membership of a group as defined … A group may be based upon a characteristic common to its members, such as real or perceived race, national or ethnic origin, language, colour, religion, sex, age, mental or physical disability, sexual orientation, or other similar factor.'[7]

While the discriminatory selection model of legislation avoids the problem for prosecutors of proving the causal nexus between an offender's motives and the commission of their act, relying instead on the less testing need to demonstrate that the victim was targeted on account of a particular aspect of their identity, it rules out the many instances of offences that are not premeditated, even on the spur of the moment, but instead occur in the unfolding of other conflicts and disputes where the offender's bigotry is weighed in to aggravate the situation. Such instances are taken into account in provisions in the UK where there is the even less testing requirement for the prosecution to prove that the offender demonstrates hostility towards the victim, either while committing the offence, or immediately before or afterwards, towards a member (or presumed member) of a racial group, a religious group, or on the basis of the victim's actual or presumed sexual orientation or disability.[8] The legislative lexicon on 'hate crime' is expanded considerably in the UK by that very inclusive word 'hostility'. And it is notable that the word 'hate', or the words 'prejudice' and 'bias' favoured by some scholars, do not appear in the legislation in question.

A victim-centred approach to defining 'hate crime'

Looking deep into offenders' souls for whether 'hate' or prejudice is at work arguably does not bring us close to the lived reality of 'hate crime' as experienced by victims. While 'hate crime' offenders manifest a variety of impulses and victims are subject to an array of incidents that occur in interpersonal offending more widely, there is a common denominator in that 'hate crimes' hurt more than the same types of crimes where offenders are acting on other impulses. The notion that 'hate crimes' inflict greater harms upon their victims therefore arguably provides a fundamental dimension in the conceptualisation of 'hate crime'. Furthermore, persons who are victimised in actual acts of 'hate crimes' are just the initial victims as the consequences extend to many others. These greater harms are acknowledged in legislation by providing the justification for penalty enhancement – or the greater punishment of 'hate crime' offenders – as will be discussed below. Before the harms are considered though, it is instructive to ask 'who are the perpetrators' of 'hate crime'?

From extreme to everyday offending

It is sometimes noted in the literature on racist violence in the UK (cf. Gadd and Jefferson 2007; Webster 2008), and on 'hate crime' more broadly conceived (cf. Chakraborti and Garland 2009), that compared with research on victims of 'hate crime', there has been relatively little research, and consequent understanding about, offenders and their motivating impulses and behaviour. Yet in the case of the 'niche' or 'enclave' (Blazak 2009a: xiv) of far-right, skinhead and white supremacist offenders a considerable body of research evidence and other scholarly literature has now accumulated. Such offenders might be labelled 'extremists' because they articulate their bigotry with a greater consciousness and clarity than most other people. And, because of the value attached to the use of violence in particular subcultures, such as skinhead groups (Simi 2009), some engage in more extreme, intense and excessive violence. The extreme transgressive drama of such offenders has proved attractive for the news and entertainment media. The main character in the 1999 film *American History X*, Derek Vineyard, played by the actor Edward Norton, for instance, represents the extreme racist of whom nightmares are made: a skinheaded, Nazi-tattooed, charismatic leader of a group of young people subscribing to white supremacy who is jailed for a particularly brutal hate-fuelled murder.

The drama of such characters has provided an attraction for scholars too. Hate crime texts published in the United States generally contain the seemingly obligatory chapter on extremist offenders (cf. Perry 2001; Levin and McDevitt 2002; Gerstenfeld and Grant 2004; Blazak 2009c). Texts produced by scholars in the UK have also joined the trend (cf. Hall 2005). And elsewhere in Europe there has been a tradition in the scholarly literature on racist violence against immigrants, refugees and asylum seekers of framing the problem as organised violence by the extreme right and by neo-Nazi skinheads (cf. Björgo and Witte 1993; Björgo 1995; van Donselaar and Wagenaar 2007). In some cases this focus on extremist offenders has been highly valuable in humanising offenders to indicate that it is too simplistic to draw a hard distinction between 'extremists' and 'ordinary' people, as extremists have their very ordinary lives too (cf. Blazak 2009b). It has also offered an understanding of the grievances extreme offenders express about their sense of exclusion in diverse multicultural society and what Blazak calls their 'ethnic envy' – their perceived lack of opportunity, compared with minorities, to express their 'white identity' (Blazak 2008).

Even though extremist offenders articulate their bigotry with a greater cogency than most other people, their views are shared by many who do not articulate them with the same intensity. Almost two decades ago, research involving economically marginalised youths in New York City (Pinderhughes 1993) demonstrated that given limited job prospects, many saw themselves as victims of policies and practices that favoured minorities: policies of affirmative action and reverse discrimination, and growing minority political power in the city. Against this background where they perceived that they were under siege, racist violence was used instrumentally to defend one of the few things over which they could act to try to exercise control – the space in which they lived. A decade later, research with convicted racist offenders, who were either unemployed or working in low-paid, casual and insecure jobs, in contact with the probation service in Greater Manchester, England, revealed how some offenders articulated their offending in terms of the sense of shame and failure they felt about their social and economic marginalisation. In the context of the 'routine, taken-for-granted racism that characterised their neighbourhoods' and also 'in the context of a shared sense of being invisible and ignored' (Ray et al. 2003: 125) their victims were scapegoated and blamed for their marginalisation. The significance of the background context of social and economic disadvantage for 'race-hate' crime has also been indicated by Dixon et al. (cf. Gadd et al. 2005; Dixon and Gadd 2006), using a small research sample of racist offenders, as they highlight the preponderance of offenders with mental health problems and other social disadvantages.

Paradoxically, though, it might serve as an emotional comfort to think that hate crime offenders are 'extremists', an aberration, confined to the ideological margins of society. Instead, it could be somewhat more disturbing to admit that they are nearer the core, acting out the values and attitudes shared by many. From this more challenging perspective, the occurrence of 'hate crime' can be seen as a barometer of the prevailing strength of those values and the strong prevalence of 'hate crime' (as will be discussed below) indicates the banality of 'hate': the intricate weaving of various forms of bigotry into the structural fabric[9] of society.

Given these structural foundations, 'hate crime' might be regarded as entirely normal and rational behaviour (Perry 2005: 126). Offenders are acting on and conveying sentiments shared by many and taking them to their logical conclusion. Those who commit acts of 'hate crime' might be different from others in the respect that they act on their attitudes whereas others don't. But in the case of racist incidents, Rae Sibbitt has suggested that there is a 'reciprocal relationship' between the racist attitudes of perpetrators and the wider communities from which offenders are drawn. According to Sibbitt 'perpetrators see this as legitimising their actions. In turn, the wider community not only spawns such perpetrators, but fails to condemn them and actively reinforces their behaviour' (Sibbitt 1997: vii). Sibbitt therefore very aptly suggested that the wider community can be regarded as the *'perpetrator community'* (Sibbitt 1997: 101) as there is in effect a 'critical, mutually supportive relationship between the individual perpetrator and the wider community' (Sibbitt 1997: 101). While the wider community shapes and legitimises the perpetrator's racism, the offender in turn serves the community 'in a vicarious fashion by taking their collective views to their logical conclusion and acting them out' (Sibbitt 1997: 101). As already noted, such a process has been conceptualised by Barbara Perry (2001) as 'doing difference'. But in going further, echoing elements of 'structured action theory', Perry proposes that by their actions hate crime offenders are not only acting out these notions of difference: they are also at the same time reconstructing the prevailing structures of oppression and reinforcing the boundaries of difference.

A limitation with such a perspective, however, is that it casts hate crime offenders as merely puppets of the social structure, automatons instrumentally acting out the bigotry woven into the structural fabric. It does not account for individual agency or explain why some people offend and others who are similarly placed in the social structure do not. To enhance the notion of 'doing difference' by addressing these limitations there is a need again to step outside of the offender's mind and also to step outside of the collective conscience that shapes it, and step into the foreground and the situational contexts of offending as reported by victims and witnesses. By scrutinising the foreground of 'hate' incidents it will not be possible to reach into the offender's soul, but it is possible to grasp some of the impulses for offending and in some cases identify the triggers at work.

In applying such an approach in an analysis which began with an unravelling of the situational dynamics of anti-Jewish incidents reported to London's Metropolitan Police Service (MPS) (Iganski et al. 2005) and then extended to news media reporting of anti-Muslim incidents following the 2005 London bombings, and developed further by drawing on qualitative research on racist incidents and survey findings on homophobic and disablist incidents, Iganski (2008) demonstrates that many 'hate crime' offenders are not 'extremists' consciously acting on their bigotry, targeting their victims in premeditated violent attacks. Instead, many 'hate crime' offenders are 'ordinary people' who offend in the unfolding contexts of their everyday lives: people like 'us', our friends, relatives, neighbours and work colleagues, passers-by in the street, people out shopping, people using public transport, people driving their cars, people at work and children at school. The ubiquity of offending indicates the banality of bigotry in various guises as many offences are not prompted by a particular ideological conviction or volition but instead in their expressive character they reveal sentiments that lie beneath the surface of everyday cognition for many people. They rise to the surface for some people when the opportunity to vent their simmering bigotry presents itself, or it is often triggered by a grievance, an irritation or conflict: the routine incivilities of everyday life. In some respects the ordinariness of everyday offending is not dissimilar to less frequent but more intense extremist offending. Pete Simi (2009), for instance, demonstrates how racist skinheads are often likely to be involved in opportunistic, situational and spontaneous violence, often fuelled by real or manufactured interpersonal disputes, in which the targets are based on convenience rather than carefully premeditated attacks in which they are acting out their bigotry with deliberation and aforethought.

The harms of 'hate crime'

To turn from the perpetrators to the victims of 'hate crime' it is clear that individual victims suffer distinct harms compared with victims of similar crimes that are not motivated or aggravated by an offender's bigotry, bias or prejudice, and the consequences spread well beyond the victimised individual (Iganski 2001). 'Hate crimes' can terrorise communities. Other people who share the victim's identity and live in the neighbourhood – and even beyond – and who hear about the crime are likely to be fearful that they could be targeted too. A similar sense of fear can be spread among other communities who are commonly victims of 'hate crime'. More diffusely, each act of 'hate crime' also brings particular society-wide consequences.

It is useful to examine each of these consequences of 'hate crime' more finely as they are fundamental to conceptualising hate crime and also fundamental to the legislative and criminal justice response as will be discussed below. To take the victimised individual first, Eva Tiby argues that victims of 'hate crime' experience more severe consequences than victims of crime in general for a number of reasons: the potential for self-blame on the part of the victim, the questioning of their own worth, strong feelings of vulnerability and 'a lack of trust in the support provided by society to the members of the group to which one belongs' (Tiby 2009: 36). Respondents in Tiby's surveys and interviews with victims of homophobic crime in Sweden reported having nightmares, feelings of grief and a greater fear of future victimisation. Some respondents reported that victimisation placed strains on their relationships (see also on this point Noelle 2009: 93–6) and Tiby suggests that the 'most far-reaching consequences relate to losing faith in one's fellow human beings' (Tiby 2009: 38). The way that victims of anti-LGBT hate crime manage their victimisation can be affected by the extent to which they have 'come out', although the impact can be variable: some victims will question their sexual identity and others will come out more strongly (Noelle 2009: 86–9).

While most victims of crime suffer psychological and emotional effects, the available research evidence clearly indicates that higher proportions of 'hate crime' victims report symptoms. Victims of racist incidents captured by the British Crime Survey are more likely, when compared with victims of the same crimes that occur for other reasons, to report psychological and emotional symptoms. Statistically significant higher proportions of victims in incidents that are believed to be racially motivated, compared with other crimes, report feelings of 'shock', 'fear', 'depression', 'anxiety' and 'panic attacks', and feelings of a 'loss of confidence' and 'feeling vulnerable' (Iganski 2008: 82, table 4.2). The same pattern of difference holds even when controlling for the type of crime experienced (Iganski 2008: 12–13, tables 1.4 and 1.5), possibly because previous experiences of victimisation and knowledge about the victimisation of others provide a context for the consequences inflicted by any incident.

The psychological impacts upon victims are unravelled in depth in the case of 'race-hate crime' by Kellina Craig-Henderson (2009). One significant consequence observed is that victims of 'hate crime' may experience 'feelings of deviancy' (Craig-Henderson 2009: 22). The experience of 'hate crime' may be perceived by victims as marking them out as being different from others and foster a negative self-image. Craig-Henderson suggests that while victims of crime in general are encouraged to 'take comfort in knowing that what happened to them could have happened to anyone' (Craig-Henderson 2009: 22), 'hate crime' victims come to recognise that what happened to them happened because of who they are. After an initial shock period this painful realisation will begin to sink in. For minority victims of 'hate crime' this realisation will closely resonate with, and be compounded by, their knowledge of the stigmatised and marginalised status of their group, increasing their sense of alienation.

Individual victims of 'hate crime' also exhibit behavioural reactions to their victimisation. In reporting on her research into homophobic crime in Sweden Eva Tiby suggests that the experience of victimisation may lead the victim 'to start using avoidance strategies, which may in turn lead to meeting fewer open LGBT people, on one hand, and to meeting LGBT people who are "on guard" and apparently ready to be attacked on the other' (Tiby 2009: 37). Avoidance strategies include the victim concealing their sexual orientation and identity (by not holding hands or being otherwise intimate in public with their partner) and even moving home away from nearby perpetrators.

Many victims of crime manifest behavioural reactions as a consequence of their experience. However, the British Crime Survey shows that statistically significant higher proportions of victims of incidents believed to be racially motivated, compared with victims of non-racially motivated crimes, report behavioural consequences in that they had 'Started to avoid walking in/going to certain places', and higher proportions of victims of racially motivated crime report having moved home (Iganski 2008: 79, table 4.1).

To compound the consequences even further, the actual process of victimisation may not be confined solely to the incident of the 'hate crime' for some victims. Those who encounter a less than sympathetic response from the police and the criminal justice system, and sometimes even abuse, will be subject to 'secondary victimisation' (Noelle 2009: 79–81). Complaints from minority ethnic communities about the policing of racist incidents in the UK were particularly prevalent prior to the publication of the Macpherson Inquiry report (1999) into the flawed police investigation of the murder of Stephen Lawrence (Iganski 2008: 89–91). Similar complaints have been voiced more recently about the policing of 'hate crimes' against people with a disability and the strength of the evidence indicates that some victims are being revictimised by the very agencies that should be expected to support them (cf. Mind 2007; Scope 2008).

In thinking beyond the individual, or the initial person targeted, each act of 'hate crime' potentially inflicts wider victimisation by terrorising and intimidating persons who share the same identity characteristics as the victim. This has been demonstrated, for instance, in the narratives of interviews conducted by Helen Ahn Lim with Asian Americans in the United States. Members of targeted communities understand that attacks are not personal –

against the individual person targeted – they are attacks against the community to which the victim belongs: the individual is attacked as a symbol of their community. Victims are therefore interchangeable. Members of victimised communities understand that they could be the next person targeted or targeted at some point in the future: 'hate crimes' are consequently 'message crimes' in the message of intimidation sent to victimised communities. This terroristic impact cannot be avoided unless potential victims can manage and seek to conceal their identity: as Helen Ahn Lim neatly puts it, 'members of the targeted community carry with them the reason for their potential victimization' (2009: 116). Such indirect victimisation cannot be captured by crime surveys of individual victims. It is also a process of victimisation that spreads well beyond the immediate neighbourhood in which acts of 'hate crime' occur, especially when extreme incidents attract extensive news media coverage. As Monique Noelle's in-depth qualitative interviews have revealed in the case of the 'ripple-effect' of the 1998 murder of the young gay student Matthew Shepard in the United States, persons who share a minority group identity with the direct victim of a 'hate crime' can be indirectly profoundly traumatised, and experience the same type of victimisation impacts as the direct victim (Noelle 2002).

Lastly, each act of 'hate crime' can be considered to inflict society-wide consequences. 'Hate crimes' offend against societal commitments to equality, diversity and a respect for difference. Although the extent of offending indicates that a substantial number of people do not share these commitments, such values are deeply embedded into the legal and political cultures of many nations (on this point see Lawrence 1994: 35, 1999: 43, 2006: 3).

Conclusion: the need for policy learning

Although 'hate crime' statistics as such are not published in the UK, evidence of crimes and incidents motivated or aggravated by offenders' bigotry, bias or prejudice indicate that 'hate crime' is a significant social problem. The number of racially motivated incidents was estimated at 184,000 incidents for the 12-month period covered by the 2006/7 British Crime Survey (BCS) (Jones and Singer 2008: 10). Data are not yet published on information collected by recently introduced questions in the BCS about whether victims of crime thought the incident was religiously motivated or motivated on account of the victim's sexual orientation or disability. However, the 'Gay British Crime Survey' commissioned by Stonewall in 2008 reported that one in eight lesbian and gay people had experienced a homophobic hate crime or incident in the last year (Dick 2008: 5). A recent report produced for the Equality and Human Rights Commission noted that 'there is compelling evidence that disabled people are at higher risk of targeted violence, harassment and abuse in comparison with non-disabled people' (Office for Public Management (OPM 2009)). For some targeted communities, upsurges in incidents are triggered by political events. Small-scale surveys of Muslims in Britain shortly after the July 2005 London bombings revealed widespread hostility and abuse. Incidents against Jews in Britain also appear to have escalated at the time of the Israeli attack on Gaza in December 2008 and January 2009, as they have done with previous upsurges in the Israel–Palestine conflict.

There is now a considerable scholarly and policy literature on the problem of 'hate crime'. While there is a need to further develop understanding of the consequences of victimisation, and also a need to further understand the motivations and behaviours of offenders, there is a relative lack of shared understanding about how to effectively manage the problem of 'hate crime'. There is a voluminous literature on the dilemmas and conflicts involved in criminalising 'hate', but hardly any by comparison on other means of managing offenders. There is even less on supporting victims. There is a strong need therefore for careful evaluation of the numerous localised initiatives that have been established so that learning can be achieved from the successes and from the limitations of the plethora of projects underway: that is the challenge that now lies ahead.

Selected further reading

One of the earliest and most influential texts, which provides a very accessible introduction to the topic, is Levin and McDevitt's *Hate Crimes: The Rising Tide of Bigotry and Bloodshed* (1993) which was revised and updated as *Hate Crimes (Revisited): America's War on Those Who Are Different* (2002). Jacobs and Potter's *Hate Crimes: Criminal Law and Identity Politics* (1998) and Lawrence's *Punishing Hate: Bias Crimes Under American Law* (1999) provide competing perspectives on the justifiability of hate crime laws. The different sides of the debate are also provided in Iganski's edited collection *The Hate Debate: Should Hate Be Punished as a Crime?* (2002). Perry's *In the Name of Hate: Understanding Hate Crime* (2001) provides a theoretical framework for thinking about hate crime, and Iganski's *Hate Crime and the City* (2008) combines empirical research and theory. Ehrlich's recent book *Hate Crimes and Ethnoviolence* (2009) includes some very useful material on hate crime and the news media. Two collections of readings, Perry's *Hate and Bias Crime: A Reader* (2003) and Gerstenfeld and Grant's *Crimes of Hate: Selected Readings* (2004) provide a valuable set of materials. Useful textbooks are offered particularly for readers in the UK by Hall's *Hate Crime* (2005) and Chakraborti and Garland's *Hate Crime: Impact, Causes and Responses* (2009). The *Journal of Interpersonal Violence* is also a very useful source for articles on hate crime.

Notes

1 US Department of Justice, Federal Bureau of Investigation, 'About *Hate Crime Statistics'*. Online at: http://www.fbi.gov/ucr/hc2007/abouthcs.htm (last accessed 21 November 2009).
2 See OSCE Office for Democratic Institutions and Human Rights, 'ODIHR Helps States to Tackle Hate Crime with New Legal Guidelines'. Online at: http://www.osce.org/odihr/item_2_30631.html (last accessed 21 November 2009).
3 See Human Rights First, *2008 Hate Crime Survey*. Online at: http://www.humanrightsfirst.org/discrimination/pages.aspx?id=157 (last accessed 21 November 2009).
4 See: http://www.homeoffice.gov.uk/crime-victims/reducing-crime/hate-crime/ (last accessed 21 November 2007).

5 This author prefers to surround the words 'hate crime' with quotation marks to signify that although 'hate' may not often figure in the crimes so labelled, the concept of 'hate crime' is not entirely devoid of utility.
6 Anti-Defamation League, *Hate Crime Laws*. Online at: http://www.adl.org/99hatecrime/text_legis.asp (last accessed 21 November 2009).
7 Office for Democratic Institutions and Human Rights, *Hate Crime*. Online at: http://www.osce.org/odihr/20052.html (last accessed 21 November 2009).
8 For the specific details of the legislation see Iganski (2008: 127–9).
9 This notion of structure contrasts with the orthodox sociological notion of structure as a patterning of social relations, embodied in the familiar terms 'class structure' and 'structural inequality', for instance, which conceive of structure in terms of the arrangement of material, economic and institutional resources, and systems of dominance derived from such arrangements.

References

Allport, G. (1954/1979) *The Nature of Prejudice*. Reading, MA: Addison-Wesley.
Association of Chief Police Officers (2005) *Hate Crime: Delivering a Quality Service: Good Practice and Tactical Guidance*. London: ACPO.
Björgo, T. (ed.) (1995) *Terror from the Extreme Right*. London: Frank Cass.
Björgo, T. and Witte, R. (eds) (1993) *Racist Violence in Europe*. Basingstoke: Macmillan.
Blazak, R. (2008) 'Ethnic envy: how teens construct whiteness in globalized America', in D. C. Brotherton and M. Flynn (eds), *Globalizing the Streets*. New York: Columbia University Press, pp. 169–84.
Blazak, R. (2009a) 'Introduction', in R. Blazak (ed.), *Hate Crimes: Hate Crime Offenders*. Westport, CT: Praeger, pp. xiii–xvii.
Blazak, R. (2009b) 'Interview with a hate offender', in R. Blazak (ed.), *Hate Crimes: Hate Crime Offenders*. Westport, CT: Praeger, pp. 189–205.
Blazak, R. (ed.) (2009c) *Hate Crimes: Hate Crime Offenders*. Westport, CT: Praeger.
Chakraborti, N. and Garland, J. (2009) *Hate Crime: Impact, Causes and Responses*. London: Sage.
Craig-Henderson, K. M. (2009) 'The psychological harms of hate: implications and interventions', in P. Iganski (ed.), *Hate Crimes. The Consequences of Hate Crime*. Westport, CT: Praeger, pp. 15–30.
Dick, S. (2008) *Homophobic Hate Crime: The Gay British Crime Survey 2008*. London: Stonewall.
Dixon, J. and Gadd, D. (2006) 'Getting the message? "New" Labour and the criminalization of "hate"', *Criminology and Criminal Justice*, 6 (3): 309–28.
Ehrlich, H. J. (2009) *Hate Crimes and Ethnoviolence*. Boulder, CO: Westview Press.
Gadd, D. and Jefferson, T. (2007) *Psychosocial Criminology*. Los Angeles: Sage.
Gadd, D., Dixon, B. and Jefferson, T. (2005) *Why Do They Do It? Racial Harassment in North Staffordshire. Key Findings*. Keele: Centre for Criminological Research, Keele University.
Gerstenfeld, P. B. and Grant, D. R. (eds) (2004) *Crimes of Hate: Selected Readings*. Thousand Oaks, CA: Sage.
Hall, N. (2005) *Hate Crime*. Cullompton: Willan.
Iganski, P. (2001) 'Hate crimes hurt more', *American Behavioral Scientist*, 45 (4): 626–38.
Iganski, P. (ed.) (2002) *The Hate Debate: Should Hate Be Punished as a Crime?* London: Profile.
Iganski, P. (2008) *Hate Crime and the City*. Bristol: Policy Press.

Iganski, P., Kielinger, V. and Paterson, S. (2005) *Hate Crimes Against London's Jews*. London: Institute for Jewish Policy Research and the Metropolitan Police Service.

Jacobs, J. and Potter, K. (1998) *Hate Crimes: Criminal Law and Identity Politics*. Oxford: Oxford University Press.

Jenness, V. and Grattet, R. (2001) *Making Hate a Crime. From Social Movement to Law Enforcement*. New York: Russell Sage Foundation.

Jones, A. and Singer, L. (2008) *Statistics on Race and the Criminal Justice System 2006/7*. London: Ministry of Justice.

Lawrence, F. (1994) 'The punishment of hate: towards a normative theory of bias-motivated crimes', *Michigan Law Review*, 93: 320–81.

Lawrence, F. (1999) *Punishing Hate: Bias Crimes under American Law*. Cambridge, MA: Harvard University Press.

Lawrence, F. (2006) *The Hate Crime Project and Its Limitations: Evaluating the Societal Gains and Risk in Bias Crime Law Enforcement*, Working Paper No. 216. Washington, DC: George Washington University Law School.

Levin, J. and McDevitt, J. (1993) *Hate Crimes: The Rising Tide of Bigotry and Bloodshed*. New York: Plenum Press.

Levin, J. and McDevitt, J. (2002) *Hate Crimes Revisited: America's War on Those Who Are Different*. Boulder, CO: Westview Press.

Lim, H. A. (2009) 'Beyond the immediate victim: understanding hate crimes as message crimes', in P. Iganski (ed.), *Hate Crimes. The Consequences of Hate Crime*. Westport, CT: Praeger, pp. 15–30.

McDevitt, J., Levin, J. and Bennett, S. (2002) 'Hate crime offenders: an expanded typology,' *Journal of Social Issues*, 58 (2): 303–18.

MacPherson, Sir W. (1999) *The Stephen Lawrence Inquiry*. London: Stationery Office.

Mind (2007) *Another Assault*. London: Mind the National Association for Mental Health.

Noelle, M. (2002) 'The ripple effect of the Matthew Shepard murder: impact upon the assumptive worlds of members of the targeted group', *American Behavioral Scientist*, 46 (1): 27–50.

Noelle, M. (2009) 'The psychological and social effects of antibisexual, antigay, and antilesbian violence and harassment', in P. Iganski (ed.), *Hate Crimes: The Consequences of Hate Crime*. Westport, CT: Praeger, pp. 73–105.

Office for Public Management (OPM) (2009) *Disabled People's Experiences of Targeted Violence, Harassment and Abuse*. London: OPM.

Perry, B. (2001) *In the Name of Hate*. New York: Routledge.

Perry, B. (2003) *Hate and Bias Crime: A Reader*. New York: Routledge.

Perry, B. (2005) 'A crime by any other name: the semantics of "hate"', *Journal of Hate Studies*, 4 (1): 121–37.

Perry, B. and Olsson, P. (2009) 'Hate crime as a human rights violation', in P. Iganski (ed.), *Hate Crimes: The Consequences of Hate Crime*. Westport, CT: Praeger, pp. 175–91.

Pinderhughes, H. (1993) 'The anatomy of racially motivated violence in New York City: a case study of youth in Southern Brooklyn', *Social Problems*, 40 (4): 478–92.

Ray, L., Smith, D. and Wastell, L. (2003) 'Understanding racist violence', in E. A. Stanko (ed.), *The Meanings of Violence*. London: Routledge, pp. 112–29.

Scope (2008) *Getting Away with Murder. Disabled People's Experiences of Hate Crime in the UK*. London: Scope.

Sibbitt, R. (1997) *The Perpetrators of Racial Harassment and Racial Violence*, Research Study No. 176. London: Home Office.

Simi, P. (2009) 'Skinhead street violence', in R. Blazak (ed.), *Hate Crimes: Hate Crime Offenders*. Westport, CT: Praeger, pp. 157–70.

Tiby, E. (2009) 'Homophobic hate crimes in Sweden: questions and consequences', in P. Iganski (ed.), *Hate Crimes. The Consequences of Hate Crime*. Westport, CT: Praeger, pp. 31–48.

van Donselaar, J. and Wagenaar, W. (eds) (2007) *Racism and Extremism Monitor: Racial Violence and Violence Incited by the Extreme Right in 2006*. Amsterdam: Anne Frank Stuchting and Leiden: Leiden University.

Webster, C. (2008) 'Racist victimisation in England and Wales', in J. A. Winterdyk and G. A. Antonopoulos (eds), *Racist Victimisation: International Reflections and Perspectives*. Aldershot: Ashgate.

Chapter 19

Stalking and harassment

Victoria Heckels and Karl Roberts

This chapter will define stalking, consider the prevalence of stalking, review what is known about the characteristics of stalkers and victims of stalking, examine the behaviour carried out by stalkers and look at some of the responses to stalking. The chapter will begin with a historical review of the concept of stalking.

History

For many years the term 'stalking' described the activity of hunters pursuing animal prey. More recently, it has become the label for a pattern of persistent pursuit and intrusive behaviour directed by one person towards another that is unwanted and can continue for several months or even years. It is only in the last decade that this behaviour has been recognised as a significant social problem.

The label 'stalking,' used to describe harassing behaviours occurred first in the late 1980s with media reports describing the persistent pursuit of celebrities by obsessed fans. The most common behaviours directed by stalkers towards their victims include repeated telephone calls, visiting the victim's home or workplace, letter writing, following the victim, sending unwanted gifts, making threats against the victim, face-to-face confrontations and physical violence (Meloy 1998; Mullen *et al*. 2000).

Stalking first became classified as a criminal offence in 1990 in California. The impetus was the 1989 murder in California of actress Rebecca Schaeffer by a fan who had pursued her for a number of years (Anderson 1993). While not explicitly using the term 'Stalking', the legislation outlawed persistent malicious harassment. Other jurisdictions have also enacted similar legislation, including all states in the USA, Australia, Canada, the United Kingdom and many European states (e.g. Mullen *et al*. 2000).

In the United Kingdom the Protection from Harassment Act was enacted in 1997. Here there are three elements to an offence of harassment: that the offender pursued a course of conduct amounting to harassment of another person and knew or ought to know that the course of conduct amounted to harassment. Harassment is defined as causing alarm or distress and a course of conduct is behaviour that is capable of causing distress that occurred on at least two occasions. Alarm or distress felt by the victim is subject to a reasonableness test – a reasonable person would when experiencing such a course of conduct respond with distress. This Act covers all forms of harassment including racial and other forms of discrimination as well as stalking behaviour. The legislation does not explicitly refer to stalking.

Although legislation exists throughout the world, one of the problems for those who attempt to carry out research on stalking is that this form of criminal behaviour is notoriously difficult to define in an unambiguous manner. It is to the problem of definition that we now move.

Definition of stalking

It is important to provide a rigorous definition of what actually constitutes stalking so that it is clear what is being discussed (Sheridan and Davies 2001). Currently there is little consensus regarding such a definition. One of the difficulties in this is that many of the behaviours commonly carried out by stalkers can be considered routine or even harmless (Cupach and Spitzberg 2000; Sheridan and Davies 2001). Consider more common stalking behaviours – making telephone calls, sending e-mails, sending letters and gifts. Most of these are socially acceptable activities; it is only when they are unwanted and form a persistent long-term pattern that they become more sinister, especially if the victim suffers fear and distress as a result.

There has been some debate as to what constitutes a 'persistent pattern of behaviour'. Many authors and most legal definitions of stalking have defined this as two or more separate acts of harassment (Mullen *et al.* 2000). In defining a persistent pattern of behaviour in this way there is a danger of over-attributing the label of stalking to other more innocuous behaviours. A low threshold such as two separate acts may lead to many activities becoming classed as stalking. For example, a potential suitor who makes two unwanted telephone calls to his beloved could be guilty of stalking her, as would other more extreme and less socially acceptable behaviour such as an individual who sends hundreds of letters and makes hundreds of telephone calls to his ex-partner.

A related problem is the duration of the unwanted attention. Few definitions of stalking explicitly state how long the harassment needs to continue to become stalking resulting in similar dangers of over-attributing the label of stalking. For example, looking at someone in the street on two or more separate occasions on the same day, if it engendered fear in the recipient, could be classified as stalking, as would two acts of harassment separated by a number of years.

Mullen *et al.* argue that the number of harassing acts and the duration of the harassment should reflect the purpose for which the behaviour is to be labelled as stalking. For legal purposes a low number of acts is perhaps optimum to give maximum likelihood of a swift response by law enforcement to the victim's distress. Most of the definitions in the literature were framed to mirror legal definitions and as such have a low threshold for defining a long-term pattern. For research purposes Mullen *et al.* (2000) suggest that tighter criteria should be set so as to minimise the risk of over-attributing behaviours as stalking.

Mullen and his colleagues (e.g. Mullen *et al.* 2000) offered a definition of stalking which attempted to address some of the problems described above. They defined stalking as

> a constellation of behaviours in which one individual inflicts on another repeated unwanted intrusions and communications.

In an attempt to operationalise their definition Mullen *et al.* (2000) added temporal and numerical considerations – for behaviour to be classified as stalking it must involve at least ten separate behavioural intrusions and/ or communications and must have continued for a period of at least four weeks.

Within many legal definitions of stalking the notion of victim fear is important. Generally the test is whether or not the victim's fear is reasonable given the context of the stalking. Fear would perhaps be an expected response from a victim of a direct physical attack or explicit threats of violence, and these experiences have often been central to the judgment within criminal justice of the reasonableness of a victim's fear (e.g. Mullen *et al.* 2000). To mirror legal definitions of stalking many researchers have made the experience of fear in response to threats and/or physical attacks central to their definition of stalking (e.g. Meloy 1998). The issue of reasonable fear is, however, problematic, especially for victims who do not experience direct threats or violent and other criminal acts. Indeed, it is possible that individuals may experience fear without explicit threats being made, for example activities such as sending unwanted gifts or making unwanted telephone calls may themselves become threatening and induce fear if repeated on a number of occasions (Spitzberg and Cupach 2003).

Stalking appears, then, to be a difficult concept to define. The notion that definitions of stalking should be related to the purpose for which they are being made is a sound one and so legal definitions perhaps should stress victim fear, perpetrator intent to cause fear and a small number of behaviours to constitute stalking. Definitions of this kind maximise the speed by which a suffering victim can be dealt with by the legal system. For researchers interested in clearly differentiating stalking from other behaviours, however, tighter criteria seem to be necessary to ensure that what researchers are considering is in fact stalking and not some unrelated innocuous behaviour.

How common is stalking?

Spitzberg and Cupach (2003) report an incidence rate of self-reported stalking of 21.2 per cent. Most studies they considered, however, used samples of undergraduate students or clinical and forensic patients as participants. These authors also reported that the incidence of stalking appears to be higher in forensic and clinical samples (32.6 per cent) than in ordinary samples (13.9 per cent). In surveys of representative community samples the incidence rate is lower, rates of 8 per cent for females and 2 per cent for males have been found in the USA (Tjaden and Thoennes 1998) and in the United Kingdom Budd *et al.* (2000) found a lifetime prevalence of 12 per cent in England and Wales (16 per cent female, 7 per cent males); similar rates have been found in other English-speaking western countries (e.g. Australian Bureau of Statistics 1996). These findings demonstrate that stalking is relatively common and as such is a significant social problem deserving the attention of policymakers, researchers and law enforcement.

Having identified what stalking is and how common it is, it is useful to consider what it is that stalkers do. The next section will move on to consider the tactics used by stalkers.

What do stalkers do?

Stalking tactics are the specific behaviours that stalkers direct towards their victims, a number of which have been observed. Spitzberg and Cupach (2003) identified five clusters of stalking tactics. These were labelled:

hyperintimacy tactics – including sending letters, emails and text messages, making telephone calls to the victim;
pursuit or proximity tactics – including following the victim and hanging around the victim's home or workplace;
invasion tactics – including breaking into or otherwise gaining access to the victim's property;
intimidation tactics – including making threats against the victim; and
violent tactics – including assault of the victim.

Stalkers may use one or more of these tactics.

It is not clear if stalking tactics are more or less related to different motives for stalking and this is an area requiring future research. One issue when examining stalking tactics is the likelihood of violence against the victim. Many victims report that it is the fear of violence that is most damaging to them (Mullen *et al.* 2001) and it is the association between stalking and violence that we now consider.

Stalking and violence perpetration

The majority of stalkers appear to make threats of violence towards the victim; however, only a minority appear to carry them out (e.g. Meloy 1998). Similarly, while Meloy (1998) reports that the frequency of violence toward stalking victims ranges from 25 per cent to 35 per cent of cases, stalking violence is generally of a relatively minor nature such as damage to property and minor assaults resulting in minor injuries (Meloy 1998; Mullen *et al.* 2000).

The risk of serious physical violence, such as murder, rape or aggravated harm, does not appear to be particularly high – indeed the homicide rate among victims of stalking is less than 2 per cent (Meloy 1998). Despite this the fear of violence has been shown to seriously impact upon the psychological and physical health of stalking victims (Westrup *et al.* 1999).

Former romantic partners who stalk are more likely than strangers or acquaintances to be violent towards their victims (Kienlen *et al.* 1997; Bjerregaard 2000; Farnham *et al.* 2000), especially if the relationship was characterised by domestic violence, controlling behaviours by the stalker and jealousy (e.g. Roberts 2002, 2005).

It seems then that there is a relatively low risk of serious violence in stalking offences, but the fear of violence in victims is significant. We now move on to consider who are the victims of stalking?

Characteristics of stalking victims

Stalking affects both males and females from all social classes, cultural backgrounds, occupations and age groups, although females are generally more at risk of victimisation than males (Spitzberg and Cupach 2003). The risk of stalking victimisation appears to be greater in certain groups, in particular young women, undergraduates, individuals who live alone, those who live in rented accommodation and those who have a criminal history and/or suffer from mental health problems (Fremouw *et al.* 1997; Logan *et al.* 2000). The likelihood of becoming a stalking victim may be related to the opportunity a potential stalker has to gain access to a victim. This applies to young people in particular. Most young people are more likely to engage in dating, go to nightclubs and to have wide circles of acquaintances than older people. This raises the risk of them crossing the path of a potential stalker. Similarly, individuals suffering mental health problems or who become involved with the criminal justice system are more likely than the average person, to come into contact with other individuals with mental health and other psychological problems, some of whom may have a propensity to stalk them.

Studies comparing stalking victims with non-victims have generally failed to find differences between them in terms of a range of social variables. For example, Bjerregaard (2000) compared student stalking victims and non-victims and found no differences between them in terms of age, education level, household income and marital status.

Stalking does not appear to be focused upon any particular group of society; rather it appears that victims may be drawn from any walk of life, gender and age group, although young females are more at risk. Moving on we will now consider what is known about the characteristics of stalkers.

Characteristics of stalkers

There appears to be no single demographic profile of stalkers (Mullen *et al.* 2000). Indeed, the only consistent finding related to the demographic characteristics of stalkers is that men are more likely than women to be stalkers. Female stalkers are more likely to target someone they have known, males are less likely to pursue other men while females will often target other females (e.g. Zona *et al.* 1993; Spitzberg and Cupach 2003). There does not appear to be a difference between the genders in the duration of stalking. While the contexts and motives for stalking appear to differ between males and females, the intrusiveness of the behaviours and the impact upon victims does not (e.g. Mullen *et al.* 2000).

Within offender populations stalkers tend to be older than other offenders (Zona *et al.* 1993; Meloy and Gothard 1995), more likely to be single, separated or divorced (Harmon *et al.* 1995), better educated (Meloy and Gothard 1995), and more intelligent (Meloy and Gothard 1995) and are often unemployed at the time of their offences (Kienlen *et al.* 1997). Other research has, however, failed to find significant demographic differences between stalkers and other comparison groups (Coleman 1997).

Psychosocial characteristics of stalkers

Lewis *et al.* (2001) found that stalkers scored higher on measures of insecure attachment and borderline personality features. The authors suggested that stalkers would be likely to exhibit a general pattern of inadequate interpersonal attachments, were more likely to have difficulty in forming and maintaining relationships, were likely to be emotionally labile and unstable, and would be most likely to experience difficulties regarding their interpersonal relationships.

Mental illness

Studies have attempted to assess the prevalence of mental illness and psychological disorders within samples of stalkers (Westrup and Fremouw 1998). A study by the Canadian Department of Justice (Gill and Brockman 1996) examined the records of 601 offenders charged under Canada's anti-stalking legislation and found that 14 per cent of the sample of 601 had a history of 'mental health problems' although the nature of these was not specified. Other research has attempted to identify the prevalence of specific disorders in stalker samples.

Erotomania is a delusional disorder in which the individual believes that another individual loves him or her. This belief frequently results in the pursuit of the love object (Mullen *et al.* 2000). Within samples of stalkers most studies have found relatively low prevalence rates for erotomania, with rates from 4–12 per cent within samples of forensic patients referred for stalking-related offences (e.g. Zona *et al.* 1993; Kienlen *et al.* 1997). Therefore, while some stalkers do exhibit this disorder, erotomania is not a particularly common disorder within stalker groups. Thus the presence of erotomania is unlikely to be an explanation for all stalking behaviour.

Schizophrenia has been found to be relatively common in forensic samples of stalkers (Harmon *et al.* 1995; Kienlen *et al.* 1997; Mullen and Pathe 1994; Sandberg *et al.* 1998), although it appears to be less common in stalkers as compared with other non-stalking mentally disordered offenders (Meloy and Gothard 1995). Mood disorders such as dysthymia, major depression or bipolar disorder have also been found in groups of stalkers (Kienlen *et al.* 1997; Meloy and Gothard 1995; Mullen and Pathe 1994; Sandberg *et al.* 1998). Studies have identified relatively high rates of personality disorder within forensic samples of stalkers, with cluster B personality disorders (antisocial, histrionic, borderline and narcissistic personality disorders) most common (McGuire and Wraith 2000).

Substance abuse has been found among stalkers, although there is some variation in the results between studies. Estimates of the prevalence of substance abuse in forensic samples of stalkers ranging from 2 per cent (Harmon *et al.* 1995) to 70 per cent (Meloy and Gothard 1995) have been found. Some studies have found substance abuse to be more common among stalkers compared to other groups of offenders while other studies have found no differences with other types of offender (Meloy and Gothard 1995). Stalking victimisation of former romantic partners has been found to be associated with frequent alcohol use by the stalker (Logan *et al.* 2000).

It therefore appears that stalker samples show a raised incidence of various forms of mental health problem, although by no means do all stalkers suffer such problems and so the presence of mental health problems appears to be neither necessary nor sufficient as an explanation for stalking (Meloy 1998). We now move on to consider other possible reasons for stalking.

Stalking and domestic violence

There is an association between stalking and domestic violence within an intimate relationship with stalking victims likely to have encountered physical, sexual and emotional abuse during their relationship with their former partner (e.g. Coleman 1997; Roberts 2002).

Stalking and attachment

There is also an association between stalking and relationship attachment problems (e.g. Meloy 1996; Roberts 2002). Bowlby (1980) defined attachment as a strong enduring affectional bond between individuals. Attachment behaviour begins during childhood and continues throughout the lifespan and in later life attachments are formed between adults.

Bartholomew described four adult attachment styles (Bartholomew and Horowitz 1991):

Secure attachment involves a positive view of the self and of others and general confidence and comfort in close adult relationships.

Preoccupied attachment involves a poor self-image and a positive image of others leading such individuals to devalue themselves and actively seek approval and validation from others.

Dismissing attachment involves a positive self-image that is maintained by remaining emotionally distant from others and viewing relationships as unimportant.

Fearful attachment involves experiencing ambivalence between a desire for interpersonal relationships and distrust of others and fear of rejection.

Meloy (1996) suggested stalking could be an abnormal attachment pattern similar to the preoccupied attachment style. Such individuals may indulge in approach and stalking behaviour because they overvalue others and perceive that contact with others is a means by which they can gain personal validation to challenge negative views of the self (Meloy 1998). There is also some evidence (e.g. Roberts 2002) that the fearful attachment style is associated with stalking of former partners either during the relationship or after a relationship is terminated – a fearful attachment style is characterised by a simultaneous desire to maintain a relationship and fear of rejection. This fear might lead to a need to monitor a romantic partner's behaviour to ensure that rejection will not happen leading to stalking within a relationship and potentially a desire to maintain the relationship even after it has ended.

Jealousy and anger

An association between jealousy, anger and stalking behaviour has been found (e.g. Langhinrischen-Rohling *et al.* 2000; Roberts 2002). Jealousy often appears within relationships perceived to be under threat and serves to intensify the concern and increase the contact the jealous person has with their partner. A propensity towards anger and jealousy has been found within stalkers who stalk former intimates (Davis *et al.* 2000). It is likely that jealousy, anger and violence may be the behavioural outcomes of attachment-related problems.

The research evidence appears then to show a range of motivations and characteristics of stalkers with some important gender differences. In the next section we move on to consider different types of motivation for stalking and different types of stalker.

Types of stalkers and stalking patterns

Mullen *et al.* (2001) described six categories of stalker based upon victim characteristics and the assumed motivation of the stalker. It is important to note that these are not mutually exclusive classes; indeed, many stalkers begin with one set of motives and move on to others. For example, some stalkers begin by desiring a relationship with their victim but over time their feelings may change into feelings of hatred and resentment as the stalker's romantic entreaties are perceived to be failing (e.g. Meloy 1998). The placement of a particular individual into a particular class is therefore likely to be a matter of judgment and valid for that particular time. Nonetheless the classes do have some utility as they give an insight into general patterns and motives for stalking. The six classes are: rejected stalker, resentful stalker, predatory stalker, intimacy seeker, incompetent suitor, and the erotomaniac and morbidly infatuated. We will now move on and consider each of these classes in turn.

Rejected stalker

This is the most common, persistent and intrusive of all stalkers. The target is a former romantic partner or friend who has ended the relationship with the stalker or has indicated that he or she intends to end the relationship. Depending on the responses of the victim, the goals of rejected stalkers might vary. Typically, the rejected stalker wrestles with the complex desire for both reconciliation and revenge. Mullen *et al.* characterise this type of stalker as having poor social skills and few friends and social contacts. Of all the sub-types of stalker this type is most likely to try to harm the victim and to employ intimidation and assault in their pursuit.

Resentful stalker

The resentful stalker is an individual who is attempting to gain revenge against another individual for some perceived slight. The whole aim of the stalking is to frighten the victim and to cause them distress. In some cases the victim may not have personally upset the stalker but may be regarded as representative of someone or some group of people who have upset them in the past. Stalkers of this type can be among the most obsessive and enduring and are most likely to threaten the victim. However, they are the least likely to use physical force. Threats, complaints and verbal abuse, damage to property, theft and injuries to or killing of pets are among the common tactics employed by these individuals.

Predatory stalker

This is the least common type of stalker who uses stalking as a tactic in the service of wider offending that ultimately aims to physically attack the victim. They appear mostly motivated by a desire for power and sexual gratification over their victim. Frequently this type of stalker exhibits personality disorders – most often psychopathy – and may also exhibit a range of paraphilic sexual interests. Frequently, they will not have any direct contact with the victim while stalking them. Typically, this stalker may engage in activities such as surveillance of the victim, obscene phone calls and voyeurism. The victim may be either someone the stalker knows or a complete stranger.

Intimacy seeker

This type of stalker is motivated by a desire to establish an intimate, loving relationship with their victim. Any responses from the victim, including abuse or legal sanctions, are for this type of stalker often interpreted as encouragement – any contact is good. This type of stalker typically writes letters, sends gifts and may use any means to contact the victim. Some stalkers of this type may come to believe that the victim owes them a relationship because of the investment that they have put in. Intimacy seekers are very resistant to changing their beliefs, although should they recognise that they are being rejected they may become threatening and try to harm the victim – they may change motive and become a rejected stalker. This type of stalker may be jealous of existing or new relationships that their victim is engaged in. The intimacy seeker is one of the most persistent types of stalker and is usually unresponsive to legal sanctions, often viewing them as challenges to be overcome that help to show their victim that their love is true.

Incompetent suitor

This type of stalker is characterised by a desire to form a romantic or intimate relationship with their victim. However, they often lack the social skills with which to achieve this. These individuals frequently lack the ability to understand the impact that their behaviour has upon the victim and to recognise the victim's suffering, and often fail to understand why the victim rejects their overtures. Typically, this type of stalker will repeatedly ask for dates and contact the victim by telephone, e-mail or text, even after being rejected. They may attempt physical contact, trying to touch the victim, to hold their hand or kiss the victim. However, this type of stalker is rarely physically violent towards the victim. The incompetent suitor is generally less persistent than other types of stalker but have often stalked many other people in the past in their attempts to gain a relationship. Frequently, incompetent suitors will stop stalking a victim when threatened with police or legal action or after psychiatric or counselling intervention.

Erotomaniac and morbidly infatuated

This is a delusional disorder described earlier in this chapter and is relatively rare. Often the victim is someone who has higher social status than the stalker such as a doctor, politician or celebrity. Stalkers of this type will typically approach and try to communicate with their victim and will be unresponsive to any kind of attempt to make them desist. In the absence of any psychological intervention this type of stalker is likely to continue with their activities.

This typology of stalkers, while suffering from overlapping catagories, does give a sense of the general patterns of stalker and their general behaviour towards their victims that may be of use in the police investigation of stalking and in the treatment and management of stalkers.

Relationships between stalker and victim

Some work has examined the relationship between the stalker and victim prior to the onset of stalking. Findings from this research indicate that stalkers are more likely to have had some pre-existing relationship with the victim than to have been a complete stranger, the most likely pre-existing relationship between stalker and victim being one of prior romantic partners (e.g. Spitzberg and Cupach 2003). Some writers have attempted to produce a typology of stalking victims; Mullen *et al.* (2001) provide a succinct description of different types of victim that are fairly self-explanatory and shown in Table 19.1.

When an individual has experienced stalking it is important to consider possible responses to it. Essentially what are the common responses to stalking and are there ways of effectively managing stalking incidents? We will consider this in the next section.

Responses to stalking

Research has shown that the experience of stalking has a significant health impact upon victims. Kernsmith *et al.* (2005) found evidence for post-traumatic stress disorder, depression and other anxiety-related symptoms in victims of stalking, with women being more likely than men to report their symptoms and to seek help from mental health professionals. Roberts, in an unpublished study, also found a high incidence of anxiety-related symptoms in samples of self-reported stalkers in Spain and the United Kingdom.

Cupach and Spitzburg (1998) explored the impact of different victim responses on the nature and duration of stalking. They found that direct methods of coping such as reporting the stalking to the police, taking legal action and/or attempting to confront the stalker had little impact upon the nature and duration of the stalking. These authors also found that passive styles of responding such as ignoring the stalker had limited impact upon the stalking, although some anecdotal evidence does suggest that ignoring stalkers is a better coping strategy than confrontation as some types of stalker will become encouraged by any response even abuse. Kernsmith *et al.* (2005) found that there were some gender differences in responses to stalking with men more likely to take active steps such as buying guns and confronting the stalker than women who were more likely to consult with friends and to seek law enforcement help.

Future research does need to qualify how different responses to stalking impact upon the behaviour of the stalker, in particular how different stalker types respond. Research might also explore how different coping strategies might impact upon the psychological outcome for the victim.

Table 19.1 Stalker–victim relationships

Relationship
Ex-intimates
Family members
Friends and acquaintances
Workplace contacts
Strangers

Source: Mullen *et al.* (2001).

Conclusions and future directions

Stalking is a significant social problem that affects individuals from all walks of life. As with many types of offending females are more at risk of becoming victims of stalking and men are more likely to be perpetrators. Some groups appear to be more at risk of becoming a victim – single young females and students – and this seems to be a reflection of lifestyle making victimisation more likely. There is no specific profile for stalkers although stalkers are most likely to be former romantic partners or acquaintances of victims. The motives for stalking appear most likely related to a desire to obtain or to maintain a romantic relationship with another individual. The tactics used by stalkers are frequently attempts to contact the victim by sending letters, telephone calls, text messages and e-mails, although many stalkers make explicit threats of violence. Despite making threats, direct violence towards victims is unlikely and the violence that is directed towards the victim is most often non-injurious. Injurious violence is most likely when there was a pre-existing romantic relationship between stalker and victim. Stalking does cause significant distress and suffering to the victims, with anxiety and depression being a common response to victimisation. Stalkers are more likely than others to exhibit psychological problems, in particular difficulties with adult attachment, jealousy and anger, and to suffer various mental health problems, although there is not one specific disorder that appears specific to stalking. Sadly society has so far failed to find a wholly successful response to stalking.

While research has been able to conceptualise stalking, the perpetrators, their behaviour and the victims there is still much that is not known and more research is required. First, as most research has been done in western nations, it is not immediately clear if stalking is a more general cross-cultural phenomenon. Research has also not explored the links between stalking tactics and motives for stalking in any systematic way. Research needs to examine the association between different stalking tactics and the risk for violence against the victim and the links between this and the social and behavioural characteristics of the stalker. Different stalker types might respond differently to various responses to stalking and work is required here.

To conclude, research has identified stalking as a significant social problem and has described some of the common features of stalkers, their behaviour and the situations where stalking occurs. What is now needed is more systematic research that may allow society to improve the identification of stalking, to design treatment strategies for stalkers and to produce methods that may aid in the early identification of stalkers before they harm the victim.

Selected further reading

There are many books and papers on the subject of stalking and harassment though no one book or paper really covers every aspect of this developing literature. A very good introduction is provided by Mullen *et al.* (2000) in their very readable *Stalkers and Their Victims*. Boon and Sheridan (2002) have edited an excellent collection of papers that cover most of the major issues in stalking in *Stalking and Psychosexual Obsession: Prevention, Policing and Treatment*. Finally one of the first books in the field is still an excellent resource from which to explore the identification of stalking as a crime and the early development of research in the area: Meloy's (1998) *The Psychology of Stalking*.

References

Anderson, S. C. (1993) 'Anti-stalking laws', *Law and Psychological Review*, 17: 171–85.

Australian Bureau of Statistics (1996) *Women's Safety*. Canberra: Commonwealth of Australia.

Bartholomew, K. and Horowitz, L. M. (1991) 'Attachment styles among young adults', *Journal of Personality and Social Psychology*, 61: 226–44.

Bjerregaard, B. (2000) 'An empirical study of stalking victimization', *Violence and Victims*, 15 (4): 389–407.

Boon, J. and Sheridan, L. (eds) (2002) *Stalking and Psychosexual Obsession: Prevention, Policing and Treatment*. Chichester: Wiley.

Bowlby, J. (1980) *Attachment and Loss: Vol. III Loss, Sadness and Depression*. New York: Basic Books.

Budd, T., Mattinson, J. and Myhill, A. (2000) *The Extent and Nature of Stalking: Findings from the 1998 British Crime Survey*, Home Office Research Study No. 210. London: Home Office Research, Development and Statistics Directorate.

Coleman, F. L. (1997) 'Stalking behaviour and the cycle of domestic violence', *Journal of Interpersonal Violence*, 12: 420–32.

Cupach, W. R. and Spitzberg, B. H. (1998) *The Dark Side of Close Relationships*. Mahwah, NJ: Lawrence Erlbaum Associates.

Cupach, W. R. and Spitzberg, B. H. (2000) 'Obsessive relational intrusion', *Violence and Victims*, 15 (4): 357–73

Davis, K. E., Ace, A. and Andra, M. (2000) 'Stalking perpetrators and psychological maltreatment of partners', *Violence and Victims*, 15 (4): 407–26.

Farnham, F., James, D. and Cantrell, P. (2000) 'Association between violence, psychosis, and relationship to victim in stalkers', *The Lancet*, 355: 199.

Fremouw, W.J., Westrup, D. and Pennypacker, J. (1997) 'Stalking on campus', *Journal of Forensic Science*, 42 (4): 666–9.

Gill, R. and Brockman, J. (1996) *A Review of Section 264 (Criminal Harassment) of the Criminal Code of Canada*. Ottawa: Department of Justice Canada.

Harmon, R. B., Rosner, R. and Owens, H. (1995) 'Obsessional harassment and erotomania in a criminal court population', *Journal of Forensic Sciences*, 40: 188–96.

Kernsmith, R., Wilczak, A. and Kalaian, S. (2005) *Gender Differences in Response to Stalking Victimization*. Paper presented at the annual meeting of the American Society of Criminology, Royal York, Toronto.

Kienlen, K. K., Birmingham, D. L., Solberg, K. B., O'Regan, J. T. and Meloy, J. R. (1997) 'A comparative study of psychotic and non-psychotic stalking', *Journal of the American Academy of Psychiatry and Law*, 25: 317–34.

Kong, R. (1996) 'Criminal harassment', *Juristat*, 16 (12): 1–13.

Langhinrischen-Rohling, J., Palera, R. E., Cohen, J. and Rohling, M. L. (2000) 'Breaking up is hard to do', *Violence and Victims*, 15 (1): 73–90.

Lewis, S., Frenmouw, W. J., Del Ben, K. and Farr, C. (2001) 'An investigation of the psychological characteristics of stalkers', *Journal of Forensic Sciences*, 46 (1): 80–4.

Logan, T. K., Leukefeld, C. and Walker, B. (2000) 'Stalking as a variant of intimate violence', *Violence and Victims*, 15 (1): 91–111.

McGuire, B. and Wraith, A. (2000) 'Legal and psychological aspects of stalking', *Journal of Forensic Psychiatry*, 11 (2): 316–27.

Meloy, J. R. (1996) 'Stalking (obsessional following)', *Aggression and Violent Behaviour*, 1: 147–62.

Meloy, J. R. (1998) *The Psychology of Stalking*. San Diego: Academic Press.

Meloy, J. R. and Gothard, S. (1995) 'A demographic and clinical comparison of obsessional following and offenders with mental disorders', *American Journal of Psychiatry*, 152: 258–63.

Mullen, P. E. and Pathe, M. (1994) 'Stalking and the pathologies of love', *Australian and New Zealand Journal of Psychiatry*, 28: 469–77.

Mullen, P. E., Pathe, M. and Purcell, R. (2000) *Stalkers and Their Victims*. Cambridge: Cambridge University Press.

Mullen, P. E., Pathé, M. and Purcell, R. (2001) 'The management of stalkers', *Advances in Psychiatric Treatment*, 7: 335–42.

Roberts, K. A. (2002) 'Stalking following the break-up of romantic relationships', *Journal of Forensic Sciences*, 47 (5): 1070–8.

Roberts, K. A. (2005) 'Women's experience of violence during stalking by former romantic partners: factors predictive of stalking violence', *Violence against Women*, 11: 89–115.

Sandberg, D. A., McNeil, D. E. and Binder, R. L. (1998) 'Characteristics of psychiatric patients who stalk, threaten, or harass hospital staff after discharge', *American Journal of Psychiatry*, 155: 1102–5.

Sheridan, L. and Davies, G. M. (2001) 'Stalking: the elusive crime', *Legal and Criminological Psychology*, 6 (2): 133–48.

Spitzberg, B. H. and Cupach, W. R. (2003) 'What mad pursuit? Obsessive relational intrusion and stalking related phenomena', *Aggression and Violent Behaviour*, 8 (4): 345–75.

Tjaden, P. and Thoennes, N. (1998) *Stalking in America: Findings From the National Violence Against Women Survey*. Washington, DC: National Institute of Justice and Centers for Disease Control and Prevention.

Westrup, D. and Fremouw, W. J. (1998) 'Stalking behavior: a literature review and suggested functional analytic assessment technology', *Aggression and Violent Behaviour*, 3: 255–74.

Westrup, D., Fremouw, W. J., Thompson, R. N. and Lewis, S. F. (1999) 'The psychological impact of stalking on female undergraduates', *Journal of Forensic Sciences*, 44 (3): 554–7.

Zona, M. A., Sharma, K. K. and Lane, J. (1993) 'A comparative study of erotomanic and obsessional subjects in a forensic sample', *Journal of Forensic Sciences*, 38 (4): 894–903.

Chapter 20

Arson

Emma J. Palmer, Clive R. Hollin, Ruth M. Hatcher and Tammy C. Ayres

Introduction

Arson accounts for a significant number of fires responded to by the Fire and Rescue Service. Nearly half (43 per cent) of all primary fires[1] attended by the UK fire service in 2006 were deliberately[2] started. In fact, arson remains the largest single cause of fire in the UK (Department for Communities and Local Government 2006a; Office of the Deputy Prime Minister 2006a).

Two organisations collect data on arson or deliberate firesetting in the UK: the fire service and the police. The fire service recorded 72,545 deliberate primary fires in the UK in 2006 (Department for Communities and Local Government 2008). This represents a 9 per cent drop since 2005 and continues the trend of the last five years, which has seen incidents of deliberate firesetting fall by 41 per cent since their peak in 2001. In contrast police statistics state that there were 43,100 arson offences recorded in 2006/7, representing a 6 per cent reduction since 2005/6 (Nicholas *et al.* 2007).

Although the figures from both organisations indicate a downward trend in the prevalence of arson and deliberate firesetting, the figures recorded by the police and the fire service differ significantly. Although this is a crude analysis, these figures indicate that the police record just over half of deliberately set fires attended by the fire service, which supports estimates made by the Home Office (2006b). This discrepancy is due to a number of factors, the most important of which is different recording practices by each organisation. The fire service only needs to suspect deliberate ignition to categorise a fire as being deliberately started. However, the police require a higher burden of proof before a charge of arson can be brought.

Certain types of building are more prone to arson attacks. Of the 72,545 deliberate fires recorded in the UK, 32 per cent (22,923) occurred in buildings, of which 10,110 were dwellings[3] and 12,813 other buildings such as schools, hospitals and businesses. Arson is also clustered in geographical areas: statistics indicate that people are more likely to be a victim of arson in socially deprived, poorer areas (Home Office 2006b).

Despite statistics indicating a downward trend in the incidence of arson and deliberate firesetting, the cost remains high both in financial and non-financial terms. Overall, arson is estimated to cost £2.53 billion annually in England and Wales (Department for Communities and Local Government 2006b). Deliberate firesetting costs the fire service an estimated £536 million a year (Office of the Deputy Prime Minister 2006b). Furthermore, it is estimated that arson cost the criminal justice system £95 million in 2004 (Office of the Deputy Prime Minister 2006b). Aside from these 'direct' costs of arson, there are also longer-term consequences of arson. For example, it is estimated that the majority of businesses (75–80 per cent) who are victims of arson never recover (Department for Communities and Local Government 2006b).

In human terms, arson causes in excess of 1,600 primary fires, 50 serious injuries and 2 deaths a week (Department for Communities and Local Government 2006b). Although dwelling fires make up only 14 per cent of all deliberate fires in the UK, they account for the highest number of fatal (58 per cent) and non-fatal injuries (70 per cent) caused by deliberate firesetting. In 2006, 68 people died in a deliberate dwelling fire, while 1,902 were injured (Department for Communities and Local Government 2008). A recent example of the devastation to human life caused by arson is the deliberately started bushfires in Victoria, Australia in February 2009, which claimed over 200 lives. Therefore arson and firesetting constitute a serious problem which requires attention from both policymakers and practitioners in order to reduce its incidence.

Criminal statistics for 2007 show that there were 1,550 convictions for arson (Ministry of Justice 2008). Of these offenders the vast majority (83.0 per cent) were males. About half of the convictions (50.3 per cent) were for offenders under 21 years, and over a third (36.6 per cent) were offenders under 18 years of age.

Explanations for firesetting and arson

Unlike some offence types, such as sexual offending, there is not a vast literature on theories for arson. In places there are theoretical accounts of arson that stress the symbolic importance of fire (Topp 1973) or the association between firesetting and sexual drives/impulses (Fras 1983). There are also behavioural accounts that consider the functions of the act (Jackson *et al.* 1987). Given the paucity of developed theories the motives for arson are probably more informative than theoretical speculation, although in practice the actual motivation in any given case may be difficult to ascertain. Prins (1994) lists six different motives:

- *vandalism* – typically perpetrated by male adolescents, with schools and public buildings typical targets;
- *playing with fire* – typically young children at home or school;
- *crime concealment* – adolescent and older males after joyriding in a stolen car;
- *revenge* – no typical age or gender, principally against dwellings;

- *fraud* – typically insurance policyholders with their own business premises; and
- *political* – as with terrorist attacks, protests, riots and racist acts of violence.

Mental illness and arson

Mental illness is often assumed to be a contributory factor in some arson, and it is worth considering the association between these in more detail. Studies with psychiatric populations suggest arson may be associated with several psychiatric conditions including schizophrenia (Ritchie and Huff 1999), personality disorder (Hurley and Monahan 1969), depression (O'Sullivan and Kelleher 1987), mood disorder (Geller 1992), and learning disability (Ritchie and Huff 1999). There is less evidence with respect to any putative relationship between arson and neurological disorders such as epilepsy (Byrne and Walsh 1989), EEG abnormality (Powers and Gunderman 1978), head trauma (Hurley and Monahan 1969), or brain tumours (Geller 1992). There is also a psychiatric condition of *pyromania*, which is described by DSM-IV (APA 1994) as a morbid fascination with setting fires as a source of pleasure, tension release and fascination.

The association between psychiatric condition and arson is illustrated in a UK study by Jayaraman and Frazer (2006). Pre-trial psychiatric reports for 34 arsonists revealed high levels of mental disorder, including personality disorder, with strong indications of alcohol and drug use before and during the arson. A similar Finnish study considered 90 arson recidivists referred for pre-trial psychiatric assessment (Lindberg *et al*. 2005). Across the Finnish sample, there were high levels (50 per cent or more) of personality disorder and co-morbid alcohol abuse and dependency, with 68 per cent of the sample having carried out the arson while in a condition of acute alcohol intoxication. There was less evidence (around 20 per cent of the sample) of low IQ and psychosis, and 12 members of the sample satisfied the DSM-IV-R criteria for pyromania. Just less than one half of the sample were 'specialists' in that they had not been convicted for any offence other than arson.

Overall, the association between arson and mental illness is inconclusive, as research typically involves psychiatric samples rather than taking an epidemiological approach and examining the prevalence of arson among both individuals with a clinically diagnosed psychiatric disorder and those with no clinical diagnosis. Furthermore, even among arsonists with a psychiatric diagnosis, their mental illness itself may not necessarily be a contributory factor in their arson.

Characteristics of arsonists

Given the lack of well articulated theoretical accounts of arson, it is useful to consider the characteristics of arsonists. In the absence of a theoretical explanation for arson, identification of risk factors associated with arson can provide information as to targets for interventions to work with arsonists.

The population of arsonists may be divided into two broad categories: first, children below the age of criminal responsibility, generally referred to as *firesetters* within the research literature, and adults as defined by law who constitute *arsonists*. The reasons or motives for setting fires vary across and within each group. In describing these juvenile and adult populations, it should be noted that most research concerns young firesetters rather than adult arsonists. In addition, the literature principally looks at populations within the USA, with fewer studies conducted in Europe and Australia.

Juvenile firesetters

Research has identified a range of characteristics of juvenile firesetters. Firesetters are more likely to be male (Kolko 1985). A number of studies have shown firesetters to have a disturbed education, with increased levels of academic underachievement and suspensions/expulsions from school (Hollin *et al.* 2002). The child's firesetting may also be associated with a lack of parental supervision and lax or inconsistent discipline to the point of maltreatment or abuse (Kolko and Kazdin 1990), and parental relationships characterised by conflict and personal difficulties and stresses (Kolko and Kazdin 1991).

Firesetting in young people is often associated with other problematic behaviours such as violence and highly antisocial behaviour, cruelty to animals and high levels of drug and alcohol abuse (e.g. Kolko 1985; Martin, *et al.* 2004; Repo and Virkkunen 1997). A range of psychological factors have been associated with firesetting in children and adolescents, including poor interpersonal skills such as impulsivity, low levels of assertion skills, an inability to resolve conflicts and psychiatric problems (e.g. Kolko and Kazdin 1988; Räsänen *et al.* 1995).

The complexity of juvenile firesetting can be seen in several studies that have examined a range of different variables. An American study of firesetters reported by Slavkin (2004) assessed 78 children aged 3–6 years, 240 children aged 7–10 years, 157 early adolescents aged 11–14 years, and 413 late adolescents aged 15–18 years. Slavkin described five types of young firesetter:

- *curiosity firesetters* – who were younger, with low levels of delinquency and few problems in socialising or expressing emotions;
- *accidental firesetters* – had low levels of delinquency and psychopathology, and few social or emotional problems;
- *cry-for-help firesetters* – were typically young females with problems in socialising and expressing emotions, although with low levels of psychopathology;
- *delinquent firesetters* – were older with high levels of delinquent behaviour, although with low levels of psychopathology and few problems in socialising or expressing emotions;
- *severely disturbed firesetters* – showed low levels of delinquency and high levels of psychopathology.

An American study by McCarty and McMahon (2005) assessed 361 children prior to 4th grade and again between 4th and 6th grade. The firesetters, who were more likely to be boys, showed higher levels of antisocial behaviour and more experience of harsh parenting, including physical abuse. The persistence of firesetting over time was associated with increased parental depressive symptoms, parental conflict and ineffective discipline. Another American study by MacKay *et al.* (2006) involved 192 male firesetters aged 6 to 17 years, most of whom had been involved in multiple incidents of firesetting. MacKay *et al.* noted that antisocial behaviour problems and fire interest were strongly associated with the frequency and versatility of involvement with firesetting.

An Australian study with 1,359 children aged from 4 to 9 years by Dadds and Fraser (2006) reported a higher prevalence of fire interest and match- and fire-play for boys than for girls, with higher rates for older boys than young boys. Firesetting was associated with parental stress and with a range of problematic behaviours including conduct disorder, hyperactivity and cruelty to animals. For the girls who set fires, there was evidence of problems with anxiety and depression.

While knowledge of juvenile firesetters is reasonably well advanced, there are two key issues that remain to be addressed. First, given the strong overlap between the social and psychological characteristics of juvenile firesetters and mainstream juvenile delinquents, what are the critical factors that are antecedent *specifically* to setting fires? Second, what is the degree of continuity between childhood firesetting and arson in adulthood? These issues indicate the need for further research, particularly longitudinal research.

Adult arsonists

The majority of research with adult arsonists has been conducted with psychiatric populations; however, there are some studies of arsonists within the mainstream criminal justice system. A UK study reported by Soothill *et al.* (2004) compared 74 arsonists convicted in 1951 with cohorts of arsonists convicted in 1963–5 (N = 1,352), 1980–1 (N = 5,584), and 2000–1 (N = 3,335). There were several notable changes over time in the profile of arsonists:

• an increase in the number of females;
• a rise in mean age for both males and females; and
• previous convictions for violence and criminal damage (including arson) were more evident in the later cohorts.

Over the fifty years spanned by the study, the reconvictions for arson had more than doubled from 4.5 per cent in the 1951 cohort to 10.7 per cent in the 2000–1 cohort.

Canter and Fritzon (1998) examined behavioural patterns of arson and suggested that there are four distinct themes of arson: two themes relate to expressive acts, arson targeted at a person and arson targeted at an object; and two themes relate to instrumental acts targeted at a person or targeted at an object. These findings have been replicated by Santilla *et al.* (2003) and Almond *et al.* (2005).

Edwards and Grace (2006) used police files to look at 44 serial arsonists, mostly male, in New Zealand. The environmental range for the arsonists' offending fell into two broad types, with the arsonists equally divided between the two types. One set of arsonists were termed 'marauders' as they moved within the location in which they lived, their 'home base', to set fires. The other set of arsonists were termed 'commuters' as they travelled away from their home base to set fires, so that there was no obvious relationship between where they lived and the distance they travelled to offend.

Prevention

As with all crime, there are a number of strategies that can be used to prevent arson. Punishment through sentences imposed by the criminal justice system and situational crime prevention are considered here, while interventions to change the offender are discussed in the next section.

Situational crime prevention

Theories of situational crime prevention propose that a crime occurs when a rational offender and a victim/target come together in a place which provides the offender with a low-risk opportunity to offend (Clarke 1983). Thus, to reduce the incidence of arson, it is necessary to manipulate the environment to limit the number of fire-setting opportunities and to increase the risk of detection. Primary situational crime prevention measures aim to alter the environment within which arson has the potential to occur. Secondary intervention strategies involve 'target hardening' of potential victims or targets in order to reduce not only the likelihood of an offence, but also the impact of the offence should it occur.

Situational crime prevention in relation to arson typically involves a thorough risk assessment of the property or area to identify any vulnerability or fire hazards. Such hazards could be abandoned vehicles or piles of flammable refuse, or in relation to a commercial unit a gap in security which could be exploited by an arsonist. Next, steps are taken to eliminate, control or avoid any threat to the area or building: this may involve the removal of flammable liquids and refuse or abandoned cars. Finally, the existing security measures are reviewed, for example, is access to the site controlled, is the perimeter of the site protected sufficiently, is CCTV installed, are fire detectors, smoke alarms and anti-arson mailboxes installed? Such measures reduce the possibility of arson through the removal of opportunity and increasing the risk of detection (Home Office n.d.) and aim to limit the damage should an attack occur (Maguire and Brookman 2005).

An early example of the implementation of situational crime prevention measures for arson in the UK was undertaken by Northumbria Police and Tyne and Wear Fire Service. An arson task force was set up in the region in 1998 to reduce the high level of arson in the west of Newcastle. A number of short-term environmental initiatives such as the removal of refuse, the boarding up of empty properties and the removal of abandoned vehicles were implemented, alongside more long-term educational and diversionary programmes.

Such interventions are now evident throughout the country and are overseen by the Arson Control Forum (ACF), a government-led national body which encourages inter-agency working between the fire service, local authorities, the police, insurance companies and government departments in an attempt to reduce arson and deaths, injuries and damages stemming from such acts. Under the ACF's New Projects Initiative, such partnerships have received government grants to invest in local arson prevention schemes (Home Office 2006a).

Sentencing policy

Under section 1 of the Criminal Damage Act 1971, a person committed for damaging or destroying property by fire can be charged with arson. The seriousness of the charge, however, depends on the act committed: 'simple arson' covers more minor acts of arson, 'reckless arson' covers those offences that were reckless as to whether a life was endangered, and 'arson with intent' relates to those acts which intentionally endanger a life or lives (Crown Prosecution Service n.d.). Offenders found guilty of these offences can face sentences ranging from an antisocial behaviour order (ASBO), through community sentences, to life imprisonment. The severity of the sentence will, of course, depend on the nature of the act, the damage caused and the intention behind the act.

Interventions

Interventions to address firesetting and arson typically use one of two approaches. First, *educational* interventions aim to teach fire-safety skills by providing information about the dangers associated with fire and providing fire-safety skills. Second, *psychosocial* interventions target the psychological and social factors associated with firesetting and arson. Educational approaches are used as both a preventative and intervention measure, whereas psychosocial approaches are typically used as an intervention for known firesetters or arsonists. As the majority of interventions are with young firesetters, the literature on interventions will be reviewed separately for children/young people and adult arsonists.

Children and young people

Interventions for young firesetters have used both the educational and psychosocial approaches (see Kolko 2002). There are a number of examples of educational interventions with young firesetters. Within England and Wales, the Fire and Rescue Service has been involved in running interventions, often in partnership with youth offending agencies. One example is the Fire Awareness Child Education (FACE) programme set up by Merseyside Fire and Rescue Service, which has also been used by other fire services across the country (Canter and Almond 2002). Liverpool's Youth Justice Department later worked with the fire service to adapt this intervention for use with convicted young arsonists aged 10–17 years as 'FACE UP'. However, the effectiveness of these two interventions has not been systematically evaluated.

Other British Fire and Rescue Services have adopted an intervention approach that was developed by an educational psychologist, Andrew Muckley. These approaches are more counselling-oriented and emphasise the importance of appropriate referral and psychological assessment (Muckley 1997). Although Canter and Almond (2002) estimated that about one-third of fire and rescue services in England and Wales use approaches based on Muckley's work, again there has been no rigorous evaluation of their impact on firesetting behaviours.

More recently, the Arson Control Forum (2006) reported that 33 of the 47 fire services in England and Wales were running schemes with young firesetters, with 332 interventions in total. Most of these interventions were aimed at diversionary prevention and early prevention of firesetting behaviour. This report noted that there was plenty of good practice within services, but that there was no coherent intervention strategy at a local or national level.

There is a similar picture in North America, with educational interventions being provided by fire services. A few small-scale evaluations of these interventions have been reported. The Federal Emergency Management Agency (FEMA 1983) and Faranda et al. (2001) reported low rates of recidivism among juvenile firesetters who had attended educational fire safety workshops (1.25 per cent and 2.1 per cent respectively). However, these studies did not have control groups. Two studies which did include a control group were reported by Franklin et al. (2002) and Cole et al. (2004). After a one-day educational programme Franklin et al. (2002) reported that 1/132 (0.8 per cent) of participants reoffended as compared to 37/102 (36.3 per cent) of the control group. Cole et al. (2004) evaluated a multimedia fire safety educational programme for pre-school children, in which at a one-month follow-up the participants showed significantly greater knowledge and fire-safety skills than the control group. Although these interventions had a positive effect on firesetting, these studies are limited by small sample sizes and short follow-up periods.

Interventions with young firesetters based on behavioural approaches, such as satiation procedures and aversive techniques, have also been reported in North America (Hardesty and Gayton 2000; Kolko 1983). There are also a few instances of psychosocial interventions with young firesetters, although these have used a wide range of techniques: behavioural family therapy (e.g. Cox-Jones et al. 1990), cognitive-behavioural skills training to address inappropriate anger expression (Kolko and Ammerman 1988) and contingency management strategies (Adler et al. 1994). Other interventions have incorporated a range of techniques and treatment targets, such as that reported by Schwartzman et al. (1998). This fire service-delivered intervention for adolescent firesetters targeted coping skills, anger management and assertiveness in a group setting. At a one-year follow-up only 7 per cent of the participants had committed a further arson offence.

A few studies have examined the comparative effectiveness of different intervention approaches with young firesetters. In Australia, Adler et al. (1994) conducted a random control trial with young firesetters, half of whom received a home visit from fire and rescue service staff and educational material on fire safety. Participants in the other group received a multi-component intervention comprising three visits from fire and rescue service staff, educational material on fire safety, application of a graphing technique, behavioural satiation and parental training to respond to firesetting behaviours. At a one-year follow-up the frequency and severity of firesetting had decreased equally in both groups, suggesting that the multi-component intervention was as effective as the educational and home visit package.

Kolko (2001) randomly assigned young firesetters to three intervention groups: fire safety education (FSE), home visit from a firefighter (HVF) and cognitive behavioural treatment (CBT). At post-treatment and one-year follow-up all three groups showed significant improvements on self- and parent-reports of firesetting and matchplay. However, the CBT and FSE groups' improvements were greater than those of the HVF group. Specifically, the FSE group had better fire-safety skills while the CBT group showed the largest decrease in fire interest. A more detailed analysis revealed that the differential targets of FSE and CBT were reflected in the impact of the two interventions on the outcome measures (Kolko et al. 2006). FSE had a greater impact on the fire knowledge and fire interest measure, while CBT impacted specifically on positive social problem-solving skills. Furthermore, the effectiveness of the interventions was moderated by various child and family factors, including level of exposure to fire materials/models, fire knowledge and family dysfunction, suggesting a need to ensure interventions are appropriately matched to the needs and characteristics of young firesetters and their families.

Adult arsonists

There is far less research on interventions with adult arsonists and the literature that is available focuses on cognitive-behavioural approaches with learning disabled samples. Taylor et al. (2002) reported that following a 40-session cognitive-behavioural programme, their sample of 14 adult male and female firesetters with a mild learning disability showed reduced fire interest and attitudes supportive of firesetting, and improved risk management and coping skills. A case study approach was used by Taylor et al. (2004) with four male firesetters with developmental disabilities who received a 31-session cognitive-behavioural intervention. However, none of the patients showed post-treatment improvements on fire-related measures. More positive results were reported for this programme with six female patients with learning disabilities. Not only did they show improvements on fire-related measures, none of the participants had set a fire at a two-year follow-up (Taylor et al. 2006).

As this section shows, the majority of interventions reported in the literature are with young firesetters rather than with adult arsonists. Recent reviews of the literature have been conducted by Haines et al. (2006) and Palmer et al. (2007). As Haines et al. note, the different approaches to intervention appear to impact differentially on outcome measures: fire-safety education increases fire-safety knowledge, while cognitive-behavioural interventions have a positive impact on the psychosocial factors associated with firesetting and arson, a conclusion that supports the study reported by Kolko et al. (2006). However, despite these reviews it is difficult to draw firm conclusions as to what works to reduce and prevent future firesetting/arson.

Conclusion

Although there is a fair amount of research on the characteristics of young firesetters, the literature on adult arsonists is sparse, with much of the adult research focusing on psychiatric samples. Moreover, for both children/adolescents and adults there is no comprehensive theoretical account of firesetting and/or arson. Explanatory evidence-based theories of these behaviours are important in order to design interventions that target the risk factors associated with firesetting/arson. Another key issue is the lack of rigorous long-term evaluations of the effectiveness of interventions among young firesetters and adult arsonists, meaning that we cannot be certain that these interventions work to reduce or prevent future firesetting behaviours and arson. Therefore, further research is required to address these points and inform practice in the future.

Selected further reading

There is not a large literature on arson, and that which does exist tends to focus on firesetting among children and young people. Prins' *Fire-Raising: Its Motivation and Management* (1994) provides a good introduction to the area; Kolko's *Handbook on Firesetting in Children and Youth* (2002) provides a comprehensive account of firesetting behaviour in children and young people. A good review article on interventions with arsonists and young firesetters, along with an examination of national provision in England and Wales, can be found in Palmer *et al.*'s article 'Interventions with arsonists and young firesetters: a survey of the national picture in England and Wales' (2007). There is also material available on the Department for Communities and Local Government website: http://www.communities.gov.uk/fire/about/ and the Home Office website: http://www.crimereduction.homeoffice.gov.uk/arson/arsonminisite01. htm.

Notes

1 Primary fires are those involving buildings and structures, vehicles, storage, plant and machinery; fires involving casualties, rescues or escapes; fires where significant fire service resources are employed.
2 Deliberate fires include those where deliberate ignition was merely suspected and recorded by the fire service as 'doubtful'.
3 Buildings occupied by households as permanent dwellings, including caravans, houseboats and other non-building structures used solely as permanent dwellings, but excluding hotels, hostels and residential institutions.

References

Adler, R. G., Nunn, R. J., Lebnan, V. M. and Northam, E. A. (1994) 'Secondary prevention of childhood fire-setting', *Journal of the American Academy of Child and Adolescent Psychiatry*, 33: 1194–202.

Almond, L., Duggan, L., Shine, J. and Canter, D. (2005) 'Test of the arson action system model in an incarcerated population', *Psychology, Crime, and Law*, 11: 1–15.

APA (1994) *Diagnostic and Statistical Manual IV*. Washington, DC: American Psychological Association.

Arson Control Forum (2006) *Youth Training and Diversion Schemes*, Arson Control Forum Research Bulletin No. 8. London: Office of the Deputy Prime Minister.

Byrne, A. and Walsh, J. B. (1989) 'The epileptic arsonist', *British Journal of Psychiatry*, 155: 268–71.

Canter, D. V. and Almond, L. (2002) *The Burning Issue: Research and Strategies for Reducing Arson*, Report for the Arson Control Forum. London: Office of the Deputy Prime Minister.

Canter, D. V. and Fritzon, K. (1998) 'Differentiating arsonists: a model of firesetting actions and characteristics', *Legal and Criminological Psychology*, 3: 73–96.

Clarke, R. V. (1983) 'Situational crime prevention: its theoretical basis and practical scope', *Crime and Justice: A Review of Research*, 4: 225–56.

Cole, R. E., Crandall, R. and Kourofsky, C. (2004) 'We can teach young children fire safety', *Young Children*, 59 (2): 14–18.

Cox-Jones, C., Lubetsky, M., Fultz, S. A. and Kolko, D. J. (1990) 'Inpatient treatment of a young recidivist firesetter', *Journal of the American Academy of Child and Adolescent Psychiatry*, 29: 936–41.

Crown Prosecution Service (n.d.) *Sentencing Manual*. Online at: http://www.cps.gov.uk/legal/s_to_u/sentencing_manual/ (accessed 23 November 2008).

Dadds, M. R. and Fraser, J. A. (2006) 'Fire interest, fire setting and psychopathology in Australian children: a normative study', *Australian and New Zealand Journal of Psychiatry*, 40: 581–6.

Department for Communities and Local Government (2006a) *Arson Control Forum Annual Report 2006*. London: Communities and Local Government.

Department for Communities and Local Government (2006b) *A Special Report from the Arson Control Forum: Good Practice Conference*. London: Corrine Fleming Associates.

Department for Communities and Local Government (2008) *Fire Statistics, United Kingdom 2006*. London: Department for Communities and Local Government.

Edwards, M. J. and Grace, R. C. (2006) 'Analysing the offence locations and residential base of serial arsonists in New Zealand', *Australian Psychologist*, 41: 219–26.

Faranda, D. M., Katsikas, S. L. and Lim, N. (2001) 'Communities working together: an evaluation of the intervention program for juvenile firesetters and arsonists in Broward County, Florida', *American Journal of Forensic Psychology*, 19: 37–62.

Federal Emergency Management Authority (1983) *Juvenile Firesetters Handbook: Dealing with Children Ages 7–13 Years*. Washington, DC: US Government Printing Office.

Franklin, G. A., Pucci, P. S., Arbabi, S., Brandt, M.-M., Wahl, W. L. and Taheri, P. A. (2002) 'Decreased juvenile arson and firesetting recidivism after implementation of a multi-disciplinary prevention program', *Journal of Trauma, Injury, Infection and Critical Care*, 53: 260–6.

Fras, I. (1983) 'Fire-setting (pyromania) and its relationship to sexuality', in L. B. Schlesinger and E. Revich (eds), *Sexual Dynamics of Anti-Social Behavior*. Springfield, IL: C. C. Thomas.

Geller, J. L. (1992) 'Arson in review', *Clinical Forensic Psychiatry*, 15: 623–45.

Haines, S., Lambie, I. and Seymour, F. (2006) *International Approaches to Reducing Deliberately Set Fires: Prevention Programmes*, New Zealand Fire Service Commission Research Report No. 63. Auckland: New Zealand Fire Service Commission.

Hardesty, V. A. and Gayton, W. F. (2000) 'The problem of children setting fire', in D. J. Kolko (eds), *Handbook on Firesetting in Children and Youth*. London: Academic Press, pp. 1–13.

Hollin, C. R., Epps, K. and Swaffer, T. (2002) 'Adolescent firesetters: findings from an analysis of 47 cases', *Pakistan Journal of Psychological Research*, 17: 1–16.

Home Office (2006a) *Tackling Arson: Home Office Guide*. London: Home Office.

Home Office (2006b) *The Arson Control Forum Update*. Online at: http://www.crimereduction.homeoffice.gov.uk/arson/arsonminisite03.htm (accessed 23 November 2008).

Home Office (n.d.) *Crime Reduction Toolkits: Arson*. Online at: http://www.crimereduction.homeoffice.gov.uk/toolkits/an00.htm (acessed 23 November 2008).

Hurley, W. and Monahan, T. M. (1969) 'Arson: the criminal and the crime', *British Journal of Criminology*, 9: 145–55.

Jackson, H. F., Glass, C. and Hope, S. (1987) 'A functional analysis of recidivistic arson', *British Journal of Clinical Psychology*, 26: 175–85.

Jayaraman, A. and Frazer, J. (2006) 'Arson: a growing inferno', *Medicine, Science, and the Law*, 46: 295–300.

Kolko, D. J. (1983) 'Multicomponent parental treatment of firesetting in a six year old boy', *Journal of Behavior and Experimental Psychology*, 14: 349–54.

Kolko, D. J. (1985) 'Juvenile firesetting: a review and methodological critique', *Clinical Psychology Review*, 5: 345–76.

Kolko, D. J. (2001) 'Efficacy of cognitive-behavioral treatment and fire safety education for children who set fires: initial and follow-up outcomes', *Journal of Child Psychology and Psychiatry*, 42: 359–69.

Kolko, D. J. (eds) (2002) *Handbook on Firesetting in Children and Youth*. London: Academic Press.

Kolko, D. J. and Ammerman, R. T. (1988) 'Firesetting', in M. Hersen and C. G. Last (eds), *Child Behavior Therapy Casebook*. New York: Plenum Press, pp. 243–62.

Kolko, D. J. and Kazdin, A. E. (1988) 'Prevalence of firesetting and related behaviors among child psychiatric patients', *Journal of Consulting and Clinical Psychology*, 56: 628–30.

Kolko, D. J. and Kazdin, A. E. (1990) 'Matchplay and firesetting in children: relationship to parent, marital and family dysfunction', *Journal of Clinical Child Psychology*, 19: 229–38.

Kolko, D. J. and Kazdin, A. E. (1991) 'Motives of childhood firesetters: firesetting characteristics and psychological correlates', *Journal of Child Psychology and Psychiatry*, 32: 535–50.

Kolko, D. J., Herschell, A. D. and Scharf, D. M. (2006) 'Education and treatment for boys who set fires: specificity, moderators, and predictors of recidivism', *Journal of Emotional and Behavioral Disorders*, 14 (4): 227–39.

Lindberg, N., Holi, M. M., Tani, P. and Virkkunen, M. (2005) 'Looking for pyromania: characteristics of a consecutive sample of Finnish male criminals with histories of recidivist fire-setting between 1973 and 1993', *BMC Psychiatry*, 5: 47.

McCarty, C. A. and McMahon, R. (2005) 'Domains of risk in the developmental continuity of fire setting', *Behavior Therapy*, 36: 185–95.

MacKay, S., Henderson, J., Del Bove, G., Marton, P., Warling, D. and Root, C. (2006) 'Fire interest and antisociality as risk factors in the severity and persistence of juvenile firesetting', *Journal of American Academy of Child and Adolescent Psychiatry*, 43 (9): 1077–84.

Maguire, M. and Brookman, F. (2005) 'Violent and sexual crime', in N. Tilley (ed.), *Handbook of Crime Prevention and Community Safety*. Cullompton: Willan, pp. 516–62.

Martin, G., Bergen, H. A., Richardson, A. S., Roeger, L. and Allison, S. (2004) 'Correlates of firesetting in a community sample of young adolescents', *Australian and New Zealand Journal of Psychiatry*, 38: 148–54.

Ministry of Justice (2008) *Criminal Statistics England and Wales 2007*. London: Ministry of Justice.

Muckley, A. (1997) *Addressing Firesetting Behaviour in Children, Young People and Adults* (a resource and training manual).

Nicholas, S., Kershaw, C. and Walker, A. (2007) *Crime in England and Wales 2006/07*, 4th edn. London: RDSD.

O'Sullivan, G. H. and Kelleher, M. J. (1987) 'A study of firesetters in the southwest of Ireland', *British Journal of Psychiatry*, 151: 818–23.

Office of the Deputy Prime Minister (2005) *Arson Terminology: Research Findings*. London: Office of the Deputy Prime Minister.

Office of the Deputy Prime Minister (2006a) *The Fire and Rescue National Framework: 2006–08*. London: Office of the Deputy Prime Minister.

Office of the Deputy Prime Minister (2006b) *The Economic Cost of Fire: Estimates for 2004*. London: Office of the Deputy Prime Minister.

Palmer, E. J., Caulfield, L. S. and Hollin, C. R. (2007) 'Interventions with arsonists and young firesetters: a survey of the national picture in England and Wales', *Legal and Criminological Psychology*, 12: 101–16.

Powers, P. S. and Gunderman, R. (1978) 'Kleine-Levin syndrome associated with firesetting', *Pediatrics and Adolescent Medicine*, 132: 786–92.

Prins, H. (1994) *Fire-Raising: Its Motivation and Management*. London: Routledge.

Räsänen, P., Hirvenoja, R., Hakko, H. and Vaeisaenen, E. (1995) 'A portrait of the juvenile arsonist', *Forensic Science International*, 73: 41–7.

Repo, E. and Virkkunen, M. (1997) 'Young arsonists: history of conduct disorder, psychiatric diagnosis and criminal recidivism', *Journal of Forensic Psychiatry*, 8: 311–20.

Ritchie, E. C. and Huff, T. G. (1999) 'Psychiatric aspects of arsonists', *Journal of Forensic Science*, 44: 733–40.

Santilla, P., Häkkänen, H., Alison, L. and White, C. (2003) 'Juvenile firesetters: crime scene actions and offender characteristics', *Legal and Criminological Psychology*, 8: 1–20.

Schwartzman, P., Stambaugh, H. and Kimball, J. (1998) *Arson and Juveniles: Responding to the Violence*. Online at: http://sosfires.com/arson%20and%20juveniles-responding%20to%20the%20violence.htm.

Slavkin, M. L. (2004) 'Characteristics of juvenile firesetting across childhood and adolescence', *Forensic Examiner*, Winter, pp. 6–18.

Soothill, K., Ackerley, E. and Francis, B. (2004) 'The criminal careers of arsonists', *Medicine, Science, and the Law*, 44: 27–40.

Taylor, J. L., Thorne, I. and Slavkin, M. L. (2004) 'Treatment of fire-setting behaviour', in W. R. Lindsay, J. L. Taylor and P. Sturmey (eds), *Offenders with Developmental Disabilities*. Chichester: John Wiley & Sons, pp. 221–40.

Taylor, J. L., Thorne, I., Robertson, A. and Avery, G. (2002) 'Evaluation of a group intervention for convicted arsonists with mild and borderline disabilities', *Criminal Behaviour and Mental Health*, 12: 282–93.

Taylor, J. L., Robertson, A., Thorne, I., Belshaw, T. and Watson, A. (2006) 'Responses of female fire-setters with mild and borderline intellectual disabilities to a group intervention', *Journal of Applied Research in Intellectual Disabilities*, 19: 179–90.

Topp, D. O. (1973) 'Fire as a symbol and as a weapon of death', *Medicine Science and the Law*, 13: 79–86.

Chapter 21

Blackmail, kidnapping and threats to kill

Keith Soothill and Brian Francis

Introduction

This chapter is concerned with blackmail, kidnapping and threats to kill, which are all relatively unusual but quite serious offences, with the possibility of attracting sentences of long-term imprisonment. The three offences tend to be neglected by criminologists, but can often attract considerable media publicity. Moreover, all three offences have been increasing in England and Wales in recent years. Beyond that, however, they are very different offences with very different origins. We start with their origins, move on to the contemporary legal categories which cover these offences, then identify patterns and trends in the numbers convicted of blackmail, kidnapping or threats to kill. Next we focus more directly on the offenders in terms of what we know about them and their criminal careers and, finally, we try to assess the future danger from those already convicted of these offences.

Origins and legal definitions

Blackmail, kidnapping and threats to kill are offences which have a long history and which continue to be of contemporary interest.

Blackmail

The classic text, *Smith & Hogan: Criminal Law* (11th edn, Ormerod 2005) provides some clues in relation to blackmail, pointing to the origins of the term, how it was used interchangeably with other offences and then how the offence of blackmail gained its own identity.

In fact, 'originally the word blackmail was used to describe the tribute paid to Scottish chieftains by landowners in the border counties in order to secure immunity from raids on their lands' (ibid.: 800), but in the early days of its development the crime of blackmail was regarded as much the same as robbery or attempted robbery. Gradually the term captured its own meaning so that, rather than straightforward robbery, 'over the years the definition has been extended to embrace more subtle forms of extortion' (ibid.).

Other jurisdictions make a distinction between extortion, where there is an independent underlying criminal act, and blackmail, where there is none. In English law, however, the term blackmail encompasses all acts of extortion. To confuse matters further, in Scottish law, the term extortion encompasses blackmail. Hobbs, in Chapter 36 of this volume, discusses some particular forms of 'extortion' (understood in a social rather than strictly legal sense), namely those practised by organised criminal groups using threats of violence in socio-economic systems where the state is weak. This chapter focuses mainly on offences of blackmail by individuals in England and Wales, including those where no violence is threatened.

English law is set out in section 21 of the Theft Act 1968. The maximum sentence is 14 years. The legal language is complicated but essentially blackmail involves making an unwarranted demand with menaces with the intention either to gain or to cause loss. The notions of loss and gain encompassed in the Theft Act 1968 seem to emphasise the importance of protecting property, but in many cases blackmail should be more appropriately considered as an offence against privacy. Alldridge (1993), in writing about this, has the arresting title of 'Attempted murder of the soul: blackmail, privacy and secrets' which illustrates the potential seriousness of the crime in this respect.

Legal authorities stress that a demand with menaces may take any form and may be implicit as well as explicit. Ormerod stresses that a demand 'extends well beyond the obvious "£1,000 or I will publish the photographs exposing your adultery"' (2005: 801). However, there are limits to what is captured by the offence of blackmail. So, for instance, demands for sexual intercourse or other acts of a sexual nature are not within the scope of the offence and are dealt with under the Sexual Offences Act 2003.

The careful use of language is fascinating. The word 'menaces' is used rather than 'threats' as the former word is thought to be stronger than 'threats'. For most people, there is probably little difference between the terms, but the distinction allows there to be a limit below which conduct will not be regarded as a menace. Clearly, lawyers can benefit in trying to distinguish a mere threat from demanding with menaces.

Importantly, not every demand accompanied by a menace amounts to blackmail. Hence, demanding the payment of a debt and to threaten civil proceedings in the event of a failure to comply would not be regarded as blackmail. In other words, one can make a perfectly lawful demand accompanied by a justifiable threat.

Finally, while the crime has a long history, the crime is certainly not out of date. We consider trends later but, as Ormerod stresses, 'the ease with which demands can be communicated via e-mail and mobile phones ... renders the opportunity for blackmail ever greater' (2005: 801).

Kidnapping

Kidnapping is an aggravated form of false imprisonment (Ormerod 2005: 575), so one needs first to consider false imprisonment. Article 5 of the European Convention on Human Rights provides a guarantee against arbitrary deprivation of movement, but that has been interpreted more narrowly than simply restricting movement. The distinction between *deprivation* of liberty and mere *restrictions* on freedom of movement are not always easy to identify and various authorities suggest that the difference is 'merely one of degree or intensity, and not one of nature or substance'. False imprisonment in English law is taken to be the unlawful and intentional or reckless detention of a person against his will. Kidnapping, in contrast, has the additional element of taking the person away to another place. The maximum sentence for kidnapping in England and Wales is life imprisonment, but in some jurisdictions it remains a capital offence.

The most recent definition of kidnapping was provided by Lord Brandon in 1984 and contains four ingredients: (1) the taking or carrying away of one person by another, (2) by force or by fraud, (3) without the consent of the person so taken or carried away and (4) without lawful excuse (Lord Brandon in *R* v. *D* [1984] AC 778, 800). In providing this authoritative account of the law of kidnapping the House of Lords remarked on the changes in society over time. Thus it is now possible for a father to be found guilty of kidnapping his own child, as a father's authority in a family is now considered not to be absolute.

Curiously, when the division of criminal offences into the two categories of felonies and misdemeanours was extant,[1] the offence of kidnapping was categorised by the common law as a misdemeanour only. Nevertheless, despite this legal anomaly, kidnapping was always regarded as a grave offence. However, there were constraints on the use of the term which have since become obsolete – for example, it involved the taking or carrying away from a place within the jurisdiction to another place outside it, and there was the notion of secreting a person (Ormerod 2005: 575–6).

The four ingredients outlined above which frame the current understanding of the term kidnapping also have their problems which feature in legal textbooks. Indeed, Ormerod (2005: 575) still insists that 'kidnapping has never been satisfactorily defined'. Mainly the problems revolve around the issues of fraud, force and consent. So, for example, if there is trivial force involved, does this invalidate the notion that the act was carried out 'without consent'? In other words, must there be force or fraud *and* an absence of consent in all cases? What is 'without lawful excuse' and so on? The possibilities for lawyers to engage are great, but there is also a common-sense understanding of kidnapping so that the public, in broad terms, understand when a person has been kidnapped.

Threats to kill

Ormerod makes the point (2005: 809) that there are numerous offences based on threats. He mentions threats to kill, threats to damage property, threats to food terrorism, threats of violence for the purpose of securing entry to premises, sending malicious communications and demanding payment for unsolicited goods with threats. Threats to 'expose' (or blackmail) is, of course, another important possibility. Ormerod notes that 'there is little coherence in English Law's approach to threat offences'. However, our focus is simply on 'threats to kill'.

While threats to kill is a criminal offence, the other person must genuinely fear the act will be carried out. Hence, casual remarks not said seriously between friends or associates will not therefore be considered an offence. Furthermore, there is a defence to the charge – that there is a lawful excuse for making the threat. So, for example, if the threat was made in a self-defence situation, then this may be a lawful excuse.

People must have made threats to kill from time immemorial, but section 16 of the Offences Against the Person Act 1861 actually created an offence of making written threats to murder. The Criminal Law Act 1977, Sch. 12, replaces that provision with a new and broader section 16 (Ormerod 2005: 490). Nowadays the threat to kill may take any form. The maximum sentence is ten years' imprisonment.

Proving a threat to kill is often difficult. So, for example, two men arrested in August 2008 with rifles, sniper scopes and an alleged desire to kill the then presidential candidate Barack Obama were at the time on a methamphetamine binge. The US Attorney, Troy Eid, said at a packed news conference, 'The law recognizes a difference between a true threat – that's one that can be carried out – and the reported racist rants of drug abusers' (http://www.truthout. org/article/threat-kill-obama-downplayed).

Nevertheless, despite difficulties in proving the offence, there seems likely to be more rather than less of the act in future, for the scope from different types of communication is increasing. So, for instance, threats to kill in England and Wales made by e-mails from abroad have been sufficient in number for the activity to be identified as an offence (Ormerod 2005: 491).

Measuring the three offences

Offences can be considered at two stages of the criminal justice process – either when crime is *reported to and/or recorded by* the police, or through examination of *court convictions* resulting from successful prosecutions.[2] There is a substantial decrease in cases between these two stages, as not all recorded crime is solved, solved crime may not be prosecuted and only a proportion of cases brought to court result in successful prosecutions.

For England and Wales, information for all three offences is relatively widely available. In the US, in contrast, the National Incident-Based Reporting System (NIBRS) is voluntary and in 2004 covered only about 20 per cent of the US population, with many states not currently contributing data. Moreover, while it records 'Kidnappings and abductions', 'Extortions and blackmail', and 'Intimidation' as separate categories, these terms have rather different meanings in the US (particularly intimidation, which covers threats to bodily harm as well as threats to kill). Australia presents another kind of difficulty. There are reports on 'Kidnapping/abduction' and 'Blackmail/ extortion' in the National Offence categorisation but not on threats to kill.

The offence of blackmail is coded as 35 in *Criminal Statistics: England and Wales* (see, for example, Table 3.19, Ministry of Justice 2008) and is straightforward. However, the other two offences need some discussion.

The offence termed as 'kidnapping etc.' and coded 36 is, in fact, a combination of three offences, all of which have maximum life sentences. First, there is the offence properly termed as kidnapping (36.1). Closely connected with this is false imprisonment (36.3). Both of these make up the bulk of reported 'kidnapping etc.' cases each year. The far rarer offence of hijacking (36.2) completes this trio of offences; this latter offence relates to behaviour on aircraft, ships and Channel Tunnel trains, and includes not only taking control of an aircraft, ship or train, but also causing damage to or destroying an aircraft, ship or train, or endangering the safety of an aircraft. Offences such as abduction and child abduction are not necessarily included in 'kidnapping', but have their own separate classifications.[3] However, serious child abduction cases which have the ingredients of kidnapping can be prosecuted as kidnapping. As Crew and Lammers (2001) state in relation to the US, 'By far the largest category of incidents that meet the legal criteria for kidnapping are child abductions by noncustodial parents involved in a custody dispute' (p. 349), but go on to point out that 'many of these abductions do not appear in the UCR or victimization data' (p. 349). In England and Wales, the distinction is quite clear and the data we will be considering does not include 'routine' child abduction cases.

'Threat or conspiracy to murder' coded 3 in *Criminal Statistics* is, again, a combination of three offences. Firstly, there is making threats to kill (3.1), covered by the Offences against the Person Act 1861, where the threat is such that 'the other would fear it would be carried out'. Conspiracy or soliciting to commit murder (3.2) is a much rarer offence, also covered by the Offences against the Person Act 1861 and the Criminal Law Act 1977. The third of this trio of offences is assisting an offender by impeding apprehension or prosecution in a case of murder, formally termed as accessory after the fact to murder (3.3). This too is a rare offence, covered by the Criminal Law Act 1977.

Nature of the offences and their representation in the media

Kidnapping

Recognising a particular offence as becoming a significant problem can have various origins and outcomes. Perhaps most commonly, concern will be heightened if a high-profile case, perhaps involving a celebrity, comes to public notice. This is especially evident with kidnapping cases. Certainly the kidnap and the subsequent murder of Charles Lindbergh's baby in the US (Campbell 2003) was a major news story in the 1930s and publicity surrounding this case helped to establish the Federal Kidnapping Act, allowing kidnappers to be followed across state boundaries. More recently, the alleged kidnap of 3-year-old Madeleine McCann while holidaying in Portugal in 2007 has brought to wide notice the horrors of this offence. Sometimes, the sad outcome of a death – which happened in the Lindbergh case – can further prolong or intensify the media coverage. Both of these cases, coming 75 years apart, had widespread publicity and an international audience was made much more aware of the crime.

Kidnapping for ransom or political gain has also become widespread over the past few decades. Indeed, patterns of kidnapping have changed so much that, as Rice-Oxley (2008) points out, 'it is easy to forget that 30 years ago it was the world's rich nations that suffered most'. He reminds us that 'in the 1970s, the proliferation of leftwing guerrilla groups from the US to Germany, Spain and Italy determined to wage war on wealth, capitalism and the established political order left a trail of victims and instilled fear among the rich and famous that anyone was a target.' Certainly, Rice-Oxley's list is a disturbing one – Patty Hearst, an American newspaper heiress, was seized in 1974 by urban guerrillas known as the Symbionese Liberation Army and went on to join her captors; Peter Lorenz, a conservative candidate for mayor of Berlin, was abducted and freed in 1975; Hanns Martin Schleyer, a German industrialist, was kidnapped in 1977, held for 43 days while ransom demands were made, then murdered; the Red Army Faction, behind the abduction, also counted leading bankers Alfred Herrhausen and Karl Heinz Beckurts among its victims; in Italy the communist Red Brigades kidnapped Christian Democratic leader Aldo Moro in 1978, killing him after a 55-day stand-off; Spain, through Eta and a left-wing group known as Grapo, also resorted to abductions. Undoubtedly, kidnapping and the like can capture the world stage. The hostage-taking at the Munich Olympics in 1972, leading to the deaths of 11 Israeli athletes, brought the activity to the media world stage as never before.

There have been attempts to draw up typologies of the offence. Alix (1978), in an analysis of a hundred kidnapping cases reported in the *New York Times*, identified 15 distinct types of kidnapping crimes, distinguished by the methods and motives of the criminals. Summarised by Crew and Lammers (2001), six of the categories involve ransom: classic ransom kidnapping, developmental ransom kidnapping, skyjacking, ransom hoaxes, conspiracy to kidnap for ransom and kidnapping as extortion threat. The first two perhaps need explanation. Classic ransom kidnapping involves a situation in which a victim is targeted, captured and held, and a demand for ransom is made. Developmental ransom kidnapping occurs when a ransom develops out of another crime already in progress, such as a burglar who decides to hold a victim for ransom.

As Crew and Lammers note, other types include incidents where kidnapping is instrumental to the commission of another crime, such as rape, murder or robbery. Hostage situations occur when an offender takes a victim for protection or to facilitate an escape. White slavery is the kidnapping of women for commercial prostitution.

The possibilities in this typology seem endless. 'Romantic kidnapping' is identified as those cases in which a juvenile, usually a female, voluntarily accompanies an offender against her parents' wishes. 'Domestic relations kidnapping' occurs when a child is taken by a divorced parent in violation of a custody decree. 'Child stealing' is a residual category to cover the taking of a child for reasons not covered in the other categories.

While interesting, this early classification is rather unwieldy and also biased towards high-profile cases. More recently, Concannon *et al.* (2008) devised a classification of seven distinct types based primarily on motive:

- *domestic kidnapping* – taking place within the family;
- *political kidnapping* – with a political motive;
- *predatory kidnapping of a child* – with a sexual motive;
- *predatory kidnapping of an adult* – with a sexual motive;
- *profit kidnapping* – with the aim of gaining money or goods;
- *revenge kidnapping* – where the aim is to right a perceived wrong by taking revenge on the victim;
- *staged kidnapping* – where the aim is to distract from another crime or activity.

This latter classification is more useful, although the motive for some of the aforementioned political kidnappings can also be financial, so this will belong in more than one class. Producing mutually exclusive categories is rarely achieved in developing typologies.

The offence of kidnapping has produced some memorable cases, some of which have been mentioned above. Recent high-profile kidnap cases in the UK include the conspiracy to kidnap Victoria Beckham and the kidnap in Dewsbury of Shannon Matthews, a nine-year-old girl, by family relatives, with the two cases demonstrating how both the rich and the socially deprived can be involved in high-profile kidnapping.

Blackmail

High-profile blackmail cases also have considerable variety – in the past year, for example, four animal rights activists involved in a hate campaign were found guilty of blackmail, and there was also an attempt to blackmail a member of the Royal Family. In fact, prominent cases of blackmail have historically sought to obtain money or other material gain through threats to reveal sexual secrets or to destroy the reputation of the victim (Hepworth 1975). McLaren (2002), however, makes the point that sexual blackmail is becoming less prevalent with changing societal mores and greater sexual honesty. Nevertheless, sexual blackmail can still produce widespread interest when there are some titillating ingredients. The just mentioned recent Royal blackmail case suitably fits this bill, for it was essentially an attempt to blackmail a relative of the Royal Family over alleged drug taking and sexual behaviour (BBC News Online 2007). Royalty have always been at risk from blackmailers with cases involving the Duke of Clarence (son of King Edward VII), Prince Ludwig of Bavaria, Victor Emmanuel III of Italy and Louis XVI of France (who paid off London criminals who threatened to publish sexual libels about his queen, Marie Antoinette) brought to light by diligent historians (Wainwright 2007).

Blackmail can be classified in a wide number of dimensions – the nature of the threat, the task required of the victim and the motivation. Rosenberg (2008) identifies two types of blackmail – hush money blackmail, where money is demanded from the victim, and behaviour modification blackmail, where the blackmailer demands some other action from the victim, such as a job or a passport or inside information. We have already discussed that, if the underlying threatened action is criminal, then the crime is labelled as extortion in some jurisdictions and this provides another typology (Lindgren 1984).

Companies are being increasingly targeted. A typical and prominent case involved the supermarket Tesco in 2007. The blackmailer McHugh threatened to poison yogurt with caustic soda and later threatened to bomb stores, with a one million pound ransom being demanded (Meikle 2008). Another recent case – a behaviour modification extortion – involved four animal rights campaigners who targeted suppliers of the Huntingdon Life Sciences Laboratory, threatening them with threats of violence and hoax bomb threats, with the intention of persuading the companies to cease supplying (Siddique 2008). Blackmailers are also starting to exploit the power of the Internet, by threatening 'denial of service' attacks against company websites and online betting sites unless a ransom is paid (see Williams, Chapter 11 of this volume). Again, although it is an ancient crime, new forms continue to emerge.

Threats to kill

In contrast to blackmail and kidnapping, the offence of threats to kill seems to have a less high-profile media coverage. Nevertheless, in one month (December 2008) there were stories in the UK tabloid press about death threats to the Hollywood actors Katie Holmes and Tom Cruise by groups opposed to Scientology, an alleged domestic threat by an ex-Ireland international soccer star to kill his wife, a revenge threat to kill in Ireland by a father against his son's presumed killers, and an alleged threat by two bankers to kill a London pleasure cruise boatman before starting a fatal assault. Again the diversity of the cases is an interesting feature.

The range of motives for threats to kill therefore appears to be as wide as that for kidnapping and blackmail, encompassing revenge and political and domestic threats. Barnes *et al.* (2001) identified two groups among those charged with threatening to kill and referred for assessment – those receiving criminal sanctions were more likely to threaten family members, whereas those receiving a psychiatric disposal were more likely to threaten strangers and health professionals. The possible link between making a threat to kill and prior contact with public mental health services has recently been explored by Warren and colleagues (2008). Of a total of 613 individuals convicted of threats to kill, 252 (or 41 per cent) had had prior contact with public mental health services at the time of their offence of making a threat to kill.

Prevalence of the three offences

Table 21.1 shows the prevalence rates for England and Wales per 100,000 population in 2006/7 for the three offences. The rates for murder and manslaughter are included in Table 21.1 for comparison.

Table 21.1 Prevalence of the three offences per 100,000 population in England and Wales and Australia in 2006

	Murder and manslaughter	Kidnapping and abduction	Blackmail and extortion	Threats and conspiracy to murder
England and Wales*	1.4	4.4	2.2*	23.9
Australia	1.6	3.5	2.1	n/a

*2007 figures taken as 2006 figures distorted by large number of reports relating to one case (see text).

Sources: *England and Wales*: Home Office Statistics Bulletin 03.08: Homicides, Firearm Offences and Intimate Violence 2006/07, Table 1.07; Police recorded crime statistics 2006/7. *Australia*: 4510.0 – Recorded Crime – Victims, Australia, 2006.

There are 4.4 kidnapping and adult abductions for every 100,000 population (this increases to 5.7 per 100,000 if child abduction is also included). Blackmail rates are around half at 2.2 per 100,000 population. The prevalence rates for kidnap are about three times the yearly prevalence rates for homicide. Rates for threats and conspiracy to murder are around five times greater than the kidnapping rates, at 23.9 per 100,000.

Owing partly to the definitional issues already discussed, it is difficult to obtain reliable rates for other countries. However, included in Table 21.1 are prevalence rates for Australia. The kidnapping rates are not strictly comparable, as the Australian definition includes kidnapping for a sexual motive (excluded for England and Wales) and excludes false imprisonment (which is included in the England and Wales figures). Nevertheless, the figures for kidnapping are broadly similar. Furthermore, rates for blackmail and extortion are comparable to those for England and Wales.

Trends over time

For the rest of this chapter we focus exclusively on England and Wales. Different offences have different trajectories. A sudden increase in a particular crime may produce general outrage, while a steadier increase may need an astute commentator to bring the shift to public notice. As Figure 21.1 shows, kidnapping (code 36) and threats or conspiracy to murder (code 3) have both shown a dramatic increase in the *recorded* figures since the 1980s reaching a peak in the early part of the twenty-first century before showing a decline.

For kidnapping, there were 70 recorded offences in 1979. The totals rose to a peak of over 3,000 in 2001/2 before declining to 2,000 offences in 2007/8. For threats to murder etc., the recorded offences have increased from 425 offences in 1979 to a peak of 23,758 in 2004/5 before halving to just under 10,000 in 2007/8. This latter decline can partially be explained by changes in guidance issued to police forces in recording threats to kill – the victim now must have a real fear that their life was at risk (Walker *et al.* 2006: 69).

Blackmail has shown a lesser increase, doubling from 533 offences in 1979 to 1,197 cases in 2007/8. However, there was a sudden spike of 2,481 offences in 2006/7,which was due to a very large number of police contacts from shareholders of GlaxoSmithKline who were targeted by threatening letters from an animal rights organisation (BBC News Online 2006; Nicholas *et al.* 2007: 27).

Offender convictions – which relate to the successful outcome of a court process for the prosecution – indicate a slightly different story. We used the Offenders Index (Home Office 1998) which contains a record of the convictions for all standard-list offences,[4] extracting all kidnappings, blackmail and threats to murder between 1979 and 2001. Our figures give all convictions for the offences in question whether or not there was a more serious conviction for the offender at the same court process – and thus give a more accurate picture than those given in *Criminal Statistics*.

Figure 21.1 shows that yearly convictions for blackmail hardly changed between 1979 and 2001, with around 350 cases per year. In contrast, total kidnapping convictions increased nearly tenfold over the same period from 82 to 678, and total convictions for threats to murder etc. increased nearly fivefold from 143 to 700.

More recent figures are available from the publication *Criminal Statistics* (Ministry of Justice 2008) and relate to both cautions and court convictions. Moreover, the figures refer to the principal caution or conviction only (thus a blackmail conviction with a manslaughter conviction at the same court proceedings would no longer count as a blackmail conviction). There were 125 principal cautions or convictions for blackmail in 2001 rising to 161 in 2007, for kidnapping there were 365 principal cautions or convictions in 2001 rising to 437 in 2007, and there were 637 principal cautions or convictions for threats or conspiracy to murder in 2001, rising to 827 in 2007. This latter group, unlike the figures extracted from the Offenders Index, also includes incitement, persuasion and conspiracy to commit murder and thus is also not comparable in offence definition. Nevertheless, these more recent figures suggest that each of the offences of interest have risen in the early years of this century and, thus, should attract more interest than they do among criminologists.

In comparing convictions to police recorded crime, it needs to be recognised that the police recorded crime figures are victim-based – if one blackmailer makes a threat to a large number of people, or a sequence of threats to the same person, this will be recorded separately for each threat. Convictions, in contrast, do not necessarily prosecute separately for each crime recorded.

Offenders

What do we know about the characteristics of the offenders convicted of blackmail, kidnapping or threats to kill in England and Wales? Based on all those convicted of one or more of these three offences between 1979 and 2001, we consider their age and gender profiles.

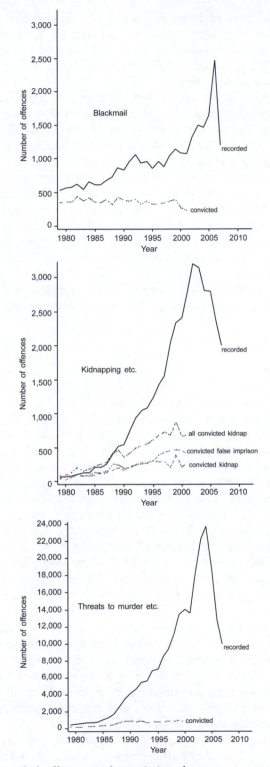

Figure 21.1 Recorded offences and convictions by year

Overall, the mean ages of those convicted for the three offences between 1979 and 2001 show that blackmail and kidnapping have a younger age profile than threats to kill – those convicted of blackmail being 25.1 years, of kidnapping being 27.6 years, and of threats to kill being 31.9 years. However, there have been changes over time.

Figure 21.2 shows the mean age of conviction by age and year for the three offences, with a superimposed linear trend.[5] Blackmail shows a significant increase in age over the period examined for both males and females, but with no difference between males and females. In contrast, for threats to kill and for kidnapping, there is no significant change over time – however, there are significant differences between males and females for both offences, with females on average being three years younger for kidnapping and three and a half years younger for threats to kill. The increase in mean age for blackmail can partially be accounted for by the decline in those under 20 being brought to court – moving from around 200 cases a year in the early 1980s to around half that figure in 2001 – whereas convictions for those 20 and above have remained more stable.

Now moving on to their criminal profiles, we consider the nature of the previous and subsequent convictions of those involved in the three offences of interest.

Previous convictions

What are the types of offences that offenders convicted of each of blackmail, kidnapping or threats to kill are likely to have committed in the past? For this purpose we considered those offenders convicted in the last three years of the period for which we have information (that is 1999–2001) as these would provide the longest 'window' to consider their previous convictions. This 'window' goes back to 1963 so, for anyone aged 46 or younger, this analysis focuses on their complete criminal history for standard-list offences.

In fact, the similarities rather than the differences between the offences is the feature which characterises Table 21.2. Among the males, approaching 60 per cent of those convicted of blackmail and those convicted of kidnapping have at least one conviction for a standard-list offence prior to their conviction for the target offences; a higher proportion – approaching two-thirds – of those convicted of threats to kill have a previous conviction for a standard-list offence.

The proportions with a previous criminal record seem lower for females – around 50 per cent for those convicted of blackmail and those convicted of threats to kill and approaching 40 per cent for kidnapping – but we suspect that these lower proportions for females may be an artefact of the construction of the Offenders Index where identification by name and date of birth are the crucial identifiers and the prevalence of name changes among females may create a problem (Francis and Crosland 2002).

So, broadly speaking, Table 21.2 indicates how the perpetrators of these three offences fall into two major categories – those with a known previous criminal history and those with no previous history for a standard-list offence.

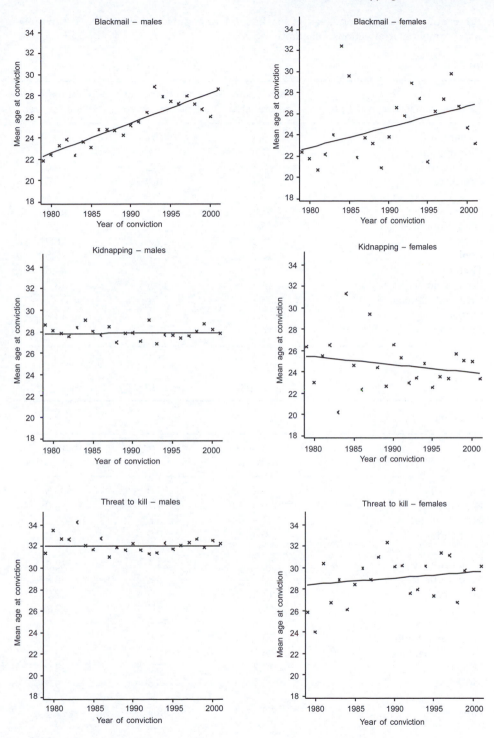

Figure 21.2 Mean age at conviction by year

Table 21.2 Offenders convicted of blackmail, kidnapping and threats to kill in 1999–2001 – previous convictions (standard list)

(a) Males

Type of previous conviction	Blackmail % convicted	Kidnapping % convicted	Threats to kill % convicted
Blackmail	5.3	0.6	0.5
Kidnapping	1.0	4.1	0.9
Threats to kill	0.8	1.2	4.6
Homicide	0.4	0.4	0.5
Violence	35.8	36.9	43.1
Sexual offences	3.1	5.3	4.5
Burglary	26.2	29.7	28.9
Robbery	11.6	11.7	7.5
Theft	41.1	42.7	44.0
Fraud and forgery	14.6	13.5	13.3
Criminal damage	23.4	27.1	36.2
Drugs	15.6	16.3	12.2
Motoring	17.1	19.5	18.9
Any	57.9	58.7	64.2
	(n = 508)	(n = 1524)	(n = 1625)

(b) Females

Type of previous conviction	Blackmail % convicted	Kidnapping % convicted	Threats to kill % convicted
Blackmail	1.9	0.0	0.8
Kidnapping	0.0	1.7	0.0
Threats to kill	1.9	0.0	5.6
Homicide	0.0	0.0	0.0
Violence	28.3	23.3	32.5
Sexual offences	0.0	0.8	0.8
Burglary	13.2	8.3	7.9
Robbery	11.3	2.5	3.3
Theft	45.3	25.0	31.7
Fraud and forgery	22.6	10.0	9.5
Criminal damage	24.5	16.7	23.8
Drugs	13.2	5.0	4.0
Motoring	3.8	5.8	4.8
Any	52.8	38.3	47.9
	(n = 53)	(n = 120)	(n = 126)

The majority of the males involved in the three offences have a known previous criminal history, while the females are more evenly split.

Among those with previous criminal convictions, the criminal profiles of males and females are similar. While theft predominates, a high proportion in each of the series have been previously convicted of violence, while among the males over one quarter of each series have been convicted of burglary.

Criminal careers of those convicted of blackmail, kidnapping or threats to kill

There are two features that this section focuses upon. Firstly, to what extent are blackmail, kidnapping or threats to kill recidivating offences? In other words, how many or what proportion get reconvicted of the same offence? This is essentially about the criminological issue of specialisation. The second feature which we consider is the interrelationship of these offences. So, for instance, how many of those who are convicted of blackmail go on to be subsequently convicted of kidnapping?

The notion of specialisation in criminology is a contentious issue. There are those who point to specialisation among offenders and there are those who stress that specialisation among offenders is marginal with most offenders being 'generalists'.

Put simply, specialisation in criminal careers is the degree to which offenders specialise in a single crime or a collection of crimes. Hence, a specialist offender might specialise in burglary or the offender might specialise *within* burglary, ignoring domestic homes and focusing efforts on commercial premises and breaking into shops. Specialist burglars might also involve themselves in other crimes to a greater or lesser degree. Nevertheless, their preferred offending will involve burglary (see Chapter 6 on specialisation in Soothill *et al.* 2009). So how does all this relate to offenders convicted of threats to kill, kidnapping or blackmail?

With these offenders the problem is much more to do with data sources rather than grasping conceptual distinctions. In other words, while one might make distinctions between different types of kidnapping or blackmail or ways of making threats to kill and so ask questions at the more micro-level of which types of kidnapping, blackmail or threats to kill an offender might specialise in, the data available will not allow us to deliver. Data sources with reasonable numbers of such offenders tend to have minimal information on the nature of these offences. Usually there is simply information that the offender has been convicted of such an offence with no further detail. Hence at a basic level there is only scope to consider whether these offenders get reconvicted of these offences.

Table 21.2 presents the *previous* convictions (standard-list offences) of all those convicted of blackmail (n = 508), of kidnapping (n = 1,524), or of threats to kill (n = 1,625) at the start of the twenty-first century. How many had previously been convicted of the offence of interest? In broad terms, the proportions are very similar – around 1 in 20 (or 5 per cent) of the males and about 1 in 50 (or 2 per cent) of the females have prior convictions for the same offence. Not unexpectedly, fewer females than males are repeating the offence – or at least getting prosecuted and convicted. The exception is for threats to kill, where about 1 in 20 (or 5.6 per cent) of the females have a prior threat to kill conviction.

So what happens *after* being convicted of one of these offences? Table 21.3 shows a 20-year follow-up for each of the three offences following a relevant conviction in 1979–81. We notice that the offences differ in their degree of subsequent specialist recidivism. Among the males, kidnapping has the lowest rate, with 3.9 per cent going on to be convicted of another kidnapping offence within the subsequent 20 year window. Blackmail has a larger specialist recidivism rate of 5.8 per cent, and threats to kill has the highest, with 7.2 per cent going on to be convicted again of that offence.

Among the females, there are fewer cases, but the offences differ in the same ways as for the males. There are no subsequent convictions for kidnapping, a specialist recidivism rate of 6.0 per cent for blackmail (nearly identical to the males) and the highest specialist recidivism rate of 11.8 per cent for threats to

Table 21.3 Offenders convicted of blackmail, kidnapping and threats to kill (in 1979–81) – subsequent convictions (standard list)

(a) Males

Type of previous conviction	Blackmail % convicted	Kidnapping % convicted	Threats to kill % convicted
Blackmail	5.8	0.8	0.2
Kidnapping	0.7	3.9	0.9
Threats to kill	1.3	1.9	7.2
Homicide	1.4	1.5	1.7
Any violence	41.8	37.1	35.3
	(n = 843)	(n = 259)	(n = 458)

(b) Females

Type of previous conviction	Blackmail % convicted	Kidnapping % convicted	Threats to kill % convicted
Blackmail	6.0	0.0	2.9
Kidnapping	0.0	0.0	0.0
Threats to kill	0.0	0.0	11.8
Homicide	1.5	0.0	0.0
Any violence	14.9	21.4	36.4
	(n = 67)	(n=14)	(n=34)

kill. Bearing in mind the difficulty of obtaining a conviction for this type of offence, the last figure is a remarkably high specialist recidivism rate.

We now turn our attention to the interrelationships between the three offences. Tables 21.2 and 21.3 also contain information on the proportions of each series who have a prior or a subsequent conviction for one of the other offences under consideration. In general, the proportions of offenders who involve themselves with another of the trio of offences is small and amounts to around one per cent of offenders for each offence, whether previous or subsequent offences are examined.

The seriousness of the offence

Up to now there has been no discussion about the seriousness of the offence. While intrinsically each of the three offences can be regarded as coming within the 'serious' category (for being caught at such activity would never be regarded as trivial), nevertheless there are still different degrees of seriousness which, in turn, merit different kinds of severity in terms of punishment. Indeed, punishment can range widely for each of these offences – from a life sentence for kidnapping, a 14-year prison sentence for blackmail and a ten-year prison sentence for threats to kill right through to all kinds of non-custodial sentences for each of the three offences.

Figure 21.3 shows the proportion of custodial sentences for each of the offences by year over a 23-year period from 1979 to 2001. In broad terms, it shows that the proportion of custodial sentences awarded have tended to rise over time. Custodial sentences for blackmail have risen from around 45 per cent of offences to approaching 70 per cent; similarly, threats to kill has increased from under 30 per cent to around 45 per cent; kidnapping, in contrast, shows a slower rise from about 70 per cent to around 75 per cent.

Certainly a problem of using severity of sentencing as a way of measuring the *seriousness* of an offence is that sentencing is basically the outcome of both the nature of the offence and the person's previous criminal history. An interpretation could be that those more recently convicted of these three offences have a higher proportion of previous convictions – and, of course, having previous convictions influences the severity of the sentencing. However, this type of shift seems unlikely. Another interpretation is that these offences have, indeed, become more serious over the years, that is there has been a behavioural change. One suspects, however, it is more likely that these offences have been regarded in an increasingly serious light over the years. In other words, it is probably much more of a perceptual issue on the part of the courts rather than a behavioural change.

How dangerous are these offenders?

Dangerousness is yet another contentious issue in criminology. Its definition is often vague, rarely specifying either the seriousness of the offences that it is

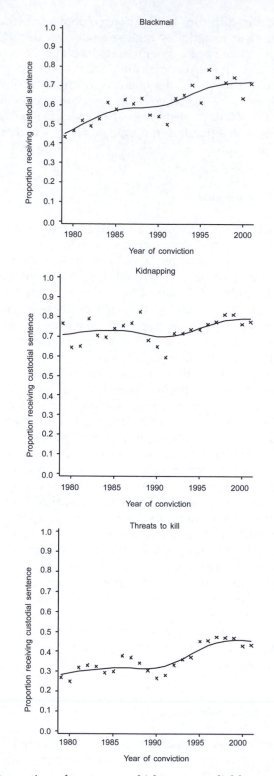

Figure 21.3 Proportion of sentences which are custodial by year

feared a person may commit or the degree of likelihood that they will do so in order for them to merit the label 'dangerous'. Rather than enter the choppy waters of definition, we have used two measures of future dangerousness – namely, a future violence conviction and a measure of extreme dangerousness that is a future homicide conviction (i.e. murder or manslaughter).

Subsequent conviction for violence

Table 21.3 shows that there is a significant minority of offenders for each of the three series who are likely to be convicted of a future violent offence within 20 years. For males around four out of every ten offenders are so convicted. However, for females, threats to kill appear to be similar to males whereas kidnapping and blackmail have a lower rate – but for all three series numbers are small.

Subsequent conviction for homicide

Table 21.3 also shows that, for males, rates of future homicide conviction are very similar for each of the three series, being around 1.5 per cent or 1 in 66 offenders over a 20-year period. This is a remarkably high figure especially when one compares it with the likelihood of members of the general population – or even of other categories of offender – being so convicted. The figure of 1 in 66 compares with the likelihood of around one in 3,000 *male* members of the general population being convicted for homicide over a 20-year follow-up period and an estimated 1 in 400 for homicide following a sexual conviction (Francis and Soothill 2000).

For females, the picture is much less clear. Only one female was convicted of homicide following one of these offences but – to re-emphasise – numbers are very low.

Conclusions

This chapter has focused on three offences which do not receive the attention from criminologists that they perhaps deserve. For the victim the three offences are undoubtedly unpleasant, even though they can range widely in terms of seriousness. Each of the offences has a long history but they are certainly not becoming obsolescent. Indeed, technological changes, such as the development of the Internet, mean that national boundaries are more easily breached. E-mails from abroad provide scope for both blackmail and threats to kill. Even the hands-on offence of kidnapping provides evidence of the importance of globalisation. The recent claim that 'a surge in extortion rackets organized by foreign gangs has substantially increased the number of kidnappings in the capital [London]' was supported by the police asserting that 'half of all kidnappers and victims in the capital are foreign nationals' (*The Guardian*, 22 June 2005). The trends of recorded crime relating to these three offences are significantly upwards over the past two decades, while the levels of convictions are much more stable. The increasing discrepancy in England and Wales between recorded offences and convictions should be a matter of concern – even taking into account the fact that some offenders have multiple victims (so *some* discrepancy is to be expected).

We have highlighted how cross-national comparisons in relation to these three important offences are problematic. Valid measurement is closely allied to definitions that are comparable so, until this issue is sorted out internationally, criminologists cannot provide a considered analysis. Hence, when cases such as the kidnapping of Madeleine McCann while on holiday in Portugal excite international media attention, there are clear dangers that journalists will make unjustified claims and comparisons in trying to provide background stories.

Nevertheless, having said all that, criminologists can do much more using the information which is available. We have tried to probe the standard criminological variables of age, sex and previous convictions. In most respects, it is the similarities rather than the differences between the offenders committing these offences which is striking. Certainly on the fraught criminological issue of specialisation, there are comparatively few who are convicted on two separate occasions for the same offence – least likely to happen for kidnapping, more likely for blackmail and most likely for threats to kill. With the latter offence of threats to kill, females are marginally more likely than males to repeat the offence: for females about 1 in 10 and for males about 1 in 15. As this is a very tight definition – they could, of course, be convicted of other serious offences – there is little doubt that there is an important minority who will continue to be troublesome in the future at a serious level.

In terms of dangerousness, our analysis also shows that a large minority of males and a smaller minority of females are likely to be subsequently reconvicted of violence. Using a tighter definition – whether or not they are subsequently convicted of homicide – this provides further evidence that there is a minority who continue to be dangerous. Those committing one of these offences are over 45 times more likely than members of the general population to be subsequently convicted of homicide, and six times more likely than those convicted of a sexual offence. Even so, while we have flagged that some of these offenders should be regarded as more dangerous than perhaps has been considered hitherto, it should be emphasised that most will not be subsequently a danger.

Acknowledgments

This work was partially supported by the Economic and Social Research Council under its National Centre for Research Methods initiative (grant number RES-576-25-0019). We are grateful for the help of Jiayi Liu who provided some of the analysis.

Selected further reading

There is no text that simply focuses on these three rather different offences. However, each of the offences has its own literature. An early classic on blackmail is Hepworth's (1975) *Blackmail: Publicity and Secrecy in Everyday Life*, while McLaren's (2002) *Sexual Blackmail: A Modern History* provides a thought-provoking history of social attitudes and sexual taboos. Books on kidnapping tend to focus on particular crimes, such as the Lindbergh kidnapping (Campbell 2003) or the Patty Hearst kidnapping (Graebner 2008), but Concannon *et al.*'s (2008) *Kidnapping: An Investigator's Guide to Profiling* is an important overview. Threats to kill have had less coverage, but recently there has been more interest in the academic literature (e.g. Barnes *et al.* 2001; Warren *et al.* 2008), while Morewitz's (2008) *Death Threats and Violence: New Research and Clinical Perspectives* offers a well-rounded assessment of the issues.

Notes

1 This division was abolished in 1967 (see section 1 of the Criminal Law Act 1967).
2 It is also possible to use crime survey data to look at victimisation prevalence. However, these unusual offences are rarely covered by such surveys. An exception is 'threats to kill', which is one of the offences covered in the British Crime Survey.
3 In England and Wales, the offence of child abduction is part of the Violence Against the Person category of police recorded crime. In 2002/3 child abduction was just 0.1 per cent of that category. The offence of child abduction is defined under the terms of the Child Abduction Act 1984, which allows for two types of abduction – abduction of a child by a parent and abduction of a child by other persons. Police recorded offences of abduction increased by 45 per cent from 2001/2 to 2002/3 (Newiss and Fairbrother 2004).
4 Broadly speaking, the 'standard list' consists of all indictable offences and the more serious summary offences. Summary offences are those which are triable summarily, i.e. without formal indictment.
5 Fitted using a weighted least squares regression model, weighted by the number of convictions.

References

Alix, E. K. (1978) *Ransom Kidnapping in America, 1874–1974: The Creation of a Capital Crime*. Southern Carbondale, IL: Southern Illinois University Press.

Alldridge, P. (1993) 'Attempted murder of the soul: blackmail, privacy and secrets', *Oxford Journal of Legal Studies*, 13: 368–87

Alldridge, P. (1994) 'Threats offences: a case for reform', *Criminal Law Review*, 176–87.

Barnes, M. T., Gordon, W. C. and Hudson, S. M. (2001) 'The crime of threatening to kill', *Journal of Interpersonal Violence*, 16 (4): 312–19.

BBC News Online (2006) 'Glaxo wins injuction over threat', 9 May. Online at: http://news.bbc.co.uk/1/hi/business/4756381.stm.

BBC News Online (2007) 'Royal targeted by blackmailers', 28 October. Online at: http://news.bbc.co.uk/1/hi/uk/7065942.stm.

Campbell, G. A. (2003) *Famous Trials: The Lindbergh Kidnapping*. San Diego: Lucent Books.

Concannon, D. M. with Fain, B., Fain, D., Honeycutt, A. B., Price-Sharps, J. and Sharps, M. (2008) *Kidnapping: An Investigator's Guide to Profiling*. Burlington, MA: Academic Press.

Crew, B. K. and Lammers, M. (2001) 'Kidnapping', in C. D. Bryant, (ed.), *Encyclopedia of Criminology and Deviant Behavior*, Vol. II. Philadelphia: Brunner-Routledge.

Francis, B. and Crosland, P. (2002) *The Police National Computer and the Offenders Index: Can They Be Combined for Research Purposes?* London: Home Office. Full report online at: http://www.homeoffice.gov.uk/rds/pdfs2/pncandoir170.pdf.

Francis, B. and Soothill, K. (2000) 'Does sex offending lead to homicide?' *Journal of Forensic Psychiatry and Psychology*, 11 (1): 49–61.

Graebner, W. (2008) *Patty's Got a Gun: Patricia Hearst in 1970s America.* Chicago: University of Chicago Press.

Hepworth, M. (1975) *Blackmail: Publicity and Secrecy in Everyday Life.* London: Routledge & Kegan Paul.

Home Office (1998) *Offenders Index – A Users Guide.* London: Home Office. Online at: http://rds.homeoffice.gov.uk/rds/pdfs/oiusers.pdf.

Horder, J. (2002) 'Criminal law and legal positivism', *Legal Theory*, 8: 221–41.

Lindgren, J. (1984) 'Unravelling the paradox of blackmail', *Columbia Law Review*, 670: 673–6.

McLaren, A. (2002) *Sexual Blackmail: A Modern History.* Cambridge, MA: Harvard University Press.

Meikle, J. (2008) 'Tesco bomb hoaxer jailed for six years', *The Guardian*, 29 January.

Ministry of Justice (2008) *Criminal Statistics: England and Wales 2007: Statistics Bulletin.* London: Ministry of Justice.

Morewitz, S. J. (2008) *Death Threats and Violence: New Research and Clinical Perspectives.* New York: Springer.

Newiss, G. and Fairbrother. L. (2004) *Child Abduction: Understanding Police Recorded Crime Statistics*, Findings No. 225. London: Home Office Research, Development and Statistics Directorate.

Nicholas, S., Kershaw, C. and Walker, A. (2007) *Crime in England and Wales 2006/7*, 4th edn. London: Home Office. Online at: http://www.homeoffice.gov.uk/rds/pdfs07/hosb1107.pdf.

Ormerod, D. (2005) *Smith & Hogan: Criminal Law*, 11th edn. Oxford: Oxford University Press.

Rice-Oxley, M. (2008) 'After 30 years, the truth behind Cruyff's World Cup absence', *The Guardian*, 29 October. Online at: http://www.guardian.co.uk/football/2008/apr/17/newsstory.sport.

Rosenberg, B. E. (2008) 'Debate: another reason for criminalising blackmail', *Journal of Political Philosophy*, 16 (3): 356–69.

Siddique, H. (2008) 'Animal rights activists guilty of blackmailing research lab suppliers', *The Guardian*, 3 December.

Soothill, K., Fitzpatrick, C. and Francis, B. (2009) *Understanding Criminal Careers.* Cullompton: Willan.

Soothill, K., Francis, B. and Liu, J. (2008) 'Does serious offending lead to homicide? Exploring the interrelationships and sequencing of serious crime', *British Journal of Criminology*, 48 (4): 522–37.

Wainwright, M. (2007) 'A brief history of blue blood extortion', *The Guardian*, 29 October.

Walker, A., Nicholas, S. and Kershaw, K. (eds) (2006) *Crime in England and Wales 2006/7*, 4th edn. London: Home Office. Online at: http://www.homeoffice.gov.uk/rds/pdfs06/hosb1206.pdf.

Warren, L. J., Mullen, P. E., Thomas, D. M., Ogloff, R. P. and Burgess, P. M. (2008) 'Threats to kill: a follow-up study', *Psychological Medicine*, 38: 599–605.

Winder, W. H. D. (1941) 'The development of blackmail', *Modern Law Review*, 21: 36–41.

Chapter 22

Elder abuse

John Williams

Introduction

All the indications are that we live longer and that this trend will continue. We have an ageing population and this creates challenges, not least the provision of pensions and social welfare benefits. In addition, older people will encounter crime and the criminal justice system as victims, potential victims and offenders. Criminology has paid less attention to older people than to juveniles and other groups, yet there are many issues where age or ageing is a distinct feature. Older prisoners are the fastest growing group within the prison system (HMIP 2004, 2008). The fear of crime among older people is, within some older groups, disproportionate to the reality (see, for example, Chadee and Ditton 2003; Chivite-Matthews and Maggs 2002; Zedner 2002). The impact of a criminal act against an older person may be devastating and in the extreme lead to premature death (Donaldson 2003). All of these invite more research from a criminological perspective. However, this chapter concentrates on one relatively neglected topic for criminological research, namely elder abuse. Although it is increasingly a subject that attracts research into the social welfare dimension, it is rarely considered within a criminal context.

Definitions

Until recently there was a paucity of data on the prevalence of elder abuse in the United Kingdom, largely because of imprecise definitions (Glendenning 1997: 13–41; Moskowitz 1998: 94). This chapter will not rehearse the debate on what is meant by 'elder' or 'old', but will adopt a pragmatic age of sixty years. Definitions of elder abuse, or more typically 'vulnerable adult abuse', are many and varied. The English and the Welsh guidance on developing and implementing multi-agency policy and procedures to protect vulnerable adults from abuse, No Secrets and In Safe Hands (Department of Health 2000;

Social Services Inspectorate Wales 2000), adopts the definition proposed in the Lord Chancellor's Consultation Paper, Who Decides? (Lord Chancellor's Department 1997). This definition provides that a 'vulnerable person' is one

> ... who is or may be in need of community care services by reason of mental or other disability, age or illness; and who is or may be unable to take care of him or herself, or unable to protect him or herself against significant harm or exploitation.

In one sense this is a convenient definition for local authorities as it links protection policies to a client group already identified, or easily identifiable, for the purposes of community care. However, whether a person is in need of community care services under the National Health Service and Community Care Act 1990 is irrelevant as to whether they are vulnerable to abuse. It is conceivable that an older person is vulnerable but not in need of community care services and unlikely ever to be so in need. Similarly, the older person could be in need of community care services but not vulnerable. A physically and mentally fit older person, who is coerced into parting with money by an abusing relative, is in need of protection; the need for community care services is possibly non-existent and arguably irrelevant. He or she may be ineligible for community care services under the 1990 Act. Some forms of psychological abuse may be driven by the strength of the abuser's personality rather than the need of the abused person for community care services. The link with community care services reinforces the welfare approach to elder abuse and its decriminalisation by society.

The second part of the definition deals with an essential component of vulnerability, namely the inability to protect against 'significant harm or exploitation'. The inability to protect arises because of the physical or mental frailty of the individual and the relative power of the abuser in relation to the abused person. This may be because of financial dependency, care dependency or the dominant personality of the abuser.

This narrow definition in the guidance is barely fit for purpose and reinforces the belief that a predominately welfare definition is appropriate. A similar debate took place within Scotland, which eventually led to the passing of the Adult Support and Protection (Scotland) Act 2007. In rejecting a broader based definition of 'vulnerable', the Scottish Law Commission stated:

> A much narrower definition of vulnerable was said to be needed, many respondents commenting that at some point in their lives almost everyone was vulnerable in the sense we used in our discussion paper. We appreciate the force of this criticism. A wide definition would place too great a strain on local authority resources and would make it impossible for the local authority to confine its attentions to those genuinely in need of them. (Scottish Law Commission 1997: para. 2.15)

The first sentence makes a reasonable point; vulnerability is something that we all experience, very often only temporarily. However, the second sentence exposes the underlying fear of government of the resource implications of the investigation and prevention of vulnerable adult abuse. The Commission conceded that there was a need to restrict the definition in recognition of the resource implications of a more broadly based approach. This restricted definition of vulnerability is driven by the peculiarities of the funding of social care and is regrettable. The danger is that this narrow definition also dictates the response of the criminal law enforcement agencies and the criminal justice system. Cases of actual elder abuse may be excluded from the criminal justice system because they do not fall within a social welfare definition driven by a resource allocation model.

The English and Welsh guidance defines 'abuse' widely as being

... a violation of an in individual's human and civil rights by any other person or persons. (para. 2.5 and para 7.4)

This is useful, albeit vague and includes stranger crime. However, English and Welsh guidance does not consider that stranger crime will feature within the procedure other than in exceptional circumstances. The guidance states:

Stranger abuse will warrant a different kind of response than the response to abuse within an ongoing relationship or care setting. Nevertheless in some instances it may be appropriate to use the locally agreed inter-agency adult protection procedures to ensure that the vulnerable adult receives the services and support that they need. Such procedures may also be used when there is the potential for harm to other vulnerable people. (para. 2.13 and para 7.17)

The definition recognises that abuse violates the rights under the European Convention on Human Rights to life, protection from inhuman and degrading treatment and to dignity as part of the right to a private life.

What the above discussion demonstrates is that the definitional debate on elder abuse focuses on welfare support almost to the exclusion of the criminal dimension. Action on Elder Abuse (1995) take a broader view and include the element of abuse of trust. They define abuse as:

A single or repeated act or lack of appropriate action occurring within any relationship where there is an expectation of trust which causes harm or distress to an older person.

Elder abuse takes many, often multiple, forms. The most obvious are physical and sexual abuse. Financial and material abuse includes theft, fraud and exploitation. These may involve transfers of property and money obtained through deception or threats of violence. Straightforward theft is also included. Psychological abuse includes emotional abuse, threats of harm or abandonment, deprivation of contact, humiliation, blaming, controlling, intimidation, coercion, harassment, verbal abuse, isolation or withdrawal from services or supportive networks. Neglect and acts of omission include ignoring medical or physical care needs, failure to provide access to appropriate health, social care or educational services, and the withholding of necessities such as medication, adequate nutrition and heating. Within each of these categories the behaviour of the abuser will constitute 'abuse' in the sense defined in the guidance; however, it will invariably also constitute a criminal offence. For example, the Domestic Violence Crime and Victims Act 2004 introduced the offence of causing or allowing the death of a child or vulnerable adult. There are many offences against the person including murder, assault, actual bodily harm, grievous bodily harm and rape; section 58 of the Medicines Act 1968 makes it an offence to administer drugs that have been prescribed for someone else. The Sexual Offences Act 2003 introduced a range of new offences in relation to sexual conduct with a person with a mental disorder impeding choice. The Mental Capacity Act 2005 makes it a criminal offence to ill treat or wilfully neglect a person lacking capacity or reasonably believed by the perpetrator to lack capacity. Section 2 of the Protection from Harassment Act 1997 states that a 'person whose course of conduct causes another to fear, on at least two occasions, that violence will be used against him or her, is guilty of an offence'. Conduct includes verbal abuse. A range of property and finance offences exist including theft and offences of obtaining through deception.

Recognition of the criminal nature of most, if not all, acts of elder abuse is critical in ensuring that society's response does not deny older people the protection of the criminal law. Article 3 of the European Convention on Human Rights imposes a positive duty on states to protect against inhuman or degrading treatment. In X v. Netherlands and A v. UK the European Court of Human Rights emphasised that this duty applies regardless of the locus of the abuse (a private care home or a family home) and the identity of the perpetrator; it also emphasised that the duty under the article is more compelling when vulnerable people are involved. To deny an older person who is the victim of abuse an effective remedy through the criminal courts is a violation of their Convention rights.

A number of factors can be identified in seeking to establish a broader definition that is not entirely focused on the welfarist response to elder abuse. They include:

1 the scale and intensity of vulnerability bearing in mind that not all older people are vulnerable;

2 the categories of abuse – financial, sexual, physical, psychological, social; neglect; the relatively private nature of the space in which abuse is committed;

3 the criminal nature of most acts of abuse and the recognition that such criminal activity should not be covertly or overtly excluded from the criminal justice system;

4 the importance of breach of trust as an element of elder abuse that distinguishes it from stranger crime.

Of these (3) is particularly important and absent from current definitions. These components provide helpful prompts in formulating a definition appropriate for researchers and practitioners in social welfare and the criminal justice sectors.

Patterns and trends

Attitudes towards elder abuse are ambivalent. It is effectively decriminalised and regarded as a welfare issue. Elder abuse is under-reported. Typically it occurs in private space – the person's own home, a care home, a nursing home or a hospital. Brogden and Nijhar (2000) express concern about such under-reporting.

> A signal failure of victim surveys is not just inadequate documentation of household abuse but also because they rarely include care and nursing home respondents, where victimisation may be rampant. (p. 63)

Lack of societal recognition of elder abuse as criminal activity emphasises its private nature, inviting at best welfare-based responses. A recent study of elder abuse by Mowlam *et al.* (2007) involving 2,100 older people (66 years or over) in England, Scotland, Wales and Northern Ireland provided data on the prevalence of elder abuse in domestic settings. It excluded older people in institutions (hospitals or care homes) and those with dementia. Their 'Prevalence Study of Elder Abuse' identified significant elder abuse within older people's own homes (4 per cent aged 66 years and over – approximately 342,000 people), often perpetrated by close family members. Partners (35 per cent), other family members (33 per cent) and neighbours/acquaintances (33 per cent) are the primary abusers, with domiciliary care workers accounting for 9 per cent and friends 3 per cent. Most abusers are men; 74 per cent for physical abuse, 56 per cent for theft and 80 per cent for other forms of abuse. A significant number of victims (30 per cent) did not report the abuse. Only 4 per cent reported the abuse to the police. Worryingly none of the victims mentioned the adult protection procedures for investigating cases of suspected abuse. The prevalence of elder abuse is highest in Wales (6 per cent) and lowest in Northern Ireland (3 per cent).

The abuser may be a relative, informal carer, friend, spouse, partner or professional. The existence of an expectation of trust, stressed in the Action on Elder Abuse definition, distinguishes the act from stranger crime. However, that relationship should not decriminalise the conduct. A crime against person or property by a spouse, partner or carer is as much a criminal offence as stranger crime. Arguably, it is an aggravated crime given that it also involves a breach of trust between abuser and abused. It is, therefore, odd that it is rarely treated as criminal. Indeed, the term 'elder abuse' suggests that it is different from a crime and should be treated differently (Williams 2008).

Responses

Analogies with domestic violence are revealing. It is only relatively recently that society accepted that domestic violence is also a crime rather than a purely 'social', 'domestic' or 'welfare' matter (Cretney and Davis 1996). Police involvement in the investigation of elder abuse is critical. They are an integral part of the joint agency response to elder abuse under the English and Welsh guidance noted above. The need for the police to investigate any alleged criminal offence is emphasised in the guidance:

> Accordingly, when complaints about alleged abuse suggest that a criminal offence may have been committed it is imperative that reference should be made to the police as a matter of urgency. Criminal investigation by the police takes priority over all other lines of enquiry. (para. 2.8 and para. 7.8)

Early involvement of the police is desirable as they can ensure that forensic evidence is not destroyed or contaminated. In some cases of elder abuse, forensic evidence may be the sole evidence before the court, particularly where the older person has restricted or no legal capacity. Police expertise may also be helpful in investigating the allegations and interviewing victims. Early involvement may minimise the risk of repeat interviews of the victim. Police interviews can proceed alongside those geared towards health and social care issues (Department of Health 2000: para. 6.7).

One major weakness in the current arrangements is the lack of any general power of access for social workers or health care professionals to vulnerable older people whom they suspect are being abused or neglected. A warrant is obtainable under section 135 of the Mental Health Act 1983 authorising a constable to enter premises where there is reasonable cause to suspect that a person believed to be suffering from mental disorder is being ill treated, or to enter premises to retake a patient already detained under the Act. The person must be taken to a place of safety for a period not exceeding 72 hours. These provisions, although involving the police, are again welfare based and enable the person either to be assessed or returned to hospital. Furthermore, they only apply to people thought to have a mental disorder and not to all older people. Under section 18(1)(e) of the Police and Criminal Evidence Act 1984, a police officer may enter and search any premises, without a warrant, for the purpose of saving life or limb, or preventing damage to property. Section 25 of the Act enables a police officer, where there are reasonable grounds, to arrest a person to prevent them from causing physical injury to another person, or to protect a child or other vulnerable person. The availability of these powers emphasise the importance of involving the police in inter-disciplinary vulnerable adult protection procedures.

Too close a comparison between child abuse and elder abuse can produce false paradigms. In an American context, Oberloh argues that you can derive a satisfactory definition from an alteration of the child abuse legislation. He states:

> By simply replacing 'parent, guardian, or custodian' with 'care giver' and 'child' with 'elder,' the definition would cover any abandonment, mistreatment, abuse, failure to provide necessary medical care, emotional harm, or mental injury committed against an elder by a care giver. If medical professionals can effectively diagnose and report abuse of children by following [child protection laws], there is no reason to think that requiring them to diagnose and report elder abuse will be any less effective. (Oberloh 2000: 666)

The Law Commission for England and Wales (1995) report, *Mental Incapacity*, proposed a public law to protect vulnerable adults from abuse. It was modelled largely on the Children Act 1989, including the use of 'significant harm' as a key concept. The government rejected the report, arguing that the proposals would interfere with the 'right of individuals to live in isolation' (Lord Chancellor's Department, 1997: para. 8.6). Instead the Department of Health and the Welsh Assembly issued the guidance for multi-agency bodies including social services, police and health on adult protection procedures (Department of Health 2000; Social Services Inspectorate Wales 2000). A key difference between the state's reaction to child abuse and elder abuse is the absence of a statutory duty to investigate elder abuse and of a statutory framework for intervention by public authorities (Williams 2008). An additional difference is the low rate of prosecutions for elder abuse. In 2007, there were 2,192 prosecutions in England and Wales for offences relating to child abuse (Hansard 2009). Prosecution is not inevitable following child abuse investigations, but where it happens it punishes offenders and may be a deterrent to others. In the absence of reliable data, anecdotal evidence suggests that prosecutions for elder abuse remain low.

The decision to prosecute rests with the Crown Prosecution Service (CPS) acting under its policy and guidance on prosecuting crimes against older people (CPS 2008a, 2008b). The policy document recognises the importance of prosecutions for elder abuse:

Stopping crimes against older people and bringing perpetrators to justice must therefore be a priority for our society and for the CPS. The CPS recognises its role in protecting older people's human rights by prosecuting offenders effectively. (CPS 2008a: para. 10)

It emphasises the need to recognise the diversity of older people:

Whatever the age of a victim or witness, their needs and case management issues should be assessed on an individual basis. Reliance should not be placed on pre-conceived or stereotypical notions and norms about older people in general. (CPS 2008b: para. 7)

The Code for Crown Prosecutors (CPS 2004) requires prosecutors to apply the Full Code Test, which consists of two stages. Stage 1 is the evidential test: is there enough evidence to provide a 'realistic prospect of conviction'? Here the admissibility and reliability of the evidence is assessed. Will the witness 'stand up at trial'? Although this is difficult to assess, it may be particularly difficult in the case of a vulnerable older person. The assumption may be that an older person will not 'stand up at trial' because of perceived frailty, poor memory or borderline capacity. In addition, ageist assumptions may be made about the robustness of an older person required to provide oral testimony. To overcome such discrimination, Sanders *et al.* in their study of victims with learning disabilities proposed that the test for vulnerable witnesses should be 'would there be a realistic prospect of conviction if one assumes that the witness "stands up"?' (Saunders *et al.* 1997: 85).

Once satisfied that the evidential test is met, the CPS considers Stage 2, namely whether a prosecution is needed in the public interest. The factors identified include:

Prosecution is more likely if:

- the defendant was in a position of trust;
- the victim was vulnerable, has been put in considerable fear, or suffered personal attack, damage or disturbance;
- there are grounds for believing that the offence is likely to be continued or repeated (e.g. a history of recurring conduct);
- a prosecution would have a significant positive impact on maintaining community confidence.

(CPS 2004: para. 5.9)

Prosecution is less likely if:

- prosecution is likely to have a bad effect on the victim's physical or mental health, always bearing in mind the seriousness of the offence.

(CPS 2004: para. 5.10)

The only reference to 'elderly' is to the age of the defendant; if the defendant is 'elderly' it is a factor making a prosecution less likely, subject to the seriousness of the offence and the possibility of repetition (para. 5.10). A welfarist response to elder abuse may lead to an assumption that a decision not to prosecute represents the 'public interest' as it avoids exposing victims to the criminal justice system, thus providing a pretext for welfare intervention. 'Well-intentioned ageism' can deny older people the protection of the criminal law and violate their human rights.

The Youth Justice and Criminal Evidence Act 1999 (YJCEA 1999) provides for special measures to assist eligible people presenting evidence at a criminal trial where their vulnerability affects the quality of their evidence. Under section 16, YJCEA 1999, a person is eligible for assistance on the grounds of incapacity. 'Incapacity' covers situations where the court concludes that the quality of the evidence 'is likely to be diminished' for one or more specified reason (section 16, YJCEA 1999). These are that the witness suffers from a mental disorder within the meaning of the Mental Health Act 1983, has a significant impairment of intelligence and social functioning, or has a physical disability or disorder. Older people are more likely to fit into these categories (Breeze *et al.* 2002). Under section 17, YJCEA 1999, a person is eligible for assistance if the court is satisfied that the quality of their evidence is likely to be diminished because of fear or distress on their part. Among the factors to be taken into consideration under section 17 is the age of the witness. The special measures available are

- *screens* – to protect the witness from the defendant;
- *video-recorded evidence-in-chief* – the witness's evidence-in-chief in court;
- *live television link* – witness gives evidence from outside the courtroom;
- *clearing the public gallery of the court;*

- *allowing the witness to use communication aids;*
- *video-recorded pre-trial cross-examination and re-examination* (unlikely to be implemented); and
- *intermediaries* – an approved intermediary to help a witness communicate with legal representatives and the court. Research highlights their potential for reducing stress for child witnesses.

Goodman *et al.* (1998) in their American study examined the effects of using closed-circuit television on the testimony of children and found that open court testimony was associated with children experiencing greater pre-trial anxiety. The Vulnerable Witness Survey found that of the 49 witnesses who used the live video link, all but three found it helpful (Kitchen and Elliott 2001).

However, do special measures violate the defendant's right to a fair trial? Is it 'fair' to depart from established procedures to address witness vulnerability? The criminal justice system is more concerned with the quality of evidence than the impact on a vulnerable older person. Ellison (2003: 10) argues that the 'principle of orality is the foundation of the adversarial trial' as it exposes inconsistency, inaccuracy and fabrication. This appears to have been recognised in PS v. Germany (2003), where the alleged victim did not provide evidence; instead, the court heard evidence from her mother and a police officer who interviewed her, and from an expert who commented on her credibility. As the accused did not have the opportunity to cross-examine the person making the allegations, the court found that the defendant's Article 6 right was violated (PS v. Germany 2003: paras 23–26). In contrast, the House of Lords in R (on the application of D) v. Camberwell Green Youth Court; R (on the application of the Director of Public Prosecutions) v. Camberwell Green Youth Court (2005) concluded that special measures do not disadvantage defendants in that evidence is produced in front of the accused, albeit it in pre-recorded form or by live video transmission and the accused can question the witnesses at trial.

Special measures should increase the use of the criminal law and challenge the almost sole reliance on a welfare response to elder abuse. Whether the use of special measures is eventually challenged under the European Convention on Human Rights as undermining the oral nature of criminal proceedings in the United Kingdom remains to be seen. Balancing the interests of the defendant and victim is complex. Arguably, special measures could lead to miscarriages of justice because they are unduly prejudicial to the right to a fair hearing.

Other aids to the greater use of the criminal law centre on the investigative process. The small number of cases of suspected abuse reported to the police identified by the Mowlam study is disturbing. In America 42 states and the District of Columbia have introduced legislation imposing a legal duty on professionals and other individuals to report cases of suspected vulnerable adult abuse (the law in most states concentrates on vulnerable older people). Mandatory reporting may be an option as it would ensure that more cases are thoroughly investigated by the law enforcement agencies. However, it raises the question of whether it would be too intrusive and violate the right of capacitated adults to autonomy. For child abuse mandatory reporting is consistent with the welfare principle enshrined in the Children Act 1989. For adults, as indeed for Gillick ([1986] AC112) competent children, it risks secondary victimisation (Hanna 1996; Williams 2002).

Conclusion

As with older prisoners, older victims of stranger crime and the fear of crime, there is a compelling case for greater criminological research into the causes, effects and responses to elder abuse. This is not to argue that every case should be prosecuted or even investigated by the police. The intervention of the police should be proportionate and appropriate. However, the debate on elder abuse needs to be extended beyond the predominately welfare-based one within which it is currently located.

Selected further reading

The literature on elder abuse from the perspective of a criminologist is not extensive. Brogden and Nijhar (2000) provide an excellent comprehensive account of the way in which the criminal justice system affects the lives of older people and the extent to which they are marginalised by the system. Clearly elder abuse forms a part of the discussion. The most comprehensive review of elder abuse in the United Kingdom is the study by Mowlam et al. (2007). For the first time we have clear data on prevalence, forms of abuse and identity of abusers. This has already had a significant impact on the role of the law, including the criminal law, in providing protection for the considerable number of older people who are abused. The limitations of the study are that it does not include older people in institutional settings, nor does it include people with dementia. Ellison (2003) engages in a fascinating debate on the impact of the special measures for vulnerable witnesses giving evidence in criminal trials. Her work reminds us that the use of special measures may compromise other safeguards within the criminal justice system, in particular the right of the accused to a fair hearing. These measures also challenge the oral nature of criminal trials in this country. Comparisons with America are useful as most of the States have in place legislation designed to protect vulnerable adults, in particular older people. Weed (1997) discusses the American experience and identifies many issues relevant to discussion in our jurisdictions. Finally, Williams (2002) considers the case for a new public law allowing intervention in the lives of older people who are being abused.

References

Action on Elder Abuse (1995) Online at: http://www.elderabuse.org.uk/What%20is%20abuse/what_is_abuse%20define.htm (accessed 10 July 2009).

Breeze, E., Grundy, C., Fletch, A., Wilkinson, P., Jones, D. and Bulpitt, P. (2002) *Inequalities in Quality of Life Among People Aged 75 years and Over in Great Britain*, Research Findings 1. Sheffield: ESRC.

Brogden, M. and Nijhar, P. (2000) *Crime, Abuse and the Elderly*. Cullompton: Willan.

Chadee, D. and Ditton, J. (2003) 'Are older people most afraid of crime?', *British Journal of Criminology*, 43: 417–33.

Chivite-Matthews, N. and Maggs, P. (2002) *Crime, Policing and Justice: The Experience of Older People*. London: Home Office.

CPS (2004) *Code for Crown Prosecutors*. London: Crown Prosecution Service.

CPS (2008a) *Crimes Against Older People – CPS Prosecutions Policy*. London: Crown Prosecution Service. Online at: http://www.cps.gov.uk/publications/docs/caop_policy.pdf (accessed 10 July 2009).

CPS (2008b) *Guidance on Prosecuting Crimes Against Older People*. London: Crown Prosecution Service.

Cretney, A. and Davis, G. (1996) 'Prosecuting "domestic" assault', *Criminal Law Review*, 162.

Department of Health (2000) *No Secrets: Guidance on Developing and Implementing Multi-Agency Policies and Procedures to Protect Vulnerable Adults from Abuse*. London: Department of Health.

Donaldson, R. (2003) *Experiences of Older Burglary Victims*, Home Office Findings No. 198. London: Home Office.

Ellison, L. (2003) *The Adversarial Process and the Vulnerable Witness*. Oxford: Oxford University Press.

Glendenning, F. (1997) 'What is elder abuse and neglect?', in P. Decalmer and F. Glendenning (eds), *The Mistreatment of Elderly People*. London: Sage.

Goodman, G. S., Tobey, A. E., Batterman-Faunce, J. M., Orcutt, H., Thomas, S., Shapiro, C. and Sachsenmaier, T. (1998) 'Face-to-face confrontation: effects of closed-circuit technology on children's eyewitness testimony and jurors' decisions', *Law and Human Behaviour*, 22: 165–203.

Hanna, C. (1996) 'No right to choose: mandated victim participation in domestic violence prosecutions', *Harvard Law Review*, 109 (8): 1849–910.

Hansard (2009) HC, 3rd March 2009, col. 1497W. Written answer by Maria Eagle MP. Online at: http://www.publications.parliament.uk/pa/cm200809/cmhansrd/cm090303/text/90303w0025.htm#09030420006384 (accessed 10th July 2009).

HMIP (2004) *Her Majesty's Inspectorate of Prisons, No Problems – Old and Quiet: Older Prisoners in England and Wales*. London: Her Majesty's Inspector of Prisons.

HMIP (2008) *Older Prisoners in England and Wales: A Follow-up to the 2004 Thematic Review by HM Chief Inspector of Prisons*. London: Her Majesty's Inspectorate of Prisons.

Kitchen, S. and Elliott, R. (2001) *Key Findings from the Vulnerable Witness Survey*, Home Office Findings No. 147. London: Home Office.

Law Commission (1995) *Report on Mental Incapacity*, Law Commission Report No. 231. London: HMSO.

Lord Chancellor's Department (1997) *Who Decides: Making Decisions on Behalf of Mentally Incapacitated Adults*. London: HMSO.

Moskowitz, S. (1998) 'Saving granny from the wolf: elder abuse and neglect – the legal framework', *Connecticut Law Review*, 31: 77.

Mowlam, A., Tennant, R., Dixon, J. and McCreadie, C. (2007) *UK Study of Abuse and Neglect of Older People: Qualitative Findings*. London: Department of Health and Comic Relief.

Oberloh, H. R. (2000) 'A call to legislative action: protecting our elders from abuse', *South Dakota Law Review*, 45: 655–69.

Saunders, A., Creaton, J., Bird, S. and Weber, L. (1997) *Victims with Learning Disabilities*, Occasional Paper No. 17. Oxford: University of Oxford Centre for Criminological Research.

Scottish Law Commission (1997) *Report on Vulnerable Adults*, Scottish Law Com No. 158. Edinburgh: TSO.

Social Services Inspectorate Wales (2000) *In Safe Hands*. Cardiff: Welsh National Assembly.

Weed, M. C. (1997) 'Law enforcement intervention on behalf of endangered adults', *Pacific Law Journal*, 28: 899–903.

Williams, J. (2002) 'Public law protection of vulnerable adults: the debate continues, so does the abuse', *Journal of Social Work*, 2 (3): 293–316.

Williams, J. (2008) 'State responsibility and the abuse of vulnerable older people: is there a case for a public law to protect vulnerable older people from abuse?', in J. Bridgeman, H. Keating and C. Lind (eds), *Responsibility, Law and the Family*. Aldershot: Ashgate, pp. 81–105.

Zedner, L. (2002) 'Victims', in M. Maguire, R. Morgan and R. Reiner (eds), *The Oxford Handbook of Criminology*, 3rd edn. Oxford: Oxford University Press, pp. 419–56.

Cases cited

A v. UK [1998] 2 FLR 959

PS v. Germany (2003) 36 EHRR

R (on the application of D) v. Camberwell Green Youth Court; R (on the application of the Director of Public Prosecutions) v. Camberwell Green Youth Court (2005) [2005] 1 All ER 999

X v. *Netherlands* (1986) 8 EHRR 2

Chapter 23

School bullying: risk factors, theories and interventions

Maria M. Ttofi and David P. Farrington

Introduction

School bullying is an important social problem with serious consequences. Many studies show that involvement in bullying (as a perpetrator or a victim) is associated with negative short-term effects on the physical and psychological health of children and with long-term effects on their future psychosocial adjustment as adults (Ttofi and Farrington 2008a). For example, in a school-based survey of 16,410 Finnish adolescents aged 14–16, Kaltiala-Heino *et al.* (1999) showed that adolescents who were bullied and those who were bullies had an increased risk of depression and severe suicidal ideation. In a review of existing literature, Salmon *et al.* (2000) found that being bullied was frequently a factor influencing the referral of adolescents to psychiatric services, with depression being diagnosed in over 70 per cent of cases.

Bullying others has also been identified as a risk factor for other types of later antisocial behaviour such as excessive drinking and substance use (Kaltiala-Heino *et al.* 2000) and later offending (Farrington 1993; Sourander *et al.* 2006; White and Loeber 2008). Follow-up studies in Norway, for example, indicate that, of those originally identified as bullies in the sixth to the ninth grades, 70 per cent were convicted of at least one crime by the age of 24 (Olweus 1997). Given the link between bullying and later offending, bullying prevention should lead to a later reduction in crime.

This chapter provides an overview of current empirical knowledge about school bullying. In order to explain the varying prevalence rates found in bullying research, the chapter begins by discussing the definition and measurement of school bullying. It also reports research on trends in bullying over time. It then reviews individual and family risk factors that predict children's involvement in bullying as bullies, victims or both (bully-victims). Current theoretical perspectives are then reviewed. The effectiveness of anti-bullying programmes, based on a recent detailed systematic and meta-analytic review, and the necessity to have theory-informed bullying prevention, are two topics further elaborated. The chapter concludes with implications for policy and directions for future research.

427

Definition and measurement

The definition of school bullying includes several key elements: physical, verbal or psychological attack or intimidation that is intended to cause fear, distress or harm to the victim; an imbalance of power (psychological or physical), with a more powerful child (or children) oppressing less powerful ones; and repeated incidents between the same children over a prolonged period (Farrington 1993; Olweus 1993a). Research has also emphasised the absence of provocation by the victim (Greene 2000). School bullying can occur in school or on the way to or from school. It is not considered bullying when two persons of the same strength (physical, psychological or verbal) victimise each other.

Bullying is a type of aggressive behaviour. However, it should not be equated with aggression or violence. Not all aggression or violence involves bullying, and not all bullying involves aggression or violence. For example, bullying includes being called nasty names, being rejected, ostracised or excluded from activities, having rumours spread about you, having belongings taken away, being teased and threatened (Baldry and Farrington 1999). Many studies that are allegedly concerned with bullying in fact focus not on bullying (specifically) but on peer aggression. We have been very careful to review research on bullying (specifically) in this chapter.

Several methods have been used to measure bullying, such as self-reports, peer and teacher nominations and direct observation. The assessment of bullying by self-reports is the most usual method. Established self-report questionnaires include the Peer Relations Questionnaire (PRQ; Rigby and Slee 1993b), the Peer Relations Assessment Questionnaire (PRAQ; Rigby 1997), the Revised Bully/Victim Questionnaire (Revised BVQ; Olweus 1996) and the Self-Reported Bullying, Fighting, and Victimization Scale (Espelage and Holt 2001). Peer and teacher nominations are two other methods employed for the assessment of bullying, although the instruments used are not specific to bullying. Examples include the Peer Nomination Instrument (Crick and Grotpeter 1995), the Participant Role Scale (Salmivalli *et al.* 1996) and the Aggressive Behavior-Teacher Checklist (Dodge and Coie 1987). Direct observation is rarely used because of the methodological or practical challenges accompanying it. However, Craig and Pepler (1998) in Canada observed bullying and victimisation in the schoolyard. Another example of a study that utilised this method is by Pellegrini and Long (2002), who used direct observation by trained observers to follow up the same individuals at least once a week for a period of a whole school year.

Special methods are needed to study bullying in different countries because of the problem of capturing the term 'bullying' in different languages (Arora 1996). Peter Smith *et al.* (2002) reviewed the meaning of bullying in 14 different countries in an attempt to examine how the use of global terms (such as 'bullying') can affect the measured prevalence. They give a nice example of how even similar terms within the same language (e.g. bullying, teasing, harassment, abuse) can have different connotations and may be understood differently by persons answering questionnaires. An alternative to using global terms such as 'bullying' in surveys is to ask for information about particular acts, such as 'hit him/her on the face' or 'excluded him/her from games' (Smith *et al.* 2002: 1131), and this is what researchers often do (e.g. Pateraki and Houndoumadi 2001: 174).

The majority of projects have used definitions of bullying and victimisation derived from researchers such as Olweus (1993a). It may be the case that students and teachers have different perceptions from researchers about the defining characteristics of bullying, but very few projects have addressed this issue (e.g. Boulton 1997). For example, a survey of 166 12-year-old Irish students by Guerin and Hennessy (2002) found that 'repetition', 'intention' and a 'lack of provocation' were not that central to students' definitions of bullying. Another study of 225 teachers and 1,820 students across 51 UK secondary schools indicated that teachers' and students' perceptions of school bullying were significantly different, with teachers having more wide-ranging ideas (Naylor *et al.* 2006).

Prevalence and trends

The prevalence of bullying depends on the time period inquired about and on the frequency criterion used (e.g. once or twice, sometimes, weekly or more often). Different researchers use different cut-off points on bullying items for prevalence estimation and this is a major reason for the considerable variability in bully/victim estimates in the literature. Choosing the 'appropriate' cut-off point for prevalence estimation is a procedure that should be carefully followed based on objective criteria since it has the potential to affect further analyses (Solberg and Olweus 2003). Nevertheless, bullying is surprisingly common (for a review of prevalence results, see Griffin and Gross 2004). Due *et al.* (2005) carried out perhaps the largest study of the prevalence of being bullied (sometimes or more often during this school term) among nationally representative samples of 11–15 year olds in 28 western industrialised countries (surveying over 4,000 students per country on average). Overall 18 per cent of boys and 15 per cent of girls were bullied according to this fairly demanding criterion. In the United States 16 per cent of boys and 11 per cent of girls were bullied. In the UK, 9 per cent of boys and 7 per cent of girls were bullied.

The prevalence of bullying decreases with age, with younger children typically being victimised by older children (Olweus 1993a; Smith *et al.* 1999a). Previous research has also suggested an increase in bullying during the transition between schools – from primary to secondary – which could be ascribed, among other factors, to changes in social hierarchies (Pellegrini and Long 2002). Gender differences in the prevalence of bullying – and, mainly, for different subtypes of bullying – are also found (Craig 1998; Olweus 1994). In particular, girls are more likely to use and experience more 'indirect' methods of bullying such as ostracising, exclusion from activities and spreading rumours (Bjorkqvist *et al.* 1992; Lagerspetz *et al.* 1988). In England, Rivers and Smith (1994) found that gender differences in direct and indirect bullying decreased during the teenage years while, in Finland, Salmivalli *et al.* (1998) reported that bullying was more stable across time for boys compared to girls.

Apparently the only national UK information on time trends in bullying derives from one question about being bullied in the Health Related Behaviour Questionnaire of the School Health Education Unit (2004), which shows a slightly declining trend from 1997 to 2003. There is national UK information on time trends in adolescent conduct problems (including bullying, fighting, stealing, lying, etc.). Collishaw *et al.* (2004) reported that the prevalence of conduct problems (according to parent ratings) increased substantially between 1974 and 1999, from 6.8 per cent to 14.9 per cent. There is local UK information on time trends in bullying. In Leicestershire, Bosley (2009) found that self-reported victimisation decreased by 15 per cent in primary schools and by 10 per cent in secondary schools between 2002/3 and 2005/6.

There is some national information on time trends in bullying in other countries. O'Moore *et al.* (1997) and Minton and O'Moore (2008) reported on the results of two nationwide surveys of bullying in Ireland. They found that, between 1993/4 and 2003/4, self-reported bullying and victimisation decreased in primary schools but increased in secondary schools. In the United States, information about being bullied was published from the School Crime Supplement to the National Crime Victimization Survey up to 2003, but there were no clear time trends between 1999 and 2003 (De Voe *et al.* 2004: 21). The rate of self-reported violent victimisation in US schools (Dinkes *et al.* 2007: 11) decreased steadily from 1992 (48 per 1,000) to 2005 (24 per 1000). In Finland, the School Health Promotion Study surveys over 75,000 students each year in secondary schools. There were no clear time trends in bullying or being bullied (weekly or more often) from 1998 to 2007 (Salmivalli 2009).

Characteristics of bullies and victims

Individual risk factors are variables that are characteristic of individuals, including age, gender, intelligence, empathy and the like. Risk factors predict a high probability of a negative outcome such as bullying. This section is concerned with changeable risk factors only – such as empathy, self-esteem and academic performance – since these may have implications for the prevention and treatment of bullying. Research often shows the predictive efficiency of risk factors, but it is difficult to determine whether a factor (e.g. self-esteem, anxiety, academic performance) is a cause or an effect of bullying behaviour, or both, when seen in a developmental sequence (Farrington and Baldry 2005). It is also difficult to establish whether bullying and particular risk factors are all indicators of the same underlying theoretical construct such as antisocial personality. To give a concrete example, research has found a link between Oppositional Defiant Disorder (ODD) and bullying: high ODD students tended to be bullies (Kokkinos and Panayiotou 2004: 528). However, given that ODD is a pattern of negative, disobedient and hostile behaviours (McMahon and Frick 2005: 478), it stands to reason that bullies would have a tendency to defy, just as defiant children would have a tendency to bully.

There is considerable evidence that bullying is associated with academic performance (e.g. Andreou and Metallidou 2004; Kaukiainen *et al.* 2002; Srabstein and Piazza 2008). In the Cambridge Study in Delinquent Development

(Farrington and Baldry 2005), which is a prospective longitudinal survey of 411 London boys, low intelligence and low attainment at age 8–10 predicted bullying at age 14. Olweus (1978) found that self-reported bullies were only slightly below average, although they had negative attitudes toward schoolwork and teachers. More recent research usually indicates a significant negative relationship between academic performance and involvement in bullying (Stephenson and Smith 1989), though some studies still find no significant difference in school achievement between bullies and non-bullies (e.g. Baldry and Farrington 1998).

Typical findings are as follows. In Seattle, Glew *et al.* (2005), in a study comparing victims, bully-victims and bystanders, found that victims and bully-victims were more likely to have low academic achievement than bystanders. In Hertfordshire and North London, Woods and Wolke (2004), in a survey of 1,016 primary school students, discovered that higher academic achievement in school year 2 predicted bullying others indirectly (e.g. using social exclusion) in school year 4. Nansel *et al.* (2001), in a survey of a representative sample of 15,686 US students (grades 6 through 10), showed that poor academic achievement predicted children's involvement in bullying as either bullies or bully-victims. In Los Angeles, Toblin *et al.* (2005) reported a significant main effect of bully/victim status on low academic performance (measured by grade point average), with aggressive victims being significantly different from passive victims, bullies and normative children.

The cluster of personality traits that fall under the heading of 'hyperactivity-impulsivity-attention deficit' are important personality factors that predict bullying. Bullies are more likely to possess an impulsive temperament (Bernstein and Watson 1997). Research has also indicated a strong link between hyperactivity and bullying (e.g. Toblin *et al.* 2005). In the Cambridge Study (Farrington and Baldry 2005), hyperactivity at aged 8–10 (based on teacher ratings) significantly predicted bullying at age 14, while impulsivity (measured in psychomotor tests) was not significantly predictive. Ando *et al.* (2005), in a survey of 2,923 Japanese adolescents in grades 7 through 9, found that impulsiveness was associated with physical, verbal and indirect bullying. Similarly, Espelage *et al.* (2001), in a study of 516 American middle-school students in grades 6–8, discovered that higher levels of impulsivity were associated with greater levels of bullying over time. Baldry (2001), comparing bullies and delinquents with non-involved children in an Italian survey of 679 male high-school students, found a strong impulsiveness trait in bullies, delinquents and students categorised as both bullies and delinquents, compared with non-involved children.

Attention-Deficit Hyperactivity Disorder (ADHD) and low self-control have also been investigated as possible risk factors that might explain children's involvement in bullying. Unnever and Cornell (2003), in a project on 1,315 American middle-school students, discovered that students who reported taking medication for ADHD were at increased risk for bullying as well as victimisation, although the relationship between the two variables could be explained by low self-esteem. In a study by Bacchini *et al.* (2008) with a sample of 195 children in grades 4 and 5, temperamental variables had a direct relationship to ADHD symptoms, which in turn had a direct relationship to bullying in males and to victimisation in females.

Some studies have reported a link between low self-control and bullying (e.g. Ando *et al.* 2005; Nofziger 2001; Unnever 2005). For example, Unnever and Cornell (2003) found a direct effect of self-control on bullying but not on victimisation. Interestingly, they also reported that ADHD had only an indirect effect on bullying via self-control. Haynie *et al.* (2001) found that middle-school bullies scored lower on a seven-item self-control scale than did victims or comparison students. Bullies generally see themselves as impulsive and lacking in self-control (Bjorkqvist *et al.* 1982). Moon *et al.* (2008), using longitudinal data from 655 Korean middle-school students in three schools, reported that there was a significant positive association between bullying and low self-control (measured on the scale by Grasmick *et al.* 1993).

Impulsiveness, attention problems, low intelligence and low achievement could all be linked to deficits in the executive functions of the brain and to neuropsychological deficits which are associated with antisocial behaviour and youth violence (Morgan and Lilienfeld 2000). Studies in both the US (Coolidge *et al.* 2004) and the UK (Monks *et al.* 2005) suggest that bullying is correlated with measures of neuropsychological dysfunction and deficits in executive functioning.

Self-esteem is another risk factor that has been investigated in bullying research (Spade 2007). In an English survey of 904 students aged 12–17, Salmon *et al.* (1998) found a non-significant association between self-esteem and both bullying and victimisation. Also, Tritt and Duncan (1997) reported similar levels of self-esteem in young adults who were childhood bullies, bully-victims or non-involved. However, Baldry and Farrington (1998) in Rome found that victims (but not bullies) had low self-esteem. Also, O'Moore and Kirkham (2001), in a study of 8,249 Irish schoolchildren aged 8 to 18, concluded that children of both primary and post-primary age who were bullies, victims or bully-victims had significantly lower global self-esteem than did children who were not involved. The more frequently children bullied others or were victimised, the lower was their global self-esteem, while the bully-victims had the lowest self-esteem of all the subgroups in the study.

In a survey of 377 English primary-school students on the impact of both self-esteem and response style on victimisation, Sharp (1996) concluded that students with both high and low self-esteem had experienced bullying by their peers. However, students with low self-esteem and passive response styles had been bullied more extensively and experienced greater stress as a result of this. In a study of 181 Greek primary school students, Andreou (2004b) found that the higher children scored on either bullying or victimisation the lower they scored on self-esteem. In the United States, Duncan (1999b) reported that bullies had high anxiety and also high self-esteem, but in Australia Rigby and Slee (1993a) concluded that bullies had above-average self-esteem. A survey of 245 English schoolchildren aged 14–15 by Johnson and Lewis (1999) also concluded that the typical bully had relatively high self-esteem.

Existing research suggests that there may be important gender differences in the relationship between self-esteem and bullying and/or victimisation. Salmivalli *et al.* (1999) in Finland found that adolescents' self-esteem profiles were associated with their behaviour in bullying situations, but these connections were stronger among boys than among girls. Bullying others and reinforcing the bully were typical of adolescents with defensive self-esteem, while defending the bully was typical of adolescents with high self-esteem. Being victimised by peers was most typical of adolescents with low self-esteem and, among girls, of those in the cluster of 'humble pride'. In an Australian survey, Rigby and Cox (1996) discovered that among girls, but not among boys, low levels of self-esteem were associated with self-reported bullying.

It is undoubtedly true that victims of bullying tend to be unpopular, rejected or neglected by other children, lonely and with few friends (e.g. Eslea *et al.* 2003; Nansel *et al.* 2001). Whether the same is true for bullies is less clear. In Illinois, Espelage and Holt (2001) reported that bullies tended to be popular, and three-quarters of bullies nominated fellow bullies as friends. In their large-scale surveys, both Eslea *et al.* (2003) in seven countries and Nansel *et al.* (2001) in the United States found that self-reported bullies were not different from comparison children in feeling left alone or having few friends. However, in Sheffield Boulton and Smith (1994) discovered that peer-rated bullies tended to be rejected by other children, and O'Moore and Hillery (1991) in Dublin found that self-reported bullies were unpopular. Similarly, Salmivalli *et al.* (1996) in Finland found that peer-rated bullies tended to be socially rejected: only 10 per cent of bullies were popular, compared with 30 per cent of comparison children.

It is widely believed that bullies tend to have low empathy. In fact, it has been suggested that low empathy and bullying may be causally related (Olweus 1991; Rigby 1996). Given the link between empathy and bullying (e.g. Bernstein and Watson 1997; Espelage *et al.* 2004), existing research on bullying prevention has often targeted empathy (e.g. Rock *et al.* 2002; Woods *et al.* 2003). In a study carried out in Italy and England, Menesini *et al.* (1997) found that bullies were less upset at observing bullying than were comparison children. In a Norwegian survey of 2,286 6–9th graders, Endresen and Olweus (2001) discovered a negative relationship between empathy and bullying and argued that it is the tendency to respond with empathic concern when exposed to another person in distress that may have an inhibitory effect on bullying.

In a project of 1,173 children in grades 4 (mean age 9.7) and 8 (mean age 13.1) from one Spanish and two Italian cities, Menesini *et al.* (2003b) investigated differences between bullies, victims and outsiders in the attribution of moral emotions to the self in a bullying scenario. They discovered that peer-rated bullies tended to be egocentric and emotionally disengaged about bullying compared to victims and outsiders. Another Italian study of 318 adolescents (mean age 13.2) by Gini *et al.* (2007) concluded that low levels of empathic responsiveness were associated with students' involvement in bullying others, while empathy was positively associated with actively helping victimised schoolmates. However, the findings were applicable to boys only.

Warden and Mackinnon (2003) examined the link between children's sociometric status, empathy and social problem-solving strategies. Based on a sample of 131 schoolchildren aged 9–10, prosocial children showed greater empathic awareness than either bullies or victims, with gender being the most significant source of variance. The observed difference in empathy between bullies and prosocial children mainly reflected the difference between males and females, with girls bullying less and having much higher empathy. The higher empathy of girls is a common finding (Lennon and Eisenberg 1987).

In Hertfordshire, the findings of a survey by Jolliffe and Farrington (2006) support the idea that self-reported bullies tend to have low affective empathy (the ability to feel or share the emotional state of another) but not low cognitive empathy (the ability to understand another's emotional state). Research on the differentiation between affective and cognitive empathy —as well as how these two types of empathy are related to bullying— has provided some interesting findings. Sutton *et al.* (1999b) examined children's understanding of cognitions and emotions in relation to their roles in bullying. Their results show that bullies have the ability to understand the emotional state of others in hypothetical scenarios but fail to experience the emotional state of others. Sutton *et al.* (1999b) concluded that the bully was a cold, manipulative and Machiavellian expert in social situations, and this finding has been replicated in other studies. For instance, Sutton and Keogh (2000) in England and Andreou (2004a) in Greece found that bullies tended to be Machiavellian and manipulative in specific social contexts.

In another study by Wolke *et al.* (2000) with 1,982 primary-school children, it was concluded that relational (indirect) bullies had the lowest behaviour problem scores but were rated as the least prosocially inclined children, consistent with the concept of a cool manipulator. It is not unreasonable to predict that bullies would tend to be high on the three dimensions of childhood psychopathy (Farrington 2005): a deficient interpersonal style (e.g. manipulative, lying, conning), deficient affective experience (e.g. low guilt, low empathy, low remorse, callous) and an impulsive or irresponsible behavioural style (e.g. failing to think before acting, excitement-seeking). A survey with 315 Spanish students aged 10–15 (Ramirez 2001) on the relationship between bullying and some personality variables (e.g. psychoticism, measured by Eysenck's EPQ-J; and self-esteem, measured by Rosenberg's Self-Esteem Inventory) partially supported the above hypothesis. The study discovered that bullies scored higher in psychoticism, sincerity and leadership, while victims scored higher in self-control and anxiety, with psychoticism being the main discriminator between the two groups. It has been suggested that Eysenck's 'psychoticism' scale should be regarded as a measure of psychopathy (Farrington and Jolliffe 2001).

Family influences

Many studies show that family factors are linked to children's involvement in bullying as perpetrators, victims and bully-victims (for recent reviews see Smith and Myron-Wilson 1998; Smith 2005). Several family characteristics have been investigated, such as criminal parents (Farrington and Baldry 2005), parental discipline practices (e.g. Baldry and Farrington 1998; Olweus 1993b), parental conflict in the home and family disharmony in general (e.g. Schwartz *et al.* 1997; Stevens *et al.* 2002), family cohesion (e.g. Berdondini and Smith 1996; Bowers *et al.* 1992), family size (Ma 2001) and maltreatment by family members (Duncan 1999a; Shields and Cicchetti 2001).

In Australia, Rigby (1993) used the Family Functioning in Adolescence Questionnaire in order to examine the family background of children involved in bullying. He found that bullying was significantly associated with poorer family functioning and that this correlation was stronger for boys than for girls. For girls, but not for boys, being victimised was associated with poorer family functioning. In a later study including bullies, victims, bully-victims and controls, Rigby (1994) concluded that male bully-victims scored lowest on family functioning and both bullies and bully-victims scored significantly lower than controls. Male victims were similar to controls. For girls, both bullies and victims scored lower than controls on family functioning.

Other researchers have examined whether parents' involvement in children's lives is related to bullying. In the US, Espelage et al. (2000) found that the time spent by children without adult supervision was positively related to their bullying. Flouri and Buchanan (2002) reported that father involvement in the family was a protective factor against victimisation. In a later study, Flouri and Buchanan (2003) concluded that low father and mother involvement contributed significantly and independently to adolescent bullying. Father and mother involvement also had interactive effects, in that high involvement by one parent could compensate for low involvement by the other. Low involvement by both parents was the best predictor of bullying. Spriggs et al. (2007), in a survey of 11,000 US adolescents regarding predictors of bullying, found that low parent–school involvement (e.g. helping with homework) predicted both bully and victim status in white and black but not Hispanic students.

Parental involvement could be seen as a measure of the quality of the parent–child relationship. Several studies have addressed this topic and the extent to which children's perceptions of their relationships with parents are related to bullying (e.g. Rican 1995; Ttofi and Farrington 2008a, 2008b). In Norway, Roland and Galloway (2002) found that positive family relationships (based on class-level estimates of family conditions) were negatively related to bullying others. In Belgium, Stevens et al. (2002: 423) reported that children who were not involved in bullying said that they had a better personal relationship with their parents compared to bullies and bully-victims.

In the Australian study by Rigby (1993), bullies reported poor relationships with their fathers. Male bullies reported negative relationships with their mothers, while female victims tended to have negative attitudes to and poor relationships with their mothers. In an Irish survey by Connolly and O'Moore (2003), children who bullied had an ambivalent relationship with their siblings, mothers and fathers while children who were not involved had a positive relationship with other members of their families. Spriggs et al. (2007) reported that ease of communication with the parents was the strongest predictor of bullying involvement. Children involved in bullying as either bullies or victims were more likely to report having difficulties in communicating with their parents.

Good family relations are important not only for the parent–child dyad but also between siblings. Several projects have reported a positive link between sibling and peer bullying (e.g. Duncan 1999b; Ttofi and Farrington 2008a, 2008b). In the UK, Wolke and Samara (2004) found that more than half of victims of bullying by siblings (50.7 per cent) were also involved in bullying at school, compared to only 12.4 per cent of those not victimised by siblings, indicating a strong link between intrafamilial and extrafamilial peer relationships.

Bowers *et al.* (1992, 1994) measured family cohesion and power relations among family members using the Family Systems Test (FAST). The researchers also measured children's perceptions of the parenting styles used by their parents in a questionnaire. They found that perceptions of cohesion and power among family members were significantly different between bullies, victims, bully-victims and non-involved children. Victims tended to have positive involvement with other family members and very close relationships with siblings. Children involved in bullying as either bullies or bully-victims were more likely to perceive other family members as distant. Bullies had negative relationships with siblings who they saw as more powerful. Bully-victims showed the most troubled relationships with parents. Non-involved children said that their families were cohesive but they were not as overprotected as victims. Non-involved children also scored low on parental punitiveness and neglect. A replication of the above two studies in England with a sample of children aged 8–11 yielded similar results (Berdondini and Smith 1996).

The relationship between parental discipline and bullying has also been investigated. Curtner-Smith (2000) examined mechanisms by which family processes might contribute to bullying by 10- to 13-year-old boys. Inappropriate discipline by parents, marital satisfaction and social support by spouses and friends (based on mother reports) were the strongest predictors of boys' bullying (based on peer nominations, teacher and mother reports). Olweus (1980) carried out in-depth interviews with parents of children involved in bullying and reported that the parents of male bullies had high permissiveness towards aggression and harsh discipline. Espelage *et al.* (2000) also found a positive relationship between parental physical discipline and bullying. The way that parents shame children after their wrongdoing (reintegrative versus disintegrative; see later) is also strongly linked to bullying (e.g. Ahmed and Braithwaite 2004b, 2005; Ttofi and Farrington 2008b). Parents should be concerned about the type of sanctioning they give to children since previous research has found that children's perceptions of the fairness of parental sanctions predict sibling bullying via the mediating effects of defiant or compliant reactions (Ttofi and Farrington 2008a).

Parenting styles have also been investigated. In Rome, Baldry and Farrington (1998) discovered that an authoritarian parenting style predicted more involvement as a bully or a victim, while punitive parenting especially predicted being a bully-victim. Baldry and Farrington (2000: 25) reported that bullies differed significantly from non-bullies in having authoritarian, highly punitive and low supportive parents who disagreed with each other. Bullies differed from non-bullies also in disagreeing more with both their mothers and fathers. Curtner-Smith *et al.* (2006) showed that mothers' inappropriate developmental expectations for children, as well as their need to exert power over children rather than grant them independence, were related to relational (indirect) bullying. Olweus (1980) found that the parents of male bullies tended to use power-assertive child-rearing methods. Similarly, in the research of Ahmed and Braithwaite (2004a), parents of bullies and bully-victims were more likely to have an authoritarian child-rearing style than parents of victims and non-involved children.

Georgiou (2008a), in a study of 252 Greek Cypriot children and their mothers, concluded that maternal responsiveness was negatively related to bullying, while overprotective mothering was associated with a high degree of victimisation. In a study with 377 Greek Cypriot children (mean age 11.6 years), Georgiou (2008b) reported that permissive mothers had children with the highest mean scores on victimisation, compared with neglectful, authoritarian or authoritative mothers. In a sample of Swedish boys aged 13 and 16, Olweus (1993b) found that a child's weak temperament predicted overprotectiveness in mothers, which in turn predicted victimisation. He also found that the father's negativism predicted a lack of identification with the father, which in turn predicted victimisation. Overall, Olweus (1993b) argued that a sensitive boy who was overprotected by his mother or who had a critical and distant father was most likely to become a victim of bullying.

Other family factors that have been related to bullying include large family size, parental maltreatment and parental depression. Ma (2001) found that children from larger families were more likely to become bullies than victims. Georgiou (2008a) reported that maternal depressiveness was positively related to both bullying and victimisation. Curtner-Smith (2000) discovered that maternal anger and maternal depression were positively related to bullying (for boys only). In a study comparing maltreated with non-maltreated children, Shields and Cicchetti (2001) showed that children who were maltreated by caregivers were more likely to bully others and to experience victimisation by peers. They also found that gender did not moderate these findings, in that maltreated boys and girls appeared to be at similar risk for bullying and victimisation.

Theories of bullying

Several theoretical perspectives have been proposed – and, more rarely, tested – in order to explain bullying (in particular) and victimisation (more rarely); see Monks et al. (2009). Previous theoretical frameworks have placed emphasis both on cognitive processes (e.g. social information processing theory, theory of mind) and social mechanisms (e.g. social dominance theory, family systems theory). These will be presented next. Wherever possible, brief references to existing research supporting these perspectives will be made. It should be noted that there is currently no *general theory of bullying or victimisation* that has been specifically developed. Instead, the theories so far are based on transferring the framework of existing theoretical models (of aggression, delinquency and, even, crime) to the context of school bullying.

The social information processing theory (SIP), originally developed by Dodge (1986) and redefined by Crick and Dodge (1994), suggests that aggressive individuals select a negative behavioural response in social situations (e.g. responding aggressively, fighting back, etc.) because of their poor ability to process social information accurately. In line with the general concept of the social skills deficit model, aggressive children suffer from hostile attributional biases. They tend to interpret ambiguous situations in an aggressive way (e.g. attributing hostile intent to other individuals) more than their non-aggressive counterparts because of social cognition deficits in sequential stages of processing social information. Previous research on aggressive behaviour has provided support for this model (e.g. Dodge *et al.* 1990).

An attempt was made to transfer the social skills deficit model to the context of school bullying (e.g. Boulton and Smith 1994; Slee 1993), and this was supported by several studies (e.g. Camodeca *et al.* 2003; Losel *et al.* 2007). Existing research within this framework suggests that social cognitive deficits are the outcome of environmental influences (e.g. McKeough *et al.* 1994), whereby children who are exposed to neglect within the family are likely to develop cognitive models of human relationships that are not healthy and are conducive to bullying.

In agreement with the postulates of SIP theory, Perry *et al.* (2001) have proposed the 'Family-Relational Schema Model' in order to explain victimisation by peers. Based on their theoretical schema, children represent family experiences in the form of 'relational schemas' (or 'cognitive structures') that they carry with them into peer interactions and that contribute to their victimisation by peers. Under certain circumstances, 'these cognitive structures and associated scripts are activated and serve to guide social perception and behaviour' (Perry *et al.* 2001: 87).

The view of the bully as an 'oaf' child has been challenged by the 'theory of mind' approach. Theory of mind (ToM), the biggest rival to the social skills deficit model, is a theoretical perspective that has changed 'the toddler from a literal observer of human behaviour to a folk psychologist, capable of making complex mental-state attributions, engaging in elaborate social and communicative games, and even deception' (Slaughter and Repacholi 2003: 1). 'Theory of mind' refers to the ability of an individual to predict and explain the behaviour and feelings of others by reference to mental states like beliefs, desires and perceptions (Astington 1993).

Social information processing theory and theory of mind could be seen as two ends of the same continuum. Whereas SIP attributes aggressive behaviour to the absence of adequate cognitive skills, ToM ascribes aggressive behaviour to the presence of advanced cognitive skills. ToM argues that aggressive individuals behave in this way not because they are intellectually simple but because they possess a 'superior theory of mind'. They are socially skilled individuals who take advantage of their advanced cognitive competence (e.g. their mind-reading abilities) to achieve personal benefits, such as leadership within a group, in an aggressive way.

ToM has been transferred to the framework of school bullying with promising results (e.g. Sutton 2003; Sutton *et al.* 1999a, 1999b). The application of ToM has uncovered interesting age differences (e.g. Rivers and Smith 1994; Sutton *et al.* 1999a, 1999b) and gender differences (e.g. Bjorkqvist *et al.* 1992), with females and older children performing better than males and younger children respectively on mind-reading abilities. These are abilities that they use while engaging in indirect rather than direct methods of bullying. Within the ToM perspective, differences in theory of mind skills have been attributed to family variables such as parenting styles (e.g. Ruffman *et al.* 1999; Vinden 1997), maternal education (e.g. Cutting and Dunn 1999) and attachment security (e.g. Symons and Clark 2000). The debate between SIP and ToM is ongoing.

The ToM perspective has been challenged by Arsenio and Lemerise (2001), who argued that advanced cognitive skills can lead to engagement not only in antisocial behaviour but also in highly prosocial behaviour. Having a superior theory of mind says nothing about how this cognitive competence will be utilised. Arsenio and Lemerise (2001) have also attempted to bridge the gap between SIP and ToM by shedding light on the impact of moral emotions on bullying. Irrespective of whether bullies are 'social inadequates' – as suggested by SIP – or 'Machiavellian schemers' – as proposed by ToM – a promising alternative approach is to pay attention to the kinds of values that guide bullies' conduct rather than their higher or lower ability in social information processing. Using an 'Integrated Model of Emotion Processes and Cognition' (Arsenio and Lemerise 2004; Lemerise and Arsenio 2000) an attempt was made to show how individual differences in emotionality and emotion regulation can explain differences in social information processing and, subsequently, in behaviour.

Transferring this concept to the framework of bullying research, the argument would be that variations in bullying are concordant with individual differences in emotion regulation. This hypothesis has been supported by research. As mentioned earlier, several studies have indicated a link between moral emotions such as low empathy and school bullying (e.g. Gini *et al.* 2004; Jolliffe and Farrington 2006; Olweus and Endresen 1998) as well as a link between maladaptive forms of emotional regulation – e.g. unacknowledged shame – and bullying (Ahmed 2006; Ahmed and Braithwaite 2006; Ttofi and Farrington 2008b). Research has also shown that bullies utilise moral disengagement mechanisms more and show higher levels of egocentric reasoning than non-involved peers (Hymmel *et al.* 2005; Menesini *et al.* 2003a, 2003b).

Social dominance theory (Sidanius 1993; Sidanius and Pratto 1999) is another theoretical perspective that has been used to explain bullying. According to some researchers (e.g. Espelage and Swearer 2003; Nishina 2004), this theory can help to explain the increase in bullying during the transition to middle school. According to social dominance theory, human beings are predisposed to create social dominance hierarchies and this can be ascribed to evolutionary processes. Historically, clearly defined hierarchies within the group would encourage the cohesion, stability and, subsequently, the survival of the group. Within the social group, some individuals are more dominant while others are more submissive and/or withdrawn. This is tolerated because, rather than threatening group cohesion, it actually promotes a clear hierarchical organisation within the group.

Transferring this concept to the framework of bullying, the argument is that some bullying might be seen as a method of establishing the social hierarchy and status within the peer group. Findings of previous surveys on bullying could be interpreted within the framework of this theory (Pellegrini and Bartini 2001; Pellegrini and Long 2002). For instance, Pellegrini (2002) argued that the transition to middle school entails renegotiating dominance relationships and hierarchy within the peer group and that bullying is a 'tool' that some students use in order to attain dominance in newly formed peer groups. Conversely, dominance hierarchies, when they are established, serve the important function of reducing in-group aggression (Pelegrini and Long 2004: 110; Vaughn 1999). Using data from a Canadian study, Bukowski and Sippola (2001: 362) discussed the functional role of harassment for the group. The researchers argued that individuals who are perceived to impede or hinder the achievement of the group's goals are more likely to become victims because they do not contribute to the welfare of the group. These individuals are 'forced out' by more dominant members of the group and this is tolerated because it facilitates the survival of the group.

Within the field of criminology, two theories of crime – Braithwaite's reintegrative shaming theory (RST) and Sherman's defiance theory— have been most notably used to explain bullying.

RST places great emphasis on the feeling of shame and the impact of shame on offending at both the micro (individual) and macro (community) levels of analysis. Shame can be triggered through shaming, the social process of expressing disapproval for wrongdoing (Braithwaite 1989: 100). Shaming –which is the pivotal concept of the theory – has a 'conscience building effect' (Braithwaite 1989: 73) and can be used as a powerful regulatory practice. From an early age, through either being the recipient of shaming or disapproving of other people's wrongdoing, the individual learns what is considered right and wrong in society and, hence, internalises social norms. The impact of shaming on offending depends not only on the cultural commitment of each society to shaming (Braithwaite 1989: 55), but also on the way in which shaming is delivered. Shaming must be offered in a reintegrative way (Braithwaite 1989: 101), in a way that communicates disapproval of the wrongdoing rather than the wrongdoer, combined with respect. Despite the strong potential of reintegrative shaming to control offending, an important condition for its success is the existence of strong social bonds between individuals (Braithwaite 1989: 81).

The applicability of RST to crime in general (e.g. Hay 1998, 2001; Zhang and Zhang 2004) and to bullying in particular is promising, with studies showing how strong social bonds, different types of shaming and different types of shame management are related to bullying (e.g. Ahmed 2001; Ahmed and Braithwaite 2005; Ttofi and Farrington 2008b). Morrison (2006) incorporated three theories (i.e. Scheff's theory of unacknowledged shame, Braithwaite's reintegrative shaming theory, and Tyler's procedural justice theory) in a restorative justice framework to explain the role of respect, pride and shame in predicting bullying. The study found significant differences in the mean level of shame management (acknowledged vs. unacknowledged shame) among bullies, victims, bully-victims and non-involved children.

Ttofi and Farrington (2008a) tested the applicability of Sherman's (1993) defiance theory to sibling and peer bullying. In line with the postulates of the theory, they found that bonding to the sanctioning agent (i.e. the parents), perceptions of fairness regarding parental sanctions, unacknowledged shame over the sanctions imposed and stigmatised sanctioning were related to defiant or compliant reactions. Defiance was the mediating theoretical construct explaining the link between family factors and sibling-targeted bullying. Similar results were obtained in a further test of the theory, aiming to explain teacher-targeted bullying by students (Ttofi and Farrington 2009a). In the study, approximately 1,000 students were randomly allocated to four experimental conditions. The type of sanctioning offered by the teacher (respectful versus disrespectful) and the intentionality of wrongdoing by the perpetrator (intentional versus unintentional) were systematically manipulated in a vignette (a 2 × 2 factorial design) in order to encourage different perceptions regarding the fairness of the sanctions imposed and the legitimacy of the authority figure (i.e. the teacher). The study findings confirm that defiance theory is a useful analytical tool for the explanation of bullying. The data fitted the theoretical model.

This overview of existing theoretical perspectives on bullying clearly indicates the contribution of both individual and social factors to the occurrence of bullying. This is acknowledged by Swearer and Doll (2001), who emphasise the necessity of an 'ecological framework' for the explanation and prevention of bullying. The 'ecological model of bullying' (Swearer and Doll 2001: 9; Swearer and Espelage 2004: 4) borrows heavily from the ecological systems perspective of Bronfenbrenner (1977, 1979). This is based on the general idea that multiple environments influence individuals and that these environments should be taken into account in explaining human development. When the ecological perspective is applied to bullying, 'a bullying interaction occurs not only because of individual characteristics of the child who is bullying, but also because of actions of peers, actions of teachers and other adult caretakers at school, physical characteristics of the school grounds, family factors, cultural characteristics and even community factors' (Swearer and Doll 2001: 10). Swearer and Espelage (2004) argue that this social ecology theory should be taken into account in devising methods of bullying prevention.

Effectiveness of anti-bullying programmes

Given the serious short-term and long-term effects of bullying on children's physical and mental health (Ttofi and Farrington 2008a), it is understandable why school bullying has increasingly become a topic of both public concern and research efforts. Research on school bullying has expanded worldwide (Smith et al. 1999b) with a variety of intervention programmes being implemented (Smith et al. 2004) and with some countries legally requiring schools to have an anti-bullying policy (Ananiadou and Smith 2002).

Many school-based intervention programmes have been devised and implemented in an attempt to reduce bullying. These have been targeted on bullies, victims, peers, teachers or on the school in general. Many programmes seem to have been based on common-sense ideas about what might reduce bullying rather than on empirically validated theories of why children bully, why children become victims or why bullying events occur.

The first large-scale anti-bullying programme was implemented nationally in Norway in 1983, following three well-publicised suicides of Norwegian boys that were attributed to bullying. A more intensive version of the national programme was evaluated in Bergen by Olweus (1991). This evaluation showed a dramatic decrease in victimisation (being bullied) of roughly half after the programme. Since then, many other large-scale anti-bullying programmes, some inspired by Olweus and some based on other principles, have been implemented and evaluated in many countries.

The most informative single source of reports of anti-bullying programmes is the book edited by Peter Smith *et al.* (2004), which contains descriptions of 13 programmes implemented in 11 different countries. There are also some reviews containing summaries of major anti-bullying programmes (e.g. Baldry and Farrington 2007; Ortega 2006; Rigby 2002).

The most relevant systematic and/or meta-analytic reviews are by David Smith *et al.* (2004), Vreeman and Carroll (2007), Ferguson *et al.* (2007) and Merrell *et al.* (2008). David Smith *et al.* (2004) reviewed 14 evaluations up to 2002, six of which were uncontrolled. Vreeman and Carroll (2007) reviewed 26 evaluations up to 2004, of which only ten involved controlled evaluations with bullying as the outcome measure. The review by Ferguson *et al.* (2007: 407) included outcome variables that measured 'some element of bullying behaviour or aggression toward peers, including direct aggressive behaviour toward children in a school setting'. Therefore, this review was not focused specifically on bullying. The meta-analytic review by Merrell *et al.* (2008) included 16 evaluations, of which four were based on the same programme (the Flemish Anti-bullying Programme), two were uncontrolled and one measured aggression in general and not bullying in particular.

In a research project for the Campbell Collaboration and the Swedish National Council for Crime Prevention (Farrington and Ttofi 2009; Ttofi and Farrington 2009b; Ttofi *et al.* 2008), we attempted to go beyond existing reviews by:

- doing much more extensive searches for evaluations, such as hand-searching all volumes of 35 journals from 1983 up to the end of April 2008;

- searching for international evaluations in 18 electronic databases and in languages other than English;

- carrying out much more extensive meta-analyses (including correlating effect sizes with study features and research design);

- focusing only on programmes that were specifically designed to reduce bullying and not aggressive behaviour (i.e. where the outcome variables specifically measured bullying).

This systematic and meta-analytic review focused on the 30 highest quality evaluations (i.e. controlled studies) of anti-bullying programmes (concerning 59 out of 593 reports included in the systematic review). Only the four highest-quality methodological designs (i.e. randomised experiments, before-after experimental control designs, other experimental control designs and age-cohort designs) were included in the meta-analysis. Farrington and Ttofi (2009) concluded that school-based anti-bullying programmes are generally effective in reducing bullying and victimisation. The results indicated that bullying and victimisation were reduced by an average of 20–23 per cent in experimental schools compared with control schools.

An attempt was made to correlate the effect sizes of each anti-bullying programme with the intervention components and evaluation features (Ttofi and Farrington 2009b). The researchers received positive feedback from the evaluators of 24 out of 30 anti-bullying programmes regarding the way the intervention components were coded. The most important programme elements that were associated with a decrease in bullying were disciplinary methods, parent training, improved playground supervision, information for parents, school conferences, classroom rules and classroom management. In addition, the total number of elements, and the duration and intensity of the programme for children and teachers, were significantly associated with a decrease in bullying. Also, programmes inspired by the work of Olweus worked best. The programmes worked better with older children, in Norway specifically and in Europe more generally. Older programmes, and those in which the outcome measure of bullying was two times per month or more, also yielded better results.

The most important programme elements that were associated with a decrease in victimisation (being bullied) were videos, disciplinary methods, parent training, and cooperative group work. In addition, the duration and intensity of the programme for children and teachers were significantly associated with a decrease in victimisation. The programmes worked better in Norway specifically and in Europe more generally, and they were less effective in the USA. Older programmes, those in which the outcome measure was two times per month or more, and those with other experimental control and age cohort designs, also yielded better results.

Policy implications

In developing new policies and practices to reduce bullying, policymakers and practitioners should draw upon high-quality evidence-based programmes that have been proved to be effective. New anti-bullying initiatives should be inspired by existing successful programmes such as the Olweus Bullying Prevention Programme (OBPP), but should be modified in light of the key programme elements that we have found to be most effective. It should be borne in mind, however, that we have discovered the programme elements that are most highly correlated with effectiveness. This does not prove that they cause effectiveness, but this is the best evidence available at present.

We recommend that a system of accrediting effective anti-bullying programmes should be developed. In England and Wales in 1996, a system of accrediting effective programmes in prison and probation was established (McGuire 2001). For a programme to be accredited, it had to meet explicit criteria based on knowledge about what worked to reduce offending. Only accredited programmes can be used in England and Wales, and similar systems have been developed in other countries such as Scotland and Canada. A similar procedure should be developed for accrediting anti-bullying programmes in schools to ensure that the programmes contain elements that have been proved to be effective in high-quality evaluations. This accreditation system could perhaps be organised by an international body such as the International Observatory on Violence in Schools.

Our results show that the intensity and duration of a programme are directly linked to its effectiveness, and Olweus (2005) also found a 'dose–response' relationship between the number of components of a programme that were implemented in a school and its effect on bullying. For example, even though teacher training was only marginally significantly related to the reduction of bullying, both the duration (number of meetings of teachers and experts) and intensity (number of hours) of teacher training were. Similarly, the intensity (number of hours) and duration (number of days) of the programme for children were significantly related to the reduction of bullying and victimisation. What these findings show is that programmes need to be intensive and long-lasting in order to have an impact on this troubling problem. A considerable time period may be needed in order to build up an appropriate school ethos that efficiently tackles bullying.

New anti-bullying initiatives should also pay attention to enhancing playground supervision. It is plausible that this is effective since a lot of bullying occurs during playtime. Improving the school playground environment (e.g. through reorganisation and/or identification of 'hot spots') may also be a promising and low-cost intervention component.

Disciplinary methods (i.e. firm methods for tackling bullying) was an intervention component that was significantly related to both bullying and victimisation. To some extent, this finding may be attributable to the big effects of the Olweus programme, which included a range of firm sanctions including serious talks with bullies, sending them to the principal, making them stay close to the teacher during playtime and depriving them of privileges.

New anti-bullying initiatives should go beyond the scope of the school and target wider systemic factors such as the family. Studies indicate that bullied children often do not communicate their problem to anyone while parents and teachers often do not talk to bullies about their conduct (e.g. Fekkes *et al.* 2005). In our systematic review, parent training was significantly related to a decrease in both bullying and victimisation. Our findings suggest that efforts should be made to sensitise parents about the issue of school bullying through educational presentations and teacher–parent meetings.

Importantly, cost-benefit analyses of anti-bullying programmes should be carried out to investigate how much money is saved for the money expended (Welsh *et al.* 2001). Saving money is a powerful argument to convince policymakers and practitioners to implement intervention programmes (Farrington 2009). There never has been a cost-benefit analysis of an anti-bullying programme.

Finally, anti-bullying programmes should be based more on theories of bullying and victimisation. Most past programmes have been based on general social learning ideas. Future programmes could be based on newer theories such as defiance theory and restorative justice approaches (Ttofi and Farrington 2008a, 2008b). For example, poor social relationships at school can be repaired through restorative justice approaches that involve bringing together all children (bullies, victims and other children) 'in a participatory process that addresses wrongdoing while offering respect to the parties involved' (Morrison 2007: 198). Defiance theory is useful because it places emphasis on improving bonding to the sanctioner, shame management and legitimate, respectful sanctioning of antisocial behaviour.

Directions for future research

Future research on bullying and victimisation should aim to study and disentangle the different types of bullying (e.g. physical aggression, verbal aggression, social exclusion). While they may all be interrelated, some risk factors, some theories and some interventions may be more applicable to one type of bullying than another. Researchers should be more concerned with issues of reliability and validity of measurement. For example, they should seek to validate self-reports concurrently and predictively against school records and teacher reports. More efforts should be made to specify how the prevalence of bullying and victimisation, and the prevalence of bully-victims, varies with the definition and measurement (e.g. the cut-off points for frequency). More research, especially using national surveys, is needed on time trends in bullying, using surveys focusing specifically on bullying.

Longitudinal research is needed on careers of bullying and victimisation: when they begin, how long they persist and when they end. In addition, variables that influence onset, persistence and desistance should be studied. More research is needed on the predictive efficiency of individual risk factors that are contentious (such as the self-esteem and popularity of bullies) and especially on whether causal effects can be identified (see Murray *et al.* 2009). It is also important to assess promotive factors that predict a low probability of bullying or victimisation, and protective factors that buffer or nullify the impact of risk factors. Cross-cultural comparisons of bullying and victimisation would be useful in attempting to establish cultural influences.

In future, theories and interventions should be based on systematic reviews of knowledge about risk, and on promotive and protective factors. In particular, theories should seek to explain well-established findings (e.g. the low self-esteem of victims, the low empathy of bullies or the importance of family disharmony and authoritarian parents).

Research is needed to develop and test better theories of bullying and victimisation. In particular, attempts should be made to explain not only the development of the potential to become a bully or a victim, but also how the potential becomes the actuality in situations and environments that provide opportunities for bullying. In other words, more research is needed on the interaction between the individual and the environment. Vignettes could be used in research designed to investigate what factors promote or prevent bullying. The results might provide indications about ways potential victims might behave in order to reduce their chances of being victimised. Similarly, more research is needed on developmental sequences, for example where a person who is victimised at a young age becomes a bully at an older age.

Future evaluations of anti-bullying programmes should provide key information about features of evaluations according to a checklist that should be developed (inspired perhaps by the CONSORT Statement for medical research: Altman *et al.* 2001; Moher *et al.* 2001). Information about key elements of programmes, and about the implementation of programmes, should be provided. For the 20 programme elements that we coded (Farrington and Ttofi 2009; Ttofi and Farrington 2009b) only one evaluation (Fekkes *et al.* 2006) reported the percentage of intervention and control schools that actually implemented these elements. Where bullying and victimisation are measured on five-point scales, the full 5×2 table should be presented, so that the area under the Receiver Operating Characteristic curve (Area under the ROC curve) could be used as a measure of effectiveness (Farrington *et al.* 2008). This would avoid the problem of results varying according to the particular cut-off points that are chosen.

High-quality evaluations are needed. In future, it is important to develop methodological quality standards for evaluation research that can be used by systematic reviewers, scholars, policymakers, the mass media and the general public in assessing the validity of conclusions about the effectiveness of interventions in reducing crime (Farrington 2003: 66). Such quality standards could include guidelines to programme evaluators with regard to what elements of the intervention should be included in published reports perhaps under the aegis of the Campbell Collaboration Crime and Justice Group (Farrington and Petrosino 2001; Farrington and Weisburd 2007).

A great deal has been learned about prevalence, risk factors, theories and interventions for bullying and victimisation. The time is ripe to mount a major coordinated cross-national programme of research to advance knowledge about all these topics and help to reduce the troubling social problem of school bullying.

Selected further reading

Perhaps the most cited book on bullying is the 1993 volume by Dan Olweus, namely *Bullying in Schools: What We Know and What We Can Do*. A 1993 essay by David Farrington, 'Understanding and preventing bullying', presents an overview of key issues – empirical, methodological, theoretical and the like – regarding bullying. Readers interested in the work carried out internationally on school bullying should consult the 1999 book edited by Peter Smith and colleagues entitled *The Nature of School Bullying: A Cross-National Perspective*, in which established researchers from all over the world present the main body of bullying research conducted in their country. Another book edited by Peter Smith and colleagues (2004) entitled *Bullying in Schools: How Successful Can Interventions Be?* offers an overview of the work done so far to tackle bullying in both the industrial and developing worlds. Maria Ttofi and colleagues, in *Effectiveness of Programmes to Reduce School Bullying: A Systematic Review* (2008), present a comprehensive systematic and meta-analytic review of the effectiveness of anti-bullying programmes from 1983 up to 2008.

References

Ahmed, E. (2001) 'Shame management: regulating bullying', in E. Ahmed, N. Harris, J. Braithwaite and V. Braithwaite (eds), *Shame Management Through Reintegration*. Cambridge: Cambridge University Press, pp. 211–311.

Ahmed, E. (2006) 'Understanding bullying from a shame management perspective: findings from a three-year follow-up study', *Educational and Child Psychology*, 23: 25–39.

Ahmed, E. and Braithwaite, V. (2004a) 'Bullying and victimization: cause for concern for both families and schools', *Social Psychology of Education*, 7: 35–54.

Ahmed, E. and Braithwaite, V. (2004b) 'What, me ashamed? Shame management and school bullying', *Journal of Research in Crime and Delinquency*, 41: 269–94.

Ahmed, E. and Braithwaite, J. (2005) 'Forgiveness, shaming, shame and bullying', *Australian and New Zealand Journal of Criminology*, 38: 298–323.

Ahmed, E. and Braithwaite, V. (2006) 'Forgiveness, reconciliation, and shame: three key variables in reducing school bullying', *Journal of Social Issues*, 62: 347–70.

Altman, D. G., Schulz, K. F., Moher, D., Egger, M., Davidoff, F., Elbourne, D., Gotzsche, P. C. and Lang, T. (2001) 'The revised CONSORT Statement for reporting randomized trials: explanation and elaboration', *Annals of Internal Medicine*, 8: 663–94.

Ananiadou, K. and Smith, K. (2002) 'Legal requirements and nationally circulated materials against school bullying in European countries', *Criminal Justice*, 2: 471–91.

Ando, M., Asakura, T. and Simons-Morton, B. (2005) 'Psychosocial influences on physical, verbal and indirect bullying among Japanese early adolescents', *Journal of Early Adolescence*, 25 (3): 268–97.

Andreou, E. (2004a) 'Bully/victim problems and their association with Machiavellianism and self-efficacy in Greek primary school children', *British Journal of Educational Psychology*, 74: 297–309.

Andreou, E. (2004b) 'Bully/victim problems and their association with psychological constructs in 8- to 12-year-old Greek schoolchildren', *Aggressive Behavior*, 26: 49–56.

Andreou, E. and Metallidou, P. (2004) 'The relationship of academic and social cognition to behaviour in bullying situations among Greek primary school children', *Educational Psychology*, 24 (1): 27–41.

Arora, C. M. J. (1996) 'Defining bullying: towards a clearer general understanding and more effective intervention strategies', *School Psychology International*, 17: 317–29.

Arsenio, W. F. and Lemerise, E. A. (2001) 'Varieties of childhood bullying: values, emotion processes and social competence', *Social Development*, 10 (1): 59–73.

Arsenio, W. F. and Lemerise, E. A. (2004) 'Aggression and moral development: integrating social information processing and moral domain models', *Child Development*, 75 (4): 987–1002.

Astington, J. (1993) *The Child's Discovery of the Mind*. Cambridge, MA: Harvard University Press.

Bacchini, D., Affuso, G. and Trotta, T. (2008) 'Temperament, ADHD and peer relations among schoolchildren: the mediating role of school bullying', *Aggressive Behavior*, 34: 447–59.

Baldry, A. C. (2001) 'Fattori individuali dei ragazzi prevaricatori e con tendenze devianti' ['Individual characteristics of adolescents who bully and manifest deviant behaviors'], *Giornale Italiano di Psicologia*, 28 (3): 643–9.

Baldry, A. C. and Farrington, D. P. (1998) 'Parenting influences on bullying and victimization', *Legal and Criminological Psychology*, 3: 237–54.

Baldry, A. C. and Farrington, D. P. (1999) 'Types of bullying among Italian school children', *Journal of Adolescence*, 22: 423–6.

Baldry, A. C. and Farrington, D. P. (2000) 'Bullies and delinquents: personal characteristics and parental styles', *Journal of Community and Applied Social Psychology*, 10 (1): 17–31.

Baldry, A. C. and Farrington, D. P. (2007) 'Effectiveness of programs to prevent school bullying', *Victims and Offenders*, 2: 183–204.

Berdondini, L. and Smith, P. K. (1996) 'Cohesion and power in the families of children involved in bully/victim problems at school: an Italian replication', *Journal of Family Therapy*, 18: 99–162.

Bernstein, J. Y. and Watson, M. W. (1997) 'Children who are targets of bullying', *Journal of Interpersonal Violence*, 12 (4): 483–98.

Bjorkqvist, K., Ekman, K. and Lagerspetz, K. (1982) 'Bullies and victims: their ego picture, ideal ego picture and normative ego picture', *Scandinavian Journal of Psychology*, 23: 307–13.

Bjorkqvist, K., Lagerspetz, K. M. J. and Kaukiainen, A. (1992) 'Do girls manipulate and boys fight? Developmental trends in regard to direct and indirect aggression', *Aggressive Behavior*, 18: 117–27.

Bosley, S. (2009) Personal communication, 26 March.

Boulton, M. J. (1997) 'Teachers' views on bullying: definitions, attitudes and ability to cope', *British Journal of Educational Psychology*, 67: 223–33.

Boulton, M. J. and Smith, P. K. (1994) 'Bully/victim problems in middle-school children: stability, self-perceived competence, peer perceptions and peer acceptance', *British Journal of Developmental Psychology*, 12: 315–29.

Bowers, L., Smith, P. K. and Binney, V. (1992) 'Cohesion and power in the families of children involved in bully/victim problems at school', *Journal of Family Therapy*, 14: 371–87.

Bowers, L., Smith, P. K. and Binney, V. (1994) 'Perceived family relationships of bullies, victims and bully/victims in the middle childhood', *Journal of Social and Personal Relationships*, 11: 215–32.

Braithwaite, J. (1989) *Crime, Shame and Reintegration*. New York: Cambridge University Press.

Bronfenbrenner, U. (1977) 'Toward an experimental ecology of human development', *American Psychologist*, 32: 513–31.

Bronfenbrenner, U. (1979) *The Ecology of Human Development: Experiments by Nature and Design*. Cambridge, MA: Harvard University Press.

Bukowski, W. M. and Sippola, L. K. (2001) 'Groups, individuals, and victimization: a view of the peer system', in J. Juvonen and S. Graham (eds), *Peer Harassment in School: The Plight of the Vulnerable and Victimized*. New York: Guilford Press, pp. 355–77.

Camodeca, M., Goossens, F. A., Schuengel, C. and Terwogt, M. M. (2003) 'Links between social information processing in middle childhood and involvement in bullying', *Aggressive Behavior*, 29: 116–27.

Collishaw, S., Maughan, B., Goodman, R. and Pickles, A. (2004) 'Time trends in adolescent mental health', *Journal of Child Psychology and Psychiatry*, 45: 1350–62.

Connolly, I. and O'Moore, M. (2003) 'Personality and family relations of children who bully', *Personality and Individual Differences*, 35: 559–67.

Coolidge, F. L., DenBoer, J. W. and Segal, D. L. (2004) 'Personality and neuropsychological correlates of bullying behavior', *Personality and Individual Differences*, 36: 1559–69.

Craig, W. M. (1998) 'The relationship among bullying, victimization, depression, anxiety, and aggression in elementary school children', *Personality and Individual Differences*, 24 (1): 123–30.

Craig, W. M. and Pepler, D. J. (1998) 'Observations of bullying and victimization in the school yard', *Canadian Journal of School Psychology*, 13 (2): 41–59.

Crick, N. R. and Dodge, K. A. (1994) 'A review and reformulation of social information-processing mechanisms in children's social adjustment', *Psychological Bulletin*, 115: 74–101.

Crick, N. R. and Grotpeter, J. K. (1995) 'Relational aggression, gender, and social-psychological adjustment', *Child Development*, 66: 710–22.

Curtner-Smith, M. E. (2000) 'Mechanisms by which family processes contribute to school-age boys' bullying', *Child Study Journal*, 30: 169–86.

Curtner-Smith, M. E., Culp, A. M., Culp, R., Scheib, C., Owen, K., Tilley, A., Murphy, M., Parkman, L. and Coleman, P. W. (2006) 'Mothers' parenting and young economically disadvantaged children's relational and overt bullying', *Journal of Child and Family Studies*, 15 (2): 181–93.

Cutting, A. L. and Dunn, J. (1999) 'Theory of mind, emotion understanding, language, and family background: individual differences and interrelations', *Child Development*, 70: 853–65.

De Voe, J. F., Peter, K., Kaufman, P., Miller, A., Noonan, M., Snyder, T. D. and Baum, K. (2004) *Indicators of School Crime and Safety, 2004*. Washington, DC: US Government Printing Office (NCES 2005-002, NCJ 205290).

Dinkes, R., Cataldi, E. F. and Lin-Kelly, W. (2007) *Indicators of School Crime and Safety, 2007*. Washington, DC: National Center for Education Statistics (NCES 2008-021/NCJ 219553).

Dodge, K. A. (1986) 'A social information processing model of social competence in children', in M. Perlmutter (ed.), *The Minnesota Symposium on Child Psychology*, Vol. 18. Hillsdale, NJ: Lawrence Erlbaum, pp. 77–125.

Dodge, K. A. and Coie, J. D. (1987) 'Social information-processing factors in reactive and proactive aggression in children's peer groups', *Journal of Personality and Social Psychology*, 53: 1146–58.

Dodge, K. A., Bates, J. and Pettit, G. (1990) 'Mechanisms in the cycle of violence', *Science*, 250: 1678–83.

Due, P., Holstein, B. E., Lynch, J., Diderichsen, F., Gabhain, S. N., Scheidt, P., Currie, C. and The Health Behaviour in School-Aged Children Bullying Working Group (2005) 'Bullying and symptoms among school-aged children: international comparative cross-sectional study in 28 countries', *European Journal of Public Health*, 15: 128–32.

Duncan, R. D. (1999a) 'Maltreatment by parents and peers: the relationship between child abuse, bully victimization, and psychological distress', *Child Maltreatment*, 4: 45–55.

Duncan, R. D. (1999b) 'Peer and sibling aggression: an investigation of intra- and extra-familial bullying', *Journal of Interpersonal Violence*, 14: 871–86.

Endresen, I. M. and Olweus, D. (2001) 'Self-reported empathy in Norwegian adolescents: sex differences, age trends, and relationship to bullying', in A. C. Bohart and D. J. Stipek (eds), *Constructive and Destructive Behavior: Implications for Family, School and Society*. Washington, DC: American Psychological Association, pp. 147–65.

Eslea, M., Menesini, E., Morita, Y., O'Moore, M., Mora-Merchan, J. A., Pereira, B. and Smith, P. K. (2003) 'Friendship and loneliness among bullies and victims: data from seven countries', *Aggressive Behavior*, 30: 71–83.

Espelage, D. L. and Holt, M. K. (2001) 'Bullying and victimization during early adolescence: peer influences and psychosocial correlates', *Journal of Emotional Abuse*, 2 (2/3): 123–42.

Espelage, D. L. and Swearer, S. M. (2003) 'Research on school bullying and victimization: what have we learnt and where do we go from here?', *School Psychology Review*, 32 (3): 365–83.

Espelage, D. L., Bosworth, K. and Simon, T. R. (2000) 'Examining the social context of bullying behaviors in early adolescence', *Journal of Counseling and Development*, 78 (3): 326–33.

Espelage, D. L., Bosworth, K. and Simon, T. R. (2001) 'Short-term stability and prospective correlates of bullying in middle-school students: an examination of potential demographic, psychosocial, and environmental influences', *Violence and Victims*, 16 (4): 411–26.

Espelage, D. L., Mebane, S. E. and Adams, R. S. (2004) 'Empathy, caring and bullying: towards an understanding of complex associations', in D. L. Espelage and S. M. Swearer (eds), *Bullying in American Schools: A Social-Ecological Perspective on Prevention and Intervention*. Mahwah, NJ: Lawrence Erlbaum, pp. 37–61.

Farrington, D. P. (1993) 'Understanding and preventing bullying', in M. Tonry (ed.), *Crime and Justice*, Vol. 17. Chicago: University of Chicago Press, pp. 381–458.

Farrington, D. P. (2003) 'Methodological quality standards for evaluation research', *Annals of the American Academy of Political and Social Science*, 587: 49–68.

Farrington, D. P. (2005) 'The importance of child and adolescent psychopathy', *Journal of Abnormal Child Psychology*, 33: 489–97.

Farrington, D. P. (2009) 'Conduct disorder, aggression, and delinquency', in R. M. Lerner and L. Steinberg (eds), *Handbook of Adolescent Psychology*, 3rd edn. Hoboken, NJ: Wiley, 1: 683–722.

Farrington, D. P. and Baldry, A. C. (2005) 'Individual risk factors for school violence', in A. Serrano (ed.), *Acoso y Violencia en la Escuela*. Valencia: Queen Sofia Center for the Study of Violence.

Farrington, D. P. and Jolliffe, D. (2001) 'Personality and crime', in N. Smelser and P. B. Baltes (eds), *International Encyclopedia of the Social and Behavioral Sciences*, Vol. 16. Amsterdam: Elsevier, pp. 11260–4.

Farrington, D. P. and Petrosino, A. (2001) 'The Campbell Collaboration Crime and Justice Group', *Annals of the American Academy of Political and Social Science*, 578: 35–49.

Farrington, D. P. and Ttofi, M. M. (2009) 'Reducing school bullying: evidence-based implications for policy', in M. Tonry (ed.), *Crime and Justice*, Vol. 38. Chicago: University of Chicago Press, pp. 281–345.

Farrington, D. P. and Weisburd, D. (2007) 'The Campbell Collaboration Crime and Justice Group', *The Criminologist*, 32 (1): 1–5.

Farrington, D. P., Jolliffe, D. and Johnstone, L. (2008) *Assessing Violence Risk: A Framework for Practice*. Edinburgh: Risk Management Authority Scotland.

Fekkes, M., Pijpers, F. I. M. and Verloove-Vanhorick, P. S. (2005) 'Bullying: who does what, when and where? Involvement of children, teachers and parents in bullying behavior', *Health Education Research*, 20: 81–91.

Fekkes, M., Pijpers, F. I. M. and Verloove-Vanhorick, S. P. (2006) 'Effects of antibullying school program on bullying and health complaints', *Archives of Pediatrics and Adolescent Medicine*, 160: 638–44.

Ferguson, C. J., Miguel, C. S., Kilburn, J. C. and Sanchez, P. (2007) 'The effectiveness of school-based anti-bullying programs: a meta-analytic review', *Criminal Justice Review*, 32: 401–14.

Flouri, E. and Buchanan, A. (2002) 'Life satisfaction in teenage boys: the moderating role of father involvement and bullying', *Aggressive Behavior*, 28: 126–33.

Flouri, E. and Buchanan, A. (2003) 'The role of mother involvement and father involvement in adolescent bullying behavior', *Journal of Interpersonal Violence*, 18: 634–44.

Georgiou, S. N. (2008a) 'Bullying and victimization at school: the role of mothers', *British Journal of Educational Psychology*, 78: 109–25.

Georgiou, S. N. (2008b) 'Parental style and child bullying and victimization experiences at school', *Social Psychology of Education*, 11: 213–27.

Gilmartin, B. G. (1987) 'Peer group antecedents of severe love-shyness in males', *Journal of Personality*, 55: 467–89.

Gini, G., Albiero, P. and Benelli, B. (2004) *Relazioni tra bullismo, empatia, imagine di se ed autoefficacia percepita in un campione di adolescenti [Relations Between Bullying, Empathy, Self-Image, and Self-Efficacy in Adolescents]*. Poster presented at the 18th National Conference of Developmental Psychology, Sciacca, Italy.

Gini, G., Albiero, P., Benelli, B. and Altoe, G. (2007) 'Does empathy predict adolescents' bullying and defending behavior?', *Aggressive Behavior*, 33: 467–76.

Glew, G. M., Fan, M.-Y., Katon, W., Rivara, F. P. and Kernic, M. A. (2005) 'Bullying, psychosocial adjustment, and academic performance in elementary school', *Archives of Pediatrics and Adolescent Medicine*, 159: 1026–31.

Grasmick, H., Tittle, C., Bursik, R. J. and Arneklev, B. J. (1993) 'Testing the core empirical implications of Gottfredson and Hirschi's general theory of crime', *Journal of Research in Crime and Delinquency*, 30: 5–29.

Greene, M. B. (2000) 'Bullying and harassment in schools', in R. S. Moser and C. E. Franz (eds), *Shocking Violence: Youth Perpetrators and Victims – A Multidisciplinary Perspective*. Springfield, IL: Charles C Thomas, pp. 72–101.

Griffin, R. S. and Gross, A. M. (2004) 'Childhood bullying: current empirical findings and future directions for research', *Aggression and Violent Behavior*, 9: 379–400.

Guerin, S. and Hennessy, E. (2002) 'Pupils' definitions of bullying', *European Journal of Psychology of Education*, 17 (3): 249–61.

Hay, C. (1998) 'Parental sanctions and delinquent behavior: towards clarification of Braithwaite's theory of reintegrative shaming', *Theoretical Criminology*, 2: 419–43.

Hay, C. (2001) 'An exploratory test of Braithwaite's reintegrative shaming theory', *Journal of Research in Crime and Delinquency*, 38: 132–53.

Haynie, D. L., Nansel, T., Eitel, P., Crump, A., Saylor, K., Yu, K. and Simons-Morton, B. (2001) 'Bullies, victims and bully/victims: distinct groups of at-risk youth', *Journal of Early Adolescence*, 21: 29–49.

Hymmel, S., Rocke-Henderson, N. and Bonanno, R. A. (2005) 'Moral disengagement: a framework for understanding bullying among adolescents', *Journal of Social Sciences*, Special Issue, 8: 1–11.

Johnson, D. and Lewis, G. (1999) 'Do you like what you see? Self-perceptions of adolescent bullies', *British Educational Research Journal*, 25 (5): 665–78.

Jolliffe, D. and Farrington, D. P. (2006) 'Examining the relationship between low empathy and bullying', *Aggressive Behavior*, 32: 540–50.

Kaltiala-Heino, R., Rimpela, M., Rantanen, P. and Rimpela, A. (2000) 'Bullying at school: an indicator of adolescents at risk for mental disorders', *Journal of Adolescence*, 23: 661–74.

Kaltiala-Heino, R., Rimpela, M., Marttunen, M., Rimpela, A. and Rantanen, P. (1999) 'Bullying, depression, and suicidal ideation in Finnish adolescents: school survey', *British Medical Journal*, 319: 348–51.

Kaukiainen, A., Salmivalli, C., Lagerspetz, K., Tamminen, M., Vauras, M., Maki, H. and Poskiparta, E. (2002) 'Learning difficulties, social intelligence, and self-concept: connections to bully-victim problems', *Scandinavian Journal of Psychology*, 43 (3): 269–78.

Kokkinos, C. M. and Panayiotou, G. (2004) 'Predicting bullying and victimization among early adolescents: associations with disruptive behavior disorders', *Aggressive Behavior*, 30 (6): 520–33.

Lagerspetz, K. M. J., Bjorkqvist, K. L. and Peltonen, T. (1988) 'Is indirect aggression typical of females? Gender differences in aggressiveness in 11- to 12-year-old children', *Aggressive Behavior*, 14: 403–14.

Lemerise, E. A. and Arsenio, W. F. (2000) 'An integrated model of emotion processes and cognition in social information processing', *Child Development*, 71 (1): 107–18.

Lennon, R. and Eisenberg, N. (1987) 'Gender and age differences in empathy and sympathy', in N. Eisenberg and J. Strayer (eds), *Empathy and Its Development*. New York: Cambridge University Press, pp. 195–217.

Losel, F., Bliesener, T. and Bender, D. (2007) 'Social information processing, experiences of aggression in social contexts, and aggressive behavior in adolescents', *Criminal Justice and Behavior*, 34: 330–47.

Ma, X. (2001) 'Bullying and being bullied: to what extent are bullies also victims?', *American Educational Research Journal*, 38: 351–70.

McGuire, J. (2001) 'What works in correctional intervention? Evidence and practical implications', in G. A. Bernfeld, D. P. Farrington and A. W. Leschield (eds), *Offender Rehabilitation in Practice: Implementing and Evaluating Effective Programs*. Chichester: Wiley, pp. 25–43.

McKeough, A., Yates, T. and Marini, A. (1994) 'Intentional reasoning: a developmental study of behaviorally aggressive and normal boys', *Development and Psychopathology*, 6: 285–304.

McMahon, R. J. and Frick, P. J. (2005) 'Evidence-based assessment of conduct problems in children and adolescents', *Journal of Clinical Child and Adolescent Psychology*, 34 (3): 477–505.

Menesini, E., Codecasa, E., Benelli, B. and Cowie, H. (2003a) 'Enhancing children's responsibility to take action against bullying: evaluation of a befriending intervention in Italian middle schools', *Aggressive Behavior*, 29: 1–14.

Menesini, E., Eslea, M., Smith, P. K., Genta, M. L., Giannetti, E., Fonzi, A. and Constabile, A. (1997) 'Cross-national comparison of children's attitudes towards bully/victim problems in school', *Aggressive Behavior*, 23: 245–57.

Menesini, E., Sanchez, V., Fonzi, A., Ortega, R., Costabile, A. and Lo-Feudo, G. (2003b) 'Moral emotions and bullying: a cross-national comparison of differences between bullies, victims and outsiders', *Aggressive Behavior*, 29: 515–30.

Merrell, K. W., Gueldner, B. A., Ross, S. W. and Isava, D. M. (2008) 'How effective are school bullying intervention programs? A meta-analysis of intervention research', *School Psychology Quarterly*, 23: 26–42.

Miller, P. A. and Eisenberg, N. (1988) 'The relationship of empathy to aggressive and externalizing/antisocial behavior', *Psychological Bulletin*, 103: 324–44.

Minton, S. J. and O'Moore, A. M. (2008) 'The effectiveness of a nationwide intervention programme to prevent and counter school bullying in Ireland', *International Journal of Psychology and Psychological Therapy*, 8 (1): 1–12.

Moher, D., Schulz, K. F. and Altman, D. (2001) 'The CONSORT statement: revised recommendations for improving the quality of reports of parallel-group randomized trials', *Journal of the American Medical Association*, 285: 1987–91.

Monks, C. P., Smith, P. K. and Swettenham, J. (2005) 'The psychological correlates of peer victimization in preschool: social cognitive skills, executive function and attachment profiles', *Aggressive Behavior*, 31 (6): 571–88.

Monks, C. P., Smith, P. K., Naylor, P., Barter, C., Ireland, J. L. and Coyne, I. (2009) 'Bullying in different contexts: commonalities, differences and the role of theory', *Aggression and Violent Behavior*, 14: 146–56.

Moon, B., Hwang, H.-W. and McCluskey, J. D. (2008) 'Causes of school bullying: empirical test of a general theory of crime, differential association theory, and general strain theory', *Crime and Delinquency*, 20 May. Online first.

Morgan, A. B. and Lilienfeld, S. O. (2000) 'A meta-analytic review of the relation between antisocial behavior and neuropsychological measures of executive function', *Clinical Psychology Review*, 20: 113–36.

Morrison, B. (2006) 'School bullying and restorative justice: toward a theoretical understanding of the role of respect, pride and shame', *Journal of Social Issues*, 62 (2): 371–92.

Morrison, B. (2007) *Restoring Safe School Communities: A Whole School Response to Bullying, Violence and Alienation*. Sydney: Federation Press.

Murray, J., Farrington, D. P. and Eisner, M. P. (2009) 'Drawing conclusions about causes from systematic reviews of risk factors: the Cambridge Quality Checklists', *Journal of Experimental Criminology*, 5: 1–23.

Nansel, T. R., Overpeck, M., Pilla, R. S., Ruan, W. J., Simons-Morton, B. and Sceidt, P. (2001) 'Bullying behaviors among US youth: prevalence and association with psychosocial adjustment', *Journal of the American Medical Association*, 285 (16): 2094–100.

Naylor, P., Cowie, H., Cossin, F., de Bettencourt, R. and Lemme, F. (2006) 'Teachers' and pupils' definitions of bullying', *British Journal of Educational Psychology*, 76 (3): 553–76.

Nishina, A. (2004) 'A theoretical review of bullying: can it be eliminated?', in C. E. Sanders and G. D. Phye (eds), *Bullying: Implications for the Classroom*. San Diego, CA: Elsevier Academics, pp. 35–62.

Nofziger, S. (2001) *Bullies, Fights, and Guns: Testing Self-Control Theory with Juveniles*. New York: LFB Scholarly Publishing.

O'Moore, M. and Hillery, B. (1991) 'What do teachers need to know?', in M. Elliot (ed.), *Bullying: A Practical Guide to Coping for Schools*. Harlow: Longman, pp. 56–69.

O'Moore, M. and Kirkham, C. (2001) 'Self-esteem and its relationship to bullying behavior', *Aggressive Behavior*, 27: 269–83.

O'Moore, M., Kirkham, C. and Smith, M. (1997) 'Bullying behaviour in Irish schools: a nationwide study', *Irish Journal of Psychology*, 18: 141–69.

Olweus, D. (1978) *Aggression in the Schools: Bullies and Whipping-boys*. Washington, DC: Hemisphere.

Olweus, D. (1980) 'Familial and temperamental determinants of aggressive behavior in adolescent boys: a causal analysis', *Developmental Psychology*, 16: 644–60.

Olweus, D. (1991) 'Bully/victim problems among school children: basic facts and effects of a school-based intervention program', in D. J. Pepler and K. H. Rubin (eds), *The Development and Treatment of Childhood Aggression*. Hillsdale, NJ: Lawrence Erlbaum, pp. 411–48.

Olweus, D. (1993a) *Bullying at School: What We Know and What We Can Do*. Oxford: Blackwell.

Olweus, D. (1993b) 'Victimization by peers: antecedents and long-term outcomes', in K. H. Rubin and J. B. Asendorpf (eds), *Social Withdrawal, Inhibition and Shyness in Childhood*. Hillsdale, NJ: Lawrence Erlbaum, pp. 315–42.

Olweus, D. (1994) 'Annotation: bullying at school: basic facts and effects of a school based intervention programme', *Journal of Child Psychology and Psychiatry*, 35 (7): 1171–90.

Olweus, D. (1996) *The Revised Olweus Bully/Victim Questionnaire*. Bergen: Research Center for Health Promotion (HEMIL Center), University of Bergen.

Olweus, D. (1997) 'Bully/victim problems in school: facts and intervention', *European Journal of Psychology of Education*, 12 (4): 495–510.

Olweus, D. (2005) 'A useful evaluation design, and effects of the Olweus bullying prevention program', *Psychology, Crime and Law*, 11: 389–402.

Olweus, D. and Endresen, I. M. (1998) 'The importance of sex-of-stimulus objects: age trends and sex differences in empathic responsiveness', *Social Development*, 7: 370–88.

Ortega, R. (2006) 'Prevention programs for pupils', in A. Serano (ed.), *Acoso y Violencia en la Escuela*. Valencia: Queen Sofia Center for the Study of Violence.

Pateraki, L. and Houndoumadi, A. (2001) 'Bullying among primary school children in Athens, Greece', *Educational Psychology*, 21: 167–75.

Pellegrini, A. D. (2002) 'Bullying and victimization in middle school: a dominance relations perspective', *Educational Psychologist*, 37: 151–63.

Pellegrini, A. D. and Bartini, M. (2001) 'Dominance in early adolescent boys: affiliative and aggressive dimensions and possible functions', *Merrill-Palmer Quarterly*, 47: 142–63.

Pellegrini, A. D. and Long, J. (2002) 'A longitudinal study of bullying, dominance, and victimization during the transition from primary to secondary school', *British Journal of Developmental Psychology*, 20: 259–80.

Pellegrini, A. D. and Long, J. (2004) 'Part of the solution, part of the problem: the role of peers in bullying, dominance, and victimization during the transition from primary school through secondary school', in D. L. Espelage and S. M. Swearer (eds), *Bullying in American Schools: A Social-Ecological Perspective on Prevention and Intervention*. Mahwah, NJ: Lawrence Erlbaum, pp. 107–18.

Perry, D. G., Hodges, E. V. E. and Egan, S. K. (2001) 'Determinants of chronic victimization by peers: a review and a new model of family influence', in J. Juvonen and S. Graham (eds), *Peer Harassment in School: The Plight of the Vulnerable and Victimized*. New York: Guilford Press, pp. 73–104.

Ramirez, F. C. (2001) 'Variables de personalidad asociadas en la dinamica bullying (aggressores versus victimas) en niños y niñas de 10 a 15 años' ['Personality variables associated with bullying (aggressors versus victims) in 10 to 15 year-old schoolers'], *Anales de Psicología*, 17 (1): 37–43.

Rican, P. (1995) 'Family values may be responsible for bullying', *Studia Psychologica*, 37: 31–6.

Rigby, K. (1993) 'School children's perceptions of their families and parents as a function of peer relations', *Journal of Genetic Psychology*, 154: 501–13.

Rigby, K. (1994) 'Psychosocial functioning in families of Australian adolescent school children involved in bully/victim problems', *Journal of Family Therapy*, 16: 173–87.

Rigby, K. (1996) *Bullying in Schools and What to Do About It*. London: Jessica Kingsley.

Rigby, K. (1997) *The Peer Relations Assessment Questionnaire*. Point Lonsdale, Vic.: Professional Reading Guide.

Rigby, K. (2002) *A Meta-Evaluation of Methods and Approaches to Reducing Bullying in Preschools and Early Primary School in Australia*. Canberra: Attorney General's Department, Crime Prevention Branch.

Rigby, K. and Cox, I. (1996) 'The contribution of bullying at school and low self-esteem to acts of delinquency among Australian teenagers', *Personality and Individual Differences*, 21: 609–12.

Rigby, K. and Slee, P. T. (1993a) 'Dimensions of interpersonal relating among Australian schoolchildren and implications for psychological well-being', *Journal of Social Psychology*, 133: 33–42.

Rigby, K. and Slee, P. T. (1993b) *The Peer Relations Questionnaire*. Point Lonsdale, Vic.: Professional Reading Guide.

Rivers, I. and Smith, P. K. (1994) 'Types of bullying behaviour and their correlates', *Aggressive Behavior*, 20: 359–68.

Rock, E. A., Hammond, M. and Rasmussen, S. (2002) *School Based Program to Teach Children Empathy and Bully Prevention*. Paper presented at the 110th Annual Conference of the American Psychological Association, Chicago, 22–25 August.

Roland, E. and Galloway, D. (2002) 'Classroom influences on bullying', *Educational Research*, 44 (3): 299–312.

Ruffman, T., Perner, J. and Parkin, L. (1999) 'How parenting style affects false belief understanding', *Social Development*, 8: 395–411.

Salmivalli, C. (2009) Personal communication, 26 March.

Salmivalli, C., Kaukiainen, A., Kaistaniemi, L. and Lagerspetz, K. M. J. (1999) 'Self-evaluated self-esteem, peer-evaluated self-esteem, and defensive egotism as predictors of adolescents' participation in bullying situation', *Personality and Social Psychology Bulletin*, 25 (10): 1268–78.

Salmivalli, C., Lappainen, M. and Lagerspetz, K. M. J. (1998) 'Stability and change of behavior in connection with bullying in schools: a two-year follow up', *Aggressive Behavior*, 24: 205–18.

Salmivalli, C., Lagerspetz, K., Bjorkqvist, K., Österman, K. and Kaukiainen, A. (1996) 'Bullying as a group process: participant roles and their relations to social status within the group', *Aggressive Behavior*, 22: 1–15.

Salmon, G., James, A. and Smith, D. M. (1998) 'Bullying in schools: self-reported anxiety, depression, and self-esteem in secondary school children', *British Medical Journal*, 317: 924–5.

Salmon, G., James, A., Cassidy, E. L. and Javaloyes, M. A. (2000) 'Bullying – a review: presentations to an adolescent psychiatric service and within a school for emotionally and behaviorally disturbed children', *Clinical Child Psychology and Psychiatry*, 5: 563–79.

School Health Education Unit (2004) *Trends: Young People and Emotional Health and Well-Being (Including Bullying), 1983–2003*. Exeter: Schools Health Education Unit.

Schwartz, D., Dodge, K. A., Pettit, G. S. and Bates, J. E. (1997) 'The early socialization of aggressive victims of bullying', *Child Development*, 68: 665–75.

Sharp, S. (1996) 'Self-esteem, response style and victimization: possible ways of preventing victimization through parenting and school based training programmes', *School Psychology International*, 17 (4): 347–57.

Sherman, L. W. (1993) 'Defiance, deterrence and irrelevance: a theory of the criminal sanction', *Journal of Research in Crime and Delinquency*, 30 (4): 445–73.

Shields, A. and Cicchetti, D. (2001) 'Parental maltreatment and emotion dysregulation as risk factors for bullying and victimization in middle childhood', *Journal of Clinical Child Psychology*, 30 (3): 349–63.

Sidanius, J. (1993) 'The psychology of group conflict and the dynamics of oppression: a social dominance perspective', in S. Iyengar and W. J. McGuire (eds), *Explorations in Political Psychology*. Durham, NC: Duke University Press, pp. 183–219.

Sidanius, J. and Pratto, F. (1999) *Social Dominance: An Intergroup Theory of Social Hierarchy and Oppression*. New York: Cambridge University Press.

Slaughter, V. and Repacholi, B. (2003) 'Introduction: individual differences in theory of mind. What are we investigating?', in. B. Repacholi and V. Slaughter (eds), *Individual Differences in Theory of Mind: Implications for Typical and Atypical Development*. New York: Psychology Press/Taylor & Francis Group, pp. 1–12.

Slee, P. T. (1993) 'Bullying: a preliminary investigation of the nature and effects on social cognition', *Early Child Development and Care*, 87: 47–57.

Smith, J. D., Schneider, B. Smith, P. K. and Ananiadou, K. (2004) 'The effectiveness of whole-school anti-bullying programs: a synthesis of evaluation research', *School Psychology Review*, 33: 548–61.

Smith, P. K. (2005) 'School violence and bullying: familial risk factors', in A. Serrano (ed.), *Acoso y Violencia en la Escuela*. Valencia: Queen Sofia Center for the Study of Violence.

Smith, P. K. and Ananiadou, K. (2003) 'The nature of school bullying and the effectiveness of school-based interventions', *Journal of Applied Psychoanalytic Studies*, 5: 189–209.

Smith, P. K. and Myron-Wilson, R. (1998) 'Parenting and school bullying', *Clinical Child Psychology and Psychiatry*, 3: 405–17.

Smith, P. K., Madsen, K. C. and Moody, J. C. (1999a) 'What causes the age decline in reports of being bullied at school? Toward a developmental analysis of risks of being bullied', *Educational Research*, 41: 267–85.

Smith, P. K., Pepler, D. and Rigby, K. (eds) (2004) *Bullying in Schools: How Successful Can Interventions Be?* Cambridge: Cambridge University Press.

Smith, P. K., Cowie, H., Olafsson, R. F. and Liefooghe, A. P. D. (2002) 'Definitions of bullying: a comparison of terms used, and age and gender differences, in a fourteen-country international comparison', *Child Development*, 73: 1119–33.

Smith, P. K., Morita, J., Junger-Tas, D., Olweus, D., Catalano, R. and Slee, P. T. (eds), (1999b) *The Nature of School Bullying: A Cross-National Perspective*. London: Routledge.

Solberg, M. E. and Olweus, D. (2003) 'Prevalence estimates of school bullying with the Olweus Bully/Victim Questionnaire', *Aggressive Behavior*, 29: 239–68.

Sourander, A., Elonheimo, H., Niemela, S., Nuutila, A., Helenius, H., Sillanmaki, L., Piha, J., Tamminen, T., Kumpulainen, K., Moilenen, I. and Almiqvistt, F. (2006) 'Childhood predictors of male criminality: a prospective population-based follow-up study from age 8 to late adolescence', *Journal of the American Academy of Child and Adolescent Psychiatry*, 45: 578–86.

Spade, J. A. (2007) 'The Relationship Between Student Bullying Behaviors and Self-Esteem'. Unpublished PhD thesis, Bowling Green State University, KY, USA.

Spriggs, A. L., Iannotti, R. J., Nansel, T. R. and Haynie, D. L. (2007) 'Adolescent bullying involvement and perceived family, peer and school relations: commonalities and differences across race/ethnicity', *Journal of Adolescent Health*, 41: 283–93.

Srabstein, J. and Piazza, T. (2008) 'Public health, safety, and educational risks associated with bullying behaviors in American adolescents', *International Journal of Adolescent Medicine and Health*, 20 (2): 223–33.

Stephenson, P. and Smith, D. (1989) 'Bullying in the junior school', in D. Tattum and D. Lane (eds), *Bullying in Schools*. Stoke-on-Trent: Trentham, pp. 45–57.

Stevens, V., De Bourdeaudhuij, I. and Van Ooost, P. (2002) 'Relationship of the family environment to children's involvement in bully/victim problems at school', *Journal of Youth and Adolescence*, 31 (6): 419–28.

Sutton, J. (2003) 'ToM goes to school: social cognition and social values in bullying', in B. Repacholi and V. Slaughter (eds), *Individual Differences in Theory of Mind: Implications for Typical and Atypical Development*. New York: Psychology Press/Taylor & Francis Group, pp. 99–120.

Sutton, J. and Keogh, E. (2000) 'Social competition in school: relationships with bullying, Machiavellianism and personality', *British Journal of Educational Psychology*, 70: 443–56.

Sutton, J., Smith, P. K. and Swettenham, J. (1999a) 'Bullying and "theory of mind": a critique of the "social skills deficit" view of anti-social behaviour', *Social Development*, 8: 117–34.

Sutton, J., Smith, P. K. and Swettenham, J. (1999b) 'Social cognition and bullying: social inadequacy or skilled manipulation?', *British Journal of Developmental Psychology*, 17: 435–50.

Swearer, S. M. and Doll, B. (2001) 'Bullying in schools: an ecological framework', *Journal of Emotional Abuse*, 2 (2/3): 7–23.

Swearer, S. M. and Espelage, D. L. (2004) 'Introduction: a social-ecological framework of bullying among youth', in D. L. Espelage and S. M. Swearer (eds), *Bullying in American Schools: A Social-Ecological Perspective on Prevention and Intervention*. Mahwah, NJ: Lawrence Erlbaum, pp. 1–12.

Symons, D. K. and Clark, S. E. (2000) 'A longitudinal study of mother–child relationships and theory of mind in preschool period', *Social Development*, 9 (1): 3–23.

Toblin, R. L., Schwartz, D., Gorman, A. H. and Abou-ezzeddine, T. (2005) 'Social-cognitive and behavioural attributes of aggressive victims of bullying', *Applied Developmental Psychology*, 26: 329–46.

Tritt, C. and Duncan, R. D. (1997) 'The relationship between childhood bullying and young adult self-esteem and loneliness', *Journal of Humanistic Education and Development*, 36 (1): 35–44.

Ttofi, M. M. and Farrington, D. P. (2008a) 'Bullying: short-term and long-term effects, and the importance of Defiance Theory in explanation and prevention', *Victims and Offenders*, 3 (2/3): 289–312.

Ttofi, M. M. and Farrington, D. P. (2008b) 'Reintegrative shaming theory, moral emotions and bullying behavior', *Aggressive Behavior*, 34 (4): 352–68.

Ttofi, M. M. and Farrington, D. P. (2009a) 'Explaining Teacher Victimization by Secondary School Students: A Randomized Experiment on Defiance Theory'. Unpublished manuscript.

Ttofi, M. M. and Farrington, D. P. (2009b) 'What works in preventing bullying? Effective elements of anti-bullying programmes', *Journal of Aggression, Conflict and Peace Research*, 1: 13–24.

Ttofi, M. M., Farrington, D. P. and Baldry, A. C. (2008) *Effectiveness of Programmes to Reduce School Bullying: A Systematic Review*. Stockholm: Swedish National Council for Crime Prevention.

Unnever, J. D. (2005) 'Bullies, aggressive victims, and victims: are they distinct groups?', *Aggressive Behavior*, 31: 153–71.

Unnever, J. D. and Cornell, D. G. (2003) 'Bullying, self-control, and ADHD', *Journal of Interpersonal Violence*, 18: 129–47.

Vaughn, B. E. (1999) 'Power is knowledge (and vice versa): a commentary on winning some and losing some: a social relations approach to social dominance in toddlers', *Merrill-Palmer Quarterly*, 45: 215–25.

Vinden, P. G. (1997) *Parenting and Theory of Mind*. Paper presented at the biennial meeting of the Society for Research in Child Development, Washington, DC, April.

Vreeman, R. C. and Carroll, A. E. (2007) 'A systematic review of school-based interventions to prevent bullying', *Archives of Pediatrics and Adolescent Medicine*, 161: 78–88.

Warden, D. and Mackinnon, S. (2003) 'Prosocial children, bullies and victims: an investigation of their sociometric status, empathy and social problem-solving strategies', *British Journal of Developmental Psychology*, 21: 367–85.

Welsh, B. C., Farrington, D. P. and Sherman, L. W. (eds) (2001) *Costs and Benefits of Preventing Crime*. Boulder, CO: Westview Press.

White, N. A. and Loeber, R. (2008) 'Bullying and special education as predictors of serious delinquency', *Journal of Research in Crime and Delinquency*, 45 (4): 380–97.

Wolke, D. and Samara, M. M. (2004) 'Bullied by siblings: the association with peer victimization and behaviour problems in Israeli lower secondary school children', *Journal of Child Psychology and Psychiatry*, 45: 1015–29.

Wolke, D., Woods, S., Bloomfield, L. and Karstadt, L. (2000) 'The association between direct and relational bullying and behavior problems among primary school children', *Journal of Child Psychology and Psychiatry*, 41 (8): 989–1002.

Woods, S. and Wolke, D. (2004) 'Direct and relational bullying among primary school children and academic achievement', *Journal of School Psychology*, 42: 135–55.

Woods, S., Hall, L., Sobral, D., Dautenhahn, K. and Wolke, D. (2003) *A Study into the Believability of Animated Characters in the Context of Bullying Intervention*. Paper presented at the 4th International Working Conference on Intelligent Virtual Agents (IVA), Kloster Irsee, Germany.

Zhang, L. and Zhang, S. (2004) 'Reintegrative shaming and predatory delinquency', *Journal of Research in Crime and Delinquency*, 41: 433–53.

Chapter 24

Institutional abuse and children's homes

Jonathan Evans

Introduction

The abuse of children within institutional settings has been well-documented across a range of organisations and domains (Butler 2007; Gallagher 1999a), including custodial institutions (Carlile 2006; Goldson 2008), hospitals (Kendrick and Taylor 2000) and faith communities (Commission to Inquire into Child Abuse 2005). The focus of this chapter, however, is on the abuse of children 'looked after' by local authorities in residential units. It will be shown that such abuse can take a variety of forms, ranging from the physical to the emotional; can be inflicted deliberately, unthinkingly or by neglect; and can be perpetrated by peers, individual staff or, in some senses, by the 'system' itself. Like other forms of 'closed institution' (Goffman 1961), children's homes place their residents (who are anyway likely to be vulnerable as a result of past experiences) in a largely powerless position, often with little opportunity to complain and hence potentially at serious risk of harm from abusive behaviour.

The chapter begins by describing the social work context and giving initial consideration to different definitions of institutional abuse. It highlights the problem of quantifying the extent of such abuse before delineating the inherent risks of residential care for an already vulnerable population. The various types of abuse to which children can be subjected in this setting are explored and competing explanations of the crime are discussed alongside recent measures designed to enhance children's safety. The chapter concludes by locating institutional abuse against the background of wider power relations between children and adults in British society.

Gil (1982: 9) defines the institutional abuse of children as involving

> ... any system, programme, policy or procedure or individual interaction with a child in placement that abuses, neglects or is detrimental to the child's health, safety or emotional and physical well-being, or in any way exploits or violates the child's basic rights.

Like Gil, Stein (2006) expands the definition of institutional abuse beyond the physical site of the children's home to include the wider welfare system of which it is a part. In addition to the categories of individual direct abuse, sanctioned abuse and organised systematic abuse he cites 'system outcome abuse'. This can refer not only to the poor outcomes of care leavers (Social Exclusion Unit (SEU 2005)), but also the corporate neglect of young people represented by planning blight and 'case drift'. Given that the overwhelming majority of children in public care in the United Kingdom are placed outside residential units, mainly in foster care or with members of their extended family, this systemic dimension should not be overlooked. The wider context of public care will therefore be revisited at various points in the account that follows.

In England and Wales there are basically three main groups of young people 'looked after' by the local authority: those accommodated with the voluntary agreement of their parents/carers (Section 20, Children Act 1989); those subject to Care Orders (Section 31, Children Act 1989); and those accommodated compulsorily in relation to either Emergency Protection Orders (Section 44 Children Act 1989) or criminal proceedings (remands for trial and sentencing).

It is worth dwelling for a moment on the Care Order, because it introduces us to the current legal-professional discourse surrounding definitions of abuse and the threshold of harm that must be suffered by a child before robust statutory intervention can be considered. For a Care Order to be made, the court has to be satisfied that '... the child concerned is suffering, or is likely to suffer significant harm' (Section 31(2)(a), Children Act 1989). Judgments about actual or potential 'significant harm' are generally made in relation to one or more of the following categories of child ill treatment: physical injury, sexual abuse, emotional abuse and neglect (Department of Health 1991). The point should be made that children who are accommodated with the voluntary agreement of their parents may also have suffered abuse and neglect. However, because their parents have agreed to cooperate with social services, in some cases applications for Care Orders may not have been considered necessary by the local authority. One should therefore be cautious about delineating hierarchies of vulnerability based solely on young people's legal status within the care system.

While social workers are required to work in partnership with children, families and other agencies (Department of Health 1991, 1999; Department for Education and Skills 2004) it is important to acknowledge that the balance of power is weighted in favour of the professional. Thus, when a Care Order is made, the rhetoric of partnership is invoked because parental responsibility is 'shared' between parents and the local authority. Nevertheless, no one leaves the courtroom doubting that the senior partners in this legal arrangement are social workers. Power can, of course, also be exercised without a court order. The chill shadow cast by the implied threat of a Care Order may sometimes be sufficient to persuade recalcitrant parents to change their child-rearing practices and general behaviour. Moreover, there will be some cases where parents simply concede defeat to professional power without a fight, their sense of relative powerlessness persuading them that it is better to consent 'freely' to a child being accommodated than a Care Order being made. This is not a criticism of social work practice per se; rather it is intended as a plain description of the typical dynamics at work between – on the one hand – middle-class professionals charged with the weighty responsibility of protecting and promoting the welfare of vulnerable children and – on the other – generally poor working-class parents struggling with acute financial hardship and often complex sets of associated problems such as addiction, physical ill health and mental illness. Social workers are thus required to make nuanced judgments about whether a child's interests are best served by removal from the family or concerted efforts to stabilise chaotic and potentially dangerous home circumstances through the provision of more support in the community. Seldom are these choices straightforward and whichever decision is taken will result in some negative outcomes.

As will be apparent from the foregoing account, social work is a necessarily messy business. It is also, as Pithouse (1998) describes it, an 'invisible trade' in which the tricky negotiations and risky compromises of daily practice are for the most part concealed from public view. Like all street-level bureaucrats (Lipsky 1980) social workers occupy the shadowlands of social policy: a difficult and dimly lit terrain where 'clear' legal principles must be interpreted and applied in the confusing emotional and evidential fog that surrounds practice. Official guidance can never really provide definitive route maps for practitioners, the boundaries between consent and coercion being continuously redrawn and smudged. In social work, professional judgment is the imperfect compass that must guide the practitioner.

There is, however, another dimension to the ambiguity that lies at the heart of the social work enterprise. There is a sense of ambivalence in wider British society in respect of the uneasy nexus of relationships that exists between adults, children and the state. There appears to be a residual cultural resistance to the idea of children possessing rights independently of adults in general and parents in particular. It is partly for this reason that suspicion is aroused when the state seeks to intervene in family life. It should be recalled that social workers are not only criticised for failing to protect vulnerable children (Colwell Report 1974; Laming 2003), but also for overly zealous intervention (Clyde Report 1992; Secretary of State for Social Services 1988). Indeed, the shortcomings and inadequacies of the unloved childcare professional generate more public and media comment than the state of adult–child power relations in society at large.

One further aspect of adults' relationship with children should be mentioned at this juncture: the language of child maltreatment. Morgan and Zedner (1992) have pointed out that child victims are marginalised by the use of the euphemism 'abuse' rather than the clear and unequivocal description of such criminal acts as physical assault, sexual assault and rape. The current discourse of abuse risks softening the true impact of the crimes committed against children by adults and, by implication, mitigating the culpability of those responsible. Writing in another context, Cohen (1985: 276) has described the use of 'special vocabularies' as a means of obscuring and disguising meaning. As far as the subject under discussion is concerned, it is certainly possible for something to be lost in translation between welfare and criminal justice discourses. It is worth reflecting on whether the language we use throws a blanket over the uncomfortable truths of child victimisation, leaving children in the traditional British position of being seen and not heard. Children in public care, particularly those in residential units, undoubtedly suffer from low visibility. While it is true that their welfare is duly overseen and regulated by the appropriate inspectorates and 'institutional watchdogs' (Brandstrom and Kuipers 2003: 281), they generally occupy the peripheral vision of the public eye. This places them in a particularly vulnerable position. The themes of children's visibility and voice are therefore particularly important in any discussion of institutional abuse.

Scale, patterns and trends

The nature and extent of child abuse is difficult to assess as it is generally perpetrated in the private or semi-private domains of family and substitute care. While awareness of child cruelty developed in the nineteenth century, it virtually disappeared from view in the inter-war years of the twentieth century (Sen *et al.* 2008), the notable exception being a Home Office Committee in 1926 that considered sexual offences against young people (Parker 1995: 5). In 1944 concerns about the quality of the public care system were famously raised in a letter from Lady Allen of Hurtwood to *The Times* and a subsequent pamphlet she authored entitled *Whose Children?* (Allen 1944). She argued that staff were insensitive, inexperienced and ill-equipped to deal with the emotional and physical needs of children in their care. Moreover, the children's homes appeared to be organised around the convenience of staff rather than the needs of young people. The process of institutionalisation was also extended to depriving children of their own personal belongings. The themes highlighted in this early pamphlet anticipated some of the concerns that would be articulated in later reports and inquiries.

The subsequent establishment of government inquiries into the state of residential provision (Hendrick 1994) investigated some of these concerns. The findings of the Curtis Committee (1946) in England and Wales and the Clyde Committee (1946) in Scotland duly influenced the subsequent drafting of the Children Act 1948. Both Committees expressed a clear preference for foster care over residential provision. Ironically, this followed the widely reported death of a 13-year-old child at the hands of his foster parents (Monckton 1945). Despite the vulnerability of children to abuse in other care settings (Gallagher 1999b; White 2003), the ideological conviction that residential care should be a 'last resort' remains something of an article of faith for many child welfare policymakers and practitioners.

While awareness of child abuse within family settings was subsequently raised by a series of public inquiries into child deaths, particularly following the case of Maria Colwell (Colwell 1974), abuse within residential settings began to come to light with a series of scandals that broke in the 1980s and 1990s (Levy and Kahan 1991; Williams and McCreadie 1992; Kirkwood 1993; Utting 1997; Waterhouse 2000). As a result, any discussion of residential care is overshadowed by the history of the scandals of recent history (Butler and

Drakeford 2005). Despite this, the concept of institutional abuse has only belatedly entered the discourse of child protection practice and research in the UK (Barter 2003: 2; Butler 2007: 182–2), although greater awareness of the issue has been evident in the USA for some time (Garrett 1979).

Barter (2003) and Gallagher (2000) have noted the methodological problems that beset attempts to estimate the numbers of those affected by institutional abuse. Nevertheless, studies in the USA (Rindfleisch and Rabb 1984; Powers et al. 1990; Blatt 1992; New York State Commission 1992) and the UK (Westcott and Clement 1992) conclude that the incidence of child abuse within institutions is higher than that within the wider population of children living in the community. It is also assumed, of course, that much abuse goes undetected and unreported, a point highlighted in the Waterhouse Report (2000), an inquiry that investigated 259 complaints in relation to physical assault, emotional abuse and the sexual exploitation of children in the residential care of Clwyd and Gwynedd County Councils between 1974 and 1990. Rindfleisch and Rabb (1984) found in their study an institutional abuse incidence rate of 10 per thousand. The New York State Commission (1992), meanwhile, estimated a higher rate of abuse in residential institutions at 87 per thousand children compared with 28 per thousand in the general child population. These estimates must, however, be treated with considerable caution. Moreover, given differences between the USA and UK in legal and professional terminology, comparative analysis is difficult. What does seem to be clear, though, is that the pattern of abuse is gendered, with girls more likely to be subjected to sexual assault and boys to physical abuse (Rosenthal et al. 1991; Westcott and Clement 1992). The gendered nature of abuse within residential settings nevertheless remains an under-researched area (Green 2005, 2006).

It should be mentioned here that some have questioned the safety of the convictions of residential workers involved in institutional abuse cases (Beckett 2002; Webster 2005; Smith 2008). Particular concern has been expressed over the use of 'trawling' techniques by the police in historic abuse cases, as in the North Wales inquiry. It has also been argued that some former residents may have been motivated to fabricate stories of abuse in order to gain financial compensation. While it is reasonable to question the police methods used in some cases, it is worth weighing against this concern the fact that very few prosecutions for perverting the course of justice have been brought by the police (Home Affairs Committee 2002: para. 20). Moreover, given the number of public inquiries that have taken place since 1985 it should also be borne in mind that no legal actions or claims for damages have been lodged in the intervening period (Butler and Drakeford 2005). For a fuller discussion on this whole subject, readers are referred to Sen and colleagues (2008).

The institutional context and the population at risk

In both the eighteenth and nineteenth centuries socially problematic populations tended to be dealt with via institutional means: the mentally ill were accommodated in asylums, criminals in penitentiaries and the poor in workhouses, while from 1854 delinquent children could be sent to reformatories. However, Mary Carpenter's horizons extended beyond those young people who broke the criminal code. The Industrial Schools Act 1857 (and the 1866 consolidating measure) was the formal embodiment of the concern felt for those young people at risk of offending: children in 'need of care and protection' (1866 Act, cited in May 1973: 110) and those who were 'beyond their parents' control' (1857 Act, cited in May 1973: 111). These embryonic Care Orders effectively brought a wide range of working-class children under the disciplinary control of the missionary middle classes. While the classificatory integrity of the 'child in need of care and protection', the 'moral orphan' and the 'juvenile delinquent' may have been difficult to maintain in practice, the fact remains that 'troubled children' as well as 'children in trouble' were targeted for institutional intervention of one sort or another.

While the nineteenth century witnessed enthusiasm for institutional solutions to childcare problems in England and Wales (in Scotland the tradition of 'boarding out' was generally favoured), after the Second World War there was a clear policy preference for fostering. It was in the last quarter of the twentieth century, though, that the residential care sector declined sharply, partly due to the scandals that came to light in the 1980s and 1990s (Butler and Drakeford 2005). The present position is that over 70 per cent of all young people in care in the UK are in foster care while some 10–12 per cent are accommodated in residential units (DCSF 2009). At any given time, therefore, the population in the residential sector hovers somewhere between 8,000 and 9,000. Taylor (2006) points out that care careers vary enormously. Many children will, for example, only be accommodated in residential settings for comparatively short periods while others will be long-stay residents. Most of these children live in small units with good staff–resident ratios. As the average number of residents per unit is currently only seven (Taylor 2006) it is important to dispel those evocative folk memories of large, gloomy and forbidding Dickensian institutions. As in other public service domains, a mixed economy of welfare prevails, with the private sector often providing more specialist therapeutic environments. The residential sector is diverse and heterogeneous in terms of regime, ethos and therapeutic rationale. The quality of provision is also extremely variable (Sinclair and Gibbs 1998). It is important to stress that good work with young people is undertaken in many children's homes. For some children, therefore, residential placements represent a positive choice rather than a 'last resort'. Indeed, because of their own troubled backgrounds some prefer an emotionally neutral atmosphere to the dynamics of family life in a foster placement. There are also young people who regard foster care as undermining loyalties and relationships to birth families (Save the Children 2001; Sinclair and Gibbs 1998). Some well-managed residential establishments can therefore provide forms of support to young people that both respect and promote their sense of personal autonomy. The simplistic formula of 'foster care good, residential bad' should therefore be abjured.

Nevertheless, the overall reduction in the size of the residential sector has had some deleterious effects on the quality of provision available to young people (Utting 1997; Hayden et al. 1999) and consequently on the risks of abuse. Firstly, there has been a reduction in the placement choice available, so that some residential units are accommodating children with radically different profiles and very diverse needs. This can result in units failing to serve the interests of many of their residents, with some children at risk of being preyed upon by more damaged, delinquent or sophisticated peers. Secondly, young people are more likely to live at a greater distance away from their families and communities. Thirdly, as Green (2005: 454) observes:

> The age of the children who live in residential child-care establishments has been increasing as the number of homes available is decreasing (in conjunction with the ideological preference for fostering). The group catered for currently in residential care is, therefore, now disproportionately adolescent, manifesting challenging behaviour, psychological problems and having experienced disrupted and often abusive family backgrounds.

Many of these young people will also have care histories that include failed foster placements. For them, therefore, the residential unit really is a 'last resort'.

Most importantly, whatever their route into public care, the personal histories of residents of children's homes are likely to involve family backgrounds in which episodes of abuse (physical, sexual and/or emotional) or extended periods of neglect have played a significant part. Others will be accommodated because their parents simply cannot cope with the demands of child-rearing, in some cases due to disability, ill health and bereavement within the family. Clearly, these are children who have experienced varying degrees of trauma and emotional disorientation and as such they are not only likely to exhibit major emotional and behavioural problems, but are particularly vulnerable to further abuse and exploitation. Those with a history of sexual abuse, for example, are at a higher risk of repeat victimisation (Colton and Vanstone 1996; Macleod 1999). Those with disabilities (Crosse *et al.* 1993) are also in an extremely vulnerable position.

Inherent risks in residential care

Sadly, there are certain aspects of the looked-after system that replicate the chaotic, neglectful and abusive home circumstances from which the children who populate it have been 'rescued'. Many looked-after children's care careers are characterised by multiple placements (Brandon and Thorburn 2008; Jackson 2002; DfES 2003) and, because of high staff turnover, many changes in social worker. It is against the background of a fragile economy of welfare services that planning blight and case drift can easily occur. At a time when the literature is emphasising the beneficial influence that can be brought to bear on young people by mentors and 'trusted adults' (SEU: 2005), it is a matter for concern that children in care experience difficulty in forming secure attachments with both family members and social work staff (Taylor 2006).

More specifically, residential units present a number of inherent risks to those living in them. Indeed, there are some institutional parallels between children's homes and custodial facilities. First of all, they share the basic characteristics of all 'closed institutions' as described by Goffman (1961) and others: limited rights, voicelessness and vulnerability to staff who have virtually total power over them. Although it is generally easier to abscond from a children's home than escape from a prison, it should be remembered that when young people are eventually caught they are returned to the care of the local authority. In some cases these young people will be placed in secure accommodation. While such secure placements are undoubtedly underpinned by welfare principles, they are also unquestionably total institutions. There is a fine dividing line between 'protective' institutional care and 'punitive' custody. While institutional regimes can be informed by contrasting philosophies – *soft-centred* treatment on the one hand and *hard-edged* disciplinary training on the other – what they have in common is the turn of a key. Child confinement is just one area of practice where *welfare* and *punishment* can appear indistinguishable, especially to the child behind the locked door.

Secondly, in common with prison, living in a residential unit can lead to the attenuation of family and community ties. Like the first-time prisoner, the young person entering a residential unit has to negotiate a *modus vivendi* with the existing peer culture. If the young person is fortunate, the culture of the unit will be prosocial. Typically, though, a children's home will include young people with a range of problems, difficulties and challenging behaviours. There is research evidence which suggests that some units are dominated by a macho and delinquent culture (Barter *et al.* 2004; Green 2005). What needs to be recognised here is that it is young people's priority to enjoy a good relationship with the other residents. One young person in Taylor's (2006: 87) study expressed this well:

> ... you've got to get on with the people who live there 'cos you're living there 24 hours a day. I mean staff, you get staff that help, you get staff that don't help, but staff that help are only there like certain days a week. There's no one there constant ... the only people who are there constant are the people who are living there, so that's who you've got to get on with.

This can quite often lead to young people engaging in substance misuse, violence, unsafe sex and criminal activity (Barter *et al.* 2004; Green 2005; Taylor 2006). In extreme cases an aggressive and intimidating peer culture within a residential unit can generate chronic peer abuse. The pecking orders and macho hierarchies of some children's homes have been rendered vividly (Barter *et al.* 2004; Green 2005). These hierarchies can be enforced brutally through physical and sexual assaults, although such abuse may be regarded by the perpetrators – and sometimes even the victims – as normative behaviour, sometimes linked to initiation rites. Green (2005: 470), for example, cites one female ex-resident who says:

> I've woken up a few times in care ... and there's been a lad trying to put his penis in my mouth ... they did it for a joke ... mainly to the new girls who came in.

Although the type of behaviours described above will take place when staff are not present, residential units are nevertheless an environment within which young people are closely observed. The welfare spotlight trained by social work staff on children, like Foucault's (1973, 1977) 'clinical gaze', is not always benign. The insights offered by the literature on labelling (Becker 1963; Lemert 1951) and deviancy amplification (Wilkins 1964; Cohen 1972) help our understanding of some of the processes at work in this institutional setting. Thus, 'problematic' actions and behaviours that in other settings would go unobserved are here recorded, analysed and reported to field social workers and case conferences. Those behaviours, moreover, risk being explained in terms of what is already known about the background of the young people concerned. This can lead to the 'identification' of pathologies and the application of diagnostic labels to behaviour that in another context might be regarded as fairly normal adolescent conduct – in some cases sparking a reaction ('kicking off') that leads to further control measures and so on.

Furthermore, one of the under-reported scandals of residential child care is the way in which young people's challenging behaviour can be criminalised (NACRO 2003; Taylor 2006; Darker *et al.* 2008). It is inconceivable that most families would involve the police when a child breaks a cup or damages a door, yet this still seems to be the practice of many local authorities who are acting *in loco parentis*. The safety of residential staff is a serious issue, but to divert vulnerable children from the domain of welfare into a criminal justice system that could prove toxic to their safety and welfare is a risk that some local authority personnel in children's services are clearly still prepared to countenance. It is difficult to understand how such practices can ever be squared with the Children Act 1989 or the UN Convention on the Rights of the Child. It is encouraging to know that some local authorities address challenging behaviour in children's homes without recourse to criminal justice remedies (NACRO 2003).

Abuse by staff

The foregoing discussion has identified some of the inherent dangers of grouping together damaged and difficult young people. Even under the supervision of well trained and caring staff, further damage may still be inflicted on them by wider systemic weaknesses or the abusive behaviour of peers, while unreflective staff responses to misbehaviour may push them unnecessarily into the criminal justice system. However, as serious as all these forms of abuse can be, there is little doubt that the worst cases of institutional abuse are those in which children have been directly abused by staff – particularly those where it has happened repeatedly and over long periods. Abuse by staff can come in a number of forms. It can involve physical, sexual and emotional abuse; it can be committed by individuals or by groups acting in concert; and it can involve different degrees of intent. Let us first consider both the degree of intent (*mens rea*) present and the extent to which responsibility for the crimes committed can be attributed to identifiable individuals.

As far as the issue of intent is concerned, it is clear that physical assaults and sexual offences are often committed with conscious purpose, although some physical assaults may be perpetrated in the belief that 'reasonable' physical restraints are being applied to the challenging behaviour of difficult young people. Those who engage in emotional abuse can sometimes be woefully unaware of the effect their behaviour is having on children, but equally such behaviour can be deliberate and calculated. Likewise neglect can be knowing or the result of ignorance and incompetence.

Responsibility, meanwhile, can be considered at both individual and corporate levels. The residential worker who abuses a 'looked-after' child is clearly responsible as an individual, although questions may be asked about whether there is any corporate culpability on the part of the local authority in terms of recruitment, staff supervision and the implementation of policies designed to safeguard children. In some instances, where there is a clear failure to discharge statutory responsibilities, it may be possible to hold a local authority to account for the corporate neglect of children in its care. Corporate sins of omission, where responsibility is dispersed, can result in the dilution of culpability. Nevertheless, individuals who work within child welfare systems should not be absolved. As Thomas (1990: 10) reminds us, these are '... inert structures awaiting human operationalisation'. The animating role of human agency in social structures should therefore never be forgotten.

A helpful distinction can be made between 'organised abuse' and those forms of abuse supported by belief systems or peculiar variants of occupational and organisational culture. According to Bibby (1996: 5–6) organised abuse is conducted in a systematic way by more than one individual and is characterised by '... the degree of planning in the purposeful, secret targeting, seduction and silencing of the subjects'. Butler (2007: 184) cites the case of Frank Beck in Leicestershire as an example of organised abuse. Beck, a predatory paedophile, used the organisational cover of a residential setting to perpetrate a series of sexual offences against children. The abuse scandal in North Wales children's homes documented in the Waterhouse Report (2000) would also fall into this category. In many respects it is unsurprising that some paedophiles target employment opportunities where they can have access to socially isolated and vulnerable young people (Barter 2003). Although some research has been done on the characteristics of such predatory offenders (Green 2001) there is clearly a need for further work in this area

The scandal in Staffordshire children's homes in the 1980s (Staffordshire County Council 1991), however, represents a set of abusive practices that are qualitatively different. The case is instructive and worth considering in detail because it contains elements of programme abuse that were supported by an organisational and occupational culture which somehow failed to recognise that the abuse was taking place. Programme abuse typically includes routine practices that are supposedly founded upon 'expert knowledge' or practice wisdom. It might take the form of managing difficult behaviour with the inappropriate use of medication (Shaughnessy 1984) or the zealous implementation of 'therapeutic' practices based on dubious research evidence. Programme abuse can on occasion illustrate perfectly the Shavian notion of professions being conspiracies against the laity. That the conspirators may often believe in what they are doing is not disputed. Good intentions and passionately held principles do not necessarily prevent the infliction of harmful therapies on a captive clientele.

Drakeford and Butler (2007) identify two main types of scandal in the field of social welfare. There are those scandals that '... arise from a single dramatic event and are immediately and unavoidably apparent to those involved in them' (p. 220) and then there are others, like the Pindown scandal (Staffordshire County Council 1991), that arise

> ... not from incidents, but from institutions. This sort of scandal ... exposes not sudden and traumatic events, but the shining of light onto practices which had, in most cases, gone on for a long time and, in some, with considerable official approval. (Drakeford and Butler 2007: 220–1)

The Pindown regime that was implemented in a number of Staffordshire children's homes between 1983 and 1989 was essentially a set of practices that developed to address challenging behaviour by children and young people. The term 'Pindown' was first coined by Tony Latham, the principal exponent of the regime, when he apparently explained that 'we must pin down the problem' while at the same time 'he gestured with his forefinger pointing towards the floor' (Staffordshire County Council 1991: 12.18). However, the underlying rationale was presumably meant to be helpful to the young people rather than punitive. This is reflected in the use of the term 'therapeutic pindown' (Butler and Drakeford 2005: 195) on some occasions. While residents experienced the regime as restrictive and humiliating, the underlying aim of the programme was seemingly to provide clear boundaries and structure for residents. As described in the official inquiry report (Staffordshire County Council 1991), it had four key elements:

> Firstly isolation for part of the time in a children's home cordoned off as a 'special' or Pindown unit; secondly removal of ordinary clothing for part of the time and the enforced wearing of shorts or night clothes; thirdly being told of having to earn 'privileges'; and fourthly being allowed to attend school or a 'school room' in the unit, and changing back into shorts or night clothes from school. (para. 2.15)

The reality of this regime is brought home vividly in evidence given to the inquiry by three male residents who had been found by the police after they had absconded from a Staffordshire children's home:

> Each recalled that after being handed over by the police, they had their clothes removed, probably at The Birches, and were then taken to 245 Hartshill Road in their underpants without shoes ... The boys were all put into the same room. This had initially been empty but after ...

they moved the furniture, it contained a table and upright chairs. They were required to have a cold shower, then ½ hour to keep fit ... They were given cheese on toast, tea and 'even a fag' ... They then went to bed, sleeping in a second room on mattresses on the floor with no other bedding ... the next morning they were required to do physical exercises outdoors in their underwear ... the boys were told ... they would have to earn back their clothes. (paras 4.40–4.42)

It is worth recalling that these children were not criminals; they were in the care of the local authority in order that their welfare could be promoted.

There was, of course, a huge gap between what practitioners thought they were doing and the perceptions of the children. The report observes that:

... in the vast majority of cases the children perceived Pindown with its supposed panoply of meetings, reviews, contracts and attempts to establish a structure of understanding and trust, as a narrow, punitive and harshly restrictive experience. We think their perceptions are correct. (para. 12.5)

Although Tony Latham was the persuasive advocate of Pindown, the regime depended upon a willing group of staff to implement the practices described above. There is no hint of these being 'crimes of obedience' committed by a defeated, demoralised or deferential workforce. These were true believers.

Tony Latham, with an excess of enthusiasm and energy, hoped to control those he saw as difficult adolescents by use of a system designed to provide individualised programming and the development of social skills. The grim reality, however, was quite different ... We can only think that Tony Latham, a person of drive, energy and ability, who had contributed much in other areas of Staffordshire, lost sight of ... minimum standards of behaviour and professional practice which are essential to a fair and sympathetic approach to children in care ... It is a matter of great regret, in our opinion, that so many were prepared to be enthusiastic practitioners of Pindown. We would hope that the frank and explicit nature of the records and comments in the logbooks only represent a temporary aberration on their part. (para. 22.2)

What is really troubling, though, is that the Pindown regime appears to have operated with the tacit approval of both management and staff within the local authority (Butler and Drakeford 2005: 195–220). The scandal did not come to light as a result of a whistleblower from practice or management. Nor did any concerns emerge as a result of an Inspectorate Report. The scandal was exposed through work undertaken by a local solicitor and the subsequent interest taken by a local newspaper. At a later stage the National Association of Young People in Care took up some of the issues that arose from the case. The failure of professional people to recognise abuse within their own organisation is, in many respects, the most puzzling and disturbing aspect of the case. In cases like Pindown it takes someone from outside the institution, organisation or profession to shine a light on the abusive practices that have somehow become normative. Perpetrators and their collaborators emerge blinking and bewildered in the bright light, seemingly wondering what all the fuss is about.

Explanations of abuse

Explanations for the type of abuse represented by the Pindown case are more difficult to explain than, for example, the infiltration of residential units by determined paedophiles, although, of course, the aetiological accounts of sex offending against children is in itself extremely complex. Clearly, though, explanations for such cases as Pindown should consider the literature on occupational socialisation (Jenne and Kersting 1998; Welland 2001), organisations (Gouldner 1954) and institutional life (Goffman 1961). Hierarchical structures, bureaucratic procedures and managerial philosophies are likely to impact on the individual worker's belief systems as much as professional training and personal values. It has been a long-standing complaint that the majority of those working in residential units are less well trained that their fieldwork counterparts (Levy and Kahan 1991; Utting 1991). In the 'disciplined organisation', though, even well qualified practitioners are seemingly capable of being brought into line. It is also important to recognise that residential institutions are not gender-neutral entities (Green 2005). The perpetrators of physical and sexual abuse are overwhelmingly male (Rosenthal *et al.* 1991; Blatt 1992; Westcott and Clement 1992; Barter 1997; Macleod 1999). The role of 'macho' management cultures that encourage leadership without listening may also contribute indirectly to institutional abuse. Indeed, power imbalances in relation to gender, sexuality, age and ethnicity are central to understanding the dynamics of children's homes and the wider organisations to which they belong.

It is a matter of debate whether most residential units fall into the category of 'total institutions' (Goffman 1961). Clearly local authority secure accommodation units are, by definition, such institutions. While many residents will be admitted to secure accommodation for offending behaviour, others are placed there because they are self-harming or likely to put themselves at risk of harm if they live in the community. Interestingly, O'Neill (2001) found that the majority of boys entered secure units via a criminal justice route whereas most girls arrived from the welfare system. Such a mixed population of residents not only raises issues about safety and risk, but also about the contested nature of the regime's dominant ethos. Goldson (2002) has, indeed, expressed concern about secure units being dominated by criminal justice concerns.

In most residential units children are able to leave the premises to attend school, maintain contact with family, visit friends and engage in community-based activities. Nevertheless, the children's home represents a large, if not defining, feature of their lives. Inevitably, therefore, some characteristics of the 'total institution' will leave an imprint on the social identities of both residents and workers. Some young people from children's homes certainly report feeling different to their peers and believe they are treated differently by teachers and other children. Lindsay has written about 'careism' as a form of discrimination (Lindsay 1996). Whether the experience of residential care leads to the 'mortification of the self' as described by Goffman (1961) will depend largely on the nature of the institution and the resilience of the child concerned. Nevertheless, the social identities of both staff and children cannot be entirely unaffected when so much time is spent in an institutional environment.

Residential units for children also occupy a point of intersection between private and public domains. For the resident the unit is meant to be a 'home': a personal and domestic space. Even for committed, skilled and sensitive members of staff the children's home is by contrast ultimately a workplace. Daily life in a residential unit thus becomes an ongoing negotiation about where the boundaries between these two worlds should be drawn. Even in a well-managed home with a democratic ethos, the tensions at the heart of such an institution can never be resolved completely. In a home where the staff take a more authoritarian line, sometimes for understandable reasons, the dynamics can assume the character of a bitter power struggle. In such circumstances, of course, there is also the risk of abusive practices developing.

Living and working in an institution can lead to a distorted sense of perspective. The outside world may sometimes seem remote. Yet despite the feeling of insularity and sometimes the development of a bunker mentality, it is important to recognise that institutions are not islands; they are socially and culturally situated. As Butler (2007: 181) observes, '... institutional practices are embedded in the prevailing social construction of childhood and in the dominant professional cultures of the period.' In other words, there is a relationship between what happens within the walls of a residential unit and what happens to children in the rest of society. Thus, if a series of physical assaults on a child that are considered 'capable of causing any social services department concern' are then sanctioned by the Civil Appeal Court on the grounds that the 'reasonable physical chastisement of children by parents is not yet unlawful in this country' (BBC News 2009), then we should not be too surprised if this is reflected to some degree by the way residential staff manage difficult children in their charge. In the case of Pindown one may also wish to reflect on whether some public school alumni would be less shocked than others by the robust management of delinquent behaviour that took place in Staffordshire.

It has been suggested Britain is a place that doesn't like young people (Haines and Drakeford 1998; Pearson 1983, 1993, 1994); a view apparently echoed by the UN Committee on the Rights of the Child (2008) and the Council of Europe (2008). The work of Hendrick (1994, 1997) would suggest we have a tendency to over-sentimentalise some of our children while simultaneously demonising others. Jenks (1996) identifies Apollonian and Dionysian discourses at work in the social construction of childhood: on the one hand the innocent in need of protection, on the other the hedonist requiring discipline and control.

Even if children are not constructed as angels or devils, they are often represented in terms of transition or perceived deficits. Rather than being valued as children and young people with developing competences they are instead represented as incomplete adults, as 'human becomings' rather than 'human beings' (Qvortrup 1994). This view of childhood lends itself to a paternalistic approach to child protection and welfare. While the Children Act 1989 does promote the idea of consulting children on their views, this goes against the cultural grain. The abuse of children in the UK therefore needs to be understood in this wider social context. Although the UK is a signatory to the UN Convention on the Rights of the Child, unlike the countries of Scandinavia it does not really possess a mature and active children's rights culture (Butler and Drakeford 2005). Young people enjoy only conditional citizenship: they are not really trusted to exercise their rights responsibly and are thus excluded routinely from matters that should concern them. When they do speak children are often not listened to, and when they complain, they tend not to be believed.

If the general position of children in Britain is one of relative powerlessness, partly because of the way we construct them, then the situation of young people in care is considerably worse. At best public attitudes to children in residential care appear to be ambivalent. It has already been argued that perceptions of these children have been tainted by historical associations stretching back to the Poor Law. Although there has always been sympathy for the abandoned and abused child, the street urchin living by wit and petty crime has tended to elicit more authoritarian and disciplinary responses. The perennial problem for the British has been one of classification. Who deserves our protection and who needs to be punished? In the case of children in care, this simplistic binary worldview has come under increasing pressure.

The 1908 Children Act eroded the boundaries between the old industrial schools (for neglected children) and the reformatories (for young offenders). In doing this it facilitated movement between these two populations (Stewart 1995). Thus there developed a more ambiguous public and professional reaction to young people in the care system. This ambiguity was further intensified later in the century by the 1969 Children and Young Persons Act which gave magistrates the power to effectively 'sentence' children to Care Orders for criminal acts. As Hayden et al. (1999: 24) observe: 'Children in care (particularly residential care) began to be seen as young criminals being given an easy ride by the courts rather than as those deserving of public sympathy.' It could be argued that the sense of stigma described here has survived the abolition of those sentencing powers. Young people in care, particularly teenagers in residential units, still tend to be associated with trouble rather than vulnerability.

Responses to institutional abuse

Revelations of institutional abuse since the mid-1980s have led to prosecutions, civil actions on the part of victims and a long string of public inquiries. Most of the inquiry reports have concentrated on safeguarding children by improving management systems, staff supervision and complaints and whistleblowing procedures. They have also sharpened the focus of inspection arrangements. While many of these recommendations have been unobjectionable and generally worthy, there is a danger of responding to complex issues with proceduralist solutions. In fairness, though, there has been a raft of government-led initiatives designed to improve child welfare, of which services to looked-after children are integral. These include *Quality Protects* (DoH 1998), *Children First* (Welsh Assembly Government, Children First website n.d.), *Every Child Matters* (DfES 2004) and the Children Act 2004. The Leaving Care Act 2000 also represents a serious effort to extend support to vulnerable young people as they negotiate the difficult transition from public care to independent living.

The government has recently signalled its continuing concern about the state of residential care and, at the time of writing, is giving active consideration to alternative means of supporting looked-after children (Gentleman 2009). These include securing places for looked-after children in private boarding schools (which would be less expensive than maintaining them in residential units), an American-style foster carer support scheme and social pedagogy. Social pedagogy is an educational model favoured in some parts of continental Europe, notably in Germany and Denmark. There are various models applied in different countries, but Petrie *et al.* (2006: 22), identify a set of core principles that include a holistic view of the child, the recognition of children's rights and the establishment of genuinely warm and stable relationships between staff and residents where '... children and staff are seen as inhabiting the same life space, not as existing in separate hierarchical domains'.

The social work profession can certainly learn some lessons from social pedagogy, but given the recent history of scandal in Britain's children's homes it is important that another bout of therapeutic optimism does not cloud our judgment. It should not prevent us from recognising that the risks of institutional abuse would still remain.

The ability of practitioners to make nuanced and independent professional judgments on the basis of carefully weighted evidence is widely appreciated. Consequently, the need to improve the quality of social work practice is reprised in most public inquiry reports that deal with the ill-treatment or murder of children. In response to these concerns social work education and training has been reviewed and reformed in recent years, but whether it has really moved much beyond a reductive, competence-based approach remains to be seen.

Given the way in which unsuitable people have been appointed to positions of power and responsibility in the childcare field, a key issue has been the recruitment, vetting and registration of staff. Although assessing whether a person is suitable for work with children is not a straightforward matter, rigorous and regular enhanced criminal record checks are an important first step. In the circumstances, the Care Standards Act 2000 is to be welcomed. The General Social Care Council (and its counterparts in the Celtic nations) established by the Act monitors and maintains a register of social work staff.

While the above developments represent important reforms and improvements, probably the most effective safeguard for children's welfare is to ensure their voices are heard. To that end more attention has been given in recent years to developing advocacy services for young people in care. The current provision can probably be best described as uneven, but evaluative work on what constitutes effective practice has been undertaken (Boylan and Ing 2005; Emond 2008).

The Waterhouse Report (2000) also recognised the vital importance of listening to young people in care, something that had not happened in the North Wales children's homes covered by the inquiry. The key recommendation of appointing an ombudsperson or children's champion was duly accepted and implemented: the first independent Children's Commissioner in the UK was appointed in Wales. The role extended beyond the care system to include all children in Wales (Seneviratne 2001). The other countries of the UK subsequently followed suit by appointing their own Commissioners on much the same basis. These are encouraging developments, but there is still a long way to go before it can be claimed that an active children's rights culture is rooted in everyday practice. When young people from care are routinely participating in inspections of children's homes (Stevens 2006) then we will know that progress is being made. If there is one clear message that emerges from the truly depressing history of institutional abuse, it is that the effective protection of children is inextricably connected to their empowerment (Butler 2007).

Selected further reading

Butler (2007) provides an authoritative overview on the subject of institutional abuse in children's residential settings while Sen *et al.* (2008) review the lessons learnt from the abuse of young people in Scottish children's homes. The contributors to Courtney and Iwaniec's (2009) *Residential Care of Children*, meanwhile, present a comparative picture of the wider issues involved in working with children in institutional settings. Although by no means devoted exclusively to the abuse of young people in children's homes, Butler and Drakeford's book (2005) provides a highly engaging account of the role played by public inquiries in scandal generation and the development of social policy. Barter *et al.* (2004) and Green (2005) depict vividly the often violent and intimidating culture that can apparently flourish in some children's homes. Attention is duly drawn to gender relations; Green, in particular, highlights the role of conquestual, hegemonic modes of masculinity among both residents and staff members. Taylor (2006) also explores residential unit cultures, but with particular reference to the relationship between public care and the criminal justice system.

As far as websites are concerned, official government sources provide reliable information and useful links: England (http://www.dcsf.gov.uk), Wales (http://wales.gov.uk/topics/childrenyoungpeople) and Scotland (http://www.scotland.gov.uk/topics/Young-People). Websites designed to provide independent advice and assistance to young people include Voices from Care (http://www.vfcc.org.uk) and the Who Cares? Trust (http://www.thewhocarestrust.org.uk).

References

Allen, M. (1944) *Whose Children?* London: Simkin Marshall.
Barter, C. (1997) 'Who's to blame: conceptualising institutional abuse by children', *Early Child Development and Care*, 133: 101–4.

Barter, C. (2003) *Abuse of Children in Residential Care*, NSPCC Information Briefing, October. Online at: http://www.nspcc.org.uk/inform.

Barter, C., Renold, E., Berridge, D. and Cawson, P. (2004) *Peer Violence in Children's Residential Care*. Basingstoke: Palgrave Macmillan.

BBC News (2009) 'Judges rule on child discipline', 1 August. Online at: http://news.bbc.co.uk/go/pr/fr/-hi/wales/8179613.stm.

Becker, H. (1963) *Outsiders: Studies in the Sociology of Deviance*. New York: Free Press.

Beckett, C. (2002) 'The witch-hunt metaphor (and accusations against child residential care workers)', *British Journal of Social Work*, 32: 621–8.

Bibby, P. C. (1996) *Organised Abuse: The Current Debate*. Aldershot: Arena.

Blatt, E. (1992) 'Factors associated with child abuse and neglect in residential care settings', *Children and Youth Services Review*, 14: 493–517.

Boylan, J. and Ing, P. (2005) '"Seen but not heard" – young people's experience of advocacy', *International Journal of Social Welfare*, 14 (1): 2–12.

Brandon, M. and Thorburn, J. (2008) 'Safeguarding children in the UK: a longitudinal study of services to children suffering or likely to suffer significant harm', *Child and Family Social Work*, 13: 365–77.

Brandstrom, A. and Kuipers, S. (2003) 'From "normal incidents" to poetical crises: understanding the selective politicisation of policy failures', *Government and Opposition*, 38: 279–306

Butler, I. (2007) 'Abuse in institutional settings', in K. Wilson and A. James (eds), *The Child Protection Handbook*. Edinburgh: Ballière Tindall, pp. 181–92.

Butler, I. and Drakeford, M. (2005) *Scandal, Social Policy and Social Welfare*. Basingstoke: Palgrave Macmillan.

Carlile, Lord A. (2006) *An Independent Inquiry into the Use of Physical Restraint, Solitary Confinement and Forcible Strip Searching of Children in Prisons, Secure Training Centres and Local Authority Children's Homes*. London: Howard League for Penal Reform.

Clyde Report (1992) *Report of the Inquiry into the Removal of Children in Orkney in February 1991*. Edinburgh: HMSO.

Cohen, S. (1972) *Folk Devils and Moral Panics*. London: MacGibbon & Kee.

Cohen, S. (1985) *Visions of Social Control: Crime, Punishment and Classification*. Cambridge: Polity Press.

Colton, M. and Vanstone, M. (1996) *Betrayal of Trust: Sexual Abuse by Men Who Work with Children ... in Their Own Words*. London: Free Association Press.

Colwell Report (1974) *Report of the Committee of Inquiry into the Care and Supervision Provided in Relation to Maria Colwell*. London: HMSO.

Commission to Inquire into Child Abuse (2005) Online at: http://www.childabusecommission.ie.

Council of Europe (2008) *Memorandum (17/10/2008) by Thomas Hammarberg, Commissioner for Human Rights, following his visit to the UK*. Strasbourg: Council of Europe.

Courtney, M. E. and Iwaniec, D. (eds), (2009) *Residential Care of Children: Comparative Perspectives*. Oxford: Oxford University Press.

Crosse, S. B., Kaye, E. and Ratnofsky, A. C. (1993) *A Report on the Maltreatment of Children with Disabilities*. Washington, DC: National Center on Child Abuse and Neglect.

Curtis Committee (1946) *Report of the Care of Children Committee*, Cmnd. 6922. London: HMSO.

Darker, I., Ward, H. and Caulfield, L. (2008) 'An analysis of offending by young people looked after by local authorities', *Youth Justice*, 8 (2): 134–48.

Department for Education and Skills (2003) *Every Child Matters*. London: Stationery Office.

Department for Education and Skills (2004) *Every Child Matters: Change for Children in Social Care*. London: Stationery Office.

Department of Children, Schools and Families (2009) Online at: http://www.dcsf.gov.uk.

Department of Health (1991) *Working Together Under the Children Act 1989*. London: HMSO.

Department of Health (1998) *Quality Protects: Objectives for Social Services for Children*. London: DoH.

Department of Health (1999) *Working Together to Safeguard Children*. London: Stationery Office.

Drakeford, M. and Butler, I. (2007) 'Everyday tragedies: justice, scandal and young people in contemporary Britain', *Howard Journal*, 46 (3): 219–35.

Emond, R. (2008) 'Children's voice, children's rights', in A. Kendrick (ed.), *Residential Child Care: Prospects and Challenges*. London: Jessica Kingsley, pp. 183–96.

Foucault, M. (1973) *The Birth of the Clinic: An Archaeology of Medical Perception*. London: Tavistock.

Foucault, M. (1977) *Discipline and Punish: The Birth of the Modern Prison*. London: Allen Lane.

Gallagher, B. (1999a) 'The abuse of children in public care', *Child Abuse Review*, 8: 357–65.

Gallagher, B. (1999b) 'Institutional abuse', in N. Parton and C. Wattram (eds), *Child Sexual Abuse: Responding to the Experiences of Children*. Chichester: Wiley.

Gallagher, B. (2000) 'The extent and nature of known cases of institutional child sexual abuse', *British Journal of Social Work*, 30: 795–817.

Garrett, J. R. (1979) 'Institutional maltreatment of children: an emerging public issue', *Residential and Community Child Care Administration*, 1: 57–68.

Garrett, P. (1999) 'Producing the moral citizen: the "looking after children" system and the regulation of children and young people in public care', *Critical Social Policy*, 19 (3): 291–311.

Gentleman, A. (2009) 'Children in care: experts fly in to help tackle crisis', *The Guardian*, Tuesday, 21 April, pp. 1 and 10–11.

Gil, E. (1982) 'Institutional abuse of children in out-of-home care', in R. Hanson (ed.), *Institutional Abuse of Children and Youth*. New York: Haworth Press.

Goffman, E. (1961) *Asylums: Essays on the Social Situation of Mental Patients and Other Inmates*. New York: Doubleday.

Goldson, B. (2002) 'New punitiveness – the politics of child incarceration', in J. Muncie, G. Hughes and E. McLaughlin (eds), *Youth Justice – Critical Readings*. London: Sage, pp. 386–400.

Goldson, B. (2008) 'Child incarceration: institutional abuse, the violent state and the politics of impunity', in P. Scraton and J. McCulloch (eds), *The Violence of Incarceration*. London: Routledge.

Gouldner, A. (1954) *Patterns of Industrial Democracy: A Case Study of Modern Factory Administration*. New York: Free Press.

Green, L. (2001) 'Analysing the sexual abuse of children by workers in residential care homes: characteristics, dynamics and contributory factors', *Journal of Sexual Aggression*, 7 (2): 5–24.

Green, L. (2005) 'Theorizing sexuality, sexual abuse and residential children's homes: adding gender to the equation', *British Journal of Social Work*, 35: 453–81.

Green, L. (2006) 'An overwhelming sense of injustice? An exploration of child sexual abuse in relation to the concept of justice?', *Critical Social Policy*, 26 (1): 74–100.

Haines, K. and Drakeford, M. (1998) *Young People and Youth Justice*. Basingstoke: Macmillan.

Hayden, C., Goddard, J., Gorin, S. and van Der Spek, N. (1999) *State Child Care – Looking After Children?* London: Jessica Kingsley.

Hendrick, H. (1994) *Child Welfare: England 1872–1989.* Glasgow: Routledge.

Hendrick, H. (1997) 'Constitutional reconstructions of British Childhood: an interpretive survey 1800 to the present', in A. James and A. Prout (eds), *Constructing and Reconstructing Childhood.* London: Falmer.

Home Affairs Committee (2002) *The Conduct of Investigations into Past Cases of Abuse in Children's Homes,* Report No. 4. London: House of Commons.

Jackson, S. (2002) 'Promoting stability and continuity in care away from home', in D. McNeish, T. Newman and H. Roberts (eds), *What Works for Children.* Buckingham: Oxford University Press.

Jenks, C. (1996) *Childhood.* London: Routledge.

Jenne, D. L. and Kersting, R .C. C. (1998) 'Gender, power and reciprocity in the correctional setting', *Prison Journal,* 78 (2): 166–85.

Kendrick, A. and Taylor, J. (2000) 'Hidden on the ward: the abuse of children in hospitals', *Journal of Advanced Nursing,* 31: 565–73.

Kirkwood, A. (1993) *The Leicestershire Inquiry 1992.* Leicester: Leicestershire County Council.

Laming, H. (2003) *The Victoria Climbié Inquiry: Report of an Inquiry by Lord Laming.* London: HMSO.

Lemert, E. (1951) *Social Pathology.* New York: McGraw-Hill.

Levy, A. and Kahan, B. (1991) *The Pindown Experience and the Protection of Children.* Stafford: Staffordshire County Council.

Lindsay, M. (1996) *Towards a Theory of 'Careism' – Discrimination Against Young People in Care.* Paper given at the International Conference on Residential Child Care, Glasgow (cited in Taylor 2006).

Lipsky, M. (1980) *Street-Level Bureaucracy: Dilemmas of the Individual in Public Services.* New York: Russell Sage Foundation.

Macleod, M. (1999) 'The abuse of children in institutional settings: children's perspectives', in M. Stanley, J. Manthorpe and J. Penhale (eds), *Institutional Abuse – Perspectives across the Lifecourse.* London: Routledge.

May, M. (1973) 'Innocence and experience: the evolution of the concept of juvenile delinquency in the mid-nineteenth century', *Victorian Studies,* 17 (1): 7–29.

Milham, S., Bullock, R., Hosie, K. and Haak, M. (1978) *Lost in Care.* Aldershot: Gower.

Monckton, W. (1945) *Report on the Circumstances which Led to the Boarding Out of Dennis and Terence O'Neill at Bank Farm, Minsterley, and the Steps Taken to Supervise Their Welfare.* London: Home Office.

Morgan, J. and Zedner, L. (1992) *Child Victims.* Oxford: Clarendon.

NACRO (2003) *Reducing Offending by Looked After Children: A Good Practice Guide.* London: Nacro.

New York State Commission (1992) *Child Abuse and Neglect in New York State Office of Mental Health and Office of Mental Retardation and Developmental Disabilities Residential Programs.* New York: New York State Commission on Quality of Care for the Mentally Disabled.

O'Neill, T. (2001) *Children in Secure Accommodation: A Gendered Exploration of Locked Institutional Care for Children in Trouble.* London: Jessica Kingsley.

Parker, R. (1995) 'A brief history of child protection', in E. Farmer and M. Owen (eds), *Child Protection Practice: Private Risk and Public Remedies.* London: HMSO.

Pearson, G. (1983) *Hooligan: A History of Respectable Fears.* London: Macmillan.

Pearson, G. (1993) 'Youth crime and moral decline: permissiveness and tradition', *The Magistrate,* December 1993/January 1994, pp. 190–2.

Pearson, G. (1994) 'Youth, crime and society', in M. Maguire, R. Morgan and R. Reiner (eds), *The Oxford Handbook of Criminology*. Oxford: Oxford University Press.

Petrie, P., Boddy, J., Cameron, C., Wigfall, V. and Simon, A. (2006) *Working with Children in Care: European Perspectives*. Maidenhead: McGraw-Hill & Open University Press.

Pithouse, A. (1998) *Social Work: The Social Organisation of an Invisible Trade*. Aldershot: Ashgate.

Powers, J.L., Mooney, A. and Nunno, M. (1990) 'Institutional abuse – a review of the literature', *Journal of Child and Youth Care*, 4: 81–95.

Qvortrup, J. (1994) *Childhood Matters*. Aldershot: Avebury.

Rindfleisch, N. and Rabb, J. (1984) 'Dilemmas in planning for the protection of children in and youths in residential facilities', *Child Welfare*, 63: 205–15.

Rosenthal, J., Motz, J., Edmondson, D. and Groze, V. (1991) 'A descriptive study of abuse and neglect in out of home placement', *Child Abuse and Neglect: The International Journal*, 15: 249–60.

Save the Children (2001) *A Sense of Purpose: Care Leavers' Views and Experiences of Growing Up*. Edinburgh: Save the Children.

Secretary of State for Social Services (1988) *Report of the Inquiry into Child Abuse in Cleveland*, Cmnd 412. London: HMSO.

Sen, R., Kendrick, A., Milligan, I. and Hawthorn, M. (2008) 'Lessons learnt? Abuse in residential child care in Scotland', *Child and Family Social Work*, 13: 411–22.

Seneviratne, M. (2001) 'Ombudsmen for children', *Journal of Social Welfare and Family Law*, 23 (2): 217–25.

Shaughnessy, M. F. (1984) 'Institutional child abuse', *Children and Youth Services Review*, 6: 311–18.

Sinclair, I. and Gibbs, I. (1998) 'Children's homes: a study in diversity', in DoH (ed.), *Caring for Children Away from Home – Messages from Research*. Chichester: Wiley.

Smith, M. (2008) 'Historical abuse in residential child care: an alternative view', *Practice: Social Work in Action*, 20: 29–41.

Social Exclusion Unit (2005) *Transitions – Young Adults with Complex Needs – A Social Exclusion Unit Final Report*. London: Office of the Deputy Prime Minister.

Staffordshire County Council (1991) See Levy and Kahan (1991).

Stein, M. (2006) 'Missing years of abuse in children's homes', *Child and Family Social Work*, 11 (1): 11–21.

Stevens, J. (2006) 'Consulting youth about residential care environments in Scotland', *Children, Youth and Environments*, 16: 51–74.

Stewart, J. (1995) 'Children, parents and the state: the Children Act 1908', *Children and Society*, 9 (1): 90–9.

Taylor, C. (2006) *Young People in Care and Criminal Behaviour*. London: Jessica Kingsley.

Thomas, G. (1990) 'Institutional child abuse: the making and prevention of an un-problem', *Journal of Child and Youth Care*, 4 (6): 1–22.

United Nations Committee on the Rights of the Child (2008) *Consideration of Reports Submitted by States Parties under Article 44 of the Convention, Concluding Observations, United Kingdom of Great Britain and Northern Ireland*, 3 October. New York: United Nations.

Utting, W. (1991) *Children in the Public Care: A Review of Residential Child Care*. London: HMSO.

Utting, W. (1997) *People Like Us: The Report of the Review of the Safeguards for Children Living Away from Home*. London: Stationery Office.

Waterhouse, S. (2000) *Lost in Care: Report of the Tribunal of the Inquiry into the Abuse of Children in Care in the Former County Council Areas of Gwynedd and Clwyd since 1974*. London: Stationery Office.

Webster, R. (2005) *The Secret of Bryn Estyn: The Making of a Modern Witch Hunt*. Oxford: Orwell Press.

Welland, T. (2001) 'Living in the "empire of the gaze": time, enclosure and surveillance in a theological college', *Sociological Review*, 49 (1): 117–35.

Welsh Assembly Government (n.d.) Children First website: http:wales.gov.uk/topics/childrenyoungpeople/childrenfirst/?lang=en.

Westcott, H. and Clement, M. (1992) *NSPCC Experience of Child Abuse in Residential Care and Educational Placements: Results of a Survey*. London: NSPCC.

White, K. (2003) 'The ideology of residential care and fostering', in K. White (ed.), *Reframing Children's Services*. London: NCVCCO.

Wilkins, L. (1964) *Social Deviancy*. London: Tavistock.

Williams, G. and McCreadie, J. (1992) *Ty Mawr Community Home Inquiry*. Cwmbran: Gwent County Council.

Chapter 25

Animal abuse

Harriet Pierpoint and Jennifer Maher[1]

Introduction

Animal abuse has largely been ignored in criminological research and literature. This oversight is surprising given links between animal abuse and human criminality and the long-standing concern for animal welfare in our legal history. For example, it has been nearly 40 years since a link between animal abuse and interpersonal violence was reported (e.g. Tapia 1971), particularly with reference to serial and mass murderers and interfamilial abuse. The black-market sale of exotic and endangered animals and animal products is the third largest illegal trade in the world, after drugs and weapons, and is one of the most profitable crimes of today (Coonan 2006). Dog fighting and the use of dangerous dogs have been tied to general deviance and other organised offences such as drug dealing (Barnes *et al.* 2006) membership has been linked to general animal abuse. Youth gangs (McVie 2007). Moreover there is an increasing recognition that animals are sentient beings worthy of moral consideration and protection (Eurogroup for Animals 2009) and therefore animal abuse is a serious problem deserving of attention irrespective of its relationship to human violence (Flynn 2001).

This chapter considers animal abuse, both in its own right as a criminal offence and as a further way to understand and identify interpersonal violence. The range of animal abuse offences is too great to discuss in any detail and, as a result, two offence categories – domestic animal and wildlife abuse – have been selected to be the main focus of the chapter. Although it is recognised that other animals (e.g. livestock, captive wild animals, laboratory animals) can frequently be the victims of abuse, domestic animals are most likely to be victims (according to RSPCA data discussed below) and, internationally, crimes against wildlife are the most profitable offences (see HSUS 2007). The chapter begins by addressing the problem of defining animal abuse and identifying the current offences which relate to animal abuse in the UK. The prevalence of animal abuse and the problems of its measurement are then considered. The chapter then turns to explanations for animal abuse by detailing a range of motivations and attitudes which may influence offending, including the implications for human as well as animal welfare. The discussion then considers detection, enforcement, prevention and intervention in relation to the said offences in the UK.

Defining animal abuse

As with other crimes, what we consider animal abuse to be will vary according to many dimensions but perhaps most notably over time (e.g. fox hunting with dogs), between countries, cultures (e.g. differing views on bull fighting) and religions (e.g. non-kosher or halal methods of slaughter). Consequently, there have been a number of attempts to define the terms animal abuse and cruelty and typologise different types of abuse (e.g. Vermeulen and Odendaal 1993; Baldry 2004).

The following definition captures features common to most efforts: 'socially unacceptable behavior [sic] that intentionally causes unnecessary pain, suffering, or distress to and/or death of an animal' (Ascione, 1993: 228). This definition excludes certain practices that some may think should be included. Firstly, Ascione's (1993) definition does not include harm caused to animals unintentionally, such as neglecting to provide adequate food, shelter, exercise or medical care owing to ignorance (e.g. hoarding). Secondly, he purposefully omits practices that may cause harm to animals yet are socially condoned (e.g. killing animals for food). He explains that this is because the status of a particular animal may vary from one culture to another so the definition takes into account the social contexts that help determine what is considered animal abuse (e.g. killing dogs for consumption is acceptable in some countries). Hence, whether an action on an animal will be conceived as abuse will depend on the species, perpetrator and context.

It is possible to identify three broad positions on the treatment of animals which influence the definition of animal abuse – the animal as a commodity, the animal welfare and the animal rights approaches. The first position would argue that there is no such thing as animal abuse. Kantian theorists, for example, would suggest that animals hold no intrinsic value, they are simply commodities – a 'means to an end' – and incapable of being abused (Regan 2004). The second position – the animal welfare position – holds that there is nothing inherently wrong with using animals as commodities, research and even entertainment, if it is done for the greater good and in a humane way that minimises unnecessary suffering (Singer 1995). From this perspective, cruelty to animals is where the infliction of pain or suffering on animals is as an end in and of itself as opposed to for the aforementioned purposes. On the other hand, according to the third position – the animal rights approach – the words 'humane', 'unnecessary' and 'suffering' can be subject to different interpretations and the only way to ensure protection for animals is to end their status as commodities. As Ryder (1989) argues, discrimination on the basis of speciesism is wrong. Therefore, all animal use which could cause suffering and harm is seen as abuse.

Current legislation used against animal cruelty tends to follow the welfare approach (with added protection for endangered species) some of which is considered below. However, a large proportion of laws are actually concerned with protecting humans against disease and food contamination (e.g. the Welfare of Animals (Slaughter and Killing) (Amendment) Regulations 1999) or land owners' property (e.g. the Night Poaching Act 1828) rather than preventing cruelty. Nevertheless, they have implications for animal welfare. Moreover, some green criminologists have argued that we should think more broadly about animal abuse and not just consider legal offences against animals but broader social harms, like threatening the environment in which animals live (e.g. South 1998). There are some legal protections against harming animals in these ways (see the section on Wildlife Crimes below) but, for green criminologists and others, they are too limited. Lynch and Stretesky (2003) point out that some great crimes may not be in 'violation of any existing laws' (e.g. vivisection).

Legal offences against animals

In 1822, Richard Martin MP piloted the first anti-cruelty bill giving cattle, horses and sheep a degree of protection through parliament (RSPCA 2009a). Since then, countless pieces of legislation have been enacted creating offences of cruelty to animals and to protect wildlife and the welfare of livestock. Table 25.1 below replicates the legislation listed under the first two of these headings in the current RSPCA's Inspectors' Legal Handbook (RSPCA n.d.).

Crimes under the Animal Welfare Act 2006

Despite the long list of legislation in Table 25.1, much of the law concerning animal welfare is now contained in the Animal Welfare Act 2006.[2] This applies to all 'protected animals',[3] whether they be pets, livestock or other captive animals.[4] The offences against these animals fall into six main categories:

- section 4 Causing unnecessary suffering;
- section 5 Mutilation;
- section 6 Dog tail docking;
- section 7 Administration of poisonous or injurious drugs or substances to an animal;
- section 8 Animal fighting;
- section 9 Failing to ensure the needs of an animal are met.

Sections 4 and 9 are considered in more detail below as, according to court statistics, there have been more cautions and convictions under these sections as opposed to the other sections under the Animal Welfare Act 2006. Additionally, offences under section 8 will also be considered owing to the significant rise in complaints recorded by the RSPCA (2009b).

Causing unnecessary suffering

It is an offence to cause unnecessary suffering to an animal by an act or failure to act or, for a person responsible for an animal, to permit or fail to take steps to prevent unnecessary suffering by an act or failure to act by another person (e.g. kicking or withholding medical treatment).[5]

Table 25.1 Legislation listed in the RSPCA's Inspector's Legal Handbook

Cruelty to animals	
Animal Welfare Act 2006	Control of Pollution (Anglers' Lead Weights) Regulations 1986
Animals (Scientific Procedures) Act 1986	Docking of Working Dogs' Tails (England) Regulations 2007 Docking of Working Dogs' Tails (Wales) Regulations 2007
Docking and Nicking of Horses Act 1949	Mutilations (Permitted Procedures) (England) Regulations 2007
Farriers (Registration) Act 1975	Mutilations (Permitted Procedures) (Wales) Regulations 2007
Night Poaching Act 1828	
Protection of Animals (Amendment) Act 1954	
Veterinary Surgeons Act 1966	Veterinary Surgery (Blood Sampling) Order 1983
	Veterinary Surgery (Exemptions) Order 1962
	Veterinary Surgery (Exemptions) Order 1970
	Veterinary Surgery (Exemptions) Order 1973

Protection of wildlife	
Agriculture (Miscellaneous Provisions) Act 1972	Animals (Cruel Poisons) Regulations 1963
Agriculture Act 1947	Conservation (Natural Habitats) Regulations 1994
Animal (Cruel Poisons) Act 1962	Control of Pesticides Regulations 1986
Conservation of Seals Act 1970	Control of Trade in Endangered Species (Enforcement) Regulations 1997
Deer Act 1991	Environmental Protection (Restriction on Use of Lead Shot) (England) Regulations 1999
Destructive Imported Animals Act 1932	Environmental Protection (Restriction on Use of Lead Shot) (Wales) Regulations 2002
Endangered Species (Import and Export) Act 1976	Heather and Grass etc. Burning (England) Regulations 2007
Game Act 1831	Heather and Grass etc. Burning (Wales) Regulations 2008
Ground Game Act 1880	Mink (Keeping) Regulations 1975
Hares Preservation Act 1892	Wildlife and Countryside (Registration and Ringing of Certain Captive Birds) Regulations 1982
Hunting Act 2004	
Pests Act 1954	Wildlife and Countryside (Registration to Sell etc. Certain Dead Wild Birds) Regulations 1982
Protection of Animals Act 1911	
Protection of Badgers Act 1992	Wildlife and Countryside (Registration, Ringing and Marking of Certain Captive Birds) (Wales) Regulations 2003
Wild Mammals (Protection) Act 1996	
Wildlife and Countryside Act 1981	Wildlife and Countryside (Ringing of Certain Birds) Regulations 1982
	Conservation of Seals (England) Order 1999
	Coypus (Prohibition on Keeping) Order 1987
	Grey Squirrels (Prohibition of Importation and Keeping) Order 1937
	Grey Squirrels (Warfarin) Order 1973
	Mink Keeping (Prohibition) (England) Order 2004
	Musk Rats (Prohibition of Importation and Keeping) Order 1933
	Small Ground Vermin Traps Order 1955
	Spring Traps (Approval) Order 1995
	Convention on International Trade in Endangered Species of Wild Fauna and Flora

Animal fighting
There are a number of offences relating to animal fighting. These include: training an animal to fight, taking part as an organiser, publicist or spectator (including making or accepting a bet) in a fight, providing premises or possessing associated paraphernalia (e.g. scales to weigh or match animals for a fight).

Failing to ensure the needs of an animal are met
The most significant development brought about by the Animal Welfare Act 2006 is the creation of a new offence of failing to ensure the needs of an animal are met. Under section 9(1), 'a person commits an offence if he does not take such steps as are reasonable in all the circumstances to ensure that the needs of an animal for which he is responsible are met to the extent required by good practice.' Basic needs include food, water and prompt veterinary treatment. There is no need to prove suffering or circumstances likely to lead to suffering and it creates a duty of care on those responsible for animals who do not necessarily have to be owners.

Wildlife crimes

There are over 150 offences relating to wildlife in domestic and international law which can be categorised into three main types:

1 crimes involving native species which are endangered or of conservation concern;
2 crimes of cruelty against wildlife species;
3 illegal trading in endangered species.

The aim here is to give some examples of the legalisation and the associated offences.

Crimes involving endangered native species
The principal legislative protection to wild birds and some wild animals and their habitats is provided by the Wildlife and Countryside Act 1981. Wild birds, all species of bat, species of dolphin, amphibians including all species of newt, species of frog and toad, reptiles, porpoise, otter, many species of insects and others are included. Although there are many exceptions, crimes against protected species include killing, injuring or taking them from the wild, collecting their eggs or skins for personal collections, trading in them and destroying nests, bat roosts and other protected breeding sites and habitats. Many methods of killing, taking, poisoning, snaring and trapping wild animals (section 11) and birds (section 5) are also outlawed.

Crimes of cruelty to wildlife species
It is an offence to mutilate, kick, beat, nail or otherwise impale, stab, stone, crush, drown, drag or asphyxiate any wild mammal with intent to inflict unnecessary suffering under the Wild Mammals (Protection) Act 1996 section 1. Additional protection is given to particular species, such as the Deer Act 1991 and the Protection of Badgers Act 1992. According to the latter, it is an

offence to kill, injure or take a badger, or to damage or interfere with a sett unless a licence is obtained from a statutory body. These offences can occur within the context of badger digging and baiting which involves sending small terriers down a sett to locate and hold a badger at bay. The baiters then dig their way down, destroying the sett and dragging the badger out (Naturewatch 2009).[6]

Illegal trading in endangered species
The import, export and re-export of many threatened species of wild fauna and flora is controlled through European Regulations implementing the Convention on International Trade in Endangered Species of Wild Fauna and Flora (CITES). This includes the import, export and re-export of animals and parts and products derived from them, such as medicines and skins (e.g. chimpanzees, African grey parrots and two-toed sloths).[7] Internal trade in these species is controlled by the Control of Trade in Endangered Species (Enforcement) Regulations 1997 (COTES). It established a series of offences and penalties for infringements of the aforementioned EU regulations within the UK. The whole system of international trade in endangered species depends on the proper issue and use of the forms accompanying the export and import of the animals concerned. Hence offences mainly concern false statements in relation to these forms and the misuse or forgery of permits. Early prosecutions under these regulations have usually been against shops or importers operating illegally, but a recent case was successfully brought against an eBay trader for illegally trading stuffed animals and birds (CPS 2005).

In attempting to define animal abuse one can look at academic, legal and animal interest groups' definitions. Although animal welfare organisations (e.g. the Dog Trust and the RSPCA) have been instrumental in legislative development such as the Animal Welfare Act 2006, there remains some distance between legal and interest groups' definitions. For example, the humane destruction of both domestic animals and wildlife remains legal and routinely practised. Local authority dog pounds sanction the destruction of stray dogs if not claimed after seven days; this practice is in clear opposition to the non-destruction policies of some dogs charities (e.g. Dogs Trust 2009). Likewise the licensed culling of badgers and experimentation on animals[8] is legal. This demonstrates the tension between the animal welfare and the animal rights positions discussed above.

Prevalence of animal abuse

Methodological difficulties and changing definitions of animal abuse have greatly impacted upon the information available on incident rates of animal abuse (Zilney and Zilney 2005). The little that we know about the prevalence of animal abuse and the characteristics of offenders in this area is derived from court statistics, data collected from animal welfare charities (e.g. the RSPCA) and vets and academic studies. Animal cruelty offences recorded by the police are not collected centrally by the Home Office. This section will focus on the first two data sources as they are collated on an annual basis and provide the most comprehensive figures (see Pierpoint and Maher, in preparation, for further analysis).

The problem of the 'dark figure' of animal abuse offences is particularly acute for this range of offences as there is unlikely to be a human victim involved who could report the incident. This may be even more so the case for crimes against wildlife where the offences may be committed against animals which are largely invisible to the public. For example, we can see from Table 25.2 below that the number of people cautioned, proceeded against and sentenced for individual wildlife offences are exceedingly low.

Incidence of animal abuse and trends over time

The Office for Criminal Justice Reform (OCJR) Evidence and Analysis unit can extract court statistics back as far as 1993. However, the RSPCA has recorded the total number of convictions resulting from its prosecutions and 'assist cases'[9] since 1832, as shown in Figure 25.1.

Figure 25.1 shows that the number of recorded convictions peaked in 1903 at 8,798. The increase in convictions reflected the number of prosecutions brought by the RSPCA which practically doubled each decade between 1830 and 1900 owing to the establishment of nationwide branches outside London and an expansion in the inspectorate, from two inspectors in 1838 to 120 in 1897 (Radford 2001). The decline in convictions which followed can probably be attributed to the two world wars (1914–45). Since the 1950s, convictions peaked in 1993 with 3,065 and 1998 with 3,114. Long-term trends show that crime generally, and violent crime specifically, as measured by the British Crime Survey peaked in 1995. Crime then fell substantially until 2004/5 and, since then, has shown little overall change (Nicholas *et al.* 2007). Convictions reported by the RSPCA dropped in 2006, reflecting a drop in BCS crime generally the previous year.[10] In recent years convictions have been rising again. The latest data for 2008 shows there were 2,574 convictions.

However, this figure does not account for all convictions because, although the RSPCA brings the majority of prosecutions, defendants can be prosecuted by other agencies (e.g. local authorities, the CPS). Moreover, there will be many incidences of animal abuse which do not result in a conviction. It is, therefore, useful to look at other measures which may shed some light on the extent of animal abuse in England and Wales. None of these measures, including those used in Figure 25.2 are perfect indicators of the incidence of animal abuse. For example, phone calls to the RSPCA can be for advice about animal welfare as well as about concern for it, complaints about alleged animal cruelty may be unfounded and animals may be collected because they are not coping living stray as opposed to any individual(s) perpetrating abuse on them. However, the multiple line chart in Figure 25.2 does show that there was a peak in all three measures between 1999/2000 after the 1998 peak in convictions shown in Figure 25.2. It is possible that the increased convictions resulted in greater public awareness around animal welfare prompting more telephone calls and complaints to the RSPCA. Recently, complaints have gone up while rescues and phone calls have gone down. It is possible that

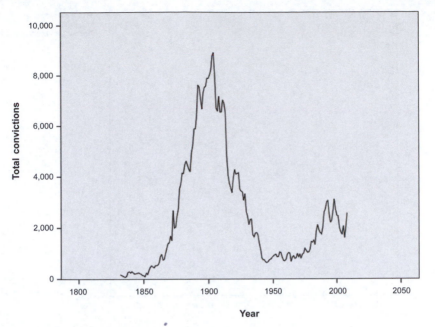

Figure 25.1   Total convictions recorded by the RSPCA
Source: Data provided by RSPCA.

phone calls are being replaced with the public using the Internet for advice instead.

Characteristics of offenders

Unlike the RSPCA data, the court statistics do include the sex of offenders and whether the offender is aged 10 to 18 or older.[11] Ethnicity data are not available. However, this data is not readily available and has to be requested from the OCJR. Although there are reams of acts under which animal cruelty offences can be prosecuted (see Table 25.1 above), in focusing on the main acts under which offences against domestic animal abuse are prosecuted, more men are cautioned and found guilty than women (see Figure 25.3 below). Perpetrators of other types of violent crime are also more likely to be male than female (Levi *et al*. 2007). More people over the age of 18 are cautioned and found guilty of these animal abuse offences than those between 10 and 17 years old (see Figure 25.4 below). Of course, court statistics do not account for children under the age of criminal responsibility.

Characteristics of victims

RSPCA data, unlike court statistics, records whether convictions relate to dogs, cats, equines, sheep, cattle, pigs or other types of animal. RSPCA data show that, over the last 15 years (1994–2008), convictions have related to animals in the following order of propensity: dogs are victimised most frequently, followed by other animals, then sheep, then cattle, and pigs have been victimised the least.

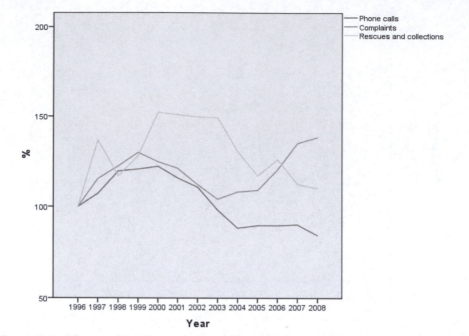

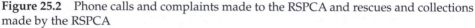

Figure 25.2 Phone calls and complaints made to the RSPCA and rescues and collections made by the RSPCA

Source: Data provided by the RSPCA.

Note: The measures have been scaled so that 1996 = 100%. This allows us to compare trends in the three variables on the same graph despite the large differences in the actual numbers.

However, court statistics do record the legislation under which the offence comes, which sometimes indicates the type of animal (e.g. Protection of Badgers Act 1992). Table 25.2 shows that overall the numbers of domestic offences against wildlife are very small. For example, no defendants have been proceeded against since 2002 under the Wildlife and Countryside Act 1981, section 11. However, there has been an increase in proceeded against offences against badgers, which could be the result of: (1) an increase in incidents involving violence towards badgers, particularly by groups of young people, reported by some police forces and charities (e.g. the Scottish Badgers charity, Strathclyde Police, Cumbria Police); (2) campaigns to increase awareness of badger baiting (e.g. Naturewatch Badger Campaign, Crime Stoppers); and/or (3) reporting of this in the media (e.g. BBC, Cynon Leader).

The figures are greater for illegal trading in endangered species and parts. For example, in 2004/5 7,846 live animals and birds were seized along with 332,043 parts and derivatives under CITES (HM Revenue and Customs 2005). Estimates of the value of the illegal trade in animals and plants vary between £5 and £13 billion a year (Operation Charm 2008; Interpol, as cited by *The Telegraph* 2009). This demonstrates the difficulty in assessing the financial value of wildlife crime. The extent of wildlife crime and indeed offences against animals more generally are equally as difficult to measure. In sum, none of the data discussed above is satisfactory in terms of assessing the extent to which animal abuse takes place and the nature of it.

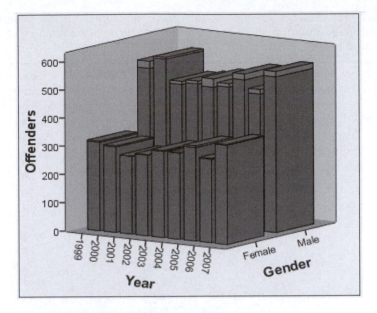

Figure 25.3 Court statistics on gender of offenders
Source: OCJR Evidence and Analysis Unit.
Note: This graph is based on offenders cautioned, receiving reprimands or final warnings or found guilty under the Protection of Animals Act 1911 (as amended), Protection of Animals (Amendment) Act 1954 and Animal Welfare Act 2006, ss. 4, 6, 9 and 32.

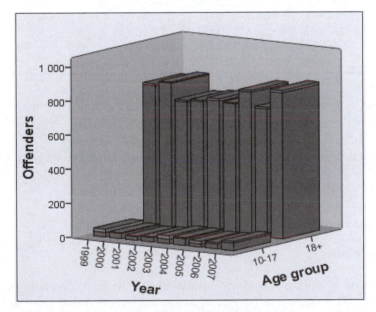

Figure 25.4 Court statistics on age of offenders
Source: OCJR Evidence and Analysis Unit.
Note: This graph is based on offenders cautioned, receiving reprimands or final warnings or found guilty under the Protection of Animals Act 1911 (as amended), Protection of Animals (Amendment) Act 1954 and Animal Welfare Act 2006, ss. 4, 6, 9 and 32.

Table 25.2 The number of persons cautioned, proceeded against at magistrates' courts and found guilty at all courts, by result, under selected offences of cruelty to wildlife, 2002 to 2007

Statute	Year	Cautioned	Proceeded against	Found guilty
Protection of Badgers Act 1992 (except s.13)	2002	1	18	5
	2003	3	4	4
	2004	–	12	4
	2005	–	30	11
	2006	3	10	3
	2007	8	20	6
Wildlife and Countryside Act 1981, s.5	2002	1	4	4
	2003	3	3	3
	2004	–	4	1
	2005	1	5	3
	2006	–	–	4
	2007	–	4	1
Wildlife and Countryside Act 1981, s.11	2002	2	2	–
	2003	1	–	–
	2004	1	–	–
	2005	1	–	–
	2006	4	–	2
	2007	1	–	–
Wild Mammals (Protection) Act 1996	2002	–	–	3
	2003	–	–	5
	2004	–	4	3
	2005	1	3	1
	2006	4	7	4
	2007	3	7	3

Notes:
* The statistics relate to persons for whom these offences were the principal offences for which they were dealt with. When a defendant has been cautioned for two or more offences at the same time the principal offence is the more serious offence.

* From 1 June 2000 the Crime and Disorder Act 1998 came into force nationally and removed the use of cautions for persons under 18 and replaced them with reprimands and warnings. These figures have been included in the totals.

* – = Nil
Source: OCJR Evidence and Analysis Unit

Explaining animal abuse

According to some philosophical positions, animals hold no intrinsic value in society (Regan 2004). It follows that no action against them can be defined as abuse and therefore, as Nell (2006) argues, it could be suggested that there is no need for motivational or neurobiological explanations for the prevalence of animal abuse. This position may explain the sparcity of criminological theories that have been specifically developed to explain animal abuse. Little attention has been given to explaining the illegal trade in wildlife. However, existing criminological explanations for international organised crime, such as rational choice theory (Cornish and Clarke 2002), may explain its growing appeal. For example, rational choice theory requires the presence of a suitable target (e.g. wildlife abuse is largely a hidden and seemingly victimless[12] crime), a motivated offender (e.g. a bear gall bladder can be worth more than heroin or gold by weight – HSUS 2007; Operation Charm 2008) and the absence of a suitable guardian (e.g. the difficultly in detecting and thereafter limited punishment for offenders). Although more attention has been given to explaining domestic animal abuse, the scope is fairly limited. For example, little attention has been given to broader structural explanations which may play a part in explaining domestic animal abuse whereby poverty or ignorance could explain the failure to meet an animal's medical or other needs. Explanations for domestic animal abuse (1) in the context of domestic violence households and (2) in the development of youth and adolescent animal abuse to adult interpersonal violence and crime – as discussed below – have received most attention.

Domestic violence

The relationship between domestic violence and the abuse of domestic animals has received much attention (Faver and Strand 2003). For example, higher rates of violence towards pets were found in domestic violent households than non-violent households (Volant et al. 2008) and more forms of and greater use of interpersonal violence and controlling behaviours were used by partners who abused pets (Simmons and Lehmann 2007). A UK study (Hutton 1983, cited in Frasch 2000) found that 83 per cent of families reported by social service agencies for animal abuse had been identified as at-risk families for child abuse and other violations. In addition to partner violence, children from domestic violence households may copy the abuse witnessed or abuse animals to exhibit their feelings of frustration, anger and helplessness (Lockwood and Ascione 1998). More generally, Levinson's (1989) study identified a cultural pattern of violence; in societies in which animal cruelty is present, the violence experienced by domestic violence victims was more serious in nature.

Feminist theory, in particular the influence of patriarchal culture, has been central to understanding the use of violence to exert control and coerce women and children in domestic settings. Findings from research in the UK (Hackett and Uprichard 2007) and US (Flynn 2000) support this theory's use for explaining animal abuse. They found that companion animals can be used in anger or revenge to teach submission, exert psychological control and maintain power over women and children in domestic violence. The suggested use of pets as an instrument of control in abusive relationships was also supported by Faver and Strand (2003) who reported women remained in the violent situation longer out of concern for their pets. As DeViney et al. (1983) and Ascione et al. (1997) identify, animal abuse is part of the constellation and continuum of family abuse.

Development from animal abuse to interpersonal violence

Age is an important variable for understanding animal abuse. Unlike other criminal behaviour, late adolescent and early adulthood are common times for the perpetration of animal cruelty (Flynn 2001). Ascione's (2001) typology identifies different levels of and motivation for animal abuse by the perpetrator's age: (1) exploratory/curious animal abuse (youngest, pre-school); (2) pathological animal abuse (young but usually older than the first group); and (3) delinquent animal abuse (oldest, adolescence). Animal abuse by children is often viewed as a precursor to serious interpersonal violence (e.g. serial killers and mass murderers) and antisocial behaviour (e.g. fire setting). Essentially the animal abuse is identified as a 'red flag' (e.g. of domestic violence in the household – as discussed above) or a risk factor in current/past abuse or in predicting future interpersonal violence (e.g. the MacDonald Triad)[13] (Fleming et al. 2002). Animal cruelty has been directly linked to psychological disorder. For example, it has been part of the criteria (being one of the earliest symptoms) for conduct disorder (CD) in the last two editions of the diagnostic and statistical manual of mental disorder (DSM) (American Psychiatric Association 1987, 1994) and 'there is evidence that it may be a particularly pernicious symptom' (Dadds et al. 2004: 321).

Much of the research on the link focuses on personality disorders and mental health, although some look at social and family circumstances (Beirne 1999). Zilney and Zilney (2005) found antisocial children who abused animals often came from violent and abusive homes and found animal abuse in follow-up studies two to nine years later, while DeViney et al. (1983) found 60 per cent of families on child abuse and neglect charges also abused pets (some of which included youth's abuse of pets). Another study found sexual abuse victims were also more likely than non-abused to abuse animals (Friedrich et al. 1992). These studies support Petersen and Farrington's (2007) use of strain theory (e.g. the abuse of animals to reduce stress or seek revenge due to poor family ties) and social learning theory (e.g. the exposure to abuse reinforces animal abuse and disregard for others' feelings) (Agnew 1998) to explain animal cruelty among youths.

Animal abuse among youths and adults is often linked back to childhood (as in the graduation hypothesis) or linked to a general criminal lifestyle (as in deviance generalisation). Research in the UK by Becker and French (2004) found that a fifth of children who sexually abused other children and committed other violent acts had a history of sexually abusing animals. This is explained by graduation thesis which suggests animal abuse precedes more serious interpersonal violence (Lockwood and Ascione 1998). However, recent studies have disputed this hypothesis (Arluke et al. 1999; Flynn 1999). Findings from Arluke et al.'s (1999) study identified animal abusers were 5.3 times more likely to have a record of violent crime, in addition to four times more likely to be arrested for property crime and 3.5 times more likely to be arrested for drug offences and disorderly behaviour. He suggests these findings are better explained using deviance generalisation hypothesis, which identifies that animal abuse may precede or follow other offences, as it is just one element of a unified phenomenon of antisocial and violent behaviour (Arluke *et al.* 1999).

Deviance generalisation hypothesis may explain adolescent and adult animal abuse in the form of dog fighting and the ownership of dangerous, 'status' or 'bling' dogs (often identified as such for their reputed[14] aggression) – which has received increased attention in the UK (*The Independent* 2009). For example, a tentative link between gang membership and animal abuse (unspecified) was found by McVie (2007) who found animal abusers were more likely to report being a gang member. The RSPCA recorded a five-fold increase in dog fighting in the UK between 2004 and 2006; of the 137 fights, 82 involved youths fighting their dogs in a park or the street. Ownership of 'status' dogs can be viewed as an extension of a gang's 'subculture of violence' (Wolfgang and Ferracuti 1967) in that the animal can be used as a powerful[15] weapon and a clear statement of intent and an individual's status (being hard, tough and deserving of respect) (RSPCA, cited in Timesonline 2008a). We have recorded this in our current research on the use and abuse of animals among youth gangs and groups, in which we are interviewing practitioners and young people (Maher and Pierpoint 2009a; 2009b). Our interviewees reported that dogs, and exotic animals, were being used in a variety of ways, including in dog breeding and dog 'rolling'/fighting and for a range of reasons including companionship, but also gang entry, protection and status. As one practitioner reported of young people:

> [They want] anything that's a status symbol … these dogs that've got [akitas, staffies, American bulldogs], because they know that they have the jaw power and they just frighten people because they know that that dog is going to rip into somebody and it's not going to stop until it's got what it wants. It can be very very frightening, I mean we've seen footage of stuff and it takes your hair off your head.

In sum, a common link between motivations for interpersonal and animal offences is notable in the examples given – indicating animal abuse is an important strand in understanding, explaining and researching crime. Each of the explanations for animal abuse discussed focus on the meaning of the behaviour rather than the behaviour itself. The context is fundamental in explaining animal abuse; similar acts of abuse may have very different meaning depending on the cultural norms and status of the animal (e.g. the explanation for a child experimenting on a pet rabbit will differ to that of a scientist experimenting on lab rabbits). And yet conflict theorists suggest these explanations are redundant when the more significant harms done legally to animals through hunting, farming, medical, entertainment, breeding and educational practices in our society are considered. According to philosophical debate animal abuse is simply a reflection of a culture's moral standard (Frasch 2000). Therefore youth's 'dirty play' (abuse) goes beyond psychological defects, control and empowerment to 'being a reflection of, rather than separate from, the value of society' (Arluke 2002: 428).

Responses to animal abuse

Animal abuse involves multiple offences which span local, national and international boundaries. This multifaceted offence has required multiple responses. Responding to animal abuse begins with the official recognition of an offence – the nature of the UK legal framework of animal abuse has been summarised above (see the Eurogroup for Animals 2009 for a summary of EU legislation). Two further responses are evident in the UK – (1) detection and enforcement of these offences; and (2) prevention and intervention, which will now be discussed with particular focus on domestic animals and wildlife.

Detection and enforcement

The UK has a long history of legislation (since the first anti-cruelty bill in 1822 to the current day – see Table 25.1 above) and interest group involvement (e.g. the RSPCA since 1824) in protecting animals. The detection and prosecution of animal abuse within the UK often falls to the RSPCA (and similar agencies). They rely heavily on members of the public to report abuse (getting a call reporting abuse every 25 seconds – RSPCA 2009a). Customs and Excise and the wildlife crime officer in the police focus on detecting specific types of animal abuse. However, as wildlife offences are not notifiable offences (they are not reported to the Home Office), they are excluded from publicly available statistics that compare the performance of each constabulary, providing little incentive for detection. Moreover, the investment in wildlife crime police officers is patchy, resulting in 82 per cent of wildlife crime officers reporting that there are too few involved (Naturewatch 2009). Two recent improvements in the detection and reporting of domestic animal abuse come in the form of (1) cross-reporting abuse through multi-agency work and (2) the development of veterinary practices to include training in identifying animal abuse.

Cross-reporting between child and animal welfare agencies has existed in the US for decades and reportedly has resulted in higher detection rates for all types of family and animal abuses (Lockwood 2001; Zilney and Zilney 2005). First Strike Scotland is a prime example of UK multi-agency work aimed at detecting and prosecuting offenders through cross-training, educating and cross-reporting between domestic violence prevention professions (e.g. social workers, the police, the Scottish Society for the Prevention of Cruelty to Children (SSPCC), the Scottish Society for the Prevention of Cruelty to Animals (SSPCA), domestic violence agencies). In terms of wildlife crime, PAW (2008) is an example of a multi-agency response. The agency comprises representatives of statutory and non-government organisations who oversee the enforcement activity, education and investigation of wildlife crimes in the UK. While these are clear examples of multi-agency work in the UK, the majority of animal protection organisations still work in isolation.

There is no mandatory reporting of animal abuse by UK veterinarians (Defra 2008). Who the vet is primarily responsible to (the animal patient or their paying customer) is an ongoing ethical dilemma. In contrast, the American Veterinary Medical Association declares that the welfare of the patient should transcend any personal advantage or monetary gain in therapeutic decisions

(Arkow 1998). Without mandatory reporting by veterinarians, a reliable and rich database for identifying and investigating animal abuse is lost, particularly given improvements in training of veterinary students on animal abuse through the Forging Link group (Intervet, RSPCA and private practice). This is a similar argument to that of using accident and emergency data to establish the prevalence of violence (e.g. Maguire and Nettleton 2003).

When abuse has been detected, it is notable that the enforcement of animal offences has been severely criticised: 'It may not be enough to criminalise animal abuse without ensuring that animal abuse will be taken seriously by both the general and legal communities, especially the latter enforcement arm ...' (Frasch 2000: 344). Perhaps one of the clearest signs that the courts have not taken animal abuse seriously in the past comes from a report by the RSPCA which identifies a rise (34 per cent) in dog cruelty convictions following the Animal Welfare Act 2006 (Timesonline 2008b). This figure may not reflect an actual increase in cruelty but in the way it is being tried. The Act makes it easier to bring charges against animal abusers and makes the courts accountable for their decision-making. Now courts are obliged to explain their reasons for not imposing a ban on guilty offenders, which has resulted in a 25 per cent increase in banning orders in 2007 (Timesonline 2008b). That said, magistrates still do not always give an explanation and sometimes are not aware that they have to. Moreover, serious sanctions are rarely imposed when convictions do occur (Zilney and Zilney 2005: 50). An analysis of court statistics show that offenders can receive a range of sentences from discharges to immediate custody, although immediate custody is very rare. Treatment programmes for sentenced offenders of animal abuse, unlike domestic, child and sexual abuse, are few and far between. In contrast programmes for those deemed at risk of abusing animals are developing at a greater rate as discussed below.

Prevention and intervention

Numerous charities such as the Dogs Trust, TRAFFIC (the wildlife trade mentoring network) and the RSPCA and some government agencies (e.g. Defra) campaign to prevent animal abuse through education and intervention. Educational programmes based in schools (Dogs Trust) and the community (RSPCA – The People with Dogs project) aim to create responsible owners and prevent general and specific (dog fighting) animal abuse. BARK (Brent Action for Responsible K9s), for example, educates the community on dog welfare and responsible pet ownership, reduces the incidents where dogs are misused and investigates antisocial behaviour linked with the misuse of dogs (Metropolitan Police 2009). Multi-agency groups such as First Strike Scotland focus on preventing animal abuse and interpersonal violence by identifying at risk families – simply, cross-reporting can result in early detection of family violence (Barnes et al. 2006).

Support and intervention is recommended (Hackett and Uprichard 2007) for youths identified as intentional animal abusers ranging from low-level educative work to more intense programmes (e.g. within a cognitive behavioural framework) which seek to address multiple issues (e.g. victimisation, trauma, aggression). Humane education programmes often target at-risk children and seek to teach empathy and gentleness with animals. For example, TLC (Teaching Love and Compassion) uses dog training with at-risk youths. Such therapeutic education in residential treatment for children with ADHD or other conduct disorders has been associated with reducing behaviour pathologies (Katcher and Wilkins 2000). The key problem with these prevention and intervention methods is the lack of assessment which can clearly identify success rates. As animal abuse has largely been ignored by criminologists and crime professionals it is difficult to identify which responses are most successful (Flynn 2000).

Conclusion

A common theme emerges from this discussion of the definition, prevalence, explanation of and responses to animal abuse – animal abuse is an issue of low priority. For example, for at least some legislation, the animal welfare provisions are incidental to those concerning human health or property rights. The recording and enforcement of offences related to animals are not prioritised by agencies such as the Home Office, police and courts. The majority of attempts to explain the phenomenon focus on the relationship of animal abuse to human violence and not on the abuse per se and how that might be caused by broader, structural circumstances. That said, there are a growing number of examples of increased prioritisation of the issue, such as the expansion of animal abuse offences under the Animal Welfare Act 2006, the cross-reporting of abuse and multi-agency work, improved vet training and preventative initiatives. However, there remains a fine line between animal abuse offences and sanctioned and socially acceptable animal abuse (in, for example, hunting, experimentation, farming and entertainment – which is supported by institutions such as the government, religion and education) and this tends to complicate our understanding and response to animal abuse.

Selected further reading

Lockwood and Ascione (1998) have brought together a collection of papers mainly from the US on the various links between animal cruelty and interpersonal violence, which is a useful place to start reading. Petersen and Farrington's (2007) journal article provides the most up-to-date summary of research on animal abuse and interpersonal violence while Hackett and Uprichard's (2007) NSPCC report provides an overview of the literature and research conducted on the link between animal abuse and child abuse. From a philosophical and political perspective Regan (2004) in *The Case for Animal Rights* and Singer (1995) in *Animal Liberation* discuss the ethical and moral standpoint for increased animal rights and welfare. Radford (2001) provides an account of UK animal legislation in *Animal Welfare Law in Britain: Regulation and Responsibility*, but before the introduction of the Animal Welfare Act 2006. Further information on international legislation and welfare issues can be found on the websites of DEFRA (http://www. defra.gov.uk), the Eurogroup for Animals (http://www.eurogroupanimalwelfare.org)

and the World Animal Network (http://www.worldanimal.net/). A large number of relevant articles covering the spectrum of issues discussed herein can be found in both the *Journal of Interpersonal Violence* and *Society and Animals*.

Notes

1   The authors wish to thank Hamish Rogers and Sue Collin of the RSPCA and Professor Trevor Bennett for their advice and comments on the paper and the RSPCA for providing the RSPCA data for analysis.

2   Since 6 April 2007, the Animal Welfare Act 2006 has repealed and replaced the majority of the Protection of Animals Act 1911 and a number of other pieces of legislation including the Abandonment of Animals Act 1960.

3   The Act currently defines an 'animal' as a vertebrate other than man (section 1(1)) and creates three categories of protected animals (section 2):
    (a)   animals commonly domesticated in the British Islands;
    (b)   animals under the control of man whether on a permanent or temporary basis; or
    (c)   animals not living in a wild state (e.g. an escaped zoo animal)

4   The Animals (Scientific Procedures) Act 1986 allows for licensed procedures on laboratory animals.

5   The question is whether the person's actions are proportionate and, in all the circumstances, that of a reasonably competent humane person, so it might be acceptable not to take a dog with a thorn in its paw to the vet immediately, but unacceptable to delay taking a dog with a broken leg.

6   Baiters may then either shoot the badger or allow the dogs and badger to fight there or take them to another venue to participate in blood sports, which would be an animal fighting offence under the Animal Welfare Act 2006, section 8.

7   Animal (and plant) species are subject to different levels of controls depending on how threatened they are in the wild and in which of the three Appendices they are listed. For example, species listed on Appendix I are considered threatened with extinction and are banned from trade (e.g. chimpanzees, giant pandas and the Lear's macaw). The EU has implemented CITES in the Wildlife Trade Regulations (EC338/97). The regulations list species in a series of Annexes (A, B and C) which broadly correspond to CITES Appendices I, II and III. However, the EU Annexes upgrade some species from a lower appendix to a higher one and include certain non-CITES species of European concern. For example, all native European birds of prey and owls are listed in Annex A, although they are not all in Appendix I.

8   See note 4.

9   These are cases where the RSPCA has assisted another agency (e.g. a local authority) but the other agency actually brought the prosecution. In 2008, the RSPCA changed the way it recorded convictions and excluded 'assist cases' to make matters more clear and transparent.

10   See note 9.

11   It is important to note that these data have been extracted from large administrative data systems generated by the police forces. As a consequence, care should be taken to ensure data collection processes and their inevitable limitations are taken into account when those data are used.

12   If one chooses to discount the pain and suffering of the animals, a victim of the offence is not always clear – for example, the death of rangers protecting the animals, the inevitable destruction of our environment and fauna and the consequences for local people, the spread of diseases among the animal kingdom

between animals and to humans (for example, Avian flu or H5N1 – see Newman and Padula 2005).

13 Macdonald (1963) suggests the combined behaviour of animal cruelty, fire-setting and bedwetting (after the age of five) by children is a predictor of future sociopathic behaviour.

14 The reputation for aggression often stems from the animal's natural instinct to protect and guard and some of these breeds were bred to fight in blood sports or for the control of other animals. That said, while the breed of a dog is an important factor that contributes to a dog's temperament, this alone is not the best gauge for determining how dangerous the dog is.

15 Once the youth is not in possession of a banned breed they can legally 'carry' this potentially lethal weapon around.

References

Agnew, R. (1998) 'The causes of animal abuse: a social psychological analysis', *Theoretical Criminology*, 2 (2): 177–209.

American Psychiatric Association (1987) *Diagnostic and Statistical Manual of Mental Disorders*, DSM-III-R. Washington, DC: American Psychiatric Publishing.

American Psychiatric Association (1994) *Diagnostic and Statistical Manual of Mental Disorders*, DSM-IV. Washington, DC: American Psychiatric Publishing.

Arkow, P. (1998) 'Application of ethics to animal welfare', *Applied Animal Behaviour Science*, 59 (1–3): 193–200.

Arluke, A. (2002) 'Animal abuse as dirty play', *Symbolic Interaction*, 25 (4): 405–30.

Arluke, A., Levin, J., Luke, C. and Ascione, F. (1999) 'The relationship of animal abuse to violence and other forms of antisocial behavior', *Journal of Interpersonal Violence*, 14: 963–75.

Ascione, F. R. (1993) 'Children who are cruel to animals – a review of research and implications for developmental psychopathology', *Anthrozoos*, 6 (4): 226–47.

Ascione, F. R. (2001) 'Animal abuse and youth violence', *Juvenile Justice Bulletin*. Washington, DC: Office of Juvenile Justice and Delinquency Prevention.

Ascione, F. R., Thompson, T.M. and Black, T. (1997) 'Childhood cruelty to animals: assessing cruelty dimensions and motivations', *Anthrozoos*, 10 (4): 170-7.

Baldry, A. C. (2004) 'The development of the PET scale for the measurement of physical and emotional tormenting against animals in adolescents', *Society and Animals*, 12 (1): 1–17.

Barnes, J. E., Putnam, F. W., Dates, H. F. and Mahlman, A. R. (2006) 'Ownership of high-risk ("vicious") dogs as a marker for deviant behaviors – implications for risk assessment', *Journal of Interpersonal Violence*, 21 (12): 1616–34.

Becker, F. and French, L. (2004) 'Making the links: child abuse, animal cruelty and domestic violence', *Child Abuse Review*, 13 (6): 399–415.

Beirne, P. (1999) 'For a nonspeciesist criminology: animal abuse as an object of study', *Criminology*, 37 (1): 117–47.

Coonan, C. (2006) 'Illegal wildlife trade is worth £6bn a year'. Online at: http://www.independent.co.uk/environment/illegal-wildlife-trade-is-worth-1636bn-a-year-409623.html (accessed 6 June 2009).

Cornish, D. B. and Clarke, R. V. (eds) (1986) *The Reasoning Criminal*. New York: Springer-Verlag.

Cornish, D. B. and Clarke, R. V. (2002) 'Analyzing organized crimes', in A. Piquero and S. G. Tibbetts (eds), *Rational Choice and Criminal Behavior: Recent Research and Future Challenges*. New York: Garland, pp. 41–62.

Crown Prosecution Service (CPS) (2005) 'CPS welcomes sentencing on illegal internet trading in wildlife products', press release 2 December 2005. Online at: http://www.cps.gov.uk/news/press_releases/165_05/ (accessed 4 August 2009).

Dadds, M. R., Whiting, C., Bunn, P., Fraser, J. A., Charlson, J. H. and Pirola-Merlo, A. (2004) 'Measurement of cruelty in children: the cruelty to animals inventory', *Journal of Abnormal Child Psychology*, 32 (3): 321–34.

Defra (2008) *Veterinary Surgeons Act 1966*. Online at: http://www.defra.gov.uk/animalh/ahws/vservices/act.htm (accessed 1 March 2009).

DeViney, E., Dickert, J. and Lockwood, R. (1983) 'The care of pets within child abusing families', *International Journal for the Study of Animal Problems*, 4: 321–9.

Dogs Trust (2009) *About Dogs Trust*. Online at: http://www.dogstrust.org.uk/topnavigation/about_us/ (accessed 6 June 2009).

Eurogroup for Animals (2009) *The Treaty and Animal Welfare*. Online at: http://www.eurogroupanimalwelfare.org/legislation/legislation_more1.htm?#art1 (accessed 6 April 2009).

Faver, C. A. and Strand, E. B. (2003) 'Domestic violence and animal cruelty: untangling the web of abuse', *Journal of Social Work Education*, 39 (2): 237–53.

Fleming, W. M., Jory, B. and Burton, D. L. (2002) 'Characteristics of juvenile offenders admitting to sexual activity with nonhuman animals', *Society and Animals*, 10 (1): 31–45.

Flynn, C. P. (1999) 'Animal abuse in childhood and later support for interpersonal violence in families', *Society and Animals*, 7 (2): 161–72.

Flynn, C. P. (2000) 'Why family professionals can no longer ignore violence toward animals', *Family Relations*, 49 (1): 87–95.

Flynn, C. P. (2001) 'Acknowledging the "zoological connection": a sociological analysis of animal cruelty – commentary', *Society and Animals*, 9 (1): 71–87.

Frasch, P. D. (2000) 'Addressing animal abuse: the complementary roles of religion, secular ethics, and the law', *Society and Animals*, 8 (3): 331–48.

Friedrich, W. N., Grambsch, P., Damon, L., Hewitt, S. K., Koverola, C., Lang, R. A., Wolfe, V. and Broughton, D. (1992) 'Child sexual behavior inventory: normative and clinical comparisons', *Psychological Assessment*, 4: 303–11.

Hackett, S. and Uprichard, E. (2007) 'Animal abuse and child maltreatment: a review of the literature and findings from a UK study. Executive summary', *NSPCC*, October.

HM Revenue and Customs C (2005) *HM Revenue and Customs Annual Report 2004–5*, Cm 6691. Norwich: The Stationery Office. Online at: http://customs.hmrc.gov.uk/channelsPortalWebApp/channelsPortalWebApp.portal?_nfpb=true&_pageLabel=pageLibrary_ShowContent&id=HMCE_PROD1_025022&propertyType=document (accessed 1 October 2009).

Humane Society of the United States (HSUS) (2007) 'Congress aims to end the black market trade in bear parts'. Online at: http://www.hsus.org/press_and_publications/press_releases/congress_aims_to_end_the.html (accessed 26 January 2009).

Independent, The (2009) 'Lethal weapons', Independent Magazine, 4 April, p. 18.

Intervet UK (2003) *Forging the Link: How to Recognize Animal Abuse in Your Practice*. Walton: Intervet UK.

Katcher, A. H. and Wilkins, G. G. (2000) 'The centaur's lessons: therapeutic education through care of animals and nature study', in A. H. Fine (ed.), *Handbook on Animal-Assisted Therapy: Theoretical Foundations and Guidelines for Practice*. San Diego, CA: Academic Press, pp. 153–77.

Levi, M., Maguire, M. and Brookman, F. (2007) 'Violent crime', in M. Maguire, R. Morgan and R. Reiner (eds), *The Oxford Handbook of Criminology*. Oxford: Oxford University Press, pp. 687–732.

Levinson, D. (1989) *Family Violence in Cross-Cultural Perspective*. Newbury Park, CA: Sage.

Lockwood, R. (2001) *Animal Abuse and Human Violence*. SOTAL: World Small Animal Veterinary Association World Congress, Vancouver.

Lockwood, R. and Ascione F. R. (1998) *Cruelty to Animals and Interpersonal Violence*. West Lafayette, IN: Purdue University Press.

Lynch, M. and Stretesky P. B. (2003) 'The meaning of green: contrasting criminological perspectives', *Theoretical Criminology*, 7 (2): 217–39.

McVie, S. (2007) *Animal Abuse Amongst Young People Aged 13 to 17: Trends, Trajectories and Links with Other Offending*. Edinburgh: RSPCA.

MacDonald, J. M. (1963) 'The threat to kill', *American Journal of Psychiatry*, 120: 125–30.

Maguire, M. and Nettleton, H. (2003) *Reducing Alcohol-Related Violence and Disorder: An Evaluation of the 'TASC' Project*, Home Office Research Study No. 265. London: Home Office.

Maher, J. and Pierpoint, H. (2009a) 'Weapon, Armour or Prey: The Use and Abuse of Animals among UK Youth Groups and Gangs' (Poster presented at the American Society of Criminology Conference 2009, 4th–7th November 2009, Philadelphia Marriott Downtown Hotel, Pennsylvania, USA). Available at http://hass.glam.ac.uk/media/files/documents/2009-11-19/Preservation_Weapon_or_Prey.pdf

Maher, J. and Pierpoint, H. (2009b) 'The Use and Abuse of Animals in Youth Gangs and Groups' (Paper presented at the Welsh Criminology Conference 2009, 6th–7th April 2009, Gregynog, UK). Available at: http://criminology.research.glam.ac.uk/media/files/documents/2009-04-21/Gregynog_Maher_and_Pierpoint.pdf

Metropolitan Police (2009) *BARK: Brent Action for Responsible K9s*. Online at: http://cms.met.police.uk/met/boroughs/brent/03working_with_the_community/bark_brent_action_for_responsible_k9s (accessed 23 May 2009).

Miller, K. S. and Knutson, J. F. (1997) 'Reports of severe physical punishment and exposure to animal cruelty by inmates convicted of felonies and by university students', *Child Abuse and Neglect*, 21 (1): 59–82.

Naturewatch (2009) Naturewatch website online at: http://www.naturewatch.org/ (accessed 4 August 2009).

Nell, V. (2006) 'Cruelty and the psychology of history – author's response', *Behavioral and Brain Sciences*, 29 (3): 246–57.

Newman, S. and Padula, V. (2005) *Avian Influenza Fact Sheet*. Wildlife Trust.

Nicholas, S., Kershaw, C. and Walker, A. (2007) Crime in England and Wales 2006/07 (Home Office Statistical Bulletin 11/07. Available at http://www.homeoffice.gov.uk/rds/pdfs07/nosb1107.pdf (accessed 15 December 2009).

Operation Charm (2008) *Illegal Wildlife Trade*. Online at: http://www.operationcharm.org/illegalwildlifetrade/ (accessed 30 March 2009).

PAW (2008) *What is PAW*. Online at: http://www.defra.gov.uk/paw/what/default.htm (accessed 30 March 2009).

Petersen, M. L. and Farrington, D. (2007) 'Cruelty to animals and violence to people', *Victims and Offenders*, 2 (1): 21–44.

Pierpoint, H. and Maher, J. (in preparation) 'Measuring animal abuse', *Society and Animals*, submitted.

Radford, M. (2001) *Animal Welfare Law in Britain: Regulation and Responsibility*. Oxford: Oxford University Press.

Regan, T. (2004) *The Case for Animal Rights*. Berkeley, CA: University of California Press.

Royal Society for the Prevention of Cruelty to Animals (RSPCA) (2009a) *RSPCA Online*. Online at: http://www.rspca.org.uk/ (accessed 4 August 2009).

Royal Society for the Prevention of Cruelty to Animals (RSPCA) (2009b) 'New RSPCA figures show shocking rise in dog fighting on our streets', News from the Press Office, 21 May.

Royal Society for the Prevention of Cruelty to Animals (RSPCA) (undated) *RSPCA's Inspector's Legal Handbook*. Sussex: RSPCA.

Ryder, R. (1989) *Animal Revolution: Changing Attitudes Towards Speciesism*. Oxford: Basil Blackwell.

Simmons, C. A. and Lehmann, P. (2007) 'Exploring the link between pet abuse and controlling behaviors in violent relationships', *Journal of Interpersonal Violence*, 22 (9): 1211–22.

Singer, P. (1995) *Animal Liberation*, 2nd edn. London: Pimlico.

South, N. (1998) 'A green field for criminology? A proposal for a perspective', *Theoretical Criminology*, 2 (2): 211–33.

Tapia, F. (1971) 'Children who are cruel to animals', *Journal of the American Academy of Child Psychiatry*, 22: 68–72.

Telegraph, The (2009) 'Inside the world of 'Wildlife CSI', 3 February. Online at: http://www.telegraph.co.uk/technology/4436586/Inside-the-world-of-Wildlife-CSI.html (accessed 15 March 2009).

Timesonline (2008a) 'Youths turn to aggressive dogs as the weapons of street status', 28 February. Online at: http://www.timesonline.co.uk/tol/news/uk/article3446273.ece (accessed 23 August 2008).

Timesonline (2008b) 'Animal cruelty cases soaring, says RSPCA', 30 July. Online at: http://www.timesonline.co.uk/tol/news/uk/article4428985.ece (accessed 23 August 2008).

Vermeulen, H. and Odendaal J. S. J. (1993) 'Proposed typology of companion animal abuse', *Anthrozoos*, 6 (4): 248–57.

Vigil, J. D. (1988) *Barrio Gangs*. Austin, TX: University of Texas Press.

Vigil, J. D. (2003) 'Urban violence and street gangs', *Annual Review of Anthropology*, 32: 225–42.

Volant, A. M., Johnson, J. A., Gullone, E. and Grahame, J. (2008) 'The relationship between domestic violence and animal abuse: an Australian study', *Journal of Interpersonal Violence*, 23 (9): 1277–95.

Wolfgang, M. E. and Ferracuti, F. (1967) *The Subculture of Violence: Towards an Integrated Theory in Criminology*. London: Tavistock.

Zilney, L. A. and Zilney M. (2005) 'Reunification of child and animal welfare agencies: cross-reporting of abuse in Wellington County, Ontario', *Child Welfare*, 84 (1): 47–66.

Part IV

Sex-Related Crime

The chapters in this section are concerned with various forms of sex-related crime and include a diverse set of behaviours ranging from 'non-contact' offences such as voyeurism, through preparatory offences such as sexual grooming, to acts involving physical violence, as with sexual assault and rape or, in the extreme, 'sexual murder' (though not defined as such in law). Each of the authors recognises that advances in technology have given rise to new forms of sex-related offending (e.g. sexual grooming via the Internet). At the same time, the ever-evolving law on sex-related crime plays its part in shaping the context in which these offences occur. And as with many other chapters in this book, the role of the economy in facilitating and shaping the nature of sex-related crime looms large. For example, Brooks-Gordon argues that, following the 2008–9 economic slump, the sex industry is likely to show a downward trend as clients have less money to spend, while at the same time the number of sex workers is likely to increase due to loss of jobs in other sectors.

Hollin, Palmer and Hatcher consider, in two separate chapters, sexual offending against adults and against children. As with many of the violent crimes referred to in the previous section, they point out that accurate data about the scale of sexual offending is lacking as much remains hidden from official view. They note that children in particular often fail to report sexual abuse as they may be unaware that they are in fact victims of abuse or lack the physical or psychological resources to report it. The authors note that explanations of sexual offending have become increasingly complex but still find difficulty in accounting for the differing behaviours of what is a heterogeneous group of offenders. For example, theories about why some men offend sexually against adults (mainly women) may be unhelpful in explaining why others sexually abuse children. Moreover, how to respond most effectively to this disparate group of offenders presents numerous challenges. The authors discuss various approaches aimed at preventing sexual offences, ranging from situational crime prevention, to incarceration, to changing the motivation of individual offenders – with particular attention paid to the difficulties of evaluating their effectiveness.

In her chapter on sex work, Brooks-Gordon opens by noting that while prostitution itself is not illegal, almost every aspect of the way in which someone works in the sex industry has become criminalised (including loitering or soliciting in a public place for prostitution, having sex in a public lavatory, managing a brothel or placing adverts for prostitution in a public telephone kiosk). She argues that the legislation surrounding sex work is problematic in that it is so broad that 'ordinary ways of living are drawn into the nebulous concept of control' and many women who wish to separate or hide their sex work from their families or rent rooms to other women for safety become 'sexual offenders' even though they represent no danger to the community. She notes that the majority of research has been on a minority of those in sex work working in the street sex markets, thereby ignoring the less visible off-street sex industry and distorting the reality of the phenomenon as a whole. Finally, the chapter draws attention to two contrasting ideological positions on sex work: (1) prostitution as exploitation and (2) sex work as work, and reveals the tensions between the two. There are also some interesting discussions on the main policy responses that have emerged from these distinct perspectives including prohibition and criminalisation on the one hand and regulation and decriminalisation on the other. The concern is raised that further developments in the direction of criminalising prostitution could have a harmful impact on sex workers and a negative impact on the criminal justice system.

Chapter 26

Sexual offences against adults

Clive R. Hollin, Ruth M. Hatcher and Emma J. Palmer

Introduction

What, exactly, is a sexual offence? This ostensibly straightforward question masks a definitional complexity that encompasses morality, law and technology. In as much as the law reflects a society's moral values at a given time, so laws change as societal values shift over time. This point is particularly pertinent with regard to the laws governing sexual behaviour and exactly how such behaviour is defined as an illegal act. There are several recent examples of changes in this aspect of law that may reflect shifts in public morality. As Myhill and Allen (2002) note, in England and Wales since the mid-1950s these changes include: 'notably the legalisation of homosexuality in 1967 and the criminalisation of rape within marriage in 1994. The legal definition of rape was also altered in 1994 to include penile penetration of the anus. Thus the offence of male rape has only been part of the criminal law for a short period of time, despite being recognised in the academic literature for some years (p. 1)'. Further, the age of consent of 21 years for homosexual males, as laid down by the 1967 Sexual Offences Act, was later reduced to 18 years by the Criminal Justice and Public Order Act 1994. The Parliament Act 1911 was later invoked to ensure the passage of the Sexual Offences (Amendment) Act 2000 which equalised the age of consent at 16 years for both homosexual and heterosexual behaviours.

There are other examples of legislative change in this context, for example the change with regard to the principle of marital rape exemption. This principle which can be traced to Chief Justice Hale in 1736 – that through marriage women agree to sexual intercourse in marriage and cannot retract that consent – was abolished in England and Wales in 1991 by the House of Lords. The fast moving pace of technological development is another catalyst for legal change. For example, as Beech *et al.* (2008) note, the Internet can be used to abuse children sexually in three ways: '(1) to disseminate images for personal and/or commercial reasons; (2) to establish and engage in social networks with other individuals who have a sexual interest in children; and (3) to engage in inappropriate sexual communication with children and/or to locate children to abuse' (p. 217). Indeed, Sheldon and Howitt (2007) take the view that the widespread availability of the Internet has produced a new category of sex offender, the 'internet sex offender'. This style of offending, which pays no heed to parochial rules of ethics or law, poses new challenges to jurisprudence.

Where are we now?

Given the above, where do we currently stand? In England and Wales the Sexual Offences Act 2003 provides the definitive list of sexual acts that are prohibited by law (Stevenson *et al.* 2003). The Sentencing Council Guidelines for the 2003 Sexual Offences Act (Sentencing Guidelines Secretariat 2007) categorises sexual offences as shown in Table 26.1. The 2003 Act introduced new offences relating to sexual activity with a child less than 16 years of age.

Table 26.1 Sexual Offences in 2003 Act (after Sentencing Guidelines)

Non-consensual offences
    Rape and assault by penetration
    Sexual assault
    Causing or inciting sexual activity
    Other non-consensual offences

Offences involving ostensible consent
    Offences involving children
    Offences against vulnerable adults

Preparatory offences
    Sexual grooming
    Committing another offence with intent
    Trespass with intent
    Administering a substance with intent

Other offences
    Sex with an adult relative
    Sexual activity in a public lavatory
    Exposure
    Voyeurism
    Intercourse with an animal
    Sexual penetration of a corpse

Exploitation offences
    Indecent photographs of children
    Abuse of children through prostitution and pornography
    Exploitation of prostitution
    Trafficking

As is evident from Table 26.1, sexual offending includes a diverse set of behaviours ranging from 'non contact' offences such as voyeurism to acts involving physical violence, as with sexual assault and rape. There is also an act of extreme violence where sex is attached to murder, giving rise to 'sexual murder' (Proulx *et al.* 2007), although sexual murder is not defined as such in law.

There are women who commit sexual offences (Gannon *et al.* 2008a) and sexual offences can be perpetrated against men. However, the overwhelming volume of sexual offences are carried out by men against women and children and this is where the research and theory is most developed. The focus of the current chapter is offences by men against non-consenting adult women, with offences against children discussed in the following chapter. However, in the sex offender literature, particularly the treatment evaluation studies, the distinction between sexual offenders against women and sexual offenders against children is not always made explicit.

Guided by the Sexual Offences Act 2003, the sexual offences against women of concern here include rape, assault by penetration and sexual assault. Briefly, a man commits *rape* if he intentionally penetrates the vagina, anus or mouth of a non-consenting person with his penis; *assault by penetration* if he intentionally penetrates the vagina or anus of another person with a part of his body or an object; and *sexual assault* if he intentionally touches another person and the touching is sexual.

Sex or violence?

The consequences of rape and sexual assault may be far-reaching for the woman, affecting her physical health, psychological state and relationships and lifestyle (Culbertson and Dehle 2001). Why do men inflict such injuries on women? The obvious answer is that the offence can be explained in terms of the man's sexual drive. However, in sexual crimes there is, to a greater or lesser extent, a fusion of violent and sexual behaviour. This mixture of violence and sex is reflected in typologies of rape. Groth (1979) suggested three categories of rape – anger rape, power rape and sadistic rape – characterised by varying levels of the man's exercise of power and use of violence. Following interviews with convicted rapists, Scully and Marolla (1985) described five types of rape:

- the man's concern is with revenge and punishment;
- the rape is a 'bonus' to another offence, such as burglary, when a women is vulnerable;
- so-called 'date rape';
- where the man said he enjoyed the experience of power and domination;
- where a group of men rape as an act of recreation.

The complexities evident in these contrasting accounts of apparently the same offence are evident in the theories below. However, before considering theory, we turn to the prevalence of sexual offences.

Sexual offending against women: facts and figures

The amount of crime can be estimated in a number of ways by utilising different sources of data. For example, the British Crime Survey (BCS) asks large samples of the general public about their personal experiences of victimisation. From the public's responses the BCS can estimate the prevalence of different types of crime. However, surveys may not be completely reliable with regard to sexual offences (Hoare and Povey 2008). Surveys may be conducted through face-to-face interviews and respondents may be unwilling to disclose experience of various sensitive crimes such as domestic violence and sexual offences. The use of confidential self-completion questionnaires may help resolve this difficulty. The BCS introduced this procedure to investigate intimate violence, requesting information about experiences of serious sexual assault (rape or assault by penetration) since the age of 16 years and in the last 12 months. The data suggested that 3 per cent of the sample (5.5 per cent of females and 0.6 per cent of males) aged 16 to 59 years had been subject to a serious sexual assault since the age of 16, with most offences (78 per cent) occurring between the ages of 16 and 29 (Hoare and Povey 2008). Less serious sexual assaults were more common, especially amongst females: almost one quarter of females, compared with 3.4 per cent of males, reported this type of experience since the age of 16. The figures for the previous 12 months suggested that about 3 per cent of women and less than 1 per cent of men reported any type of sexual assault, with lower figures (0.6 per cent of females and 0.1 per cent of males) for a serious sexual assault.

An alternative to surveys lies in estimates derived from routine police recording of reported incidents. The difficulty here is that, for a variety of reasons, victims do not always report the crime, while reported incidents are not always recorded by the police. Kershaw *et al.* (2008) noted that for 2007–8 twice as many crimes were estimated by the BCS (10.1 million) than were reported to the police (5 million). It is highly likely that sexual offences are less likely to be reported than other crimes. Hoare and Jansson (2007) estimated that only 11 per cent of victims of serious sexual assault reported the crime to the police. The reasons for not reporting were not wishing to feel humiliated, thinking that the police could not help or that it was a family matter so the police were not needed. Kelly *et al.* (2005) note that when crimes are reported to the police some reports may be 'lost'. This loss is not sinister: it may be that on investigation the police correctly concluded that no sexual offence took place, or that a crime had taken place but there was no supportive evidence, or the complainant later withdrew their complaint. Overall, it is highly likely that the official figures underestimate the true prevalence of sexual offences (Koss 1992).

From police data it appears that the prevalence of sexual offences in England and Wales is in decline: there were just over 62,000 offences in 2005–6 falling to 53,500 in 2007–8, a reduction of almost 15 per cent (Hoare and Povey 2008). However, the BCS suggests a more static picture for sexual offending, with figures close to 3 per cent of females and 0.6 per cent of males in the 2004–5, 2005–6 and 2006–7 surveys (Povey *et al.* 2008). This disparity may be due to unwillingness to report the crime, or lack of belief that with this type of crime the criminal justice system can successfully investigate and convict. This belief may, indeed, be accurate: Thomas (2005) makes the comment that 'A joint report of the Crown Prosecution Service and HM Inspectorate of Constabulary has further reported a fall in the number of prosecutions [since 2000] and a "marked decline" in the percentage of successful prosecutions for rape offences' (p. 250).

Theories of sexual offending

Feminist theories

Feminist theories view rape as a form of patriarchal hegemony used to subjugate and oppress women (Brownmiller 1975; Murmen *et al.* 2002). Rape is seen as a consequence of the way men are socialised and is maintained by societal attitudes and values that are supportive of rape. Evidence for feminist theories is found in studies that show that cultures with a high prevalence of rape are more accepting of macho attitudes and have a higher level of segregation between males and females, and that individuals within these cultures hold attitudes and beliefs that support male superiority and dominance over women (Reiss 1986; Sanday 1981). Although feminist theories offer an often neglected cultural perspective on rape, they do not account for individual differences to help explain why only some men, indeed the minority of men, commit rape.

Evolutionary theories

Evolutionary theories view rape as an evolutionary strategy, although they differ in terms of the specific strategies that are seen as causing rape (Malamuth and Heilman 1998; Quinsey and Lalumiere 1995; Thornhill and Palmer 2000). Rape may be seen as a consequence of a *direct* adaptation of human behaviour in our ancestral history: for example, men who raped were reproductively more successful. Alternatively, rape may be a result of *indirect* adaptation of behaviour: for example, sexual promiscuity may lead to increased reproductive success so that coerced sex becomes a by-product of this behaviour.

The natural history theory of rape proposed by Thornhill and Palmer (2000) draws on evolutionary psychology and incorporates both direct and indirect explanations of rape. This theory proposes that rape is a consequence of mating strategies that increased male reproductive success (*direct* explanation), acknowledging that these are not the only mating strategies. In addition, rape may occur as a by-product of adaptive strategies for gaining sexual access to a consenting female (*indirect* explanation). Thornhill and Palmer note that rape as a strategy to obtain sexual access is only used in situations in which it is seen to be 'favourable' as, for example, when sexual access cannot be obtained in other ways.

Thornhill and Palmer's theory does not offer a systematic detailed explanation of why and how rape occurs, nor does it take account of the role of factors such as an individual's learning and cognitions and the

509

effect of sociocultural influences. However, evolutionary explanations of behaviour continue to advance, as seen with gene-culture co-evolutionary theory and niche construction (Odling-Smee *et al.* 2003). Gene-culture theory proposes that human evolution results from genetic, individual learning and cultural processes, so attempting to deal with some criticisms of traditional evolutionary theory. In their work on gene-culture theory, Odling-Smee *et al.* (2003) focus on niche construction, which refers to the way in which all living organisms 'construct, modify, and select important components of their local environments' (Day *et al.* 2003: 80). Ward *et al.* (2006) suggest that this approach to rape allows the interaction of genetic predispositions, individual learning, and cultural processes to create specific 'mating domains' in which some men will be 'rape-prone'.

Social-cognitive theories

Cognitive distortions

Cognitive distortions refer to aspects of thinking, such as attitudes and beliefs that are supportive of sexual offending. In the context of sex offending, the term *cognitive distortion* was first used by Abel *et al.* (1984) who proposed that cognitive distortions may be involved in the aetiology and maintenance of child sexual abuse. Thus the development of a view of women as available for sex may play a role in the background of men who rape. Further, cognitive distortions may be seen in rapists' post-offence justifications that rationalise or excuse their behaviour (Gannon *et al.* 2007).

The empirical evidence regarding cognitive distortions among sexual offenders is mixed. Research typically uses questionnaires to ask respondents about their level of agreement for statements supportive of sex offences. The responses of sex offender and control groups are then compared. The reviews conclude that sex offenders show less disagreement with these statements than comparison groups, but that they do *not* necessarily agree with the statements (Gannon and Polaschek 2006). It may be that the questionnaires are too transparent and so respondents, aware of what is being asked, give the 'correct' socially desirable response. However, there is no firm evidence that responses on cognitive distortion measures are correlated with social desirability measures (e.g. Bumby 1996). Nonetheless, there are anecdotal clinical reports that some sex offenders give distorted views about their offending and, indeed, cognitive distortions are a common target in interventions with sex offenders (Ward *et al.* 2006).

The phenomenon of cognitive distortions has been considered within an information-processing approach, with a particular focus on *schema* theories. Schemas are cognitive structures that contain information based on our previous experiences and may guide our interpretation of social cues when we are in similar situations to those previously encountered. A theory has been proposed which suggests that the cognitive distortions of sex offenders are products of schema, or 'causal theories', with respect to the individual's beliefs about themselves and other people (Ward 2000). As these cognitions are normally outside conscious awareness, Ward refers to them as 'implicit theories'. Based on interviews with sex offenders implicit theories have been described for both rapists and child sexual offenders. Polaschek and Ward (2002) have suggested five implicit theories for rapists (see Table 26.2).

Table 26.2   Implicit theories of rapists (after Polaschek and Ward 2002)

---

1. Women are unknowable. Women are different to men and so men cannot understand them so that heterosexual relations are by definition adversarial and women will try to deceive men about their needs/wishes.
2. Women are sex objects. Women are always receptive to men's' sexual needs, even if they don't realise it.
3. The male sex drive is uncontrollable. Men need sexual release or their sexual energy can increase to dangerous levels: once sexually aroused men need to reach orgasm.
4. Entitlement. The belief that one's needs are more important than other people's: thus, men are entitled to sexual access to women and if it is not forthcoming then they are entitled to take it by force.
5. Dangerous world. The world is perceived to be a hostile place so there is a need to act in a pre-emptive way to avoid rejection and hostility.

Implicit theories may develop during childhood and are later applied to the sexual 'domain' as the individual becomes sexually active (Ward 2000). While interviews with rapists provide some support for the presence of implicit theories among rapists (e.g. Polaschek and Gannon 2004), there is as yet no detailed explanations of how sexual *offending* is a consequence of implicit theories.

Empathy deficits
Empathy refers to the ability to be aware of and share the emotions of other people (Jolliffe and Farrington 2004). The distinction may be made between *cognitive* empathy, the ability to understand another's emotions, and *affective* empathy, as in 'sharing' another's emotions. It has been suggested that sexual offenders, like other types of offender, lack empathy: this lack of empathy, evident in other aspects of the offender's life, may be a causal factor for offending (Marshall and Barbaree 1990). However, the empirical evidence shows little difference in empathy between sex offender, non-sex offender and non-offender groups (see Polaschek 2003).

Rather than global deficits in empathy, sex offenders may have specific empathy deficits for their victim group (i.e. women or children). While victim-specific empathy deficits appear to be stable over time, the deficit appears to be strongest for the offender's actual victim rather than for all members of the victim group (Marshall *et al.* 2001). A meta-analysis examining the relationship between empathy and offending confirms that the association is not straightforward and that for sex offenders there is a relatively weak relationship between empathy and sexual offending (Jolliffe and Farrington 2004).

It has been proposed that empathy deficits are a type of cognitive distortion specifically about victim harm (Marshall *et al.* 1999; Ward and Beech 2006) indicating that the cognitive aspect of empathy is involved. Jolliffe and Farrington (2004) supported this view in showing that sex offenders have a greater discrepancy for cognitive empathy than for affective empathy than non sex-offenders.

Deviant sexual preferences

The notion has been advanced (Lalumiere and Quinsey 1994) that sexual offending is a consequence of the offender's deviant sexual preferences, as in preferring coerced to consensual sex. A great deal of the literature concerning deviant sexual preferences applies to offences against both adults and children and will be discussed in the following chapter.

Intimacy deficits

Problems with establishing and maintaining intimate relationships have been associated with sexual offending against women and children and are discussed in the following chapter.

Complex integrationist theories

There have been several attempts to integrate the evidence into complex theories or models of sexual offending against adults. Marshall and Barbaree (1990) developed a general theory of sexual offending, applied to child sexual abuse, rape and other forms of sexual deviance. They propose that sex offending is a consequence of the development of psychological vulnerabilities in childhood and the social and biological changes during puberty that may interact with disinhibiting factors when the opportunity to offend presents itself. According to Marshall and Barbaree, psychological vulnerabilities, such as poor interpersonal skills and problems with emotional self-regulation, can develop from adverse early experiences. In turn, these vulnerabilities may precipitate difficulties in forming social, emotional and sexual attachments to other people. Thus the vulnerabilities may cause problems for the adolescent male in that his poor social skills lead to rejection of genuine attempts at sexual intimacy; this rejection then leads to the development of deviant sexual fantasies. Further, as aggression and sex are associated with the same neural substrates, so they lead to similar feelings which can become confused. If the adolescent male does not learn to distinguish his feelings of aggression and sexual interest then, given the right circumstances, there is an increased likelihood of sexually aggressive behaviour.

Marshall and Barbaree suggest that for a sex offence to occur the male's vulnerabilities interact with situational and emotional disinhibitors such as substance use, anger, sexual frustration or rejection and loneliness, the availability of a victim and the opportunity to offend. Continued sex offending can be accounted for by direct reinforcement of the offence behaviour and by the cognitive distortions the offender uses to rationalise his behaviour. The complex explanation of the development of sex offending proposed by Marshall and Barbaree does not give specific explanations for different types of sexual offending.

The confluence model of sexual aggression advanced by Malamuth *et al.* (1993) draws on evolutionary, feminist and social learning theories. From an evolutionary perspective, it is proposed that sexual aggression has both *ultimate* and *proximal* causes. Ultimate causes provide an explanation of why humans as a species have developed certain behaviour patterns. Malamuth *et al.* outline two pathways relating to the evolutionary drive among men to increase reproductive success that are associated with sexual aggressive behaviour towards women. The first pathway is *sexual promiscuity*: a preference for impersonal sex with lots of partners which may at times involve coercion. The second is *hostile masculinity*: the use of aggression and coercion to obtain sex when in relationships with women and to achieve dominance over women more generally. Sexual aggression is the result of the convergence of these two pathways.

In contrast, proximal causes explain how patterns of behaviour develop in individuals. Malamuth *et al.* suggest that the proximal causes of sexual aggression are based on four assumptions. First, sexual aggression against women results from a convergence of risk factors which act to motivate, disinhibit and provide the context for the aggression to occur. Second, these risk factors will predict aggression against women but not against other men. Third, the risk factors will also account for other aggressive and 'dominance' behaviour towards women. Fourth, the likelihood of sexually aggressive behaviour is also influenced by environmental factors such as childhood experiences and situational factors. Malamuth *et al.* outline six types of proximal risk factors for sexual aggression against women:

- sexual responsiveness to rape;
- dominance and control as motives for sex;
- general hostility towards women;
- cognitive distortions that support sexual aggression;
- antisocial personality characteristics; and
- previous sexual experiences.

There is empirical support for these risk factors (Malamuth *et al.* 1995; Wheeler *et al.* 2002), and the theory has predictive utility for a range of sexually aggressive behaviours (Malamuth *et al.* 1995).

Ward and Beech (2006) incorporate biological, neuropsychological and ecological factors into their 'integrated theory of sexual offending'. This view maintains that brain development is influenced by genetics, evolutionary processes and neurobiological processes which can lead to 'vulnerabilities' that predispose an individual to sexual offending. Other vulnerabilities may arise due to ecological factors, such as an individual's social, cultural and physical environment and their personal circumstances. Brain development and ecological factors are proposed to affect an individual's neuropsychological functioning, with a focus on the three interrelated systems of motivation and emotion, action selection and control, and perception and memory. The characteristics, or *state factors*, of sex offenders – deviant sexual arousal, cognitive distortions, emotional dysregulation – are seen as the consequences of an interaction between genes, neurological systems and social learning. However, the integrated theory remains untested empirically.

Prevention

There is a variety of strategies that may be employed to prevent crime, including sexual crime, such as punishing the offender, situational crime prevention and changing the offender. The use of effective crime prevention strategies has advantages if they can reduce both the personal and financial costs associated with crime (Welsh *et al.* 2001). Cohen (2005) suggested that there are three types of cost associated with crime. First, there are *victim costs*: the consequences of a sex offence may include adverse effects on the woman's psychological and physical health, on her close relationships and on her working and social life. Second, there are *third-party costs*: for example, family members may be affected as the consequences of coping with the woman's distress may have adverse effects on personal relationships and may bring about financial loss. Third, there are *society costs*: as with health care, an employer's loss of an employee and, for apprehended offenders, the criminal justice system costs of a court prosecution and the police, prison and probation services.

Situational crime prevention

Situational crime prevention encompasses a range of approaches with a focus on reducing opportunities for crime to take place (Clarke 1997). If criminal behaviour is reliably associated with certain times and places or with specific target vulnerabilities, then by changing the characteristics of the environment or the target the opportunity for successful offending can be reduced. Situational crime prevention is perhaps most widely associated with property crimes, such as burglary and car theft (Felson and Clarke 1998), although the principles arguably extend to crimes against the person, including sex offending (e.g. Wortley and Smallbone 2006). However, Hayward (2007) puts the opposite view, arguing that situational crime prevention may have some utility in reducing property or acquisitive crime but is of limited value in the context of 'expressive crimes' including sexual offending.

Situational approaches to reducing sex offences against women (and children) may seek to increase levels of protection when women are at increased risk of being potential 'targets'. Thus situational methods to reduce the opportunity for sex offending may include improved surveillance, the presence of authority figures such as police officers and the provision of safe transport. Of course, this approach to prevention is principally relevant only to a 'public' environment and does not address the behaviour of the offender, rather relying on potential victims to manage their own behaviour. Sexual crimes against women (and children) occur in other environments, including the home (Fossi *et al.* 2005), where preventative strategies are less likely to be applicable.

Alongside environmental change, measures can be introduced to heighten the individual's awareness of risk. Thus educational programmes may seek to inform potential targets, perhaps particularly children, how to make the distinction between appropriate and inappropriate sexual behaviour and how to develop strategies for recognising and dealing with inappropriate behaviour. This type of educational programme may be delivered in several ways:

- through school education;
- through formal school procedures, reflected in policies and programmes designed to assist in the prevention of sexual abuse;

- through educational programmes for parents, children and teachers to show how technologies, such as the Internet, can be used for sexual harassment and offending and which provide advice on prevention strategies.

Punishment

One of the functions of the criminal justice system is to deliver retribution through punishment to convicted offenders. This punitive function is primarily served by taking something away from the offender, typically their assets through financial penalty or their liberty through incarceration. In some jurisdictions life itself is taken away through administration of the death penalty.

There are various sources of statistical information on the numbers of sex offenders punished by the courts. For sex offences generally, Home Offices figures show a rise in males sentenced to custody from just under 4,000 in 1995 to just over 6,000 in 2005 (Home Office 2006). As noted previously, some caution should be exercised in reading such statistics as changes in legislation and reporting conventions can misleadingly make it appear that actual crime rates are changing.

Does punishing sex offenders work?

The answer to this question, of course, depends on what is meant by 'work'. Imprisoning sex offenders does protect the public (although not prison staff or other prisoners) while the offender is incarcerated. However, once released from custody does the experience of imprisonment make sex offenders less likely to reoffend? The overall reoffending rate after two years for adult men released from prison in England and Wales is around 65 per cent, varying by year, type of offence and so on (Cunliffe and Shepherd 2007). Set against this baseline level, the reconviction rates in England and Wales for serious sex offenders are considerably lower, at around 10 per cent, even with follow-up periods of up to six years (Craig et al. 2008; Friendship and Thornton 2001; Hood et al. 2002). It appears that the reconviction rates in England and Wales are not out of step with other countries (Harris and Hanson 2004).

The broad picture to emerge from the reconviction studies is that, while they may commit other types of crime, after being convicted most sex offenders do not reoffend sexually. In particular, 'first-time' sexual offenders are less likely to be reconvicted for a sex offence than individuals with a history of convictions for sex offences, and reoffending is less likely when offenders are past 50 years of age.

Do recidivism rates of sex offenders vary by the type of offence? Harris and Hanson show that, in increasing order, 'boy-victim' child molesters, rapists, 'girl-victim' and incest offenders are reconvicted at significantly different rates. Reconviction rates may also be influenced by the interaction between the type of offence and the offender's age. Drawing on data from a large sample, Hanson (2001) reported that rapists (mean age 32.1 years) were younger than both extra-familial child molesters (37.1 years) and incest offenders (38.9 years). The recidivism risk of the rapists decreased as they grew older but the extra-familial child molesters showed little reduction in recidivism risk until they reached 50 years of age. Parenthetically, while the mean ages suggest that sex offenders are in their 30s, this should not mask the fact that there is a population of adolescent sex offenders (Barbaree *et al.* 1993; Hudson and Ward 2001). Understanding young sex offenders is important with respect to gaining a greater appreciation of the link between abuse and abusing.

One of the issues associated with the low rates of recidivism for sex offences lies in determining the success of interventions intended to reduce reoffending. This issue is particularly pertinent when considering the effects of initiatives with the individual sex offender.

Changing the offender

The literature does not lend itself easily to disentangling the effects of treatment according to whether the sex offence was committed against an adult or a child. As Lösel and Schmucker (2005) point out: 'Most treatment programmes combined individuals with different types of sex offense' (p. 126).

In their meta-analysis of the effectiveness of treatments for sex offenders (against both adults and children), Lösel and Schmucker distinguish seven approaches to intervention: two interventions based on biological treatment, hormonal medication and surgical castration; two based on methods of behaviour change, 'classic behavioural' and cognitive-behavioural; and three psychotherapeutic based on psychosocial methods, insight orientated treatment and therapeutic communities. The focus here is on treatment effectiveness; issues related to outcome research are discussed in the following chapter.

Biological intervention

The two methods of biological intervention are surgical castration (e.g. Willie and Beier 1989) and hormonal medication (e.g. Maletzky and Field 2003). Lösel and Schmucker coded eight studies of surgical castration and six studies of hormonal medication (none of which were conducted in the UK) and suggested that both the biological-based interventions had substantial effects on recidivism. Given due caution regarding the quality of the research base, the negative side effects of the intervention and the legal and ethical implications of these interventions, Lösel and Schmucker suggest that this approach should not be abandoned. When combined with psychological treatments biological intervention may have a maximum effect.

Psychosocial intervention

A psychosocial intervention brings together psychological and behavioural change in order to reduce sex offending (Gannon *et al.* 2008b; Marshall *et al.* 1999). An example of this style of intervention is provided by the Sex Offender Treatment Programme.

Sex Offender Treatment Programme
In the 1990s the English and Welsh Prison Service developed a manualised treatment programme specifically for sex offenders – the Sex Offender

Treatment Programme (SOTP; Grubin and Thornton 1994) – based on cognitive-behavioural methods of behaviour change. Mann and Fernandez (2006) provide an overview of the development of SOTP into a set of treatment programmes for various subgroups of sex offenders. Programmes such as SOTP are *multimodal* in that they address a range of targets associated with sex offending. Mann and Fernandez note that targets may be patterns of sexual arousal, attitudes tolerant of sexual assault, interpersonal problems and self-regulation deficits. The delivery of SOTP, typically with a group of offenders, is led by trained prison staff, including psychologists, with quality of delivery carefully monitored and managed. The methods of behaviour change used in SOTP, in keeping with its cognitive-behavioural orientation, include education, role-play, social problem-solving skills training, social skills and assertiveness training and relapse prevention techniques.

As well as prison-based programmes, there are community-based treatment programmes for sex offenders. Community programmes were first implemented in England and Wales during the 1990s (Barker and Morgan 1993) and several more have subsequently been developed for use by the Probation Service in England and Wales (Mandeville-Norden and Beech 2004). In community provision, unlike prisons, it can be difficult to ensure that the offenders attend treatment with the desired frequency.

What works with sex offenders?

There are two basic strategies to evaluate the outcome of interventions with sex offenders. The first is to consider the effects on reoffending of specific interventions such as SOTP; the second is to review the aggregated outcomes from a substantial number of individual studies.

Evaluation of SOTP and community programmes

Friendship *et al.* (2003) compared the two-year reconviction rates for sex offences of 647 men who had completed the prison-based SOTP with a comparison group of 1,910 men serving custodial sentences for a sex offence but who had not participated in SOTP. The reconviction rate for sex offences was low for both the SOTP group (2.6 per cent) and the comparison group (2.8 per cent). The low reconviction rates make it impossible to draw any conclusions with respect to the effectiveness of SOTP. (The 'low base rate' issue was discussed previously.) Friendship *et al.* also compared the sexual *and* violent offending of the two groups, reporting a trend towards a lower reconviction rate for offenders who had participated in SOTP.

Beech *et al.* (2001) reported a six-year follow-up of 53 child molesters who had previously engaged in community-based treatment (Beckett *et al.* 1994). The overall reconviction rate was 15 per cent; however, only 10 per cent of those offenders 'benefiting from treatment' (based on change on psychometric measures) were reconvicted as compared to 23 per cent of offenders who had 'not responded to treatment'.

Reviews and meta-analyses

The traditional literature review has been augmented by meta-analysis, a method that enables statistically rigorous conclusions to be drawn from large bodies of evidence. As Marshall and McGuire (2003) explain, a meta-analysis generates an *effect size* which is the magnitude of the effect of an independent variable, say treatment, on a dependent variable, say reconviction. An individual meta-analysis can generate an array of effect sizes to determine, for example, how the independent variable affects the dependent variable according to factors such as type of offender, type of treatment and length of follow-up. An effect size can range from 0 to 1: following Cohen (1962), an effect size of 0.2 and below is small, around 0.5 is medium and 0.8 and above is large.

There are several traditional reviews of the sex offender treatment literature (e.g. Alexander 1999; Friendship and Beech 2005; Furby *et al.* 1989; Marshall *et al.* 1991). Alexander (1999) reported a quantitative review of 79 treatment outcome studies involving a total of 10,988 sex offenders. Alexander noted a recidivism rate of 20.1 per cent for treated rapists (N = 393) against 23.7 per cent for untreated rapists (N = 135), and a recidivism rate of 14.4 per cent for treated child molesters (N = 1,676) compared to 25.8 per cent for untreated child molesters (N = 461). Overall, for the two types of sex offending, the recidivism rate was 15.5 per cent with treatment and 25.3 per cent without. Marshall and McGuire note that this equates to an effect size of 0.10.

The first meta-analyses of the effects of intervention with sexual offenders were published in the mid-1990s with more in the early 2000s (Gallagher *et al.* 1999; Hall 1995; Hanson *et al.* 2002; Lösel and Schmucker 2005; Polizzi *et al.* 1999).

Hall (1995) reported the first meta-analysis of the sex offender treatment studies, encompassing 12 individual studies with a total of 1,313 sex offenders. Hall reported an overall effect size of 0.24: the recidivism rate for treated offenders was 19 per cent compared to 27 per cent for untreated offenders. A larger effect size was reported when studies had long follow-up periods (greater than five years) and when the treatment employed cognitive-behavioural methods or biological interventions (castration and hormonal). Further, the presence of rapists in a treatment population did not impact on the size of the treatment effect.

Gallagher *et al.* (1999) reported a qualitative synthesis of 25 outcome studies of sex offender treatment. Comparing treatment and no treatment conditions, the overall effect size was 0.43. Gallagher *et al.* took a base rate of 15 per cent recidivism for sex offenders against which to compare the recidivism rates for different treatment modalities: they recorded a recidivism rate of 7 per cent for cognitive-behavioural treatment, with an effect size of 0.47.

Polizzi *et al.* (1999) reported an evaluation of 21 sex offender programmes, setting categories of scientific rigour for coding the studies. Polizzi *et al.* did not report a mean effect size across all the studies; however, they comment that of the studies reaching minimum standards of experimental rigour (N = 13), six 'showed statistically significant findings in favour of treatment' (p. 371). Polizzi *et al.* gave positive effect sizes ranging from 0.03 to 0.67, concluding that non-prison-based treatments for sex offenders using cognitive-behavioural treatments have the strongest evidence base in terms of effectiveness.

Hanson *et al.* (2002) reported a meta-analysis of 43 psychological treatment studies for sex offenders. This study is particularly notable for the rigour of its procedures for study selection, data coding (across no fewer than 250 variables) and statistical analysis. Across all the studies, Hanson *et al.* note that the rate of recidivism for sexual offences, at an average 46-month follow-up, was lower for the treated (12.3 per cent, N = 5,078) than for the untreated offenders (16.8 per cent, N = 4,376). Hanson *et al.* reported this difference in terms of an odds ratio of 0.81, which Marshall and McGuire have converted to an effect size of 0.11. Hanson *et al.* coded studies as 'current' if they were based on cognitive-behavioural or systemic therapies, the evidence-based treatment of choice. The current studies consistently produced higher odds ratios than the other studies: thus current treatment with adult offenders produced an odds ratio of 0.62 (or, as Marshall and McGuire note, an effect size of 0.28). Thus, as Marshall and McGuire point out, sex offender treatment can produce reasonable effect sizes. Indeed, the effect sizes from sex offender treatment stand comparison with those found for standard treatments of physical heath problems such as bypass surgery (effect size = 0.15) and aspirin for myocardial infarction (effect size = 0.03).

Conclusion

Alongside changing legislation, theories of sexual offending have become increasingly complex, taking account of a range of aetiological factors. Given that sex offenders are a heterogeneous group, it is important to develop theories that are firmly based in empirical research. Furthermore, theories need to attend to the issue of why some men offend sexually against adults and others against children (Gannon *et al.* 2008b). There are problems in estimating the extent of sexual offending but it is highly likely that the official figures are an underestimation of the true rate. Of the strategies to reduce sex offending there is reasonable evidence for tertiary prevention. While this is important, further attention to primary and secondary prevention strategies is needed.

Selected further reading

As the literature often deals with sex offences generally and not always specifically with sex offences against children or against women, the following suggestions for further reading apply to both Chapter 26 and Chapter 27.

A range of theories have been applied to help in understanding sex offending. An overview of theories is given by Tony Ward, Devon Polaschek and Anthony Beech in their book *Theories of Sexual Offending* (2006). For those interested in treatment, William L. Marshall, Dana Anderson and Yolanda Fernandez give an excellent overview of the range and scope of practice in their text *Cognitive Behavioural Treatment of Sexual Offenders* (1999). The theme of treatment is also addressed by William L. Marshall, Yolanda Fernandez, Liam E. Marshall and Geris A. Serran in an edited text, *Sexual Offender Treatment: Controversial Issues* (2006). Sex offenders are of great concern to the

Home Office whose website gives a wide range of statistical and legislative information, along with details of several research projects concerned with sex offending: there is a wealth of information across the whole site (http://www.homeoffice.gov.uk) and in particular at http://www.homeoffice.gov.uk/science-research/RDS//science-research/RDS/.

References

Abel, G. G., Becker, J. V. and Cunningham-Rathner, J. (1984) 'Complications, consent, and cognitions in sex between children and adults', *International Journal of Law and Psychiatry*, 7: 89–103.

Alexander, M. A. (1999) 'Sexual offender treatment efficacy revisited', *Sexual Abuse: A Journal of Research and Treatment*, 11: 101–16.

Barbaree, H. E., Marshall, W. L. and Hudson, S. M. (eds) (1993) *The Juvenile Sex Offender*. New York: Guildford Press.

Barker, M. and Morgan, R. (1993) *Sex Offenders: A Framework for the Evaluation of Community-Based Treatment*. London: Home Office.

Beckett, R. C., Beech, A. R., Fisher, D. and Fordham, A. S. (1994) *Community-Based Treatment for Sex Offenders: An Evaluation of Seven Treatment Programmes*. London: Home Office.

Beech, A. R., Elliott, I. A., Birgden, A. and Findlater, D. (2008) 'The internet and child sexual offending: a criminological review', *Aggression and Violent Behavior*, 13: 216–28.

Beech, A. R., Erikson, M., Friendship, C. and Ditchfield, J. (2001) *A Six-Year Follow-Up of Men Going Through Probation-Based Sex Offender Treatment Programmes*, Home Office Research Findings No. 144. London: Home Office.

Brownmiller, S. (1975) *Against Our Will: Men, Women and Rape*. New York: Simon & Schuster.

Bumby, K. M. (1996) 'Assessing the cognitive distortions of child molesters and rapists: development and validation of the MOLEST and RAPE scales', *Sexual Abuse: A Journal of Research and Treatment*, 8: 37–54.

Clarke, R. V. (ed.) (1997) *Situational Crime Prevention: Successful Case Studies*, 2nd edn. New York: Harrow & Heston.

Cohen, J. (1962) 'The statistical power of abnormal-social psychological research: a review', *Journal of Abnormal and Social Psychology*, 65: 145–53.

Cohen, M. A. (2005) *The Costs of Crime and Justice*. New York: Routledge.

Craig, L. A., Browne, K. D., Stringer, I. and Hogue, T. E. (2008) 'Sexual reconviction rates in the United Kingdom and actuarial risk estimates', *Child Abuse and Neglect*, 32: 121–38.

Culbertson, K. and Dehle, C. (2001) 'Impact of sexual assault as a function of perpetrator type', *Journal of Interpersonal Violence*, 16: 992–1007.

Cunliffe, J. and Shepherd, A. (2007) *Re-offending of Adults: Results from the 2004 Cohort*, Home Office Statistical Bulletin 06/07. London: Home Office.

Day, R. L., Laland, K. N. and Odling-Smee, J. (2003) 'Rethinking adaptation: the niche construction perspective', *Perspectives in Biology and Medicine*, 46: 80–95.

Felson, M. and Clarke, R. V. (1998) *Opportunity Makes the Thief*, Police Research Series Paper 98. London: Home Office.

Fossi, J. J., Clarke, D. D. and Lawrence, C. (2005) 'Bedroom rape: sequences of sexual behavior in stranger assaults', *Journal of Interpersonal Violence*, 20: 1444–66.

Friendship, C. and Beech, A. R. (2005) 'Reconviction of sexual offenders in England and Wales: an overview of research', *Journal of Sexual Aggression*, 11: 209–23.

Friendship, C. and Thornton, D. (2001) 'Sexual reconviction for sexual offenders discharged from prison in England and Wales', *British Journal of Criminology*, 41: 285–92.

Friendship, C., Mann, R. E. and Beech, A. R. (2003) *The Prison-Based Sex Offender Treatment Programme – An Evaluation*, Home Office Research Findings No. 205. London: Home Office.

Furby, L., Weinrott, M. R. and Blackshaw, L. (1989) 'Sex offender recidivism: a review', *Psychological Bulletin*, 105: 3–30.

Gallagher, C. A., Wilson, D. B., Hirschfield, P., Coggeshall, M. B. and MacKenzie, D. L. (1999) 'A quantitative review of the effects of sex offender treatment on sexual reoffending', *Corrections Management Quarterly*, 3: 19–29.

Gannon, T. A. and Polaschek, D. L. L. (2006) 'Cognitive distortions in child molesters: a re-examination of key theories and research', *Clinical Psychology Review*, 26: 1000–19.

Gannon, T. A., Rose, M. R. and Ward, T. (2008a) 'A descriptive model of the offense process for female sexual offenders', *Sexual Abuse: A Journal of Research and Treatment*, 20: 352–74.

Gannon, T. A., Ward, T. and Collie, R. M. (2007) 'Cognitive distortions in child molesters: theoretical and research developments over the past two decades', *Aggression and Violent Behavior*, 12: 402–16.

Gannon, T. A., Collie, R. M., Ward, T. and Thakker, J. (2008b) 'Rape: psychopathology, theory and treatment', *Clinical Psychology Review*, 28: 982–1008.

Groth, A. N. (1979) *Men Who Rape: The Psychology of the Offender*. New York: Plenum Press.

Grubin, D. and Thornton, D. M. (1994) 'A national programme for the assessment and treatment of sex offenders in the English prison system', *Criminal Justice and Behavior*, 21: 55–71.

Hall, G. C. N. (1995) 'Sexual offender recidivism revisited: a meta-analysis of recent treatment studies', *Journal of Consulting and Clinical Psychology*, 63: 802–9.

Hanson, R. K. (2001) *Age and Sexual Recidivism: A Comparison of Rapists and Child Molesters*, Report No. 2001-01. Canadian Correctional Service, Canada.

Hanson, R. K., Gordon, A., Harris, A. J. R., Marques, J. K., Murphy, W., Quinsey, V. L. and Seto, M. C. (2002) 'First report on the collaborative outcome data project on the effectiveness of psychological treatment for sex offenders', *Sexual Abuse: A Journal of Research and Treatment*, 14: 169–94.

Harris, A. J. R. and Hanson, R. K. (2004) *Sex Offender Recidivism: A Simple Question*, Report No. 2004-03. Canadian Correctional Service, Canada.

Hayward, K. (2007) 'Situational crime prevention and its discontents: rational choice theory versus the "culture of now"', *Social Policy and Administration*, 41: 232–50.

Hoare, J. and Jansson, K. (2007) 'Extent of intimate violence, nature of partner abuse and serious sexual assault, 2004/05, 2005/06, 2006/07 BCS', in D. Povey, K. Coleman, P. Kaiza, J. Hoare and K. Jansson (eds), *Homicides, Firearm Offences and Intimate Violence 2006/07*, 3rd edn, Home Office Statistical Bulletin 03/08. London: Home Office.

Hoare, J. and Povey, D. (2008) 'Violent and sexual crime', in C. Kershaw, S. Nicholas and A. Walker (eds), *Crime in England and Wales 2007/08*, Home Office Statistical Bulletin 07/08. London: Home Office.

Home Office (2006) *Offender Management Caseload Statistics 2005*, Home Office Statistical Bulletin 18/06. London: Home Office.

Hood, R., Shute, S., Feilzer, M. and Wilcox, A. (2002) 'Sex offenders emerging from long-term imprisonment: a study of their long-term reconviction rates and of Parole Board members' judgements of their risk', *British Journal of Criminology*, 42: 371–94.

Hudson, S. M. and Ward, T. (2001) 'Adolescent sexual offenders: assessment and treatment', in C. R. Hollin (ed.), *Handbook of Offender Assessment and Treatment*. Chichester: John Wiley & Sons, pp. 363–77.

Jolliffe, D. and Farrington, D. P. (2004) 'Empathy and offending: a systematic review and meta-analysis', *Aggression and Violent Behavior*, 9: 441–76.

Kelly, L., Lovett, J. and Regan, L. (2005) *A Gap or a Chasm? Attrition in Reported Rape Cases*, Research Study No. 293. London: Home Office.

Kershaw, C., Nicholas, S. and Walker, A. (eds) (2008) *Crime in England and Wales 2007/08*, Home Office Statistical Bulletin 07/08. London: Home Office.

Koss, M. (1992) 'The underdetection of rape: methodological choices influence incidence estimates', *Journal of Social Issues*, 48: 61–75.

Lalumiere, M. L. and Quinsey, V. L. (1994) 'The discriminability of rapists from non-sex-offenders using phallometric measures: a meta-analysis', *Criminal Justice and Behavior*, 21: 150–75.

Lösel, F. and Schmucker, M. (2005) 'The effectiveness of treatment for sexual offenders: a comprehensive meta-analysis', *Journal of Experimental Criminology*, 1: 117–46.

Malamuth, N. M. and Heilman, M. F. (1998) 'Evolutionary psychology and sexual aggression', in C. B. Crawford and D. L. Krebs (eds), *Handbook of Evolutionary Psychology: Ideas, Issues, and Applications*. Mahwah, NJ: Lawrence Erlbaum & Associates, pp. 515–42.

Malamuth, N. M., Heavey, C. L. and Linz, D. (1993) 'Predicting men's antisocial behavior against women: the interaction model of sexual aggression', in G. C. N. Hall, R. Hirschmann, J. R. Graham and M. S. Zaragoza (eds), *Sexual Aggression: Issues in Etiology, Assessment, and Treatment*. Washington, DC: Taylor & Francis, pp. 63–97.

Malamuth, N. M., Linz, D., Heavey, C. L., Barnes, G. and Acker, M. (1995) 'Using the confluence model of sexual aggression to predict men's conflict with women: a ten year follow-up study', *Journal of Personality and Social Psychology*, 69: 353–69.

Maletzky, B. M. and Field, G. (2003) 'The biological treatment of dangerous sex offenders: a review and preliminary report of the Oregon pilot depo-Provera program', *Aggression and Violent Behavior*, 8: 391–412.

Mandeville-Norden, R. and Beech, A. R. (2004) 'Community-based treatment of sex offenders', *Journal of Sexual Aggression*, 10: 193–214.

Mann, R. E. and Fernandez, Y. M. (2006). 'Sex offender programmes: concept, theory, and practice', in C. R. Hollin and E. J. Palmer (eds), *Offending Behaviour Programmes: Development, Application, and Controversies*. Chichester: John Wiley & Sons, pp. 155–77.

Marshall, W. L. and Barbaree, H. E. (1990) 'An integrated theory of the etiology of sexual offending', in W. L. Marshall, D. R. Laws and H. E. Barbaree (eds), *Handbook of Sexual Assault: Issues, Theories, and Treatment of the Offender*. New York: Plenum Press, pp. 257–75.

Marshall, W. L. and McGuire, J. (2003) 'Effect sizes in the treatment of sexual offenders', *International Journal of Offender Therapy and Comparative Criminology*, 47: 653–63.

Marshall, W. L., Anderson, D. and Fernandez, Y. (1999) *Cognitive Behavioural Treatment of Sexual Offenders*. Chichester: John Wiley & Sons.

Marshall, W. L., Hamilton, K. and Fernandez, Y. M. (2001) 'Empathy deficits and cognitive distortions in child molesters', *Sexual Abuse: A Journal of Research and Treatment*, 13: 123–30.

Marshall, W. L., Fernandez, Y. M., Marshall, L. E. and Serran, G. A. (eds) (2006) *Sexual Offender Treatment: Controversial Issues*. Chichester: John Wiley & Sons.

Marshall, W. L., Jones, R., Ward, T., Johnston, P. and Barbaree, H. E. (1991) 'Treatment outcome with sex offenders', *Clinical Psychology Review*, 11: 465–85.

Murmen, S. K., Wright, C. and Kalunzy, G. (2002) 'If "boys will be boys", then girls will be victims? A meta-analytic review of the research that relates masculine ideology to sexual aggression', *Sex Roles*, 46: 359–75.

Myhill, A. and Allen, J. (2002) *Rape and Sexual Assault of Women: The Extent and Nature of the Problem. Findings from the British Crime Survey*, Home Office Research Study No. 237. London: Home Office.

Odling-Smee, F. J., Laland, K. N. and Feldman, M. W. (2003) *Niche Construction: The Neglected Process in Evolution*. Princeton, NJ: Princeton University Press.

Polaschek, D. L. L. (2003) 'Classification', in T. Ward, D. R. Laws and S. M. Hudson (eds), *Sexual Deviance: Issues and Controversies*. Thousand Oaks, CA: Sage, pp. 154–71.

Polaschek, D. L. L. and Gannon, T. A. (2004) 'The implicit theories of rapists: what convicted offenders tell us', *Sexual Abuse: A Journal of Research and Treatment*, 16: 299–314.

Polaschek, D. L. L. and Ward, T. (2002) 'The implicit theories of potential rapists: what our questionnaires tell us', *Aggression and Violent Behavior*, 7: 385–406.

Polizzi, D. M., MacKenzie, D. L. and Hickman, L. J. (1999) 'What works in adult sex offender treatment? A review of prison- and non-prison-based treatment programmes', *International Journal of Offender Therapy and Comparative Criminology*, 43: 357–74.

Povey, D., Coleman, K., Kaiza, P., Hoare, J. and Jansson, K. (2008) *Homicides, Firearm Offences and Intimate Violence 2006/07*, Home Office Statistical Bulletin 03/08. London: Home Office.

Proulx, J., Beauregard, E., Cusson, M. and Nicole, A. (eds) (2007) *Sexual Murderers: A Comparative Analysis and New Perspectives*. Chichester: John Wiley & Sons.

Quinsey, V. L. and Lalumiere, M. L. (1995) 'Evolutionary perspectives on sexual offending', *Sexual Abuse: A Journal of Research and Treatment*, 7: 301–15.

Reiss, L. L. (1986) *Journey into Sexuality: An Exploratory Voyage*. Englewood Cliffs, NJ: Prentice-Hall.

Sanday, P. R. (1981) 'The socio-cultural context of rape: a cross-cultural study', *Journal of Social Issues*, 37: 5–27.

Scully, D. and Marolla, J. (1985) '"Riding the bull at Gilley's": convicted rapists describe the rewards of rape', *Social Problems*, 32: 251–63.

Sentencing Guidelines Secretariat (2007) *Sexual Offences Act 2003. Definitive Guideline*. London: Sentencing Guidelines Secretariat..

Sheldon, K. and Howitt, D. (2007) *Sex Offenders and the Internet*. Chichester: John Wiley & Sons.

Stevenson, K., Davies, A. and Gunn, M. (2003) *Blackstone's Guide to the Sexual Offences Act 2003*. Oxford: Oxford University Press.

Thomas, T. (2005) 'Sex crime', in C. Hale, K. Hayward, A. Wahidin and E. Wincup (eds), *Criminology*. Oxford: Oxford University Press, pp. 245–65.

Thornhill, R. and Palmer, C. T. (2000) *A Natural History of Rape: Biological Bases of Sexual Coercion*. Boston: MIT Press.

Ward, T. (2000) 'Sexual offenders' cognitive distortions as implicit theories', *Aggression and Violent Behavior*, 5: 491–507.

Ward, T. and Beech, A. R. (2006) 'An integrated theory of sexual offending', *Aggression and Violent Behavior*, 11: 44–63.

Ward, T., Polaschek, D. L. L. and Beech, A. R. (2006) *Theories of Sexual Offending*. Chichester: John Wiley & Sons.

Welsh, B. C., Farrington, D. P. and Sherman, L. W. (eds) (2001) *Costs and Benefits of Preventing Crime*. Boulder, CO: Westview Press.

Wheeler, J. G., George, W. H. and Dahl, B. J. (2002) 'Sexually aggressive college males: empathy as a moderator in the "confluence model" of sexual aggression', *Personality and Individual Differences*, 33: 759–77.

Willie, R. and Beier, K. M. (1989) 'Castration in Germany', *Annals of Sex Research*, 2: 103–33.

Wortley, R. and Smallbone, S. (eds) (2006) *Situational Prevention of Child Sexual Abuse*, Crime Prevention Studies Vol. 19. Monsey, NY: Criminal Justice Press.

Chapter 27

Sexual offences against children

Clive R. Hollin, Emma J. Palmer and Ruth M. Hatcher

Introduction

Although one of the first texts on child sexual assault was published in 1857 by Auguste Ambroise Tardieu (1818–79), a French pathologist and forensic medical scientist, it is highly likely that adult sexual activity with children has been prevalent for centuries. The growth in concern about the involvement of children in sexual activity led many countries to enact laws, as seen with the introduction of an age of consent for sexual activity, to reflect society's changing moral values. However, the difficult issue in practice is to say at what age children stop being children and have the capacity knowingly to consent to sex. Thus, staying with the example of age of consent, the practical consequences of legally defining 'child' is seen in changes in the age of consent over time and in current international variations in the age of consent.

In the mid-nineteenth century children aged as young as ten could legally consent to (hetero)sexual acts: this age has increased over time so that currently 15 to 18 years of age is the range in most western societies. There are still variations be to seen: for example, in England and Wales the age of consent is 16 years, in Turkey it is 18 years, and in Spain it is 13 years. Of course, there are caveats associated with the legislation regarding, for example, the child's mental capacity and whether the consent is to a heterosexual or homosexual act.

As with other forms of crime, the legal definition of a sexual offence against a child has shifted and changed over time. As outlined in Table 27.1 the Sentencing Council Guidelines for the 2003 Sexual Offences Act (Sentencing Guidelines Secretariat 2007) categorises sexual offences against children under a number of headings. These headings encompass a range of types of offence including rape committed against females and males, physically violent assaults, offences committed within the family and the use of images on the Internet.

With regard to sexual offences against children, the 2003 Act removed an ambiguity that previously allowed those accused of child rape to argue

Table 27.1 Sexual offences in 2003 Act (after Sentencing Guidelines)

Rape and other offences against children under 13
- Rape of a child under 13
- Assault of a child under 13 by penetration
- Sexual assault of a child under 13
- Causing or inciting a child under 13 to engage in sexual activity

Child sex offences
- Sexual activity with a child
- Causing or inciting a child to engage in sexual activity
- Engaging in sexual activity in the presence of a child
- Causing a child to watch a sexual act
- Child sex offences committed by children or young persons
- Arranging or facilitating commission of a child sex offence
- Meeting a child following sexual grooming etc.

Abuse of position of trust
- Sexual activity with a child
- Causing or inciting a child to engage in sexual activity
- Sexual activity in the presence of a child
- Causing a child to watch a sexual act

Familial child sex offences
- Sexual activity with a child family member
- Inciting a child family member to engage in sexual activity
- Family relationships

Indecent photographs of children
- Indecent photographs of persons aged 16 or 17

Abuse of children through prostitution and pornography
- Paying for sexual services of a child
- Causing or inciting child prostitution or pornography
- Controlling a child prostitute or a child involved in pornography
- Arranging or facilitating child prostitution or pornography

that the child consented to the sexual act. From the implementation of the 2003 Act, sexual intercourse with a child under 13 years of age is treated as rape. The 2003 Act also introduced the new offences of adult sexual activity, involving both physical and non-physical contact, with a child under the age of 16 years. The Act also takes cognisance of the fact that children may commit sexual crimes against other children so that some offences also apply to those under 18 years of age as well as to adults.

One of the many points to note about the 2003 Act is that while the more familiar sexual crimes, such as rape and sexual assault (familial and non-familial) are present, there is also the inclusion of acts that rely on technology. It is invariably true that as technology advances, so crime will keep pace: this observation is as true for sexual crimes as it is for identity theft, credit card scams and online fraud (Baker 1999; Chen *et al.* 2006), types of offending that are rapidly gaining in sophistication (Grazioli 2004). The 2003 Act took heed of the increasing use of technology, principally the Internet, by adults making inappropriate approaches to children with the aim of encouraging initial agreement to physical contact and so to sexual contact. A new offence was introduced to account for acts of meeting a child following sexual grooming: this offence is one in which an adult becomes friendly with a child, over time establishes an online rapport with the child and then arranges a meeting with the intent of sexual abuse. This type of offence may be countered with a civil preventative order, called a Risk of Sexual Harm Order, which prohibits an adult from engaging in inappropriate behaviours such as sexual online conversations with children. The offence carries a maximum sentence of ten years' imprisonment.

Alongside grooming, the Internet can be used to distribute sexual images of children and as a means of communication between adults with a sexual interest in children (Beech et al. 2008; Sheldon and Howitt 2007; Taylor and Quayle 2006).

The distribution of images of children is of concern not just because it perpetuates a sexual view of children but also because it is likely that children will have been abused in making the images. Taylor et al. (2001) have developed a nine-level typology to describe paedophile picture collections: the typology ranges from pictures of children wearing normal everyday clothes, through explicit erotic posing, to pictures depicting gross sexual assault, sadistic acts and bestiality. The images of children are sometimes produced in large numbers and then made available through the Internet: several researchers have commented on the phenomenon of 'collecting' where adults electronically store large numbers of images of children from the same set (Sheldon and Howitt 2007; Taylor and Quayle 2003). While some adults may restrict their sexual interest in children to the virtual world, others will 'cross over' to physical acts of abuse (Marshall 2000).

The Internet knows no international boundaries so allowing virtual communities, or networks, to form that consist of adults with a sexual interest in children. Beech et al. (2008) describe several such networks and suggest that they exist in order to allow members to trade in images (including filmed images), pass information and function as a location for online discussion (see also Chapter 11 this volume).

The concept of 'crossover' has been applied to the types of crime committed by sexual offenders. While the distinction can be made between sex offences against adults and sex offences against children, it is not the case that every sex offender falls neatly into one of these categories. Some offenders will cross a range of boundaries in their sexual offending: these boundaries may be age, as in whether the offence takes place against adults or children; or gender, with offences against females and males; or type of relationship, as in offending against family members, acquaintances and strangers.

A study carried out in England and Wales investigated the extent of crossover in a sample of 1,345 adult male sex offenders. Cann et al. (2007) reported that 330 (24.5 per cent) of the offenders had a criminal history that showed evidence of crossover. Of these 330 offenders, 108 had offended against both adults and children, 121 had offended against females and males and 189 had offended both within and outside their own family. A smaller number of offenders (74) had crossed at two boundaries and seven had crossed all three (age, gender and relationship). As assessed using the Static-99 risk assessment

(Hanson and Thornton 1999), the crossover offenders were of significantly greater risk of reoffending than the non-crossover offenders.

Finally, not all those who commit sex offences against children are adults: there are sexual offences committed against children by other juveniles (Barbaree *et al.* 1993). As with crime generally, and perhaps sex offences specifically, it is difficult to know exactly what percentage of sex offences are committed by juveniles. Hudson and Ward (2001) suggest that: 'Estimates of the incidents of sexual assaults perpetrated by adolescents range from 20 per cent to 30 per cent of rapes and from 30 per cent to 60 per cent of instances of child molestation' (p. 364). The point made by Hudson and Ward is true of sex offences generally where precise figures and estimates are notoriously difficult to find.

Sexual offending against children: facts and figures

Determining the prevalence of sexual offences committed against children raises similar problems to those discussed in the previous chapter with regard to sex offences against adults. The official statistics are incomplete, hiding the 'dark figure' of unidentified crime. As with sexual offences against adults, an unknown number of sex offences against children remain unreported and, obviously, will not appear in the official crime figures (Grubin 1998). In the case of sex offences against children, however, the picture is further complicated as it may be more difficult for children to report their involvement in sex offences. Children may lack an understanding of the criminal nature of the acts perpetrated against them or they may not have the physical or psychological resources to report abuse. Finally, the British Crime Survey (BCS), which is informative with respect to a large number of offences, is less useful in determining the prevalence of sexual offences against children. The BCS only asks individuals over the age of 16 years about their experience as victims, and for adults it asks only about offences experienced after the age of 16.

The estimation of the prevalence of sex offences against children in England and Wales has therefore rested largely upon crime statistics derived from police recording of reported crime. The Sexual Offences Act 2003 changed the definition of many sexual offences, particularly those relating to children, so that the comparison of data before and after the Act is problematic. Since 2004, the crime figures recorded by police are available for sexual assault on males and females under 13 years old, sexual assault on males and females aged 13 or over, rape of a female or male child aged under 13 and rape of a female or male child aged under 16, sexual activity involving a child under 13, sexual activity involving a child under 16. Additionally, data are also available on the abuse of children through prostitution or pornography and sexual grooming (Home Office n.d.). The figures for the year 2007/8 are summarised in Table 27.2.

The most prevalent recorded crime is sexual assault on a female aged 13 years or over: between 2004 and 2008 there were 15,000 to 17,000 of these crimes reported annually. These figures include females aged 13 years and

Table 27.2 Recorded crime 2007/8: sexual offences against children (adapted from Home Office n.d.)

	Against males	Against females
Sexual assault on individual aged 13 and over	1,315	15,790
Sexual assault on a child aged under 16	1,118	3,976
Rape of a child aged under 13	427	1,472
Rape of a child aged under 16	235	2,418
Sexual activity involving a child under 13	1,836[1]	
Sexual activity involving a child under 16	3,100[1]	
Sexual grooming	272[1]	
Abuse of children through prostitution or pornography	110[1]	

[1]These offences are not gender specific so separate figures are not available for males and females.

over so that they include adults as well children. Nonetheless, it is clear from these data that female children are far more likely to be the victims of sex offences than male children. For sexual assault under the age of 16 years and rape under the age of 13 years, three times as many females as males reported such offences. This gender difference is even more pronounced for the (reported) offence of rape of a child aged under the age of 16 years: ten times as many females as males between the ages of 13 and 16 years reported being a victim of rape.

These estimates of crime prevalence based on official statistics can be supplemented by the findings from population surveys. The survey data provides a more rounded picture of the nature of sexual offences against children: a number of localised surveys have thrown up findings which supplement and, in some cases, challenge the reliability of estimates based just on police recorded crime. For example, a study of students aged 16–21 years in England, Scotland and Wales reported that over one half of the sample of females and one quarter of males reported an unwanted sexual incident or interaction before the age of 18 years (Burton *et al.* 1989). This type of finding demonstrates that police data may significantly underestimate the occurrence of such offences.

The data from population surveys can also provide information on the perpetrators of sexual offences against children. Grubin (1998) reports that the surveys have provided information in relation to gender: the vast majority of reported offences against females have been perpetrated by males, while the studies of offences against males are less conclusive. Population surveys can also provide information about the relationship of the offender to the child. A study conducted on behalf of the NSPCC (Cawson *et al.* 2000) reported that abuse is most commonly perpetrated by people known to the victim (other than family): 11 per cent of the sample have been sexually abused in this way, of which 8 per cent involved physical contact and 3 per cent non-contact abuse. In addition, 4 per cent of the sample had been abused, mainly through contact abuse by parents, carers or relatives. Sexual offences by strangers or short-lived acquaintances were reported by 4 per cent of the sample. Thus the research suggests that the perpetrators of sexual offences against children are most likely to be relatives or acquaintances (Burton *et al*. 1989; Fergusson *et al*. 1996; Grubin 1998).

Theories of sexual offending against children

Feminist theories

As noted in the previous chapter, feminist theories are important in highlighting the importance of culture on child sexual abuse. Although feminist theories are predominately concerned with rape, there are attempts to offer a feminist approach to explaining why child sexual abuse occurs (for a review see Ward *et al*. 2006). Feminist theories may consider the role of patriarchy, gender and power in explaining child sexual abuse (e.g. Breckenridge 1992; Featherstone and Fawcett 1994), although different traditions view the role of these factors in different ways.

Cossins (2000) has proposed a power/powerless theory to help explain child sexual abuse. Cossins suggests that child sexual abuse is a means by which some men deal with their feelings of powerlessness or perceived threats to their masculinity and power. Sexuality is seen as playing a vital role in the construction of men's masculinity and power, as sexual behaviours can be important in the establishment of power relationships. Sexually exploitative behaviour, including child sexual abuse, is seen to be part of normative masculine sexuality: the abusive behaviours may occur when a man experiences feelings of powerlessness.

Social-cognitive theories

Cognitive distortions
As noted in Chapter 26 (this volume) cognitive distortion is a term that refers to aspects of cognition, such as attitudes and beliefs, which are supportive of sexual offending. To recap briefly, Abel *et al*. (1984, 1987) proposed that cognitive distortions might be involved in both the development and maintenance of sexual offending. Research among sexual offenders using pen and paper measures asking respondents to indicate their agreement with statements of sexual offence-supportive beliefs provides mixed evidence (for a review see Gannon and Polaschek 2006).

A more recent approach to studying cognitive distortions among sexual offenders has focused on schema theory. Schemas are held to be cognitive structures that contain information based on our previous experiences; in similar situations they may guide how we interpret social cues and respond to the situation. Ward's (2000) implicit theories model is a schema theory that conceptualises sexual offenders' cognitive distortions as products of schema or 'causal theories' about their and others' beliefs and desires. (More detail is provided about Ward's approach in Chapter 26 this volume).

Alongside the implicit theories that have been proposed for rapists, Ward and Keenan (1999) proposed five implicit theories held by child sexual offenders:

- *Children as sexual beings* – children enjoy and even seek opportunities for sex with adults.

- *Nature of harm* – sexual relations between children and adults do not harm children, harm only comes from physical injuries and children recover from these quickly.

- *Uncontrollability* – the offender has little control over events that happen to them and their behaviour is caused by uncontrollable emotions and urges.

- *Entitlement* – evident in the belief that their personal superiority means they are entitled to have their needs met by others, including children meeting their sexual needs.

- *Dangerous world* – the world is full of hostile individuals so if adults are perceived as rejecting and hostile then children may be perceived as 'safe'.

Some studies examining implicit theories have used interview data and the results do provide some support for implicit theories among child sex offenders (e.g. Marziano *et al.* 2006). Other studies have used an experimental approach and provide equivocal support (Gray *et al.* 2005; Keown *et al.* 2008; Milhailides *et al.* 2004).

Empathy deficits
The role of empathy deficits in sex offending was discussed in Chapter 26, this volume. A great deal of this literature applies to both child sex offenders and rapists.

Deviant sexual preferences
Sex offending may be seen as a consequence of offenders having deviant sexual preferences (Lalumiere and Quinsey 1994). In other words, child sex abusers may have a sexual preference for children, while rapists prefer coerced, rather than consensual, sex with women. It has been argued that sexual preference is learnt through classical and operant conditioning processes, as sexual arousal becomes associated with and reinforced by specific stimuli (Laws and Marshall 1990). An individual's acquisition of deviant sexual preferences – remembering that what is considered 'deviant' is dependent upon time and place – is said to result from exposure to or experience of deviant sexual stimuli in childhood. If through classical conditioning these stimuli become associated with sexual arousal, then sexual arousal will become a conditioned response to these stimuli. However, this explanation does not account for individual differences: not everyone who is exposed to or experiences deviant stimuli will develop deviant sexual preferences and, by implication, commit sex offences.

Sexual fantasy is given an important role in maintaining deviant sexual interests, as it allows cognitive rehearsal of the arousing stimuli. If a deviant sexual fantasy is paired with sexual arousal, as through the use of pornography and masturbation, then the arousal will be reinforced. As sexual fantasies grow and develop over time it is possible that, given the opportunity, the individual will act out their fantasies in real life. There is evidence that some sex offenders are aroused by their deviant sexual fantasies: Abel *et al.* (1987) reported that over one half of a sample of sex offenders said that they had been sexually aroused by offence-related deviant sexual fantasies. Similarly, Marshall and Eccles (1991) found that by the age of 20 years two-fifths of child sex offenders had deviant sexual fantasies. While sexual fantasies may have some explanatory power, the figures indicate that deviant fantasies are not always characteristic of sex offenders.

The research that attempts directly to assess sexually deviant preferences faces the methodological issue of how these preferences can be measured. The penile plethysmograph (PPG) is a commonly used method of physiologically measuring sexual preference. In PPG testing the subject attends to a variety of stimuli (audible, visual or both) and the PPG equipment measures concomitant changes in penile length and volume. As with other types of physiological assessment with sex offenders, such as the polygraph (Meijer *et al.* 2008), the research provides mixed support for the effectiveness of PPG assessment (Marshall and Fernandez 2000).

Questions have been raised as to what, exactly, the PPG measures: does the PPG assess sexual preference, sexual interest or sexual arousal? Notwithstanding these issues, a meta-analysis of the predictors of sexual recidivism found that deviant sexual arousal, as assessed by the PPG, was the single largest predictor of reoffending (Hanson and Bussière 1998).

Intimacy deficits
It is frequently noted that many sex offenders have problems in their personal lives with forming and maintaining intimate relationships. According to Marshall (1989), these intimacy deficits arise because of an insecure attachment with parents in childhood. Marshall proposes that the development of an insecure attachment style in childhood can lead to low self-esteem, poor social skills and a perception of the world as rejecting and hostile. These factors make it harder to establish and then maintain intimate relationships as an adult resulting in emotional loneliness. Marshall argues that the interaction of attachment style with social and cultural influences, such as media images, macho attitudes and pornography, can exacerbate an insecure attachment style. This combination may lead to inappropriate intimate behaviours such as seeking intimacy with children as they are perceived to be less rejecting than adults.

In support of this view, there is evidence that sexual offenders are more likely to have an insecure attachment style (Browne and Herbert 1997; Marshall *et al.* 2000; Rich 2006). Furthermore, the childhood of sex offenders may contain events, such as neglect, violence and family disruption, associated with the development of an insecure attachment to parents (Craissati *et al.* 2002). Simons *et al.* (2008) compared the developmental experiences of rapists and child sex offenders and reported that most sex offenders said that they had problematic parental attachment. The rapists were more likely than the child sex offenders to have experienced physical abuse while the child sex offenders had more sexualised experiences at an early age, such as exposure to pornography during childhood and masturbation.

There is empirical support for the role of intimacy deficits in at least some sex offences. Higher levels of emotional loneliness and isolation have also been reported among sexual offenders (Bumby and Hansen 1997; Fisher *et al.* 1999).

Complex integrationist theories

In attempts to integrate the research evidence, a number of complex theories or models of sex offending against children have been proposed. Marshall and Barbaree's (1990) integrated theory and Ward and Beech's (2006) integrated theory of sex offending offer explanations of child sexual abuse. As these theories were discussed in Chapter 26 (this volume) they will not be repeated here. However, there are several other complex models to consider in the context of sex offending against children.

Finkelhor's 'four preconditions' model

Based on empirical research, Finkelhor (1984) developed one of the first theories that acknowledged that child sexual abuse is a complex phenomenon with multiple causes. Finkelhor proposed that four preconditions come together to produce child sex abuse. These four conditions form a temporal sequence, such that each creates the necessary conditions for the following condition and each condition cannot occur without the preceding conditions being met. The four preconditions are: (1) motivation to abuse sexually; (2) overcoming internal inhibitions; (3) the presence of external factors that facilitate offending; and (4) overcoming the child's resistance.

With respect to the first precondition, motivation, Finkelhor proposed three motives for child sexual abuse, each of which has its own background and developmental pathway. The first is deviant sexual arousal, whereby an offender is sexually aroused by children. The second is emotional congruence with children, in which the offender's emotional needs match what children can provide. Third, is 'blockage', when an offender does not have access to appropriate sexual or emotional expression with another adult. A blockage may be temporary or persistent: for example, a temporary blockage might occur due to marital problems, while a persistent blockage might be due to a fear of intimacy. According to Finkelhor, these motives can occur separately or they can interact to produce the motivation for child sexual abuse.

However, motivation alone is not sufficient to lead to child sex abuse. The offender also needs to overcome their internal inhibitions against committing a sexually abusive act. Finkelhor describes a range of factors, some temporary others more enduring, that can lower, or *disinhibit*, a man's internal inhibitions. Disinhibitors include cognitive distortions supportive of sex with children, the effects of drugs or alcohol, some forms of mental illness or senility and current experience of a high level of stress.

Once internal inhibitions have been lowered, it is necessary for external obstacles to be overcome. Negotiating external obstacles may involve systematic planning, although not in all cases. For example, some offenders may work over a period of time to gain the trust of the child, and sometimes also trust of the family, prior to the abuse. In other situations, the offender is alone with the child and the abuse follows. Finally, the offender needs to overcome the child's resistance. There are various strategies the adult may use to gain the trust of the child, including grooming by giving attention and gifts or by gradually desensitising the child to ideas of sexual contact. In other situations, the offender may use threats or force to facilitate sexual abuse.

Finkelhor's model is important, particularly in the way it draws together a variety of factors to explain child sexual abuse. However, it does not offer an explanation of the developmental antecedents that lead to the adult's motivations to sexually abuse children.

Hall and Hirschmann's quadripartite model

Hall and Hirschmann's (1992) account of child sexual abuse focuses on the roles of inappropriate physiological sexual arousal, cognitive distortions, poor emotional control and issues of personality. This model proposes that adverse experiences in childhood can lead to the development of personality problems that, in turn, can produce a predisposition to sex offending against children. This predisposition is only triggered in certain circumstances, as, for example, when an individual experiences poor emotional control. When the predisposition is triggered, the individual can experience deviant sexual arousal, emotional disturbance and enact beliefs supportive of child sexual abuse. If this psychological state is combined with the opportunity to offend, then there is an increased likelihood that child sexual abuse will occur.

Hall and Hirschmann's model states that child sexual abusers will experience varying levels of problems with each factor. In individual cases one problem is likely to be predominant: for example, some men may have higher levels of deviant sexual arousal, others have stronger offence-supportive beliefs. The individual's predominant factor is labelled the 'primary motivation precursor' so that, the model suggests, there may be various subtypes of offenders. The practical implication is that different subtypes may require different treatment strategies.

Hall and Hirschmann (1992) also suggest that child sexual abusers have a 'threshold' for committing an offence: this threshold is reached when the benefits from the abuse are perceived to outweigh the risks. The risks may be related to the self, as with being caught, or to the victim, as with hurting the child. Therefore, it is possible that a man has a 'predisposition' to child sex abuse but does not commit an offence as he has a high 'threshold'. This concept is useful in explaining why some men offend whereas others do not. The research that has examined the risk factors for child sexual abuse supports the propositions within this model.

Ward and Siegert's pathways model

The model of child sexual abuse put forward by Ward and Siegert (2002) is based on 'knitting' together other models, specifically Finkelhor's precondition model, Marshall and Barbaree's integrated theory and Hall and Hirschmann's quadripartite model. The pathways model proposes that there are four separate but interacting psychological mechanisms that lead to child sexual abuse: (1) intimacy and social skills deficits; (2) distorted sexual scripts; (3) emotional dysregulation; and (4) cognitive distortions. The pathways model argues that all four components are involved in sexual offences against children, but that for the individual offender one is dominant and so determines the 'pathway' into child sex offending.

The first pathway focuses on intimacy and social skills deficits. Fear of intimacy is seen as a consequence of an insecure attachment style following early abusive experiences. An insecure attachment style leads the individual to view the world as a hostile place and to expect that becoming emotionally close to other people will lead to rejection. Insecure attachment styles may also affect the development of social skills within adult intimate relationships. It is proposed that this type of offender has normal sexual interests: however, in some situations their fear of intimacy with other adults and lack of social skills can lead them to seek intimacy with a child.

The second pathway highlights the role of deviant sexual scripts in child sex abuse. Sexual scripts are held to be acquired cognitive patterns based on the individual's learning history and which govern behaviour in sexual situations. According to Ward and Siegert, these offenders have distorted beliefs relating to the *context* of sexual behaviour rather than their preferred sexual partner. These distortions lead men to view sex as a physical release that is not associated with intimacy so that the offender seeks impersonal sex. If this strategy leads to rejection from other adults then the man may turn to children for sexual gratification.

The third pathway concerns problems with emotional regulation, i.e. an individual's ability to identify their emotions and those of other people, and to moderate and control their own emotions. These problems are held to be caused by inappropriate experiences and/or an absence of modelling of emotional skills by others. Poor emotional regulation may lead to the individual not being able to recognise other people's emotional responses, such as a child's response to sexual abuse, which act as a disinhibitor for child sex offending.

The fourth pathway focuses on the role of cognitive distortions in child sexual abuse. In this instance, offenders are hypothesised to have attitudes and beliefs supportive of offending in general, not just sexual offending. As such, these offenders are 'generalists' rather than 'specialist' sex offenders. Ward and Keenan (1999) suggested that schemas are responsible for the cognitive distortions shown by child sex abusers. These schemas are proposed to be coherent sets of beliefs that underpin behaviour and are referred to as *implicit theories* (see cognitive distortions above).

Ward and Siegert (2002) have suggested a fifth pathway where offenders – held to be 'pure' paedophiles – have problems in multiple areas, although deviant sexual scripts are at the heart of the matter.

While the pathways model is useful in suggesting that there are several routes that lead to child sex offending, it lacks an evidence base so that it cannot inform evidence-based practice.

Broad conclusions

The complex models of child sex abuse involve a range of factors to attempt to explain this offence. Although there is a growing number of these complex models, there is commonality as each involves distorted cognitive processes such as attitudes, beliefs and empathy, deviant sexual arousal, emotional and impulse dysregulation, and problems such as social skills and intimacy deficits in relating to other people. Further, the models refer to the role of childhood adversity in the development of adult problems. While some models are reasonably well established, others require substantial empirical work to establish their validity. However, as noted in Chapter 26 (this volume), some models seek to explain all types of sexual offending but are not always very clear on the differences between men who offend sexually against children and men who commit rape against adult women. This issue is an obvious target for future empirical research.

Researching prevention

In the previous chapter various approaches aimed at preventing sexual offences – ranging from situational crime prevention, incarceration and changing the individual offender – were discussed. The point was made that it is difficult to separate the effects of interventions according to the nature of the offence. Gannon *et al.* (2008) make the same point in specifically discussing the effects of treatment for rapists. This point is further reinforced by the figures noted above regarding 'crossover', meaning that it is not straightforward to focus on measures intended to reduce sexual offending against adults as opposed to sexual offending against children. As discussed in the previous chapter, there have been six meta-analyses of the sex offender literature: McGuire (2008) gives a full account of the findings from the meta-analyses in reducing violence, including sexual violence. However, nested within the broad findings from the meta-analyses, there is an important issue with regard to the design of the individual studies included in the meta-analyses which is important with respect to the way the literature is interpreted and understood.

It is widely held that the randomised control trial (RCT) is the 'gold standard' in research design as it gives high levels of internal validity. However, there are other types of validity, primarily *external* validity (the wider applicability of the findings), that may be adversely affected by the use of an RCT (see Hollin 2008). To maintain internal validity the conduct of an RCT demands high levels of control over selection, intervention methods and procedures and so on. In treatment with sex offenders the inherent risk in striving for high levels of internal control is that external validity is compromised. In other words, factors such as too strict criteria for admission into the treatment and a style of delivery that is too prescribed via treatment protocols may produce such an artificial set of conditions that the findings cannot be generalised to other settings.

An RCT design requires that participants are randomly allocated to experimental and control conditions. In the case of sex offenders this raises specific ethical and legal issues. If there are grounds for believing that an intervention will be effective in reducing sex offending then, arguably, to withhold this intervention from some sex offenders and to allow others to participate is akin to playing the lottery with future rates of victimisation as the stakes. Further, if decision-making within the prison and probation services regarding the use of custody, levels of security and parole is, in part at least, influenced by the offender's participation in an intervention, then a decision to withhold the intervention on research grounds would be open to legal challenge. These issues have been the subject of exchanges within the sex offender literature.

In the context of sex offender treatment, Marshall and Marshall (2007) posed the question of whether the RCT is the 'gold standard or an inappropriate strategy'. They took the view, based on a critique of the research literature and, in particular, an RCT of sex offender treatment – the Sex Offender Treatment and Evaluation Programme (SOTEP; Marques *et al.* 2005) – that the design itself poses practical and ethical problems for practitioners. Marshall and Marshall's article drew a response from other researchers in the sex offender field who argued that RCTs are the optimum design for evaluative research (Seto *et al.* 2008). In their reply, Marshall and Marshall (2008) respond to the points raised by Seto *et al.*, maintaining their position that there are doubts about using RCTs in the particular context of the evaluation of sex offender treatment. Marshall and Marshall raise the interesting point that when RCTs are conducted over a long period of time (SOTEP was started in the 1980s) the content of the intervention must remain unchanged, regardless of advances in the field, as to change the intervention would violate the design. This provides an excellent example of research into effectiveness working against effective practice! It is not possible to say how the above debate will play out, although it is worth noting that questions about the 'gold standard' of RCTs are being asked in other fields (e.g. Tucker and Reed 2008) as well as in mainstream criminology (Goldkamp 2008).

Conclusion

As with sex offences against adults, sex offending against children raises legal and practical concerns. The law continues to evolve, particularly in the light of technological advances such as the Internet that give new ways and means for child sex offenders to operate. It is impossible to be precise about the extent of sex offending against children. It is likely that a great deal of sexual abuse of children remains unreported and hidden from statistical records. While complex models of sexual offending have been advanced, this complexity is not always matched by a strong evidence base. There are a number of strategies that have been used with some success to prevent sex offending. However, disentangling the specific effects against children and against adults remains a task for future preventative research.

Selected further reading

As the literature often deals with sex offences generally and not always specifically with sex offences against children or against women, the following suggestions for further reading apply to both Chapter 26 and Chapter 27.

A range of theories have been applied to help in understanding sex offending. An overview of theories is given by Tony Ward, Devon Polaschek and Anthony Beech in their book *Theories of Sexual Offending* (2006). For those interested in treatment, William L. Marshall, Dana Anderson and Yolanda Fernandez give an excellent overview of the range and scope of practice in their text *Cognitive Behavioural Treatment of Sexual Offenders* (1999). The theme of treatment is also addressed by William L. Marshall, Yolanda Fernandez, Liam E. Marshall and Geris A. Serran in an edited text, *Sexual Offender Treatment: Controversial Issues* (2006). Sex offenders are of great concern to the Home Office whose website gives a wide range of statistical and legislative information, along with details of several research projects concerned with sex offending: there is a wealth of information across the whole site (http://www.homeoffice.gov.uk) and in particular at http://www.homeoffice.gov.uk/science-research/RDS//science-research/RDS/.

References

Abel, G. G., Becker, J. V. and Cunningham-Rathner, J. (1984) 'Complications, consent, and cognitions in sex between children and adults', *International Journal of Law and Psychiatry*, 7: 89–103.

Abel, G. G., Becker, J. V., Cunningham-Rathner, J., Mittelman, M. S., Murphy, W. D. and Rouleau, J. L. (1987) 'Self-reported sex crimes of nonincarcerated paraphiliacs', *Journal of Interpersonal Violence*, 2: 3–25.

Abel, G. G., Gore, D. K., Holland, C. L., Camp, N., Becker, J. and Rathner, J. (1989) 'The measurement of the cognitive distortions of child molesters', *Annals of Sex Research*, 2: 135–53.

Baker, C. R. (1999) 'An analysis of fraud on the internet', *Internet Research: Networking Applications and Policy*, 9: 348–59.

Barbaree, H. E., Marshall, W. L. and Hudson, S. M. (eds) (1993) *The Juvenile Sex Offender*. New York: Guildford Press.

Beech, A. R., Elliott, I. A., Birgden, A. and Findlater, D. (2008) 'The Internet and child sexual offending: a criminological review', *Aggression and Violent Behavior*, 13: 216–28.

Breckenridge, J. (1992) 'An exotic phenomenon? Incest and child rape', in J. Breckenridge and M. Carmody (eds), *Crimes of Violence: Australian Responses to Rape and Child Sexual Assault*. Sydney: Allen & Unwin, pp. 18–37.

Browne, K. D. and Herbert, M. (1997) *Preventing Family Violence*. Chichester: John Wiley & Sons.

Bumby, K. M. and Hansen, D. J. (1997) 'Intimacy deficits, fear of intimacy and loneliness among sexual offenders', *Criminal Justice and Behavior*, 24: 315–31.

Burton, S., Kelly, L. and Regan, L. (1989) *An Exploratory Study of the Prevalence of Sexual Abuse in a Sample of 16–21 Year Olds*. London: CWASU, London Metropolitan University.

Cann, J., Friendship, C. and Gozna, L. (2007) 'Assessing crossover in a sample of sexual offenders with multiple victims', *Legal and Criminological Psychology*, 12: 149–63.

Cawson, P., Wattam, C., Brooker, S. and Kelly, G. (2000) *Child Maltreatment in the United Kingdom: A Study of the Prevalence of Abuse and Neglect*. London: NSPCC.

Chen, Y., Chen, P. S., Hwang, J., Korba, L, Song, R. and Yee, G. (2006) 'An analysis of online gaming crime characteristics', *Internet Research*, 16: 246–61.

Cossins, A. (2000) *Masculinities, Sexualities and Child Sexual Abuse*. The Hague: Kluwer Law International.

Craissati, J., McClurg, G. and Browne, K. D. (2002) 'Characteristics of perpetrators of child sexual abuse who have been sexually victimized as children', *Sexual Abuse: A Journal of Research and Treatment*, 14: 225–40.

Featherstone, B. and Fawcett, B. (1994) 'Feminism and child abuse: opening up some possibilities?', *Critical Social Policy*, 42: 61–80.

Fergusson, D. M., Horwood, L. J. and Lynskey, M. T. (1996) 'Childhood sexual abuse and psychiatric disorder in young adulthood: I. Prevalence of sexual abuse and factors associated with sexual abuse', *Journal of the American Academy of Child and Adolescent Psychiatry*, 35: 1355–64.

Finkelhor, D. (1984) *Child Sexual Abuse: New Theory and Research*. New York: Free Press.

Fisher, D., Beech, A. R. and Browne, K. D. (1999) 'Comparison of sex offenders to non-sex offenders on selected psychometric measures', *International Journal of Offender Therapy and Comparative Criminology*, 43: 473–91.

Gannon, T. A. and Polaschek, D. L. L. (2006) 'Cognitive distortions in child molesters: a re-examination of key theories and research', *Clinical Psychology Review*, 26: 1000–9.

Gannon, T. A., Collie, R. M., Ward, T. and Thakker, J. (2008) 'Rape: psychopathology, theory and treatment', *Clinical Psychology Review*, 28: 982–1008.

Goldkamp, J. S. (2008) 'Missing the target and missing the point: 'successful' random assignment but misleading results', *Journal of Experimental Criminology*, 4: 83–115.

Gray, N. S., Brown, A. S., MacCulloch, M. J., Smith, J. and Snowden, R. J. (2005) 'An implicit test of the association between children and sex in paedophiles', *Journal of Abnormal Psychology*, 114: 304–8.

Grazioli, S. (2004) 'Where did they go wrong? An analysis of the failure of knowledgeable internet consumers to detect deception over the internet', *Group Decision and Negotiation*, 13: 149–72.

Grubin, D. (1998) *Sex Offending Against Children: Understanding the Risk*, Police Research Series Paper No. 99 London: Home Office.

Hall, G. C. N. and Hirschmann, R. (1992) 'Sexual aggression against children: a conceptual perspective of etiology', *Criminal Justice and Behavior*, 19: 8–23.

Hanson, R. K. and Bussière, M. T. (1998) 'Predicting relapse: a meta-analysis of sexual offender recidivism studies', *Journal of Consulting and Clinical Psychology*, 66: 348–62.

Hanson, R. K. and Thornton, D. (1999) *Static-99: Improving Actuarial Risk Assessments for Sex Offenders*, User Report 99-02. Ottawa: Department of the Solicitor General of Canada.

Hollin, C. R. (2008) 'Evaluating offending behaviour programmes: does only randomisation glister?', *Criminology and Criminal Justice*, 8: 89–106.

Home Office (n.d.) A *Summary of Recorded Crime Data from 2002/03 to 2007/08*. Online at: http://www.homeoffice.gov.uk/rds/recordedcrime1.html (accessed 20 November 2008).

Hudson, S. M. and Ward, T. (2001) 'Adolescent sexual offenders: assessment and treatment', in C. R. Hollin (ed.), *Handbook of Offender Assessment and Treatment*. Chichester: John Wiley & Sons, pp. 363–77.

Keown, K., Gannon, T. A. and Ward, T. (2008) 'What were they thinking? An exploration of child sexual offenders' beliefs using a lexical decision task', *Psychology, Crime, and Law*, 14: 317–37.

Lalumiere, M. L. and Quinsey, V. L. (1994) 'The discriminability of rapists from non-sex-offenders using phallometric measures: a meta-analysis', *Criminal Justice and Behavior*, 21: 150–75.

Laws, D. R. and Marshall, W. L. (1990) 'A conditioning theory of the etiology and maintenance of deviant sexual preference and behavior', in W. L. Marshall, D. R. Laws and H. E. Barbaree (eds), *Handbook of Sexual Assault: Issues, Theories, and Treatment of the Offender*. New York: Plenum Press, pp. 209–30.

McGuire, J. (2008) 'A review of effective interventions for reducing aggression and violence', *Philosophical Transactions of the Royal Society*, 1503: 2577–97.

Marques, J., Wiederanders, M., Day, D. M., Nelson, C. and van Ommeren, A. (2005) 'Effects of a relapse prevention program on sexual recidivism: final results from California's Sex Offender Treatment and Evaluation Project (SOTEP)', *Sexual Abuse: A Journal of Research and Treatment*, 17: 79–107.

Marshall, W. L. (1989) 'Invited essay: intimacy, loneliness and sexual offenders', *Behaviour Research and Therapy*, 27: 491–503.

Marshall, W. L. (2000) 'Revisiting the use of pornography by sexual offenders: implications for theory and practice', *Journal of Sexual Aggression*, 6: 67–78.

Marshall, W. L. and Barbaree, H. E. (1990) 'An integrated theory of the etiology of sexual offending', in W. L. Marshall, D. R. Laws and H. E. Barbaree (eds), *Handbook of Sexual Assault: Issues, Theories, and Treatment of the Offender*. New York: Plenum Press, pp. 257–75.

Marshall, W. L. and Eccles, A. (1991) 'Issues in clinical practice with sex offenders', *Journal of Interpersonal Violence*, 6: 68–93.

Marshall, W. L. and Fernandez, Y. M. (2000) 'Phallometric testing with sexual offenders: limits to its value', *Clinical Psychology Review*, 20: 807–22.

Marshall, W. L. and Marshall, L. E. (2007) 'The utility of the random controlled trial for evaluating sexual offender treatment: the gold standard or an inappropriate strategy?', *Sexual Abuse: A Journal of Research and Treatment*, 19: 175–91.

Marshall, W. L. and Marshall, L. E. (2008) 'Good clinical practice and the evaluation of treatment: a response to Seto et al.', *Sexual Abuse: A Journal of Research and Treatment*, 20: 256–60.

Marshall, W. L., Anderson, D. and Fernandez, Y. (1999) *Cognitive Behavioural Treatment of Sex Offenders*. Chichester: Wiley.

Marshall, W. L., Serran, G. and Cortoni, F. A. (2000) 'Childhood attachments, sexual abuse, and their relationship to adult coping in child molesters', *Sexual Abuse: A Journal of Research and Treatment*, 12: 17–26.

Marshall, W. L., Fernandez, Y. M., Marshall, L. E. and Serran, G. A. (eds) (2006) *Sexual Offender Treatment: Controversial Issues*. Chichester: John Wiley & Sons.

Marziano, V., Ward, T., Beech, A. R. and Pattison, P. (2006) 'Identification of five fundamental implicit theories underlying cognitive distortions in child abusers: a preliminary study', *Psychology, Crime and Law*, 12: 97–105.

Meijer, E. H., Verschuere, B., Merckelbach, H. L. G. J. and Crombez, G. (2008) 'Sex offender management using the polygraph: a critical review', *International Journal of Law and Psychiatry*, 31: 423–9.

Milhailides, S., Devilly, G. J. and Ward, T. (2004) 'Implicit cognitive distortions and sexual offending', *Sexual Abuse: A Journal of Research and Treatment*, 16: 333–50.

Rich, P. (2006) *Attachment and Sexual Offending*. Chichester: John Wiley & Sons.

Sentencing Guidelines Secretariat (2007) *Sexual Offences Act 2003. Definitive Guideline*. London: Sentencing Guidelines Secretariat.

Seto, M. C., Marques, J. K., Harris, G. T. *et al.* (2008) 'Good science and progress in sex offender treatment are intertwined: a response to Marshall and Marshall (2007)', *Sexual Abuse: A Journal of Research and Treatment*, 20: 247–55.

Sheldon, K. and Howitt, D. (2007) *Sex Offenders and the Internet*. Chichester: John Wiley & Sons.

Simons, D. A., Wurtele, S. K. and Durham, R. L. (2008) 'Developmental experiences of child sexual abusers and rapists', *Child Abuse and Neglect*, 32: 549–60.

Taylor, M. and Quayle, E. (2003) *Child Pornography: An Internet Crime*. Hove: Brunner-Routledge.

Taylor, M., Holland, G. and Quayle, M. (2001) 'Typology of paedophile picture collections', *Police Journal*, 74: 97–107.

Tucker, J. A. and Reed, J. M. (2008) 'Evidentiary pluralism as a strategy for research and evidence-based practice in rehabilitation psychology', *Rehabilitation Psychology*, 53: 279–93.

Ward, T. (2000) 'Sexual offenders' cognitive distortions as implicit theories', *Aggression and Violent Behavior*, 5: 491–507.

Ward, T. and Beech, A. R. (2006) 'An integrated theory of sexual offending', *Aggression and Violent Behavior*, 11: 44–63.

Ward, T. and Keenan, T. (1999) 'Child molesters' implicit theories', *Journal of Interpersonal Violence*, 14: 821–38.

Ward, T. and Siegert, R. J. (2002) 'Towards a comprehensive theory of child sexual abuse: a theory knitting perspective', *Psychology, Crime and Law*, 8: 319–51.

Ward, T., Polaschek, D. L. L. and Beech, A. R. (2006) *Theories of Sexual Offending*. Chichester: John Wiley & Sons.

Chapter 28

Sex work

Belinda Brooks-Gordon

Defining prostitution

Prostitution is the exchange of sex for money or other goods. Prostitution is not a crime but many of the activities surrounding it, however, are criminal offences. The legal definition of a 'common prostitute' is a man or woman who 'on at least one occasion and whether or not compelled to do so, offers or provides sexual services to another person in return for payment or a promise of payment to them or a third person'.[1] Payment or gain is *any* financial advantage or the provision of goods or services (including sexual services) gratuitously or at a discount.[2] Gain can also include the goodwill of any person likely to bring financial advantage. Although prostitution is not illegal almost every way someone works in the sex industry has become criminalised. There are currently 24 offences with maximum punishments of 14 years to life imprisonment used against people in the sex industry. At the time of writing the Policing and Crime Bill 2009 contains provisions for further offences, making at least 26 possible offences to punish people involved in prostitution. In this chapter I will show how these laws are defined as well as the main patterns, trends and characteristics of those involved in prostitution. This will be followed by explanations of the phenomena and recent policy responses to sex work.

Offences related to sex work

People in the sex industry are subjected to a broad range of punitive offences which are shown in Table 28.1. It is an offence in England and Wales[3] to loiter or solicit in a public place for prostitution. This includes any kind of tempting or alluring of prospective customers in words, winks, glances or smiles and includes wearing revealing clothing in a red light area or 'beat' (Release 2005). A street or public place includes any bridge, lane or alley and it includes working from windows or balconies.[4] It is an arrestable offence to solicit from, or close to, a vehicle, either persistently or in a way to cause nuisance or annoyance. Loitering and soliciting were defined fifty years ago[5]

Table 28.1 Offences associated with sex work

Public offences	Maximum penalties
Soliciting[i]	Fine
Kerb crawling[ii]	Fine. Loss of driving licence, exposure to family and friends
Sex in a public lavatory[iii]	Fine or 6 months sentence
Disorderly behaviour[iv]	Fine
Anti-Social Behaviour Orders[v]	Ban on any behaviour, association, exclusion from any area, for between 2 years and life
Controlling offences	
Causing or inciting prostitution for gain[vi]	7 years
Controlling prostitution for gain[vii]	7 years
Keeping a brothel	7 years
Indoor offences	
Breach of planning regulations	Fine
Keeping a disorderly house[viii]	Fine and/or imprisonment at discretion of court
Allowing children in brothels[ix]	6 months and/or fine
Landlord knowingly allowing use of premises as brothel[x]	6 months and/or fine
Tenant knowingly allowing use of premises as a brothel or for prostitution by a single person[xi]	6 months and/or fine
Breach of tenancy agreement[xii]	Repossession of property, litigation for damages
Breach of licensing requirements	Revocation of licence
Advertising offences	
Graphic advertising likely to 'deprave or corrupt'[xiii]	3 years and/or fine
Placing adverts for prostitution in public telephone[xiv]	6 months and/or fine
Criminal damage[xv]	6 months and/or fine

i. Street Offences Act 1959, as amended by the Sexual Offences Act 2003.
ii. Sexual Offences Act 1985, s.1(4).
iii. Sexual Offences Act 2003, s.71.
iv. Public Order Act 1986, s.5.
v. Crime and Disorder Act 1998.
vi. Sexual Offences Act 2003, s.52.
vii. Sexual Offences Act 2003, s.53.
viii. Disorderly Houses Act 1751, s.8 (and common law).
ix. Children and Young Persons Act 1933, s.3.
x. Sexual Offences Act 1956, s.34.
xi. Sexual Offences Act 1956, s.35.
xii. Sexual Offences Act 1956, s.36.
xiii. Obscene Publications Act 1959.
xiv. Criminal Justice and Police Act 2001, s. 46.
xv. Town and Country Planning (Control of Advertisements) Regulations 1992.

and although these are 'nuisance' offences the activity of waiting on the street is no different to waiting for a bus or a lift. Despite its presumed nuisance value, it is the commercial sexual activity that *follows* the waiting that is the substance of the offence. Similarly kerb-crawling[6] is the act of looking for someone and giving them a lift elsewhere. There is therefore an interesting conceptual slippage between how the activity is defined, i.e. by 'nuisance', and what is criminalised.

It is also an offence for any individual to have any sexual activity in a public lavatory or to use threatening, abusive or insulting words or behaviour. For any of these offences, civil orders designed for anti-social behaviour (ASBOs) may also be applied (see Burney 2005; Collins and Cattermole 2006; Sagar 2007) and breaching these can result in criminal charges.

'Controlling' offences

The offences of causing or inciting prostitution for gain apply to both street and indoor work. These laws were passed in the controversial Sexual Offences Act (SOA) 2003 and are committed where a person intentionally causes or incites a person to become a prostitute in any part of the world for, or in the expectation of, gain for themselves or a third person (see Bainham and Brooks-Gordon 2004). Controlling is where someone intentionally controls any of the activities of another person relating to prostitution in any part of the world for, or in the expectation of, gain. The tariff of seven years can be applied to any person, including family members, boyfriends, girlfriends or maids. It is possible to be charged with aiding and abetting someone to commit these offences and the nebulous concept of 'control' must be proven beyond reasonable doubt.

While it is not illegal to work in a brothel it is illegal to 'to keep, manage, or act or assist in the management' of a brothel. A brothel can be a private flat, sauna or massage parlour if it is used by more than one man or woman for the purposes of heterosexual or homosexual prostitution. If premises are shared between two people and they work on different days of the week, the premises still count as a brothel even if only one person is present on any one day. Where rooms or flats in one building are let separately to different people, the building may be regarded as a brothel if the people are working together. Management includes any type of administrative activity such as having a say in what services would be offered, taking clients' money and entering amounts in a ledger, putting up adverts, paying bills, selecting staff, supplying materials or taking money to the bank or post office. The law prevents any type of collaborative or collective working by turning it into brothel-keeping and groups who wish to work together for safety become liable to brothel-keeping laws. A major failing of the law is that it provides no way to work safely with others and avoid prosecution and seizure of assets.

Brothel-keepers and parlour managers are prosecuted under the Proceeds of Crime Act 2002, which allows significant police disruption of, and encroachment into, off-street sex workers' lives.[7] The police have a share in the proceeds of sex workers' earnings as a result of the intrusion giving the police a powerful vested interest in maintaining the criminality of sex work-related activities as a result of the Serious and Organised Crime and Police Act 2005. This allows for assets from brothel-keeping offences to be seized, and as police keep a proportion (min. 25 per cent) of the assets seized there is a large financial inducement to raid brothels where people are working contentedly and safely. This inducement represents a serious conflict of interest in the policing of brothels.

Prosecutions under the Proceeds of Crime Act frequently fail, however, on 'abuse of process' arguments. When the police are aware of the existence of a sauna or parlour for several years, visit the premises numerous times and never tell them to close, brothels might legitimately expect not to be prosecuted. For example *R v. Green and others* [2008] was a 13-handed prosecution (as a result of Police Operation Pentameter 1) involving the running of one of the biggest brothels in the UK. The indictment was stayed after a successful abuse of process argument.

For those who are convicted the consequences are far-reaching, and because brothel-keeping offences are cast as sexual offences perpetrators become 'sexual offenders'. The Sentencing Guidelines Council states that 'the sentences for public protection must be considered in all cases'. The guidelines aim to ensure that 'sexual offenders' are not released into the community if they present 'a significant risk of serious harm'. The controlling offences are therefore highly problematic, and as they are so broad ordinary ways of living are drawn into the nebulous concept of control and many women who wish to hide or separate their sex work from their families by renting premises or who rent rooms to other women for safety become 'sexual offenders' even though they represent no danger to the community. The Sentencing Guidelines Council recommends a starting tariff for brothel-keepers of two years' imprisonment.[8] This not only encourages net-widening of the criminal law into adult consensual sexual activity, but militates against sex workers working together for company and safety. In few other areas in democratic society is the right to freedom of association so impinged upon. It also shows penalties under the criminal law to be at odds with the civil law where judgements in VAT cases recognise that workers in the wider sex industry such as escort agencies and lap dancing clubs do a legitimate job and have agency to work for themselves.[9]

Additional indoor offences

A breach of planning regulations is possible if residential premises are used, depending on the amount of space given to the business – even if a sex worker is working from home alone. It is also an offence to keep a 'disorderly house' frequented by the public. A house is 'disorderly' if it is 'not regulated by the restraints of morality' under the antiquated Disorderly Houses Act 1751 used when there are public complaints about sex shows, bondage, domination, sadism and masochism (BDSM) practices, even if no conduct is visible from the outside. Whoever 'appears' to keep the house, irrespective of whether they are the real owner, is charged under this law.

It is an offence to allow a child between the ages of 4 and 15 years to reside in or frequent a brothel even if nothing is going on there. It is an offence for a landlord to let or continue to let premises knowing they will be used as a brothel. A tenant or occupier of premises knowingly permitting them to be used as a brothel commits an offence. It is an offence for a tenant knowingly to allow their premises to be used for prostitution by a single person even if the person is not doing anything illegal. Using premises for prostitution constitutes a breach of a tenancy agreement if the agreement prohibits 'illegal or immoral' use.[10] The law therefore defines and controls prostitution differently to other businesses operating in indoor premises.

Advertising and maiding

It is an offence to place advertisements that could 'deprave or corrupt' or to place advertisements for prostitution in or near a public telephone. People employed to place advertising cards (carders) risk being prosecuted for unauthorised advertising or criminal damage. If sexual services are advertised on the Internet this can be criminal depending on which country it is viewed in, but if *time* is offered with clients then no offence is committed. With such laws there is the danger of legal anomalies such as *Shaw* v. *DPP*[11] or *Knuller* v. *DPP*.[12] Sex workers can legally employ a maid or housekeeper to assist them and for safety but maids or housekeepers run the risk of being accused of keeping a brothel if they have any say in how things are run (Adams 2008).[13] In addition, there can be entrapment where police pose as clients, and although the police may act as an agent provocateur, this gives no defence for the sex worker.

Trafficking for sexual exploitation

Trafficking for sexual exploitation offences are designed to protect people of all ages. None of the offences which came into force under the Sexual Offences Act 2003[14] in Table 28.2 require proof that the offender acted 'for gain' so prosecution cannot be avoided by someone not standing to benefit from their involvement.[15] There is no requirement for anyone to have been forced into sex work and allegations of trafficking may be made about migration where no fear, force or fraud took place (Release 2005).[16]

It is possible to be imprisoned under section 58 for giving a prostitute a free lift to her brothel at her own request.[17] The Sentencing Guidelines Council recommends that custodial sentences *must* be considered in *all* cases, despite

Table 28.2 Trafficking for 'sexual exploitation'

Offences	Maximum penalties
To arrange or facilitate arrival in UK[i]	14 years' imprisonment
To arrange of facilitate travel in UK[ii]	14 years' imprisonment
To arrange of facilitate departure from UK[iii]	14 years' imprisonment

i. Sexual Offences Act 2003, s.57.
ii. Sexual Offences Act 2003, s.58.
iii. Sexual Offences Act 2003, s.59.

cases where there was evidence that all involved were consensually selling sexual services.[18]

Child prostitution offences

The activities of anyone involved in the sex work of youths under 18 years of age is criminalised except the young person.[19] Four main offences include: paying for sexual services of anyone under 18 years,[20] causing or inciting prostitution involving anyone under 18 years,[21] controlling prostitution involving anyone under 18 years,[22] arranging or facilitating prostitution involving anyone under 18 years.[23] The offences have maximum penalties of 14 years' imprisonment to life imprisonment. It means that two 17 year olds who help each other with advice and support or lifts could be liable for a life sentence on indictment. It is questionable how easy these laws are to police and gather intelligence on when the rest of the adult consensual sex industry is increasingly criminalised and alienated from the police services.[24]

Patterns and trends

Historically the selling and buying of sexual services was regulated through a variety of means in the civil and criminal courts, and also the canonical courts.[25] Offences have been constructed through history from Vagrancy Acts dating back to Henry VIII (1530–1), Contagious Diseases Acts (1964–9), the recommendations of the Wolfenden Report, and subsequent Sexual Offences Acts (1956, 1959, 1967, 1985 and 2003). Prior to 2003, prostitution offences were minor, low-level offences. Table 28.3 shows conviction levels for prostitution offences. The main thing to note in these contemporary patterns and trends is that the number of offences are counted rather than offenders so that a large number of offences often pertains to a small number of offenders.

Offences

Figures for prosecutions of the main street-based offences show a reduction from the previous decade overall. Prosecutions for loitering and soliciting went down by nearly two-thirds over the decade from 10,459 prosecutions in 1990 to 3,065 in 2001 in England and Wales. Convictions went down by over two-thirds from 10,020 in 1990 to 2,781 in 2001 (Offending and Criminal Justice Group, Home Office 2003). Prosecutions and convictions for kerb-crawling and persistent solicitation of women went down by nearly a third from 70 in 1990 to 51 in 2001. Soliciting offences have remained stable throughout the past decade peaking at 2,111 offences in 2002/3. Since that time soliciting offences have fallen year on year to a recent total of 1,258 recorded offences in 2007/8.

Prosecutions of sex workers in indoor locations were rare in the past and convictions for running a brothel or for living on the earnings of a prostitute were more likely; however, even the latter were very low and went down from two prosecutions in 1990 to none in 2001. At the same time, parliamentary and Home Office debates represented a mismatch between low prevalence of the

Table 28.3 Prostitution offences in England and Wales 1997–2007/8*

	1997	1997/8	1998/9	1999/0	2000/1	2001/2	2002/3	2003/4	2004/5	2005/6	2006/7	2007/8	% change 2006/7– 2007/8
Soliciting for purposes of prostitution	–	–	1,107	973	1,028	1,655	2,111	1,944	1,821	1,640	1,290	1,258	–2
Exploitation of prostitution	131	142	215	138	129	129	127	186	117	153	190	183	–4
Trafficking for prostitution	–	–	–	–	–	–	–	–	21	33	43	56	30
Abuse of children through prostitution	–	–	–	–	–	–	–	–	99	124	101	110	9

*Chris Kershaw, Sian Nicholas and Alison Walker (eds) (2008) *Crime in England and Wales 2007/08: Findings from the British Crime Survey and Police Recorded Crime*, Home Office Statistical Bulletin 07/08. London: Home Office.

offences and government attention to them. The catch-all term 'exploitation' makes it difficult to disaggregate these offences. Not surprisingly, there was a large rise in these offences in 2003/4 with the implementation of the SOA 2003, followed by a drop in the number of offences. A subsequent rise in 2006/7 accompanied the financial inducement provided to police following the Serious Organised Crime and Police Act (SOCA) 2005.

Trafficking offences, the spectre through which prostitution is framed in political debates, are, despite yearly increases since the SOA 2003, comparatively low compared to the numbers of people said to be trafficked. Since the SOA 2003 there have been 90 convictions for trafficking for sexual exploitation (Hansard, col. 587W, 19 November 2008).

Estimates of trafficking vary: in 2000 the Home Office gave widely varying estimates of between 142 and 1,420 women trafficked into the UK. The Home Office told the Joint Committtee on Human Rights that it estimated 4,000 people had been trafficked into prostitution in the UK in 2003 at any one time,[26] while prohibitionist politician Denis McShane stated 25,000 people had been trafficked.[27] Yet the official report on trafficking from the police operation Pentameter 1 shows that despite 55 forces hunting for them, only 88 people were trafficked. If it is accepted that 80,000 work in the sex industry, then only a tiny proportion, 0.11 per cent of people in the sex industry, were trafficked.[28] A subsequent operation, Pentameter 2, found 167 trafficked people, which is still only 0.21 per cent, and in this case some of these people were not in the sex industry but in domestic service.[29] The people found in Pentameter 1 and Pentameter 2 in 2007 were the result of over 1,337 raids of more than 1,300 premises raided and targeted by the police and thought likely to be abusive, yet less than 5 per cent were 'rescued' by police raids. The total convictions for trafficking since it became a crime in the SOA 2003 amounts only to 153 people. Because of the broad definition of trafficking in the SOA 2003, however, it is impossible to know how many of these offences are for serious (i.e. coercive or violent) trafficking and how many were sex workers helping other or migrant workers with lifts or accommodation.

Convictions for trafficking for sexual exploitation halved in the last year from what was an already low and declining rate (Hansard, 4 December 2008, col. 161). Impressions that the sex industry is rife with trafficked people or traffickers is highly misleading. Concern about trafficking was used by the government as the reason for its punitive proposals against sex workers and their clients. At the same time, the government announced cuts in funding to the Metropolitan Police's human trafficking unit and budget cuts for Her Majesty's Court Service (HMCS) and probation (where the lack of increase for years represents a 25 per cent cut for the HMCS and probation service). A similar conflict of interests, when the prisons are full and budgets are being cut, is for assets to be seized under SOCA 2005 and divided up to some of these services.[30]

The abuse of children through prostitution is linked in the official terminology to pornography so it is impossible to disaggregate how many of these offences relate to under-18s in prostitution and how many offences are for the distribution of child pornography. It is interesting, however, that from a peak of 124 offences recorded in 2005/6 the number of offences fell to 110 over the next two years in 2007/8. This drop by a fifth occurs at the same time as the increase in other convictions above following the financial inducements for the police, court services and the Home Office. It has to be questioned whether this drop is linked to the increased criminalisation of adults in sex work which results in worse relationships with the police and a concomitant reduction in intelligence and prosecution of underage offences.

Following the 2008 economic slump, the service sector is in sharp decline[31] and the sex industry may show a downward trend as clients have less money to spend. If, on the other hand, there is an increase in the number of sex workers owing to the loss of jobs in other sectors, then it is possible that only prices will fall even if client numbers are fewer but that the offences may rise with more people going into the sex industry. The combination of lower prices, fewer clients and increased policing could make sex workers' lives more difficult.

Characteristics of offenders, victims, and the 'offence'

Although criminalisation is a relatively recent phenomenon, elements of the historical construction(s) remain in current debates around prostitution and sex work. Traditionally, prostitution was characterised in terms of the depraved woman leading the innocent client astray. In the Wolfenden Report[32] street prostitution was characterised as a public nuisance while off-street prostitution was characterised as an issue of private morality which was not the place of the criminal law. Most notably the behaviour was gender-specific with prostitutes being female and clients male. Current statutes dictate that prostitution is gender neutral yet policy debates still use 'prostitute' to mean a female seller of sexual services and 'client' to refer to a male buyer of services. In government press releases and media coverage grotesque caricatures of abusive clients and abused sex workers are routinely made. The characterisation of participants in the sex industry as either 'offenders' or 'victims' is a false dichotomy when there are workers who are 'offenders' but who could equally be seen as 'victims' of a perversely punitive system.

Sex workers

In recent policy debates it has been repeatedly suggested that there are 80,000 sex workers in the UK. This estimate was produced by Europap-UK[33] in a survey carried out by the European Network for HIV/STD Prevention in Prostitution (Kinnell 1999). The gender distribution showed 85–90 per cent of sex workers were female, with the rest male and transgender. A high proportion (30–40 per cent) of the male sex workers were in central London. One decade later, in a recent replication, the same methodology was used to calculate from projects the current numbers of active adult sex workers and provided a tentative estimate of between 35,870 and 48,393[34] people now working in the UK sex industry (Cusick *et al.* 2009). This is a sex worker population who may never have offended. One of the characteristics of sex work is its mundanity (e.g. Kinnell 1989; Ward and Day 2007). Legal cases, from that of Cynthia Payne to Max Mosley,[35] are characterised by the ordinariness – from cups of tea with clients to luncheon vouchers – of the daily routines of the sex industry. Sex workers illustrate the relational inter-dependence of sex workers and clients:

> Many ladies like me depend on their clients to be able to live and boosts the treasury's coffers too (I pay taxes, have my health checked) so what harm are we doing? It isn't always an easy job, but what is? At least I know I am valued by my gents and I value them. (Marcey, personal correspondence, 16 April 2008)

Perversely the majority of research has been on a minority of those in sex work working in the street sex markets. This is partly because they are the most accessible, most likely to come into contact with the criminal justice system or the least able to refuse the advances of determined interviewers. The majority of those in the sex industry who are self-employed indoor workers have nothing to gain by assisting researchers – especially those who aim to prohibit their activities. However, empirical studies on indoor markets illustrates the choices sex workers have made and their fight for rights (e.g. Bernstein 2007; Gaffney 2008; IUSW Rights of Sex Workers Report 2009; Rhodes *et al.* 2008; Sanders 2006).

Clients

The NATSAL 2000 survey was a probability study of 11,161 men which showed that 4.2 per cent of the male population had paid for commercial sex in the previous five years. This proportion rose from 2 per cent in 1990, though statistical analysis shows that the increase could be due to sampling error (see Weitzer 2005). Outside London, 3.5 per cent of men had paid for sex in the past five years, and only in London, the teeming metropolis (which also has the majority of the UK's male sex worker population), were proportions larger at 8.9 per cent of men (Ward *et al.* 2005).[36] The men who had paid for sex in the previous five years were more likely to be aged 25–34 years, to be previously or never married and to be resident in London. Given that the rate of divorce has increased and the number of men who were previously or never married has also increased, then this too, state the authors, could account for any increase between 1990 and 2000.[37] When the same question is asked over the past year, only 1.3 per cent of men reported paying for sex in the previous 12 months. Although women also pay for sex, the NATSAL survey omitted to ask women the question.

In an analysis of lifetime recourse to prostitution (LRP) Jeannin *et al.* (2008) carried out nine repeated representative cross-sectional surveys from 1987 to 2000 and age-specific estimates of LRP were made. They reported that: 'There was no consistent increasing or decreasing trend over the years' (p. 557). The authors suggest it is possible

> to reconcile the observed stability trend-wise, with the anecdotal evidence of increased recourse to prostitution. First, in the presence of population growth in the relevant age classes, one may find a higher

absolute number of clients despite stability in relative numbers. Second, if anecdotal reports of the decreasing price of paid sex are true, existing clients may increase their buying frequency without a noticeable increase in LRP. Third, the increase in the number of clients may be due to men above the age range [17–45 years] covered in our study. (Jeannin *et al.* 2008: 558).

In a retrospective case note review study Groom and Nandwani (2006) found that of 258 men who had paid for sex, three had also been paid for sex. Over half (51 per cent) had paid for sex abroad, 11 per cent paid somewhere else in the UK while 40 per cent in their own city, either on the streets or in saunas. The majority of the men (93 per cent) paid female sex workers and 4.3 per cent paid men for sex; others paid both. This was a clinic sample so the proportion of those paying for sex is likely to be higher than a general probability sample.

The prevalence of men who are clients of female sex workers varies across continents. In a study on 78 national household surveys, nine city-based surveys and behavioural surveillance surveys totalling 54 countries by Careal *et al.* (2006), prevalence was lowest in Western Europe[38] with 3 per cent of men going to sex workers.[39] Other low-prevalence countries included Vietnam 3 per cent, the Caribbean 3–7 per cent; South Asia Pacific Islands 3–5 per cent; Latin America 2.5 per cent. In Cambodia it was 5–10 per cent, the USA and Australia was 6 per cent; Russia and Southern Africa 7 per cent; West Africa 9 per cent; and Eastern Africa[40] 10 per cent. In China and Hong Kong it was 11 per cent; Central Africa 15 per cent; and in Zimbabwe 29 per cent. In Rwandan and Zambian truck drivers prevalence was high at 47 per cent and 30 per cent respectively. Also in urban areas where incomes were higher, men with high mobility occupations such as migrant workers, police, military, drivers and truckers more men paid for sex (25–30 per cent). In an exploration of patterns of lifetime payment for sex in a general population (in Switzerland) Jeannin *et al.* (2008) found there to be an age effect with an increase in the younger age groups (17–30 years and 31–45 years) which plateaued at 40 years before declining.

Client diversity

Clients of sex workers may be gay, straight or bisexual. They may be female, male or transgender. They may be single, married, divorced or widowed. Approximately 25 per cent of men who paid for sex reported having sex with men (Careal *et al.* 2006). As Humphreys' (1970) classic study showed, many heterosexually married men have homosexual liaisons, so not only do gay men pay for sex but otherwise heterosexual clients pay for gay sex. Clients may also be able-bodied or disabled or sensorily impaired. Sanders (2005) illustrates the disabled communities and it is apparent that men with physical and sensory impairments are a core group of clients who visit female sex workers and sexual surrogates.[41] One sex worker illustrates the reality of a disabled client's experience:

This week I saw a client with Spina Bifida. I had to lift him from his wheelchair, position him (not just dump him) on the bed, undress him, then later, redress him, and place him back in the wheelchair. I was lucky he only weighed 5 stone. Its one of the reasons why more than one lady on the premises can be a good idea. (Penny, 16 February 2008)

Such insights into the client/sex worker relationship shows how the concepts of 'offenders' and 'victims' are blurred or redundant when applied to the reality of many sex workers' and clients' lives. One sex worker described her clients thus:

I wish the likes of Ms Harman[42] could meet with ladies like myself – this week alone I have helped a gent left with injuries after a major motor-cycle accident, a man unfortunate enough to have been born a dwarf, a nice fella who loves cross-dressing (and had nowhere to do it away from his wife – she would divorce him and deprive him of his family life if she knew of his preferences). Yesterday, I met again with a lovely gent – who was virtually a virgin at the age of 60+ when we met for the first time a year or so back. (Glenda 2008)

In a qualitative study on 50 indoor clients Sanders (2008) shows how relationships between male clients and female sex workers are not necessarily exploitative, damaging or disrespectful but that sexual and social scripts performed by male clients are normative and can be used to make sex work a responsible industry. She questions whether there are not economic, material and social capital trade-offs in all relationships. Similarly Earle and Sharpe (2008) describe how some of the similar discourses exist in commercial as non-commercial sex. Analysis of police data on kerb-crawlers found clients to have a lower level of criminality than the general population with only 11 out of 518 men having a prior criminal record (Brooks-Gordon 2006). Kinnell (2008) noted how violent men will adopt the 'client disguise' and mimic clients until they have manoeuvred a sex worker into a vulnerable position to attack her and that it is not unusual for serial predators to target sex workers just because they are easy to attack (Kinnell 2008). This has to be factored in whenever drawing retrospective assumptions from client populations, i.e. that it is not necessarily clients who are violent but the situation in which sex workers operate which renders them vulnerable to violence from others including men who masquerade as clients, the police, the community, as well as vigilantes.

Explanations of prostitution

The historical explanation of prostitution was a perspective devised by men which pathologised prostitute women as being of bad character and 'abnormal' (e.g. Lombroso 1885). More recently, in the Sexual Offences Acts 1956 and 1959, prostitution was explained as a public order offence in the soliciting and kerb-crawling laws (see Self 2003). Public order has become a minor strand in current debates and two explanations of the behaviour have greater predominance in contemporary explanations of prostitution: one is 'exploitation' and the other 'work'.

Prostitution as exploitation

The perspective which holds that prostitution is 'exploitation' regards the sale of any type of sexual service as violence, that prostitutes cannot consent to having their bodies 'invaded' and thus 'exploited', and that prostitution is a symptom of patriarchal society. Those who argue from this perspective campaign for the prohibition of prostitution and for the criminalisation of clients in the belief that prostitution can be eradicted. The view is supported by few academics (e.g. Farley and Raymond in the US; Kelly in England and Barry in Australia). The core claims of the exploitation hypothesis also propose that all customers and traffickers are evil and that sex work and trafficking are inextricably linked. While these claims have been shown to be exaggerated, unverifiable or demonstrably false, the institutionalisation of the moral crusade discourse occurred in US policymaking and practice under the Bush administration (Weitzer 2007). Similarly, institutionalisation of the prohibitionist stance occurred in official discourses in England and Wales[43] where passionate prohibitionist arguments manipulated debates and policy on sex work in the UK from the Sexual Offences Review in 1999 to gain supremacy between 2001 and 2008. This was facilitated by the 'global gag rule' which meant that the US government led an agenda on abstinence and prohibition which influenced many areas of sexuality research. It meant that essential services, advocacy and advice on sexual health, HIV and sex work were prevented as it affected all government-funded research on prostitution between 2001 and 2008[44] in both the USA and UK as many ideologically driven but empirically unsound studies were published on abortion, sexuality and prostitution in an agenda based on denial of choice.

Ideological underpinning of prostitution as exploitation hypothesis

The exploitation hypothesis is informed by three strands of ideological thought. The first is radical separatist lesbian feminism which argues that *all* heterosexual sex is exploitation (Dworkin 1987).[45] The second strand of thought is Marxist feminism which argues that all work is exploitation, and indeed ministers responsible for policy such as Harriet Harman and Fiona McTaggart came from Marxist feminist backgrounds. The final strand is religious evangelism which argues that all non-procreational sex is wrong.[46] The uneasy alliance of separatist feminists and the religious Right that led to the calamitous Meese Commission are replicated in this alliance but with some important differences.[47] One is a critical mass of female parliamentarians eager to be seen to be doing something for women.[48] Others include the politicisation of senior police officers who, using pseudo-scare tactics, lobbied for more power (e.g. Brain *et al.* 1999), the vested interests of pressure groups influenced by US prohibition research and supported by the UK government,[49] and the use of trafficking rhetoric and inflated trafficking figures which exploits migration fears and masks immigration statistics and practices, as well as a news media dependent on 'client journalism' and news agencies producing 'churnalism' from government press releases (Davies 2008).[50] The perspective does not readily accept homosexual and transgender sex work, and the exploitation hypothesis was pursued through the argument that selling sex causes psychological trauma. However, when the argument was explored empirically, the British Psychological Society (BPS) found it was based on untested, unsubstantiated measures and the application of unvalidated and unwarranted 'treatment' (BPS 2008).[51]

Sex work as work

The second current perspective is that sex work is work and exists as labour. While this perspective acknowledges that some sex workers are vulnerable, these vulnerabilities can either be designed out,[52] dealt with by stable housing, employment and welfare support, or addressed in ways other than the criminal law. This perspective argues that sex work is a specific form of labour which should be accorded the full rights and dignity accorded to other types of labour.[53] Large studies carried out by many independent academics and researchers support this perspective (e.g. Brooks-Gordon 2006; Kinnell 2008; Munro and Della Giusta 2008; Sanders 2006; Sanders and Campbell 2007, 2008; Scambler and Scambler 1997; Self 2003, 2006; Ward and Day 2007) as well as clinicians delivering Genito-Urinary services and medical research (Goodyear and Cusick 2007; Jeal *et al.* 2008; Ward *et al.* 2005; Ward and Day 2007) and legal scholars (Scoular and O'Neill 2007; Bainham and Brooks-Gordon 2006; Brooks-Gordon 2006). A variety of different groups including sex worker groups such as the ECP, IUSW and Xtalk campaign for sex work to be recognised as work, and for sex workers to be able to organise (and unionise) in order to make their working lives safer.[54]

This perspective argues that when prostitution is subject to the criminal law, it creates greater vulnerability. De facto criminalisation makes sex workers vulnerable to exploitation and less likely to report any violence (irrespective of how or by whom perpetrated) or access wider health or social services, and puts them, their families and their partners at risk. When sex work is criminalised sex workers are targeted by a variety of criminals and it starts a downward spiral into criminality and prison which inhibits exit from prostitution for those who wish to do other work.[55]

Ideological underpinning of sex work as work

The ideology of sex work as work is informed by traditional liberal principles (e.g. J. S. Mill 'over himself, over his own body and mind, the individual is sovereign') according to which it is not the place of the state to police personal morality. Just because some people disapprove of prostitution or find it distasteful this is no basis to constrain freedoms in a liberal democracy. Sex work is the exchange of money for sex, and because there is nothing wrong with earning money, and there is nothing wrong with having sex, there is nothing wrong with selling or paying for sex. In a modern context, between consenting adults there is no philosophical difference between paid sex and any other sex between adults (casual sex, swinger sex, gay sex, unmarried sex, etc.). Physical sexual pleasure is a joyful thing and may be part of love and attachment but it exists on it own and this can be in a commercial context.

The ideology is also informed by a historical socio-legal perspective which shows how damaging alternative perspectives have been to the safety of those in prostitution and how prohibition has failed historically. For example, brothels have been illegal since 1885 and they have not gone away. Following the Criminal Law Amendment Act of 1885 the National Vigilance Association pursued private prosecutions to get them closed. The result was an increase in street prostitution and pimping (then called bullies) which resulted in the Vagrants Act 1898, making 'living on the earnings of prostitution' illegal (Self 2003). This has been the pattern ever since, with new problems addressed by new legislation which, in turn, creates more, not less, vulnerability. The law in its present form creates vulnerability, and the only solution to the problem of the disempowerment of those who choose to do the work is in empowering them to work safely. The ideology of sex as work is informed by the peer-reviewed medical literature on harm-reduction and HIV (e.g. Aggleton 1998; Goodyear 2007; Goodyear and Cusick 2007; Ward and Day 2007), queer theory and acceptance of alternative lifestyles (Weeks 2008) which acknowledges and respects same-sex and trans-sex work, as well as psychological and sociological empirical work showing the diversity of sex work (e.g. Brooks-Gordon 2005; Sanders 2006, 2008).

Tension between the two ideologies

The exploitation message gathered currency with a new generation of feminists who grew up with the 'transformation of intimacy' (Giddens 1992) or the idealisation of modern love (Beck 1992). It provided a fertile climate for pressure groups to conflate sex work with exploitation, adultery and trafficking, a parallel world where the mere act of being a client was thought to cause 'demand' for trafficking, and ordinary economic migration patterns were conflated as campaigners argued that the influx of migrants from Eastern European states who, faced with discrimination and poor pay in other sectors, chose sex work over other forms of employment. However, methodologically sound empirical studies showed sex workers in the UK to be motivated more by the flexibility of sex work for balancing childcare responsibilities, lifestyle choice, freedom and the relatively high pay compared to other sectors. For example, Sanders (2004) showed nearly half (48 per cent) of indoor workers had a degree or nursing, caring or teaching qualification. And Agustín (2005, 2007) illustrates that in more marginalised spheres sex work can be a free choice or a rational 'resistance' and courageous choice in the face of poverty.

The two ideological positions give rise to four main policy reponses and the effect of each response is shown in Table 28.4. The prohibitionist approach which underpins formal policy in Thailand and in many US states such as New York is often linked to corruption in Thailand and New York where prohibitionist policies are practised against prostitution.[56] The consequences of prohibition result in symbolic or status law, seen in the prohibition of alcohol in the US. It also leads to institutional evasion, evidenced in England previously in divorce and abortion law.

Table 28.4 Policy responses to prostitution and their effects

Characterisation	Response	Aim	Policy	Effect
Exploitation	Prohibition	Eradication	Criminalisation of clients Criminalisation/'rehabilitative penalties' of sex workers	Institutionalised evasion Symbolic law Corruption Witch-hunts Increased danger and death of street sex workers Blackmail of sex worker and clients Distrust of police, intelligence breakdown Industry goes underground Proliferation of pimping Increased imprisonment leading to family breakdown (sex workers and clients) Hard to exit as criminalisation traps sex workers into prostitution
Exploitation	Partial criminalisation	Containment	Criminalisation of clients/decriminalisation of sex workers	Confusion Incoherent legal framework Impossible to police (as star witnesses won't testify) Danger to sex workers as clients more nervous on streets Blackmail of clients Distrust of police Effectively creates criminalisation

Table 28.4 continues overleaf

Table 28.4 continued

Characterisation	Response	Aim	Policy	Effect
Work	Regulation	Containment of street work Labour and human rights/harm reduction	Decriminalisation of sex workers, clients, brothels; safety or tolerance zones for street sex workers Full labour regulation similar to other service sector work including site inspections of premises Licensing of brothels	Partial containment of street work Less danger and fewer deaths of street workers Better health and safety for indoor workers Bad brothels/businesses closed down Better condom use Creates two-tier system if not all allowed to register
Work	Decriminalisation	Self-governance Full labour and human rights/harm reduction	Decriminalisation of both sex workers and clients, brothels Premises subject to same regulations as other service sector work	Empowerment of sex workers Best health and safety of sex workers Improved ability to exit sex work Best cooperation with police Least violence Best harm reduction

While prohibition is a simple policy, easily understood by those who have to police or prosecute it, many objectors argue that, on pragmatic grounds, it is a known policy failure (Meadowcroft 2008). It is impossible to enforce, as no one has a vested interest in coming forward with evidence, and it gives rise to many other problems such as corruption in states where it is formal policy. Partial criminalisation is another policy response with known failings. This intellectually incoherent policy was introduced under controversial circumstances in Sweden in 1999 and despite independent evaluation of its incipient danger to street sex workers (Justis-og Politidepartmentet 2004). This policy response has a lone academic supporter who promotes it as policy for England and Wales (i.e. Matthews 2008).[57]

On the other hand there is the regulationist approach which accompanies legalisation and occurs in many parts of Europe such as Spain, Switzerland, Germany and Austria. It is also seen in differing forms in Nevada and the Netherlands, where partial regulation systems are in place and only those who are entitled to register can do so. This can result in a two-tier system (Netherlands) or allows brothels to operate but not street prostitution (Nevada, USA), which leaves those who work in brothels better off than in regions without them, but excludes those unable to work in brothels who are much worse off. So regulationism, while vastly safer than criminalisation or partial criminalisation, is not as safe, effective or fair as either full legalisation as in Switzerland or decriminalisation.

Decriminalisation, however, has emerged as a step forward for change and empowerment in New Zealand. The Prostitution Reform Act 2003 (PRA) decriminalised prostitution without 'endorsing or morally sanctioning it or its use'. It sought to safeguard the human rights of sex workers, promote their health and safety, contribute to public health and prohibit under-18s from prostitution. The new law led to improvements in health, safety and human rights of sex workers. A rigorous five-year evaluation revealed that over 90 per cent of sex workers felt they had legal rights under the PRA, and more than 60 per cent felt they were more able to refuse sexual services. Prior to the enactment of the PRA, the industry's illegal status meant sex workers were open to coercion and exploitation. The impact of the Prostitution Reform Act 2003 in New Zealand shows that decriminalisation cuts violence, gives greater empowerment to workers and results in better cooperation with police against attempts at coercion. The PRA empowered sex workers by removing the 'taint of criminality' so they can take control of their employment relationships. Such deregulation is part of the richer historical tradition of feminist concern for those in the sex industry espoused by the social reformer Josephine Butler and her 1869 campaign which led to the repeal in 1883 of the Contagious Diseases Acts. To be workable, policy on sex work has to be based, not on moral authoritarianism, but on sound psychological and legal principles and robust evidence that respects the civil liberties and human rights of both sex workers and clients.

Contemporary policy proposals in England and Wales

The Policing and Crime Bill (2009) contains provisions for a new strict liability offence of paying for sexual services with someone controlled for gain, punitive measures against loitering and soliciting including the forced 'rehabilitation' of sex workers and closure orders for indoor premises.[58] Downing Street argues it will: 'protect vulnerable groups, particularly women and children by tackling demand for prostitution'; 'prevent low level crime and disorder taking root in our communities by tightening controls around lap dancing clubs'; and 'strengthen our ability to fight serious and organized crime through improved recovery of criminal assets and improved international judicial co-operation.'[59] The stated purpose of these clauses in the Policing and Crime Bill 2009 is the prevention of violence, abuse and trafficking into prostitution, yet to date there have been no provisions which explicitly address violence.

The Bill comes a short time after harsh sanctions were imposed on sex workers, and those who help them, in the Sexual Offences Act (SOA) 2003. The Sexual Offences Act was followed by the consultation document *Paying the Price* in July 2004[60] and the controversial Home Office document *A Coordinated Prostitution Strategy* (Home Office 2006)[61] which recommended tackling the 'demand' for prostitution with punitive measures against clients.[62] The Bill reintroduces provisions (cl.123–5) removed the previous year from the Criminal Justice and Immigration Bill 2008. These clauses and the creation of enforced rehabilitation of sex workers would have negative consequences for sex workers' lives and for major sections of the criminal justice system.[63] Following the expression of significant concerns, the clauses on prostitution were withdrawn from the Bill, only to return in the Policing and Crime Bill 2008 (following a lamentably short eight-day deadline for comments) and before the results from *Tackling the Demand for Prostitution: A Review* (Home Office 2008) were published.[64]

Criminalising payment for sex

The most controversial part in the new Bill is the strict liability offence of 'paying for services of a prostitute controlled for gain' (cl.13). It will be irrelevant whether the client 'is, or ought to be, aware that any of B's activities are controlled for gain' (cl.13(2)b).[65] The creation of a new offence would criminalise virtually all clients because of the existing broad definitions of 'controlling' and 'for gain' discussed above. All prostitution is for gain, otherwise it is just sex. And the strict liability means that prosecutors would not have to prove that a client knew that the prostitute they had hired was trafficked or pimped. Prosecutors would simply have to show that the prostitute was 'trafficked' and that money changed hands.[66] Thus the proposals would criminalise all clients and the situation would be like that of Sweden where it is more dangerous for sex workers on the streets and results in an increase in off-street work. The Police Federation have argued that it would be impossible to police because clients and sex workers won't testify against each other. The proposals would mean that the clients who currently contact the police if they have concerns about a sex worker's situation would not do so for fear of being criminalised. If a woman had been trafficked, escaped and continued to work in sex work for herself the proposals would criminalise her clients. Any acts involving those who cannot consent are already illegal[67] and critics have argued that the Home Office should focus on helping sex working women to bring charges against any violent man or woman to justice with extant laws rather than bringing in dangerous new ones (Longstaff 2008).[68] For sex workers this provision would render them liable to all of the inchoate offences in English law such as incitement, accessory and procurement to make them more vulnerable.

Given that 25 per cent of men who pay for sex have sex with other men, to criminalise male clients of male sex workers would return to the pre-Wolfenden days of criminalising same-sex activity in private just because money changes hands. It would be a gross infringement of civil liberties and natural justice. For disabled groups, according to European (case) law rulings, one's sex life is the most intimate part of one's private life. For disabled clients (men and women) paying a sex worker sometimes to lose their virginity or for the first non-medical touch in their lives conflicts with the spirit of European Human Rights Law.[69]

Loitering or soliciting and forced rehabilitation

While there is a positive move to remove the term 'common prostitute' (cl.15),[70] a clause redefines soliciting behaviour taking place on two or more occasions in any period of three months as 'persistently'. Such infrequency can only be described as occasional.[71] Clause 16 brings in compulsory and forced 'rehabilitative penalties' for sex workers in an amendment to cl.57 of the Street Offences Act 1959 requiring anyone arrested for loitering or soliciting to attend three meetings with a supervisor approved by the court. Failure to comply would result in a summons back to court and 72 hours imprisonment. The compulsory rehabilitation order under section 1(2A) of the Street Offences Act 1959 intended to address the 'causes of their offending'. The provisions in the Bill and much of the media discussion[72] were based on extrapolations from limited evidence from street sector samples (Weitzer 2007), which form a small part of the sex industry,[73] and applied to all sections of the industry. Yet the majority of women, men and trans workers in the sex industry are based indoors (Sanders 2005). Compulsory rehabilitation schemes, rather than helping to address complex and diverse needs, often penalise vulnerable people, including street-based sex workers.[74] The research evidence also shows that rehabilitation schemes for complex needs should be voluntary. Coercion into rehabilitation, where motivation is important, is not an appropriate or effective way to deliver treatment. Linking service provision with the criminal justice system can have a negative impact on the relationship of trust between project staff and service users.[75] The proposals in the Bill, rather than ensuring the welfare of workers, could further disenfranchise them.

Soliciting (re)defined

Clause 18(1) criminalises soliciting by anyone of anyone else for prostitution. This draconian measure would remove the need for either persistence or annoyance/nuisance to anyone solicited or in the neighbourhood. Anyone could be charged for merely asking a sex worker for business. If one sex worker spoke to another about a client who wished to see both of them, both sex workers could be criminalised. The provision would therefore severely affect sex workers' right to association. This clause also overlaps with kerb-crawling laws in the SOA 1985 because it encompasses soliciting in a vehicle.[76] This is a recycling of the Shelton Bill which sought to remove persistence but was filibustered out of Parliament in 1990 following recognition that it would cause more vulnerability and herald in a new 'sus' law for police to stop Irish or immigrant men, or anyone the police wanted to stop for any other purposes.[77] Enforcement against kerb-crawlers results in greater danger to sex workers as they are removed from usual forms of support and have less time to negotiate safer sex, prices and terms.[78] The government Strategy on Prostitution of January 2006 resulted in police clampdowns against kerb-crawlers in cities which made things more dangerous for street workers and ended in the murder of five young women in Ipswich during November and December 2006.[79] Legal groups also argue that this 'will have no tangible effect on the sort of crime that really does affect our communities (violent crime and crimes against property). Critics argue that it will further distort policing methods and crime figures, and ultimately undermine confidence in the criminal justice system' (response to HO proposals, Release 2008).

Closure orders

Clause 20 puts forward a new civil order to close premises such as brothels. These closure orders could be applied retrospectively and on the hearsay evidence of one person. The provision would give the police enormous power to seal premises on suspicion (i.e. without any proof) that a wide range of activities related to prostitution have happened or may happen. The consequences for sex workers of closure orders are far reaching and dangerous. They remove the protection of the law from many people in the indoor industry as people will not call the police if they know doing so risks closing the premises so they are likely to suffer increased violence, robbery and rape.[80] The laws on brothel-keeping with a penalty of seven years' imprisonment on criminal indictment are already the most punitive in Europe.[81] Closure orders are made through civil proceedings, upon application to the police, based upon the balance of probabilities in which hearsay evidence is admissible. Breach of a closure order is, however, a criminal offence. This represents a blurring of the lines between civil and criminal proceedings. Orders can be obtained on the most tenuous evidence and commonly leads to the displacement of vulnerable people. Where sex workers share their home with others the result of the order will be homelessness and displacement with sex workers moving to increasingly dangerous environments. It would create a 'spiralling down' through the criminal justice system for sex workers and others in the sex industry as they are criminalised and made homeless. This is an obvious outcome and it should be possible to learn from the effects of ASBOs on street workers which have resulted in many more (non-violent) women in prison away from home, more broken families and an increase in the prison population. This is especially worrying as with more private prisons there are more corporations and NGOs with a vested interest in locking up more people. Many sex workers' families do not know they are in sex work. These orders could mean that families would fracture following police raids and prosecutions. The police already have a vested interest in policing and shutting down brothels under current legislation and this gives them a further powerful interest that could interfere with due process.

The provisions in the Police and Crime Bill 2008 are incoherent, dangerous and abusive and will result in more, not less, exploitation.[82] Not only are the contemporary proposals in conflict with empirical evidence showing how sex work could be made less 'problematic' to the law,[83] but they conflict with other government policies and recommendations in the Corston Report that women who represent no danger to the community should not go to prison.

One alternative option would be to redefine a brothel as premises where four or more workers work. Alternatively local authorities should be empowered to allow two or three sex workers to work together in indoor premises for greater personal safety and statute aimed at empowering the women and men working as sex workers, not removing their safe working spaces.

The government argued that 'paying for sex fuels the demand for trafficked women' but there is no evidence either way to state whether sex markets are demand-driven or supply-led. Indeed, with the government targets of 50 per cent of students in higher education, coupled with the increase of students in the sex industry (given its flexible hours and relatively high pay, it is work that many students choose to do while studying for their degree), it could equally be argued that the government is fuelling supply. The then Equalities Minister Harriet Harman was responsible for cuts to lone-parent benefits in November 1997, so if lone-parents (the majority of whom are women) go into sex work through lack of money to bring up their children, then it could be said that Ms Harman negatively impacted on the finances of those women and arguably helped to fuel supply in the sex industry. A newspaper ban imposed by Ms Harman on sex workers' advertisements and pressure on the Newspaper Society made lives more difficult for sex workers so they were not able to advertise for themselves which could be said to 'fuel' the demand for go-betweens, i.e. pimps.[84] Ms Harman maintained that tackling domestic violence was a priority yet made the financial situation harder for women who wished to escape a violent partner through the reduction of these same benefits. Violence is often used as the excuse for greater state intervention in sex work yet it is shown above that the number of violent men among clients is tiny at 2 per cent (Brooks-Gordon 2006), a prevalence far lower than in the general population. More violence occurs in marriage, but no attempt has been made to criminalise marriage, so questions have to be asked about the focus in contemporary crime policy on prostitution.

Trafficking and migration

Trafficking is used as the reason for promoting the punishment of sex workers and enforcing the prohibition of prostitution. The 'rescue industry' offers a dehumanising view of migrants, but the majority of migrants in the sex industry do not want to be 'rescued' and there are many grass roots rebellions against being 'rescued'.[85] The US-led neo-conservative 'war' against prostitution resembled a puritanical 'white woman's burden' (Rothschild 2008) while policy on trafficking in England and Wales does not acknowledge that migrants can exercise choice, that the decision to leave one's country of origin in order to seek a better life shows control over one's life as an active post-colonial agent (Agustín 2007). Distortion comes in the misleading term 'sexual exploitation' when used for 'prostitution' or 'sex work'. It is used by some groups carrying out studies, and there is confusion in one report between those in prostitution and those sexually abused in domestic service (see Zimmerman *et al.* 2006). It has been suggested that these statistics could be used to mask migration figures and the government has been criticised by the Royal Statistical Society for manipulating the way migration figures are presented.[86] The government has a vested interested in distorting the trafficking figures to hide the migration figures. Migration increased from the accession states of Europe, and it arises in all agricultural work, whether cabbage, cockle or carrot picking. It is possible to appreciate the motivations of such migrants (such as transvestite workers escaping police violence in Serbia (Brooks-Gordon 2008b) or young men from Poland, where the conservative Prime Minister banned the Gay Pride parade and called homosexuality an abomination to be stamped out) who leave their home state for other parts of Europe for a few years and sell sex.

Notwithstanding the confusion about migration and trafficking, these proposals are put forward in the wider context of erosion of civil liberties whereby the 'mission creep' of laws brought in for one purpose are used against citizens in everyday life. For example, laws on surveillance brought in under the 'threat' of terrorism have been used by councils using anti-terrorist legislation to spy on parents suspected of lying about school catchment areas and the police have used anti-terrorist measures against environmental or anti-war protesters (Pantazis 2008). Leading up to the debates on the Police and Crime Bill, the House of Lords passed a counter-terrorism Bill on 17 November 2008 to allow the power of entry and search of any business premises without a warrant. There are already 1,039 powers of entry, and given the almost constant use of legislation for purposes for which it was not initially drafted and the conflict of interest inherent in assets seizure,[87] civil liberties and fundamental concepts of a free society become undermined.[88] Trafficking legislation is used to criminalise consenting adults' sex lives and to police sex workers' lives.

Sex workers and their clients are bellwether citizens. This has already been seen in the laws around DNA sampling, and where the erosion of such workers' and clients' liberties start, that of others will follow,[89] providing an indicator of how the state will treat the rest of society a few years later.[90]

Discussion

Prostitution is not in and of itself a crime. There are, however, 24 offences on the statute book that relate to sex work and broad definitions used in many offences such as 'control' and 'gain' mean that contemporary provisions lack clear purpose for workable policy and the recognition of sex workers as entitled to the same civil and human rights as other citizens. Prostitution policy legislation has suffered from a flawed consultation process (see Brooks-Gordon 2006), a misdirected remit and unsustainable assumptions.[91] Policy to support people who sell sex has been marred by divisions in perspectives and guidance and marked by a conservative approach to 'abstinence' and the de facto criminalisation of prostitution. New provisions, if implemented, could change the whole tenor of the law on prostitution from nuisance to prohibition by means of a raft of punitive and potentially damaging proposals and interventions. These would not only be dangerous for workers but also have a negative impact on the criminal justice, probation and prison systems.

Selected further reading

Helen Self's book *Prostitution, Women and the Misuse of the Law* (2006) is essential reading to understand the basis of current policy on sex work. This highly readable history shows, through the individuals involved, how contemporary policy is based on Wolfenden and it provides a salutary reminder how cyclical moral panics and their supposed solutions are. Sanders (2008) *Paying for Pleasure: Men Who Buy Sex* is useful to understand the (male) client, while Day (2007) shows the everyday tapestry of sex workers' lives rather than simply viewing sex workers as no more than the job they do. Kinnell (2008) provides insight into the violence that sex workers suffer and how policy allows that to flourish. Brooks-Gordon (2006) shows the tension for police who would rather be protecting the truly vulnerable than chasing after kerb-crawlers at taxpayers' expense. This text is also the first to attempt to show what a good law on sex work would be like. Weitzer (2005) shows how flawed theory and method skews research studies and is required reading before carrying out research into sex work, while Weitzer's (2007) paper on trafficking is essential reading to understand how the language of lobby groups and vested interests can create the environment in which research and policy are made, and then become part of a government's official discourse and agenda.

Notes

1 Sexual Offences Act 2003, section 51.
2 Sexual Offences Act 2003, section 51(3).
3 In Scotland the law is different; the Scottish Prostitution Act of 2007 created an even more punitive legislative environment than in England and Wales.
4 A public place can be anywhere the public may wander, irrespective of their right to be there.
5 Sexual Offences Acts 1956 and 1959.
6 Sexual Offences Act 1985.
7 The Proceeds of Crime Act 2002 established the Assets Recovery Agency to seize assets from a defendant with a criminal lifestyle if the assets are recoverable. It was intended for serious crimes such as drug trafficking and terrorism, but the Serious Organised Crime and Police Act 2005 brought brothel-keeping under its

remit and extended powers for civil recovery of assets (for example, sections 245A, 245B). In section 110 the power of arrest is extended to enable police (or community warden) to arrest without warrant (Police and Criminal Evidence Act (PACE) 1984, section 24A) anyone for any offence, or on suspicion that an offence might be committed, however trivial (sections 116, 117, 119). See further Brooks-Gordon (2008a).

8 When the offence was summary only, few people ever went to prison.

9 The High Court held, in *Spearmint Rhino Ventures (UK) Limited* v. *HMRC* [2007] EWHC 613, that entertainment services in Spearmint Rhino's clubs are supplied by the dancer to the customer on her own behalf and not as agent for the club. The case, led by David Milne QC, demonstrated that the dancer made the engagement with the customer and performed in her own right. This has also been established in a number of tribunal decisions such as *Portman Escort Agency* v. *HMRC* [2006] UKVAT V19728, and that of *Leapmagic Ltd* v. *CCE* (1991) VATD 6441 regarding the agency of self-employed hostesses who entertain customers at a club.

10 In London, workers advertising massage services must have a licence under the London and Local Authorities Act 1991. This licence can be refused if there is likelihood of nuisance, or the person is not considered a fit and proper person, or if the premises are being improperly conducted.

11 [1961] 2 All ER 446.

12 [1972] 2 All ER 898, [1972] 3 WLR 143. The defendant, who has published a book of advertisements by people selling sexual services, was convicted of corrupting public morals. These cases are controversial because the services (heterosexual and homosexual) sold and being advertised were not and are not illegal.

13 Because sex workers are liable to declare their earnings and pay tax, including VAT, the Inland Revenue frequently work with the police, accompanying them on raids.

14 It has never been stated why the laws on trafficking or controlling were needed in 2003 because there were already laws in existence to deal with these issues. The International Criminal Courts Act 2001, section 51 states that 'it is an offence against the law of England and Wales for a person to commit genocide, a crime against humanity or a war crime'. Among the acts defined as against humanity are enforced prostitution. These are triable in the International Criminal Court and carry a 30-year sentence anywhere in the world (see further Brooks-Gordon 2006). In addition, clarification which would have brought the SOA trafficking laws closer to their professed aim was rejected by the government.

15 Any financial gain is added as an aggravating factor in sentencing.

16 If these statutes are compared with Article 3 of the Palermo Protocol it is possible to see the disjuncture between it and the Palermo Protocol because the law in England and Wales ignores the actions of harbouring, transfer and receipt of people, for example, focusing purely on transport, and treats the entire adult population like the international community does its children by omitting the 'by means of' clauses of Article 3 of the Palermo Protocol on Trafficking (A/RES/55/25 (2001), Annexe II (commonly referred to as the 'Palermo Protocol').

17 One could be liable to imprisonment for up to 14 years for giving someone a lift to a public lavatory knowing they intend to have consensual sex in it.

18 Where someone has profited from their involvement in the prostitution of others, the Sentencing Guidelines Council recommend: 'The courts should always consider making a confiscation order approximately equivalent to the profits enjoyed.'

19 This comes in part from much investment by children's charities in the past two decades to ameliorate the situation of children and young people in prostitution.

20 Sexual Offences Act 2003, section 47.

21 Sexual Offences Act 2003, section 48.
22 Sexual Offences Act 2003, section 49.
23 Sexual Offences Act 2003, section 50.
24 This expansion follows the general tendency to criminalise since New Labour came into office in 1997 (see Pantazis 2008).
25 Where, for example, it was not illegal to buy or sell sex unless either the prostitute or the client was married, in which case it contravened the sacrament that marriage was believed to be and was tried in the ecclesiastical courts as fornication.
26 Joint Committee on Human Rights Twenty-Sixth Report. Online at: http://www.publications.parliament.uk/pa/jt200506/jtselect/jtrights/245/24507.htm.
27 To great public criticism (see O'Connell-Davidson 2007; BBC, *More or Less* programme, 12 January 2008).
28 Pentameter 1 – see: http://www.homeoffice.gov.uk/rds/pdfs08/horr07b.pdf.
29 See: http://www.homeoffice.gov.uk/about-us/news/pentameter-2; http://www.publications.parliament.uk/pa/cm200708/cmhansrd/cm080715/text/80715w0010.htm
30 Cuts of £22 million in 2009–10 and £17 million in 2010–11 to the National Offender Management Service (NOMS) were also announced (written answer to David Howarth MP by Angela Eagle, Minister). Similarly Minister of Justice Jack Straw admitted that the budget will be reduced by £1 bn over three years (written answers, 17 November 2008, col. 20W).
31 See: http://www.guardian.co.uk/business/2008/dec/03/recession-economics.
32 Report of the Committee on Homosexual Offences and Prostitution (1957), Cmnd. 247.
33 Europap: European Network for HIV/STD Prevention in Prostitution. A network of agencies and academics from all countries of Europe, funded from the EU Europe Against AIDS programme (DG V) from 1993 to 2002.
34 This study replicated Kinnell (1999).
35 *Max Mosley* v. *The News Group Newspapers Limited* [2008] EWHC 1777 (QB).
36 It is likely that in cities where the overall rate of men paying for sex is high, a proportion of these are paying men for sex.
37 Given what we know about social trends, e.g. that the UK has an ageing population more generally with a declining mortality rate, there is a tendency for wives to outlive husbands and divorcees take on average three years to remarry. Indeed, official projections from the Office of National Statistics suggest that 16 per cent of men born in 1964 will neither have married nor be in a cohabiting union by the time they reach their fifties, compared with 8 per cent of men born in 1946. This factor would lead to a projected increase in the client population.
38 Aggregated data from nine countries.
39 This is the median figure; the mean was 3.5 per cent. Unless otherwise stated, subsequent means and medians are the same.
40 Data from six countries.
41 This is not necessarily just because they have an impairment or because of discrimination in the social world. Like non-disabled men they have unfulfilled sexual desires for a range of reasons (Sanders 2007).
42 Harriet Harman MP, Minister for Women and Equality.
43 For example, following the Government Strategy on Prostitution in January 2006 the Home Office launched a kerb-crawler 'marketing' campaign which was arguably a morality campaign. See: http://www.homeoffice.gov.uk/documents/paying_the_price.pdf?view=Binary.
44 The rule was rescinded on 23 January 2009 by President Barack Obama.
45 Indeed many of the current lobby groups are headed by separatists (see PYE 2009).

46 The ideological and political alliance is an interesting one because the three groups take conflicting views on issues like abortion or same-sex partnerships.

47 Examples of this alliance included a new All Party Parliamentary Group on Prostitution chaired by ex-minister Fiona McTaggart funded by a fundamentalist Christian anti-prostitution group. The first meeting was addressed by a radical separatist feminist from Sweden whose expenses were met by the Christian group.

48 Including Equalities Minister Harriet Harman, Home Secretary Jacqui Smith, Solicitor General Vera Baird, and Barbara Follet, ex-minister Fiona McTaggart and Maria Eagle. These female parliamentarians are fiercely loyal to each other and, Harriet Harman in particular, was keen to regain feminist credentials after removing benefits from single parents in 1997 and later cutting pensions, moves which disproportionately affected women.

49 For example, the Home Office gave £5.8 million of public money to the Poppy Project (Charities Commission 2008), enabling it to lobby the government, write numerous studies on 'exploitation' and furnish the public with prohibitionist tools such as 'objector packs' against lap-dancing clubs. Both the Home Office and the Equalities Office were linked to the project through studies commissioned or drawn upon heavily for policy despite the methodological critiques made of the reports (cf. the Big Brothel Report by Sanders *et al.* 2008; Brooks-Gordon 2005; Soothill and Sanders 2004; Home Office 2009).

50 This situation is ably described by Davies (2008) who shows how cuts in newsroom budgets for journalistic investigation, fact-checking of sources and stories, a high turnover of staff, hungry 24-hour news cycles and increases in press releases and the numbers of news agencies such as Bloomberg and Reuters have changed the shape of the news, enabling headline-catching scare stories to flourish and grow.

51 Indeed there is no intrinsic reason why prostitution should be exploitative, either between client and sex worker or between the sex worker and indirect sex workers, often referred to as pimps. There are, of course, exploitative clients, sex workers and (especially) indirect sex workers, but at the same time all can be valid stakeholders, the latter notoriously providing important de facto security and meeting other needs. The question among adults is whether coercion or deceit takes place, whether arrangements are freely entered into by the parties and whether they can be freely terminated by them (Patterson 2008).

52 Sanders and Campbell (2007: 1).

53 Not all sex work is seen as invasive because (a) it can be non-contact (e.g. sex chat lines), (b) it can be non-penetrative such as bondage, domination or many S & M practices or erotic massage ('hand relief'), and (c) sex workers separate their sex work from the sexual activity they have with non-commercial partners in a variety of ways.

54 International Union of Sex Workers (IUSW) website (http:www.iusw.org).

55 A number of respected think tanks (e.g. Liberal Vision, the Institute of Economic Affairs – for example Meadowcroft (2008)), MPs and civil liberties groups such as Liberty and Justice across traditional political divides also argue that not only does prohibition not work but it makes the sex worker more vulnerable.

56 Most notably seen in the New York moral crusade against escort agencies recently discussed in media coverage of the Eliot Spitzer case.

57 A Ministerial group (including Vernon Coaker, Under-Secretary at the Home Office, and Barbara Follett, Under-Secretary for Equalities) went to Sweden in January 2008 and returned saying that it was not the policy answer for England and Wales.

58 The Policing and Crime Bill will amend the Sexual Offences Acts 1959 and 2003.

59 See: http://www.number10.gov.uk/Page17673.

60 For a critical analysis of the consultation see B. Brooks-Gordon, 'Clients and commercial sex' [2006] Crim LR 425. Subsequently, Katherine Raymond, a special advisor to the then Home Secretary David Blunkett from 2001 to 2004 and who helped prepare the Green Paper *Paying the Price*, later stated that they 'forensically examined the prostitution laws' and asked for people's views on legalised brothels and locally authority-sponsored red light districts. The results were not welcomed by Downing Street fearful of a hostile media response. In 2006 Raymond wrote: 'Brothels, giving women a safer place to work, should be made legal, and subject to licensing conditions. In Australia and New Zealand, brothels are regulated like other businesses … red light zones have their problems. But their existence can help reduce crime, and enhance women's safety. If more public servants were as honest about commercial sex the government would not be heading so swiftly towards further repression and danger for sex workers. There are no groups of active sex workers who support the prohibitionist stance and criminalisation of clients' (politics.co.uk, 8 September 2008).

61 Specifically this aimed to 'prevent people becoming involved in prostitution, reduce demand, remove opportunities for street prostitution, get people to leave prostitution, prosecute people who are violent to people involved in prostitution, tackle trafficking and "take action on" indoor prostitution.' The Strategy is explored in Brooks-Gordon (2006).

62 Following the implementation of such measures on clients of street workers in January 2006, the death of five sex workers followed in Ipswich in December 2006. Media coverage of the subsequent trial accompanied the reading of the Bill.

63 Not least the Safety First Coalition (which includes members of the church, the RCN, medical consultants, National Association of Probation Officers (NAPO, or the Trade Union and Professional Association for Family Court and Probation Officers), drug and prison reformers, anti-rape and anti-poverty organisations, residents from red light areas, sex workers, sex work projects and disability rights groups), the International Union of Sex Workers and others working in harm-reduction programmes. There was concern that broadening the definition of persistence would increase the vulnerability of sex workers and would also result in net-widening, drawing more women in particular into the criminal justice system.

64 During passage of the Bill, medical service providers, academics and sex worker advocates provided evidence to the House of Commons and House of Lords and received considerable support from a number of politicians and parliamentarians (including John McDonnell MP, Evan Harris MP, Lord Faulkner, Baroness Stern, Baroness Howe, Baroness Miller). Decriminalisation of prostitution, based on the research evidence and a human rights perspective is official Liberal Democrat policy.

65 There was no mention of trafficking in the Bill despite much rhetoric about it by the then Home Secretary Jacqui Smith and the Leader of the House of Commons Harriet Harman.

66 People convicted under the new law would face a fine of up to £1,000 and receive a criminal record.

67 There are already numerous offences against kidnap, rape, trafficking, etc.

68 The loss of their driving licences can already mean the loss of their jobs for clients, but the expansion of the law under the proposals would lead to more marital breakdown.

69 *Niemietz* v. *Germany* (1993) 16 EHRR 97.

70 Questions have to be asked as to why, however, when this change was put forward by Ralph Lucas in the House of Lords during the Sexual Offences Act

2003, the government rejected such a change (see Amendment 362A Revised Fifth Marshalled List of Amendments to be Moved in Committee, Sexual Offences Bill [HL Bill 26-V (Rev) 53/2, 12th May 2003]).

71 In practice persistence is currently interpreted as two or more occasions of soliciting in the same evening.

72 Clauses 15–17 are expanded versions of clauses that the government removed from the previous year's Criminal Justice and Immigration Bill.

73 Estimated by most studies to be no more than 10–15 per cent of the entire industry.

74 See Pitcher *et al.* (2006).

75 See Campbell and O'Neill (2006).

76 The removal of 'persistence' represents a gross widening. The police used to interpret persistence as soliciting on two or more occasions in the same evening whereas this means that anyone stopping to ask directions could be caught under this provision.

77 Sir William Shelton proposed the Sexual Offences Bill 1990, a Private Member's Bill for the removal of 'persistence' in kerb-crawling legislation. The Bill was, however, talked out by Ken Livingstone who recognised that the removal of 'persistence' would be less safe for sex workers and could provide a Trojan horse with which to bring in a new 'sus' law to use against Irish, Black or immigrant people who the police might want to charge for other purposes. See Brooks-Gordon and Gelsthorpe (2003).

78 See Brooks-Gordon (2006).

79 If the kerb-crawler client is convicted a fine is imposed, which if unpaid could lead to loss of liberty through imprisonment. This would be the case for an incident that causes no nuisance or annoyance to anyone in the pursuance of a legal activity. Policing kerb-crawling in this manner is open to abuse by the current system of target-led policing.

80 Many prosecutions against well-run parlours have failed on 'abuse of process' whereby judges accept that the police were previously aware of the existence of a brothel and had visited the premises, thus the brothel owner might legitimately have expected not to be prosecuted. While the Home Office has been criticised for the cost of this to the wider public in terms of the burden to the taxpayer of an expensive waste of public money when such cases fail, it is an indictment on the government that they address this with a further extension of state power over private property rather than rectifying their procedures so that well-run parlours and saunas are held as exemplars of safe working practices. These orders will affect premises raided and assets taken after the Serious Organised Crime and Police Act 2005 brought brothel-keeping under the Assets Recovery Agency remit. This new legislation would allow cases such as those previously thrown out of court on abuse of process grounds back through the system.

81 Indeed brothel-keeping is not an offence at all in many parts of Europe, e.g. Switzerland, Germany, Spain.

82 At a public meeting in parliament on 25 November 2008, the Safety First Coalition told how it had been inundated by women who had been raided, arrested and charged, and face imprisonment for running safe, discreet premises where no coercion was taking place, with anti-trafficking legislation used to justify these raids.

83 See, for example, Scoular *et al.* (2007: 11).

84 This was despite the fact that a poll by IPSOS Mori (2008) and funded by the Ministry for Women and Equality, commissioned by Mrs Harman herself, found that 59 per cent (six out of ten) people feel 'prostitution is a perfectly reasonable

choice that women should be free to make'. Despite the use of 'push-polling' questions and the fact that only women were mentioned, nearly two-thirds of people stated that prostitution was an acceptable choice for women to make. Had the questions mentioned male or trans sex workers the figures would have been even higher. Despite a juxtaposition of negative terms like trafficking in other questions the survey shows the public to be pro-choice, pro-sex work in the main. The immediate context of the survey was negative. Derogatory stereotypes, words and imagery 'such as trafficking' were used. The survey mentioned only heterosexual prostitution and not same-sex or trans workers, which are statistically well-represented in the industry. Such terms are all known to make a difference and if the survey represented the industry as the industry actually exists then the responses would have been even more liberal than here. Indeed the wider context of predominantly negative media and government slant given to drug use and street work, about which many sex workers have complained, was the one in which this survey was carried out.

85 See, for example, http://www.empowerfoundation.org/ and http://www.rhrealitycheck.org/blog/2008/08/07/sex-workers-iac-listen-us.

86 See: http://www.rss.org.uk/pdf/Home_Office_Press_Office_RSS_President_to_Chair_of_Authority.pdf; http://www.telegraph.co.uk/news/newstopics/politics/2977230/Home-Office-accused-of-burying-bad-news-over-immigration.html; http://www.dailymail.co.uk/news/article-1057116/Home-Office-apologises-Minister-accused-hijacking-spin-free-immigration-briefing.html.

87 On 17 November 2008 judges spoke out against the conflict of interest inherent in the reliance on court fines for court funding.

88 The obscure common law offence of 'aiding and abetting misconduct in a public office' was used to arrest Damian Green MP. He was questioned for nine hours and his homes and Commons office were searched after being arrested on 27 November 2008. Mr Green had been given information about migration leaked by a member of Home Office staff. The case is highly unusual and illustrates the degree to which the erosion of civil liberties and fundamental freedoms has occurred and the sensitivity of the Home Office about its migration policies.

89 The Metropolitan Police were ordered to destroy DNA samples collected from kerb-crawlers and held unlawfully prior to the Police and Criminal Justice Act 2001.

90 The expansion of the DNA database to include innocent people was ruled unlawful in December 2008 by the European Court of Human Rights. The progression was logical, predictable and very worrying.

91 Home Office Ministers and the Equalities Minister are already linked to organisations carrying out flawed and unethical research practices. As a result the government policy on prostitution is built on sensationalist studies that are inaccurate (see Butterworth 2008).

References

Adams, N. (2008) Talk to Parliamentary Public Meeting, House of Commons, 25 November.

Aggleton, P. (1998) *Men Who Sell Sex: International Perspectives on Male Prostitution and HIV/AIDS*. London: Routledge.

Agustín, L. (2005) 'Migrants in the mistress's house: other voices in the "trafficking" debate', *Social Politics*, 12 (1): 96–117.

Agustín, L. (2007) *Sex at the Margins: Migration, Labour Markets and the Rescue Industry.* London: Zed Books.

Bainham, A. and Brooks-Gordon, B. M. (2006) 'Reforming the law on sexual offences', in B. M. Brooks-Gordon, L. R. Gelsthorpe, M. H. Johnson and A. Bainham (eds), *Sexuality Repositioned: Diversity and the Law.* Oxford: Hart.

Beck, U. (1992) *Risk Society.* London: Sage.

Bernstein, E. (2007) 'Sex work for the middle classes', *Sexualities*, 10: 473–88.

Brain, T., Davis, T. and Philips, A. (1999) *National Strategy for Policing Prostitution: Guidelines for Dealing with Abuse and Exploitation through Prostitution.*

British Psychological Society (2008) Memorandum of Evidence on the Criminal Justice and Immigration Bill, No. 388. Heard at Scrutiny Committee, 9th Sitting, 20 November 2007.

Brooks-Gordon, B. M. (2000) 'Sexism in the city', *Psychology of Women Review*, 2 (1): 5–15.

Brooks-Gordon, B. M. (2005) 'Clients and commercial sex: reflections on "paying the price": a consultation paper on prostitution', *Criminal Law Review*, June, pp. 425–43.

Brooks-Gordon, B. M. (2006) *The Price of Sex: Prostitution, Policy, and Society.* Cullompton: Willan.

Brooks-Gordon, B. M. (2008a) 'The Criminal Justice and Immigration Bill 2008 and prostitution law reform', *Archbold News*, 3: 4–6.

Brooks-Gordon, B. M. (2008b) 'State violence towards sex workers', *British Medical Journal*, 337: a908.

Brooks-Gordon, B. M. (2008c) 'We don't need McCarthyism in the bedroom', Opinion, *Daily Telegraph*, 21 November, p. 27. Online at: http://www.telegraph.co.uk/opinion/main.jhtml?xml=/opinion/2008/11/21/do2108.xml.

Brooks-Gordon, B. M. (2008d) 'Playing politics with sex workers', *Guardian.co.uk*, Comment is Free, 16 October. Online at: http://www.guardian.co.uk/commentisfree/2008/oct/16/law-jacquismith.

Brooks-Gordon, B. M. and Gelsthorpe, L. R. (2003) 'Prostitutes' clients, Ken Livingstone, and a new Trojan horse', *Howard Journal of Criminal Justice*, 42 (5): 437–51

Bruce-Lockhart, A. (2008) 'What's wrong with paying for sex?', *GuardianWeekly. co.uk*, 13 November. Online at: http://www.guardianweekly.co.uk/?page=editorial&id=818&catID=21.

Burney, E. (2005) *Making People Behave: Anti-Social Behaviour, Politics, and Policy.* Cullompton: Willan.

Butterworth, S. (2008) 'Open Door: The readers' editor on the studious reader's approach to "studies"', *Guardian.co.uk*, 8 December 2008. Online at: http://www.guardian.co.uk/commentisfree/2008/dec/08/prostitution-open-door.

Careal, M., Slaymaker, E., Lyerla, R. and Sarker, S. (2006) 'Clients of sex workers in different regions of the world: hard to count', *Sexually Transmitted Infections*, 82: 26–33.

Charities Commission (2008) *Accounts for Eaves Housing (incorporating Poppy Project).* Online at: http://www.charitycommission.gov.uk/registeredcharities/ScannedAccounts/Ends48/0000275048_ac_20080331_e_c.pdf.

Collins, S. and Cattermole, R. (2006) *Anti-Social Behaviour and Disorder. Powers and Remedies*, 2nd edn. London: Sweet & Maxwell.

Cusick, L., Kinnell, H., Brooks-Gordon, B. and Campbell, R. (2009) 'Wild guesses and conflated meanings: estimating the size of the sex worker population in Britain', *Journal of Critical Social Policy*, Vol. 29 (4), pp. 703–19.

Daily Mail (2008) http://www.dailymail.co.uk/debate/polls/poll.html?pollId=1004981 $1239427.htm.

Davies, N. (2008) *Flat Earth News*. London: Random House.

Day (2007) *On The Game*. London: Pluto Press.

Dworkin, A. (1987) *Intercourse*. London Secker & Warburg.

Earle, S. and Sharpe, K. (2008) 'Intimacy, pleasure, and the men who pay for sex', in G. Letherby, K. Williams, P. Birch, and M. Cain (eds), *Sex As Crime?* Cullompton: Willan.

Evans, L. (2008) IQ2 debate: 'It's wrong to pay for sex', *The Spectator*, 15 November, p. 26. Online at: http://www.spectator.co.uk/the-magazine/features/2626376/part_2/iq2-debate-its-wrong-to-pay-for-sex.thtml.

Gaffney, J. (2008) *The Challenges of Delivering Innovative Services to Male Sex Workers Through a Partnership Approach*. Presentation to Capita's 3rd Annual Tackling Prostitution Conference, 11 December 2007.

Giddens, A. (1992) *The Transformation of Intimacy*. Cambridge: Polity.

Goodyear, M. (2007) 'Public health policy must be based on sound evidence', *British Medical Journal*, 334: 863–4.

Goodyear, M. (2008) 'Incarceration of female sex workers in China and STI/HIV programmes that are not rights based are doomed to fail', *Sexually Transmitted Infections*, 84 (1): 1–2.

Goodyear, M. and Cusick, L. (2007) 'Protection of sex workers', *British Medical Journal*, 334: 52–3.

Groom, T. M. and Nandwani, R. (2006) 'Characteristics of men who pay for sex: a UK sexual health clinic survey', *Sexually Transmitted Infections*, 82: 364–7.

Harman, H. MP (2008) Speech to NFWI Conference on International Day for the Elimination of Violence Against Women, Mary Sumner House, 25 November.

Home Office (2003) *Offending and Criminal Justice Group*. London: HMSO.

Home Office (2006) *A Coordinated Prostitution Strategy*. Online at: http://www.homeoffice.gov.uk/documents/cons-paying-the-price/.

Home Office (2008) *Trafficking for Sexual Exploitation: A Process Review of Operation Pentameter*, compiled by Julie Avenell, Research Report 7. Online at: http://www.homeoffice.gov.uk/rds/pdfs08/horr07b.pdf.

Home Office (2009) *Tackling Demand for Prostitution: A Rapid Evidence Assessment of the published research literature*, Research Report 37.

House of Commons, Hansard, col. 587W, 19 November 2008.

House of Commons, Hansard, col. 161W, 4 December 2008.

Humphreys, L. (1970) *The Tearoom Trade: Impersonal Sex in Public Places*. London: Duckworth.

IPSOS Mori (2008) Online at: http://www.equalities.gov.uk/pdf/Attitudestowardsprostitutionsurvey%20June2008.pdf.

IUSW (2009) *Declaration of the Rights of Sex Workers*. Online at: http://www.iusw.org/.

Jeal, N. and Salisbury, C. (2004) 'A health needs assessment of street-based prostitutes: cross-sectional survey', *Journal of Public Health*, 26 (2). Online at: http://jpubhealth.oxfordjournals.org/cgi/content/abstract/26/2/147.

Jeal, N., Salisbury, C. and Turner, K. (2008) 'The multiplicity and interdepency of factors influencing the health of street-based workers: a qualitative study', *Sexually Transmitted Infections*, 2 July. Online at: http://sti.bmj.com/cgi/content/abstract/sti.2008.030841v1.

Jeannin, A., Rousson, V., Meystre-Agustoni, G. and Dubois-Arber, F. (2008) 'Patterns of sex work contact among men in the general population of Switzerland, 1987–2000', *Sexually Transmitted Infections*, 84: 556–9.

Justis-og Politidepartmentet (2004) *Purchasing Sexual Services in Sweden and the Netherlands: Legal Regulation and Experiences*. Ministry of Justice and the Police. Sweden.

Online at: http://www.regjeringen.no/upload/kilde/jd/rap/2004/0034/ddd/ pdfv/232216-purchasing_sexual_services_in_sweden_and_the_nederlands.pdf.

Kershaw, C., Nicholas, S. and Walker, A. (eds) (2008) *Crime in England and Wales 2007/08: Findings from the British Crime Survey and Police Recorded Crime*, Home Office Statistical Bulletin. London: Home Office.

Kinnell, H. (1989) 'Male clients of female prostitutes in Birmingham, England: a bridge for transmission of HIV?', *Report of 5th International Conference on AIDS*, Montreal, June.

Kinnell, H. (1999) *Sex Workers in England and Wales*, Europap-UK briefing paper for Department of Health, National Sexual Health Strategy.

Kinnell, H. (2008) *Violence and Sex Work in Britain*. Cullompton: Willan.

Lipsett, A. (2008) 'Big Brothel research seriously flawed', *The Guardian*, Guardian Education, 3 October. Online at: http://www.guardian.co.uk/education/2008/ oct/03/research.women.

Lombroso, C. ([1885] 1997) *The Criminal Woman and the Prostitute*, trans. L. Melville. Milan: M. St Auben.

Longstaff, L. (2008) 'Accused: British legal system that fails to protect women', *Tribune*, 15 February.

Marrin, M. (2008) 'Slithery Jacqui Smith wants a backdoor ban on prostitution', *Times Online*. Online at: http://www.timesonline.co.uk/tol/comment/columnists/minette_ marrin/article5213486.ece.

Matthews, R. (2008) *Prostitution, Politics, and Policy*. Oxford: Routledge-Cavendish.

Meadowcroft, J. (2008) 'Prostitution', in J. Meadowcroft (ed.), *Prohibition*. London: Institute of Economic Affairs, pp. 178–95.

Munro, V. E. and Della Giusta, M. (2008) *Demanding Sex: Critical Reflections on the Regulation of Prostitution*. Aldershot: Ashgate.

O'Connell-Davidson, J. (2007) 'Sex slaves and the reality of prostitution', *The Guardian*, Letters, 27 December, p. 43. Online at: http://politics.guardian.co.uk/homeaffairs/ story/0,,2232720,00.html.

Pantazis, C. (2008) 'The problem of criminalisation', *Criminal Justice Matters*, 74: 10–12.

Patterson, S. (2008) 'An Anthology of English Pros', Evidence to Public Bill Committee on the Policing and Crime Bill. Online at: http://stephenpaterson.wordpress. com/2009/01/.

Pitcher, J., Campbell, R., Hubbard, P., O'Neill, M. and Scoular, J. (2006) *Living and Working in Areas of Street Sex Work: From Conflict to Coexistence*. Bristol: Policy Press.

Politics.co.uk (2008a) 'Massive Support for Legalisation of Prostitution', 27 November. Online at: http://www.politics.co.uk/news/opinion-former-index/policing-and- crime/massive-support-legalisation-prostitution-$1251359.htm.

Politics.co.uk (2008b) 'Prostitutes United', 8 September. Online at: http://www.politics. co.uk/analysis/opinion-former-index/policing-and-crime/feature-prostitutes- united-$1239427.htm.

PRA (2007) 'Prostitution Reform Act', Report of the Prostitution Law Review Committee, New Zealand. Online at: http://www.justice.govt.nz/prostitution-law- review-committee/index.html.

PYE (2009) 'Political lesbianism', *Guardian.co.uk*, Women, 30 January. Online at: http:// www.guardian.co.uk/lifeandstyle/2009/jan/30/women-gayrights.

Raymond, K. (2006) 'Brothels and safe red light areas are the only way forward', *Guardian. co.uk*, 17 December. Online at: http://www.guardian.co.uk/commentisfree/2006/ dec/17/comment.politics3.

Release (2005) *Sex Workers and the Law: Drugs, the Law and Human Rights*. London: Release.

Release (2008) *Response to Home Office Proposals*. London: Release.

Rhodes, T., Simič, M., Baroš, S., Platt, L. and Žikič, B. (2008) 'Police violence and sexual risk among female and transvestite prostitutes in Serbia: qualitative study', *British Medical Journal*, 337: a811.

Roberts, R., Bergstrom, S. and La Rooy, D. (2007) 'Commentary – UK students and sex work: current knowledge and research issues', *Journal of Community and Applied Social Psychology*, 17: 141–6.

Rothschild, N. (2008) 'Prostituting women's solidarity: the UK government's call to British women to help combat "sex trafficking" amounts to a crackdown on immigration', *Spiked*, 27 November. Online at: http://www.spiked-online.com/index.php?/site/article/5973/.

Royal College of Nursing (2007) Memorandum of Evidence on the Criminal Justice and Immigration Bill, 2nd Reading, 8 October.

Sagar, T. (2007) 'Tackling on-street sex work', *Criminology and Criminal Justice*, 7 (2): 153–68.

Sanders, T. (2005) 'The politics of sexual citizenship: commercial sex and disability', *Disability and Society*, 22 (5): 439–55.

Sanders, T. (2006) *Sex Work: A Risky Business*. Cullompton: Willan.

Sanders, T. (2008) *Paying for Pleasure: Men Who Buy Sex*. Cullompton: Willan.

Sanders, T. and Campbell, R. (2007) 'Designing out vulnerability, building in respect: violence, safety and sex work policy', *British Journal of Sociology*, 58 (1): 1–19.

Sanders, T. and Campbell, R. (2008) 'What's criminal about indoor sex work?', in G. Letherby, K. Williams, P. Birch and M. Cain (eds), *Sex as Crime?* Cullompton: Willan.

Sanders, T., Pitcher, J., Campbell, R., Brooks-Gordon, B., O'Neil, M. *et al.* (2008) 'A Response to "Big Brothel" by Julie Bindel and Helen Atkins, Poppy Project'. Unpublished.

Scambler, G. and Scambler, A. (eds) (1997) *Rethinking Prostitution in the 1990s*. London: Sage.

Scoular, J. and O'Neill, M. (2007) 'Social inclusion, responsibilization and the politics of prostitution reform', *British Journal of Criminology*, 14 (2). Online at: http://bjc.oxfordjournals.org/cgi/content/abstract/azm014v2.

Scoular, J., Pitcher, J., Campbell, R., Hubbard, P. and O'Neill, M. (2007) 'What's anti-social about sex work? Governance, discourse and the changing representation of prostitution's incivility', *Community Safety Journal*, 6 (1): 11–17.

Self, H. (2003) *Prostitution, Women, and Misuse of the Law*. London: Frank Cass.

Self, H. (2006) 'Regulating prostitution', in B. M. Brooks-Gordon and M. Freeman (eds), *Law and Psychology: Current Legal Issues*. Oxford: Oxford University Press.

Sentencing Guidelines Council (2007) *Sexual Offences Act 2003, Definitive Guideline*. Sentencing Guidelines Secretariat. Online at: http://www.sentencing-guidelines.gov.uk/docs/82083-COI-SCG_final.pdf.

Soothill, K. and Sanders, T. (2004) 'Calling the tune? Some observations on *Paying the Price*: a consultation paper on prostitution', *Journal of Forensic Psychiatry and Psychology*, 15 (4): 1–18.

Ward, H. and Day, S. (2007) *On the Game*. London: Pluto Press.

Ward, H., Mercer, C. H., Wellings, K., Fenton, K., Erens, B., Copas, A. and Johnson, A. M. (2005) 'Who pays for sex: an analysis of the increasing prevalence of female commercial sex contacts among men in Britain', *Sexually Transmitted Infections*, 81: 467–76.

Weeks, J. (2008) *The World We Have Won*. London and New York: Routledge.

Weitzer, R. (2005) 'Flawed theory and method in studies of prostitution', *Violence Against Women*, 2 (7): 934–49.

Weitzer, R. (2007) 'The social construction of sex trafficking: ideology and institutionalization of a moral crusade', *Politics and Society*, 35: 447–75.

Zimmerman, C., Hossain, M., Yun, K., Roche, B., Morison, L. and Watts, C. (2006) *Stolen Smiles: A Summary Report on the Physical and Psychological Health Consequences of Women and Adolescents Trafficked into Europe*. Report produced in conjunction with Animus Assoc. Foundation, International Organization for Migration, La Strada, On The Road and the Poppy Project.

Part V

Drug-related crime

This section covers various aspects of what we have termed 'drug-related crime'. Although reference is made to legal drugs – especially alcohol – where appropriate, the focus here is on criminal behaviour related to illegal drugs. Discussion of alcohol-related violence and disorder can be found in Part III.

The broadest definition of drug-related crime is that it comprises three main elements. The first covers the various criminal offences that define the ways in which drugs are proscribed in law, such as drug possession and supply. The second covers those offences that might be directly caused by drug misuse, including robberies and thefts to fund drug purchases and assaults and other forms of violence following drug consumption. The third comprises systemic offences linked to the distribution of drugs and drug markets such as punishment violence and money laundering. The three chapters in this section examine these three main forms of drug-related crime. McSweeney, Turnbull and May discuss drug offences relating to possession and supply. Bennett and Holloway deal with those offences that might be directly caused by drug misuse. Paoli, Spapens and Fijnaut consider drug trafficking and the various methods used for smuggling illegal drugs across and within countries.

In combination, these three chapters provide a succinct overview of the many connections between drug use and crime. McSweeney and colleagues describe the rather relentless rise in the supply of all classes of drugs over the last 30 years and the predominance of heroin and crack cocaine at one end of the scale and cannabis at the other. A similar picture emerges for drug possession, showing a steady increase over the last half century with a slight, more recent reduction. The authors conclude that trends in supply and demand for drugs appear to have little to do with the severity of laws or level of policing activity. Bennett and Holloway get to grips with the concept of crimes committed as a consequence of drug misuse and the problems involved in measuring offences motivated by drugs. They note that this has led to some wild speculation about the numbers of offences connected to substance misuse. They conclude that there is still a lot to learn about the drugs–crime connection and a good place to start is to define it. Paoli and colleagues provide a useful map of drug smuggling with the focus on Europe as a destination. They provide detailed descriptions of the process of drug trafficking from the production of illegal drugs to cross-border smuggling, as well as internal trafficking to the end user. They conclude that large drug-trafficking enterprises are born in countries in which governments are unable to enforce international prohibitions and because of this international organisations need to provide realistic goals.

Overall, this section of the book identifies contemporary forms of crime that have emerged out of the demand and supply of drugs. These are often hard to define and hidden from view. They can also be particularly difficult to understand and tackle. Many are committed in the underworld of criminal networks, their victims are often offenders, and neither victims nor offenders are likely to seek out the formal control system to resolve disputes. Nevertheless, the section shows that good progress is being made in addressing these issues among criminologists and others interested in drug crime.

Chapter 29

Drug- and alcohol-related crime

Trevor Bennett and Katy Holloway

Introduction

The concepts of drug-related crime and alcohol-related crime are not clearly defined in the literature. In practice, the terms tend to refer to one or more of three conceptually distinct ways in which drug and alcohol use might be connected to crime.

The first is that various substances might be linked to crime by the drug and alcohol offences that define them as criminal in law. In relation to drugs, for example, they would cover all offences specified in the drugs legislation, such as drug possession and supply. The same might apply to alcohol in relation to the offences covered under the alcohol legislation, such as under-age consumption or purchase. The second connection refers to offences that are in some way caused directly by drug or alcohol use. In the case of drugs, this would include robberies or shopliftings committed by drug users seeking funds for drug purchases. A similar meaning could be applied to alcohol-related crime in that some offences such as assault and other forms of violence might be caused directly by alcohol consumption. The third connection comprises those offences that are indirectly associated with drug or alcohol misuse such as systemic violence associated with drug markets or the laundering of the proceeds of drug sales. In relation to alcohol use, it might refer to violence associated with drinking subcultures.

In order to investigate possible meanings of drug-related crime, it is useful to begin by looking at how the government defines it in drugs policy documents and reports. The term 'drug-related crime' was first used in a drug policy document in 1994 (Home Office 1994) and was defined as '... not only the offence of supply and possession of illegal drugs, but also other criminal activity directly or indirectly associated with drug misuse'. The definition was elaborated in a follow-up document published in 1995 (Home Office 1995) in which it was stated that drug-related crime included offences committed under the Misuse of Drugs Act 1971 and offences committed by persons acting as a consequence of drug misuse. This latter group included crimes directly connected to drug use such as burglary and theft and crimes indirectly connected such as laundering of profits of drug sales and systemic crimes associated with drug trafficking. It is clear that the early use of the term in government policy documents encompassed all three potential connections between drugs and crime.

More recent government reports have tended to use a more limited version of the concept. In the consultation paper *Drugs: Our Community, Your Say* published in 2007, it is reported that 'drug-related crime is falling' and cites as evidence figures for recorded acquisitive crime (Home Office 2007b). In this case, the concept of drug-related crime is taken to mean the second of the three options discussed above which refers to crimes directly caused by drug misuse. A similar kind of focus has taken place in relation to alcohol-related crime. In its strategy document *Alcohol Harm Reduction Strategy for England* (Cabinet Office 2004) the government defined the term to refer to crime and disorder in which alcohol use is implicated. In other words, attention is drawn to those crimes directly caused by alcohol misuse.

There is nothing wrong in using the more restricted version of the definition. In some ways, it makes more sense to identify three different kinds of connection. In the case of drugs, these would include 'drug offences' which refer to crimes covered by drug legislation, 'drug-related crime' which refers to crimes committed as a direct consequence of drug use and 'systemic' crimes which refer to offences indirectly caused by drug use. In fact, this is the favoured definition used in this book and the three chapters in this section are selected to cover these three elements. The phrase 'drug crime' might be used to encompass all three connections. The main problem that exists with this approach is the way in which the concepts of drug-related and alcohol-related crimes are operationalised in practice. The problem is similar for both drugs and alcohol and the following will focus the discussion mainly on drug-related crime.

It is understandable that there are no 'ready-made' measures of drug-related crime that could be used to summarise all crimes directly caused as a consequence of drug use. As a result, the government has chosen 'acquisitive crime' as the main current measure of drug-related crime. It is almost certainly the case that a large number of drug-related crimes are contained in the statistics on acquisitive crime. However, there is no way of knowing which are and which are not drug-related. This is not meant to be a criticism of the practice of using an existing crime category as a measure. The problem is more fundamental than this and concerns the intricacies and nature of drug-related crime.

The first fundamental problem is that the concept of drug-related crime requires some knowledge of motivation. The concept makes most sense when the offender is motivated to commit the crime because of drug use. It also fits most precisely the government definition of the term which involves '... offences committed by persons acting as a consequence of drug misuse' (Home Office 1995). If the offender would have committed the crime anyway for other reasons, then the idea that the offence was drug-related loses its meaning. This implies that it cannot be assumed that a crime is drug-related simply because it is committed by a drug user or simply because it is an acquisitive crime. The uncertainty about the role of motivation in defining the term is highlighted in the operation of mandatory drug-testing of arrestees. In the case of 'non-trigger offences', officers of inspector rank or above have the discretion to request a test, but only when they suspect that a Class A drug use was *a causal or contributory factor* in the commission of the crime (Home Office 2007a). In the case of 'trigger offences', knowledge of offender motivation is not required.

The second problem is that drug-related crimes might include non-acquisitive offences. This is based on the definition of drug-related crimes as crimes that are a direct consequence of drug misuse. There is nothing in this definition that requires that the drug-related crime has to be an acquisitive crime (Bennett and Holloway 2007). In practice, research has shown that drug misuse is connected to several types of non-acquisitive crimes including homicides, robberies and assaults. Limiting the measure to acquisitive crimes excludes a proportion of all drug-related crimes.

The third problem concerns the nature of the motivation for the offence. According to policy documents, an offence is drug-related if drug use provided an economic motivation for the offence (Home Office 2007b). This assumption is consistent with the use of acquisitive crime as a measure of drug-related crime. However, research has shown that one of the main connections between drug use and crime is pharmacological (Bennett and Holloway 2005). In practice, the pharmacological effect of the drug might lead to various kinds of offences including those not involving financial gain such as violence, sex offences, criminal damage or disorder. A single offence might also be committed for different motives. A robbery, for example, might be committed for economic, expressive or systemic reasons.

The fourth problem is that the concept of 'acquisitive crime' is itself unclear. Home Office reports provide different lists of offences that might be included under this heading. According to Kershaw *et al.* (2008), acquisitive crime includes both household acquisitive crime (such as burglary in a dwelling, theft in a dwelling and theft of vehicles) and personal acquisitive crime (such as theft from the person and robbery). The Home Office website states that acquisitive crime also includes commercial acquisitive crime such as shoplifting.

While government reports and Home Office statements have been used to illustrate the problems of defining drug- and alcohol-related crime, these problems are not confined to government sources. Instead, they permeate research and theory more widely. Nevertheless, in order to take the discussion forward, it is necessary to put these conceptual problems to one side and use the current evidence available to find out more about the extent and nature of substance-related crime.

Patterns and trends

There are no national level data on the extent of drug- and alcohol-related crime as mentioned above. As a result, various other methods have to be used to find out the prevalence of these offences.

There is a debate currently emerging concerning the use of expert estimates of the proportion of all crime that is drug-related. One of the beliefs driving the current drug strategy is that a high proportion of all crime is caused by drug use. The absence of reliable evidence for this has made it difficult to determine how much crime is drug-related. Stevens noted that an 'arbitrary figure' of 'about half' is often cited in government reports as the proportion of all crime that is caused by drug use (Stevens 2007). This proportion can be found in the policy document *Tackling Drugs to Build a Better Britain* which reported that '... many police forces estimate that around half of all recorded crime has some drug-related element to it, whether in terms of individual consumption or supply of drugs, or the consequent impact of it on criminal behaviour ...' (Home Office 1998: 18). This estimate is more or less repeated in the 2008 drug strategy document which states that: 'We know from the latest available evidence that ... between a third and a half of acquisitive crime is estimated to be drug related' (Home Office 2008: 8). Stevens identifies as the original source of these estimates research conducted in the US and the UK on the proportion of drug-misusing offenders in custody. The fact that these estimates relate to the proportion of incarcerated offenders who take drugs rather than the proportion of offences that are caused by drugs has led to what he refers to as a serious overestimation of the prevalence of drug-related crime (Stevens 2007: 78).

What evidence is there that can provide a better estimate of the amount of drug-related or alcohol-related offending? In relation to some offences (usually violent offences) the use of drugs or alcohol by the victim or suspect is sometimes recorded by the police. In these cases, when the data are reported in government documents or research findings, it is possible to estimate the prevalence of the drug- or alcohol-related crime in relation to these specific offences.

According to research based on the Homicide Index, approximately 9 per cent of the suspects of homicides during the period 1995–9 were under the influence of alcohol at the time of the offence and about 1 per cent were under the influence of drugs (Brookman and Maguire 2003). However, the authors note that the Homicide Index substantially underestimates the involvement of alcohol and drugs as this information is not always collected. A study conducted on homicide in Scotland based on homicides recorded by Scottish police forces during the period 2007–8 found that 22 per cent of those accused of homicide were drunk, 9 per cent were on drugs and 14 per cent were both drunk and on drugs (Scottish Government 2008). Unfortunately, in 42 per cent of cases the intoxication status of the offender was unknown. Research on violence has also provided information on the proportion of offenders who had consumed alcohol or drugs prior to the offence. A Home Office report on the findings of the British Crime Survey found that in over half (53 per cent) of all incidents of stranger violence the victim described the perpetrator as being under the influence of alcohol and in 16 per cent of cases under the influence of drugs (Mattinson 2001). There are no published figures that could be used to assess the prevalence of drug or alcohol involvement in relation to acquisitive crimes.

It is difficult to determine trends in drug-related crime for the reasons already mentioned. It is hard to define and hard to measure. Some attempt to do this has been made by the government through the use of acquisitive crimes. The Home Office consultation document mentioned earlier claimed that drug-related crime is decreasing and stated that 'recorded acquisitive crime has fallen by 20 per cent since the introduction of the Drug Interventions Programme' (Home Office 2007b: 30). The source of this figure appears to be the British Crime Survey (BCS) which showed that the number of incidents of household acquisitive crime reduced over this period by this amount. In fact, household acquisitive crime makes up a sizeable proportion of all crime and both BCS and police estimates have shown that the number of total crimes has reduced over the last few years. However, it is a leap of faith to assume that this means that drug-related crime has also reduced over this period. It is possible that it has reduced in line with all acquisitive crime or even by a greater amount. But it is also possible that it has not. Until a better measure is used, it is not possible to determine trends in all drug-related crime.

While there are no systematically collected data available on trends in the overall number of drug-related offences, there is some evidence available in relation to homicide. The Scottish report mentioned earlier showed that from 2003–4 to 2007–8 the number of persons accused of alcohol-related homicides in Scotland fell from 65 to 54 (17 per cent), whereas the total number of persons accused of all homicides fell from 155 to 148 (5 per cent) (Scottish Government 2008). During the same period, the number of persons accused of drug-related homicides increased from 29 to 34 (17 per cent). These changes have to be treated with caution as the alcohol or drug status of the accused was not known in 17–45 per cent of all homicides.

Over the last few years, there have been several surveys conducted on drug use and crime among arrestees. These surveys provide various measures (some better than others) of drug involvement in crime, including drug use at the time of arrest, reported intoxication at the time of the offence, reported drug use during the period covered by the offence and offenders' perceptions of the causal role that drug use played in the commission of their recent crimes. The main disadvantage of arrestee surveys is that the results relate to the proportion of offenders whose drug use is related to crime rather than the proportion of crimes that are related to drug use. Nevertheless, they provide another source of information that can be assessed alongside other sources.

Holloway et al. (2004) used NEW-ADAM data to investigate trends in drug-related crime over the three-year period of the programme from 1999 to 2002. One measure of drug involvement in crime used was whether people currently arrested for an offence (often committed shortly before the time of the arrest) tested positive for drugs. Over the period of the research, the proportion of positive tests for any drug remained constant and the proportion of positive tests for opiates (including heroin) and cocaine (including crack) increased significantly from 25 per cent to 28 per cent in the case of opiates and 15 per cent to 23 per cent in the case of cocaine. Unfortunately, it is not possible to translate these figures into total numbers of drug-related crimes for various reasons.

The NEW-ADAM survey was superseded by the Arrestee Survey which provided more recent information on changes in drug use and crime among arrestees. The report of the first three years of the programme (2003 to 2006) did not discuss trends in drug-related crime (Boreham *et al.* 2007). However, similar analyses were conducted as those above. During the period 2003/4 to 2005/6 the proportion of arrestees testing positive for opiates showed a reduction from 19 per cent to 15 per cent and the proportion testing positive for cocaine also reduced from 15 per cent to 13 per cent. As the sampling and testing methods used were different across the NEW-ADAM programme and the Arrestee Survey, the two sets of results are not directly comparable. Nevertheless, it is interesting to note that together they show an increase followed by a later decrease in the proportion of drug-using offenders – which is more or less the recent trend in police recorded crime. It cannot be determined, of course, from this data whether the two are causally connected.

Characteristics of the offence

In a general sense drug and alcohol-related crime can be any crime in which substance use played a part. It is plausible, therefore, that drug- and alcohol-related crime is no different from other forms of crime, apart from the involvement of substance use. It is not possible in a short chapter to summarise the characteristics of all crime. However, it might be the case that the characteristics of drug and alcohol-related offences are different from other offences. This could be in terms of the types of offences committed or ways in which they are committed.

There is some evidence available in relation to offences in which substance involvement is commonly recorded by the police. One fact that emerged from the Scottish research on homicide mentioned earlier was that drugs used by the accused were more likely to be consumed in combination with alcohol (14 per cent) than alone (9 per cent), whereas alcohol was more likely to be consumed alone (22 per cent) than in combination with drugs (14 per cent) (Scottish Government 2008). As the substance-using status of the accused was unknown in 42 per cent of homicides, the significance of these differences is uncertain.

A more relevant question is whether there are any differences in the characteristics of substance-related homicides compared with non-substance related homicides. There is little routinely collected data available that can be used to assess this. However, there is one recent doctoral dissertation which looked specifically at substance-related homicides in England and Wales. The study was based on data compiled from the Homicide Index and supplementary data from police case files (Chapple 2008). Some differences were found in relation to both alcohol and drug-related homicides. Offenders convicted of *alcohol-related* homicides were more likely than other homicide suspects to be white (92 per cent compared with 80 per cent). There were no differences in relation to gender or age. Offenders convicted of *drug-related* homicides were more likely to be younger (aged under 36) than other homicide offenders (82 per cent compared with 70 per cent) and more likely to be black (25 per cent compared with 11 per cent). The research also found some variation in the contextual factors in both alcohol- and drug-related homicides. Alcohol-related homicides were more likely than other homicides to involve a friend or past friend, no weapon use and some kind of quarrel or dispute. Drug-related homicides were more likely than other homicides to involve an acquaintance, shooting the victim and economic motivation.

Another method of determining differences among substance-related and non-substance-related crimes is to ask offenders. Information on drug use and crime among arrestees is available from the results of the NEW-ADAM surveys (Bennett and Holloway 2007) and the Arrestee Survey (Boreham *et al.* 2007). It is acknowledged, of course, that arrestees do not necessarily represent all offenders and that the characteristics of offenders are not the same as the characteristics of offences.

Bennett and Holloway (2007) found some differences among drug-using and non-drug-using arrestees. Generally speaking, drug-using offenders committed crimes at a higher rate than non-drug-using offenders and heroin and crack cocaine users committed crimes at the highest rate of all. They also found that the most prolific drug using and offenders were significantly more likely than their less involved counterparts to be female, to be aged over 20 years, to be white, to have left school before age 17 and to be in receipt of social security benefits. There were also differences noted in their choice of offences. Drug-misusing prolific offenders were more likely than other offenders to report committing shoplifting, handling, theft from a person and drug supply offences.

The Arrestee Survey investigated differences among drug-using and non-drug-using offenders in terms of their involvement in acquisitive crime (Boreham *et al.* 2007). The study defined acquisitive crime as comprising any one of a long list of offences including: shoplifting, handling, vehicle crime, burglary, robbery, theft from a person, fraud, deception, other theft, and prostitution. They found that regular heroin and crack cocaine users were substantially more likely than other arrestees (31 per cent compared with 3 per cent) to report committing acquisitive crime in the last year at a high rate (366 or more acquisitive crimes in the last 12 months).

Information on the characteristics of alcohol- and drug-related crime is disappointingly scant. Ideally, it would be useful to know if substance-related crime was fundamentally different from other crime in terms of, say, modus operandi, levels of violence, amount stolen, choice of targets and so on. Unfortunately, current research can only hint at these differences. It is clear that substance-related crime focuses on some offence types more than others. Drug-related crimes are associated primarily with a small group of income-generating crimes and alcohol-related crimes encompass particular forms of assault and some more serious forms of violence. There appear to be demographic differences among substance-using and non-using offenders and behavioural differences in terms of their rates of offending.

Explanations

The current UK drugs strategy is based on the belief that drug use causes crime. One of the stated aims of the strategy is to reduce crime by reducing the availability of drugs. According to one government definition, drug-related crime comprises offences committed by persons acting 'as a consequence' of drug misuse (Home Office 1998). The idea that drug use might provide the motivation to offend is central to the government's strategy and the concept of drug-related crime. It would be useful to know, therefore, whether drug use actually leads to crime.

Is the relationship between drugs and crime causal?

It is argued that because drug use and crime are often found together it does not necessarily mean that one causes the other. Instead, the relationship might be spurious or the product of other factors. It is generally accepted that a causal connection involves something more than a statistical association. Moser and Kalton (1993) argue that three types of evidence are required to establish causality: there must be an association between the variables, the cause must occur before the effect and the connection must not disappear when other variables are taken into account. In other words, one of the variables must precede the other and no other variables must independently cause the relationship.

There has been some longitudinal research that has investigated the impact of changes in drug use on changes in crime over time. Ball *et al.* (1981) examined changes in drug use and crime among a sample of opiate addicts drawn from police files in the USA. The results showed that there were substantially more crime-days during periods of addiction than during periods of abstinence (248 days per year compared with 41 days per year). They concluded that, 'criminality decreased markedly during the months or years that these addicts were not dependent on heroin and other opiates' (Ball *et al.* 1981: 60). Nurco *et al.* (1984) in a similar study found that the number of crime-days per year was significantly higher during periods of addiction than periods of non-addiction (280 in the last period of addiction and 62 during the last period of non-addiction). These studies suggest that changes in drug use can sometimes precede changes in crime and that this finding holds up over different time periods and under different conditions. However, in the absence of more detailed information on the way in which the two are linked, it remains unclear how drug use causes offending.

Another approach to determine whether drug use and crime are causally linked is to ask drug users or offenders. Studies of arrestees have provided some information on the causal connection. Makkai and Payne (2003) interviewed incarcerated offenders in Australia and asked them whether their use of alcohol or drugs had an effect on their criminal activities. Among the offenders who answered, 71 per cent thought that drugs or alcohol were connected to their offending. The results from the NEW-ADAM programme showed that 61 per cent of drug-using arrestees said that there was a connection between their drug use and offending (Bennett and Holloway 2007). Liriano and Ramsay (2003) in a survey of prisoners in the UK asked inmates whether they thought that their drug use and crime were connected in the period immediately before incarceration. Fifty-five per cent said that they thought that their drug use and crime were connected. Hammersley and Morrison (1987) conducted a study of active heroin users and found that 'almost all' of them said that their offending and drug-misuse were causally connected. There is some evidence, therefore, that drug use and crime at least some of the time are causally connected. The next question to ask is whether drug use causes crime.

Does drug use cause crime or crime cause drug use?

The government's drug strategy is based on the assumption that drug use causes crime. However, the research literature suggests that there might be several kinds of relationship. Overall, there are five common relationships: the 'drug-use-causes-crime' relationship, the 'crime-causes-drug-use' relationship, the 'reciprocal' relationship, the 'common-cause' relationship and the 'coincidence' relationship (Bennett and Holloway 2005). The first two models ('drug use causes crime' and 'crime causes drug use') are fairly straightforward and suggest the relationships described by their names. The third model (the 'reciprocal' relationship) proposes that drug use sometimes causes crime and crime sometimes causes drug use. Illegal behaviour might lead to the initiation of drug use and serious drug use might lead to the continuity of illegal behaviour (Bennett and Holloway 2005). The fourth model (the 'common-cause' relationship) proposes that drug use does not cause crime nor does crime cause drug use. Instead, they are both caused by a common variable. The fifth model (the 'coincidence' relationship) is described as a spuriousness model whereby drug use and crime are not causally linked but exist within a nexus of problematic behaviours.

There has been some empirical research that has investigated causal order in practice. Bennett and Holloway (2007) asked arrestees who said that there was a connection between their drug use and crime about the nature of the connection. The main explanations given fell within the 'drug-use-causes-crime' category. These include committing crimes for money for drugs (given by 85 per cent of arrestees mentioning a connection) and judgment impairment (mentioned by 22 per cent of arrestees). A smaller proportion of arrestees gave explanations that fell under the heading of 'crime causes drug use'. Six per cent of arrestees said that surplus cash from crime was sometimes used for celebratory purposes including the purchase of drugs. Liriano and Ramsay (2003) in their study of prisoners found that the most frequently given explanations for the drug use and crime connection fell into the 'drug-use-causes-crime' category.

The research tends to show that the main reason given for the drugs–crime connection is that drug use causes crime. A small number of respondents mentioned crime causing drug use and (perhaps understandably) none mentioned common variable causes or reciprocal relationships.

How are drug use and crime causally linked?

Within each of the broad categories of relationship between drug use and crime are more detailed mechanisms that explain the connection. Some of these relationships have been discussed in the research literature.

One of the most influential explanations of drug-related crime was developed by Goldstein in a series of articles published in the late 1980s (Goldstein 1985; Goldstein *et al.* 1989). Goldstein proposed a tripartite conceptual framework which divided explanations of the connection into three models: 'economic-compulsive', 'psychopharmacological' and 'systemic'. 'Economic compulsive' crime was committed as a means of generating money to support drug use. 'Psychopharmacological' crime occurred when the use of drugs resulted in change or impairment in cognitive functioning. 'Systemic' crime was associated with crime that occurred as part of the system of drug distribution and use (Bennett and Holloway 2005). More detailed information on the mechanisms involved in each of the three main categories can be found in qualitative studies of offenders and drug users.

Economic compulsive

Several studies have described in detail the way in which economic necessity to purchase drugs might lead to the commission of crime. Erikson *et al.* (2000) explored the effect of crack dependence on women in Toronto involved in the sex trade. The authors concluded that '... it is clear that they work in the sex trade to get money and/or crack to support their own usage when few other sources of income are available to them' (p. 784). Brain *et al.* (1998) interviewed crack cocaine users in the north of England about the links between drug use and shoplifting. The study showed that dependent drug users required large sums of money and often committed shoplifting offences every day or more than once a day to fund their drug use. In an ethnographic study conducted in New York City, Sommers *et al.* (2000) investigated the lives of women drug dealers in two neighbourhoods and found that most of the women (63 per cent) said that they became dealers wholly in order to support their personal drug use.

Psychopharmacological

The psychopharmacological relationship is based on the idea that the cognitive effects of certain drugs on the individual can lead to the commission of crime. The link may be direct (or almost direct) whereby the drug generates the immediate motivation for crime. The consumption of alcohol, for example, might lead directly to aggression and violent crime. The link may also be indirect whereby drug use affects judgment which in turn affects decision-making. Drug use might result in the decision to commit a risky burglary that might not otherwise have been attempted. There are several studies that have identified these kinds of motives for offending. Cromwell *et al.* (1991) found that drug use often impaired judgment which not only affected the decision to offend but also the risks that might be taken in selecting the potential target. Wright and Decker (1997) in a study of currently active armed robbers found that the proceeds of robbery were often used for pleasure-seeking purposes which typically included drug use.

Systemic crime

The final explanation concerns the way in which drug use causes crime as part of the process of buying and selling drugs. Drug users often have to operate in a world of criminals in order to obtain illegal drugs. As a result, criminal opportunities are presented and crimes (such as retributive violence) sometimes have to be committed. Goldstein *et al.*'s (1989) original study of drug-related homicides in New York City found that systemic violence was the main cause of drug-related homicide. Other studies have identified drug lifestyle factors that might contribute to offending. Parent and Brochu (2002) conducted a study in Canada that explored the drugs–crime relationship among 42 male regular cocaine users. One of the respondents described the way in which drug users need to inhabit the criminal world and how this can result in criminality: '… to keep on using you have to hang round in places where it's being sold. People who sell dope are all criminals. Because they're all criminals, you get into that yourself and automatically become a criminal too' (Parent and Brochu 2002: 145).

Other mechanisms

Within each of the tripartite categories mentioned by Goldstein there are many different mechanisms operating which explain the connection between drug use and crime. Some of the more detailed mechanisms linking drug use and crime were outlined in a recent study of imprisoned offenders (Bennett and Holloway 2009). The study argued that Goldstein's tripartite system covered only some of the causal mechanisms that linked drug use and crime. Economic compulsive crime might include shoplifting to raise money for drugs. However, it might also include shoplifting to save legally obtained money for drug purchases, stealing drugs directly or paying for them with other goods or services. Psychopharmacological influences might include committing violent offences as a result of drug- or alcohol-induced aggression or untypical burglaries as a result of judgment impairment. It also might include taking drugs that give courage or otherwise assist the commission of an offence already planned. Systemic crimes might result from the association with drug users in the criminal world. It can also result from association with criminals in the drug user world or as a result of other problems associated with chaotic lives and deviant lifestyles. For example, one of the offenders interviewed committed an offence in order to get arrested and be provided with drug treatment from within the criminal justice system (Bennett and Holloway 2009).

Explaining the drug-related crime

The research evidence suggests that some crimes committed by drug users are causally connected to their drug use and that some crimes are not. This is based on findings that show that a proportion of drug users say that a proportion of their crimes are connected to their drug use. Some say that the connection is based on their drug use causing crime and some say that it was a result of crime causing drug use. It is not possible with any confidence to place numbers on these proportions or to extrapolate from numbers of offenders to numbers of crimes. Nevertheless, it appears from the research evidence that drug use on some (and perhaps many) occasions causes crime.

Responses

The current government drugs policy is summarised in the 2008 strategy document titled *Drugs: Protecting Families and Communities* (Home Office 2008). The main aim of the strategy is to reduce the harms associated with drug misuse, including drug-related crime. The main approaches used are enforcement through prosecution and seizures, drug treatment and reintegration, harm prevention in relation to children and families, and communication and education. The main method used to reduce drug-related crime is to provide treatment to drug-misusing offenders during their contact with the criminal justice system. The main way in which this is implemented is through the Drug Interventions Programme (DIP).

The DIP is based on the provision of treatment to drug-misusing offenders and on maintaining support to these offenders through the criminal justice system and upon release. The programme aims to reduce drug-related crime by encouraging offenders to stop using drugs and by assisting them to stay off drugs. Offenders receive treatment through specific interventions operating at the various stages of the criminal justice process. A distinction is usually made between interventions operating within prisons and interventions operating within the community. At the prison level, offenders are selected for treatment as part of the CARAT (Counselling, Assessment, Referral, Advice and Throughcare) scheme and the Integrated Drug Treatment System (IDTS) (Home Office 2008). At the community level, offenders are referred into treatment through mandatory drug testing at arrest or charge, restrictions on bail (RoB), conditional cautioning, Drug Treatment and Testing Orders (DTTOs), Drug Rehabilitation Requirements (DRRs), the Offender Substance Abuse Programme (OSAP), the Addressing Substance Related Offending (ASRO) behavioural change programmes and drug courts.

The treatment received as a result of these referrals is made available through a separate body of providers who are commissioned to supply services to drug users. Treatment providers might be involved in providing services to both offenders and non-offenders and in most cases they exist independently of the criminal justice system. There are several types of treatment offered depending on whether the offenders are serving a prison sentence or a community sentence. Prison-based provision is limited to treatment that can be implemented in a prison context, whereas community-based provision can include the wide range of services available at the local level. Prison-based treatment typically includes detoxification, maintenance prescribing, psycho-social support, motivational support, a 12-step treatment programme, cognitive behavioural therapy, supervision and support, and therapeutic communities (UK Drug Policy Commission 2008). Community-based treatment provided within DIP includes almost any programmes available at the local level. In practice, the kinds of treatment offered include the approved programmes listed in the UK guidelines on the clinical management of drug misusers

(Department of Health (England) and the Developed Administrations 2007). These comprise pharmacological interventions (such as detoxification and prescribing) and a wide range of psychosocial interventions (such as motivational enhancement techniques, advice and support, cognitive behavioural treatment, family therapy and interventions designed to improve health and social skills).

What is known about the effectiveness of these kinds of programmes? In order to answer this question the distinction referred to above between programmes of referral (such as drug testing and drug courts) and programmes of treatment (such as methadone prescribing and cognitive behavioural therapy) needs to be borne in mind.

Referral programmes

A recent thematic review of the effectiveness of referral programmes has been conducted by the Institute for Criminal Policy Research on behalf of the UK Drug Policy Commission (McSweeney *et al.* 2008). The review of the research on the effectiveness of *drug testing* concluded that the results were equivocal. The authors thought that there was no evidence that drug testing was effective in reducing drug use or offending. However, it was suggested that drug testing might play a motivating role when coupled with other measures. The results of research on the *restrictions on bail* pilots concluded that the impact of the programme was unclear. Those exposed to the intervention generally fared less well than those exposed to other interventions. Research on the effectiveness of *criminal justice integrated teams* showed some reduction in drug use and offending. However, the reviewers noted that the number of referrals was no different from under the previous arrest referral scheme (McSweeney *et al.* 2008). The review also looked at evaluations of the effectiveness of *DTTOs* and *DRRs*. The research showed that over half of offenders failed to complete these orders and those that did continued to have high reconviction rates. It was noted, however, that those completing the order generally had lower reconviction rates than those who did not. The evidence on the effectiveness of *drug courts* was more encouraging, with most studies showing a reduction in rearrest or reconviction. There is also some evidence of additional benefits relating to health and social functioning. However, to date, most of these studies have been conducted in the United States. The authors reported that the early results of the pilot schemes in the United Kingdom have been inconclusive in part as a result of implementation difficulties.

Treatment programmes

There are considerably more evaluations of treatment programmes than referral programmes. In fact, there are so many that it is common to summarise the results based on numbers of systematic reviews (and in some cases systematic reviews of systematic reviews) rather than numbers of evaluations. There have been at least six systematic reviews of the effectiveness of drug use treatment programmes that have investigated offending behaviour as an outcome variable. Marsch (1998), for example, evaluated the impact of methadone maintenance programmes on various problem behaviours including crime.

Seventeen of the 24 studies that included criminal behaviour as an outcome variable showed a positive and significant effect. Prendergast *et al.* (2002) conducted a meta-analysis of 25 studies on the impact of various kinds of drug treatment on criminal behaviour including methadone maintenance, therapeutic communities, outpatient drug-free programmes, detoxification programmes and private sector treatment. They concluded that drug treatment overall was effective in reducing criminal behaviour. However, there were no significant differences in effect across the different treatment types. Mitchell *et al.* (2006) conducted a meta-analysis of incarceration-based drug treatment programmes including therapeutic communities, group counselling, boot camps and methadone maintenance. They found that there was reduction in offending in relation to therapeutic communities and group counselling programmes but no significant reduction in relation to boot camps or methadone maintenance. Overall, the results of these reviews have been encouraging. However, they have also been variable in relation to the outcomes of specific types of programmes.

A recent systematic review of the effectiveness of a broad range of drug treatment and referral programmes on offending showed that some programmes were more effective than others in reducing offending. The study was based on selecting studies that matched pre-established selection criteria relating to the types of programmes evaluated and the quality of methods use (Holloway *et al.* 2008). In total, 75 evaluations were included in the review. Most of the studies (53) were conducted in the USA. The others were conducted in the UK (15), Australia (4), Scotland (1), Sweden (1) and Switzerland (1). Two methods were used to summarise the results of the selected studies.

The first method was a *narrative review*, which presents descriptive summaries of the results obtained, and the second was a *meta-analysis*, which involves recalculating the published findings to produce a standardised effect size for each study. The results of the narrative review showed that 68 per cent of all outcomes were classified as positive (the treatment group performed better than the comparison group in terms of subsequent criminal behaviour). However, there was some variation in the effectiveness of different types of interventions. The most effective programmes in terms of reducing offending were psychosocial approaches (100 per cent positive, n = 5) and therapeutic communities (88 per cent positive, n = 16), whereas the least effective programmes were 'other' (usually alternative) treatment programmes (33 per cent positive, n = 6) and 'other' (usually a generalised category of 'coercive') criminal justice programmes (25 per cent positive, n = 4). The second method was a meta analysis. In some ways, this is a superior method of analysis compared with the narrative review in that the size of the effect can be taken into account. It is also possible to calculate a mean effect size across all studies or groups of studies. Overall, the results of the meta analysis showed that treatment interventions were associated with favourable changes in crime. The mean effect size for all studies combined showed that following the intervention crime decreased by 26 per cent in the experimental groups compared with the comparison groups. The meta analysis also investigated differences in outcomes across different types of intervention. The results showed that while most of the programme types showed favourable changes only therapeutic communities and supervision had a statistically significant effect on criminal behaviour.

Effectiveness of interventions

Overall, the results of evaluations of referral programmes (such as drug testing and DTTOs) are generally unfavourable in terms of offending. The main notable exception is in relation to drug courts which consistently show favourable outcomes. The results of evaluations of treatment programmes (such as therapeutic communities and cognitive behavioural therapy) are generally favourable in showing a reduction in offending. The main exception is in relation to evaluations of methadone maintenance which have produced more variable results. As interventions involve individual and social processes it is perhaps too much to expect that any single programme will always be effective and, as a result, there will always be some variation in results. This makes it hard to draw any firm conclusions from the results. Nevertheless, there is a significant amount of evidence to show that treatment programmes are often effective in reducing criminal behaviour. Conversely, there is much less evidence to show that referral programmes are effective (with the exception of drug courts). This result might appear surprising bearing in mind that referral programmes use treatment programmes as part of the intervention. One possible explanation is implementation failure at the level of referral. In other words, criminal justice programmes might not always succeed in getting offenders into treatment. There is some evidence that supports this view and shows that many of the early pilot schemes experienced implementation problems. There is also evidence that a proportion (sometimes a high proportion) of offenders referred to these schemes drop out before completion (McSweeney *et al.* 2008).

Discussion and conclusion

There is no agreed definition or list of what constitutes drug-related or alcohol-related crime. Almost any crime could be drug or alcohol related if it were shown to be connected to these substances in some meaningful way. There is some variation in the literature in the ways in which these substances might be linked to crime. The broad definition that substance-related crime includes everything from drug or alcohol offences through to systemic and contextual crimes is probably too wide to be useful. It was proposed in this chapter that the concepts make most sense when they referred to offences committed as a consequence of use of these substances.

Uncertainties about the definition of drug- and alcohol-related crime do not help when it comes to determining trends in these offences over time. The current preferred measure of drug-related crime is acquisitive crime which itself is hard to define. Using this measure suggests that drug-related crime is falling. However, this does not take into account the unknown extent of drug-related violent crime. Data from the Homicide Index is too unreliable to make a confident estimate. However, the evidence that does exist suggests that over the last few years there has been a slight fall in alcohol-related homicides but a slight increase in drug-related homicides.

The assumption of government policy that drug use causes crime rather than crime causes drug use has not until recently been properly tested. It might be considered fortunate that recent research on drug-misusing offenders shows that this assumption is probably more or less correct. However, there remains a proportion of all drug-related crime that is the result of crime stimulating drug use rather than the other way around. The linked assumption that drug use causes crime because of economic motives also seems to be supported by recent research. The majority of drug-misusing offenders report that their crimes are caused by drugs and that the main reason for the connection is economic necessity. It is important to acknowledge, however, that a certain amount of substance-related crime is caused by the pharmacological effects of these drugs.

The government can also claim some success in its assumptions about the suitability of reducing drug misuse among offenders through drug treatment programmes. The research on the effectiveness of drug treatment shows that some of the most common kinds of treatment can reduce drug misuse and criminal behaviour. There are other forms of treatment where the research results are less clear but are sufficiently promising to justify their continued use. The main downside with the government's strategy lies with the referral programmes that link the offender to treatment. The research evidence is almost unanimous in showing that many of the current pilot programmes established in recent years are suffering from various kinds of implementation failure.

Overall, the debate about drug and alcohol-related crime is largely a policy debate. The concepts have their origins in policy as do the methods used to prevent them. While the government has to some extent operated ahead of the insights of research, the results of studies now emerging provide some support for its broad principles. The main work that needs to be done is to devise a clearer definition of substance-related crime and the accepted methods for measuring it, as well as selecting and making available the most effective treatment programmes for reducing it.

Selected further reading

No single text comprehensively covers the concept of drug-related crime. There are, however, a number of useful sources that provide some information on the subject. It is recommended that the reader refers to the various UK strategy documents in order to observe the changing definition of drug-related crime over time (e.g. Home Office 1994, 1995, 1998, 2002, 2008). Bennett and Holloway's (2007) *Drug–Crime Connections* and Boreham *et al.*'s (2007) *The Arrestee Survey: 2003–2006* provide useful results on patterns and trends in drug-related crime as well as information on the characteristics of offenders. Stevens' (2007) article 'When two dark figures collide' neatly explains the socio-political construction of drug-related crime and the difficulties involved in determining how much crime is drug related. Goldstein's (1985) seminal article 'The drugs/violence nexus' and Bennett and Holloway's (2009) 'The causal connection between drug use and crime' include useful discussions on the causal relationship between drug misuse and crime. McSweeney *et al.*'s (2008) *The Treatment and Supervision of Drug-Dependent Offenders: A Review of the Literature* is a particularly helpful source of information on what works in reducing drug-related crime.

References

Ball, J. C., Rosen, L., Fluceck, J. A. and Nurco, D. N. (1981) 'The criminality of heroin addicts when addicted and when off opiates', in J. A. Inciardi (ed.), *The Drugs–Crime Connection*. Beverly Hills, CA: Sage, pp. 39–65.

Bennett, T. H. and Holloway, K. R. (2005) *Understanding Drugs, Alcohol and Crime*. Buckingham: McGraw-Hill/Open University Press.

Bennett, T. H. and Holloway, K. R. (2007) *Drug–Crime Connections*. New York: Cambridge University Press.

Bennett, T. H. and Holloway, K. R. (2009) 'The causal connection between drug use and crime', *British Journal of Criminology*, 49 (4): 513–31.

Boreham, R., Cronberg, A., Dollin, L. and Pudney, S. (2007) *The Arrestee Survey: 2003–2006*, Home Office Statistical Bulletin12/07. London: Home Office.

Brain, K., Howard, P. and Bottomley, T. (1998) *Evolving Crack Cocaine Careers: New Users, Quitters and Long Term Combination Drug Users in N.W. England*. Manchester: University of Manchester.

Brookman, F. and Maguire, M. (2003) *Reducing Homicide: Summary of a Review of the Possibilities*, RDS Occasional Paper No. 84. London: Home Office.

Cabinet Office (2004) *Alcohol Harm Reduction Strategy for England*. London: Cabinet Office.

Chapple, C. (2008) 'Substance-Related Homicide in England and Wales: Pathways, Processes, and Events', unpublished doctoral dissertation. Manchester: University of Manchester.

Cromwell, P. F., Olson, J. N., Avary, D. W. and Marks, A. (1991) 'How drugs affect decisions by burglars', *International Journal of Offender Therapy and Comparative Criminology*, 35 (4): 310–21.

Department of Health (England) and the Developed Administrations (2007) *Drug Misuse and Dependence: UK Guidelines on Clinical Management*. London: Department of Health (England), the Scottish Government, Welsh Assembly Government and Northern Ireland Executive.

Erickson, P. G., Butters, J., McGillicuddy, P. and Hallgren, A. (2000) 'Crack and prostitution: gender, myths and experiences', *Journal of Drug Issues*, 30 (4): 767–88.

Goldstein, P. J. (1985) 'The drugs/violence nexus: a tripartite conceptual framework', *Journal of Drug Issues*, 39: 143–74.

Goldstein, P. J., Brownstein, H. H., Ryan, P. J. and Bellucci, P. A. (1989) 'Crack and homicide in New York City, 1988: a conceptually based event analysis', *Contemporary Drug Problems*, 16: 651–87.

Hammersley, R. and Morrison, V. (1987) 'Effects of polydrug use on the criminal activities of heroin-users', *British Journal of Addiction*, 82: 899–906.

Holloway, K., Bennett, T. H. and Farrington, D. P. (2008) *Effectiveness of Drug Treatment Programmes in Reducing Criminal Behaviour*. Stockholm: National Council on Crime Prevention.

Holloway, K., Bennett, T. H. and Williams, T. (2004) *Trends in Drug Use and Crime: The Results of the NEW-ADAM Programme 1999–2002*, Research Findings No. 219. London: Home Office.

Home Office (1994) *Tackling Drugs Together: A Consultation Document on a Strategy for England 1995–98*. London: HMSO.

Home Office (1995) *Tackling Drugs Together: A Strategy for England 1995–1998*. London: HMSO.

Home Office (1998) *Tackling Drugs Together to Build a Better Britain*. London: HMSO.

Home Office (2002) *Updated Drug Strategy 2002*. London: Home Office.

Home Office (2007a) *Operational Process Guidance for Implementation of Testing on Arrest, Required Assessment and Restriction on Bail*. London: Home Office.

Home Office (2007b) *Drugs: Our Community, Your Say: A Consultation Paper*. London: Home Office.

Home Office (2008) *Drugs: Protecting Families and Communities: The 2008 Drug Strategy*. London: Home Office.

Kershaw, C., Nicholas, S. and Walker, A. (2008) *Crime in England and Wales 2007/08: Findings from the British Crime Survey and Police Recorded Crime*, Home Office Statistical Bulletin 07/08: London: Home Office.

Liriano, S. and Ramsay, M. (2003) 'Prisoners' drug use before prison and the links with crime', in M. Ramsay (ed.), *Prisoners' Drug Use and Treatment: Seven Research Studies*, Home Office Research Study 267. London: Home Office.

McSweeney, T., Turnbull, P. and Hough, M. (2008) *The Treatment and Supervision of Drug-Dependent Offenders: A Review of the Literature Prepared for the UK Drug Policy Commission*. London: UKDPC.

Makkai, T. and Payne, J. (2003) *Drugs and Crime: A Study of Incarcerated Male Offenders*, Research and Public Policy Series No. 52. Canberra: Australian Institute of Criminology.

Marsch, L. (1998) 'The efficacy of methadone maintenance interventions in reducing illicit opiate use, HIV risk behaviour and criminality: a meta-analysis', *Addiction*, 93 (4): 515–32.

Mattinson, J. (2001) *Stranger and Acquaintance Violence: Practice Messages from the British Crime Survey*, Home Office Briefing Note No. 7/01. London: Home Office.

Mitchell, O., MacKenzie, D. L. and Wilson, D. B. (2006) 'Incarceration-based drug treatment', in B. C. Welsh and D. P. Farrington (eds), *Preventing Crime: What Works for Children, Offenders, Victims and Places?* Dordrecht: Springer, pp. 103–16.

Moser, C. A. and Kalton, G. (1993) *Survey Methods in Social Investigation*. Aldershot: Dartmouth.

National Treatment Agency for Substance Misuse (2009) *Criminal Justice: Treatment for Offenders*. Online at: http://www.nta.nhs.uk/areas/criminal_justice/default.aspx (accessed 30 March 2009).

Nurco, D. N., Shaffer, J. W., Ball, J. C. and Kinlock, T. W. (1984) 'Trends in the commission of crime among narcotic addicts over successive periods of addiction and non-addiction', *American Journal of Drug and Alcohol Abuse*, 10: 481–9.

Parent, I. and Brochu, S. (2002) 'Drug/crime pathways among cocaine users', in S. Brochu, C. Da Agra and M. Cousineau (eds), *Drugs and Crime Deviant Pathways*. Aldershot: Ashgate.

Prendergast, M., Podus, D., Chang, E. and Urada, D. (2002) 'The effectiveness of drug abuse treatment: a meta-analysis of comparison group studies', *Drug and Alcohol Dependence*, 67 (1): 53–72.

Scottish Government (2008) *Homicide in Scotland, 2007–08*. Edinburgh: Scottish Government National Statistics.

Sommers, I., Baskin, D. and Fagan, J. (2000) *Workin' Hard for the Money: The Social and Economic Lives of Women Drug Sellers*. New York: Nova Science.

Stevens, A. (2007) 'When two dark figures collide: evidence and discourse on drug-related crime', *Critical Social Policy*, 27 (1): 77–99.

UK Drug Policy Commission (2008) *Reducing Drug Use, Reducing Reoffending: Are Programmes for Problem Drug-Using Offenders in the UK Supported by the Evidence?* London: UKDPC.

Wright, R. and Decker, S. (1997) *Armed Robbers in Action: Stickups and Street Culture.* Boston: Northeastern University Press.

Chapter 30

Drug supply and possession

Tim McSweeney, Paul J. Turnbull and Tiggey May

Introduction

The World Drug Report suggests that the number of people reporting recent use of illicit drugs has remained stable over the last decade; however, there has been a surge in the cultivation, trafficking and supply of drugs (United Nations Office on Drugs and Crime 2008). In particular opium cultivation, which eventually finds its way on to the streets of the UK as heroin, has risen by 17 per cent since 2006 to 235,700 hectares of land under cultivation. Similar increases in coca production (16 per cent) in South America have also been observed.

Illicit drug use is largely a hidden activity making it difficult to provide reliable statistics on trends. However, the European Monitoring Centre for Drugs and Drug Addiction (EMCDDA) has produced estimates for the number of users of illicit drugs based on the available evidence (see Table 30.1). Quite clearly cannabis is the most widely used drug in Europe, followed by cocaine and amphetamine. The use of heroin is not considered to be widespread; it is estimated that there are between one and six problem users per 1,000 of the adult population in European Union countries.

Illicit drug use in the UK

The British Crime Survey (BCS) provides measurements of drug use in England and Wales (Scotland and Northern Ireland conduct their own crime surveys) for at least part of the adult general population,[1] and the National Centre for Social Research (NatCen) and the National Foundation for Education Research (NFER) provide useful information about drug use in the school population. It was not, however, until 1996 that the BCS included a comparable self-completion module on drug use which has meant that trend data, since this time, has become a fairly reliable indicator of the general population's illicit drug use.

Table 30.1 Use of illicit drugs among EU citizens aged between 15 and 64 years

Drug	Lifetime use (millions) (%)	Use in the last 12 months (millions) (%)
Cannabis	71 (21)	23 (6.5)
Amphetamine	11 (3.3)	2 (0.6)
Ecstasy	9.5 (2.8)	2.6 (0.76)
Cocaine	12 (3.6)	4 (1.1)

Source: Data from EMCDDA (2008a).

From the 1980s to the 2000s

Illicit drug use escalated during the 1980s. The increase in consumption was predominated by cannabis and amphetamine, but also increasingly heroin. Prior to the 1980s cheap pure heroin was relatively difficult to purchase; however, towards the end of the late 1970s heroin from South West Asia (Iran, Pakistan and Afghanistan) started to be imported into Britain. The new purer heroin was able to be smoked which, for many users, lessened the fear and stigma associated with injecting. The consequence of this was an emergence of a new wave of heroin users across England in the early 1980s (Parker *et al.* 1988; Pearson 1987). At around the same time the UK saw a growing trend in users smoking (and some injecting) crack cocaine. By the end of the 1980s crack cocaine had become firmly entrenched in many inner-city drug markets and was starting to become a particular concern for both the police and health professionals alike.

During the 1990s reported drug use increased year on year. Data from the 2000 BCS[2] showed that by the end of the 1990s around a third of those aged 16 to 59 had tried at least one illicit substance in their lifetime. While lifetime prevalence rates might be viewed as quite high, the proportions using drugs in the last year and last month tended to be much lower, with only 11 per cent disclosing they had used an illicit substance in the previous year and 6 per cent reporting using in the previous month. Rates of use of 'any drug' were generally higher in young people; the figures for 16- to 29-year-olds were 50 per cent for lifetime use, 25 per cent for use in the last year and 16 per cent for use in the last month. Based on the 2000 BCS findings it is estimated that of the 9.5 million young people aged 16 to 29 in England and Wales, at least 2.3 million would have used a prohibited drug in the previous year. Men were more likely to report the use of drugs than women. While cannabis was the most commonly used drug, with just over a fifth of young people aged 16 to 29 reporting use within the last year, heroin use remained low at around 1 per cent for the under 30 age group. Cocaine use, however, appeared more common, with 5 per cent of the 16–29 age group reporting use within the last year – a level similar to ecstasy (Ramsay *et al*. 2001).

Unsurprisingly, London has consistently higher rates of drug use than any other region in England and Wales for any drug. Drug consumption rates, reported by Ramsay and colleagues, tend to be more highly concentrated (or disclosed) in the 16–29 year age group residing in affluent urban areas. Heroin use, however, was significantly higher in the poorest income group (3 per cent compared with less than 0.5 per cent in the intermediate and richest groups). Single people and those living in rented accommodation were more likely to have taken drugs. Drug use was also more common for those who visited pubs and clubs and drank alcohol more frequently (ibid.). During the 1990s there was a decline in amphetamine, LSD and amyl nitrite ('popper') use. Use of any illicit drug in the last year, by 16- to 19-year-olds, also fell from around a third in 1994 to just over a quarter by 2000. Reported heroin use continued to be particularly low across all age ranges and both sexes throughout the 1990s. Before 2000, cocaine use was reported to be more prevalent among the unemployed but, in 2000, its use was as common among those with or without a job. Lifetime use of any drug among those aged 16 to 59 was greatest in the white population (34 per cent), followed by 28 per cent of black people, 15 per cent of Indians and 10 per cent of Pakistani/Bangladeshis. This was the same for all age groups (ibid.).

By 2006/7 overall illicit (drug use) prevalence rates (as recorded by the BCS) were at their lowest since recording began in 1995. The drop in prevalence rates was largely due to the reported decline in cannabis use, the drug most commonly used by all age groups (Murphy and Roe 2007). In 2007/8 the BCS estimated that about 11.5 million people aged 16–59 in England and Wales had ever used an illicit drug, which equates to around one in three adults disclosing having ever tried an illicit substance. Of these, it was estimated that just under 3 million had used an illicit substance in the year prior to being surveyed (about one in 10) and around 1.7 million in the last month (one in 20). Class A drug use is far less common with the BCS reporting that nearly 4.5 million people aged 16–59 are estimated to have ever used a Class A drug (13.9 per cent of those surveyed), with just under one million people having used them in the last year (3 per cent of those surveyed) and just over 400,000 in the last month (1.3 per cent of those surveyed). Cocaine powder and ecstasy are the most commonly used Class A drugs (Hoare and Flatley 2008). Cannabis continues to be the most widely used illicit drug. In 2006/7 just over nine and a half million people aged 16–59 were estimated to have ever used cannabis, around 2.3 million in the last year (7.4 per cent of those surveyed) and about 1.3 million in the last month. Since 1995, the reported consumption of cannabis has, however, decreased from 26 per cent to just under 18 per cent among the 16–24-year-old age group.

Young people and drug use
Results from a Department of Health survey conducted in 2003 of over 10,000 secondary schoolchildren aged 11–15 years found that 21 per cent disclosed that they had taken an illicit substance during the previous 12–month period and 12 per cent had done so in the month before the survey. Thirteen per

cent had used cannabis, but only 4 per cent had use a Class A drug in the previous 12 months (Department of Health 2004). A more recent NHS Information Centre survey *Drug Use, Smoking and Drinking Among Young People in England 2007* reported that, from a sample of 8,000 11–15 year olds, 25 per cent had consumed an illicit substance, down from 29 per cent in 2001 (NHS Information Centre 2008). In the Ofsted/Department for Children, Schools and Families (DCSF) *TellUs3* survey undertaken during 2008, 86 per cent of 13 and 15-year-old children questioned said they had never used drugs, compared to 80 per cent in the previous year's survey.

Drugs and the law

The EMCDDA has recently described a tendency for European countries to make a clear distinction in law between those who use drugs and those who traffic or sell them (EMCDDA 2008a). Some countries (Belgium, Germany, Holland, Italy, Portugal, Spain and Switzerland) have removed altogether criminal penalties for users found in possession of drugs which are considered of small enough quantity to be for their own personal use. A recent evaluation of this approach concluded that it had enabled Portugal to more effectively manage drug use and related problems (e.g. drug-related overdoses, HIV infections and deaths) than most other nations dealing with possession and consumption as a criminal offence (Greenwald 2009). However, in most jurisdictions it is quite often difficult to distinguish between users and small-scale drug sellers (Hughes and Stevens 2007: 7).

Despite this, between 2001 and 2006 there was a 36 per cent rise in the number of drug law offences across Europe, with drug possession offences increasing by over half (51 per cent) (EMCDDA 2008a). The greatest increase in possession offences were those related to cocaine (up 61 per cent) and cannabis (up 34 per cent). Only the number of heroin-related offences dropped over this period – falling by 14 per cent. Drug supply offences also increased during this period, but only by 12 per cent. These data clearly indicate that most drug enforcement activities are conducted against users of drugs rather than sellers, suppliers, traffickers or producers.

International treaties and UK law

February 2009 marked 100 years since the First Opium Commission in Shanghai. This was effectively the beginning of what became global drug prohibition. The most important international treaty in recent times was introduced in 1961: the United Nations (UN) Single Convention on Narcotic Drugs brought together all existing multilateral treaties on drug control and extended them to include the cultivation of plants. This has become the bedrock of the international drug control system. Section 36 of the convention requires signatory countries to ensure that within the constitutional limitations of individual countries:

... the cultivation, production, manufacture, extraction, preparation, possession, offering, offering for sale, distribution, purchase, sale, delivery ... shall be punishable offences ... and that serious offences shall be liable to adequate punishment, particularly by imprisonment.

It introduced a global penal response to controlled drug production, supply and possession. In 1971 a further convention was introduced to cover new psychotropic drugs such as MDMA, LSD and amphetamines.

The 1971 Misuse of Drugs Act brought UK legislation into line with UN conventions and placed restrictions on drugs because of the harm they were believed to cause. These are known as controlled drugs. The 1971 Act categorises controlled drugs in Classes A, B and C; Class A drugs are considered to be the most harmful and Class C the least harmful (though the extent to which the classification system accurately assesses levels of harm has subsequently been questioned by the House of Commons Science and Technology Committee (2006)). Table 30.2 shows the class in which individual drugs are currently placed.

The penalties applied for the possession, supply and production of controlled drugs are related to the class they fall within and, by implication, the perceived level of harm they cause. Table 30.3 shows the maximum sentences by class of drug, although in most cases this will not reflect the actual sentence given.

Table 30.2 Classification of drugs

Class A	Class B	Class C
	Certain class B drugs are reclassified as class A if they have been prepared for injection	
Cocaine	Barbiturates	Steroids
Crack	Dihydrocodine	Buprenorphine
Ecstasy	Cannabis	Ketamine
Magic mushrooms	Amphetamine	GHB
Methamphetamine		

Source: Information from http://www.homeoffice.gov.uk.

Table 30.3 Maximum sentences for possession, supply and production

Class of drug	Possession	Supply	Production
Class A	7 years' imprisonment or a fine or both	Life imprisonment or a fine or both	Life imprisonment or a fine or both
Class B	5 years' imprisonment or a fine or both	14 years' imprisonment or a fine or both	14 years' imprisonment or a fine or both
Class C	2 years' imprisonment or a fine or both	14 years' imprisonment or a fine or both	14 years' imprisonment or a fine or both

Source: Information from http//www.homeoffice.gov.uk.

Drug laws: debate and reform

Recently there has been considerable debate among academics, policymakers and their advisory bodies, enforcement agencies and drug treatment services about the appropriateness of the drug classification system. In their detailed report on drug policy the Royal Society of Arts Commission on Illegal Drugs, Communities and Public Policy argued that the 1971 Misuse of Drugs Act is no longer fit for purpose and should be replaced with a new Misuse of Substances Act (RSA 2007). The Commission suggested that a new Act should aim to:

- set drugs in a wider context of substance misuse (including alcohol and tobacco);
- provide a stronger link to an evidence base in which an assessment of the relative risks of harm of different substances can be made; and
- ensure that the focus of punishment should be mainly on harmful behaviours stemming from drug use rather than drug possession.

There has been a particularly protracted debate over both the harms associated with cannabis use and its appropriate classification. In 2004, cannabis was downgraded from Class B to Class C only to be regraded to Class B in early 2009 because of uncertainties about the potential impact of a perceived increase in the strength of some forms of cannabis available to UK users (a further detailed discussion is provided later in this chapter). In regrading cannabis as a Class B drug the government failed to implement the main recommendation from its advisory body on drug issues, the Advisory Council on the Misuse of Drugs (ACMD 2008).

There is also a growing debate about the effectiveness of the drug control system as a whole, both at an international and a national level. Opponents of the current system argue that not only does the approach fundamentally fail to distinguish between drug use harms and drug policy harms, but that it has failed to regulate or reduce the numbers using drugs and the scale of drug production (see, for example, the Transform Drug Policy Foundation (TDPF)[3]). Indeed it has been argued that the 'war on drugs' has had a number of unintended consequences which have increased harms:

- at the level of individual users (for example, through the use of adulterated drugs, risk of imprisonment, risk of infection, overdose);
- communities (acquisitive crime committed by some drug users to support their use); and
- internationally (via organised crime and criminal organisation profiteering, and its destabilising influence in producer countries and along trafficking routes, e.g. Mexico and Afghanistan).

Some reformers argue that if drug production and sales were brought within a regulatory system this would reduce the impact of most of the unintended consequences and produce some benefits (Transform 2009). Opponents argue that such moves would increase the number of people using drugs or that many of these benefits could be achieved via an expansion of heroin prescribing, for example.

The rest of this chapter is divided into two main sections looking in detail at drug supply and drug possession in the UK. Most of the data are drawn from government or official sources and population-based surveys and therefore have a number of limitations (for example, only representing successful police activity and the drug use of those interviewed in households).

Drug supply

Patterns and trends

Patterns and trends in illicit drug seizures

Over the last 25 years, the number of seizures by UK law enforcement agencies of controlled and illicit drugs has increased by 956 per cent: from 17,617 seizures in 1980[4] (Home Office 1986: 13) to 186,054 in 2005[5] (Reed 2007: 1; Scottish Executive 2007: 3). Seizures of Class A drugs – such as heroin, cocaine, crack and ecstasy – increased by 1,898 per cent over this period (from 2,196 to 43,875). With the exception of LSD (which saw seizure rates fall by 23 per cent), there were considerable increases in the *number* of seizures for all the main illicit drugs, including:

- cocaine (up 2,854 per cent from 445 seizures in 1980 to 13,146 in 2005);
- heroin (up 2,268 per cent from 697 to 16,506);
- crack (up 1,956 per cent from 316[6] to 6,498);
- ecstasy (up 1,696 per cent from 399[7] to 7,165);
- amphetamines (up 1,063 per cent from 729 to 8,477); and
- cannabis (up 748 per cent from 15,726 to 133,350) (Home Office 1986: 13, 1991: 20; Corkery 2002: 49; Reed 2007: tables A3 and A5; Scottish Executive 2007: 9–10).

Cannabis has accounted for the bulk of illicit drug seizures in the UK: ranging from 90 per cent in 1990 (Home Office 1991: 1) to just under three-quarters (72 per cent) of all confiscations in Britain during 2005 (Reed 2007: 1; Scottish Executive 2007: 10). Figure 30.1 below charts the increase in the number of UK seizures across the different classes of drug over a twenty-year period and highlights the dominance of cannabis (a Class B drug during this time) in most enforcement-related seizures.

There were commensurate increases in the total *quantity* (measured in kilograms) of illicit drugs being confiscated each year between 1980 and 2005. This included considerable increases in the annual amounts being seized by law enforcement agencies for substances such as:

- amphetamines (up 44,696 per cent from 5 kg in 1980 to 2,240 kg in 2005);
- cocaine (up 9,499 per cent from 40 to 3,840 kg);
- heroin (up 5,063 per cent from 38 to 1,926 kg);

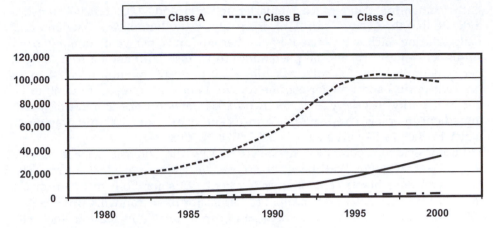

Figure 30.1 Number of UK seizures by class (1980–2000)
Source: Data from Home Office (1986: 13) and Corkery (2002: 50).

- crack (up 5,100 per cent from 1 to 52 kg); and
- cannabis (up 180 per cent from 26,300 to 73,662).

Previously unpublished analysis by HM Treasury (subsequently released under the Freedom of Information Act) concluded that these increased seizures and interceptions were likely to reflect 'rising volumes of drug imports rather than greatly increased shares: increased effectiveness being countered by increased sophistication and scale on the trafficker's part' in order to meet growing levels of demand (*The Economist* 2008: 35–6; TDPF 2008: 11–12).

The sheer scale of the increases in both the number and quantity of drug seizures is therefore more indicative of the growth in global production of opium and coca and subsequent availability of illicit drugs in the UK during the last 25 years than the sophistication and effectiveness of law enforcement activities. It is worth noting that the police are responsible for most seizures of controlled drugs in the UK. In contrast to HM Revenue and Customs, for example, local police forces in England and Wales accounted for 96 per cent of all seizures in 2000 and 2005 (Reed 2007: table S1) which tended to involve only small quantities of drugs: most seizures of heroin (74 per cent), crack (70 per cent) and cocaine (61 per cent) during 2005 were less than one gram in weight (ibid.: table 5).

The impact of seizures on prices and purity
There are, though, two other proxy measures of increased availability: drug prices and purity levels. Since 2000, average street prices in the UK have fallen consistently for heroin (from £70 a gram in 2000 to £45 in 2007), cocaine (from £65 a gram in 2000 to between £30 and £50 in 2007, depending on purity levels) and ecstasy (from £9 in December 2000 to £3 in 2007) (SOCA 2008: 32–4). Between 2000 and 2004 the average price (per ounce) also fell for skunk (from £145 to £121), cannabis resin (from £85 to £61) and herbal cannabis (from £82 to £72) (Pudney *et al.* 2006: 63).

By comparing data for each quarter in 1995 and 2005, official statistics indicate that the average purity of drugs seized by the police in England and Wales during each year increased for heroin (up 4 per cent; ranging from 40–48 per cent purity) and amphetamines (up 1 per cent; ranging from 7 to 12 per cent purity), but fell for crack (down 20 per cent; ranging from 64 to 87 per cent purity) and powder cocaine (down 8 per cent; ranging from 40 to 54 per cent purity) (Corkery 2002: 59; Reed 2007: table 6). The amount of active ingredient in ecstasy has also fallen in recent years: from 100 milligrams per tablet in 2000 to 54 milligrams in 2007 (SOCA 2008: 34).

Recent evidence submitted to the ACMD by the Forensic Science Service indicated that there had been no consistent change in the mean THC (tetrahydrocannabinol) content during recent years for both resin (from 6.1 in 1998 to 4.5 in 2007) and traditional herbal forms of cannabis (from 3.9 in 1995 to 2.6 in 2007). However, there had been a notable increase in the THC content of sinsemilla between 1995 and 2000 (from 5.8 to 10.4) which appears to have remained broadly stable since then (ACMD 2008: 23–4).

Data on the purity of police seizures tends to be variable and inconsistent and thus needs to be interpreted with some caution. As Reed observes, 'the purity from HM Revenue and Customs seizures is higher than that of the police force seizures, reflecting the fact that their seizures will tend to be made higher in the supply chain and before "cutting" occurs (the addition of active agents to increase profit margins)' (2007: 5) (cf. Matrix Knowledge Group 2007).

Estimates of the size of the UK market

The size of the UK illicit drugs market – estimated to be worth £5.3 billion during 2003/4 (Pudney *et al*. 2006: 46) – means it is extremely lucrative for drug traffickers and dealers – both in scale and in terms of the profits that can be generated. For example, estimated lifetime prevalence of cannabis use is estimated to be higher among the adult population in the UK (30 per cent) than in 22 neighbouring European Union Member States (EMCDDA 2008a: table GPS-8).[8] The UK is also thought to have a higher proportion of problem drug users within the adult population than any of its European neighbours[9] (EMCDDA 2007).

Over half the estimated market expenditure on illicit drugs in the UK during 2003/4 was devoted to crack (28 per cent) and heroin (23 per cent). Cannabis (20 per cent) and powder cocaine (18 per cent) accounted for two-fifths of this market activity. The contribution of amphetamines (6 per cent) and ecstasy (5 per cent) were much smaller by comparison (Pudney *et al*. 2006: 46).

Importation seizure information

In terms of volume, the estimated UK market for heroin during 2003/4 was sized at 20 tonnes; for powder cocaine it was 18 tonnes and for crack 16 tonnes. The figures for cannabis and ecstasy were 412 tonnes and 60 million tablets respectively (ibid.: 76). Using these figures, the market share of heroin and cocaine (including crack) seized was estimated by Pudney and colleagues to be 12 and 9 per cent respectively, as illustrated in Figure 30.2 (ibid.: 46

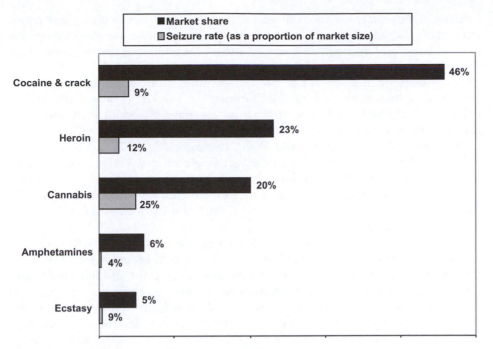

Figure 30.2   Market share and seizure rates (2003/4)
Source: Data from Pudney *et al*. (2006: 46 and 83).

and 83). At 25 per cent, cannabis had the highest interception rate and amphetamines the lowest at 4 per cent.

In 2003, British Cabinet Office analysts presented the Prime Minister and senior Cabinet Ministers with their assessment of the considerable challenges posed by attempts to tackle illicit drug markets and trafficking networks. They concluded that sustained seizure rates in the region of 60 to 80 per cent would be required to put major traffickers and dealers out of business (Strategy Unit 2003: 73). Their report went on to note that seizure rates on this scale have never been achieved anywhere in the world, and both attaining and sustaining them would have major logistical and resource implications for law enforcement agencies.

Cannabis cultivation

There has in recent years been concern about a shift from the importation of cannabis to home-grown forms cultivated using hydroponic systems. Offences for the unlawful production and cultivation of cannabis[10] increased by 14 per cent between 1980[11] and 2004:[12] from 2,173 to 2,480 offences (but had peaked at 4,960 offences in 1995 – up 128 per cent on the figures for 1980) (Home Office 1991: 31; Mwenda 2005: 13). While considering the implications of the changes then being proposed to the laws on cannabis for offences of cultivation, Hough *et al.* (2003) made two important observations. Firstly, they noted how UK police forces varied considerably in their responses to cannabis cultivators: where some issued cautions others would routinely charge suspects with production offences (or a lesser offence of cultivation). Secondly, the motives of these different 'types' of cultivator varied in a number of important ways: from 'sole-use growers cultivating cannabis as a money-saving hobby, for personal use and use with friends' to more 'commercial growers cultivating cannabis to make money, selling to any potential customer' (ibid.: 2).

As a consequence there has been a commensurate growth in both the size and sophistication of cannabis 'farming' in the UK (Bryne 2008), to the extent that cannabis 'factories' or 'farms' are now an established source of production of cannabis on a commercial scale in parts of the UK. Around 2,000 were raided in England and Wales during 2007 (ACPO 2008), and well over half the cannabis now consumed in England and Wales is thought to be grown here (ACMD 2008; Hough *et al.* 2003). This was one of the main reasons that led the Association of Chief Police Officers to advise the ACMD that, in its view, cannabis should revert from Class C to Class B (ACPO 2008; see also HM Government 2008: 18).

However, the implications for illicit drug markets in the UK from the hydroponic cultivation of cannabis are only starting to become clear. The same cannot be said about effective enforcement strategies for dealing with these developments or how pending changes to the law on cannabis offences will allow for a more appropriate response aimed at different 'types' of cultivator, thus ensuring that, as much as possible, illicit markets for cannabis are kept separate from those for heroin and crack (Hough *et al.* 2003; McSweeney *et al.* 2008a; May *et al.* 2007).

Characteristics of offenders and victims

Distribution networks

There is no single accepted definition of a drug market that emerges from the international research literature. A review of the recent evidence on behalf of the UK Drug Policy Commission (McSweeney *et al.* 2008a) described how previous studies had tended to conceptualise two distinct types of distribution system: a pyramidical one and a more fragmented, non-hierarchical and entrepreneurial free market. However, while noting the difficultly of judging which system is dominant in the UK, it drew on research which indicates that there has been 'a shift from historical affiliations and ties with hierarchical structures among some ethnic groups, towards more open and entrepreneurial networks of individuals who lack any formal connections with traditional syndicates' (ibid.: 8).

The market is also usually described as having three levels: an international trafficking level (Dorn *et al.* 2005), a local retail level (May and Hough 2004), and between these a loosely defined 'middle market' at national and regional levels (Pearson and Hobbs 2001). However, the research evidence tends to emphasise how the lines between the different levels in the supply chain are far from clear and that the various roles within them are often fluid and interchangeable (Matrix Knowledge Group 2007).

Domestic local drug markets

UK retail-level drug markets are often described as being either open (e.g. street dealing), semi-open (e.g. pub- and club-based) or closed structures (e.g. where access is restricted to only known and trusted participants)

(May and Hough 2004). The 1990s also saw the emergence of 'crack houses' or 'dealing houses' in many inner cities involving a range of residential, uninhabited or semi-derelict properties from which drugs were sold. More recently UK research has focused on the development of 'social network markets' for drugs such as cannabis (Duffy *et al.* 2007; Hough *et al.* 2003). These are primarily based around friendship and social networks and serve to insulate participants from the risks posed by more overtly criminal drug markets. Supply of illicit drugs within these sorts of market tends to have little to do with commercial gain.

Description of suppliers and dealers
The most recently published figures on known drug offenders are for England and Wales during 2004 and based on data from 'police cautions, court proceedings and HM Revenue and Customs compounding (where payment is made of a compound settlement in lieu of prosecution for minor cannabis possession offences) for drug offences' (Mwenda 2005: 2). This Home Office report notes that between 1994 and 2004 the majority of known drug offenders were male. Men accounted for 85 per cent of dealing offences in 2004 and 83 per cent of production/import/export offences. The distribution of known offenders by age indicated that dealing offences tended to be committed by those over the age of 25 (60 per cent) while most production/import/export offences involved people aged 30 years or over (61 per cent). However, there is very little published comparative data available to inform a discussion on the changing profiles of those involved in drug supply offences over an extended period of time.

Previous research had suggested that the UK market was divided along racial lines with much of the more precarious and comparatively poorly paid work being undertaken by young black males at the retail level (Ruggiero and South 1995). More recent work by Pearson and Hobbs (2001) also noted the importance of kinship and ethnicity in sustaining networks at the lower end of the UK supply chain.

Victims
The illicit drugs trade creates victims along the entire supply chain. Illicit drugs are a major source of violence, instability and corruption at source/production (see Schweich (2008) for a recent assessment of the situation in Afghanistan) and along trafficking routes (there are estimated to have been more than 7,600 killings in Mexico since 2007 linked to the drugs trade there) (Carroll 2009), and expose users to a considerable range of drug-related harms, including arrest and imprisonment, violence, overdose, infection (e.g. hepatitis and HIV) and death. The 'collateral damage' from the 'war on drugs' also ranges from executions and extrajudicial killings of farmers, dealers and users in countries such as Thailand and Columbia, to the economic and social hardships endured by rural workers in a number of source countries, such as Myanmar (Stevens 2007: 79).

Closer to home the broader economic and social costs to society of Class A drug use in England and Wales were estimated to be around £15.4 billion in 2003/4 (Gordon *et al.* 2006: 41). 'Drug-related' crime accounted for

90 per cent of the costs associated with 'problematic' drug use. The illicit drugs trade in the UK, and enforcement efforts against it, have far-reaching political, cultural and economic ramifications, and impacts negatively upon prison populations (Liriano and Ramsay 2003), levels of gun crime (Hales *et al.* 2006), social exclusion (Buchanan 2004), and public health (Lister *et al.* 2008) and community safety (Lupton *et al.* 2002). A review by McSweeney and colleagues observed how drug law enforcement efforts can have

> a significant negative impact on the nature and extent of harms associated with illicit drugs by (unintentionally) increasing threats to public health and public safety, and by altering both the behaviour of individual drug users and the stability and operation of drug markets (e.g. by displacing dealers and related activity elsewhere or increasing the incidence of violence as displaced dealers clash with established ones). (McSweeney *et al.* 2008a: 12)

These consequences and impacts are experienced disproportionately by the urban poor and minority ethnic groups. For example, research has established the disparity of imprisonment rates for drug offences among these groups, both in the UK and elsewhere (Ministry of Justice 2008: 73; Morgan and Liebling 2007: 1122; Radosh 2008: 174). As Reuter and Stevens (2007: 52) have noted, this raises important questions about the enforcement of drugs laws against particular groups and communities.

Explanations of the crime

Profit margins

The available evidence suggests that dealers and operatives at all levels of the market tend to display a fair degree of adaptability and responsiveness to changing market conditions. In the main many seem unconcerned about legal penalties and the risks associated with police enforcement activities (see McSweeney *et al.* (2008a) for a recent review). Indeed, given the apparent minimal entry barriers to the market, the limited deterrent effect of law enforcement and the sheer scale of the revenues and profits that can be generated (with some estimates calculating the mark-ups for heroin entering the UK and its street-level retail price to be in excess of 250 per cent), recent research studies have concluded that illicit drug markets in the UK have considerable scope for growth within established and mature structures which, to date, have proven highly resilient to enforcement activity (Matrix Knowledge Group 2007; Lupton *et al.* 2002).

Access to legitimate opportunities

Both the social context and meaning attributed to drug use and involvement in the illicit drugs trade have featured prominently in much sociological research and theory (see Seddon (2006) for a recent British overview). Some theories have emphasised how participants, when faced with two opportunity structures – the legitimate and illegitimate – might come to reject both conventional cultural goals of success and the legitimate means of achieving them. Others see participation in illicit drug markets as a perceived solution to problems of status and identity associated with social and economic exclusion and highlight the positive social and economic pay-offs in different subcultures (e.g. the status acquired from drug dealing) (Preble and Casey 1969; Auld *et al.* 1986; Burr 1987; Pearson 1987; May *et al.* 2005).

Clearly, the various models and explanations that have been developed are not mutually exclusive or incompatible with others. They are also likely to have only limited explanatory power in terms of understanding forms of drug distribution higher up the supply chain and those embedded within, or related to, licit business organisations and organised forms of crime (for example, see Dorn *et al.* 2005). Nevertheless, in terms of developing communities' resilience to drug markets at a local level, May and colleagues (2005: ix) have argued that it is important to appreciate the limited or constrained choices that are open to many participants and residents. These constraints on capacity for action are associated with:

- the use of violence in drug markets;
- the limited legitimate opportunities open to many residents, especially young people; and
- the impact of family or peer pressure on young people.

Different responses and explanations for involvement in the illicit drugs trade will therefore be required for different times, places and spaces and take into consideration changing social, cultural and economic conditions.

Economic, social and subcultural influences

The heroin outbreaks of the 1980s and 1990s emerged in areas experiencing high levels of unemployment and deprivation.[13] As Seddon notes, 'for the first time in Britain, heroin use was very strongly connected with social disadvantage' and 'saw a newly forged drugs–crime connection'. As a consequence 'neighbourhoods affected by a heroin outbreak typically experienced a clustering together of social difficulties: high unemployment, high crime rates, heroin dealing and heroin use' (2006: 683). He goes on to describe how 'some observers at the time certainly saw the new heroin problem as linked to wider social issues ... economic recession and a period of de-industrialization in which many working-class areas were devastated by high unemployment' (2006: 684).

While the initial outbreaks may have been linked to deprivation the opposite is true for the subsequent growth in availability, experimentation, use and acceptability of illicit drugs documented by Parker and colleagues (1998). Such increases have since been located within the 'new late-modern experience of adolescence in which consumption has achieved a cultural and economic centrality' to the extent that the 'conspicuous consumption of pleasurable commodities, including recreational drugs, is now part of how young people today create and establish their identities' (Seddon *et al.* 2008: 823). Such conspicuous consumption also featured prominently in the accounts offered by a small number of English and Welsh street robbers interviewed by Wright *et al.* in order to explain how they had committed many of their offences 'not to sustain the offenders' lives, but rather to maintain a particular sort of hedonistic lifestyle that rejects "rationality and long-range planning … in favour of enjoying the moment"' (2006: 12). Drugs formed an integral part of this lifestyle.

The picture that emerges then in relation to economic and social influences on involvement in the illicit drugs trade, particularly at lower levels of the supply chain, is a complex one. As Seddon has observed 'individuals respond differently to the structural difficulties with which they are faced and make active choices about the actions they take … what needs to be understood is a three-way relationship between structure, culture and agency' (2006: 691–2).

Responses to the crime

Sentencing of suppliers and dealers

Laws against the non-medical use of drugs have been 'justified on the basis that the criminal law seeks to protect fundamental interests, including the ability to seek one's welfare and exercise autonomy' (Shiner 2003: 774). McKeganey has argued:

> UK drug laws present a means through which society differentiates between those substances that are accepted and those that are proscribed. In doing so such laws conveys a kind of societal morality. Irrespective of whether one acts in accordance with or in breach of those laws the laws themselves send out a clear message that illegal drug use is not an acceptable behaviour. (2007: 569)

While the illegal status of some drugs is likely to have contained their availability and use to some extent (though this has yet to be quantified, measured or even estimated in an accurate way), their illicit status appears to have only a marginal effect on decision-making about whether to use illicit drugs – with concerns about health, harm and utility featuring much more prominently (European Commission 2004: 32–3; Police Foundation 2000: 34; Pearson and Shiner 2002; Shiner 2003: 788–90) – or as a deterrent to continued involvement in the drugs trade (Dorn et al. 1998; Matrix Knowledge Group 2007; May et al. 2000: vi). Of the estimated 70,000 street-level drug dealers (ibid.: 2), there were fewer than 11,000 people convicted for possession with intent to supply (6,300) or unlawful supply (4,500) offences in England and Wales during 2004 (Mwenda 2005: 13). The estimated 6 per cent incarceration rate for Class A drug dealers calculated by Reuter and Stevens (2008: 471) is consistent with the estimated risk of arrest for cannabis users from eight countries during 2005, which never exceeded 5 per cent (Room et al. 2008: 81).

This is despite the fact that the number of offenders imprisoned for drugs offences increased from 1,000 in 1982 to 3,200 in 1990 (Home Office 1991: 18) – equivalent to 2 and 7 per cent of the prison population during these periods (Home Office 1983: 11, 1992: 9). By October 2005 the number of imprisoned drug offenders had increased by 288 per cent and stood at 12,400 (Ministry of Justice 2007). This was equivalent to 15 per cent of the 81,812 people held in prisons in England and Wales at this time.

The average length of prison sentences imposed for drugs offences doubled from 16 months[14] in 1980 to 32 months[15] in 2004 (Home Office 1991: 38; Mwenda 2005: 5). As Reuter and Stevens commented, 'the proportion of imprisoned offenders who are given longer prison sentences has ... been increasing for all offences ... [but] use of imprisonment has grown especially rapidly for drug dealers and distributors' (2007: 59). These growing throughputs place increased pressure on an already overstretched criminal justice system but appear to have done little to deter the supply of illicit drugs to meet growing demand.

Figure 30.3 below charts the increase in the numbers found guilty, cautioned or dealt with by compounding for supply-related offences in the UK between 1980 and 2000. It illustrates how the number of people dealt with for offences involving possession with intent to supply unlawfully increased in the UK by 1,176 per cent over this period: from 572 to 7,296. Offences for unlawful supply increased from 892 to 5,742 – up 544 per cent. While those dealt with for unlawful import and export offences increased by 26 per cent (from 1,186 to 1,490), the numbers involved in unlawful production offences fluctuated considerably over the period (falling by 1 per cent overall, but peaking at 5,337 offenders in 1995 – up 145 per cent since 1980). Ninety-five per cent (11,140) of the 11,675 people convicted, cautioned, fined or dealt with by compounding over this 20-year period for such offences were sentenced for the production and/or cultivation of cannabis. Overall, the number of people processed for drug trafficking and 'dealing' offences[16] in the UK increased by 245 per cent: from 4,830 in 1980 to 16,684 in 2000 (Home Office 1991: 31; Corkery 2002: 63).

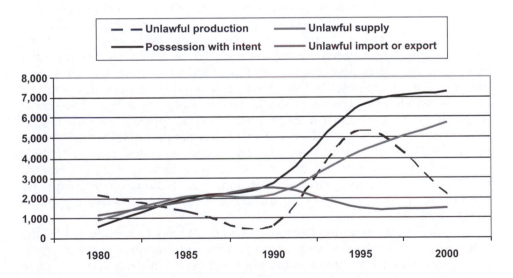

Figure 30.3 Persons found guilty, cautioned, fined or dealt with by compounding for drug dealing or supply offences (1980–2000)
Source: Data from Home Office (1991: 31) and Corkery (2002: 63).

National and local law enforcement

In their recent review of the literature, McSweeney *et al.* noted that the UK government had 'allocated just under £1.5 billion in order to deliver the aims of the drug strategy in 2005/06. Around a quarter of these funds (£380 million) were dedicated to reducing the supply of drugs, compared with 39 per cent (£573 million) for drug treatment' (2008a: 36). This is what might be considered 'labelled drug-related expenditure', that is, the 'voluntary commitment of the state in the field of drugs' (EMCDDA 2008b: 11). Efforts to accurately calculate the proportion of government expenditure devoted to enforcement are confounded, however, by the sheer range of governmental departments and initiatives engaged in this and related activities, and by the reactive nature of much drug-related expenditure (ibid.: 11). An obvious example of broader 'non-labelled drug-related expenditure' devoted to enforcement would include the considerable criminal justice costs of dealing with 'drug-related' crime (e.g. detection, prosecution and sentencing), which were estimated to be in the region of £4 billion in 2003/4 for the crime associated with Class A drug use alone (Gordon *et al.* 2006: 44).

Working in partnership with a wide range of other local, national and international agencies, the Serious Organised Crime Agency (SOCA) leads on higher-level UK enforcement activities aimed at tackling distribution networks within the UK's borders. Formed following an amalgamation of the National Crime Squad and the National Criminal Intelligence Service, SOCA became operational on 1 April 2006. It also assumed HM Revenue and Customs' responsibility for drugs trafficking and associated criminal finance. In April 2008 the Asset Recovery Agency's asset recovering functions were also transferred over to SOCA.

Following its inception the government set out SOCA's priorities during its first three years of operations. Tackling Class A drug trafficking was deemed its first priority and its board set a target of directing 40 per cent of the Agency's operational efforts towards meeting this objective. To date there has been no independent assessment of SOCA's work. However, its first annual report to Parliament described involvement in a range of activities resulting in some considerable seizures during 2006/7 in which its activity had been a contributory factor (whether through intelligence or a physical seizure) (SOCA 2007: 22). More recently HM Inspectorate of Constabulary (HMIC) have noted that the national response to tackling serious and organised criminal groups – the majority of whom are involved in drug trafficking – is undermined by 'the lack of a unifying strategic direction, inadequate covert capacity and under-investment in intelligence gathering, analysis and proactive capability' (HMIC 2009: 2).

At a local or regional level enforcement operations are usually led by the police, sometimes in partnership with statutory and voluntary sector agencies like SOCA. When measured against rates of arrest and drug seizures, these activities can certainly appear to achieve some considerable successes. However, there is rarely any independent assessment of their impact on how markets might continue to function and operate, on the subsequent availability, price and purity of illicit drugs, or on broader harm reduction outcomes as a result of enforcement action (notable exceptions include Webster *et al.* (2001), Best and colleagues (2001), and Parker and Egginton (2004)).

Demand reduction strategies

Demand reduction strategies such as drug education and treatment have been developed in recognition that supply reduction and enforcement in isolation are insufficient as an effective response (McSweeney *et al.* 2008a). Instead, enforcement and demand reduction strategies need to be combined in a complementary way. However, previous reviews of the available international and UK literature have concluded that there is little evidence to suggest that drug education and prevention – as currently practised, at least – has had any significant impact on levels of illicit drug use or engagement with the illicit drugs trade (for example, see Reuter and Stevens 2007).

By contrast there is a much stronger evidence base to support the effectiveness and cost-effectiveness of various drug treatment approaches for those who have developed 'problematic' patterns of illicit drug use, including a range of criminal justice-based interventions (UKDPC 2008; McSweeney *et al.* 2008b). However:

> In the UK, as in many other countries, the effectiveness of drug treatment as a demand reduction measure is undermined by high programme attrition rates and low levels of treatment completion, inconsistencies regarding the quality and availability of different treatment options, and ongoing concerns about its scope for facilitating recovery and reintegration among problem drug users. (McSweeney *et al.* 2008a: 11)

Drug possession

As mentioned in the introduction to this chapter, the 1971 Misuse of Drugs Act places restrictions on certain 'controlled drugs' and categorises them under Classes A, B or C. Controlled drugs are those drugs that Parliament considers harmful and therefore makes illegal to possess, supply, produce or cultivate. The (A, B, C) classification system is based on the concept of 'relative harm'. Class A drugs are deemed the most harmful and Class C drugs the least harmful. For the police to arrest for a possession offence they must be satisfied (and prove) that:

- the illicit substance found is an illegal controlled substance;
- it is the property of the individual they have apprehended and that the individual is aware that they have the substance; and
- they know that the substance is an illegal drug.

If the defendant can prove that their intention was to destroy the substance as soon as was practicable, or hand it to a police officer to destroy, both arguments can be used as a defence against a possession charge.

The different levels of punishments that offences attract are specified for Classes A, B and C. Punishments for possession range from police warnings through to imprisonment. For simple possession of a Class A drug the maximum penalty available to a court is seven years' imprisonment, a fine or both. For a Class B drug the maximum penalty is five years' imprisonment, a fine or both, and for a Class C drug the maximum penalty is two years' imprisonment, a fine or both. Besides incarceration there are a variety of penalties that either a court or the police can impose on an adult found guilty of a possession offence. These include: a community order, a fine, a warning or a caution. For juveniles (those aged 17 and under) the police must adhere to the Crime and Disorder Act 1998 and give a reprimand, finally warn or charge for a possession offence.

Policing possession offences

Over the last 30 years the number of possession offences has increased year on year. In 1979, the number of persons found guilty of, or cautioned for, possession offences was just over 12,000, 89 per cent of which were cannabis possession offenders and 4 per cent were heroin offenders. During the 1970s about one in six offenders sentenced for a possession offence received a custodial sentence. In mid-1979 there were 772 people serving a custodial sentence for a drug offence, of these, 10 per cent were imprisoned for unlawful possession (Home Office 1980). During the 1980s the majority of people coming to the attention of the police and courts for a possession offence were cannabis users. By 1984 the number of people found guilty or cautioned for any drug offence had risen to about 25,000 (86 per cent of whom had been arrested for a possession offence). Heroin offences continued to rise and by 1984 the number of offences involving heroin was 2,450 – three times what it had been in 1981. During the 1980s the number of people being processed for a drug possession offence rose year on year; this rise was, however, mirrored by the rise in the number of people who received a police caution for a drug offence as opposed to a court disposal.

Throughout the 1990s the number of drug offenders continued to rise. In 1990, there were 44,900 individuals dealt with for a drug offence, 90 per cent of which were possession offences, the majority (40,200) of which were cannabis possession. The use of police cautioning also continued to rise and in 1990 more people were cautioned than were fined (40 per cent and 35 per cent respectively). Immediate custody was used in less than 10 per cent of cases. By 1997, the number of drug offenders had risen to 113,000, a rise of 19 per cent on the previous year. Like previous years almost 90 per cent of offenders were arrested for a possession offence, again mainly cannabis possession offences. Between 1987 and 1997 possession offences accounted for between 84 and 89 per cent of all drug offenders. By 1997, just over half (54 per cent) of those arrested for a possession offence were cautioned, a fifth were fined and 10 per cent were sentenced to immediate custody. By the end of the 1990s first-time offenders found in possession of a Class B or C drug were more likely than any other drug offender to receive a caution (Corkery 2002).

By 2004, the number of recorded drug offences had declined to 105,570, which represented a fall of 21 per cent from the previous year. Class A drug offences had, however, risen by 2 per cent to 36,350. In total there were

7,260 Class B offences and 59,050 Class C offences (Mwenda 2005). In the ten-year period from 1994 to 2004 cocaine offenders had risen from 2 per cent of all drug offenders to 10 per cent, 8 per cent of whom were arrested for a possession offence. In 2004 those found in possession of crack cocaine accounted for 2 per cent of all drug offenders, heroin possession offenders accounted for 13 per cent and ecstasy possession offenders 5 per cent. The inclusion of cannabis offences in the Class C category in 2004 increased the proportion of Class C offences from less than one per cent (prior to 2004) to 60 per cent in 2004. In 1994 just under 81 per cent of all drug offenders were cannabis offenders; this fell to 66 per cent (66,410 offenders) in 2001 and 60 per cent in 2004 (49,840 offenders). In 2004, 55 per cent of all drug offenders were cannabis possession offenders.

In 2004 a caution was the most commonly used disposal for a possession offence, used in 44 per cent of cases. Fines were used in just over a fifth of cases (22 per cent) and 11 per cent of offenders were given an absolute discharge. Only 5 per cent were sentenced to immediate custody. In addition, formal warnings data for cannabis possession have been available since April 2004. Police issued 27,520 formal warnings between April and December 2004 (Mwenda 2005).

The cannabis issue

The road to reclassifying cannabis from a Class B to a Class C drug and then back to Class B was a long and tortuous one. Although the cannabis laws have been a contentious issue in Britain for the last 40 years, the 1971 Misuse of Drugs Act remained largely unchanged until 2001 when the then Home Secretary David Blunkett, announced his intention to reclassify cannabis to a Class C drug. If reclassification had gone ahead without any other legislative change, the power of arrest for cannabis possession offences would have been removed. However, removing the power of arrest attracted disquiet among some police officers and politicians as well as sections of the media. In response, the government announced a compromise, whereby cannabis would be reclassified as a Class C drug, but possession offences would remain an arrestable offence where aggravating factors were present. Reclassification eventually took effect in January 2004. The power of arrest was retained for possession offences, but in parallel the Association of Chief Police Officers issued guidance urging front-line officers to issue cannabis warnings for first-time offenders rather than arrest.

Following reclassification in 2004 as a Class C drug, cautions or convictions for Class B drugs dropped from just under 67,000 in 2003 to around 6,500 in 2006. However, since 2004 there has been a steady increase in the number of people cautioned or convicted for Class C drugs from 663 in 2003 to over 30,000 in 2006. Prior to reclassification cautions and convictions for Class C offences between 1998 and 2003 were between 264 and 663 for each year. It seems, therefore, safe to assume that the steep rise in Class C offences can be attributed to cannabis. These changes are likely to be a result of reclassification. Also, the rise in the use of cannabis warnings has been dramatic. Between 2005 and 2006 there were an additional 27,000 warnings given, resulting in excess of 80,000 cannabis warnings in 2006. Given there has been no evidence of growth in the prevalence of cannabis use over this period (in fact it has declined according to the British Crime Survey), the increasing number of police contacts for cannabis suggests two possible explanations: (1) that the police are now targeting cannabis users and giving them cannabis warnings; and/or (2) that many cannabis contacts are now recorded as a cannabis warning when previously they would have been dealt with informally. This means that since reclassification more cannabis users have been dealt with formally by the criminal justice system than were previously when cannabis was a Class B drug, a process known as net-widening.

In 2008, Jacqui Smith, then Home Secretary, against the advice of the ACMD, announced her intention to reclassify cannabis back to a Class B drug. She explained that her decision was based upon the classification of cannabis needing to be more in line with the overarching aims of the government's 10-year drug strategy. She also suggested that the move to reclassify cannabis reflected the fact that 'skunk', a much stronger version of the drug, now dominates the UK's cannabis market. It is, however, unclear as to where this information comes from. The reclassification back to a Class B drug means that those who are caught more than once are unlikely to receive more than one cannabis warning. The changes now mean that those caught with cannabis could still get a cannabis warning on a first offence, but on a second offence they are likely to face a fine of £80 and if caught a third time they could be arrested. For young people the position remains the same as it always has been. Those aged 17 years and under, if caught, will be arrested and taken to a police station where they will receive a reprimand, final warning or charge depending on the seriousness and circumstances of the offence (see Turnbull (2009) for a more detailed discussion of the impact of reclassification).

Discussion

Trends in use, supply and production of drugs appear to have little to do with local laws, enforcement or policing activities (Van het Loo *et al.* 2003). Although this conclusion is most often reached with reference to cannabis, is it likely that the same is true for other commonly used illegal drugs? The available evidence described in this chapter would indicate so; while drug laws have remained largely unchanged for over thirty years and enforcement efforts have increased internationally, nationally and locally, the numbers reporting having used illicit drugs and their availability has dramatically increased during the same period. Additionally, it should be remembered that data reported in this chapter on supply, possession and consumption are based on imperfect measures. At best they reflect enforcement agencies 'successful' activities in disrupting supply, sale and use. As reported earlier, estimates have been made suggesting that enforcement activities only disrupt between 4 and 25 per cent of the supply of individual drugs. As for individual reports of drug consumption, they are likely to be an underestimate of the numbers of people who use, as well as the frequency and quantities used. Individuals are often reticent to disclose illegal drug-taking activity and have difficulty (particularly if they are regular users) recalling the details of drug-using episodes.

Some drug law reformers have for some time now been calling for the state to impose a system of legal regulation and control over the production and distribution of – initially some but perhaps eventually all – currently illicit drugs in the same way it does for both alcohol (though not very successfully many would argue) and tobacco, and a wide range of prescription drugs – including, on a limited basis in parts of the UK, heroin – for medical or therapeutic use. Commentators have in the past dismissed such calls because 'proposals for a full-blown "market solution" are not thought through, politically naive, and (worst of all) a waste of an opportunity to intervene positively in public policy-making' (Dorn and South 1990: 186). In the intervening years these alternative models – and the case against prohibition – have been further developed and refined in the UK (Rolles *et al.* 2006), North America (Haden 2004; King County Bar Association 2005) and elsewhere (Wodak and Owens 1996).[17] During the same period there have also been calls for greater engagement from criminologists on this issue since:

> scholars of crime and law enforcement, have a particular obligation to think and analyze the language, character, and underlying assumptions of drug prohibition more critically and without undue deference to the prohibitionist ideologies and institutions currently in power. No other scholarly discipline is so defined by the state's legislative, judicial, and regulatory decisions. (Nadelmann 2004: 1003)

The UK Government (Lords Hansard 2007) has consistently rejected moves towards reform because:

- Its obligations as signatories to various UN conventions prevent them from doing so.[18]

- It believes that (1) the current system of prohibition constrains and contains levels of substance use[19] and (2) forms of legal regulation and control would lead to increased availability and use.

- It is extremely difficult to accurately estimate the likely impact and consequences of such a move which it believes would potentially outweigh any benefits (see also MacCoun and Reuter 2001).

Furthermore, there appears to be little public appetite for such change. Having reviewed the international evidence, Newcombe believes that 'it can reasonably be concluded that support for relaxing the laws on cannabis has grown considerably over the last decade … However, support for legalisation of any other drug has rarely climbed above 10 per cent in general population surveys'[20] (2004: 82–3). These findings are entirely consistent with the results from a more recent survey conducted for the European Commission. This questioned 12,000 15- to 24-year-olds (the peak age for illicit drug use) from 28 European countries about their views and experiences of drugs. Between 94 and 97 per cent felt that drugs like heroin, cocaine and ecstasy should remain banned (European Commission 2008). Such findings are likely to have an important bearing on the direction of drugs law and policy since, as the Independent Inquiry into the Misuse of Drugs Act observed, the law should reflect 'the social and cultural attitudes of modern British society' (Police Foundation 2000: 1).

Given the levels of synergy required between public opinion and political will to prompt drug policy reform, it seems that realpolitik will ensure, in the short to medium term at least, that incremental tweaking of the current system of drug prohibition is a more likely prospect than radical reform (see Hough *et al.* (2003) for a broader discussion on options for reassessing the UN conventions). Yet the new Obama administration in the United States, the current global economic crisis and a pending general election in Britain could all present important opportunities that shape and influence the future direction of domestic and international responses to tackling the issue of illicit drugs.

Selected further reading

Perhaps one of the most important recent contributions to our knowledge in this area is derived from data obtained from interviews with a self-selecting sample of 222 convicted drug dealers and traffickers held in prison establishments throughout the UK (Matrix Knowledge Group 2007). Funded by the Home Office this study employed an analytical framework informed by business, economic and social networks perspectives.

The UK Drug Policy Commission (UKDPC) also published the findings from an extensive review of the international research literature (McSweeney *et al.* 2008a). This work sought to describe both the nature and extent of the UK drug markets and the law enforcement responses which sought to disrupt or dismantle them. The review then collated and examined the existing evidence for the effectiveness of existing strategies aimed at dealing with these issues, before finally highlighting the gaps in our knowledge and understanding. The findings from this review formed the basis of a subsequent thematic report by the UKDPC which considered the scope for refocusing drug law enforcement efforts to better tackle and address a range of related harms associated with drug market activity.

More recently an international team of academic experts produced a report for the European Commission, edited by Reuter and Trautmann (2009), in an effort to provide a comprehensive overview of the nature and extent of global illicit drug markets and assess the impact of policy responses which have sought to respond both appropriately and effectively.

Contemporary debate and commentary relevant to both UK and international drug policy reform can be found on the Transform Drug Policy Foundation website: http://www.tdpf.org.uk/.

Notes

1 Those under the age of 16, prisoners, the homeless and individuals in residential care settings are not currently included in the BCS.
2 Ramsay *et al.* (2001).

3 http://www.tdpf.org.uk/
4 Figures for the United Kingdom.
5 Figures for Scotland, England and Wales.
6 Crack figures only available from 1990.
7 Ecstasy figures only available from 1990.
8 Only the French (31 per cent) and Danish (37 per cent) report higher lifetime prevalence rates.
9 These figures need to be interpreted with caution as concerns have been raised about the comparability of such data and the reliability of the estimates provided by many countries.
10 As Hough et al. note, 'Home Office statistics do not distinguish between production and cultivation offences, recording all as production' (2003: 2).
11 Figures for the United Kingdom.
12 Figures for England and Wales only.
13 These outbreaks and the emergence of crack cocaine in Britain during the 1990s were also aided by more effective distribution systems facilitated by transport infrastructure and technology (e.g. mobile phones) and developed in response to changing supply routes from South America, the Caribbean and other prominent areas (Seddon 2006; Seddon et al. 2008).
14 Figures for the United Kingdom.
15 Figures for England and Wales only.
16 Including offences of unlawful production of drugs, unlawful supply, possession with intent to supply unlawfully and unlawful import or export.
17 See also the International Journal of Drug Policy, 14 (2) (April 2003) for a broader discussion on the UN conventions.
18 As Hunt notes, 'evidence in this area cannot be produced as policies involving regulated forms of drug distribution are prohibited under the UN Conventions of 1961 [narcotic drugs], 1971 [psychotropic drugs] and 1988 [illicit trafficking] and therefore cannot be evaluated. In effect, the Conventions prohibit the production of knowledge and evidence regarding the impact of different policies involving different, regulated supply systems' (2004: 233).
19 The House of Commons Science and Technology Committee 'found no convincing evidence for the deterrent effect, which is widely seen as underpinning the Government's classification policy, and have criticised the Government for failing to meet its commitments to evidence based policy making in this area' (2006: 3).
20 Newcombe also warns that such surveys need to be more explicit and consistent in the range of terms and definitions which they employ.

References

Advisory Council on the Misuse of Drugs (ACMD) (2008) Cannabis: Classification and Public Health. London: Home Office.

Association of Chief Police Officers of England, Wales and Northern Ireland (ACPO) (2008) ACPO Recommends Cannabis Classification. Press release, 5 February.

Auld, J., Dorn, N. and South, N. (1986) 'Irregular work, irregular pleasures: heroin in the 1980s', in R. Matthews and J. Young (eds), Confronting Crime. London: Sage, pp. 166–87.

Best, D., Strang, J., Beswick, T. and Gossop, M. (2001) 'Assessment of a concentrated, high-profile police operation. No discernible impact on drug availability, price or purity', British Journal of Criminology, 41 (4): 738–45.

Bryne, S. (2008) *Submission of Evidence on the Classification of Cannabis: An ACPO Review for the Advisory Council on the Misuse of Drugs*. London: ACPO.

Buchanan, J. (2004) 'Missing links: problem drug use and social exclusion', *Probation Journal*, 51 (4): 387–97.

Burr, A. (1987) 'Chasing the dragon: heroin misuse, delinquency and crime in the context of South London Culture', *British Journal of Criminology*, 27 (4): 333–57.

Carroll, R. (2009) 'Death in Mexico', *The Guardian*, 20 May.

Corkery, J. (2002) *Drug Seizure and Offender Statistics, United Kingdom 2000*. London: Home Office.

Department of Health (2004) *Smoking, Drinking and Drug Use among Young People, 2003*. London: Department of Health.

Dorn, N. and South, N. (1990) 'Drug markets and law enforcement', *British Journal of Criminology*, 30 (2): 171–88.

Dorn, N., Levi, M. and King, L. (2005) *Literature Review on Upper Level Drug Trafficking*, Home Office Online Report 22/05. London: Home Office.

Dorn, N., Oette, L. and White, S. (1998) 'Drugs importation and the bifurcation of risk: capitalization, cut outs and organized crime', *British Journal of Criminology*, 38 (4): 537–60.

Duffy, M., Schafer, N., Coomber, R. and O'Connell, L. (2007) *'It's a Social Thing': Cannabis Supply and Young People*. York: Joseph Rowntree Foundation.

The Economist (2008) 'Hard to swallow', 9 February.

European Commission (2004) *Young People and Drugs. Flash Eurobarometer 158*. Brussels: European Commission.

European Commission (2008) *Young People and Drugs. Flash Eurobarometer 233*. Brussels: European Commission.

European Monitoring Centre for Drugs and Drug Addiction (EMCDDA) (2007) *Annual Report 2007: The State of the Drugs Problem in Europe*. Luxembourg: Office for Official Publications of the European Communities.

European Monitoring Centre for Drugs and Drug Addiction (EMCDDA) (2008a) *Annual Report 2008: The State of the Drugs Problem in Europe*. Luxembourg: Office for Official Publications of the European Communities.

European Monitoring Centre for Drugs and Drug Addiction (EMCDDA) (2008b) *Towards a Better Understanding of Drug-Related Public Expenditure in Europe*. Luxembourg: Office for Official Publications of the European Communities.

Gordon, L., Tinsley, L., Godfrey, C. and Parrott, S. (2006) 'The economic and social costs of Class A drug use in England and Wales, 2003/04', in N. Singleton, R. Murray and L. Tinsley (eds), *Measuring Different Aspects of Problem Drug Use: Methodological Developments*, Home Office Online Report 16/06. London: Home Office, pp. 41–5.

Greenwald, G. (2009) *Drug Decriminalization in Portugal: Lessons for Creating Fair and Successful Drug Policies*. Washington, DC: Cato Institute.

Haden, M. (2004) 'Regulation illegal drugs: an exploration of public health tools', *International Journal of Drug Policy*, 15 (4): 225–30.

Hales, G., Lewis, C. and Silverstone, D. (2006) *Gun Crime: The Market in and Use of Illegal Firearms*, Home Office Research Findings No. 279. London: Home Office.

HM Inspectorate of Constabulary (HMIC) (2009) *Her Majesty's Inspectorate of Constabulary – Getting Organised*. London: Home Office.

HM Government (2008) *Drugs: Protecting Families and Communities. The 2008 Drug Strategy*, 1st edn. London: COI.

Hoare, J. and Flatley, J. (2008) *Drug Misuse Declared: Findings from the 2007/08 British Crime Survey (England and Wales)*, Home Office Statistical Bulletin 13/08. London: Home Office.

Home Office (1980) *Statistics of the Misuse of Drugs in the United Kingdom, 1979,* Statistical Bulletin 11/80. London: Home Office.

Home Office (1983) *Prison Statistics England and Wales 1982.* London: HMSO.

Home Office (1986) *Statistics of the Misuse of Drugs in the United Kingdom, 1985,* Statistical Bulletin 28/86. London: Home Office.

Home Office (1991) *Statistics of the Misuse of Drugs: Seizures and Offenders Dealt With, United Kingdom, 1990.* London: HMSO.

Home Office (1992) *Prison Statistics England and Wales 1990.* London: HMSO.

Hough, M., Warburton, H., Few, B., May, T., Man, L. and Turnbull, P. J. (2003) *A Growing Market: The Domestic Cultivation of Cannabis.* York: Joseph Rowntree Foundation.

House of Commons Science and Technology Committee (2006) *Drug Classification: Making a Hash of It?* Fifth Report of Session 2005–06. London: The Stationery Office.

Hughes, C. and Stevens, A. (2007) *The Effects of Decriminalization of Drug Use in Portugal,* Briefing Paper 14. Oxford: Beckley Foundation Drug Policy Programme.

Hunt, N. (2004) 'Public health or human rights: what comes first?', *International Journal of Drug Policy,* 15 (4): 231–7.

King County Bar Association (2005) *Effective Drug Control: Toward A New Legal Framework. State-Level Regulation as a Workable Alternative to the 'War on Drugs'.* Washington, DC: King County Bar Association.

Liriano, S. and Ramsay M. (2003) 'Prisoners' drug use before prison and the links with crime', in M. Ramsay (ed.), *Prisoners' Drug Use and Treatment: Seven Research Studies,* Home Office Research Study No. 267. London: Home Office, pp. 7–23.

Lister, S., Seddon, T., Wincup, E., Barrett, S. and Traynor, P. (2008) *Street Policing of Problem Drug Users.* York: Joseph Rowntree Foundation.

Lords Hansard (2007) *Drugs: Government Consultation Paper,* col. 1286, 29 October. London: Home Office.

Lupton, R., Wilson, A., May, T., Warburton, H. and Turnbull, P. J. (2002) *Drug Markets in Deprived Neighbourhoods,* Home Office Research Findings No. 167. London: Home Office.

MacCoun, R. J. and Reuter, P. (2001) *Drug War Heresies: Learning from Other Vices, Times and Places.* Cambridge: Cambridge University Press.

McKeganey, N. (2007) 'The challenge to UK drug policy', *Drugs: Education, Prevention and Policy,* 14 (6): 559–71.

McKeganey, N., Neale, J., Lloyd, C. and Hay, G. (2007) 'Drugs in the future: a response to Frisher', *Drugs: Education, Prevention and Policy,* 14 (5): 467–70.

McSweeney, T., Turnbull, P. J. and Hough, M. (2008a) *Tackling Drug Markets and Distribution Networks in the UK: A Review of Recent Literature.* London: UK Drug Policy Commission.

McSweeney, T., Turnbull, P. J. and Hough, M. (2008b) *The Treatment and Supervision of Drug-Dependent Offenders.* London: UK Drug Policy Commission.

Matrix Knowledge Group (2007) *The Illicit Drug Trade in the United Kingdom,* Home Office Online Report 20/07. London: Home Office.

May, T. and Hough, M. (2004) 'Drug markets and distribution systems', *Addiction Research and Theory,* 12 (6): 549–63.

May, T., Duffy, M., Few, B. and Hough, M. (2005) *Understanding Drug Selling in Communities: Insider or Outsider Trading?* York: Joseph Rowntree Foundation.

May, T., Duffy, M., Warburton, H. and Hough, M. (2007) *Policing Cannabis as a Class C Drug: An Arresting Change?* York: Joseph Rowntree Foundation.

May, T., Harocopos, A., Turnbull, P. J. and Hough, M. (2000) *Serving Up: The Impact of Low-Level Police Enforcement on Drug Markets,* Police Research Series Paper 133. London: Home Office.

Ministry of Justice (2007) *Population in Custody – October 2007*. London: Ministry of Justice.

Ministry of Justice (2008) *Statistics on Race and the Criminal Justice System – 2006/7*. London: Ministry of Justice.

Morgan, R. and Liebling, A. (2007) 'Imprisonment: an expanding scene', in M. Maguire, R. Morgan and R. Reiner (eds), *The Handbook of Criminology*, 4th edn. Oxford: Oxford University Press, pp. 1101–38.

Murphy, R. and Roe, S. (2007) *Drug Misuse Declared: Findings from the 2006/07 British Crime Survey (England and Wales)*, Home Office Statistical Bulletin 18/07. London: Home Office.

Mwenda, L. (2005) *Drug Offenders in England and Wales, 2004*, Statistical Bulletin 23/05. London: Home Office.

Nadelmann, E. A. (2004) 'Criminologists and punitive drug prohibition: to serve or to challenge?', *Criminology and Public Policy*, 3 (3): 441–50.

Newcombe, R. (2004) *Attitudes to Drug Policy and Drug Laws: A Review of the International Evidence*. Liverpool: 3D Research Bureau.

NHS Information Centre for Health and Social Care (2008) *Drug Use, Smoking and Drinking Among Young People in England 2007*. London: Department of Health.

Office for Standards in Education, Children's Services and Skills (Ofsted) (2008) *TellUs3 National Report*. London: Ofsted.

Parker, H. and Egginton, R. (2004) *Managing Local Heroin-Crack Problems: Hard Lessons About Policing Drug Markets and Treating Problem Users. Final Report from the Derbyshire Drug Market Project*. Leicester: Anchor Print.

Parker, H., Aldridge, J. and Measham, F. (1998) *Illegal Leisure: The Normalisation of Adolescent Recreational Drug Use*. London: Routledge.

Parker, H., Bakx, K. and Newcombe, R. (1988) *Living with Heroin: The Impact of a Drugs 'Epidemic' on an English Community*. Milton Keynes: Open University Press.

Pearson, G. (1987) *The New Heroin Users*. Oxford: Blackwell.

Pearson, G. and Hobbs, D. (2001) *Middle Market Drug Distribution*, Home Office Research Study No. 227. London: Home Office.

Pearson, G. and Shiner, M. (2002) 'Rethinking the generation gap: attitudes to illicit drugs among young people and adults', *Criminology and Criminal Justice*, 2 (1): 71–86.

Police Foundation (2000) *Drugs and the Law: Report of the Independent Inquiry into the Misuse of Drugs Act 1971*. London: Police Foundation.

Preble, E. and Casey, J. J. (1969) 'Taking care of business', *International Journal of the Addictions*, 4 (1): 1–24.

Pudney, S., Badillo, C., Bryan, M., Burton, J., Conti, G. and Iacovou, M. (2006) 'Estimating the size of the UK illicit drug market', in N. Singleton, R. Murray and L. Tinsley (eds), *Measuring Different Aspects of Problem Drug Use: Methodological Developments*, Home Office Online Report 16/06. London: Home Office, pp. 46–85.

Radosh, P. F. (2008) 'War on drugs: gender and race inequities in crime control strategies', *Criminal Justice Studies*, 21 (2): 167–78.

Ramsay, M., Baker, P., Goulden, C., Sharp, C. and Sondhi, A. (2001) *Drug Misuse Declared in 2000: Results from the British Crime Survey*, Home Office Research Study No. 224. London: Home Office.

Reed, E. (2007) *Seizures of Drugs in England and Wales, 2005*, Home Office Statistical Bulletin 17/07. London: Home Office.

Reuter, P. and Stevens, A. (2008) 'Assessing UK drug policy from a crime control perspective', *Criminology and Criminal Justice*, 8 (4): 461–82.

Reuter, P. and Stevens, A. (2007) *An Analysis of UK Drug Policy: A Monograph Prepared for the UK Drug Policy Commission*. London: UK Drug Policy Commission.

Reuter, P. and Trautmann, F. (eds) (2009) *A Report on Global Illicit Drug Markets 1998–2007*. European Commission.

Rolles, S., Kushlick, D. and Jay, M. (2006) *After the War on Drugs, Options for Control*. Bristol: Transform Drug Policy Foundation.

Room, R., Fischer, B., Hall, W., Lenton, S. and Reuter, P. (2008) *Cannabis Policy: Moving Beyond Stalemate. The Global Cannabis Commission Report*. Oxford: Beckley Foundation.

Royal Society of Arts (RSA) (2007) *Drugs – Facing Facts: The Report of the RSA Commission on Illegal Drugs, Communities and Public Policy*. London: RSA.

Ruggiero, V. and South, N. (1995) *Eurodrugs: Drug Use, Markets and Trafficking in Europe*. London: UCL Press.

Schweich, T. (2008) 'Is Afghanistan a nacro-state?', *International Herald Tribune*, 24 July.

Scottish Executive (2007) *Drug Seizures by Scottish Police Forces, 2004/5 and 2005/6*, Crime and Justice Series. Edinburgh: Scottish Executive.

Seddon, T. (2006) 'Drugs, crime and social exclusion: social context and social theory in British drugs–crime research', *British Journal of Criminology*, 46 (4): 680–703.

Seddon, T., Ralphs, R. and Williams, L. (2008) 'Risk, security and the "criminalization" of British drug policy', *British Journal of Criminology*, 48 (6): 818–34.

Serious Organised Crime Agency (SOCA) (2007) *SOCA Annual Report 2006/07*. London: The Stationery Office.

Serious Organised Crime Agency (SOCA) (2008) *The United Kingdom Threat Assessment of Serious Organised Crime 2008/9*. London: The Stationery Office.

Shiner, S. (2003) 'Out of harm's way? Illicit drug use, medicalization and the law', *British Journal of Criminology*, 43 (4): 772–96.

Stevens, A. (2007) 'When two dark figures collide: evidence and discourse on drug related crime', *Critical Social Policy*, 27 (1): 77–99.

Strategy Unit (2003) *SU Drugs Project Phase 1 Report: Understanding the Issues*. Online at: http://image.guardian.co.uk/sys-files/Guardian/documents/2005/07/05/Report.pdf.

Transform Drug Policy Foundation (TDPF) (2008) *Forward Notice Briefing: New UK Drug Strategy Publication*. Bristol: TDPF.

Transform Drug Policy Foundation (TDPF) (2009) *A Comparison of the Cost-Effectiveness of the Prohibition and Regulation of Drugs*. Bristol: TDPF.

Turnbull, P. J. (2009) 'The great cannabis classification debacle: what are the likely consequences for policing cannabis possession in England and Wales?', *Drug and Alcohol Review*, 28 (1): 191–8.

UK Drug Policy Commission (UKDPC) (2008) *Reducing Drug Use, Reducing Reoffending: Are Programmes for Problem Drug-Using Offenders in the UK Supported by the Evidence?* London: UK Drug Policy Commission.

United Nations Office on Drugs and Crime (UNODC) (2008) *World Drug Report 2008*. Vienna: United Nations Publications.

Van het Loo, M., Hoovens, S., Van't Hof, C. and Kahan, J. (2003) *Cannabis Policy*. Santa Monica, CA: Rand Europe.

Webster, R., Hough, M. and Clancy, A. (2001) *An Evaluation of the Impact of Operation Crackdown*. London: Criminal Policy Research Unit, South Bank University.

Wodak, A. and Owens, R. (1996) *Drug Prohibition: A Call for Change*. Sydney: UNSW Press.

Wright, R., Brookman, F. and Bennett, T. (2006) 'The foreground dynamics of street robbery in Britain', *British Journal of Criminology*, 46 (1): 1–15.

Chapter 31

Drug trafficking

Letizia Paoli, Toine Spapens and Cyrille Fijnaut

Introduction

Nowadays, the trafficking of illegal narcotics and other psychoactive drugs is considered one of the prototypical activities of organised crime and is a matter of serious concern worldwide. Despite the lack of reliable estimates regarding other illegal markets, the markets fed by drug trafficking most probably constitute the world's 'largest' illegal markets in terms of both financial turnover and the number of people involved as end users.

Both the concern about drug trafficking and the size of contemporary illegal drug markets are relatively new phenomena. Until the early twentieth century, some of the drugs now considered most dangerous – such as heroin and cocaine, as well as the substances from which they are derived (opium and coca) – were freely traded and consumed, not only in Asia and Latin America, but also in western countries. Their production, trade and consumption began to be regulated and then largely prohibited (except for limited medical purposes) only after the first International Opium Convention was signed in The Hague in 1912. During the 1930s, the consumption of opium and coca derivatives drastically declined in most western countries and it was only a resurgence of their consumption and that of a few other prohibited psychoactive substances during the 1960s that led to the upsurge of today's illegal drug markets. In turn, growing demand fostered the expansion of illegal production and trafficking.

None of the three UN conventions constituting the pillars of the contemporary drug control regime explicitly defines what should be meant by illegal drug trafficking. In the Convention against Illicit Traffic in Narcotic Drugs and Psychotropic Substances of 1988, for example, Article 1 ('Definition') merely states that 'illicit traffic' means the offences set forth in the following Article 3 and these virtually include all aspects of the production, transportation and distribution of illegal drugs. According to Article. 3, paragraph 1(a), in fact, the Parties should establish the following activities, if committed intentionally, as criminal offences under their domestic law:

The production, manufacture, extraction, preparation, offering, offering for sale, distribution, sale, delivery on any terms whatsoever, brokerage, dispatch, dispatch in transit, transport, importation or exportation of any narcotic drug or any psychotropic substance contrary to the provisions of the 1961 Convention, the 1961 Convention as amended or the 1971 Convention.

Pursuant to the official broad definition, in this article we not only discuss the wholesale and retail trafficking in drugs but we also include drug production in our analysis and thus adopt a worldwide perspective, although we pay special attention to the wholesale and retail distribution of illegal drugs in Europe. The next section presents some basic figures on the size of contemporary drug markets while the following section outlines the emergence of the international drug control regime and the expansion of illegal drug markets from the 1960s onwards. We then go on to analyse the production and smuggling of the most common illegal drugs, focusing on four classes of drugs: heroin, cocaine, synthetic drugs and cannabis. The subsequent section analyses drug distribution. The final section sketches the main policies currently pursued in Europe and worldwide against drug trafficking and rounds off with a few concluding remarks.

Illegal drug markets today: some figures

The *2005 World Drug Report* of the United Nations Office on Drugs and Crime (UNODC) includes the most recent systematic efforts to estimate the turnover of contemporary drug markets. For illicit drugs as a whole, the UNODC estimates a total of almost US$322 bn in retail sales in 2003, US$94 bn in wholesale revenues, and US$13 bn in producer sales (UNODC 2005: 123–43).

The largest market, according to the UN calculations, is cannabis herb (normally called marijuana), which has a retail market size of US$113 bn. Marijuana is followed by cocaine (US$71 bn), the opiates (including both raw opium and its derivatives, primarily heroin: US$65 bn) and cannabis resin (popularly called hashish, with US$29 bn). The markets for synthetic drugs (properly called amphetamine-type stimulants and including methamphetamine, amphetamine and ecstasy) total about US$44 bn. Though derived from an economic model, these figures are actually guesstimates and must be treated with great caution. The basic inputs that are needed for such calculations – data on production, prices, quantities exported, imported and consumed – are themselves often estimates and frequently based on deficient data.

Compared with global licit exports or global gross domestic product (GDP) (US$7,503 bn and US$35,765 bn respectively in 2003), the estimated size of the global illicit drug market may not seem to be very large. Total retail drug expenditures correspond to 0.9 per cent of global GDP and drug wholesale revenues represent only 1.3 per cent of global export measures. The size of the global illicit drug market is not insubstantial, however. Illicit drug wholesale revenues account for 14 per cent of global agricultural products and are much

627

higher than the export value of most licit agricultural commodities (UNODC 2005: 127).

The global drug market also involves a considerable number of people. According to the UNODC (2008a: 9) estimates, about 200 million people currently use illicit drugs at least once a year (about 5 per cent of the world population aged 15–64). Cannabis is by far the most popular and widespread illegal drug: out of the total of 200 million, 166 million are cannabis users. Cannabis is followed by synthetic drugs (some 35 million people), which include amphetamines (used by 25 million people) and ecstasy (almost 10 million people). The number of opiate users is estimated at 17 million, of which 12 million are heroin users. Around 16 million people also use cocaine at least once a year.

A large proportion of drug users can be found in Asia. More than 60 per cent of the world's amphetamine or methamphetamine users and more than half of opiate users reside there (UNODC 2008a). Asia accounts for only a small proportion of total retail expenditures, however: US$35 bn or 11 per cent. With US$142 bn (or 44 per cent) and US$106 bn (or 33 per cent) respectively, North America and Europe account for the bulk of total retail expenditure estimates (UNODC 2005), simply because retail drug prices are much higher there than in developing nations.

The rise of the international drug control regime and the expansion of illegal drug markets

Opium, coca and cannabis have been consumed for centuries in their traditional areas of production and elsewhere. Opium, for example, has been used and valued for its analgesic and other medicinal properties throughout Asia and Europe since ancient times. Likewise, coca has been chewed for centuries in the Andes and, with its stimulant and appetite-suppressant properties, it long helped the Indios withstand altitude sickness and harsh living conditions (Courtwright 2001).

While opium was the cornerstone of self-medication in many western countries (Courtwright 1982; Berridge 1999), coca, as well as the semi-synthetic derivatives of both opium (primarily morphine, codeine and heroin) and coca (i.e. cocaine), also became available in the West from the mid-nineteenth century and began to be used for both medicinal and recreational purposes. In the United States, for example, the spread of morphine created a serious opiate problem in the late nineteenth century (Musto 1987). According to Courtwright (1982: 9), the rate of opiate addiction reached a maximum of 4.6 per thousand in the 1890s – almost 50 per cent higher than the contemporary rate of chronic users (slightly more than 3 per thousand; ONDCP 2001).[1]

The country with the largest opium-using population was China, however. Newman (1995) estimates that total opium consumption in China in 1879 amounted to about 25,000 metric tonnes. By 1906, according to the same source, total consumption in China had almost doubled, reaching the extraordinary figure of more than 48,000 metric tonnes. Concerns about the large and growing Chinese opium market and the spread of natural and semi-synthetic opium and coca derivatives were among the factors that led to a change in the perception of these drugs and the emergence of an international control regime at the beginning of the twentieth century. Other factors included western developments in medical practice and organisation, technological progress, changes in commercial interests, revised political views, pressures from social reform movements and cultural anxieties. Both the changed perception and the new international regime, in turn, contributed to the introduction of national regulations and prohibitions.

As already mentioned, the first International Opium Convention of 1912 is usually considered the cornerstone of the current international drug control regime. The Hague Convention, however, mainly focused on regulation and it was only during the 1920s, and especially after the Second World War, that the tone and provisions of international treaties became increasingly prohibitionist, mainly at the insistence of the United States (for an overview, see McAllister 2001 and Paoli *et al.* 2009). The new international drug control regime, enforcement of which was entrusted to the League of Nations post-First World War and to the United Nations post-Second World War, seemed quite successful at first. During the 1920s, 1930s and 1940s consumption of all prohibited substances declined rapidly in the United States, Europe and many Asian nations. However, according to several scholars (Courtwright 2001; Berridge 1999; Paoli *et al.* 2009), the interwar decline can be attributed not so much to increasing prohibition as to other factors, above all changing medical and public attitudes toward drugs. Under pressure from the United States, cannabis trade and possession were also increasingly restricted and, finally, subjected to the international drug control regime in the early 1960s.

From the 1960s onwards, demand for heroin, cocaine and cannabis rose again, first in the United States and then in Western Europe. Ecstasy and other amphetamine products followed from the late 1980s onwards. Consumption of illegal drugs also spread in the former Warsaw Pact countries after 1989 (e.g. Paoli 2005). The post-war expansion of illicit drug use was caused by both contingent events – such as the Vietnam War, which brought thousands of young American soldiers into contact with heroin – and macro-social changes. Two of these changes are particularly important: (1) the rise of a mass youth subculture, which resorts to illegal psychoactive substances to distinguish itself from the mainstream culture; and (2) technological progress, which has made communication, travel and trade in both legal and illegal goods and services easier and faster.

The rising demand for illegal drugs has fostered illicit drug production, mostly in poor and weakly governed countries, the development of an international drug trade from producer to consumer countries and the emergence of nationwide drug distribution systems in virtually all countries, with the partial exception of Africa.

Production of major illegal drugs

This section focuses on the production of the main types of illicit drugs: heroin, cocaine, synthetic drugs and cannabis. The production process for each of these is outlined and the production countries discussed.

Production of heroin

Heroin is a semi-synthetic opioid synthesised from morphine, a derivative of the opium poppy. Roughly ten kilograms of opium gum are necessary to produce, through a chemical process, a kilogram of morphine, which can then be further refined into a kilogram of heroin (UNODC 2007: 40).

Afghanistan and Myanmar have been responsible since 1980 for 70–95 per cent of the world's opium supply. After 2001, Afghanistan accounted for an increasing share of world production, up to 92 per cent in 2007. Myanmar's share, with 460 tonnes, had meanwhile declined to a mere 5 per cent. Heroin processing has also become increasingly concentrated in Afghanistan.

Although it accounted in 2007 for only 1.5 per cent of the world's heroin production, Mexico has been since the 1970s an important source of heroin for the US market. For about a decade from the mid-1990s onwards, Colombia was also one of the major suppliers of the US market – and the only country entering the illicit opiate industry since the Second World War. Heroin production in Colombia, however, has declined dramatically since 2005, at least according to the official data of the Colombian government. During the last quarter of the twentieth century, some major illicit opium-producing countries gradually dropped out of the international market, possibly the result of both policy changes and increasing wealth. Turkey did so in the early 1970s and Pakistan and Thailand followed suit in the 1990s, though Pakistan has more recently resumed production. Laos, which used to be a traditional producer of opium, has also drastically reduced its opium output since 2003 (UNODC 2008a: 37–44; see Paoli *et al.* 2009).

Although the country does not appear in the official UNODC statistics, India may also be a major illicit opium producer. However, India's contribution derives from significant diversion from licit cultivation. For several decades India has been the main licit producer and sole supplier of opium (as a final product) to the world pharmaceutical market (INCB 2008: 72). Paoli *et al.* (2009) estimate that Indian producers annually diverted quantities of 200 to 300 tonnes of opium to the black market in the past years. This makes India the largest producer of illicit opium after Afghanistan and Myanmar. However, India is routinely ignored when the supply of heroin is considered. This may be explained by the assumption that this diverted production is absorbed by the country's internal demand.

Of all the drug producing countries, the Afghan economy is by far the most dependent on the illegal drug industry. Over 3 million people, or 14.3 per cent of the total Afghan population, are directly involved in opium cultivation, with many hundreds of thousands indirectly profiting from opium cultivation, refining and trafficking. According to the UNODC (2008a: 225), in 2007 the total export value of opiates to neighbouring countries, estimated at about US$4 bn, added over 50 per cent to Afghanistan's legitimate GDP. The opium industry – coupled with the uncoordinated efforts made to repress it by several NATO countries active in Afghanistan, and particularly by the United States – has become a major obstacle to the political stabilisation of the country. In fact, drug money not only feeds corruption at all levels of government but – perhaps more crucially – the efforts made to repress the industry also weaken the legitimacy of the nascent Afghan state apparatus and the rule of law, as opium producers and traffickers are prompted to seek the protection of the resurgent Taliban and maverick politicians (Paoli *et al.* 2009).

Production of cocaine

Cocaine is derived from the coca plant. Coca leaves are picked by hand and dried in the sun. The leaves are then chemically processed, firstly into coca paste, secondly into cocaine base and thirdly into cocaine hydrochloride. After crystallisation, cocaine is obtained (see Zaitch 2001).

Like heroin, cocaine is produced in a small number of countries. Virtually all cultivation of the coca bush is concentrated in three Andean countries: Colombia, Peru and Bolivia. According to the UNODC (2008a: 66), potential manufacture of cocaine is by far the largest in Colombia (600 metric tonnes in 2007), followed by Peru (290 metric tonnes) and Bolivia (104 metric tonnes). Most cocaine hydrochloride is processed in Colombia and from there exported to the United States and Europe (UNODC 2007: 65–71).

In 2006 no fewer than 6,390 laboratories, where one or more steps in the cocaine production process were carried out, were located and dismantled (UNODC 2008a: 68). The production of cocaine from coca leaves is a labour-intensive process but it does not require any special equipment. The laboratories where coca paste and cocaine base are made are therefore usually small and improvised. Ninety-nine per cent of the dismantled laboratories were in the three aforementioned countries (UNODC 2007: 65). Laboratories in Bolivia and Peru nearly always produced coca paste or cocaine base, whereas the laboratories producing cocaine hydrochloride were mainly in Colombia. Of the 210 laboratories where cocaine was made, 163 were in Colombia, 33 in other South American countries and only 14 in other parts of the world.

One surprising fact is that 11 of the laboratories were found in Spain (UNODC 2007: 65). In the past years, several cocaine laboratories, where cocaine paste or cocaine base were processed, were also discovered in the Netherlands. Experts suggest that this is done because the penalties for trafficking semi-manufactures are far less severe. These substances are also cheaper, thus financial losses, if a shipment is intercepted, are smaller (Gruter and Van de Mheen 2005: 60).

Coca-producing countries, like opium-producing countries, also suffer from the adverse consequences of the illegal drug industry, the most serious being political instability. In fact, due to its visibility, illegal drug cultivation tends to concentrate in areas where there is no or only very lax enforcement of international drug prohibitions. Even if the industry did not create these pockets of instability in the first place, it certainly perpetuates them. Colombia, for example, has attracted a growing and now preponderant share of coca cultivation and processing from Bolivia and Peru since the late 1990s, precisely because these activities could be relocated to those vast tracts of the country controlled by guerrilla organisations and paramilitary groups, which finance their activities with drug money. Today, for example, the largest Colombian guerrilla organisation, the Revolutionary Armed Forces of Colombia (known by its Spanish acronym FARC), not only extorts protection money from the peasants growing coca and poppies and the traffickers trading in the semi-finished products, but has also become a key player in the refinement and sale of coca paste. According to journalists' estimates, roughly half of FARC's US$300–500 million annual income is believed to come from drug profits (Miller 2002; Thoumi 2003).

Production of synthetic drugs

Synthetic drugs exist in many forms. There are dozens of chemical compounds that have mind-altering effects: in the early 1990s the American Alexander Shulgin described no fewer than 179 of them (Shulgin and Shulgin 1991). Moreover, chemical drugs can be made using various synthesis methods. It would, of course, be well outside our scope to describe all types of synthetic drugs and their production methods. We shall therefore confine ourselves to the drugs that are currently most common: amphetamine, MDMA (ecstasy or XTC) and methamphetamine (pervitine).

Synthetic drugs are made in a laboratory, which may be extremely simple and small-scale, for example in the form of a 'kitchen lab', but may also be more professional and large-scale. The requisite raw materials differ according to drug type and the way in which the synthesis process is carried out. On the one hand, chemicals that have many industrial uses are often involved, such as acetone, sulphuric acid or methylamine. Common raw materials, such as microcellulose (filler), are also used to make pills (Spapens 2006). On the other hand, precursors that have fewer or absolutely no conventional uses are also used, the main ones being benzyl methyl ketone (BMK), piperonyl methyl ketone (PMK) and ephedrine or pseudo-ephedrine. BMK is mainly used in the manufacture of amphetamine. PMK is the main raw material for MDMA, the active ingredient in ecstasy. Ephedrine and pseudo-ephedrine are the main precursors of methamphetamine. These substances have been brought under a control regime by the United Nations and, consequently, cannot be legally produced or sold, or at least not without a licence.

Ecstasy is mainly consumed in pill form, amphetamine usually in powder form and methamphetamine in both powder and pill form. The pills must be manufactured separately. They are composed of a specific quantity of active ingredient – an ecstasy pill contains, for example, 80 or 100 milligrams of MDMA – as well as a filler. The pills are made in machines that can also be used for other applications, such as the manufacture of ordinary pills or sweets.

In so far as any information is available, amphetamine is mainly produced in Europe, particularly in the Netherlands and Poland, as well as in the Baltic states and Belgium (UNODC 2007: 131). The UNODC estimated the scale of production in 2005 to be 88 metric tonnes.

Ecstasy production is also concentrated in the Netherlands as well as in Belgium. An estimated 113 metric tonnes was made in 2005. There are signs, however, that in the past few years the US market has been increasingly supplied by Chinese criminal groups which produce ecstasy in Canada. The Netherlands and Belgium – and in the case of the latter, it is often Dutch people who have taken refuge over the border who are involved – mainly supply the European and Australian markets. There has also been an apparent downturn in production as a result of a decline in the popularity of ecstasy.

Methamphetamine is now produced mainly in China and South East Asia (Myanmar, Philippines). Annual production was estimated at 278 metric tonnes in 2005. The US was also regarded as an important producer until a few years ago. The number of larger laboratories (known as 'super-labs') dismantled there has fallen dramatically in recent years, however, from 244 in 2001 to 130 in 2003 and to just 35 in 2005 (UNODC 2007: 127).[2] This decline is thought to be mainly due to measures taken to limit the availability of ephedrine and pseudo-ephedrine.

Production of cannabis

The cannabis market is undoubtedly the largest drug market. It exists in two forms: cannabis herb and cannabis resin.

Herbal cannabis (marijuana) consists of the chopped dried flowering tops of the female hemp plant. The plant is cultivated, harvested and dried, and the flowering tops are then chopped and ground. In principle, the end product is then ready. It can also be pressed into blocks and vacuum sealed to make it easier to transport and to increase its keeping quality (Spapens et al. 2007).

Cannabis resin (hashish) is made from the resin crystals found on the buds and part of the leaves of the flowering plant. The crystals are removed mechanically – for example using a centrifuge – or by other methods and then pressed into blocks.

In countries where the climate permits it, the plants are grown in the open air. Since the early 1990s, however, indoor cultivation of cannabis herb has also been an increasingly common occurrence in colder areas – not only in greenhouses, but also, for example, in commercial hangars, farm buildings and houses or garden sheds.

The indoor cultivation method was developed in the United States. Americans who emigrated to escape the crackdown in their own country introduced this method into Western Europe at the beginning of the 1990s. Within just a few years, this substantially increased domestic production of cannabis herb, particularly in the Netherlands. The plants were also selectively bred, by Dutch agricultural students among others. The concentration of active ingredient (THC) was increased from 8 to 20 per cent or more. Varieties were also developed that grew faster, or had a shorter stem. This latter property enabled the plant to be grown more easily in rooms with a low ceiling, such as attics or basements in houses.

Both indoor and outdoor, cannabis herb is produced all over the world. This widespread propagation is primarily due to the tremendous adaptability of the cannabis plant, which grows well in virtually every inhabited region of the world and can be cultivated with little maintenance. In addition, unlike most other illicit drugs, cannabis products can be consumed with little processing after harvesting. Thanks to these two characteristics, users can feasibly grow their own supply even in countries that rigorously apply the world prohibition regime. The US authorities, for example, report that about two-thirds of the cannabis consumed in the country, predominantly in the form of marijuana, is domestically produced (UNODC 2005: 82).

The UNODC estimated global cannabis herb production in 2006 at 41,400 metric tonnes. Africa accounted for 22 per cent, North America for 31 per cent, South America and the Caribbean for 24 per cent, and Asia for 16 per cent. Europe was a relatively small producer, with 6 per cent of the total. Lastly, Oceania was responsible for 1 per cent of global production (UNODC 2008a: 96–7).

Compared with cannabis herb, cannabis resin is made in only a limited number of countries, the main producers being Morocco, Afghanistan and Pakistan. Global production was estimated at 6,000 metric tonnes in 2006 (UNODC 2008a: 100). Morocco is by far the main source country for cannabis resin, with an estimated 27 per cent of global production in 2006. Other important source countries are Afghanistan and Pakistan (9 per cent) and Nepal and India (8.5 per cent) (UNODC 2008a: 100).

Cross-border trafficking of drugs

This section looks at how narcotics are smuggled across international borders from drug-producing countries to drug-consuming countries. Smuggling routes span the globe, of course. The emphasis here, however, will be on shipments of drugs to and from Europe.

Following the expansion of demand in the mid-1960s, illegal drugs were often imported into western countries by users themselves, who used some and sold the rest within a close circle of friends. This was a sort of 'ants' trafficking'. Soon, however, in both the United States and Western Europe the professional role of the drug trafficker and dealer began to consolidate. Since the early 1970s in the Western world and the early 1990s in the eastern part of the 'Old Continent', this role has emerged to link producers to consumers and to regularly supply large urban centres with a variety of illegal drugs from distant regions. From the late 1970s on, professional criminals in most Western European countries began to deal in drugs, realising that they could earn much more and risk less than they would in their traditional occupations (Paoli and Fijnaut 2004: 612).

It has long been assumed that drug smuggling is based on a supply chain approach (Wright 2006: 76). In other words, large shipments of drugs are sent from the countries where they are produced to the countries where they are consumed, either directly or indirectly. Upon arrival the shipment is sold in smaller quantities to middlemen who in turn supply retail dealers. In recent years, however, drug smuggling has become more direct and smaller-scale, even long-distance smuggling. Small dealers in the destination countries seem to be increasingly able to obtain drugs directly from source countries, or from countries like the Netherlands which serve as a marketplace. In parallel with the more hierarchically organised supply chains, a growing number of small-scale point-to-point smuggling flows have emerged (Spapens 2008).

The sharp increase in international mobility, the ease of electronic communications and the increasingly diverse migration flows that have created all kinds of new links between source and destination countries are important explanatory factors for this development. Small-scale smuggling to overseas destinations is usually done by air using couriers who hide the drugs in their luggage or clothes, strap them to their body or use their body as a container. Often there are family or friendship ties between the suppliers in the production or transit countries and the recipients in the destination countries.

The removal of systematic border controls within the European Union is another factor. With the reduced risk of checks being carried out, few protective measures need to be taken. Couriers carry relatively small quantities each time, usually in private vehicles. Additional measures are required only where drugs are being smuggled into the UK, due to the system of border checks that is still in place and the relatively small number of entry points into the country. The shipments are larger and are often transported in trucks with secret storage compartments.

Smuggling of heroin

Since the late 1970s, Turkey has emerged as the main gateway for Afghan heroin on its way to Western European markets. To a considerable extent, Turkish criminal groups and gangs are also in charge of the wholesale distribution of heroin in Western Europe, as they can hide easily among the large, and for the most part unaware, Turkish diaspora. Profits derived from the heroin trade have become a relevant source of finance for both the Kurdish separatist movement and the paramilitary groups and clans supported by the Turkish government in the fight against the Kurds (Bovenkerk and Yesilgöz 2007).

It is important to stress, however, that Turkish heroin entrepreneurs have never constituted a single trafficking organisation; instead they constitute a myriad of independently dealing enterprises. Some of these are made up of just a few friends or associates. Many are family businesses, sometimes quite stable ones, that rely upon a large but changing pool of more recently arrived Turkish collaborators to do the more menial and risky tasks. Additionally, there are a few large criminal organisations capable of organising shipments of several hundred kilograms from Turkey to Western Europe (Paoli 2000: 65–6; see also Bovenkerk and Yesilgöz 2007 and Fijnaut et al. 1998: 86).

From Turkey, heroin is primarily transported to Western Europe along what is known as the Balkan route, which originally traversed Bulgaria and the former Yugoslavia and, since 1989, has acquired numerous alternative – northern and southern – paths, including a sea route from Greece and Albania into Southern Italy. Except for this route heroin is usually smuggled by road. Entrepreneurs located along these routes, and particularly the Albanians, increasingly play an important role in heroin smuggling and the wholesale distribution of the drug in the EU countries. The size of the shipments tends to decrease as opiates move from east to west. Multi-tonne seizures are often made in both Iran and Turkey: in April 2002, for example, a record 7.5 metric tonnes of morphine base was seized in a depot close to Istanbul (Paoli et al. 2009). In the rest of Europe, seizures rarely exceed a few hundred kilograms.

A second major route emerged in 1991 – often called the Silk Route – which services the booming Russian and Eastern European market via Tajikistan and the other Central Asian states. Although heroin was largely unknown up to the mid-1990s, Tajikistan now rivals Afghanistan for the unenviable title of the country most dependent on the illicit drug industry. According to the calculations of Paoli *et al.* (2009), it is unlikely that opiate trafficking adds less than 30 per cent to the recorded gross domestic product (GDP).

Through Central Asia, heroin is smuggled in both large and small shipments. Contrary to the general trend, however, the Central Asian countries have recorded a shift from small-scale to large-scale trafficking. Whereas drug 'swallowers' were most prominent in bringing heroin into Russia up to 2001–2, since then an increasing quantity of heroin has also been shipped in large consignments in freight trains and trucks, particularly those transporting cotton and aluminium, Tajikistan's main legitimate export goods. The increasing size of heroin shipments leaving Tajikistan must be connected with the consolidation of large drug trafficking organisations, which currently dominate the market as a result of the protection and even direct involvement in drug trafficking of high-ranking politicians and civil servants (Paoli *et al.* 2007).

According to Interpol, the heroin smuggling routes from Afghanistan to Africa run mainly via Pakistan or India (Interpol n.d.). The North American market is principally supplied from Mexico and Colombia. Heroin destined for China and Australia comes chiefly from South East Asia, though the recent sharp decline in Myanmar's heroin production may lead to larger imports from Afghanistan (Jelsma and Kramer 2008).

Smuggling of cocaine

The main market for cocaine is still the United States but, judging by the quantities seized, Europe is becoming an increasingly important destination. There are also indications that young Europeans often prefer cocaine to synthetic drugs like amphetamine or ecstasy as a result of its ready availability and low price (EMCDDA 2007).

Cocaine destined for the US is smuggled through various Central American and Caribbean countries. As a result of intensive law enforcement measures, the large Colombian cocaine cartels of the 1980s have been eliminated and succeeded by numerous smaller criminal groups (UNODC 2007: 175). Most of the cocaine is transported by sea craft, e.g. speedboats or fishing trawlers. Small private aircraft are also used for smuggling purposes.

Large-scale smuggling to European destinations also occurs via maritime vessels for the most part. The main entry points are ports in Spain (especially Galicia in the north-west), the Netherlands and Belgium. The shipments concerned weigh between several hundred and several thousand kilograms. Ordinary cargo vessels are mostly used, with the necessary measures being taken to avoid attention from customs officials. The cargo must be valuable enough to be profitable to transport it to Europe from a South American country (Colombia is often avoided because every shipment from that country is automatically suspect). All sorts of 'cover loads' are used, such as bananas or fruit juice. The smugglers are also highly creative in finding ways to hide cocaine in other goods, such as washing machines, cameras, statuettes, cable drums, etc. (Gruter and Van de Mheen 2005: 58). In addition to cargo ships, private yachts are also regularly used.

Finally, significant quantities of cocaine are brought into the European Union by couriers travelling by air, who smuggle in anything up to a few dozen kilograms by hiding the drugs on or in their body – known as 'body packing' or 'balloon swallowing' – or in their luggage. In the Netherlands, it transpired that these transport jobs were often organised by immigrants from the Caribbean who had got mixed up in drug dealing. With the help of relatives still living in the country of origin, the more entrepreneurial types had switched to importing cocaine themselves instead of buying it from middlemen in the Netherlands.

Although both law enforcement agencies (Europol 2005: 11) and independent researchers (Zaitch 2001) agree that Colombian traffickers dominate the import of cocaine in both Europe and the United States, it would be a great mistake to consider these groups of traffickers as monolithic blocs. In his ethnographic study of Colombian traffickers in the Netherlands, Damian Zaitch (2001), for example, identified different types of Colombian smugglers and importers, stressing that they are very heterogeneous with respect to social background and prestige, vulnerability, infrastructure, organisation and size of their enterprises, and connections with Colombian exporters, non-Colombian importers and other Colombian immigrants.

Smuggling of synthetic drugs

As mentioned earlier, synthetic drugs include amphetamine, ecstasy and methamphetamine. These three main types of synthetic drugs are smuggled via various routes.

Most seizures of amphetamine are in Europe and the Near and Middle East/South West Asia region (UNODC 2008a: 142). These regions accounted for 84 per cent of amphetamine seizures from 2000 to 2006 (UNODC 2008a: 142). The European countries with proportionately the most users are the UK, Scandinavia, the Baltic states and Spain (EMCDDA 2007: 51), with the Netherlands, Poland and the Baltic states being the main producers of amphetamines in Europe. In general, amphetamine is not transported over long distances (UNODC 2008a: 148), though there is one documented exception: it is smuggled to Japan and Australia from Canada. The Netherlands, Poland and the Baltic states are the main source countries for amphetamine in Europe (KLPD 2005a: 51).

Ecstasy is a product that is regularly smuggled from one continent to another. Besides Europe, the United States and Australia are important destination countries. The largest European market for ecstasy is the UK. In the past few years ecstasy has also become increasingly popular in, for example, the Czech Republic, Slovakia and Ireland. Ecstasy use is also relatively high in Latvia (EMCDDA 2007: 53). Elsewhere in Western Europe, however, ecstasy has been waning in popularity in recent years. This drug is mainly still used at large dance parties (raves), but also, for example, in holiday resorts that attract a lot of young people, such as the Spanish costas and the Turkish Riviera.

Large-scale smuggling of ecstasy from the Netherlands or Belgium is mainly destined for Australia at the moment. Shipments of several hundred thousand and upwards of a million ecstasy pills have regularly been intercepted in the past few years. These were hidden, for example, in a pizza oven (intended for a restaurant), a safe and in a cargo of chandeliers (Spapens 2006).

Until the beginning of the twenty-first century, the US was a very important destination country for ecstasy produced in the Netherlands or Belgium. This market is now served by Chinese criminal groups who manufacture the ecstasy in Canada (Spapens 2008).

Last but not least, methamphetamine is mainly used in Asia, where Japan is the major market, and also in North America. Levels of methamphetamine use in Europe are limited but seem to be growing. The Czech Republic is currently the main European market for this drug (where it is called pervitine) (EMCDDA 2007: 51). Methamphetamine is not smuggled over long distances. Myanmar, for example, supplies the rest of South East Asia and Oceania, while most of Mexico's production is exported to the US and Canada (UNODC 2008a: 140–2).

Finally, in relation to the production of synthetic drugs, the smuggling of precursor chemicals must also be considered. China is by far the biggest producer of BMK and PMK. These precursors for amphetamine and ecstasy respectively are smuggled mainly by container, hidden among legitimate goods such as soap, soya sauce or cooking oil, to important production countries like the Netherlands and Belgium (KLPD 2005b: 46).

Little is known about smuggling ephedrine and pseudo-ephedrine, the main precursors of methamphetamine.

Smuggling of cannabis

Cannabis herb is not usually smuggled over long distances. This is because the plant can be grown just about anywhere, either in the open air or indoors. There are exceptions, however: cannabis herb is smuggled from Africa to Western and Central Europe, from Central Asia (Russian Federation) to Central Europe, and from South America (especially Colombia) to North America (UNODC 2007).

Based on the number of seizures, the main market for cannabis resin is Western and Central Europe. The most important smuggling route runs from Morocco, via Spain, to the north. Transportation is by road, mainly in trucks with secret storage compartments, but other vehicles are also used. The quantities involved are substantial: single shipments of several hundred or several thousand kilograms are no exception (Spapens 2008).

Cannabis resin is also smuggled from Pakistan to overseas destinations such as the Netherlands, usually by ship. In the 1980s and 1990s Dutch smugglers generally used coasters which were specially purchased for the task. The drugs were hidden in secret storage compartments or in torpedo-like containers suspended under the vessels. Divers employed by the criminal organisations would later retrieve these.

Drug distribution

Once illegal drugs have entered the final country of destination, they reach customers through a system of distribution. In a seminal study of the New York heroin market in the late 1960s, Preble and Casey (1969) identified six different levels ranging from importers to retail users. However, given the trend towards importing smaller consignments of drugs and the fact that synthetic drugs and cannabis are often distributed in the production countries themselves, the number of transactions necessary to link importers/producers and end users is frequently much lower than originally established by Preble and Casey. For instance, more and more users from the countries surrounding the Netherlands nowadays cross the border in order to buy small quantities of drugs and then smuggle them back into their own country. A quantity of 5 grams of cannabis per person can be bought at coffee shops, which is tolerated by the Dutch government. However, larger quantities of cannabis, as well as different types of hard drugs, are also sold to foreign users by illegal dealers. In addition, local drug dealers, mostly from Germany, Belgium and France, but also from other countries on the European continent, are directly supplied by Dutch dealers. Regular shipments, often comprising different types of drugs, are then delivered by couriers (Spapens 2008).

In these cases, there is *strictu sensu* no national distribution system at all, as wholesale and middle-market dealers in the destination countries are bypassed by these entrepreneurial 'user-importers' or retail dealers who are directly supplied from abroad. The same is true when users grow their own cannabis. Even when drugs are imported from the Netherlands or other European countries by professional dealers, a few transactions are sufficient to pass the illegal merchandise from the importer to the end user (Duprez and Kokoreff 1997; Paoli 2000: 50–2; see also Matrix Knowledge Group 2007).

Empirical research in various western cities shows that the vast majority of drug deals, even those involving large quantities of drugs, tend to be carried out by numerous, relatively small and often ephemeral enterprises (Adler 1985; Johnson *et al.* 1985; Reuter and Haaga 1989; Dorn *et al.* 1992; Ruggiero and South 1995; Paoli 2000; Pearson and Hobbs 2001; Dorn *et al.* 2005; Matrix Knowledge Group 2007).

This is explained firstly by the fact that drug entrepreneurs cannot resort to state institutions to enforce contracts and have breaches of contract prosecuted. As a result, property rights are poorly protected, employment contracts cannot be formalised and the development of large, formally organised, long-lasting companies is strongly discouraged (Reuter 1985). Secondly, in developed countries with effective governments all drug suppliers are forced to operate under the constant threat of arrest and confiscation of their assets by law enforcement agencies. They will thus try to organise their activities in such a way as to ensure that the risk of police detection is minimised. Incorporating drug transactions into kinship and friendship networks and reducing the number of customers and employees are two of the most frequent strategies illegal entrepreneurs employ to reduce their vulnerability to law enforcement moves (Reuter 1985). These constraints have largely prevented the emergence of large, hierarchically organised firms to mediate economic transactions in the illegal marketplace of developed countries.

Some of the drug trafficking enterprises are family businesses, i.e. they are run by the members of a blood family, who may opportunistically resort to a network of non-kin to carry out the most dangerous tasks. Some are non-kin groups, formed around a more or less charismatic leader, which then acquire a certain degree of stability and develop a rudimentary division of labour. Others are short-term partnerships or collaborations: loose associations of people which form, split and come together again as the opportunity arises. Especially at the intermediate and lower level, many dealers work alone, either to finance their own drug habits or, more rarely, to earn fast money. Most of these retail drug entrepreneurs have no ties whatsoever with the underworld but are often inconspicuous individuals who are indistinguishable from 'normal' people.

Drugs are sold to end users in four main ways. First of all, they are sold at open-air markets. In effect this means certain streets or areas in larger cities, or stations or parks, where dealers hang around and meet buyers. The dealers can also, for example, frequent certain discotheques to build up contacts or sell drugs to customers on the premises.

The second option is drug-dealing houses. In this case, the dealers work from fixed locations, where customers come to buy and/or try out the goods. In principle, drug-dealing houses can be found anywhere in cities or smaller towns. This practice makes the dealers less visible, of course, so one option is for them to use a network of drug runners who 'recruit' customers and bring them to the dealing house.

Thirdly, there are itinerant vendors. They might make appointments with customers by phone, for instance, and then meet them at a prearranged place. Because of the risk of these phone calls being tapped, other methods are also used. In one such example, a dealer always walked along the same route through the city at specific times. The customer only needed to wait somewhere en route until the vendor passed by (Spapens and Fijnaut 2005: 142).

Lastly, drugs are traditionally sold within closed social networks. In this case, the dealer sells his wares within a circle of friends and acquaintances and only accepts new customers when they are introduced by one of the members of the network. Generally speaking, this form of drug dealing is relatively small-scale.

In many contemporary cities, the street drug market is largely dominated by foreign dealers. Since the 1980s a veritable substitution process has taken place in many European cities at a varying pace: the lowliest and most dangerous positions, which used to be occupied by the most marginalised domestic drug users, have been taken over by members of ethnic minorities, especially those who have immigrated recently, have applied for political asylum or do not have a residence permit (Paoli and Reuter 2008). It is not just recent immigrants who are at risk, however. Long-established migrant communities also suffer from the combination of low socio-economic status and cultural marginalisation (Fijnaut et al. 1998: 84–5). Despite the visibility of ethnic minority dealers, in most cities native-born hard-drug addicts also continue to operate as sellers on street markets (Paoli 2000; Braun *et al.* 2001; Blickmann *et al.* 2003: 29).

Though most foreign street dealers also strive to abandon the open drug scene and move to safer, closed settings, existing studies show that closed-scene dealing is still largely carried out by indigenous people or by second or third-generation immigrants, who were born and raised in a western European country (Paoli 2000: 61–4). Unlike recent immigrants, in fact, only local people possess the 'social and cultural capital' (Bourdieu 1986) necessary to carry out closed-scene deals. They have a network of friends and acquaintances among whom they can at least initially sell drugs. They know the local language and social rules, which makes them appear inconspicuous and avoid police detection. They visit the cafés, bars and public places where potential customers gather, as part of their routine activities. Thanks to these skills, which can be acquired only slowly through socialisation, local people have been able to retain the lion's share of retail and middle drug dealing in private settings.

Given the abundance of dealers and the variety of their dealing techniques, it is no wonder that in most European cities the relationships between drug-dealing enterprises are based more on competition than on collusion. Although some suppliers may occasionally enjoy a considerable monopolistic power over a local (usually small) market, most drug enterprises in Europe seem to be price-takers rather than price-givers. In other words, none of them is able to influence the commodity's price appreciably by varying the quantity of the output sold. The continuing decline in prices over a twenty-year period at all levels of the market in heroin and cocaine in many of the major consumer countries (see UNODC 2006: 363–7) is proof of that.

Policies against drug trafficking

The cornerstone of the contemporary drug control regime is represented by the UN Single Convention on Narcotic Drugs which was opened for signature in 1961 and amended in 1972. This convention for the first time explicitly prohibited the cultivation, import, export, traffic, possession and use of the derivatives of the opium poppy, coca and cannabis, except for restricted medical and scientific purposes. The convention also set up the International Narcotics Control Board (INCB). In 1971, the UN Convention on Psychotropic Substances increased the controls of hallucinogens such as LSD and amphetamines. The further growth of cross-border trafficking in both agriculturally based and synthetic drugs led to the Convention against Illicit Traffic in Narcotic Drugs and Psychotropic Substances being adopted by the UN in 1988. Its special objective was to end the safe havens for people who are involved in international drug trafficking. While the first two conventions are already predominantly prohibitionist, the last convention is completely inspired by a repressive view of the approach to drug problems. This is exemplified by Article 3 in which the Parties are asked to apply penal sanctions not only to production and trafficking offences but also the purchase, possession and cultivation of illegal drugs for personal use.

While the convention of 1988 particularly concerns the fight against illegal drug trafficking, its objective, of course, was not merely the harmonisation of the penal stipulations in the affiliated countries. Indeed, their harmonisation is only a strategic condition for closer criminal law collaboration. The provisions that matter most in this regard – alongside the articles concerning the confiscation of the proceeds of drug trafficking, the extradition of persons and the transfer of penal procedures – are primarily the provisions concerning the exchange of information between the Parties, the granting of mutual assistance by means of legal-assistance requests and the application of controlled deliveries. Furthermore, the Parties are asked to prevent, with the help of the chemical and pharmaceutical industry, the use of legal substances (the so-called precursors) for the production of illegal drugs and, together with transportation companies and postal services, the use of parcel post and letters for cross-border drug trafficking. The Parties are also called to do their utmost to restrict the smuggling of illegal drugs across the world's oceans as well as via free-trade zones and free ports (De Ruyver *et al.* 2002).

These rigid conventions, cast in terms of criminal law, did not prevent the gradual development of broader and more comprehensive drug control approaches, even at the UN level. Since the late 1980s even the UNODC and the INCB have increasingly realised that the demand for illegal drugs has to be reduced as much as possible reduced by ways other than those offered by the criminal law. In its 2007 report, for example, the INCB (2008) emphasises the relevance of youth prevention campaigns, medical provisions for drug addicts and efforts to reintegrate the latter into society. In other words, even the very conservative watchdog of the conventions admits the fact that the criminal law approach must be complemented by a healthcare approach for drug users. While most of the INCB recommendations still concern the strengthening of supply-side interventions, a number of them also concern demand reduction. In the foreword, the INCB explicitly states: 'Governments should recognize that reducing illicit drug demand and reducing illicit drug supply are complementary and mutually reinforcing' (INCB 2008).

Realising the difficulties of cutting down drug production, the size of the world drug markets and the availability of most drugs in final consumer countries, the question inevitably arises whether it is not necessary to launch a fundamental discussion over the current drug control regime. The INCB will certainly do its utmost to block such a decision. It aims at an uncurtailed reinforcement of the current policies and, in its annual reports, declares itself dead set against any form of drug legislation, decriminalisation or even depenalisation. This refusal to bring up the current policy for discussion, however, is diametrically opposed to the readiness of the European Union to do so in 2012.

The European Union published the first Drugs Action Plan (2000–4) in 2000, accepted the second Drugs Action Plan (2005–8) in 2005 and is presently preparing the Third Drugs Action Plan (2009–12). The last two action plans have to be seen in the light of the European Union Drugs Strategy 2005–12 (Council of the European Union 2004). This document first defines the two major objectives the European Union is pursuing with its drug control policy:

- 'a high level of health protection, well-being and social cohesion by complementing the efforts of the Member States to prevent and to reduce drug use, dependence and drug-related harms to health and society';

- 'a high level of security for the general public by fighting drug production, crossborder trafficking in drugs and the diversion of precursors used in drug production, and by intensifying preventive action against drug-related crime, through effective cooperation embedded in a joint approach'.

The sequence in which these objectives are presented shows that the European Union is certainly not distancing itself from the policy of the UN – it also could not do so – but that it gives priority to demand over supply reduction. As for demand reduction, the strategy emphasises the importance of prevention, intervention and treatment programmes. As regards supply reduction, particularly in the sphere of international police and judicial cooperation between the member states, priorities are assigned to reinforcing their mutual collaboration and to intensifying law enforcement efforts with respect to non-EU countries that are major drug-producing or transit countries. Further, this strategy stresses the need to defend a balanced view of drug problems in international forums and to assist third countries in all kinds of ways in the context of the foreign policy of the European Union. It also commits the member states to expand further the knowledge infrastructure in the European Union and to promote scientific research into the evolution of drug problems.

These objectives are concretised in numerous ways in the second Drugs Action Plan (European Union 2005). It is beyond the scope of this chapter to list here all the operational measures. Let it suffice to give an indication of what kinds of measure are involved. For demand reduction, it is a question not only of preventive measures with regard to young people in general but also of measures aimed at special risk groups such as HIV/AIDS patients and at the professionals who deal with these groups in order to reinforce initiatives concerned with the quality of the treatment of drug addicts, the development of alternatives to imprisonment and the reduction in the number of drug-related deaths. In the area of supply reduction, measures are included in this action plan to promote cooperation between the member states, Europol and Eurojust to reinforce the control of the importation of drugs at the outer borders of the European Union, to curb the production of synthetic drugs in the member states and to counter the laundering of drug revenues by, among other things, intensifying the exchange of information between the Financial Intelligence Units in the member states and a further expansion of the liaison officers' networks of the member states in third countries.

Now, of course, it is one thing for states to ratify treaties and subscribe to action plans and another for them actually to assign people and allocate resources to carry out the obligations they enter into with each other. If only in this respect, it is praiseworthy that, in the European Union Drugs Strategy, it is expressly stated that the European Commission in 2012 'will organise an overall evaluation of the EU Drugs Strategy and Action Plans … for the Council and the European Parliament'. In this document it is not indicated how this evaluation will occur but that it will be thorough is certain, at least if the Commission allows itself to be led in this evaluation by its provisional assessment of the situation. Indeed, this judgment comes down to the following: 'Progress has been made in achieving some of the targets of the current Strategy, although the available data does not suggest that there has been a significant reduction in the prevalence of drug use or that the availability of drugs has been substantially reduced.'

This assessment means that the European Union has a concept of the efficacy of the present drug control policy that stands in large measure directly in opposition to the concepts of the INCB. And this crucial difference of opinion of itself already implies that the European Commission is obliged to conduct very thorough research into the drug problems in the European Union and into the drug policy that has hitherto been applied by itself and by the Member States. Such research will necessarily have to comprise more than an inventorying of the measures that the Member States have taken over, nominally or not, into their national policies. In particular, it will have to be related to the personnel and material resources that have been assigned to execute these measures in practice. The primary question that then arises here is, of course, this: do these resources have to be substantially increased in order to level up significantly the effectiveness of the policy applied in these areas, or must this policy itself be first and foremost reconsidered before there can be talk of investing more resources? Obviously, this question cannot yet be answered.

Concluding remarks

The danger that the contemporary illegal drugs industry represents for the world society and economy is not limited to its turnover, the number of people involved as producers, traffickers and users and the harms resulting from heavy drug use. Two further aspects also need to be considered. The industry is a major source of corruption, violence and instability in a number of drug-producing and transit countries – its collateral effects being frequently reinforced by the war on drugs itself. Moreover, the international routes and networks that have been developed for the transportation of illegal drugs from source countries to the final consumer nations (and for bringing back the money) can be used for a multiplicity of other illicit goals, ranging from human smuggling and trafficking to the financing of terrorism.

Since the beginning of the twentieth century an international drug control regime has complemented national policies in trying to reduce the supply of, and the demand for, illegal drugs with a persistent focus on supply-reduction interventions (McAllister 2001). Nonetheless, as recently admitted even by the European Union authorities, the available data do not suggest that there has been a significant reduction in either the prevalence of drug use or the availability of illegal narcotics themselves.

It is a common opinion among scholars and independent observers that supply-side interventions are particularly unlikely to achieve their main goal, namely a reduction of drug availability by curbing illegal drug production and trafficking. At the end of a lengthy project on the world heroin market, for example, Paoli *et al.* (2009) conclude that opiate production may be cut locally or regionally but that lasting global reductions are unlikely. In other words, strengthening the institutions and the legitimate economies of producing countries such as Afghanistan or Myanmar could lead ultimately to a shift in production to other countries. This is the so-called 'balloon effect' (that is the notion that squeezing the opiate industry in one location will shift it elsewhere).

According to these three authors, it is even more difficult to curb international trafficking itself: the most effective solution to this problem with regard to specific countries or regions may be an intervention against production or consumption in neighbouring countries or regions. Trafficking, in fact, tends to gravitate to those countries in close proximity to producing or consuming nations, particularly to those with strong demographic or economic ties. Some countries seem almost predestined to become important transit countries because of their geographic location. Prominent examples are Thailand for Burmese opiates; Pakistan, Iran and, more recently, Tajikistan with regard to Afghan opiates; and, at the opposite end of the supply chain, Mexico for the US market.

Only under exceptional circumstances (such as islands) can drug routes be shifted as, for instance, in the case of the Netherlands Antilles. There, by implementing a 100 per cent search policy for airline passengers in March 2004, the Dutch government boosted cocaine seizures and sharply reduced shipments to Schiphol, the Netherlands' main airport (UNODC and World Bank 2007; Reuter 2009). However, success was largely determined by the fact that the Netherlands Antilles are islands and because the drugs were smuggled by couriers travelling by airplane. Therefore replicating this positive experience in a different context will be very difficult (Paoli *et al.* 2009). Moreover, instead of taking the direct route from the Netherlands Antilles to the Netherlands, smugglers now depart from other South American and Caribbean airports and fly to destinations throughout the European Union. From there, the drugs are transported further over land.

This does not mean, however, that interventions in the supply chain hold no value. On the contrary, they may well affect the size, the organisation and the operating methods of trafficking enterprises and may thus reduce the negative impact of the drug industry on society as a whole. Enforcing prohibitions with sufficient rigour will prevent the development of large and stable criminal enterprises that are able to infiltrate or systematically corrupt government apparatuses or, alternatively, to challenge state authority by using excessive violence or insurgent plans (Paoli *et al.* 2009).

This article has shown that large and particularly threatening drug-trafficking enterprises tend to emerge in countries where governments are unable to enforce the international prohibitions on drug production and trafficking strictly. Instead, in states with a properly functioning legal order, drugs tend to be produced and traded by relatively small and ephemeral criminal enterprises that have no political ambitions and only occasionally resort to violence. These benefits though, have to be weighed against the costs, negative, intended or unintended, consequences of the repressive interventions themselves.

This sober picture leads us to question the effectiveness of the persistent focus of the United Nations on supply reduction. Even if one does not want to advocate a radical transformation of the current international regime it would be advisable to redefine the goals of supply-side controls in terms that are more realistic. Since the 1990s, it has become clear that besides reducing the supply and availability of illicit narcotics, harm reduction is also an essential part of informed drug-demand policies (see Ritter and Cameron 2006). In practice, this would imply that supply-oriented drug control policy should no longer be focused exclusively on reducing drug production and availability and that a reduction of the negative consequences of drug production trafficking and drug control interventions, such as violence, corruption and instability, should be placed higher on the agenda.

Selected further reading

There is a large body of popular, grey and academic literature on production, trafficking and dealing in illegal narcotic drugs. However, even in the United States and Europe research has not been carried out systematically; the base is so thin that it is hard to provide strong general statements. A good starting point is represented by the *World Drug Report*, annually issued by the United Nations Office on Drugs and Crime. Hamid Ghodse (2008), the current chairman of the International Narcotics Control Board, provides an overview of international drug control policies and their future. A review of global illicit drug markets and drug policies was edited in 2009 by Peter Reuter and Frank Trautmann (2009) on behalf of the European Commission.

With regard to the production and trafficking of specific types of drugs, Paoli *et al.* (2009) analyse extensively the world heroin market, focusing on production and international trafficking. Thoumi published in 2003 a comparative analysis of Latin American cocaine-producing countries, while Zaitch (2001) made an ethnographic study of cocaine trafficking to the Netherlands. With regard to cannabis, global issues and local experiences are described in the EMCDDA's (2008) *Cannabis Reader*. The UNODC (2008b) provides an assessment of the world markets for amphetamines and ecstasy, while the European production and trafficking of ecstasy has been investigated in Gruppo Abele (2003).

After Patricia Adler's seminal ethnographic study of an upper-level dealing and smuggling community in California during the 1970s (1985), studies involving interviews with convicted drug traffickers were carried out in the United States (Reuter and Haaga 1989; Decker and Townsend Chapman 2008), the United Kingdom (Pearson and Hobbs 2001; Matrix Knowledge Group 2007) and Canada (DesRoches 2005). In addition to several other studies on high-level drug trafficking with a more limited primary data collection and a bourgeoning journalistic literature, a substantial body of field research has accumulated over the past two decades describing characteristics of various low-level markets, primarily for cocaine and heroin. A summary of that literature can be found in Natarajan and Hough (2000) and Dorn *et al.* (2005).

Notes

1 It must be stressed, however, that the current figure is only for heroin and does not include other opioids, such as OxyContin. If the household survey data is to be trusted, taking the consumption of other opioids into account would double the current number of chronic users.
2 'Super-labs' are defined as clandestine laboratories capable of producing more than 5 kg in 24 hours.

References

Adler, P. A. (1985) *Wheeling and Dealing. An Ethnography of an Upper-Level Drug Dealing and Smuggling Community*. New York: Columbia University Press.

Berridge, V. (1999) *Opium and the People: Opiate Use and Drug Control Policy in Nineteenth and Early-Twentieth Century England*. London: Free Association Books.

Blickman, T., Korf, D. J., Siegel, D. and Zaitch, D. (2003) 'Synthetic drug trafficking in Amsterdam', in Gruppo Abele (ed.), *Synthetic Drugs Trafficking in Three European Cities: Major Trends and the Involvement of Organised Crime*. Turin: Gipiangrafica.

Bourdieu, P. (1986) 'The forms of capital', in J. G. Richardson (ed.), *Handbook for Theory and Research for the Sociology of Education*. New York: Greenwood.

Bovenkerk, F. and Yesilgöz, Y. (2007) *The Turkish Mafia: A History of the Heroin Godfathers*. Preston: Milo.

Braun, N., Nydegger-Lory, B., Berger, R. and Zahner, C. (2001) *Illegale Märkte für Heroin und Kokain*. Bern: Haupt.

Council of the European Union (2004) *EU Drugs Strategy (2005–2012)*. Brussels. Online at: http://register.consilium.europa.eu.

Courtwright, D. T. (1982) *Dark Paradise: Opiate Addiction in America before 1940*. Cambridge, MA: Harvard University Press.

Courtwright, D. T. (2001) *Forces of Habit: Drugs and the Making of the Modern World*. Cambridge, MA: Harvard University Press.

De Ruyver, B., Vermeulen, G., Vander Beken, T., Vander Laenen, F. and Geenens, K. (2002) *Multidisciplinary Drug Policies and the UN Drug Treaties*. Antwerp: Maklu.

Decker, S. and Townsend Chapman, M. (2008) *Drug Smugglers on Drug Smuggling*. Philadelphia, PA: Temple University Press.

Desroches, F. (2005) *The Crime That Pays: Drug Trafficking and Organized Crime in Canada*. Toronto: Canadian Scholar's Press.

Dorn, N., Levi, M. and King, L. (2005) *Literature Review on Upper Level Drug Trafficking*, Home Office Online Report 22/05. Online at: http://www.homeoffice.gov.uk/rds/pdfs05/rdsolr2205.pdf.

Dorn, N., Murji, K. and South, N. (1992) *Traffickers: Drug Markets and Law Enforcement*. London: Routledge.

Duprez, D. and Kokoreff, M. (1997) 'Drug trafficking and deprived neighbourhoods', in D. J. Korf and H. Riper (eds), *Illicit Drugs in Europe*. Amsterdam: Siswo, pp. 176–83.

European Monitoring Centre for Drugs and Drug Addiction (EMCDDA) (2007) *Annual Report 2007*. Lisbon: EMCDDA. Online at: http://www.emcdda.europa.eu/ (accessed 9 September 2008).

European Monitoring Centre for Drugs and Drug Addiction (EMCDDA) (2008) *A Cannabis Reader: Global Issues and Local Experiences*. Lisbon: EMCDDA. Online at: http://www.emcdda.europa.eu/publications/monographs/cannabis.

European Union (2005) *EU Drugs Action Plan (2005–2008)*. Brussels: Official Journal of the European Union, 2005/C168/01. Online at: http://eur-lex.europa.eu/ (accessed 14 October 2008).

Europol (2005) *EU Organised Crime Report*. The Hague, Europol. Online at: http://www.europol.eu.int/publications/EUOrganisedCrimeSitRep/2005/EU_OrganisedCrimeReport2005.pdf (accessed October 2006).

Fijnaut, C., Bovenkerk, F., Bruinsma, G. and van de Bunt, H. (1998) *Organized Crime in the Netherlands*. The Hague: Kluwer Law International.

Ghodse, H. (2008) *International Drug Control into the 21st Century*. Aldershot: Ashgate.

Gruppo Abele (2003) *Synthetic Drugs Trafficking in Three European Cities: Major Trends and the Involvement of Organised Crime*. Turin: Gipiangrafica.

Gruter, P. and Van de Mheen, D. (2005) *Cocaïnehandel in Nederland, impressies van deelnemers aan drugsdistributienetwerken*. Rotterdam: IVO.

International Narcotics Control Board (INCB) (2008) *Report of the International Narcotics Control Board 2007*. New York: United Nations. Online at: http://www.incb.org/ (accessed 14 October 2008).

Interpol (n.d.) *Heroin*. Online at: http://www.interpol.int/Public/Drugs/heroin/default.asp (accessed 26 September 2008).

Jelsma, M. and Kramer, T. (2008) *Withdrawal Symptoms: Changes in the Southeast Asian Drugs Market*, Drugs and Conflict Debate Papers No. 16. Amsterdam: Transnational Institute.

Johnson, B. D., Goldstein, P. J., Preble, E., Schmeidler, J., Lipton, D. S., Spunt, B. and Miller, T. (1985) *Taking Care of Business: The Economics of Crime by Heroin Abusers*. Lexington, MA: Lexington Books.

KLPD (2005a) *Criminaliteitsbeeldanalyse synthetische drugs 2002–2004*. Driebergen: Dienst Nationale Recherche.

KLPD (2005b) *Criminaliteitsbeeld 2005*. Driebergen: Dienst Nationale Recherche.

McAllister, W. (2001) *Drug Diplomacy in the Twentieth Century*. London: Routledge.

Matrix Knowledge Group (2007) *The Illicit Drug Trade in the United Kingdom*, Home Office Online Report 20/07. London: Home Office. Online at: http://www.homeoffice.gov.uk/rds/pdfs07/rdsolr2007.pdf (accessed 23 September 2008).

Miller, C. (2002) 'Rebels push Colombia toward anarchy', *Los Angeles Times*, 29 June, p. 1-1.

Musto, D. F. (1987) *The American Disease: Origins of Narcotics Control*. New York: Oxford University Press.

Natarajan, M. and Hough, M. (2000) *Illegal Drug Markets: From Research to Prevention Policy*. Monsey, NY: Criminal Justice Press.

Newman, R. K. (1995) 'Opium smoking in late imperial China', *Modern Asian Studies*, 29: 765–94.

Office of National Drug Control Policy (ONDCP) (2001) *What America's Users Spend on Illegal Drugs, 1988–2000*. Washington, DC: ONDCP. Online at: http://www.whitehousedrugpolicy.gov/publications/pdf/american_users_spend_2002.pdf (accessed 30 May 2007).

Paoli, L. (2000) *Pilot Project to Describe and Analyse Local Drug Markets – First Phase Final Report: Illegal Drug Markets in Frankfurt and Milan*. Lisbon: EMCDDA. Online at: http://www.emcdda.org (accessed 30 May 2007).

Paoli, L. (2005) 'The ugly side of capitalism and democracy: the development of the illegal drug market in post-Soviet Russia', in W. A. Pridemore (ed.), *Ruling Russia: Crime, Law and Justice in Post-Soviet Russia*. Lanham, MD: Rowman & Littlefield.

Paoli, L. and Fijnaut, C. (2004) 'Comparative synthesis of Part II', in C. Fijnaut and L. Paoli (eds), *Organised Crime in Europe, Concepts, Patterns and Control Policies in the European Union and Beyond*. Dordrecht: Springer.

Paoli, L. and Reuter, P. (2008) 'Ethnic minorities and drug trafficking', *European Journal of Criminology*, 5: 13–37.

Paoli, L., Greenfield, V. and Reuter, P. (2009) *The World Heroin Market: Can Policy Reduce Supply?* New York: Oxford University Press.

Paoli, L., Rabkov, I., Greenfield, V. and Reuter, P. (2007) 'Tajikistan: the rise of a narco-state', *Journal of Drug Issues*, 37 (4): 951–80.

Pearson, G. and Hobbs, D. (2001) *Middle Market Drug Distribution*. London: Home Office Research, Development and Statistics Directorate. Online at: http://www.homeoffice.gov.uk/rds/pdfs/hors227.pdf.

Preble, E. and Casey, J. J. (1969) 'Taking care of business: the heroin user's life on the street', *International Journal of the Addiction*, 4: 1–24.

Reuter, P. (1985) *The Organization of Illegal Markets: An Economic Analysis*. Washington, DC: National Institute of Justice.

Reuter, P. (2009) 'Do no harm', *American Interest*, IV (4): 46–52.

Reuter, P. and Haaga, J. (1989) *The Organization of High-Level Drug Markets: An Exploratory Study*. Santa Monica, CA: Rand.

Reuter, P. and Pain, E. with Greenfield, V. (2003) *The Effects of Drug Trafficking on Central Asia*. Mimeo.

Reuter, P. and Trautmann, F. (eds) (2009) *A Report on Global Illicit Drug Markets 1998–2007*. Online at: http://ec.europa.eu/justice_home/doc_centre/drugs/studies/doc/report_10_03_09_en.pdf.

Ritter, A. and Cameron, J. (2006) 'A review of the efficacy and effectiveness of harm reduction strategies for alcohol, tobacco and illicit drugs', *Drug and Alcohol Review*, 25 November 2009, 25 (6): 611–24.

Ruggiero, V. and South, N. (1995) *Eurodrugs: Drug Use, Markets and Trafficking in Europe*. London: UCL Press.

Shulgin A. and Shulgin, A. (1991) *PIHKAL, A Chemical Love Story*. Berkeley, CA: Transform Press.

Spapens, T. (2006) *Interactie tussen criminaliteit en opsporing. De gevolgen van opsporingsactiviteiten voor de organisatie en afscherming van XTC-productie en -handel in Nederland*. Antwerp/Oxford: Intersentia.

Spapens, T. (2008) *Georganiseerde criminaliteit en strafrechtelijke samenwerking in de Nederlandse grensgebieden*. Antwerp/Oxford: Intersentia.

Spapens, T. and Fijnaut, C. (2005) *Criminaliteit en rechtshandhaving in de Euregio Maas-Rijn deel 1*. Antwerp/Oxford: Intersentia.

Spapens, T., van de Bunt, H. and Rastovac, L. (2007) *De wereld achter de wietteelt*. The Hague: Boom Juridische Uitgevers.

Thoumi, F. E. (2003) *Illegal Drugs, Economy and Society in the Andes*. Washington, DC: Woodrow Wilson Center.

United Nations Office on Drugs and Crime (UNODC) (2005) *2005 World Drug Report*. Vienna: United Nations Office on Drugs and Crime. Online at: http://www.unodc.org/ (accessed 9 September 2008).

United Nations Office on Drugs and Crime (UNODC) (2006) *2006 World Drug Report*. Vienna: United Nations Office on Drugs and Crime. Online at http://www.unodc.org/ (accessed 9 September 2008).

United Nations Office on Drugs and Crime (UNODC) (2007) *2007 World Drug Report*. Vienna: United Nations Office on Drugs and Crime. Online at: http://www.unodc.org/ (accessed 9 September 2008).

United Nations Office on Drugs and Crime (UNODC) (2008a) *2008 World Drug Report*. Vienna: United Nations Office on Drugs and Crime. Online at: http://www.unodc.org/ (accessed 9 September 2008).

United Nations Office on Drugs and Crime (UNODC) (2008b) *Amphetamines and Ecstasy. 2008 Global ATS Assessment*. Vienna: United Nations Office on Drugs and

Crime. Online at: http://www.unodc.org/documents/scientific/ATS/Global-ATS-Assessment-2008-Web.pdf.

United Nations Office on Drugs and Crime (UNODC) (annual) *World Drug Report*. Vienna: United Nations Office on Drugs and Crime. Online at: http://www.unodc.org/unodc/en/data-and-analysis/WDR-2007.html.

United Nations Office on Drugs and Crime and World Bank (2007) *Crime, Violence, and Development: Trends, Costs, and Policy Options in the Caribbean*. Vienna and Washington.

Wright, A. (2006) *Organised Crime*. Cullompton: Willan.

Zaitch, D. (2001) *Trafficking Cocaine, Colombian Drug Entrepreneurs in the Netherlands*. The Hague, London and New York: Kluwer Law International.

Suggested websites

Drug Enforcement Administration: http://www.usdoj.gov/dea

European Monitoring Centre for Drugs and Drug Addiction: http://www.emcdda.europa.eu

Interpol: http://www.interpol.int

United Nations Office on Drugs and Crime: http://www.unodc.org

Part VI

Organised and Business Crime

The chapters in this section relate to serious crimes committed by members of organisations. The organisations discussed vary widely in size, complexity, legitimacy and permanence. In some cases, indeed, the offences are legally and/or socially defined as having been committed by the organisation itself rather than by individuals. All five authors note that, despite the seriousness and scale of the activities they discuss, there is a dearth of reliable information about them and they have received surprisingly little attention from criminologists.

Minkes' and Croall's chapters discuss financial crimes committed by members of apparently legitimate business organisations, Minkes focusing mainly on large corporations and Croall on small and 'middle-range' businesses. Minkes argues that corporate crime not only involves sums far in excess of the totality stolen through conventional property offences, but is more damaging to the social fabric: it therefore deserves much more attention from both theorists and policymakers. Croall notes that a great deal of theft and fraud committed by smaller businesses can also be highly damaging to victims but – especially where the owners manage to present themselves as 'respectable' rather than 'rogue' traders – is often under-regulated by the criminal justice system and unexplored by criminologists. She gives examples from the fields of farming and food production, car service and sales, and 'cowboy' builders, and surmises that such crime may increase as a result of the economic downturn.

The other three chapters cover specific types of crime committed by organised criminal groups, namely human trafficking, money laundering and extortion. These may or may not be committed under the cover of legitimate business activities. Goodey's chapter on human trafficking argues that organised crime groups have taken advantage of new opportunities created by, on the one hand, the poverty and social dislocation created by the break-up of the Soviet Union and, on the other, burgeoning sex markets in the West. She places particular emphasis on the impact on victims and calls for much greater attention to the problem by policymakers.

Hicks describes various forms of money laundering which organised crime groups employ to conceal the proceeds of illegal activities and give them the appearance of legitimacy. He argues that any serious attempts to combat it need both international governmental and police collaboration and the cooperation of banks and other financial institutions. He notes that such cooperation has grown significantly over recent years, but there remain fundamental gaps in knowledge and disagreements about the relative effectiveness of preventive and investigative strategies.

Finally, Hobbs discusses the phenomenon of extortion, arguing that it is an activity that thrives in political systems where the state is weak or in transition, giving criminal gangs (or in some cases corrupt state agents) an opportunity to exploit a market in violence for their own gain. He gives historical and contemporary examples, including the Sicilian Mafia and Russian gangs. He also argues that extortion can flourish in areas of cities where the public police do not have a monopoly over violence, such as areas with socially marginalised populations or with an unregulated 'night-time economy' of clubs and pubs, where policing is left largely in the hands of 'bouncers'.

Chapter 32

Corporate financial crimes

John Minkes

Introduction

This chapter deals with financial crimes committed by large organisations. It will discuss the nature, prevalence and costs of such crimes and show that they do more damage and represent a greater threat to the fabric of capitalist society than do conventional property crimes such as burglary and street robbery. It will then review the debate about the causes of corporate financial crimes, contrasting attempts to apply traditional criminological theories to corporate misconduct with explanations that are rooted more in business and management studies, and focus particularly on the nature of organisational behaviour. In this discussion, particular attention will be paid to the boundaries between individual and organisational fault and the chapter will move on from there to look at formal responses to corporate misconduct which raise similar issues about individual versus corporate liability.

Even in its narrowest sense, the term 'corporate financial crimes' covers a considerable range of offence types: examples include conspiring with competitors to fix prices, false accounting to conceal the true financial status of a company, illegal operations to increase a company's share price and misuse of corporate funds.[1] However, it is important to emphasise that many of the rule-breaking activities discussed in the criminological literature under the general rubric of 'corporate *crime*' are not defined or handled as breaches of criminal law. Sutherland (1949) famously had to anonymise the case examples he used in his groundbreaking study *White-Collar Crime* because much of the corporate misconduct he described was not formally defined as crime. Instead, it was regarded as breaching regulations or administrative rules and dealt with by tribunals or regulatory agencies rather than criminal courts. To Sutherland, this was not because of the nature of the conduct concerned but because people with status and wealth were able to influence both legislation and its enforcement; their conduct was really no different to that of conventional offenders. He was unmoved by a fierce debate with Tappan (1947) who insisted that sociological investigations of crime should concern themselves solely with acts defined in law as criminal. Nevertheless, the likelihood of libel actions against Sutherland and his college left him little option but to remove the names of the companies from his text (they were restored when the book was republished in 1983, under the protection of the Statute of Limitations).

Nelken (2007) discusses Sutherland's use of the term 'corporate crime' and points out that if one follows him in including misbehaviours which attract only civil or administrative penalties, then there is no sound reason to exclude other behaviours which break no formal rules or attract no sanctions at all. In fact, some commentators, such as those who have developed the concept of 'social harm' (Hillyard *et al.* 2004) would broaden the definition to include unethical behaviour and legal but harmful actions such as closing a business down. However, while recognising the artificiality of the boundaries drawn between crime, breaches of regulations and unethical behaviour, the focus in this chapter is primarily upon behaviour which breaches either criminal law or administrative regulations. Both kinds of breach will be discussed here – as is common in the literature – under the general heading of corporate (financial) crime, but at times it will be appropriate for the sake of clarity to use a more accurate umbrella term such as 'corporate misconduct', which can cover any breach of regulations and rules as well as laws.

There is a further debate over the use of the term 'white-collar crime', which frequently appears in discussions about financial offences. Although Sutherland (1949) used this term as the title of his book, and defined it as crimes committed by 'offenders of high social status', he actually dealt with offences committed within large organisations, *almost exclusively for the benefit of the organisation*. As already noted, such offences are now more usually referred to as corporate crime (or, of course, corporate misconduct). The term white-collar crime is used more commonly for offences such as embezzlement, which may be connected with employment in a corporation but where the primary beneficiary is an individual, or for non-violent financial offences committed outside a corporate context, such as income tax evasion and other kinds of fraud (Weisburd and Waring 2001; Weisburd *et al.* 2008; see also Chapters 5 and 6, in this volume).

History

Corporate financial crime is not a new phenomenon. Robb (1992) charts the rise of the modern corporation in the United Kingdom from the Railway Mania of the 1840s to the Great Crash in 1929. Drawing on case studies and broader empirical studies, he shows how each new financial development was vulnerable to abuse. The concepts of laissez-faire (i.e. that the government should not interfere in the conduct of business) and *caveat emptor* ('let the buyer beware') were used to resist legislation for most of the nineteenth century. At this time, companies were not even required to keep paper accounts, so prosecution for fraud was virtually impossible. The turning point was a series of financial scandals and disasters from 1866 on, although the process of change was very slow; the first Companies Act was not passed until

1900, and it was only in 1948 that the UK adopted a vigorous regulatory system comparable to those of the United States and other European countries.

In the United States, robust investigative journalism brought to light the activities of corrupt leaders of industry, the so-called robber barons, in the late nineteenth century. Their crimes included fraud, theft, bribery, corruption and murder (Snider 1993). In addition, concerns about monopolisation of markets led to legislation designed to control mergers and prevent collusion between competitors (the Sherman Anti-Trust Act of 1890), and the creation of federal agencies with powers over banking and transport (Simpson 2002).

The most comprehensive account of corporate financial crimes in the early twentieth century is provided by the pioneering work of Sutherland (1949). Drawing on newspaper accounts and records of courts and administrative sanctions, Sutherland established that many of America's major corporations had committed offences and some of them were frequent offenders. Their misconduct included price-fixing, restraint of trade, abuses of the patent system, fraudulent manipulation of accounts, illegal labour practices, false advertising and breaches of wartime price controls in both world wars. A similar survey by Clinard and Yeager (1980) in the 1970s showed that the problem had not gone away. Unfortunately, there is no comparable systematic study of corporate financial crimes in the UK.

The scale and costs of corporate financial crimes

Estimates of the scale and costs of corporate crime are fraught with difficulty, even more so than the costs of conventional crimes. It is well known that the scale of conventional crimes is understated by official statistics because they are not always reported to, or recorded by, the police (Maguire 2007). But corporate misconduct is even harder to quantify. Conventional crimes such as burglary, robbery and car crime are highly visible to both victims and investigators. Leaving aside the debate about what is or is not a crime and what should or should not be included, corporate crimes are far less visible and therefore much harder to detect than conventional crime (this is also true of corporate violence, as discussed by Tombs in Chapter 44). Corporate financial crimes typically take place behind closed doors and are concealed by complex accounting procedures. The victims may be unaware that they have been victimised: for example, in price-fixing cases, customers are unlikely to realise that the prices they are paying have been fixed by companies who are supposed to be in competition. Robert Maxwell's theft of over £500 million from his companies' pension funds was only revealed after his sudden death (Punch 2008). Major frauds such as Enron (discussed below) involve complicated networks of genuine and fake companies, often constructed by professionals who are well aware of the best ways to conceal illicit transactions. Furthermore, even when they are detected, such crimes are often dealt with by administrative or civil procedures rather than criminal prosecutions, and they are processed by a variety of agencies whose records are never aggregated.

There are thus no reliable estimates of either the extent or, importantly, the total costs of corporate financial crime. However, there is general agreement among criminologists that the costs far exceed those of conventional crimes. For example, Slapper and Tombs (1999) compare the annual average for cases dealt with by the Serious Fraud Office in England and Wales of £5 billion with the average annual cost of burglary, put at £1 billion. In the United States in the mid 1980s, according to Simpson (2002), the average monetary loss in corporate crimes was $565,000 while the average burglary offence involved $1,000 and simple larceny $400. Snider (1993) gives overall crime figures for the United States, noting that street crime cost $4 billion a year, less than 5 per cent of the total for corporate crime. It will also be apparent from some of the cases referred to in the next section that individual corporate crimes can involve huge amounts of money, far beyond the sums involved in even the biggest of conventional robberies. And there is another, more insidious harm. In his presidential address to the American Sociological Association, Sutherland (1940) referred to the social damage caused by corporate crimes when they destroy *trust* in the financial institutions which are the very foundations of the capitalist economy. This threat has been recognised by some governments which generally favour deregulation but have responded to financial scandals by insisting on a stricter regime (Snider 2007). Nevertheless, the reputation of business is again tarnished at the time of writing, particularly in the United States, where commentators note the coincidence of the current banking crisis and a major FBI investigation into fraud by major financial institutions.[2]

Recent cases

The globalisation of corporate crime

In the era of globalisation, corporate misconduct persists and occurs around the world. Case examples described by Snider (2008) include: Bre-X, a Canadian mining company whose worth was vastly inflated on the back of bogus claims to have found substantial reserves of gold in Indonesia; Parmalat, the Italian food and dairy giant which lost hundreds of millions of euros in a high-risk investment fund and hundreds more through offshore liquidity transfers, and concealed its true financial position for years until it collapsed with debts of $17.38 billion, leading to bankruptcy and criminal charges (see also Hamilton and Micklethwait 2006; Kellens *et al.* 2007); Enron, one of a number of major American companies brought down by fraud at the beginning of the current decade; and Barings, the British merchant bank which was bankrupted by the illicit stock market dealing of the 'rogue trader', Nick Leeson (Enron and Barings are described below). Corporate crime can also be truly international; one of the most famous cases concerned the Bank of Credit and Commerce International (BCCI) which operated over 400 branches in 78 countries. Originally an honest business, BCCI became totally corrupt. It used small investors' money to speculate and make unsecured loans, moving money around to obscure losses (Doig 2006), but investigations by the Bank of England revealed that it was also involved in money-laundering, tax evasion, bribery and arms trafficking, in addition to rampant illegal accounting practices. By the time BCCI was closed down, total losses had mounted to some $20 billion.

The Savings & Loan scandal

In the United States, two of the most costly and notorious cases are the Savings and Loan (S&L) debacle and Enron. Calavita and Pontell (1990) describe the SandL as a sequel to the financial deregulation of the Reagan government in the 1980s. S&Ls (also known as 'thrifts') were the equivalent of British building societies; until the 1970s, their main business was extending loans to home buyers. Deregulation was seen as the answer to problems they experienced in the 1970s when they could not coexist with high levels of inflation, but it opened them up to fraud. Thrift owners conspired together to lend each other money with no intention of repayment; land used as security for loans was deliberately overvalued to inflate the apparent value of business; and false accounting was employed to hide the losses. Inevitably, the losses mounted and thrifts began to fail. By 1986, the federal agency which underwrote them had closed or merged so many insolvent thrifts that it was itself insolvent. In 1990, estimates of the total losses ranged from $325 *billion* to four times that amount. The General Attorney's Office estimated that criminal activity was a factor in 70 to 80 per cent of failures. Worse still, many politicians and officials were implicated in the scandal through overlooking wrongdoing or using political influence to obstruct investigations.

Enron

Enron is probably the most written-about financial scandal of recent times; media coverage was extensive on both sides of the Atlantic, many first-hand accounts have been published (e.g. Cruver 2003), as well as academic discussions (e.g. Kellens *et al*. 2007; Snider 2008). The company started out as a regional gas supplier but under the stewardship of Kenneth Lay, it became a major global player in natural gas and electricity before diversifying into many new ventures. However, some of the new schemes were poorly conceived and went badly wrong. Enron's financial position worsened but this was concealed by a series of fraudulent accounting practices. Executives whose remuneration packages included company shares conspired to keep the share price rising by pretending that business was still booming, aided by Wall Street analysts whose supposedly independent advice was effectively being paid for by Enron. Other senior personnel obtained illegal personal loans from the company or created fake subsidiaries which were simply used to divert company funds to their own accounts. Eventually, the losses could no longer be hidden and the company collapsed, leaving honest shareholders and company pension scheme members with huge losses. At around the same time, several other major American companies (e.g. Worldcom, Tyco) folded in broadly similar circumstances. Ken Lay, Chief Executive Officer of Enron, and Bernie Ebbers, Chief Executive of Worldcom, were both sentenced to long prison terms, although Lay died suddenly while on bail pending appeal.

Guinness

In Britain, three of the most significant cases of the last 25 years have been the Guinness case, the pensions scandal and Barings Bank. In the Guinness case, directors and senior executives of the brewing company conspired in an illegal share support operation in order to boost the value of their offer to buy another company, Distillers – the offer included Guinness shares so Guinness gave their associates money to buy their shares and force the share price up (Kochan and Pym 1987). The chief executive of Guinness, Ernest Saunders, was sent to prison for five years (he was subsequently released early on grounds of ill health) and three other participants were convicted, though they fought their conviction all the way to the European Court.

The pensions scandal

The pensions scandal arose after financial deregulation in the 1980s allowed employees to opt out of occupational pension schemes and choose private pensions instead. It involved many of the most reputable financial corporations. Potential customers were falsely advised that private pension schemes would give them better returns than the occupational schemes to which they belonged; it is estimated that there were 2.4 million victims and the final costs totalled £11 billion (Slapper and Tombs 1999). In a recent echo of this case, a number of British banks were fined by the Financial Services Authority (FSA) for mis-selling payment protection insurance (policies paid for by borrowers which protect the lenders against default). By October 2008, the FSA had taken action against 19 firms, culminating in a record fine of £7 million imposed on Alliance & Leicester which the FSA said had trained its staff to put pressure on customers who questioned the inclusion of supposedly optional policies in their quotes (BBC News 2008b).

Barings Bank

Barings was a traditional and rather old-fashioned London banking company which diversified into complex stock market dealings in the Far East. Nick Leeson, originally sent from London to Singapore to deal with an administrative problem, took a leading role in this new business. However, he started to incur huge losses which he concealed in a hidden account. The bank continued to send him large amounts of money without question and by the time he walked out of his office, he had lost £780 million. Barings collapsed and was later sold to a Dutch bank for £1. Leeson was sent to prison in Singapore but the subsequent inquiry by the Bank of England also blamed the non-existence of internal control systems in Barings and the failure of the bank's auditors and the regulatory authorities to uncover his activities (Punch 2008).

Dairy product price-fixing

Corporate misconduct can involve more mundane items. In 2007, following an investigation by the Office of Fair Trading, several of Britain's leading supermarket chains, Sainsbury's, Asda and Safeway (since taken over by

Morrisons) and several major dairy processors, Dairy Crest, Wiseman and the Cheese Company, admitted colluding to increase retail prices of milk, butter and cheese. The cost to each individual customer was small – about three pence on each pound of butter – but the total amount was substantial and the companies agreed to pay between them £116 million in penalties (OFT 2007).

Finally, it should not be assumed that only profit-making corporations break the rules. For example, in 2008, the BBC, a non-profit public service corporation, was fined £400,000 by the media regulator, Ofcom, for encouraging viewers and listeners to phone in and enter competitions which they had no chance of winning (BBC News 2008c). As this suggests, explanations of corporate misconduct which focus only on the profit motive inevitably overlook the existence of other pressures which are common to all target-driven organisations.

Corporate crimes: individual or organisational?

In cases such as those described above, the question arises as to who is to blame? Who should take responsibility and be punished? This is sometimes presented as a simple issue: all organisations are made up of individuals and decisions are taken by individuals; how can an organisation take decisions? On the other hand, we often attribute actions to, for example, 'the government' or 'the university', without acknowledging that we are referring to the complex networks of decisions and actions by the individuals which ultimately constitute organisational behaviour (Minkes and Minkes 2005).

There is considerable debate among management scholars about the process of decision-making in large organisations (Loasby 2008), and this is often overlooked by criminologists (Punch 1996, 2008 is an exception). Legal assignation of responsibility has been an equally controversial issue (Wells 2001; Gobert and Punch 2003; Gobert 2008); although many European countries and, increasingly, the United States, have developed legislation which permits corporations to be prosecuted, the law in England and Wales, especially the criminal law, has tended to focus on individuals, as typified by Baron Thurlow's famous dictum that a corporation cannot be prosecuted because it has 'no soul to be damned and no body to be kicked.'[3]

In fact, such questions about the division of responsibility between individuals and organisations are highly important. They arose perhaps most famously in the Nuremberg war crimes trials but they are also extremely relevant to current debates about corporate criminal responsibility. Harding (2007) makes it clear that the 'methodological individualism' adopted in British law and exemplified by Baron Thurlow is based on a misconception of the nature of organisations. They are not simply a collection of individuals. Large organisations have three distinct characteristics which make them more than just the sum of their parts: they have a clear organisational structure; there are organisational goals which create a sense of shared mission; and the individuals who work in them can be replaced by other individuals without changing the nature of the organisation. Organisational employees are therefore rarely autonomous: they follow prescribed routines and their decision-making is influenced by organisational cultures and power structures. Responsibility can thus be attributed to both individuals and the organisations in which they work. From a criminological perspective, therefore, it is necessary to consider both when discussing corporate crime and its causes.

To return to some of the examples discussed earlier, there are cases where responsibility is widely spread throughout the organisation. As described in the account by Geis (1967) of price-fixing in the heavy electrical equipment industry in the USA in the 1950s and 1960s, executives at all levels of the corporations took part in illegal conferences, concealed telephone contacts and conspired to fix the market. Newly appointed managers were introduced to systematic and ingrained deviance and expected to participate.

Superficially, in the case of Barings Bank, Nick Leeson acted alone; essentially he was gambling with other people's money. But there was also system failure: the checks and balances which should have prevented him losing £780 million and destroying the bank were all absent. He was allowed to supervise himself; his seniors in London did not fully understand the new style of business he was involved in and broke rules in advancing him more money without question; and the Bank of England allowed transfers well in excess of permissible limits. Thus Punch (2008) states that 'the organisation did it' and the blame must be shared.

In contrast, there have been some cases in which it seems the individual is wholly to blame. Certainly the jury which acquitted Robert Maxwell's son Kevin of conspiracy appears to have believed that Maxwell senior had controlled his businesses so tightly that even his son was deceived about his depredations of the company pension fund (*The Times* 1996).

Explanations

This section deals firstly with conventional criminological theories of causation, social and individual, as applied to corporate crime, then with structural theories which explain corporate crime as an inevitable consequence of the capitalist mode of production, and finally explanations which pay more attention to organisational factors.

Theoretical development has undoubtedly been hampered by a lack of research, especially in Britain; apart from the preoccupation of government and academics with conventional crimes, funding is difficult to obtain and business is (perhaps understandably) reluctant to open its doors to critical criminological scrutiny. Tombs and Whyte (2002: 218) lament this, concluding that '... the past quarter of a century has been one in which the ability of the powerful to protect themselves from critical scrutiny has been augmented.' They paint a depressing picture of research being handicapped by limited access and suppression of unwelcome findings, and complain that the research community has acquiesced. In addition, what research there is deals almost exclusively with misconduct; more studies of corporations that comply with the rules might throw useful light on their motivation (and might be more palatable to the business community). Theoretical work has therefore been based to a great extent on case studies or (auto)biographical accounts, which provide valuable insights but arguably are not a foundation for generalisation.

Social and environmental causes

Nevertheless, since the earliest days of the study of corporate crime, it has been seen as intensely relevant to theoretical development in criminology. Sutherland (1940) made it clear that his purpose in highlighting the wrongdoings of people of high status was to change criminology, not to attack the American way of life. He complained that the dominant theories of causation were all based on statistics that implied that only the poor and disadvantaged committed crime and therefore blamed such factors as poverty, poor education, inadequate housing or immigration. His research showed that wealthy and successful people also broke the rules and therefore, if there was to be a general theory of the cause of crime, it would have to account for their conduct as well. Consequently, he advanced the theory of *differential association* which suggested that people become offenders if a preponderance of the people with whom they associate favour offending, and that this applies to all sectors of society. Thus, for example, new employees who join a company where price-fixing agreements are the norm will be drawn into the practice. The theory also rested on the concept of social disorganisation, a lack of, or conflicts in, moral standards in society; monopolies and big organisations had replaced competition and family firms as the mainstays of the economy and neither law nor culture had kept pace, so business behaviour was not restrained by social values.

There is some support for Sutherland's views in autobiographical accounts of business careers (Geis and Goff 1983) and Langan (1996) cites Clinard and Yeager's finding that 40 per cent of corporations had a clean record – clearly some companies have a culture of honesty, while in others, everyone is involved in misconduct and new employees are rapidly drawn in. Some employees may resist (restrained by wider social influences outside work) but others will use justifications such as loyalty or 'business is business'. They may also have less to lose.

However, as Nelken (2007) points out, differential association is subject to the same criticism as all general theories of crime, particularly that it cannot satisfactorily explain why some people are able to resist the influence. Lee Iacocca, later Chief Executive of General Motors, recalled that in his early career at Ford, he found that colleagues 'played fast and loose with the rules [...] As an idealistic, freshly-scrubbed kid just a year out of college, I was shocked' (Iacocca 1984: 35), but he avoided getting drawn in. Furthermore, it seems only to explain the persistence of wrongdoing rather than how it starts in the first place.

Another attempt to fit corporate crime into a general theory of causation is made by Gottfredson and Hirschi (1990). They argue that all crime, including what they refer to as white-collar crime, is caused primarily by poor self-control and failure to restrain our need for immediate self-gratification. Human beings naturally pursue self-interest and if they do not learn self-control in early childhood (mainly through effective parenting), they are likely to engage in criminal or other anti-social forms of behaviour into adulthood. According to their 'general theory of crime', the explanation for white-collar crime is no different – offenders benefit either directly or indirectly through the success of the corporation on whose behalf they break the law. Gottfredson and Hirschi explicitly discount consideration of the organisational context; the only difference they acknowledge between white-collar and conventional criminals is that the former are in employment, and dishonesty is the same regardless of the employment status of the dishonest person. In criminological terms, therefore, they argue that white-collar crime has no distinct value and can thus be included in their theory.

The main weakness of this approach is its focus on a single factor to the virtual exclusion of other social and environmental causes, but they are also on thin ice when they apply it specifically to white-collar crime. Since low self-control and the need for immediate gratification are the opposite of the qualities needed to succeed in white-collar employment, their theory predicts low levels of white-collar crime. So they take issue with the claims of Sutherland and others that white-collar crime is common and refer to 'the extraordinarily high level of law-abiding conduct found among many white-collar workers' (1990: 198). This is a weak argument, however, as they admit elsewhere that there is little evidence either way and its relevance is further reduced by their emphasis on crimes which damage the organisation; despite citing Geis and Sutherland, they barely deal with those that benefit the organisation.

A different approach is taken by Box (1983), who applies aspects of Merton's *theory of anomie* to corporations.[4] Merton had argued that crime occurred as a result of 'strain' created when individuals or groups in society found their legitimate aspirations for material or personal success blocked by unequal opportunities. One possible response was to seek to achieve those aspirations by illegitimate means. Similarly, Box suggests, capitalist corporations sometimes resort to illegality when legitimate opportunities to make profits are blocked. He identified five problem areas for businesses: their competitors, government rules and regulations, employees' demands for better wages or working conditions, the behaviour of consumers, and pressures from the general public, especially environmental campaigners, all of which create uncertainty and threaten profits. Hopkins Burke (2001) adds that the theory is also applicable to individuals involved in white-collar crime without much amendment – why should it only be the poor who feel aggrieved about their rewards?

Box (1983) also suggests that individuals working in corporations display a form of anomie more related to Durkheim's original concept of anomie as an absence of norms: successful individuals move beyond moral limits into normlessness. Top jobs go to people who are ambitious, shrewd and slightly immoral – just the kind of person who will turn to crime to further the organisation's goals. For instance, Hamilton and Micklethwait describe the recruitment policies of BSL, Barings' Far East subsidiary, as follows (2006: 18): 'BSL hiring criteria were personality, self-assurance and drive – or desire to make money. These qualities were judged to be more important than the education, professional experience or management expertise which Barings valued.' But both versions of anomie put forward by Box have the same limitation as Merton's original concept, which is that they have difficulty explaining why some of those whose aspirations are blocked choose crime and others react in different ways.

Another concept from general criminological theory which has been applied to corporate misconduct is that of *techniques of neutralisation*. This was originally developed by Sykes and Matza (1957) to explain the involvement of young people in crime; contrary to contemporary theories about deviant subcultures, they did not reject society's values but drifted in and out of delinquency. In order to preserve their self-image as law-abiding, they developed a number of ways of minimising or denying the illegality or the impact of their behaviour. For example, they would say that 'everybody does it' or 'the victim deserved it'. The same sort of technique is apparent in the following exchange from the United States Senate Subcommittee hearings on price-fixing in the heavy electrical equipment industry, quoted in Geis (1967):

Committee Attorney: Did you know that these meetings with competitors were illegal?

Witness: Illegal? Yes, but not criminal. I did not find that out until I read the indictment ... I assumed that criminal action meant damaging someone, and we did not do that ... I thought that we were more or less working on a survival basis in order to try and keep our plant and our employees.

More recently, Sainsbury's, in the price-fixing case referred to above, effectively protested their innocence despite having agreed a settlement of £26 million with the OFT, stating in a press release (J. Sainsbury plc 2007):

We are disappointed that we have been penalised for actions that were intended to help British farmers [...] at a time of considerable economic pressure and public debate about whether farmers were getting a fair price for their products.

Box's comment (1983: 54) that managers have 'a library of verbal techniques for neutralizing the moral bind of laws against corporate behaviour' seems apposite here. Misconduct may be justified by portraying regulations as interference with necessary business practices rather than legitimate restraints on wrongdoing, for example, and examples of such conduct abound. Once again, though, this is a better *post-facto* explanation of why some corporations offend than a general theory to account for their offending in the first place.

Writing from a business studies perspective, Anand *et al.* (2004) interestingly put forward similar arguments, combining elements of techniques of neutralisation and differential association (without actually using these criminological terms). They explain participation in corrupt practice as the result of *rationalisation* and *socialisation*. Executives compromise on their principles to win favour and participate in practices that are 'good for business'; their membership of a special group enables them to become cocooned from reality and ignore the discontinuity between their norms in work and outside it. Newcomers are drawn into small and easily rationalised actions at first and then it escalates, so the deviant system is perpetuated.

Finally, two innovative, if empirically untested, theses are put forward respectively by Shover (2007) and Newton (2006). Shover (2007) focuses on the class background of corporate offenders who are, by definition, middle-class. In his view, white-collar crime can be explained by attitudes learnt in childhood. Middle-class children are brought up to be competitive. They also question authority and expect benefits and this can turn into a pervasive ethos of entitlement; they believe that their contribution to society entitles them to cut corners and claim perks. Success only brings insecurity and the desire to hang on and gain more. And class differences mean that the middle classes are much better at neutralisation, trying to be seen as respectable, choosing criminal options without adopting a criminal identity and getting others to empathise with them.

Newton (2006) takes a more moral stance, blaming the development of liberalism which she defines (2006: 11–12) as

> ... the thesis that, in general, adults should be allowed to follow their desires wherever they lead, including the desire for accumulation of wealth beyond all reason, without limit and without social sanction.

She traces this back to philosophers of the seventeenth and eighteenth centuries such as John Locke and Adam Smith and the nineteenth-century Utilitarians and their abandonment of the sense of community in favour of the individual's desire and right to further their own interests. Thus she explains corporate crime as part of a wider failure of fundamental morality: moral standards have fallen in all aspects of life, not just in business. The 1980s in particular were characterised by greed, ostentation and excess, and the press made celebrities of the very rich. Historically, we lived in small communities where our behaviour was controlled because there were always witnesses; modern society lacks such communities so our behaviour goes unrestrained.

Gender and corporate crime

Another aspect to be considered is gender. The corporate world is still largely male-dominated and Snider (1993) cites the work of Messerschmidt on gender and crime, suggesting that corporations are particularly male structures, rewarding 'masculine' behaviour. This raises the question as to whether having more women managers would make a difference.

Dodge (2007) also points out that men dominate high-status jobs and therefore white-collar crime (this is also illustrated in Coates and Herbert's (2008) study of City traders, discussed below, where only 4 out of 260 traders on the trading floor they studied were female). But women who do get to the top experience discriminatory treatment; for example, women who display the aggression that men get rewarded for are likely to be pilloried for violating gender roles. Media coverage can also focus unduly on gender. In June 2003, for example, major New York newspapers carried 1,279 stories about Martha Stewart, who was being indicted for tax evasion, and only 23 on Ken Lay, the Chief Executive Officer of Enron. Dodge notes that it was thought that Stewart was made an example of because she was a woman in a man's world.

She cites a number of surveys which suggest that women in corporate boardrooms behave differently to men: they are more ethical and less focused on money and power. However, there are also contradictory research findings that suggest that morals and ethics are determined more by situational context than gender. Dodge concludes that some women may commit white-collar crimes to be 'one of the boys' or under pressure to conform, but essentially women in a male-dominated world may share the same motivations as the men.

In line with a general perception that 'masculine' qualities such as aggression and ruthlessness are valued in the business world, Shover (2007: 90) suggests that such behaviours may lie behind corporate misconduct. In his view, unbridled competition is at its most corrosive where most participants are young men: 'Patriarchal notions of masculinity and competitors of privileged background predominate in worlds that breed tempted individuals and predisposed organizations.'

Another perspective on gender is put forward by Coates and Herbert (2008). They measured steroid levels in a small sample of male City of London traders and found that testosterone levels rose on days when traders made more than average profits. Testosterone is linked to confidence and successful risk-taking, but previous studies have shown that too much can lead to irrational decision-making by increasing impulsivity and sensation-seeking. Another hormone, cortisol, reacts to economic uncertainty and may decrease appetite for risk, so risk-averse behaviour may increase when the market is going down. Thus steroid levels are affected by performance and may in turn have an impact on the quality of financial decision-making. It is clear from their work and the others cited above that the role of gender in corporate misconduct deserves greater scrutiny.

Individual explanations

In common with theorising about conventional crime, some commentators have focused on the characters of individuals rather than the company as a whole. Sutherland (1949) discouraged this when he ridiculed the idea that corporate offenders broke the law because they had had unhappy childhoods. Nevertheless, greed, ruthlessness and unscrupulousness are popular images of corporate offenders (Langan 1996). Such explanations are tempting in cases such as Robert Maxwell. Even Punch, despite his main emphasis on organisational factors, nevertheless states (1996: 233) that:

> Certain personality types make it into corporate leadership where their dominating style – related to power, control and egoism – can lead to rule-breaking by themselves, or by subordinates on their behalf. Of course, psychotic megalomaniacs are not confined to business …

Babiak and Hare (2006) offer a more extreme explanation in their character-isation of some business executives as psychopaths. But leaving aside the controversy over the term psychopath, simply identifying greed as the cause begs more questions than it answers. Why are some executives greedy and not others? Why do some break the law for the benefit of their employers and others steal from them? Why do corporations not restrain the activities of such individuals? The fact is that individual explanations inevitably overlook the organisational context which allows or provides the opportunity for the dishonest or misguided individual to break rules.

Hamilton and Micklethwait (2006) do blame corporate failure on greed, hubris and the desire for power, asserting (2006: 4) that: 'People tend to be naturally greedy, rarely content with what they have achieved' and that chief executive officers may be allowed to dominate: '... sometimes maverick behaviour [is] excused in order not to disturb the profit-making genius.' But they use a series of case studies to go beyond individual factors and set them in a broader explanation of business failure (it should be noted that not all their cases involved criminal activities). Companies also failed because of poor strategic decision-making, over-expansion and ill-judged acquisitions, ineffectual or ineffective boards of directors and, ultimately, the failure of internal controls at all levels. Some of these factors were clearly present in cases such as Enron and Barings.

Capitalism is criminogenic

Before moving on to theories derived from studies of organisational behaviour, mention must be made of those who argue that corporate crime is embedded in capitalist societies. Pearce (1976) and Slapper and Tombs (1999) write from an avowedly socialist perspective, according to which capitalism is criminogenic because corporations put profits before all other considerations such as honesty or the welfare of consumers or employees. Generally, radical writers in the 1970s and 1980s argued that companies will turn to crime when profitability is threatened. To some extent, this echoes Box's (1983) application of anomie to corporations but it is more openly political, with the implicit assumption that such things would not happen in a socialist society.

Glasbeek (2002, 2007) also links corporate power to crime, although from a slightly less explicitly political perspective. In his view, the corporation as a legal entity exists mainly to protect the owners from responsibility for their actions and misdeeds:

> ... the corporation is a device that irresponsible profiteers use to their benefit, because through it they can avoid being subjugated to the norms and the values that the rest of us have to accept. (Glasbeek 2002: 177)

The very same diffusion and delegation of responsibility which underpins efficiency also enables owners to avoid blame. He goes on to say that corporations are criminogenic because they are 'legally constructed so as to become a site of irresponsibility and, thereby, criminogenic' (2002: 142, emphasis in the original). Furthermore, in large corporations, internal structures make deviance logical in pursuit of profit regardless of any costs. Deviance may start as recklessness or carelessness, but is then concealed by lying; more often, however, it is planned. Corporations are rational calculators and the capitalist agenda is criminogenic.

This argument seems to imply that only capitalism generates crime within its organisational forms. Clearly, this is not consistent with history. In fairness, Snider (1993), while arguing that capitalism is criminogenic, acknowledges that so are feudalism and socialism, albeit in different ways. The problem with capitalism is that everything is valued purely in economic terms, the process of commodification. Capitalism is based on exploitation of workers and requires everyone to be ruthless and impersonal and pursue self-interest single-mindedly. So while it is very successful at generating a high standard of living, it also generates widespread corporate crime.

Leaving aside the existence of crime in other forms of society, the assertion that corporations are amoral rational calculators is the weakest point of these radical explanations of corporate crime. Although it is a feature of some economic models of the corporation, the rational actor model is far too simplistic to explain corporate decision-making. As will be seen in the following discussion, decision-making is a far more complex process, influenced by the availability of information and the internal processes and structures of the organisation.

The organisational context

An important insight into the behaviour of managers in large corporations is given by Jackall (1988). Although not concerned with corporate misconduct, his work nevertheless is a necessary corrective to theories based on the rational actor model. Jackall's study, based on interviews with over 100 managers in American corporations, shows that modern managers' priority in their work is usually to please their superior(s). Their short-term aim is not to increase profits but to secure their own position. He quotes a former vice-president of a large firm:

> What is right in the corporation is not what is right in a man's home or his church. *What is right in the corporation is what the guy above you wants from you.* That's what morality is in the corporation. (1988: 6, emphasis in the original)

As an example, he records that if a company's chief executive officer is due to visit one of the company's plants, the whole plant may be painted and a special book of photographs and illustrations costing thousands of dollars prepared as a memento for him – an irrational expenditure apparently, but one that makes sense according to the corporate social standards.

Generally, Jackall (1988) argues that managers are driven by expediency. In all the corporations he studied, managers saw themselves as under siege – from environmentalists, from regulators, from labour activists, etc. – and they responded by caricaturing all their critics. They learn 'dexterity with symbols' – that is, they find the right way to present things, knowing what can and cannot be said. He thus convincingly portrays a world which is very far removed from the supposition that all corporate decisions are based on fully-informed, rational strategies designed to maximise profits.

It is also necessary here to introduce the concept of *bounded rationality* (Simon 1957) as another corrective to the model of corporations as rational actors. The rational actor model assumes that all the information necessary to make a fully rational decision is always available, but the reality is that decision-makers may be confronted with more information than they can assimilate, or alternatively, that information is diffused around the organisation and is not all available when and where needed. Consequently, decision-makers do not maximise but *satisfice*, to use Simon's term: they settle for solutions which are 'good enough'. Simon also makes another important point about decision-makers in large organisations, that they make their decisions with one eye on the decision itself and the other on its organisational consequences.

These more realistic representations of corporate life inform the work of a number of recent writers who have applied them to the study of corporate crime. Chief among these are Punch (1996) and Gobert and Punch (2007). Punch focuses on the pressures which push managers in large organisations into misconduct (1996: 67–8):

> An underlying assumption is that *pressure* – to get work done, to deliver the goods, to bring in a contract, to raise economic performance, to achieve financial goals, and to amass personal fortunes – in some way generates motivation and willingness to break or bend rules and the law.

Punch (1996: 239) further argues that 'the condition of work shapes moral consciousness and [...] ordinary people are induced in an organisational setting to violate laws and rules ...' Business deviance has to be considered in terms of the opportunities, means, incentives and rationalisations that companies provide (Punch 1996; Gobert and Punch 2007). Gobert and Punch (2007) identify three categories of misconduct: deliberate and conscious wrongdoing such as price-fixing, fraudulent accounting and tax evasion; conscious actions with unintended outcomes and 'hidden illegality', as in the case of Barings Bank; and situations in which the law is ambiguous and offenders deny law-breaking, such as the Guinness case where previous experience may have led some of the perpetrators to believe that their actions were legal. But all of these have to be seen in the context of the pressures to which Punch alludes. And this is not restricted to capitalist enterprises; Punch (1996: 223) suggests that the evidence is that

> ... it could be argued that all organizations – capitalist or socialist, governmental or private – experience pressure to resort to illegal means of goal attainment when legitimate means are blocked ...

Explanations that deal with the organisational pressures clearly have a great deal to offer, given the debate referred to earlier about corporate versus individual responsibility. Of course, individuals respond in different ways and it is possible that the most fruitful way forward in deepening our understanding of corporate misconduct will be to combine understanding of the organisational context with understanding of the reasons why some individuals resist pressures and temptations and others do not.

Responses

There is no consensus on the most effective response to corporate crime. As noted above, radical criminologists regard capitalism as criminogenic per se and see major structural change in society as the only answer. Short of this, the main argument is between those who favour *compliance* – regulatory agencies working in partnership with business to improve standards by education and persuasion – and those who advocate *coercion* – the use of prosecution and severe sanctions in the criminal or civil courts to deter offending. To some extent, these two camps are influenced by their beliefs about the causes: those who follow the rational actor model are likely to advocate deterrence on the grounds that corporations and the individuals who work in them weigh up the consequences of wrongdoing as part of their decision-making process and will be deterred by the threat of severe sanctions, while those who stress the organisational context of misconduct believe that improvements in knowledge and ethical awareness will change business behaviour. In recent years, however, conservative and radical thinkers have both tended to call for increased sanctions, the former in line with their support for harsher penalties for conventional crimes and the latter in line with their conviction that powerful corporations and individuals have been escaping their due punishment (Simpson 2002).

Deterrence and punitive strategies

Those who favour the deterrence argument often seem to take it for granted that corporations (or those who run them) are rational actors and can therefore be deterred by the threat of sanctions. For the Harvard Law Review (1979), the choice is merely between criminal and civil action. In their view, civil sanctions are more appropriate because what is being punished is 'not in and of itself morally blameworthy, and indeed in some cases [there is] an absence of fault' (1979: 1369).[5] The only problem was that current penalties were not sufficient but larger civil penalties would be both appropriate and effective.

Coffee (1981) also looks at deterrence but notes that it does not appear to work because the rational calculator model is so inaccurate. Companies do not know the consequences, may not realise they are breaking the law or may calculate that the potential penalties are small and it is worth the risk, while for the individual managers involved, the fear of losing their jobs may outweigh the risks. In addition, the financial costs usually fall on shareholders, employees and consumers rather than the firm itself, and it is possible that judges mitigate penalties to avoid harming the corporation. Rather than abandon deterrence, however, Coffee suggests ways of making it work better such as equity fines (requiring the company to give the government a stake in its shares) and adverse publicity aimed at the culpable officers rather than the company as a whole. He also discusses civil actions which often cost companies more than criminal cases and looks at incentives for people to sue, although success usually depends on some form of prior formal action as proof of damage. All these measures, in his view, would increase corporate deterrence without serious social consequences.

Davis's (2004) review of research on the impact of different responses, mainly based on surveys of managers' motivations, focused on health and safety matters but it is reasonable to suppose that the findings may also be applied to financial offences. She concluded firmly that the evidence was in favour of the use of legal sanctions as it was the threat of such penalties that weighed most heavily with managers and was therefore most likely to affect their decisions. Russell and Gilbert (1999) also draw on studies of managers' behaviour but reach a less firm conclusion, suggesting that deterrence can work, but only in certain circumstances. Criminal sanctions appear to operate by increasing executives' perception of risk to the corporation and by providing a greater sense of personal liability for corporate crime among executives. They also have an impact on executives who are less restrained by a personal sense of shame and need the threat of formal sanctions to influence their decisions. This suggests that a uniform approach is not appropriate; but how are regulatory and sentencing authorities to know what will work, and could an individualised approach be fair?

Simpson (2002) noted a trend towards greater use of criminal courts in the USA[6] but her review of the evidence on deterrence suggests that it is weak. There has been little research specifically about the effectiveness of deterrence in restraining corporate behaviour and the findings, though somewhat inconsistent, suggest that other factors such as informal sanctions (including disapproval from colleagues, friends and family) are more important than formal sanctions. Her own research used vignettes with postgraduate management students and suggested that offending decisions are complex and mostly personal (based on consideration of morals, shame and personal gain) but also take into account the organisational context of such controls whether they are following instructions, or the risk to the organisation's reputation. Managers do feel protected from the law by the impenetrable facade of the corporation but they also fear formal legal sanctions. There was support for informal controls but also for ethics and self-regulation. Like Russell and Gilbert (1999), Simpson concluded that there are also differences between individuals – some respond to persuasion, some to punishment.

Simpson (2002) also considers more broadly the reasons why deterrence appears not to work. In common with Box (1983), she points out that the chances of getting caught and punished are very small (in this respect, corporate crime is actually very similar to most conventional crimes). But she also refers to the nature of organisations and the problems of group decision-making as discussed above, and also the problems of changing staff who are uninformed about the impact of sanctions. She considers that insufficient thought has been given to whether deterrent policies should be aimed at individuals or the corporation as a whole. And while some writers hold that corporations should be forced to publicise their convictions[7] because they will be deterred by the thought of the damage to their reputations, the low likelihood of prosecution must limit the potential impact of such scandal and disgrace, and even where companies have been publicly shamed, the effect seems very limited (Box 1983). The same argument can be applied to the idea that criminal sanctions will achieve more because they stigmatise the offender in a way that civil or administrative penalties do not. There is, however, a persuasive moral argument in favour of employing criminal sanctions purely in order to make a symbolic statement of social disapproval – and indeed to emphasise that there is no reason why corporate dishonesty should be met with less disapproval than other forms of dishonesty (Wells 2001).

There are pragmatic reasons, though, for favouring alternatives to criminal prosecution. Corporate financial crimes are often complex, expensive to prosecute and difficult to prove (Simpson 2002). Civil and administrative remedies may be swifter, more focused on the needs of the victims and easier to conclude. Corporations have access to expert legal advice and may contest criminal charges but be willing to negotiate with regulators in less formal, less accusatory procedures.[8] Furthermore, Makkai and Braithwaite (1994), in their study of the regulation of Australian nursing homes, suggest that punitive enforcement risks reducing respect for the law and regulators which would be counterproductive. Capitalist economies also depend on business being profitable, so governments also have to balance their desire to control business behaviour against the need to encourage business and foster a thriving economy (Punch 1996).

Compliance

Regulatory agencies may choose to avoid confrontational and coercive stances and rely instead on compliance. Punch (1996: 83) defines compliance as 'encouraging and stimulating corporations to conform to the rules, and investing in self-regulation as a matter of self-interest, rather than having controls imposed from the outside' and suggests that it may work better than regulation by outside agencies. Self-regulation relies on corporations taking responsibility for their own conduct; in return for satisfying regulators that they have robust procedures in place to discourage misconduct and take firm action if they discover it, they may be offered a lighter touch regime of inspection and oversight by the regulatory agencies. Many corporations have adopted Codes of Ethics which are publicised to all employees as evidence of good intentions. There are a number of writers who focus on such aspects of corporate culture, most of them arguing that the key to prevention is strong ethical leadership. Clinard (1983), drawing on his interviews with retired middle managers from large American corporations, concluded that prevention is better than cure and highlighted the importance of strong ethical control from top managers; they must adopt high standards and make them clear to everyone else in the firm. This needs to be combined with frequent issuing of guidelines on regulation, compliance checks and training on ethics and regulations for middle managers.

Sonnenfeld and Lawrence (1978) also focused on the potential of internal controls. They blamed the problem of price-fixing partly on market conditions and argued that companies should choose legitimate responses such as pulling out of unprofitable markets. But they also emphasised the need for tighter central oversight over decisions, better legal training and proactive legal departments, and a clearer code of ethics and leadership from the top. Anand *et al.* (2004) reached similar conclusions, suggesting the fostering of awareness among employees, but also added that their performance should be evaluated not only on whether they achieved their targets but also how they achieved them. They too stress the importance of an ethical environment and good role modelling by top management.

There are, of course, sceptical views on the power of ethics and ethical codes to improve business behaviour. Allinson (2008) regards the term 'business ethics' as an oxymoron: how can a capitalist corporation prioritise ethics when it must always choose the most profitable option? Glasbeek (2002, 2007) similarly asserts that attempts to change the behaviour of corporations by making them more socially responsible are doomed because they contradict the fundamental nature of the corporation. For him, too, the problem is with capitalism itself, though he stops short of advocating revolution and argues instead for the democratisation of corporations, with greater participation by workers and small shareholders.

The Harvard Law Review (2003) also reviews the potential of corporate codes of ethics which have become very popular in the United States. The incentive for good codes, made available to the public, is said to be that investors and customers will favour firms they think they can trust. But they predict that companies will simply write nebulous codes so that it will be difficult to prove that they have breached them. However, this argument seems to overlook the role of regulators in overseeing the content of codes. A more worrying observation comes from Punch (1996: x) who relates his experiences in teaching postgraduate management students; they all professed to be in favour of ethical behaviour in principle but when given simulated cases to role play, their ethics deserted them and they favoured the risky options.

The most cogent response to this problem comes from the writing of Braithwaite, set out especially in the book by Fisse and Braithwaite (1993) which argues for an enforced self-regulation model. Every firm must have compliance procedures which are externally approved, with effective internal systems supported by top management and effective communication and training. The crux of their ideas is the oft-cited 'pyramid of enforcement'. Under this model, companies that breach rules infrequently and in minor ways may be treated leniently, while severe sanctions are reserved for those which offend seriously, blatantly and repeatedly. These principles have been incorporated into American sentencing guidelines: companies that have reasonable compliance systems may have sentences reduced and those that do not may be put on probation with a requirement to develop one. As Simpson (2002) notes, Braithwaite acknowledges that there are problems with his proposals but his belief in the power of informal social control exerted by conscience, values and fear of shame outweighs them. She concludes (2002: 102) that self-regulation is 'an idea whose time has come'. Less convinced is Snider (1993) who argues that the problem with current laws is not that they do not exist but that they are weakly enforced, so she doubts that a regime based on compliance will be any more effective.

Conclusion

Corporate financial crimes deserve far more attention from policymakers and agents of criminal justice. The financial losses to the victims and the potential threat to the integrity and success of the economy demand a response at least equal to that given to conventional crimes. Criminology too needs to focus more on developing theoretical explanations of the causes, in order to lend stronger underpinning to efforts to prevent corporate misconduct. In particular, more consideration needs to be given to developing understanding of the way that organisations influence and control the behaviour of those who work in them, which is surely crucial to understanding this phenomenon. Furthermore, the study of how corporate actors respond to institutional pressures may help us to learn about the behaviour of conventional offenders, many of whom are also subject to pressure from their peers and the groups and cultures to which they belong. Thus Sutherland's intention that criminology should be changed by the study of the crimes of people of high status may yet be achieved, albeit with a different theoretical perspective.[9]

Selected further reading

There are few texts which focus specifically on corporate financial crimes as opposed to corporate misconduct generally, so texts recommended here may overlap with those suggested elsewhere in this volume.

Despite its age, Box's *Power, Crime and Mystification* (1983) is still an inspirational text, covering corporate crime in the course of an incisive exposé of the crimes of the powerful. Punch's *Dirty Business: Exploring Corporate Misconduct* (1996), while less colourful, nevertheless combines detailed and illuminating case studies with penetrating theoretical analysis. Slapper and Tombs cover much of the same ground in their *Corporate Crime* (1999) though from a more avowedly socialist perspective. Two recent edited collections which include chapters on corporate financial crimes as well as a general discussion of theory and related issues are Minkes and Minkes's *Corporate and White-Collar Crime* (2008) and Pontell and Geis's much lengthier *International Handbook of White-Collar and Corporate Crime* (2007). The former advocates a multidisciplinary approach to the understanding of corporate misconduct while those interested in the legal aspects of corporate crime will find Wells's *Corporations and Criminal Responsibility* (2001) and Gobert and Punch's *Rethinking Corporate Crime* (2003) essential if sometimes challenging reading. Two other academic disciplines are represented by the organisational sociologist Jackall's *Moral Mazes: The World of Corporate Managers* (1988), a fascinating account of corporate life in America, and Hamilton and Micklethwait's *Greed and Corporate Failure* (2006), a series of case studies written primarily from a management and accounting perspective.

Notes

1 Corporations are, of course, also involved in breaches of health and safety rules and environmental regulations (see Chapters 43 and 44) but this chapter is concerned solely with financial crimes.
2 See, for example, BBC News (2008a). British responses have tended to focus on the 'culture of greed' rather than alleging criminality (e.g. Treanor 2009).
3 Baron Thurlow was Lord Chancellor from 1778 to 1792. The comment is very widely cited, in particular by Coffee (1981) who took it for the title of his article, though there is apparently some doubt about its provenance (Nicholls 2005). Some British legislation permits prosecution of corporations, most notably the recent Corporate Manslaughter and Corporate Homicide Act 2007, but this relates solely to health and safety issues.
4 Box (in common with some other writers making similar points) refers here to Merton's theory of 'anomie', but it might have been more accurate to use the term 'strain theory'. In Merton's writings, anomie usually refers to a de-institutionalisation of norms (a state of 'normlessness') that occurs when there is a disjunction between cultural goals and institutional means, while his strain theory explains deviant behaviour by arguing that people are more likely to pursue illegitimate means to attain culturally prescribed goals when they are blocked from accessing the institutionalised means to these goals (see Featherstone and Deflem 2003).
5 Presumably they have in mind offences of strict liability, where guilt does not depend on intention. However, these often involve negligence, which some commentators (e.g. Reiman 2006) regard as potentially just as blameworthy as deliberate actions.
6 Had she been writing after the sentencing in the Enron and other cases, she might also have noted a trend to wards more punitive sentences as well. American courts have consistently taken a tougher line with convicted corporate offenders than British courts but it is unclear whether their aim is deterrence or simply retribution.
7 The Corporate Manslaughter and Corporate Homicide Act 2007 gives courts in England and Wales and Scotland power to order this but only in respect of manslaughter. There have as yet been no convictions under this legislation.
8 A recent example of this is the case of Balfour Beatty who agreed to pay £2.25 million to settle bribery allegations relating to an overseas contract. The payment followed a three-year investigation by the Serious Fraud Office (SFO) which stated: 'By proceeding in this way, the SFO has been able to impose a significant sanction on a major UK company whilst avoiding the extensive cost to the public purse of lengthy court proceedings' (Leigh and Evans 2008).
9 I am grateful to Professor Leonard Minkes for his comments on the first draft of this chapter, especially in relation to the concept of satisficing and the work of H. A. Simon.

References

Allinson, R. E. (2008) 'The foundation of business ethics', in J. Minkes and L. Minkes (eds), *Corporate and White-Collar Crime*. London: Sage.
Anand, V., Ashforth, B. and Joshi, M. (2004) 'Business as usual: the acceptance and perpetuation of corruption in organizations', *Academy of Management Executive*, 18 (2): 39–53.

Babiak, P. and Hare, R. (2006) *Snakes in Suits: When Psychopaths Go to Work*. New York: HarperCollins.

BBC News (2008a) *FBI Investigates Sub-prime Crisis*. Online at: http://news.bbc.co.uk/1/hi/business/7216602.stm (accessed 23 March 2009).

BBC News (2008b) *Record Fine for PPI Mis-selling*. Online at: http://news.bbc.co.uk/1/hi/business/7657446.stm (accessed 8 October 2008).

BBC News (2008c) *Record Fine over BBC's Phone-ins*. Online at: http://news.bbc.co.uk/1/hi/entertainment/7497168.stm (accessed 30 July 2008).

Box, S. (1983) *Power, Crime and Mystification*. London: Tavistock.

Calavita, K. and Pontell, H. (1990) 'Savings and Loan fraud as organized crime: towards a conceptual typology of corporate illegality', *Criminology*, 31 (4): 519–48.

Clinard, M. B. (1983) *Corporate Ethics and Crime*. Beverley Hills, CA: Sage.

Clinard, M. B. and Yeager, P. C. (1980) *Corporate Crime*. New York: Free Press.

Coates, J. M. and Herbert, J. (2008) 'Endogenous steroids and financial risk taking in London trading floor', *National Academy of Sciences of the USA*, 104 (16): 6167–72.

Coffee, J. C. (1981) '"No soul to damn – no body to kick?": an unscandalized inquiry into the problem of corporate punishment', *Michigan Law Review*, 79: 386–459.

Cruver, B. (2003) *Anatomy of Greed: The Unshredded Truth from an Enron Insider*. New York: Carroll & Graf.

Davis, C. (2004) *Making Companies Safe: What Works?* London: Centre for Corporate Accountability.

Dodge, M. (2007) 'From pink to white with various shades of embezzlement: women who commit white-collar crimes', in H. N. Pontell and G. Geis (eds), *International Handbook of White-Collar and Corporate Crime*. New York: Springer.

Doig, A. (2006) *Fraud*. Cullompton: Willan.

Featherstone, M. and Deflem, M. (2003) 'Anomie and strain: context and consequences of Merton's two theories', *Sociological Inquiry*, 73 (4): 471–89.

Fisse, B. and Braithwaite, J. (1993) *Corporations, Crime and Accountability*. Cambridge: Cambridge University Press.

Geis, G. (1967) 'White-collar crime: the heavy electrical equipment antitrust cases of 1961', in M. B. Clinard and R. Quinney (1967) *Criminal Behavior Systems: A Typology*. New York: Holt, Rinehart & Winston.

Geis, G. and Goff, C. (1983) 'Introduction', to E. Sutherland (1983) *White Collar Crime: The Uncut Version*. New York: Yale University Press.

Glasbeek, H. (2002) *Wealth by Stealth: Corporate Crime, Corporate Law and the Perversion of Democracy*. Toronto: Between the Lines.

Glasbeek, H. (2007) 'The corporation as a legally created site of irresponsibility', in H. N. Pontell and G. Geis (eds), *International Handbook of White-Collar and Corporate Crime*. New York: Springer.

Gobert, J. (2008) 'The evolving legal test of corporate liability', in J. Minkes and L. Minkes (eds), *Corporate and White-Collar Crime*. London: Sage.

Gobert, J. and Punch, M. (2003) *Rethinking Corporate Crime*. Cambridge: Cambridge University Press.

Gobert, J. and Punch, M. (2007) 'Because they can: motivations and intent of white-collar criminals', in H. N. Pontell and G. Geis (eds), *International Handbook of White-Collar and Corporate Crime*. New York: Springer.

Gottfredson, M. R. and Hirschi, T. (1990) *A General Theory of Crime*. Stanford, CA: Stanford University Press.

Hamilton, S. and Micklethwait, A. (2006) *Greed and Corporate Failure*. Basingstoke: Palgrave Macmillan.

Harding, C. (2007) *Criminal Enterprise: Individuals, Organisations and Criminal Responsibility*. Cullompton: Willan.

Harvard Law Review (1979) 'Developments in the law – corporate crime: regulating corporate behavior through criminal sanctions', *Harvard Law Review*, 92 (6): 1227–375.

Harvard Law Review (2003) 'The good, the bad and their corporate codes of ethics: Enron, Sarbanes-Oxley and the problems with legislating good behaviour', *Harvard Law Review*, 116: 2123–41.

Hillyard, P., Pantazis, C., Tombs, S., Gordon D. and Dorling, D. (2004) *Criminal Obsessions*. London: Crime and Society Foundation.

Hopkins Burke, R. (2001) *An Introduction to Criminological Theory*. Cullompton: Willan.

Iacocca, L. (with William Novak) (1984) *Iacocca: An Autobiography*. New York: Bantam Books.

J. Sainsbury plc (2007) *Company News: OFT Dairy Investigation Concluded*. Online at: http://www.j-sainsbury.com/index.asp?PageID=418andsubsection=andYear=2007an dNewsID=996 (accessed 30 July 2008).

Jackall, R. (1988) *Moral Mazes: The World of Corporate Managers*. New York and London: Oxford University Press.

Kellens, G., Dantinne, M. and Demonceau, B. (2007) 'Enron, Lemont and Hauspie and Parmalat: comparative case studies', in H. N. Pontell and G. Geis (eds), *International Handbook of White-Collar and Corporate Crime*. New York: Springer.

Kochan, N. and Pym, H. (1987) *The Guinness Affair: Anatomy of a Scandal*. London: Christopher Helm.

Langan, M. (1996) 'Hidden and respectable: crime and the market', in J. Muncie and E. McLaughlin (eds), *The Problem of Crime*. London: Sage/Open University.

Leigh, D. and Evans, R. (2008) 'Balfour Beatty agrees to pay £2.25m over allegations of bribery in Egypt', *The Guardian*, 7 October. Online at: http://www.guardian.co.uk/business/2008/oct07/balfourbeatty.egypt (accessed 7 October 2008).

Loasby, B. (2008) 'Organizational decision-making: economic and managerial considerations', in J. Minkes and L. Minkes (eds), *Corporate and White-Collar Crime*. London: Sage.

Maguire, M. (2007) 'Crime data and statistics', in M. Maguire, R. Morgan and R. Reiner (eds), *The Oxford Handbook of Criminology*, 4th edn. Oxford: Oxford University Press.

Makkai, T. and Braithwaite, J. (1994) 'Reintegrative shaming and compliance with regulatory standards', *Criminology*, 32: 361–86.

Minkes, J. and Minkes, L. (2005) 'Decentralisation, responsibility and ethical dilemmas', *Social Responsibility*, 1 (1/2): 16–20.

Minkes, J. and Minkes, L. (eds) (2008) *Corporate and White-Collar Crime*. London: Sage.

Nelken, D. (2007) 'White-collar crime', in M. Maguire, R. Morgan and R. Reiner (eds), *The Oxford Handbook of Criminology*, 4th edn. Oxford: Oxford University Press.

Newton, L. H. (2006) *Permission to Steal*. Maldon, MA: Blackwell.

Nicholls, C. (2005) *Corporate Law*. Toronto: Emond Montgomery.

Office of Fair Trading (OFT) (2007) 'OFT welcomes early resolution agreements and agrees over £116m penalties'. Online at: http://www.oft.gov.uk/news/press/2007170-07 (accessed 4 April 2008).

Pearce, F. (1976) *Crimes of the Powerful*. London: Pluto Press.

Pontell, H. N. and Geis, G. (2007) *International Handbook of White-Collar and Corporate Crime*. New York: Springer.

Punch, M. (1996) *Dirty Business: Exploring Corporate Misconduct*. London: Sage.

Punch, M. (2008) 'The organization did it: individuals, corporations and crime', in J. Minkes and L. Minkes (eds), *Corporate and White-Collar Crime*. London: Sage.

Reiman, J. (2006) *The Rich Get Rich and the Poor Get Prison*, 7th edn. New York: Allyn & Bacon.

Robb, G. (1992) *White-collar Crime in Modern England: Financial Fraud and Business Morality 1845–1929*. Cambridge: Cambridge University Press.

Russell, S. and Gilbert, M. (1999) 'Truman's revenge: social control and corporate crime', *Crime, Law and Social Change*, 32: 59–82.

Shover, N. (2007) 'Generative worlds of white-collar crime', in H. N. Pontell and G. Geis (eds), *International Handbook of White-Collar and Corporate Crime*. New York: Springer.

Simon, H. A. (1957) *Administrative Behaviour*, 2nd edn. New York/London: Free Press/Collier Macmillan.

Simpson, S. (2002) *Corporate Crime, Law and Social Control*. Cambridge: Cambridge University Press.

Slapper, G. and Tombs, S. (1999) *Corporate Crime*. Harlow: Longman.

Snider, L. (1993) *Bad Business: Corporate Crime in Canada*. Scarborough, Ont.: Nelson.

Snider, L. (2007) '"This time we really mean it": cracking down on stock market fraud', in H. N. Pontell and G. Geis (eds), *International Handbook of White-Collar and Corporate Crime*. New York: Springer.

Snider, L. (2008) 'Corporate economic crimes', in J. Minkes and L. Minkes (eds), *Corporate and White-Collar Crime*. London: Sage.

Sonnenfeld, J. and Lawrence, P. (1978) 'Why do companies succumb to price-fixing?', *Harvard Business Review*, 56 (4): 145–57.

Sutherland, E. (1940) 'White collar criminality', *American Sociological Review*, 5 (1): 1–12.

Sutherland, E. (1949) *White-collar Crime*. New York: Yale University Press; reprinted (1983) as *White-Collar Crime: The Uncut Version*.

Sykes, G. and Matza, D. (1957) 'Techniques of neutralization: a theory of delinquency', *American Sociological Review*, 22: 664–70.

Tappan, P. W. (1947) 'Who is the criminal?', *American Sociological Review*, 12: 96–102.

The Times (1996) 'Maxwell brothers are cleared; what they said about outcome of the hearing', 20 January, p. 1.

Tombs, S. and Whyte, D. (2002) 'Unmasking the crimes of the powerful', *Critical Criminology*, 11: 217–36.

Treanor, J. (2009) 'Regulator under pressure to investigate "culture of greed" at RBS', *The Guardian*, 22 March. Online at: http://www.guardian.co.uk/business/2009/mar/22/royalbankofscotlandgroup-sir-fred-goodwin (accessed 24 March 2009).

Weisburd, D. and Waring, E. with Chayet, E. (2001) *White-Collar Crime and Criminal Careers*. Cambridge: Cambridge University Press.

Weisburd, D., Waring, E. and Piquero, N. (2008) 'Getting beyond the moral drama of crime: what we learn from studying white-collar criminal careers', in J. Minkes and L. Minkes (eds), *Corporate and White-Collar Crime*. London: Sage.

Wells, C. (2001) *Corporations and Criminal Responsibility*. Oxford: Oxford University Press.

Chapter 33

Middle-range business crime: rogue and respectable businesses, family firms and entrepreneurs

Hazel Croall

This chapter will focus on a group of crimes often rendered invisible by being subsumed into categories of organised, corporate or white-collar crime. While most often associated with large corporations and elite offenders, with 'Mr Bigs' and large criminal cartels, these categories contain many offences committed by or within smaller and medium-size businesses, 'family firms' and crime enterprises. The chapter will start by looking at how this area of crime can be conceptualised and researched before detailing examples of offences and offenders and their impact on victims. It will then explore issues of analysis and regulation.

Defining and conceptualising 'middle-range business crimes'

'Middle range business crime' is not a widely recognised criminological category and is not found in standard criminological texts such as *The Sage Dictionary of Criminology* (McLaughlin and Muncie 2005) or *The Oxford Handbook of Criminology* (Maguire *et al.* 2007). Google searches produce references to 'middle market drug distribution' which lies in between importation and street level drugs,[1] and to Karstedt and Farrall's (2006) work on the everyday crimes of the middle classes lying in between 'street' and 'suite' crime. 'Middle' can therefore refer to status or function, but also to size, thus directing attention to the often misunderstood term 'business crime'. This has variously been used to refer to crimes *against* and crimes committed *by* businesses, and indeed to 'criminal businesses', confusions which have generally discouraged its use (Croall 2001a).

The offences of small and medium businesses are generally located, if not always highlighted, in work on the more widely recognised areas of white-collar, corporate, organised or enterprise crimes, sometimes described as economic crime. This involves a conceptual minefield, as the definitions of all of these areas, and the borderlines between them, are highly contested (Croall 2001a; Wright 2006; Levi 2007; Nelken 2007). Many difficulties go back to the pioneering work of Sutherland (1949) who distinguished between *white-collar* crime, associated with offenders of 'respectable' social status in the course of their legitimate occupations, and the activities of the largely 'non-respectable' offenders engaged in *'professional'* and 'organized' crime. These definitions include characteristics of both offences and offenders, activities and actors (Croall 2001a; Ruggiero 1996, 2000) and in essence distinguish between two major categories of crime on the basis of the 'respectability' (however this could be defined) of offenders and the legitimacy of their activities. This has proved a difficult distinction to maintain with further issues arising out of the popular and criminological association of both kinds of crime with 'big business' in the form of large, multinational corporations or the Mafia and large criminal cartels.

A number of empirical studies nonetheless suggest that a sizeable proportion of these kinds of crime are associated with smaller and medium-size enterprises. Much so called 'white-collar' crime has been shown to involve lower middle-class offenders (Weisburd *et al.* 1991), and many offenders implicated in 'corporate' crime (such as environmental, safety or consumer crime – see Tombs this volume, and Minkes this volume) are directors or employees of smaller businesses, including, for example, farmers (Smith 2004, 2009a), bakers, butchers or builders (Croall 1989; 2001b). As well as challenging the mythology of 'Mr Bigs' and the Mafia, many now question the concept of organised crime itself, arguing that it can be described more accurately as disorganised crime, being characterised by loosely organised networks of smaller firms, 'family firms' (Hobbs 2002), criminal enterprises or crime entrepreneurs (van Duyne 2003; Wright 2006; Levi 2007).

It is also difficult to draw any clear lines between legitimate and illegitimate businesses or markets, with some commentators arguing that there is little distinction as they all seek to enhance profits by breaking, neglecting or avoiding the law. The offenders involved (which may be individuals or the business as an entity) differ from so called 'conventional' criminals in respect of their continuing organisation around these goals and the non-predatory but profit-seeking nature of their crimes (Naylor 2003). All businesses have to develop a division of labour and relationships with producers, suppliers and consumers (Levi 2007), and distinctions between 'shady', unfair and illegal practices are blurred (Karstedt *et al.* 2006). Many writers in this field find the concept of *entrepreneurship* useful, although difficult to define. It has, however, been associated with exploiting gaps in markets, either legally or illegally, and providing a desired service on a more or less regular basis (Smith 2009b). It has for long been associated with innovative and 'maverick' or 'sharp' business practices, straddling and often challenging the borderline between legitimacy and criminality (Ruggiero 1996) and operating on the frontiers of the permissible (Smith 2004).

Moreover, some markets and individual businesses encompass both legitimate and illegitimate activities. What would be regarded as unambiguously 'fraudulent' businesses, such as those set up to perpetrate long firm frauds, use legitimate fronts as a cover to attract customers and obtain goods, while legitimate businesses owned by professional criminals are a crucial vehicle for money laundering. Ruggiero (1996) argues that organised crime can provide a service to legitimate enterprises as is the case, for example, with waste dumping, the provision of illegal labour and supplying illegal goods. Legitimate industries in turn provide services to organised crime by, for example, enabling money laundering, and there are also joint enterprises.

It is extremely difficult therefore to delineate tight boundaries between legal and illegal businesses and this, largely exploratory, chapter will adopt an inclusive approach by incorporating both. A hard and fast definition of 'middle-range business crime' will not be offered, in part to avoid adding to the plethora of confusing definitions. In common with customarily used, if often criticised, definitions of organised crime, it will include the activities of businesses which have continuing operations involving the same group of people, or which have a sizeable turnover and which are distinct from 'one-off' projects (Wright 2006; Levi 2007). It will include what would be described as small or medium-size legitimate businesses, defined by a combination of: their primarily local and regional as opposed to national and multinational operations; the employment of some staff (normally up to 250); and/or having a sizeable turnover or number of customers. It will include small business 'firms' set up with primarily 'criminal' intent, along with those whose activities cut across conventional dividing lines of the legal and illegal. It will also include the activities of offenders – often described as crime entrepreneurs – who can be located between 'low-level' participants in the criminal labour market and larger, 'serious' criminal businesses (Hobbs 2002; Hornsby and Hobbs 2007).

Research issues and assessing trends and patterns

It is extremely difficult to assess trends and patterns for this group of crimes, particularly in view of its relative invisibility and its failure to be recognised as a 'crime' problem. It shares all the research problems widely associated with the study of organised, white-collar and corporate crime (Slapper and Tombs 1999; Croall 2001b; Tombs and Whyte 2003). Apart from difficulties of obtaining research funding and access, crimes in this area are not included in standard victim surveys such as the British Crime Survey and there is no central information source.

Many offences are not reported as 'crime' for a variety of reasons. Offences which involve health and safety, environmental or consumer regulations are difficult to detect by the general public who often cannot judge for themselves the contents or safety of food or mass produced goods or the risks associated with air or water. Other offences, such as the systematic sale of underweight goods by small amounts, have, as Sutherland (1949) pointed out, a 'rippling effect' in which individual victims lose very little. In offences where victims are aware of harm, they may not define it as crime or report it to relevant authorities. A host of different enforcement agencies are involved and complainants may be unsure of their responsibilities. Other offences involve the sale of largely illegal goods or services or cheap goods for which there is high demand. These are effectively crimes without victims, with low reporting rates. In yet other offences, ranging from serious fraud to situations in which victims feel 'conned' or 'ripped off', they may be unwilling to complain, feeling embarrassed or that they are themselves to blame (see Mackenzie this volume).

Where cases are reported to enforcers, they may not be counted as 'crimes' but as 'complaints' or, as is the case with health and safety, as injuries or fatalities (Tombs 2000, and this volume), not all of which are offences. As Tombs argues, reaching any reliable estimate of offences leading to workplace deaths would involve reading across a wide range of statistics and estimating how many 'complaints' or incidents are attributable to negligence or deliberate breaches of rules or standards. A further problem is that the size of a business is often not recorded. Moreover, as will be seen below, few cases lead to prosecution.

There are nonetheless some invaluable sources of information about these kinds of crime, often lying outside standard criminological sources. Enforcement agencies do record incidents, complaints and prosecutions, and also carry out research, hold seminars and seek to publicise their activities. While not widely regarded as 'crime', many of the activities are seen as scandals or issues, receive some publicity and form the subject of campaigns by relevant interest groups. In relation, for example, to industrial health and safety, trade unions, pressure groups and victim support groups all carry out research and conduct campaigns (Tombs and Whyte 2007) as is also the case with environmental and consumer issues. These groups collect and publish information and may welcome research. Case studies can be used for analysis (Tombs and Whyte 2007). Investigative journalism forms another valuable source of information and the growth of the Internet has made many of these sources more readily accessible. Care must be taken, however, to critically evaluate all sources, recognising the purpose for which the information has been gathered.

Offences, offenders and victims

The area of crime identified is vast, with the activities of a wide range of offenders affecting many individual victims directly along with having a diffuse effect on individuals and communities (Croall 2009b). This section will provide some examples to illustrate the significance of these offences. Space necessitates a highly selective approach as medium-size businesses are found in virtually all sectors of business, commerce and financial services, all of which contain recognisable 'rogue' or 'cowboy' operators. Professional groups, such as lawyers, accountants, dentists or pharmacists, often organised in small, indeed 'family' firms, have all been associated with frauds (Croall 2001a). Offenders from medium-size businesses are also found in many other chapters in this collection including, for example, scams and swindles, tax and benefit frauds, fakes and forgeries and cybercrimes. They are involved in drug and human trafficking, and, as seen above, in various categories of corporate crime, corporate violence and environmental and eco-crime. While unnecessary overlap will be avoided, some mention will inevitably be made of these categories. This section will start with examples taken from the main regulatory areas of safety, the environment and consumer legislation, moving on to more illegal businesses.

'Safety crimes'

The often serious impact of these kind of offences is well illustrated in cases involving 'safety crime' (Tombs and Whyte 2007) or 'corporate violence' (Tombs 2007 and this volume) in which, along with large corporations, smaller firms have been convicted of offences occasioning death and injury. One of the few successful convictions in England and Wales, in 1994, for corporate manslaughter involved the owner and director of OLL, a small company running an adventure centre. This followed the drowning of four teenagers in Lyme Bay after which it was revealed that the director had ignored persistent warnings about risks (Slapper and Tombs 1999). In Glasgow, six employees were killed and 40 injured following an explosion in the family-owned 'Stockline' factory, which was subsequently convicted under health and safety legislation in 2007 on the grounds that it had failed to maintain underground gas piping (*The Scotsman*, 29 August 2007). Tombs and Whyte (2007) point to the high rates of fatalities, over five times the industry average, in the construction industry, which is made up of large numbers of small firms and self-employed builders. Some firms operate on the fringes of legality, working, for example, for 'cash in hand' in the informal economy, and some rely on the employment of illegal immigrants – all features which, they argue, contribute to a less safe working environment.

Immigrant labour has been associated with low pay and exploitation by gangmasters, traffickers and smugglers in other sectors. Examples have included the employment, in private care homes, of nurses who have had passports confiscated, been forced to sign illegal contracts and work for over 60 hours per week for £4 per hour (Croall 2007a). The most serious instance was the drowning, in February 2004, of 23 Chinese cockle pickers in Morecambe Bay. They had been smuggled into Britain and were organised by a gangmaster, subsequently convicted of manslaughter. These examples illustrate the involvement of the primarily legal employing business along with illegal traffickers and smugglers and gangmasters, whose legal status has been problematic (Tombs and Whyte 2007). Similar problems are found in relation to other industries.

Farming and food production

Farming and food production, in which medium-sized businesses play a significant part, can give rise to a wide variety of criminal and regulatory offences, including crimes against the environment, breaches of health and safety laws and misuse of subsidies. Such offences may be committed by primarily legitimate farmers, food producers, butchers or restaurateurs, along with a variety of 'rural rogues' (Smith 2004, 2009a).

Among the most notorious farming-related crimes have been subsidies frauds involving the Common Agricultural Policy (CAP) of the European Union, whose extent has proved difficult to estimate (Passas and Nelken 1993; Doig 1995, 2006). Examples have included a Devon farmer who was imprisoned for two and a half years having been given £130,000 subsidies for non-existent land, for which he provided fictitious map references in Greenland and Iceland (Watt 2002). Farmers were also convicted, following the foot-and-mouth epidemic, for claiming for animals which did not exist (Elliot 2001). Pollution of rivers, beaches and waterways with slurry and sewage has also led to prosecutions and has involved the death of fish (Croall 2007b). Subsidies frauds have been found to involve both primarily legal and illegal organisations (Passas and Nelken 1993) and, like construction, farming, food packing and distribution are heavily dependent on the use of cheap, immigrant labour, sometimes involving gangmasters (Lawrence 2004).

Smith (2004, 2009a) provides some interesting examples of 'rural rogues' including the illegal trade in 'smokies' and what he describes as 'illegal pluriactivity' in the farming community. The lucrative trade in 'smokies', illegally slaughtered 'halal' meat, emerged out of the high costs of producing this meat in the small number of licensed abbatoirs and the high demand for it. This gap was filled by a supply network involving largely legitimate transport hauliers, slaughtermen and labourers, and butchers and restaurateurs who sold the meat. What he describes as 'criminal entrepreneurs', drawn from primarily 'bona fide' farmers, financed and organised the operation, and the livestock and location for the illegal slaughter were provided by a group widely recognised within the community as 'rogue' farmers, many of whom had previous convictions. This particular trade declined, but he provides other examples of illegal 'diversification', including the theft of cattle, the use and sale of so called 'red diesel', the sale of out-of-date animal medicines and illegal businesses in pedigree dogs. Offences ranged from what he describes as 'gentlemen farmers' and 'petit bourgeoisie' to 'likeable' and 'dislikeable' rogues. Most retained a primary identity as 'farmers' rather than as 'criminals' and their activities straddled the disparate worlds of farming and crime.

Meat can also be 'laundered' with meat unfit for human consumption, often illegally slaughtered, being passed into the food chain and meat products being adulterated and falsely described – often in smaller food processing operations (Croall 2007b). Some of these trades are cross-border, with reports of, for example, illegally imported, frozen meat being 'tumbled', injected with illegal amounts of water and additives, and exported (Lawrence 2004). Products can be falsely described as 'organic' and others contain a mixture of meats not declared on the label. In one case, what was described as a 'criminal gang' led by 'Maggot Pete' were convicted following the sale of unfit meat intended as pet food to hospitals, schools and supermarkets carrying risks of hepatitis, Staphylococci and E. coli into the food chain (Lawrence 2004).

Inattention to food hygiene and modern food processing techniques have been associated with food poisoning, which can cause death, long-term illness and, at the very least, extreme discomfort for victims. Very often these cases are associated with individual restaurants and food establishments. In one of the most serious cases in Scotland, 21 old-age pensioners died following the consumption of meat prepared in the premises of one local butcher who supplied meat to care institutions and clubs for the elderly. He was subsequently convicted under the Food Acts (Croall 2007b). A *Which?* (2004) investigation revealed that around 42 per cent of UK food businesses visited by environmental health organisations in 2001 failed to comply fully with food law. Prosecutions are relatively rare as it is notoriously difficult to establish the necessary 'chain' of evidence to link the poisoning to the outlet.

Finally, smaller retail outlets have been prosecuted for a range of offences including selling out-of-date food, misrepresenting the contents of food and for a number of seemingly trivial offences under weights and measures legislation, in which for example, bakers have sold bread which is underweight or which fails to comply with regulations about its contents. Publicans have long been associated with the sale of short measure drinks which produce higher profits and lower taxes (Croall 2007b).

Crimes against consumers

Safety risks and fraudulent practices are found in many other consumer goods and services industries, and while many are associated, rightly, with large corporations, many others are attributable to smaller businesses and to enterprises whose activities lie in the grey area between legality and illegality (Croall 2009a). Regulations have only recently been tightened up to deal, for example, with the activities of the 'cosmetic cowboys' who used illegally obtained Botox in unlicensed parlours or Botox parties (Hall 2005). This section will focus on the two areas which feature most strongly in consumer complaints: car sales, repairs and servicing; and home maintenance repairs and servicing (Biswell 2004).

Car sales, repairs and servicing

The car industry has long been characterised as 'criminogenic' (Leonard and Weber 1970), particularly in respect of the second-hand car sales and car repairs associated with individual dealers and garages. In the United States, it has been estimated that auto repair shops cheat customers out of around $57 million every day (Rosoff *et al.* 1998). In Britain a 'mystery shopping exercise', involving car servicing and repair, carried out by trading standards officers in 2002, rated over half of garages as 'poor' or 'very poor'. Seventeen per cent carried out unnecessary work, 40 per cent missed or did not replace at least one item on the service schedule, 86 per cent missed at least one fault and 43 per cent provided no accurate quotes (Department of Trade and Industry 2002). The National Consumer Council (NCC) has calculated that the individual consumer typically loses £235 for each unsatisfactory repair or service (National Consumer Council 2004). Car 'clocking', the turning back of odometers to suggest that the car has done fewer miles than it has, is also a major problem as is the safety of second-hand cars and the practice of reconstructing vehicles from damaged cars, associated with deaths and injuries (Croall 2009a).

'Cowboy' builders

Home repairs and maintenance are also subject to considerable complaint and in one British study, carried out by a major insurance company, plumbers, builders, roofers and plasterers were found to have victimised an estimated total of nearly five million people (Peake 2004). The effects of victimisation can be severe, not only in terms of financial loss, but also emotionally, with reports of sleepless nights, feelings that homes have been invaded and needing to take time off work. Some groups of perpetrators have been described as 'gangs' – one case involved a 'gang' who targeted old people and are said to have marched victims to the bank after falsely claiming that their homes could collapse (Penrose 2003).

Criminal enterprises: the case of cigarette smuggling

As seen above, so called crime entrepreneurs exploit niches in markets, some of which involve heterogeneous networks of smaller businesses many of whom cannot be properly described as 'organised crime'. An interesting example of this is the trade in 'bootleg' cigarettes, which emerged out of the disparities in revenue across different European countries (van Duyne 2003; Hornsby and Hobbs 2007). Research suggests that these often start with individuals, often unemployed, importing cheap cigarettes which are sold in car boots or local markets. High demand and an initially low risk of capture lead to expansion, often by employing friends and family and utilising a wider range of networks in the underground market. These 'middle-level' traders could be classified as 'criminal organisations' and, although their links with so called organised crime were not strong, they did on occasion interact with 'intermediate' and 'higher' trade levels (van Duyne 2003). Hornsby and Hobbs (2007) describe the growth of an entrepreneurial criminal firm which expanded from 'pensioner days out', through employing friends and acquaintances to a well organised, efficient and highly profitable smuggling and distribution network. The business ceased as it became threatened by competition, including the use of violence, from more 'serious' members of the criminal fraternity seeking to diversify.

Long firm fraud

While different kinds of fraud are the subject of other chapters, some businesses are set up mainly to perpetrate frauds. These include the long firm frauds, which also involve bankruptcy and insolvency frauds, described by Levi (1981, 2008) in which the perpetrators set up one or more businesses with the initial or subsequent aim of defrauding creditors from whom goods have been ordered with no real attempt to sell them. As Levi points out, while often regarded as an example of criminal business, they span the worlds of white-collar and so-called organised crime and, while it is often assumed that the business is primarily illegal, involve a range of different kinds of offences and offenders. Thus Levi (1981) distinguishes between pre-planned frauds in which the business is set up for fraudulent purposes and which can involve so-called professional criminals, intermediate frauds where the business starts out as legal but later becomes fraudulent and 'slippery-slope' frauds in which deceptions spiral to save an essentially insolvent business. Long firm frauds continue to exact a high toll with, in 2000, a total of 71 offences being investigated by 20 police forces with estimated total losses of £35 million. Individual cases involve sums at risk ranging from £18,000 to £10 million. Other frauds, including scams and swindles and advance fee frauds, some perpetrated via the Internet, in which services are offered but not subsequently provided (Doig 2006; Mackenzie this volume; M. Williams this volume), also constitute examples of middle-range business crime.

Offenders

On the basis of these albeit selective examples, middle-range business crime clearly involves an extremely diverse group of offenders who appear to defy classification, as it is difficult to fit them into specific boxes. Many, such as those involving farmers or long firm fraudsters, span the worlds of legitimate and illegitimate businesses (Smith 2004; Levi 2008) and Hobbs (2002) rejects any hierarchical model differentiating between street and corporate crime which to him normalises business and pathologises crime. Moreover, as he also points out, and as is seen in the example of cigarette smuggling or the 'smokies' trade, different permutations develop and trades expand and decline – indicating a dynamic rather than static picture.

Nonetheless, broad distinctions can be discerned. Terms such as 'rogues' and 'cowboys' are widely used and differentiate what have been described as 'shady operators' (Sutton and Wild 1985) from, on the one hand, one of the 'petite bourgeoisie' of small, largely reputable businesses and, on the other, more overtly 'criminal' businesses. Naylor (2003) distinguishes between *predatory* forms of profit-driven crime involving largely conventional criminals, *market based* offences involving illicit trades in largely prohibited goods and services, and *commercial* offences, involving largely legitimate organisations and primarily legal goods and services. Many of the above examples involve what would be widely recognised as primarily legitimate businesses, committing only regulatory offences seen in most cases as 'not really criminal'. These can be broadly contrasted with the more unambiguously 'criminal' activities and legal status of other businesses. In between lie those who engage in both legitimate and illegitimate activities and whose 'criminal' status is often contestable and culturally and subculturally tolerated. Culturally recognisable characterisations of offenders, such as 'petit bourgeois' or rogues, reflect perceptions of social status which approximate to Sutherland's (much criticised) use of 'respectability' which is in turn associated with a variety of factors including social and economic capital. It could be tentatively suggested that offenders can be distinguished by a combination of their social status, perceptions of the 'criminality' of their activities and the legitimacy of their businesses – producing the different groups sketched out below:

- The label *petite bourgeoisie* (Croall 1989, 2001a; Smith 2009a) refers to 'reputable' businesses, largely involved in breaches of regulatory laws with an ambivalent criminal status. This group contains the farmers, butchers, bakers, shopkeepers and small manufacturers outlined above.

- Less 'respectable', but nonetheless engaged in primarily legitimate businesses, are the *rogues* found across economic sectors. In this group lie the 'cowboy' builders, 'rogue' farmers and second-hand car dealers, whose activities are more likely to be seen as 'cons', 'swindles' or 'sharp practice' indicating the very narrow dividing line between such subculturally tolerated activities and 'fraud' or 'crime'.

- Very little, other than the primarily legitimate nature of their business, divides this group from the *crime entrepreneurs* and others whose activities span both the legitimate and illegitimate, like the cigarette smugglers and the networks involving a mixture of legal and illegal enterprises. Many of these entrepreneurs move between categories as businesses expand, develop and contract.

- In contrast, are those whose businesses are more overtly set up for primarily illegal ends and whose activities are more widely regarded as 'fraud' or 'crime' – such as the long firm fraudsters, or those who deliberately set out, as is the case with some Internet crimes and advance fee frauds, to defraud.

These broad groupings are closely interconnected with differences in the way in which offences and offenders are subject to criminalisation and dealt with in the criminal justice process, which will be considered below.

The examples also reveal the substantial impact of these crimes. As outlined above, many victims are unaware of any specific harm and others do not experience the trauma associated with direct victimisation. Some offences could well be characterised as 'crimes without victims' as they involve the sale of desirable but illegal goods and services such as the cheap cigarettes sold by bootleggers. Others, however, have an extremely serious impact including, as is the case for safety offences or food poisoning, death, injury and illness. In yet others, while the harm may be primarily economic, psychological effects such as feelings of invasion or sleepless nights may result as is the case with victims of cowboy builders and also with victims of serious fraud, the experience of which has been likened by Levi (1999) to that of rape.

It could also be argued (Croall 2001b, 2009a) that victimisation from these kinds of crime exceeds that from many forms of conventional crime, and the vast majority of citizens are likely to be repeat or multiple victims. Despite this universality, however, victimisation also reflects wider patterns of inequality as some groups are more vulnerable to some crimes, and other groups can better protect themselves. Safety crimes in the workplace are more likely to affect workers, particularly, as seen in relation to the construction industry, casual workers with little choice but to work in unsafe environments. As was also seen, immigrant labour is particularly vulnerable to exploitative practices. Women may be more at risk from some consumer offences, especially those involving cosmetics, diets or car repairs and servicing, where the assumption that they know little about cars makes them more likely targets. The elderly are often seen to be the targets of fraudsters and 'cons' which play on the fear of fraud or crime – although Titus (2001) warns against such stereotypes having found that older people are no more likely to be defrauded from a range of consumer frauds – as they have got older, he argues, they may also have got smarter. And, while the most affluent present more attractive targets to fraudsters, their 'cultural capital' may make them more aware of risks and their economic capital enables them to avoid the problems posed by cowboy builders, second-hand car dealers or unsafe and risky workplaces.

Explanations and analyses

Given its relative invisibility, there have been few attempts to analyse, let alone explain, middle-range business crime although, following analyses of white-collar and other economic crimes, some criminological perspectives can be applied. As suggested above, the primarily profit-driven nature of offending suggests rational choice theories, and particular markets and industries could also be regarded as crime-prone. Reference has also been made to the cultural and subcultural tolerance accorded to many of the activities, and, as for other crimes, structural theories such as anomie can be applied. Difficulties of detection and prosecution also create a regulatory environment which can, particularly for international trades, provide space for a variety of illegal activities to flourish. A variety of approaches can therefore be drawn on, albeit applying differently to different forms of crime.

Business persons are often portrayed as 'amoral calculators', whose decisions prioritise profit over other, particularly social, considerations, which suggests that rational choice theories – in which crime results from choices weighing the benefits of crime against its costs – are appropriate. Instituting systems to ensure compliance can be costly for the legitimate business, and the low chance of being caught, convicted or severely punished can create a situation in which offending becomes cost-effective. Crime entrepreneurs also 'rationally' exploit niches in markets. Theoretical models have been drawn up of business offending which aim to take into account not only these 'rational' economic factors but which also include considerations of business reputation and perceptions of morality (Paternoster and Simpson 1993). Nonetheless, economic models have not been found to predict offending in some sectors (Braithwaite and Makkai 1991). Not all decisions to offend can be seen as rational as discovery of criminal activity can endanger the survival of a business; not all are simply driven by profit but can be, for example, a desire to escape boredom (van Duyne 2003); and, as is the case for other crimes, rational choice theories have been criticised for neglecting the wider economic, social structural and cultural environment within which choices may be perceived as rational or otherwise (Slapper and Tombs 1999; Croall 2001a).

Other approaches have sought to establish whether some characteristics of businesses, such as size, make them more crime-prone (Croall 2001a; Punch 1996). In general terms neither smaller nor larger businesses appear any more likely to offend, although different factors affect different sizes of business. The division of labour and its associated 'diffusion of responsibility' within large organisations make it easier for individuals to 'pass the buck' and blame superiors or subordinates. On the other hand, larger companies can employ experts such as accountants, lawyers, or other scientific and technical experts to advise on aspects of compliance, an option unavailable to smaller companies for whom the costs of purchasing necessary equipment or improving premises may be prohibitive. For some smaller companies, this may be compounded by a lack of knowledge of appropriate regulations, thus starting the 'slippery slope' to offending.

Different considerations apply to the crime entrepreneurs and primarily criminal businesses for which Levi (2007) argues, 'small is beautiful'. In the kind of criminal networks described above, the less participants know about the involvement of others, the less they can tell enforcement agencies. Trust is crucial – a factor reflected in the preference for 'family firms' and businesses based on local networks of friends, acquaintances and geographical areas (Levi 2007; van Duyne 2003). Levi argues that in many countries, networked crime, as opposed to large cartels, is more efficient than 'hierarchical planned centralism' for survival.

Criminogenic markets may produce what Leonard and Weber (1970) describe as 'coerced' economic crime among smaller businesses. In their analysis of the car industry, cited above, they argue that the high investment necessary to develop new models and the high concentration of car manufacturing placed such high pressure on car dealers to meet sales quotas that there was little profit in new car sales. This led to a variety of 'rackets' on the part of dealers and mechanics such as 'forcing' sales of accessories and parts, used car mark-ups and service gouging (overcharging). The relative ignorance of the consumer about the inner workings of a car also make it easier to persuade them that work needs to be done – making for a 'fiddle-prone' occupation (Mars 1982).

Tombs and Whyte's (2007) account of the construction industry also suggests a criminogenic environment in which the predominantly small to medium companies operating locally and regionally face competition from the informal economy. This, along with the prominence of short-term projects, leads to pressures to cut corners and limits the effectiveness of safety training. This is exacerbated by a culture which accepts the dangerousness of the industry and downplays the importance of safety precautions. Similar analyses could be applied to farming and food production. The precariousness of farming forms the context for 'diversification' into illegal activity, as does a culture within rural and farming communities in which 'sharp' practice is a virtue (Smith 2009a). The food industry, like the car industry, illustrates the pressures placed on smaller businesses by the practices of 'global giant' producers and the major supermarket chains in the UK (Lawrence 2004; Jones *et al.* 2005; Croall 2007b). Many concerns have been voiced about the pressures, including bullying, which supermarkets exert on smaller suppliers to cut costs and to supply food 'just in time', or 'buy one get one free' offers at a loss (Lawrence 2004). As seen above, this provides an environment in which a reliance on low-paid, immigrant and casual labour becomes a necessity.

Wider structural and cultural factors are also important and anomie or strain theory has been applied to economic crime (Box 1983; Passas 1990). Businesses, whether large or small, face the 'strain' between profitability and, particularly for primarily legitimate firms, the need to comply with regulations which are often seen as burdensome. Particularly in periods of recession, cutting corners on compliance can become part of a 'struggle for survival' (Croall 1989). The activities of crime enterprises have been interpreted as 'innovative' (Ruggiero 1996) and have also been related to the decline of traditional crafts and trades and the growth of unemployment in lower-class communities (Hobbs 1995, 2002). Involvement in the illegal economy can become a means of obtaining employment, escaping boredom and achieving status.

In these circumstances, turning to crime may be more likely where there is cultural and subcultural support for the activities involved. A major feature in analyses of white-collar crime is its ambivalent criminal status and perceptions of regulatory crime as 'not really criminal' have been reinforced by the prevailing assumption, associated with the deregulatory climate of recent decades, that business is *over-regulated* and that regulations create too much 'red tape' which hampers enterprise. Similar arguments have been made about tax avoidance (Cook 1989) and recent work has also highlighted cultural support for the 'crimes of everyday life' (Karstedt and Farrall 2006) of those who consider themselves as 'respectable' citizens, such as not paying TV licence fees, avoiding taxes or making false insurance claims. The 'cash in hand' basis of some businesses reflects these attitudes and many crime enterprises are based, like the example of cigarette smuggling, on activities which, while recognised as illegal, are not perceived as 'criminal' (van Duyne 2003). To Hobbs (1995), working-class criminal entrepreneurs draw on a male working-class culture which has always adapted to formal and informal economies, in which the use of violence is a sign of status and, as cited above, which values entrepreneurship and 'sharp practice'.

These attitudes can be seen in the wider context of capitalism and more recently in the wider ideological context of neo-liberalism and its associated deregulatory policies (Tombs and Whyte 2007), highlighted dramatically in recent financial markets. Sociologists looking at white-collar crime have related it to, for example, the culture of competition (Coleman 1987) and, in the latter part of the twentieth century, to the sentiments of the enterprise culture and its slogan 'greed is good' (Punch 1996). Many analyses point to the importance of the favourable regulatory environment in which difficulties of detection and prosecution have been exacerbated by reductions in the resources available for many regulatory inspections. Some of the crime enterprises, particularly those involving cross-border operations, have exploited regulatory 'voids' or 'spaces between laws' (Gilbert and Russell 2002). The different tax levels across Europe have created opportunities for cigarette smuggling (van Duyne 2003) along with 'bootleg' luxury goods and alcohol. Regulation therefore is a key issue.

Responses

It has long been assumed that business and corporate offenders are treated more favourably than others within the criminal justice process. To what extent, therefore, do medium-size businesses share these advantages? It could also be hypothesised that responses will vary for the different kinds of offenders outlined above, with the more 'respectable' businesses being more favourably dealt with than the 'rogues'. Indeed, underlying many discussions of the advantages of the regulatory as opposed to the criminal law is the assumption that the majority of businesses are reputable and do not need criminal sanctions, as opposed to the minority of unscrupulous 'rogues' for whom they are necessary (Croall 2004).

The distinction between perceptions of criminality and the legality of different kinds of businesses is clearly evident in relation to criminalisation and to Sutherland (1949), a major factor distinguishing white-collar criminals was the different legal and administrative procedures applied to their activities. Primarily illegal businesses, such as those involved in long firm or advance fee frauds, are mainly dealt with by the police and prosecuted under criminal laws with a high chance of a prison sentence. The offences of more 'legitimate' businesses on the other hand, such as those jeopardising safety, consumers or the environment, are generally dealt with under so called 'regulatory' law, for long associated with 'compliance' strategies based on persuasion and negotiation, with low rates of detection and prosecution and monetary as opposed to custodial sentences. Somewhere in between lie the activities of the criminal enterprises which span the legitimate and illegitimate, some of whose activities may cut across the responsibilities of the police and different agencies such as Trading Standards, Food Standards, Ministry Vets and Animal Health Officers, and are often not a priority for the police (Smith 2004). Indeed, some deliberately exploit regulatory 'voids' and loopholes in the law and regulation.

Smaller legitimate businesses may nonetheless be disadvantaged in some areas of law, in that it has been found easier to convict smaller companies under criminal law. As seen above, within larger companies it is more difficult to identify who is legally responsible for an offence and a company as such cannot be said to have a 'mind' capable of being 'guilty'. The difficulties of establishing the necessary *mens rea* to obtain a criminal conviction has led to the use, in England and other legal systems, of the 'doctrine of identification' which requires that in order to convict a company, an individual, assumed to be its 'hands or mind', must also be convicted (Slapper and Tombs 1999; Gobert and Punch 2003; Tombs and Whyte 2007). This can pose considerable difficulties in large organisations whereas in smaller ones, the owner or director is more immediately identifiable, is more likely to have been there at the time and to have been aware of, if not actively encouraging, non-compliance and can less easily claim in defence that they had systems of risk management in place. As was the case with OLL, cited above, this makes the small company more vulnerable to prosecution, conviction and relatively heavier sentencing as it is easier to identify and 'blame' the person responsible. Disparities in how the law applied to large and small companies, along with the difficulties posed by the doctrine of identification, led to the attempt, in the recent Corporate Manslaughter and Corporate Homicide Act of 2007, to modify this doctrine by holding the organisation guilty of an offence if the way in which its activities are managed or organised by its senior management is a substantial element in any breach and including, among the factors which may be considered, any evidence of 'attitudes, policies, systems or accepted practices' that could have encouraged or tolerated the breach. It remains to be seen, however, whether this will make the prosecution of larger companies any easier as the definition of 'senior management' may in itself be problematic (Gobert 2008).

Small companies' offences can also be more easily detected as their activities are more readily visible. Enforcers' attention can be drawn by, for example, evident signs of non-compliance such as dangerous scaffolding, food displays or, quite literally, a 'nasty smell' (Hutter 1986; Croall 1989). Like the police, enforcers have stereotypes of the kinds of businesses more likely to offend, and offenders more readily categorised as 'rogues' can be subject to more attention and perceptions that they are more recalcitrant and dishonest and therefore more 'deserving' of prosecution. This is likely to become even more significant as agencies move away from routine inspections to those based on assessments of 'risk'. Some of these considerations also apply to smaller crime enterprises or illegitimate businesses. As seen above, smaller businesses based on kinship or community networks may be preferable but, at the same time, more 'serious' and persistent organised criminals may avoid detection by delegating the more visible functions of retail or distribution which, by having to deal with the public, have a greater chance of being detected.

Smaller businesses are also disadvantaged in relation to prosecution and court appearances. Larger businesses can use their resources to contest prosecution by negotiating plea bargains and out-of-court settlements. Technical experts, lawyers or accountants can also be used in court to present strong mitigation for offences arguing that they are 'not really criminal' or are 'one-off' incidents in an otherwise blame-free record (Croall 1988). While some smaller businesses, particularly those characterised as the 'petite bourgeoisie', can also use these tactics, others cannot. Some offenders, like second-hand car dealers, are less likely to be regarded as 'respectable', may be less articulate, may have committed offences more likely to be perceived as 'criminal' and may be less likely to seek legal advice.

Similar differences affect sentencing (Croall 2005; Tombs and Whyte 2007). While it is generally argued that white-collar offenders and companies receive lenient sentences with, particularly for cases involving death and injury, fines being regarded as 'derisory', monetary penalties have a differential impact on different companies. Large fines such as the 'record' £15 million given to Transco constitute only a small proportion of their resources, in that case a mere one per cent of annual turnover, whereas even a relatively small fine can threaten the survival of a smaller business. Monetary penalties do little to remedy the situation which has led to offences, nor do they always satisfy popular demands and victims' desires to see that the 'guilty' have been punished. Moreover, while being convicted as a company may reduce the eventual penalty as the 'corporate veil' may conceal culpability, the owners or directors of smaller companies are more liable to be seen as personally to blame. While enjoying some of the benefits of the larger company therefore, the medium or smaller company may also be disadvantaged. Those falling into the 'rogue' or crime enterprise categories are more likely to be imprisoned. Car dealers constitute a major group among those sentenced for Trade Descriptions offences. And 'Maggot Pete' and at least one 'gang' of builders victimising elderly householders were also imprisoned, as have been long firm fraudsters.

Conclusions

The above discussion has drawn attention to a vast range of crime often neglected by criminologists in favour of the 'big' business crimes of criminal cartels or multinational corporations. While only being able to cover a small selection, it indicates that the offences associated with smaller and medium-size businesses are not only extensive but have a considerable impact causing deaths, injuries, illnesses, emotional trauma and serious financial losses. Moreover, as the current recession deepens, it could be hypothesised that such crime is likely to increase, as smaller businesses engaged in a 'struggle for survival' see non-compliance with regulations as a means of staying in business and start to descend the 'slippery slope' to criminal behaviour. Similarly, rising unemployment may encourage those, like the 'bored and unemployed' offenders described by van Duyne or the 'rural rogues' described by Smith, to seek alternative means of employment and diversification, exploiting new market niches.

Exploring middle-range business crime also challenges criminological categorisations and draws attention to the dangers of drawing tight lines around organised or corporate crime based on the characteristics of either offences or offenders. At the same time, while legitimate and illegitimate business offences show similar characteristics, broad groups can be identified, and there are clear differences between those who can generally be characterised as 'respectable' and 'rogue' businesses, those who are often described as crime entrepreneurs and more clearly criminal businesses. A complex interrelationship between different factors distinguishes these groups, including offenders' status and respectability, which are in turn related to their economic and social capital, the legitimacy or otherwise of their businesses and the extent to which their activities are considered to be 'criminal', 'legal' or as lying on the very fuzzy line in between. These in turn reflect and reinforce very clear differences in criminalisation and in the way in which they are subject to control and regulation. Those considered to be 'respectable' or 'petit bourgeois' enjoy some but not all the advantages associated with white-collar and corporate offenders, whereas rogues are more likely to be dealt with more severely and others present particular problems of policing and prosecution. These must in turn be placed in the wider ideological and political context of how some business activities come to be regarded as legitimate or illegitimate and subjected to more or less severe forms of regulation, illustrated well in the many discussions of and changes in regulation likely to follow the current financial crisis.

Selected further reading

As middle-range business crime is not an established category and crosses over several criminological areas, no source covers the area comprehensively. Many of the activities involved are covered in Croall's (2001a) *Understanding White-Collar Crime*, which discusses the wide range of offences and offenders to be found within this more established, although difficult to define, area. A more recent account of victimisation from a range of consumer crimes can be found in Croall (2009a) 'White collar crime, consumers and victimization'. The newly issued revised edition of Levi's *Phantom Capitalists* (2008) contains a fascinating account of long-firm fraudsters along with an insightful analysis of the relationship between this and other forms of crime. Hobbs' (2002) article, 'The firm: organizational logic and criminal culture on a shifting terrain', looks at local organised crime 'firms' in the context of social and economic change and van Duyne's (2003) case study of cigarette smuggling well illustrates the emergence of the one-person entrepreneur.

Note

1 http://www.crimereduction.homeoffice.gov.uk/drugsalcohol/drugsalcohol44.htm (accessed 26 September 2008).

References

Biswell, K. (2004) 'Consumers and standards: increasing influence', *Consumer Policy Review*, 14: 177–85.

Box, S. (1983) *Power, Crime and Mystification*. London: Tavistock.

Braithwaite, J. and Makkai, T. (1991) 'Testing an expected utility model of corporate deterrence', *Law and Society Review*, 25: 7–39.

Coleman, J. W. (1987) 'Toward an integrated theory of white-collar crime', *American Journal of Sociology*, 93: 406–39.

Cook, D. (1989) *Rich Law, Poor Law: Different Responses to Tax and Supplementary Benefit Fraud*. Milton Keynes: Open University Press.

Croall, H. (1988) 'Mistakes, accidents and someone else's fault: the trading offender in court', *Journal of Law and Society*, 15 (3): 293–315.

Croall, H. (1989) 'Who is the white-collar criminal?', *British Journal of Criminology*, 29 (2): 157–74.

Croall, H. (2001a) *Understanding White-Collar Crime*. Milton Keynes: Open University Press.

Croall, H. (2001b) 'The victims of white-collar crime', in S.-A. Lindgren (ed.), *White-Collar Crime Research. Old Views and Future Potentials: Lectures and Papers from a Scandinavian Seminar*. Stockholm: National Council for Crime Prevention, Brottsforebyggande radet, pp. 35–54.

Croall, H. (2004) 'Combating financial crime: regulatory versus crime control approaches', *Journal of Financial Crime*, 11 (1): 45.

Croall, H. (2005) 'Penalties for Corporate Homicide', Annex to Scottish Executive Expert Group on Corporate Homicide. Online at: http://www.scotland.gov.uk/Publications/2005/11/14133559/36003.

Croall, H. (2007a) 'Victims of white-collar and corporate crime', in P. Davies, P. Francis and C. Greer (eds), *Victims, Crime and Society*. London: Sage.

Croall, H. (2007b) 'Food crime', in P. Beirne and N. South (eds), *Issues in Green Criminology*. Cullompton: Willan.

Croall, H. (2009a) 'White collar crime, consumers and victimization', *Crime, Law and Social Change*, 51: 127–46.

Croall, H. (2009b) 'Community safety and economic crime', *Criminology and Criminal Justice*, 9: 165–85.

Department of Trade and Industry (2002) *Car Servicing and Repairs: Mystery Shopping Research*. London: Department of Trade and Industry.

Doig, A (1995) 'A fragmented organizational approach to fraud in a European context', *European Journal of Criminal Policy*, 3 (2): 48–74.

Doig, A. (2006) *Fraud*. Cullompton: Willan

Elliot, V. (2001) 'Fraud spurs change in farming payouts', *The Times*, 31 July, p. 1.

Gilbert, M. and Russell, S. (2002) 'Globalization of criminal justice in the corporate context', *Crime, Law and Social Change*, 38 (3): 211–38.

Gobert, J. (2008) 'The evolving test of corporate liability', in J. Minkes and L. Minkes (eds), *Corporate and White Collar Crime*. London: Sage.

Gobert, J. and Punch, M. (2003) *Rethinking Corporate Crime*. London: Butterworths, LexisNexis.

Hall, C. (2005) 'Health crackdown on beauty clinics and Botox parties', *Daily Telegraph*, 29 January, p. 5.

Hobbs, D. (1995) *Bad Business: Professional Crime in Modern Britain*. Oxford: Oxford University Press.

Hobbs, D. (2002) 'The firm: organizational logic and criminal culture on a shifting terrain', *British Journal of Criminology*, 42 (1): 549–60.

Hornsby, R. and Hobbs, D. (2007) 'A zone of ambiguity: the political economy of cigarette bootlegging', *British Journal of Criminology*, 47 (4): 551–72.

Hutter, B. (1986) 'An inspector calls', *British Journal of Criminology*, 26 (2): 4–28.

Jones, P., Comfort, D., Hillier, D. and Eastwood, I. (2005) 'Corporate social responsibility: a case study of the UK's leading food retailers', *British Food Journal*, 107 (6): 423–5.

Karstedt, S. and Farrall, S. (2006) 'The moral economy of everyday crime: markets, consumers and citizens', *British Journal of Criminology*, 46 (6): 1011–36.

Karstedt, S., Levi, M. and Godfrey, B. (2006) 'Introduction', *British Journal of Criminology*, 46 (6): 971–5.

Lawrence, F. (2004) *Not on the Label! What Really Goes into the Food on Your Plate*. London: Penguin Books.

Leonard, W. and Weber, M. (1970) 'Auto makers and dealers: a study of criminogenic market forces', *Law and Society Review*, 4 (3): 407–24.

Levi, M. (1981) *The Phantom Capitalists: The Organization and Control of Long-Firm Fraud*. London: Heinemann.

Levi, M. (1999) 'The impact of fraud', *Criminal Justice Matters*, 36 (summer): 5–7.

Levi, M. (2007) 'Organized crime and terrorism', in M. Maguire, R. Morgan and R. Reiner (eds), *The Oxford Handbook of Criminology*, 4th edn. Oxford: Oxford University Press.

Levi, M. (2008) *The Phantom Capitalists: The Organization and Control of Long-Firm Fraud*, revised edn. Aldershot: Ashgate.

McLaughlin, E. and Muncie, J. (eds) (2005) *The Sage Dictionary of Criminology*, 2nd edn. London: Sage.

Maguire, M., Morgan, R. and Reiner, R. (eds) (2007) *The Oxford Handbook of Criminology*, 4th edn. Oxford: Oxford University Press.

Mars, G. (1982) *Cheats at Work: An Anthropology of Workplace Crime*. London: George Allen & Unwin.

National Consumer Council (2004) *Car Repairs and Servicing: Key Facts*, Fact Sheet, April. London: National Consumer Council.

Naylor, R.T. (2003) 'Toward a general theory of profit-driven crimes', *British Journal of Criminology*, 43 (1): 81–101.

Nelken, D. (2007) 'White collar crime', in M. Maguire, R. Morgan and R. Reiner (eds), *The Oxford Handbook of Criminology*, 4th edn. Oxford: Oxford University Press.

Passas, N. (1990) 'Anomie and corporate deviance', *Contemporary Crises*, 4: 157–78.

Passas, N. and Nelken, D. (1993) 'The thin line between legitimate and criminal enterprises: subsidy frauds in the European Community', *Crime, Law and Social Change*, 19: 223–43.

Paternoster, R. and Simpson, S. (1993) 'A rational choice theory of corporate crime', in R. V. Clarke and M. Felson (eds), *Advances in Criminological Theory: Routine Activity and Rational Choice*. New Brunswick, NJ: Transaction Books, pp. 37–58.

Peake, A. (2004) 'Cowboy builders take us for £1bn', *The Sun*, London, 19 October, p. 15.

Penrose, J. (2003) 'Cowboys jailed over £1m scam on elderly', *The Sun*, London, 25 October, p. 23.

Punch, M. (1996) *Dirty Business: Exploring Corporate Misconduct*. London: Sage.

Rosoff, S., Pontell, H. and Tillman, R. (1998) *Profit without Honor: White Collar Crime and the Looting of America*. Upper Saddle River, NJ: Prentice Hall.

Ruggiero, V. (1996) *Organized and Corporate Crime in Europe: Offers That Can't Be Refused*. Aldershot: Dartmouth.

Ruggiero, V. (2000) *Crime and Markets*. Oxford: Oxford University Press.

Slapper, G. and Tombs, S. (1999) *Corporate Crime*. London: Addison-Wesley-Longman.

Smith, R. (2004) 'Rural rogues: a case story on the "smokies" trade', *International Journal of Entrepreneurial Behaviour and Research*, 10 (4): 277–94.

Smith, R. (2009a) 'A Case Study on "Illegal Pluriactivity" in the Farming Community'. Unpublished paper.

Smith, R. (2009b) 'Understanding entrepreneurial behaviour in organised criminals', *Journal of Enterprising Communities*, 3 (3): in print.

Sutherland, E. (1949) *White Collar Crime*. NewYork: Holt, Reinhart & Winston.

Sutton, A. and Wild, R. (1985) 'Small business: white collar villains or victims?', *International Journal of the Sociology of Law*, 13: 247–59.

Titus, R. M. (2001) 'Personal fraud and its victims', in N. Shover and J. P. Wright (eds), *Crimes of Privilege: Readings in White-Collar Crime*. New York and Oxford: Oxford University Press.

Tombs, S. (2000) 'Official statistics and hidden crimes: researching health and safety crimes', in V. Jupp, P. Davies and P. Francis (eds), *Doing Criminological Research*. London: Sage, pp. 64–81.

Tombs, S. (2007) 'Violence, safety crimes and criminology', *British Journal of Criminology*, 47 (4): 531–50.

Tombs, S. and Whyte, D. (2003) 'Scrutinizing the powerful: crime, contemporary political economy, and critical social research', in S. Tombs and D. Whyte (eds), *Unmasking the Crimes of the Powerful*. New York: Lang, pp. 3–48.

Tombs, S. and Whyte, D. (2007) *Safety Crime*. Cullompton: Willan.

van Duyne, P. C. (2003) 'Organizing cigarette smuggling and policy making, ending up in smoke', *Crime, Law and Social Change*, 39: 285–317.

Watt, N. (2002) 'Olive growers ditch tradition for subsidies: EU cash has encouraged intensive farming and fraud', *Daily Telegraph*, 10 July, p.12.

Weisburd, D., Wheeler, S., Waring, E. and Bode, N. (1991) *Crimes of the Middle Classes: White-Collar Offenders in the Federal Courts*. New Haven, CT and London: Yale University Press.

Which? (2004) 'Food safety'. February. Online at: http://www.which.co.uk.

Wright, A. (2006) *Organized Crime*. Cullompton: Willan.

Chapter 34

Human trafficking

Jo Goodey[1]

Introducing the crime of human trafficking

The year 2007 marked the 200th anniversary of the abolition of the slave trade in Britain's colonies, yet the crime of human trafficking remains a reality in the twenty-first century and, as such, is often described as 'modern-day slavery'.

Human trafficking refers to the recruitment, transport, receipt, harbouring and selling of people through exploitative means such as fraud, force, threat and deception. It is both a cross-border crime and one that can occur within a country's borders, and variously encompasses the crimes of slavery, forced labour and services, exploitative prostitution and other sexual services. In this regard, it is the exploitative nature of trafficking that distinguishes it from human smuggling. However, human smuggling becomes trafficking when the smuggled person is exploited at some point, for example if, having paid a sum of money to be smuggled across international borders, the smuggled person finds him or herself subject to some form of debt bondage at their destination. By default, children are victims of trafficking because the process involves the exploitation of a minor who cannot give their consent (regardless of whether their parents or guardian gave their consent).

While the crime of slavery has a long history of legal recognition, the United Nations 1949 Convention on the Suppression of Trafficking in Women and the Exploitation of the Prostitution of Others was the first UN Convention to address the specific crime of 'trafficking'. More recently, trafficking has been defined in international law under the United Nations (UN) 2000 Protocol to Prevent, Suppress and Punish Trafficking in Persons, Especially Women and Children,[1] which covers forced labour and services, prostitution and other sexual services, as well as the removal of organs. Since the very end of the 1980s to the beginning of the 1990s, when post-Communist Europe was confronted with the increasing problem of trafficking in women (and children) for sexual exploitation, legal recognition of trafficking has been growing among European legislators. In 1989, the European Parliament adopted its first resolution on the exploitation of prostitution and trafficking in human beings, which was followed in 1993 by a resolution calling for international cooperation to combat trafficking in women and to address responses to its victims.

Legal and policy responses to trafficking have continued throughout the 1990s and 2000s as a reflection of the fact that trafficking is an ongoing problem. Given the wide scope of human trafficking as a crime on a global scale, this chapter can only provide a brief introduction to the phenomenon of trafficking and responses to it. With this in mind, the chapter will focus on trafficking in women (and children) for sexual exploitation in the context of the UK and the European Union.

Extent, patterns and trends

No accurate figures exist on the extent of human trafficking. In this regard, trafficking is no different to many other offences that are connected with organised crime as it is difficult to gauge its extent with any accuracy. In comparison, it is easier to describe the nature of the offence.

The vulnerable position of trafficking victims, who are working in the criminal underworld of prostitution and forced labour and are often illegal immigrants, means that they are not in a position to report their victimisation. This situation is made worse when victims are children. As a result, trafficking remains severely under-reported. In addition, police forces and other agencies that encounter trafficking cases, such as border control and immigration, are often not trained to recognise trafficking as a distinct crime. In the case of women who are trafficked for sexual exploitation, the typical policing and immigration response in Europe has been, until recently, to criminalise trafficked women as prostitutes and illegal immigrants and to return victims as soon as possible to their country of origin.

While human trafficking cannot be accurately counted, numbers are regularly employed by governments, intergovernmental organisations (IGOs) and non-governmental organisations (NGOs) alike to highlight the problem of trafficking. In 1990s Europe, when trafficking was increasingly coming to public attention, a common figure that was often cited, which has variously been attributed to the International Organisation for Migration (IOM), was 500,000 women and children being trafficking annually into the 'old' 15 Member States of the European Union (EU) (Aromaa and Lehti 2007). In 2008, the United Nations (UN) used the same approach to draw attention to the crime of human trafficking, with the introduction to a publication for the UN Global Initiative to Fight Human Trafficking (UN.GIFT) stating: 'Billions of dollars are being made at the expense of millions of victims of trafficking.'[3]

Efforts have been made or are underway to try and more accurately count the scale of the problem. The UN's International Labour Office (ILO) has produced a number of reports that attempt to tease out different methodological approaches for counting trafficking, which place equal emphasis on trafficking for labour exploitation as well as sexual exploitation (De Cock 2007; Ghinararu and van der Linden 2004). According to the ILO's own methodologies for counting, anything within a range of 275,068 to 508,931 people are actively being trafficked within and between nations at any point in time, and a further 2.45 million, at least, are caught by trafficking globally. In contrast, the US government has produced figures indicating that between 600,000 and 800,000 people are trafficked across international borders each year (Danilova-Trainor and Belser 2006). Different methodologies for counting do not allow for data comparisons, but it is clear from these various estimates that the crime exists on a large scale.

Whereas the true extent of trafficking is difficult to gauge, patterns in trafficking have been identified with some accuracy with respect to victims' countries of origin, transit and destination. In 2006 the UN Office on Drugs and Crime (UNODC) published the report *Trafficking in Persons: Global Patterns*,[4] which used content analysis of print material to develop a citation index of how often countries are referred to as places of origin, transit and destination. According to the report, Belgium, Germany, Greece, Italy and the Netherlands are ranked *very high* as destination countries in Europe, and Austria, Bosnia and Herzegovina, the Czech Republic, Denmark, France, Kosovo, Poland, Spain, Switzerland and the UK are ranked *high*. However, this methodology over-represents countries that have an active government, research and NGO response that records and publishes information about the problem of trafficking, and under-represents those countries where trafficking is a real problem but where there is an absence of documentation for citation. Recognising this fact, the UNODC report stressed that its role was to map known patterns in trafficking rather than to provide a count of the scale of the problem. To this end the report usefully provides maps and indicators about trafficking flows around the world, and shows that Europe – encompassing the 'old' west, the countries of central and eastern Europe, and the Balkans – contains origin, transit and destination countries.

Alongside the UN's work, other IGOs, together with NGOs, have provided a wealth of information about trafficking movements and emergent trends. The International Organisation for Migration (IOM) is the largest organisation working to assist trafficking victims and return them to their countries of origin and is particularly active in Europe. In the Balkans, the IOM's regional clearing point for data collection on trafficking cases revealed a decrease in trafficking cases in this region in the mid-2000s. However, the causes of this decrease are difficult to determine. They could reflect on the one hand an actual decrease in trafficking cases or, on the other hand, the ability of traffickers to evade detection. Alternatively, the downturn could reveal the failure of the IOM to encourage victims to take up their services, particularly in those cases where victims do not want to return to their country of origin.

Where government agencies currently do not accurately record trafficking cases, alternative data collection sources, like NGOs, cannot be expected to fill this gap given that the mainstay of their resources are devoted to providing services for trafficking victims. However, the work of NGOs – such as La Strada, the Coalition against Trafficking in Women (CATW) and the Global Alliance against Trafficking in Women (GAATW) – plays an important role in mapping European trafficking patterns. These NGOs have documented the movement of women from central and eastern Europe and the Balkans into western Europe, as well as the more recent trend of moving women within and between central and eastern European countries and the Balkans. In turn, NGOs report the movement of women from as far away as Brazil and the Philippines to the brothels of the Netherlands, Germany and Italy (to name just a handful of countries of origin and destination). The evidence supplied by NGOs, gathered through the testimonies of trafficking victims, is supported by a few reports from the police and other government agencies that are available in the public domain. Notable among these are the annual reports from the Dutch National Rapporteur on Trafficking and Germany's federal police, the Bundeskriminalamt (which will be referred to in the next section).

Characteristics of the offence, victims and offenders

As already explained, trafficking is by definition a crime involving a range of exploitative elements. According to the testimonies of women trafficked for the sex industry, their exploitation can take the form of deception and debt bondage, through to mental, physical and sexual abuse. The following description of the trafficking process, from recruitment to prostitution, and of its victims and offenders, reflects accounts provided from a range of sources such as governments (Home Office 2007; Dutch National Rapporteur[5]), inter-governmental organisations (OSCE 2008; European Commission Expert Group[6]), research (such as Friman and Reich 2007; Surtees 2008; van den Anker and Doomernik 2006), including the author's own work (Goodey 2003, 2005a), as well as NGOs.[7]

The offence

Women's initial recruitment is often part of a scam where they are offered work in seemingly legitimate and lucrative jobs – such as au-pair work or as dancers. Recruitment can take the form of adverts in the local press or meetings with recruiters who are on the lookout for young women from poor regions who are often naive to the dangers of job offers that might seem 'too good to be true'. At the same time, some NGOs report that a number of women are aware of the dangers involved but are willing to take the risk given the dire financial situation they find themselves in. One of the reasons why women take these risks is because recruiters are often known to them, being family members or acquaintances, and in some cases 'boyfriends'. Women are also recruiters, some having been victims of trafficking themselves who are under threat of harm being done to them or their families should they fail to cooperate with the traffickers.

In turn, there are cases where women have suspected or known that they are being recruited for prostitution but have not known the abuse and exploitation they would suffer during the trafficking process and at their final destination. And finally, there are those women who have been trafficked and returned to their countries of origin by organisations such as the IOM, only to be retrafficked at some later point. This retrafficking can occur when traffickers find women and threaten to expose the nature of their 'work' to family and friends unless they return to prostitution. Traffickers can also threaten to traffic another member of a woman's family, including children, unless she cooperates. If a woman's 'work' is revealed this serves to make her prospects of regular employment and marriage impossible in what are often conservative communities. Hence, once back home, trafficked women are often easy prey for traffickers to re-exploit.

The actual trafficking process involves moving women from one place to another, both within a country and across borders. This can be done using any means of transport and often seemingly legitimate covers are used to evade any suspicion of trafficking, such as a man and woman travelling together as a 'couple' rather than a man or men travelling with a group of young women. Where women are trafficked across borders, and particularly where they are illegally trafficked, the removal of their passport is a means often used by traffickers to control any attempts of escape during the trafficking process and at the final destination. The degree of violence used against trafficked women various from one trafficking ring to the next, with some reports indicating that the use of violence is more prevalent among some nationalities than others. Some traffickers do not physically or sexually harm women during trafficking as this reduces the value of trafficked women as 'goods', while other traffickers abuse women into a status of submission. Working as prostitutes, women are liable to service as many clients as the brothel owner requires, and either receive no or little money for this, the argument being that they are in debt to the traffickers and the brothel owner. Women can be sold from one brothel to the next, the advantage being that with each sale a woman can be advertised as 'new' to clients.

Victims and offenders

More is known about the nature of victims and their experiences of the trafficking process than is known about the nature of offenders and how they become involved in trafficking. This reflects the fact that more victims come to light, and as a result their testimonies are collected, than traffickers are identified and prosecuted. As part of their role to assist and return victims to their country of origin, the IOM[8] has collected perhaps the most extensive record of trafficking cases in Europe.

NGO and police reports indicate consistently that trafficked women (and girls) are young, typically ranging in age from 16 to 25. Underage girls, and some boys, are also victims of trafficking, but in the main the evidence points to the fact that victims are predominantly young women. A characteristic that is shared among trafficking victims is their financial hardship, which recruiters exploit with promises of good jobs. Victims' relative poverty is reflected in their countries of origin. The 2007 report by the Dutch National Rapporteur on Trafficking,[9] which refers to 2005 data collected from the police, the prosecutor's office and the Foundation against Trafficking in Women, indicates that of the 424 victims of trafficking registered in the Netherlands in 2005, the main countries of origin, after internal cases of Dutch victims of trafficking, were Bulgaria, Russia and Nigeria. In previous reports, Romanian victims were also recorded in high numbers. A similar pattern emerges in the reports of the German Federal Police (Bundeskriminalamt – BKA[10]). The BKA's 2005 report, referring to 2004 police data, indicates that of 972 victims 127 were German nationals, with the remainder originating from countries such as Bulgaria, Romania, Russia and the Ukraine.

In the UK, detailed information about the nature of trafficking victims (and offenders) is not available in the form of annual reports. A 2000 report for the Home Office by Kelly and Regan was the first major government publication that attempted to estimate the scale of the trafficking problem and to document the characteristics of victims. Acknowledging the limitations of official police figures on trafficking cases, Kelly and Regan's report took available police data and estimated that there could be anywhere between 142 and 1,420 trafficked women in the UK in 1998. More recently, the UK police have released some limited information about the countries of origin of possible trafficking victims in connection with the largest anti-trafficking raids carried out in the UK on brothels and massage parlours – Operation Pentameter in 2006 and Pentameter II in 2007.[11] Once again, central and east European countries dominate countries of origin, but with victims coming from as far away as South America and the Indian sub-continent too, so reflecting the UK's and particularly London's pull as a global hub offering lucrative opportunities for the sex industry.

The Dutch National Rapporteur and German BKA reports also offer insights into the origin of trafficking suspects – with Dutch nationals the predominant group in the Netherlands and German nationals the predominant group in Germany. Foreign suspects are often the same nationality as victims; that is, typically, Bulgarian, Romanian, Russian and Ukrainian. However, the 2007 Dutch National Rapporteur report indicates that after people born in the Netherlands, Moroccan and Turkish suspects were the next largest suspect groups – which reflects the make-up of the country's significant immigrant populations. Just as victims' countries of origin can shift from one year to the next, so traffickers' nationalities can change. Yet, interpreting these changes, as with any crime statistics, demands not only that an analysis of dominant criminal networks is undertaken, but also that careful consideration is given to any developments in policing practices and recording patterns from one year to the next. For example, an increase in suspects from a particular country may reflect increased police efforts to target the criminal activities of criminals from certain communities.

Where information about traffickers does exist, as in reports by the Dutch National Rapporteur and the German BKA, it throws up some facts that appear to contradict established wisdom about trafficking as organised crime, namely that many traffickers appear to be working alone and would seem to be loosely connected with organised crime. Herein, the focus on trafficking as part of organised crime is not incorrect, but reflects more the legislative approach to trafficking that has placed it within or alongside laws searching to eliminate cross-border organised crime – such as the UN Protocol on Trafficking which comes under the UN Convention on Transnational Organised Crime.

Explanations of the crime

Explanations of human trafficking are typically constructed around 'push' and 'pull' factors in recruitment, transport and destination countries. Herein, consideration is given to the push factors of high unemployment and lack of state support in countries of recruitment, and of the demand side and economic viability of prostitution in destination countries. In the context of Europe, the disintegration of the old order in the former communist bloc at the end of the 1980s and beginning of the 1990s created a widening gap between rich and poor and provided ample opportunities for crime, which included trafficking in women to the economically wealthy sex markets of Western Europe. At the same time, the break-up of the former Yugoslavia also offered lucrative markets for both supply of and demand for trafficked women in the Balkans region, including demand for prostitutes from UNMIK[12] and NATO[13] peacekeepers working for the very missions that were supposed to be upholding international human rights in the region[14] (Amnesty International 2006).

When looking to understand the causes of and markets for sex trafficking, what cannot be overlooked is the gendered nature of this crime and, more generally, of prostitution – wherein men are typically the traffickers and clients of both trafficked and non-trafficked prostitutes, and women are predominantly prostitutes and hence victims of trafficking. Although women are involved in aspects of recruitment for trafficking, particularly in some countries such as Moldova, the worst excesses of trafficking, involving actual violence and sexual violence, remain the preserve of male perpetrators. While a great deal is now known about trafficking victims and to a lesser extent about traffickers, much less is known about the men who use prostitutes and encounter trafficking victims. Reflecting this situation, prevention initiatives focus on warning young women about the dangers of trafficking and little regard is given to targeting male clients. This response is understandable if one considers the seemingly insurmountable causes of trafficking that include the gendered nature of prostitution and relative poverty.

At the heart of explanations of this gendered crime lie considerations about women's poverty. In the case of Europe, the collapse of communist regimes saw women suffer in terms of relative poverty (Nikolić-Ristanović 2002). Former state-subsidised welfare, including provision for childcare, and support for women's place in the workforce were undermined in post-Communist countries in the absence of ideological and financial backing. As a result, women became particularly vulnerable to economic sexual exploitation in the absence of financial alternatives. This vulnerability was exacerbated because of a lack of awareness among many women, particularly those from rural communities in central and eastern Europe, about the dangers of accepting certain job offers – those with good pay but with minimum experience or qualifications needed. In the same way, men from economically poor regions are trafficked for labour exploitation as they are often deceived into thinking that golden opportunities for work lie abroad.

In destination countries in Europe, such as the UK, the Netherlands and Germany, economic wealth and a booming sex industry are able to support and create demand for trafficked women. Abolitionists, who like the anti-slave traders before them call for the prohibition of prostitution, would contend that governments' tacit acceptance of prostitution serves to support the industry – and hence support the demand for trafficked women. So far the evidence is inconclusive as to whether abolition or some form of regulation of prostitution would either serve to increase or decrease demand for prostitution. On the one hand there is the approach of the Dutch government that recognises prostitution as work in need of regulation to combat its worst excesses and to protect women, while others, such as the Swedish government, have outlawed the purchasing of prostitution as a violation of women's equality. Whereas condemnation of the worst aspects of prostitution, such as child prostitution, is a point on which governments and NGOs can agree, there is a high level of disagreement in some quarters about how best to respond to prostitution, which has implications for trafficking victims.

With the accession of twelve 'new' Member States to the European Union since 2004 and the opening up of Europe's borders within the Schengen zone, it has become easier for more Europeans to move around unencumbered within the EU. Freedom of movement of European citizens lies at the heart of the European model, but while this benefits the mainstay of the law-abiding public it also presents increased opportunities for criminals to move trafficked people around without detection. In this regard, established criminological insights about opportunities to commit crime versus risk of detection apply to the crime of sex trafficking. Traffickers exploit a market situation where supply and demand for trafficked women is high, but where internal border controls within the Union are relaxed and the risks of detection are low relative to the economic gains that can be made through the exploitation of women (and girls) in the sex industry.

Responses to the crime

Writing about the Balkans, Lindstrom (2007) characterises four different *policy* approaches to trafficking by the international community; namely: (1) the migration-focused approach adopted by organisations such as the IOM; (2) the law enforcement approach of policing, immigration and border control; (3) the human rights approach of NGOs; and (4) the economic approach that focuses on the root causes of trafficking. These four approaches can be reconsidered as two distinct responses – the first driven by concerns about the criminality of trafficking in relation to traffickers, illegal immigrants and law enforcement responses, and the second by recognition of trafficking as a human rights violation with deep-seated roots in inequality. In turn, three *practical* responses to trafficking can be characterised, namely: (1) prevention of trafficking; (2) protection and support of victims; and (3) prosecution of traffickers. Prevention and protection are essentially victim-centred and have been offered in the main by NGOs. In comparison, law enforcement and immigration have focused typically on the *need to* prosecute traffickers and not on the *needs of* trafficking victims.

Whether these distinct responses to trafficking can be recognised today is questionable as, more recently, a third 'P' has been added in the response of inter-governmental agencies, and others, to trafficking – namely the need for 'partnerships' between different actors in the fight against trafficking. The growth throughout the 1990s and 2000s of 'victim-centred' justice, which sought to recognise victims' place in the criminal justice process and to treat them respectfully and with due care, has meant that trafficking victims, alongside other victims, have seen changes in how they are responded to by law enforcement (Goodey 2005b). In parallel, as calls were stepped up in the 1990s and 2000s to prosecute traffickers, the need for victim assistance emerged as a means of enhancing victim cooperation in testifying against traffickers. One way to gain this cooperation was to offer various levels of support to victims, such as a period of reflection prior to testifying and residence permits in the run up to and for the duration of any trial. To this end, in 2004 the Justice and Home Affairs Council of the EU adopted a limited directive on residence permits for trafficking victims. In this way, law enforcement goals to prosecute traffickers can be wedded with human rights goals to assist victims – and hence a more victim-centred approach has gradually emerged as beneficial to all parties.

The European Commission has been active in its response to trafficking in the context of general concerns to address crime, and in particular organised crime, and the problems of illegal immigration. Herein, human smuggling and trafficking are often responded to as part of the same problem, just as offenders and victims are wrapped up in the same policy responses that are increasingly packaged as both crime-fighting and victim-centred. Notable policy responses and legislation that have emerged from the EU, and which variously address the need to fight crime and recognise victims, include the following: the 1997 Joint Action by the Council of the European Union to combat trafficking in human beings and the sexual exploitation of children; the more weighty 2002 Council Framework Decision on combating trafficking in human beings, which was followed in 2003 by the Framework Decision on combating the sexual exploitation of children and child pornography which makes specific reference to child trafficking; and the 2004 Council Directive that deals with residence permits for third-country nationals who are trafficking victims and agree to cooperate with the authorities in their efforts to prosecute traffickers. In May 2009 the Commission, subsequent to a review of existing legislation, entered new proposals for the Council Framework Decision on preventing and combating trafficking in human beings and the Council Framework Decision on combating the sexual exploitation of children.

In addition to legislative developments, the EU has launched a number of crime-fighting programmes since the 1990s that have funded various practical law-enforcement and victim-centred initiatives addressing trafficking; namely, the DAPHNE programme concerning violence against women and children, and the STOP and AGIS programmes that have focused on policing and judicial cooperation.[15]

In England and Wales, which is subject to EU-wide legislation, legal developments addressing trafficking include recognition of the offence of trafficking for prostitution in the 2002 Nationality, Immigration and Asylum Act, along with the 2003 Sexual Offences Act, which went beyond the scope of the UN Trafficking Protocol by not stipulating the use of coercion, force or threat by traffickers for the crime of trafficking to have occurred. Notable practical responses to trafficking include the establishment in 2006 of the Sheffield-based Human Trafficking Centre, which was formed in response to the need for a coordinated approach to tackling trafficking from the police, the prosecution service, immigration and NGOs. At the same time, the police conducted two UK-wide raids on locations with suspected trafficking victims under the name of Operation Pentameter in 2006 and Pentameter II in 2007. The success of these raids has been questioned by some commentators who contend that victims still receive less than adequate treatment as the focus remains with law and immigration enforcement rather than victim assistance. However, while the practical outcomes of law enforcement interventions can be criticised, the policy direction of the government's 2007 Action Plan on Trafficking is squarely victim-centred with respect to both its content and the language it adopts.

More recently, attention has turned in the UK to the issue of trafficked children in the care of social services. A 2007 report by End Child Prostitution, Child Pornography and the Trafficking of Children (ECPAT) indicated that three regions alone in the UK reported 80 cases of known or suspected victims of child trafficking, with a staggering 48 of these cases involving children who had disappeared from the care of social services. While it is unclear whether these children were trafficked for sexual exploitation, the findings of this report, together with other publications (CEOP 2007) and the 2007 UK Home Office Action Plan on Trafficking, are that children in care, and particularly unaccompanied minors, are particularly vulnerable to exploitation by traffickers. The focus on child victims of trafficking who are 'in care' serves to highlight particularly vulnerable groups and locations for trafficking that have hitherto been overlooked in research and policy responses. At the same time, the enactment of the Asylum and Immigration Act 2004 in England and Wales, which included legislation on trafficking for labour exploitation, is illustrative of this wider recognition of trafficking in all its guises.

Although international legislation has recognised trafficking with respect to both sexual and labour exploitation, it is evident that labour exploitation has taken second place in comparison with the attention and policy responses that have been devoted over the years to sexual exploitation of women (and children). To some extent this skewed focus on trafficking for sexual exploitation can be explained because of the public's long held fascination with the idea of 'sex slavery', which provides more scope for newspaper headlines and evokes more public sympathy than tales of exploited illegal workers. In this regard sex trafficking will inevitably remain at the heart of policy and practical responses to trafficking, but there are signs that other areas, such as trafficking for labour exploitation, are gaining in recognition (Craig *et al.* 2007).

Concluding comments

Human trafficking is both an ancient crime and one that has re-emerged in new guises in the light of opportunities to exploit other human beings as a result of economic inequalities, socio-political upheaval and a seemingly unstoppable demand for cheap labour, including sexual services. In recognition of human trafficking as a growing problem, legal and policy responses have grown apace in recent years in an effort to stem the tide of trafficking. Yet, unlike conventional crimes such as burglary and car crime, what we know about the extent and nature of trafficking is limited because of severe under-reporting by victims and under-recording by criminal justice personnel. In turn, the focus of responses to trafficking has been on sex trafficking and less so on other manifestations of trafficking in the labour market. As a reflection of the uneven nature of knowledge about and responses to trafficking, the chapter concentrated on the area where most is known about this crime, namely sex trafficking. Having described the scope, nature of and responses to trafficking in the chapter, two themes have emerged.

First, it is apparent that sex trafficking cannot be understood in the context of conventional crime and with respect to experiences in a single country (the UK). Given the cross-border nature of much of sex trafficking – as a process involving countries of origin, transit and destination, and victims and offenders of various nationalities – the chapter explored the nature of and responses to trafficking in the context of Europe and, more specifically, the UK. From the evidence available, trafficking would appear to be a crime that is loosely connected to organised criminal networks, but is perhaps better understood as part of a process that extends from one place and one country to another in the form of recruiters, traffickers, brothel owners, clients and trafficking victims.

Describing the crime of trafficking serves to highlight an area where, until recently, criminology and criminal justice has devoted little attention. In comparison, the work of international organisations such as the IOM and the humanitarian efforts of NGOs working with victims have served to draw attention to a crime that was long below the radar of conventional research and policy interventions. To some extent a lack of focus on trafficking – its offenders and victims – reflects the relatively marginal role in criminology of renewed approaches in the 1990s to exploring organised crime and its related phenomena such as trafficking.

Second, describing and accounting for the crime of sex trafficking highlights the need to see and respond to crime as victim-centred as well as a criminal event. Although criminology is essentially concerned with the essence of offending – its patterns, explanations, and criminal justice responses to it – the victim has increasingly come to be placed centre-stage in responses to crime. This is particularly important for crimes where there are discernible victims and where they suffer extreme harm – as in the case of sex trafficking. Also, where the cooperation of the victim plays a central part in the prosecution of offenders, the requirement to effectively recognise and respond to victims' needs in the criminal justice process has become increasingly important, whereas previously trafficking victims themselves were often criminalised by law enforcement and immigration as part of a crime-immigration scourge. In this regard, trafficking is recognised in the Charter of Fundamental Rights of the European Union as a human rights abuse and therefore cannot be addressed without consideration of the centrality of victims' experiences.

In sum, this chapter has presented a limited introduction to human trafficking with respect to sex trafficking. In so doing it has attempted to alert the reader to the extent and nature of this crime and legislative and policy responses to it, while giving due recognition to the need for a victim-centred approach to sex trafficking as a gendered and human rights abuse.

Selected further reading

For an introduction to the scope and global reach of human trafficking, including the latest legislative and policy responses to the problem, readers should look at the 'human trafficking and migrant smuggling' part of the United Nations Office on Drugs and Crime (UNODC) website.[16] The International Labour Organisation (ILO) also produces some interesting reports on the theme of trafficking for forced labour;[17] thereby offering an alternative to the predominant focus on trafficking in women and children for sexual exploitation. In the UK, the UK Action Plan on Tackling Human Trafficking[18] presents the government's approach to the problem and can be read alongside the work of the Sheffield-based UK Human Trafficking Centre[19] that sets out to offer a multi-agency response to trafficking. For an overview of legislative and policy responses in the specific area of child trafficking, the 2009 Report on Child Trafficking[20] by the European Union Agency for Fundamental Rights (FRA) provides information on the situation in the EU's 27 member states. For further information on child trafficking, readers are advised to look at the reports of the NGO ECPAT,[21] which present a thorough overview of what is largely a hidden problem.

Notes

1 The opinions of the author expressed in this chapter do not represent those of the European Union Agency for Fundamental Rights (FRA).
2 The Trafficking Protocol, together with a separate protocol on the Smuggling of Migrants by Land, Sea and Air, supplements the 2000 UN Convention against Transnational Organised Crime.
3 http://www.ungift.org/docs/ungift/pdf/knowledge/ebook.pdf
4 http://www.ungift.org/docs/ungift/pdf/knowledge/trafficking inpersons_report_2006ver2.pdf
5 http://english.bnrm.nl/reports/fifth – Trafficking in Human Beings: Fifth Report of the Dutch National Rapporteur.
6 Report of the Experts Group on Trafficking in Human Beings (2004). Online at: http://ec.europa.eu/justice_home/doc_centre/crime/trafficking/doc/report_expert_group_1204_en.pdf.
7 NGO 'La Strada' – http://www.lastradainternational.org/?main=home; NGO 'The Coalition against Trafficking in Women' – http://www.catwinternational.org/; NGO 'The Global Alliance against Trafficking in Women' – http://www.gaatw.net/.
8 http://www.iom.int/jahia/Jahia/pid/748
9 http://english.bnrm.nl/reports/fifth/
10 http://www.bka.de/lageberichte/mh/2004/lagebildmh_en.pdf
11 http://www.pentameter.police.uk/docs/pentameter.pdf
12 UNMIK – United Nations Mission in Kosovo
13 NATO – North Atlantic Treaty Organisation

14 In a Council of Europe publication on the 'Octopus Programme' (2004), which partly explored the issue of trafficking, the list of bars that were classified as 'off limits' to UNMIK and KFOR staff because of the premises' suspected involvement in trafficking went from 18 in late 1999 to 75 in January 2001 and 200+ in January 2004.

15 http://ec.europa.eu/justice_home/fsj/intro/fsj_intro_en.htm – this site provides information about the Commission's various programmes that address either directly or indirectly human trafficking.

16 http://www.unodc.org/unodc/en/human-trafficking/index.html

17 http://www.ilo.org/sapfl/Informationresources/ILOPublications/lang--en/docName--WCMS_090548/index.htm

18 http://www.homeoffice.gov.uk/documents/human-traffick-action-plan

19 http://www.ukhtc.org/

20 http://fra.europa.eu/fraWebsite/attachments/Pub_Child_Trafficking_09_en.pdf

21 http://www.ecpat.org.uk/publications.html

References

Amnesty International (2006) 'The UN in Kosova – A Legacy of Impunity'. Online at: http://www.amnesty.org/en/library/asset/EUR70/015/2006/en/dom-EUR700152006en.pdf.

Aromaa, K. and Lehti, M. (2007) 'Trafficking in human beings: policy problems and recommendations', in P. C. van Duyne, A. Maljevic, M. van Dijck, K. van Lampe and J. Harvey (eds), *Crime Business and Crime Money in Europe: The Dirty Linen of Illicit Enterprise*. Nijmegen: Wolf Legal Publishers, pp. 97–109.

Child Exploitation and Online Protection Centre (CEOP) (2007) *A Scoping Project on Child Trafficking in the UK*. London: CEOP.

Craig, G., Gaus, A., Wilkinson, M., Skrivankova, K. and McQuade, A. (2007) *Contemporary Slavery in the UK*. York: Joseph Rowntree Foundation.

Danilova-Trainor, G. and Belser, P. (2006) *Globalization and the Illicit Market for Human Trafficking: An Empirical Analysis of Supply and Demand*. Geneva: International Labour Office (ILO).

De Cock, M. (2007) *Directions for National and International Data Collection on Forced Labour*. Geneva: International Labour Office (ILO).

ECPAT (2007) *Missing Out: A Study of Child Trafficking in the North-West, North-East and West Midlands*. London: ECPAT UK.

Friman, H. R. and Reich, S. (eds) (2007) *Human Trafficking, Human Security and the Balkans*. Pittsburgh, PA: University of Pittsburgh Press. Online at: http://www.maxwell.syr.edu/moynihan/programs/ces/pcconfpdfs/lindstrom.pdf.

Ghinararu, C. and van der Linden, M. N. J. (2004) *Trafficking of Migrant Workers from Romania: Issues of Labour and Sexual Exploitation*. Geneva: International Labour Office (ILO).

Goodey, J. (2003) 'Recognising organised crime's victims: the case of sex trafficking in the EU', in A. Edwards and P. Gill (eds), *Transnational Organised Crime: Perspectives on Global Security*. London: Routledge, pp. 157–73.

Goodey, J. (2005a) 'Sex trafficking in the European Union', in J. Sheptycki and A. Wardak (eds), *Transnational and Comparative Criminology*. London: Cavendish, pp. 269–85.

Goodey, J. (2005b) *Victims and Victimology: Research, Policy and Practice*. Harlow: Pearson.

Home Office (2007) *UK Action Plan on Tackling Human Trafficking*. London: Home Office.

Kelly, L. and Regan, L. (2000) *Stopping Traffic: Exploring the Extent of, and Responses to, Trafficking in Women for Sexual Exploitation in the UK*, Home Office Police Research Series Paper No. 125. London: Home Office.

Lindstrom, N. (2007) 'Transnational responses to human trafficking: the politics of anti-trafficking in the Balkans', in H. Richard Friman and Simon Reich *(eds)*, *Human Trafficking, Human Security and the Balkans*. Pittsburgh, PA: University of Pittsburgh Press. Available on line at: http://www.maxwell.syr.edu/moynihan/programs/ces/pcconfpdfs/lindstrom.pdf.

Nikolić-Ristanović, V. (2002) 'War and post-war victimization of women', *European Journal of Crime, Criminal Law and Criminal Justice*, 10 (2–3): 138–45.

OSCE (2008) *Human Trafficking for Labour Exploitation/Forced and Bonded Labour: Identification, Prevention and Prosecution*. Vienna: OSCE.

Surtees, R. (2008) 'Traffickers and trafficking in Southern and Eastern Europe: considering the other side of human trafficking', *European Journal of Criminology*, 5 (1): 39–68.

van den Anker, C. L. and Doomernik, J. (eds) (2006) *Trafficking and Women's Rights*. Basingstoke: Palgrave.

Chapter 35

Money laundering

David C. Hicks[1]

Introduction

This chapter aims to offer insights into a specialist topic, the crime of money laundering. It will begin with a definition of the concept, including discussion of the Proceeds of Crime Act (POCA) of 2002 in the United Kingdom and the implications of its definition. Then it turns to evidence on the scope and magnitude of the phenomenon drawn from various international bodies such as the United Nations, the Financial Action Task Force (FATF), the International Monetary Fund (IMF) and other sources. The chapter subsequently addresses types of predicate or underlying offending that are commonly associated with proceeds of crime and discusses several of the methods used to launder money.

Attention then turns to key developments in the responses to this crime, inclusive of those introduced by the United States, the UN, the FATF, the European Union (EU) and the Egmont Group. Such developments over the past few decades have led to concerted efforts to implement anti-money laundering (AML) regimes. These are often represented in the institutional form of national financial intelligence units (FIUs), which receive, analyse and disseminate pertinent information. Since 2006 in the UK, many of the AML functions and additional institutional measures to target proceeds of crime and those involved have been integrated into the Serious Organised Crime Agency (SOCA).

The limited space allotted for this chapter necessitates a rather selective overview of key aspects and issues. A core issue that will be noted is the progressive expansion of money-laundering definitions to potentially include most underlying offending as well as virtually any interaction with the proceeds of crime. Nonetheless, the impacts of these expansionary initiatives in reducing the targeted phenomena are not clear.

Definition

In simple terms, money laundering refers to efforts to convert or conceal the 'financial' proceeds of crime, that is efforts to give them the appearance of legitimacy. The standard definition and understanding of money laundering tends to presuppose substantive criminal involvement linked to organised crime activities, if not the possible presence of professional launderers. Nevertheless, international conventions and domestic responses (more below) tend toward the inclusion of a broad range of underlying or predicate offences and an even broader range of methods that may be considered as money laundering. This inclusive approach is not without boundaries.

For instance, some argue that the AML agenda exposes the (international) inclination to target tax evasion or avoidance (Beare 2002). Nevertheless, tax issues represent one area of concern that has been resistant to explicit inclusion under international money-laundering efforts and cross-border data sharing. This resistance has continued even though several governments may explicitly and in some cases aggressively use such controls to target tax issues within their jurisdiction (e.g. Australia, the United Kingdom, the United States).

While the range of predicate offences has been subject to expansion over time (from drugs and designated crimes to all serious crimes) so has the definition of the activities that constitute money laundering. In many cases, the latter definition has been expanded to include virtually any disposition of the proceeds of crime (Alldridge 2008; van Duyne 2003). The Proceeds of Crime Act (POCA) of 2002 in the UK exemplifies this point. The Act covers the diverse range of:

- concealing in the form of attempts, conspiracy, incitement, aiding, abetting, counselling or procuring the commission of virtually any interaction with criminal property or its removal from the country;

- arrangements that indicate knowing or suspecting that one is facilitating another in the 'beneficial' ownership of criminal property; and

- acquisition, use and possession of criminal property which also constitutes an offence of money laundering.

What is more, the legislation has extra-territorial reach in that activities committed outside the country are also criminalised where those activities would constitute money laundering if committed within the UK. This definition is so broad that it apparently does not require deliberate efforts to obscure illegitimate funds and property, and instead criminalises virtually any interaction with the proceeds of crime. Law-abiding members of society may well be concerned that inadvertent interaction with the proceeds of crime may result in criminal liability. However, POCA offers some protection in that citizens may escape criminal liability by reporting suspicious activity to a competent authority, or they may be exempt where their acquisition, use or possession of criminal property is obtained for 'adequate consideration' (i.e. something close to the market value of the property).

Scope of the problem

Since the 1990s it has become increasingly popular to articulate the threat of serious and organised crime in terms of its *raison d'être*, that is money. The FATF began the charge with its 1990 estimate of US $300 billion in global illicit drug proceeds, the bulk of which was deemed to be available for laundering (van Duyne 2002: 62). The IMF followed with the estimate that 2–5 per cent of global gross domestic product (GDP) represents laundered funds involving some US $500 billion in the study year (Quirk 1996). The UN topped the debate with an estimate that organised crime syndicates worldwide gross US $1.5 trillion per year with, presumably, a substantial portion of this available for laundering (UN Development Programme 1999: 42; UN International Drug Control Programme 1997: 123–4). These estimates are impressive in their (escalating) valuations and their impact upon the 'common sense' views of decision-makers and perhaps the public; however, the methodological foundations are far from compelling.

The FATF estimate is linked to the examples submitted by member states, but these might not offer a representative sample of cases. The IMF paper provides some interesting ideas but it appears to derive its 2–5 per cent figure from a newspaper article and unreferenced data from the US Internal Revenue Service (Quirk 1996: 16). The UN estimate is only indicative as it derives from a basket of indicators. In summary, the estimates of money laundering often suffer from non-existent or questionable methodologies, indirect indicators of supply and demand with large margins of error and mathematical incoherence combined with the generation of 'facts by repetition' (Passas 1999; van Duyne 2002). The 2–5 per cent claim has had particular resonance as an accepted fact among decision-makers. It has the benefit of a built-in tendency toward the expansion of the money laundering problem over time, notwithstanding the lack of empirical inquiry into how laundering may parallel or contrast patterns of economic growth and contraction in the 'legitimate' economy. Much of the suggested growth in laundering can also be attributed to the expansion of definitional boundaries, from an early focus on drugs and designated offences to the wide domain of all serious crime.

Reuter and Truman (2004: 9–24) offer a helpful overview of the academic literature relating to the macroeconomic and microeconomic estimates of money laundering. The former is a broad category that refers to all untaxed revenue from illegal and legal activity, including tax evasion and avoidance. The latter is a narrow category that refers to estimates of earnings from criminal activity, excluding tax evasion and avoidance. A key macroeconomic approach is to examine variables associated with the known gross domestic product (GDP) and its relationship to currency demand, with gaps assumed to reflect the unknown or underground GDP. While offering an indicative insight into the possible size of the underground economy, the monetary focus may tend to overemphasise cash-intensive businesses such as illicit drugs at the expense of frauds. The microeconomic approach focuses on estimating the possible revenues of particular crime activities. Obtaining valid and reliable estimates is clearly problematic given the context-dependent nature of profitability for particular activities and products. The unavoidable conclusion appears to be that 'the macroeconomic estimates are methodologically flawed, while the available microeconomic estimates lack credible empirical foundations' (Reuter and Truman 2004: 10).

Much of the available (imperfect) knowledge about money laundering comes from cases that are revealed through regulatory and compliance activities, civil actions, enforcement investigations and happenstance or luck. The examples that come to official attention all too often reflect the priorities, interests and budgetary realities of those who inquire into such problems. Little attention has been devoted to constructing a systematic evidence base integrating macro and micro levels of analysis. This would include studying the differential distribution of the tangible and intangible costs and benefits (inclusive of realisable revenue following depreciation etc.) across various types of crime activities in different contexts (Levi and Osofsky 1995). More detailed analytical insights into how different money-laundering schemes intersect with legitimate economic sectors would be helpful alongside analysis of the vulnerability or resilience of various sectors. In the absence of detailed and systematic research evidence, the tendency is toward an ever-expanding net of assumed (but often under-researched) risk and more entities recruited into providing reports to pertinent authorities on suspicious and large cash transactions. In European countries and many others, the reporting of suspicious and other transactions has expanded from banks and financial institutions to include businesses such as car dealers, casinos and jewellers, and professionals such as accountants and lawyers.

Selected money laundering methods

Theoretically, there are no limits to the possibilities for laundering save offender ingenuity and the time to learn and design new methods. The range could include squirrelling away some cannabis-related cash in a biscuit tin or running a multi-billion pound international Ponzi (or pyramid) fraud scheme over many years. The former is a self-evident, though uninspired, attempt to conceal. The latter involves the creation of a programme where the money of new investors goes toward paying the high-yield returns promised to existing investors. Despite the mafia-octopus imagery that may attach to official and common-sense thinking about money laundering, much of this activity will only be as organised as it needs to be (Levi and Maguire 2004: 458). Indeed, the vast majority of cases are do-it-yourself (DIY) where those involved in the predicate offence perform the laundering and oftentimes the proceeds of crime may go toward day-to-day and lifestyle expenses.

Reuter and Truman (2004: 33) reviewed cases (N = 580) drawn from the FATF typology reports 1998–2004 and an Egmont Group report in 2000. This does not provide a representative international sample. The secretive nature of this type of criminal activity and the secretive nature of those who respond to it make it particularly difficult to envisage how to obtain a truly representative sample.

Nevertheless, the authors found that three offences accounted for 70 per cent of cases: drug trafficking (32 per cent), fraud (22 per cent), and non-drug smuggling (16 per cent). The bulk of the remaining 30 per cent of cases related to terrorism, unknown crimes, blue-collar crimes such as prostitution and illegal gambling, bribery/corruption and tax evasion.

For all predicate offences the authors found that nearly 70 per cent of the laundering methods involved eight techniques, with wire transfers (23 per cent), and the use of a front company/organisation (13 per cent) comprising the largest categories. The remaining techniques included the use of accountants and financial officers (6 per cent), purchase of high-value goods (6 per cent), shell corporations (6 per cent), money orders and cashiers' checks (5 per cent), real estate (5 per cent), and offshore accounts (5 per cent). Across the three dominant predicate offences, the laundering methods of wire transfer and use of a front company/organisation are the largest single categories. Nonetheless, the focus of laundering methods does vary according to the nature of the underlying predicate offence. For instance, drug-related laundering appears to place greater focus on (in descending order) the purchase of high-value goods, real estate, use of financial instruments and use of lawyers and accountants. In contrast, fraud tends to focus more on (in descending order) shell corporations, use of lawyers and accountants and securities.

Individuals or groups involved in producing and/or trafficking illicit drugs represent a clear example of the placement, layering and integration sequence that may be useful to explaining laundering activity and complexity. Drug activities are capable of generating large volumes of cash, tens or hundreds of thousands of pounds depending on the size of the trafficking operation. The drugs and the proceeds of crime are vulnerable to potential 'theft' by criminal rivals and the state (forfeiture), and participants are at personal risk of harm and the loss of liberty (Matrix Knowledge Group 2007). To reduce such risks, the drug entrepreneur(s) may seek to 'place' the proceeds of crime into convertible and portable instruments: for instance, depositing proceeds into their bank account and/or obtaining a money order or cashiers' cheque to deposit into other accounts. Movements of tens and hundreds of thousands of pounds should be atypical for most persons and may arouse suspicions from financial institutions. Suspicion may be reduced through techniques such as 'smurfing' (making smaller deposits at multiple institutions and perhaps using a number of people) and 'structuring' (making smaller deposits over a longer period). Once placed into the financial system, the security of proceeds can be further increased by 'layering' transactions to obscure the criminal origins of the funds. Wire transfers out of the host country and then between several countries (such as tax havens) offer an effective means of complicating enforcement efforts to trace and seize proceeds of crime. Assuming the two previous steps are conducted with some care and attention, criminals should be able to 'integrate' the proceeds of crime into otherwise legitimate assets or investments without attracting the interest of law enforcement.

Frauds may tend to flatten the discrete divisions between placement, layering and integration as well as the detection capabilities of AML systems. This is because the proceeds of fraud can be generated from within a set of transactions. Such monies may already be placed within the financial or economic system in which they have been generated, are readily available for layering which also may occur in generating such processes, and/or they may already be integrated into securities or other financial products. Transfer pricing (de Boyrie *et al.* 2005; Pak *et al.* 2003) offers one method of laundering where businesses can launder monies between countries with relatively little risk of detection by AML systems that tend to focus on suspicious activities or the physical/electronic movement of large amounts of cash across borders. Imagine two businesses who wish to launder money, with A in one country and B in another country. The former may sell the latter legitimate goods at an undervalued price that can be subsequently sold on for profit. Typically, the supplementary value of the exchange or the good itself constitutes the laundered portion. Such trade-based laundering is difficult to detect where parties maintain otherwise real and modest transactions, and especially where it involves a non-standardised commodity such as jewellery (as opposed to razor blades), whose true value cannot be assessed in a mechanical fashion by weight or volume.

Terrorist finance bears some similarities to money laundering where revenues for the former are derived from criminal activities and intended to support terrorist operations. It is different where otherwise legitimate activities such as charitable fund-raising may be used to generate terrorist finance. In either case, unless the charity or the recipient of the funds is on a national or international terror watch-list or under active surveillance and investigation, the reader may rightly presume that it is difficult to identify monies that are 'intended' for criminal/terrorist use. Thus the concepts of placement, layering and integration seem somewhat moot in the case of terrorist finance.

Response

The foundations to target money laundering were established during the 1970s and 1980s, though the substantive international drive began, in earnest, from the 1990s. This has involved a range of domestic and international bodies and, while supported by many, the United States has inspired and provided much of the underpinning in the fight against organised crime, drugs and money laundering (Andreas and Nadelmann 2006).

United States

Money-laundering controls were pioneered in the United States with two pieces of 1970 legislation: the Bank Secrecy Act (BSA) and the Racketeer-Influenced Corrupt Organizations (RICO) Act. The former served to limit bank secrecy in that financial institutions operating in the United States were compelled, under the threat of criminal penalties for non-compliance, to file currency transaction reports (CTRs) to the Department of the Treasury for cash transactions of $10,000 or more. The latter targeted persons involved in enterprise linked to a set of serious federal and state crimes, and provided enhanced controls (restraining orders on ill-gotten assets), penalties such as fines and up to 20 years in prison for each individual racketeering count and the forfeiture of ill-gotten gains upon conviction. It further affords private entities such as individuals and businesses, which have been harmed by racketeering activities, the opportunity to sue individuals involved in such criminal enterprises. Those convicted under the criminal and civil provisions of the RICO Act are liable to paying treble damages, that is three times the amount of the damages linked to the racketeering activity. The Money Laundering Control Act of 1986 provides under section 18 USC § 1956 and 1957 a consolidation of previous controls, it makes money laundering a federal crime and criminalises efforts to structure transactions to avoid reporting requirements.

The inspiration for these three US responses was varied. The BSA focus was on tax evasion (and other potential crimes) via foreign banks within the United States, RICO was part of a broader initiative under the Organized Crime Control Act 1970 to target those involved in organised crime, and the Money Laundering Control Act was clearly inspired by the war on drugs (Levi and Reuter 2006). The various provisions began to be used in a more focused manner during the 1980s and 1990s to target significant organised crime activity, and these provisions have contributed to the attack upon and declining influence of traditional organised crime groups in the United States (Reuter 1995). It is perhaps not surprising that these provisions have increasingly been used to target a diverse range of actors, many of whom do not correspond to stereotypical images of organised crime.

International bodies

The 1988 United Nations Convention Against Illicit Traffic in Narcotic Drugs and Psychotropic Substances (also known as the Vienna Convention) aimed to create an international set of standards in tackling illicit drugs and the organisation of criminal enterprise linked to such activities. Building upon previous international drug conventions from 1961 and 1971, the 1988 development included provisions for signatory nation states to engage in complementary controls to permit the tracing and seizure of 'drug-related' assets. The Vienna Convention fostered money-laundering reporting requirements by financial institutions, confiscation of the proceeds of drug-related offences and mutual legal assistance inclusive of extradition between countries in drug-related cases.

The group of seven (G7) leading industrial nations formed the Financial Action Task Force (FATF) in 1989. This intergovernmental body specifies the benchmark standards for money-laundering controls. It released its 40 recommendations to tackle money laundering in 1990 and offered subsequent revisions to address changing understanding of the phenomenon. The recommendations include, *inter alia*, criminalising money laundering, requiring financial institutions and other relevant entities to perform due diligence in knowing your customers (KYC) and maintaining relevant records, supporting international cooperation and submitting required reports to the competent authority. The competent authority is typically a financial intelligence unit (FIU) – an institution that is discussed below in some detail – that receives reports and provides intelligence for investigations.

Nation-state compliance with the 1999 United Nations International Convention for the Suppression of the Financing of Terrorism was afforded urgent salience following the terrorist attacks in the United States in 2001. In the month following these attacks, the FATF issued eight special recommendations to address terrorist financing and a ninth recommendation was added in 2004. These special recommendations include the ratification and implementation of UN instruments, criminalising, freezing and confiscating funds and assets linked to terrorism and terrorists, reporting of suspicious transactions and a focus on issues such as alternative remittance systems such as hawala (Passas 1999), wire transfers and non-profit charitable organisations. The FATF promotes domestic policymaking consistent with the recommendations and fosters such consistency with a (potentially) formidable enforcement mechanism. Members are subject to periodic mutual evaluation and parties may be blacklisted as Non-Cooperative Countries and Territories (NCCT) where they are deemed non-compliant with the recommendations. NCCT status can result in a range of sanctions, including denial of access to international financial networks and additional scrutiny of financial transactions connected to NCCT-designated states. This may substantially impact upon a given state, though in practice NCCT status and sanctions have tended to be imposed upon developing and transition countries, prompting possible charges of imperialistic bias (Levi and Gilmore 2002).

The European Union (EU) has issued money laundering directives to foster member state compliance with UN Conventions and the FATF recommendations. The first was issued in 1991, with subsequent directives issued in 2001 and 2005. The EU directives demonstrate a progressive expansion from requiring member states to criminalise money laundering and enlisting financial institution participation in the AML regime, to expanding coverage to service professionals (lawyers, tax advisers, auditors) and enhanced due diligence with respect to beneficial owners.

The Egmont Group was established in 1995 from the meetings of several FIUs attempting to share information and support their respective efforts to address money laundering. As of 2009, 116 agencies around the world are members of Egmont. It acts as a vehicle for data sharing and policy discussion as well as the elaboration of standards for member and would-be member institutions.

The expansionary tendencies of efforts to target the proceeds of crime may have reached a zenith with the 2000 United Nations Convention Against Transnational Organised Crime (also known as the Palermo Convention). Primarily, this was achieved by broadly defining the concept of the organised criminal group and by targeting four activities specified in the convention and all 'serious crimes'. The convention focuses its definition to include a structured group of at least three members, involving formal or informal association and/or roles, and acting in concert to commit crimes specified in the convention or 'serious crimes' for financial or material benefit. The convention applies to four specific offences (participation in a criminal organisation, laundering the proceeds of crime, corruption and obstruction of justice) and all 'serious crimes', defined as those offences punishable by four or more years imprisonment as a maximum penalty. The initial focus on drugs and designated offences has given way to wide definitions that make it difficult to identify examples of criminal activities that would be immune to the choice of a given state to potentially target for proceeds of crime and money laundering.

Anti-money laundering (AML) regimes

Levi and Reuter (2006) offer a generic structure that can be helpfully used to understand the possibilities and limitations of AML systems. The generic structure broadly involves prevention and enforcement. The prevention portion includes customer due diligence (knowing your clients), reporting of suspicious and prescribed transactions (e.g. wire transfers and the physical or electronic transport of large volumes of cash, typically 10,000 or more units of local currency across the border), regulation and supervision, and administrative or regulatory sanctions for non-compliance. The enforcement component includes a focus on the underlying predicate offences associated with money laundering, investigation, prosecution and punishment, and civil and criminal confiscation and forfeiture. While the industrialised nations will have many if not all of these components, the specific configurations are indicative of the possibilities and the limitations experienced in each jurisdiction.

Although hybrid examples exist, there are three main types of FIUs: administrative, enforcement and judicial. The administrative model is characterised by a civilian agency that is typically accountable to, and subsumed under, a department of the treasury, finance or a central bank. Such institutions exercise variable independence but are notably not accountable to law enforcement bodies and often act as a buffer between such agencies and reporting entities. The enforcement model may involve a separate agency, but the FIU is a part of the law enforcement matrix and is accountable to departments that oversee policing. The judicial model is most common in civil law and inquisitorial systems where prosecutorial and judicial functions are combined.

The choice of which model to use reflects particular cultural and legal rules, but it also represents a choice with respect to the advantages and disadvantages of the three models (International Monetary Fund 2004: 9–16). For instance, judicial FIUs may act more speedily given that they combine the various functions of receiving suspicious and prescribed reports, investigation, arrests, freezing and seizing assets and prosecution. While having less concentration of powers than the judicial model, enforcement FIUs have similar advantages in terms of investigative efficiency due to established integration within the criminal justice system. The two models also share the disadvantages of tending to focus on the investigation rather than the prevention of money laundering and potential legal problems of data sharing with non-judicial/enforcement FIUs. Moreover, reporting entities may have a less 'open' relationship with such FIUs and the former may perhaps be less likely to disclose information that could be used for investigative purposes beyond inquiries into possible money laundering. Administrative FIUs may present difficulties in terms of investigative efficiency and the timeliness of asset seizures, but such agencies do have several advantages. They act as a neutral party between reporting entities and law enforcement, can maintain a more 'open' regulatory relationship with reporting entities, more readily share data with other types of FIUs and limit disclosures to information relevant to laundering investigations. The distinctions discussed above are helpful in understanding particular FIU structures, such as the model used in the United Kingdom.

AML in the United Kingdom

Like other industrialised nations, the organisation of higher-level UK policing focused on organised crime often associated with illicit drugs activity. This was evident in the formation of Regional Crime Squads in the 1960s and, through various organisational iterations and committee reports, a trend emerged toward the centralisation of intelligence (in particular) and policing of organised crime. The Drug Trafficking Offences Act (DTOA) of 1986 targeted the drug-related proceeds of crime and introduced measures to counter money laundering, inclusive of monitoring orders to trace transactions on specified accounts, the freezing of assets of those under investigation and the confiscation of illegally acquired assets upon conviction. In 1992, the National Criminal Intelligence Service (NCIS) was created to gather and disseminate intelligence relating to drugs, immigration, firearms and organised crime. It acted as the national FIU receiving information on suspected money laundering. The NCIS also liaised with domestic and international stakeholders such as Interpol, Europol and counterpart agencies in various countries. In 1998, the National Crime Squad (NCS) was created from the previous regional crime squads. The remit of this organisation was policing related to organised crime, drug trafficking, money laundering and a range of serious crimes. It is estimated that the NCIS and NCS focused perhaps three-quarters of their efforts on illicit drugs (Lee and South 2008: 502).

The Proceeds of Crime Act (POCA) of 2002 extended and enhanced the provisions first introduced under the DTOA and integrated non-drug proceeds of crime covered under the Criminal Justice Act 1988 as amended. POCA adopted a more aggressive approach to targeting the proceeds of crime for a range of serious crime, inclusive of tax evasion. In addition to criminal prosecution and confiscation, individuals may face civil action to target the proceeds of crime. The Act created the Assets Recovery Agency (ARA) to initiate, upon receiving referrals from partner agencies, cases to recover proceeds of crime assets based on the civil law standard. The civil standard means that investigators need only prove to the High Court that on a 'balance of probabilities' (rather than the criminal standard of beyond a reasonable doubt) that the assets are linked to proceeds of crime in order for forfeiture to take place.

The UK Serious Organised Crime Agency (SOCA) came into formal legal existence in April 2006. This new mega-agency involved the merger of the NCS, the NCIS, the drug trafficking and criminal finance sections of HM Revenue and Customs and the organised immigration section of UK Immigration. The Assets Recovery Agency (ARA) was not included in the initial merger but was absorbed into the collective in April 2008.

SOCA is an interesting development in the structure of British policing given that the agency is officially deemed not to be a police organisation. Rather it describes itself as 'an intelligence-led agency with law enforcement powers and harm reduction responsibilities' in reducing the damage that serious organised crime may cause to people and communities. While the Home Secretary may assess the efforts of SOCA and involve him or herself in setting strategic priorities, the agency is a non-departmental public body with autonomy to plan how it will exercise and measure the implementation of its statutory functions.

Prior to its absorption into SOCA, the NCIS was an enforcement-style FIU embedded in a matrix of police and quasi-police institutions. Under the SOCA umbrella, Britain's FIU may be becoming more of a hybrid model but it is difficult not to characterise it as an enforcement-based model. Unlike its contemporaries in Australia, Canada and the United States, money-laundering compliance (much of the prevention elements discussed above) in Britain is a function delegated to the Financial Services Authority (FSA). On the other hand, SOCA's integration of seemingly all of the previous enforcement components, inclusive of criminal and civil investigative powers, should sufficiently empower it to fulfil its mandate. Of course, this is dependent upon whether it can 'rise above the legacies of its constituent elements to become truly more than the sum of its parts' (Harfield 2006: 759). The benefits of integration seem clear: interoperable and/or combined databases should be able to better leverage overall holdings while systematic case management between previously separate agencies should result in greater efficiency as well as more effective targeting of the proceeds of crime, money laundering and those involved using criminal, civil and taxation powers.

In its third year of existence, SOCA (2009/10: 32) documented outputs of £4.5 million in cash forfeitures, £29.7 million in confiscation order payments and £16.7 million in civil recovery, set against a budget of £494 million in resource and capital funding.

The overall rate of forfeiture/confiscation is thus over 10 per cent of budgetary expenses, although this may significantly rise as the growing pool of proceeds of crime seizures progress through the investigation and court process. At 35 per cent, the rate of forfeiture/confiscation against budgetary expenses was higher within the former Assets Recovery Agency (ARA): £23 million in recovered assets against £65 million in programme costs from 2003 to 2006 (National Audit Office 2007). It is not clear that this area of crime control can become self-financing from proceeds of crime forfeitures alone and that the UK response will continue to require considerable ongoing public financial support. Nonetheless, there is scope to extend and enhance the UK initiative given the £20–40 billion in estimated social and economic 'harm' caused every year by organised crime, and the recognition of the need, among other things, to make fuller use of existing enforcement powers and skills and further build regional capacity (Home Office 2009: 3, 34–42).

While organisational and programme integration seems to hold many potential advantages, it may tend to complicate systematic assessment of the value-added of its component parts to the overall initiative. The contribution that AML offers in targeting individuals, groups and illicit markets involved in generating and disposing of the proceeds of crime may become (further) obscured in the UK under the SOCA umbrella.

Conclusion

This chapter has offered a selective overview of the crime of money laundering. Although there are some areas such as cross-border tax issues that are resistant to inclusion in AML regimes, the overall trend is toward very broad definitions including all 'serious crimes' and the inclusion of virtually any interaction with the proceeds of crime as constituting money laundering. Notwithstanding the generalised absence of methodologically sound empirical studies, unsubstantiated claims continue to dominate the official and common-sense debate on the size and scope of the money laundering problem. The United States has been a pioneer and key driver in the development of AML controls and its diffusion to other jurisdictions. This diffusion has proceeded rapidly since the late 1980s as advanced by international bodies such as the United Nations, the FATF, the European Union and the Egmont Group. AML regimes typically include a prevention and an enforcement component, although this mix varies depending on whether the respective national FIU is administrative, enforcement or judicial in nature. The UK has an enforcement-type FIU that is focused on contributing toward investigations, whereas FIUs in the United States and other countries include more prevention and regulatory compliance functions.

Some authors view the AML regime and FIUs as an exemplar of flexible domestic and cross-border responses to organised crime, money laundering and proceeds of crime (Slaughter 2004). Nevertheless, perhaps one of the major impediments to greater effectiveness is that money laundering controls have tended to act as a supplement that is grafted onto traditional investigative and criminal justice approaches. This illustrates a distinct tendency for AML to be drafted into substantially more 'rowing' than 'steering' (Garland 2001) in addressing money laundering, the proceeds of crime and relationships to serious and organised crime (Beare and Schneider 2007; Cuellar 2003; Fleming 2005; Levi and Reuter 2006).

Selected further reading

Reuter and Truman's (2004) *Chasing Dirty Money* offers a comprehensive overview of key money-laundering issues and Levi and Reuter (2006) helpfully extend this work in *Crime and Justice*. For helpful single volumes and edited collections, see the series from van Duyne (2008) and colleagues published by Wolf Legal Publishers. Levi (1991, 2007) provides a review and analysis of the development of the UK AML programme. Readers looking for a critical discussion of the possibilities and limitations of AML should find Cuellar (2003) to be of particular interest.

Readers who wish to review previous and ongoing developments in UK policy and practice should consult the Home Office website (http://www.homeoffice.gov. uk/crime-victims/reducing-crime/organised-crime/), including the July 2009 policy document *Extending Our Reach* (http://www.homeoffice.gov.uk/documents/extending-our-reach/) and the Serious Organised Crime Agency (http://www.soca.gov.uk/). International developments in policy and practice are available on the websites of the United Nations (http://www.unodc.org/unodc/en/money-laundering/index.html), the Financial Action Task Force (http://www.fatf-gafi.org/), the European Union (http://ec.europa.eu/justice_home/fsj/crime/laundering/fsj_crime_laundering_en.htm) and the Egmont Group (http://www.egmontgroup.org/) that also includes links to many financial intelligence units around the world.

Note

1 Thanks to Mike Levi for helpful comments on a previous draft of this article.

References

Alldridge, P. (2008) 'Money laundering and globalization', *Journal of Law and Society*, 35 (4): 437–63.

Andreas, P. and Nadelmann, E. (2006) *Policing the Globe: Criminalization and Crime Control in International Relations*. New York: Oxford University Press.

Beare, M. E. (2002) 'Searching for wayward dollars: money-laundering or tax evasion – which dollars are we really after?', *Journal of Financial Crime*, 9 (3): 259–67.

Beare, M. E. and Schneider, S. R. (2007) *Money Laundering in Canada: Chasing Dirty and Dangerous Dollars*. Toronto: University of Toronto Press.

Cuellar, M. (2003) 'Criminal law: the tenuous relationship between the fight against money laundering and the disruption of criminal finance', *Journal of Criminal Law and Criminology*, 93 (2/3): 311–465.

de Boyrie, M., Pak, S. J. and Zdanowicz, J. S. (2005) 'The impact of Switzerland's money laundering law on capital flows through abnormal pricing in international trade', *Applied Financial Economics*, 15: 217–30.

Fleming, M. H. (2005) *UK Law Enforcement Agency Use and Management of Suspicious Activity Reports: Towards Determining the Value of the Regime*. London: University College London.

Garland, D. (2001) *The Culture of Control: Crime and Social Order in Contemporary Society*. Oxford: Oxford University Press.

Harfield, C. (2006) 'SOCA: a paradigm shift in British policing', *British Journal of Criminology*, 46: 743–61.

Home Office (2009) *Extending Our Reach: A Comprehensive Approach to Tackling Serious Organised Crime*. London: Home Office, Cabinet Office and Strategy Unit.

International Monetary Fund (IMF) (2004) *Financial Intelligence Units: An Overview*. Washington, DC: IMF.

Lee, M. and South, N. (2008) 'Drugs policing', in T. Newburn (ed.), *Handbook of Policing*, 2nd edn. Cullompton: Willan.

Levi, M. (1991) 'Pecunia non olet: cleansing the money launderers from the temple', *Crime, Law and Social Change*, 16: 217–302.

Levi, M. (2007) 'Pecunia non olet? The control of money laundering revisited', in F. Bovenkerk and M. Levi (eds), *The Organized Crime Community*. New York: Springer, pp. 161–82.

Levi, M. and Gilmore, W. (2002) 'Terrorist finance, money laundering and the rise and rise of mutual evaluation: a new paradigm for crime control?', *European Journal of Law Reform*, 4 (2): 337–64.

Levi, M. and Maguire, M. (2004) 'Reducing and preventing organised crime: an evidence-based critique', *Crime, Law and Social Change*, 41 (5): 397–469.

Levi, M. and Osofsky, L. (1995) *Investigating, Seizing and Confiscating the Proceeds of Crime*, Crime Detection and Prevention Series Paper 61. London: Home Office, Police Research Group.

Levi, M. and Reuter, P. (2006) 'Money laundering', *Crime and Justice: A Review of Research*, 34: 1–90.

Matrix Knowledge Group (2007) *The Illicit Drug Trade in the United Kingdom*, 2nd edn. London: Home Office.

National Audit Office (NAO) (2007) *The Assets Recovery Agency*. London: NAO.

Pak, S. J., Zanakis, S. H. and Zdanowicz, J. S. (2003) 'Detecting abnormal pricing in international trade: the Greece–USA case', *Interfaces*, 33 (2): 54–64.

Passas, N. (1999) *Informal Value Transfer Systems and Criminal Organizations: A Study into So-Called Underground Banking Networks*. The Hague: Ministry of Justice, Research and Documentation Centre.

Quirk, P. J. (1996) *Macroeconomic Implications of Money Laundering*, IMF Working Paper WP/96/66. Washington, DC: IMF.

Reuter, P. (1995) 'The decline of the American Mafia', *Public Interest*, 120 (89): 89–99.

Reuter, P. and Truman, E. M. (2004) *Chasing Dirty Money: The Fight Against Money Laundering*. Washington, DC: Institute for International Economics.

Serious Organised Crime Agency (SOCA) (2009) *SOCA Annual Report 2009/10*. London: SOCA.

Slaughter, A. (2004) *A New World Order*. Princeton, NJ: Princeton University Press.

United Nations Development Programme (UNDP) (1999) *Human Development Report 1999*. New York: Oxford University Press.

United Nations International Drug Control Programme (UNDCP) (1997) *World Drug Report*. Oxford: Oxford University Press.

van Duyne, P. C. (2002) 'Crime-entrepreneurs and financial management', in P. C. van Duyne, K. von Lampe and N. Passas (eds), *Upperworld and Underworld in Cross-Border Crime*. Nijmegen: Wolf Legal Publishers, pp. 61–83.

van Duyne, P. C. (2003) 'Money laundering policy: facts and fears', in P. C. van Duyne, K. von Lampe and J. L. Newell (eds), *Criminal Finances and Organising Crime in Europe*. Nijmegen: Wolf Legal Publishers, pp. 67–104.

van Duyne, P. C. and de Miranda, H. (1999) 'The emperor's clothes of disclosure: hot money and suspect disclosures', *Crime, Law and Social Change*, 31 (3): 245–71.

van Duyne, P. C., Harvey, J., Maljevic, A. and von Lampe, K. (2008) *European Crime-Markets at Cross-Roads: Extended and Extending Criminal Europe*. Nijmegen: Wolf Legal Publishers.

Chapter 36

Extortion

Dick Hobbs

Introduction

Extortion is the unlawful demand for property or money through the threat of force, and has long been an entry-level activity both for individuals embarking on criminal careers and for collaborations of criminals seeking to establish a monopoly or 'protected enclave' (Arlacchi 1986: 195). Extortion involves the marketing of a threat, and at its core lies coercive, but not exclusively violent, potential as an essentially pragmatic resource (Gambetta 1993: 2), a resource that has proved to be highly adaptable for the establishment of both legal and illegal enterprise.

Extortion is a growth industry 'in insecure and competitive market societies' (Taylor 1999: 169) and the ability of organised crime groups to 'guarantee that individuals and firms yield to their demands' (Jacobs 1999: 118) clearly constitutes a potent form of economic power, affording the criminal entrepreneur an essence of authority that informs how he is received within both licit and illicit enterprise. This authority forges the essential essence of the extortioner, an essence that exists independent of observable behaviour (Katz 1975: 1371) but features violent potential as a form of moral licence involving the possession of a special competence (ibid.: 1381).

In this brief chapter I will concentrate upon extortion as an activity that thrives in socio-economic systems, or in segments of a socio-economic system where the state is weak and where agents of the state do not have a monopoly over the means of violence, or where state agents utilise the threat of state-licensed coercion for personal gain. I shall begin with some general comments on the marketing of violence as a commodity before turning to the archetypal example of the development of the Sicilian Mafia to illustrate the vulnerability of weak states to exploitation by criminal groups. I will proceed to highlight various ways in which extortion is manifested by actors connected to the state and the legitimate economy before examining extortion's role as a primary economic relationship within both transitory states and excluded communities.

The marketing of violence as a commodity

Extortion (Gambetta 1988) is a sphere through which violence is commodified, and is a means of establishing a sheltered territory within which patterns of protection and extortion can be or are replicated in a modern urban setting (Block 1983: 239; Paoli 2003: 140). For Schelling (1976), extortion is primarily an activity that targets other criminals, and is the means by which a monopoly is both established and maintained. Illegal enterprises are unable to turn to state agencies for protection (Reuter 1983), and organised criminals emerge as entrepreneurs of trust via the threat and utility of violence. Schelling (1984) regards the practice as central to organised crime – the illegal trader must '... pay to stay in business' (185), but the protection on offer is only against other extortionists that seek to gain a monopoly over the protection of illegal business (Buchanan 1973). Consequently the protection is somewhat bogus, based upon a perception of the extortioner as more violent than his rivals in the securing of trust. Indeed, '... one of the structural ... features of protection is the toughness of the supplier ... a Mafioso who hits harder can be expected to be a far more reliable protector. The most credible proof he can offer, in fact, consists in eliminating his competitors altogether' (Gambetta 1988: 140).

As Falcone indicates (1993: 116), extortion is a highly effective vehicle for consolidating control over territory (see also Behan 1996: 110–12). While the majority of commodities are traded in terms of continuous quantities and prices, protection is contingent upon violence, which as Gambetta points out is a 'dychotomous variable, i.e. if not you then me' (1988: 141). Violence not price is the key, and the more visceral level of competence will attract the entire market within a given territory. 'He who beats hardest not only does away with the beaten competitors, but advertises himself as an adequate protector' (ibid.: 140).

The Sicilian Mafia

Traditional Sicilian society was constructed around a unique set of social arrangements. Predominantly feudal with absentee landlords ruling the land from afar (Blok 1974), national systems of power emerged without usurping entrenched local systems. As a consequence the state failed to gain a monopoly over the use of force and gaps in the social order were conspicuous, particularly during the crucial period when feudalism was declining and democracy was in its infancy (Gambetta 1988). The protection of the large estates and the retention of landworkers in a state of feudal submission was paramount, and in the absence of a competent agent of state-sanctioned violence, landowners explored an alternative method of consolidating their interests by turning to local 'Men of Respect' (Catanzaro 1992).

'What earned these men 'respect' was, first, their capacity to coerce with physical violence and thus invoke fear in others' (Blok 1974: 62). Given the impotence of public authorities in Sicily, the Mafia emerged as an 'expression of a need for order' (Falcone 1993: 56), which in turn was imposed by 'persons who had a reputation for violence and who eschewed recourse to public authorities ... Others less skilled in the realm of violence turned to them for protection' (Blok 1974: 211).

The emergent pattern of extortionate interdependencies relied heavily upon men skilled in the practice and threat of violence (Ruggiero 1993: 145), with careers kick-started by the establishment of reputations forged in the redressing of personal wrongs (Blok 1974: 101). As the large estates were broken up in what was a late transition to the market economy, Sicilian society was typified by a poor definition of property rights, and no centralisation of violence by state institutions. Consequently the new non-aristocratic landowners, bereft of any effective recourse to the monopoly of violence which is central to state sovereignty (Elias 1994), also turned to 'Men of Respect' who in time became leaders of the community and 'supplied protection to absentee landlords from resentful peasants, while exploiting the peasants for their own profit' (Ianni and Ianni 1972: 36).

The ability to extort money in return for a level of relative security from landworkers and local bandits as well as landowners relied heavily upon a brokerage of power both congruent with local cultural precedent (Falcone 1993: 52) and functional to the needs of a state whose ability to impose its will was limited on the island of Sicily. Therefore the dominant economic system was buttressed through the use of private violence (Catanzaro 1992). However, in the absence of effective state regulation, the locally phrased power domains that such a practice creates also become markets for extortion. Non-existent threats to property and livestock were created, but if ignored the threat would become reality (Catanzaro 1992: 21–3; Blok 1974: 151), and non-interference pacts with other Mafiosi created a monopoly of violence and a form of social order that could not be guaranteed by the state. Consequently, extortion functioned as a means of mediation between local culture and national interests, becoming a vehicle for wealth accumulation (Catanzaro 1992: 31).

The police

Agents of the state are also prone to extortionate activity, and while not opposed to the threat of violence, are able to invoke the coercive power of the state as a negotiating tool with illegal businesses. Indeed the relationship between professional criminals and detectives has been portrayed as symbiotic in that both operate according to a version of market principles in relation to the trading of information (Hobbs 1988: 62–83). What is normatively categorised as corruption ignores the overwhelming advantage often held by detectives in their ability to wield the full force of the state, and there can be a fine line between monetary reward for the organisational returns of information and the cultural remuneration of status (Hobbs 1988: 197–216).

During the 1960s and 1970s businesses dealing in pornography were extorted by the police in exchange for allowing the pornographers to continue their activities (Cox et al. 1977). Armed robbers were rampant partly as a result of their close relationships with local detectives (Ball et al. 1978), and gangsters imposed a form of local order for as long as they could maintain local police officers 'on the firm' (Pearson 1973). The distinction between police corruption and extortion is extremely fine (see Newburn 1999 for a review of the literature), but we should not hide from the potential of the state power that the police brings to the table when negotiating with criminals. This power is fully recognised by criminal entrepreneurs seeking an advantage in the marketplace, and state power is embedded in all such commercial exchanges, making the powers of the police implicitly extortionate when they are placed in a business-related environment (Mollen Commission 1994). Further, such arrangements go beyond the stereotypical activities of thieves, ponces and gangsters. For instance, recent examination of official documents relating to London's Richardson brothers indicate that the frauds so successfully carried out by Charlie Richardson were made possible by paying a weekly retainer to a senior detective for allowing the frauds to continue on his patch. Here the so called 'gangster' is being extorted, and who was on whose firm is debatable.[1]

Careers

The establishment of the role of protector/extortionist relies upon the provider of security being more violent than his clients, and this is particularly crucial in the case of criminal clients who may also be prone to violence. However, the establishment of extortionate relations is not confined to illegal business, and particularly in those enterprises situated alongside businesses based on vice extortion is often accepted as an informal tax. Importantly, the careers of many notable organised crime figures were initially propelled by their successful involvement in extorting money from bars, and clubs (Lambrianou 1992: 32–3, 36–7; Donoghue and Short 1995: 23–4). In Britain, the Kray twins, having first established themselves as exceptionally violent individuals both in the boxing ring and on the street, in the beginning extorted money from a billiard hall and local pubs and clubs (Pearson 1973: 80–1; Ward and Gray 1974: 152) before, under the mentorship of underworld icon Billy Hill (Hill 1955), moving upmarket into London's West End providing 'security' for illegal gambling clubs (Pearson 1973: 124–5). Having penetrated this market, the legalisation of gambling in Britain in 1960 enabled the Krays to evolve into semi-legal activities, but they continued to use their regularly enhanced reputations for extreme violence to extort clubs, pubs and legitimate businesses (Pearson 1973: 133–4) as well as successful thieves (Pearson 1973: 80, 2001: 45; Donoghue and Short 1995: 58–75).

During the same era the South London-based Richardson brothers, with a similar reputation forged in the boxing ring and on the street but with an entrepreneurial imagination far superior to the Krays, were busy providing an interesting example of how extortion can subtly mutate (Richardson 1992). Atlantic Machines, which was run by Eddie Richardson and Frank Fraser, was a business providing gaming machines to licensed premises and was heavily reliant upon the violent reputations of both Richardson and Fraser (Fraser 1994: 192–6, 199–203; Richardson 2005: 77–81). With violence and potential violence mediating trust between supplier and client, gaming machines were provided to venues all over the UK, and both potential competitors or anyone disrupting the smooth running of clients' business were subjected to violent sanctions (Parker 1981: 151–4).

Night-time economy

We now explore a somewhat different example of how violence and extortion will thrive in environments where the state does not have a monopoly over the means of violence – that of criminal activities associated with the growth of the 'night-time economy'. Here, as with the case of Sicily, the context for the emergence of extortion as a routine means of coordinating trust and security is all important, and clearly intertwined with marked changes in the legitimate political economy.

The decline of British manufacturing had created an economic crisis that local governments were tasked to address (Hobbs *et al.* 2003) and, along with a liberalisation of commercial restraint (Hadfield 2006), free-market forces were allowed to dominate British social and economic life in accord with the dominant neo-conservative ethos (see Winlow this volume). In an economic zone where violence was normalised (Winlow and Hall 2006), the night-time resources available to the public police remained at the same level as during the industrial era, when drinking had been severely restricted by formal licensing in order to maintain a sober workforce and therefore protect production. The exponential increase in public disorder generated by the night-time economy produced a demand for security that is not met by state institutions, and which in turn has severely damaged the credibility of neo-liberal institutions tasked with incorporation and market coherence. This produced the conditions for a new security market requiring precisely those muscular resources that constitute the core of traditional organised crime (Hobbs *et al.* 2003: 211–42).

In the night-time economy extortion is often accepted as an informal tax (Winlow 2001: 147–53), and with potential violence constituting the legitimate marketable service, the fine line between security and protection is particularly marked, as in both spheres coercion is commodified, creating locally phrased power domains that are difficult to distinguish from markets for extortion. As in the case of Sicily, non-existent threats can be created which can, in turn, become a reality. For, as they were periodically required to demonstrate, these extortion firms were only as strong as their reputations[2] (McLean 1998: 75; Hobbs *et al.* 2003: 241–2).

These extortionate networks can reduce uncertainties and enforce market stability (see Gambetta and Reuter 1995: 116–35), and criminal door firms and individual security 'consultants' (New York State Organized Crime Task Force 1988: 66) also engaged in a form of labour-leasing, acting as intermediaries between door staff and venue management (Neff 1989). Legitimate security companies, brewers and leisure corporations 'faced with the constant threat of cut-throat competition are subject to easy temptation to pay gangsters for protection against competitors' (Lippman 1962: 61), and often liaise with local crime groups to resolve situations before working on a contract. Further, where venues are drug rather than alcohol orientated, bouncers can operate as 'gatekeepers' for the drug trade (Hobbs 1995: 74–80; O'Mahoney 1997; Hobbs *at al*. 2003: 228–9), extorting money from dealers as a licensing fee for allowing the sale of drugs in specific venues (Silverstone forthcoming).

By encouraging the night-time economy without taking full responsibility for its regulation, the British state exposed the liberal conceit that violence is a subordinate element in society (Hobbs *et al*. 2005). Extortion, based upon violent potential, is embedded in the dominant socio-economic structure (Arlacchi 1986: 115) via 'systems of accumulated expertise' (Giddens 1991: 3), and features the cultural inheritance of traditional criminogenic locales (Arlacchi 1986: 227).

Extortion enables violence to become located within the ambit of market exchange, 'where the state is weak or its rationalizing minions are held in contempt' (Courtwright 1996: 29), and as a consequence entrepreneurs, seeking to protect and consolidate their interests, turn to '… the forces of law and disorder' (Wilson 2002: 223) in precisely the same manner that landowners of Sicily turned to local 'Men of Respect' (Wilson 2002: 238), and bouncers, like the Sicilian Mafia, become, in effect, unofficial instruments of the dominant economic order through the use of private violence.

Labour and management

The establishment of violence as a resource in the conflictual zone of labour and management disputes illustrates another way in which extortion creates an entrée for organised crime groups into the legitimate political economy. Conflictual relations between labour and capital create a market for violence and men with well established violent reputations are perfectly placed to exploit this market (Moldea 1978; Neff 1989). 'As labor padrones to organise construction gangs, or as strikebreakers during the years of nascent unionism, or as general mediators between labor and industry, criminals took advantage of their reputation for violence and insinuated themselves into strategic roles within the constant of labor and management strife' (Block 1994: 51). Here extortion became a refinement of mundane violent oppression, with crime groups first penetrating both employers and labour by the provision of a service, before creating more insidious relationships with both groups via extortion.

By controlling the unions via violence, criminals held down wages and were paid off by employers (Block and Chambliss 1981; Potter and Jenkins 1985). Similarly employers used organised criminals as 'labor disciplinarians' (Block 1983: 195) who utilised violence to suppress efforts by workers to unionise, to break strikes and to protect blackleg (strikebreaking) labour (Pearce 1976). Indeed as gangs that supplied violent labour were also involved in the corruption of politicians who in turn were allied to the police, a powerful urban coalition of organised crime, business, politicians and police based upon violence and refined by extortion was created (Block 1983: 163–99).

Via their infiltration of the unions, organised crime was able to extort employers by threatening strikes. Further, the pension and welfare funds of union members were plundered by organised crime, providing capital for both criminal and non-criminal enterprise (Quinney 1975: 145; Moldea 1978: 263–4; Neff 1989; Block 1991: part 3). In an attempt to fight fire with fire, unions would often actively seek alliances with organised crime to assist in disputes with other unions or to impose discipline within their own organisation (Brill 1978; Moldea 1978; Friedman and Schwarz 1989).

The resultant extortionate arrangements can dictate contract protocols and police illegal trade agreements designed to restrict competition. As Reuter (1983) indicates, such activity may not involve actual violence but 'it seems reasonable to infer that the racketeers provide a credible continuing threat of violence that ensures compliance …' (ibid.: 11). While the threat of violence remains a constant, mutations of legitimate business practice in the form of both competition and labour rigging are enabled before the circle is completed by organised crime's penetration of legal trade and commerce (Anderson 1979; Moore 1987; Reuter 1987), which in turn can manufacture further extortionate business opportunities which are policed by the threat of violence (Kwitny 1979; Block and Scarpitti 1985).

Extortion enables considerable advantages in the so called legitimate marketplace (Falcone 1993: 78–81), and although actual violence exacted against legitimate business is rare, 'The organised crime families' reputations for ruthless violence guaranteed that individuals and firms would yield to their demands' (Jacobs 1999: 118). Such reputations enable organised crime to extort a favourable advantage in tendering processes (Gambetta 1993: 214–20; Falcone 1993: 133–4), discourage competition, hold down wages and provide access to financial resources (Arlacchi 1986: 91–2).

States in transition

As Rawlinson (2009) indicates, in Russia, physical violence has always been a central resource of criminal economies, and the violence that has accompanied the former Soviet Union's transition from a communist to a capitalist economy should be regarded to some extent as an extension of the brutalisation of Russian society under its various authoritarian regimes. Rawlinson draws our attention to the highly competitive world of illegal protection during Russia's transition period, where 'Anton', the head of a criminal group in St Petersburg, brought a matter-of-fact philosophy to the use of violence even when threatened by the presence of a rival group: 'If we are forced to use violence then we will resort to it. But this is pretty rare as it's a serious issue … Then we stop making money and everything is diverted to this conflict' (Rawlinson 2009: ch. 5; Volkov 2002).

The proliferation of extortion in Russia, where three-quarters of private enterprises are forced to pay 10–20 per cent of their earnings to crime groups (*The Economist* 1994: 57; see also Rawlinson 2009) indicates that this most traditional of acquisitional crime has remained fashionable. Indeed, as with the Sicilian Mafia, extortion in Russia has proved to be an enduring example of criminal modernisation, and Varese (2001) illustrates this process by showing how small businesses were forced to pay a protection fee to avoid having their premises burnt down. This system developed into a relatively sophisticated form of law and contract enforcement, incorporating debt recovery, the settlement of tax and payment arrears and the negotiation of business issues with bureaucracies on behalf of the 'protected'.

Excluded communities

This normalisation of extortion within states in transition can also be replicated in cultures that are isolated within host communities whose language, commercial practices, etc. are literally alien. In these situations immigrant cultures become marginalised, and lean heavily upon their cultural inheritance and practices. 'He fell back on a system that he brought with him' (Ianni and Ianni 1971: 47), becoming oblivious to the normative, often potentially corrosive practices of the host culture (Zorbaugh 1929: 152). Cut off from the family structures that often sustain concepts of personal security and unable to communicate with the indigenous population or its institutions, 'the new immigrants clustered in ethnic enclaves in the large cities ... Within the cities, the Italians settled in well-defined Little Italies, and within these colonies they tended to congregate with others from the same province and even the same village' (Ianni and Ianni 1971: 44). The standards for immigrant culture were often set by the culture of the old country, and suspicion of indigenous institutions and in particular the police (Landesco [1929] 1968: 117) placed a particular emphasis upon the kind of informal resolution that had been central to the function of 'Men of Honour' in the old country discussed above (Park and Miller 1921).

These are the conditions that created 'a chaotic and pernicious social milieu in which victimisers and victims frequently negotiate the criteria for "normal" extortion' (Chin 1996: 77) among New York's Chinese community where Kelly et al. (1993) have estimated that 70 per cent of businesses are subjected to extortion. The institutionalisation of extortion among immigrant communities (Nelli 1976; Chin 1996: 59–77) becomes part of an unofficial system of taxation that is often integral to the everyday political economy of the homeland (Landesco [1929] 1968: 108–9), but is adapted to the particular field conditions generated by the host culture (Chin 1996: 78–99).

Among this excluded category are included trafficked and smuggled individuals, who are forced into 'bonded work' (van der Kleij 2002; Pearson 2003; Piper 2004) or coerced into prostitution or other forms of dubious labour by organised criminals (Kelly 2005) as a means of payment (see Goodey on human trafficking, this volume). Their illegal status renders them unable to turn to the police of the host country, and the victims are confronted with large debts which are generally to be repaid through prostitution (Council of Europe 2004: 23).

It is in such environments where citizens mistrust legal/rational authority and are socially excluded from access to institutions that may or may not be capable or inclined to assist them that extortion will thrive. Mistrust, misunderstanding or ignorance with regard to the official authority structure of their new home can also play a part. However, colluding with extortion can also be based upon a clear understanding of the corrupt, racist and exclusionary practices that predominate in the host country. Either way, they do not trust the police and have no faith in the ability of the police to help them.

Conclusion

Extortion is business with the gloves off and thrives in formative, tentative, illegal or frontier milieus. Until victims can trust that reporting extortion will result in an appropriate and effective legal response, and that state institutions and not criminal entrepreneurs have a monopoly over violence, extortion will remain both an entry-level crime for career criminals and a foundation block of ongoing criminal enterprise. Extortion thrives not only in transitory societies or within communities of marginal or excluded individuals where established economic protocols are absent or underdeveloped. It also thrives in frontier environments within long established socio-economic milieus, where the protocols of normative business are inappropriate or the essences of these protocols are exposed as essentially predatory. Whether we are considering the state, or groups linked to peasant and proletarian traditions, the ability to intimidate is an essential tool for gaining power and resources across the entire 'spectrum of legitimacy' (Smith 1980).

Selected further reading

A combination of Gambetta (1993) and Catanzaro (1992) will give a historical foundation for an understanding of the evolution of extortion and its fundamental importance to organised crime while Arlacchi (1986) expresses its importance to the contemporary model. Cox *et al.* (1977) and Ball *et al.* (1978) present vivid narratives of police involvement in extortion. Jacobs (1999) describes the role of extortion within legitimate enterprise and Hobbs *et al.* (2003) and Volkov (2002) highlight the thin line between extortion and security and extortion's subsequent role in economic development.

Notes

1 Richardson employed individuals with long-standing professional relationships with the police, such as ex-pickpockets, specifically to perform this task (Hobbs in progress).
2 http://www.manchestereveningnews.co.uk/news/s/1042125_protection_racket_

References

Anderson, A. (1979) *The Business of Organised Crime*. Stanford, CA: Hoover Institute Press.
Arlacchi, P. (1986) *Mafia Business: The Mafia Ethic and the Spirit of Capitalism*. London: Verso.

Ball, J., Chester, L. and Perrott, R. (1978) *Cops and Robbers*. London: André Deutsch.

Behan, T. (1996) *The Camorra*. London: Routledge.

Block, A. (1983) *East Side–West Side: Organizing Crime in New York, 1930–1950*. Newark, NJ: Transaction.

Block, A. (1991) *The Business of Crime*. Colorado: Westview Press.

Block, A. (1994) *Space Time and Organised Crime*. New Brunswick, NJ: Transaction.

Block, A. and Chambliss, W. (1981) *Organizing Crime*. New York: Elsevier.

Block, A. and Scarpitti, F. (1985) *Poisoning for Profit: The Mafia and Toxic Waste*. New York: William Morrow.

Blok, A. (1974) *The Mafia of a Sicilian Village*. New York: Harper.

Brill, S. (1978) *Teamsters*. New York: Simon & Schuster.

Buchanan, J. (1973) 'A defense of organised crime', in R. Andreano and J. Siegfried (eds), *The Economics of Organised Crime*. Cambridge, MA: Schenkman.

Catanzaro, R. (1992) *Men of Respect: A Social History of the Sicilian Mafia*. New York: Free Press.

Chambliss, W. (1978) *On the Take*. Bloomington, IN: Indiana University Press.

Chin, K. (1996) *Chinatown Gangs*. New York: Oxford University Press.

Council of Europe (2004) *Organised Crime Situation Report*. Strasbourg: Council of Europe.

Courtwright, D. (1996) *Violent Land*. Cambridge, MA: Harvard University Press.

Cox, B., Shirley, J. and Short, M. (1977) *The Fall of Scotland Yard*. Harmondsworth: Penguin.

Donoghue, A. and Short, M. (1995) *The Krays' Lieutenant*. London: Blake.

The Economist (1994) 'The high price of freeing markets', 19 February, p. 57.

Elias, N. (1994) *The Civilizing Process: The History of Manners*, Vol. 1. Oxford: Blackwell.

Falcone, G. (1993) *Men of Honour*. London: Mainstream Publishing.

Fraser, F. (1994) *Mad Frank*. London: Little, Brown.

Friedman, A. and Schwarz, T. (1989) *Power and Greed: Inside the Teamsters' Empire of Corruption*. New York: Scholastic Library Publishing.

Gambetta, D. (1988) 'Fragments of an economic theory of the Mafia', *Archives Européennes de Sociologie*, 29: 127–45.

Gambetta, D. (1993) *The Sicilian Mafia: The Business of Private Protection*. Cambridge, MA: Harvard University Press.

Gambetta, D. and Reuter, P. (1995) 'Conspiracy among the many: the Mafia in legitimate industries', in G. Fiorentini and S. Peltzman (eds), *The Economics of Organised Crime*. Cambridge: Cambridge University Press, pp. 116–39.

Giddens, A. (1991) *Modernity and Self-Identity*. Cambridge: Polity.

Hadfield, P. (2006) *Bar Wars*. Oxford: Oxford University Press.

Hill, B. (1955) *Boss of Britain's Underworld*. London: Naldrett.

Hobbs, D. (1988) *Doing the Business: Entrepreneurship, Detectives and the Working Class in the East End of London*. Oxford: Clarendon Press.

Hobbs, D. (1995) *Bad Business: Professional Crime in Modern Britain*. Oxford: Oxford University Press.

Hobbs, D. (in progress) *Populating the Underworld*. Cambridge: Polity.

Hobbs, D., Hadfield, P., Lister, S. and Winlow, S. (2003) *Bouncers: Violence and Governance in the Night-time Economy*. Oxford: Oxford University Press.

Hobbs, D., Winlow, S., Hadfield, P. and Lister, S. (2005) 'Violent hypocrisy: post-industrialism and the night-time economy', *European Journal of Criminology*, 2: 161–83.

Hobsbawm, E. (1959) *Primitive Rebels: Studies in Archaic Forms of Social Movement during the Nineteenth and Twentieth Centuries*. Manchester: Manchester University Press.

Ianni, F. and Ianni, E. R (1972) *A Family Business: Kinship and Social Control in Organized Crime*. New York: Russell Sage Foundation.

Jacobs, J. B. (1999) *Gotham Unbound*. New York: New York University Press.

Katz, J. (1975) 'Essences as moral identities', *American Journal of Sociology*, 80 (6): 1369–90.

Kelly, E. (2005) '"You can find anything you want": a critical reflection on research on trafficking in persons within and into Europe', in IOM (ed.), *Data and Research on Human Trafficking: A Global Survey*. Geneva: IOM.

Kelly, R. J., Chin, K.-L. and Fagan, J. A. (1993) 'The dragon breathes fire: Chinese organized crime in New York City', *Crime, Law and Social Change*, 19 (3): 245–69.

Kwitny, J. (1979) *Vicious Circles: The Mafia in the Marketplace*. New York: Norton.

Kyvig, D. (1979) *Repealing National Prohibition*. Chicago: University of Chicago Press.

Lambrianou, T. (1992) *Inside the Firm*. London: Pan.

Landesco, J. ([1929] 1968) *Organised Crime in Chicago*, 2nd edn. Chicago: University of Chicago Press.

Lippman, W. (1962) 'The underworld as servant', in G. Tyler (ed.), *Organized Crime in America*. Ann Arbor, MI: University of Michigan Press; article originally published in 1931.

McLean, L. (1998) *Guv'nor*. London: Blake Publishing.

Moldea, D. (1978) *The Hoffa Wars: Teamsters, Rebels, Politicians, and the Mob*. New York: Paddington Press.

Mollen Commission (1994) *Report of the Commission to Investigate Allegations of Police Corruption and the Anti-Corruption Procedures of the Police Department*. City of New York: Mollen Commission.

Moore, M. (1987) 'Organized crime as a business enterprise', in H. Edelhertz (ed.), *Major Issues in Organized Crime*. Washington, DC: National Institute of Justice, pp. 51–63.

Neff, J. (1989) *Mobbed Up*. New York: Atlantic Monthly Press.

Nelli, H. (1976) *The Business of Crime*. New York: Oxford University Press.

New York State Organized Crime Task Force (1988) *Corruption and Racketeering in the New York City Construction Industry: Final Report*. New York: New York University Press.

Newburn, T. (1999) *Understanding and Preventing Police Corruption: Lessons from the Literature*, Police Research Series Paper No. 110. London: Home Office RDS.

O'Mahoney, B. (1997) *So This Is Ecstasy?* Edinburgh: Mainstream Publishing.

Paoli, L. (2003) *Mafia Brotherhoods. Organized Crime, Italian Style*. Oxford: Oxford University Press.

Park, R. and Miller, H. (1921) *Old World Traits Transplanted*. New York: Harper & Bros.

Parker, R. (1981) *Rough Justice*. London: Fontana.

Pearce, F. (1976) *Crimes of the Powerful*. London: Pluto.

Pearson, E. (2003) *Study on Trafficking in Women in East Africa*. Eschborn: GTZ. Online at: http://www.gtz.de/traffickinginwomen.

Pearson, J. (1973) *The Profession of Violence*. London: Granada.

Pearson, J. (2001) *The Cult of Violence*. London: Orion.

Piper, N. (2004) 'A problem by a different name? A review of research on trafficking in South-East Asia and Oceania', in IOM (ed.), *Data and Research on Human Trafficking: A Global Survey*. Geneva: IOM.

Potter, G. and Jenkins, P. (1985) *The City and the Syndicate*. Lexington, MA: Ginn Press.

Quinney, R. (1975) *Critique of Legal Order: Crime Control in Capitalist Society*. Boston: Little, Brown.

Rawlinson, P. (2009) *From Fear to Fraternity: A Russian Tale of Crime, Economy and Modernity*. London: Pluto Press.

Reuter, P. (1983) *Disorganised Crime*. Cambridge, MA: MIT Press.

Reuter, P. (1987) *Racketeering in Legitimate Industries: A Study in the Economics of Intimidation*. Santa Monica, CA: Rand Corporation.

Richardson, C. (1992) *My Manor*. London: Pan.

Richardson, E. (2005) *The Last Word: My Life as a Gangland Boss*. London: Headline.

Ruggiero, V. (1993) 'Brixton, London: a drug culture without a drug economy?', *International Journal of Drug Policy*, 4 (2): 83–90.

Schelling, T. (1976) 'What is the business of organized crime?', in F. Ianni and E. Ruess-Ianni (eds), *The Crime Society – Organized Crime and Corruption in America*. New York: Times-Mirror, pp. 69–82.

Schelling, T. (1984) *Choice and Consequences*. Cambridge, MA: Harvard University Press.

Short, M. (1991) *Lundy: The Destruction of Scotland Yard's Finest Detective*. London: Grafton Books.

Silverstone, D. (forthcoming) *Night Clubbing: Drugs, Clubs and Regulation*. Cullompton: Willan.

Smith, D. Jr (1980) 'Paragons, pariahs, and pirates: a spectrum-based theory of enterprise', *Crime and Delinquency*, 26: 358–86.

Taylor, I. (1999) *Crime in Context*. Cambridge: Polity.

van der Kleij, A. (2002) *Provisions for Victims of Trafficking in Bonded Sexual Labour, i.e. Prostitution – in 6 European Countries. Final Report*. Bonded Labour in Netherlands, Amsterdam Online at: http://www.humanitas.nl/project/Blinn_Final_Report.pdf.

Varese, F. (2001) *The Russian Mafia: Private Protection in a New Market Economy*. Oxford: Oxford University Press.

Volkov, V. (2002) *Violent Entrepreneurs: The Use of Force in the Making of Russian Capitalism*. New York: Cornell University Press.

Ward, H. and Gray, T. (1974) *Buller*. London: Hodder & Stoughton.

Wilson, A. H. (2002) *24-Hour Party People: What the Sleeve Notes Never Tell You*. London: Channel 4 Books.

Winlow, S. (2001) *Badfellas*. Oxford: Berg.

Winlow, S. and Hall, S. (2006) *Violent Night*. Oxford: Berg.

Zorbaugh, H. (1929) *The Gold Coast and the Slum*. Chicago: Chicago University Press.

Part VII

State, Political and War Crimes

The penultimate section of the book covers what may be broadly characterised as 'political' crimes in that they are in most cases tied up with struggles to maintain or achieve political power. They may occur in the context of war, including civil war, but are also committed in conditions of apparent peace and stability, and under democratic as well as autocratic governments. The main focus here is on major crimes perpetrated by regimes already in power, although two chapters discuss crime by groups challenging the state. As in Part VI, the contributors draw attention to the dearth of criminological literature on such topics.

Of course, crime committed by those in power is among the most difficult to prevent or punish, at least until they have lost their power, and if it goes unchecked can escalate into massive abuses of human rights and ultimately 'crimes against humanity'. In many cases, international action is necessary to bring perpetrators to justice. Williams' chapter presents a broad introduction to these issues, as well as distinguishing different types of state crime and addressing key problems of definition. The other chapters focus on specific forms of behaviour.

Aitchison discusses what many would agree to be the gravest crime of all: genocide. He shows that attempts to destroy whole populations can be found throughout history. However, it was not until the revelations of the Nazi atrocities that the term 'genocide' was coined and international legal frameworks were created to allow perpetrators to be brought to justice – albeit with continuing weaknesses in practice. In this context he considers more recent examples and responses to them, including the 'ethnic cleansing' that occurred following the break-up of Yugoslavia.

Morgan's chapter considers definitions of torture, who uses it to what purposes, and why the practice persists. He also analyses arguments which have been used to justify torture, including the 'ticking bomb' scenario, as well as noting the ease with which torture can become 'normalised'. His chapter is highly topical, with comments on recent controversies surrounding the 'rendition' of terrorist suspects.

Cain tackles a subject that has rarely been addressed in a criminological context: what she calls 'crimes of the global state'. By this she means harms committed by powerful transnational financial bodies such as the International Monetary Fund and the World Bank which, she claims, have wilfully ignored evidence about the disastrous impact of their policies on some countries, particularly in the Third World. She argues that their activities should be regulated by the United Nations. She also raises questions – discussed also in Part VIII – about distinctions between 'crimes' and 'harms'.

The last two chapters discuss actions by opponents of established orders. Waddington discusses the complex relationship of political protest to crime. He uses examples such as the civil rights movement in the USA and demonstrations against global capitalism to explore issues around media labelling and court responses, as well as raising fundamental questions about civil liberties in democratic societies. Finally, Weston and Innes focus on 'terrorism'. Like Waddington, they stress the importance of media labelling and the threats to civil liberties caused by government reactions to major terrorist attacks. They also show how a variety of academic disciplines have shed light on the understanding of the causes and consequences of such events.

Chapter 37

State crime

Katherine S. Williams

Introduction and definition

Although debated in classic works by moral philosophers and political economists, including Adam Smith's *The Wealth of Nations* (1776), and despite its importance to a full understanding of the relationship between individuals and the state, the topic of state crime has been studied in depth by relatively few criminologists. Nevertheless, a growing body of literature has emerged since the 1970s, mainly but not exclusively, from writers on the left (see, for example, Schwendinger and Schwendinger 1970; Block and Chambliss 1981; Faulk 1988; Chambliss 1989; Luyt 1989; Scott 1989; Barak 1990; Tunnell 1993; Johns and Johnson 1994; Kramer 1994; Kauzlarich and Kramer 1998; Rose-Ackermann 1999; Ross 2000a, 2000b; Cohen 2002; Green and Ward 2004; Bovenkerk and Levi 2007). This chapter draws on this work to provide a basic overview of state crime: what it is and the different forms it takes; which criminological explanations throw light on its occurrence; and the national, international and other controls which are, or might be, used to counter it.

Throughout history states have committed crimes which dwarf those of 'conventional' offenders or even organised criminal groups; their actions have often been costly, exceptionally violent and destructive of both property and people. This applies to a wide range of criminal behaviour: violence, acquisitive crime, exploitation, corruption, political offences, crimes of oppression or removal of freedoms, rights and dignity. If we concentrate merely on state violence, in the modern era Rummel (1994) estimated that between 1900 and 1987 over 168 million people were murdered by governments (excluding about 35 million deaths in war, legitimate judicial executions and killing of armed opponents or criminals using legitimate force). Many regimes and dictators have also stolen from their peoples. For example, General Sani Abacha, the Nigerian leader between 1993 and 1998, was accused of stealing £2.5–3 billion from his country and the Military Junta in Burma (Myanmar) keeps its people in poverty while allegedly using Burma's wealth for its own ends. From the outset it is important to recognise that, while these are extreme examples, 'state crime' is not confined simply to a few 'rogue' states or to third-world countries with authoritarian regimes. It can be found in all states, albeit some more than others and some more openly than others; no state has 'clean hands'.

Before any of these claims can be assessed a clear definition is necessary. The narrowest is acts which breach state criminal law and are committed by states, generally through their organisations and/or servants, in order to achieve or further a political interest for the state or the government of that state. Legally a criminal act is a breach of a legal rule which has criminal consequences attached to it, namely prosecution in a criminal court and, if found guilty, the possibility of punishment. If servants of the state commit offences when carrying out orders or even in acting out an overzealous interpretation of such orders they can trigger the criminal law. However, these individual or low-level acts do not embrace the worst state crimes and violations of human rights, which are unlikely to be caught by internal criminal laws. The problem arises because, at least in western democracies, the state itself is seen as the instrument to fight crime. Going back to social contract conceptions of states (Hobbes, Leviathan, 1651; Locke, Second Treatise on Government, 1689; Rousseau The Social Contract, 1762) one of the main reasons for giving up absolute freedom and joining with others in a community was protection both from those outside the community (state) and from those who breach one's rights within the community (state). Clearly, if the state is to successfully fulfil its role as protector of individuals in its territory there will be times when it needs to use force to preserve the social order. Max Weber in Politics as Vocation (1919) went further, arguing that 'a state is a human community that (successfully) claims the monopoly of the legitimate use of physical force within a given territory'. That does not mean all state force is justified but that the considered and proportionate use of force to maintain or restore social order is legitimate. However, this is an ends-based definition: an act is a legitimate use of force if it is both sanctioned by the state and tends to restore social order. This is unsatisfactory both because it takes the state as the point of departure for legitimising its own behaviour and because the restoration of order is subjective. Who decides which social order to restore and whether force is legitimate? The state is the principal protector; in this role the state both defines most crimes and is the authority under which crimes are prosecuted. Understandably states tend not to define damaging acts they will participate in as criminal or to prosecute themselves, though the acts of their servants are sometimes prosecuted. This allows the worst atrocities to go unpunished and any centrally orchestrated state crime escapes national criminal prosecution. Clearly a wider definition is necessary.

There are a number of more objective definitions in circulation. For example, 'state crime' may be seen as an act or failure to act that breaks either internal criminal law or public international law (Ross 2000b). Seen narrowly that might merely encapsulate the international rules enforced by nations such as those which are acted on by the United Nations. Being set by states these too are limited so a definition might legitimately go wider and encapsulate concepts which are accepted at a level beyond the individual state. Green and Ward (2004) thus defined 'state crime' as state organised deviance involving the violation of human rights. Here these definitions will be amalgamated:

'State crime' is a state organised act or failure to act that breaks either the internal criminal laws or public international laws or is a form of organised deviance (by omission or commission) involving the violation of human rights or the destruction either of the interests of peoples or of their economies.

Some aspects of this definition require closer scrutiny. Firstly, a state is the elected (or otherwise constituted) central power along with appointed officials, bureaucrats and institutions, organisations and agencies which allow the ruling group to run the country: the apparatus of government (Ross 2000b). Green and Ward (2004) see it as a legitimate power, sufficiently organised to be able to sustain social order (through legitimate force if necessary), punish wrongdoing, dispense justice, collect taxes and control a wide geographic area under its jurisdiction. It is an entity recognised (though maybe not either welcomed or accepted) as such by its people and maybe also by international law or other nations. However, modern states are complex structures, many have federal systems and local and federal elements may have different, sometimes conflicting, interests. Even a unitary state requires many agencies and institutions to conduct its business and each will have slightly differing goals. Each agency has subgroups, specialist units or geographically defined powers; each of these may set different goals and act separately. To complicate things further, neo-liberal states, where there has been a move from government towards governance, also operate through private (and sometimes even charitable) organisations. If these transgress on state business some might morally class that as state crime but legally states may avoid accountability: the above definition would include such cases. Clearly, some actions by agents of the state, even when ostensibly on state business, may be merely individual crimes committed for personal reasons or personal gain. To be a state crime it is necessary for the action or failure to act to be state-organised or to further some organisational end (or the ends of a unit within an organisation) and where it is more individual for it to be at least tolerated or condoned by the organisation or unit. Green and Ward (2004) give the example of a soldier who, for personal gratification, rapes one of the enemy; that act might further the interests of the state or part of it through ethnic cleansing or degradation of the enemy and if colleagues do nothing they have colluded and it is state crime. This recognises a number of things: it will not always be possible to claim that a state crime has been committed at the behest of the state or of a senior agent of the state; promotions often follow the occurrence of state crime as those who commit them advance the interests of the state or a state unit and have shown loyalty even without being asked; the ethos within a unit, or even the broader population, may be one of disinterest in or support for goals of the state which violate the rights of others.

Secondly, ideally state crime involves the breach of a legal rule: national or international. Above there was some consideration of breaches of internal criminal laws. Transgression of international laws is rather more complex. Generally international law is a system of agreements that bind nation states to recognised values and standards; here the declarations of the United

Nations are of particular importance. However, for these to apply states have to be recognised by the relevant international body and have to agree to be bound by the convention or declaration. Also international legal standards are delineated by states; they may fail to criminalise some of the harms they commit or to recognise them as crimes under their own regimes. States have been slow to move towards holding their own agents responsible for wrongdoing or holding each other responsible for wrongdoing. As Ross (2000a, 2000b) notes, states have slowly moved from being the protectors from harm (providing punishment for criminal transgressions and protection from external intrusions) through being victims to being perpetrators. The journey has been slow and is incomplete so one can never rely wholly on state-imposed recognition of actions for our definition of state crime. It is for this reason that Green and Ward (2004) added organised deviance involving the violation of human rights.

Thirdly, organised deviance: building on Becker's (1963) concept of deviance Green and Ward (2004: 4) define it as an act which a significant proportion in a community (an audience) believe violates a standard of behaviour (a rule) and would apply a significant sanction to that violation. Rules include internal and international legal rules (including standards such as the rule of law) and also international standards of behaviour (human rights) and other moral standards (e.g. justice) as interpreted by an audience. The audience or community which delineates the rules might be one's own citizens (organised or not), international organisations, other domestic state agencies, other states, domestic civic society (those groups such as intellectuals, media, political pressure groups and others that lie between the state and private individuals/families) or transnational civic society (groups such as non-governmental organisations which operate on an international stage). The sanctions may be legal (domestic or international punishment), anger or uprising from within the state, censure by any of the bodies which might harm the state's reputation (academics, media, NGOs), or diplomatic, economic, military, sporting or political sanctions imposed by other states or international organisations. Again it must be remembered that state crime only arises out of organised actions, as delineated above, where the state (or part of it) gains.

State crime includes failure to act. There are many occasions where a failure to act on the part of the state should and does attract censure. For example, where the state has used its force to imprison someone it has a duty to take steps to ensure that they do not harm themselves. Ballinger (2003) gives the example of a failure to carefully investigate a crime which results in wrongful conviction and, in her examples, execution of individuals. It might also include failure to help people following a national disaster, e.g. Burma following the cyclone in 2008.

Finally, the definition covers human rights and similar high moral standards. These rights include, though may be broader than, those which may be acknowledged by states in UN conventions and include economic norms such as those which might be enforced by the World Bank. It is necessary to tie the definition of state crime to something other than law in order to provide an independent theoretical base, one which is an accepted standard, not tied to the tyranny of moral majorities or the power of states.

It does not necessarily include every transgression of rights – this would equate it with protection from social harm. State crime causes criminal-level harm or gives rise to institutionalised harms such as racism and sexism (Schwendinger and Schwendinger 1970). The use of power to victimise another person by suppressing, controlling or reducing their power or their sense of self is criminalised. This opens the possibility of a dynamic conception of state crime (Henry and Milovanovic 1996) one which aims to protect the physical person, human dignity and social psychological well-being from the excesses of the state and its organs of power. For example, law would have problems recognising and dealing with atrocities resulting partly from natural disasters but exacerbated by governmental policies or which are unintended consequences of economic and social policies, for example the Chinese Famine of 1959–60 or the Great Depression of the 1930s. Human rights would view these as crimes, especially if the policies continue once their effects are known (Marcus 2003), while national and international law would see it as an accident, the result of inadequate, inequitable, exploitative policies (Vasak, with Alston 1982).

Patterns and examples

The incidence of state crime is high but does not form part of official records, so rates and trends are hard to assess. Therefore this section will focus on patterns and examples rather than trends. Torture, disappearances, summary arrests and executions have been widely used by states throughout history to terrorise groups and individuals into obedience to the dominant ideology. Taking a few examples from Europe: from the Tudor oppression of Catholics through the French Revolution to the twentieth-century experiences of the Stalinist regime in the Soviet Union, the Nazi regime in Germany and Slobodan Milošević's Serbia, oppression has been frequent and, in the twentieth century, almost ever-present (see Aitchison, this volume). Another example from Europe is the oppression and enslavement of colonised peoples and the unwillingness, until very recently, to recognise women as people possessing equal rights or to recognise children's rights. Oppression has been used by both third-world states with authoritarian regimes and first-world democratic states. Some atrocities such as the 1970s 'dirty war' in Argentina and the current oppression in Burma (Myanmar) and Zimbabwe involve a state's oppression of its own people. Others involve interference by one state in the affairs of another. Sometimes such interference is open such as the illegal US invasion of Panama in December 1989; which Johns and Johnson (1994) and Trent (1992) depict as part of US attempts to 'roll back' to a pre-communist world and establish free-market capitalism, but the US claim was to deliver democracy. In the invasion the US used deadly force, often against civilians, carried out executions, systematically burned buildings (including homes and villages), herded people into refugee camps and repressed opponents. At other times the interference is more subtle such as the CIA funding of the Contras guerrilla warfare against the Sandinista regime in Nicaragua. Again part of the reason behind the intervention was the 'roll back' and the desire to promote capitalism, especially on the US doorstep; the official reason was again to promote democracy and to remove corrupt regimes so that aid would be more effective. These examples serve to show both direct and indirect actions in both internal and external state crimes. While such actions have been present throughout history they are arguably more prevalent in the modern and post-modern era.

The above are major abuses but orchestrated breaches, even by the central state, can be smaller; they can occur wherever agencies have a legitimate possibility of physical force such as the use of 'reasonable force'. Within states these exist most commonly in police and punishment agencies; police violence, or that of the punishment agencies, can result in intimidation of the population and may be used by states to retain control. Even in otherwise democratic states these tactics can sometimes be orchestrated: some claim that this was the situation in the policing of the 1984/5 miners' strike in Britain when various police forces, the prisons, the courts, the security services and the military were coordinated (from central government) in a deviant strategy designed to undermine the power of the unions; this violated both the proper roles of these state agencies and human rights (Callinicos and Simons 1985; Fine and Millar 1985; Green 1990). Therefore, in a time of economic and political crisis, democratic capitalist states might be driven to using state crime while claiming to defend the existing order. Examples can be found in Kretzmer's 2007 discussion of torture in Israel and the case of *Ireland* v. *United Kingdom* (1978–9) 2 EHRR 25 which found the UK's use of the 'five techniques' to be inhuman and degrading treatment which occurred because of fears of terrorist attacks in Northern Ireland. Certain types of state violence may even exist on an international, state-orchestrated level, as is claimed for the system of rendition (Council of Europe 2008: European Parliament 2006a, 2006b, 2009) involving the USA and states in which torture is not illegal and committed with the collusion, if not help and support, of certain European states, including the UK, whereby terrorist suspects were tortured in order to try to obtain information about networks and possible attacks. This internationally orchestrated state crime is particularly worrying as it leaves no one except the national, international and transnational civil society to monitor and uncover such activities (see Statewatch, n.d.). It is likely that secret organisations worldwide (e.g. MI5, MI6 and the CIA) have always operated this type of criminality at some level. Precise calculations of its prevalence are difficult but, as with most other areas of state crime, it seems to be increasing.

State crime involving violence or deprivation of liberty also occurs at a less politically charged level. In some states excessive use of force is at a much lower level and not orchestrated (Sherman 1980; Jacobs and O'Brien 1998; Phillips and Smith 2000). Many recent academic and other research studies report appalling conditions in the modern penal system: at the very least overcrowding, poor infrastructure, unsanitary conditions, poorly trained staff, unacceptable use of solitary confinement, inadequate legal support, poor health and education services, little work and exercise and long periods of confinement to cells; at worst inhuman treatment, violence from staff and/or inmates, torture and killing (Cassese 1996; Davis 2005; Goldson and Coles

2005; Stanley 2008). Here the example of deaths in custody in the UK will be used. INQUEST note that 2,120 men, women and children died in prison and police custody between 1995 and 2005 (558 died after contact with police and 1,562 in prison). A number of HM Inspector of Prisons Reports on various establishments over the last 4–5 years have detailed regimes of violence in establishments and high levels of fear among prisoners. The 2007 Safety Report produced by HM Chief Inspector of Prisons found high levels of staff violence and negative attitudes were central to prisoner's feelings of fear and insecurity. Deaths in custody have resulted from medical neglect following use of force by police or prison officers and homicides in prison. All of these clearly display a violent environment. Some prisoners committed suicide so appear not to be state crimes; however, suicides often result from conditions of incarceration or institutional and psychological violence within the system (Goldson and Coles 2005) so their deaths too are the result of an ever more punitive society and are therefore, on the above definition, instances of state crime. Clearly some deaths in custody result from natural causes.

Not all state crime involves violence or repression; much is economic, usually involving corruption (inducement of a public official by improper means (bribery) to violate duty). It has always existed and been important within and between states. Traditionally, corruption is depicted as the illegitimate individual abuse of a position of power for personal gain and is thereby portrayed as an individual offence. However, much corruption occurs in order to further the interests or goals of the state or is tolerated by state organs because there is some state or institutional interest being served. The corruption may directly promote an organisational goal; it may serve organisational goals to tacitly permit or tolerate corruption, or the pursuit of profit through corruption may become the goal of the state or of an arm of the state. As with acts of violence, corruption may occur at every level of government and in all aspects of society; it permeates dealings with individuals, corporations and states and exists in all areas of policy including economics and the financial community (Tombs and Whyte 2003). The link between corruption and state crime is complex and particularly interesting as, at its highest level, much state criminality is committed to fulfil ideals, often in the western world the ideal of democracy and/or capitalism, and yet state corruption at these central state levels may be challenging democracy and economic globalisation through its undermining of accountable government.

Corruption is often depicted as low-level, street-level, where the interests being served are likely to be those of an agency of the state or part of such an agency. The International Crime Victims Survey is one of the most reliable estimates of this type of offending. As with earlier surveys in 2005 they found that in most developed countries victimisation rates from corruption were below 0.5 per cent (some of these would be purely individual corruption), whereas for developing states the figure was over 13 per cent and included more structural, officially permitted or encouraged cases.

Not all corruption is either individual or low-level; some is chronic in departments or units of government and is therefore pervasive of the agency or of the whole state apparatus. The rate at which this occurs is very difficult to calculate. The International Crime Victim Survey is not well-placed to assess it but notes that it is likely to exist in states or parts of states where they find high rates of victimisation from corruption, for example Maputo (over 30 per cent) or Phnom Penh (29 per cent). Better situated to assess this pervasive corruption is Transparency International, whose Corruption Perception Index calculates annual rates of corruption. Their index is based on the perception of corruption as assessed by expert assessments and opinion surveys. They found that Denmark, New Zealand and Sweden are least likely to be corrupt whereas Somalia, Iraq and Burma (Myanmar) are most corrupt. They also note that Bulgaria, Burundi, the Maldives, Norway and the United Kingdom are becoming more corrupt (the UK moved from 12th cleanest to 16th). Huguette Labelle, Chair of Transparency International, stated:

> In the poorest countries, corruption levels can mean the difference between life and death, when money for hospitals or clean water is in play ...

> The continuing high levels of corruption and poverty plaguing many of the world's societies amount to an ongoing humanitarian disaster and cannot be tolerated. But even in more privileged countries, with enforcement disturbingly uneven, a tougher approach to tackling corruption is needed.

In the worst systems corruption and therefore state crime might be seen as part of the whole system – i.e. it is a structural phenomenon, something at least supported by, maybe even encouraged or ordered by, the government. This will tend to occur where the political system is powerful and structures which might question its actions, such as civil society (academics, the media, etc.) are insufficiently free or influential to alter the system, allowing it to become increasingly corrupt and to require bribery for the delivery of services, benefits or licenses which should be free to those who qualify. Here often commercial enterprises collude in the system by buying favours or contracts from the state (Morris 1991) and therefore state crime and commercial crime go hand in hand. In certain circumstances, usually when corruption is part of the fabric of a state or of a unit of the state, the extortion and bribery will also embrace organised crime, for example in relation to trade in illegal drugs, and become part of the mechanism for maintaining power (Sterling 1994; Jordan 1999) – structural corruption. Jordan (1999) notes that some governments even control drug trafficking, or the whole drug production chain, as being the most lucrative criminal activity. He also documents instances where part of a government may be managing the system while another section is allied with, or in corrupt relationships with, illegal traffickers and the two sections of state may thereby be in opposition so causing an unstable situation, one which may dissolve into civil war. He even suggests that this connection between criminal activity and state may, through global capitalism, infect more markets so opening up the possibility of global conflicts based on competing corrupt states' links with criminal activity, and that this might threaten democratic stability and international political power relations. All these areas of corruption are increasing as global markets offer more possibilities for it to take hold.

The last area of economic crimes involves states which use ostensibly legitimate financial means (offshore tax havens, offshore banking and secret financial havens) to boost their economy in the knowledge that these also help to sustain organised crime and breaches of criminal laws elsewhere. At an international level such activities are increasingly being recognised as assisting organised crime, undermining international financial stability and undermining tax and social welfare systems so being unacceptable, even criminal, and states are pressured into relinquishing them; they serve to violate human rights so, on the above definition, are forms of state crime. Furthermore, often such practices are accompanied by high levels of corruption and other financial state crimes. These states are driven by purely financial ends: in many cases it is their main means of economic stability, and their state structure is based on undermining the economies of other states.

Finally, there is computer crime. Usually this merely facilitates the occurrence of other state crime or is the means by which it is committed, but there is also cyberterrorism and cyberwar. These new activities could be used to interfere with or paralyse vital infrastructures or critical safety systems (possibly killing many people), to freeze computer systems in other states or to impede vital services such as transport and communications infrastructure so interfering with the ability to govern (Denning 2001; McGuire 2007). However, at the moment such attacks do not appear to be common and the danger of major attacks is low because where states have greatest capacity (rich western states) they claim to be against its use, while where states are more inclined to use it they lack the capacity for a large-scale attack (Denning 2007). Lower-level attacks may be occurring but as yet there are no reliable measures. One other area where computers may be involved is the way in which states control computer crime (and other offences): some measures, particularly data collection and retention and the blocking of the Web, interfere with human rights of individuals and might, themselves, constitute state crimes (Williams 2009).

Overall, most writers in the field agree that state crime is increasing, though there are fluctuations in when it occurs, which states are perpetrators and which peoples fall victim. More work needs to be done to calculate levels of state crime and its impact on victims but it is clear that the most common victims are inhabitants of the violating state. As will be seen below, these are also the most difficult to protect.

Explanations of state crime

Most people cannot conceive of a situation in which they would take bribes or commit other forms of corruption if they were in a position of power, even less torture, kill, inhumanly treat, abduct or use excessive violence against another human being. However, Sir Nigel Rodley, the UN's Special Rapporteur on Terrorism from 1993 to 2001, stated:

> When you meet torturers you realise that they're not doing it because they enjoy it, they torture people because it's a way of getting promotion

and pay rises. They want to get confessions and convictions because they see that as meeting the wishes of the institution.

There is a process of culturisation, where torturers are made to stop seeing their victim as human. But if they didn't think they'd be rewarded, they wouldn't do it. (Quoted by Coughlan 2003)

They are not mentally disturbed nor suffering from any personality disorder; they are the people next door, ordinary (Post 1998, 2001, 2005).

State crime occurs in wealthy, poor, tyrannical and democratic states. Where it is highly orchestrated a single person, group or class is behind it and it is conducted in order to maintain or extend power or control or ensure that certain cultural, political, economic or other state aims are achieved. For example, the US intervention in Nicaragua was clearly led by Reagan's administration and connected to US desire to extend capitalism and democracy. State corruption, violence and repression of oppositions and media are all committed to ensure continued power (Adams 2004a, 2004b; Freedom House 2008).

In some cases although leaders of the central state may not commit the crimes they may turn a blind eye where unlawful practices are perceived, however erroneously, to permit them to retain power or serve other political aims such as the desire to restore order or guarantee the status quo. Examples include abuse of powers in policing or punishment. States are particularly likely to resort to such measures or to turn the other way when they are under pressure, and they may then be willing to abandon the rule of law in the name of 'necessity'. The present 'war on terror' has created such a situation, whereby in trying to protect their citizens many nations pass laws or allow practices which violate human rights. This includes states which would not normally take part in acts such as torture, nor sit back while others do, but are willing to be involved because they believe, however erroneously, that it will give them the information they need to deliver safety within their own borders. Here the few (those suspected of links with terrorism) suffer and are sacrificed in the hope of delivering safety to the wider population. In extreme cases state violence may also grow out of the desire of factions to take power or a response to such actions (Luconi 2007).

A further major contributor in some cases has been a collapse of the state leaving factions free to impose order in various sections of the former state or a foreign power to take control (many atrocities committed by colonial powers might fall into this category: Cunneen 2007). Very often the worst atrocities occur to sustain a failing state. Interestingly, state violence or oppression is often caused by or causes kickbacks (bribes) or even revenge or reprisals, some of which may be violent and spawn violent regimes (Kaarthikeyan 2005), while the kickbacks merely cause more repressive action so building a spiral of violence and/or civil war. For example, Mugabe came to power in Zimbabwe ostensibly to bring peace where there had been violence between the rich white and poor black populations, but his rule led to excessive violence and oppression first to deliver on ideological policies and then to ensure continued power, with the result that state crime and violence became almost the essence of the regime. Power struggles can also be a catalyst for external powers to sustain or refuse to intervene in violent state control. Some states capitalise on terrorist groups to keep a society in fear and controlled, while sometimes normal foreign policy may support terrorist activities in certain states or support another state's repression of its people (Bjorgo 2005: chapters 14–16; Martin 2006: chapter 4).

A major driving factor, particularly behind corruption and other financial state crimes, is economics. While it is tempting to link atrocities to poverty and economic deprivation and, much of the worst types of state violence occur in such conditions, Malecková (2005) suggests that connections between poverty and terrorism and orchestrated violence are weak; the participants are not the poor but those with a higher living standard, those with government positions. Of course in a poor state this may be a way of stamping authority over others. It may be that the financial or other repressive factors are the backdrop where the sense of hopelessness is overwhelming and the move to act to take control becomes the central focus. Interestingly mounting debts and internationally agreed debt repayment schemes may cause state crime by placing too great a financial burden on poor nations which are then driven to collusion with corporations (often in the form of bribery for reduced regulations, e.g. lower environmental protections) or which may be destabilised and, in order to retain power, driven to allowing corrupt corporations and organised crime to take hold while using powerful authoritarianism to control the people; this often leads to the worst atrocities of torture and even genocide (Green and Ward 2004). In such cases the trigger may arise from a loan agreement set by the International Monetary Fund (IMF), which has broadly the same membership as the UN, and is focused on delivering economic stability. The IMF's critics say that this is often at the expense of democracy, human rights (nutrition, healthcare and education are often the first to be sacrificed) and labour rights. Critics see the IMF as sharing criminal responsibility by virtually forcing poor states to turn to corruption, authoritarian government and maybe even torture or worse (Green and Ward 2004). Who is responsible, the state or the IMF and, by implication, the international community?

In some cases state terrorism is born of fast-growing wealth, wealth which alters the nature of the society so that the ruling regime and their controls are no longer relevant and they have to participate in financial crime or repress, often violently, claims for change in order to retain control. Some of the excessive corruption and control found in Eastern European states is explained from this perspective though many such as Romania and Bulgaria are fighting hard to control the problem. Some states' whole economies rely on offshore havens, a lot of which encourage or help sustain criminal activities. This is purely economic sustenance for the whole nation, but it has often very negative repercussions elsewhere.

General social factors may also be involved. Mohammad (2005), in explaining developments in the Middle East, weaves a complex link to the social factors underlying extreme violence (especially terror, some state inflicted), some of which can be applied on a world stage to the reason why regimes may turn to tyrannical measures and why they may succeed. Most important among these are the beliefs and ideas 'fed' to the 'people' so as to encourage their support. These shared beliefs are instilled through hegemony. The means of mass communication are controlled or their managers are persuaded to 'sell' the requisite ideas to the citizens so they appear to be obviously right, with no credible alternative. This may help explain individual participation and general apathy to preventing state crime. It happens in a number of ways, two of which will be mentioned briefly here.

First is the absence or suppression of dissent. Most people will do nothing and allow things to happen in their name; these pose no threat to state crime and their passivity means tacit support for the tyranny. As Burke is supposed to have said '... the only thing necessary for the triumph of evil is for good men to do nothing' (Alvarez 2001). A few individuals dissent and are silenced by tyrannical regimes. Sometimes, too, democracies silence them: Tombs and Whyte (2003) refer to the silencing of dissenting academics in the USA following 9/11.

Secondly, the creation of groups is important. Many communities create 'in-groups' and 'out-groups' (Hall et al. 1978). The latter, which may include racial or religious minorities, the homeless, asylum seekers, offenders, prisoners, terrorists, the disabled and so on, tend to be denigrated and excluded from benefits, rights and dignity. Leaders can exploit this and cultivate it to give rise to superior, dominant groups and inferior powerless groups. 'Out-groups' may be portrayed as lacking intelligence, utility or morals, a threat to the dominant culture; even if people do not participate in crimes against them they may hand them over to the authorities (Alvarez 2001) or merely not bother to help them (Post 2005; Kaarthikeyan 2005; Reinares 2005; Finlay 2007; Fraser 2007). The negative image of these groups may arise at work, in the press or media, in films or in discussions with family and friends; once fixed and accepted they become less human and ripe for lesser treatment and eventually state crime. A powerful example can be drawn from Rwanda where in 1994 the government, run by the minority Hutus, used a radio station to broadcast anti-Tutsi messages, likening them to rats and blaming them for all ills; it was a factor in the massacre of over 800,000 Tutsis and moderate Hutus. This is not an isolated example: in 1971 Zimbardo carried out the Stanford Prison experiment where fellow students became either prisoners or prison guards. Within five days the guards became all powerful, lacking in compassion and using physical and verbal aggression, humiliating the prisoners or treating them inhumanely; the prisoners became totally powerless (Haney et al. 1973a, 1973b; Haney and Zimbardo 1998; Zimbardo 2005a, 2005b, 2007; see also Zimbardo n.d.). One can see exact parallels in the dehumanisation of and brutality against prisoners in Iraqi gaols (Provance 2005), in Guantanamo and in normal prisons (Cassese 1996; Davis 2005). It also suggests how ethnically mixed communities where people know each other and have lived together can be turned into communities of racial conflict as happened in the former Yugoslavia (see Aitchison this volume). The Chinese Cultural Revolution and Nazi Germany show how this can even split families. Therefore empathy between groups is essential to the prevention of state crime; its absence breeds or at least permits these offences. Many organisations work hard to ensure that all people are treated with equal respect; where they do not, state crime is likely to arise.

There is agreement that state crimes are committed by normal people. How do they become involved? Where there is personal gain all the normal explanations might apply, and here we will only consider instances where that is missing. One explanation may be deindividuation – the transformation of apparently rational and responsible individuals into unruly and irresponsible people. In a crowd inner restraints are lost when people are no longer seen as individuals and they become a puppet of the group or its leader (Le Bon 1895). More recently theorists have linked deindividuation to anonymity and lack of self-awareness, so reducing self-restraint (Postmes and Spears 1998). Zimbardo (1969) showed that people were more likely to administer a stronger electric shock when they were hooded and therefore unknown. However, the links between deindividuation and negative behaviour are not particularly strong (Postmes and Spears 1998).

Most people wrongly believe they would not follow an immoral order. However, Milgram's (1963, 1965 and 1974) experiments indicated that 65 per cent of ordinary people would administer a fatal electric shock if the researcher took responsibility for any consequences. These results have been partially replicated by Burger (2009). The usual reason given by ordinary individuals as to why they tortured or massacred individuals is 'we were only following orders'; this was used, though rejected, as a defence at the Nuremburg trials, by the Serbs in the former Yugoslavia and by the Hutus in Rwanda. Burger's 2009 study suggests that this may be an excuse and not an explanation as his subjects chose to administer the shock rather than being ordered to.

To conclude, state crime is underpinned by a plethora of explanations, some individual but many political and economic. Here a flavour has been given and it is clear that while some state crime relies on extreme evil the more worrying truth is the normality underlying both the individual and structural explanations. Many state crimes are based on intentions to avert what are seen as greater evils and represent an illegitimate use of force in a situation where some force may be legitimate by overzealous individuals or states whose intentions may be good.

Responses to state crime

States do not tend to criminalise their own activities; they rarely protect their people against terror committed by themselves or their servants. However, most states do control the actions of their servants in an effort to prevent state crimes. Control may be through criminal laws where state acts or those of its servants fall within the definitions. However, the apparatus of enforcement is rarely used against state agents. Control is more likely to be achieved through internal disciplinary procedures possibly leading to loss of promotional opportunities. The level at which this occurs may depend on the morality of the government and its people, something which fluctuates often unintentionally by merely not being as vigilant. In emergencies internal enforcement mechanisms may fail: governments choose not to prosecute as in the former Yugoslavia, or national institutions may have collapsed as happened in Rwanda. To avoid internal control some states move activities out of the jurisdiction of their normal control systems, e.g. Abu Ghraib and Guantánamo, both located in places where rights could be restricted and each using civilian private guards so that accountability was diffuse. To prevent this type of loophole control must be actively pursued. There are also states where all internal controls are crushed. For example, Freedom House notes that in Burma (Myanmar) the military government:

> ... rules by decree; controls all executive, legislative, and judicial powers; suppresses nearly all basic rights; and commits human rights abuses with impunity ... military officers hold most cabinet positions, and active or retired officers hold most top posts in all ministries, as well as key positions in the private sector ... In a system that lacks both transparency and accountability, official corruption is rampant at both the national and local levels. (Freedom House 2008)

When internal control fails or proves insufficient, international controls are necessary. These are wielded by international or regional organisations such as the United Nations or the Council of Europe. Their official systems are generally limited to interactions between states. They rely on a plethora of pieces of legislation: each has main human rights documents, e.g. the United Nations Declaration of Human Rights 1948 and the International Covenant on Civil and Political Rights (ICCPR) 1966 or the European Convention on Human Rights 1950; each also has particular conventions, e.g. Standard Minimum Rules for the Treatment of Prisoners (SMR) 1955. Compliance procedures are complex; for example, the UN Human Rights Committee receives annual reports from each of its member states concerning their own human rights record. It also examines complaints about violations and, under the First Protocol to the ICCPR, individuals can petition if their state has ratified (e.g. *Mukong* v. *Kameroon*, Communication No. 458/1991, UN Doc. CCPR/C/51/D/458/1991 (1994) where standards in prison were questioned). There are also special procedures, structures (e.g. UN Human Rights Council) or posts for particular types of transgressions (e.g. the Special Rapporteur of the UN Commission on Human Rights). Each is intended to toughen the controls to protect human rights. States can also be tried at the International Court of Justice. Despite all these possibilities the international community still often fails (it only intervenes once the breaches of rights reach a high enough threshold), or fails to deal appropriately or effectively with abuses: for example on 27 May 2009 it passed a resolution about Sri Lanka but failed to address many of the worst atrocities. These failures are indicative of the complex political web which surrounds international controls. Furthermore, the international community is still uncomfortable with holding states responsible (Jorgensen 2003) – it relies on unofficial denunciation of activities to deal with atrocities which occur inside a state by a government on its own people and often for problems between states. At international law states are not criminally responsible, though they may be persuaded or pushed into altering their policies.

International law holds individuals responsible, in particular through War Crimes Tribunals (based on humanitarian law) and the International Criminal Court (based on human rights), though some states including the USA have not signed the Rome statute so its nationals cannot be prosecuted.

These emphasise individual responsibility and hold individuals to account for their actions, because if individuals were not willing to commit atrocities state crime would not occur. They both use normal punishment systems, mostly imprisonment. Both are also feared by those who commit atrocities. Sir Nigel Rodley, the UN's Special Rapporteur on Terrorism from 1993 to 2001, 'saw "heads of police sweating profusely" at the prospect of their actions being brought out into the daylight' (Coughlan 2003). Each will only hold people to account where the human rights suffering is sufficiently egregious (*Prosecutor* v. *Blagojević and Jokić* (Case no. IT-02-60 (trial chamber) 7 January 2005) and it is a crime against a people or group not just against an individual (Drumbl 2007).

Further inadequacies of international law are uncovered because governments increasingly rely on private bodies to deliver policies, e.g. security in both Guantánamo Bay and in Iraq. As the perpetrators are not state actors the state cannot be held accountable for their acts and they escape prosecution (Alston 2005). The international regime needs to adapt to deal with modern situations.

The last real protection is a strong internal, international and transnational civil society, one which will question the actions of states, call them to account (sometimes through whistle-blowers) and not accept that ends justify means. Internal publicising of abuse can trigger control and prevent abuse becoming institutionalised. However, when groups such as the media and academics are legally or brutally silenced by the state, action has to be taken by international media and NGOs such as Amnesty, Human Rights Watch and Statewatch and citizen journalism through the Internet; their input and vigilance in bringing abuses out into the open and keeping them on the world agenda is vital and is not dampened by political pressures. While civil society has no power to prevent or punish abuse it can organise protests and boycotts (Green and Ward 2004) and publicity can move or shame the national or international community into acting. Building on information academic research brings understanding so uncovering mechanisms which might prevent or control abuses; this has been powerful in preventing economic violations (Alvesalo and Virta 2003). Through ensuring moral standards are recognised these mechanisms help prevention and by explaining the activities and so prompting official action or designing new controls they are also supportive of enforcement.

Often it takes a complex web of responses before abuse is stopped. For example, to stop the Reagan administration's supply of weapons, training and money to Nicaragua took a number of measures. The Boland Intervention by the US Congress in 1982, extended in 1984, prevented direct intervention. US support for the Contras was also attacked by the International Court of Justice in *Nicaragua* v. *United States* (1984 ICJ REP. 392, June 27 1986) which found against the US and called on them to refrain from the unlawful use of force against Nicaragua. The administration moved from direct to more covert provision of aid to the Contras; this was stopped when the Iran-Contra scandal headed by Oliver North was uncovered (through a leak from an Iranian to a Lebanese newspaper) and Reagan was forced to admit responsibility though still denied any direct knowledge of it. Interestingly, it was the actions by Congress and the reporting of the Iran-Contra scandal more than the international condemnation that brought the policy to an end.

Conclusion

States, particularly modern democratic ones, work to protect their citizens from being victimised by crime, and they take their duty to deliver security very seriously. Ideally constitutions, even unwritten ones, support this and provide legal restraint on state power, but constitutions can be rewritten (as in Burma). Even where constitutional protections exist they may not be enforceable in the face of an emergency or when the state is intent on the use of terror for political ends or claims extreme use of force in the name of protecting the majority (as is evident in powers to fight terrorism). The best states take clear, and in some cases fairly effective, steps to protect individuals from state crimes, usually by controlling servants of the state through disciplinary procedures. Even they do not recognise state crime at any more than an individual level. The worst use state power to oppress individuals in every aspect of their lives and control the judiciary and the media and oppress opponents to ensure continued power.

For this reason, and because even international organisations may be implicated in abuses (as in the case of the IMF above), it is necessary to define state crime by recognising it both as seen from within state and international law but also through objective, generally accepted values such as human rights. Only once it is defined and understood can it be uncovered and dealt with. This further marks the importance of extra-legal controls: law can never fully deal with criminal states, it needs the support of civil society to call states and individuals to account for more general human rights breaches.

This brief discussion has served to uncover a few examples of state crime and to indicate its existence in some of the worst atrocities in the world as well as its existence in the everyday occurrences within every state. Recognition that our own states have failed to treat people with respect and dignity and have breached human rights in their treatment of prisoners, suspected terrorists, illegal immigrants and other, largely excluded, groups is important. Recognition of their collusion and sometimes active participation in economic crimes and of their failure to deal with corruption is also important. If such failure can take place in western democratic states with little outcry from the population then it is difficult to see how worse atrocities will be stopped elsewhere. Change will only come when we recognise our own failings: through our silence we are complicit in the crimes our state perpetrates in our name and of much worse atrocities worldwide. While states do hold individuals to account and pressurise each other into respect for human rights they constantly need to be reminded of their duty. Only if civil society vociferously denunciates human rights abuses will states vigorously control them and actively respect the human rights of all citizens.

Selected further reading

One of the most comprehensive introductory works in this area is Green and Ward's *State Crime: Governments, Violence and Corruption* (2004) which provides a full and theoretically satisfying discussion of state crime and an excellent foundation for understanding what might release or encourage states to offend. While it also considers non-legal controls this is its weakest area and legal controls are almost completely absent. For a more comprehensive, though often rather more dated consideration, Friedrichs's two-volume collection of already published work *State Crime* (1998) draws together a broad range of excellent pieces to define, explore and explain state crime (Vol. 1) and to look at sanctions and preventative strategies (Vol. 2). For a comprehensive consideration of the international controls and their shortcomings see Drumbl, *Atrocity, Punishment and International Law* (2007) or, for a slightly less legalistic and broader consideration of controls, see Ross (2000b), *Varieties of State Crime and Its Control*. One of the best ways to keep up-to-date on actual state crimes is through the civil society websites such as Freedom House, especially their annual world reports (http://www.freedomhouse.org/template.cfm?page=15). Also worth noting are Statewatch (http://www.statewatch.org/ (for Europe)), Human Rights Watch (http://www.hrw.org/ (global)), Amnesty International (http://www.amnesty.org/ (global)); and Transparency International's Corruption Perception Index for information about corruption (http://www.transparency.org/policy_research/surveys_indices/cpi). As well as this extra reading there is a very informative, visually powerful though rather dated documentary film entitled *The Panama Deception* (see Trent, 1992) which provides a useful historical overview to the illegal invasion of Panama by the USA and juxtaposes US policy statements against those from the people of Panama. It also documents the sanitised and inadequate coverage of the invasion by the US media and the reaction of the international community to what was clearly an illegal act (note that some scenes depict distressing images).

References

Adams, B. (2004a) Quoted in Burma Democratic Concern. Online at: http://www.bdcburma.org/Humanrights.asp (accessed March 2009).

Adams, B. (2004b) *Statement to the European Union Development Committee*. Reproduced in Human Rights Watch online at: http://hrw.org/english/docs/2004/09/01/burma9290.htm (accessed March 2009).

Alston, P. (2005) *Non-state Actors and Human Rights*. Oxford: Oxford University Press.

Alvarez, A. (2001) *Governments, Citizens and Genocide*. Indiana, IN: Indiana University Press.

Alvesalo, A. and Virta, E. (2003) 'Researching regulators and paradoxes of access', in S. Tombs and D. Whyte (eds), *Unmasking the Crimes of the Powerful*. New York: Peter Lang.

Ballinger, A. (2003) 'Researching and redefining state crime', in S. Tombs and D. Whyte (eds), *Unmasking the Crimes of the Powerful*. New York: Peter Lang.

Barak, G. (ed.) (1990) *Crimes by the Capitalist State: An Introduction to State Criminality*. Albany, NY: State University of New York Press.

Becker, H. (1963) *Outsiders*. Glencoe, IL: Free Press.

Bjorgo, T. (2005) *Route Causes of Terrorism: Myths Realities and Ways Forward*. Abingdon: Routledge.

Block, A. and Chambliss, W. (1981) *Organizing Crime*. New York: Elsivier.

Bovenkerk, F. and Levi, M. (2007) *The Organized Crime Community: Essays in Honour of Alan Block*. New York: Springer.

Burger, J. M. (2009) 'Replicating Milgram: would people still obey today?', *American Psychologist*, 64 (1): 1–11.

Callinicos, A. and Simons, M. (1985) 'The tragedy of Nottinghamshire', in Socialist Worker, *The Great Strike: The Miners' Strike of 1984–85 and Its Lessons*. London: Socialist Worker, pp. 47–81.

Cassese, A. (1996) *Inhuman States: Imprisonment, Detention and Torture in Europe Today*. Cambridge: Polity Press.

Chambliss, W. (1989) 'State organised crime', *Criminology*, 27 (2): 183–208.

Cohen, S. (2002) 'Human rights and crimes of the state: the culture of denial', in E. McLaughlin, J. Muncie and G. Hughes (eds), *Criminological Perspectives*, 2nd edn. London: Sage.

Coughlan, S. (2003) 'Do human rights stand a chance post 9/11?', *Times Higher Education Supplement*, 29 August. Online at: http://www.timeshighereducation.co.uk/story. asp?sectioncode=26&storycode=178828 (accessed March 2009).

Council of Europe (2008) *CIA above the law? Secret Detentions and Unlawful Inter-state Transfers of Detainees in Europe*. Council of Europe.

Cunneen, C. (2007) 'The effects of colonial policy: genocide, racism and aboriginal people in Australia', in M. Prum, B. Deschamps and M.-C. Barbier (eds), *Racial, Ethnic and Homophobic Violence: Killing in the Name of Otherness*. New York: Routledge Cavendish.

Davis, A. Y. (2005) *Abolition Democracy: Beyond Empire, Prisons and Torture*. New York: Seven Stories Press.

Denning, D. E. (2001) *Is Cyber Terror Next?* New York: US Social Science Research Council. Online at: http://www.ssrc.org/sept11/essays/denning.htm (accessed March 2009).

Denning, D. E. (2007) 'Assessing the CNO threat of foreign countries', in J. Arquilla and D. Borer (eds), *Information Strategy and Warfare*. London: Routledge.

Drumbl, M. A. (2007) *Atrocity, Punishment and International Law*. Cambridge: Cambridge University Press.

European Parliament (2006a) *Interim Report on the Alleged Use of European Countries by the CIA for the Transportation and Illegal Detention of Prisoners* (2006/2027(INI) Rapporteur: Giovanni Claudio Fava (A6-9999/2006). Online at: http://www. statewatch.org/rendition/rendition.html.

European Parliament (2006b) Final edition: Extraordinary rendition, Thursday, 6 July, Strasbourg. Online at: http://www.europarl.europa.eu/sides/getDoc.do?pubRef=-//EP//TEXT+TA+P6-TA-2006-0316+0+DOC+XML+V0//EN&language=EN (accessed March 2009).

European Parliament (2009) Resolution of 19 February 2009. Online at: http://www. europarl.europa.eu/sides/getDoc.do?pubRef=-//EP//TEXT+TA+P6-TA-2009-0073+0+DOC+XML+V0//EN&language=EN (accessed March 2009)

Faulk, R. (1988) *Revolutionaries and Functionaries: The Dual Face of Terrorism*. New York: E. P. Hutton.

Fine, B. and Millar, R. (eds) (1985) *Policing the Miners' Strike*. London: Lawrence & Wishart.

Finlay, W. M. L. (2007) 'The propaganda of extreme hostility: denunciation and the regulation of the group', *British Journal of Social Psychology*, 46: 323–41.

Fraser, D. (2007) 'Roma sacer: constructing the gypsy other in British political and legal discourse', in M. Prum, B. Deschamps and M.-C. Barbier (eds), *Racial, Ethnic and Homophobic Violence: Killing in the name of Otherness*. New York: Routledge Cavendish.

Freedom House (2008) The Freedom in the World 2008 Country Report. Online at: http://www.freedomhouse.org/template.cfm?page=22&country=7363&year=2008.

Friedrichs, D. O. (ed.) (1998) *State Crime*, 2 vols. Aldershot: Dartmouth.

Goldson, B. and Coles, D. (2005) *In the Care of the State?* London: INQUEST.

Green, P. (1990) *The Enemy Without: Policing and Class Consciousness in the Miners' Strike*. Milton Keynes: Open University Press.

Green, P. and Ward, T. (2004) *State Crime: Governments, Violence and Corruption*. London: Pluto Press.

Hall, S., Critcher, C., Jefferson, T., Clarke, J. and Roberts, B. (1978) *Policing the Crisis*. Basingstoke: Macmillan.

Haney, C. and Zimbardo, P. G. (1998) 'The past and future of U.S. prison policy: twenty-five years after the Stanford Prison Experiment', *American Psychologist*, 53: 709–27.

Haney, C., Banks, W. C. and Zimbardo, P. G. (1973a) 'Interpersonal dynamics in a simulated prison', *International Journal of Criminology and Penology*, 1: 69–97.

Haney, C., Banks, W. C. and Zimbardo, P. G. (1973b) 'Study of prisoners and guards in a simulated prison', *Naval Research Reviews*, 9: 1–17. Washington, DC: Office of Naval Research.

Henry, S. and Milovanovic, D. (1996) *Constitutive Criminology: Beyond Postmodernism*. London: Sage.

HM Chief inspector of Prisons (2007) *Safety Report*. London: Home Office. Online at: http://inspectorates.homeoffice.gov.uk/hmiprisons/thematic-reports1/Prisoner_safety_in_HM_priso1.pdf.

Jacobs, D. and O'Brien, R. M. (1998) 'The determinants of deadly force: a structural analysis of police violence', *American Journal of Sociology*, 103 (4): 837–62.

Johns, C. J. and Johnson, P. W. (1994) *State Crime, the Media, and the Invasion of Panama*. Westport, CT: Praeger.

Jordan, D. C. (1999) *Drug Politics: Dirty Money and Democracies*. Norman, OK: University of Oklahoma Press.

Jorgensen, N. (2003) *The Responsibility of States for International Crimes*. Oxford: Oxford University Press.

Kaarthikeyan, S. D. R. (2005) 'Root causes of terrorism? A case study of the Tamil insurgency and the LTTE', in T. Bjorgo (ed.), *Root Causes of Terrorism: Myths Realities and Ways Forward*. Abingdon: Routledge.

Kauzlarich, D. and Kramer, R. C. (1998) *Crimes of the American Nuclear State: At Home and Abroad*. Boston: Northeastern University Press.

Kramer, R. C. (1994) 'State violence and violent crime', *Peace Review*, 6 (2): 171–5.

Kretzmer, D. (2007) 'The torture debate: Israel and beyond', in D. Downes, P. Rock, C. Chinkin and C. Gearty (eds), *Crime, Social Control and Human Rights: From Moral Panics to States of Denial*. Cullompton: Willan.

Le Bon, G. (1895) *The Crowd: A Study of the Popular Mind*, reprinted in 1995. London: Transaction Publishers.

Luconi, S. (2007) 'Italian Americans and the racialisation of ethnic violence in the United States', in M. Prum, B. Deschamps and M.-C. Barbier (eds), *Racial, Ethnic and Homophobic Violence: Killing in the Name of Otherness*. New York: Routledge Cavendish.

Luyt, C. (1989) 'The killing fields: South Africa's human rights record in Southern Africa', *Social Justice*, 16 (2): 89–115

McGuire, M. (2007) *Hypercrime: The New Geometry of Harm*. Abingdon: Routledge Cavendish.

Malecková, J. (2005) 'Impoverished terrorists: stereotype or reality?', in T. Bjorgo (ed.), *Root Causes of Terrorism: Myths Realities and Ways Forward*. Abingdon: Routledge.

Marcus, D. (2003) 'Famine crimes in international law', *American Journal of International Law*, 97 (2): 245–81.

Martin, G. (2006) *Understanding Terrorism: Challenges, Perspectives and Issues*. Thousand Oaks, CA: Sage.

Milgram, S. (1963) 'Behavioral study of obedience', *Journal of Abnormal and Social Psychology*, 67: 371–78.

Milgram, S. (1965) 'Some conditions of obedience and disobedience to authority', *Human Relations*, 18: 57–76.

Milgram, S. (1974) *Obedience to Authority: An Experimental View*. New York: Harper & Row.

Mohammad, A. S. (2005) 'Roots of terrorism in the Middle East: international pressures and international constraints', in T. Bjorgo (ed.), *Root Causes of Terrorism: Myths Realities and Ways Forward*. Abingdon: Routledge.

Morris, S. D. (1991) *Corruption and Politics in Contemporary Mexico*. Tuscaloosa, AL: University of Alabama Press.

Phillips, T. and Smith, P. (2000) 'Police violence occasioning citizen complaint', *British Journal of Criminology*, 40: 480–96.

Post, J. M. (1998) 'Terrorist psycho-logic: terrorist behaviour as a product of psychological forces', in W. Reich (ed.), *Origins of Terrorism*. Baltimore, MD: Johns Hopkins University Press.

Post, J. M. (2001) *Washington Post*, Monday, 22 October.

Post, J. M. (2005) '"When hatred is bred in the bone": the socio-cultural underpinnings of terrorist', in T. Bjorgo (ed.), *Root Causes of Terrorism: Myths Realities and Ways Forward*. Abingdon: Routledge.

Postmes, T. and Spears, R. (1998) 'Deindividuation and anti-normative behavior: a meta-analysis', *Psychological Bulletin*, 123: 238–59.

Provance, S. (2005) Sgt Sam Provance statement to Congress. Online at: http://www. humanrightsfirst.info/pdf/06214-usls-provance-statment.pdf.

Reinares, F. (2005) 'Nationalist separatism and terrorism in comparative perspective', in T. Bjorgo (ed.), *Root Causes of Terrorism: Myths Realities and Ways Forward*. Abingdon: Routledge.

Rose-Ackerman, S. (1999) *Corruption and Government: Causes, Consequences and Reform*. Cambridge: Cambridge University Press.

Ross, J. I. (ed.) (2000a) *Controlling State Crime*, 2nd edn. New Brunswick, NJ: Transaction Publishers.

Ross, J. I. (ed.) (2000b) *Varieties of State Crime and Its Control*. Monsey, NJ: Criminal Justice.

Rummel, R. J. (1994) 'Demicide in totalitarian states: mortocracies and megamurders', in I. W. Chany (ed.), *Genocide: A Critical Bibliographic Review*, Vol. 3. New Brunswick, NJ: Transaction Publishers.

Schwendinger, H. and Schwendinger, J. (1970) 'Defenders of order or guardians of human rights?', *Issues in Criminology*, 5 (2) (Summer): 123–57 .

Scott, P. (1989) 'Northwards without North: Bush, counterterrorism and the continuation of secret power', *Social Justice*, 16 (2): 1–30.

Sherman, L. W. (1980) 'Causes of police behaviour: the current state of quantitative research', *Journal of Research in Crime and Delinquency*, 17 (1): 69–100.

Stanley, E. (2008) 'Torture and terror', in T. Anthony and C. Cunneen (eds), *The Critical Criminology Companion*. Sydney: Federation Press.

Statewatch (n.d.) Online at: http://www.statewatch.org/rendition/rendition.html (accessed March 2009).

Sterling, C. H. (1994) *Thieves' World*. New York: Simon & Schuster.

Tombs, S. and Whyte, D. (2003) *Unmasking the Crimes of the Powerful: Scrutinizing States and Corporations*. New York: Peter Lang.

Transparency International (1995–2008) *Corruption Perception Index: Annual Survey*. Online at: http://www.transparency.org/policy_research/surveys_indices/cpi (accessed March 2009).

Trent, B. (Director) (1992) *The Panama Deception*, written and edited by David Kasper. Empowerment Project, Chapel Hill, NC: A Rhino Home Video Release. 91 minutes.

Tunnell, K. D. (1993) *Political Crime in Contemporary America: A Critical Approach*. New York: Garland.

Vasak, K. (ed.) revised and edited for the English version by Alston, P. (1982) *The International Dimensions of Human Rights*. Westport, CT: Greenwood Press.

Williams, K. S. (2009) 'Trans-national developments in Internet law', in Y. Jewkes and M. Yar (eds), *The Handbook of Internet Crime*. Collumpton: Willan.

Zimbardo, P. G. (1969) 'The human choice: reason and order versus impulse and chaos', *Nebrasca Symposium on Motivation*, 17: 237.

Zimbardo, P. G. (2005a) *Liberation Psychology in a Time of Terror*. Speech to accept the Dagmar and Václav Havel Foundation VIZ 97 Award for 2005. Online at: http://www.prisonexp.org/pdf/havelprize.pdf (accessed March 2009).

Zimbardo, P. G. (2005b) *Stanford Prison Experiment: A Simulation Study of the Psychology of Imprisonment Conducted at Stanford University*. Online at: http://www.prisonexp.org/.

Zimbardo, P. G. (2007) *The Lucifer Effect: Understanding How Good People Turn Evil*. New York: Random House.

Zimbardo, P. G. (n.d.) Stanford Prison Experiment. Online at: http://www.prisonexp.org/ (accessed March 2009).

Chapter 38

Genocide and 'ethnic cleansing'

Andy Aitchison

Introduction

The term 'genocide' was first coined by Raphael Lemkin in 1944 to label a range of acts which had, since 1933, involved the increasingly systematic destruction of targeted ethnic or national groups, including Jews, Poles and Gypsies in Germany, German occupied territory and other Axis states in Europe (Lemkin 1944). The importance and originality of Lemkin's analysis was recognised immediately (Kuhn 1945: 361) and genocide was soon recognised as a crime by the nascent UN (UNGA 1946). Over two years the Convention on the Prevention and Punishment of the Crime of Genocide turned this initial declaration into a more detailed instrument which ultimately came into force early in 1951. While the term is of relatively recent invention, it was recognised that it described an 'ancient practice in its modern manifestation' (Kuhn 1945: 361) and has allowed the subsequent re-examination of the historical fates of a number of groups. Examples include the Armenians in Anatolia (Bloxham 2003), the Herero in German South West Africa (Madley 2005), indigenous populations of Australia (Van Krieken 1999) and further groups stretching back to antiquity (Chalk and Jonassohn 1990). Since the 1990s a further term, 'ethnic cleansing', translated directly from the Serbian/Croatian *etničko čišćenje* and having been applied to the forced population transfers and mass killings that followed the break-up of the former Yugoslavia, has come into increasingly common use to describe particular forms of genocide.

As will be discussed later, a core characteristic of genocide is the intent to destroy, wholly or in part, targeted racial, ethnic, religious or national groups; in this respect, it might be considered as one criminal episode. However, it is almost always composed of an immense number of offences (ranging from theft, robbery, criminal damage, arson, through major sexual offences to murder), committed in a sustained and organised fashion, which taken together may threaten the existence of the target group. It is, in this sense, a 'composite crime': indeed, Lemkin hoped that this would allow genocidal acts on the part of the Axis powers to be punished under existing laws (1947: 150).

The consequences of such a composite offence, alongside other 'egregious' international offences (Yacoubian 2000: 8), are clearly of great significance; yet as a discipline, criminology stands accused of giving insufficient analytical attention to this 'crime of crimes' (Yacoubian 2000; Day and Vandiver 2000; Cohen 1996, 2001). Acknowledging all murder as a form of violent death, and thus wishing to avoid trivialisation of any form it takes, Yehuda Bauer nevertheless observes not only that mass-murder demands special attention but that different forms of mass-murder demand different responses, and as such the attempt to define, analyse and understand genocide is more than simply an intellectual exercise in categorisation (1999: 31–2). In this spirit the chapter will seek to consider some of the ways in which legal, historical and sociological scholarship has sought to understand genocide. Such a discussion is essential before any detailed consideration may be given to questions of the prevalence of genocide. This question is revisited towards the end of the chapter.

The chapter starts by sketching out the specific historical parameters in which genocide will be examined before going on to examine genocide in three distinct frameworks. Firstly, in a legal framework, genocide can be understood as a crime distinct from a broader category of war crimes, and can be isolated from a broader category of political killings. Three specific elements of the legal category of genocide will be examined: the quantitative threshold of genocide, the question of intent and the more recent incorporation of ethnic cleansing as a form of genocide. The moral and political use of the term will then be explored briefly. Thirdly historical and sociological efforts to define and explain genocide in terms of perpetrators, victims and the relationship between the two will be examined. The chapter concludes with a discussion of the challenge of assessing the prevalence of genocide, even within a strictly bounded period, and touches on recent developments in the response to genocide and other crimes against humanity.

Historical parameters

As stated, genocide is a recent invention as a concept and as a legal category, yet the concept lends itself to retrospective application by historians and by groups with historical experience of persecution. As such the term has been applied to numerous events prior to the widespread killings and persecutions carried out by Axis powers. Perhaps the most famous of these is the *Armenian Genocide* during the course of the First World War, but in their history of genocide, Chalk and Jonassohn (1990) consider possible applications of the term as far back as Old Testament accounts of conflict between the Israelites and Amalekites, Assyrian campaigns in the ninth century BCE, and the Athenian attack on Melos in the fifth century BCE. On the basis of multiple cases from antiquity and the near total absence of evidence of various civilisations, including the Hittites, they conclude that genocide may not have been exceptional. These ancient genocides focused their destructive energies on external enemies. Later mass killings in the colonial period are defined by an economic and territorial rationale (see, for example, Chalk and Jonassohn 1990: 36). When Kuhn (1945) described Lemkin's analyses as indicative of a modern manifestation of an ancient practice, he prefigured much of the analysis that differentiates the Holocaust and many subsequent genocides from the mass killings that preceded them. Arguably, many of the mass killings which have occurred since the 1930s are qualitatively different from ancient or colonial genocides. In the twentieth and early twenty-first centuries genocide victims often exist within the perpetrating state or society and are targeted for ideological rather than purely economic reasons. These genocides, seeking to 'cleanse' or 'purify' a nation or society by eliminating groups which are portrayed as alien to its ideals or obstructive to its progress, have been characterised as modern phenomena (Bauman 2000). The source material for the chapter is based on such modern genocides, particularly those occurring since 1933, including those that inspired the term, namely the widespread persecutions perpetrated by Nazi Germany and collaborating regimes against Jewish and other populations in Europe.

Defining genocide: law, morality, history and sociology

A fundamental question in the study of genocide is what defines the phenomenon and what, if anything, differentiates it from mass killing. The term combines Greek and Latin elements: the former provides *genos*, indicating a race, nation or tribe, and the Latin suffix *-cide* denotes the act of killing (Lemkin 1947: 147). Lemkin's formulation of the concept followed on from his earlier efforts to have crimes of barbarity and vandalism recognised in international law, encompassing a range of punishable acts stemming from hatred towards or desire to destroy a 'racial, religious, or social collectivity'. These were taken to include acts against 'life, bodily integrity, liberty, dignity or economic existence' of members of the collectivity (barbarity) and destruction of cultural and artistic works (vandalism) (Lemkin 1947: 146, note 3). In highlighting his earlier use of the broad term 'social collectivity' as opposed to a narrower concept of *genos*, Lemkin flags up one of the enduring debates in analyses of genocide as a social and legal phenomenon, namely how the act of genocide is delimited in terms of the kinds of groups targeted. This and other definitional issues are addressed in a range of sources: international and domestic law, including the original Genocide Convention and a growing body of case law from international tribunals and domestic courts; less explicitly in moral and popular discourse; and in a significant body of historical and sociological analyses of the phenomenon. Each of these will be considered in turn.

Law and genocide

Law and legal scholarship is less concerned with explaining genocide than it is with defining the crime and creating a framework through which it can be prosecuted. The legal framework begins with Resolution 96(1) of the UN General Assembly which declared genocide to be a crime shocking to the conscience of mankind and against moral law. This crime was analogous to homicide, in that while the latter denied the individual the right to live, genocide represented a denial of the right to existence of entire groups. Groups were conceived of in racial, religious or political terms (UNGA 1946). The resolution underpins the subsequent Convention on the Prevention and Punishment of Genocide (1948) which defines genocide more precisely as an act committed with intent to destroy in whole, or in part, groups defined in terms of nationality, ethnicity, race or religion. The subcategory of attempts to destroy groups defined politically, subsequently named *politicide*, was removed in the drafting process (Robinson 1960: 59). Article 2 of the convention lists a series of acts which, when 'committed with intent to destroy in whole or in part a national, ethnical, racial or religious group, as such' constitute genocide:

- killing members of the group;
- causing serious bodily or mental harm to members of the group;
- deliberately inflicting on the group conditions of life calculated to bring about its physical destruction in whole or in part;
- imposing measures intended to prevent births within the group;
- forcibly transferring children of the group to another group.

The convention has provided the legal basis for prosecutions of genocide in a number of international and special domestic tribunals, including ad hoc tribunals for the former Yugoslavia (Updated Statute of the ICTY 2008: Art. 4), Rwanda (Statute of the ICTR 2007: Art. 2), Cambodia (Law on the Establishment of Extraordinary Chambers 2004: Art. 4) and the International Criminal Court (Rome Statute: Art. 6), as well as the domestic legislation of a number of states (for the UK, see the 1969 Genocide Act and the 2001 International Criminal Court Act and International Criminal Court (Scotland) Act). The last two decades have witnessed a growing body of prosecutions and subsequent case law on genocide, particularly from international tribunals but also from domestic courts including those of Ethiopia, France, Germany, the Netherlands and Spain. This can be used to build an understanding of genocide as a category within criminal law. There is not scope to go into a full analysis of the development of legal practice around genocide, but a number of difficulties in applying the legal definition can be highlighted here: the relationship between genocide and war crimes; quantitative assessments of killings; the question of intent; and politicide and ethnic cleansing as forms of genocide, indicating possible expansions of the legal concept.

Genocide as distinct from war crimes

While the term genocide was coined during war to describe activities taking place primarily in the wartime context of Axis occupied Europe, it is worth underlining that genocide is a crime independent of war crimes. The Genocide Convention states that it is a crime 'whether committed in war or in peace' (Art. 1) but the International Military Tribunal (IMT) at Nuremberg may have muddied the water somewhat. The Tribunal's charter outlines three sets of acts which fall within its jurisdiction: crimes against peace, war crimes and crimes against humanity. While genocide is not mentioned explicitly in any of these categories, the latter two include acts which, when conducted with an aim of group destruction, would constitute genocide. These two categories form the basis, respectively, of the third and fourth counts in the Nuremberg indictment. The third count, war crimes, included murder and ill-treatment of civilian populations, including 'systematic genocide, viz., the extermination of racial and national groups, against the civilian population of certain occupied territories in order to destroy particular races and classes of people and national, racial or religious groups' (reproduced in Marrus 1997: 65). This related to those territories subject to military occupation, and as such does not cover the genocide in totality, which included widespread persecution and murder of German Jews. Indeed, where British prosecutors Shawcross and Maxwell-Fyfe referred to genocide in the course of the trial, it was often in relation to German policy towards native populations, Jewish, Slavic or otherwise, in occupied territories (Nuremberg Trial Proceedings 1946, particularly 25 June §§60–4, 27 July §§493–4, 496–8).

Yet the beginnings of genocide can be traced back to earlier pre-war laws targeting Germany's Jewish population, removing them from the category of *Reichsbürger* to the lesser category of *Staatsangehörigen* (Garner 1936). At the time, these laws were recognised as part of an intensifying combination of legislative, administrative and party action against the 'non-Aryan' population of Germany leading to a 'catastrophic development of conditions' in which German Jews were faced with pauperisation or exile (James G. McDonald, League of Nations High Commissioner for Refugees, quoted in Stowell 1936: 102–3). McDonald was moved to say, when resigning from his position in the League, that in many parts of the country the punitive effect of discriminatory laws, which removed Jews from their livelihoods and from their relations with other Germans, amounted to 'a systematic attempt at starvation of the Jewish population' (in Stowell 1936: 103).

The fourth count of the IMT indictment, crimes against humanity, included the persecution of political, racial and religious groups, covering the persecution and murder of hundreds of thousands of German Jews between 1933 and 1939, and the escalation of this process and its extension to occupied territories from September 1939 onwards (reproduced in Marrus 1977: 70). The term genocide is not used in this count. While the war extended the area across which genocide could be conducted, there is a strong argument for separating this particular crime from broader German war aims. Yet the bench declined to make a statement on acts prior to September 1939, arguing that although the persecution, repression and murder of civilians, particularly German Jews, were established satisfactorily 'to constitute crimes against humanity, the acts relied on before the outbreak of war must have been in execution of, or in connection with, any crime within the jurisdiction of the trial' (IMT Judgment and Sentences 1947: 249), thus demanding a clear link to crimes against peace or war crimes.

Politicide

While the Genocide Convention excluded political groups from those protected, this is not a distinction that is universally recognised, even in law. The Ethiopian adoption of genocide as a crime in domestic law includes groups defined by political affiliation, and these laws have been instrumental in trials of Mengistu and other former members of the Derg and the government of the subsequent People's Democratic Republic of Ethiopia (Article 281 of the Ethiopian Penal Code of 1957, 269 in the revised 2004 Criminal Code; for a full discussion of the law and the genocide trials in Ethiopia see Tiba 2007).

The quantitative threshold: 'in whole or in part'

The Genocide Convention identifies the need to establish an intent to destroy a group in whole or in part (Art. 2), which begs the question how much of a group one need intend to destroy before the threshold of genocide is breached. Robinson interprets this as meaning that the intent to destroy a 'part of a group either within a country, or within a region, or within a single community' constitutes genocide, 'provided the number is substantial' (1960: 63). The 'substantial' qualification is left to the courts' discretion as to whether a number is sufficiently large. Arguably, this quantitative threshold requires elaboration. There may be groups in existence who are sufficiently small that even the destruction of a limited number of individuals may result in the dying out of the whole group, and so the number should be interpreted in two complementary ways: firstly as an integer indicating an absolute level of destruction; and secondly as a fraction indicating the proportion of the group targeted with destruction.

In the *Kayishema* judgment the International Criminal Tribunal for Rwanda (ICTR) chamber interpreted 'in part' to mean a 'considerable number of individuals who are part of the group' where they are targeted solely on the grounds of group membership. Arguably, this makes little advance on 'substantial', although the court also took into account earlier work of the Genocide Subcommittee of the International Law Commission which could imply 'a reasonably significant number, relative to the total of the group as a whole, or else a significant section of a group such as its leadership' (§§ 96–7). In the case of Rwanda, the number of Tutsi victims, estimated at 800,000 to 1 million or one in seven of the country's total population, was seen as compelling (§§289–91), and the number killed in particular massacres with which Kayishema was charged was also seen as evidence of his own genocidal intent (§§531–3). This judgment has, in turn, informed the deliberations of the International Criminal Tribunal for the former Yugoslavia (ICTY). In *Jelisić*, concerning the destruction of Muslims as a group in the Brčko region, the chamber went further, drawing on Lemkin and other authorities to argue that genocidal intent may be inferred from an attack on a smaller number of group members who are of special significance to that group and whose removal brings into question the ongoing survival of the group (§82). The chamber noted that the geographical area in which a group is targeted for destruction may be limited (§83). In *Krstić* the issue was examined again as the defence contended that the seven or eight thousand men killed over a few days in Srebrenica constituted a substantial proportion of neither the overall Muslim population of Bosnia and Herzegovina (1.4 million) nor the Muslim population of Srebrenica (40,000). A first instance finding of genocide was supported by the Appeals Chamber, who noted that numbers were not, in themselves, enough to dismiss or accept a finding of genocide, and that the Muslims of Srebrenica had, by their inclusion in a designated safe area, and through international media, gained a special significance. As such the Appeals Chamber found that 'the fate of the Bosnian Muslims of Srebrenica would be emblematic of that of all Bosnian Muslims' (§16). The targeting of adult males was also taken to be significant where the target group was seen to be traditionally patriarchal in structures of authority (§§91–2).

Intent

In a commentary on the convention, destruction which is carried out from motives of profit is not taken to fall within the legal definition, understood as a particular intent to destroy the group as a group on account of its characteristics (Robinson 1960: 60). The implications of such a narrow definition might undermine attempts to recognise as genocide the destruction of native Amazonian groups through incursions associated with commercial deforestation and the expansion of transport infrastructure, as here the motive is primarily economic development. It may also imply the need for a re-evaluation of the acts of Axis powers and their allies in Europe between 1939 and 1945. While it is apparent that Jews throughout Europe, Serbs in the Independent State of Croatia, and Roma and Sinti were targeted specifically as groups, the mass killings and other acts undermining national groups in Poland and Czechoslovakia as part of a strategy to create *Lebensraum* might be understood through different forms of intent, that is the intent to expand the *Reich*. Yet in the absence of military defeat, had these acts been pursued to a logical and long-term conclusion the end results would have been the destruction of non-German national groups in these territories.

Ethnic cleansing as a recently recognised form of genocide

While not covered by article 2 of the genocide convention, ethnic cleansing, understood as a policy of mass expulsion of civilians and other acts designed to block their return, was recognised as a form of genocide by the UN General Assembly (1992) in the course of the war in Bosnia and Herzegovina. This was drawn upon in the judgment in *Krstić* as the court sought to elaborate its understanding of steps taken towards the destruction of a group and the qualification of such actions as genocide. They recognise that while physical destruction 'is the most obvious method', similar ends may be pursued by 'purposeful eradication of its culture and identity resulting in the eventual extinction of the group as an entity distinct from the remainder of the community' (§§574 and 578). As such they consider a ruling by Germany's Federal Constitutional Court which found that the law on genocide (article 220a of the *Strafgesetzbuch*) did not 'compel the interpretation that the culprit's intent must be to exterminate physically at least a substantial number of the members of the group' and that an intent to destroy could extend 'beyond physical and biological extermination' (cited in *Krstić*: §579). The ICTY chamber did not fully endorse the German position, taking a cautious approach to anything which might expand the legal interpretation of genocide. However, they did draw upon evidence of ethnic cleansing, particularly in the form of destruction of the homes and cultural and religious property of persecuted groups to support inferences of the intent to physically destroy those groups. Thus it can be seen that understandings of genocide, in the legal sphere, are by no means static, and the legal concept has been developing over time with tensions between decisions which seek to take a broad notion of genocide from statutory instruments and conventions, and those which seek to interpret those instruments more narrowly. It will be seen, after a brief discussion of moral and political uses of the term genocide, that such tendencies towards broader and narrow conceptualisations of genocide are by no means unique to the legal sphere and emerge also in historical and sociological research.

Genocide as a moral concept

Bloxham observes that the term 'war criminal' is employed as much as a moral category as it is a legal one (2006: 180), using the lack of moral equivalence to obscure criminality on one side or the other. Genocide too has a strong moral dimension which can exist independently of its legal or social-scientific dimensions (Huttenbach 1988: 297; see also Lemarchand 1996 for a discussion of the consequences in Rwanda and Burundi). Yet social scientists fear that the use of the language of genocide in everyday discourse, indicating disapproval through association, risks obscuring, through emotive and evaluative understandings of the term, cognitive and analytical content in studies of genocide (Chalk and Jonassohn 1990: 3). In the earliest days of the conflict between Georgia and Russia over the territory of South Ossetia, the two governments exchanged accusations of genocide and ethnic cleansing (Percival and Meikle 2008; President of Russia 2008a, 2008b). These accusations were accompanied by the initiation of legal procedures: the creation of an Investigative Committee by Russia and the location of criminal investigators in the field (President of Russia 2008c); and the instituting of procedures at the International Court of Justice by Georgia, drawing on obligations in the International Convention on the Elimination of All Forms of Racial Discrimination (ICJ 2008). The outcome of such legal procedures remains to be seen, but in the meantime, the claims and counterclaims of political leaders may also serve as part of a strategy to legitimate certain activities and to delegitimate those of others.

Political use of the term genocide might diverge from more rigorous legal or social scientific applications, but their value should not be immediately discounted as mere politicking. The cry of genocide can call international attention and scrutiny to particular sites of conflict. Elsewhere Fein has noted that disinterested comparison between contemporary events and past genocides has had beneficial effects in encouraging preventative action to be taken (1990: 56) – arguably even a partisan cry of genocide may serve this purpose. The balance is a difficult one and 'the banalization of the cry of genocide in political rhetoric' is likened to 'crying wolf' (Fein 1990: 4). More immediately pressing is the concern expressed by one international human rights agency that the exaggeration of casualty figures and accompanying use of the terminology of genocide can feed into retributive attacks (Anna Neistat of Human Rights Watch, in Parfitt 2008). Retributive attacks may, in turn, escalate into a cycle of genocide or genocidal massacres. The idea of genocide as 'retribution' or as a response to real or perceived threats from another group is recognised in the literature (e.g. Fein 1990; Chalk and Jonassohn

1990) and in the case of Burundi has been well documented by Lemarchand (1996; and with Martin 1974).

Genocide as a historical and sociological concept

Although Bloxham has located genocide, first and foremost, as a legal term designed for courtroom judgment (2003: 189), there is a significant body of work spanning the disciplines of history and sociology which takes genocide as its central object of analysis. Some, like Kuper, regret the shortcomings of the Genocide Convention but nonetheless use it as a basis for analysis, given that it provides a degree of international agreement and therefore a possible platform for action (1981: 39). Evident from further scholarly work on genocide, illustrated in Table 38.1, is a distinct lack of consensus around how the concept of genocide might be defined for analytical purposes and what elements are essential to that definition. In the three examples shown, it can be seen that the victim group is defined narrowly in terms of ethnicity and nationality (Bauer), through the eyes of the perpetrator (Chalk and Jonassohn) or simply as a collectivity (Fein), although elsewhere Fein has observed that victims are generally members of 'real' groups and recognise their membership in those groups (1990: 14). Killing is either an essential accompanying indicator of genocide, defines genocide as a necessary and central aspect or is simply one possibility, the presence of which is not necessary to achieve genocidal ends in light of other biological possibilities such as sterilisation. Other elements are variously included and understood differently, or left out of definitions, including the perpetrator (absent in Bauer's concise definition) and the relationship between perpetrator and victim. The following section will examine these particular issues, not necessarily to arrive at a new or composite definition, but to understand the implications of adopting the existing definitions.

Table 38.1 Definitions of genocide

Definition	Source
... a purposeful attempt to eliminate an ethnicity or a nation, accompanied by the murder of large numbers of the targeted group	Bauer (1999: 36)
... a form of one sided mass killing in which a state or other authority intends to destroy a group, as that group and membership in it are defined by the perpetrator	Chalk and Jonassohn (1990: 23)
... sustained purposeful action by a perpetrator to physically destroy a collectivity directly or indirectly, through interdiction of the biological and social reproduction of group members, sustained regardless of surrender or lack of threat offered by the victims	Fein (1990: 24)

Perpetrators: genocide defined as a state crime

Literature on genocide displays a strong tendency to take the state as instrumental to genocide, either as an organising force or at the very least in condoning or failing to respond to genocide where it is the responsible authority (e.g. Chalk and Jonassohn 1990; Chorbajian 1999; Fein 1990; Lemarchand 2003; see Huttenbach 1988 for a discussion of non-state-sponsored genocide).[1] It is unsurprising that a body which lays claim to a monopoly of legitimate force (Weber 1947; Elias 1996) and which exists in a centralised and coordinated form to exercise control over a territorially defined entity is usually implicated in cases involving such large-scale organised violence, as it may be one of very few organisations which have the capacity to implement genocidal programmes. For example, the linking of bureaucracy, military, industry and party through the modern state were necessary for the extensive programme of persecution and murders making up the Holocaust (Bauman 2000: 13). However, certain cases flag up a need to qualify this, and to acknowledge that potential states and emerging polities may also be capable of organising and implementing genocide. Poggi (1990) notes that a fundamental element of the concept of state is recognition in the context of a system of states; this may be problematic in the case of long-standing autonomous yet unrecognised territorial units such as Taiwan, yet in an important sense recognition differentiates states and non-states in terms of their relations with other participants in a system of states and with international bodies whose membership is reserved for states.

Two cases merit attention here: the violence surrounding the partition of the British Indian Empire; and the conflict over the territory of Bosnia and Herzegovina from 1992 to 1995. Hansen (2003) has examined violence in the Punjab between 1937 and 1947 in which an estimated 500,000 died and around 10 million were displaced across new borders, part of a process in which access to power and statehood were the subjects of struggle and contestation. He cites Kuper as one authority who considered the case and defined it outside the category of genocide on account of the absence of state involvement. Nonetheless Hansen's analysis of riots and precision attacks on trains indicate organisation as opposed to spontaneous action which characterised 'traditional' communal violence (Hansen 2003: 101–2). The new forms of violence observed are linked intrinsically to state formation (Hansen 2003: 115–16) but exist separately from recognised states as perpetrators. The Republic of the Serbian People of BiH, later *Republika Srpska*, presents the same challenge in relation to the Yugoslavian secessionist conflicts. Over the course of 1992, and particularly after the declaration of BiH's independence, this new Serb republic came to take on many institutions of a state, including presidency, judicial structures, police functions and an interior ministry, and armed forces (details are examined in the *Krajišnik* judgment 2006), but without recognition and participation in a system of states. The trappings of state were certainly instrumental to genocidal acts, such as those that took place at Srebrenica (see the *Erdemović* judgment for examples of police and military cooperation), yet statehood had not been attained.

Victims: genocide defined by target groups

To a certain extent the differences around who might be included in the category of victims of genocide (as opposed to other forms of mass killing) mirror those of the parties drafting the Genocide Convention. The Convention secured an internationally agreed definition, but more open-ended academic debate continues to provide varying interpretations of genocide in terms of victim groups. At the heart of the concept is the idea that victims are selected not as individuals, but specifically as members of the group which is the target of the genocide. Bauer seeks to retain the etymological content of the word, restricting the victims to ethnic or national groupings. In doing so, he is not merely advocating linguistic fidelity, but wishes to distinguish genocide as a crime carried out against groups that have no 'avenue of escape', theoretical or otherwise (1999: 35). He posits that the groupings of Armenian, Turk, Azeri, Jew, German, Roma and black rest upon a presumption of a common genetic or hereditary origin and thus are defined by birth, by physical characteristics or by both. Whether fixed by the meanings ascribed to physical attributes through social processes or by the records kept by state bureaucracies, such forms of identity are not easily shed. By contrast, he suggests that in the Third Reich communists could abjure their politics and Jehovah's Witnesses could join the army to escape persecution, or in Soviet Russia aristocrats and bourgeoisie might support the regime or change their lifestyle. Returning to the question of etymology, the term *genos* carried a particular significance to Lemkin in that the distinction between mass murder and genocide is that the latter concept involves an attempt to convey 'the specific losses to civilization in the form of cultural contributions which can be made only by groups of people united through national, racial or cultural characteristics' (1947: 147). Yet Lemkin's claim applies to groups that are united by other characteristics (for example, religious or ideological) and who make, or create conditions which encourage, significant contributions to civilisation.

Fein limits herself to the phrase 'collectivity' but does argue that the victims are 'generally members of *real* groups, whether conceived of as collectivities, races or classes' (1990: 14, my emphasis). Some 'Jews' identified as such by German authorities may not have accepted this classification. However, without an identifiable Jewish community with institutions there would have been no way to define and thus to target them. In this sense, she is aligned with Kuper who notes the importance of an 'identifiable group' (1981: 53). Chalk and Jonassohn's focus on groups as defined by perpetrators is one way to handle Bauer's concern with the absence of an avenue for escape, in that their schema recognises arbitrary classifications such as class enemy, wrecker or kulak. Fein argues that this labelling process is more useful in thinking about the social control of population within a state as opposed to the extermination of particular groups (1990: 14). Taking Fein's comments on board, one might still argue that the genocidal state's power to categorise and to decide fates, serves as a tool to control those who, in the meantime, have been identified as the people of a more homogenous unit. As such the creation of target groups by a process of labelling may be best distinguished from the definition of what is essential to the act of genocide, and Fein's collectivity might be qualified, after Kuper (1981), as an identifiable one.

The implication of adopting each of these definitions can be examined in relation to a case identified as genocide elsewhere (see Table 38.2 below). Kaufman (1999) focuses on the 'Dirty War' waged from 1976 to 1983 by the Argentinean government through the means of disappearances and extra-judicial executions. Over the seven-year period, she estimates that somewhere between 9,000 and 30,000 deaths and disappearances took place, targeting political opponents. This would not appear to meet Bauer's strict ethno-racial criteria, although Kaufman notes that the 'war' had an anti-semitic edge to it and that Jews formed 12 per cent of the victims but only one per cent of the general population. The nature of the victims was examined in the report of the official Argentinean National Commission on the Disappearance of Persons, *Nunca Más*. They included members of trade and student unions, journalists, members of 'suspicious' professions, pacifists, members of the clergy and religious orders and many others associated with these individuals (CONADEP 1984).

The extent to which this represents a 'collectivity', recalling Fein's focus on 'real' groups and Kuper's requirement that groups be identifiable, is limited. The label 'opposition' is problematic as it need not correspond to the kind of community institutions Fein identified at the heart of Nazi persecution of Jews, or the identifiable party structure that informed Indonesian persecution of Communists in the 1960s. In this instance there is a multitude of target groups connected by antipathy or hostility to a government but not united by any other common foundation. Chalk and Jonassohn's definition of a group 'as that group and membership are defined by the perpetrator' would allow the recognition of the Dirty War as genocide; however, this would remain dependent on evidence that the intent was to destroy the defined 'opposition' group, not merely to control a diverse opposition through fear and repression.

So far the focus has been on victims understood as part of a collectivity, whether defined by heritable characteristics such as race and ethnicity or other characteristics such as political allegiance. It is worth giving some attention to gender and biological sex and the role that they play in experiences of genocide. Huttenbach has been somewhat dismissive of efforts to introduce sex as a dimension in genocide studies, stating that:

> There have been no incidents of genocide against women *per se* ... to segregate them from the male victims is not only to distort reality by pretending that there was a distinct 'female' experience of the Holocaust, but to create an ahistoric category of genocide that never took place but according to commonsense probably never will take place. (Huttenbach 1988: 295)

Bauer commented similarly that there has never been a 'wholesale murder campaign against women [as women]' (1999: 34). Recognising that a campaign to eliminate one or other biological sex is necessarily a campaign to eliminate both, this does not mean that there has never been a distinct and gendered experience in the history of genocide. Certainly, the systematic use of rape to destroy communities was observed during the war in Bosnia and

Herzegovina and expressed in terms of the Genocide Convention provisions on serious bodily or mental harm, conditions of life calculated to bring about the destruction of a group, and forcible measures to prevent births within the group (Art. 2, paras b–d; see Poust 1994: 88). Beyond the legal sphere the act of rape is understood sociologically as an attempt to destroy the identity of the victim and to widen the victimisation through undermining their connectedness with others, the bonds that hold families and communities together (Doubt 2000: 63, 65). This 'psychosexual destruction' (Quindlen 1993) has been broken down in terms of its functions by Catherine MacKinnon, who recognises a reproductive element in strategic rape policies, but also identifies a wider range of logics: 'rape to make you leave your home and never go back … rape as spectacle … rape to drive a wedge through a community, to shatter a society, to destroy a people' (1994: 11; for a broad-ranging discussion of genocidal rape in the former Yugoslavia, see Allen 1996). The examples drawn from Bosnia-Herzegovina post-date Huttenbach's claims denying a distinctive female experience of the Holocaust by a matter of a couple of years, but Hansen's (2003) analysis of new, genocidal forms of violence in the Punjab between 1937 and 1947 show that women experienced genocide in particular ways, and that this was a distinctive aspect of the violence, differentiating it from earlier traditional forms.

Relationship between victim and perpetrator
Returning to the definitions of genocide in Table 38.1, Bauer's (1999) definition suggests that there is little significance in the relationship between victim and perpetrator in genocide other than their membership in mutually exclusive ethno-racial categories. However, both Chalk and Jonassohn (1990) and Fein (1990) specify certain relationships in that killing is one-sided or is sustained regardless of the threat that the victim presents to the perpetrator. Chalk and Jonassohn's definition would exclude what Kopf and Hansen (1999) term the 'reciprocal genocidal massacres' which accompanied the partition of the Punjab. Accepting genocide as characterised by an objective to destroy a collectivity (regardless of how that may be defined) it seems unreasonable to exclude cases on the grounds of an active and mutual animosity marked by the desire to annihilate an enemy group. Fein's focus on the continuation of attacks regardless of whether the target group poses any threat means that these cases are not so easily dismissed, but at the same time serves to exclude mass killings such as the widespread bombing of German cities and the atomic attacks on Hiroshima and Nagasaki. Arguably these represent war crimes (see Bloxham 2006), but the fact that surrender on the part of Germany and Japan was followed by a cessation of hostilities suggests the acts were committed in pursuit of limited goals. Ultimately, genocide is defined by its exterminatory end.

Explaining genocide

Historical and sociological analysis is used not only to define the phenomenon of genocide, but also offers explanatory frameworks, both at the level of the propensity of particular states or types of states to engage in genocidal acts and the participation of individuals in such crimes. This section considers both these levels of analysis.

Explaining the genocidal state

Accepting that states, state-like bodies or emerging states have been implicated as prime, if not exclusive, perpetrators of genocidal violence, the seemingly innate capacity of the state for genocide clearly does not mean that this potential will be released in every state and the question is begged, are certain forms of state more prone to genocide? The nature of genocidal states may vary with time. Smith (1999) observes that in antiquity genocide was a fate befalling peoples who happened to be in the path of conquering armies, while later genocides were linked to the colonial expansion of imperial states. The focus here, however, is on the somewhat different manifestations of genocide that have been in evidence in the modern world, and in particular since 1933.

In his study of the Holocaust as a peculiarly modern phenomenon, Bauman observes the importance of Nazi destruction of pluralism, in the political science sense of the word, creating an absolute power free from 'effective social control' (2000: 165). Fein (1993) has provided an analysis of genocides and genocidal massacres since the Second World War which supports a more general claim regarding non-democratic government and an increased propensity to commit genocide. Totalitarian regimes, exemplified by Communist ideologies, show an even greater propensity towards genocide (Fein 1993: 92). Further analysis, following Kuper (1981), relates genocidal propensity to the exclusion of subordinate groups in stratified societies, particularly where stratification is linked to ethnicity. The relationship is indirect via increased probabilities of rebellion and genocidal responses, subsequent or pre-emptive (Fein 1993: 98). Finally, Fein notes a number of repeat offenders: eight of eleven perpetrator states had conducted genocides or massacres either under separate governments or against different target groups (1993: 86).

While states and other emerging authorities may provide the organisational framework for genocide, as a composite crime it is inseparable from the myriad persecutions, acts of violence and attacks in various forms which are visited upon the victim group. The implications are starkly illustrated in the case of Rwanda where William Schabas noted that plans for *Gacaca* courts revealed that there may have been as many as one million participants in the genocide. Excluding those too young to be held criminally responsible, this represented 'an indictment of perhaps one third of the country's adult population' (2005: 881–2). The wide base of perpetrators of genocide encompasses those who envisage and advocate the extermination of a particular group as a social and political goal, those who provide the planning and logistics for extermination, those who implement that plan, participating directly in the murder of victims, and those who put the tools in their hands, whether pangas[2] or prussic acid.[3] The Israeli court which tried Adolf Eichmann struggled with the responsibility of individuals in light of the enormity of the crime in terms of both victims and perpetrators, but noted a general trend whereby 'the degree of responsibility increases as we draw further away from the man who uses the fatal instrument with his own hands' (quoted in Arendt 2006: 247).

Explaining individual participation in genocide

What makes a perpetrator of genocide is perhaps one of the most taxing questions in the study of genocide, particularly in light of the extent of participation and the degree of inhumanity involved. There is not necessarily a general theory that will explain the participation of so many in such different roles and representing different degrees of commitment and enthusiasm. Browning (1992) has studied a variety of perpetrators including bureaucrats, doctors and police reservists providing the logistics, intellectual justification and manpower required for Nazi plans to annihilate Europe's Jewish population. His detailed study of Police Reserve Battalion 101 sheds light on a range of explanatory theories involving wartime brutalisation, racism, the segmentation and routinisation of murder, special selection procedures, obedience and deference, ideological indoctrination, conformity or some combination of these (2001: 159). Some theories can be dismissed by examining the background of the reservists who participated in the Józefów massacre and subsequent mass killings. Reserve Battalion 101 had no experience of front-line service and the men, predominantly from Hamburg with employment histories that would indicate links to unions and socialist and communist politics, were of an age where their political identities would have been formed before the Nazi capture of power. They were neither war hardened soldiers nor obvious choices in terms of pro-Nazi sympathies (2001: 45).

While the police reservists, whose tasks included shooting, at point blank range, defenceless people of all ages, could not distance themselves from the killing in the way that bureaucrats might, efforts were made to divide labour in a way that desensitised people to the logical end of their tasks. Browning notes that it was easier, psychologically, to round up Jews and load them on to trains destined for Treblinka than it was to be involved directly in shootings (2001: 162). In his analysis, Browning does not seek to isolate a single cause, but drawing on a range of sources, including Milgram and Zimbardo, sketches out a context in which relatively normal patterns of deference to authority and fear of social isolation combined with government policy backed by 'a deluge of racist and anti-semitic propaganda'. This enabled most reservists to participate in shooting assignments when it was asked of them, but the majority did not actively seek selection for the task and avoided it where possible.

Assessing the prevalence of genocide

Having elaborated some legal and sociological perspectives on the defining features of genocide, it is possible to turn to the question of prevalence. Table 38.2 is drawn from two sources (Charny 1999 and Chalk and Jonassohn 1990) and indicates a range of potentially genocidal events. It summarises

Table 38.2 Proposed genocides 1933–99

Location	Dates	Victims	Perpetrators
(a) Africa			
Biafra/Nigeria	1966–69	Ibo	Domestic government, mobs
Burundi	1972	Hutu	Domestic (Tutsi dominated) government
Burundi	1993	Tutsi; Hutu	Hutu peasantry and militia, Tutsi-dominated army
Congo	1996	Hutu	Rwandan Army
Ethiopia	1974–9	Political opposition	Domestic government (Derg)
Ethiopia	1984–6	Ethiopians	Domestic government (Derg)
Mozambique	1973–94	Mozambicans	Renamo and Portuguese military
Rwanda	1994	Tutsi	Domestic government, army and Interehamwe militia
Sudan	From 1956	Southern Animist and Christian populations, Dinka, Nuba	Domestic government
(b) Americas			
Amazon	1973ff.	Indigenous tribes	Domestic government, settlers, commercial interests
Argentina	1976–83	Political opposition	Domestic government
Guatemala	1982	Mayan peasants	Domestic government
(c) Asia			
Afghanistan	1978–9	Political opposition, Pashtun population	Domestic government, Soviet Union
East Pakistan (Bangladesh)	1971	Bengalis, particularly Hindus	West Pakistani government
Cambodia	1975–9	Urban and professional populations, disproportionately Chinese and Vietnamese	Domestic (Khmer-Rouge)

Table 38.2 continues overleaf

Table 38.2 continued

Location	Dates	Victims	Perpetrators
China	20th century	Various, at various times	Japan, Chinese nationalists, Communist Party
East Timor	1975–91	East Timorese	Indonesia
Indonesia	1965–6	Communists	Domestic government and militia
Iraq (and other areas)	1988 (and other times)	Kurds	At various periods, Iran, Iraq and Turkey
Punjab	1946–48	Hindus, Muslims, Sikhs	Communal mobs
Sri Lanka	1978	Tamils	Government, military and mobs
Tibet	From 1956	Tibetans, Buddhists	China
(d) Australasia			
Australia	To 1988	Indigenous population	Domestic government
(e) Europe			
Continental Europe	1933–45	Mentally and physically disabled, Jews, Roma/Sinti and other national groups	Nazi Germany and collaborating regimes
Soviet Union	To 1960s	Various economic classes, political groups and nationalities	Soviet government
Yugoslavia	1992–5	Bosnian Muslims, Bosnian Croats	Armies of Republika Srpska, Croatia and Croat Defence Groups in BiH

Adapted from Chalk and Jonassohn (1990) and Charny (1999).

the authors' observation of event, victim groups and perpetrators in as much as these are made clear. These are indicative of 'headline' events and do not include a number of genocides which have been subsumed elsewhere under the heading of genocides against indigenous peoples (Charny 1999). This accounts for a further seven in Africa, seven in South and Central America and six in Asia, all occurring after 1965. The purpose of presenting the table here is not necessarily to say that these cases are examples of genocide or that this is a definitive list of genocides in the period covered. Certainly, the table includes cases which would not be counted as genocide under certain legal or sociological definitions examined above. Those where the victim group is defined politically are prime examples, and it is notable that the initial charge laid by the investigative judge in the case of Adolfo Scilingo, a participant in Argentina's Dirty War was dropped by the Audiencia Nacional in Spain which proceeded on the basis of crimes against humanity (Gil Gil 2005: 1083). Other challenging examples are those where the targeting of specific ethnic groups, including Cham, Chinese and Vietnamese in Cambodia, has accompanied attacks on a wider civilian population. In order to understand the genocidal process, it may be necessary to isolate the attacks on each of these specific groups from those on urban or educated groups during the reign of the Khmer Rouge, much as scholars seek analytical clarity in separating out the multiple genocides occurring in Europe between 1933 and 1945. Where multiple and overlapping group memberships can be maintained, for example where Chinese and Vietnamese Cambodians were strongly represented in urban economies, this becomes more complicated. The table also includes cases where the methods employed do not necessarily involve murder, such as that of twentieth-century Australia where the forced removal of children from Aboriginal families is seen as an attack on the group's ability to reproduce in a meaningful sense of the word (Tatz 1999).

It is clear from Table 38.2 that mass killings, whether categorised as genocide or taken as having an affinity with genocide, punctuated the twentieth century. Yet to enter into an exercise which seeks to define the act merely to indicate its prevalence seems somewhat perverse. Those scholars who have sought to define and categorise genocide have done so with the admirable aim of understanding the crime with a view to prevention (Bauer 1999; Chalk and Jonassohn 1990; Fein 1990; Kuper 1981), and to apply this to calculate prevalence may be an act of bad faith. Ruggiero (2006) has proposed that criminology might turn its attention to warfare, becoming in the process of challenging authorised state violence 'criminology as ceasefire'. As observed above and as is apparent from the recurrence of domestic governments as perpetrators in Table 38.2, genocide is not limited to conditions of warfare and state-authorised killing is not limited to genocide. Arguably state killing may be the proper object of criminological analysis, with the proviso that the concept of state is constructed with enough flexibility to account for nascent or apparently emerging states and other formal, organised and public structures of authority. Table 38.2 is only a partial list of such acts, covering a period of 60–70 years; that it lists 'only' 26 incidents disguises the multiple victim groups in certain events and the mass victimisation in every case.

Concluding remarks: responses to genocide

The failure to respond in a strong way to the Armenian genocide has been directly related to Hitler's confidence that his attacks on European Jews would go unpunished (Fein 1990: 2). Arguably, the failure to respond adequately to a continuing history of genocide, mass killings and acts conducive to the destruction of social groups may, in part, underpin the continuing resort to such methods by governing authorities, whether recognised as states or not. The ad hoc tribunals in The Hague and Arusha, the genesis of an International Criminal Court and the growing number of domestic prosecutions suggest a shift in attitudes, although not a universal one by any means. Moreover, these developments do suggest the possibility of a more uniform and internationally collaborative approach to the recognition and prosecution of genocide than may have been the case in the aftermath of the Second World War. As it becomes possible to speak of a more serious and consistent legal approach to the recognition of genocide, it is desirable to see a stronger engagement with genocide as an object of criminological study in line with calls by Yacoubian (2000) and Day and Vandiver (2000). This chapter has sought to outline a number of the challenges in identifying and understanding genocide as a particular form of persecution and murder and has suggested that a broader focus is justified. There are many more questions that demand scholarly attention, including the impact of plea bargaining in cases where the accused has been indicted for genocide (see *Plavšić*), and the development of associated forms of criminality such as genocide denial. Genocide is undeniably an extreme form of harmful behaviour, but the idea that genocide, and crimes with a close affinity to genocide, are somehow exceptional, and as such peripheral to criminological inquiry, is no longer tenable.

Selected further reading

A number of texts gather together historical accounts of various genocidal episodes and, as secondary data, these can be usefully employed in comparative conceptual and theoretical work on the question of what constitutes, and what facilitates or obstructs, genocide. Israel Charny's edited *Encyclopedia of Genocide* (1999) has uneven coverage but provides some useful and thought-provoking material, while Chalk and Jonassohn's *History and Sociology of Genocide* (1990) offers accounts of various episodes alongside their own conceptual analysis. Helen Fein's (1990) 'Genocide: a sociological perspective' also offers a strong conceptual examination of genocide. In contrast to the broad scope of these comparative works, Browning's *Ordinary Men* (2001) is a fine example of a more narrowly defined analytical focus, in this case on a German reserve police battalion in Poland. The nature of Browning's work makes it possible to examine the motivation of the individuals whose actions are essential to the realisation of genocidal potential in state structures.

A wide range of documentary material is now also available in the form of judgments, transcripts and evidence submissions from the International Criminal Tribunals in The Hague and Arusha (http://www.icty.org; http://www.ictr.org).

Notes

1 In *Jelisić* the court considered the theoretical possibility of an individual holding a plan to exterminate a protected group without the support of an organisation for this intent (§100).
2 The *panga* is 'a large, heavy knife with a long, broad blade, used for cutting undergrowth and firewood or as a weapon' (Oxford English Dictionary), and was indicative of the 'low- tech' means by which massacres were carried out in Rwanda (Maogoto 2004: 188).
3 A recent case at the District Court in The Hague, accepting the material evidence of genocide in Iraqi attacks on Kurds in 1988, found the Dutch trader Frans van Anraat guilty of supplying chemicals to the Iraqi regime knowing that they were to be used in chemical weapons (Penketh and Verkaik 2005).

Cases

International Criminal Tribunal for the former Yugoslavia, *Prosecutor* v. *Erdemović*, IT-96-22-T (29 November 1996).
International Criminal Tribunal for the former Yugoslavia, *Prosecutor* v. *Jelisić*, IT-95-10-T (14 December 1999).
International Criminal Tribunal for Rwanda, *Prosecutor* v. *Kayishema*, ICTR-95-1-T (21 May 1999).
International Criminal Tribunal for the former Yugoslavia, *Prosecutor* v. *Krajišnik*, IT-00-39-T (27 September 2006).
International Criminal Tribunal for the former Yugoslavia, *Prosecutor* v. *Krstić*, IT-98-33-T (2 August 2001).
International Criminal Tribunal for the former Yugoslavia, *Prosecutor* v. *Krstić*, IT-98-33-A (19 April 2004).
International Criminal Tribunal for the former Yugoslavia, *Prosecutor* v *Plavšić*, IT-00-39&40/1-S (27 February 2003).

References

Allen, B. (1996) *Rape Warfare: The Hidden Genocide in Bosnia-Herzegovina and Croatia.* Minneapolis, MN: University of Minnesota Press.
Arendt, H. (2006) *Eichmann in Jerusalem: A Report on the Banality of Evil.* London: Penguin.
Bauer, Y. (1999) 'Comparison of genocides', in L. Chorbajian and G. Shirinian (eds), *Studies in Comparative Genocide.* London: Macmillan, pp. 31–43.
Bauman, Z. (2000) *Modernity and the Holocaust.* Cambridge: Polity.
Bloxham, D. (2003) 'The Armenian genocide of 1915–1916: cumulative radicalization and the development of a destruction policy', *Past and Present*, 181: 141–91.
Bloxham, D. (2006) 'Dresden as a war crime', in P. Addison and J. A. Crang (eds), *Firestorm: The Bombing of Dresden 1945.* London: Pimlico, pp. 180–208.
Browning, C. R. (1992) *The Path to Genocide: Essays on Launching the Final Solution.* Cambridge: Cambridge University Press.
Browning, C. R. (2001) *Ordinary Men: Reserve Police Battalion 101 and the Final Solution in Poland.* London: Penguin.
Cambodia Law on the Establishment of Extraordinary Chambers in the Courts of Cambodia for the Prosecution of Crimes Committed during the Period of Democratic Kampuchea (amended version) (2004) NS/RKM/1004/006.

Chalk, F. and Jonassohn, K. (1990) *The History and Sociology of Genocide*. London: Yale University Press.

Charny, I. W. (ed.) (1999) *Encyclopedia of Genocide*. Santa Barbara, CA: ABC-CLIO. Online at: http://ebooks.abc-clio.com/?bookid=9781576074466&loc=50&format=page (accessed 7 August 2008).

Chorbajian, L. (1999) 'Introduction', in L. Chorbajian and G. Shirinian (eds), *Studies in Comparative Genocide*. London: Macmillan, pp. xv–xxxv.

Cohen, S. (1996) 'Crime and politics: spot the difference', *British Journal of Sociology*, 47 (1): 2–21.

Cohen, S. (2001) *States of Denial: Knowing about Atrocities and Suffering*. Cambridge: Polity.

CONADEP (National Commission on the Disappearance of Persons) (1984) *Nunca Más*. Reproduced online at: http://nuncamas.org.

Day, L. E. and Vandiver, M. (2000) 'Criminology and genocide studies: notes on what might have been and what still could be', *Crime, Law and Social Change*, 34 (1): 43–59.

Doubt, K. (2000) *Sociology after Bosnia and Kosovo: Recovering Justice*. Lanham, MD: Rowman & Littlefield.

Elias, N. (1996) *The Germans: Power Struggles and the Development of Habitus in the Nineteenth and Twentieth Centuries*. New York: Columbia University Press.

Fein, H. (1990) 'Genocide: a sociological perspective', *Current Sociology*, 38 (1): 1–126.

Fein, H. (1993) 'Accounting for genocide after 1945: theories and some findings', *International Journal on Group Rights*, 1 (2): 79–106.

Garner, J. W. (1936) 'Recent German nationality legislation', *American Journal of International Law*, 30 (1): 96–9.

Gil Gil, A. (2005) 'The flaws of the Scilingo judgment', *Journal of International Criminal Law*, 3 (5): 1082–91.

Hansen, A. B. (2003) 'The Punjab 1937–47 – a case of genocide?', in S. L. B. Jensen (ed.), *Genocide: Cases, Comparisons and Contemporary Debates*. Copenhagen: Danish Centre for Holocaust and Genocide Studies, pp. 83–122.

Huttenbach, H. H. (1988) 'Locating the Holocaust on the genocide spectrum: towards a methodology of definition and categorisation', *Holocaust and Genocide Studies*, 3 (3): 289–303.

International Court of Justice (2008) *Georgia Institutes Proceedings against Russia for Violations of the Convention on the Elimination of all Forms of Racial Discrimination* (The Hague). Online at: http://icj-ccj.org/docket/files/140/14659.pdf (accessed 22 August 2008).

International Military Tribunal (Nuremberg) Judgment and Sentences (1947) Reproduced in *American Journal of International Law*, 41 (1): 172–333.

Kaufman, E. (1999) 'Argentina: the "Dirty War" of disappearances, 1976–1983', in I. W. Charny (ed.), *Encyclopedia of Genocide*. Santa Barbara, CA: ABC-CLIO. Online at: http://ebooks.abc-clio.com/?bookid=9781576074466&loc=50&format=page (accessed 7 August 2008).

Kopf, D. and Hansen, A. (1999) 'Genocide of Sikhs', in I. W. Charny (ed.), *Encyclopedia of Genocide*. Santa Barbara, CA: ABC-CLIO. Online at: http://ebooks.abc-clio.com/?bookid=9781576074466&loc=50&format=page (accessed 7 August 2008).

Kuhn, A. (1945) 'Review of *Axis Rule in Occupied Europe* by Raphael Lemkin', in *American Journal of International Law*, 39 (2): 360–2.

Kuper, L. (1981) *Genocide: Its Political Use in the Twentieth Century*. New Haven, CT: Yale University Press.

Lemarchand, R. (1996) *Burundi: Genocide Forgotten, Invented and Anticipated*. Copenhagen: Centre for African Studies, University of Copenhagen.

Lemarchand, R. (2003) 'Comparing the killing fields: Rwanda, Cambodia and Bosnia', in S. L. B. Jensen (ed.), *Genocide: Cases, Comparisons and Contemporary Debates*. (Copenhagen: Danish Centre for Holocaust and Genocide Studies), pp. 141–74.

Lemarchand, R. and Martin, D. (1974) *Selective Genocide in Burundi*. London: Minority Rights Group.

Lemkin, R. (1944) *Axis Rule in Occupied Europe: Laws of Occupation, Analysis of Government, Proposals for Redress*. Washington, DC: Carnegie Endowment for International Peace.

Lemkin, R. (1947) 'Genocide as a crime under international law', *American Journal of International Law*, 41 (1): 145–51.

MacKinnon, C. (1994) 'Rape, genocide and women's rights', *Harvard Women's Law Journal*, 17: 5–16.

Madley, B. (2005) 'From Africa to Auschwitz: how German South West Africa incubated ideas and methods adopted and developed by the Nazis in Eastern Europe', *European History Quarterly*, 35 (3): 429–64.

Maogoto, J. N. (2004) 'The International Criminal Tribunal for Rwanda: a paper umbrella in the rain? Initial pitfalls and brighter prospects', *Nordic Journal of International Law*, 72 (2): 187–221.

Marrus, M. (1997) *The Nuremberg War Crimes Trial 1945–46: A Documentary History*. Boston: Bedford.

Nuremberg Trial Proceedings (1946) Reproduced by Avalon Project, Yale School of Law. Online at: http://www.yale.edu/lawweb/avalon/imt/imt.htm (accessed 27 August 2008).

Parfitt, T. (2008) 'Human Rights Watch: Russia inflating casualty figures', *guardian.co.uk*, 14 August. Online at: http://www.guardian.co.uk/world/2008/aug/14/georgia.russia1 (accessed 26 August 2008).

Penketh, A. and Verkaik, R. (2005) 'Dutch court says gassing of Iraqi Kurds was "genocide"', *The Independent*, 24 December. Online at: http://www.independent.co.uk/news/world/europe/dutch-court-says-gassing-of-iraqi-kurds-was-genocide-520599.html (accessed 11 September 2008).

Percival, J. and Meikle, J. (2008) 'Georgia agrees to ceasefire with Russia', *guardian.co.uk*, 15 August. Online at: http://www.guardian.co.uk/world/2008/aug/15/georgia.russia2 (accessed 22 August 2008).

Poggi, G. (1990) *The State: Its Nature, Development and Prospects*. Cambridge: Polity.

Poust, J. (1994) 'Correspondence', *American Journal of International Law*, 88 (1): 88.

President of Russia (2008a) 'Dmitry Medvedev had a telephone conversation with President of the United States George W. Bush', in *News* (Moscow). Online at: http://president.kremlin.ru/eng/sdocs/news.shtml#205091 (accessed 11 August 2008).

President of Russia (2008b) 'Georgia is guilty of genocide – Medvedev', in *News* (Moscow). Online at: http://president.kremlin.ru/eng/sdocs/news.shtml#205091 (accessed 11 August 2008).

President of Russia (2008c) 'Dmitry Medvedev instructed the Russian Federation Prosecutor General's Office Committee of Inquiry to document crimes committed in South Ossetia in order to prosecute the perpetrators', in *News* (Moscow). Online at: http://president.kremlin.ru/eng/sdocs/news.shtml#205091 (accessed 11 August 2008).

Quindlen, A. (1993) 'Gynocide', *New York Times*, 10 March. Online at: http://query.nytimes.com/gst/fullpage.html?res=9F0CE5DE153BF933A25750C0A965958260&scp=1&sq=gynocide&st=cse (accessed 14 August 2008).

Robinson, N. (1960) *The Genocide Convention: A Commentary*. New York: Institute of Jewish Affairs.

Rome Statute of the International Criminal Court (2002) A/CONF.183/9.

Ruggiero, V. (2006) *Understanding Political Violence: A Criminological Analysis.* Maidenhead: Open University Press.

Schabas, W. (2005) 'Genocide trials and Gacaca courts', *Journal of International Criminal Justice*, 3 (4): 879–95.

Smith, R. W. (1999) 'State power and genocidal intent: on the uses of genocide in the twentieth century', in L. Chorbajian and G. Shirinian (eds), *Studies in Comparative Genocide*. London: Macmillan, pp. 3–14.

Statute of the International Criminal Tribunal for Rwanda (2007), reproduced in Basic Documents (Arusha, ICTR). Online at: http://69.94.11.53/ENGLISH/basicdocs/statute/2007.pdf (accessed 28 August 2008).

Stowell, E. C. (1936) 'Intercession against persecution of Jews', *American Journal of International Law*, 30 (1): 102–6.

Tatz, C. (1999) 'Genocide of Australian Aboriginals', in I. W. Charny (ed.), *Encyclopedia of Genocide*. Santa Barbara, CA: ABC-CLIO. Online at: http://ebooks.abc-clio.com/?bookid=9781576074466&loc=50&format=page (accessed 7 August 2008).

Tiba, F. K. (2007) 'The Mengistu genocide trial in Ethiopia', *Journal of International Criminal Justice*, 5 (2): 513–28.

United Nations General Assembly (1946) Resolution 96(1), 55th Plenary Meeting, 11 December. Online at: http://daccessdds.un.org/doc/RESOLUTION/GEN/NR0/033/47/IMG/NR003347.pdf?OpenElement (accessed 6 August 2008).

United Nations General Assembly (1992) Resolution 47(121), 91st Plenary Meeting, 18 December. Online at: http://daccessdds.un.org/doc/GEN/N93/213/52/IMG/N9321352.pdf?OpenElement (accessed 1 September 2008).

Updated Statute of the International Criminal Tribunal for the Former Yugoslavia (2008) The Hague: ICTY. Online at: http://www.un.org/icty/legaldoc-e/basic/statut/statute-feb08-e.pdf (accessed 28 August 2008).

Van Krieken, R. (1999) 'The "stolen generations" and cultural genocide: the forced removal of Australian indigenous children from their families and its implications for the sociology of childhood', *Childhood*, 6 (3): 297–311.

Weber, M. (1947) 'Politics as a vocation', in H. H. Gerth and C. Wright Mills (eds), *From Max Weber: Essays in Sociology*. London: Kegan Paul, Trench & Trubner, pp. 77–128.

Yacoubian, G. S. (2000) 'The (in)significance of genocidal behavior to the discipline of criminology', *Crime, Law and Social Change*, 34 (1): 7–19.

Chapter 39

Torture

Rod Morgan

Introduction

At the time of writing, April 2009, the Attorney General for England and Wales has referred to the police for investigation the case of Binyam Mohamed. Mohamed was detained and allegedly tortured in Pakistan in 2002, was questioned by MI5 before being 'rendered' to Morocco, where it is alleged he was further tortured. He was then flown to Afghanistan where he claims he was tortured by the Americans before being transferred to Guantánamo Bay, Cuba, from which he was released without charge and returned to Britain in February 2009. Mohamed's case is one of several currently being looked into in Britain. Meanwhile evidence regarding what is alleged to be the widespread use of torture, either by American security personnel, or by allies of the United States with the complicity of American security personnel, is accumulating in the USA where incoming President Obama is distancing himself from the policies authorised by his predecessor George W. Bush, not least by announcing that the detention facilities at Guantánamo Bay will be closed. The revelations of torture that are emerging are arguably as shocking to contemporary world opinion as those which emerged from the Algerian War of Independence 1954–62, from Greece following the military *coup d'état* in 1967 and from various postcolonial struggles since the Second World War when, in the wake of the torturous practices of the Bolsheviks in Russia, the Fascists in Italy and Spain and the Nazis in Germany, the United Nations was established and by international treaty torture was proscribed in customary international law.

The abolition of torture in every modern state was generally considered to be one of the principal accomplishments of the Enlightenment. In 1874 Victor Hugo felt able to announce that 'torture had ceased to exist' (Peters 1996: 5). It proved not to be so. Torture persisted, albeit it now became a practice carried out mostly in secret. Amnesty International, established in the wake of the revelations emerging from Greece in the 1960s, regularly announces that torture continues to be a practice carried out in a significant proportion of UN member states, including some of the richest and the most democratic. For example, its 2006 report concluded that 104 out of the 150 countries it examined had tortured or ill-treated people, despite most of them being party to the UN Convention against torture and other ill-treatment (Amnesty International 2006), and the most recent report recorded torture or other ill-treatment in 14 of the G20 countries (Amnesty International 2009). Now, it is becoming apparent, the most powerful nation on earth, ostensibly in its pursuit of 'freedom' while conducting a 'War on Terror', has been allowing practices generally agreed to constitute torture, though the USA has throughout maintained that it is not so.

In this chapter we shall consider at a broad level what constitutes torture, who is involved, to what purpose and why the practice persists. The chapter begins with a brief summary of definitions of torture used in major international declarations and conventions. This is followed by a discussion of how and why numerous states, including signatories to such conventions, have either turned a blind eye to or publicly condoned behaviour by their own police, security services or armed forces which clearly breaches them. Particular attention is paid here to the utilitarian argument that such behaviour can be justified on the grounds of preventing a greater evil. It is then shown how torture is often facilitated by a process of normalisation, whereby it is supported by bureaucratic systems and 'regulated' by psychologists and other professionls, and is practised not by 'monsters' but by ordinary people whose training gradually dehumanises their view of those they are interrogating.

Torture in international law

The prohibition of torture is arguably the most well attested of the entire human rights catalogue. The Universal Declaration of Human Rights (UDHR) Article 5 proclaims that:

> No one shall be subjected to torture or to cruel, inhuman or degrading treatment or punishment.

The UDHR is not itself a source of legal obligation. But the wording of Article 5 has repeatedly been used since 1948, most notably in the European Convention of Human Rights 1950, Article 3, the 1984 UN Convention Against Torture and the 1987 European Convention for the Prevention of Torture and Inhuman or Degrading Treatment or Punishment. But what is torture? Answers to that question have filled many pages and will likely continue to do so. For working purposes torture may be understood to be the officially sanctioned infliction of intense suffering, aimed at forcing someone to do or say something against his or her will. The UN Convention Against Torture Article 1 elaborates this as:

> any act by which severe pain or suffering, whether physical or mental, is intentionally inflicted on a person for such purposes as obtaining from him or a third person information or a confession, punishing him

for an act he or a third person has committed or is suspected of having committed, or intimidating or coercing him or a third person, or for any reason based on discrimination of any kind, when such pain or suffering is inflicted by or at the instigation or with the consent or acquiescence of a public official or other person acting in an official capacity. It does not include pain or suffering arising only from, inherent in or incidental to lawful sanctions.

This extended definition contains several terms – 'severe', 'pain', 'suffering', 'intentionally' – more than sufficient to generate argument about particular cases. Since the definition was formulated it is clear that different legal authorities have, with the passage of time, creatively developed their view as to what constitutes torture (for discussions see, for example, Evans and Morgan 1998; Rodley 2002). Within Europe, by way of example, the jurisprudence of the European Court of Human Rights makes it clear that torture is considered to lie at the apex of a pyramid of suffering below which stands inhuman and degrading treatment, below which stands degrading treatment. This progressive, definitional approach has the attraction of underlining the view that acts of torture are particularly serious. It also diverts attention from questions of purpose and justification. What it fails to acknowledge is that criteria are arguably needed to differentiate the categories of torture and inhuman and/or degrading treatment. By way of contrast the inspection committee (the Committee for the Prevention of Torture (CPT)) established under the European Convention for the Prevention of Torture has developed what we may term a branched definitional approach, torture being used where severe ill-treatment of a purposive, premeditated nature involving particular techniques for the extraction of information (particularly by the police) is involved, inhuman or degrading treatment being reserved for bad custodial conditions, often cumulative in nature. However, the following practices have been found by all legal and other bodies to constitute torture:

Suspension by the arms or wrists; electric shocks to sensitive parts of the body; squeezing the testicles; beating the soles of the feet; hosing with pressurised cold water; incarceration for lengthy periods in very small, dark or unventilated cells; threats of torture or other form of serious ill-treatment to the person detained or others related to him; temporary asphyxiation with a plastic bag or being immersed in water; severe psychological humiliation.

In 1978 the European Court of Human Rights famously found that the five oppressive interrogation techniques used by the British military in Northern Ireland – prolonged, stressful wall-standing, hooding, exposure to white noise, bread and water diet and sleep deprivation – did not comprise torture but was inhuman and degrading treatment. It is widely agreed that were that case brought before the Court today the five techniques, used in combination, would be found to comprise torture. Similar techniques were employed by the Israeli General Security Services (GSS) against Palestinian suspects in the 1990s and though 'moderate physical pressure' of this nature was initially approved by a government commission, the Landau Commission, as falling short of torture, in 1999 the Israeli Supreme Court found that shaking, prolonged use of certain physical stress positions, loud music and sleep deprivation were torture (see Morgan 2000). This is the backcloth to the now notorious advice given in early 2002 to and accepted by President Bush by the Office of Legal Counsel in the United States Justice Department to the effect that torture:

> covers only extreme acts. Severe pain is generally of the kind difficult for the victim to endure. Where the pain is physical, it must be of an intensity which accompanies serious physical injury such as death or organ failure. (Danner 2004: 155; Geenberg and Dratel 2004: 213–40)

It was on this basis that 'water-boarding', partial asphyxiation by simulated drowning, was permitted by the US authorities, a practice that most commentators now agree is torture (Danner 2009).

It is clear that despite all the human rights proscriptions against torture when states are faced with what they perceive to be imminent threats, when the 'gloves come off' as they did in the wake of the 9/11 attack on the Twin Towers, utilitarian arguments come to the fore. The boundary as to what constitutes torture is pushed back or torture is resorted to covertly. For this reason it remains pertinent to consider the utilitarian case for employing interrogation techniques constituting torture or bordering on it.

Torture: the utilitarian case

The efficacy of torture for establishing truth has from the earliest times been doubted. By the same token whenever the use of torture has been justified it has generally been on the grounds that either its subjects, because of their individual or class characteristics or their organisational adherence, will not without such methods be persuaded to provide essential information. Extreme situations, the argument goes, demand that extreme defensive measures be taken. The state and its innocent citizens have a right to defend themselves. As the *Newsweek* headline had it in the wake of 9/11 it's 'Time to Think About Torture' (Alter 2001).

The test, invariably apocryphal but nonetheless telling, always cited by utilitarian apologists is the ticking bomb scenario or its equivalent. A bomb has been placed in a crowded, but unidentified, public place and could explode at any moment. The perpetrator, or a knowledgeable collaborator, is captured. What methods is the interrogator justified in using in order to obtain information as to the whereabouts of the bomb?

Jeremy Bentham (1997), in an essay unpublished in his lifetime, posed this question and answered it unequivocally: in order to rescue innocents from extreme violence no scruple should be had about applying equal or greater violence to him whose intelligence might save them. The Israeli Landau Commission (1987: para. 3.15), investigating the excesses of the Israeli General Security Services (GSS) during the 1980s, considered the answer self-evident: pressurising suspects would be the lesser evil. Vice President Dick Cheyney and Donald Rumsfeld, when asked about water-boarding considered use of the technique a 'no-brainer' (Sands 2008). Jay Bybee, now a judge, and Alberto Gonzales, then Counsel to President George Bush and subsequently Attorney General, referred to the 'choice of evils' arising from such scenarios and found the evil of international terrorism sufficiently compelling to advocate that a variety of safeguards for prisoners be abandoned and more coercive interrogation methods used (Greenberg and Dratel 2004: Memos 6, 7, 14 and 15). The reasoning is clear, and its resonances with arguments debated over two centuries earlier are so strong that it makes sense to address these issues largely without regard to time or place.

In the eighteenth century, at a time when torture remained legal and in widespread use, Bentham argued for its retention subject to certain rules:

- it ought not to be used 'without good proof of its being in the power of the prisoner to do what is required of him';
- it should be used only 'in cases which admit of no delay';
- the harm to be averted, even in urgent cases, must be great;
- the severity of the torture must be proportionate to the harm to be prevented;
- the use of torture should be regulated and limited by law; and
- the type of torture used should be such as to have the fewest long-term effects – that is, it should be of the sort where the 'pain goes off the soonest'. (Bentham 1997: 313–5)

Bentham's advice has effectively been followed in more recent times. In the 1930s the US police employed what were termed 'third-degree methods', which the Wickersham Commission typified as torture, against organised crime suspects: their use had to be approved by senior officers qualified to judge the seriousness of the threat allegedly posed (Chaffee *et al.* 1931: 174–80). Likewise in the 1980s the Israeli Landau Commission insisted that 'moderate physical pressure' falling short of torture was justified by the criminal law defence of 'necessity': the methods should be regulated, albeit both the methods that were sanctioned and the agreed regulatory procedure remained secret. In the US Michael Ignatieff (2004) has controversially argued that facing up to 'lesser evils' is something the age of terrorism makes imperative – though he also insists that he is contemplating coercive interrogation methods falling short of torture. Like Bentham, Ignatieff wants whatever is to be allowed to be regulated by law. Likewise, Alan Dershowitz (2001), the Harvard human rights lawyer, has argued that since, given a 'ticking bomb situation', US security agents would torture 'anyway', it would be better were the practice regulated through the issue of 'torture warrants'. And, as we have seen, unusual coercive interrogation methods, and the circumstances in which they can officially be used, were in early 2002 approved by the Office of Legal Counsel in the United States Justice Department. All of which makes it appropriate that we examine Bentham's criteria closely.

Bentham argued that if through torture we could be certain that the subject would do that which it is in the public interest that he be made to do, torture would be more efficacious, and therefore justified on utilitarian grounds, than punishment. The problem with punishment, whose utilitarian justification is deterrence or rehabilitation, is the risk, the future being uncertain, that it won't work, that insufficient or inappropriate punishment will be applied. With torture, he argued, there is no such risk. The torture stops immediately the subject complies. But herein also lies the difficulty. The torturer can *never* be certain that the subject *can* comply. Or that he or she *has*. We can never be certain that the subject knows that which we have an interest in knowing and, as Aristotle put it, 'those under compulsion are as likely to give false evidence as true' (*Rhetoric*, 1376b–1377a).

The obvious response to these objections is that we can never be certain about anything, which is why Bentham argued that the investigator should be as certain as he can be: he should apply an evidential test similar to that sufficient to convict for a serious crime. But how is such a test to be applied in circumstances 'which admit of no delay', while the bomb ticks? In most advanced states convictions for serious crimes are arrived at with deliberation, following full, thorough and transparent examinations of all the available evidence. These are the very opposite of the frenetic circumstances arising from a ticking bomb. Which is why, as Luban convincingly argues, the ticking bomb scenario is a rhetorical red herring, a 'picture that bewitches us':

> The real debate is not between one guilty man's pain and hundreds of innocent lives. It is the debate between the certainty of anguish and the mere possibility of learning something vital and saving lives. (Luban 2006: 46–7)

Necessity, as the old adage has it, knows no law. It is the most lawless of legal doctrines. An *individual* may do something out of necessity, in the heat of the moment, making an emergency judgement in extreme circumstances. An *individual* may subsequently advance *necessity* in his defence, something Ignatieff (2004) considers we should more explicitly acknowledge. That is one thing. But to attempt to justify a regular state practice on this basis means standardising allegedly compelling circumstances incapable of standardisation and effective regulation. It means granting security or police personnel a general discretion to use extreme coercive methods: in individual cases where there is no necessary urgency; where no specific harm by gathering intelligence from a particular subject can precisely be identified or averted; where the guilt of the subject has not been proved; and where the suspect's capacity to provide information about the alleged threat has to be assumed, possibly reasonably, but not independently tested.

Secondly, even if a genuine ticking bomb situation were to arise and force were to be used in order to obtain information to dispel the imminent threat, and even were the conduct of the security forces or police subsequently to be excused, that would not mean that the evidence derived from the exercise could subsequently be used in criminal proceedings for past crimes. There is a fundamental difference between averting a future harm and punishing an old one. Allowing evidence collected by force to be used in criminal proceedings creates an *incentive* to apply coercive means to *all* suspects resisting interrogation. It means allowing the security forces and police to treat suspects in a way which, if done by others, constitutes a criminal offence. This was the objection which Lord Donaldson had to the interrogation methods used by the British army against terrorist suspects in Northern Ireland in the early 1970s (Parker Report 1972). It means licensing the police to use the very practices which the criminal law prohibits and the criminal justice system is ostensibly designed to prevent. This can only mean bringing the system generally into contempt. If the use of force is to be allowed to the police against citizens subject to the presumption of innocence and wishing to preserve their right to silence, it will no longer be clear to citizens that their security is being safeguarded by the system. How will the behaviour of the security forces be distinguishable from that of criminals?

In the case of the detainees at Guantánamo Bay, the US authorities under Bush clearly considered several of the above objections, which makes the policies they adopted all the more cynical. They determined that the detainees were not covered by the Geneva Conventions, which given the open-ended nature of the undeclared non-inter-state nature of the so-called 'War Against Terror' meant, in the absence of the US courts determining the policy unconstitutional, they could be detained and coercively interrogated without limit of time, with no right of access to the US domestic courts and the forum of public opinion which would accompany such access. They also determined that any criminal proceedings against the detainees should be by way of specially constituted military tribunals without certain protections afforded by the US domestic courts. As Alberto Gonzales advised President Bush when recommending these measures, the President would thus have maximum flexibility in how to deal with these and subsequent detainees and the threat of domestic criminal prosecution would be reduced. The suggestion that these policies would bring criticism from the United States' allies was 'undoubtedly true' but the US would continue to be able 'to bring war crimes charges against anyone who mistreats U.S. personnel' and most allies, they argued, would be reassured by claims that the treatment at Guantánamo was humane (Greenberg and Dratel 2004: Memo 7). It is clear that even the United States' staunchest and most supine ally, the UK, was *not* reassured, even if it took four years for a British Cabinet minister, Lord Falconer, the Lord Chancellor, to declare that the legal black hole represented by the Guantánamo arrangements were a 'shocking affront to the principles of democracy' (Falconer 2006). Even so, Lord Falconer failed to comment on the conditions and the interrogation methods in use at Guantánamo Bay.

Thirdly, Israel in the 1980s and the US under Bush set limits to the amount of coercion and pain that could be applied, allowing techniques not dissimilar to those used by the British in Northern Ireland (Greenberg and Dratel 2004: Memo 26; Sands 2008; Danner 2009). By contrast Bentham set no upper limit to the torture that might be inflicted other than that it should be proportionate and of the sort where the 'pain goes off the soonest'. But why, on utilitarian grounds, should any upper limit be set? There seems no good reason so long as the torture is the lesser of the two evils, the other being the harm prevented. One possible utilitarian reason – that the application of extreme pain might produce unreliable evidence – is implausible. There is now a sufficient corpus of research and case study evidence to demonstrate that even the mildest pressure – pressure so mild that the ordinary citizen would probably not interpret it as pressure – is capable of eliciting from some vulnerable or suggestible subjects false confessions or misleading information (Royal Commission 1981: 25–6; Gudjonsson 1996).

Rather, contemporary utilitarians tend to fall back on the prevailing human rights culture and the reputation of the state, limits being set so as to contend that the coercion falls short of torture and thus the state is in conformity with its international treaty obligations and international public opinion. This was the position taken by the British in Northern Ireland, by the Landau Commission in Israel and by the US authorities under Bush.

But once coercive interrogation methods – sleep deprivation, hooding, dietary manipulation, subjection to temperature extremes, white noise, forcible use of physical stress postures, physical slaps and punches, water-boarding, or threats of all this and worse – have been authorised the evidence suggests that setting upper limits becomes a mere fig leaf. Once the dog is off the leash legal regulatory frameworks of the type argued for by Dershowitz and Ignatieff do not work, particularly in a 'War on Terror' doomsday climate of the sort that Ignatieff suggests we now inhabit. Trained, committed terrorists do not succumb to 'moderate physical pressure'. They are prepared to resist, not least because they often risk worse treatment from their own organisations if they succumb: this much is clear from the experience of Algeria, Northern Ireland and Palestine. When moderately or even severely coercive methods don't work and the amber light has been given, all the case studies indicate that the security forces go further, much further. The senior US Justice Department officials who prepared the legal advice on interrogation methods for President Bush in 2002 were not inept lawyers. They were highly qualified lawyer advisors who fully understood the operational interpretation likely to be put on their tough-minded memorandum about the lack of terrorist suspect detainees' rights (Luban 2006).

The evidence that has already emerged from events in Iraq, Afghanistan and Guantánamo is compelling (ICRC 2007; Sands 2008). Near-torture or 'torture-lite' spills over into practices that unequivocally comprise torture, however torture is defined. It is not credible that security forces, operating largely in secret or in theatres where minimal public accountability can routinely be applied, will abide by upper limits. Licensed now to employ coercive methods the rationale for which is the speedy breaking down of detainees' resistance, they step over the line. Lowering the psychological threshold for the use of force almost inevitably leads the dam to be swept away. As one commentator on the Landau Commission's findings has put it: 'If a suspect's body is no longer taboo, what is one blow relative to the sanctity of the cause?' (Kremnitzer 1989: 254). The qualitative Rubicon will be crossed. The suspect is no longer a subject but an object, not a person but a body, not a citizen but an alien, a reservoir of information to be tapped, a means to an end (Scarry 1985). What begins with tidy intellectual debates about the public interest and lesser evils ends with dirty, hole-in-the-corner contests of will waged in sordid environments by underground officials against demonised *others* whose assumed *evil* and *inhumanity* means they do not count in a calculus where, gradually, almost anything goes.

This leads to the ultimate utilitarian objection to torture: it corrosively deligitimates the state, which is Dershowitz's and Ignatieff's rationale for legally regulating more coercive practices. They seek to safeguard the reputation of the state whilst defending its citizenry from major serious harm. But Dershowitz sells the pass: he seeks to regulate practices he argues the state, *in extremis*, will resort to anyway – that is, to regulate that which he concedes is not effectively susceptible to regulation. Ignatieff, by contrast, believes that upper limits can be fixed on the lesser evil of coercive interrogation, thereby protecting the integrity of the state. But Ignatieff deals in generalities. He opposes use of torture – 'if you want to create terrorists, torture is a pretty sure way to do so' (Ignatieff 2004) – but fails to engage the detail as to what torture comprises. He pirouettes on the slippery semantic slopes of pre-emptive strikes and coercive interrogation.

Because near torture almost inevitably leads to torture and because the truth eventually leaks out, the repercussions ultimately discredit the state. Use of force may initially be supported by popular demand that threats be neutralised and fears assuaged, but the *other* is ultimately never capable of precise definition and identification in practice. There is always general fallout – the massacre of the innocents, the false confessions, the mistaken identities, the miscarriages of a justice system that no longer seems to deserve the name. This fallout is then capable of being exploited by precisely the groups against whom the state seeks to defend itself. If some suspects are tortured then those who seek to discredit the state routinely claim that they have been. And if all insurgents claim they have been tortured, why should the police not do that of which they will be accused anyway? One might as well be hung for a sheep as a lamb. Thus is promoted a cycle of disinformation and mistrust. If there are no limits, if the state is engaged in dirty tricks, why should trust be invested in the state and its authority acknowledged?

The practice of torture cannot be justified on utilitarian grounds. There is no consolation for those unconvinced by human rights arguments.

Facilitating torture

Who becomes a torturer? To torture is so abhorrent that it is easy to assume that perpetrators are inherently evil. Nothing could be further from the truth. The evidence suggests that torturers are not originally out of the ordinary and that situational circumstances are sufficiently powerful as to turn ordinary persons into custodians capable of inflicting severe pain on their fellow human beings, an aspect of what Hannah Arendt (1970) terms the 'banality of evil'.

Social psychologists have observed that people have a tendency to underestimate the power of situational forces. This is linked with their tendency to overestimate the role of personality in producing behaviour, a misattribution referred to as the 'fundamental attribution error' (Ross 1977). On the basis of interviews with executioners under military regimes in Greece and Brazil (Huggins *et al.* 2002) it does not seem that torturers are selected for their psychopathic or sadistic tendencies. They take quite routine training and career routes. They are typically young recruits to the police or military drawn from rural and politically conservative areas, eventually selected for entry into elite units where specific torture training takes place. They enjoy privileges not available to their peers and their selection is presented as an honour, though their training may also be harsh, as in Brazil. This desensitises them to pain and suffering, promotes total obedience to authority, creates an acceptance of the state's ideology, and energises them to root out and destroy enemies of the state (Huggins *et al.* 2007: 237). Through such means normal men (and women) can be shaped into torturers.

During the Brazilian military regime the torture and execution of citizens found its justification in propaganda centred on a national security ideology which led to the development of supporting organisational structures to carry out the repression:

> The military regime did what most repressive governments do: it created enemies of the state who must be identified, searched out, collected in secure settings, interrogated if they might have information of value, tortured if they do not comply, and executed when they are of no further value to the state's mission. (Huggins *et al.* 2007: 244)

The social psychological processes involved in this transformation involve: the creation of a new morality to override previous moral considerations; mandating blind obedience; dehumanising victims; and neutralising personal and social accountability. The personal standards which guide our behaviour can be changed if normal constraints are absent, a process termed moral disengagement (Bandura 1990). This can occur when the perpetrators of violence have a distorted perception of the humanity of their victims, seeing them as subhuman enemies against whom violent actions can be taken with impunity. The kind of authoritarian regimes in which torture flourishes demand blind obedience. This can absolve participants in state-sponsored violence from a sense of responsibility for what they have done, encouraging further moral disengagement.

Laboratory experiments have shown that under the right social conditions untrained, ordinary people will display blind obedience. Milgram notoriously created a laboratory experiment whereby subjects were informed that they were taking part in a memory training exercise (Milgram 1974). They were shown an electric apparatus that allegedly delivered shocks ranging on a scale from a mild jolt (15 volts) up to a dangerous level (450 volts) to be applied incrementally each time the learner in the experiment made an error. The learner was out of sight in another room, but could be heard responding to the shocks delivered by the subject. The learners never got the answers right and the subjects were required to go on progressively delivering greater shocks. Prior to the experiment Milgram invited 40 psychiatrists to offer their estimate of the likelihood of participants going to the maximum shock level. The average estimate was 1 per cent. In fact almost two-thirds of the students taking part delivered the maximum shock. Milgram replicated this experiment using over 1,000 people drawn from all walks of American life. In some versions of the experiment the obedience level reached 90 per cent thereby demonstrating the power of situational forces in shaping behavioural obedience. The failure of the psychiatrists accurately to predict the outcome is an example of the fundamental attribution error.

Torture and execution become more possible when victims are dehumanised, no longer persons but 'animals', 'vermin', 'cockroaches', 'terrorists', 'communists' and other labels serving to erase their humanity. The absence of accountability results in a process which Zimbardo (1970) terms deindividuation. Anonymity provides a situation where normal restraints are suspended.

Laboratory support for the influence of these four processes was found in the Stanford Prison Experiment (Zimbardo *et al.* 1973). Here college student volunteers assessed as normal on the basis of psychological tests, clinical interviews and background reports were randomly assigned to play the role of either prisoner or prison guard. By the end of the experiment the roles assigned for each set of participants led to totally contrasting behaviours. Those subjects assigned to be prisoners were arrested by the city police at their place of residence and booked at the local police station for various felonies before being transferred to a mock prison in the basement of the Stanford University psychology department. Here the subjects were issued with uniforms and given rules created by the guards to follow. The prisoners remained in their cells but the guards worked eight-hour shifts. The experiment was designed to run for two weeks but was terminated after only six days because the simulated prison had become too real. The guards behaved in authoritarian and in some cases even sadistic ways, while the prisoners became passive and submissive, experiencing extreme stress reactions. One prisoner had to be released after only 36 hours. The observed process involved the guards dehumanising the prisoners through punishment and harassment and, according to Zimbardo and his colleagues, a process of deindividuation, dehumanisation and moral disengagement unfolded. When combined with the results of Milgram's experiment the Stanford study points to a psychological process whereby the behaviour of ordinary people can be shaped by situational forces such that they are willing to harm and degrade others known to be totally innocent.

Zimbardo and his colleagues point out that the behaviour in their experiment occurred in a context where there were many other actors – city police, a local TV station photographer, a Roman Catholic priest who interviewed the prisoners in the presence of the guards and heard their complaints, and parents and friends who visited – whose involvement was intended to lend credibility to the experiment. Despite the ragged appearance of the detainees, these participants did nothing to demand the prisoners' release. The use of torture and summary executions in Brazil likewise did not occur in social isolation. Many other actors were peripherally involved: the trainers who instructed the recruits in the use of torture; the supervisors who selected the officers for this kind of work; the command structure; the technical and maintenance staff who created, serviced and equipped the facilities where torture took place; and the military officers who created the propaganda of a state under threat from enemies who could only be dealt with by recourse to extra-judicial methods. There are social psychological processes that clearly enable ordinary people to turn a blind eye to or be transformed to commit acts involving extreme inhumanity: that is, 'anyone could become a torturer or an executioner under a set of quite well-known conditions' (Huggins *et al.* 2002: 267).

The transformation of ordinary people into torturers is also shaped by the socio-political climate. This is briefly illustrated by the arrangements made by the United States government following the events of 9/11, and in particular the role of actors such as psychologists and psychiatrists in the interrogation process. Where state-sponsored terrorism occurs torturers may have the assistance of other professionals who have forsaken their professional ethics in order to take part in dealing with the hated enemy. Medical doctors may be present to revive the victim of torture and nurses may be present to give injections. Consider the following logged incidents from the account of the International Committee of the Red Cross (ICRC) of Abu Zubaydah, allegedly a senior al-Qaeda operative, captured in Pakhistan and apparently held in secret locations in Thailand, Afghanistan, Morocco, Poland and Romania before being transferred to Guantánamo Bay:

- A trauma surgeon from Johns Hopkins University, Baltimore is flown by the CIA to a military hospital in Lahore to provide treatment to injuries sustained by the suspect when captured.

- At various times the suspect is stripped and made to wear a diaper for prolonged periods such that he has to urinate and defecate into the diaper; is blindfolded and made to wear goggles; has earphones placed over his ears and loud music played; is handcuffed in physical stress positions; is deprived of sleep; is placed in a coffin-like box; is repeatedly swung against a plywood-plated wall by means of a towel placed around his neck: and periodically, between times, his condition is checked by a medical doctor, or medical personnel are present during the procedures, observing. (Danner 2009)

Or, as illustrated by the case of al-Qahtani, the minutely detailed accounts of suspects' reactions to their interrogation sessions maintained by the US Army:

Detainee began to cry. Visibly shaken, Very emotional. Detainee cried. Disturbed. Detainee began to cry. Detainee butted SGT R in the eye. Detainee bit the IV tube completely in two. Started moaning. Uncomfortable. Moaning. Turned his head from left to right. Began crying hard spontaneously. Crying and praying. Began to cry. Claimed to have been pressured into making a confession. Falling asleep. Very uncomfortable. On the verge of breaking. Angry. Detainee struggled ... (Cole 2008: 20–2, quoted from Sands 2008)

Psychologists, psychiatrists and medical doctors are involved in advising interrogators on interrogation proceedings. That is, they are 'reverse-engineering' the resistance training formerly offered to American special forces at risk of being captured and subjected themselves to torture.

What should be the role of psychologists and psychiatrists in interrogating detainees? There is controversy. Different professional bodies have taken different positions on the involvement of members. The most unambiguous statement has been provided by the American Medical Association:

> Physicians must not conduct, directly participate in, or monitor an interrogation with an intent to intervene, because this undermines the physician's role as healer.

Likewise the American Psychiatric Association holds that:

> No psychiatrist should participate directly in the interrogation of a person held in custody by military or civilian investigative or law enforcement authorities, whether in the United States or elsewhere. Direct participation includes being present in the interrogation room, asking or suggesting questions, or advising authorities on the use of specific techniques of interrogation with particular detainees.

More controversial is the position of the American Psychological Association (APA). It does see a role for psychologists, providing it is consistent with the Association's Code of Ethics:

> Psychologists may serve in various national security-related roles, such as a consultant to an interrogation, in a manner that is consistent with the Ethics Code, and when doing so psychologists are mindful of factors unique to these roles and contexts that require special ethical consideration.

Given that the controversy is linked to the legal ambiguity of places like Guantánamo Bay this places APA members in a difficult position. The debate within the APA has been fuelled by the fact that six out of ten members of a presidential task force endorsed by the APA had ties with the military, four of them having been involved either at Guantánamo Bay, at Abu Ghraib Prison, Iraq or at detention facilities in Afghanistan. The report stated that psychologists could act as consultants to interrogations, but they must report any instances of torture or degrading treatment and are forbidden from mixing the roles of healthcare provider and interrogation consultant.

The dilemma is that if psychologists and psychiatrists are excluded from providing advice on interrogations, the practice of interrogators may be crude, ineffective and violate basic human rights. Alternatively some psychologists and psychiatrists may become so involved with the process that their advice leads to violations of basic human rights. The position of the British Psychological Society is that their members are bound by a code of ethics that does not set out specific ethical guidelines on issues such as involvement in interrogation (BPS 2006). At the time of writing the Royal College of Psychiatrists has yet to announce its policy.

Because of the secretive nature of these security-related interrogations and the closed nature of any military commissions or legal proceedings that follow, it is unlikely that the quality of the interrogation or the advice given by psychologists or psychiatrists will ever be open to critical examination. There therefore seems very little that can be done to monitor the role of these professionals and consider whether their advice is consistent with psychological principles held by the wider psychological or psychiatric communities. The easy option would be to follow the American Psychiatric Association and American Medical Association position and forbid participation in interrogation. The problem resulting from permitting participation is that the regulatory systems are so weak that there is little control during the interrogation, no opportunity for independent evaluation of what took place and, in the unlikely event of evidence of malpractice by a professional ever coming to public light, the disciplinary procedures of the various associations and societies would be a weak and ineffective means of sanction. We are therefore likely to see the continuing involvement of both psychologists and (outside the US) psychiatrists in the interrogation of suspects with the risk that this political endorsement becomes another contextual factor that facilitates the moral disengagement of interrogators. Their practices will have been designed – and sanctioned – by powerful authority figures in the form of psychologists and psychiatrists.

Conclusion

The torturous practices and the maintenance of places of detention, secret or disclosed but operating in a legal vacuum, sanctioned by President George Bush inflicted great damage on the international reputation of the United States. They have arguably also stimulated the terrorist urges of those groups opposed to the foreign policy of the United States and its closest allies, which include the UK. If human rights considerations are set aside – as behind the scenes they often are – this, ultimately, is the strongest utilitarian argument against resort to torture: it undermines the very security of those states who claim to defend human rights. Further, the more social scientists and the medical profession collude in such practices the more likely it is that ordinary mortals will be drawn into torturing their fellow humans.

Selected further reading

Peters' *Torture* (1996) provides the best general discussion of the use of and debate about torture both historically and contemporaneously. Evans and Morgan's *Preventing Torture* (1998) and Rodley's *The Treatment of Prisoners Under International Law* (1999) provide authoritative accounts of the development of international human rights obligations and standards relating to torture and inhuman and degrading treatment or punishment: both texts include the most relevant key documents as appendices. By contrast Scarry's *The Body in Pain* (1985) provides the most eloquent account of what torture means and how it is made possible. A huge amount of material has recently emerged about the use of torture associated with the wars in Iraq and Afghanistan. Sands' *Torture Team* (2008) provides a fascinating account of how the political decisions in the USA came to be made and by whom. There is no alternative to Amnesty International's annual yearbook for a detailed account of what abuses are being perpetrated where in the world.

References

Alter, J. (2001) 'Time to think about torture', *Newsweek*, 5 November.

Amnesty International (2006) *Amnesty International Report 2006: The State of the World's Human Rights*. London: Amnesty International, International Secretariat. Online at: http://www.amnesty.org/en/library/info/POL10/023/2006.

Amnesty International (2009) *Amnesty International Report 2009: The State of the World's Human Rights*. London: Amnesty International, International Secretariat. Online at: http://thereport.amnesty.org/sites/report2009.amnesty.org/files/documents/air09-en.pdf.

Arendt, H. (1970) *Eichmann in Jerusalem: A Report on the Banality of Evil*. London. Viking Press.

Bandura, A. (1990) 'Mechanisms of moral disengagement', in W. Reich (ed.), *Origins of Terrorism. Psychologies, Ideologies, Theologies, States of Mind*. New York: Cambridge University Press.

Bentham, J. (1777–9) 'Of torture': previously unpublished manuscript edited by W. L. Twining and P. E. Twining in 'Bentham on torture', *Northern Ireland Legal Quarterly* (1997) 24 (3): 307–56.

British Psychological Society (2006) 'Controversy over psychologists' role in national security', *The Psychologist*, 19 (10): 580–5.

Chaffee, Z., Pollock, W. H. and Stern, C. S. (1931) 'The third degree: report on lawlessness in law enforcement', *National Commission on Law Observance and Enforcement*, Vol. IV, No. II. Washington, DC: Government Printing Office.

Cole, D. (2008) 'What to do about the torturers?', *New York Review of Books*, 15 January, pp. 20–4.

Danner, M. (2004) *Torture and Truth: America, Abu Ghraib and the War on Terror*. London: Granta.

Danner, M. (2009) 'US torture: voices from the black sites', *New York Review of Books*, 9 April, pp. 69–77.

Dershowitz, A. (2001) 'America needs torture warrants', *Los Angeles Times*, 8 November.

Evans, D. and Morgan, R. (1998) *Preventing Torture: A Study of the European Convention for the Prevention of Torture and Inhuman or Degrading Treatment or Punishment*. Oxford: Clarendon Press.

Falconer, Lord (2006) *The Role of Judges in a Modern Democracy*, Magna Carta Lecture, Sydney, Australia, 13 September.

Greenberg, K. J. and Dratel, J. L. (2004) *The Torture Papers: The Road to Abu Ghraib*. New York: Cambridge University Press.

Gudjonsson, G. (1996) 'Custodial confinement, interrogation and coerced confessions', in D. Forrest (ed.), *A Glimpse of Hell: Reports on Torture Worldwide*. London: Amnesty International.

Huggins, M. K., Garitos-Fatouros, M. and Zimbardo, P. G. (2002) *Violence Workers. Police Torturers and Murderers Reconstruct Brazilian Atrocities*. Berkeley, CA: University of California Press.

ICRC (2007) *Report on the Treatment of Fourteen 'High Value Detainees' in CIA Custody*. Geneva: ICRC.

Ignatieff, M. (2004) *The Lesser Evil: Political Ethics in and Age of Terror*. Princeton, NJ: Princeton University Press.

Kremnitzer, M. (1989) 'The Landau Commmission Report: was the security service subordinated to the law, or the law to the "needs" of the security service?', *Israeli Law Review*, 24: 216–79.

Landau Commission (1987) *Report of the Commission of Inquiry into the Methods of Investigation of the General Security Service Regarding Hostile Terrorist Activity: Part One*. Jerusalem: Israeli Government.

Luban, D. (2006) 'Liberalism, torture and the ticking bomb', in K. L. Greenberg (ed.), *The Torture Debate in America*. New York: Cambridge University Press.

Milgram, S. (1974) *Obedience to Authority: An Experimental View*. New York: Taylor & Francis.

Morgan, R. (2000) 'The utilitarian justification of torture: denial, desert and disinformation', *Punishment and Society*, 2 (2): 180–96.

Parker Report (1972) *Report of the Committee of Privy Councillors Appointed to Consider Authorised Procedures for the Interrogation of Persons Suspected of Terrorism* (Chairman Lord Parker), Cmnd 4981. London: HMSO.

Peters, E. (1996) *Torture*, 2nd edn. Pennsylvania, PA: University of Pennsylvania Press.

Rodley, N. S. (1999) *The Treatment of Prisoners Under International Law*, 2nd edn. Oxford: Oxford University Press.

Rodley, N. S. (2002) 'The definition of torture in international law', *Current Legal Problems*, 55: 467.

Ross, L. (1977) 'The intuitive psychologist and his shortcomings. Distortions in the attribution process', in L. Berkowitz (ed.), *Advances in Experimental Social Psychology*. New York: Academic Press.

Royal Commission (1981) *Report of the Royal Commission on Criminal Procedure*. London: HMSO.

Sands, P. (2008) *Torture Team: Rumsfeld's Memo and the Betrayal of American Values*. London: Palgrave Macmillan.

Scarry, E. (1985) *The Body in Pain*. New York: Oxford University Press.

Zimbardo, P. G. (1970) 'The human choice: individuation, reason, and order versus deindividuation, impulse and chaos', in W. J. Arnold and D. Levine (eds), *1969 Nebraska Symposium on Motivation*. Lincoln, NE: University of Nebraska Press.

Zimbardo, P. G., Haney, C., Banks, W. C. and Jaffe, D. (1973) 'The mind is a formidable jailer: a Pirandellian prison', *New York Times Magazine*, 8 April, pp. 38ff.

Chapter 40

Crimes of the global state

Maureen Cain

Introduction

In this paper I start by elaborating a concept of the global state, first in a common-sense and then in a theoretical way. This section highlights the problem of the non-accountability of the economic arm of the global state. Later sections document the social harms resulting from the economic policies adopted by the International Monetary Fund (IMF) and the World Bank in particular. The question of whether the global state agencies are culpable (responsible in a strong sense) for the harms they cause is based on both the familiar distinction between crimes and harms and a jurisprudential discussion of what constitutes a just state. It is argued that the global state fails to pass both the criminological and the jurisprudential tests, having disregarded a strong body of evidence as to the effects of its policies. The issue of what should be done to prevent future harms and to ameliorate existing ones is then considered. The responses of the global state itself are revealed as inadequate before constructive 'next steps' are suggested, and the value of moving beyond existing crime prevention measures made clear.

What is the global state?

The global state has economic, political/legal, and cultural/ideological powers, each embedded in a set of institutions. Global economic powers are located in a triumvirate of institutions, two of which were established in 1944 at a meeting in Bretton Woods, USA, the purpose of which was to plan for post-Second World War reconstruction. At this meeting the World Bank was set up to finance development and the International Monetary Fund (IMF) was set up to provide shorter-term loans to deal with temporary instabilities in national finances. The role of the Fund changed in 1975 when a sudden rise in the price of oil led to financial turmoil for the oil-consuming nations. Many newly independent nations of the developing world sought loans from the IMF at this time and, as will be seen, some of those loans have turned out to be of almost infinite duration.

The third global economic agency began life in 1948 as the General Agreement on Tariffs and Trade (GATT), negotiating both bilateral and multi-lateral international trading deals and rules. Following the 'Uruguay Round' of negotiations (September 1986 – April 1994) this morphed in 1995 into the World Trade Organisation, embodying in its trade policies the particular ethos of freedom which by this time had also come to dominate the economic strategies governing the 'conditionalities' or terms upon which the World Bank and the IMF would be prepared to lend money.

In addition to these global economic agencies there exists also the United Nations Organisation (UN), governed by a General Assembly of all the nations of the world and its Security Council on which China, France, the Russian Federation, the United Kingdom and the USA have permanent seats, supplemented by ten non-permanent members.[1] The great Conventions setting global standards in such areas as Civil and Political Rights, Human, Social and Economic Rights, Rights of the Child, and Women's Rights (CEDAW)[2] emanate from the General Assembly of the United Nations. Their moral force derives from the fact that the nations and peoples of the world have agreed about them.[3]

The tasks arising from these global treaties are carried out by Standing Committees with their bureaucracies and a plethora of service institutions which report to these committees. For the purposes of this paper it is useful to recognise UNCTAD[4] (dealing with Trade and Development), WHO (World Health Organisation), UNIFEM[5] (dealing with the condition of women), ILO (International Labour Organisation) and UNHCR (the UN High Commission for Refugees). The UN, primarily through UNESCO,[6] also has cultural/ ideological responsibilities. The United Nations and its agents and agencies, I argue, are also constitutive of the global state.

Between them, therefore, the agencies so far described fulfil the economic, political/legal and cultural/ideological functions conventionally ascribed to states. They have power to make rules which have the potential capacity for global reach, and to monitor and encourage compliance.[7]

One value of this formulation is that it immediately highlights an anomaly. One sector of the global state (the UN and its agencies) is democratic insofar as its leading institution, the General Assembly, is constituted on the principle of one nation, one vote. This arrangement connects the UN in a public way to the policies of the governments of its constituent members, most of which these days derive their legitimacy from some form of democratic process. However, the Security Council, with sole power to decide on the legality of war, is not a democratic institution, because although the permanent members are outnumbered by the non-permanent members, the latter rarely vote as a block. The sociology of this is that the permanent members are better informed because they have permanent background staff in their New York embassies, because they know each other better and therefore know the bases for forging possible alliances, and because the temporary members may be seeking grounds of alliance (perhaps 'deals' is too harsh a term) with one or more of these powerful nations (Harris-Short 2001). So the UN is not yet a fully democratic institution. It is, however, (1) the best global institution that we have, and (2) capable of succumbing to political pressure as national democracies have had to do.[8]

None of this is the case for the IMF/World Bank. The constitutions of these institutions are modelled on those of private companies, insofar as the national members 'buy' shares based on their financial contributions. Voting rights, as in a publicly floated company, are in proportion to the number of shares held. While this weighting in favour of the rich might be cause for concern, it at least has its own consistent logic. However, in the case of the IMF/World Bank there is a further worrying constitutional twist. The free market logic which the IMF/World Bank apply so unsparingly elsewhere, as we shall see, is not applied to their own constitutions, for there is no 'market' in IMF/World Bank shares: they are not freely tradable. Rather, existing members decide, on grounds which are not made public, whether or not an applicant nation may increase its shareholding and therefore its voting capacity. In 2008 India was allowed to do this. Japan has recently had an application rejected. There is no external control over this decision-making, either by a superordinate power or by the market. The IMF and the World Bank as institutions are accountable to no nation and to no agency. They 'belong' to their member states in proportion to their voting rights. Currently the United States of America holds 16.77 per cent[9] of the shares, giving a very considerable influence to the free-market economic policies which were favoured in that nation from the mid-1970s to the demise of George W. Bush, the banking failures of 2008 and the near collapse of the global economic system. The combined voting power of the 27 EU nations amounts to a further 24.97 per cent. Japan, China, Israel, and Saudi Arabia all hold more than 3 per cent of the votes.[10] At the other extreme, three-quarters of the nation-state members (141 of 186) hold less than one per cent of the votes each.

In spite of this, as I write, these same agencies, the World Bank and the IMF, are proposing solutions to the global economic crisis, including an increase in the amount of money available to lend to the developing world, as agreed at the G20 meeting in April 2009. Such proposals demand the most careful scrutiny, bearing in mind the economic concerns of the majority shareholding group.

This is the formal structure. However, even these formal arrangements do not tell the full story. As Kirton's painstaking and insightful analysis of the minutes reveals, decisions as to which nations will be allowed to increase their shareholding are negotiated in meetings of the G8,[11] unashamedly (and on the whole usefully) meetings of heads of state and their senior advisors from the world's 'old' economies (Kirton 2001). A greater influence for India and China, both G20 nations, has recently been widely trumpeted (McRae 2009). It seems likely to be some time, however, before these nations will be in a position to match the influence and voting power of the developed world.

These are the agencies which, together with the World Trade Organisation, have governance of the global economy: undemocratic, secretive and weighted against the poor. What, then, has all this to do with criminology?

The policies of the global financial institutions and their criminogenic effects

The damaging effects of 'structural adjustment' policies on the economies and infrastructure of developing countries are now well known. However, it is necessary to describe at least some of these negative consequences once again in order to establish that these effects are global harms in the criminological sense (Cain and Howe 2008). For this to be the case it is necessary that the harmful effects could have been foreseen, that they are not just the unfortunate and unexpected results of a well intentioned policy. In other words, it will be necessary to establish that these are culpable harms.[12] Criminology does not concern itself with understandable mistakes.

The evidence that global economic policies have been harming rather than helping the developing world is plentiful and long-standing. Robinson (1996), for example, using official UN data, documented a growing global polarisation, noting that by 1991 the top 20 per cent of nations were 61.1 per cent richer than the poorest 20 per cent and that, if people rather than nations are considered, the richest 20 per cent get 150 times more than the poorest 20 per cent – 'the ratio of inequality between the global rich and the global poor is 150:1' (p. 22: based on UNDP data). Chossudovsky (1997) produces even more compelling evidence, noting that as a result of the policies of the global financial institutions 'by the mid 1980s, developing countries had become net exporters of capital in favour of rich countries' (p. 45).

The first connection between structural adjustment policies and an increased level of recorded crime within a nation state was made by Cain and Birju (1992), documenting the impact of the first structural adjustment loan taken out by Trinidad and Tobago in 1987 as a consequence of a fall in that nation's oil revenues. These data were elaborated more fully in the Sampson Report of 1994 (Sampson 1994), and the data most central to this argument are reproduced yet again in Tables 40.1 and 40.2 below (see also Cain 2008).

An immediate result of these 'adjustments' is that the society is economically polarised. Both the mean and, more tellingly, the median income levels fall, for both men and women. The median, of course, is that figure which bisects the population, with half earning more than the median level and the other half earning less. Therefore if the median falls, half the population now fall below a new and lower measure. Likewise, in Table 40.1 it can be seen that for each sex the number of people in the top income bracket goes up, but that at the same time there is a far greater increase in the numbers of people in the bottom income bracket. For women the change is extreme, increasing from 4,600 in the lowest income bracket in 1987 (less than TT$250 pcm – roughly £25 per month at the time) to 10,900 five years later in 1991. As Castells so succinctly put it in 1998, such polarisation is 'a specific process of inequality when the ends grow faster than the middle' (p. 71). In sum, Table 40.1 reveals a relatively stable society being pulled apart economically within the space of five years as a result of the implementation of structural adjustment conditionalities.

Non-oil-producing nations – the vast majority – experienced structural adjustment earlier than Trinidad and Tobago. For these nations it was the

Table 40.1 Earnings of those employed in Trinidad and Tobago 1987–91*

Loan year	Mean income per month (TT$)		Median income per month (TT$)		Numbers in top income bracket		Numbers in bottom income bracket	
	M	F	M	F	M	F	M	F
1987	1,800	1,500	1,500	1,200	5,600	700	6,000	4,600
1988	1,700	1,500	1,500	1,200	5,500	800	6,700	4,600
1989	1,700	1,400	1,300	1,200	6,600	800	5,800	4,300
1990	1,600	1,400	1,300	1,200	7,000	1,200	6,200	3,900
1991	1,700	1,400	1,400	1,100	8,000	1,400	9,200	10,900

*Data re-analysed by the author for the Sampson Committee (Sampson 1994).
Source: Annual Statistical Digest of Trinidad and Tobago (1991).

sharp increase in the price of oil in the 1970s, a problem compounded for a number of African nations by their inability to pay for the armaments which they were encouraged to buy by both sides during the Cold War (Campaign Against the Arms Trade 1989), that precipitated economic crises and the need for a loan. The evidence of a growing polarisation within and between nations which have undergone structural adjustment has been there for all to see for almost thirty years.

What, then, is structural adjustment? It is the name given to a particular set of conditions upon which a loan will be made to an applicant nation by either the World Bank or the IMF. These conditions ('conditionalities') are premised on the principles that markets in money and in goods and services should be 'free': outside governmental control, as should markets in labour. These freedoms were deemed to be international for money and goods, but a more limited conception was applied to labour: here 'freedom' meant no organised trade unions, not freedom to export one's labour to another country.

More concretely, the conditionalities applied in Trinidad and Tobago in 1987 (Cain 2001/2, 2008; Cain and Birju 1992) are typical: the 'downsizing' of parts of the public sector (e.g. health care, the public service) and the privatisation of public utilities (electricity and water); flattening the tax structure by reducing the higher rates of income tax while at the same time introducing a purchase tax ('value added tax' if ever there was a misnomer) on all consumer goods except essentials such as basic foodstuffs and children's clothing; and floating the currency on the international market so that the value of the local currency (the TT$) fell. The effect of the change in the tax structure is to leave high wage and salary earners better off, while imposing a larger proportion of the overall tax burden on the poor who, being the majority, in aggregate pay disproportionately more of the new purchase tax. The effect of the removal of currency controls is to make imported goods more expensive, while capital is exported to places where its value is safer and the interest it can earn greater. Local investment declines. In many places unemployment increases as the state sector is 'downsized':[13] workers are laid off in an attempt to make the newly 'adjusted' industries either profitable, as in the case of public utilities, or cheaper, as in the case of health, education and social welfare. As Table 40.1 shows, the society is polarised. These outcomes have been even more marked in nations lacking the oil and natural gas resources which enabled Trinidad and Tobago to avoid long-term indebtedness.

In addition, it can be demonstrated that the sudden immiseration which results from structural adjustment is correlated with increases in recorded offending. Four processes appear to be at work here: instrumental crime, self-assertive crime, embedding and compounding. The first three of these are indicated in the same set of data from Trinidad and Tobago discussed above and by evidence from Jamaica. The concept of 'compounding' is derived from Lea and Young's (1984) analysis of the outcomes of the UK's programme of structural adjustment carried out by the government of Margaret Thatcher in the early 1980s. However, although the illustrations are particular, at some level each of these four processes can be observed in all structurally adjusted nations for which data are available. In the global context these processes together lead to what Castells (1998) calls 'perverse integration': 'income generating activities that are normatively declared to be crime and are accordingly prosecuted in a given institutional context' (p. 76). I expand the concept to include non-legal and societally damaging patterns of connection with the global economy, global politics, and global cultural patterns.

Instrumental crime is directed to making up shortfalls in income arising from a sudden loss of earnings. In Trinidad and Tobago, as Table 40.2 shows, property crime increased as an immediate consequence of structural adjustment, and after a few years the rate stabilised, albeit at higher than the pre-adjustment level. An individual example of this phenomenon is offered by Green (1998) who cites the case of a school teacher in Nigeria, unemployed following 'downsizing' of public services in that nation as part of an 'adjustment' programme, who had found an alternative source of income in the drugs trade. People have to make ends meet. Home-based industries such as cake making or selling garden produce expand. 'Higgling' and informal sector trading of all kinds expand, some selling legal goods, others illegal items; some are trading lawfully in authorised markets, others are engaged in street vending which may itself be unlawful. Lawful or not, these are readily understandable responses to a sudden loss of income. Notably, many more women engage in these grey-area activities following adjustment as they carry heavier domestic burdens, not only if their men lose their jobs, but also because they have to fill the spaces caused by half-time schooling and a reduction in health care (Deere et al. 1990; Ellis 2003; Sparr 1994). From the perspective of victimisation, Dorling (2004), using the hardest data he could find, documents that the risk of being murdered rose dramatically for young men leaving school into the workless, structurally adjusted world of Britain in the early 1980s, and that the risk for this age cohort continues to be abnormally high throughout their lives.

The concept of self-assertive crime enables us to understand the growth in offences against the person/crimes of violence. In the case of both Trinidad and Tobago and the UK this growth continues even after the level of property crime has steadied or, in the case of the UK, declined. To explain this it is necessary to return to a paper by Lynette Brown (1994), discussing the consequences of

Table 40.2 Serious offences reported to the police (excluding traffic offences) in Trinidad and Tobago 1980–92

Year	Offences against persons	Breaking and entering	Other offences against property	Forgery	Other offences	Total
1980	439	5,463	6,262	56	18	12,238*
1981	595	6,306	4,678	34	8	11,621
1982	691	6,877	3,018	94	17	10,697
1983	716	7,261	3,287	94	38	11,396
1984	643	7,743	3,542	83	14	11,725
1985	686	9,089	3,978	216	10	13,979
1986	741	8,861	4,603	125	31	14,361
1987	844	8,707	6,021	136	524**	16,232
1988	976	9,352	7,723	164	1,167	19,385
1989	1,171	8,278	7,436	187	911	17,983
1990	1,098	7,543	5,916	129	1,516	16,202
1991	1,161	7,313	3,280	245	1,406	16,157
1992	1,254	7,938	7,267	236	985	17,680

* The published total is 12,233. This appears to be an error.

** Part way through 1987 certain drug offences were reclassified as serious rather than minor crimes. For comparability the annual totals should therefore be adjusted down. This was not done here because exact numbers are unknown.

Source: Taken in part from Cain and Birju (1992: 143). Data from Central Statistical Office, re-analysed by the author for the Sampson Committee (Sampson 1994).

an early experiment with structural adjustment conditionalities from the time when Jamaica sought its first IMF loan in 1977, up to 1989. Brown carried out research on values in Jamaica, and is therefore able to give a before-and-after comparison. Crucially, she found that whereas in the pre-adjustment world certain values were deemed to be ends in themselves, in the post-adjustment situation values were relative. Thus whereas education had previously been valued as an end in itself, in the post-adjustment world education became solely a means to a high income. Similarly, and as occurred in the UK also, the old professional occupations which once carried high status, such as teaching, lost standing when status itself became liquid, something that could only be evaluated in terms of the universal measure of money. Thus, as Lea and Young also noted more than 20 years ago (Lea and Young 1984), industrial craft skills also lose their integral value as a source of self-worth. In such a liquid world identity and self-worth are at risk.

The argument here (see also Cain and Howe 2008) is that violence is one way of asserting identity, of insisting upon being noticed: commanding 'respect', as the saying goes. There is long-standing evidence for such a relationship. Franz Fanon (1961/5) observed a similar phenomenon among the freedom fighters in the Algerian War of Independence: I bleed, therefore I am; I kill, therefore I am; I die, therefore .... Peter and Favert write of a surge in murders by women ('ogresses') after the French Revolution, a time when the sign of signs, the king, was negated in a 'prodigious reversal of all signs' (1973/8: 186). Liquid identity demands a moment in which it can be fixed, perhaps for eternity.

The two problems, of securing material necessities and of fixing identity, which arise for those at the bottom when a society is polarised, can be addressed by 'criminal' means. There is, however, a third process, discussed most clearly in Harriott's work, also on Jamaica, and this process he calls 'embedding' (Harriott 1996). Harriott's data relate to the embedding of violence in particular urban constellations, in a situation where politics has always been territorial (rather than class-based as in the UK, or ethnicity based as in Trinidad and Tobago). Perverse integration was facilitated in Jamaica by its proximity to the USA, by the residence of many people of Jamaican origin in the US, and by the possibility within the US for anyone to buy a gun over the counter, without any licensing system. Kin and friendship ties enabled the easy – if illegal – importation of both guns and drugs into and out of Jamaica. This was mapped onto the territorial bases of local and political power, and the violence engendered by the sudden immiseration became embedded. Whether or not it still involves identity issues, it is now also and primarily a means of securing a position in a highly competitive and lucrative trade in illegal narcotics. As a result of embedding, self-assertive crime acquires an instrumental dimension as well as its primary expressive one.

Compounding occurs when these processes impact negatively upon each other, as for example when someone contributing to a family by illegal means is imprisoned, thereby reducing the family's income and adding to the workload of women who will now have to add prison visiting to their list; or when someone makes contacts in prison which enhance his ability to engage in illegal activities on release; or when illegal earnings are so much more profitable than legal ones – particularly so in the case of criminal justice workers in a cash-strapped state – that the perversion of formal justice by bribery ensues (Griffiths 1996, 1997); or when such a perversion leads to the withdrawal of respect or consent so that illegal money-making can seem justified. And round again.

The point is, of course, that once embedding and compounding set in, the process cannot simply be reversed by an improved economic situation (although that last is of course, a prerequisite for any reversal).

The four processes of a rise in instrumental crime, an increase in violence as a response to a liquefied identity, the embedding of either or both, and the compounding of these problems, vary from region to region, from nation to nation. In the next section I explore the ways in which the capacity of structurally adjusted societies to deal with these issues has also been weakened.

Structural adjustment and the nation state

The conditionalities of structural adjustment loans from the IMF and the World Bank weaken the central state itself in the nations which borrow funds from these global lending institutions. Some of this weakening is intended, since the ideology governing the IMF/World Bank through the 1980s and 1990s to the late 2000s was that of a free market supported by a small state. This ideology, of course, ignored the significant role of public enterprises in regimes of 'all political persuasions' and not least in the more recently industrialised countries, such as India, Brazil, Mexico and even Taiwan in its early industrialising years (Chang 2003: 201). The role of the Chinese state in planning and orchestrating industrial development and foreign investment is also well known. Nonetheless, the ideology of a self-adjusting free market has been central to the IMF/World Bank lending policies.

For this reason the sale of public service industries, such as water and electricity supply, has been a conditionality of all structural adjustment loans, with one short-term result being an increase in unemployment. Another result has been the transfer of the responsibility for finding investment capital from the central state to the consumer. In post-adjustment nations where taxation bands have been flattened out and taxes on purchases imposed instead, this means that lower-paid workers as a whole now have to meet a greater proportion of future investment costs than was the case when these costs were met by governments funded by more steeply graduated taxation regimes.

A more immediate result is the shrinking or partial privatisation of essential public services such as health and education in recipient nations. These changes have exacerbated the inequalities of well-being within as well as between nations. Such changes inevitably involve harm to children, women, the aged and the already poor. In a position paper for the Human Development Report of 2003, Pettifor and Greenhill (2002/3) point out that of the nations borrowing under the 'Highly Indebted Poor Countries Initiative' (HIPC) the goal of halving the number of undernourished citizens by the millennium had been reached by only one (Ghana). Sixteen other nations were 'on track', two 'lagging', twelve 'far behind', and seven 'slipping back' having made some progress. In relation to the goal of 'sustainable access to drinking water' one billion people still have no safe supply while 'almost three billion people – half the world's population – lack adequate sanitation' (p. 29). All this is in spite of 15 documented multilateral 'debt reduction' and loan initiatives between 1969 and 1999, following each other with increasing frequency, with two different initiatives in both 1996 and 1999. *None of these loan schemes, however, suspended the terms under which the loans were granted –* the infamous conditionalities. Pettifor and Greenhill conclude that 'attempts by creditors to resolve the sovereign debt crisis' have 'failed miserably', mainly because the underlying ideology has not changed, and the donor agencies themselves have not been sensitive to the priorities of the recipient nations.[14]

There is a policy implication here too. In the same year (2002) Birdsall *et al.* note that 'in spite of reschedulings and reductions' in debt service in the years leading up to and just after the millennium, in fact 'debt service owed to official creditors [had] risen' (p. 6): in particular the proportion of debt owed to the multilateral agencies. Repayments had to be squeezed from domestic budgets, the alternative being borrowing more money to make repayments on the books, thereby increasing the total debt outstanding, and round again.

Bilateral donors, to avoid this outcome, increasingly gave grants for specific projects. This strategy, however, while avoiding the worst of the economic knock-on effects, created a problem in situations where the projects 'reflected donor priorities more than government priorities' (Birdsall *et al.* 2002: 7).

In this way the central states of nations which owe money to the agencies of the global state are weakened not only by the loss of functions, the loss of personnel owing to 'right sizing' and the loss of taxation revenue as the rich pay less and the poor also pay less if they are not employed. They are also weakened by the methods of donation used by their would-be helpers. Deborah Brautigam (2000) argues that both multilateral and in particular bilateral donors have, by lending directly to, or for the use of, particular regional authorities or state agencies, weakened both democracy and the state itself. Monies donated for specific purposes in this way do not have to pass through parliament: when a substantial part of the national spend is not debated in and approved by parliament, the most important agency of the central state – the true site of democracy – is weakened; when a substantial part of the national spend does not pass through the treasury, i.e. is 'off the books' of the national government, a space is created for the subversion of central state priorities, for non-accountable spending and, at worst, for corruption. In other words, Brautigam argues that the IMF/World Bank and the bilateral national and transnational funders are, in their historic mistrust of the state, deploying criminogenic lending strategies. First-world lending strategies are causing both immiseration and corruption on a scale not observed before that intervention.

Equally important from the criminological point of view is the strain put upon the social control agencies of the state by the increased number of crimes, and by the change in the types of crime that structural adjustment has brought about. The data from Trinidad and Tobago, presented in Table 40.2, reveal the suddenness of the changes. The impact on a justice system which simultaneously was denied the resources to expand was, in some Caribbean nations, little short of disastrous (Griffiths 1996, 1997). One result was deteriorating conditions for accused and convicted alike: longer waiting periods for a trial in an already overcrowded remand prison; eight convicted men or more to a prison cell without internal sanitation (Hagley 1996). If even an adequate prison environment can provide an education in criminality, the circumstances described above would surely enhance the probability of recidivism. And in addition to these inevitable consequences of a rising crime rate, Cain and Birju (1992) present data indicating that longer sentences, i.e. an increase in punitiveness, were another consequence of these dramatic structural changes in that society.

These problems are shared worldwide, although the scale of them and the resources available to cope with them vary. Griffiths (1996, 1997) notes that corruption of police and court personnel is also not unusual – a sign that the state has not so much overreached itself as been overreached by events. The response of donor agencies has been to pour money into policing – both training and the 'placing' of UK officers to bolster the structure at key points. This has had limited success in Jamaica (Harriott 2000). The evidence from Trinidad and Tobago is not yet available. The ambiguity in relation to whether this strengthens or further weakens the local state is obvious: all depends on the level and appropriateness of the skills transfer.

Beyond even these harms to the democratic institutions of nations which have experienced structural adjustment is the harm wrought in any nation by civil war. Trinidad and Tobago experienced a successful but short-lived coup by a Muslim faction four years after being structurally adjusted (1990). Fitzgerald (1999) noted, as we have done, that sudden changes in economic circumstances cause economic uncertainty and create a perceived injustice on the part of particular ethnic or other social groups or regions, while at the same time weakening the capacity of the central state to deliver order. He points out that of the 48 least developed countries identified by the United Nations, 24 have had serious conflicts in the last 30 years, and that one in three of the low-income countries identified by the World Bank have also had this experience. The nation state, unable any longer to deliver public well-being, loses its legitimacy and is vulnerable to internal attack and the development of 'perverse' forms of integration such as drug trading or gun running (Castells 2003: 350). Because of the state's inability to redistribute income between regions it is vulnerable to schism (Fitzgerald 1999).

More recently Abouharb and Cingranelli (2007) have explored the impact of structural adjustment programmes (SAPs) on human rights, their main finding being that economic and social rights are adversely affected by SAPs, but not civil and political rights. The findings from their statistical analysis support the earlier results of Fitzgerald: 'Countries that entered into structural adjustment agreements with the World Bank or IMF faced an increased probability of rebellion' (1999: 165). In addition, these weakened states had a higher incidence of low-level protest and violence than matched countries with no such agreement. Moreover, the longer a nation is subject to an SAP the more 'years of anti-government demonstrations, riots, and rebellion' they experience (p. 166).

Why is this the case? Partly it is so because the people have experienced a falling standard of living, poorer health and education services, and a greater personal insecurity because of the increase in crimes of violence which always occurs after structural adjustment. In other words, the people have real grievances and they express them. But beyond this, these adjusted states, especially after long periods of adjustment as these data demonstrate, lack the capacity either to take firm action or to remedy the social ills which are the cause of the disaffection. These states, as a direct result of the new focus on alleviation for the poor, increasingly lack the capacity to make long-term investments which will change the situation for the future. Loans now come with specific poverty alleviation objectives. The nations which have suffered deep and long-term adjustment can no longer choose, say, to build a road to attract investment and create jobs. Their policies are determined by the donors. The policymaking parliamentary machinery is thereby bypassed; the state's best personnel leave to work for international aid agencies where the pay is better and where their skills can be put to use, while the only organ that has the potential for producing a democratically chosen path is further weakened, from within as well as without. Abouharb and Cingranelli's results should come as no surprise.

If the ideological aim of the donor agencies was to weaken states to allow the free play of capital, then that aim has in some part been achieved, although capital itself eschews those regions with unstable or vulnerable governments. As a strategy for development, therefore, this one was doomed from the outset.

The harms 'achieved' by these policies do not stop here. Del Olmo (1998), for example, documents the environmental harm caused in Latin America by drug cropping, and in particular by the policing of drug cropping using intensive sprays. If drugs were not illegal and the price of drugs were consequently lower, much of this could be avoided. When the health of a population is ravaged by the AIDS virus and the government lacks the resource either to mount an educational campaign or to supply anti-retroviral drugs, then the harm arising from such a misallocation of resources amounts to genocide by default.

And so the tragic story goes on.

Of crimes, harms and culpability

Edwin Sutherland's famous definition of a social harm (1949/61) requires a 'legal description of the act as socially harmful' and the 'legal provision of a penalty' (p. 31). These descriptions and provisions do not have to be part of the criminal law: any use of harm language, whether noun or adjective, in any branch of the law will suffice; in addition to 'crime' he cites terms such as 'infringement', 'misdemeanour', 'discrimination', 'wilful appropriation' and 'false'. Law is concerned, he argues, with 'the common welfare of society' (p. 32) and all actions described as contrary to this in a legal document constitute social harm. This conception of a social harm is supplemented and strengthened by the further requirement (p. 36) that a penal sanction be provided for any breach. Typically, Sutherland's conception of a sanction is equally broad: not just a criminal sentence but also sanctions for non-compliance with a civil order, or applications to the court for enforcement of an order (p. 36). In other words, for Sutherland a 'harm' is legally constituted by both rule and sanction. Such harms are the proper objects of criminological study, since what becomes a matter of criminal law and what remains subject to other legal rules is a matter of politics not intellectual value.

Sutherland's concept of a social harm has re-emerged in the work of progressive criminologists over the years (recent examples include Green and Ward 2000, and Hillyard *et al.* 2004, who both eschewed the legal criterion). The harm concept persists in criminology because it is grounded in a traditional, but still important, jurisprudential principle: it is grounded in 'the common welfare of society' (Sutherland 1949/61: 86). What that common welfare or good itself consists in is open to debate: indeed, it is a familiar enough exam question in jurisprudence. All are agreed, however, that the common good requires that different parts of a society, as recognisable collectivities, must all participate in and shape that good. According to Finnis (1980), for example, a society which polarises its citizens, and excludes whole sections of them from what are self-evidently 'basic forms of ... human well-being' (p. 45), such as access to knowledge or spirituality or life and health, or 'practical reasonableness', could not be just. Crucially, in the context of structural adjustment, Finnis argues that in a just society, one which seeks the maximisation of all human goods,[15] 'impartiality' is essential. It would be contrary to the 'good of practical reasonableness' to favour any one 'good' above another: all must be held in balance within each life and within a society. Crucially in the context of the current argument, he also argues that 'impartiality between the subjects' who may be partakers of the goods is also essential. The self-realisation of one person (or a group of people) cannot be at the expense of another. Societies which are internally polarised are unjust.

By the same token it may be argued that an institution of world governance which denies the 'good' of life itself to some nations or some citizens (e.g. access to clean drinking water or to knowledge about and medication for AIDS) is unjust. The institutions of global economic governance, therefore, in bringing about the progressive immiseration of certain global citizens – albeit some others fare better – stand condemned as unjust, as perpetrating acts of injustice on a global scale as measured by these most rigorous intellectual criteria.

The question that must therefore be asked is: did these global agencies, acting on our collective behalf, realise what unjust outcomes their policies were (and are) bringing about? Or did they have the opportunity to find out what outcomes their policies were producing? We cannot claim that the global agencies are guilty of either global crime or global deviance unless it can be demonstrated that they knew what the effects of their policies would be at the time these policies were put into practice, at the time a loan was granted only upon the condition of implementing 'structural adjustment'. If it can be shown that they knew, or could/should have known, the effects of their policies, then they have perpetrated culpable harms. If a sanction is available, then these harms, following Sutherland (1949/61), could best be described as global crimes. This would be the case for war crimes arising from a conflict made possible and more likely by the weakening of a central state apparatus. In the light of the findings of Fitzgerald (1999) and Abouharb and Cingranelli (2007) it even seems possible that the global state agencies may be indirectly responsible for war crimes. However, it is the actual perpetrator – rather than the creators of the situation which generates the crime – who alone, as I understand it, has the capacity to be charged with a war crime. Even in a case of being ultimately responsible for a war crime, therefore, neither the leading shareholders nor the officials of the global state agencies can be deemed responsible for a global crime according to Sutherland's very strict conception, including the availability of a penal sanction. By now, 2009, the evidence is clear and global censure certain. Technically, therefore, this is global deviance as defined by Green and Ward (2000) – a concept that most surely seems inadequate to the harm, the war crime, indirectly but so surely perpetrated. It is not the concept which is at fault, however. The feeling that the technical concept 'deviance' does not capture the horror of what is alleged demonstrates most powerfully the risks – the deathly dangers – of leaving governance of the world's economies to an organisation which is accountable only to its most powerful members.

To develop the analysis further, a failure by a poor signatory state to implement the Convention on the Rights of the Child would most probably be dealt with by relatively gentle censure and the assistance of officials of the Committee (Hamarberg 1995). The censure and the publication of the report would rightly bring such a case within the definition of a global crime, being dealt with by restorative justice. The point is clear: the agencies of the United Nations, the – more or less – democratic organisation of global governance, respond in an appropriate way to global crimes and can be held to account by their members if they fail to do so. The self-governing agencies of the economic arm of the global state answer to no one.

The unanswered question in this connection is: did the economic agencies of the global state, the IMF and the World Bank in particular, know or have the opportunity to know how disastrous for the poor the outcomes of their policy would be? There are two kinds of suggestive evidence that they did indeed know. The first is the development of one reform to the Highly Indebted Poor Countries Initiative after another throughout the 1980s and 1990s, as we have already discussed (Birdsall *et al.* 2002). They knew that something in the formula was not working, and yet, whatever other tinkering with the formula took place, the basic tenets of structural adjustment programmes remained the same: shrink the state, both at its central core and in its service delivery agencies; privatise public utilities; eradicate steeply graduated taxation and replace with a tax (VAT) which the poor pay too; insist upon non-reciprocal opening of borders to imported goods (not all export products from the developing world are allowed to compete freely in the US); float the exchange rate, and so on. Surely, when all the changes that could otherwise be made had been tried, it should have occurred to someone, whether politician or official, to query these basic tenets? It occurred most certainly to those on the receiving end, as the nations involved in the SAPRIN Report (2002/4) attempted to show.

SAPRIN (the Structural Adjustment Participatory Review International Network) based their research on deep consultation with a wide range of civil society organisations. In the Introduction (p. 4) the authors note that although the 'so called Washington Consensus' behind the structural adjustment policies was at the time of the review already 'dissolving', 'the main components of aid programmes remain firmly in place as conditions of continued lending by aid agencies' (p. 4). This seems to suggest that the World Bank/IMF knew the harm they were doing and continued to do it. In the end, the report is a well documented account of the failure of these policies across the nine participating countries.

In spite of having approved the methodology for what was to have been a joint report, the Bank began to withdraw from its commitment as soon as the largely negative results of the evaluation were made known to it, and 'senior Bank managers failed to participate in discussions of the report's findings with the twenty SAPRIN representatives who had travelled to Washington for the meeting, and the Bank officially withdrew from SAPRIN as the report was delivered'.

The qualitative method of collecting evidence, by hearing direct experiences in meetings and various public fora, may not have appealed to the Bank, although they certainly had early notification of it. It seems more likely, however, that they withdrew because they did not like the results, because they wanted to distance themselves from them, or even to be in a position to say that they had not heard them officially, the formal connection having been broken in the nick of time to prevent this (SAPRIN 2002/4: 33). The poor in person, I suppose, are always discomforting to the rich.

It is, of course, the major donor nations who have most votes, as we have seen, and therefore determine the policies that officials follow. And clearly if the officials did not receive the report then there is no way that their paymasters could know about it – at least officially. It may also be the case that the methodology, while known in advance, was not trusted. On the other hand, there is in the academic literature some, cautiously presented, evidence that at least one senior official of the World Bank was not, by the turn of the millennium, one hundred per cent committed to the structural adjustment recipe. There is also ample evidence derived from sophisticated econometric models which demonstrates that structural adjustment, so far from assisting recipient nations, is actually causing their economies to deteriorate. Finally, there is circumstantial evidence that the policymaking nations themselves were, and at the time of writing still are, in denial as to the reasons for their policies so often producing deterioration rather than improvement in the economies of recipient nations. The evidence on these three points is presented briefly below.

William Easterly, whose 2006 book *The White Man's Burden* makes clear his view that structural adjustment conditionalities have damaged the nations to whom the loans were given, appears to have held similar views when working as a senior official in the IMF. In 2000, Easterly concluded that as a result of adjustment conditionalities, the ability of the poor within a given nation to reap benefits from a growing economy would be reduced and that this 'might increase the support of the poor for populist experiments at re-distributing income',[16] which I interpret as enhancing the possibility of civil unrest. In 2005 another careful analysis by Easterly found no evidence of 'per capita growth' improving with repeated structural adjustment loans (p. 7), and the other objectives such as improving tax collection, reducing corruption, or reforming 'inefficient and loss prone financial systems' did not occur (p. 20). By 2006 he records actual harm, as opposed to failure to achieve success. The point is a simple one, that Easterly's views would have been known to his colleagues at the IMF and doubtless also at the World Bank. Of the IMF/World Bank's internal practices for processing knowledge nothing is known. However, these clues suggest that the push to continue with these policies may have come from the political masters, the major shareholding nations, rather than the senior staff of these institutions. In either case, the question 'why the blindness' occurs.

Perhaps the agencies of the global state found the evidence cited so far in this paper unconvincing. Perhaps they can accept only sophisticated econometric analyses? That could explain their failure to accept the SAPRIN report, even though they agreed the methodology with the Network in advance. Perhaps the correlations between structural adjustment, declining standards of health and increased probabilities of civil strife did not convince them. Perhaps

Easterly, despite his senior position, was regarded internally as a maverick. Perhaps those working for UN agencies are regarded as biased, although a bias in favour of democracy and social welfare might be adjudged by others to be a good thing. But even if one grants them all these implausible points there remains no justification for not knowing the negative effects of their policies. This is because there are at least three first-class, methodologically impeccable, econometric studies which document the economic effects of structural adjustment, which demonstrate that even the economic outcomes which were (and are) sought after have not been achieved. Indeed, on these economic indicators too, structural adjustment programmes have demonstrably made matters worse.

What is the evidence? Lundberg and Squire (2003) show that, as in the UK, inequality can increase even while an economy grows. The methods are impeccable and the findings clear. At an even earlier date (2000) Garuda published his findings that nations under structural adjustment both increased inequalities – polarised societies as in Trinidad and Tobago – and reduced the incomes for the poor, compared with counterpart countries which did not 'enter the Fund': in effect that structural adjustment makes inequality greater and poverty worse.

Also in 2000 Przeworski and Vreeland demonstrated that:

1 'countries which never experienced IMF programmes grew the fastest' (p. 402);

2 'for any number of years already under the programme (1–8) the observed rates of growth during the next four years were lower if it remained under than if it left' (p. 402);

3 'these programmes reduce growth while countries remain under (the programme) and do not return benefits that would compensate the losses once they leave' (p. 403);

4 'once countries leave the programme they grow faster than if they had remained, but not faster than they would have without participation' (p. 385), i.e. they do not grow fast enough to compensate for their losses while under the programme;

5 there is no evidence of policy change within the agencies apart from a 1993 statement by the Executive Board of the IMF to the effect that in 1991 it had decided that the 1979 guidelines on conditionalities 'remain broadly appropriate' (p. 404).

In sum, the data the IMF/World Bank needed in order to recognise that their policies were, and are, failing have been around for almost a decade. They have tinkered with many aspects of their programmes, but as yet they have neither abandoned nor modified the structural adjustment conditionalities. I conclude that these agencies are guilty of committing culpable harms.

Further evidence that the global policymakers – the major donors to the IMF/World Bank – are in denial as to the harms that demonstrably arise as a direct result of their policies also comes from a background paper for the Human Development Report Office of the UNDP (Pettifor and Greenhill 2002/3). For a start, 'by 2000 developing countries as a whole were paying out seven times more in debt service than they were receiving in aid, a sharp increase from the ratio of only 3.6 in 1995' (p. 6). But this is by now a familiar story, and some waiving of arrears has since taken place. I repeat, what have not changed to date are the conditionalities themselves. In 1996 the global funding agencies launched the Highly Indebted Poor Countries Initiative, which allowed the cancellation of multilateral debts. By 1999 the Jubilee 2000 campaign for debt cancellation was underway, and HIPC II (the 'enhanced' HIPC initiative) was launched, with a focus on 'poverty reduction' (p. 15), and President Clinton, closely followed by the leaders of other developed nations, led the way in debt cancellation. In 2001 the HIPC programme was 'topped up' (p. 13). So the story goes, and so the situation for the poorest nations deteriorates, for structural adjustment remains the condition for receiving help. It is this constant repetition of more of the same old conditionalities, the same belief in the same failed recipe which fails to set the jam, raise the cake or even adequately to fry the chips. So far, despite arguments and evidence from NGOs, academics and the poor themselves, there has been an absolute refusal to cancel the anti-state conditionalities which undermine the effectiveness of any loan offered by incapacitating the very organisation which alone could ensure the application of a sustained policy – the nation state. Instead, policy is made by donors, who may insist that all the money donated is diverted to the poor, when perhaps a longer-term solution to the problem might be to spend it on the building of infrastructure to attract industry or to assist agriculture. The poor of Africa, in particular, are quite literally by now being killed by western kindness.

Reforms of the global lending arrangements and why they do not work

So far this chapter has demonstrated the long duration of the processes of immiseration which have moved so many nations from the status of less developed but developing to highly indebted and poor. Evidence has been produced revealing not only that structural adjustment loan conditionalities have been the cause of this epidemic of poverty, but also that this evidence was in large part of a kind that would satisfy the strict methodological criteria deployed these days in economics and econometric research. The voices of the poor have also been available to be heard by the lending institutions, not only as interpreted by western NGOs,[17] but also directly via the pathbreaking research methodologies designed by SAPRIN to capture directly their sentiments and their lived experiences. Both large-scale academic studies and those based on smaller samples have revealed that this wanton immiseration has encouraged tribalism, ethnic violence and segmentation, as well as raised levels of 'everyday' disorder and criminality. Over this thirty years of policy-led immiseration some of these patterns of violence and crime have become structurated, or embedded. Whatever the next steps may be, the problems to be solved now are worse than those which started in the 1970s, and subsequently got worse year on year as a fully developed economic ideology, flying in the face of emergent evidence, was brought to bear upon them. This evidence shows that both by criminological criteria and by jurisprudential criteria the global lending agencies are culpable: either they made a choice to continue with policies which they knew would wreak economic havoc, or they actively or by default chose to disregard the evidence. That the latter has been the case is suggested by Pettifor and Greenhill (2002/3). Debt cancellation, first attempted in 1978 by means of 'retroactive terms adjustments' (p. 13) continued under various schemes launched by the United States and the World Bank. However, these schemes did little to assist the recipients. Indeed, the bilateral US 'Brady Plan' of 1989 'did little to reduce the debt burden. It simply decreased the burden of commercial debt – and thus the exposure of commercial banks – while increasing debts owed to multilateral institutions' (p. 14). Behind the scenes there was private commercial capital. This suggests that private capital, behind the scenes but becoming visible briefly here, may be a driver of these counterproductive policies.

After Brady came the first HIPC (Highly Indebted Poor Countries) initiative in 1996, 'a comprehensive debt relief initiative' (p. 14) which proved to be 'completely ineffective, largely as a result of falls in the price of the commodities produced by poorer countries', now prohibited under free-trade rules from keeping the price up by supply-side controls. By now the world had got the message, and the calls from civil society to cancel debt were much harder to ignore. HIPC II was introduced, coupled to 'Poverty Reduction Strategies', which were still pegged to the requirements of donors rather than to the needs of the immiserated citizens of recipient countries. The structural adjustment conditionalities which have so incapacitated nation states remained.

This – the bankers' focus – has been the problem of all multilateral lending. If you are a bank it is your job to get your money back over the long term and, indeed, to make a profit. World Bank/IMF 'profits' are not redistributed to donor nation shareholders as in a commercial bank, but the model of doing business is the same. The alternative model for assistance would be to ask 'how much would be needed and for how long to achieve this specific objective?' Such a lending strategy could monitor concrete progress and defer repayment until the objective had been achieved – i.e. project-specific loans but for social welfare projects, ideally those chosen by the parliament of the recipient nation: every child has five years of primary education, for example, with learning materials in the child's own language. This could connect with Brautigam's strategy, discussed earlier, leading to a strengthening of the Department of Education, both centrally and locally, as part of the scheme. The projects would have to be ordered into a priority sequence by the national governments. Or would all this look too much like a Five Year Plan, dreaded since the emergence of the old Soviet Union as a world power after the Second World War? The current clean drinking water project is led by NGOs, most health projects by the World Health Organisation. Targeting appears to be effective when sustained over the long haul, but for the continuation of success into the indefinite future a simultaneous strengthening of the nation state is essential.

More on what is to be done? Towards control of the global lending agencies

The conclusion of this argument is that the economic institutions of the global state have been culpably deviant over at least twenty years, allowing for a decade before the failure of the structural adjustment conditionalities for lending became apparent. It is now time to devise a mechanism to hold them to account.

As I write, nations with fewer shares and therefore fewer votes in the IMF/World Bank are demanding a bigger voice, and this would plainly help to rebalance the lending policies of the two global multilaterals. It would help these institutions to make better judgments; it would help too if it led to better representation of developing nations on the staff, preferably on a medium-term temporary basis. But such changes would not amount to the kind of democratic structure required to invent a system of global banking which puts the needs of developing and indebted countries at its heart, while still maintaining its viability as a bank. It is also time to resituate the global economic institutions within a democratic framework, for their non-accountable status will always leave them vulnerable to the latest fashionable theory. Pettifor and Greenhill (2002/3: 36–8) offer a plausible starting point for reform, which, crucially, also advocates formal connections with other agencies. Below I paraphrase, expand and comment on their proposals.

In the first place, the resolution of a sovereign nation's debt crisis should be treated in an ad hoc, case-by-case way and this dispute resolution process should be overseen by the Secretary General of the UN.

In this way the sovereignty of the debtor nation(s) would be acknowledged, as well as each nation's particular needs in relation to honouring its international obligations (rights of the child; treatment of prisoners), while the entitlements of the donor agencies would also be acknowledged and explored. Recipient nations could move to resolving their debts.

A court drawn from a UN-agreed panel and with personnel approved by both parties would guarantee the rights of the parties, propose solutions and, crucially, be responsible for monitoring the progress of the agreement. Pettifor and Greenhill (2002/3: 36) suggest the court should have enforcement powers. As earlier discussed, this is not the UN way. But both the UN and its agencies have many powers to nudge and cajole, to name and shame. In extreme cases, a panel of the General Assembly should be the final court of appeal. Donor nations also have powers to withhold payments, or a UN-backed monitoring group could be placed alongside officials of a recalcitrant nation state. The powers of the UN are indeed both huge and gentle – a truly earth-moving Suffolk Punch of an organisation, and I say that with affection.

The third proposal (p. 36) is that sovereign debtors should have 'an unconditional right to petition the UN via the Secretary General for protection from creditors'. Such a petition would set in train the process described above.

The fourth is that it will be the responsibility of the Secretary General to oversee appointments panels, ensuring fair representation for each party, to oversee the panels' work using human rights standards, and to publish reports of petition, process and outcome. In so managing and overseeing the process the Secretary General would conduct an independent assessment of the debtor nation's 'debt sustainability', and of the debtor nation's rate of progress towards the new universal minimum standard, the Millennium Development Goals.

A difficult issue will be location; Europe and the United States as sites of such procedures advantage wealthy states-parties, as they can afford to support a large staff in an expensive location (Harris-Short 2001). A less expensive location which still provides all the amenities for complex negotiations and long-term security guarantees is required. Perhaps it is time for the UN to set up one of its agencies in the East.

A role for the IMF is proposed as an interim donor when a sovereign debtor petitions for a 'standstill' in its debt repayments, pending a full adjudicator process (Pettifor and Greenhill 2002/3). A court as described above could guarantee that the IMF be repaid first when the crisis is past and, crucially, should also ensure equity in the conditions of any such loan. The final two points proposed deal with the details of debt rescheduling and immunity.

A move towards the establishment of such a restorative justice process under the auspices of the United Nations would have the following advantages:

1 The procedure would be public.
2 The procedure would be democratic: under the procedure rich and poor nations would negotiate as formal equals.
3 The objectives of the process would be clear: the achievement of internationally established goals by a non-confrontational process.
4 Decisions of the global economic agencies would be subject to scrutiny on grounds of justice and equitability in the event of a dispute.
5 The publicity surrounding the process would encourage both justice and compliance by the parties to the dispute.
6 The United Nations itself would benefit in terms of credibility and prestige if the court came to be regarded as a fair and final arbiter in economic matters.

In the end, the incipient democracy of the UN is our only ground of hope for global justice. It is not perfect, but by using it we strengthen and shape it to the needs of the twenty-first century. Any other site for global justice would weaken it further. In truth, we have no choice, but we are fortunate in the one choice that we do have.

Selected further reading

This paper will be more useful to students who become familiar with the two concepts which underpin this discussion: the concept of state crime and the (much earlier) concept of social harm. A third concept, that of the global state, has its roots in Marxist theory of the 1970s rather than in criminology.

Stan Cohen first developed the concept of 'crimes of the state' in 1993, a concept which has been elaborated most notably by Green and Ward (2004) and again by Green (2008). The discussion turns on the distinction between crime and deviance, and the presence or absence of a superordinate political capacity to define the actions of states as criminal, that is to say a law-making capacity. Key texts are Cohen's (1993) 'Human rights and crimes of the state: the culture of denial', Green's (2008) 'Women and natural disasters: state crime and discourses in vulnerability' in M. Cain and A. Howe (eds). See also Green and Ward's (2004) *State Crime: Governments, Violence and Corruption*.

The criminological concept of social harm was developed by Edwin Sutherland, whose work is cited in the text and references. A valuable recent discussion and elaboration of the concept can be found in the editorial Introduction to Hillyard *et al.* (2004) *Beyond Criminology: Taking Harm Seriously*. In this text harm is pegged definitionally to the *experience of victims*. The difference between this and the definition of Sutherland (1948) and, much later, of Cain and Howe (2008) is between those who seek a legal definition of harm, however broadly 'legal' may be defined, and those who argue that harms are best identified and defined by the victims. Green and Ward's work, defining social rather than legal definitions of harm as deviance even when a state is the perpetrator, offers a third option. This is an important debate between scholars who all agree, as Hillyard *et al.* so cogently put it, that 'much harm is the wreckage of neo-liberal globalisation' (Hillyard *et al.* 2004: 3), and that those constellations of power known as states perpetrate most of it.

The concept of the *global state*, used but scarcely developed here, has its roots in 1970s Marxism and the concepts of state apparatuses defined in terms of their dominant practice (or 'function', in the language of the day). Nicos Poulantzas' work may be a difficult place to start for those not familiar with the theoretical idiom of the time, but his influence undeniably remains in my own thinking (Poulantzas 1974/5). At an even deeper level, and perhaps less immediately applicable, is the work of Antonio Gramsci, who aided the sociological analysis of emergent state forms (such as the global state) empirically as well as theoretically by pointing out in *Selections from the Prison Notebooks* (1971: 186) that every new form of state develops a new type of functionary alongside the old. Sociologists and criminologists are particularly skilled in studying types of functionary, and research in this area, as well as theoretical development, is urgently needed (see also Cain 1983). Over to you, Reader.

Notes

1 At the time of writing (October 2008) these were Belgium, Burkino Faso, Costa Rica, Croatia, Indonesia, Italy, Libyan Arab Republic, Panama, South Africa and Vietnam.

2 Convention on the Elimination of all forms of Discrimination Against Women (1979).

3 Varying numbers of signatories are required for a Convention or Treaty to become law, as specified within each document. Ratification commits a state to abide by the terms of the document. The Convention on the Rights of the Child (1989) has been ratified by more nations than any other Convention. To date only Somalia has not ratified. See Sedley (2005) on the basis of the moral force of treaty rights.

4 UNCTAD: United Nations Conference on Trade and Development.

5 UNIFEM: United Nations Development Fund for Women.

6 UNESCO: United Nations Educational, Social and Cultural Organisation.

7 The publication of Committee findings of non-compliance is the main sanction, leaving international politics to take their course based upon this 'naming and shaming'. Permanent officials serving the Committees are available for guidance. There is also the more positive incentive of project funding.

8 In the UK, it must be remembered, between 1688 when Parliamentary Sovereignty was conceded by the Crown in the Bill of Rights, to 1928 when full female suffrage was granted on an equal basis with men, there was, as with the UN, the potential for democracy but not its realisation. Ongoing changes in the constitution of the House of Lords reveal that the process of democratisation is still – and perhaps always will be – incomplete.

9 As at 14 October 2009.

10 Japan at 6.02 per cent has the largest single nation holding after the United States.

11 Canada, France, Germany, Italy, Japan, Russia, the UK, the US. Note the absence of China and India. The most recent addition (to the former G7) was Russia.

12 Cain (2008: 26) argues that the repetition of economic policies known to be harmful is 'nothing less than a moral outrage perpetrated on the poor'.

13 This did not happen to a marked degree in Trinidad and Tobago; see Cain and Birju (1992: table 2). The presence of the oil industry in Trinidad, and of strong trades unions, may explain this anomaly.

14 A new round of talks about restructuring the restructuring process was scheduled for the 2009 meeting of the G20 in London. Instead of pressure for changes in the conditionalities, a greater influence for the large and newly prosperous nations such as Brazil, India and China has been mooted, although no specific information has been given (McRae 2008).

15 The seven 'Goods' identified by Finnis are Knowledge, Friendship/sociability, Spirituality/religion/sanctity, Play, Art or aesthetic experience, Life, and Practical reasonableness. I would have added Work/labour.

16 Unnumbered pages.

17 Non-governmental organisations.

References

Abouharb, M. and Cingranelli, C. (2007) *Human Rights and Structural Adjustment.* Cambridge: Cambridge University Press.

Birdsall, N., Claessens, S. and Diwan, I. (2002) *Will HIPC Matter? The Debt Game and Donor Behaviour in Africa.* United Nations, World Institute for Development Economics Research (WIDER).

Brautigam, D. (2000) *Aid Dependence and Governance.* Stockholm: Ministry of Foreign Affairs, Expert Group on Dependence and Governance, Expert Group on Development Issues (EGDI). Distributed by Almquist & Wiksell International, Stockholm.

Brown, L. (1994) 'Crisis, adjustment, and social change: the middle class under adjustment', in E. Le Franc (ed.), *Consequences of Structural Adjustment: A Review of the Jamaican Experience.* Jamaica: Canoe Press.

Cain, M. (1983) 'Towards an understanding of the international state', *International Journal of the Sociology of Law,* 11 (1): 1–10.

Cain, M. (2001/2) 'International crime and globalisation', *Criminal Justice Matters,* 46, Winter, pp. 34–5.

Cain, M. (2008) 'Criminogenesis and the war against drugs', in M. Cain and A. Howe (eds), *Women, Crime and Social Harm: Towards a Criminology for the Global Age.* Oxford: Hart, pp. 21–36.

Cain, M. and Birju, A. (1992) 'Crime and structural adjustment in Trinidad and Tobago', *Caribbean Affairs,* 5 (2): 141–53.

Cain, M. and Howe, A. (2008) 'Introduction', in M. Cain and A. Howe (eds), *Women, Crime and Social Harm: Towards a Criminology for the Global Age*. Oxford: Hart, pp. 1–18.

Campaign Against the Arms Trade (1989) *Death on Delivery: The Impact of the Arms Trade on the Third World*. London: Campaign Against the Arms Trade.

Castells, M. (1998) *End of Millennium*, Vol. III of *The Information Age: Economy, Society and Culture*. Oxford: Blackwell.

Castells, M. (2003) 'The rise of the fourth world', in D. Held and A. McGraw (eds), *The Global Transformations Reader*. Cambridge: Polity, pp. 348–54.

Chang, H.-J. (2003) *Globalisation, Economic Development, and the Role of the State*. London: Zed Books.

Chossudovsky, M. (1997) *The Globalisation of Poverty*. London: Zed Books.

Cohen, S. (1993) 'Human rights and crimes of the state: the culture of denial', *Australian and New Zealand Journal of Criminology*, 26 (1): 97–115.

Deere, C. *et al.* (1990) *In the Shadows of the Sun: Caribbean Development Alternatives and US Policy*. San Francisco: Westview Press.

Del Olmo, R. (1998) 'The economic impact of illicit drug cultivation and crop eradication programmes in Latin America', *Theoretical Criminology*, 2 (2): 269–78.

Dorling, D. (2004) 'Prime suspect: murder in Britain', in P. Hillyard, C. Pantazis, S. Tombs and D. Gordon (eds), *Beyond Criminology: Taking Harm Seriously*. London: Pluto, pp. 178–91.

Easterly, W. (2000) 'The effect of IMF and World Bank programs on poverty'. Online at: http://www.imf.org/external/Pubs/FT/staffp/2000/00-00/e.pdf. (accessed November 2005).

Easterly, W. (2005) 'What did structural adjustment adjust? The association of policies and growth with repeated IMF and World Bank adjustment loans', *Journal of Development Economics*, 76: 1–22.

Easterly, W. (2006) *The White Man's Burden: Why the West's Efforts to Aid the Rest Have Done So Much Ill and So Little Good*. Oxford: Oxford University Press

Ellis, P. (2003) *Women, Gender, and Development in the Caribbean*. London: Zed Books.

Fanon, F. (1961/1965) *The Wretched of the Earth*. Harmondsworth: Penguin.

Finnis, J. (1980) *Natural Law and Natural Rights*. Oxford: Clarendon Press.

Fitzgerald, V. (1999) 'Global linkages, vulnerable economies, and the outbreak of conflict', *Development*, 42 (3): 57–64.

Garuda, G. (2000) 'The distributional effects of IMF programs: a cross country analysis', *World Development*, 28 (6): 1031–57.

Gramsci, A. *Selections from the Prison Notebooks*. London: Lawrence Wishart.

Green, P. (1998) *Drugs, Trafficking, and Criminal Policy*. Winchester: Waterside Press.

Green, P. (2008) 'Women and natural disasters: state crime and discourses in vulnerability', in M. Cain and A. Howe (eds), *Women, Crime, and Social Harm: Towards a Criminology for the Global Age*. Oxford: Hart.

Green, P. and Ward, T. (2000) 'State crime, human rights, and the limits of criminology', *Social Justice*, 27 (1): 101–15.

Green P. and Ward, T. (2004) *State Crime: Governments, Violence and Corruption*. London: Pluto.

Griffiths, I. (1996) 'Drugs and criminal justice in the Caribbean', in M. Cain (ed.), *For a Caribbean Criminology*, a special issue of *Caribbean Quarterly*, 42: 23.

Griffiths, I. (1997) *Drugs and Security in the Caribbean: Sovereignty under Siege*. Pennsylvania: University of Pennsylvania Press.

Hagley, L. (1996) 'How the inside affects the outside: prisoners and survivors in Trinidad and Tobago', *Caribbean Quarterly*, 42 (2–3): 131–57.

Hamarberg, T. (1995) 'Foreword', in J. Himes (ed.), *Implementing the Convention on the Rights of the Child: Resource Mobilization in Low Income Countries*. The Hague: Martinus Nijhoff and UNICEF.

Harriott, A. (1996) 'The changing social organisation of crime and criminals in Jamaica', in M. Cain (ed.), *For a Caribbean Criminology*, a special issue of *Caribbean Quarterly*, 42 (23): 54–71.

Harriott, A. (2000) *Police and Crime Control in Jamaica: Problems of Reforming Ex Colonial Constabularies*. Kingston: UWI Press.

Harris-Short, S. (2001) 'Listening to "the Other": THE Convention on the Rights of the Child', *Melbourne Journal of International Law*, 2 (2): 304–50.

Hillyard, P., Pantazis, C., Tombs, S. and Gordon, D. (2004) *Beyond Criminology: Taking Harm Seriously*. London: Pluto.

Kirton, J. (2001) 'Guiding global economic governance: the G20, the G7, and the International Monetary Fund at century's dawn', in J. Kirton and G. von Furstenberg (eds), *New Directions in Global Economic Governance: Managing Globalisation in the Twenty-First Century*. Aldershot: Ashgate, pp. 143–67.

Lea, J. and Young, J. (1984) *What Is to Be Done About Law and Order?* Harmondsworth: Penguin.

Lundberg, M. and Squire, L. (2003) 'The simultaneous evolution of growth and inequality', *Economic Journal*, 113: 326–44.

McRae, H. (2009) 'This recession will hasten the shift to a new economic world order', *The Independent* [London], 17 April, p. 41.

Peter, J.-P. and Favert, J. (1973/1978) 'Comment', in M. Foucault (ed.), *I, Pierre Rivière, Having Slaughtered My Mother, My Sister, and My Brother* ... Harmondsworth: Penguin, pp. 174–98.

Pettifor, A. and Greenhill, R. (2002/3) *Debt Relief and the Millennium Development Goals*, background paper for Human Development Report 2003. Geneva: United Nations Development Programme.

Poulantzas (1974/5) *Classes in Contemporary Capitalism*. London: New Left Books.

Przeworski, A. and Vreeland, J. (2000) 'The effect of IMF programs on economic growth', *Journal of Development Economics*, 62: 385–421.

Robinson, W. (1996) 'Globalisation: nine theses in our epoch', *Race and Class*, 38 (2): 13–31.

Sampson, J. (1994) *Report of the Cabinet Appointed Committee to Examine the Juvenile Delinquency and Youth Crime Situation in Trinidad and Tobago*. Port of Spain: Ministry of Social Development.

SAPRIN (2002/4) *Structural Adjustment: The Policy Roots of Economic Crisis, Poverty, and Inequality*. London: Zed Books.

Sedley, S. (2005) 'Are human rights universal and does it matter?' Holdsworth Club Presidential Address by the Rt Hon. Lord Justice Sedley, University of Birmingham, November.

Sparr, P. (1994) 'Feminist critiques of structural adjustment', in P. Sparr (ed.), *Mortgaging Women's Lives: Feminist Critiques of Structural Adjustment*. London: Zed Books.

Sutherland, E. H. (1949/61) *White Collar Crime*. New York: Holt Rinehart & Winston.

United Nations (1990) *Poverty*, World Development Report 1990. Oxford: Oxford University Press.

Chapter 41

Political protest and crime

P.A.J. Waddington[1]

Introduction: key issues

The relationship of protest to crime is problematic mainly in democratic states (and to an extent their clients): in authoritarian and totalitarian states protest is almost invariably criminal ('counter-revolutionary') activity that is suppressed with hardly any reflection upon its justifiability. It is in democratic societies that espouse a commitment to freedom of speech and assembly that the relationship between protest and crime becomes problematic and it is the purpose of this chapter to explain just how problematic it can become.

Akin to many other topics discussed in this volume, there is no legal category of 'protest crime'. Instead the relationship of protest to crime is complex and fluid. Offences committed in the course of protest span the entire breadth of the law. The least serious tend to be by far the most prevalent: obstructing the highway, failing to give notification of a procession, disorderly behaviour. The most serious are thankfully rare: desecrating a grave, vandalism, intimidation and threats of violence. What gives them their unity and profoundly affects who commits the offence, how, and with what effect is the motivation that lies behind it – political protest. Viewing the 'martyrdom video' of Mohammed Sadique Khan (the leader of the 7 July 2005 London bombers) there can be little doubt as to his political purpose in committing that atrocity.

Motivation, as a defining element, gives rise to three major issues: first, the vast majority of those motivated to protest do so lawfully – indeed it is a civic *virtue*. Doughty protesters are sometime valorised, like Brian Haw whose solitary encampment in Parliament Square in opposition to the Iraq War propelled him to celebrity status. Yet actions that in one context would be virtuous, in another can become heinous: a rhetorical stance can be inspiring or racist demagogy, or, worse still, 'glorification of terrorism'.

Secondly, 'protest crime' is doubly indefinite, because in 'contentious politics' (Tilly 1979, 2004), whether an activity is or is not a crime often becomes a contested issue in itself. For example, in September 1975 four men attempted to rob the 'Spaghetti House' restaurant in London, but were cornered by police, whereupon they took staff hostage at gun-point and a siege ensued. The robbers claimed to be members of the 'Black Liberation Army', demanded an aircraft to take them to Jamaica, and at their eventual trial they refused to acknowledge the legitimacy of the court. They were sentenced to between 17 and 22 years for attempted robbery and no more was heard of this 'terrorist' group in Britain, if it ever existed.[2] Just a couple of months later, four Provisional IRA terrorists were cornered in Balcombe Street, London, where they too took hostages and a siege ensued. They were convicted, but their political motives were never in doubt and they were eventually freed in April 1999 under the terms of the 'Good Friday Agreement'. Thus whether or not a criminal act is *deemed* to be politically motivated, how and by whom, often has a direct and profound impact on how the perpetrators are regarded and treated, even within the criminal justice system, which is *not* to say that those with political motives are necessary treated more leniently.

The same goes for police action to circumscribe or prevent protest: on many occasions arrests are entirely unproblematic, but on others allegations of illegality are directed at the police. One example was the forced removal of banners and flags from those protesting at the visit of President Jiang Zemin in October 1999. Accusations of illegality are frequently exchanged between protesters and the police. This tussle between virtue and depravity is a theme that runs throughout the remainder of this discussion.

A third issue that needs to be highlighted at the outset is that the prominence and political impact of an incident can far eclipse its legal significance. In September 2004 eight protesters gained access to the floor of the House of Commons while legislation to ban hunting with hounds was being debated. The debate was suspended in chaos and confusion as the men were arrested by police. The incident led the broadcast news and was headlines in the newspapers. It was a significant political moment and a very effective act of protest that propelled the issue of the hunting ban to the top of the news agenda. However, the men were charged and eventually convicted of only the most minor public order offences.

Together, these three issues mean that there is no clear subset of protest activity that is distinctively 'criminal'. 'Protest' is a political activity, whether criminal or not, that is explained by *political* processes. So this chapter is located at the intersection of criminology and political science. It draws mainly on that body of literature called 'social movements'. It is my purpose in writing this to draw to the attention of a wider audience the extent of that overlap and the fascinating issues that it arouses. Therefore, as far as possible, I will follow the same outline as other contributions to this volume.

Patterns and trends

About what do people protest, sometimes illegally? Again, the spectrum is indefinite from major global issues to parochial concerns. Protests also span the ideological spectrum, for example proponents and opponents of fox hunting. Protest may reflect secular or religious adherence. It may be directed at foreign states, domestic government policies, private organisations or individuals. Very few protests acquire prominence – the vast majority enjoy only a brief existence in obscurity.

The emergence of modern protest

Yet, amid this diversity and idiosyncrasy, there are discernible patterns, the most striking of which is the emergence of modern forms of protest in the eighteenth century. Before this period protest was almost exclusively localised, mediated by appeals to local notables, exploiting holidays and events that brought people together such as funerals and hangings, and was reactionary – seeking the restoration of the traditional order (Critchley 1970). In less than a lifetime, this traditional template was transformed into protest that was overwhelmingly national, independent, organised and principled – imagining a world better than that which existed and seeking to achieve it through political change (Tilly 1978, 1995). This earth-shaking transformation was facilitated by rapid industrialisation and urbanisation, the spread of literacy, and the rise of the war-fighting imperial state that increasingly intruded into the lives of the population and gave them something to grumble about (Tilly 2004). However, while the growth of the state created new reasons for and provided opportunities to exert influence through protest, so it also protected itself by the growth of laws that could be used to repress protest. So political protest (as we now understand it) and the use of the institutions of criminal justice to regulate it is decidedly a modern phenomenon.

Protest cycles

Just as there are 'crime waves', so too there are periods of intense protest, often accompanied by acute political concerns about 'mob rule', disorder and insecurity. According to Tarrow (1989, 1994), the phenomenon of 'protest cycles' was epitomised by the period during the late 1960s and throughout the 1970s when politics across the western world was thrown into turmoil by mass street protest, governmental instability and political violence. Issues tumbled over one another and left a legacy of new political movements that influenced the political agenda for the remainder of the twentieth century and beyond – minority ethnic civil rights, feminism, gay rights, environmentalism, anti-nuclear and many more. Tarrow argues that such periods have their own 'natural history': the cycle begins with the articulation of new issues by new constituents employing novel tactics that catch the authorities unprepared. Many of these tactics contravene existing law, but others may be so novel that legislators must catch up. These 'early risers' form the kernel around which protest grows as other issues and constituencies attach themselves to the movement.

Growth comes at a price, however, for the issues and constituencies that are attracted to the burgeoning movement tend to be more moderate than those espoused by the 'early risers' and have their own established advocates who strive to regain control of the movement so that it serves their own and their members' interests. Thus the 1960s/1970s protest cycle was initiated by students in the newly expanded higher education sector in America and Europe, but later attracted industrial workers and their trade unions (Tarrow

827

1989; della Porta 1995). These mainstream and established interests added momentum to the movement but were easily bought off by compromises negotiated by political elites. As the movement lost momentum radical factions began to compete to retain influence and did so by becoming ever more militant than their competitors, frequently committing serious criminal offences, especially street-fighting against police and right-wing opponents. Means tended to become substituted for ends, and militants glorified nihilistic violence as well as attracting to their ranks new adherents for whom participation in violence was valued for its own sake.

The end of the cycle was one in which only the hardest militant core remained, as the movement's members generally found the upsurge of violence progressively unpalatable. It concluded with tiny cells of inward-looking militant groups – for instance, the 'Weathermen'/'Weather Underground', 'Red Army Faction', 'Red Brigades' – divorced from and repudiated by the mainstream and hunted down by the police and internal security forces throughout Europe (della Porta 1995). This account of the 1960s and 1970s has striking echoes of David Matza's criminology, with its emphasis on 'drift' and 'labelling' (Wilkins 1964; Matza 1969), as well as notions of 'deviancy amplification' (Young 1971), because in its later stages the pressure exerted by law enforcement created what amounted to a 'private war' between militants and the state in which violence was increasingly used by the militants to rescue captured colleagues or wreak revenge for the deaths of comrades at the hands of the state, which then justified still more violent state repression.

The issue is whether the 1960s and 1970s were *sui generis* or exemplified a more common process. It seemed for a while as though a new protest cycle was beginning to acquire momentum in the 1990s as issues of environmentalism, animal rights, opposition to genetic engineering of crops and global justice began to coalesce. There is a plausible argument that affluence and the collapse of traditional class structures had created new constituencies that spawned 'New Social Movements' with concern for moral issues rather than class interest (Melucci 1989). The 'early risers' of these movements created novel forms of protest such as opponents of the building of roads and airport runways occupying tree tops and constructing tunnels on private land that blurred the distinction between private and public domains and thus the responsibilities of the police and private security (Button and John 2002; Button *et al*. 2002). However, it was not novel tactics that propelled this nascent protest movement onto the political agenda, but a traditional protest demonstration that became a riot – the so-called 'Battle of Seattle' in 1999 (Gillham and Marx 2000; Smith 2001; Waddington 2007). Successive violent protests accompanied meetings of various international organisations such as the World Trade Organisation, the International Monetary Fund and the G8. Then the movement suddenly lost momentum following the infamous attacks of '9/11'. Quite why this atrocity had such a dramatic effect continues to fascinate political analysts (Hadden and Tarrow 2007), but perhaps it testifies most eloquently to the interconnection between protest and wider political events.

Political opportunities

That interconnection is conceptualised as political opportunity structures, perhaps best exemplified by McAdam's analysis of the Civil Rights Movement in the USA (McAdam 1982, 1983, 1986, 1988). This was a movement that, we should remind ourselves, challenged a deeply entrenched mode of domination and did so by committing non-violent breaches of segregationist laws.

There was nothing new about the oppression of African Americans in the Deep South of the USA that explains the eruption of activism during the 1950s and 1960s. What, then, explains the blossoming of that movement? McAdam's answer is that a series of political opportunities arose (some of them paradoxically) that facilitated political mobilisation. First, the cotton industry had undergone changes that weakened the economic and social infrastructure that sustained segregation. Cotton was no longer a staple industry that national political elites needed to support. It was also rapidly becoming mechanised and no longer relied upon a large rural labour force resulting in the migration of African Americans into the towns and cities of the South and further afield to the smokestack industries of the North. Either way, they were no longer so vulnerable to the control of segregationists, for in the cities they concentrated in poor neighbourhoods and were too numerous to control through traditional methods of intimidation such as lynching. In the northern cities they also became a significant political constituency to whom national politicians sought to appeal. Secondly, the Civil Rights Movement reaped the benefit of segregationist institutions, most notably segregated black colleges and churches in which there flourished an African American elite that gave the Civil Rights Movement its embryonic leadership under Martin Luther King. Finally, the time was right: the superpowers were competing internationally for the allegiance of the newly independent former colonies of the European powers, which left America vulnerable to the accusation that oppression of its own citizens was neo-colonial. Legal institutions also played a direct role: the 1954 Supreme Court judgment in *Brown* v. *Board of Education* not only desegregated schooling, but also de-legitimated segregationist ideology (Scheingold 1974).

When Rosa Parks illegally occupied a 'whites only' seat on a Montgomery bus, structural opportunities beckoned: she belonged to the local chapter of the National Association for the Advancement of Colored People whose leadership locally was able to capitalise on her treatment and mobilise a bus boycott, which was emulated as the word spread through informal networks. Spontaneous action taken in one town after another ignited sympathetic action elsewhere (Killian 1984). Needing to avoid disillusioning its African American supporters in northern cities and alienating international opinion, the Kennedy-Johnson administrations felt compelled to support civil rights. Then political opportunities began to contract: the ghetto riots that punctuated the summer months in cities across the USA and the rise of 'black power' militancy frightened the white electorate who were mobilised under the banner of 'law and order' to support Nixon in the 1968 Presidential election. We see here how perilously poised is the identification of protesters when they engage in criminal acts. The illegal marchers of Birmingham, Alabama were regarded as 'victims' of 'Bull' Connor's oppressive policing deserving sympathy and protection; but when the ghettoes burned during the 'long hot summers' of the 1960s, white majority opinion abandoned sympathy and sought refuge in 'law and order' politics.

Characteristics of 'offenders' and 'victims'

Just as criminologists have debated whether and to what extent criminality is the product of social deprivation, so too have political scientists debated the role of deprivation in contentious politics, especially the politics of the street. Some of the earliest and most influential theorising on the topic of protest viewed the 'mob' as a threat not only to established political power, but also to civilised society. What is now popularly depicted as 'riff-raff' theory is most closely associated with Gustav Le Bon (1895) who argued that 'the crowd' acquires a mind of its own, transmitted among its constituent members through a process of contagion, that liberates the passions and overwhelms reason. This approach spawned a lengthy lineage of theory and research that emphasised the irrationality of collective protest (McPhail 1991).

There are two, not entirely consistent, themes that contributed to the perpetuation of this view: first is the notion of 'predisposition', and second that protest 'transforms' participants causing them to behave irrationally. These themes conjoin most explicitly and cogently in the theory of relative deprivation (Gurr 1968). Gurr argues that the failure of people to achieve their expectations produces feelings of frustration and aggression that are easily channelled through politicisation so that aggression is expressed in collective disorder aimed at arbitrary targets. This view elicits strong rhetorical condemnation from Gurr's opponents who wish to assert the justifiability of disorders such as the ghetto riots of 1960s America or the 'inner-city' riots witnessed in Britain in the early 1980s (see Waddington 1991: ch. 7 for a discussion). Yet while critics assert that injustices prompt disorder, they share the assumption that protest, especially disorderly protest, is the preserve of the most deprived sections of the population. The deprived have the most obvious cause for complaint and are excluded from political channels through which to pursue remedial action – riot is the 'ballot box of the poor' (Bachrach and Baratz 1970). Such a debate neatly reflects the politics of class, with conservatives wishing to demean collective action as 'mob violence and disorder' while liberals and radicals assert that such outbreaks are justified (Grimshaw and Bowen 1968; Taylor 1984).

However, this shared assumption is false, for the *middle class* are more likely to participate in all forms of political action, including protest, than are members of the most deprived and excluded sections of the population. Even in the riots of American ghettos and British inner-cities there was little evidence of involvement by the most deprived members of society (see Field and Southgate 1982 for a review). Spilerman's research found that indices of deprivation failed to account for why riots occurred in some locations and not others. A far better explanation was the proportion of African Americans in different cities (Spilerman 1970, 1971, 1976).

A variant on the 'riff-raff' theory prevalent in the 1950s and 1960s attributed middle-class adherence to right-wing and other illiberal movements to 'status inconsistency' (Gusfield 1963, 1970; Trow 1970) and other misfortunes. This too proved to be superficial and derogatory: McCarthyites emerged as well-integrated members of communities, who held deeply conservative views and were distrustful of the federal government (Polsby 1960; Wolfinger *et al.* 1964; Rogin 1967; McEvoy 1971).

The other side of the view that protest is the 'ballot box of the poor' which is aimed at the powerful. Sometimes it is, but 'deadly ethnic riots' and pogroms are most likely to target ethnic minorities (Horowitz 2001; Brass 1996); the American ghetto riots and British inner-city disorders largely wrought destruction on the area in which rioters lived (Kerner 1968; Scarman 1981); protests are as likely to target asylum-seekers, paedophiles and other out-groups as they are to attack privilege; some protesters seek to save the environment, whereas others oppose rises in the price of fossil fuel. Protest is a strategy that can serve almost any aim and mobilise any constituency.

Explanations of activism and militancy

More than representing the voice of the dispossessed, the overwhelmingly consistent pattern of protest is that it attracts young people, most notably students who tend to be drawn disproportionately from among the most affluent and well-educated sections of the population. Nor is this coincidental, for political activity of whatever kind makes the greatest demands on those characteristics that are least abundant among the poor and dispossessed – social and cultural capital – the possession of which is the theoretical focus of resource mobilisation theory (McCarthy and Zald 1977) which has proven a robustly influential paradigm.

This theoretical framework represents a profound departure from theories considered above, not least because it rests upon a counterintuitive observation: protest is more abundant during periods of affluence (rather than times of hardship) when participants have sufficient disposable income and time with which to commit to their chosen cause. This emphasis upon the resources available for protest *rather than its motivation* rests upon the challenging argument that grievances explain little or nothing about protest – protest campaigns come and go irrespective of fluctuations in any conceivable grounds for unrest.

Protest (whether lawful or not) is resource-intensive; it requires mobilising sufficient people so that their collective voice is heard, and activities (such as picketing) require organisation, which in some instances must be done in secret to avoid countermeasures from opponents. This focus on the organisation of protest awakens controversy, for it undermines the claim of so many social movements to be 'grass roots'. This raises two quite different concerns that might discredit movements: first, the role of agitators and, secondly, the influence of officials over movement strategy and tactics. Killian (1984) acknowledges that contemporary analyses of the Civil Rights Movement tacitly avoided the issue of organisation and emphasised the importance of spontaneity for fear that the leaders of the movement might have been besmirched as 'agitators' and perhaps targeted by opponents. He now accepts that while the actions of individuals and small groups (such as the Tallahassee lunch-counter sit-ins) were spontaneous, they had their impact through the organisational infrastructure that supported them and disseminated their tactics. Gamson (1975) goes further and concludes from a review of American social movements that bureaucracy allows movements to be more responsive to events, longer lived and achieve at least some of their goals. There are echoes here of Max Weber's theory of bureaucracy (Weber *et al*. 1948), for while, on the one hand, efficient organisation enables effective protest, it can, on the other, also create an 'iron cage' of its own. Piven and Cloward (1977) argue that 'poor people's movements' are ill-served by professional bureaucracy because the interests of officials diverge from that of the movement as a whole. This is a view with which McCarthy and Zald (1977) appear to agree, for they point out that professionals acquire goals different to those of the membership. Their first goal is to keep the movement organisation in being by retaining existing members and recruiting new ones. Because those beyond the core of activists are progressively less committed to the cause, and therefore their continued membership cannot be relied upon, social movement cadres focus upon the short-term goals of converting this 'soft' support into active commitment rather than bringing about radical political change. Cadres also seek to pursue their own careers, moving from one social movement to another. Like bureaucrats elsewhere (Merton 1957), there is the danger that officials focus on the means rather than the ends of the movement, which leads them to seek compromises through negotiation that the activists may consider sell-outs. Among the most successful campaigning organisations, protest becomes a 'business' like any other, in which 'stunts' are performed so as to raise public awareness of the movement and stimulate financial support (Jordan and Maloney 1997).

Recruitment and retention of members is a major obstacle to the success of any movement. As McCarthy and Zald (1977) observe, movements attract a sympathetic 'conscience constituency' of indefinite size, from among whom it seeks to convert sympathy into activism. The handicap in doing so is the 'free-rider problem' (Olson 1965): why would any rational person pay the price of membership when they will in any case benefit from gains that the movement makes? Certainly, it is true that mobilising protest actions of any kind – legal or illegal – involves tremendous attrition, for sympathy is rarely converted into committed action (Klandermans 1997). How, then, are activists recruited and retained? Olson's answer, betraying his rational-choice perspective, is that members must enjoy 'selective incentives' to compensate for short-term costs, such as favourable rates offered to trade unionists by suppliers of goods and services. However, it is less obvious that social movements such as environmentalism, animal rights and Amnesty International could offer such incentives. This has led social movement researchers into the social psychology of activism and the intrinsic rewards that derive from being among like-minded others in pursuit of a worthy cause (Wilson and Orum 1976; Oliver and Marwell 1992).

Activists become increasingly radical or militant for a wide variety of reasons. First, external circumstances may change in ways that deeply offend the established values that people hold, for instance in war pacifist values may be sorely challenged and in the past pacifists have suffered imprisonment for their refusal to be conscripted. Secondly, as people enter any milieu they tend to acquire the values common therein. Certainly, social networks are very important in mobilising activism at all levels (Snow *et al.* 1980) and moving in particular circles will make someone preferentially available for more or less haphazard recruitment into other activist networks. In many movements there is the opportunity to prove one's strength of commitment through 'high-risk/high-cost' activism (McAdam 1986, 1989). Militant groups within movements may outbid each other in the degree of militancy they espouse, implicitly (and sometimes explicitly) asking fellow activists 'Are you really committed to the cause? Then prove it!' (della Porta 1995). Militant groups may also attract support by offering the opportunity to participate in disorderly and violent protest to those for whom this is a 'selective incentive'; there are persistent, but unsubstantiated, suggestions that 'far-right' and neo-fascist organisations target soccer hooligans precisely on this basis.

However, recruiting people individually into protest movements is remarkably ineffective: few join and those that do quickly melt away (Snow *et al.* 1980; Barker 1984; Klandermans and Oegema 1987; Klandermans 1994). Hence, movements pragmatically tend to recruit from among existing members of similar movements (Klandermans 1997; Fireman and Gamson 1979; Rucht 1999), thus creating a more or less exclusive activist group. Instead of arousing the political consciousness of non-activists, campaigns on specific issues often rely on the 'block recruitment' of fellow protesters. Thus opposition to the visit of President Reagan to Berlin in 1987 followed by meetings of the IMF and World Bank a year later attracted the participation of 140 and 133 pre-existing protest groups respectively (Gerhards and Rucht 1992). This has a profound effect on how protest is conducted, first because, while the term 'rent-a-crowd' is intended as derogatory, it points to a core of committed activists, many of whom, 'far from seeking to be pillars of respectable society, are content to be on the borders of such society. They live on marginal incomes and in marginal occupations, attempting not to participate in the dominant economic and political processes' (MacQueen 1992: 70). It also means that social movements are frequently factionalised, which represents both a strength and a weakness. Strength comes from creating coalitions of experienced and committed activist groups. The weakness of such diverse arrays of groups sheltering under a common social movement umbrella is that tensions arise. Lipsky (1968, 1970) believes that social movements are characterised by attraction and repulsion between moderates and militants. Moderates need militants for the latter attract public attention to the movement and its goals ('early risers' are invariably militants); simultaneously, moderates fear that militants will, by their actions, discredit the movement.

Violence

It is because protest groups comprise so few activists when compared to the electorate that they are compelled to *force* issues onto the political agenda, which led Wilson (1976) to the conclusion that violence is a resource that protest movements deploy as part of the bargaining process. This undoubtedly occurs in some situations: picketing an enterprise inflicts costs upon an employer that are explicitly part of a bargaining process. A similar strategy is followed by animal rights activists and anti-abortionists who also aim to impose unsustainable costs upon businesses they abhor. By extension, Wilson argues that assembling a large number of volubly angry people represents a barely concealed threat: unless policies and practices of which the protesters disapprove are changed, the anger demonstrated by protesters might overflow into more tangible acts of violence. The effectiveness of this tactic depends upon the balance between the costs of protest activities and the cost of satisfying the concessions that are demanded. The anti-vivisection movement was successful in gaining concessions over the regulation of animal experimentation without recourse to violence or disruption because the concessions they sought were modest. On the other hand, campaigns by animal rights activists to close down businesses performing services crucial to the pharmaceutical industry have enjoyed much less success, despite using more disruptive and sometimes violent methods, because their demands threaten a highly profitable sector of the national economy (Garner 1993, 1998). While this approach seems applicable in some cases, there are many more instances where there is no commensurability between costs and concessions. Greenpeace activists who obstructed whalers were doubtless a nuisance but were surely incapable of inflicting sufficient costs upon the whaling industry as a whole to compel nations to agree to an international moratorium on the hunting of whales. On the other hand, the deployment of Cruise and Pershing missiles in Europe during the 1980s was opposed by a massively disruptive and sometimes violent 'peace' movement, but that did not deter NATO from this deployment (Klandermans 1991).

Violence is a perilous tactic for protesters to employ because it can distract attention from the protest message and discredit the movement. Suppression is easily justified where movements are discredited by their association with violence. So protesters must carefully calculate what is a sufficient challenge to public tranquillity, but not go so far as to cause self-inflicted damage upon the cause that they espouse. Thus in 2006, when some members of the protest group 'Fathers for Justice' were implicated in plans to kidnap the young son of Prime Minister, Tony Blair, the group officially disbanded, although it was revived later. States sometimes seek to undermine protest by employing *agents provocateur* (Marx 1974, 1979) who engage in wanton acts of violence or encourage others to do so, so as to discredit movements and justify repression.

Disruption, on the other hand, especially when accomplished through inventive forms of activism, is just as attention-grabbing as acts of violence, but not as potentially discrediting. The environmentalist protest group, Reclaim the Streets, held 'street parties' in major thoroughfares of towns and cities during the 1990s and succeeded in attracting enormous attention because this was a novel, interesting and somewhat amusing form of protest. Disrupting a sitting of the House of Commons (as did opponents of the ban on hunting with hounds, see above) publicly exposed deficiencies in security that embarrassed the authorities. Putting oneself in jeopardy draws attention to a movement's cause by a potent act of potential self-sacrifice. An environmental activist who impeded road builders in Devon in 1997 by refusing to vacate a maze of tunnels that had been excavated across the path of the A30 relief road earned celebrity status under the assumed name of 'Swampy'. Finally, performing spectacular novel acts also attracts media attention, such as the tactic of Fathers for Justice activists dressing-up as comic book 'superheroes' and performing highly public stunts, such as clambering onto a ledge at Buckingham Palace.

In calculating what forms of protest are most likely to prove effective protesters rely upon 'collective action repertoires' (Tilly 1979, 1995). Where repertoires have proven successful in the past they offer familiarity and the comfort of being able to predict the actions of others, such as internal security agencies and the mass media. However, too much familiarity contradicts the desire to attract attention and so innovation tends to be at the margins of the repertoire – more or less novel variations on familiar themes. This is facilitated by what Tilly (2004) describes as 'modularity', that is protest repertoires are disassembled into their component elements and reassembled in novel variants. The venerable street barricade of burning tyres has been reassembled as carnivalesque 'street parties' or transformed into slow mobile barriers in the form of numerous cyclists. Protest groups are quite promiscuous in the tactics they employ using what works whatever the cause. For example, hauliers protesting at the price of fuel have purloined the tactics of the environmentalist group, Critical Mass, and effectively barricaded highways by slowly driving their trucks (rather than riding bicycles) in large convoys.

There is one very important caveat to the preceding discussion, for it refers to the vast majority of protests that are means to the attainment of goals, such as obstructing the building of roads and airport runways. Not all protests are instrumental, some are motivated by symbolic causes, such as asserting the right to process along a particular route, which others find an affront. An example of this was the annual confrontation that occurred in the vicinity of Portadown in Northern Ireland, when Loyalist 'Orange' parades insisted on marching along the Garvachy Road, a Republic enclave (Jarman and Bryan 1996; North 1997; Dingley 2002). Unlike 'instrumental' protest, 'symbolic' protests tend to be 'zero-sum games' in which if one side wins, the other side must lose. In such disputes there can be no negotiation: when issues are indivisible and deeply felt both sides are motivated to press their cause with equal vigour, which is very likely to result in violence.

Responses to protest

Repression

It is too easily assumed that the inevitable response of the state to protest is repressive. Of course, repression is an option but it is almost as perilous for the state to employ in a democracy as violence is for protesters. As already noted, the political impact of protest need bear no relationship to the seriousness of any breach of the law. Protesters can bring a capital city virtually to a halt and yet have committed only minor road traffic offences. Often the inventiveness of protesters is such that legislators feel compelled to pass new criminal statutes to outlaw their actions and which can, thereby, enlist civil libertarians in opposing those powers that are seen as draconian. Equally, action is sometimes taken against protesters on legal grounds that seem disproportionate to the seriousness of any threat the protesters might pose. For instance, in September 2003 an arms fair was held in London that attracted protesters, some of whom were stopped and searched under powers conferred by anti-terrorist legislation, which allowed protesters to claim that treating them as 'terrorists' was heavy-handed.

It is precisely because of the uncertainty that surrounds 'protest crime' that the police in many jurisdictions tend to tread lightly in dealing with anything that has or might acquire political overtones (McCarthy *et al.* 2007). This involves police officers in making decisions for purely political reasons: for instance, in the aftermath of riots in British inner cities the police were officially advised to avoid the use of police dogs in such riots because of the association that senior officers saw between the use of dogs and racial oppression in the southern states of the USA 15 years previously and the then contemporary situation in South Africa. It has also markedly influenced how police approach protest gatherings, where their preference is to negotiate mutually acceptable arrangements with the protest organisers (della Porta and Reiter 1998). Following the 'Battle of Seattle' in 1999 there has been a series of violent confrontations at locations throughout the world between police and people protesting about environmental degradation and global injustice, which has led some commentators to question whether the trend towards 'negotiated management' has been reversed (Barkan 2006; della Porta *et al.* 2006; Earl and Soule 2006; Gillham and Noakes 2007; Noakes and Gillham 2007; Waddington 2007; Wood 2007; Waddington and King 2007). This argument is flawed, first because it only attends to a handful of high-profile international meetings – a biased sample of all the thousands of protests that occur throughout democracies each year. Secondly, the era in which 'negotiated management' was first identified by researchers also included occasions where violent disorder took place that was met with repressive response. My own research on public order policing in London during the early 1990s (Waddington 1994) both drew attention to the heavy reliance of the police on 'negotiated management' but also witnessed the 'poll tax riot' and other episodes of disorder forcefully repressed by police.

Thirdly, 'negotiated management' refers to a process rather than an outcome: it is perfectly possible for negotiations to fail and for police to revert to more coercive methods if they deem it necessary or expedient. Why would coercive methods be deemed necessary or expedient? On the one hand, because serious disorder unambiguously caused by protesters gives the police ample justification for their use of coercion. On the other, the police might deem that they are willing to 'die in a ditch': that is, the location of the disorder is so politically sensitive that coercion is justified. Very few locations in London during the early 1990s were regarded as sacrosanct, but any protest that in any way besmirched the Cenotaph (the memorial to the war dead in the centre of Whitehall) was regarded as an intolerable affront. Where and how deeply 'ditches' are proverbially 'dug' is continually adjusted. For instance, the diplomatic premises of friendly and powerful allies are afforded greater respect than those of less friendly and comparatively powerless countries. In some circumstances, modest levels of disorder are tolerated, but not in others. For instance, a sit-down demonstration in the vicinity of Downing Street was regarded as acceptable but not more rowdy forms of protest at that location. It is instructive that many of the post-Seattle confrontations have been at locations hosting 'internationally protected persons' who, in London, were always afforded high levels of protection, for under international treaty the police felt compelled not only to protect their persons but also their 'dignity'. Hence, state occasions were policed with zero tolerance of any form of protest.

It is undoubtedly true that police have adopted tactics of dealing with some protesters that amount to 'structural incapacitation' (Noakes and Gillham 2006). Just as protesters are compelled to innovate in order to have maximum effect, so too the police innovate in response to emerging patterns of protest. Protests in the name of 'global justice' have attracted protesters from all over the world with whom the police in any location have no lasting relationship and little opportunity to negotiate. In response the police have used tactics previously developed for dealing with another group of unruly international travellers – soccer hooligans. The type of border controls to which Noakes and Gillham draw attention are well-worn methods of incapacitating soccer hooligans; so too is the sharing of intelligence between jurisdictions.

The foregoing debate misses a more crucial issue raised by McPhail *et al.* (1998): that is that 'negotiated management' institutionalises protest and thereby blunts its edge. When protest is facilitated, yet regulated, by the state, perhaps democracy is subtly, yet dangerously, undermined.

Media 'framing'

Protesters crave the attention of the mass media because the media provide the gateway through which to influence wider audiences. Public opinion is influenced not simply by events reported in the news media but also by the meaning that is attributed to them. The news media thus provides an arena for contention in its own right in which events are dissected and their significance assessed. To be successful, protesters need media-savvy spokespeople to promote their cause in media studios, since otherwise protesters risk being dismissed as unruly hooligans. This gives a further twist to the importance of organisation and the role of professionals. Indeed, one of the features of so-called 'new social movements' is that they increasingly eschew the streets for the broadcasting studio and feature articles in newspapers.

The task of spokespeople is to 'frame' their cause so as to promote it by encouraging recruitment, support and sympathy. Framing provides explanations of: what is wrong? who is to blame? what is the remedy? The answers to these questions are designed to promote collective action by emphasising that individual woes are merely symptomatic of shared injustices that are capable of change as an act of political will (Klandermans and Goslinga 1996; Klandermans 1997). For example, environmentalists have been spectacularly successful in persuading decision-makers that climate change is bad, it's our fault, and we can prevent disaster through our own actions. What is important is that the frame should be persuasive: convincing audiences to look at the taken-for-granted world in ways that make new sense – that is, it raises consciousness.

Among adherents of social movements, such framing attempts to clothe otherwise delinquent and criminal actions in moral rectitude.

> Looting is not primarily a means of acquiring property, as it is normally viewed in disaster situations; breaking store windows and burning buildings is not merely a perverted form of amusement or immoral vengeance like the usual vandalism and arson; threats of violence and injury to persons are not simply criminal actions. All are expressions of outrage against injustice of sufficient magnitude and duration to render the resort to such exceptional means of communication understandable to the observer. (Turner 1969: 186)

Thus it becomes a moral duty to do all in one's power to obstruct the building of roads in areas of natural beauty or disrupt meetings of international organisations whose policies create global injustice. While this is a powerful spur to action – putting 'fire in the belly and iron in the soul' (Gamson 1975) – it has wider effects on diverse audiences. The inactive 'conscience constituency' tends to accept the same frames as activists. While they may not agree with all the *tactics* that activists employ, they may still sympathise with actions that they perceive to be motivated by the same *principles* to which they subscribe. In so far as social movement framing is successful, it creates a conundrum for the police, for interventions intended to prevent, mitigate or negate protest are likely themselves to be tainted by association with the wrong that activists are trying to oppose, especially when police tactics are coercive. This was illustrated by the policing of a Compassion in World Farming campaign to prevent the exportation of live animals for slaughter in abattoirs throughout Europe during 1996 (Critcher 1996; Markham and Punch 2004). The decision of the Essex police to invoke the Public Order Act and to attire in protective clothing officers escorting the trucks transporting the live animals was widely portrayed as both excessively heavy-handed and also complicit with a trade that treated animals in ways forbidden under domestic English law.

This example draws attention to how, in the arena of contention of the media studio, policing and institutions of criminal justice can be framed as issues in their own right. Often this is conducted through the 'master frame' of 'rights', but protest often involves rights in conflicts (Walker 1968). In determining whose rights should prevail, protesters and their cause may be framed as more or less 'deserving' of lenient treatment. Despised protesters, such as those affiliated to far-right social movements, may be treated relatively harshly by the police without attracting support for their rights because they lack articulate spokespeople with access to the media (Linden and Klandermans 2006).

Legal institutions as arenas of contention

Another, and increasingly important, arena of contention is the courts. The furore over live animal exports eventually led to a hearing in the High Court in which exporters challenged bans and restrictions that had been imposed on the trade by local police who were unwilling to commit sufficient resources to facilitate unfettered exports. The Court took a very different view to that which had dominated much of the public debate hitherto: the Court affirmed the legality of the trade and overturned attempts to prevent it, which were interpreted as 'surrendering to mob rule' (Critcher 1996: 55). However, this judgment was overturned by the House of Lords, albeit by that time the BSE crisis had rendered the judgment somewhat redundant. Effectively, the 'arena of contention' involved not just one court, but the entire civil justice system.

This draws attention to the growth of 'cause lawyering' (Scheingold 1997) and 'legal mobilisation' (McCann 2006) in which legal professionals become advocates of causes and sometimes advance explicitly political arguments on behalf of clients. The famous and long-running saga of the 'McLibel' case that began when the McDonald's fast-food chain sued two activists for defamation ended with a pyrrhic victory for McDonald's, and the British government being found by the European Court on Human Rights to be in breach of the Convention resulting in a review of the English law of libel. Legal institutions can also find that apparently apolitical cases can become transformed into causes célèbres with significant social, legal and political implications (Chancer 2005). The decision of a Simi Valley jury to acquit four Los Angeles police officers of charges arising from the beating of Rodney King not only prompted days of violence and disorder in the black ghettoes of Los Angeles but also a commission of inquiry that prompted reforms of the Los Angeles Police (Christopher 1991).

Legal and quasi-legal institutions can also become involved in another arena of contention – establishing the political credentials of episodes of collective disorder. When people gather at a prearranged time and place under a political banner, the political meaning of their actions is reasonably clear. However, when violence and disorder erupts spontaneously its political meaning may be highly contested. The most celebrated occasions in which courts or official inquiries acknowledged that rioters had been motivated by political grievances were during the ghetto riots in America and the inner-city riots in Britain. The authorities sought to portray these riots and those involved in them as simply criminal, whereas the Kerner Commission (Kerner 1968) and Scarman inquiry (Scarman 1981) both accepted that genuine political grievances had prompted the disorders, conclusions that had far-reaching consequences for police and government. On the other hand, when rioting erupted in some of Britain's northern towns and cities during the summer of 2000 rioters and the communities afflicted received much less sympathy (Lea 2004).

Conclusions

Protest is a *political* activity, which can be expressed legally and illegally. Because protest is the recourse of those unable to bring influence through established political channels, there are many occasions when protesters commit offences. The need to find novel means of protesting that attract the attention of the mass media tends to encourage protesters to act illegally, albeit that many offences are minor. The policing of these crimes is also deeply political: first, even if protesters are clearly committing criminal offences, they might use legal channels as arenas in which to pursue their cause. So, what would in any other circumstances be a routine matter for the police may become a source of 'grief' (Waddington 1994). Secondly, courts tend to treat leniently those who commit crimes that are genuinely motivated by acceptable political motives. Thirdly, police tend to treat occasions of political protest far more warily than non-politically sensitive events: for instance, a rowdy political march is more tolerated than an equally rowdy gathering of soccer supporters/hooligans. Fourthly, police feel that there are 'ditches' in which others oblige them to 'die' and recent confrontations between police and opponents of global capitalism would seem to fall into this category. Finally, legal institutions and mass media studios are increasingly becoming the most active arenas of contention in which protesters are able to achieve far more significant gains than was ever possible on the streets.

Finally, what does all this mean for the health of democracy? Some worry that civil liberties are being eroded by the progressive criminalisation of protest activity. For instance, a provision in the Serious Organised Crime and Police Act 2005 forbids protest in the 'vicinity of Parliament',[3] a clause that was widely regarded as a thinly disguised device for ridding the 'vicinity of Parliament' of the long-standing protest encampment maintained by Brian Haw. They may well be correct, but does this amount to a reduction in civil liberties? Here we confront the long-established distinction between the 'law in books' and the 'law in action'. In reality there has been precious little liberty to protest in the 'vicinity of Parliament' for decades, at least not when Parliament was sitting. Prior to the enactment of this provision, each of the Houses of Parliament annually passed a 'Sessional Order' instructing the Commissioner of Police to keep the highways in the vicinity of the Palace of Westminster free from obstruction. This was enforced, when required, by sections 52 and 54 of the Metropolitan Police Act 1839. This was long recognised to be a slender thread from which dangled the integrity of Parliament and the privileges of Members and Peers (Waddington 1994). When it was successfully challenged, Parliament restored the status quo ante by the provision in the Serious Organised Crime and Police Act. This would not appear to reduce de facto liberty in this respect, which is not to say that liberty elsewhere remains intact. It does, however, alert us to the danger of taking at face value the assertions or 'framing' of civil libertarian campaigners (Waddington 2005).

Selected further reading

There is no established literature on 'protest crime' as such: political scientists tend to study protests, some of which involve the commission of crimes, while criminologists have largely ignored that very small minority of crimes which are politically inspired.

Theory and research on 'social movements' is the field that aligns most closely with protest crime, but the reader needs to be aware (as few of the authors are) of the legal status of the behaviour that is often being described and analysed from a political perspective.

There are several introductions to social movements theory and research, but few better than della Porta and Diani (2006), *Social Movements: An Introduction*. Della Porta's own research *Social Movements, Political Violence, and the State* (1995) on the German and Italian student movements of the 1970s that descended into nihilistic violence is also particularly insightful.

The closest that social movements theory gets to criminology is in the study of collective violence and there is no better introduction to this than Tilly (2003) *The Politics of Collective Violence*. The other side of the coin, of course, is repression by the state, usually at the hands of the police. Two collections edited by Donatella della Porta and others show the two sides of this: della Porta and Reiter (eds) (1998), in *Policing Protest: The Control of Mass Demonstrations in Western Democracies*, paint a rather peaceful picture of police negotiating with protesters whereas in *Policing transnational protest*, written in the aftermath of the rise of anti-globalisation protest, della Porta, Peterson and Reiter (eds) (2006: 1–20) are more pessimistic. *Repression and Mobilization* by Davenport, Johnston and Mueller (eds) (2004) is also a useful collection of essays on this topic.

Law and Social Movements by McCann (ed.) (2006) is a collection of the diverse literature on the role of the law and the courts in the politics of protest, which often centres around disorder or violence. A related text is Sarat and Scheingold (1998) 'Cause lawyering and the reproduction of professional authority: an introduction', which discusses how the courts have become arenas of contention in their own right.

Notes

1 The author wishes to thank Paul Rock, Kate Moss and Martin Wright for their helpful comments on earlier drafts of this chapter.
2 A terrorist group of this name did exist in the USA during this period, but no evidence of any connection between this group and the Spaghetti House robbers was established.
3 I am indebted to Kate Moss for drawing my attention to this.

References

Bachrach, P. and Baratz, M. S. (1970) *Power and Poverty: Theory and Practice*. Oxford: Oxford University Press.

Barkan, S. E. (2006) 'Criminal prosecution and the legal control of protest', *Mobilization*, 11: 181–95.

Barker, E. (1984) *The Making of a Moonie: Choice or Brainwashing*. Oxford: Blackwell.

Brass, P. R. (1996) *Riots and Pogroms*. Basingstoke: Macmillan.

Button, M. and John, T. (2002) '"Plural policing" in action: a review of the policing of environmental protests in England and Wales', *Policing and Society*, 12: 111–21.

Button, M., John, T. and Brearley, N. (2002) 'New challenges in public order policing: the professionalisation of environmental protest and the emergence of the militant environmental activist', *International Journal of the Sociology of Law*, 30: 17–32.

Chancer, L. S. (2005) *High-Profile Crimes: When Legal Cases Become Social Causes*. Chicago and London: University of Chicago Press.

Christopher, W. C. (1991) *Report of the Independent Commission on the Los Angeles Police Department*. Los Angeles.

Critcher, C. (1996) 'On the waterfront: applying the flashpoints model to protest against live animal exports', in C. Critcher and D. Waddington (eds), *Policing Public Order: Theoretical and Practical Issues*. Aldershot: Avebury, pp. 53–70.

Critchley, T. (1970) *The Conquest of Violence*. London: Constable.

Davenport, C., Johnston, H. and Mueller, C. M. (eds) (2004) *Repression and Mobilization*. Minneapolis, MN: University of Minnesota Press.

della Porta, D. (1995) *Social Movements, Political Violence, and the State*. Cambridge: Cambridge University Press.

della Porta, D. and Diani, M. (2006) *Social Movements: An Introduction*. Malden, MA: Blackwell.

della Porta, D. and Reiter, H. (eds) (1998) *Policing Protest: The Control of Mass Demonstrations in Western Democracies*. Minneapolis, MN: University of Minnesota Press.

della Porta, D., Peterson, A. and Reiter, H. (eds) (2006) *The Policing of Transnational Protest*. Aldershot: Ashgate.

Dingley, J. (2002) 'Marching down the Garvaghy Road: Republican Tactics and state response to the Orangemen's claim to march their traditional route home after the Drumcree church service', *Terrorism and Political Violence*, 14: 42–79.

Earl, J. and Soule, S. A. (2006) 'Seeing blue: a police-centred explanation of protest policing', *Mobilization*, 11: 145–64.

Field, S. and Southgate, P. (1982) *Public Disorder: A Review of Research and a Study in One Inner City Area*. London: HMSO.

Fireman, B. and Gamson, W. A. (1979) 'Utilitarian logic in the resource mobilization perspective', in M. N. Zald and J. D. McCarthy (eds), *The Dynamics of Social Movements: Resource Mobilization, Social Control and Tactics*. Cambridge, MA: Winthrop, pp. 8–44.

Gamson, W. A. (1975) *The Strategy of Social Protest*. Homewood, IL: Dorsey.

Garner, R. (1993) *Animals, Politics and Morality*. Manchester: Manchester University Press.

Garner, R. (1998) *Political Animals: Animal Protection Politics in Britain and the United States*. London: Macmillan.

Gerhards, J. and Rucht, D. (1992) 'Mesomobilization – organizing and framing in two protest campaigns in West Germany', *American Journal of Sociology*, 98: 555–95.

Gillham, P. F. and Marx, G. T. (2000) 'Complexity and irony in policing and protesting: the World Trade Organization in Seattle', *Social Justice*, 27: 212–36.

Gillham, P. F. and Noakes, J. (2007) '"More than a march in a circle": transgressive protests and the limits of negotiated management', *Mobilization*, 13: 341–58.

Grimshaw, A. D. and Bowen, D. R. (1968) 'Three views of urban violence: civil disturbance, racial revolt, class assault', in L. H. Masotti and D. R. Bowen (eds), *Civil Violence in the Urban Community*. Beverly Hills, CA: Sage, pp. 103–19.

Gurr, T. R. (1968) *Why Men Rebel*. Princeton, NJ: Princeton University Press.

Gusfield, J. R. (1963) *Symbolic Crusade: Status Politics and the American Temperance Movement*. Urbana, IL: University of Illinois Press.

Gusfield, J. R. (1970) *Protest, Reform, and Revolt*. New York: Wiley.

Hadden, J. and Tarrow, S. (2007) 'Spillover or spillout? The Global Justice Movement in the United States after 9/11', *Mobilization*, 13: 359–76.

Horowitz, D. L. (2001) *The Deadly Ethnic Riot*. Berkley, CA: University of California Press.

Jarman, N. and Bryan, D. (1996) *Parade and Protest: A Discussion of Parading Disputes in Northern Ireland*. Coleraine: Centre for the Study of Conflict, University of Ulster.

Jordan, G. and Maloney, W. (1997) *The Protest Business? Mobilizing Campaign Groups*. Manchester: University of Manchester Press.

Kerner, O. (1968) *The Report of the National Advisory Commission on Civil Disorders*. Washington, DC: US Government Printing Office.

Killian, L. M. (1984) 'Organization, rationality and spontaneity in the civil rights movement', *American Sociological Review*, 49: 770–83.

Klandermans, B. (1991) 'The peace movement and social movement theory', in B. Klandermans (ed.), *International Social Movement Research*. Greenwich, CT: JAI, pp. 1–39.

Klandermans, B. (1994) 'Transient identities: membership patterns in the Dutch peace movement', in E. Larana, H. Johnston and J. R. Gusfield (eds), *New Social Movements: From Ideology to Identity*. Philadelphia: Temple University Press, pp. 168–84.

Klandermans, B. (1997) *The Social Psychology of Protest*. Oxford: Blackwell.

Klandermans, B. and Oegema, D. (1987) 'Potentials, networks, motivations, and barriers: steps towards participation in social movements', *American Sociological Review*, 52: 519–31.

Klandermans, B. and Goslinga, S. (1996) 'Media discourse, movement publicity, and the generation of collective action frames: theoretical and empirical exercises in meaning construction,' in D. McAdam, J. D. McCarthy and M. N. Zald (eds), *Comparative Perspectives on Social Movements*. Cambridge: Cambridge University Press, pp. 312–37.

Le Bon, G. (1895) *The Crowd*. New Brunswick, NJ: Viking.

Lea, J. (2004) 'From Brixton to Bradford: official discourse on race and urban violence in the United Kingdom' in G. Gilligan and J. Pratt (eds), *Crime, Truth and Justice: Official Inquiry, Discourse and Knowledge*. Cullompton: Willan, pp. 183–203.

Linden, A. and Klandermans, B. (2006) 'Stigmatization and repression of extreme-right activism in the Netherlands', *Mobilization*, 11: 213–28.

Lipsky, M. (1968) 'Protest as a political resource', *American Political Science Review*, 62: 1144–58.

Lipsky, M. (1970) *Protest in City Politics*. Chicago: Rand McNally.

McAdam, D. (1982) *Political Process and the Development of Black Insurgency*. Chicago: University of Chicago Press.

McAdam, D. (1983) 'Tactical innovation and the pace of insurgency', *American Sociological Review*, 48: 735–54.

McAdam, D. (1986) 'Recruitment to high-risk activism: the case of Freedom Summer', *American Journal of Sociology*, 92: 64–90.

McAdam, D. (1988) *Freedom Summer*. New York: Oxford University Press.

McAdam, D. (1989) 'The biographical consequences of activism', *American Sociological Review*, 54: 744–60.

McCann, M. (ed.) (2006) *Law and Social Movements*. Aldershot: Ashgate.

McCarthy, J. D. and Zald, M. N. (1977) 'Resource mobilization and social movements: a partial theory', *American Journal of Sociology*, 82: 1212–41.

McCarthy, J. D., Martin, A. and McPhail, C. (2007) 'Policing disorderly campus protests and convivial gatherings: the interaction of threat, social organization, and First Amendment guarantees', *Social Problems*, 54: 274–96.

McEvoy, J. (1971) *Radicals or Conservatives: The Contemporary American Right*. Chicago: Rand McNally.

McPhail, C. (1991) *The Myth of the Madding Crowd*. Hawthorne, NY: Aldine de Gruyter.

McPhail, C., Schweingruber, D. and McCarthy, J. (1998) 'Policing protest in the United States: 1960–1995', in D. della Porta and H. Reiter (eds), *Policing Protest: The Control of Mass Demonstrations in Western Democracies*. Minneapolis, MN: University of Minnesota Press, pp. 49–69.

MacQueen, G. (1992) 'Marking and binding: an interpretation of the pouring of blood in nonviolent direct action', *Peace and Change*, 17: 60–81.

Markham, G. and Punch, M. (2004) 'Animal rights, public order and police accountability: the Brightlingsea demonstrations', *International Journal of Police Science and Management*, 6: 84–96.

Marx, G. T. (1974) 'Thoughts on a neglected category of social movement participant: the agent provocateur and the informant', *American Journal of Sociology*, 80: 402–42.

Marx, G. T. (1979) 'External efforts to damage or facilitate social movements: some patterns, explanations, outcomes and complications', in J. McCarthy and M. N. Zald (eds), *The Dynamics of Social Movements*. Cambridge, MA: Winthrop, pp. 94–125.

Matza, D. (1969) *Becoming Deviant*. Englewood Cliffs, NJ: Prentice Hall.

Melucci, A. (1989) *Nomads of the Present: Social Movements and Individual Needs in Contemporary Society*. London: Hutchinson Radius.

Merton, R. K. (1957) *Social Theory and Social Structure*. New York: Free Press.

Noakes, J. and Gillham, P. F. (2006) 'Aspects of the "new penology" in the police response to major political protests in the United States, 1999–2000', in D. della Porta, A. Peterson and H. Reiter (eds), *The Policing of Transnational Protest*. Aldershot: Ashgate, pp. 97–116.

Noakes, J. and Gillham, P. F. (2007) 'Police and protester innovation since Seattle', *Mobilization*, 13: 335–40.

North, D. P. (1997) *Report of the Independent Review of Parades and Marches*. Belfast: The Stationery Office.

Oliver, P. E. and Marwell, G. (1992) 'Mobilizing technologies for collective action', in A. D. Morris and C. M. Mueller (eds), *Frontiers in Social Movement Theory*. New Haven, CT: Yale University Press, pp. 251–72.

Olson, M. (1965) *The Logic of Collective Action: Public Goods and the Theory of Groups*. Cambridge: Cambridge University Press.

Piven, F. F. and Cloward, R. A. (1977) *Poor People's Movements: Why They Succeed, How They Fail*. New York: Random House.

Polsby, N. W. (1960) 'Toward an explanation of McCarthyism', *Political Studies*, 8: 250–71.

Rogin, M. P. (1967) *The Intellectuals and McCarthy: The Radical Specter*. Cambridge, MA: MIT.

Rucht, D. (1999) 'Linking organization and mobilization: Michels's iron law of oligarchy reconsidered', *Mobilization*, 4: 151–70.

Sarat, A. and Scheingold, S. A. (1998) 'Cause lawyering and the reproduction of professional authority: an introduction', in A. Sarat and S. A. Scheingold (eds), *Cause Lawyering: Political Commitments and Professional Responsibilities*. New York: Oxford University Press, pp. 3–28.

Scarman, L., Rt Hon the Lord (1981) *The Brixton Disorders 10–12 April 1981: Report of an Inquiry by the Rt. Hon. The Lord Scarman, OBE*. London: HMSO.

Scheingold, S. A. (1974) *The Politics of Rights: Lawyers, Public Policy, and Political Change*. New Haven, CT: Yale University Press.

Scheingold, S. A. (1997) *Politics, Crime Control, and Culture*. Aldershot, UK and Brookfield, VT: Ashgate/Dartmouth.

Smith, J. (2001) 'Globalizing resistance: the Battle of Seattle and the future of social movements', *Mobilization*, 6: 1–20.

Snow, D. A., Zurcher, L. A. and Ekland-Olson, S. (1980) 'Social networks and social movements: a microstructural approach to differential recruitment', *American Sociological Review*, 45: 787–801.

Spilerman, S. (1970) 'The causes of racial disturbances: a comparison of alternative explanations', *American Sociological Review*, 35: 627–49.

Spilerman, S. (1971) 'The causes of racial disturbances: tests of an explanation', *American Sociological Review*, 36: 427–42.

Spilerman, S. (1976) 'Structural characteristics of cities and the severity of racial disorders', *American Sociological Review*, 41: 771–93.

Tarrow, S. (1989) *Democracy and Disorder: Protest Politics in Italy, 1965–1975*. Oxford: Oxford University Press.

Tarrow, S. (1994) *Power in Movement: Social Movements, Collective Action and Politics*. New York: Cambridge University Press.

Taylor, S. (1984) 'The Scarman Report and explanations of riots', in J. Benyon (ed.), *Scarman and After*. London: Pergamon, pp. 20–35.

Tilly, C. (1978) *From Mobilization to Revolution*. Reading, MA: Addison-Wesley.

Tilly, C. (1979) 'Repertoires of contention in America and Britain, 1750–1830', in M. N. Zald and J. D. Mccarthy (eds), *The Dynamics of Social Movements*. Cambridge, MA: Winthrop, pp. 126–55.

Tilly, C. (1995) *Popular Contention in Great Britain, 1758–1834*. Cambridge, MA: Harvard University Press.

Tilly, C. (2003) *The Politics of Collective Violence*. Cambridge and New York: Cambridge University Press.

Tilly, C. (2004) *Social Movements, 1768–2004*. Boulder, CO: Paradigm Publishers.

Trow, M. (1970) 'Small businessmen, political tolerance, and support for McCarthy', in J. R. Gusfield (ed.), *Protest, Reform, and Revolt*. New York: Wiley, pp. 403–18.

Turner, R. H. (1969) 'The public perception of protest', *American Sociological Review*, 32: 815–31.

Waddington, D. P. (2007) *Policing Public Disorder: Theory and Practice*. Willan: Cullompton.

Waddington, D. P. and King, M. (2007) 'The impact of the local: police public-order strategies during the G8 Justice and Home Affairs Ministerial Meetings' *Mobilization*, 12: 417–30.

Waddington, P. A. J. (1991) *The Strong Arm of the Law*. Oxford: Clarendon.

Waddington, P. A. J. (1994) *Liberty and Order: Policing Public Order in a Capital City*. London: UCL Press.

Waddington, P. A. J. (2005) 'Slippery slopes and civil libertarian pessimism', *Policing and Society*, 15: 353–75.

Walker, D. (1968) *Rights in Conflict: The Violent Confrontation of Demonstrators and Police, During the Week of the Democratic National Convention*. New York: Banton.

Weber, M., Mills, C. W. and Gerth, H. H. (1948) *From Max Weber: Essays in Sociology*. London: Kegan Paul.

Wilkins, L. T. (1964) *Social Deviance*. London: Tavistock.

Wilson, J. (1976) 'Social protest and social control', *Social Problems*, 24: 469–81.

Wilson, K. L. and Orum, A. M. (1976) 'Mobilizing people for collective political action', *Journal of Political and Military Sociology*, 4: 187–202.

Wolfinger, R. E., Wolfinger, B. K., Prewitt, K. and Rosenhack, S. (1964) 'America's Radical Right: politics and ideology', in D. E. Apter (ed.), *Ideology and Discontent*. London: Collier-Macmillan.

Wood, J. (2007) 'Breaking the wave: repression, identity, and Seattle tactics', *Mobilization*, 13: 377–88.

Young, J. (1971) 'The role of the police as amplifiers of deviancy, negotiators of reality and translators of fantasy: some consequences of our present system of drug control as seen in Notting Hill', in S. Cohen (ed.), *Images of Deviance*. Harmondsworth: Penguin, pp. 27–16.

Chapter 42

Terrorism

Nicola Weston and Martin Innes

During the mid-1990s in the United Kingdom, the United States and many countries in Western Europe, following two decades of sustained rises, recorded crime levels started to fall. Especially given the changes in the geopolitical sphere prompted by the decline of the Soviet Union and the consequent ending of the Cold War a few years prior to the decline in crime, the not unreasonable assumption that countries in the West at least were on the cusp of an era of enhanced security gained traction in some quarters.[1] Any such thoughts, though, were dramatically and viscerally smashed when, on 11 September 2001, two passenger planes were hijacked and hurled through the sky as part of a calculated attack on the Twin Towers of the World Trade Center.

The assault on the Twin Towers rapidly acquired the properties of a 'signal crime' changing the postures of citizens, institutions and states in terms of how they thought, felt and acted in relation to their security (Innes 2006; Lee 2007). In propagating a profound and pervasive social reaction that has stimulated manifest alterations in the basic conduct of the interactional and institutional orderings of social life, these attacks served to attribute to terrorism an increased salience in the hierarchy of public concerns. In an environment where the problem of recorded volume crime has become less pronounced and pressing, terrorism has seemingly occupied the space left potentially vacant: the police role, in both its 'high' and 'low' forms, has increasingly been directed to the prevention and detection of terrorists threats (Innes and Thiel 2008); legislative activity has proven occupied by introducing new categories of offence intended to mitigate the risks posed by the terrorist threats; and target-hardening measures have been increasingly designed into the physical environment around perceived targets. Accompanying such developments the world of ideas and intellectual inquiry has also been transformed, wherein 'terrorism studies' that was previously little more than a minor offshoot of international relations has been transformed into a multidisciplinary and rapidly evolving arena of study. Since 2001 when the planes literally exploded into a number of targets symbolic of western, liberal-democratic capitalism, there has also been a metaphorical 'explosion' in the number of journalistic, policy-driven and academic accounts of terrorism.

In this chapter, our main aims are to examine the slippery concept of 'terrorism', to explore some questions about its changing form and scale and to review some of the key ideas that are emanating from this rapid growth of interest in the causes and consequences of terrorism. In so doing, though, we are mindful of the fact that, while to a significant extent systematic and well-funded research into this area is new, terrorism as a social problem is not. As such, there is a need to avoid a form of what Rock (2005) has dubbed 'chronocentrism' wherein we attend more carefully to and tend to privilege 'new' ideas and concerns at the expense of longer-term and more established regularities in the social organisation of knowledge. Concern about the 'chronocentrism' of terrorism studies is especially apposite for, as we will discuss in due course, one of the most vigorous recent debates revolve around whether the attacks committed in the name of Al-Qaeda constitute a 'new' form of terrorist threat or whether they fit into a longer-term trajectory of development. Many nation states have a considerable history of dealing with 'terrorist' and 'extremist' threats of different kinds, prior to their current concerns with Islamist-inspired violent extremism, and studies of such conflicts are insightful in terms of building up a textured and nuanced picture of terrorism as a social problem (cf. Laqueur 2001).

The chapter commences by seeking to clarify what is meant by the label 'terrorism' and the implications that flow from defining an act or group of people as 'terrorist'. One of the recurring concerns of academics has been that while the category of 'terrorist' is routinely invoked in the discourses of security practitioners and politicians to describe a 'real-world' phenomenon, at a conceptual level its boundaries remain less clear and somewhat ambiguous. There is a popular adage that 'one person's terrorist is another's freedom fighter' and there is some truth in this. In examining these debates over definitional propriety, we consider how the core ideas and perspectives associated with particular academic disciplines have shaped considerations of what counts as terrorism, when, where and for whom. Having reviewed these primarily intellectual concerns we then shift to issues of aetiology and causation, focusing particularly upon explanations of how and why individuals and groups engage in activities that may be labelled as 'terrorist.' Studies grounded in political science, sociology, psychology and economics all tend to betray subtly different nuances in the explanations they proffer.

Moving the analysis forward we turn from issues of causation to matters of consequences. The chapter explores how terrorist behaviour has evolved over time and whether patterns of behaviour displayed in recent terrorist attacks constitute a new form of terrorism or simply a modification of more established principles. Of particular interest are the ways in which collective memories of historical injustices are used to ferment support for violent, politically motivated action, and how technological developments have altered how such violence can be enacted. Here we will suggest that reactions to terrorist acts are not something exogenous to terrorism, but are in fact interwoven with and integral to what acts and groups the label of terrorist is successfully applied to. As such, the conduct of counterterrorism must be seen as imbricated in terrorism. Within this discussion we address the debate around whether terrorism or the threat of terrorism has increased. For there is a sense in which it is our reactions to the perceived threat of terrorism, both perceptually and in terms of policy responses, that exhibit the greatest capacity to impact upon the conduct and organisation of social life. As such, it is important that we understand the longer-term implications of responding and reacting in particular ways to risks and threats in the short term.

Diverse analytic lenses

Writing in 1988 Schmid and Jongman were able to identify more than one hundred different and competing definitions of 'terrorism' and it likely that there are many, many more in circulation now (see Smelser 2007). Attempts at establishing an agreed upon and widely accepted definition of terrorism have been rendered difficult by subtle shifts in the meaning and usage of the term over the years. There have been multiple definitions emanating from the policy arena, frequently supported by influential institutional actors whose particular interests subtly lead them to accent certain dimensions and attend less carefully to others. Additional multiple inflections have also resulted from the fact that so many different acts, undertaken in pursuance of a variety of causes, can be classified as terrorist. Over the course of the twentieth and twenty-first centuries in Europe, acts that fulfil many of the most commonly agreed upon criteria for being terrorist have been pursued by: groups from the far left and right of the political spectrum (Wardlaw 1982); those pursuing an ethno-nationalist agenda (Laqueur 2004); in support of a purported religious ideology (Rapoport 1988; Lincoln 2006); by members of serious and organised crime groups (Levi 2007); those wishing to advocate the protection of animal rights (Monaghan 1999) and many more besides. Further complexity to the debates about definitional propriety has been caused by multiple contributions being offered from a variety of academic disciplines and perspectives. Again, these vary markedly, being inflected by disciplinary axioms about how one should seek to explain the patterns and pathologies of the world around us.

A potentially useful starting point for trying to define terrorism has been made by Donald Black (2004). As part of a wider intellectual project that he has dubbed mapping 'the geometry of social relations', Black argues that one of the problems that bedevils terrorism as an academic concept rather than a political one is that it has become freighted with the normative overtones that attend its deployment in the political sphere.

Casting an act or group as terrorist speaks to the perceived legitimacy of the claim and/or objective that is being pursued and seeks to undermine it. In an effort to circumvent such problems, he proposes that terrorism be thought of as a particular type of (usually) 'upwards' social control. For Black then, terrorist activities constitute a particular species of violent self-help utilised in pursuance of a political objective, where there is a power asymmetry between one party and the other. Although it is somewhat implicit in Black's definition, other influential accounts have placed more accent upon recognising the importance of a political dimension. In order to distinguish it from other forms of violence, they argue, it is important to explicitly acknowledge the political motivations driving the enactment of violence. One definition in this mould is propounded by Bruce Hoffman (2006) who posits 'terrorism is thus violence – or, equally important the threat of violence – used and directed in pursuit of, or in service of, a political aim'. According to Hoffman, in order for a violent act to be labelled as 'terrorism' the aim or motivation for the act must be identifiably political in nature.

These two examples help to convey how there are important differences between some of the key definitional positions that have been proposed in the study of terrorism. Any such difficulties have been further compounded by the arguments of a number of more critically oriented scholars who have suggested that the adoption of the kinds of definition outlined above has contributed to the neglect of 'state-sponsored' terrorism (Cohen 2001). Those expounding this perspective note that while the security agencies of nation states tend to promote cases where states are the target of terrorist activity, in actuality the most profligate users of terror as a political mechanism have been states themselves. This includes cases where state leaders who perceive their hold on power to be under threat have deliberately used terror tactics against their own citizenry in order to retain control, as well as cases where states have practised terror more indirectly as a way of destabilising the security of a usually more powerful territorially distinct adversary.

As noted earlier, the divergences, convergences and tensions that exist between different attempts to define the essence of what is terrorist in order to demarcate its boundary relations with other forms of violence are in part a reflection of the variety of theoretical and disciplinary approaches which make up the base intellectual architecture that underpins and guides individual studies. As such, it is useful to briefly try and summarise the key contributions to our knowledge and understanding of terrorism and terrorists that have been made by the respective disciplines.

Political science and international relations

Perhaps understandably, given how it has come to be positioned within the interplay of academic disciplines, a significant proportion of the key interventions in the study of terrorism have their roots in the domains of political science and international relations. Although by looking across the vast range of contributions emanating from this perspective one can detect significant differences between contributions, the pivotal and recurring theme that tends to provide a common sense of purpose is that of how particular groups emerge to identify particular states and their institutions as targets for terrorist actions and how the latter respond to the risks and threats created. In effect, these contributions tend to adopt an institutional level of analysis inasmuch as they tend to display a particular concern with the ideologies and actions of the terrorist group and the policy responses of those they attack. More recently, this has developed to include an interest in supranational institutions and the governance of terrorist risks and threats (cf. Jacobson 2006).

An archetypal and influential exemplar of this kind of approach is Wilkinson's (2001) *Terrorism Versus Democracy*, in which he focuses particularly upon how liberal-democratic states should seek to respond to the variety of threats and risks of terrorism that confront them. In particular, he is concerned with mapping out how states can be effective in their responses without encroaching on key institutionalised values associated with being bound by the rule of law and the protection of human rights. As he sees it:

> Democracies are clearly vulnerable to terrorist attacks because of the openness of their societies and the ease of movement across and within frontiers. It is always easy for extremists to exploit democratic freedoms with the aim of destroying democracy. (Wilkinson 2001: 220)

While acknowledging that no European democracy has seen its political system overthrown by a terrorist campaign, he does caution about the potential for subverting liberal-democratic principles when subject to prolonged conflicts between state institutions and 'asymmetric' adversaries. Drawing upon the example of Northern Ireland, he flags up how a committed campaign of violence undertaken by a relatively small group against a state can induce corrosive and long-term political, economic and social consequences.

Economics

The principal thrust of those contributions to the study of terrorism that have been informed by a conceptual framing derived from economics has been to treat the individuals and groups who engage in terrorist activity as rational actors, whose participation and conduct is enmeshed within judgments about the costs and benefits associated with adopting particular lines of action. Indeed, the notion of the rational actor is of paramount importance to this approach. It should be clarified, however, that the concern with rationality is not to do with whether terrorists enact acceptable behaviour or whether they are engaged in conduct that is likely to be successful in realising particular objectives. Rather the concept of rationality is a measure of how they react to changing risks and constraints within the environment and whether their responses are predictable in light of alterations to the social environment. The economic contribution to terrorism purports to model behaviour contingent upon certain situational and social constraints. As constructed through the analytic lens of economics, terrorists are cast as making choices about when, where and how to engage in terrorist actions on the basis of a capacity to optimise their aims given the costs and benefits to individuals and society brought about by the situation (see Sandler 1997). For example, in policy-making circles such approaches have been regularly used to inform thinking about the predicted costs of terrorism and hence whether particular modes of response or counterterrorism strategies are cost-effective ways of preventing attacks.

In particular, game theoretic approaches have been deployed to evaluate the interaction between terrorist decisions and governmental actions (e.g. Sandler and Enders 2004). This approach, originating back in 1944 and subsequently developed by many researchers, suggests that individual decision-making is largely based on the options available coupled with a prediction of how others will act in that situation (for an example see Lapan and Sandler 1988). Game theory suggests that terrorists make choices based upon evaluations of the actions taken by government, and governments make decisions based on their perceptions of the conduct of terrorists, with each seeking to negotiate a tactical advantage for themselves vis-à-vis the other's position (see Sandler and Lapan 1988; Sandler and Enders 2004; Bier 2007). The aim of each individual or group is to seek the maximum reward or beneficial outcome. Configured in this fashion, the behaviour of terrorists can be 'measured' by analysing situations and relating these to the constraints imposed upon lines of action. So, for example, if through a particular governmental intervention the quantity or quality of constraints changes, then the behaviour of the terrorist actor is expected to alter accordingly. Hence, if a government invests in 'target-hardening' security measures at airports, then it could be anticipated that this action would render terrorist attacks against such places less viable and attractive, leading to some form of action 'displacement'. Depending upon the political cause that they were mobilising around, this displacement might involve terrorists looking at similar targets in other locations, nationally or internationally, where the situational prevention measures have not been introduced, or the adoption of new, less well protected targets.

Psychology

Although by no means limited to this issue, a recurring question that appears to have animated psychological research on terrorism is that of 'how and why individuals and groups come to be involved in terrorist activities?' (cf. Horgan 2005). In tackling this question the approaches utilised can be divided between those that focus primarily upon individuals as the principal unit of analysis and the more group-oriented approach typical of social psychological studies. From the former, much of the work has examined whether any specific characteristics or dispositional traits determine whether someone will engage in terrorist activity. Thakrah (2004), for instance, investigated the possibility that terrorists 'choose' to engage in political violence as a result of encountering a disturbed relationship with their own identity. Other studies that similarly find explanatory potential in notions of abnormal personality have suggested that certain individuals are susceptible to becoming terrorists because they are possessed of a 'lack of independence' or 'absence of empathy' (Orbach 2001). Rather than rooting terrorist violence in facets of an abnormal personality, others (e.g. Piven 2002) have focused more upon the claim that disproportionate levels of mental illness are present among people who engage in forms of politically motivated violence. Such studies have been subject to extensive criticism on the basis that interviews carried out with terrorists do not tend to support the view that individuals who carry out such attacks are mentally unstable, as the acts they commit frequently require calculation and systematic planning (Reid 2002). Although subtly different in the approaches that they take, the common factor underpinning these studies is their focus upon individuals. There is, though, a second cluster of studies that, although incorporating some of the principle axioms of psychology, have been more interested in integrating considerations of group dynamics and interactions in terms of what motivates and mobilises people to participate in terrorist campaigns.

These more social psychological perspectives stress the importance of inter-group behaviour and processes of categorisation in terms of how and why certain individuals arrive at a point where they are both able and willing to utilise fairly indiscriminate forms of violence against others. This is exemplified by Tajfel and Turner's (1979, 1986) formulation of 'social identity theory', wherein they posit that group membership involves a reflex sense of 'ingroup' favouritism at the expense of any 'outgroup'. It also induces conformity to group values and norms (Hogg and Tindale 2001). Inflections of such ideas can be detected in Silke's (2008) recent theoretical account of processes of radicalisation wherein he points to how typically terrorists see themselves as heroically working for the benefit of others, not themselves. Moreover, they construct a sense of social identity figured around the notion that they are victims of a majority outgroup's aggression rather than being in the role of the aggressor themselves. This capacity to invoke and sustain self-identification as a victim who is part of a wider process of collective victimisation, seems to be a recurrent justification for the extreme violence enacted by terrorists. Cromer (2001), in seeking to explain such processes, appropriates Sykes and Matza's (1957) repertoire of 'neutralisation' techniques. Cromer maintains that the capacity to invoke 'higher motives' for their actions and to 'condemn their condemners' are centrifugal properties in terms of terrorists being able to sustain a sense of group cohesion over time and to justify the use of violent actions. These are all themes brought together and applied in Post et al.'s (2002) recent analysis of how and why some small groups are at particular risk of moving from holding a set of radical ideas to engaging in violent actions.

Sociology

Contrasted with the 'dispositional' orientations to be found in psychological studies of terrorism, the contribution of sociology tends to be more situational, placing an accent on the role of social context in explaining the causes and consequences of terrorism. In particular, many of the key contributions from a more sociological perspective can be traced back to Emile Durkheim's (1893) conceptualisation of anomie. Durkheim's proposition, empirically grounded in studies of the intertwined processes of urbanisation and industrialisation in the nineteenth century, was that periods of rapid economic, social and political change display a tendency to induce feelings of alienation and disenchantment that are, in turn, generative of wider social tensions and conflicts. Thus, 'anomic' accounts of terrorism tend to relate specific manifestations of political violence to wider processes of social change and locate them as an 'acting out' of the 'pains' of modernisation and social change. Turk (2004) for example seeks to counter the frequently made, but empirically ill-founded, claim that terrorist acts are often performed by the most economically and politically disenfranchised groups in a society. In contrast, he argues that engagement in terrorist activities frequently involves comparatively educated and affluent individuals, precisely because they are better placed to understand the (frequently yawning) gap between political ideals and social realities. The result is that they become radically disconnected from the extant political system and come to view violence enacted in pursuance of political objectives as a solution to the intrinsic and insoluble system failure.

A recent contribution that exemplifies the predispositions of the anomic perspective on terrorism is Neil Smelser's (2007) book *The Faces of Terrorism*. Establishing a broadly Durkheimian account of the pathologies of social change at the end of the twentieth century, Smelser seeks to sketch out the ways that the stresses induced in an era of pronounced and rapid development became refracted into a fundamentalist, religiously inspired ideology promoting mass indiscriminately targeted political violence. His account is particularly engaging at the points where he seeks to make connections between the broad social forces he is charting and the ways that they articulate with more specific social-psychological pressures that come to bear upon particular individuals and groups.

This connecting of base sociological and social psychological themes can be detected also in the work of Marc Sageman (2004). Whereas Smelser's lineage within sociology is theoretical and conceptual, Sageman's connection is more methodological. Utilising a form of social network analysis he has sought to map out, based upon publicly available information, the constitution of Al-Qaeda and its affiliates. The particular insight that his work affords is to distinguish between a tightly interconnected 'core' membership and a more numerous, more peripheral collection of associates whose bonds are based upon a series of 'weak ties.' This insight has proven to be profoundly influential in terms of how governments have sought to respond to the contemporary terrorist threat posed by those seeking to perform political violence as 'jihad.'

One could extend this analysis of disciplinary perspective to include law, architecture and criminology, but the above is sufficient to illustrate that the contributions that have been made by different disciplinary perspectives to understanding the social problem of terrorism have points of overlap and tension. In effect, these key intellectual positions have tended to construct the problem in slightly different ways, and consequently have been steered towards accenting certain causes and consequences. This is a tendency that has been reinforced by the differences that arise in the substantive nature of the conflicts that supply the empirical data for such studies. As Wilkinson (2001), among others, contends, it is important to recognise that each terrorist conflict tends to involve its own unique 'signature' in terms of what is being fought over or what constitutes the terrorists' or counterterrorists' preferred methodology. Nevertheless, while recognising these unique and situational qualities of each conflict, there is a concomitant and equally pressing desire for academic studies to diagnose patterns and trends.

It is set against this backdrop that the import of a number of accounts that have adopted a more self-consciously interdisciplinary and synthetic approach to the study of terrorism starts to become clear. For example, Louise Richardson's (2006) book effectively melds some of the key tenets and ideas found in different intellectual traditions and associated with particular academic disciplines to arrive at a position identifying three common factors to terrorist campaigns:

- Causation – as Richardson (2006:14) describes it '… the causes of terrorism are … a lethal cocktail containing a disaffected individual, an enabling community and a legitimizing ideology'.

- Revenge, renown and reaction – engagement in terrorist violence by individuals and groups is driven by the three, often intertwined, motivations of a desire for revenge, renown and reaction.

- Conducive surround – those terrorist campaigns that acquire traction will be situated in an environment that is somewhat amenable to mounting a sustained campaign, frequently because it affords a degree of either tacit or explicit community support.

Informed by some of the key ideas and themes identified in the intellectual cartography outlined above, in what follows we will examine three particularly significant aspects of terrorism in order to show how the adoption of an interdisciplinary perspective aids the development of a more nuanced and textured understanding of what terrorism is and how it relates to the wider social order.

The shifting scale and modes of terrorism

As is clear from the overview provided above, which acts are labelled as 'terrorism' and which individuals are ascribed the status of 'terrorists' is deeply contested. Such vagaries necessarily carry over into attempts to measure how much 'terrorism' there is and gauge how many people are engaging in terrorist acts. Several studies have attempted to chart, based upon 'open source' publicly available information, whether there has been a growth in the amount of terrorism in recent decades. For example, Pape (2005) has sought to track the number of recorded incidents of suicide bombing over recent years. While useful, such data do not supply us with an in-depth picture of terrorism, charting as they do only the use of a specific tactic. Utilising different metrics, publications such as the *Human Security Brief* (2007) attempt to provide a more global picture of the amount of terrorism worldwide. In this particular instance, they recorded a sharp net decline in the year 2007, probably as a result of reductions in fatalities in Iraq. But any such attempts are bedevilled by active and intense debates across both the academic and political communities about what precisely is an accurate and valid measure. In calibrating the terrorist threat globally, should one measure the number of attacks? Or would a more meaningful measure be the number of fatalities? What should be done about attempted attacks that are disrupted by security agencies? Should these be included in any count, on the basis that they give a measure of terrorist activity and actually in a perverse way counting only successful attacks is more an indicator of the failures of the national security apparatus? Moreover, if one is seeking to track changes in levels of threat or harm, what is an appropriate baseline against which any comparisons should be established? Those familiar with the literature on measuring crime and debates about criminal statistics will recognise the resonances with ongoing discussions in that particular domain.

Attempts to quantify and track the amount of terrorism are understandable, but as was clearly demonstrated in the attacks in New York in 2001, the power of terrorist attacks to articulate a sense of injustice and grievance and to animate political changes cannot be captured through a simple process of enumeration. Acts of terrorism are more often than not, dramaturgically freighted, directed against symbolic people, places or events in an effort to trigger a profound social reaction. Violence is performed, not just for its own sake but to communicate a message. In this sense it is interesting to reflect upon the extent to which developments in technology have been imbricated in the increasing ability of terrorists to elicit fear.

In a recent study of media coverage of terrorism, David Altheide (2006) has charted the ways in which the multiplication of media news platforms and the spread of 24/7 news broadcasting has contributed to an increased reach of acts of mass violence to shape public consciousness. But it is also the case that similar technologies have been co-opted for use by terrorist groups to disseminate their messages. Al-Qaeda in particular has been particularly effective at using the Internet to post videos of attacks undertaken in Iraq and elsewhere so their actions can be 'seen' by their current or potential supporters around the world. But technology has been influential in shaping patterns of terrorist activity in more ways than simply aiding communication. In a very real sense shifts in the modal type of attack that occur over time are products of technological developments. For example, the growth in popularity in suicide bombing as a tactic seen over the past decade (Gambetta 2005) has been facilitated by the spread of types of explosives that can be constructed as a 'bomb vest'. At a more mundane level, it has been the ability of terrorist groups to identify the potential to convert everyday technologies and situations into weapons and targets that has resulted in them being able to extend the destructive and symbolic power of their actions. Indeed there is something akin to a process of social learning evident if one maps the 'long history' of terrorist campaigns rather than focusing upon individual groups and their strategies and tactics. Over time, groups with quite different motivational agendas have borrowed and adapted tactics from earlier groups and learnt from each others' successes and failures. So while in many ways the tactical dimension of terrorism has escalated, the strategic imperatives determining why people seek to engage in terrorism, using a repertoire of tactics, remains more constant.

Capturing and acknowledging the importance of the symbolic dimension to the effects and affects of terrorist incidents is vital in terms of understanding how it shapes the ways in which publics and politicians respond to potential risks and threats that present across particular situations. For example, if one looks at the swell of academic and journalistic interest in terrorism in recent years it has gravitated significantly towards Al-Qaeda and Islamist forms of terrorist violence. But in so doing, there has been something of a neglect of other forms of terrorism, which in the world of counterterrorism practice is difficult to handle. For while the levels of public concern translate into political imperatives which shape agency agendas, on a day-to-day basis most counterterrorism agencies are facing multi-polar threats. So while public and political attention focuses upon Al-Qaeda and its affiliates, security and intelligence agencies are also seeking to intercept and interdict 'domestic extremism' bombing campaigns undertaken by far-right political groups or so-called 'lone-wolf' terrorists (such as the Una-Bomber in the United States). Understanding the particular tensions and demands created by multi-polar threat environments is something that remains largely undocumented in terms of how academic studies have approached the problem of responding to terrorism.

Social support: motivating and mobilising

In seeking to emphasise the importance of locating violent conflicts in their social context, sociology, perhaps more than is the case for the other disciplines engaged in the study of terrorists and terrorisms, clarifies the importance of levels of social support in shaping and influencing the trajectories of terrorist campaigns. Considering such matters widens the scope of analytic interest in a number of important ways. Firstly, it shifts the locus of attention from those individuals and groups who perform the violence of terrorism to those who either directly assist or facilitate such actions, as well as the more passive members of a community who nonetheless support the use of violence in pursuit of a stated political goal. Second, it brings directly into view questions about the capacity of different actors and their acts to motivate and mobilise those communities on whose behalf violence is purportedly being practised. For as much as they are intended to cause harm to the interests of the frequently more powerful adversary, violent interventions are, at least in the minds of those who perform them, also designed to generate a groundswell of support for both the ends and means of the group concerned. In both theoretical and empirical registers, such questions are important in terms of being able to gauge the social impacts of particular terrorist actions and campaigns. Such issues are largely neglected in those studies that focus more explicitly upon the terrorist individual or group.

One of the most insightful studies of the role of social support in terrorism is to be found in Slucka's (1989) ethnographic study of the Divis Flats in Belfast, Northern Ireland. Whereas in media reports of terrorist groups and the public policy rhetoric of politicians and practitioners, there is a tendency to bifurcate the situation between a small group of committed terrorists and everyone else, Slucka constructs a more complex and nuanced picture of the social reality of support and opposition to terrorism. Based upon his extensive observations of life in a particular area of Belfast, he argues that in fact there is a 'spectrum' of positions rather than just two that can be adopted by the general populace in terms of how they relate to actions that are defined by the authorities as terrorist. On the one hand there are those committed to political causes, who provide ongoing and active assistance of various kinds to those who directly commit the violent acts. At the other end of the spectrum are those who are implacably opposed to both the means and ends of the active terrorists. But of most interest to Slucka is the range of positions in between these two polarities. For it is the beliefs and attitudes of people, in the middle parts of the spectrum that are liable to ebb and flow according to the actions and reactions of the terrorists and those arrayed against them. Accordingly he charts how violence by the Provisional IRA that harmed innocent civilians would typically lead to a decline in their popular support. But by far the most significant factor shaping community attitudes and opinions were the interventions of the Royal Ulster Constabulary and the British Army. Particularly when the authorities were perceived to have overreacted to an event, this generated an increase in levels of support for the paramilitary groups.

Support for the general tenor of this argument is to be found in the work of Hillyard (1993), which is also grounded in the study of the conflict in Northern Ireland. Hillyard maintains that the tendency of the authorities to utilise a bifurcated order of reality, wherein the general public are either simply cast as being 'for' the terrorists or 'against' them, results in them operating on the basis of there being a de facto 'suspect community'. The concept of a suspect community is an important one that attempts to articulate how police and allied agencies end up treating all members of a community or group as potential terrorists and failing to try to differentiate between the 'real' terrorists and 'normal' members of the public. The results of this are that the discrimination and harassment that is consequently experienced by ordinary people leads them to express more support than they might otherwise have done for the terrorists. This theme of the consequences of overreaction in countering terrorism functioning as a motivator and mobilising force for terrorist campaigns is something we will return to in due course, when we turn to discuss the conduct of counterterrorism in more detail below.

What is especially intriguing about Slucka's account of life in Belfast during 'The Troubles' is that, as much as it is a physical conflict involving the utilisation of violence by the adversaries, it points to how terrorism and the responses to acts defined in this way is also a 'legitimacy contest'. Unless a terrorist campaign is able to tap into a reservoir of social support somewhere, then it is unlikely to be sustained over a particularly long period. Commenting upon the situation in Israel for instance, Ganor (2005) stresses the pragmatic point that the various groups who engage in terrorist activities in that setting are, in effect, in competition for general support and activists. Therefore the perceived legitimacy of the claims and counterclaims forwarded by the various groups are pivotal to their capacity to continue their opposition to the Israeli government and its policies. In Northern Ireland, the need to secure and sustain a degree of popular legitimacy led the IRA and other similar organisations to engage in activities specifically intended to try and propagate and enhance their standing in the eyes of the general public. As Slucka (1989) documents, in effect the IRA sought to provide particular 'social services' to local communities, especially relating to the social control of crime and disorder, in the belief that adopting this role in maintaining a degree of local social order would help to garner support for their principal focus.

Counterterrorism

In the preceding discussion it was noted that the perceived success of a particular terrorist attack and/or campaign is frequently determined as much by the reaction it elicits from a state's security agencies as by the intrinsic qualities of any intervention itself. This is an idea that features strongly in the game theoretic approaches common in treatments of terrorist conflicts emanating from the discipline of economics. Albeit that it tends to be rendered overly simplistically in such formulations, the fundamental proposition that the conduct of counterterrorism exhibits a profound influence upon the conduct of terrorism itself is undoubtedly correct. Steven and Gunaratna (2004) remind us that direct responses to terrorist activity span a range from military applications of force through to interventions premised upon harnessing the capacities of the criminal justice system. If one looks at the current situation in respect of countering jihadist inspired violent extremism, one can see that these two approaches are not necessarily mutually exclusive. The military interventions in the borderlands between Pakistan and Afghanistan are being utilised to try and degrade the influence of the Al-Qaeda network and particularly its core leadership hub, while in Europe the criminal justice agencies have become increasingly involved in attempts to prevent and detect the activities of those who would seek to inflict mass casualties there. But as has been demonstrated by the developments in Northern Ireland, politics also has a counterterrorist function in terms of addressing perceived grievances and injustices and 'winning hearts and minds' in such a way that any social support for terrorism is degraded.

Although it is not especially common to think in these terms the relations between counterterrorism agencies and those they oppose can be construed as one of point and counterpoint, inasmuch as each continually seeks to innovate in their operating procedures in order to secure a tactical advantage over their opponent. In effect, a group motivated to engage in terrorism is consistently trying to identify a vulnerability that can be exploited in order to increase the chances of prosecuting a successful attack. Simultaneously, the authorities are seeking to prevent, detect and disrupt any moves to exploit potential vulnerabilities. Thus, as the authorities succeed in making particular targets more difficult to harm, they may in effect shift the focus of risks and threats onto other aspects of social life. For example, the significant enhancements to security introduced into airports after the 2001 attacks and the interception of Richard Reid, the attempted 'shoe-bomber', have been followed by attacks on the public transport network in London and several planned assaults on shopping centres and nightclubs. Likewise, the attacks carried out in Mumbai in December 2008 by groups affiliated to Al-Qaeda demonstrated how, as authorities around the world had increasingly configured their assets in such a way as to mitigate the risks posed by suicide bombers, a committed group intent on causing mass casualties was able to circumvent these defensive measures by adopting a different and tactically innovative, but equally effective, method of killing.

In most western states the assets available and utilised for counter-terrorism work are divided between several different institutions. Typically the military will provide a more offensive capability, with the management of the domestic situation divided between agencies specialising in collecting, analysing and acting upon secret intelligence and the law enforcement capabilities of the police. In Britain, for example, the Security Service (MI5) tends to assume the lead role for identifying and responding to potential and active risks and threats. Their efforts are supplemented and augmented by specialist counterterrorism police located in SO15 at Scotland Yard and several Counter-Terrorism Units located around the country. Although detailed empirical research on the conduct of counterterrorism is currently notable by its absence, several available sources do suggest that such patterns of organisation tend to be driven by tensions in relation to the preferred modes of intervention of intelligence agencies and the police.

Gearty (2007) for example, suggests that those agencies whose principal focus gravitates around the use of intelligence exhibit a preference for early interventions and disrupting the activities of those believed to be planning an atrocity, oftentimes through extra-legal interventions. In contrast, the police mindset is more concerned with collecting evidence and case-building in order to utilise the criminal justice process to bring offenders to justice. Focusing more explicitly upon the current issue of Islamist-inspired violent extremism, Innes and Thiel (2008) point to a further tension within UK policing that resonates with the broader one outlined above. This involves disagreement as to whether the most effective way to respond to the current threat of Islamist extremism is one grounded in the use of specialist counterterrorism officers, operating targeted 'intelligence-led approaches' or, alternatively, whether it is more appropriate to widen the counterterrorism effort to encompass neighbourhood policing teams who are potentially better placed to deal with the myriad local injustices that may, at least according to some accounts, 'prime' certain individuals so that they are more likely to be persuaded by radical ideologies (Innes *et al.* 2007). According to Innes and Thiel (2008), recent policing policy has appeared somewhat indecisive about which strategy to adopt and has, as a result, sought to fashion an ad hoc position incorporating elements of both.

The case against widening the police involvement to formally incorporate community policing assets has been set out by Thacher (2005) and Bratton and Kelling (2006). The former suggests that the danger with involving local policing in national security issues is that they will be 'contaminated' in the eyes of minority ethnic communities, who will see them as an agency concerned not with responding to their needs as victims of crime, but as enforcers solely concerned with rooting out individuals from a 'suspect community'. Relatedly, Bratton is also concerned about the potentially negative consequences that might flow from asking local policing to focus explicitly upon countering the threats posed by Al-Qaeda inspired terrorism. But his concern is that in developing such a role, policing resources will inevitably be shifted from managing crime levels to managing terrorism risks, with the longer-term consequences that overall levels for volume and major crime will start to creep upwards. While such concerns are both pertinent and incisive, it does seem that, particularly in relation to the 'prevention' strand of counterterrorism work, the general trend seems to be to establish a role for community policing officers. This reflects a sense among senior officers that despite considerable expansion in the resources of specialist intelligence-based operatives, the levels of threat do not appear to be reducing. As such, there may be a need to configure a new approach that recognises the increasing interconnections that exist between neighbourhood and national security (Innes and Thiel 2008).

The latter point speaks to one of the defining tensions that animate the conduct of counterterrorism work. This is that while assertive, intelligence-based interventions may be effective in neutralising, or at least mitigating, potential threats, if they are not seen to be proportionate and targeted they may serve to amplify levels of public concern and antipathy towards the state and its agencies, thus effectively buttressing the terrorists' cause. With this in mind, Pickering *et al.* (2008) have suggested that any effective counter-terrorist strategy be based upon balancing the demands to reduce short-term immediately 'acute' risks and threats while also sustaining community cohesion and the fundamentals of the prevalent social order.

Conclusion

This chapter has highlighted some of the key themes and issues to be found in the academic literature on terrorism, showing how principles derived from a number of disciplinary perspectives have contributed to our growing understanding of the causes and consequences of politically motivated mass violence. At the same time it has sought to show how developments in the realm of ideas are also, in part, a response to shifts in how the conduct of terrorism is imagined and practised. Thus, as shifts in the combinations of strategy, tactics and ideas utilised by different terrorist groups have become evident, as well as the social control responses enacted, different ideas and perspectives demonstrate the capacity to offer insight into the complexities of behaviour and social change from which, in turn, emanate understanding. In a rapidly changing global world the threat of terror has already been associated with the current environmental debates around climate change and ecological development. Thus an understanding of the current threat does not mean that we are equipped either intellectually or practically to respond to the future social problems that might be sufficiently profound as to motivate and mobilise people to engage in activities that others will seek to define as 'terrorist'.

Selected further reading

There are a large number of readings dedicated to the widespread debate regarding the many facets of global terrorism some of which have been covered in this and other chapters in this edition, e.g. Chapter 37 on state crime and Chapter 40 on crimes of the global state. The literature surrounding global terrorism, society, the state and the individual is ever-changing in both the academic domain and political domain therefore readers are advised to keep up to date with the latest developments through online sources such as the Home Office's Security and Counter Terrorism Branch (http://security.homeoffice.gov.uk/). For a greater understanding of the contributions and direction of research regarding the debate around 'terror' readers may find Louise Richardson's *What Terrorists Want: Understanding the Terrorist Threat* (2006) and Walter Laqueur's *No End To War: Terrorism in the Twenty-First Century* (2004) good starting points.

Note

1 This tendency was most pithily encapsulated in Fukuyama's influential thesis on 'the end of history'.

References

Altheide, D. (2006) *Terrorism and the Politics of Fear*. Lanham, MD: Rowman & Littlefield.

Bier, V. (2007) 'Choosing what to protect', *Risk Analysis*, 27 (3): 607–20.

Black, D. (2004) 'The geometry of terrorism', *Sociological Theory*, 22 (1): 14–25.

Bratton, W. and Kelling, G. (2006) *Policing Terrorism*, Civic Bulletin No. 43. Manhattan Lust for Policy Research. Online at: http://www.manhattan-institute.org/html/cb_43.htm (accessed 6 January 2008).

Cohen, S. (2001) *States of Denial*. Cambridge: Polity.

Cromer, G. (2001) 'Terrorist tales', in G. Cromer (ed.), *Narratives of Violence*. Aldershot: Ashgate.

Durkheim, É. ([1893] 1984) *The Division of Labour in Society*. Basingstoke: Macmillan.

Fukuyama, F. (1989) 'The end of history?', *The National Interest*, Summer, pp. 13–18.

Gambetta, D. (2005) 'Can we make sense of suicide missions?', in D. Gambetta (ed.), *Making Sense of Suicide Missions*. Oxford: Oxford University Press.

Ganor, B. (2005) *The Counter-Terrorism Puzzle: A Guide for Decision-Makers*. Edison, NJ: Transaction.

Gearty, C. (2007) 'Dilemmas of terror', *Prospect*, October, pp. 34–8.

Hillyard, P. (1993) *Suspect Community: People's Experience of the Prevention of Terrorism Acts in Britain*. London: Pluto Press.

Hoffman, B. (2006) *Inside Terrorism*, 2nd edn. New York: Columbia University Press.

Hogg, M. A. and Tindale, R. S. (eds) (2001) *Blackwell Handbook in Social Psychology: Group Processes*. Oxford: Blackwell, pp. 1–30.

Horgan, J. (2005) *The Psychology of Terrorism*. London: Routledge.

Human Security Brief (2007) Simon Fraser University, School for International Studies. Online at the Human Security Report Project website: http://www.humansecuritybrief.info/ (accessed 14 September 2008.

Innes, M. (2006) 'Policing uncertainty: countering terror through community intelligence and democratic policing', *Annals of the American Academy of Political and Social Science*, 605: 222–41.

Innes, M. and D. Thiel (2008) 'Policing terror', in T. Newburn (ed.), *The Handbook of Policing*, 2nd edn. Cullompton: Willan.

Innes, M., Abbott, L., Lowe, T. and Roberts, C. (2007) *Hearts and Minds and Eyes and Ears: Reducing Radicalisation Risks Through Reassurance-Oriented Policing*. London: ACPO.

Jacobson, M. (2006) *The West at War: US and European Counterterrorism Efforts, Post-September 11*. Washington, DC: Washington Institute for Near-East Policy.

Kean, T. and Hamilton, L. (2004) *The 9/11 Commission Report*. New York: W. W. Norton.

Lapan, H. E and Sandler, T. (1988) 'To bargain or not to bargain: that is the question', *American Economic Review*, 78 (2): 16–21.

Laqueur, W. (2001) *A History of Terrorism*. New York: Transaction.

Laqueur, W. (2004) *No End To War: Terrorism in the Twenty-First Century*. New York: Continuum.

Lee, M. (2007) *Inventing Fear of Crime*. Cullompton: Willan.

Levi, M. (2007) 'Organized crime and terrorism', in M. Maguire, R. Morgan and R. Reiner (eds), *The Oxford Handbook of Criminology*, 4th edn. Oxford: Oxford University Press.

Lincoln, B. (2006) *Holy Terrors: Thinking About Religion After September 11th*, 2nd edn. Chicago: University of Chicago Press.

Monaghan, R (1999) 'Terrorism in the name of animal rights', *Terrorism and Political Violence*, 11 (4): 159–69.

Orbach, B. (2001) 'Usama Bin Laden and Al-Qa'ida: origins and doctrines', *Middle East Review of International Affairs*, 5: 54–68.

Pape, R. (2005) *Dying to Win: The Strategic Logic of Suicide Terrorism*. New York: Random House.

Pickering, S., McCulloch, J. and Wright-Neville, D. P. (2008) *Counter-terrorism Policing: Community, Cohesion and Security*. New York: Springer.

Piven, J. S. (2002) 'On the psychosis (religion) of terrorists', in C. E. Stout (ed.), *The Psychology of Terrorism: Theoretical Understandings and Perspectives (Psychological Dimension to War and Peace)*, Vol. III. Westport, CT: Praeger, pp. 120–47.

Post, J., Ruby, K. and Shaw, E. (2002) 'The radical group in context 1: an integrated framework for the analysis for group risk for terrorism', *Studies in Conflict and Terrorism*, 25 (2): 73–100.

Rapoport, D. (1988) 'Messianic sanctions for terror', *Comparative Politics*, 20: 195–213.

Reid, W. H (2002) 'Controlling political terrorism: practically (not psychology)', in C. E. Stout (ed.), *The Psychology of Terrorism: Theoretical Understandings and Perspectives (Psychological Dimension to War and Peace)*, Vol. III. Westport, CT: Praeger, pp. 120–47.

Richardson, L. (2006) *What Terrorists Want: Understanding the Terrorist Threat*. London: John Murray.

Rock, P. (2005) 'Chronocentrism and British criminology', *British Journal of Sociology*, 56 (3): 473–791.

Sageman, M. (2004) *Understanding Terror Networks*. Philadelphia: University of Pennsylvania Press.

Sandler, T. (1997) *Global Challenges: An Approach to Environmental, Political and Economic Problems*. Cambridge: Cambridge University Press.

Sandler, T. and Enders, W. (2004) 'An economic perspective on transnational terrorism', *European Journal of Political Economy*, 20: 301–16.

Sandler, T. and Lapan, H. E. (1988) 'The calculus of dissent: an analysis of terrorists' choice of targets', *Synthese*, 76 (2): 245–61.

Schmid, A. and Jongman, A. (1988) *Political Terrorism: A Research Guide to Concepts, Theories, Data Bases and Literature*. Amsterdam: North Holland.

Silke, A. (2004) 'The road less travelled: recent trends in terrorism research', in A. Silke (ed.), *Research on Terrorism: Trends, Achievements and Failures*. London: Frank Cass.

Silke, A. (2008) 'Holy warriors: exploring the psychological processes of jihadi radicalization', *European Journal of Criminology*, 5: 99–123.

Slucka, J. (1989) *Hearts and Minds, Water and Fish: Support for the IRA and INLA in a Northern Ireland Ghetto*. Greenwich, CT: JAI Press.

Smelser, N. (2007) *The Faces of Terrorism: Social and Psychological Dimensions*. Princeton, NJ: Princeton University Press.

Steven, G. and Gunaratna, R. (2004) *Counter-terrorism: A Reference Handbook*. Santa Barbara, CA: ABC-ClIO.

Sykes, G. and Matza, D. (1957) 'Techniques of neutralization: a theory of delinquency', *American Sociological Review*, 22 (6): 664–70.

Tajfel, H. and Turner, J. C. (1979) 'An integrative theory of intergroup conflict', in W. G. Austin and S. Worchel (eds), *The Social Psychology of Intergroup Relations*. Monterey, CA: Brooks-Cole.

Tajfel, H. and Turner, J. C. (1986) 'The social identity theory of inter-group behavior', in S. Worchel and L. W. Austin (eds), *Psychology of Intergroup Relations*. Chigago: Nelson-Hall.

Thacher, D. (2005) 'The local role in Homeland Security', *Law and Society Review*, 39 (5): 635–76.

Thackrah, J. R. (2004) *Dictionary of Terrorism*, 2nd edn. London: Routledge.

Turk, A. T. (2004) 'Sociology of terrorism', *Annual Review of Sociology*, 30: 271–86.

Wardlaw, G. (1982) *Political Terrorism: Theory Tactics and Counter-Measures*. Cambridge: Cambridge University Press.

Wilkinson, P. (2001) *Terrorism Versus Democracy: The Liberal State Response*. Abingdon: Frank Cass.

Part VIII

Harms, Health and Safety

The harmful actions discussed in this section - eco-crime, corporate harms and driving offences – have in common that they are often not considered to be 'real' crimes. Instead, they are typically regarded as 'accidents', 'disasters' or 'breaches' of acceptable standards and dealt with by regulatory rather than by criminal sanctions. Prosecutions for work-related fatalities and air pollution are rare, and even those cases that get to court tend to be dealt with not as criminal offences, but as breaches of environmental law or health and safety law, attracting relatively lenient penalties. The criminal law is used more often for serious driving offences, but, even in cases resulting in death, sentences are typically more lenient than for other forms of violent crime.

This is perhaps surprising given the nature and quantity of harm caused by these crimes – among the most devastating discussed in this volume. The numbers of victims involved are enormous. For example, both Walters and Tombs cite an estimate that air pollution kills up to 24,000 people a year in the UK. It is also estimated that, worldwide, 2.2 million workers die each year through work-related accidents and diseases, while Corbett notes that road deaths are predicted to become the third biggest killer by 2020. Such figures have been used by some academics to argue that 'zemiology' – the study of harms – offers a more appropriate lens than traditional criminology through which to analyse these kinds of behaviour and the responses to them.

The extent to which the boundaries of criminology should be extended to embrace 'harms' which are not normally punished through the criminal law is one of the key debates addressed in this part of the book. Both Walters and Tombs refer to 'green criminology', which includes the study of harms against humanity, the environment and animals committed both by powerful organisations (e.g. governments, transnational corporations, military forces) and by individuals. These three chapters also explore several other important questions. Firstly, how can corporate harms be explained? Tombs argues that it is unhelpful to pitch explanations simply at the levels of intention to harm or interpersonal relationships and that the role of the political economy has to be recognised in explaining the phenomenon. Secondly, what is the appropriate level of sanctions where offender culpability is low, as in 'careless' offences, but harm is as extreme as death? Corbett notes that government and Crown Prosecution Service efforts to respond to the anger of the families of road victims are not helped by the fact that no mention of a death is included in charges such as 'driving without due care and attention'. Finally, how effective is self-regulation? Walters questions whether a 'partnership model', which is industry-led and relies upon compliance and corporate good practice, works.

Overall, this collection of chapters provides an overview of the extent, causes and responses to a set of harms caused by individuals, corporations and states that are often ignored, in spite of the immense damage that they cause to health, life, wildlife, soils, water, agriculture, buildings and natural heritage.

Chapter 43

Eco-crime and air pollution[1]

Reece Walters

Introduction

Contemporary discourses in green criminology continue to engage with and critique acts that damage and destroy the environment (Beirne and South 2007; White 2008). Such debates seek to focus the criminological lens on the ways in which environmental harm is relevant to issues of crime and justice. The ongoing protection and regulation of the environment continues to witness a global increase in law and policy. Such developments have provided a new language regarding environmental harm including 'precaution', liability', 'responsibility' and 'assessment'. The rapidly expanding body of environment law that seeks to develop, protect and conserve the environment sometimes refers to 'breaches' or 'violations' of acceptable standards, but the language of 'crime' is noticeably absent (see Bodansky *et al.* 2007). From a jurisprudential viewpoint this is best explained by the simple fact that environmental offences, within the UK and abroad, are dealt with in civil courts as 'administrative matters' rather than in criminal jurisdictions. While the term 'environmental crime' is often used within academia and various activist and campaign movements, its usage within law and official government policy (notably in the UK and across Europe) is often limited to anti-social behaviour (see Home Office 2007). While the UK House of Commons Environmental Audit has discussed the problems of 'corporate environmental crime' as 'any environmental crime that has been committed by a corporate body' (House of Commons 2005: 8), such debates have focused largely on the domestic issues of water, sewerage and landfill and not transnational issues. As a result, eco-crime is a preferred term that broadens the gaze beyond legal definitions to include discourses on risk, rights and regulation. As a result, eco-crime extends existing usages of environmental crime to include licensed or lawful acts of ecological degradation committed by states and corporations (Walters 2009).

This chapter applies emerging discourses of eco-crime and green criminology to issues of air pollution. Of course there are various forms of pollution (land, sea, water, soil, space and air), but this chapter will focus on the contamination and regulation of 'the air we breathe' (the theme of the World Meteorological Day 2009).

The unacceptable levels of existing air pollution in London and other areas of the UK is a reality that is not being ignored by the European Commission. For example, in January 2009 it was widely reported that the European Union was preparing a legal case against the British government for repeatedly breaching air pollution laws (Vanhoeyvelt 2009; Vidal 2009). More than 20 UK towns and cities were emitting air pollution more than twice the UN World Health Organisation standards, notably PM10 particles from diesel engines (CCAL 2009). This latest action by the EU follows a previous infringement procedure against the UK in 2007 'for exceeding EU limits on ambient concentrations of sulphuer dioxide (SO_2), an air pollutant from industrial installations that can cause respiratory problems and aggravate cardiovascular disease' (Europa 2007: 1).

This chapter specifically examines the existing mechanisms of air pollution control and enforcement in the UK. In doing so, it identifies how criminology must continue to push new boundaries and engage with new horizons with emerging harmful acts of both local and global concern.

Air pollution and its impacts

Air is an essential ingredient of all living things. Its properties influence the quality and longevity of life. The World Health Organisation estimates that air pollution causes the annual premature death of two million people worldwide (WHO 2008). In the UK, an estimated 24,000 'die prematurely every year' because of air pollution and many thousands are hospitalised (COMEAP 2009), with London the worst affected area (London Assembly 2009). Not only are humans placed at risk, but wildlife, soils, water, agriculture, buildings and natural heritage are also damaged by air pollutants with an average annual cost to the taxpayer of £20 billion (Defra 2009a).

The European Commission aims to reduce death and environmental degradation associated with particulate matter through its Thematic Strategy. This strategy aims 'by 2020 to cut the annual number of premature deaths from air pollution-related diseases by almost 40 per cent from the 2000 level. It also aims to substantially reduce the area of forests and other ecosystems suffering damage from airborne pollutants' (Europa 2006). Yet the success of such approaches will be contingent upon the participation and compliance of member states.

Defining air pollution

In 1970, The Royal Commission on Environmental Pollution (RCEP), an independent advisory body, was established to advise on issues relating to polluting emissions. It defines pollution as:

> The introduction by Man into the environment of substances or energy liable to cause hazard to human health, harm to living resources and

ecological systems, damage to structure or amenity or interference with legitimate use of the environment. (RCEP 2006)

Therefore is it important to note that the legal regime in the UK and across Europe is not designed to monitor and regulate 'primary pollutants' or natural pollution such as carbon and sulphur produced from oceans, volcanoes, rain forests and so on, but is focused on 'secondary pollutants', notably chemically created emissions combined with atmospheric conditions (Bridgman 1990).

Sources of air pollution

The UK's National Air Quality Archive monitors the impact of eight different forms of harmful air pollution. The following list of pollutants is adapted from the Archive's database and represents a conservative estimation of the dangers and harms of air pollution.

- *Sulphur dioxide* – created from burning sulphur in fossil fuels and oil. Sulphur dioxide produces lung dysfunction when measured at moderate levels within atmospheric conditions.

- *Nitrogen oxides* – produced from vehicle emissions and the production of electricity. Nitrogen oxides compromise lung functions and cause respiratory and viral illness, notably in children.

- *Toxic organic micro-pollutants* (TOMPs) – very dangerous chemicals caused by combustible activities including using fuels such as waste from industry smokestacks, and vehicular and engine emissions. Carcinogenic chemicals such as dioxins, furans, polyaromatic hydrocarbons and polychlorinated biphenyls in small amounts are highly deleterious to humans and other lung-breathing animals causing cancer, lung disease, immune deficiency and cerebral dysfunction in young children.

- *Fine particles* – dusts, sulphates and nitrates caused by combustible sources such as road traffic and atmospheric reactions. Fine particles are carcinogenic and enter the lungs and bloodstream causing inflammation as well as more serious conditions such as heart and other disease.

- *Butadiene* – a chemical released into the atmosphere from the industrial burning of rubber and synthetics and the emissions from petrol- and diesel-operated machinery. Butadiene is responsible for a range of human health problems including birth defects, organ damage and reproductive disorders.

- *Carbon monoxide* – a poisonous gas produced by petrol engines. Carbon dioxide damages respiratory and circulatory body functions, reduces oxygen supply to major organs including the heart and causes heart disease.

- *Lead and heavy metals* – industrial areas emitting smoke and vapour waste create extremely dangerous lead and other heavy metals that damage the neural and organ development of infants and young children as well as causing deformity in the unborn. This form of highly dangerous industrial pollution also causes mental, neurological and visual problems.

- *Ozone and volatile organic compounds* – volatile organic compounds (VOCs) react with sunlight and nitrogen oxide to create vapour that is capable of travelling thousands of miles. It causes damage to the natural environment as well as human health conditions such as asthma and lung disease.

Exposure to air pollutants such as the above has been widely reported to produce pulmonary dysfunction as well as a range of neurological and vascular disorders (Ghio and Devlin 2001). Such pollutants are monitored on a daily basis using 1,500 different monitoring facilities across the UK. The results are posted on the National Air Quality Archive for public consumption. However, the pollutants listed above are often (not always) created by legal enterprises engaging in legal activities such as transport, agriculture, building, engineering, trade and so on, activities that are considered necessary for a developing and growing society. However, not all air pollution is caused by legitimate, ethical and legal means.

Crime, harm and air pollution

Air pollution is responsible for damage to human health, wildlife, agriculture, materials, buildings and natural heritage. Air pollution is the major source of global warming and climate change that reportedly kills 150 million people a year (Brown 2003; Greenpeace 2009). The illegal emission of air pollutants or the illegal acts, notably by states and corporations, that lead to atmospheric contamination has been reported within various discourses. Criminological scholars have for some time documented how high-polluting transnational corporations flout national laws by relocating to developing countries where toxic chemicals are deliberately released into the environment to the detriment of the surrounding flora and fauna (Michalowski and Kramer 1987; South 1998). Others have detailed the ways in which corporations unlawfully release toxic waste into the atmosphere and the devastating impacts it has on the environment, children and the unborn as well those living in poverty (Pearce and Tombs 1998). Moreover, acts of illegal logging, the dumping of hazardous waste, the illegal trade in ozone depleting substances, the unlawful trade in endangered species, corporate contamination of water and soil, and fuel smuggling, all contribute to the production of air pollution and other environmental damage (Hayman and Brack 2002; White 2008; Walters 2009). As a result, 'industrial disasters' that often include wilful acts of corporate negligence result in toxic chemical release, oil spills and widespread environmental contamination resulting in air pollution and fatality (Carrabine *et al.* 2004; White 2008). Moreover, it is important to recognise that a broad range of eco-crime is linked to the poverty, social dislocation as well as the mental and physical debilitation of people who are victims of corporations and states that deliberately violate environmental agreements (Hauck 2007). Such impacts on human health, culture, flora and fauna are immeasurable. Studies that attempt to link specific aspects of air pollution to financial costs are often imprecise and rife with methodological and data ambiguities (Watkiss *et al.* 2006). That said, the production, distribution, enforcement and consequences of air pollution are a multi-billion pound a year cost with widespread social and environmental harm.

It is clear that increasing air pollution is a by-product of capitalist societies. Our very way of life necessitates that we contaminate our environment in order to maintain a standard of living with luxuries and technologies that are detrimental to that environment. The rapid industrialisation of countries such as China and India has witnessed a sharp increase in air pollution (Watts 2005). The question is how much environmental damage is acceptable? At what point do agricultural, industrial and transportation-related contaminants exceed legal and moral levels that require intervention? These are broader questions about consumption and production that require debate. There are also issues pertaining to legal levels of air pollution and the ways in which laws are deliberately flouted in the pursuit of profit. Such legal levels differ according to individual national contexts.

The Environmental Protection Agency in the United States provides a list of the top ten fines meted out by US courts for 'environmental crimes'. Two of the top three include 'air pollution offences'. For example, in 1998 Louisiana Pacific Corporation, a timber mill, agreed to pay a '$31.5 million penalty for mail fraud and a $5.5 million fine for willfully conspiring to violate the Clean Air Act' (Siegal 1998). In 2001 the Koch Petroleum Group was fined $US20 million for deliberately covering up the disposal of toxic chemicals at its Texas oil refinery. This included the illegal release of ten tonnes of fumes from burning the highly dangerous and carcinogenic substance benzene (*New York Times* 2001). More recently, in October 2008, Erler Industries was convicted for 'clean air crimes' and fined US$1 million by the US District Court of Northern Illinois for 'knowingly submitting false quarterly reports' (USEPA 2008).

In December 2008, the US Environmental Protection Agency (USEPA) launched its 'most wanted' website, detailing a list of 'fugitives' at large for various environmental crimes. Many on the list include corporate entrepreneurs who have owned and operated installations that have deliberately released toxic waste into the atmosphere (USEPA 2009). It should be noted that while the language of 'crime' is used by the US regulatory authorities, most matters are dealt with in civil jurisdictions. Indeed, a Senate Bill presented in March 2008 that attempted to try environmental offences within criminal proceedings was rejected (O'Malley 2008).

The international increase in environmental offences has recently been reported as escalating rapidly. The illegal logging and trade in wildlife alone is estimated to be a £10 billion a year industry (Booth 2008). Such is the expanding nature of illegal environmental acts internationally that Interpol has committed dedicated resources to what it calls 'wildlife crime' and 'pollution crime'. It describes the latter as 'the handling, transport, trading, possessing and disposal of hazardous wastes or resources in contravention of national and international laws' (Interpol 2009a). In 2007 Interpol established the Pollution Crime Working Group which meets annually for the express purpose of sharing and consolidating databases and working in partnership with its 187 affiliated enforcement bodies to tackle the global challenges of illegal pollution (2009b). This international policing partnership comprises the latest enforcement initiative to uphold existing international, European and UK laws that regulate and control air pollution. The following section explores the existing regulatory regimes, notably in the UK and throughout Europe, for controlling and preventing air pollution.

Air pollution – regulations and preventions

The IPPC Directive

The European Environmental Agency (EEA) strategy 2004–8 emphasised an integrated view for the implementation of the sixth Action Programme that would include a series of cross-sectoral assessments on 'environmental trends and ecosystem health' (EEA 2004). The environmental policies of the EC are extensive and secondary legislation through the vast number of directives has addressed a widespread number of issues including pollution, the protection of marine life, water quality, climate change and so on. It is clear that the post-Maastricht phase has witnessed a substantial growth in environmental policy and legislation. The important question is to what extent has integration across the EC been achieved and within the national legal frameworks of member states? In relation to air pollution, it is the EU that has integrated UK policy and law, or at least, has been guided by the UK's regulatory regime.

In 1996, the European Council adopted the Integrated Pollution Prevention and Control (IPPC) Directive. The IPPC Directive was integrated into UK law through the Pollution Prevention and Control (PPC) Act 1999 and the 2000 regulations. The PPC Act 1999 did not replace the Environmental Protection Act (EPA) 1990 but was seen to embellish and complement existing mechanisms. The existing PPC regime has many differences from its predecessor. Notably it has more expansive coverage of pollution which includes waste management, landfill, farming and the food service industry. It also regulates 'installations' and not just processes, and it requires Best Available Techniques (BAT) irrespective of cost. Moreover, the PPC is a more onerous system of control that places 'more industrial processes under control by an integrated approach' (see Thornton and Beckwith 2004: 113).

The IPPC Directive attempts to harmonise pollution control mechanisms across the EU. As of October 1999, the IPPC Directive applies to all new installations in Britain. It imposes more stringent BAT requirements and because these enhanced standards may jeopardise employment markets across Europe, the IPPC Directive 'grants these installations an 11 year long transition period counting from the day that the Directive entered into force' to conform to new guidelines (Europa 2006: 1). The IPPC Directive involves a number of organisations that ensure that the Directive is implemented. For example, licensing agencies across EU countries must issue permits and oversee regulation and the European Commission monitors the Directive's integration into member state legislation. In addition, industry experts, environmental organisations, the Information Exchange Forum, the European IPPC Bureau and the IPPC Expert Group are charged with varying responsibilities to ensure that the IPPC Directive is integrated into domestic laws across the EU (Europa 2006).

The PPC (England and Wales) Regulations 2000 provide a three-tier system of pollution control. Installations must apply to the EA for permits to operate. Permit applications provide non-technical information about the operations of the proposed installation and the various mechanisms to be put in place to prevent or limit emissions. Permits may carry specified conditions that may be reviewed or varied. Moreover, revocation notices can be issued to an operator that fails to fulfil the conditions of the permits. It should be noted that installations are entrusted with the responsibility to self-regulate and manage the conditions of their designated permit. For example, the guidelines from the UK's Environment Agency to business and industry vis-à-vis applying for a PPC permit stipulate that 'you [operators] are responsible for designing and managing your installation using the best available technique (BAT) to prevent or minimise pollution. You also have to minimise waste and return the site to a satisfactory state on completion of your activities' (Environment Agency (EA) 2006: 1).

It is an offence for an operator in the UK to engage in a commercial activity that causes air pollution without a permit. In addition, the EA often uses Administrative Orders as a means of enforcing pollution control laws. These regulatory offences under IPPC can be referred to a criminal court if the operator fails to comply with the conditions of an enforcement notice (Regulation 24, PPC Regulations 2000). Corporate executives may also be prosecuted and imprisoned for breaching permits; however, this rarely occurs (see Jervis 2005). That said, existing pollution control laws in the UK, similar to those in the US, are not focused solely on criminal sanction and deterrence but on legal and environmental compliance. Therefore, a non-punitive system of governance relies upon a partnership between operator and regulator to negotiate and jointly resolve contentious issues within a culture of dispute resolution and environmental management rather then prosecution.

In June 2008, EU Directive 2008/50/EC on ambient air quality and cleaner air for Europe came into force and must be integrated into UK law by June 2010. This directive consolidates previous EU air quality law (with the exception of 2004/107/EC which will be integrated within a further EU Directive in 2010). The new directive requires member states to reduce PM2.5 in urban areas by 20 per cent by 2020 based on 2010 levels, and permits member states to submit applications for time extensions to comply (Euopa 2008).

It should be noted that the IPPC Directive within the EU was premised on an economic foundation where trade remains central to the actions of the EC and to member states. The European Court of Justice (ECJ) ruling in the case of *Procureur du Roi* v. *Dassonville* highlights the importance of promoting trade and sets standards for trade restriction. The widely quoted Dassonville formula serves to preserve and stress that community beneficial trade is the cornerstone of the EU. This formula identifies:

> All rules enacted by Member States which are capable of hindering, directly or indirectly, actually or potentially, intra-Community trade are to be considered as measures having an effect equivalent to quantitative restrictions.

The challenges that face the EC are to integrate environmental concerns into a model that has continually prioritised trade and economic prosperity for five decades (see Sands 2003).

Air pollution control in the UK

The earliest known form of air pollution regulation in the UK dates back to Royal Proclamations of the late thirteenth century that recognised the problems caused by burning sea coal (see Thornton and Beckwith 2004: 292). Further pollution control laws in Britain have their origins in the post-industrial revolution regulation based on the Best Practicable Means (BPM), the subsequent Alkali Works Regulation Act 1906 and the Clean Air Acts of 1956 and 1968. However, it was the Environmental Protection Act 1990 that created an integrated system of pollution control (IPC). The IPC is underpinned by a 'scheme of authorisation, control and enforcement of processes capable of causing pollution of the environment' (Garbutt 2000: 23). The processes subject to regulation are those that may cause harm to the environment and to any living organism (see section 1, EPA 1990). The IPC adopted a 'holistic approach' and drew upon established pollution control principles in creating a system based on the 'Best Practicable Environmental Option' and 'Best Available Techniques Not Entailing Excessive Costs' (National Society for Clean Air and Environmental Protection 2005: 3).

Air pollution is generated from a diversity of sources and atmospherically dispersed across large expanses of territory. Factors such as wind direction and speed and atmospheric stability have assisted the use of various models within 'dispersion theory' to estimate trans-boundary pollution (Colls 1997). Such theories based on the sources, diversity and movement of air pollution have assisted the development of a regulatory regime capable of capturing the various dimensions ensuring air quality. As a result, the air pollution controls in the UK involve several organisations across central and local government in the assessment, management and enforcement of numerous regulations.

The EPA 1990 provided a dual system of regulation involving two governing bodies, namely the Environment Agency and local authorities. The Environment Agency controlled industrial and commercial activities causing serious or heavy pollution (IPC) while local authorities through Local Authority Air Pollution Control (LAAPC) regulated less polluting activities. Under IPC, the operator of an activity causing pollution must seek consent and an environmental licence from either the EA or the relevant local authority (depending on the nature of the emission). Best Available Techniques Not Entailing Excessive Cost (BATNEEC) is used to assess and determine the means by which a certain emission should be controlled. Such an assessment takes into account economic and environmental advantages and disadvantages of the proposed commercial activity (see section 7, EPA 1990). In addition, the Best Practicable Environmental Option (BPEO), while not proscribed in the EPA 1990, assesses the environmental impacts and sets a range of objectives and targets that seek to maximise environmental benefits and reduce environmental harms (Thornton and Beckwith 2004: 110). The EA or the local authority (the 'enforcing agency') will stipulate terms and conditions on the licence for the pollution-causing activity. For example, an operator is not permitted to engage in the activity beyond a specified dated unless a successful application for 'authorisation' has been approved by the enforcing agency to extend the date of operations (see section 6, EPA 1990). Authorisations may also be varied or revoked (sections 10–12).

The enforcing agency also exercises powers of enforcement through issuing prohibition or enforcement notices. Section 13 identifies that an enforcement notice may be issued by the authority if an authorisation is contravened or about to be contravened. The prohibition notice constitutes a more serious process and is issued when the authority is of the opinion that the activity is at risk of causing 'serious pollution' (section 14). Furthermore, offences under section 23 of the EPA and section 110 of the Environment Act (EA) 1995 attract a list of penalties up to £20,000 for a summary conviction. The IPC relies upon operators to be self-regulatory. The ratio of licensed sites to Environment Agency inspectors is such that regulation relies upon operators to report incidents that breach or affect authorisation.

UK air pollution control laws are governed by common law principles of nuisance. The laws of statutory nuisance are referred to in Part 3 of the EPA 1990. The statutory nuisance regime covers numerous non-commercial activities as well as those pollutants emitted by industry. For example, it regulates smoke, fumes and gases from premises as well as dust, steam or smells from industry deemed to be 'prejudicial to health or a nuisance' (Thornton and Beckwith 2004: 297).

As an integrated system of regulation, pollution control in the UK intersects with transport policy and air quality strategies. For example, the Environment Act 1995 requires the Secretary of State to establish a National Air Quality Strategy (NAQS) and for local authorities to review the standards and objectives of the strategy (Jervis 2005). The NAQS serves to provide an overview of pollution-causing activities in Britain and to identify the policies and practices in place to control and prevent air pollution. In doing so, it acts as a reference point and guide to regulators and sets targets and objectives for reducing emissions. Such targets provide a framework in which regulation operates; notably to achieve, or be seen to be achieving, outcomes designed to improve air quality and enhance the protection of the environment. Local authorities are increasingly playing a more active role through the review of air quality and may declare a specified region as an 'Air Quality Management Area' (AQMA). This local air quality management may lead to the introduction of incentives to reduce emissions or congestion charges to tackle transport pollution. More than 127 local authorities have produced AQMAs, 'most of these [being] in urban areas and resulting from traffic emissions of nitrogen dioxide or fine particulates' (National Environment Technology Centre 2005: 4).

What are the prospects and pitfalls of IPC? Thornton and Beckwith (2004: 110) pose the question whether or not the IPC has been successful. How is success or failure of a regulatory regime measured? In relation to pollution control it could be argued that reductions in polluting emissions are the key indicators of success. However, such a measure is fraught with uncertainty and ambiguity. The accurate measurement of air pollution is complex and contested. It is the process of administration which is criticised by Thornton and Beckwith (2004), notably the lack of objectivity. They argue that regulators rely upon the expertise of operators rather than the enforcing agency, a criticism that exists under PPC. As a result, the regulation of air pollution in the UK is not an openly transparent process conducted by a detached and dispassionate regulatory agency, but one that relies upon trust, partnership and negotiation between the operator and the regulator. There is no public involvement or public scrutiny of regulator decisions. The enforcement agency relies upon the technical assistance of 'the regulated' in reaching its decisions.

It is clear that the UK provides an extensive system of air pollution monitoring through its Air Quality Archive. Yet the processes of enforcing the regulations identified above are negotiated by the authorities and the polluters. This 'partnership model' is very much industry-led and relies upon compliance and corporate good practice. When corporations exceed legal air pollution emissions the language of 'crime', 'offences', 'violation' or 'breach' is not used. Instead, we witness the use of the term 'exceedence' to describe unlawful levels of air pollution.

Air pollution offences in the UK

Defra regularly publishes 'statistical releases' on air quality in the UK. These news releases provide a selectively favourable interpretation of existing air quality data in the UK. Indeed, there is a sense that the slightest 'good news' is rushed to print in a seemingly desperate attempt to convey compliance with EU standards for air quality. However, what such updates fail to acknowledge is that existing levels of air contaminants continue to breach EU targets (Defra 2009b). Moreover, there is an unhelpful and misleading language that underestimates the seriousness of exposure to air pollution. Such comments as 'long-term exposure to even low levels of particulates (PM10) *may* have a significant effect on public health' (emphasis added, Defra 2009c). There is no 'may' about it, and the usage of this defensive terminology serves to neutralise criticism of bland and unflattering government statistics. Moreover, Defra concluded in its January 2009 update by stating 'both particulate and ozone concentrations are strongly influenced by weather, which will contribute to the fluctuations seen across the time serious' (p. 3). This 'good news' air quality update by Defra released on 29 January 2009 coincided with the exact day that the European Commission issued an infringement notice against the UK government for failure to respect repeated exceedence of particulate air pollution. British authorities point to the importance of the 'weather' in understanding variance in air pollution readings. Will this be the defence of the British government when pending proceedings are taken to the European Court? Rather than piecemeal presentation of manipulated 'successes', what is needed is an open and honest account of all statistical trends with comparable data on EU compliance with future projections.

There is an increasing amount of statistical data on air pollution released online. Yet the voluminous amount of facts and figures serves to skew and confound rather than provide a consistent picture of the realities of air pollution in the UK. This research encountered particular difficulty in obtaining data, notably relating to air pollution offences.[2] As mentioned above, the more serious air pollution offences in England and Wales are dealt with by the Environment Agency, by the Scottish Environment Protection Agency in Scotland and by the Industrial Pollution and Radiochemical Inspectorate within the Northern Ireland Environment Agency (NIEA).

England and Wales

Data about air pollution incidents were obtained from the Environment Agency for the years 2006–7.

The total number of air pollution incidents brought to the attention of, and investigated by, the Environment Agency UK in 2006 were 161 and 151 in 2007 (Doran 2009).

In 2006, court proceedings were initiated against 17 offending parties (12 companies and six individuals). Two of the defendants were acquitted, a further six were cautioned, eight were given fines totalling £96,500 and one individual received an unspecific custodial sentence.

Overall, the fines are very small, notably for industries with multi-million pound annual turnovers. It is also surprising that numerous offences identified by the Environment Agency as causing 'significant' air pollution were treated with a caution, for example one case involved the deliberate release of kerosene and aviation fuel into a controlled waterway. Most of the matters taken to court were breaches of licences or cases involving the illegal burning or disposal of waste.

In 2007, a further 17 defendants (11 companies and seven individuals) were taken to court – six outcomes resulted in cautions, one was acquitted and for one no penalty was recorded. Only nine defendants were convicted of air pollution offences. In the same year within the magistrates courts in England and Wales 1.74 million offenders appeared and were fined more than £255 million (Ministry of Justice 2007).

Scotland

During the past fives years (2004 to May 2009) there were 9,990 air pollution incidents brought to the attention of and investigated by the Scottish Environment Protection Agency (SEPA). Whilst the SEPA database does not provide details on outcomes for all cases (such a task requires manually searching all files) it does indicate the number of prosecutions. During the five years, three prosecutions were successfully made. A total of £15,900 in fines was ordered by the courts for 'failing to contain offensive odours' (Everitt 2009).

Northern Ireland

Between 1 April 2004 and 31 March 2009 a total of 537 air pollution incidents were brought to the attention of NIEA. In total, nine enforcement notices were issued and two prosecutions taken; all other complaints were 'dealt with by discussion and/or correspondence' (Doherty 2009). The two successful prosecutions involved a poultry farm that was fined £6,000 and a company operating three illegal incinerators without permits that was convicted on eight counts and fined £1,000. The case is still subject to an appeal.

Greening the criminological landscape

Green criminology asserts that eco-crimes should encapsulate all acts of environmental harm to human and non-human species as well as to the natural environment itself (Lynch and Stretesky 2003; Beirne and South 2007). It remains an undeveloped criminological narrative, yet its various perspectives aim to provide an interdisciplinary study committed to the protection and development of environmental resources and the prevention of illegal and harmful acts that unnecessarily threaten or damage the environment.

Two key figures in the founding of green criminology (Beirne and South 2007: xiii) argue that at its 'most abstract level' it includes 'those harms against humanity, against the environment (including space) and against non-human animals committed by both powerful organisations (e.g. governments, transnational corporations, military apparatuses) and also by ordinary people'. This broad definition acknowledges governmental understandings of individual irresponsibility (vandalism, graffiti and fly tipping), but is also capable of focusing primary attention on acts of the 'powerful' in causing widespread and long-term environmental damage. This focus is consistent with the origins of green criminology. When it was first coined by Michael Lynch in 1990 it was a term designed to harness green environmentalism and green political theories to examine 'environmental destruction as an outcome of the structure of modern capitalist production and consumption patterns' (p. 1). In this sense, green criminology has its theoretical roots embedded within the traditions of radical criminological schools of thought such as feminism, Marxism and social constructionism (these radical criminologies emerged in the late 1960s and early 1970s in the UK and the US arguing, among other things, that crime is to be found in relations of power, oppression and selective processes of criminalisation – see Muncie 2006).

White (2008) argues that there is no one green criminological theory but rather a series of 'perspectives' or narratives that draw on various philosophical, sociological, legal and scientific traditions. He argues that the three 'theoretical tendencies' that inform green criminology, are 'environmental justice', 'ecological justice' and 'species justice' (p. 15). *Environmental justice* is a human-centred or anthropocentric discourse with two distinct dimensions. It assesses the equity of access and use of environmental resources across social and cultural divides. Who has access to the benefits and profits of natural resources and why? It also explores how people are affected by natural disasters, corporate activity and state actions that damage the environment. *Ecological justice* focuses on the relationship or interaction between humans and the natural environment. When humans develop the environment for material needs (housing, agriculture, business, consumption) this approach insists that such actions be assessed within the context of damage or harm to other living things. It asserts the intrinsic value and equal status of non-humans but explores the potential for sustainability while utilising environmental resources for fundamental human needs. *Species justice* is a non-human or biocentric discourse that emphasises the importance of non-human rights. It asserts that human beings are not the only creatures with rights, nor are humans superior beings. In other words, there is no hierarchy of existence with human beings at the pinnacle. All 'living things in existence' share an equal status of importance. Beirne and South (2007) argue that to disregard non-human creatures as not of equal standing within the natural environment denies the value and worth of those species.

The above perspectives centre critical attention on the key issues of how and why certain things come to be called criminal and others not. In doing so, it opens up debate over whether certain harms should be criminalised. Importantly, green criminology is not only a response to official and scientific evidence about environmental damage and species decline, but also an engagement with emerging social movements and public opinions of resistance. In these ways, green criminology itself can be considered an evolving knowledge base that challenges mainstream disciplinary discourses as well as neo-liberal government and corporate rationalities. It questions the moral and ethical bases upon which contemporary laws permit the exploitation of nature and examines the conditions in which coexistence and inter-species cooperation can be achieved. Moreover, its globalising of the criminological lens (viewing crime beyond the local and national level to include international and global actions of criminality) permits the involvement of movements and organisations which are outside the state to contribute to emerging notions of environmental justice. In that sense, air pollution becomes a subject of criminological inquiry drawing upon different academic narratives such as law, science, sociology and development studies and embellishes such understanding with social movements and citizen participation.

Conclusion

There are numerous measures proposed, or being implemented, to reduce air pollution: the introduction of biofuels, vehicle retrofit schemes, the creation of low emission zones, solar energy and renewable resources in building schemes, educational initiatives and government incentives to encourage lifestyle changes that promote low-energy outputs (London Assembly Environment Committee 2009). All such approaches are important and worthwhile ventures. However, innovative efforts to reduce emissions must be accompanied by dynamic and effective regulatory arrangements.

Air pollution control in the UK remains a model based on trust, partnership and operator self-regulation. The involvement of operator-appointed scientific expertise to assess and process permits raises serious questions that challenge the regime's ability to make impartial judgments. The existing regulatory regime of air pollution in the UK lacks neutrality. It is a process that remains biased towards the economic imperatives of free trade over and above the centrality of environmental protection. The penalties imposed for operators breaching permits are minor in comparison to corporate profits. The more severe penalties are rarely imposed. Thus the system of regulation and control is not founded on deterrence but on incentive, partnership and dispute resolution. Regulators must be given greater resources to investigate installations to facilitate a proactive approach that sees breaches identified before damage to the environment occurs. Moreover, the existing regime must inculcate greater independence and pubic visibility. The use of autonomous scientific expertise coupled with civilian oversight should comprise a key component of future air pollution regulation in the UK. When air pollution offences are viewed as eco-crimes it is likely that the severity of such acts will become subject to great public, political and subsequently prosecutorial scrutiny. While such life-threatening offences are portrayed as mere 'exceedence' by government within an industry/polluter-dominated partnership built on trust and trade, it is difficult to envisage a decline in the harms caused by air pollution.

Finally, regulators must be given greater resources to investigate installations to facilitate a proactive approach that sees breaches identified before damage to the environment occurs. It is clear that those responsible for the investigation and enforcement of air pollution regulation in the UK operate with inadequate resources. An increase in personnel (for investigation, prosecution, research and knowledge transfer), increased sophistication of databases (for collaborating with and coordinating existing information across regulators and relevant bodies) and the production of research and new forms of information to assist the development of policy for improving practices are urgently required.

Selected further reading

For further reading on eco-crime see Walters' (2009) 'Eco crime' in Muncie *et al.* (eds) *Crime: Local and Global*. A comprehensive overview of the emerging debates in green criminology can also be found in the collection edited by Beirne and South (2007), *Issues in Green Criminology. Confronting Harms Against Environments, Humanity and Other Animals*. Moreover, White's (2008) *Crimes Against Nature. Environmental Criminology and Ecological Justice* introduces the reader to various debates within the green criminology field.

Notes

1 An earlier version of this chapter was published by the Centre for Crime and Justice Studies; see Walters, R. (2009) *Crime Is in the Air. Air Pollution and Regulation in the UK*. London: CCJS.
2 Repeated unsuccessful attempts to obtain statistical data on air pollution offences under the Freedom of Information Act from the Environment Agency necessitated a formal complaint to the Office of Information Commissioner that resulted in the expeditious release of requested information.

References

Air Quality Archive (2009) *Air Quality Data and Statistics*. Online at: www.airqaulity. co.uk/archive/data_and_statistics_home.php (accessed 16 January 2009).

Beirne, P. and South, N. (eds) (2007) *Issues in Green Criminology. Confronting Harms Against Environments, Humanity and Other Animals*. Cullompton: Willan.

Bodansky, D., Brunnee, J. and Hey, E. (eds) (2007) *The Oxford Handbook of International Environmental Law*. Oxford: Oxford University Press.

Booth, R. (2008) 'Environment criminals build $10bn empire on ivory, timber and skins', *The Guardian*, 13 October.

Bridgman, H. (1990) *Global Air Pollution – Problems for the 1990s*. London: Belhaven Press.

Brown, P. (2003) 'Global warming kills 150,000 a year', *The Guardian*, 12 December.

Campaign for Clean Air in London (2009) 'Mission'. Online at: http://www.cleanairinlondon.org/.

Carrabine, E., Iganski, P., Lee, M., Plummer, K. and South, N. (2004) *Criminology: A Sociological Introduction*. London: Routledge.

Colls, J. (1997) *Air Pollution: An Introduction*. London: Chapman & Hall.

COMEAP, (2009) *Long-Term Exposure to Air Pollution*. Online at: http://www.advisorybodies.doh.gov.uk/comeap/pdfs/finallongtermeffectsmort2009report.pdf (accessed 30 June 2009).

Defra (2009a) *Pollution Prevention and Control*. Online at: http://www.defra.gov.uk/environment/ppc/index.htm (accessed 28 June 2009).

Defra (2009b) *Statistical Release – UK Emissions of Air Pollutants – 2007 Results*, Reference 04/09, 8 January.

Defra (2009c) *Statistical Release – Air Quality Indicator for Sustainable Development 2008 Provisional Results*, Reference 15/09, 29 January.

Doherty, J. (2009) Written correspondence in response to FOI request, 2 June 2009, Reference EA09C68, Northern Ireland Environment Agency.

Doran, T. (2009) 'Air pollution incidents for 2006 and 2007'. E-mail communication from the Environment Agency, 17 February.

Environment Agency (2006) *Business and Industry – Applying for PPC Permit*. Online at: http://www.environment-agewcy.gov.uk/business/444217/444663/298441/274320/?ve...

Europa (2005) 'Commission proposes clean air strategy to protect human health and the environment'. Online at: http://europa.eu.int/comm/environment/air/cafe/index.htm; http://europa.eu.int/rapid/pressReleasesAction.do?reference=IP/05/1170&format=HTML&aged=0&language=EN&guiLanguage=en.

Europa (2006) *The IPPC Directive*. Online at: http://europa.eu.int/comm/environment/ippc/.

Europa (2007) 'Air pollution: Commission takes action over levels of sulphur dioxide and PM10 in member states', 17 October, IP/07/1537. Online at: http://europa.eu/rapid/pressReleasesAction.do?reference=IP/07/1537 (accessed 20 May 2009).

Europa (2008) 'Directives'. Online at: http://eur-lex.europa.eu/LexUriServ/LexUriServ.do?uri=OJ:L:2008:152:0001:0044:EN:PDF (accessed 31 May 2009).

European Environmental Agency (2004) *EEA Strategy 2004–2008*. Copenhagen: EEA.

Everitt, C. (2009) FOI Request, FO136281, 23 June.

Garbutt, J. (2000) *Environmental Law*, 3rd edn. Bembridge: Paladian Law Publishing.

Ghio, A. and Devlin, R. (2001) 'Inflammatory lung injury after bronchial instillation of air pollution particles', *American Journal of Respiratory and Critical Care Medicine*, 164 (4): 704–8.

Greenpeace (2009) *Climate Change*. Online at: http://www.greenpeace.org.uk/climate (accessed 26 January 2009).

Hauck, M. (2007) 'Non-compliance in small-scale fisheries: a threat to security?', in P. Beirne and N. South (eds), *Issues in Green Criminology. Confronting Harms Against Environments, Humanity and Other Animals*. Cullompton: Willan.

Hayman, G. and Brack, D. (2002) *International Environment. The Nature and Control of Environmental Black Markets*. London: Royal Institute of International Affairs.

Home Office (2007) *Environmental Crime*. Online at: http://www.homeoffice.gov.uk/anti-social-behaviour/types-of-asb/environmental-crime/ (accessed 3 June 2009).

House of Commons (2005) Environmental Audit Committee. Online at: http://www.parliament.uk/parliamentary_committees/environmentalaudit_committees.cfm (accessed 11 January 2009).

Interpol (2009a) *Pollution Crime*. Online at: http://www.interpol.int/Public/EnvironmentalCrime/Pollution/Default.asp (accessed 26 January 2009).

Interpol (2009b) *The Interpol Pollution Control Working Group*. Online at: http://www.interpol.int/Public/EnvironmentalCrime/Pollution/WorkingGroup.asp (accessed 27 January 2009).

Jervis, F. (2005) 'Pollution Control 1', Module LAM 5510, Module Notes. Department of Law, University of Wales, Aberystwyth.

London Assembly Environment Committee (2009) *Air Pollution in London*. London Assembly Environmental Committee. Online at: http://www.london.gov.uk/assembly/reports/environment.jsp (accessed 27 April 2009).

Lynch, M. (1990) 'The Greening of Criminology: a perspective for the 1990s', *The Critical Criminologist*, 2: 11–12.

Lynch, M. and Stretesky, P. (2003) 'The meaning of green: contrasting criminological perspectives', *Theoretical Criminology*, 7 (2): 217–38.

MacRory, R. (1989) 'British environmental law: major strands and characteristics', *Connecticut Journal of International Law*, 4: 287–303.

Michalowski, R. and Kramer, R. (1987) 'The space between laws: the problem of corporate crime in a transnational context', *Social Problems*, 34 (1): 34–53.

Ministry of Justice (2007) *Judicial and Court Statistics Report 2007*. Online at: http://www.justice.gov.uk/publications/6012.htm (accessed 15 June 2009).

Muncie, J. (2006) 'Radical criminologies', in E. McLaughlin and J. Muncie (eds), *The Sage Dictionary of Criminology*, 2nd edn. London: Sage.

National Environment Technology Centre (2005) *UK Air Pollution*. London: Defra Publications.

National Society for Clean Air and Environmental Protection (2005) *Pollution Handbook 2005*. Brighton: NSCA.

National Society for Clean Air and Environmental Protection (2006) *Clean Air for Europe in 2006?* Online at: http://www.nsca.org.uk/pages/index.cfm.

New York Times (2001) 'Company news: Koch Petroleum fined $20 million in pollution case', 10 April.

O'Malley, C. (2008) 'Prosecution of environmental crimes dies', *Indianapolis Business Journal*, 3 March.

Osborn, D. (1997) 'Some reflections on UK environmental policy, 1970–1995', *Journal of Environmental Law*, 9 (1): 3–22.

Pearce, F. and Tombs, S. (1998) *Toxic Capitalism. Corporate Crime and the Chemical Industry*. Aldershot: Ashgate.

Royal Commission on Environmental Pollution (2006) 'What is the Royal Commission on Environmental Pollution'. Online at: http://www.rcep.org.uk/about.htm#1.

Sands, P. (2003) *Principles of International Environmental Law*, 2nd edn. Cambridge: Cambridge University Press.

Siegal, N. (1998) '"If I believed in hell, this could be no worse" – Louisiana-Pacific Corp. sued over environmental crimes', *The Progressive*. Online at: http://findarticles.com/p/articles/mi_m1295/is_1998_Dec/ai_53281653 (accessed 27 January 2009).

South, N. (1998) 'Corporate and state crimes against the environment: foundations for a green perspective in European criminology', in V. Ruggiero, N. South and I. Taylor (eds), *The New European Criminology*. London: Routledge.

Thornton, J. and Beckwith, S. (2004) *Environmental Law*, 2nd edn. London: Sweet & Maxwell.

Tromans, S. (1991) 'Review of this common inheritance: Britain's environmental strategy', *Journal of Environmental Law*, 3 (1): 168–71.

United States Environmental Protection Agency (2008) *October 2008 Enforcement Action Summaries*. Online at: http://www.epa.gov/reg5oorc/enfactions/enfactions2009/week-200810.htm (accessed 26 January 2008).

United States Environmental Protection Agency (2009) *EPA Fugitives*. Online at: http://www.epa.gov/fugitives/ (accessed 28 January 2009).

Vanhoeyvelt, N. (2009) 'Response on behalf on Commissioner Dimas' European Commission, Directorate-General Environment. Directorate C – Climate Change and Air. DGENV C3/PolAk/nvAres 135497 (2009) 120111'. Received by e-mail on 5 June 2009.

Vidal, J. (2009) 'UK faces court case over air pollution breaches', *The Guardian*, 2 January. Online at: http://www.guardian.co.uk/environment/2009/jan/02/air-pollution-laws-britain-eu.

Walters, R. (2009) 'Eco-crime', in J. Muncie, D. Talbot and R. Walters (eds), *Crime – Local and Global*. Cullompton: Willan.

Watkiss, P., Holland, M., Hurley, F. and Pye, S. (2006) *Damage Costs for Air Pollution. Final Report to Defra*. Didcot: AEA Technology Environment.

Watts, J. (2005) 'Satellite data reveals Beijing as air pollution capital of world', *The Guardian*, 31 October.

White, R. (2008) *Crimes Against Nature. Environmental Criminology and Ecological Justice*. Cullompton: Willan.

World Health Organisation (2008) *Air Quality and Health*. Online at: http://www.who.int/mediacentre/factshhets/fs313/en/index.html (accessed 22 January 2009).

Case

Case 8/74, *Procureur du Roi* v. *Dassonville* [1974] ECR 837.

Chapter 44

Corporate violence and harm

Steve Tombs

Introduction

Though we can dispute its actual prevalence, its differential distribution and of course its causes, we can probably all agree that violent crime holds a powerful contemporary salience in the popular and political mindset. That said, there are good reasons, as this chapter shall seek to demonstrate, for thinking that contemporary discourses of violence, violent crime and the violent offender are not only partial, but in fact systematically, if not consciously, socially constructed to draw a veil across the source of the greatest form of contemporary violence – the corporation. It is with these issues that this chapter is concerned.

It begins by setting out the terrain potentially covered by the term corporate violence via an overview of some of the physical harms routinely associated with corporate activity. While attempts to quantify them are fraught with difficulty, it is clear that the harms wreaked by corporate activity far outweigh those measured by, for example, the British Crime Survey (BCS) and recorded crime statistics. Having noted the range of such harms, the chapter then focuses upon a specific subset of violence, notably deaths, injury and illness arising out of work. The chapter then seeks to establish that these corporate harms are indeed forms of 'corporate *violence*'. Having defined, set out the range and scale, then identified some of the sources of corporate violence, the chapter will then consider how and to what extent these forms of crime and harm might be explained. Typically, explanatory variables are complex and criminologists have rarely dealt with them satisfactorily. It is at this point, then, that the chapter moves 'beyond criminology'.

Varieties of corporate harm

There is no doubt that corporate activities produce a great deal of physical harm – though, to be clear, to state that corporate activity produces physically harmful consequences is not necessarily to claim that *all* such harms can legitimately be classified as violence. In this section, we shall briefly survey the range of physical harms that result from various corporate activities, before focusing in detail upon a subset of harms, namely those associated with unsafe and unhealthy workplaces.

We begin by emphasising how widespread, physical harms are routinely created in the production, distribution and consumption of goods and services in contemporary economies – often, with no law being violated. If we turn first to environmental harm, we find a chilling set of consequences of the production and distribution activities of corporations and their relationships with states.

The US is the world's largest polluter, and within the US, industry and car use are the primary and secondary contributors to air pollution – of which trucks and buses account for almost three-quarters of the estimated cancer-risk from auto-related pollution (Donohoe 2003: 575). Moreover,

> The US Environmental Protection Agency (EPA) has estimated that 250,000 cases of aggravated asthma and 15,000 deaths from cardiopulmonary diseases could be eliminated each year if the agency's standards for ozone and particulates are implemented … Unfortunately, the implementation has been blocked by heavy lobbying from oil, gas and other industries. (Donohoe 2003: 575)

In the UK, according to Department of Health estimates, the deaths of up to 24,000 people every year in the UK can be attributed to poisoning by various forms of environmental air pollution (Department of Health Committee on the Medical Effects of Air Pollutants 1998). Although the absence of accurate data makes it particularly difficult to assess, in quantitative terms, the link between corporate activities and deaths and illnesses caused by pollution, there is little doubt that the most deadly environmental forms of pollution are caused directly by corporations as opposed to private individuals (Whyte 2004).

A second example of harm caused in the production, distribution and consumption of goods focuses on deaths and illnesses arising from consumption itself. Though probably the most harmful substance consumed today is tobacco, the analysis here focuses on the production and consumption of the food we eat. There are now well-documented links between food consumption and health (Baggot 2000). The dynamics of the market and the ever-present demand to increase profits creates an environment in which concerns about food safety are hardly prioritised, so that concerns about food-related health hazards abound. For example, while the health and environmental effects of genetically modified organisms (GMOs) remain unknown, US multinationals are determined to push ahead with their production. At least 60 per cent of convenience foods now sold in the US contain genetically altered ingredients, for which 'no labelling is required' (Donohoe 2003: 580). Convenience foods are disproportionately marketed to and consumed by lower socio-economic groups.

Similarly, the consequences of prioritising profit over health are only too apparent in beef production and the subsequent development of vCJD – from which the number of 'definite and probable cases' of deaths in the UK stood at 164 by 1 September 2008 (National Creutzfeldt-Jakob Disease Surveillance Unit 2008). As with much corporate harm however, not least that cloaked in scientific uncertainty, we simply do not know the full extent of the disease. If the origins of the disease are far from clear, they appear to lie rooted within the system of food production and the lack of external control and oversight of those processes.

More generally, the full scale of food-poisoning-related deaths remains unknown. This is partly because of the lack of official figures that allow us to know about this problem, but it is also a function of the complex way that food infection affects human health. So, although between 100 and 200 people in the UK die directly as a result of salmonella and campylobacter every year, this does not capture the full scale of food-poisoning-related deaths. Food poisoning has lasting and complex effects on health: for example, it has been estimated that salmonella and campylobacter triple the average person's chances of dying from any other disease or condition within a year (Helms *et al.* 2003). Government estimates indicate that around half of all food poisoning cases in the UK can be attributed to food consumed outside the home (UK Parliament 2003), while the fourth FSA Consumer Attitudes to Food survey recorded self-reported incidence of food poisoning at 16 per cent of the sample population, 82 per cent of them claiming the source was outside the home (TNS 2004: 61).

Finally in this section, we wish to give the briefest indication of the harms which emerge as a consequence of the very differential production and distribution founded upon the ability to pay rather than human need, the central basis of a market-based system – and here we illustrate the point via reference to the pharmaceutical industry. As Cohen (2002) has noted, if the pharmaceutical industry has contributed to a 'health revolution', it is one that has resulted in considerable gains in life expectancy and health improvements in some parts of the world, while leaving most of the world's population behind.

Thus drug research and development (R&D) for diseases that disproportionately affect poor people in developing countries is at a virtual standstill. Of the 1,393 new drugs approved between 1975 and 1999, only 16 (or just over one per cent) were specifically developed for tropical diseases and tuberculosis, diseases that account for 11 per cent of the global disease burden (Cohen 2002). The 'neglected diseases' are those mainly affecting people in developing countries, for which treatment options are inadequate or do not exist, and for which R&D is insufficient or non-existent (Cohen 2002). Meanwhile, there are 'increased investments for R&D on drugs for impotence, obesity and baldness' (Corporate Watch n.d). This makes good economic sense – pharmaceutical companies top the US industry performance list for return on investment, with a 39 per cent return for shareholders, according to *Fortune* magazine (Cohen 2002).

Moreover, and more generally, despite both its successful lobbying for a global system of patent protection, and its consistent argument that it must charge high prices for its pharmaceuticals, resting on the industry's long-voiced claims about high R&D costs *and* the need to maintain innovation (Tyfield 2008), two key issues undermine these positions. First, the dominant players in the industry spend far more on marketing than they do on research and development; and, second, what often appears as innovation is the development of me-too-products, so that innovation does not at all equal therapeutic advances (Angell 2004). In other words, an industry with significant harm-mitigating potential is actually based upon ignoring harm at the altar of high rates of profitability – while lobbying to maintain a legal system which reproduces its ability to do so.

This section has only scraped the surface in terms of the extent of physical harms associated with contemporary corporate activity. Yet such harms are clearly heterogeneous and ubiquitous. It is worth, then, setting out, briefly and schematically, a typology of these, not least one that locates them in relation to a legal standard, whether law in general or criminal law in particular – an exercise useful not least given that this text is concerned with the discipline of criminology.

First, we can identify harms that are produced through the legal operation of a free-market system within which corporations, driven necessarily by a profit-maximising motive, are the key actors, albeit only ever operating within conditions of existence guaranteed by state actors. We have used the example of the pharmaceutical industry, above, to highlight the ways in which this industry, through the profit motive, reproduces mass physical harms. This is such an obvious, taken-for-granted fact of life that it rarely attracts comment. But its effect is that while such companies are the key means whereby harm-mitigating products are developed then sold the effect of the market is in fact to perpetuate ill-health, as products are developed on the basis of the ability to pay rather than need. Thus harms are produced by *the effective exclusion* of certain people – as consumers, for example – from the market system, while it should be added that this effective exclusion is generally established and maintained through a legal system overseen by states and state bodies, a classic example being the system of patents which apply to pharmaceuticals.

Second, if certain harms are produced by the effective exclusion of some workers or consumers from certain sectors of market activity, others are produced by the *effective inclusion*, or locking in, of certain populations into certain sectors of consumption or labour markets. Thus safer and healthier foods attract premiums in terms of their price (or availability) which often restrict access to the poorest populations, thus affecting their quality of life and morbidity rates. A second example can be found in the exposure to polluted land or water, in which context we know, for example, that racial minorities in the US 'are more likely to live in neighbourhoods prone to environmental hazards' (Friedrichs 1999: 149; see also the work of Lynch, Stretesky and colleagues on environmental racism/justice, for example Lynch *et al.* 2002; Stretesky and Lynch 1998, 1999; Stretesky and Hogan 1998). Third, in terms of labour markets and the distribution of hazardous work, if undocumented workers are by definition those most likely to have little or no legal protection (Pai 2008), we know that the distribution of more or less safe and healthy work closely parallels existing dimensions of labour market and occupational vulnerability (Tombs and Whyte 2007: 48–61). Quite simply, certain segments of populations are effectively *locked into* certain sectors of markets, denied the effective choice upon which market ideology rests.

Third, we can identify physical harms that arise from the provision of specific goods and services which, although legal, and often in principle at least subject to regulation, are in themselves harm-*producing* (Passas and Goodwin 2007). Most obviously, the tobacco and alcohol industries, while both clearly legal, produce a range of physical harms through their very products. Similarly, the arms and defence industries, again legal, equally produce goods which are intrinsically harmful to human life.[1]

Fourth – and note it is only here where we encounter harms that might fall within the discipline of criminology – we can identify harms that are produced through violation of legal standards in the context of essentially legal processes. These may range from the falsification of testing data or burying of known side effects in order to gain or retain a licence to market a product – of which there are numerous cases documented in relation to the pharmaceutical industry – to the violation of legal regulations in legal production processes which contravene standards of environmental or occupational safety protection or marketing practices. It is physical harms of these types that are generally the stuff of corporate crime research – and cases of specific incidents, groups of harms or industry-specific harms are numerous.

One of the clear consequences of such a typology, however provisional and schematic, is that much corporate harm is *legal*. This is certainly the case with the first category of corporate activity outlined in this typology. But it is also an issue that clouds attempts to use law in relation to corporate harms, either as a means of generating analytical categories such as 'corporate crime' or as a means of calling corporations to account. For example, if we take pollution or exposure to noxious substances in workplaces, then for the most part exposures and emissions up to a certain prescribed limit are legally permissible. This makes the line between legality and crime a very difficult one to draw. In the following section, we shall highlight further these latter issues regarding the problematic nature of the relationship between the law and corporate harm through an extended focus upon one subset of corporate harms, namely those associated with harms arising to workers and members of the public arising out of the production process.

The scale of occupational death, injury and illness

Work is a major killer across the globe. The International Labour Organisation (ILO) estimates that, at a bare minimum, 2.2 million workers die each year through work-related 'accidents' and diseases (International Labour Organisation 2005: 1). This means that annually there are more than 5,000 work-related deaths every day, while for every fatality there are another 500–2,000 injuries, depending on the type of job.

Of the 345,000 workers estimated by the ILO to have died in *incidents* (as opposed to occupational diseases and exposures) at the workplace in 2002, by far the greatest number, almost 220,000, were in Asia, with China having by far the highest number of deaths of any one Asian country – 73,595 – with the second highest number being India (48,176).[2] In Europe, Russia is the state with the highest absolute numbers of occupational fatalities – almost 7,000 – followed by Turkey, Ukraine, Poland and Romania. For Woolfson, flexibilisation – or, as he puts it, the creation of 'a deregulated low-cost, low-wage economy, where labour (preferably "union-free") is comprehensively subordinated to the needs of capital' – is the key to understanding why the states of the former Soviet Union mostly have safety records poorer than the rest of Europe: 'Figures show that, as a whole, Central and East Europeans are three times as likely to die at work than those in the EU-15 (9.6 per 100,000 persons in employment compared to 3.4)' (Woolfson 2005).

Britain is not, then, one of the most dangerous places to work in Europe. Nor, however, is it one of the very safest and, compared with EU counterparts, its safety record is deteriorating (Eurostat 2004; Health and Safety Executive n.d.). In 2006–7, the HSE recorded a total of 241 fatalities suffered by workers in Great Britain (Health and Safety Commission 2007). However, the data collated by the HSE on which this figure is based are so incomplete that they need to be reconstructed to provide a more accurate indication of the scale of the problem. If we insert into that headline figure the key, omitted data – HSE recorded deaths to members of the public (excluding suicides and trespass on railways), the Reporting of Injuries, Diseases and Dangerous Occurrences Regulations 1995 (road deaths and categories of deaths caused by working not recorded under RIDDOR)[3] – this increases the total of occupational deaths from the HSE's 'all workers' figure of 241 for 2006–7 to a figure of at least 1,400. Thus we need to apply a multiplier of between 5 and 6 to the headline figure to reach a more accurate estimate of the numbers of officially recorded occupational fatalitites. Certainly if we set the number of people killed at work alongside those recorded by the Home Office as homicides (that is, murder, manslaughter and infanticide), it is immediately apparent that the chance of being a victim of a work-related fatality is several times more likely than being a victim of homicide (Tombs and Whyte 2007, 2008).

If we turn now to non-fatal injuries, we also need to be aware that each category of *non-fatal* injury data provided by RIDDOR also suffers from significant under-reporting. A comparison of the non-fatal RIDDOR data with the more authoritative Labour Force Surveys (LFS), published by the Office for National Statistics (see below), indicates that only about a quarter of reportable non-fatal injuries to employees, and probably about 5 per cent in the case of self-employed workers, are actually reported by employers. This indicates a widespread failure on the part of employers to meet their legal obligation to report incidents, itself an offence under safety law.

Even on RIDDOR data, workplace injury is far from an uncommon experience. Typically the HSE records that 30,000 major injuries[4] are sustained by workers and 15,000 non-fatal injuries are sustained by members of the public each year.[5] Around 120,000 injuries to workers which result in more than three days off work are also typically recorded in any given year. However, if we utilise the most recent LFS data[6] – broadly equivalent to BCS data in the context of Home Office crime statistics – we find that, in 2006–7 that there were 274,000 non-fatal reportable injuries, a rate of 1,000 per 100,000 workers (1.0 per cent).[7]

Again, a comparison between occupational injury and 'crime' data is useful here. According to the 2006/7 British Crime Survey (BCS), there was a total of 2,471,000 violent offences in England and Wales, and 3.6 per cent of people experienced a violent incident. Of these, 49 per cent resulted in no injury to the victim, about one in ten (12 per cent) required medical attention and one in 50 (2 per cent) resulted in a hospital stay (Jansson *et al.* 2007). In absolute terms, this equates to some 49,420 BCS recorded incidents of violence resulting in a hospital stay. Now, we cannot disaggregate from HSE's LFS or RIDDOR injury data those which similarly require a hospital stay. But we do know that the kinds of injures defined under RIDDOR as 'major' are serious enough to warrant at least hospital treatment, while the definition of an injury to a member of the public is one that requires the injured person going straight to hospital. Thus we can reasonably set against BCS data on violence resulting in a hospital stay RIDDOR (as opposed to the much higher LFS figures) data for major injuries to workers and injuries to the public which, for 2006/7, stands at 29,450 and 17,483 such injuries respectively. Combining these two figures produces a total – 46,933 – which is virtually the same as the figure for BCS recorded violence requiring a hospital stay. And this is not even to begin to estimate the numbers of over-three-day injuries – 114,222 in 2006/7 – which resulted in hospitalisation (nor, of course, to account for the high levels of under-reporting). This comparison can also be expressed in percentage terms: again using data for 2006/7, we find the percentage of workers experiencing a major injury stands at just under 0.1 per cent (0.097 per cent, or 97.1 in 100,000); this can be compared with the 0.072 per cent of BCS respondents (the 2 per cent of the 3.6 per cent who experienced violence) resulting in a hospital stay. Although such comparisons can only be broadly indicative, they do lead us to the rather undeniable conclusion – that work is much more likely to be a source of violence in Britain than those 'real' crimes recorded by the Home Office.

To this point, none of the data include death and illness produced as a result of occupational ill-health – and here, really, is the major source of workplace harm. Mostly, then, in the sphere of occupational ill-health, we are in the realm of informed estimates. For at least a headline figure, the Labour Force Survey is again, here, instructive: it suggests that, in 2006/7, 2.2 million people were suffering from an illness they believe was caused or made worse by their current or past work. More recently, gathering together best available evidence on the scale of fatal occupational illnesses in Britain, Greater Manchester Hazards Centre has reached a total estimate of up to 50,000 killed by occupational illnesses, a figure which includes some 18,000 occupational cancers, 6,000 deaths from work-related obstructive lung disease and 20 per cent (20,000) of annual heart disease deaths (see Palmer 2008).

If we know little in general about the scale of deaths and illness as a result of exposure to substances used in the workplace, one substance about which we do have a considerable stock of knowledge – accumulated through thousands of deaths over more than a century – is asbestos, exposure to which causes a range of fatal diseases. Currently about 125 million people in the world are exposed to asbestos at the workplace (World Health Organisation 2006). The ILO estimates that 100,000 people die each year from work-related asbestos exposure (Takala 2006). In the UK, asbestos-related deaths continue to rise, on a conservative (HSE) estimate standing at 4,000 per annum, and are set to rise to a peak somewhere between 2011 and 2015; 'excess deaths in Britain from asbestos-related diseases could eventually reach 100,000' (Tweedale 2000: 276). French scientists attributed 35,000 deaths to asbestos between 1965 and 1995, and expect 'another 60,000 to 100,000 deaths' up to 2030 (Takala 2006). The ILO estimates over 21,000 deaths per annum in the US, more than 10,000 in the Russian Federation and more than 110,000 in China (ibid.). Moreover, if some states have banned the use and production of the substance – though have yet to remove asbestos safely from existing buildings – then more broadly, the global problem has simply been shifted. 'In transition and developing countries the risk is now even higher than in the established market economies and it is certain that asbestos will prove to be a health "time bomb" in these countries in 20 to 30 years' time' (Takala 2006; see also Vogel 2005: 7–8).

Corporate harm as corporate violence

Corporate activity, then, has produced, and continues to produce, a range of physical harms, the effects of which look very much like the effects of that which we most commonly understand as 'violence' – acute or premature death, injury, illness and long-term suffering through physical impairment. What is also clear is that the vast majority of these harms are not treated as violence by the criminal justice system (nor through the media, nor by academics, nor in popular and political discussions of the violence 'problem', and so on). This then begs at least two questions: can such physical harms legitimately be categorised as violence? And, if so, why are they not treated as such?

In a recent review of some key, recent approaches to violence – approaches selected for analysis precisely because each explicitly provided a critique of narrow legalistic definitions of violence – it was concluded that, while there were obviously enormous epistemological, theoretical and political differences between the approaches to violence considered, they nevertheless shared certain characteristics (Tombs 2007). And crucial within the definitions of violence deployed or included within these approaches were two central assumptions: first, a primacy granted to intention; and, second, a focus upon individual as opposed to collective sources of violence, and thus the centrality of violence as interpersonal as opposed to structural. Both of these assumptions reflect the definitions of violence which tend to be enshrined within systems of criminal law and criminal justice.

Yet if we are able to abandon an epistemological commitment to individualism, then more encompassing definitions and considerations of violence become possible. For example, among the work on the issue of workplace violence, that of Bowie stands out, since he has sought to develop the category of 'organisational violence', and although this is partially limited by some commitment to intention, it is far more useful than other definitions of violence. Thus, for Bowie, organisational violence 'involves organisations knowingly placing their workers or clients in dangerous or violent situations or allowing a climate of abuse, bullying or harassment to thrive in the workplace' (Bowie 2002: 6). If this still retains some commitment to intention, it at least moves beyond simple understandings of individual action, not least because it acknowledges how a general organisational demeanour of generating or turning a blind eye towards violence can be fostered 'in a growing economic rationalist climate of decreasing job security, massive retrenchments and expanding unemployment that pitted workers and unions against employers' (Bowie 2002: 9). Of particular interest for us is that Bowie also notes that such violence is much harder to recognise due to the tendency to 'blame' (ibid.: 6) individuals, and to develop strategies for responding to violence which are 'based on a pathology model of "mad, bad or sad" employees or clients and patients who are seen as individually responsible for the violence occurring at work' (ibid.: 8).

Similarly, Hills, in introducing a collection of case histories of 'corporate violence', defines this phenomenon as:

> Actual harm and risk of harm inflicted on consumers, workers, and the general public as a result of decisions by corporate executives or managers, from corporate negligence, the quest for profits at any cost, and wilful violations of health, safety and environmental laws. (Hills 1987a: vii)

Hills' collection presents a series of case studies which would not generally fall within the rubric of violence. These include: examples of corporate violence which victimise consumers such as in the uniquely infamous case of the Ford Pinto, the dumping of hazardous products on developing economies or the sale of patently unsafe contraceptive devices; where workers are the victims such as through exposure to carbon monoxide poisoning at a steel plant, the death of 78 men in a coal mine and the epidemic of brown lung disease through working in the textiles industry; and those forms of violence wreaked upon local communities via illegal dumping of toxic products or living in the vicinity of a nuclear power plant. In his final considerations regarding such cases, Hills concludes that such violence is understood 'not in the pathology of evil individuals but in the culture and structure of large-scale bureaucratic organisations within a particular political economy' (Hills 1987b: 190). Thus Hills' understanding of violence shifts beyond *both* intention and the interpersonal. Similar shifts can also be discerned in some other, recent criminological work which, if not explicitly couched in the language of violence, could be reframed as such – note in particular a variety of work within the rubric of 'green' criminology (Lynch and Stretesky 2003; White 2003), within which we would include the systematic (state-corporate) exploitation of whole classes of people (Walters 2006). So if the (partial) transgressing of the boundaries of dominant understandings of violence by Bowie and Hills are not unique, they are, within criminology, extremely rare.

Explaining corporate violence?

This need to transcend a problematic dominated by individualism also indicates why explanations of violence produced by corporations sit both rarely and uneasily within the theoretical frameworks that constitute criminology. If criminology has focused relatively little energy upon bringing to light corporate crimes in general, this is partly an effect of the fact that historically, and to this day, the vast majority of criminological teaching and research tends simply to assume 'crime' as an activity engaged in by *individual* men (and sometimes women). Quite remarkably for a social science, one key feature of criminological literature is that it has often taken crime as socially and legally constructed as its starting point!

I have argued elsewhere that to understand corporate crime causation we must take into account a series of factors ranging from the individual through to the structural. These will be set out here – albeit very briefly – in four analytically (though not of course empirically) distinct 'levels'. Crucially, as we move through these levels, we find that criminology has, in turn, less to say about them.

First, while acknowledging the need to consider individual actions or omissions, understanding corporate violence generally requires us to look far beyond the individual 'on the scene' – the ship's assistant bosun who did not check whether the ferry's bow doors were closed before leaving port, the chemical plant worker who attached the hose to the methylisocyanate tank at Bhopal, or the 'gangmaster' who sent out undocumented workers to their death on Morecambe Bay sands (Tombs and Whyte 2007: 7–36). This is not to deny human agency, nor that individuals at times act (or fail to act) in ways that function as decisive triggers for such crimes. But it is to argue that an understanding of the production of these crimes is rarely found at this level. For to examine incidents and offences in terms of individuals is to fail to ask the question, what kind of organisation or process is it that allows the actions or inactions of one or several low-level employees unintentionally to cause significant physical harm, as is often the case?

The actions, inactions, decisions and so on of individuals must therefore be placed in the structures within which they operate – and this means taking cognisance of their immediate work group, their workplace, their organisation/company as well as, beyond these, a far wider complex of factors. And so, if we focus on the level of the individual, we might take some account of individual personality and characteristics, but do so especially in terms of the kinds of personalities that are recruited or encouraged within the organisation, as well as 'individual' factors that are socially constructed as relevant, such as rank/position within hierarchy, age, gender and ethnicity. For example, is it relevant to inquire whether an organisation is one where being female diminishes one's social power or is one in which time served adds authority?

Certain forms of criminological theorising and research have, of course, focused upon the individual, her or his modes of calculation in terms of rational choices, or personality, characteristics, pathology and so on. But in general, in terms of the kinds of theorising I have suggested in relation to the individual as an organisational member or an object of organisational violence, criminology has had relatively little to say.

Second, in terms of explaining corporate crime in general and corporate violence in particular, we need to move to the level of the immediate work group or sub-unit within the organisation. Here we need to take account of interpersonal dynamics, the culture of the work group (and the extent to which this coheres or clashes with the culture of the wider organisation) and its location within the overall organisation, both structurally and geographically – that is, is it relatively autonomous or highly supervised, is it part of one large organisational complex, or is it geographically isolated? Again, while there are some insights to be gleaned here from some forms of sociological positivism, these are considerations into which criminology has largely failed to enter.

Third, there are also key sets of issues to be raised in relation to the organisation itself. We need to understand something of its structure, its internal lines of decision-making and accountability, its geographical scope of operations, and the nature, volume and complexity of internal transactions. Issues of organisational culture must also be addressed: is the organisation risk-taking or risk-averse? is it gendered? is it authoritarian? and is it one where a blame culture predominates? Crucially, a focus on the organisation also entails a focus upon *management* (that is, as a collective, if often highly dispersed, 'entity', rather than in terms of individual managers). Examining specific forms of corporate violence often reveals evidence of aggressive managements, or managements who ensured that warnings, usually from below, were being systematically ignored. Moreover, we are likely to find a patterned lack of management accountability for violence, where management decisions and failures to heed warnings are subject to very little external counterbalancing in terms of regulation. Indeed, corporate violence often emanates from companies that frequently offend or from sectors where recidivist employers are commonplace. These may be facilitated by remuneration systems which focus solely on the bottom line and neither monitor let alone reward compliance. Thus managerial practices – and the cultures within which these are embedded – are crucial in understanding the production of violence (Tombs and Whyte 2007).

Finally at this level, or perhaps more accurately at the interstices of the level of the organisational and the extra-organisational, are a series of key *inter-organisational* features which need to be accounted for when explaining some forms of corporate violence. These include the ways in which different parts of the same firm relate to each other (parent–subsidiary relationships, for example), agency–contractor relationships, how different firms are linked into each other within or across particular sectors, perhaps in terms of long and complex supply chains, or indeed in terms of systematic relationships between legal and illegal businesses.

Fourth, and lastly, there are key sets of questions to be broached regarding the wider economic, political and social environments within which the organisation operates. Crucial among these extra-organisational features is the nature, size and structure of the market in which the organisation operates.

These also include the norms that predominate in an industry for what is acceptable or even 'required' for how the production of goods and services is organised – characterised by Carson's (1982) classic study of the UK offshore oil industry, for example, in the 'political economy of speed', alongside a series of (more or less real, but perceived in any case) market pressures, operating locally, nationally, internationally and even globally. Different markets and different industries create quite specific demands for profitability, speed or cost-cutting.

Beyond the market *per se*, we need to take cognisance of the nature and level of law and regulation. This clearly differs significantly by the form of corporate violence upon which we are focusing and the level at which we are analysing it. But, even before we can understand contemporary law and enforcement with regard to occupational safety, for example – characterised by the terms 'under-' and 'non-enforcement' – we need to recognise that the bases of these are to be found in the ways in which legal systems have been constructed either to separate out safety crimes from real crimes or even to deny the notion of safety crimes. Thus low levels of inspection, detection, formal enforcement and sanctions ensure that safety offences are regarded as less serious than other crimes of violence, an enduring phenomenon that acts to reduce the social opprobrium that is attached to those crimes. Crucially, the way the state does – or does not – frame and respond to safety crimes shapes the extent to which such crimes are tolerated, from the boardroom to the workplace.

Thus understanding how law and regulation helps to *produce* corporate violence means also taking into account the more general nature of state–business relationships, the dominant form of political economy and concomitant societal values, including the nature and degree of pro- or anti-business sentiment. Lastly, key information is to be gleaned in any understanding of the general 'health' of the economies in which the corporation operates.

The utility and relevance of these levels of analysis can be best highlighted through reference to a specific example of corporate violence – the killing of Simon Jones. Simon Jones was a 24-year-old student, taking a year out of study before sitting his finals in social anthropology at Sussex University. In April 1998, he signed on for casual work in Brighton with a local employment agency, Personnel Selection. Simon was required to register with an employment agency under the Jobseekers Allowance scheme – part of Labour's broader Welfare to Work strategy, whereby claimants must continually demonstrate availability for and willingness to work in exchange for continued receipt of 'benefits'. His first job with Personnel Selection was at Shoreham Docks, working for Euromin Ltd, a Dutch cargo company. He went to work in a ship's hold, unloading its cargo. Within an hour of arriving for his first day of work, he was dead. His head had been crushed and partially severed when a three tonne 'crane' grab closed around it. The grab should not have been there; it certainly should not have been open. The work required chains which should have been fastened to a hook instead. Changing back between a grab and a hook costs time and therefore money.

No prosecution was ever taken against Personnel Selection, though they are covered by the legal requirement to ensure the suitability of work which they assign or offer. Initially, the CPS also declined to prosecute Euromin, the firm for which the student was working (at just over £4 an hour). This is despite the fact that on visiting the scene of the death, the HSE issued two Prohibition Notices – regarding the use of the crane – and an Improvement Notice requiring the training and supervision of new workers. Following a protracted and high-profile campaign by the Simon Jones Memorial Campaign, a judicial review, in March 2000, overturned the decisions of the DPP and CPS not to prosecute. James Martell, Euromin Ltd, and its General Manager were eventually tried for manslaughter and corporate manslaughter respectively. On 29 November 2001, Martell and Euromin Ltd were cleared of manslaughter; Euromin was fined £50,000 for two offences under health and safety law. During the trial the judge had described Euromin's and Mr Martell's attitude to safety as 'absolutely deplorable' and giving 'wholly insufficient thought and attention' to safety. He also stated that the method of attaching bags to a hook welded to the grab should never have been used (Brooks 2001).

Simon's death is not explicable at the level of individual agency – he had not received training, Martell was censured in court but not convicted, and the crane driver appears not to have spoken English, all features at the level of individuals that in different ways tell us something of how Simon's death unfolded. But there are more significant, and extra-individual factors, to be taken into account to understand this case.

If a focus on the distribution of power in workplaces and upon the nature of *management* is required, as above, then we would usefully inquire into what passes for acceptable forms of management in this industry. Were Euromin and Martell exceptional 'bad apples' (the individualising term often used in such cases), or was the 'case' of Simon Jones unusual only in the fact that it ended in death, and such a gruesome one at that, yet in fact an effect of a very commonly found set of 'causes'? Further, as we indicate below, it is surely relevant in terms of the balance of power in this industry that the sector at issue – dockworking – had been subjected to a very explicit process of casualisation in the years prior to Simon's death, increasing the structural power of management. This had transformed the standard of management that was regarded as 'acceptable' in this industry at this time.

If we look beyond the organisation which was the site of the death, here, Euromin Ltd, we can see in this case how *inter-organisational* relationships are crucial to its production: the agency–contractor relationship placed Simon Jones where he would eventually die, as Personnel Selection received financial reward for sending Simon to what appears clearly to have been inappropriate work and, ultimately, his death.

At the level of the market or industry, we noted above that different markets and different industries create quite specific demands for profitability, speed or cost-cutting. Work in docks in often strictly time limited, to be completed according to sailing schedules and turnaround times. This partly explains why the crane grab had been so fatally modified and why, following Simon's death, a co-worker in the ship's hold was told to clean up the blood so that work could continue (Simon Jones Memorial Campaign, n.d.).

Now, tellingly, the Simon Jones Memorial Campaign based its fight around the issue of casualisation – a now firmly re-entrenched feature of working life in neo-liberal Britain, where deskilled, short-term and often agency-mediated employment is a common feature of a deregulated labour market. Such a feature is bolstered by a benefits system which forces claimants to take work – even work for which they are patently 'unfit' – on threat of withdrawal of any minimal financial support from the state. Finally, the role of Personnel Selection – acting as the 'middleman' between the state and Euromin – is also symptomatic of a state contracting out its functions to the private sector. In short, Simon's death is only explicable in the context of a particular political economy, namely neo-liberalism in an era of 'globalisation'. It was quite literally neo-liberalism that, in Emma Aynsley's words, 'put [Simon] in that situation'; (cited at http://www.simonjones.org.uk/articles/bigissuesep98.htm) prior to neo-liberalism Simon Jones simply could not have been where he was to lose his life. In the heyday of the Keynesian post-1945 settlement, there would have been no compulsion to work in exchange for benefit entitlement, no role for private companies in finding that work and no chance of him working on the docks without having been certified as competent to do so under the National Dock Labour Scheme (Lavalette and Kennedy 1996). In other words, if a routine killing, Simon's death is only comprehensible in the context of wider social, political and economic trends and the prevailing modes of thought and dominant value systems within which these emerge and through which they are sustained.

Also requiring critical scrutiny, as we noted, are law and regulation. Here, the response to Simon's death was both typical and extremely rare. It was typical in that such a routine killing was not to lead to any prosecution – as is the case with the majority of the work-related fatalities in the UK. But then, it was unusual because of the high-profile and successful campaign to overturn the decision not to prosecute, and the fact that the charges eventually laid were of manslaughter. Indeed, while these both failed, even the level of fine for the health and safety offences, at £50,000, was unusual – in the year of the Simon Jones case, the average fine for a conviction following a work-related fatality was £24,586.

Corporate violence: beyond criminology?

Even this brief example should be enough to indicate that all of these levels of analysis help us to make sense of this particular 'case', though of course the extent to which some are more relevant than others varies across specific examples and indeed broad types of corporate violence. But the key points remain: we cannot understand corporate violence through restricted considerations at the levels of intention or the interpersonal.

Rather, understanding corporate violence in particular, and corporate crime in general, requires two central recognitions. First, it means understanding that the corporation is an organisation, and this means that we must generally invoke explanations which lead us beyond concrete individuals, their actions or omissions, interpersonal relationships and intentions. Thus, even where it appears possible to identify key individuals behind corporate offending, Punch argues cogently that, if organisations of course consist of individuals 'in the sense of ostensibly morally autonomous actors', '[t]hey are not individuals in a vacuum and executives are not languishing in some meadow of independent reflection and moral balancing' (Punch 2008: 104). This is not to deny agency nor to absolve individuals of responsibility, but it is to recognise the crucial fact of the corporation as an organisational sector, one which provides 'motive, opportunity and means'; and it is this that allows us to conclude, for the most part, that 'the organization did it' (ibid.: 119).

Second, and of course relatedly, it means understanding that the corporation is an organisation that exists within particular kinds of social order with certain legal bases, guarantees and powers. And these are rooted in an economic power which, within certain social orders, can be augmented or diminished. Thus, for example, under conditions of neo-globalising liberalism, with their material and ideological manifestations of deregulation, the primacy of the private sector and the valorisation of risk, corporate recklessness, including that which results in violence, is more possible than in other, more regulated, social democratic contexts.

These considerations take us, finally, to a central issue within any consideration of corporate crime in general, namely the nature and distribution of power. This issue links discussion of the production of corporate violence, its representation and its regulation, and forces us to examine the relationships between businesses, states, other organisations and populations. Given this, one finds that various forms of critical and radical criminologies—including Marxisms and feminisms – have made important contributions to our knowledge of corporate crime causation. While there are clear differences between Marxisms, feminisms and other forms of critical criminology, one characteristic these share is the theoretical commitment to move beyond the narrowest confines of criminology, in particular to deconstruct dominant categories of crime and to view these constructions, and the criminal justice systems based upon them, as both an effect of and also a means of reproducing power.

Whether examined in isolation or in combination through attempts to conceptualise the range and relative importance of such factors in terms of an overarching framework, the production of corporate crimes against health and safety therefore needs to be conceptualised at a range of micro, meso and macro levels. And this requirement for an integrated understanding of these complex levels of analysis takes us towards disciplinary areas such as organisation theory and organisation studies, economics and political science in order that we may fully understand how corporate crimes are produced in any given society. Only this shift will facilitate understanding of the production of corporate crimes against health and safety through prevailing systems of economic, social and political organisation, dominant value systems and beliefs, and the differential distribution of power. Further, we require an integrated historical and international focus – for we cannot understand such crimes in the UK, without some understanding of how these, first, have emerged, and, second, how they fit within broader market processes that are increasingly played out internationally, if not globally.

Such an approach, alongside a recognition of the embedded biases of states and criminal justice systems, forces us to think about a much more profound question in relation to regulation: whether, under capitalist social orders, corporate violence can ever be sufficiently harnessed given that states see as their primary aim the encouragement of private profit maximisation and capital growth? Given that under-regulation and an absence of controls on corporate activity appear to be as much an embedded feature of capitalist social orders as corporate harm, crime and violence themselves, our greatest challenge is to go beyond reforming the ways we might control individual corporations: much more pressing is to seek an alternative means of organising production regimes that will neither encourage nor sustain the routine killings, injuries, disease and widespread emiseration of lives wreaked by corporations.

Acknowledgements

This chapter draws together work conducted over many years with friends and colleagues, notably Paddy Hillyard, Frank Pearce and Dave Whyte. Particular thanks go to Dave for casting his always insightful and critical eye over a draft of this chapter.

Selected further reading

Still a must read for a concise, and explicitly Marxist, introduction to corporate crime – its nature, scale, opportunity structure, 'regulation' and relative invisibility – is provided by Pearce's (1976) *Crimes of the Powerful: Marxism, Crime and Deviance*. A key theme of Pearce's text is how corporate crime systematically resists the label of crime. One of the few texts to label corporate activities as violent crime is the classic collection of readings found in Hills's (1987c) *Corporate Violence: Injury and Death for Profit*. The scope for legal harms, and the often difficult-to-distinguish line between lawful and illegal corporate activities, is nicely teased out through the various contributions to Passas and Goodwin's (2007) *It's Legal But It Ain't Right: Harmful Social Consequences of Legal Industries*. Focusing on occupational safety and health violations in particular, Tombs and Whyte's (2007) *Safety Crimes* is the first UK-based book-length treatment of this subject matter. The range of factors that are set out in this chapter as necessary for explaining corporate violence are elegantly and succinctly discussed in Punch's (2000) article 'Suite violence: why managers murder and corporations kill'. Updates on cases, statistics and legal reforms in this sphere are best gleaned from http://www.hazards. org/, an award winning workers' magazine focusing on safety and health issues, as well as the website of the Centre for Corporate Accountability, a UK charity which promotes worker and public safety (http://www.corporateaccountability.org/index. htm).

Notes

1 This is not to deny that corporations in such industries themselves engage in practices which are either illegal or of dubious legality.
2 Further details can be found at International Labour Organisation (2005) and at http://www.corporateaccountability.org/international/deaths/tables/summary/ main.htm.

3 Various other categories of occupational injury are excluded.
4 According to RIDDOR reporting criteria, reportable major injuries are: fractures, other than to fingers, thumbs and toes; amputations; dislocations of the shoulder, hip, knee or spine; loss of sight (temporary or permanent); chemical or hot metal burn or any penetrating injury to the eye; injury resulting from an electric shock or electrical burn; injury leading to hypothermia or heat-induced illness requiring resuscitation or requiring admittance to hospital for more than 24 hours; unconsciousness caused by asphyxia or exposure to harmful substance or biological agent; acute illness requiring medical treatment, or loss of consciousness arising from absorption of any substance by inhalation, ingestion or through the skin; acute illness following exposure to a biological agent or toxic or infected material.
5 These injuries are those which arise from work activity which result in the injured person being taken directly to hospital.
6 The Labour Force Survey (LFS) is a sample survey of households in the UK carried out by the Office of National Statistics. The survey is organised quarterly and seeks information on respondents' employment and labour market status. It is regarded as being more reliable than RIDDOR data in some respects since it relies upon confidential self-reporting of injuries rather that the willingness of employers to report to the authorities. The level of around a quarter of all injuries being reported is supported by recent research into hospital patients commissioned by the HSE (Davies *et al.* 2007), which indicates that 30 per cent of all injuries sustained at work leading to hospital treatment are reported to the HSE. If we assume that less serious injuries, not requiring hospitalisation, are more vulnerable to under-reporting, this research confirms reporting rates of less than 30 per cent for all injuries sustained at work.
7 http://www.hse.gov.uk/statistics/index.htm

References

Angell, M. (2004) 'The truth about the drug companies', *New York Review of Books*, 51 (12), 15 July. Online at: http://www.nybooks.com/articles/17244 (accessed 1 December 2008).

Baggot, R. (2000) *Public Health. Policy and Politics*. London: Macmillan.

Bowie, V. (2002) *Workplace Violence*. New South Wales: Workcover.

Brooks, L. (2001) 'Alarm as employer cleared in death case', *The Guardian*, 30 November. Online at: http://www.guardian.co.uk/Archive/Article/0,4273,4310372,00.html (accessed 11 December 2008).

Carrabine, E., Iganski, P., Lee, M., Plummer, K. and South, N. (2004) *Criminology. A Sociological Introduction*. London: Routledge.

Carson, W. G. (1982) *The Other Price of Britain's Oil: Safety and Control in the North Sea*. Oxford: Martin Robertson.

Cohen, R. (2002) 'An epidemic of neglect: neglected diseases and the health burden in poor countries', *Multinational Monitor*, 23 (6). Online at: http://www.multinationalmonitor.org/mm2002/02june/june02corp1.html (accessed 25 September 2008).

Corporate Watch (n.d.) *Pharmaceutical Industry: Sector Overview*. Online at: http://www.corporatewatch.org/?lid=315#poor (accessed 16 September 2008).

Davies, G., Kemp, G. and Frostick, S. (2007) *An Investigation of Reporting of Workplace Accidents Under RIDDOR Using the Merseyside Accident Information Model*, Research Report RR528. Norwich: HSE Books. Online at: http://www.hse.gov.uk/research/rrpdf/rr528.pdf (accessed 11 December 2008).

Department of Health Committee on the Medical Effects of Air Pollutants (1998) *Quantification of the Effects of Air Pollution on Health in the United Kingdom*. London: The Stationery Office.

Donohoe, M. (2003) 'Causes and health consequences of environmental degradation and social injustice', *Social Science and Medicine*, 56 (3): 573–87.

Eurostat (2004) *Accidents at Work in the EU: Serious and Fatal Accidents at Work Decreasing in the EU*. Reference STAT/04/55. Online at: http://europa.eu/rapid/pressReleasesAction.do?reference=STAT/04/55&format=HTML&aged=0&language=EN&guiLanguage=en (accessed 16 September 2008).

Friedrichs, D. O. (1999) 'White-collar crime and the class-race-gender construct', in M. D. Schwartz and D. Milovanovic (eds), *Race, Gender and Class in Criminology: The Intersections*. New York: Garland, pp. 141–58.

Greater Manchester Hazards Centre (2008) *Corporate Killing: Facts and Figures*. Manchester: Greater Manchester Hazards Centre.

Health and Safety Commission (2007) *Health and Safety Statistics 2006/2007*. London: National Statistics.

Health and Safety Executive (n.d.) *Statistics of Workplace Fatalities and Injuries in Great Britain: International Comparisons 2000*. London: HSE.

Helms, M., Vastrup, P., Gerner-Smidt, P. and Molbak, K. (2003) 'Short- and long-term mortality associated with foodborne bacterial gastrointestinal infections: registry based study', *British Medical Journal*, 326: 357–60.

Hills, S. (1987a) 'Preface', in S. Hills (ed.), *Corporate Violence: Injury and Death for Profit*. Totowa, NJ: Rowman & Littlefield.

Hills, S. (1987b) 'Epilogue: corporate violence and the banality of evil', in S. Hills (ed.), *Corporate Violence: Injury and Death for Profit*. Totowa, NJ: Rowman & Littlefield.

Hills, S. (ed.) (1987c) *Corporate Violence: Injury and Death for Profit*. Totowa, NJ: Rowman & Littlefield.

International Labour Organisation (2005) *World Day for Safety and Health at Work 2005: A Background Paper*. Geneva: International Labour Office.

Jansson, K., Povey, D. and Kaiza, P. (2007) 'Violent and sexual crime', in S. Nicholas, C. Kershaw and A. Walker (eds), *Crime in England and Wales 2006/07*. London: Home Office, pp. 49–72.

Lavalette, M. and Kennedy, J. (1996) *Solidarity on the Waterfront. The Liverpool Lock-out of 1995/96*. Birkenhead: Liver Press.

Lynch, M. and Stretesky, P. (2003) 'The meaning of green: contrasting criminological perspectives', *Theoretical Criminology*, 7 (2): 217–38.

Lynch, M., Stretesky, P. and McGurrin, D. (2002) 'Toxic crimes and environmental justice: examining the hidden dangers of hazardous waste', in G. Potter (ed.), *Controversies in White-Collar Crime*. Cincinnati, OH: Anderson, pp. 109–36.

National Creutzfeldt-Jakob Disease Surveillance Unit (2008) *CJD Statistics*. Online at: http://www.cjd.ed.ac.uk/figures.htm (accessed 16 September 2008).

Pai, H.-H. (2008) *Chinese Whispers: The True Story Behind Britain's Hidden Army of Labour*. London: Penguin.

Palmer, H. (2008) 'The whole story', *Safety and Health Practitioner*, 10 December. Online at: http://www.shponline.co.uk/article.asp?pagename=features&article_id=8265 (accessed 15 December 2008).

Passas, N. and Goodwin, N. (eds) (2007) *It's Legal But It Ain't Right: Harmful Social Consequences of Legal Industries*. Ann Arbor, MI: University of Michigan Press.

Pearce, F. (1976) *Crimes of the Powerful: Marxism, Crime and Deviance*. London: Pluto.

Pearce, F. and Tombs, S. (1998) *Toxic Capitalism: Corporate Crime in the Chemical Industry*. Aldershot: Ashgate.

Pemberton, S. (2004) 'A theory of moral indifference: understanding the production of harm by capitalist society', in P. Hillyard, C. Pantazis, S. Tombs and D. Gordon (eds), *Beyond Criminology: Taking Harm Seriously*. London: Pluto, pp. 67–83.

Punch, M. (2000) 'Suite violence: why managers murder and corporations kill', *Crime, Law and Social Change*, 33: 243–80.

Punch, M. (2008) 'The organization did it: individuals, corporations and crime', in J. Minkes and L. Minkes (eds), *Corporate and White-Collar Crime*. London: Sage, pp. 102–21.

Reiman, J. (1998) *The Rich Get Richer and the Poor Get Prison*, 5th edn. Boston: Allyn & Bacon.

Simon Jones Memorial Campaign (n.d.) *Not This Time! The Story of the Simon Jones Memorial Campaign*. Online at: http://www.simonjones.org.uk/film/notthistime.mov (accessed 11 December 2008).

Snider, L. (2003) 'Captured by Neo-liberalism: regulation and risk in Walkerton, Ontario', *Risk Management: An International Journal* (Special Issue: *Globalised Crime in a Globalised Era*), 5 (2).

Stretesky, P. and Hogan, M. (1998) 'Environmental justice: an analysis of superfund sites in Florida', *Social Problems*, 45: 268–87.

Stretesky, P. and Lynch, M. (1998) 'Corporate environmental violence and racism', *Crime, Law and Social Change*, 30: 163–84.

Stretesky, P. and Lynch, M. (1999) 'Environmental justice and the predictions of distance to accidental chemical releases in Hillsborough County, Florida', *Social Science Quarterly*, 80: 830–46.

Szockyi, E. and Fox, J. G. (eds) (1996) *Corporate Victimisation of Women*. Boston: Northeastern University Press.

Takala, J. (2006) *The Iron Grip of Latency*. Geneva: ILO. Online at: http://www.ilo.org/global/About_the_ILO/Media_and_public_information/Press_releases/lang--en/WCMS_076282/index.htm (accessed 30 July 2008).

TNS (2004) *Consumer Attitudes to Food Standards Wave 4: UK Report*, prepared for Food Standards Agency and COI Communications. London: TNS. Online at: http://www.foodstandards.gov.uk/multimedia/pdfs/cas2003.pdf (accessed 30 July 2008).

Tombs, S. and Whyte, D. (2007) *Safety Crimes*. Cullompton: Willan.

Tombs, S. and Whyte, D. (2008) *A Crisis of Enforcement: The Decriminalisation of Death and Injury at Work*. London: Harm and Society Foundation.

Tombs, S. (2007) 'Violence, safety crimes and criminology', *British Journal of Criminology*, 47 (4): 531–50.

Tweedale, G. (2000) *Magic Mineral to Killer Dust: Turner and Newall and the Asbestos Hazard*. Oxford: Oxford University Press.

Tyfield, D. (2008) 'Enabling TRIPs: the pharma-biotech-university patent coalition', *Review of International Political Economy*, 15 (4): 535–66.

UK Parliament (2003) *Postnote: Food Poisoning*. London: Parliamentary Office of Science and Technology.

Vogel, L. (2005) 'Asbestos in the world', *HESA Newsletter*, No. 27, June. Online at: http://hesa.etui-rehs.org/uk/newsletter/files/Newsletter27p7-21.pdf (accessed 30 July 2008).

Walters, D., Nichols, T., Conner, J., Tasiran, A. and Cam, S. (2005) *The Role and Effectiveness of Safety Representatives in Influencing Workplace Health and Safety*, HSE Research Report 363. London: HSE Books.

Walters, R. (2006) 'Crime, bio-agriculture and the exploitation of hunger', *British Journal of Criminology*, 46 (1): 26–45.

White, R. (2003) 'Environmental issues and the criminological imagination', *Theoretical Criminology*, 7 (4): 483–506.

Whyte, D. (2004) 'Regulation and corporate crime', in J. Muncie and D. Wilson (eds), *Student Handbook of Criminal Justice and Criminology*. London: Cavendish.

Woolfson, C. (2005) 'Un-social Europe', *Transitions Online*, 10 June. Online at: http://www.tol.cz/look/TOL/article.tpl?IdLanguage=1&IdPublication=4&NrIssue=119&NrSection=4&NrArticle=14149&tpid=6 (accessed 30 July 2008).

World Health Organisation (2006) *Elimination of Asbestos-Related Diseases*. Geneva: WHO. Online at: http://www.who.int/occupational_health/publications/asbestosrelateddiseases.pdf (accessed 30 July 2008).

Chapter 45

Driving offences

Claire Corbett

Introduction

Owing to the vast array of driving offences in existence, this chapter will necessarily examine a limited selection only based on their high volume, seriousness and public concern. The first section will define what driving offences are and how they developed alongside the emerging car culture. The second section will give a general overview of patterns and trends, those most likely to engage in road traffic offending, and the kinds of explanations voiced by drivers and theoretical approaches used to explain their commission. The next three sections will follow a similar pattern and focus on speeding, bad driving and impaired driving. In addition, contemporary debates concerning each will be considered, along with official responses to each offence category.

The final section will draw the key themes together, noting the danger of work-related driving, given that up to a third of all road traffic collisions involve somebody at work at the time accounting for up to 20 fatalities and 250 serious injuries every week (DfT and HSE 2003).

Definition of 'driving offences'

There is no strict statutory definition of 'driving offences', though there is considerable case law defining what a 'driver' and 'driving' are for the purposes of interpreting road traffic legislation. Using such definitions, driving offences may be considered as acts breaching road traffic law committed by a driver of a motorised vehicle engaged in 'driving' within the ordinary meaning of that word. 'Driving offences' differ from 'vehicle offences', which is the subject of Chapter 2, in that the former concern crimes *by* drivers while the latter involve crimes *to* vehicles such as theft of and from them. Driving offences are crimes under road traffic law, which is separate from criminal law though an integral part of it. Road traffic offences encompass more than just driving offences in that not all involve driving or motorised vehicles.

While there is no hard-and-fast classification of driving offences and what these should or should not comprise, the main types of road traffic offence that involve driving follow with some examples to illustrate the category. Should driving offences be limited to 'the way the vehicle is driven', arguably the last three categories might be excluded.

- *Driving below the minimum standard required by law* (careless driving,causing death by dangerous driving, 'tailgating').
- *Driver competence and physical fitness breaches* (drink and drug offences, poor eyesight, medical conditions).
- *Speed limit breaches* (failing to observe 30 m.p.h. speed limit signs).
- *Traffic signals and signs offences* (failing to observe hatched line restrictions, red lights, no right turn signs).
- *Driving with inadequate driver documentation or vehicle documentation* (driving unlicensed, uninsured or while disqualified, having no vehicle excise licence or vehicle registration document).
- *Construction and use offences* (driving a vehicle with faulty brakes or tyres, driving an overloaded vehicle).
- *Parking and obstruction offences* (obstructing a highway; wrongful use of a disabled person's badge).

The historical and legislative context of driving offences

The first major legislation on driving offences comprised the Motor Car Act 1903 that established the offence of reckless driving, the penalty of disqualification from driving, the introduction of vehicle number plates and driving licences, and raised the speed limit to 20 m.p.h.

Careless driving and driving a vehicle while unfit through drink or drugs joined the statute book under the Road Traffic Act 1930, which became the main platform on which modern road traffic law is based. It introduced the concept of mandatory insurance and also decriminalised speeding on the grounds that road congestion would reduce and driver responsibility would increase, with both leading to fewer crashes (Emsley 1993: 25). Yet this optimism was not rewarded and speeding offences were reintroduced in 1934, along with a higher 30 m.p.h. maximum.

As car ownership became more affordable during the twentieth century and vehicle numbers rose dramatically, road fatalities peaked in 1966 when 7,985 died on the roads (compared with 2,946 in 2007). To counter this huge toll, the Road Safety Act 1967 introduced a raft of safety measures including the compulsory fitting of seat belts to all new cars, a 70 m.p.h. speed limit on previously unrestricted roads and drink-drive regulations and standards that remain largely unchanged today.

Under the Road Traffic Act 1991, reckless driving offences were replaced by dangerous driving offences that were based on the actual standard of driving rather than a subjective test of the driver's mental state at the time of the offence. That Act introduced a requirement for the worst convicted drivers to retake the driving test and provisions to allow the installation of automatic camera devices for red light and speeding offences.

As interesting is how the socio-political context of driving has evolved over time. When cars first arrived their wealthy owners fell foul of the car-less, who represented the environmental lobby angry at the pollution caused. These affluent drivers were soon in conflict with the traffic police and government at their unwarranted 'criminalisation' from enforcement of the traffic laws (Emsley 1993: 374). On one occasion, police were exhorted by the Home Secretary not to treat motorists who might be 'persons of the utmost respectability of character and position' as 'possible criminals' (ibid.).

Antipathy between drivers and others is a theme that has reverberated through much of the last century. Little has changed since other than that car owners are no longer a small elite group but have mushroomed into a large proportion of the adult population, and now comprise members of all social classes from the bottom to the top. With road transport and car use again at the centre of the environmental debate on congestion and pollution, with those choosing to drive the so-called 'gas guzzlers' cast as contemporary 'folk devils', the debate of a century ago has re-emerged but with differently configured parties.

Another theme that has weathered the years is the view that penalties for driving offences have been on the lenient side and often do not reflect the seriousness of the incident nor the harm done. Early vehicle owners largely comprised the elite, including MPs and judges, who may not have rushed to over-penalise 'minor' transgressions they personally might commit. This may give a clue why the public discourse around failing to comply with traffic laws has developed in the way it has. Using the word 'accident' to construct collisions as blameless and unpredictable events that could befall anyone would have suited the interests of the first car owners and illustrates how that early discourse of driving offences as 'minor' has endured to this day. The outcomes are that the 'thrills and spills' and 'car as king of the road' images still prevail (Corbett 2003: 29–31).

Current context

The twenty-first century arrived with the road death toll still falling since its peak in 1966, and with the British government introducing a new road safety strategy for the ensuing ten years including casualty reduction targets that were well on the way to being met by 2007 (DfT 2007b: 3).

Despite several higher maxima sentences for causing death by dangerous offences introduced in 2003, concern continued and two new offences of causing death were introduced under the Road Safety Act 2006. This long-awaited, wide-ranging and controversial Act provides for new graduated fixed penalties for speeding offences, various measures to combat unlicensed and uninsured driving and vehicle registration fraud, and several measures regarding drink-driving.

Specialist police traffic officers have been the main enforcers of these offences for much of the last century, though their numbers have been in long-term decline for the latter half of it (e.g. Gaventa 2005: 11–13). To offset this drop in specialist officers and the vastly increased volume of vehicles, traffic law enforcement is becoming strongly reliant on technology. Thus automatic speed cameras and red traffic light cameras are now commonplace, and the advent of automatic number plate recognition (ANPR) cameras has enabled the enforcement of many document offences and the detection of offenders associated with particular vehicles who are wanted for serious vehicle-related and mainstream offences.

While the news media has taken much interest in the treatment of driving offenders by speed cameras – sometimes casting drivers as 'victimised' – and considerable interest is shown in vehicle-related crime through television series on 'traffic cops' and 'vehicle theft', criminologists have largely kept well clear. This is interesting considering that vehicle stops are the second-most common context for any police–public contact (Allen *et al.* 2005: Table 2.04) and that three-quarters of the adult population in Britain hold full driving licences and are at risk of committing driving offences. One explanation is that because driving offences use the strict liability standard rather than the 'guilty mind' associated with *mens rea* for proof, they are not always regarded as 'real crime' in the same sense that burglary or robbery are (Corbett and Simon 1992: 37–42a) and tend to be ignored by most criminologists.

Patterns and trends of driving offences

No perfect measure exists by which to determine the incidence of and trends in driving offences, and other than self-report studies reliance must be placed on annually published statistics of numbers of offences dealt with by official action. Even then, such statistics are prone to the vagaries of factors that include the numbers of traffic police officers, other enforcers and automatic camera devices available to detect offences, police prosecution policies and accuracy in collating data, the readiness of the infrastructure to process detected offenders and the introduction of new legislation.

Given these caveats, the total number of driving offences dealt with by official *police* action has fallen gradually from a peak of 8.8 million in 1990 to a steady 5–6 million between 1999 to 2005, and is now under 5 million in 2006 (MoJ 2008a: Table 2). The reason for this drop is largely the result of the Road Traffic Act 1991, effective from mid-1992, which specified that parking contraventions were no longer criminal offences. Thereafter, local authorities have taken over enforcement of parking, obstruction and waiting infringements. If, however, penalty charge notices issued for these offences are included in total motoring offences dealt with by *official* action – which is often how they are reported in the media – a peak was reached in 2004 of 13.5 million (MoJ 2008a: Table A), as parking offences soared. Since then there has been a slight downturn in most categories of offence year on year (MoJ 2008a: Table 2), with a few exceptions. The main one has been a 26 per cent increase in careless driving offences between 2005–2006, resulting from a big increase in prosecuting those using a hand-held mobile phone while driving (MoJ 2008a: 7).

It is important to note the second largest offence category dealt with by official police action, that of *licence, insurance and record-keeping offences*, which totalled 1,016,400 in 2006. Before speed cameras began multiplying, this category remained the largest from 1951 until 2000. The number of processed offences in this category overall has fallen slightly since 2003 in common with others mentioned above, but its incidence is likely to be much higher as it is hard to detect. To assist with this, ANPR is now being rolled out across the country in view of its high 'hit' rate from stops for document, other traffic and mainstream offences and offenders. Research studies estimate that around 1 in 20 drivers on British roads drive without insurance (Greenaway 2006: 10) or without an appropriate licence (Knox *et al.* 2003: 47–8), and it is hoped that ANPR will help cut the numbers involved. Document offences are important despite the low penalties typically given, as those committing them tend to engage in a cocktail of other traffic and mainstream offending – some serious (e.g. Rose 2000), and such offenders have a higher crash risk than others (e.g. Knox *et al.* 2003: 61–2) and may be partly responsible for the current rise in 'hit and run' collisions where drivers fail to stop.

So overall, despite the increasing numbers of licensed vehicles on British roads (now at 30 million in 2006 – MoJ 2008a: Table A), motoring offences with or without parking offences are falling slightly since earlier peaks.

Who are the driving offenders?

Driving offences are hardly homogeneous, and a key distinction between them is whether they occur as unintended errors of omission or commission, or as deliberate violations. In the latter case, the purpose or need to be served by a particular illicit driving action may also vary. It should not be surprising therefore if different offender profiles emerge for those committing different kinds of offence.

Traffic offending, according to motoring court conviction statistics, has been and still is largely the preserve of male drivers. In 2006, male convictions considerably outstripped the female conviction rate with males responsible for 87 per cent of the total (MoJ 2008a: Table 12). This gender imbalance well reflects that for mainstream offending where men were responsible for 75 per cent of all court convictions in 2006 (MoJ 2007: Table 3.8). At face value, this suggests that the propensity to offend on and off the road may not be so different.

Despite the big difference in the gender ratio for convictions, women are slowly catching up. Women were responsible for 7 per cent in 1988, 11 per cent in 1998, 12 per cent in 2003 and 13 per cent of motoring convictions in 2006 (Home Office 1989: Table 17, 2000, 2005; MoJ 2008a). Yet this *might* be linked with their increasing representation in the fully licensed driver population rather than an increased propensity to offend, as in the same years women comprised 38 per cent, 43 per cent, 44 per cent and 44 per cent respectively of that population. The opposing argument is that indeed women drivers are acting more unlawfully, and Corbett (2007: 6–8) has presented evidence to support such a view.

Age is another important factor in traffic offending, with the bulk of evidence showing that younger men and to a lesser extent younger women tend to comply considerably less with the motoring laws than their respective older counterparts (e.g. OECD 2006; Corbett 2007: 5). Yet young drivers are not the sole culprits, and some other groups are at higher risk of traffic offending. These include mid-aged women, often working mothers in professional occupations, who were found by Dobson *et al.* (1999) to be at higher risk of poor driving including speeding, lapses and errors, and company car drivers (often older males) who were found to engage more frequently in risky behaviours like eating or drinking and using a mobile phone while driving, fatigued driving and speeding (e.g. Broughton *et al.* 2003).

Before the statistical sophistication we have now, it was wondered whether driving offenders were like Jekyll and Hyde characters, changing their mild manners once behind the wheel. The answer from recent research fails to confirm this, and indeed suggests there is considerable overlap between serious traffic and mainstream offending (Chenery *et al.* 1999; Broughton 2007). For example, Rose (2000) examined the criminal histories of large samples of offenders convicted for mainstream, car theft and serious traffic offences using the Home Office Offenders Index. The data showed a strong overlap between drink driving, dangerous driving, disqualified driving and mainstream offending, with, for example, convicted drink-drivers twice as likely and disqualified or dangerous drivers four times as likely as the general population to have a criminal record for mainstream offending.

With road deaths estimated to become the world's third biggest killer overall by 2020 (Jacobs *et al.* 2000), a pertinent question is whether there are links between road traffic offending and crash involvement. Surprisingly, relatively little research has been conducted to explore this question, but what has been done supports a correlation (e.g. Stradling 1997: 4–9). Another study showed that drivers judged to have displayed risky behaviour immediately preceding a road crash, including actions deemed careless or dangerous, were more likely to have an extensive criminal record than accident-involved 'passive' drivers (Junger *et al.* 2001).

Explanations for driving offences

Because there is less social stigma attached to road traffic offending than mainstream offending, ordinary drivers are frequently willing to give explanations for it. Key motives people cite to account for traffic offending generally follow; offence-specific reasons will come later.

- *Utility.* Many offences have utility for drivers and this is perhaps the broadest category applying to many offences and offenders. Popular explanations here include offending when 'in a hurry' and 'out of convenience or laziness' (e.g. Corbett and Simon 1992a). Utility explanations also account for documentation offences where drivers consider they are unable to afford repairs, insurance, vehicle taxation or pay for driver training (e.g. Knox *et al.* 2003) but want to drive. Marsh and Collett (1986) outlined the utility for young men of breaking traffic laws that included the opportunity to impress others – particularly the opposite sex, to express individuality, freedom, independence and defiance, and to 'play on a level playing field' against better-off drivers and better vehicles, e.g. by racing away from traffic signals.

- *Perceived low risk of detection.* The perceived likelihood of 'getting away with it' underpins much traffic offending and this is naturally linked with perceived and actual levels of enforcement (e.g. Corbett and Simon 1992a). Research shows that there must be some correspondence between perceived and actual risk of detection for an enforcement initiative to have effect (e.g. Shinar and McKnight 1985).

- *Perceived lack of danger and low risk of harm.* This is one of the most common categories to emerge in driver research, and is implicitly qualified by 'in those circumstances', as in the expression 'it's safe when I do it' (see Corbett and Simon 1992a: 30–4; Corbett *et al.* 2008).

- *Inadvertence/lack of intention.* This explanation is common to careless driving (e.g. Stradling 1997) and speeding offences especially (e.g. Corbett and Simon 1999: 52–3), and distinguishes much traffic offending from mainstream offending, the latter tending to be deliberate.

- *Thrill/excitement of risky manoeuvres or behaviours.* This a long-standing theme in driver research and is commonly but not exclusively associated with younger drivers and an intrinsic pleasure in risk-taking. It may apply especially to bad driving offences (e.g. McKenna *et al.* 1998: chapter 4, especially 21, 36).

- *Social consensus/social acceptability.* This is expressed by the view that 'everyone does it' and the notion of 'safety in numbers' (e.g. Corbett and Simon 1992a: 38), and as if legitimation of law-breaking is to be found in social consensus. Such explanations are redolent of Sykes and Matza's (1957) 'techniques of neutralisation' whereby wrongdoing or immorality is denied through such appeals to the consensus.

- *Not real crime.* This is another large category encompassing the notions that traffic rules are to be treated as guidelines (Corbett and Simon 1992a: 35–6), that driving offences are not serious or morally wrong, and are of a different quality to mainstream offending (Corbett and Simon 1992a: 38–40).

Some of the factors above have been incorporated into various general theoretical approaches to crime. These include deterrence theories, which have been tested in research on drink-drivers by, for example, Homel (1993); the rational choice perspective that has been applied to vehicle theft and joyriding (e.g. Light *et al.* 1993) and extended to other driving offences (Corbett and Simon 1992b); and the general theory of crime where a general predisposition to impulsive and risky behaviour has been applied to traffic crime by Junger *et al.* (2001). They also include *gender-based theories* within which a gendered lens has been applied to view male involvement in driving offences such as joyriding (e.g. Cohen 1955), drink-driving (Gusfield *et al.* 1981), speeding (Marsh and Collett 1986) and ram-raiding (Campbell 1993). Elements of the above have also been incorporated into *critical perspectives* where the hegemony of the car can help explain the perceived minor nature of driving offences, permitting non-compliance (Corbett 2003: 29–31). The views of some drivers that traffic laws are guidelines only to be negotiated by themselves (Corbett and Simon 1992a: 34–40) are also indices of the car's dominance in society.

Speeding: introduction

Exceeding a posted speed limit or 'speeding' is the driving offence type most commonly dealt with by official action in England and Wales (see MoJ 2008a: Table 2), among which exceeding the 30 m.p.h. limit is the most commonly actioned offence overall. 'Racing vehicles on a public highway' recently popular around the M25 is another offence and is not confined to the UK. 'Car cruise' events with 'pimped up' and other vehicles are variations of illegal road racing, and footage may be filmed and posted by offenders and spectators on popular websites.[1]

The word 'speeding' has become an emotive word for many drivers as those with some 'live' penalty points on their licences for speeding could be around 14 per cent, extrapolating from a recent large representative survey (Direct Line 2007). What irks many drivers is that speeding is not thought dangerous when they do it (see above) and many appear to suspect that the proliferation of speed cameras to enforce speeding laws has as much if not more to do with revenue generation as with improving road safety. As more become 'criminalised' through prosecution for speeding so perhaps does the risk of alienation, which could erode what has been majority support for cameras until now (e.g. Corbett and Caramlau 2006: 414). At the extremes, antipathy towards cameras can lead to their vandalisation by the disaffected, and the existence of lobby groups underlines the continuing opposition to speed cameras and speed limits by some.

Fortunately for drivers, excess or inappropriate speed rarely leads to negative consequences, which may help account for speeding having been considered a relatively minor offence by drivers (e.g. O'Connell and Whelan 1996). Yet viewed from the perspective of victims and bereaved relatives, excess and inappropriate speed are extremely harmful and were implicated in 32 per cent of fatal collisions and 20 per cent of serious injury collisions as contributory factors in Great Britain in 2006 (DfT 2007c: Table 4B). Interestingly, the potential threat from inappropriate speed is also a concern. Wood (2004: 11) showed that 43 per cent of the population found that 'speeding traffic in their local area' was regarded as a 'fairly' or 'very big' problem, and this was the most commonly mentioned community concern about antisocial behaviour. All this suggests that speeding may be constructed as a problem of the 'other driver', which view is supported by a large survey showing 62 per cent of drivers considered speeding to be a 'serious offence' – suggesting that attitudes may be changing somewhat – yet over half admitted doing it themselves (RAC 2006).

Patterns and trends

Two kinds of statistics are collected for speeding offences in England and Wales. The first comprises vehicle speed monitoring data gathered via automatic counters located at around 100 sites on different road types. The second kind comprises various statistics relating to the detection and onward processing of speed offences.

Vehicle speed monitoring data measure proportions of vehicles exceeding speed limits on different road types in free-flow conditions. There has been a downward trend for vehicles exceeding the 30 m.p.h. limit on built-up roads over the last decade – where most speed cameras are sited. In 1997, 70 per cent of cars exceeded the 30 m.p.h. limit which figure fell to 49 per cent in 2007, suggesting that the threat of penalty points does deter. However, apart from slight falls on some road types, the proportions of cars speeding on rural single carriageway roads (9 per cent in 1997 and 2007) and on motorways (54 per cent in 1997 and 53 per cent in 2007) have remained remarkably stable over this period, highlighting the challenge ahead (DTLR 2001: Tables 4 and 8; DfT 2008b: Tables 3 and 4).

Table 45.1 shows how speed limit offences actioned over the last decade have increased massively as cameras have multiplied. However, despite a big jump from 761,400 offences dealt with in 1996 to 2,118,800 in 2005, the tide may have turned as 2006 saw the first fall in numbers dealt with by fixed penalty or prosecution. Over the same decade, speed camera activity increased and comprised a higher proportion year on year of all detections dealt with from 34 per cent in 1996 to 95 per cent in 2006, while police enforcement of speed limit breaches correspondingly fell. In fact, the drop between 2005 and 2006 is largely accounted for by the police turning attention to other motoring offences, including mobile phone and careless driving offences. Police dealt with approximately 254,000 speed limit offences in 2005 but only 98,000 in 2006. It remains to be seen whether the downward trend continues.

Who does it?

Few drivers deny ever speeding though some engage in it more than others. Those prosecuted at court for speeding (the worst offences) largely comprise men, but women are catching up as their share of the licensed driver population grows (Corbett 2007). In 1988 women comprised 7 per cent, and in 2006 19 per cent of all those convicted in court for speeding. Nearly all self-report surveys confirm the greater male involvement in speeding (e.g.

Table 45.1 Numbers of speed limit offences dealt with by official action (in thousands) and the proportions detected by speed cameras: 1996–2006

	1996	1999	2002	2005	2006
Total dealt with by official police action	761.4	995.3	1,557.9	2,118.8	1,959.5
% detected by automatic camera	34%	49%	85%	88%	95%

Source: DTLR, Motoring Offences England and Wales (1996, 1999); DTLR, Motoring Offences and Breath Test Statistics England and Wales (2002); MoJ (2005, 2006)

Stradling *et al.* 2003: 1–7) and greater female compliance with speed cameras (Corbett and Caramlau 2006: 424).

Speeding like other risky road behaviours tends to decrease with age (e.g. Stradling *et al.* 2003: 58–9). It is more frequently reported among those with higher mileages and company-car drivers (Broughton *et al.* 2003). Corbett *et al.*'s (2008) survey of drivers with different patterns of penalty points supports these findings. They showed that drivers with some points for speeding compared with those reporting none were more likely to be male, to have higher mileages, to drive for work and to slow down just before a camera box. Finally, getting caught for speeding is no respecter of status. In Britain, royalty, current senior politicians, the most senior traffic police officer and various celebrities all have court convictions for speeding recently.

Specific explanations for speeding

Mirroring the 'thrills and spills' image and worldwide attraction of Formula 1 racing, 'enjoyment in driving fast' is a common cross-cultural explanation given to explain speeding behaviour by drivers (e.g. SWOV 1998: Table 5.1). 'Being in a hurry' is perhaps the most common explanation overall (e.g. Corbett *et al.* 2008), though 'inadvertently exceeding a limit' is frequently cited (ibid.). Risk compensation theories are enjoying renewed appeal as research shows that as technological advances have reduced external speed cues like noise and vibration and comfort levels have increased, high speeds seem slower and less dangerous to drivers than they are (Walker *et al.* 2006). A related hydraulic model (e.g. Wilde 1986) says that safety features like airbags, anti-lock braking systems and side impact bars have reduced actual risk to drivers, with drivers responding by seeking out more risk by driving closer or faster.

Responses to speeding

There are now around 6,000 fixed speed cameras in Britain, and detection normally brings a conditional offer of a £60 fixed penalty (as at 2008) together with a licence endorsement of 3 penalty points. Higher margins of excess speed can lead to a higher fine and up to 6 penalty points in court, or even discretionary disqualification of the driver's licence. Points stay on a driver's licence for four years, though they are 'live' for only three. Upon accumulation of 12 points, disqualification should normally occur under section 3, Road Traffic Offenders Act 1988, though this does not always transpire (Corbett *et al.* 2008: 7). It is becoming standard practice across police force areas to offer low-level speeders a once-only option of paying to attend a short 'speed awareness' course instead of forfeiting 3 penalty points. Anecdotal and research evidence of a salutary short-term positive effect is encouraging (e.g. McKenna 2004), though evidence is awaited for long-term speed reduction.

Under the Road Safety Act 2006, provisions were made to introduce a graduated points system dependent on the level of excess speed. This could mean that 6 points would accompany a higher fixed penalty for the worst breaches. A lower starting point of 2 penalty points for low levels of excess speed was dropped for fear of undermining the government's message that even small breaches can kill, e.g. hitting someone at 35 m.p.h. is twice as likely to kill than at 30 m.p.h. A second consultation on this and other matters was launched in late 2008 (DfT 2008a) with the government's response due later.

Despite the high risk of detection by speed cameras in Britain, Broughton (2008) found that proportionately very few drivers since 1994 were disqualified by accumulating 12 points solely for speeding in the next three years. Moreover, despite the huge 247 per cent increase in driver licence endorsements (without disqualification) for speeding and traffic light offences between 1996 and 2006, numbers of disqualifications from 'totting up' penalty points over the same period decreased by 19 per cent (MoJ 2008a: Table 16). This suggests that drivers are behaving as if deterred by the threat of disqualification or avoiding it by alternative means. Corbett *et al.*'s (2008) study found evidence to support both propositions, and another survey suggested that 1.5 per cent of British motorists had swapped penalty points with others (Churchill Insurance 2007).

However frequently true deterrence is achieved, studies show that speeds do reduce where cameras are installed and considerably fewer casualties result (e.g. Pilkington and Kinra 2005), demonstrating the oft-disputed effectiveness of cameras. Yet despite the research evidence many opponents remain, and in 2008 Swindon in Wiltshire became the first English town voting to withdraw fixed-spot cameras on the grounds they failed to curb excessive speed.

Cameras where the average speed between two points is calculated represent a technological advance, and a new 2009 version could work in clusters of up to 50 cameras to cover entry and exit points across wide areas to encourage compliance (*The Times* 2008b). This would be especially useful on rural roads where most road deaths occur. Intelligent Speed Adaptation (ISA) uses satellite technology to restrict vehicle speeds to the maximum allowed on a particular road and would eradicate speeding if used compulsorily nationwide. Interestingly, research indicates that most British drivers would welcome compulsory use by all drivers (Lai *et al.* 2007: x). Other attempts to control speed have come from unpopular road humps and various traffic calming measures, with education as a longer-term strategy. Speed awareness courses may be used for the 'worst' speeders who might benefit more than the usual 'low' speeding participants of such courses.

Concluding comments

Ironically, the continued global economic downturn could do more to cut speeding than many previous efforts, and incentives for commercial businesses to install ISA such as cheaper insurance and lower fuel costs could cut the speeds not only of company car drivers but also those of other drivers blocked behind. One effect of the Corporate Manslaughter and Corporate Homicide Act (CMCHA) 2007 is likely to be increased training of fleet vehicle drivers in efforts to avoid corporate liability for any gross failure in the duty of care to employees or others. Such training may also indirectly lead to lowered speeds. In the meantime, exceeding limits remains paradoxical with drivers thinking it acceptable and not dangerous when they do it, but more serious and antisocial when others do.

Bad driving: dangerous and careless offences – introduction

'Bad driving' is a generic term used to describe a range of actions that are generally classed as dangerous or careless driving offences when prosecuted. They are considered the most difficult to legislate for because of: (1) the difficulty of adequately distinguishing the elements of 'careless' and 'dangerous' behaviours and consequently of constructing offences appropriately and comprehensively to encompass the gamut of bad driving actions; and (2) the huge dilemma of setting appropriate levels of sanctions where offender culpability is low as in 'careless' offences but harm is extreme, as in death.

Those who have lost loved ones have long been angered that no mention of a death is included in the charged offence of 'driving without due care and attention', and in the magistrates' courts where such cases are heard, no mention need be made that a person has been killed as a result of the careless action (e.g. RoadPeace 2007: 4). Moreover, usually a small fine only is awarded plus a few penalty points. To compound these issues, research has found inconsistency in charging by Crown Prosecutors (Pearce *et al.* 2002: 46–51).

Various recent developments have occurred to meet these concerns. Two new offences have finally been implemented in 2008 under the Road Safety Act 2006 to join the existing offences of 'causing death by dangerous driving' and 'causing death by careless driving when under the influence of drink or drugs'.[2] These are 'causing death by careless or inconsiderate driving' and 'causing death by driving: unlicensed, disqualified or uninsured drivers', which are both either-way offences.

In 2007, the Crown Prosecution Service published a revised prosecution policy on bad driving designed to distinguish more precisely careless from dangerous offences, though road safety campaigners thought little would change as a result. The Sentencing Guidelines Council (SGC) has recommended lengthy custodial sentences of up to seven years in fatal cases involving 'prolonged, persistent and deliberate bad driving' such as reading or composing text messages, of at least seven years in fatal cases involving 'consumption of substantial amounts of drugs or alcohol', and up to 14 years if combined with other aggravating features (SGC 2008). While some offenders are likely to go to jail for longer, in practice it is unlikely many more will be imprisoned and, indeed, community sentences are recommended for deaths caused by the lowest levels of culpability (ibid. 15) where short lapses of attention or momentary negligent errors of judgment result.

New criteria for assessing dangerous and careless behaviour were introduced under the Road Traffic Act (RTA) 1991, when 'dangerous' driving offences replaced 'reckless' offences. Under this Act, the *subjective* element of determining the offending driver's state of mind was replaced by a two-prong formula based on *objective* qualities of the driving. So, now the court must decide whether the behaviour in question fell *far below* (for a dangerous offence) or *below* (for a careless offence) that expected of a 'competent and careful driver', and then whether it would have been obvious to such a driver that the behaviour would be dangerous/careless. The problem with this 'objective' measure is that most drivers think their skills above average (e.g. Svenson 1981) and most will identify with the 'careful and competent driver'. Yet among those drafting charges and deciding verdicts will be some having no problem with exceeding speed limits or other injudicious behaviours, and who may thus be less willing to concur that a driver's behaviour fell far below what a careful and competent driver would think appropriate. This could account for the far lower rate of dangerous driving to careless driving charges brought and the far higher acquittal rate of dangerous prosecutions (see Pearce *et al.* 2002: 43, 55; Corbett 2003: chapter 7). In other words, application of the objective test almost inevitably requires subjective judgment.

Other examples of behaviour that may be charged as causing death by dangerous driving include aggressive driving, racing or competitive driving, driving at inappropriate speeds for the prevailing conditions, knowingly driving a dangerously defective or overloaded vehicle, driving when too tired to stay awake, driving with impaired ability such as with a leg or arm in plaster or wearing high heels or impaired eyesight. Causing death by careless driving might include overtaking on the inside lane or tailgating, inadvertently failing to observe traffic lights and short distractions such as tuning a car radio.

Together with the arrival of the CMCHA that will allow organisations to be prosecuted where a death has been caused by 'gross negligence', all these measures are intended to recognise the harm done to victims and the bereaved and to ensure bad driving is suitably punished. A cautious welcome has been given by campaigners to these changes, yet concern continues that bad driving offences causing serious injuries (which run to many thousands each year) remain unacknowledged without a specific offence (usually still charged as 'dangerous' or 'careless' driving), and that road crash victims receive fewer funded services than other crime victims and receive poor treatment by the criminal justice system.

The vast majority of bad driving offences are discovered as a consequence of road collisions rather than proactively enforced without collision. Table 45.2 shows that processed offences of causing death by dangerous driving have remained depressingly stable since 1981, while those of dangerous driving have varied slightly over that period though have decreased since 2004. In marked contrast with both, careless driving offences have dipped and risen again considerably over that period. The fall in traffic police numbers since 1966, the diversion of 'careless' offenders to Driver Improvement Schemes

Table 45.2 Bad driving offences dealt with by official police action: England and Wales (thousands of offences)

	1981	1991	2001	2003	2004	2005	2006
Causing death or bodily harm	0.4	0.6	0.5	0.5	0.5	0.5	0.5
Dangerous driving offences	6.8	12.2	9.6	11.4	10.3	8.5	7.4
Careless driving offences	180.5	128.8	91.7	86.4	137.8	185.9	233.6

Source: MoJ (2008a) Motoring Offences and Breath Test Statistics England and Wales, 2006, Table 2.

(see below) since the late 1990s in place of prosecution and the amount of paperwork involved in prosecution could explain the reduction in careless offences until 2004. The introduction of 'driving while using a hand-held mobile phone' as a careless driving fixed-penalty offence in 2003 accounts for the considerable rise in that category since then. Even before mobile phone use was outlawed while driving, it is clear that careless offences were far more frequently charged than dangerous offences.

Who does it?

As for serious mainstream offending, males and younger drivers are over-represented among those processed for dangerous driving offences, as shown in Table 45.3. Again there is marked stability over time in these gender and age proportions. These official statistics are matched by self-report data that suggest men more frequently report deliberate and dangerous behaviours (e.g. Corbett and Simon 1999).

Police vehicle accidents

The driving public are not the only people involved in bad driving collisions. Police drivers are very occasionally convicted of dangerous or careless driving following a crash in which they were direct or indirect participants, though convictions rarely happen in this way, e.g. involving 2 per cent of police drivers in Rix *et al.*'s (1997) study. As reported by the Independent Police Complaints Commission (IPCC), fatalities arising from road traffic incidents involving police vehicles comprise the largest single group of deaths following police contact, averaging around 40 annually (IPCC 2008: 28). Research published by the IPCC into their incidence and causation patterns showed the majority of deaths were the result of police pursuits, estimated to occur in 1–11 out of 1,000 pursuits (Docking *et al.* 2007: vi). Deaths resulting from emergency journeys to attend specific locations were estimated to occur once in every 100,000 such journeys.

Findings of concern were that 50 per cent of the police drivers involved were not fully trained in pursuit, motorcycles were sometimes pursued – deemed inappropriate under ACPO guidelines – and pursuits were often conducted in inappropriate police vehicles (ibid.). Much strengthening of procedures

Table 45.3 Gender and age profile of bad driving offenders: England and Wales

	% Male			% Under 21		
	2000	2003	2006	2000	2003	2006
Causing death or bodily harm	95	94	93	25	24	32
Dangerous driving offences	97	95	96	34	34	33
Careless driving offences	84	85	86	16	18	18

Source: MoJ (2007) Motoring Offences and Breath Test Statistics England and Wales, 2006. Table 12.

was recommended, including limiting pursuits only to those where a serious crime had been committed. Though road pursuit is held to be a vital police tactic, it surely should not be at the risk and expense of people's lives.

Specific explanations

Minor errors of judgment and momentary lapses of attention underlie many careless driving prosecutions, reflecting lower culpability. By contrast, a factor suggesting impulsiveness, low self-control and a propensity for risk-taking was held to describe drivers judged at fault by risky actions immediately preceding a crash in Junger *et al.*'s (2001) study. Indeed, deliberate or intended behaviours underpin many dangerous driving prosecutions, reflecting higher culpability.

Although pulling out from a junction into the path of an oncoming vehicle is a familiar scenario for either careless or dangerous offences, 'looked but failed to see' is a common explanation for ensuing collisions and is a frequently observed contributory factor (DfT 2007c). Interestingly, modern car designs favour windscreen frames that include 'A-pillars' to enhance a sleek and stylish appearance, yet these can cause blind spots when pulling out from junctions and may therefore be implicated in 'looked but failed to see' junction collisions.

Responses to bad driving offences

As of August 2008, courts are obliged to follow the guidelines laid down by the Sentencing Guidelines Council which detail starting points, sentencing ranges for offences at different levels of seriousness and aggravating and mitigating factors for bad driving offences. This means that there is no change to the statutory maximum of 14 years for 'causing death by dangerous driving' and for 'causing death by careless driving when under the influence of drink or drugs'. The new offence of 'causing death by careless or inconsiderate driving' carries a five-year maximum and the offence of 'causing death by driving: unlicensed, disqualified or uninsured drivers' a two-year maximum. Community orders may be awarded for less serious offences of the latter two types.

Licence disqualification is mandatory for any dangerous conviction and careless offence causing death. An extended driving test is required on completion of a dangerous driving ban, while ordinary or extended retests are discretionary for other bad driving offences.

Pearce *et al.* (2002) found that previously disqualified drivers with more than ten motoring convictions were more likely to reoffend on the road than drivers with fewer convictions. More concerning was the finding that the majority of those required to pass a retest did not do so within three years of being banned (ibid.: 83). In view of the proportion who were convicted of driving while disqualified in the sample, it looks as though many dangerous drivers, especially those with the worst records, continue to drive unlicensed and unconcerned for the consequences after disqualification. Finding ways to ensure disqualified dangerous drivers either get relicensed or desist from driving thus seems imperative.

While dangerous drivers may benefit most from formal court sanctions aimed at deterrence, careless drivers may benefit most from educative penalties. With this in mind, the National Driving Improvement Scheme offered by local police forces countrywide allows attendance on a two-day training programme to those satisfying certain conditions, mainly committing offences involving minor errors of judgment or lapses of attention (but not death), in place of prosecution if drivers are willing to pay the course fee. The effectiveness of these programmes in terms of reoffending has been mixed, with Broughton *et al.* (2005) finding no effect compared with a control group. Diversion of offenders to such courses helps account for the fall in careless driving convictions from the late 1990s before mobile phone prosecutions caused a rise from 2004. Meanwhile, a proposal to introduce a fixed penalty with 3 penalty points for some careless offences was included in the 2008 government consultation (DfT 2008a).

Concluding comment

The new offence and penalty structures implemented in 2008 for dangerous and careless offences go a considerable way towards acknowledging that culpable deaths on the road are no less serious than other homicides, although there is still no specific offence for seriously injuring someone through bad driving. However, the SGC has finally tackled the most difficult sentencing decisions for 'low culpability – extreme harm' cases and has raised the tariff where there are aggravating features. Custodial sentences are likely to be given to slightly more drivers and these could be longer, though the maximum for killing someone while driving unlicensed or uninsured is still less than illegally possessing a firearm (two years v. five years).

Impaired driving: introduction

Impaired driving occurs where the level of competence required for safe driving falls below the minimum standard, leading to traffic breaches and road crashes. As yet, not all types of driver impairment can be adequately measured and minimum standards defined. The main types causing most harm are taking alcohol and/or illicit or licit drugs before driving and driving while tired, yet many others affect most drivers at some stage of their driving careers. These include restrictions to driver mobility following illness, injury or surgery, reductions to cognitive functioning such as impaired hazard perception or information processing as a natural consequence of ageing or of health conditions like dementia or Alzheimer's, and sensory impairment through defective vision or hearing. Driving while angry, upset or stressed also raises crash risk.

The most discussed and researched form of impairment is *drink-driving*, convictions for which have reduced considerably over the last three decades along with fatalities that have fallen by two-thirds since 1979, signalling educative and enforcement successes. However, 17 per cent of road fatalities still involved a driver or rider over the legal blood alcohol limit in 2006, and young drivers are considerably over-involved. This has led to calls for a zero alcohol limit for teenagers (Department of Health 2008), whose lack of driving experience compounds with alcohol and drugs to heighten risk. Technical difficulties may rule out this recommendation, though a zero limit applies to young and novice drivers in 14 European countries (ibid.).

Certainly, Britain has been reluctant to harmonise with Europe on legal blood (and breath) alcohol limits, preferring a higher limit of 80 mg alcohol in 100 ml blood rather than the 50 mg/100 ml limit adopted there. Research suggests that 65 lives and 230 injuries would be saved annually in Britain by moving to the lower limit (Allsop 2005), though government reluctance to lower the limit was still evident in 2008 on the grounds that more breath tests would be more effective than lowering the limit. Views on lowering the limit and the government proposal to grant *random* breath testing powers to police to stop drivers were added to the 2008 consultation (DfT 2008a). This power is credited with success in many countries (Peek-Asa 1999).

Road collision fatality statistics suggest a six-fold increase in *illegal drug-driving* during the 1990s from 3 per cent to 18 per cent of all those injured, with cannabis most commonly detected in two-thirds (Tunbridge *et al.* 2001). This accords with surveys that show cannabis followed by amphetamines and cocaine are commonly taken before driving by young drivers (e.g. BRAKE 2005). The problem is that a drug's presence does not prove impairment caused a crash, since cannabis, for example, remains in the body for over four weeks yet is inactive shortly after ingestion (Tunbridge 2001). Indeed, taking drugs before driving becomes a criminal offence only *if* it is proved that impairment is a consequence. This has led to the ACPO calling for a simple offence of driving after taking illegal drugs without having to prove impairment (ACPO 2007). With the imminent arrival of a roadside testing kit capable of detecting the presence of several drug groups from one saliva sample, the government was looking into ACPO's suggestion in its 2008 consultation. Currently, reliance is still placed on outmoded roadside hand–eye and motor skills coordination tests that may fail to detect impairment. Partly because of the detection and proof of impairment difficulties, less publicity has been accorded to illicit drug-driving which may lead to the perception that it is not wrong to do so if feeling fit to drive – especially if taken with alcohol below the legally permitted maximum.

Driving while under the influence of medicinal or over-the-counter (OTC) drugs (*legal drug-driving*) is also not an offence unless it is shown the driver is unfit to drive as a result. Estimates suggest considerably fewer road deaths on European roads would occur if those taking benzodiazepines or psychotropic drugs did not drive (e.g. de Gier 1993). Even impairment caused by particular OTC antihistamine drugs is estimated to be greater than that caused by driving over the legal blood alcohol concentration limit in Britain (Horne and Barrett 2004).

Drivers are not helped by occasional inconsistent labelling of medicinal drugs since it seems that information supplied on inserts giving warnings of drowsiness or other side effects are not necessarily given on the exterior packaging or vice versa, and manufacturers are not obliged to comply with the recommendations of the British National Formulary in this regard (ibid.). Conversely, drivers do not always help themselves, as a quarter of a large representative sample reported rarely or never checking the side-effects of medication before driving (Privilege Insurance 2006).

Fatigued driving is reckoned to account for a staggering 17 per cent of killed and seriously injured (KSI) road collisions, or between 3 per cent and 30 per cent depending on the road type (Flatley *et al.* 2004), yet there is no specific offence of 'tired driving'. Instead its consequences can be prosecuted under dangerous or careless driving causing death offences where its presence may be treated as an aggravating factor (SGC 2008). Tired driving often causes fatalities because drivers cannot apply brakes or take avoiding action if they have fallen asleep, though technological advances are being made to prevent this. Much currently depends on educative initiatives and encouraging better company safety policies for employees, including promoting realistic work schedules and warning of tired driving dangers. Indeed, comparing those who drive as part of their job with those who do not, the former report 'nodding off' at the wheel during the previous year twice as often as the latter – 10 per cent v. 4 per cent (BRAKE and Green Flag 2008), underlining the increased risk of work-related driving. Under the CMCHA, it is strongly hoped that any such 'deaths at work' will fall.

As things stand, the main 'at risk' tired driver groups comprise young people who stay awake all night feeling invulnerable (Horne, as reported in *The Times* 2008a), and sufferers of sleep apnoea who tend to be overweight lorry drivers with thick necks who cause around 100 fatalities annually (ibid.). Chronic sleep deficiency and night-time shift work are also big risk factors, prompting the questions of how much predictable impairment society should tolerate among the workers it strongly depends on, and how the courts will react to any such cases brought under the CHCMA.

As most research, societal concern and media interest has centred on drink-driving, the remainder of this section will focus on this despite the parallel importance of other impaired driving offences.

Patterns and trends in drink-driving

Various measures assess the extent and trends in drink-impaired driving but none is perfect. Probably the best objective measure is the number of casualties involved in drink-drive collisions derived from STATS19 and coroners' data, which in Table 45.4 shows a steady decrease from 1980 through to 1998, with a slight rise in casualties until 2002 with a drop thereafter to 2006.

The numbers of court convictions for alcohol/drug impairment offences are another gauge, and these show an overall 3 per cent drop between 1996 and 2006 with the last peak in 2004 (MoJ 2008b: Table 11). It is fair to say, therefore, that there has been considerable success in reducing drink-driving casualties since the 1980s, but there is no room for complacency as there have been rises and falls in that period in most measures used, and in 2006 there were still 14,380 casualties of which 540 were fatal. Indeed, it looks as if something more is needed to make a substantial impact to cut drink/drug-drive casualties.

Table 45.4 Estimates of all GB road accident casualties where illegal alcohol levels were found among drivers and riders, adjusted for under-reporting

	Fatal	Serious	Slight	Total
1980	1,450	7,970	20,420	29,830
1990	760	4,090	15,550	20,400
1998	460	2,520	12,610	15,580
2000	530	2,540	14,990	18,060
2002	550	2,790	16,760	20,100
2006	540	1,960	11,880	14,380

Source: DfT (2007a): Table 3a Road Casualties Great Britain 2006, Article 3: Drink and Driving Statistics.
Note: All figures are subject to rounding up.

Table 45.5 Findings of guilt for drink- or drug-driving offences by age and sex

		1996	2001	2006	% change 1996–2006	
Males	< 21 n =	8,924	10,234	10,173	+ 14	
	≥ 21 n =	79,032	66,107	71,203	− 9	− 3
	% male =	92	90	88		
Females	< 21 n =	565	669	1,067	+ 89	
	≥ 21 n =	7,185	7,732	10,228	+ 42	+ 46
	% female =	8	10	12		
All	% < 21 =	10	13	12		

Source: Offences Relating to Motor Vehicles England and Wales: Supplementary Tables, Table 17 (Home Office 1998, 2002; MoJ 2008b).

Who does it?

Table 45.5 shows that males and young people are over-represented among those convicted of drink- or drug-driving. In 2006, males comprised 56 per cent of fully-licensed drivers but 88 per cent of those convicted, and young people comprised under 3 per cent of the fully licensed but 12 per cent of those convicted. Interestingly, there has been an overall drop of 3 per cent in the numbers of men convicted for drink drug offences over the decade to 2006, but an increase of 46 per cent in numbers of women convicted over the same period, albeit from a low base. This prompts speculation that the 'ladette' culture whereby young women are said to be keen to emulate men's lifestyles and drinking habits is having an impact (see Corbett 2007).

Specific explanations

As alluded to, cultural factors may play a role in drivers' decisions to risk driving over the permitted blood alcohol limit. For women, the rise of the ladette culture and behaviour, the popularity of flavoured 'alcopops' that mask the taste of alcohol, of drinking venues more welcoming of groups of women and of 250 ml glasses of wine as the norm – one of which can lead to 'over the limit' driving, all raise the likelihood of illegal driving by women. For men, being seen among one's peers as competent to drive after a few drinks may lead to some taking risks through bravado and expectation (e.g. Homel 1993: 71–2). Indeed, feeling fit enough to drive after alcohol was the main reason for driving home among pub patrons thinking they might or would be over the legal limit in Corbett *et al.*'s (1991) study. Coupled with drivers' usual perceptions of being more skilful than the average (e.g. Svenson 1981), one can see how drink- or drug-driving occurs.

Responses to drink-driving

Driving or attempting to drive while unfit through drink or drugs or over the prescribed alcohol limit in Britain carries a mandatory 12-month minimum period of disqualification, a fine and/or six months' custody. Detection may become more likely from 2009 when approval for a new roadside breathalyser device is expected that will remove the need for a second confirmatory breath test at the police station.

To reduce the risk of reoffending, most offenders are offered the opportunity of driver retraining (paid for by the offender), satisfactory completion of which attracts up to a 25 per cent reduction in the length of disqualification. Though the better-off might be better placed to purchase a reduced disqualification period, research by Davies *et al.* (1999) showed that reconviction rates were cut by 50 per cent among those taking up the offer. The worst offenders with a blood alcohol concentration (BAC) $\geq$ 250 per cent over the permitted limit or facing a second conviction within ten years or less are usually put on the High Risk Offenders Scheme. This means they must pass a medical test to ensure they do not have a serious alcohol problem before regaining their licence at the end of the disqualification period. A technological innovation provided for under the Road Safety Act 2006 is for breath-alcohol interlock ignition devices to be fitted to the vehicles of repeat offenders who must give an alcohol-free reading before the vehicle's ignition can be switched on. Research shows these 'alcolocks' provide a useful halfway stage for those at risk of reoffending (e.g. Beirness 2004), while meters to check alcohol level are available commercially for others concerned not to drive illegally.

Concluding comment

At the root of competence to drive issues is how fit society requires its drivers to be and how much impairment it can tolerate given varying risks of harm. With regard to physical fitness issues, weighing the wishes of individuals to remain mobile against the wishes acceptable to society to remain reasonably safe is the crunch issue, and inroads are being made to help measure and evaluate levels of risk posed by differently impaired drivers. With regard to drug-driving, better means of roadside fitness tests are urgently needed to detect those risking the safety of themselves and others. With respect to drink-driving, it remains to be seen whether harmonisation with Europe will occur any time soon with regard to blood alcohol concentration limits and random breath testing.

Conclusion

Driving offences have long been regarded largely as minor offences that have received correspondingly lenient penalties. Yet as this chapter illustrates, official responses to the most serious offences where death results show that serious treatment and attention is at last being afforded by the courts. Big problems on the roads remain, however, with some behaviours such as distracted driving using mobile phones or satellite navigation technology, drink- and drug-driving, careless and dangerous driving, speeding and driving with inadequate documentation still common and linked with serious harm and increased collision risk.

Technological advances are helping police enormously in enforcement efforts with closed circuit television (CCTV) and ANPR well evident, and many more technologies are waiting for roll-out that should further encourage driver compliance with traffic laws and lead to improved security and safety for all road users and fewer casualties (Corbett 2008). This surveillance technology does, however, carry dangers such as those concerning the transparency, accountability and migration of surveillance data for purposes other than for which they were collected, and adequacy of privacy safeguards against unauthorised leakages and misuse (ibid.). Such matters deserve the criminological gaze, but with several important exceptions (e.g. Wood 2006), this topic, like the bulk concerning vehicle-related and driving offences, has been neglected by the discipline.

This marginalisation is surprising in view of the roads arguably being the most commonly shared public space and, as noted above, it being the space that will see road deaths becoming the world's third biggest killer by 2020, many of which will be judged unlawful. As Corbett (2008) has discussed, there are many grounds to support criminology's engagement with road traffic crime, theoretical reward being one of them. For instance, 'invisible' safety crimes concerning powerful elites like motor manufacturers and corporations would repay criminological attention, as would consideration of the safety cultures of employers with motorised workforces. The British government does not yet collect dedicated statistics on work-related traffic collisions, but these are estimated as the single biggest cause of sudden death at work, and research into the role of driving offences in helping to cause them is long overdue.

Selected further reading

Academic consideration of driving offences has been rather thin on the ground, though Cunningham's (2008) text on *Driving Offences: Law, Policy and Practice* may signal a broader, emerging interest in this terrain and adopts a legal perspective in considering several key offences. Corbett's earlier *Car Crime* (2003) takes up the cudgels by adopting a critical perspective from which to view many common driving offences including vehicle theft, but also brings together disparate research studies and sources. The earlier self-explanatory texts *Drivers after Sentence* (Willett 1973) and *Sentencing the Motoring Offender* (Hood 1972) are worth seeking out and still retain relevance to current discourses. The influential *Road Traffic Law Review Report* (the 'North' Report)

(Department of Transport/Home Office 1986) is a very good starting point for scholars wishing to understand the background context and multi-faceted considerations needed for any changes and improvements to road traffic law (focused on driving offences). A recommended online source is the Parliamentary Advisory Council for Transport Safety (PACTS) website providing up-to-date information on contemporary developments, *inter alia*, in road traffic law, incorporating its own research publications, links to published statistics, respected editorial comment and parliamentary debates (http://www.pacts.org.uk). The Department for Transport's (Policy, Guidance and Research) website (http://www.dft.gov.uk/pgr) provides what it says, including access to its own commissioned research reports on driving offences, related government consultations and campaigns. A useful website giving the driver's perspective on changes to driving legislation and contemporary concerns incorporating research is that of the Royal Automobile Club Foundation (http://www.racfoundation.org); two sites giving the road crash victim's perspective are those of the road safety charities RoadPeace (http://www.roadpeace.org.uk) and BRAKE (http://www.brake.org.uk).

Notes

1 Driving inappropriately fast for the prevailing conditions but under the maximum speed limit is popularly considered as 'speeding' but is not prosecuted as such. Instead this may be claimed as an aggravating factor in a dangerous driving offence and is one of the contributory causal factors for the STATS19 data routinely collected by the government with regard to injury crashes.
2 Murder, manslaughter and aggravated vehicle taking where death results may also be charged for road deaths.

References

ACPO (2007) *Drug Driving*, Press Release, 30 July 20007. Online at: http://www.acpo. police.uk/pressrelease.asp?PR_GUID={8DB6B522-2CBE-4D00-83AA-173F85CB2438}.
Allen, J., Komy, M., Lovbakke, J. and Roy, H. (2005) *Policing and the Criminal Justice System – Public Confidence and Perceptions: Findings from the 2003/04 British Crime Survey*, Home Office Online Report 31/05.
Allsop, R. (2005) *How Much Is Too Much? Lowering the Drink Driving Limit.* London: PACTS. Online at: http://www.pacts.org.uk/policy/briefings/allsopbacpaper.pdf.
Beirness, D. (2004) 'Alcohol interlocks: their use, effectiveness and future', in *Behavioural Research in Road Safety: 14th Seminar.* London: DfT, pp. 73–86.
BRAKE (2005) *One in Seven Young Drivers Drive on Drugs*, Press Release, 18 August.
BRAKE and Green Flag (2008) *One in Ten at-Work Drivers Say They Fall Asleep at the Wheel*, Press Release, 4 January. Online at: http://www.greenflag.com/news/press/asleep-at-the-wheel.html.
Broughton, J. (2007) 'The correlation between motoring and other types of offence', *Accident Analysis and Prevention*, 39 (2): 274–83.
Broughton, J. (2008) *Recent Trends for Speeding Convictions and Totting-Up Disqualifications*, Project Report PR181. Crowthorne: Transport Research Laboratory.
Broughton, J., Buckle, G., Buttress, S. And Pearce, L. (2005) *The Effects of the National Driver Improvement Scheme on Re-Offending Rates*, TRL Report 649. Crowthorne: Transport Research Laboratory.
Broughton, J., Baughan, C., Pearce, L., Smith, L and Buckle, G. (2003) *Work-Related Road Accidents*, TRL Report 582. Crowthorne: Transport Research Laboratory.

Campbell, B. (1993) *Goliath: Britain's Dangerous Places*. London: Methuen.

Chenery, S., Henshaw, C. and Pease, K. (1999) *Illegal Parking in Disabled Bays: A Means of Offender Targeting*, HORS Briefing Note 1/99. London: Home Office.

Churchill Insurance (2007) *Motorists Resort to Illegal Tactics to Escape Convictions*, Press Release, 31 May. Online at: http://www.churchill.com/pressReleases/31052007. htm.

Cohen, A. (1955) *Delinquent Boys*. New York: Free Press.

Corbett, C. (2003) *Car Crime*. Cullompton: Willan.

Corbett, C. (2007) 'Vehicle-related crime and the gender gap', *Psychology, Crime and Law*, 13 (3): 245–63.

Corbett, C. (2008) 'Techno-surveillance of the roads: high impact and low interest', *Crime Prevention and Community Safety: An International Journal*, 10 (1): 1–18.

Corbett, C. and Caramlau, I. (2006) 'Gender differences in responses to speed cameras: typology findings and implications for road safety', *Criminology and Criminal Justice*, 6 (4): 411–33.

Corbett, C. and Simon, F. (1992a) *Unlawful Driving Behaviour: A Criminological Perspective*, Contractor Report 310. Crowthorne: Transport Research Laboratory.

Corbett, C. and Simon, F. (1992b) 'Decisions to break and adhere to the rules of the road viewed from the rational choice perspective', *British Journal of Criminology*, 32 (4): 537–49.

Corbett, C. and Simon, F. (1999) *The Effects of Speed Cameras: How Drivers Respond*, Road Safety Research Report 11. London: DETR.

Corbett, C., Simon, F. and O'Connell, M. (1998) *The Deterrence of High-Speed Driving: A Criminological Perspective*, Contractor Report 296. Crowthorne: Transport Research Laboratory.

Corbett, C., Simon, F. and Hyde, G. (1991) 'Driving with excess alcohol: why some drivers do and why some don't', in G. Grayson and J. Lester (eds), *Behavioural Research in Road Safety: II*. Crowthorne: Transport Research Laboratory, pp. 108–17.

Corbett, C., Delmonte, E., Quimby, A. and Grayson, G. (2008) *Does the Threat of Disqualification Deter Drivers from Speeding?* London: DfT. Online at: http://www. dft.gov.uk/pgr/roadsafety/research/rsrr/theme2/threat.pdf.

Cunningham, S. (2008) *Driving Offences: Law, Policy and Practice*. Cullompton: Willan.

Davies, G., Harland, G. and Broughton, J. (1999) *Drink-Driver Rehabilitation Courses in England and Wales*, TRL Report 426. Crowthorne: Transport Research Laboratory.

de Gier, J. (1993) *Driving Licences and Known Use of Licit or Illicit Drugs*, IHP 93-39. Maastricht: University of Limburg, Institute for Human Psychopharmacology.

Department of Health (2008) *On the State of Public Health: Annual Report of the Chief Medical Officer 2007*. London: DoH, chapter 3.

Department of Transport/Home Office (1986) *Road Traffic Law Review Report*. London: HMSO.

Direct Line Insurance (2007) *One Million Brits Close to Driving Ban*, Press Release, 29 March 2007. Online at: http://www.directline.com/about_us/news_290307.htm.

Dobson, A., Brown, W., Ball, J., Powers, J. and McFadden, M. (1999) 'Women drivers' behaviour, socio-demographic characteristics and accidents', *Accident Analysis and Prevention*, 31 (5): 525–35.

Docking, M., Bucke, T., Grace, K. and Dady, H. (2007) *Police Road Traffic Incidents: A Study of Cases Involving Serious and Fatal Injuries*, IPCC Research and Statistics Series Paper 7. London: IPCC.

DfT (2007a) *Road Casualties Great Britain: Annual Report 2006*. London: TSO.

DfT (2007b) *Second Review of the Government's Road Safety Strategy*. London: DfT. Online at: http://www.dft.gov.uk/pgr/roadsafety/strategytargetsperformance/2ndreview/ screen.

DfT (2007c) *Contributory Factors Statistics 2006*. Online at: http://www.dft.gov.uk/1729 74/173025/221412/221549/227755/285672/article4contributoryfa1.xls.

DfT (2008a) *Road Safety Compliance Consultation*. Online at: http://www.dft.gov.uk/ consultations/closed/compliance/roadsafetyconsultation.pdf.

DfT (2008b) *Free-Flow Vehicle Speed Statistics 2007*. Online at: http://www.dft.gov.uk/17 2974/173025/221412/221546/227050/261688/vehiclespeeddata07.xls.

DfT and HSE (2003) *Driving at Work: Managing Work-Related Road Safety*. London: HSE Books.

DTLR (2001) *Transport Statistics Great Britain 2001*. London: HMSO.

Emsley, C. (1993) '"Mother, what *did* policemen do when there weren't any motors?" The law, the police and the regulation of motor traffic in England, 1900–1939', *Historical Journal*, 36 (2): 357–81.

Flatley, D., Reyner, L. and Horne, J. (2004) *Sleep-Related Crashes on Sections of Different Road Types in the UK (1995–2001)*, Road Safety Research Report No. 52. London: DfT.

Gaventa, J. (2005) *Policing Road Risk: New Technologies, Road Traffic Enforcement and Road Safety*, Occasional Research Report. London: PACTS.

Gottfredson, M. and Hirschi, T. (1990) *A General Theory of Crime*. Stanford, CA: Stanford University Press.

Gusfield, H., Kotarba, J. and Rasmussen, P. (1981) 'Managing competence: an ethnographic study of drinking-driving and the context of bars', in T. Harford and L. Gaines (eds), *Social Drinking Contexts, Research*, Monograph 7. Washington, DC: US Government Printing Office.

Greenaway, D. (2006) *Uninsured Driving in the UK*. London: DfT.

Home Office (1989) *Offences Relating to Motor Vehicles England and Wales 1988*. London: Home Office.

Home Office (2000) *Offences Relating to Motor Vehicles England and Wales 1998*. London: Home Office.

Home Office (2005) *Offences Relating to Motor Vehicles England and Wales 2003*. London: Home Office.

Homel, R. (1993) 'Drivers who drink and rational choice: random breath testing and the process of deterrence', in R. V. Clarke and M. Felson (eds), *Routine Activity and Rational Choice. Advances in Criminological Theory*, Vol. 5. New Brunswick, NJ: Transaction.

Hood, R. (1972) *Sentencing the Motoring Offender*. London: Heinemann.

Horne, J. and Barrett, P. (2004) *Over-the-Counter Medicines: Assessment of Package Warnings Liable to Cause Unwanted Sleepiness*, Road Safety Report No. 28. London: DfT.

Independent Police Complaints Commission (2008) IPCC Annual Report and Statement of Accounts 2007/08. HC898. London: TSO.

Jacobs, G., Aeron-Thomas, A. and Astrop, A. (2000) *Estimating Global Road Fatalities*, TRL Report 445. Crowthorne: Transport Research Laboratory.

Junger, M., West, R. and Timman, R. (2001) 'Crime and risky behavior in traffic: an example of cross-situational consistency', *Journal of Research in Crime and Delinquency*, 38 (4): 439–59.

Knox, D., Turner, B. and Silcock, D. (2003) *Research into Unlicensed Driving: Final Report*, Road Safety Research Report No. 48. London: DfT.

Lai, F., Chorlton, K. and Carsten, O. (2007) *Intelligent Speed Adaptation: Overall Field Trial Results*. London: Department for Transport. Online at: http://www.dft.gov.uk/ pgr/roads/vehicles/intelligentspeedadaptation/overallfieldtrial.pdf.

Light, R., Nee, C. and Ingham, H. (1993) *Car Theft: The Offender's Perspective*, HORS 130. London: Home Office.

Marsh, P. and Collett, P. (1986) *Driving Passion: The Psychology of the Car*. London: Cape.

McKenna, F. (2004) 'The Thames Valley Speeding Awareness Scheme: a comparison of high and low speed courses', in G. Grayson (ed.), *Behavioural Research in Road Safety: 14th Seminar*. London: DfT, pp. 170–81.

McKenna, F., Waylen, A. and Burkes, M. (1998) *Male and Female Drivers: How Different Are They?* Basingstoke: AA Foundation for Road Safety Research.

MoJ (2007) *Criminal Statistics 2006: England and Wales*. Online at: http://www.justice.gov.uk/docs/crim-stats-2006-tag.pdf.

MoJ (2008a) *Motoring Offences and Breath Test Statistics England and Wales 2006*. Online at: http://www.justice.gov.uk/docs/motoring-offences-and-breath-stats-2006.pdf.

MoJ (2008b) *Offences Relating to Motor Vehicles England and Wales 2006: Supplementary Tables*. Online at: http://www.justice.gov.uk/docs/offences-relating-to-motor-vehicles-2006.pdf.

O'Connell, M. and Whelan, A. (1996) 'Taking wrongs seriously: public perceptions of crime seriousness', *British Journal of Criminology*, 36 (2): 299–318.

Organisation for Economic Cooperation and Development (OECD) (2006) *Young Drivers: The Road to Safety*. Paris: OECD.

Pearce, L., Knowles, J., Davies, G. and Buttress, S. (2002) *Dangerous Driving and the Law*, Road Safety Research Report No. 26. London: DTLR.

Peek-Asa, C. (1999) 'The effect of random alcohol screening in reducing motor vehicle crash injuries', *American Journal of Preventive Medicine*, 16 (1): 57–67.

Pilkington, P. and Kinra, S. (2005) 'Effectiveness of speed cameras in preventing road traffic collisions and related casualties: systematic review', *BMJ*, 330: 331–4.

Privilege Insurance (2006) *Driving Danger from Common Medicines*, Press Release, October. Online at: http://www.privilege.com/aboutus/driver_health.htm.

RAC (2006) *Prescription to Fix Drug Driving?*, Press Release, 10 April. Online at: http://www.racfoundation.org/index.php?option=com_content&task=view&id=357&itemid=35.

Rix, B., Walker, D. and Brown, R. (1997) *A Study of Deaths and Serious Injuries Resulting from Police Vehicle Accidents*, PRG Ad Hoc Paper AH312. London: Home Office.

RoadPeace (2007) 'Prosecuting bad driving', *Safety First*, Issue 27. London: RoadPeace.

Rose, G. (2000) *The Criminal Histories of Serious Traffic Offenders*, HORS 206. London: Home Office.

Sentencing Guidelines Council (SGC) (2008) *Causing Death by Dangerous Driving: Definitive Guideline*. Online at: http://www.sentencing-guidelines.gov.uk/docs/causing_death_by_driving_definitive_guideline.pdf.

Shinar, D. and McKnight, A. (1985) 'The effects of enforcement and public information on speed compliance', in L. Evans and R. Schwing (eds), *Human Behaviour and Traffic Safety*. New York: Plenum Press.

Stradling, S. (1997) 'Violators as "crash magnets"'. in G. Grayson (ed.), *Behavioural Research in Road Safety: VII*. Crowthorne: Transport Research Laboratory, pp. 4–9.

Stradling, S., Campbell, M., Allan, I., Gorell, R., Hill, J., Winter, M., TRL Ltd, Hope, S. and NFO System Three Social Research (2003) *The Speeding Driver: Who, How And Why?*, Scottish Executive Social Research. Edinburgh: TSO.

Svenson, O. (1981 'Are we all less risky and more skilful than our fellow drivers?', *Acta Psychologica*, 47: 143–8.

SWOV (1998) *SARTRE 2: The Attitude and Behaviour of European Car Drivers to Road Safety. Part 1*. Leidschendam: SWOV.

Sykes, G. and Matza, D. (1957) 'Techniques of neutralisation: a theory of delinquency', *American Sociological Review*, 22 December, pp. 664–70.

The Times (2008a) 'Highlighting the danger of driving when you are tired' by T. Dawe, 14 February.

The Times (2008b) 'Drivers will have no escape from new speed cameras', by B. Webster, 9 October.

Tunbridge, R. (2001) 'The influence of cannabis on driving', in G. Grayson (ed.), *Behavioural Research in Road Safety: X*. London: DETR, pp. 215–29.

Tunbridge, R., Keigan, M. and James, F. (2001) *The Incidence of Drugs and Alcohol in Road Accident Fatalities*, TRL Report 495. Crowthorne: Transport Research Laboratory.

Walker, G., Stanton, N. and Young, M (2006) 'The ironies of vehicle feedback in car design', Ergonomics, 49 (2): 161–79.

Wilde, G. (1986) 'Beyond the concept of risk homeostasis: suggestions for research and application towards the prevention of accidents and lifestyle-related disease', Accident Analysis and Prevention, 18 (5): 377–401.

Willett, T. (1973) *Drivers after Sentence*. London: Heinemann.

Wood, D. M. (2004) *Perceptions and Experience of Antisocial Behaviour: Findings From the 2003/2004 British Crime Survey*, Home Office Online Report 49/04. London: Home Office.

Wood, D. M. (ed.) (2006) A Report on the Surveillance Society for the Information Commissioner by the Surveillance Studies Network. Online at: http//www.ico.gov.uk/upload/documents/library/data_protection/practical_application/surveillance_society_full_report_2006.pdf.

Index

'2 Smart' 319
9/11 attacks 788, 828, 846, 855
'419' fraud 138–9, 141, 143, 169

A Coordinated Prostitution Strategy 560
A&M Records Inc. v. Napster, Inc. (2000)
  198
Abacha, General Sani 741
Abu Ghraib 753, 797
academic performance and bullying 430–1
accidental firesetters 383
Action on Elder Abuse 417, 419
actus reus 217–18
address impersonation fraud 178
Adult Support and Protection (Scotland) Act
  2007 416
advance fee frauds see '419' fraud
advertising and maiding 546
Advertising Standards Agency 147
Afghanistan, production of opium and heroin
  630–1
age of consent 525
  homosexual males 505
aggravated burglary 3
AGIS programme 706
air pollution 865, 867–80
  control in the UK 874–6
  crime, harm and 870–2
  defining 868–9
  greening the criminological landscape
    877–9
  IPPC Directive 872–3
  offences in the UK 876–7
  sources of 869–70
Air Quality Management Areas (AQMAs)
  875
alcohol, role of in homicide 228–9

Alcohol Harm Reduction Strategy for England
  580
alcohol related crime see drug and alcohol
  related crime
alcohol-related violence, meaning of term
  332
Allport, Gordon 352
Al-Qaeda 847, 853, 855, 856, 858, 859
American History X 356
Amnesty 755
amphetamine 598, 599, 600, 606, 632–3, 637–8
amyl-nitrate 600
animal abuse 480–98
  Animal Welfare Act 2006 482–4
  characteristics of offenders 487
  characteristics of victims 487–90
  defining 481–2
  explaining 490–3
    development to interpersonal violence
      492–3
    domestic violence 491–2
  incidence of and trends 486–7
  legal offences against animals 482
  prevalence of 485–6
  response to 494–6
  wildlife crimes 484–5
animal rights activists 834
Animal Welfare Act 2006 482–4, 495
  animal fighting 484
  causing unnecessary suffering to animals
    482–4
  failing to ensure the needs of an animal
    are met 484
anomie, theory of 145, 662–3, 674n4, 688, 690,
  852–3
Anti-Defamation League (ADL) 354–5
Anti-Social Behaviour Act 2003 321

Anti-Social Behaviour Orders (ASBOs) 320
  on street workers 562
anti-social children, link with animal abuse
  492
anti-vivisection movement 834
armed robbers 294–304
  impact of drugs trade on 302
  lifestyle of 295–6
  skill and competence of 298–9
armed youth gangs 234–5
  see also youth gang crime
Armenian Genocide 763, 780
Arrestee Survey 584, 585
arson 380–9
  adult arsonists 384–5, 388–9
  children and young people 386–8
  explanations for 381–2
  juvenile firesetters 383–4
  mental illness and 382
  sentencing policy 386
  situational crime prevention 385–6
  with intent 386
assault by penetration, definition of 507
Assets Recovery Agency 721, 722
assisting an offender by impeding
  apprehension 397
Asylum and Immigration Act 2004 707
asylums 462
at-risk children and humane animal education
  programmes 496
'Atlantic Machines' 729
ATMs, interference with 167
attachment and stalking 372–3
Attention-Deficit Hyperactivity Disorder
  (ADHD) 431, 432
autobiographies of armed robbers 296–7
Automatic Number Plate Recognition (ANPR)
  42, 907, 908

bad driving: dangerous and careless offences
  915–19
  offenders 917
  police vehicle accidents 917–18
  responses to 918–19
  specific explanations 918
bag-snatching 272
Bank of Credit and Commerce International
  (BCCI) 656–7
Bank Secrecy Act (US) 717–18
Barings Bank 658, 660, 668
'Battle of Seattle' 828, 836
'Be Safe' 319
Bebo 179
Beck, Frank 467
Becker, Gary 91
Beckham, Victoria 399
behaviour modification blackmail 400
benefit fraud see income tax evasion and
  benefit fraud
Bentham, Jeremy 788, 789–90, 791
Bhopal disaster 893
'big store' con 140–1
binge drinking 333–4
biographical identifiers 177
biometric identifiers 177, 184
Black Liberation Army 826
blackmail 393–412
  criminal careers of those convicted 407–9
  dangerousness of offenders 409–11
  measuring the offence 396–7
  nature and representation in the media
    399–400
  offenders 402–4
  origin and legal definition 393–4
  prevalence 400–1
  previous convictions 404–7
  seriousness of 409
boiler room selling 139, 168
Bolivia, production of coca 631
Bosnia and Herzegovina, conflict 771, 773–4
Boston Ceasefire 321
bounded rationality, concept of 668
Brent Action for Responsible K9s (BARK) 495
Bre-X 656
Bretton Woods 801
Brinks-Mat robbery 301
British Indian Empire, violence surrounding
  partition 771
British Phonographic Industry (BPI) 130
'Brixton Against Robbery' initiative 283
brothel-keepers, prosecution of 544–5, 562
Buckle and Farrington's shoppers study 50
bullying see school bullying
bureaucracy, theory of 832
burglary see domestic burglary
Bush, President George W. 785, 789, 791, 798
'business' IPC 125–6
butadiene 869
Butler, Josephine 559
Bybee, Jay 789

Cambridge Study 430–1
cannabis 598, 599, 606
  cultivation of 607–8
  production of 633–4
  reclassification of 603, 617–18
  smuggling 638
'car cruise' events 911
car-jacking 36, 272, 280
car key burglary 6, 36
car sales, repairs and servicing 684
carbon monoxide 869
card-not-present (CNP) fraud 164, 167, 176,
  180
Care Orders 459–60, 463
Care Standards Act 2000 473

carnivalesque, concept of 341
carousel frauds 164
Carpenter, Mary 463
cash-in-transit (CIT) robberies 302
cause lawyering 839
caveat emptor, concept of 654
CCTV 61–2, 109, 283, 342, 346
CD-burning 125
challenging behaviour of young people,
  criminalisation of 466
Cheyney, Vice President Dick 788–9
child contact, conflict associated with 249,
  251
child maltreatment, language of 460
child prostitution offences 547
child stealing 398
Children Act 1908 472
Children Act 1948 461
Children Act 1989 421, 459, 466, 472
Children Act 2004 473
Children and Young Persons Act 1969 472
Children First 473
China, global centre for counterfeit goods 122
Chinese cockle pickers, drowning of 682, 893
Chip & PIN 163, 167, 175–6, 185
Chrome Project (Manchester) 323
CID 293
cigarette smuggling 685
Civil Rights Movements 829–30, 831
Clarke, Ron 17
classic ransom kidnapping 398
climate change scams 148–9
'clinical gaze' 466
Clyde Committee 461
coca 628–9
cocaine 598, 600, 606
  illicit drug seizures 604
  production of 631–2
  smuggling of 636–7
coercive interrogation methods 792
cognitive behavioural treatment (CBT) for
  firesetters 388
cognitive dissonance 143
cognitive distortions 510, 530–1
cognitive script 156
'coincidence' relationship of drug use 587
Colombia
  production of coca 631
  production of heroin 630
Colwell, Maria 461
commercial cash, stealing 290–304
  armed robbery as subculture 294–5
  big hits 300–1
  buzz 296–8
  control 299
  decline of 301–3
  fantasy and innovation 303
  growth and decline of safecracking 291–2

lifestyle 295–6
  supergrasses and police corruption
    299–300
  superior competence 298–9
  wage snatches and bank robberies 293
commercial fence supplies 68
Commercial Victimisation Survey (CVS) 50
commercial sales 69
Common Agricultural Policy (CAP) subsidies
  frauds 683
'common cause' relationship of drug use 587
Companies House 158
Compassion in World Farming campaign 838
complex integrationist theories 512–13, 533–5
component parts, of cars 33
Computer Misuse Act 1990 207
conduct disorder (CD), animal abuse a
  symptom of 492
confluence model of sexual aggression 512–13
conspiracy or soliciting to commit murder
  397
Construction Plant Action Group 41
consumer culture, rise of 335–9
Consumer Direct 147
consumer fraud, four-fold classification of
  138–40
Consumer Protection (Cancellation of
  Contracts Concluded away from Business
  Premises) Regulations 1987 147
Control of Misleading Advertising Regulations
  1988 147
Control of Trade in Endangered Species
  (Enforcement) Regulations 1997 (COTES)
  485
controlled drugs
  classification of 602, 615
  debate on classification 603
  possession offences 615–16
controlling offences 544
convenience foods 885
Convention against Illicit Traffic in Narcotic
  Drugs and Psychotropic Substances 626,
  641
Convention on Cybercrime 192, 207
Convention on International Trade in
  Endangered Species of Wild Fauna and
  Flora (CITES) 485, 488
Convention on the Prevention and
  Punishment of the Crime of Genocide
  762, 765
Copyright, Designs and Patents Act 1988 129
corporate codes of ethics 672
corporate financial crimes 653–73
  Barings Bank 658
  dairy product price-fixing 658–9
  Enron 657
  explanations 660–9
    capitalism is criminogenic 666–7

gender 664–5
individuals 665–6
organisational context 667–9
social and environmental causes 661–4
globalisation of corporate crime 656–7
Guinness 658
history 654–5
individual or organisational blame 659–60
pensions scandal 658
responses 669–73
compliance 671–3
deterrence and punitive strategies
669–71
Savings and Loan scandal 657
scale and costs of 655–6
corporate hijack 163
Corporate Manslaughter and Corporate
Homicide Act 2007 219, 692, 914
corporate violence and harm 884–900
beyond criminology 897–9
corporate harm as corporate violence
891–2
explaining corporate violence 893–7
scale of occupational death, injury and
illness 888–91
varieties of 884–8
corruption 747–8
Corruption Perception Index 748
counterfeit card fraud 164
counterfeiting
meaning of term 120
of cheques 165
counter-terrorism 858–60
cowboy builders 685
crack cocaine 599, 606
crack houses 609
'crack rentals' 280
CRAVED items 51
shoplifting 51, 61–2
stolen goods market 81
vehicle crime 39
credit fraud 153–70
investment frauds 168–70
long-firm fraud 155–64
arts of deception 156–61
changing nature of 162–4
financing and setting up 155–6
strategies to avoid arrest and conviction
161–2
payment card and cheque fraud 164–8
credit scoring 162
Crime and Disorder Act 1998 351
'crime-causes-drug-use' relationship model
587
crime screening 1
Crime (Sentences) Act 1997 19
Criminal Damage Act 1971 386
Criminal Justice Act 1988 721

Criminal Justice Act 2003 71, 321
Criminal Justice and Public Order Act 1994
505
Criminal Law Act 1977 396, 397
'crossover' concept of 527
cross-referenced frauds 158
cruelty to wildlife species, crimes of
484–5
cry-for-help firesetters 383
cryptoviral extortion 195
cultural ideology, contributing factor to
domestic violence 254
curiosity firesetters 383
Curtis Committee 461
'cut and shut' vehicle 34
cybercrime 191–211
defining 191–4
governance of 205–9
distal 205–7
proximal 208–9
prevalence and impact of 200–5
personal 204–5
specific business trends 202–4
trends in business 201–2
types of 194–200
denial of service 194–5
intellectual property violations and
online theft 198–9
online fraud 197–8
online violence 199–200
virus attacks 195–6
website and system hacking 196–7
cyber-espionage 197
cyber-stalking 199–200
cyber-terrorism 197

dairy product price fixing 658–9
DAPHNE programme 706
Data Protection Act 1998 187
deaths in custody in UK 746–7
debt bondage 701, 702
deception 156–61
decoy vehicles 41
decriminalisation of sex work 559
Dedicated Cheque and Plastic Crime Unit
(DCPCU) 168
Deer Act 1991 485
defiance theory 440, 444, 445
deindividuation 753
delinquent firesetters 383
denial of service (DoS) 194–5, 197
Department of Health and Social Security,
prosecutions by 95
Dershowitz, Alan 789, 792, 793
deterrent sentencing 282
developmental ransom kidnapping 398
deviance generalisation hypothesis 493
deviant sexual preferences 512, 531–2

differential association, theory of 661
Digital Millennium Copyright Act 1998
   (DMCA) (US) 198
'digital performances', hate related 199
Dirty War, Argentina 773, 779
Disarm Trust 320
dishonest workplace activity, definition of
   101
dismissing attachment 373
Disorderly Houses Act 1751 545
disqualification from driving 913, 914, 918
distal causes of crime 105
distraction burglary 6
distributed denial of service (DDoS) 194, 197
Divis Flats Belfast, study 856–7
doctrine of identification 691
dog fighting 493
Dogs Trust 495
domestic burglary 3–20
   background 3–4
   characteristics of offence 5–6
   characteristics of offenders 8–9
   definitions 3–4
   enactment 14–15
   explanations of crime 9–10
   patterns and trends 4–5
   reactions and response to 15–20
      detection and prevention 16–18
      impact, needs and rights of victims 16
      sentencing and legislation 18–19
   reporting to the police 7–8
   target selection 11–14
   victims and repeat victimisation 6–7
domestic kidnapping 399
domestic relations kidnapping 398
domestic violence 245–64
   and animal abuse 491–2
   characteristics of domestic offenders 248–9
   consequences of 250
   definition of 245
   explanations for 252–4
      individual level 252–3
      social–structural level 253–4
   offenders 250–1
   patterns of 246–7
   responses to 255–64
      critical analysis of the current UK
         approach 261–4
      multi-agency approaches 259–60
      policy context 255–6
      specialist domestic violence courts
         256–8
      supporting victims 260–1
   and stalking 372
   victims of 249–50
Domestic Violence Crime and Victims Act
   2004 418
drink-driving 919–20

drive-by shootings 313
driving offences 904–25
   current context 906–7
   definition of 904–5
   explanations for 909–10
   historical and legislative context of 905–6
   offenders 908–9
   patterns and trends 907–8
   see also bad driving; impaired driving;
      speeding
drug and alcohol related crime 579–95
   characteristics of the offence 584–5
   explanations 586–90
   patterns and trends 581–4
   responses 590–4
      effectiveness of interventions 593
      referral programmes 591
      treatment programmes 591–3
drug control, effectiveness of 603
drug dealers 73, 235, 588, 612–13
Drug Interventions Programme (DIP) 583,
   590
drug referral programmes 591
drug supply and possession 598–621
   characteristics of offenders and victims
      608–10
      description of suppliers and dealers
         609
      distribution networks 608
      domestic local drug markets 608–9
      victims 609–10
   debate and reform 603–4
   drugs and the law 601–2
   drug possession 615–18
      cannabis issue 617–18
      policing possession offences 616–17
   explanations of the crime 610–12
      access to legitimate opportunities
         610–11
      economic, social and subcultural
         influences 611–12
      profit margins 610
   illicit drug use in the UK 598–601
      1980s – 2000s 599–600
      young people 600–1
   patterns and trends 604–8
      cannabis cultivation 607–8
      estimated size of UK market 606
      illicit drug seizures 604–5
      impact of seizures on price and purity
         605–6
      importation seizure information 606–7
   responses to 612–15
      demand reduction strategies 615
      national and local law enforcement
         614–15
      sentencing of suppliers and dealers
         612–14

drug trafficking 626–46
cross-border trafficking 634–5
distribution 639–41
expansion of markets 628–9
illegal markets today 627–8
policies against 641–4
production of major illegal drugs 629–34
cannabis 633–4
cocaine 631–2
heroin 630–1
synthetic drugs 632–3
rise of international control 628–9
smuggling of major illegal drugs 635–8
cannabis 638
cocaine 636–7
heroin 635–6
synthetic drugs 637–8
Drug Trafficking Offences Act 1986 721
drug treatment programmes 591–3
'drug-use-causes-crime' model 587
drugs
and gangs 314–5
role in homicide 228–9
Drugs Action Plan (EU) 642–3
drugs market, three levels of 608
Drugs: Our Community, Your Say 580
Drugs: Protecting Families and Communities 590
Duluth 'coordinated community response' model 259
'dummy' transactions 157
dumpster diving 178
Dun & Bradstreet 157
Durkheim, Emile 852

Easterly, William 815–16
eBay 73, 209
eco-crime *see* air pollution
economic compulsive model 588
ecstasy 632–3, 637–6
Egmont Group 719
electronic immobilisers 36, 42, 43
elder abuse 415–24
definitions of 415–18
patterns and trends 419
responses 419–24
empathy
and bullying 433–4
deficits 511, 531
emotional abuse 248
employee theft and fraud 100–14
characteristics of 104–5
definition and context 101–2
explaining and responding to dishonesty 105–10
gender issues 110–12
patterns and trends 102–4
endangered native species, crimes involving 484

endangered species, illegal trading in 485
Enron 655, 656, 657
Enterprise Act 2002 147, 148
Entertainment and Leisure Software Producers Association (ELSPA) 130
Environment Act 1995 875
Environmental Protection Act 1990 874
Equifax 157
erotomania 371
erotomaniac and morbidly infatuated 375
eSelling 69
Estonian Cyberwar 2007 197
ethnic cleansing *see* genocide and ethnic cleansing
Eurogang, definition 308
European Convention for the Prevention of Torture and Inhuman or Degrading Treatment or Punishment 786–7
European Convention of Human Rights
Article 3 418, 786
Article 5 395
European Environmental Protection Agency (EPA) 872
European Union Drugs Strategy 642–3
euthanasia 219
Every Child Matters 473
Experian 157
extortion 726–34
careers 729–30
excluded communities 733–4
labour and management 731–2
marketing of violence as a commodity 727
night-time economy 730–1
police 728–9
Sicilian Mafia 727–8
states in transition 732–3

Facebook 179
fake drugs 123
fakes 120–33
adverse effects of faking 127–8
characteristics of IPC 125–6
detecting, regulating and preventing 130–2
explaining IPC 126–7
industrialisation and globalisation of 121–3
legal response to 129
lost tax revenue 128
policing of 129–30
physical harm caused by 128
production of 122–3
statistical evidence 123–4
Falconer, Lord 791
false identity, meaning of 173
false imprisonment 397
Family-Relational Schema Model 438

fatal shootings 228
Fathers for Justice 834, 835
fatigued driving 921
fearful attachment 373
Federation Against Software Theft (FACT) 130
fiddling, taxes and benefits 88
file-sharing 125
financial abuse 248
Financial Action Task Force (FATF) 718
Financial Intelligence Unit (FIU) 720–1
Financial Services Authority (FSA) 722
fine particles 869
Finkelhor's 'four preconditions' model 533–4
Fire Awareness Child Education (FACE) 386
fire safety education (FSE) 388
firesetters, juvenile 383–4
first degree murder 219
First Opium Commission 601
First Strike Scotland 494, 495
food poisoning 886
food safety 885
Ford Pinto 892
forged cheques 165
'forgery', meaning of term 120
Forgery and Counterfeiting Act 1981 129
fostering 463
Fraser, Frank 729
Fraud Act 2006 101, 129, 147, 186
Fraud Squad 162
fraudulently altered cheques 165
Friends Reunited 179
'front man' 156, 158, 160–1, 168, 170n1
full/permanent immersion 181
'funny money' scams 159

game theory 851
gangs
    core offences 314–15
    gang homicide 233–5, 311–12
    in-group violence 314
    intervention 319–20
    patterns of 310–11
    prevention 319
    problem of definition 322
    situational explanations 316–18
    subcultural theory 315–16
    suppression 320–2
    territorial disputes 313–14
    weapons 312–13
    youth gang crime 308–25
Gang Resistance Education and Training (GREAT) programme 309, 319
gender
    and bullying 432
    child abuse 462
    child sex offences 529
    corporate crime 664–5

domestic violence 249
driving offences 908, 917
and employee theft and fraud 110–12
homicide 225
sex workers 550
street robbery 276, 277–8
gene-culture theory of rape 510
General Agreement on Tariffs and Trade (GATT) 802
general theory of crime 661–2, 910
genetically modified organisms (GMOs) 885
genocide and 'ethnic cleansing' 762–81
    definitions of 764, 770, 774
    explaining individual participation in 776
    explaining the genocide state 775
    historical parameters 763–4
    as a historical and sociological concept 770–4
        perpetrators: genocide defined as a state crime 771
        relationship between victim and perpetrator 774
        victims: genocide defined by target groups 772–4
    law and 764–9
        distinction from war crimes 765–6
        ethnic cleansing 768–9
        intent 768
        politicide 766–7
        quantitative threshold 767–8
    as a moral concept 769–70
    prevalence of 776–9
    responses to 780
ghosting 88
Global Software Piracy Study 127
global state crimes 801–21
    crimes, harms and culpability 812–17
    definition of global state 801–3
    policies of global financial institutions and criminogenic effects 804–8
    reforms of the global lending arrangements and why they do not work 817–18
    structural adjustment and the nation state 808–12
    towards control of the global lending agencies 819–20
Goffman, Erving 143
Goldstein's tripartite conceptual framework 588–9
Gonzales, Alberto 789, 791
Good Friday Agreement 826
governance of cybercrime 205–9
    distal 205–7
    proximal 207–9
        technological control 208
        social control 208–9
graduation hypothesis 492–3

Great Train Robbery 293
green criminology 865, 867, 877–9
Greenpeace activists 834
Guantánamo Bay 753, 785, 791, 792, 797
Guinness 658, 668

hacking websites and systems 196–7, 203
hacktivists 196
Hague Convention 629
halal meat, illegal slaughter 683
handling stolen goods and the law 69–71
    see also stolen goods markets
harassment, definition of 367
    see also stalking and harassment
hate crime 351–62
    concept of 352–3
    domain of activism 353–4
    from extreme to everyday offending 356–8
    growth of the policy domain 351–2
    harms of 359–61
    legislative approach to defining 354–5
    need for policy learning 361–2
    victim-centered approach to defining
        355–6
Hate Crime 353
Hate Crime Scrutiny Panels 351
Hate Crimes: Criminal Law and Identity Politics
    353
Haw, Brian 825
hawking 69
'Herbless' 196
heroin 598, 599, 600, 606
    production of 630–1
    smuggling of 635–6
heroin outbreaks 611
hidden economy 88, 90
high-density police patrols 284–5
High Risk Offenders Scheme 923
Highly Indebted Poor Countries Initiative
    814, 817, 818
hijacking 397
HM Revenue and Customs 90, 721
    drug seizures 605, 606
    prosecutions by 95
Home Office Car Theft Index 30, 40
homicide 217–40
    characteristics of offenders and victims
        224–7
    corporate 217, 219, 692, 914
    deconstructing 217–20
    explanations for 229
        cultural influences 230–1
        micro-environment and situational
            dynamics 231–3
        structural forces 229–30
    features of homicide event 227
    gang related 233–5
    international rates 222–4

patterns and trends 220–2
    proposed three-tier law of 219–20
    responding to 235–7
Homicide Act 1957 218
Homicide Index 582, 584
homophobic hate crime 361
'honour' in gangs 316
hormonal medication 516
hostage taking 398
hot products 71, 76
'hot spot' analysis 16
'hot spots'
    alcohol-related assaults 332
    weapons related violence 236
Housing Benefit 89
Human Development Index, and homicide
    224
Human Rights Watch 755
Human Security Brief 854
human trafficking 698–709
    characteristics 701–3
        of the offence 701–2
        of victims and offenders 702–3
    explanations of the crime 704–5
    extent, patterns and trends 699–701
    responses to the crime 705–7
Human Trafficking Centre 706
Huntingdon Life Sciences Laboratory,
    blackmail target 400
Hurricane Katrina 89
Hurtwood, Lady Allen of 461
hush money blackmail 399–400
hydraulic theory of crime 65
hyperactivity-impulsivity-attention deficit 432

identification, process of 183–5
identifiers 176–80, 184
    five requirements of 184
    gaining access held by another party
        179–80
    taking from individual's possession 178–9
Identity Cards Act 2006 186
identity crime, meaning of 173
identity fraud, meaning of 173
identity theft and fraud 143, 164, 165, 172–88
    characteristics of the offence 176–82
        methods of acquiring data 177–80
        methods of using data 180–1
        offenders 181–2
        types of data targeted 176–7
        victims 182
    definition of 172–4
    explanations for 182–5
    patterns and trends 174–6
    policing and prosecution 186–7
    prevention strategies 185–6
Identity Theft and Assumption Deterrence Act
    1998 (US) 185

Ignatieff, Michael 789, 792, 793
illegal drug-driving 920
immigrant communities, extortion among
    733–4
impaired driving 919–24
    offenders 922
    patterns and trends in drink driving
        921–2
    responses to 923
    specific explanations 922–3
implicit theories of child sexual offenders
    530–1
implicit theories of rapists 510–11
In the Name of Hate 353
incapacity 422
Income Support 89
income tax evasion and benefit fraud 87–96
    amounts involved and prevalence 89–90
    causes 91–4
    nature of offending 88–9
    official responses 95
incompetent suitor 375
Independent Domestic Violence Advisors
    (IDVAs) 256, 260, 261
India, producer of opium 630
Individual Voluntary Agreement 161–2
Industrial Schools Act 1857 463
Industry Trust for IP Awareness 130
infanticide 218
Infanticide Act 1938 218
'information warfare' 197
initiation rituals in gangs 314
Inland Revenue *see* HM Revenue and
    Customs
institutional abuse and children's homes
    458–74
    abuse by staff 466–70
    explanations of abuse 470–2
    inherent risks in residential care 464–6
    population at risk 462–4
    responses to abuse 472–4
    scale, patterns and trends 461–2
Instrumental crime 806–8
insurance fraud 33
Integrated Model of Emotion Processes and
    Cognition 439
integrated theory of sexual offending 513
intellectual property violations 198–9
    see also fakes
intelligence-led approach
    burglary 16
    homicide 236
    SOCA 722
    terrorism 859
    vehicle crime reduction 41
Intelligent Speed Adaptation (ISA) 914
International Consumer Protection and
    Enforcement Network 147

International Federation of Spirit Producers
    UK 130
*International Handbook of White-Collar and
    Corporate Crime* 91
International Monetary Fund (IMF) 801–2,
    803
International Narcotics Control Board (INCB)
    641–2, 643
International Opium Convention 1912 626,
    629
International Organisation for Migration
    (IOM) 699
internet
    dating scams 141–2
    and sexual crimes 526–7
    use of to abuse children 505–6
Internet Holy Trinity 208
interpersonal violence
    age 492
    development from animal abuse 492–3
intimacy deficits 512, 532–3
intimacy seeker 374–5
involuntary manslaughter 218
Iran-Contra scandal 755

Jamaica, IMF loan 807–8
jealousy
    and anger 373
    as a predictor of domestic violence 251
Jewish population of Germany 766
Jobseeker's Allowance 89, 90
Joint Action Group on Lorry Theft 40–1
Jones, Simon 895–7
joyriding 27, 32, 37, 38

Kansas City Preventive Patrol Experiment 17
Kantian theorists and animal abuse 481
kerb-crawlers 562
Khan, Mohammed Sadique 825
kidnapping 393–412
    criminal careers of those convicted 407–9
    dangerousness of offenders 409–11
    for ransom 398
    measuring the offence 396–7
    nature and representation in the media
        397–9
    offenders 402–4
    origin and legal definition 394–5
    prevalence 400–1
    previous convictions 404–7
    seriousness of 409
knife culture 227
knowledge-based identification 184
Koch Petroleum Group 871
Kray Twins 156, 158, 729

laissez faire, concept of 654
Landau Commission 788, 789, 792

Latham, Tony 469–9
'laundered' meat 683
Lawrence, Stephen 351
Lay, Ken 665
lead and heavy metals 869
'Leap' 319
Leaving Care Act 2000 473
Leeson, Nick 660
legal mobilisation 839
Legends of Mir 3, online theft case 199
'leisure' IPC 125–6
Lemkin, Raphael 762
licence, insurance and record keeping offences 907–8
licenced killings 219
liminality, concept of 340–1
Lindbergh, Charles 397
Little Village Project: A Community Approach to the Gang Problem 321
Local Law Enforcement Hate Crimes Prevention Act 2007 (US) 355
loitering 561
London bombings 358
lone parents 89
long-firm fraud 155–6, 685–6
lost and stolen card fraud 164
Lotteries and Amusements Act 1976 147
Louisiana Pacific Corporation 871
Love Bug 195
low-density police patrols 284
LSD 600

machismo 316
Madoff, Bernie 168–9
'Maggot Pete' 683, 693
mail intercept fraud 178
mail non-receipt frauds 164
male rape 505
malware 195
Manchester Gun Project 237
Manchester Multi-Agency Gang Strategy (MMAGS) 321
Manchester United brand 128
mandatory sentencing policy 19
manslaughter 218, 220
marital rape 505
Marshall, Alfred 88
Martin, Richard 482
Martin, Tony 16
Marxist feminism 554
Matthews, Shannon 399
Maxwell, Robert 655, 660, 665
McCann, Madeleine 397, 412
McIntosh, Anne 64
McVicar, John 297
Medicines Act 1968 418
Medicines and Healthcare Products Regulatory Agency 130

Meese Commission 554
mens rea 218, 467, 691, 907
Mental Capacity Act 2005 418
Mental Health Act 1983 420, 422
mental illness
    and arson 382
    and stalking 372
methamphetamine 632–3, 637–8
Metropolitan Police Film Piracy Unit 130
Mexico, production of heroin 630
middle-range business crime 678–94
    car sales, repairs and servicing 684
    cigarette smuggling 685
    'cowboy' builders 685
    definition and concept of 678–80
    explanations and analyses 688–90
    farming and food production 682–4
    long firm fraud 685–6
    offenders and victims 686–8
    responses 691–3
    'safety crimes' 682
    trends and patterns 680–81
Milgram's experiment 753, 794–5
Military Junta, Burma 741
millennium diamonds 303
miners' strike 746
Minimum Income Guarantee 89
Missing Trader Intra-Community (MTIC) frauds 164
Misuse of Drugs Act 1971 579, 602, 603, 615, 617, 620
mobile phones, robbery involving 273–4, 276
Mohamed, Binyam 785
money laundering 712–24
    definition of 713
    response 717–23
        AML in the United Kingdom 721–3
        anti-money laundering (AML) regimes 720–21
        international bodies 718–20
        United States 717–18
    scope of the problem 714–15
    selected methods 715–17
Money Laundering Control Act 1986 (US) 718
Money Laundering Regulations (2003 and 2007) 129
mood disorders and stalking 372
moonlighting 88
Motor Car Act 1903 905
Motor Vehicle Theft Law Enforcement Act 1984 (USA) 34
Mugabe, President 750
mugging 271
multi-agency risk assessment conferences (MARACs) 259–60
Munich Olympics, hostage taking 398
murder, definition of 218

Myanmar, production of opium 630

National Air Quality Archive 870
National Air Quality Strategy (NAQS) 875
National Criminal Intelligence service (NCIS)
    721–2
National Driving Improvement Scheme 919
National High-Tech Crime Unit (NHTCU)
    200, 201, 206–7
Nationality, Immigration and Asylum Act
    2002 706
natural history theory of rape 509
NCIS Organised Vehicle Crime Programme
    33
negotiated management 836, 837
Neighbourhood Watch 17
neo-liberal economies and homicide 222
network sales 69
NEW-ADAM survey 583-4, 585
New Social Movements 828
Nigerian fraudsters *see* '419' fraud
night-time economy, extortion in 730–1
nitrogen oxides 869
non-delivery and defective products and
    services 139
North Wales children's homes, abuse scandal
    467
Northern Ireland conflict 856–7
Northern Ireland terrorist suspects 791
Not Another Drop (NAD) 321
Nuremburg trials 659, 753

Obama, President Barak 785
'occupation', burglary as 9
occupational death 888–9
occupational fraud, definition of 101
occupational ill-health 890
occupational injury 889–90
'off the shelf' companies 156
Offences Against the Person Act 1861 396,
    397
offenders
    animal abuse 487
    arson 383–5
    blackmail, kidnapping and threats to kill
        402–4
    domestic burglary 8–9
    domestic violence 250–2
    driving 908–9, 917, 922
    elder abuse 419
    employee theft and fraud 111–12
    genocide 771
    hate crime 356–8
    homicide 225–7
    human trafficking 702–3
    identity theft and fraud 181–2
    illicit drugs 608–9
    middle-range business crime 686–8

    political protest 830–1
    scams 142–3
    school bullying 430–4
    sex work 550–3
    shoplifting 52–5
    stalking 370–1
    stolen goods market 73
    street robbery 276–7
    vehicle crime 37
OLL adventure centre 682, 691
Olweus Bullying Prevention Programme
    (OBPP) 443
'On cooling the mark out' 143
online fraud 197–8
online theft 198–9
online violence 199–200
Operation Eagle Eye 285
Operation Pentameter 703, 707
Operation Trident 237
Opium 628–9
opportunist burglaries 11–12
Oppositional Defiant Disorder (ODD) 430
Organisation for Security and Cooperation in
    Europe (OSCE) 352
overpayment scams 141, 143
over-the-counter drugs and driving 920
ozone and volatile organic compounds 870

paedophile picture collections 527
Palermo Convention 719
parenting styles and bullying 436
Parks, Rosa 829
Parmalat 656
partial criminalisation of sex work 559
pathways model 534–5
patriarchal culture and animal abuse 491
PAW 494
Paying the Price 560
peer influence
    car theft 38
    shoplifting 59
penitentiaries 462
pensions scandal 658
Pentameter II 703, 707
permanent vehicle theft 27–8
personal data, safe storage of 179–80
Peru, production of coca 631
pharmaceutical industry 886, 887
pharming 197–8
phishing 179, 197–8
phoenix companies 159
physical abuse 248
pick-pocketing 272
PINcard 167–8
Pindown regime 468–70
'piracy', meaning of term 120
playground supervision and bullying 444
'plural policing' 129–30

police
corruption 299–300
proceeds of sex workers earnings 544–5,
549
vehicle accidents 917–18
Police and Criminal Evidence Act 1984
(PACE) 420
Police Central e-Crime Unit (PceU) 207
Police Reserve Battalion 101 776
Policing and Crime Bill 2009 560
policing strategies 283–5
political kidnapping 399
political protest and crime 825–41
characteristics of offenders and victims
830–1
emergence of modern protest 827
explanations of activism and militancy
831–3
key issues 825–6
patterns and trends 826–7
political opportunities 829–30
protest cycles 827–8
responses to protest 835–9
legal institutions as arenas of
contention 839
media 'framing' 837–8
repression 835–7
violence 833–5
Polo Ammond (Polar Ammon Gelignite) 291
Ponzi scheme 169, 715
see also pyramid schemes
power, concept of in domestic violence 253–4
power/powerless theory of child sexual abuse
530
predatory kidnapping
of an adult 399
of a child 399
predatory stalker 374
premium rate telephone prize scams 139
preoccupied attachment 373
preparatory knowledge 74–5
Prevalence Study of Elder Abuse 419
Proceeds of Crime Act (POCA) 2002 129,
544–5, 713, 721
profit kidnapping 399
programme abuse 467–8
prohibitionist policies of sex work 556
property investment scams 139
property marking 18, 79
prostitution 705
definition of 542
Prostitution Reform Act 2003 (NZ) 559
Protection from Harassment Act 1997 366,
418
Protection of Badgers Act 1992 485
protest cycles 827–8
provocation, defence of 220
proximal causes of crime 105

psychiatrists, role in interrogation 797–8
psychologists, role in interrogation 797–8
psychopathology, as a predictor of domestic
violence 251
psychopharmacological model 588
pump and dump schemes 139–40
Punishing Hate 353
'pyramid of enforcement' model 672
pyramid schemes 139, 140
see also Ponzi scheme

quadripartite model 534
Quality Protects 473

Racketeer-Influenced Corrupt Organizations
(US) 717–18
randomised control trial (RCT) 536–7
rape
definition of 507
five types of 507
sociological understanding of 774
rational actor theory 91–2, 668
rational choice
animal abuse 491
employee theft and fraud 105
IPC 126
middle-range business 688
shoplifting 57, 65
stolen goods 75
street robbery 279
tax and benefit fraud 94
Reagan administration, supply of weapons to
Nicaragua 755
'reciprocal' relationship of drug use 587
reckless arson 386
'Red Army Faction' 828
'Red Brigades' 828
reformatories 463
regulationist approach to sex work 559
Reid, Richard 858
reintegrative shaming theory (RST) 440
rejected stalker 374
religious evangelism 554
repeat victims, of burglary 7
rerum natura 218
resentful stalker 374
residential care 463
parallels with custodial facilities 465
residential fence supplies 69
resource mobilization theory 831–2
restorative justice approach to bullying 444–5
Retail Radio Links 63
Retail Theft Initiative 64
revenge kidnapping 399
Reynolds, Bruce 292, 296–7
Richardson gang 156, 158, 729
'ringing' 34–5
ritualised violence in gangs 314

Road Safety Act 1967 905
Road Safety Act 2006 906, 913, 923
Road Traffic Act 1930 905
Road Traffic Act 1991 905, 907
Road Traffic Offenders Act 1988 913
Rolex watches, fake 126
romantic kidnapping 398
Royal Family, attempted blackmail of 399
RSPCA 494, 495
Rumsfeld, Donald 789
Russia, extortion in 732–3
Rwanda
    genocide 765, 767, 775
    state crime 752, 753

safe-cracking 291–2
Safer Parking Initiative 43
salvage yards, registration of 41–2
'sanction' detection rates, burglary 16
SAPRIN 814–15
Savings and Loan scandal 657
Scambusters team 147
scams 137–49
    characteristics of offence, offenders and
        victims 142–3
    common 138–40
    explanation of 145–6
    OFT definition of 137
    patterns and trends 140–2
    reporting of 146
    responses to 146–8
    role of emotions in 143–4
    victim demographics 144–5
Scams Enforcement Group 147
Schaeffer, Rebecca 366
schema theories 510
schizophrenia 372
school bullying 427–46
    characteristics 430–4
    definition and measurement 428–9
    effectiveness of anti-bullying programmes
        441–3
    family influences 434–7
    future research 445–6
    policy implications 443–5
    prevalence and trends 429–30
    theories of bullying 437–41
second degree murder 219
'Second Life' 199
secure accommodation 465, 470
secure attachment 372
Secured Car Park initiative see Safer Parking
    Initiative
Security Express robbery 300–1
security measures, to prevent burglary 12
security technology, improvements in 301
self-assertive crime, concept of 806
self-esteem and bullying 432–3

self-referencing 156–8
self reported figures, stolen goods 71–2
self-service shops 57
separatist lesbian feminism 554
Serious Crime Act 2007 129
Serious Crime Prevention Orders (SCPOs)
    129
Serious Organised Crime Agency (SOCA)
    130, 169, 206–7, 614, 721–3
severely disturbed firesetters 383
Sex Offender Treatment Programme 517–18
sex work 542–71
    client diversity 552–3
    clients 551–2
    contemporary policy proposals 560–4
        closure orders 562–3
        criminalising payment for sex 560–1
        loitering or soliciting and forced
            rehabilitation 561
        soliciting (re)defined 561–2
        trafficking and migration 563–4
    explanations 553–9
        prostitution as exploitation 554–5
        sex work as work 555–6
    prostitution, definition of 542
    offences related to 542–7
        advertising and maiding 546
        additional indoor 545–6
        child prostitution 547
        controlling 544–5
        trafficking for sexual exploitation
            546–7
    patterns and trends 547–50
    sex workers 550–1
sexual abuse 248
    linked to animal abuse 492
sexual assault, definition of 507
sexual blackmail 399
sexual grooming 527
sexual images, distribution of 527
sexual murder 507
Sexual Offences Act 1967 505
Sexual Offences Act 2003 394, 418, 506,
    525–6, 528, 544, 560, 706
sexual offences against adults 505–20
    facts and figures 508–9
    outcomes 517–19
        evaluation of SOTP and community
            programmes 517–18
        reviews and meta-analyses 518–19
    prevention 513–17
        changing the offender 516–17
        punishment 515–16
        situational crime 514–15
    theories of 509–13
        evolutionary 509–10
        feminist 509
        social-cognitive 510–13

sexual offences against children 525–38
    facts and figures 528–30
    theories 530–5
        complex integrationist 533–5
        feminist 530
        social-cognitive 530–3
    researching prevention 536–7
'sharp practices' 137–8
Shipman, Harold 221
Shop Watch schemes 63
shoplifting 48–66
    explanations for 55–9
    measures taken to prevent 60–1, 62
    motives for 58
    patterns and measurement of 48–51
    profile of shoplifters 52–5
    responses to by criminal justice system
        63–4
    responses to by shops 59–63
    types of goods stolen 51–2
shrinkage 50, 102
Sicilian Mafia 727–8, 732
simple arson 386
situational crime prevention
    adult sexual offences 514–15
    arson 385–6
    domestic burglary 17–18
    scams 148
    street robbery 282–3
    vehicle crime 42–3
    in the workplace 105–6
six markets for stolen goods 68–9
skimming 179
'skunk' 605, 618
Smartwater 79
Smalls, Bertie 299–300
Smelser, Neil 853
Smith, Adam 88, 741
Smith, Razor 297
Smith, Terry 297
'smokies', illegal trade in 683
snatch thefts 271
social disorganisation, concept of 661
social dominance theory 439
social engineering 158–9
social harm, concept of 654, 812
social identity theory 852
social information processing theory (SIP)
    438–9
social learning theory 492
Social security numbers, use of fake 89
social skills deficit model 438
soliciting 561–2
South Ossetia conflict 769
special measures to assist vulnerable people
    giving evidence 422–3
specialised domestic violence courts (SDVCs)
    255, 256–8

basic features of 257
    sentencing in 258
Specialist Crime Department 6 162
speed cameras 907, 911, 913, 914
speeding 911–14
    explanations for 913
    offenders 912–13
    patterns and trends 911–12
    responses to 913–14
'splash and dash' scam 148–9
spyware 179
staff dishonesty
    Bamfields classification of 103–2
    key characteristics of 104–5
    nine key tactics 106–110, 112
Staffordshire children's homes, abuse scandal
    467–70
staged kidnapping 399
stalking and harassment 366–7
    and attachment 371–3
    characteristics of stalkers 370–1
    characteristics of victims 370
    definition of 367–8
    and domestic violence 372
    history of 366–7
    jealousy and anger 373
    mental illness 371–2
    prevalence of 368–9
    psychosocial characteristics 371
    relationships with victim 375–6
    responses to 376–7
    tactics 369
    types of stalkers and patterns 373–5
    and violence perpetration 369–70
Stanford, Sir Allen 169
Stanford Prison Experiment 752, 795
state computer crime 749
state crimes 739–57
    definition of 741–5
    explanations of 749–53
    patterns and examples 745–9
    responses to 753–5
Statewatch 755
'status' dogs, ownership of 493
status symbol, cars as 38–9
steering column locks 36, 42
Stewart, Martha 665
STEPS programme 320
Stockline factory 682
stolen goods markets 68–82
    anti-theft initiatives 80–1
    anti-theft initiatives to avoid 77–80
    characteristics of offenders 73
    consumer society 76–7
    handling and the law 69–71
    patterns and trends 71–3
    role of demand for 73–7
    six markets for 68–9

stop and search 236
STOP programme 706
store detectives 59, 62
strain theory 145, 492
stranger abuse 417
Street Crime Initiative (SCI) 285
Street Offences Act 1959 561
street robbery 270–87
    definitions of 270–2
    explanation for 278–82
        cultural 280
        empirical support 280–1
        rational choice 279
    patterns and trends 272–4
    response to 282–5
        combined approaches 285
        deterrent sentencing 282
        policing strategies 283–5
        situational crime prevention 282–3
        social crime prevention 283
    types of offence 274–6
    types of offender 276–7
    types of victim 277–8
structural adjustment, definition of 805–6
subcontracting in the building industry 88
subculture theory of violence 315–16
substance abuse
    and stalking 372
    in gangs 317
    as a predictor of domestic violence 251,
        252
suckers lists 145, 168
suicide bombing 855
sulphur dioxide 869
supergrasses 299–300, 301
surgical castration 526
surveillance, police 17
survival, burglary as a means of 10–11
Sutton, Willie 296
'Swampy' 835
synthetic drugs, production of 632–3
systemic crime model 589

Tackling Drugs to Build a Better Britain 582
Tackling Gangs Action Programme (TGAP)
    321, 323
Tackling Knives Action Programme (TKAP)
    236
Tackling the Demand for Prostitution: A Review
    560
target hardening 17
tax evasion, five types of 88
taxation, attitudes towards 92–3
techniques of neutralisation 663
temporary/partial immersion 180–1
temporary vehicle theft 27
terrorism 846–61
    counter-terrorism 858–60

definitions 848–9
economics 850–1
political science and international relations
    849–50
psychology 851–2
shifting scale and modes of 854–6
social support 856–7
sociology 852–4
Terrorism Versus Democracy 850
terrorist campaigns, three common factors
    854
Tesco, blackmail target 400
Thatcher, Margaret 335–6
The Face of Terrorism 853
The Nature of Prejudice 352
The Professional Thief 154
The Wealth of Nations 88, 741
The White Man's Burden 815
Theft Act 1968
    section 1 101
    section 1(1) 27
    section 8(1) 270
    section 9 3
    section 12(1) 27
    section 12(7) 26
    section 21 294
    section 22 69
    section 22(1) 70
    section 27 70
Theft Act 1978
    section 1(1) 64
Theory of Mind (ToM) model 438–9
'third degree methods' of torture 789
threats to kill 393–412
    criminal careers of those convicted 407–9
    dangerousness of offenders 409–11
    measuring the offence 396–7
    nature and representation in the media
        400
    offenders 402–4
    origin and legal definition 395–6
    prevalence 400–1
    previous convictions 404–7
    seriousness of 409
ticking bomb scenario 788, 790
tiger kidnap 303
Titan Rain 197
token-based identification 184
torture 785–98
    definition of 786–7
    facilitating 793–8
    in international law 786–8
    practices constituting 787–8
    regulation of 789
    upper limits of coercion 791–2
    utilitarian case 788–93
'total institution' 470
toxic organic micro-pollutants (TOMPS) 869

Trade Descriptions Act 1968 129
Trade Marks Act 1994 129
trading standards service 147
TRAFFIC 495
trafficking
    of children in care 707
    for sexual exploitation 546–7
Trafficking in persons: global patterns 700
Transco 692
Transparency International 748
travel agency frauds 158
triangle of crime 283
Trinidad and Tobago, structural adjustment
    loan 804, 805
trojans 195, 197, 198
Turkey, gateway for heroin smuggling 635–6

UN Convention Against Torture 786
UN Convention on the Rights of the Child
    466, 472
UN Convention on Psychotropic Substances
    641
UN Convention on the Suppression of
    Trafficking in Women and the Exploitation
    of the Prostitution of Others 698
UN International Convention for the
    Suppression of the Financing of Terrorism
    718–19
UN Protocol to Prevent, Suppress and Punish
    Trafficking in Persons, Especially Women
    and Children 698
UN Single Convention on Narcotic Drugs
    601–2, 642
United Nations 802
Universal Declaration of Human Rights
    (UDHR) 786
unsolicited and unwanted goods and services
    139–40
Uruguay Round of negotiations 802
US Environmental Protection Agency (USEPA)
    871

vCJD 886
vehicle crime 26–44
    characteristics of 29–37
        age profile of stolen vehicles 30
        destination of stolen vehicles 32–3
        locations of theft 31–2
        methods of theft 36
        models of car stolen 30
        profile of offenders 37
        profile of victims 36
        resale in the domestic market 34–5
        stripping cars for components 33–4
        theft for export 35–6
        theft risk by car segment 30
    explanation 37–40
        of permanent theft 39–40

        of temporary theft 37–9
    meaning of 26
    motivation for 26–9
        permanent theft 27–8
        temporary theft 27
        theft from vehicles 28–9
        vehicle interference and tampering 28
    response to 40–3
        enforcement 41–2
        situational crime prevention 42–3
        social crime prevention 41
Vehicle Crime Reduction Action Team
    (VCRAT) 40
vehicle documentation, methods of obtaining
    34–5
Vehicle Identification Numbers (VINs) 34
vehicles
    interference and tampering 28
    theft from 28
Victim Support 16
victims
    animal abuse 487–8
    domestic burglary 6–7
    domestic violence 249–50
    elder abuse 419
    employee theft and fraud 111
    faking 127–8
    genocide 772–4
    hate crime 359–61
    homicide 225–7
    human trafficking 702–3
    identity theft and fraud 182
    illicit drugs 609–10
    political protest 830–1
    scams 143–5
    school bullying 430–4
    sex work 550–3
    stalkers 370
    street robbery 277–8
    vehicle crime 36
Video Recordings Act 1984 129
Vienna Convention 718
Vietnam War, expansion of illicit drug use
    629
violence, intergenerational transmission of
    252–3
violence in the night-time economy 331–48
    context of 332–5
    control 346–7
    structural change and the rise of consumer
        cultures 335–9
    subjective 343–6
    young people and the attractions of the
        night-time economy 339–43
'virtual-rape' 200
virus attacks 195–6
voluntary liquidation 161–2
voluntary manslaughter 218

vulnerable adult abuse, mandatory reporting of 423
vulnerable person, definition of 416

wage snatches 293
Waltham Forest Gangs Intervention Project 320
War Crimes Tribunals 754
war on terror 750, 791, 792
Wasik, Professor Martin 69
waterboarding 788, 789
Waterhouse Report 467
weapons
    of homicide 227–8
    of street robbery 276
    of youth gangs 312–13
weapons-awareness courses 236
'Weathermen'/'Weather Underground' 828
Western Union 142
'Westley's Weapons Awareness' 319
White-Collar Crime 154, 653
white slavery 398
Whose Children? 461

Wickersham Commission 789
Wildlife and Countryside Act 1981 484, 488
Wildlife Crimes 484–5
Williams, Glanville 70
withdrawal against uncleared effects 165
work from home scams 139, 142
workhouses 463
World Bank 801, 803
World Intellectual Property Organisation (WIPO) 198
'World on Warcraft' 199
World Trade Organisation 802
worms 185

youth gang crime *see* gangs
Yugoslavia
    genocide 762, 765, 767, 774
    human trafficking 704
    state crime 753

Zemin, President Jiang 826
Zubaydah, Abu 796